Frommer's 96

Italy

by Darwin Porter
& Danforth Prince

D1472241

Macmillan • USA

ABOUT THE AUTHORS

A native of North Carolina, **Darwin Porter** was a bureau chief for *The Miami Herald* when he was 21, and later worked in television advertising. A veteran travel writer, he is the author of numerous bestselling Frommer Guides, notably to England, France, the Caribbean, Italy, and Spain. When not traveling (which is rare), he lives in New York City. **Danforth Prince** formerly worked at the Paris bureau of *The New York Times*.

MACMILLAN TRAVEL

A Simon & Schuster Macmillan Company
1633 Broadway
New York, NY 10019

Copyright © 1996 by Simon & Schuster, Inc.

ISBN 0-02-860628-0
ISSN 1044-2170

Design by Michele Laseau
Digital cartography: Ortelius Design

SPECIAL SALES

Bulk purchases (10 or more copies) of Frommer's Travel Guides are available to corporations at special discounts. The Special Sales Department can produce custom editions to be used as premiums and/or for sales promotion to suit individual needs. Existing editions can be produced with custom cover imprints such as a corporate logo. For more information write to: Special Sales, Simon & Schuster, 1633 Broadway, 8th floor, New York, NY 10019.

Manufactured in the United States of America

Contents

4 Introducing Rome 101

5 Where to Stay & Dine in Rome 114

6 What to See & Do in Rome 158

List of Maps

INVITATION TO THE READER

In researching this book, we discovered many wonderful places—hotels, restaurants, shops, and more. We're sure that you'll find others. Please tell us about them, so we can share the information with your fellow travelers in upcoming editions. If you were disappointed with a recommendation, we'd love to know that, too. Please write to:

Darwin Porter and Danforth Prince
Frommer's Italy '96
Macmillan Travel
1633 Broadway
New York, NY 10019

AN ADDITIONAL NOTE

Please be advised that travel information is subject to change at any time—and this is especially true of prices. We therefore suggest that you write or call ahead for confirmation when making your travel plans. The authors, editors, and publisher cannot be held responsible for the experiences of readers while traveling. Your safety is important to us, however, so we encourage you to stay alert and be aware of your surroundings. Keep a close eye on cameras, purses, and wallets, all favorite targets of thieves and pickpockets.

WHAT THE SYMBOLS MEAN

✪ Frommer's Favorites

Hotels, restaurants, attractions, and entertainment you should not miss.

⑤ Super-Special Values

Hotels and restaurants that offer great value for your money.

The following abbreviations are used for credit cards:

AE	American Express	EU	Eurocard
CB	Carte Blanche	JCB	Japan Credit Bank
DC	Diners Club	MC	MasterCard
DISC	Discover	V	Visa
ER	enRoute		

The Best of Italy

Selecting the best of what Italy has to offer is far from easy, not because the choices are limited but because, on the contrary, so many things about Italy—one of the most beautiful, diverse, and culturally rich countries in the world—can only be described in the superlative. So, while the selections below do represent the best of Italy, they by no means exhaust the list of wonderful places to see or memorable experiences to enjoy. For Italy is a land of enchanting discoveries, and each visitor may come up with his or her own favorites to add to any personal *best-of* list.

1 The Best Travel Experiences

Italy is a feast for the senses and the intellect, and some of the country's most thrilling experiences involve the simple act of living in the Italian style. Though the country is literally stuffed with the potential for memorable experiences, here is an abbreviated list of some that are, by anyone's estimate, spectacular.

- **Visiting the Art Cities of Italy.** When Italy consisted of dozens of principalities, its art treasures were concentrated in many small capitals. Each of these cities, blessed with the patronage of a papal representative or ducal family, amassed vast quantities of art. Exquisite paintings, statues, and frescoes are displayed in churches, monasteries, and palaces whose architects are world-acclaimed. Although the best-known of these troves reside in Florence, Rome, and Venice, stunning art collections are also found in the smaller-scale and often ravishingly beautiful cities of Assisi, Cremona, Genoa, Mantua, Padua, Parma, Palermo, Pisa, Siena, Taormina, Tivoli, Turin, Verona, and Vicenza.

- **A Boat Ride on the Grand Canal of Venice.** The S-shaped Grand Canal, curving for two miles along historic buildings and under ornate bridges, is the most romantic and evocative waterway in the world. Most first-timers are stunned by the variety of Gothic and Renaissance buildings, whose elaborate styles could fill a book on architecture. A ride on the canal will give you ever-changing glimpses of the city's poignant beauty. Your ride doesn't have to be on a gondola; any public vaporetto (ferry) sailing between Venice's railway station and the Piazza San Marco will provide a heart-stopping view.

- **Celebrating Mass in St. Peter's (Vatican).** With the possible exception of some sites in Jerusalem, St. Peter's is the most visible and important building in Christendom. The huge size of the church is daunting. For many visitors, the celebration of Mass here is a spiritual highlight of their lives. Your co-celebrants are likely to come from every corner of the world.

- **Eating Out.** One of the most cherished pastimes of the Italians is eating out. Regardless of how much lasagne you've had in your life, it's never better than the real thing in Italy. Each region has its own specialties, some handed down for centuries. The cuisine can be addictively delicious; and if the weather is fine, and you're dining outdoors with a view of, perhaps, a medieval church or piazza, it's the closest thing to heaven in Italy. Buon appetito!

- **Walking in Venice.** The most obvious means of transport in Venice is by boat; an even more appealing method is by foot, traversing hundreds of canals, large and small, and crossing over the arches of medieval bridges. Getting from one point to another can be like walking through a maze, but you won't be hassled by traffic, and the sense of the city's beauty, timelessness, and slow decay is almost mystical.

- **Attending an Opera.** It's estimated that more than 2,000 new operas were staged in Italy during the 18th century, and since then Italian opera fans have earned a reputation as the toughest and most demanding in the world. For a firsthand view of their devotion to this art form, consider attending an opera. Likely choices include Venice's Teatro di San Cassiano (opened in 1637 as the first opera house in Italy); Milan's La Scala (probably the most prestigious opera house in the world, especially for bel canto); and a wide assortment of outdoor settings such as The Arena in Verona, one of the largest surviving amphitheaters in the ancient world. Suitable for up to 20,000 spectators, and known for its fine acoustics, it presents operas throughout the warm season, when moonlight and the perfumed air of the Veneto add to the production's charms.

- **Opera at the Baths of Caracalla (Rome).** Few ancient ruins in Italy rival the Baths of Caracalla in their drawing power, especially at night during the summer months. Illumined dramatically and suffused, as is the area surrounding them, with the scent of mimosa and oleander, the ruins serve as the setting for major operatic performances, including the staging of Verdi's Aïda. A celebrated concert by three of the world's top tenors—José Carreras, Plácido Domingo, and Luciano Pavarotti—took place a few years ago in the baths' open-air shell.

- **Shopping in Milan.** Milan is one of the most enchanting fashion capitals of Europe. If you're assembling a wardrobe, you'll find a range of shoes, clothing, and accessories that are unequaled anywhere else in the world. Even if shopping isn't something you usually enjoy back home, a window-shopping stroll along streets bordering the via Montenapoleone offers bottomless elegance, often from the most famous designers of Europe.

- **Rejuvenating at a Spa.** Although the spas of Germany are infinitely busier, the terme (spas) of Italy enjoy a relaxed charm, a 19th-century sense of belle-époque nostalgia, and thousands of devoted aficionados. Learn why they're so passionate about "the cure" by heading to Montecatini Terme, Salsomaggiore Terme, Tabiano Terme, Saturnia Terme, Chiusi Terme, Chianchiano Terme, Castrocaro Terme, or the island of Ischia. If you're affluent and exhausted, you can opt for a regime of mud baths and immersion in the sulpherous waters bubbling out of geothermal springs. Regardless of how deeply you participate in the spa rituals, you're likely to emerge refreshed, more relaxed, and healthier than before you arrived.

- **The Grand Tour.** During the 18th and 19th centuries, enlightened schoolmasters believed that a tour through Italy was the proper conclusion to a well-rounded education. The sons of prosperous families from France, Britain, and Germany swept southward on grand loops through the Alps; the great art cities of the Veneto, Umbria, and Tuscany; the monuments and churches of Rome; and the ancient ruins of Naples and Sicily. Part of the enchantment of a grand tour of Italy is stumbling upon unexpected charms in the smaller towns, as well, as one travels the length of the country.

2 The Best Hotels

If you've just made a killing on Wall Street and the cost of your accommodations is unimportant, here's a list of upscale hotels whose beauty is nothing less than thrilling.

- **Quisisana & Grand Hotel, Capri.** Originally established as a health spa by an English doctor around 1850, in a part of the island sheltered from the sometimes annoying winds of Capri, this hotel is large (165 rooms), supremely comfortable, and intricately linked to the allure that made Capri popular with the ancient Roman emperors. The clientele comes from all over the world.
- **Miramonti Majestic, Cortina d'Ampezzo.** Designed like a massive mountain fortress, this hotel is located in the heart of Italy's most glamorous alpine resort. The clientele seems to relish the hotel's Italian panache amid the bracing air of the Dolomites. Despite the modern amenities, there's a 19th-century quality about this place, which is located in the Veneto region.
- **Albergo Splendido, Portofino.** Originally built as a monastery in the 14th century, and later abandoned because of attacks from North African pirates, this monument was rescued during the 19th century by an Italian baron and converted into a summer retreat for his family. The posh hillside retreat on the Italian Riviera now accommodates a sophisticated clientele, including many film stars. Mimosas fill a forest with their scent, and the sea views are blissful.
- **Villa d'Este, Cernobbio.** Originally built in 1568, this splendid palace in the Lake District is one of the most famous Renaissance-era hotels in the world. The interior is filled with frescoed ceilings, impeccable antiques, and many other exquisite details. Some visitors, including this writer, thrill to the 10 magnificently landscaped acres surrounding it, parts of which have been nurtured since the 1500s. Cool breezes are provided by nearby Lake Como and the proximity to the Swiss and Italian alps.
- **San Pietro, Positano.** The only marker that identifies this cliffside hotel, in the Campania region, is a 15th-century chapel set beside the winding road. The hotel doesn't advertise, protects the privacy of its guests, and offers frequent transportation into that hub of midsummer Italian glamour, Positano, less than a mile away. Bedrooms resemble suites, and offer views of the sea. Strands of bougainvillea twine around the dramatically terraced, glistening white walls of the exterior.
- **Hassler, Rome.** Hollywood mingles easily here with old European wealth. The setting (near an obelisque and a baroque renaissance church) at the top of the Spanish Steps is among the most evocative in Rome. The bar attracts an invigorating mixture of faded stars. The view from the panoramic restaurant sweeps out over Rome.

Italy

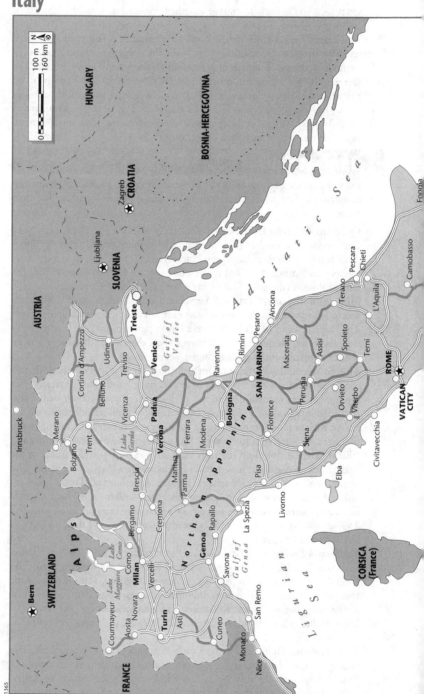

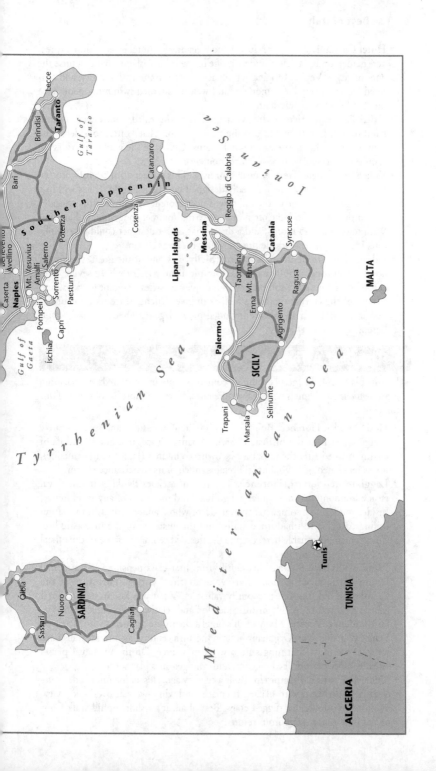

- **Hotel Cipriani, Venice.** Exclusive and elegant, this hotel is set within a three-acre garden on Isola della Giudecca, one of the calmer islands that comprise the ancient city of Venice. Originally built as a cloister in the 15th century, and centered around a very large, modern, and well-maintained swimming pool, it's a hotel redolent with grandeur.
- **Gritti Palace, Venice.** Andrea Gritti, a Doge who ruled Venice with an iron hand until his death in 1538, is the namesake for what's often considered the gem of one of the most elegant hotel chains (CIGA) in the world. Interiors are exquisite, a taste of Venice's historic opulence.
- **Villa San Michele, Fiesole, near Florence.** This former 15th-century monastery is set behind a facade reputedly designed by Michelangelo. It lies within a scented garden, in one of the hill towns near Florence. Many visitors consider it a worthy escape from the often oppressive midsummer congestion of Florence. With fewer than 45 rooms, and a decor that no set designer could ever duplicate, it evokes an aristocratic private villa with great charm.
- **Palazzo San Domenico, Taormina, Sicily.** It's one of the great, stylish old hotels of Europe, a 500-year-old Dominican monastery whose severe lines and dignified bulk are softened with antique tapestries, fragrant gardens, and a sense of the eternal that only Sicily can give. Clients since its transformation into a hotel in 1896 have included movie legends Dietrich, Garbo, and Loren.

3 The Best Affordable Hotels

If costs play a role in the planning of your trip, Italy has hundreds of charming inns, *pensiones*, and hotels with reasonable rates. Here is a short list of some of our top choices.

- **Hotel J and J, Florence.** Built in the 1500s as a monastery, and set on a rarely visited street near the historic church of Santa Croce, this hotel has lots of charm. Named after the initials of its owners' children (James and Jacqueline), it was renovated in 1990, but still retains much of its Renaissance charm.
- **Loggiato dei Serviti, Florence.** The row of arcades flanking its medieval facade is among the most quietly dignified (and soothing) of any in Florence. Inside, you'll find a somewhat spartan decor whose allure derives from soaring ceilings, thick and unadorned walls, and the austerity of the monastic life. Costs remain reasonable here, despite the frescoed ceilings in some of the otherwise very simple bedrooms.
- **Palazzo Ravizza, Siena.** This family-run, first-class pensione has a formal facade and terraced gardens that evoke another century. Furniture in the bedrooms is old (but not necessarily valuable). What you lose in decor, you'll gain in a central and richly historic location and relatively affordable costs.
- **La Residenza, Venice.** Many of this hotel's clients are art lovers who return to Venice year after year. Originally built in the 14th century, its interior walls have some of the most charming stucco work in Venice. On the medieval piazza outside, older persons feed pigeons, and younger ones play soccer.
- **Menardi, Cortina d'Ampezzo.** Built a century ago, this alpine inn exudes Austrian gemütlichkeit, with blazing fireplaces and windows that overlook a view of alpine meadows and rugged crags. Best of all, it's a short uphill walk from one of Italy's most glamorous resorts.

- **Hotel Venezia, Rome.** Set near Rome's main railway terminal, this hotel features such grace notes as Murano glass chandeliers in the bedrooms and public areas, which were recently renovated. Some units have balconies overlooking the street, and everything is clean.
- **Hotel Palazzo Bocci, in Spello, near Assisi.** Built in the late 18th century, and renovated and transformed into a hotel in 1992, this palace is posh, tasteful, and reasonably priced. Many of the public and private rooms have sweeping views of the valley below.
- **Hotel Roma, Modena.** In the 1700s this building was among the real-estate holdings of the duca d'Este. Today, it's likely to be the temporary home of whatever opera star happens to be singing in Pavarotti's hometown. Flourishing as a hotel since the 1950s, the Roma, located in the historic heart of town, is comfortable and uncomplicated.
- **Hotel Asnigo, Cernobbio.** The Asnigo embodies the Edwardian style of the age in which it was built (1914), and has the atmosphere of a genteel retreat. Set within a garden, it's clean and run in a friendly, low-key style. Some visitors return year after year.
- **Hotel Florence, Bellagio.** A private villa in the 19th century, this hotel has a dignified facade, an arbor with tumbling wisteria, and stone-sided terraces overlooking a lake. In 1990 a series of renovations brought it tastefully up to date, and Saturday night jazz concerts and an American-style bar have made it better than ever.

4 The Best Restaurants

Italy has always been known for its agricultural bounty; it's a fertile peninsula rich with olive groves and other farmland. The result has been the emergence of one of the world's premier cuisines. Here is a list of Italy's most glamorous and consistently recommended eateries.

- **Relais le Jardin, Rome.** Set within the dignified Lord Byron hotel, in an upscale residential neighborhood a short drive from the center of Rome, this place is always on the short list of the country's best. The menu varies according to the availability of what's in season at the time.
- **Harry's Bar, Venice.** It's legendary, it's lighthearted, and it's fun. First made famous by writer Ernest Hemingway, Harry's Bar still serves sublime food in the formal dining room upstairs. The Bellini (peach juice with champagne) was born here.
- **Antico Martini, Venice.** Founded in 1720 as a spot to savor the newly developed rage of coffee-drinking, this restaurant is usually cited as one of the very best in Venice. Replete with paneled walls and glittering chandeliers, Antico Martini specializes in Venetian cuisine.
- **Ristorante il Desco, Verona.** Set in a former palazzo, this restaurant is considered one of the best in the Veneto region of northeastern Italy. Its culinary repertoire emphasizes a *nuova cucina* (nouvelle cuisine) that makes use of the freshest ingredients. The wine selections are excellent.
- **Ristorante Tivoli, Cortina d'Ampezzo.** This charming and friendly restaurant, a cozy chalet on a hillside above the town, serves superb food. From the bustling kitchen emerge such dishes as stuffed rabbit in an onion sauce, filet of veal with pine nuts and basil, or else a delectable saffron-flavored salmon.

- **Ristorante Emiliano, Stresa.** Overlooking the soothing waters of Lake Garda, this restaurant caters to conservative clients from throughout Northern Europe who come to the Italian lake district for R&R. Recipes adhere to the traditions of the Emilia-Romagna region, which is known for its pastas, sausage, and cheeses.
- **Peck's Restaurant, Milan.** In the 19th century, an entrepreneur from Prague moved to Lombardy and founded the most upscale delicatessen (Peck's) in Milan. His organization also manages this sumptuously elegant restaurant. You're likely to dine surrounded by the business moguls who run Italy. The chefs are among the most skillful in Lombardy.
- **Ristorante da Vittorio, Bergamo.** Set on a busy commercial boulevard in a town known for its feudal fortifications, this restaurant stresses regional cuisine with an array of risottos, pastas, and game dishes.
- **L'Aquila Negra, Mantua.** To reach this restaurant, which used to be a Renaissance palace, you'll have to meander through a labyrinth of narrow alleyways in the historic heart of Mantua. Inside, the high-ceilinged rooms offer elegant food, served with dignified panache by a well-trained staff.
- **Ristorante Vecchia Lanterna, Turin.** Its interior is loaded with ornate 19th-century furniture, belle-époque lighting fixtures, and art nouveau accessories that have long added charm to the elegant dinners consumed here. Food is rich, savory, and permeated with a bourgeois flair.
- **Gran Grotto, Genoa.** Despite the excellence of its cuisine, this eatery manages to remain lighthearted, irreverent, and richly connected to the seafaring life of this ancient Italian port. The zuppa di pesce (a Riviera version of a Marseillaise bouillabaisse) is worth the trip to Genoa.

5 The Best Romantic Getaways

These destinations are known throughout the world as restful, enchanting, secluded places to recuperate from stress and, under optimum circumstances, rejuvenate a romance.

- **Capri.** Floating amid azure seas south of Naples, Capri is often referred to as the "Island of Dreams." Roman emperors Augustus and Tiberius both came here for R&R, and since the late 1800s, celebrities have flocked here for an escape. A boat ride around the island's rugged coastline is one of my favorite things to do in Capri.
- **Taormina, Sicily.** One of the three or four most charming places on Sicily, this resort is loaded with regional charm, chiseled stonework, and a sense of the ages. Favored by wealthy Europeans and dedicated artists, especially in midwinter when the climate is delightful, it's a fertile oasis of olive groves, grape vines, and orchards. Visitors will relish the delights of the sun, the sea, and the medieval setting.
- **Portofino.** It's probably the most famous small port in the world, largely because of the well-preserved buildings surrounding its small, circular harbor. Located 22 miles southeast of Genoa, in the heart of the Italian Riviera, it's charming, chic, and cosmopolitan. A cluster of topnotch hotels cater to the very rich and famous.
- **Ravello, Campania.** It's small, sunny, and loaded with notable buildings (such as its cathedral, founded in 1086). Despite its choice position on

the Amalfi coast, it manages to retain the aura of an old-fashioned village. Such famous residents as writer Gore Vidal live high in the hills above town.

- **Spoleto, Umbria.** It's as ancient as the Roman Empire, and as timeless as the music that is presented here every summer during its world-renowned arts festival. Considered the quintessential Umbrian hill town, its architecture has changed very little, and is centered around a core of religious buildings dating from the 13th century. It's less chic but more romantic during off-season, when the crowds are less dense.

6 The Best Castelli and Palazzi

The dynastic and territorial conflicts of Italy were among the most plentiful in European history. The warlike atmosphere forced people to fortify themselves from attacks by outsiders. As civilization progressed, the thick walls of *castelli* (fortified castles) were replaced by the *palazzi* of such Renaissance robber barons as the Medici, the Barberini, the Farnese, and the Borgia families. More or less assured of their status, these families placed less focus on defensive fortifications and more emphasis on comfort and opulence.

- **Palazzo Vecchio, Florence.** Built over a 15-year period beginning in 1299, it dominates one of the most memorable piazzas in Italy. Originally intended as an administration building, it was transformed 200 years later into the private residence of Cosimo I of the Medici family. Despite its inner luxury and the airy spaciousness of its courtyard, it has no windows on its ground floor, a reminder of the feudal sense of fortification.

- **Palazzo Ducale, Mantua.** One of Mantua's most impressive showcases, this palazzo was created in the 1500s by joining a newly built palace with a Renaissance chapel and a 200-year-old stone fortress. Inside, many of the walls and ceilings are lavishly adorned with *trompe l'oeil* frescoes and carved and gilded plaster, some of it commissioned by the palace's most legendary occupant, Isabelle d'Este, and some of it executed by Mantegna.

- **Castel Sant'Angelo, Rome.** Originating as a mausoleum in A.D. 135 for Hadrian and his family, it was enlarged by Gregory the Great in the 500s, who added a Christian chapel to its uppermost floor. Nine hundred years later, Pope Nicholas V added a brick upper story and angular towers. Later popes added a bridge across the Tiber (complete with stone angels carved by Bernini), and some of the most luxurious apartments in Christendom.

- **Villa d'Este, Tivoli.** Italian cardinal Hippolyte d'Este decided to retire in the countryside near Tivoli, outside Rome. While building his villa, he created an exquisite garden, where scores of ornate fountains and waterfalls continue to delight visitors to this day. Some travelers consider it one of their favorite spots in all of Italy.

- **Palazzo Ducale, The Doge's Palace, Venice.** Built in the 1100s, and radically upgraded between 1400 and 1550, it functioned as the court, prison, seat of government, and the residence of the Venetian doge (ruling prince) during the most glorious years of Venetian history. Designed as a massive block of pink and white geometric patterns poised atop 36 delicately carved columns, it's surpassed in grandeur only by the city's cathedral.

7 The Best Museums

Although some fans argue that the entire Italian peninsula is a display of human civilization, the country's museums are incomparable. You're likely to stumble upon many of them in out-of-the-way places, but here is a short list of the country's best.

- **Bargello Palace and Museum, Florence.** Severely angular, its 12th-century exterior is permeated with the raw power of the governing magistrate who built it in the heart of Florence. Today, its collection of sculpture and decorative accessories is without equal in Italy.

- **Pitti Palace, Florence.** The spheres of influence that dominated Florence during its most creative years revolved around the Medicis and the Pittis, two families who ruled the city from their respective banks of the Arno. The Pittis moved into this palazzo in 1560, after it was enlarged with two new wings. Today, it houses a museum containing everything from paintings by old masters (such as Raphael and Titian), to works by modern artists, and a collection of antique silver.

- **Pinacoteca di Brera, Milan.** Though Milan is usually associated with wealth and corporate power, it contains a worthy assortment of cultural icons as well. Foremost among these is the Brera Picture Gallery (Pinacoteca di Brera), whose collection—set within a 17th-century palace—is especially rich in paintings from the schools of Lombardy and Venice.

- **Museo Archeologico Nazionale (National Archeological Museum), Naples.** Naples and the region around it have yielded more sculptural treasures from the ancient Roman Empire than anywhere else in Italy. Many of these riches have been accumulated in a rambling building originally designed as a barracks for the Neapolitan cavalry in the 1500s. Today, much of the loot excavated from Pompeii and Herculaneum, as well as the Renaissance collections of the Farnese family, lie within this museum, which boasts one of the richest troves of Greco-Roman antiquities in the world.

- **Galleria Nazionale dell'Umbria (National Gallery of Umbria), Perugia.** Italian Renaissance art has roots in the Tuscan and Umbrian painting of the 1200s. This collection, set on the uppermost floor of the Palazzo dei Priori (parts of which date from the 1400s), contains a world-class collection of paintings, most executed in Tuscany or Umbria between the 13th and 18th century. The museum contains works by Perugino, Piero della Francesco, Duccio, Fra Angelico, and Benozzo Gozzoli, among others.

- **Musei Vaticani (Vatican Museums), Vatican City.** Rambling, disjointed, and unbelievably well-stocked with the artistic treasures accumulated over the centuries by the popes, this complex contains some of the most famous attractions of Italy. Among them are the Sistine Chapel, such sculptures as *Laocoön and his Sons* and the *Belvedere Apollo*, buildings whose walls were almost completely executed by Raphael, and endless collections of art which range from (very pagan) Greco-Roman antiquities to Christian art by famous European masters.

- **Galleria degli Uffizi (Uffizi Museum and Gallery), Florence.** This 16th-century Renaissance palace functioned as the administrative headquarters, or office (*uffizi*), for the Medici's administration of Florence. It's estimated that up to 90% of Italy's artistic patrimony is stored within this building, the crown jewel of Italy's museums. (The Uffizi was the target of a very destructive car bomb that caused considerable damage in 1993, but most exhibits are open.)

- **Museo Nazionale di Villa Giulia, Rome.** Mysterious and for the most part undocumented, the Etruscans were the ancestors of the ancient Romans who later conquered most of the known world. They left a legacy of bronze and marble sculpture, sarcophagi, jewelry, and representations of mythical heros, some of which were excavated at Cerveteri, an Etruscan stronghold north of Rome. Most startling about the artifacts is their sophisticated, almost mystical sense of design. The building that houses this collection was a papal villa in the 1500s.

- **Gallerie dell'Accademia (Academy of Fine Arts), Venice.** It's one of the most richly stocked art museums in Italy, boasting hundreds of paintings, many of them Venetian, executed between 1300 and 1790. Among the highlights here are works by Bellini, Giorgione, Carpaccio, and Titian.

- **Museo Poldi-Pezzoli (Poldi-Pezzoli Museum), Milan.** In 1881, this museum's namesake donated his extensive art collection to his home town, thereby creating the base for one of Italy's most influential museums. The collection includes Persian carpets, portraits by Cranach of Martin Luther and his wife, works by Botticelli and Bellini, and massive amounts of decorative art, including furniture.

8 The Best Cathedrals

As the home of many of Christianity's most important monuments, Italy has always combined a reverence for churches with a vivid sense of architectural showmanship. The result has been some of the most spectacular cathedrals in the world.

- **St. Francis' Basilica, Assisi.** St. Francis, protector of small animals and birds, was long dead when construction began on this double-tiered showcase of the Franciscan brotherhood. Interior decoration, in many cases by Cimabue and Giotto, reached a new kind of figurative realism in Italian art around 1300, long before later masters of the Renaissance carried the technique even further. Consecrated in 1253, the cathedral is considered one of the highlights of Umbria, and the site of many religious pilgrimages.

- **Il Duomo (Santa Maria del Fiore), Florence.** Begun in the final years of the 1200s, and consecrated 140 years later, it was a symbol of the prestige and wealth of Florence. With an exterior of pink, green, and white marble, and loaded with world-class art, it's one of the largest and most distinctive religious buildings in Italy. A view of its dome, erected over a 14-year period in what was at the time a radical new design by Brunelleschi, is worth the trip to Florence. Other elements of the Duomo include the Campanile (one of the most charming bell towers in Italy), and the Baptistery (a Romanesque outbuilding with renowned bronze doors and a sheath of green and white marble).

- **Il Duomo, Milan.** Begun in 1386, and finally completed in 1809 on orders of Napoleon, Il Duomo of Milan is an ornate and unusual building. Massed around a triangular gable bristling with 135 pointed and chiselled spires, it's both massive and airy at the same time. The interior is as severe as its exterior is ornate. One of the most remarkable buildings in Italy, it's often overlooked.

- **Il Duomo, Orvieto.** Considered a well-designed transition between the Romanesque and Gothic styles, this cathedral was begun in 1290 and completed in 1600. It sheltered an Italian pope (Clement VII) when Rome was sacked by French soldiers in 1527. Part of the building's mystery derives from Orvieto's role as an Etruscan stronghold long before Italy's recorded history.
- **Basilica di San Pietro (St. Peter's Basilica), The Vatican, Rome.** Its roots began with the first Christian emperor, Constantine, in A.D. 324. By 1400, the Roman basilica was in danger of collapsing, prompting the Renaissance popes to commission plans for the largest, most impressive cathedral that the world had ever seen. Amid the rich decor of gilt, marble, and mosaics, are countless art works, including Michelangelo's *Pietà.* Other sights here are a small museum of Vatican treasures and the eerie, underground grottoes containing the tombs of former popes. An elevator ride (or rigorous climb) up the tower to Michelangelo's dome provides breathtaking views of Rome.

9 The Best Ruins

During the 18th century, no self-respecting aristocrat from England or Germany would dream of entering middle age without a tour through the ruins of the ancient world, perhaps picking up a load of ancient Greek or Roman mementoes en route. Here is a list of the ruins they were bound to have visited.

- **Herculaneum (Ercolano), Campania.** Legend says that it was founded by Hercules. The historical facts tell us that it was buried under rivers of volcanic mud one fateful day in A.D. 79 after the eruption of Vesuvius. Seeping into the cracks of virtually every building in town, the scalding mud preserved the timbers of hundreds of structures that would otherwise have rotted in the normal course of time. Devote at least two hours to seeing some of the best-preserved houses to survive from the ancient world.
- **Ostia (Ostia Antica), Latium.** During the height of the Roman Empire, Ostia (whose name is "mouth" in Latin) was the harbor town set at the point where the Tiber flowed into the sea. As Rome declined, so did Ostia. By the early middle ages, with a population decimated by malaria, the town almost disappeared. In the early 1900s archaeologists excavated the ruins of hundreds of ancient buildings, many of which can be viewed.
- **Paestum, Campania.** Paestum was discovered by accident around 1750, when local bureaucrats tried to build a road across the heart of what had been a thriving ancient city. Paestum originated as a Greek colony around 600 B.C., fell to the Romans in 273 B.C., and declined into obscurity in the final days of the Empire. Today, amateur archaeologists can follow a well-marked walking tour through the excavations.
- **Pompeii, Campania.** Once it was an opulent resort filled with 25,000 wealthy Romans. In A.D. 79, the same eruption which devastated Herculaneum (see above) buried Pompeii under at least 20 feet of scalding volcanic ash. Beginning around 1750, Charles of Bourbon ordered the systematic excavation of the ruins—the treasures hauled out of Pompeii sparked a wave of interest throughout northern Europe in the neoclassical era.
- **Roman Forum (Il Foro Romano), Rome.** Two thousand years ago, most of the known world was directly affected by decisions made in the Roman Forum. Today, classicists and archaeologists wander among its ruins, conjuring up the glory that was Rome. What you'll see today is a pale, rubble-strewn version of

the site's original majesty—it's now surrounded by modern boulevards packed with whizzing cars.

- **The Palatine Hill (Il Palatino), Rome.** According to legend, this hillock was the site where Romulus and Remus (the orphaned infant twins who survived in the wild by suckling a she-wolf) eventually founded the city. Though it's one of the seven hills of ancient Rome, it's hard to distinguish it as such because of the urban congestion that rises all around it. Despite that, scholars come to pay frequent homage. The site is enhanced by the presence of the Farnese Gardens (Orti Farnesiani), laid out in the 1500s on the site of Tiberius's palace.

- **The Coliseum (Il Coliseo), Rome.** Rome boasts only a handful of other ancient monuments that survive in such well-preserved condition. A massive amphitheater set incongruously amid a maze of modern traffic, it once was the setting for gladiator combat, lion-feeding frenzies, and public entertainment whose cruelty was a noted characteristic of the Roman Empire. All three of the ancient world's classical styles (Doric, Ionic, and Corinthian) are superimposed in tiers, one above the other.

- **Hadrian's Villa (Villa Adriana), near Tivoli.** It slumbered in rural obscurity until the 1500s, when Renaissance popes ordered its excavation. Only then was the scale of this massive and very beautiful villa from A.D. 134 appreciated. Its builder was Hadrian, who had visited almost every part of his empire, and who wanted to incorporate the widespread wonders of the world into one fantastic building site.

- **Valley of the Temples (Valle dei Templi), Agrigento, Sicily.** Though most of it lies in ruins, this is one of the most beautiful and evocative classical sites in Europe, especially in February and March when the almond trees surrounding it burst into pink blossoms. One of the site's quintet of temples dates from as early as 520 B.C.; another—although never completed—ranks as one of the largest temples in the ancient world.

- **Segesta, near Trapani, Sicily.** Even its site is impressive: a rocky outcropping surrounded on most sides by a jagged ravine. Built around 430 B.C. by the Greeks, its Doric colonnade is one of the most graceful in the ancient world. Believed to have been destroyed by the Saracens (Muslim raiders) in the 11th century, Segesta is stark, mysterious, and highly evocative of the ancient world.

- **Selinunte, near Castelvetrano, Sicily.** Although its massive columns lie scattered on the ground, as if an earthquake had punished its builders, this is one of our favorite ancient ruins in Italy. Built by immigrants from Syracuse into an important trading port around 600 B.C., and a bitter rival of the neighboring city of Segesta (see above), it was destroyed around 400 B.C., and again in 250 B.C. by the Carthaginians.

10 The Best Wineries

Italy has thousands of vineyards, many of which have been run by families for generations. Here is a guide (geographically listed) to the major wine-growing regions of Italy, with a short list of the best and most interesting vineyards within each region.

- **Alto Adige.** Once considered part of the Austro-Hungarian province of the South Tyrol, this wine-growing region lies near Bolzano in Italy's extreme north. More Germanic than Italian, it clings to its Austrian traditions and folklore, and grows an Italian version of the *gewürtztraminers* (a fruity white wine) that would more often be found in Germany, Austria, and Alsace. Venerable wine grow-ers include Alois Lageder (founded in 1855), and the Schloss Turmhof, in Entiklar, both near Bolzano. This latter boasts a castle that exudes Teutonic history and some of the highest-altitude vineyards in the South Tyrol. For information, contact Alois Lageder, 235 Viale Druso, 39100 Bolzano (☎ 0471/920164) or Schloss Turmhof, Entiklar, Kurtatsch, 39040 (☎ 0471/880122).

- **Friuli-Venezia Giulia and Veneto.** Comprised of mostly white wines from ad-jacent zones in northeastern Italy, these vintages are light, fruity, and very appealing when young. One of the most important vineyards in Friuli-Venezia (near the Slovenian border) is Livio Felluga, near Gorizia. For information, con-tact Livio Felluga, 1 Via Risorgimento, Brazzano di Cormons, 34071 Gorizia (☎ 0481/630126).

  Important vineyards within the flat, humid borders of the Veneto region in-clude Nino Franco (known for its sparkling prosecco), in the hamlet of Valdobbiadene, 31049 Treviso (☎ 0423/972051). Also appealing are the vine-yards of Masi/Gargagnago di Valpolicella, whose output includes soave whites and valpolicella reds. For information, contact the region's Azienda di Promozione Turistica, 61 Via Leoncino, 37121 Verona (☎ 045/592828).

- **The Piedmont.** Most of the output includes reds with rich and complex flavors fostered by the rolling hills of this rugged region near Italy's border with France. One of the most interesting vineyards is headquartered in a 15th-century abbey near the hamlet of Alba. For information, contact the Antiche Cantine dell'Annunziata, Abbazia dell'Annunziata, La Morra, 12064 Cuneo (☎ 0173/50185).

- **Lombardy.** The fertile soil of the Po valley has always been known for its flat vistas, its midsummer humidity, and its excellent wines. The region produces everything from dry flat reds to sparkling whites whose zest resembles that of champagne. One of Italy's largest wineries (Guido Berlucchi, 4 Piazza Duranti, Borgonato di Cortefranca, 25040 Brescia [☎ 030/984381]) is especially will-ing to receive visitors.

- **Tuscany and Umbria.** Some of Italy's most scenic vineyards lie nestled among the verdant and rolling hills of two of its most stately provinces. Virtually any winery in either of the two districts is likely to be permeated with history and local character, but one of the most appealing in Umbria is Azienda Vallesant di Luigi Barberani, Azienda Agricola Vallesant, Loc. Cerreto, Baschi, 05023 Terni (☎ 0763/41820). In Tuscany, one of the province's largest vintners is the Villa Banfi, S.p.A Castello Banfi, Sant'Angelo Scalo, Montalcino, 53020 Siena (☎ 0577/840111).

- **Campania.** The wines produced in the harsh, hot landscapes of Campania, around Naples in southern Italy, seem stronger, rougher, and in many cases more powerful than those produced in gentler climes. Among the most famous are the *lacryma cristi* (Tears of Christ), a white that grows in the volcanic soil near Naples, Herculaneum, and Pompeii; a potent red (*taurasi*); and a pungent white laden with the odors of apricots and apples, the *greco di tufo*, whose scent is particularly wonderful when consumed with local anchovies and salted cheese. One of the most frequently visited vineyards of Campania is Mastroberardino, 75 via Manfredi, Atripalda, 80342 Avellino (☎ 0825/626123).

- **Sicily.** Its hot climate and volcanic soil foster the growth of more vineyards than any other region of Italy. Most of these are devoted to the production of simple table wines that are used to add bulk to blends in Italy's more prosperous north. Of the better vintages, the best-known wines are marsala and, to a lesser extent, muscat dessert wines. Marsala, a heady wine whose alcoholic content is sometimes enhanced with additives, was first discovered by 19th-century British visitors. A vineyard that produces this wine is Corvo Duca di Salaparuta, a 19th-century winery set in the hills above Palermo. For information, contact Vini Corvo, Via Nazionale, S113, Casteldaccia, 90014 Palermo (☎ 091/ 953988). A leading competitor, also near Palermo, is Regaleali, a historic enterprise maintained by the Tasca d'Alerita family. Known mainly for its still and sparkling whites (Nozze d'Oro) and to a lesser extent its reds (Rosso del Conte) and rosés, it welcomes visitors. For information, contact Regaleali, Contrada Regaleali, Vallelunga, 90020 Palermo (☎ 0921/542522).

11 The Best Countryside to Explore by Car

What's the best way to drive through the spectacular landscape of Italy? Gesticulate wildly with one hand, hold the steering wheel with the other, and do your best to avoid colliding with the hysterical traffic around you. Once you get used to the narrow roads, blind corners, and breakneck speeds, you might actually find it fun.

- **Abruzzi Massif.** A short drive southeast of Rome, amid the highest of the Apennine mountain range, this landlocked district boasts an odd, arid topography riddled with underground caverns, mountains, lakes, gullies, high plateaus, and fertile grazing fields. Looking for scenery and Italian traditions? Devote two days to circumnavigating the Abruzzi Massif, incorporating such towns as L'Aquila, Fonte Cerreto, and Castelli, and on a more southerly loop, Scanno, Pescocostanzo, Sulmona, and Castel di Sangro. Other than a peek at local culture, none of the individual towns will be overwhelmingly interesting, but the route passes through the most savage landscapes of the *Parco Nazionale d'Abruzzo*, with its bizarrely striated rock walls, clannish local families, and 155 square miles of mostly beech and maple forests.

- **The Amalfi Coast.** This road rims a wedge-shaped peninsula jutting westward from a position south of Naples. Since the days of the Roman empire, its sweeping views over rock cliffs down to the sea and its healthful climate have personified everything that is beautiful and glorious about southern Italy. There's a cliché about this road that originated during the 18th-century grand tours of the Continent: "See Amalfi and die." True, the drive is aesthetically thrilling, but because of speeding traffic and death-inducing cliffs both above and below the roadside, you'd better remain more alert along this scenic drive than almost anywhere else in Italy. The road cuts through the jagged coastline between Sorrento and Salerno. Though it's only 19 miles, it seems longer because of the wealth of panoramas that unfold along every bend. Charming (and often crowded) villages en route include Ravello, Positano, and Amalfi.

- **The Dolomite Road.** This drive follows a medieval trading route used many centuries ago through the mountainous landscapes of the Dolomites between Venice and cities of the German-speaking world. (Motorists usually consider Bolzano and Cortina d'Ampezzo as the two points of the route, and allow two days for its 130-mile transit.) It's considered one of the best examples of road engineering in Italy, traversing rugged terrain over many terraces and bridges, and through tunnels. You can detour from your drive by taking at least two cable car rides up to points of panoramic beauty (beginning at Malga Ciapela and at Ortisei, respectively), although most visitors find the view from their rented automobiles to be quite panoramic itself.

- **The Philaegrean Fields (Campi Flegrei).** Bubbling and steaming with geologic emissions, and rich in sites whose architecture was developed by the ancient Greeks and Romans, this is one of the weirdest excursions in Italy. The instability of the region (whose altitude above sea level changes by several inches at regular intervals) can be taken as a metaphor for the sociological turmoil of Naples itself, with its horrendous traffic. The two points of the 30-mile drive are Naples and the seaside village of Cuma. The route includes views of a semi-extinct volcano (Solfatara), which last erupted in the 1200s, but has belched odorous gases ever since.

  One of the region's highlights is the Greek colony of Cuma (sometimes spelled Cumae), founded in the 8th century B.C. and believed to be the oldest archaeological site in Italy. En route, you'll pass through the town of Pozzuoli, site of a massive ancient Roman amphitheater, and hometown of Sophia Loren. Lago d'Averna, another crater lake you'll see en route, was believed by Cicero to be the entrance to the Underworld.

- **Castelli Romani.** Set southeast of Rome, this district was the preferred hideaway of dozens of Roman families during the early middle ages. Escaping the growing anarchy of Rome, they founded scores of castles (*castelli*) as semi-fortified retreats. Today, these castelli are hill towns, each with a lore and legend of its own.

  Although the round-trip distance is less than 80 miles, it's worth spending an entire day in this region. Highlights include the archaeological digs of the Via Appia; Castel Gandolfo (home of the Villa Barberini, summer residence of the Pope); Nemi (site of an interesting museum); Grottaferrata, whose abbey was founded in the 1100s; Frascati, site of famous vineyards and the 17th-century Villa Aldobrandini; and Palestrina, site of a rebuilt Roman temple (Fortuna Primigenia) and the Barberini Palace.

12 The Best Offbeat Trips

As a country of individualists, Italy presents more offbeat activities than you can imagine.

- **A motor trip around the Gargano Promontory.** Only a handful of visitors take the time to explore this wild region of Italy's deep south. Set along the country's southeastern coast, directly east of Naples, it projects like a spur from the "boot" of Italy (across from what used to be known as Yugoslavia). A region of limestone caves and relative poverty, it contains unspoiled scenery and such towns as Peschici, Vieste, Mattinata, and the region's spiritual centerpiece, *Testa del Gargano*, a rocky promontory at the region's easternmost tip, which juts out into the Adriatic Sea.

- **Short-term seclusion on the Lipari (Aeolian) Islands.** Set north of Sicily and west of Italy's "toe," these islands were believed to be the home of Aeolus, the god of the winds. The island group is composed of seven members (Alicudi, Filicudi, Lipari, Panarea, Salina, Stromboli, and Vulcano), each of which evokes scenes of North Africa more than Italy. The islands that are the largest, most interesting, and most favored by wealthy Italians are Vulcano and Stromboli; both have been the site of recent investments.

- **Sailing the Seas around Italy.** The four subdivisions of the Mediterranean that surround Italy are the Ionian, the Adriatic, the Ligurian, and the Tyrrhenian. Each area abounds in ports, estuaries, and harbors that have sheltered foreign sailors for thousands of years.

  Words of advice for mariners in Italian waters: Ensure that at least one member of your yachting party speaks and understands Italian for translation of short-wave radio broadcasts and for negotiations with local harbor authorities. Schedule your visit for anytime other than August, when dock and anchorage space becomes less widely available and more expensive. And if you're interested in canoeing or kayaking, look no further than the Veneto, the flat and often humid region of northeastern Italy, where a series of lagoons, rivers, lakes, and saltwater estuaries provides ample sites for practicing your sport. These include the region around Lake Garda, near Verona, and the many lagoons along the Adriatic coast.

  For information on canoeing and kayaking (and schools that teach canoeing), contact the Federazione Italiana Canoe e Kayak, Viale Tiziano 70, 00196 Roma, Italy (☎ 06/368-58525).

- **Hiking along the Cinque Terre.** Set on a 15-mile stretch of rocky coastline along the Ligurian Sea, Cinque Terre is composed of five different fishing villages which, until recently, were accessible only by boat or donkey. Despite its charms, it remains relatively ignored by most vacationers. Its residents make a living by farming and fishing. As such, the region offers unusual insights into an old-fashioned Italian culture. Largest of the villages is Monterosso al Mare (accessible by train and car) and Manarola (accessible by car). Either of these would be suitable departure points for hikes along the clifftops to the hamlet of Vernazza, which some visitors consider the most colorful of the five villages. Lodgings are dull and basic, but there are plenty of places to buy picnic ingredients, and the views of the sea and the terraced hillsides are invigorating.

13 The Best Ski Areas

Despite the midsummer heat of the country's central and southern districts, Italy's mountainous northern regions offer lots of opportunities for skiing.

- **Cervinia, Valle d'Aosta.** Set within the shadow of the Matterhorn (whose opposite side looms over Zermatt, in Switzerland), Cervinia is modern, urbanized, and very capable of hosting glamorous holidays in the snow. Altitudes begin at over 6,500 feet above sea level, and the network of ski lifts carries enthusiasts over a wide "snow bunny" terrain.

- **Cortina d'Ampezzo, Veneto.** Set across the border from Austria, Cortina has been celebrated by skiers and climbers since the mid–19th century, when the English and Germans first discovered its charms. Today, it's a stylish enclave where everyone seems to enjoy the bracing climate and well-upholstered surroundings. Four distinctly different ski areas compete for attention.

- **Courmayeur, Valle d'Aosta.** Courmayeur lies in the center of a dozen mountain peaks, each of whose 13,000-foot altitude guarantees plenty of snowfall. Downhill skiing is supplemented by many cross-country trails, and skiing on a nearby glacier (the Gigante) is a popular activity even during the summer.

2 Getting to Know Italy

Conquerors, scholars, artists, and saints as well as curious travelers have been drawn to Italy for centuries. Across turbulent seas and stormy mountains, they came, even risking their lives to see Italy. Getting there by plane, sea, rail, or car is considerably easier today, but the age-old attraction remains.

Some have been fascinated by its people, including the novelist E. M. Forster, who wrote that the Italians were "more marvellous than the land." Others have been drawn to its artistic treasures, left by geniuses like Leonardo da Vinci and Michelangelo.

Although ancient, Italy is still a relatively modern country in terms of political unity. As late as the 19th century, the prominent Austrian statesman Prince Metternich dismissed it as no more than a "geographical expression." Unlike the rest of Europe, Italy was late in developing a national identity. It wasn't until 1870 that the country's 20 regions were united under one central government. Although Italy may be a late bloomer among European nations, its culture has flourished since antiquity, and no country in the world has as many reminders of its cultural heritage as does Italy. They range from Rome's Colosseum to Sicily's Greek ruins.

Other visitors come to Italy for the scenery. As any Italian will confide, "Italy is the world's most beautiful country," with cypress-studded landscapes, coastal coves, jagged Dolomite peaks, fishing ports, sandy beaches, and charming little hill towns whose historic cores haven't changed much in hundreds of years.

Many travelers visit Italy just to have fun, and given that country's sense of *la dolce vita*, that goal is almost guaranteed. Other, more serious visitors come here to immerse themselves in its history and culture, and most of them leave thinking Italy is one of the world's most rewarding travel destinations.

1 The Regions in Brief

Italy is about the size of the state of Arizona. The peninsula shape, however, gives visitors the impression of a much larger area; the ever-changing sea coast contributes to this feeling, as do the large islands of Sicily and Sardinia. Bordered on the northwest by France, on the north by Switzerland and Austria, and on the east by Slovenia (formerly part of Yugoslavia), Italy is still a land largely surrounded by the sea.

❓ Did You Know?

- The tomato, that quintessentially Italian vegetable, was brought to Europe from North America in the 16th century.
- About 60% of Italy's historical and artistic treasures are not on view, but are kept in storerooms and warehouses.
- Italians made the first super-spectacle, a nine-reel blockbuster, *Quo Vadis,* released in 1912.
- Spaghetti was introduced from China by Marco Polo.
- The wife of slain dictator Benito Mussolini ran a trattoria in northern Italy for many years after the end of World War II; in 1992 her granddaughter, Alessandra Mussolini, won a seat in Parliament as a member of the neo-Fascist party.
- Every 30 or 40 minutes, somewhere in Italy, a historical trophy or work of art disappears.

Two areas within the boundaries of Italy not under the control of the Italian government are the State of Vatican City and the Republic of San Marino. The 109 acres of Vatican City in Rome were established in 1929 by a concordat, or formal agreement, between Pope Pius XI and Benito Mussolini, acting as head of the Italian government; the agreement also gave the Roman Catholic religion special status in the country. The pope is the sovereign of the State of Vatican City, which has its own legal system and its own post office.

Abruzzi   Set to the east and southeast of Rome, within central Italy's rugged core, the Abruzzi is one of the poorest and least-visited regions in Italy. Arid and sun-scorched, it's the home of one of the peninsula's largest national forests (Abruzzi National Park), the Gran Sasso mountain range, and such battered resorts as L'Aquila. Prone to frequent earthquakes, the Abruzzi is proud but impoverished and visually stark. Many of its people have emigrated to more prosperous regions of the peninsula.

Aosta Valley (Val d'Aosta)   The smallest region of Italy, the Val d'Aosta is a semi-autonomous, high-altitude region of towering peaks and valleys in northwestern Italy. Known for its sunshine and the ancient French-derived dialect of its citizens, it's probably more closely linked to France (especially the French alpine region of the Savoy) than to any other region of Europe, including Italy. Rich in scenery, dairy products, and wine, its most important (and interesting) city is the ancient Roman city of Aosta. Its famous ski resorts include Courmayeur and Breuil-Cervinia. Many of the region's villages are crafted from gray rocks culled from the mountains that rise on all sides. Among these are the Matterhorn and Mont Blanc, parts of which lie across the border in Switzerland and France, respectively.

Apulia   Sun-drenched and poor, and forming the heel of the Italian boot, Apulia is the most frequently visited province of Italy's Deep South. Part of its allure lies in its string of resorts, which line the elongated seacoast. It was the site of some of the most morbid and costliest battles of the Middle Ages. Depending on the dialect you're hearing, the region is referred to as Puglia, Le Puglie, or Apulia. The li" houses of Alberobello are known for their unique cylindrical shapes and conical, flagstone-sheathed roofs. Among the region's largest cities are Bari (the capital), Foggia, and Brindisi (gateway to nearby Greece, with which the town shares many characteristics).

Basilicata   The smallest region of Italy's Deep South, Basilicata is the poorest part of the Italian peninsula, a mountain region with coastlines along both the Ionian and the Tyrrhenian Seas. The region isn't rich in Renaissance charm, but contains ample insights into a simple way of life that has disappeared in the more prosperous regions of Italy.

Calabria   The extreme southwestern region of Italy (the toe of Italy's boot) is agrarian, impoverished, cruelly hot in summertime, and, to an alarming extent, almost devoid of younger people who flee to other regions. Considered a stronghold of the Mafia (referred to locally as the *'ndrangheta)*, the region reinforces many of the southern Italian stereotypes the visitor hears about in the industrial north. Life revolves around age-old villages with a somber style of architecture. Cosenza is the district's largest city, and Reggio di Calabria its capital and a port of ferryboat embarkation for nearby Sicily. Local spokespersons hope that a handful of modest beach resorts (Locri, Rossano, Praia a Mare, Cirello, and Pizzo) will lure holidaymakers to the province.

Campania   More than any other region of Italy, Campania reverberates with the memories of the ancient Romans, who favored its strong sunlight, fertile soil, and bubbling sulphurous springs. It manages to incorporate the anarchy of Naples with the elegant beauty of Capri and the Amalfi coast. The district also contains many sites specifically identified in ancient mythology (lakes defined as the entrance to the Kingdom of the Dead, etc.), and some of the most prolific ancient ruins (including Pompeii and Herculaneum) in the world. The region is divided into five different provinces: Avellino, Benevento, Caserta, Naples, and Salerno.

Emilia-Romagna   Italians seem to agree on only one thing: That food in Emilia-Romagna is the best in Italy. Its capital, Bologna, boasts a stunning Renaissance core with plenty of majestic churches and arcades, a fine university with roots in the early middle ages, and a populace with a reputation for leftist leanings. Irrigated by the Po, it's a region of flat and fertile soil and has one of the highest standards of living in Italy. Besides Bologna, highlights include Modena (hometown of opera star Pavarotti and headquarters of Fiat), Parma (a city of magnificent monuments and world headquarters for Parmesan cheese and prosciutto), and such noteworthy art cities as Piacenza, Ferrara, and the ancient Byzantine city of Ravenna. The crowded Adriatic resort of Rimini and the medieval stronghold of San Marino are both at the edge of Emilia-Romagna.

Friuli-Venezia Giulia   Set in the extreme northeastern corner of Italy, adjacent to the border of modern-day Slovenia, this is, in its own way, one of the most cosmopolitan and culturally sophisticated regions of Italy. Set at the crossroads of the Balkans and the Teutonic world, it was highly influenced by the Austro-Hungarian empire. Its capital is the seaport of Trieste, although worthy sites of touristic interest include Udine, Gorizia, and Pordenone. The area is filled with artistic treasures from the Roman, Byzantine, and Romanesque-Gothic eras, and many of the public buildings (especially those of Trieste) might remind you more of Vienna.

Latium   The region of Latium is dominated by Rome, capital of the ancient empire and the modern nation of Italy, and Vatican City, the independent papal state. Containing vast lodes of the world's artistic treasures, Latium is a land of myth, legend, grandeur, and ironies. Much of the civilized world was once ruled from here, going back to the days when Romulus and Remus are said to have founded Rome on April 21, 753 B.C. For generations, Rome was justifiably referred to as *caput mundi* (capital of the world).

Leghorn (Liguria) and the Italian Riviera   Comprising most of the Italian Riviera, the unexpected capital of which is the steeply sloping city of Genoa, this region incorporates medieval ports known for their charm (Portofino, Ventimiglia, and San Remo), a massive naval base known for its raucousness (La Spezia), and a quintet of coastal communities (Cinque Terra) that cling tenaciously to traditional values. There is also a series of belle-époque seaside resorts (Rapallo and Santa Margherita Ligure) whose style and nonchalance are reminiscent of resorts along the nearby French Riviera. Genoa, with its traffic-clogged core, is a blend of tawdriness and splendid Renaissance majesty.

Lombardy   Flat, fertile, prosperous, and politically conservative, Lombardy is dominated by Milan in the same way that Latium is dominated by Rome. Lombardy is one of the world's leading commercial and cultural centers—it has been immersed in the mercantile ethic ever since Milan developed into Italy's gateway to northern, German-speaking Europe during the early Middle Ages. Although it's fashionable to belittle Milan for its industrial power and contempt of poorer regions of Italy's south, its fans compare some of its aspects to New York. Milan's cathedral is the third-largest in Europe, its opera house (La Scala) is the site of some of the finest performances anywhere, and its museums and churches are considered world-class. Other major cities of Lombardy—each filled with the artistic treasures that only centuries of prosperity can bring—include Bergamo, Brescia, Pavia, Cremona, and Mantua. Also appealing are the lakes of Garda and Maggiore, which lie near Lombardy's eastern edge.

The Marches   It's the easternmost province of central Italy, with an economy revolving around the beach resorts of its seacoast (the largest of which include Ancona and the relatively modern town of Pesaro) and tourism to its Renaissance gem, Urbino. The region also contains the ruins of such ancient Roman sites as Urbis Salvia and Macerata.

Molise   Set in the central core of the Italian peninsula, adjacent to the Abruzzi (with which it shares a dialect and many of its characteristics), the Molise is poor, underdeveloped, and frequently ravaged by earthquakes. Many of its older buildings have been replaced with low and unimaginative houses in the cement-block style, and other than a handful of prehistoric excavations, the artistic legacy is relatively uninspired. The province is rarely visited by non-Italians. Major population centers include Termoli, Campobasso, Capracotta, and Isernia.

Piedmont   Set at the extreme northwestern edge of Italy, sharing a set of alpine peaks with France (which in some ways it resembles), the Piedmont was the district from which Italy's dreams of unification spread in 1861. Long under the domination of the Austro-Hungarian empire, the Piedmont enjoys a cuisine laced with alpine cheeses and dairy products. It's proud of its largest city (Torino), which administers a vast industrial empire.

Regions of Italy

Sardinia   Rugged, arid, and notoriously clannish, Sardinia is the second-largest island in the Mediterranean. Certain regions (especially the Costa Smeralda) are about the most chic places to be in the world during August. Populated by a race of people genetically distinct from those inhabiting the Italian peninsula, Sardinia's capital is Cagliari. Cone-shaped towers (*nuraghi*) crafted from huge stone slabs and fortified dwellings of the earliest inhabitants dot the island.

Sicily   The largest island of the Mediterranean, Sicily is a land of beauty, mystery, and world-class monuments. It is endlessly fascinating, a bizarre mixture of bloodlines and architecture from medieval Normandy, Aragonese Spain, Moorish north Africa, and ancient Greece, Phoenicia, and Rome. Since the advent of modern times, part of the island's primitiveness has faded, as thousands of newly arrived cars clog the narrow lanes of its biggest city, Palermo. Although poverty remains widespread, the age-old stranglehold of the Mafia seems less certain because of the increasingly vocal protests of an outraged Italian public. On the eastern edge of the island is Mount Etna, the tallest active volcano in Europe. Many of Sicily's larger cities (Trapani, Catania, and Messina) are relatively unattractive, but areas of ravishing beauty and eerie historic interest include Siracusa, Taormina, Agrigento, and Selinunte.

Trentino-Alto Adige (South Tyrol)   Until this region was annexed by Italy after World War I, it considered itself an integral part of Austria. Despite the changes made almost 80 years ago in the demarcation of the Italian-Austrian border, passions continue to run deep here as family loyalties cling tenaciously to Austrian ways. The region's split personality is enhanced by the mixture of Italian and German spoken on an everyday basis. Also, the architecture dotting the rocky sides of the Dolomites seems mostly influenced by either the chalet or the Austrian *jugendstil* style. Trent is the region's major city, followed by Bolzano (Bozen) and Merano (Meran). The region's most visible resort is the endlessly stylish Cortina d'Ampezzo.

Tuscany   One of the most culturally and politically influential provinces in Italy, the development of Italy without Tuscany is simply unthinkable. Major cities visited by hundreds of thousands of art lovers every year include Florence, Siena, Lucca, and Pisa. And along with Tuscany's neighbor (Umbria, see below), the verdant countryside of this province is probably among the most desirable in the world for the rental of farmhouses and villas.

Umbria   Pastoral, hilly, and fertile, it's more similar to Tuscany than any other province, but with less of a touristic frenzy drawn to its world-class monuments. Its once fortified network of hill towns is considered the most charming in Italy. Crafted from millions of tons of gray-brown rocks, each is a testament to the masonry and architectural skills of many generations of Italian craftsmen.

Impressions

Italy: A paradise inhabited with devils.
—Sir Henry Wotton, letter to Lord Zouche, 1592

Italy is so tender—like cooked macaroni—yards and yards of soft tenderness, raveled round everything.
—D. H. Lawrence, Sea and Sardinia, 1923

Noteworthy examples include Perugia, Gubbio, Assisi, Spoleto (site of the world-renowned annual arts festival), and Orvieto, a mysterious citadel once used as a stronghold by the Etruscans.

Veneto   It sprawls across the verdant hills and flat and fertile plains of northeastern Italy, between the Adriatic, the Dolomites, Verona, and the edges of Lake Garda. Dotted with richly stocked museums and some of the best architecture in Italy, the fortunes of the Veneto revolved, for many generations, in an orbit around Venice. Although the city on the lagoon is by far the most spectacular in the region, worthy (and less frequently visited) competitors include Verona (site of the mythical romance of Romeo and Juliet), Vicenza (home to more Palladian buildings than anywhere else in the world), and Padua.

2 Italy Past & Present

Dateline

- Bronze Age Celts, Teutonic tribes, and others from the Mediterranean and Asia Minor inhabit the peninsula.
- 1000 B.C. Large colonies of Etruscans settle in Tuscany and Campania, quickly subjugating many of the Latin inhabitants of the Italian peninsula.
- 800 B.C. Rome begins to take shape, evolving from a strategically located shepherd village into a magnet for Latin tribes fleeing the Etruscans.
- 600 B.C. Etruscans occupy Rome, designating it the capital of their empire; the city grows rapidly and a major seaport opens at Ostia.
- 510 B.C. The Latin tribes, still centered in Rome, revolt against the Etruscans; alpine Gauls attack from the north; Greeks living in Sicily destroy the Etruscan navy.
- 250 B.C. The Romans, allied to the Greeks, Phoenicians, and native Sicilians, defeat the

continues

THE ETRUSCANS   Among the early inhabitants of Italy, the most significant were the Etruscans—but who were they, actually? No one knows, and the many inscriptions they left behind—mostly on graves—are of no help, since the Etruscan language has never been deciphered by modern scholars. It's thought that they arrived on the eastern coast of Umbria several centuries before Rome was built, which was around 800 B.C. Their religious rites and architecture show an obvious contact with Mesopotamia; the Etruscans may have been refugees from Asia Minor who traveled westward about 1200 to 1000 B.C. Within two centuries they had subjugated Tuscany and Campania and the Villanova tribes who lived there.

While the Etruscans built temples at Tarquinia and Caere (present-day Cerveteri), the few nervous Latin tribes who remained outside their sway gravitated to Rome, then little more than a sheepherding village. As its power grew, however, Rome increasingly profited from the strategically important Tiber crossing where the ancient Salt Way (Via Salaria) turned northeastward toward the Central Apennines.

From their base at Rome, the Latins remained free of the Etruscans until about 600 B.C. But the Etruscan advance was as inexorable, and though the tribes concentrated their forces at Rome for a last stand, they were swept away by the sophisticated Mesopotamian conquerors. The new overlords introduced gold tableware and jewelry, bronze urns and terra-cotta statuary, and the best of Greek and Asia Minor art and culture; they also made Rome the governmental seat of all Latium.

Roma is an Etruscan name, and the kings of Rome had Etruscan names: Numa, Ancus, Tarquinius, even Romulus.

The Estruscans ruled until the Roman revolt around 510 B.C., and by 250 B.C. the Romans and their Campania allies had vanquished the Etruscans, wiping out their language and religion. However, many of the former rulers' manners and beliefs remained, assimilated into the culture. Even today, certain Etruscan customs and bloodlines are believed to exist still in Italy, especially in Tuscany.

THE ROMAN REPUBLIC The Romans increased their power through conquest of neighboring communities in the highlands and became allied with other Latins of the lowlands. They gave to their Latin allies, and then to conquered peoples, partial or complete Roman citizenship, with the obligation of military service. Citizen colonies were set up as settlements of Roman farmers, and many of the famous cities of Italy today originated as colonies. The colonies were for the most part fortified, and they were linked to Rome by military roads.

The stern Roman republic was characterized by belief in the gods, the necessity of learning from the past, strength of the family, education through books and public service, and—most important—obedience. The all-powerful Senate presided as Rome defeated rival powers one after the other and grew to rule the Mediterranean. The Punic Wars with Carthage in the 3rd century B.C. cleared away a major obstacle to Rome's growth, although people said later that Rome's breaking of its treaty with Carthage (which led to the total destruction of that city) put a curse on the Italian city.

ROMAN EMPIRE By 49 B.C., Italy ruled all of the Mediterranean world either directly or indirectly, with all political, commercial, and cultural pathways leading directly to Rome. The possible wealth and glory to be found in Rome lured many there, but drained other Italian communities of human resources, while foreign imports, particularly in the field of agriculture, hurt local farmers and landowners. Municipal governments faltered and civil wars ensued. Public order was restored by the Caesars (planned by Julius but brought to fruition under Augustus). On the eve of the birth of Christ, Rome was a mighty empire whose generals

Etruscans; Rome flourishes and begins the accumulation of a vast empire.

- **49 B.C.** Italy (through Rome) controls the entire Mediterranean world.

- **44 B.C.** Julius Caesar assassinated; his successor, Augustus, transforms Rome from a city of brick to a city of marble.

- **3rd century A.D.** Rome declines under a series of incompetent and corrupt emperors.

- **4th century A.D.** Rome is fragmented politically as administrative capitals are established in such cities as Milan and Trier, Germany.

- **A.D. 395** The empire splits; Constantine establishes a "New Rome" at Constantinople (Byzantium); Goths successfully invade Rome's northern provinces.

- **410–455** Rome is sacked by barbarians.

- **475** Rome falls, leaving only the primate of the Catholic Church in control; the pope slowly adopts many of the powers once reserved for the Roman emperor.

- **800** Charlemagne is crowned Holy Roman Emperor by Pope Leo III; Italy dissolves into a series of small warring kingdoms.

- **Late 11th century** The popes function like secular princes with private armies.

- **1065** The Holy Land falls to the Muslim Turks; the Crusades are launched.

- **1303–77** Papal schism; the pope and his entourage move from Rome to Avignon.

continues

- 1377 The papacy returns to Rome.
- 1443 Brunelleschi's dome caps the Duomo in Florence as the Renaissance ("rebirth") bursts into full bloom.
- 1469–92 Lorenzo il Magnifico rules in Florence as the Medici patron of Renaissance artists.
- 1499 *The Last Supper* is completed by Leonardo da Vinci in Milan.
- 1508 Michelangelo begins work on the Vatican's Sistine Chapel.
- 1527 Rome is sacked by Charles V of Spain, who is crowned Holy Roman Emperor the following year.
- 1796–97 Napoleon's series of invasions arouses Italian nationalism.
- 1861 Establishment of the Kingdom of Italy.
- 1915–18 Italy enters World War I on the side of the Allies.
- 1922 Fascists march on Rome; Benito Mussolini becomes premier.
- 1929 Signing of a concordat between the Vatican and the Italian government delineating the rights and responsibilities of each party.
- 1935 Italian invasion of Abyssinia (Ethiopia).
- 1936 Italy signs "Axis" pact with Germany.
- 1940 Italian invasion of Greece.
- 1943 U.S. Gen. George Patton lands in Sicily and soon controls the island.
- 1945 Mussolini is killed by a mob in Milan.
- 1946 Establishment of the Republic of Italy.
- 1957 The Treaty of Rome,

continues

had brought the western world under the sway of Roman law and civilization.

The emperors, whose succession started with Augustus's principate after the death of Julius Caesar, brought Rome to new, almost giddy, heights. Augustus transformed the city from brick to marble—much the way that Napoleon III transformed Paris many centuries later. But success led to corruption. The emperors wielded autocratic power, and the centuries witnessed a steady decay in the ideals and traditions upon which the empire had been founded. The army became a fifth column of barbarian mercenaries, the tax collector became the scourge of the countryside, and for every good emperor (Augustus, Trajan, Vespasian, and Hadrian, to name a few) there were three or four incredibly corrupt and debased heads of state (Caligula, Nero, Domitian, Caracalla, and more).

The Roman citizen in the capital either lived on the public dole and spent his days at gladiatorial games and imperial baths or was a disillusioned patrician at the mercy of emperors who might murder him for his property. The 3rd century A.D. saw so many emperors that it was common to hear in the provinces of the election of an emperor together with a report on his assassination. The 4th-century reforms of Diocletian held the empire together, but at the expense of its inhabitants, who were reduced to tax units. He reinforced imperial power but paradoxically at the same time weakened Roman dominance and prestige by establishing administrative capitals at such outposts as Milan, Trier in Germany, and elsewhere. When the Emporer Constantine built his "New Rome," Constantinople (also known as Byzantium), he moved the administrative functions away from Rome altogether, partly because the menace of possible barbarian attack in the West had increased greatly.

Constantine took the best Roman artisans, politicians, and public figures with him to the new capital, creating a city renowned for its splendor, intrigue, jealousies, and passion.

THE EMPIRE FALLS   The eastern and western sections of the Roman Empire split in A.D. 395, leaving Italy without the support it once received from east of the Adriatic. When the Goths moved toward Rome in the early 5th century, citizens in the provinces, who had grown to hate and fear the cruel bureaucracy set up by Diocletian and followed by succeeding emperors, welcomed the invaders. And then the pillage began.

Rome was sacked by Alaric in 410, and after more than 40 troubled years, Attila the Hun laid siege to the once powerful capital. He was followed in 455 by Gaiseric the Vandal, who engaged in a two-week spree of looting and destruction. The empire of the West lasted for only another 20 years; it was terminated by Odovacar, a barbarian chief, who opened areas of Italy to Teutonic settlement.

Christianity, a new religion that created a new society, was probably founded in Rome about a decade after Jesus' crucifixion. Gradually gaining strength despite early persecution, it was finally accepted as the official religion of the empire. But by the end of the power of Rome in 476, the Roman popes were under the nominal auspices of an exarch from Byzantium (Constantinople).

THE MIDDLE AGES After the fall of the Western Empire, the pope took on more and more imperial powers, although there was no political unity in the country. Decades of rule by barbarians and then Goths were followed by takeovers in different parts of the country by various strong warriors, such as the Lombards. Italy was thus divided into several spheres of control. In 731, Pope Gregory II renounced Rome's dependence on Constantinople, and thus ended the twilight era of the Greek exarch who had nominally ruled Rome. Papal Rome turned toward Europe, where the papacy found a powerful ally in Charlemagne, a king of the barbarian Franks. In 800 he was crowned emperor by Pope Leo III. The capital that he established at Aachen (in French, Aix-la-Chapelle) lay deep within territory known to the Romans a half millennium ago as the heart of the barbarian world. Although Charlemagne pledged allegiance to the church and looked to Rome and its pope as the final arbiter in most religious and cultural affairs, he launched northwestern Europe on a course toward bitter political opposition to the meddling of the papacy in temporal affairs.

The successor to the empire of Charlemagne was a political entity known as the Holy Roman Empire, which lasted from 962 to 1806. The new empire defined the end of the Dark Ages, but it ushered in a period of long and bloody warfare as well. The Lombard leaders battled Franks. Magyars from Hungary invaded northeastern Lombardy and were in turn defeated by the increasingly powerful Venetians. Eventually, Normans gained military control of Sicily in the 11th century, divided it completely from the rest of Italy, and altered forever both the island's racial and ethnic makeup and its architecture.

As Italy dissolved into an increasingly fragmented collection of city-states, the papacy fell under the power of the feudal landowners of Rome. Eventually, even the selection process for determining the choice of pope came into the hands of

founding the European Community (EC), is signed by six nations.

- **1960s** The country's economy grows under the EC, but the impoverished south lags behind.
- **1970s** Italy is plagued by left-wing terrorism; former Premier Aldo Moro is kidnapped and killed.
- **1980s** Political changes in Eastern Europe induce Italy's strong Communist party to modify its program and even to change its name; the Socialists head their first post-1945 coalition government.
- **1994** A conservative coalition, led by Silvio Berlusconi, wins general elections.
- **1995** Following resignation of Berlusconi, Lamberto Dini, Treasury minister, named prime minister to head transitional government.

the increasingly Germanic Holy Roman Emperors, although this power balance would very soon shift.

Rome during the Middle Ages was a quaint, rural town. Narrow lanes with over-hanging buildings filled many areas that were originally planned as showcases of ancient imperial power, including the Campus Martius. Great basilicas were built and embellished with golden-hued mosaics. The forums, mercantile exchanges, temples, and great theaters of the imperial era slowly disintegrated and collapsed. The decay of ancient Rome was assisted by periodic earthquakes, centuries of ne-glect, and, in particular, the growing need for building materials. Rome receded into a dusty provincialism. The seat of the Roman Catholic Church, it was a state almost completely controlled by priests, with an insatiable need for new churches and convents.

By the end of the 11th century, the popes shook off control of the Roman ar-istocracy, rid themselves of what they considered the excessive influence of the emperors at Aachen, and began an aggressive expansion of church influence and acquisitions. The deliberate organization of the church into a format modeled on the hierarchies of the ancient Roman Empire put the church on a collision course with the empire and the other temporal leaders of Europe, resulting in an endless series of not-very-flattering power struggles.

THE RENAISSANCE   The story of Italy from the dawn of the Renaissance to the Age of Enlightenment in the 17th and 18th centuries is as varied and fascinat-ing as that of the rise and fall of the empire. The papacy soon became essentially a feudal state, and the pope was a medieval (later Renaissance) prince engaged in many of the worldly activities that brought criticism upon the church in later centuries. The fall of the Holy Land to the Turks in 1065 catapulted the papacy into the forefront of world politics, primarily because of the crusades, many of which the popes directly caused or encouraged (but most of which were judged military and economic disasters). During the 12th and 13th centuries the bitter rivalries that rocked the secular and spiritual bastions of Europe took their toll on the stability of the Holy Roman Empire, which grew weaker as city-states buttressed by mercantile and trade-related prosperity grew stronger, and as France emerged as a potent nation in its own right. Each investiture of a new bishop to any influential post became a cause of endless jockeying for power among many factions.

These conflicts achieved their most visible impasse in 1303 with the full-fledged removal of the papacy to the French city of Avignon. For more than 70 years, until 1377, viciously competing popes (one in Rome, another under the protection of the French kings in Avignon) made simultaneous claims to the legacy of St. Peter, underscoring as never before the degree to which the church was both a victim and a victimizer in the temporal world of European politics.

The seat of the papacy was eventually returned to Rome, where a series of popes were every bit as interesting as the Roman emperors they replaced. The great families—Barberini, Medici, Borgia—enhanced their status and fortunes impres-sively when one of their sons was elected pope.

Despite the civilizing effects of the Renaissance, and the centuries that had passed since the collapse of the Roman Empire, the age of siege was not yet over. In 1527, Charles V, king of Spain, carried out the worst sack ever. To the horror of Pope Clement VII (a Medici), the entire city was brutally pillaged by the man who was to be crowned Holy Roman Emperor the next year.

During the years of the Renaissance, Reformation, and the Counter-Reformation, Rome underwent major physical changes. The old centers of culture reverted to pastures and fields, while great churches and palaces were built with the stones of ancient Rome. This building boom, in fact, did far more damage to the temples of the Caesars than any barbarian sack had done. Rare marbles were stripped from the imperial baths and used as altarpieces or sent to lime kilns. So enthusiastic was the papal destruction of Imperial Rome that it's a miracle anything is left.

UNITED ITALY The 19th century witnessed the final collapse of the Renaissance city-states, which had existed since the end of the 13th century. These units, eventually coming under the control of a *signore* (lord), were, in effect, regional states, with mercenary soldiers, civil rights, and assistance for their friendly neighbors. Some had attained formidable power under such signori as the Este family in Ferrara, the Medici in Florence, and the Visconti and the Sforza families in Milan.

During the 17th, 18th, and 19th centuries, decades of turmoil in Italy had lasted through the many years of succession of different European dynasties; Napoleon made a bid for power in Italy beginning in 1796, fueling his war machines with what was considered a relatively easy victory. During the Congress of Vienna (1814–15), which followed Napoleon's defeat, Italy was once again divided among many different factions: Austria was given Lombardy and Venetia, and the Papal States were returned to the pope. Some duchies were put back into the hands of their hereditary rulers, and southern Italy and Sicily went to a Bourbon dynasty. One historic move, which eventually assisted in the unification of Italy, was the assignment of the former republic of Genoa to Sardinia (which at the time was governed by the House of Savoy).

Political unrest became a fact of Italian life, at least some of it encouraged by the rapid industrialization of the north and the almost total lack of industrialization in the Italian south. Despite those barriers, in 1861, thanks to the brilliant efforts of the patriots Camillo Cavour (1810–61) and Giuseppe Garibaldi (1807–82), the Kingdom of Italy was proclaimed and Victor Emmanuel (Vittorio Emanuele) II of the House of Savoy, king of Sardinia, became head of the new monarchy.

Although the hope, pushed by Europe's theocrats and some of its devout Catholics, of attaining one empire ruled by the pope and the church had long ago faded away, there was still a fight, followed by generations of hard feelings, when the Papal States—a strategically and historically important principality under the temporal jurisdiction of the pope—were confiscated by the new Kingdom of Italy.

The establishment of the kingdom, however, did not signal a complete unification of Italy, because the city of Rome was still under papal control and Venetia was still held by Austria. This was partially resolved in 1866, when Venetia joined the rest of Italy after the Seven Weeks' War between Austria and Prussia; in 1871 Rome became the capital of the newly formed country. The Vatican, however, did not yield its territory to the new order, despite guarantees of nonintervention proffered by the Italian government, and relations between the pope and the country of Italy remained rocky until 1929.

In that year, Mussolini—who had acceded to power in a Fascist coup in 1922—defined the divisions between the Italian government and the Vatican by signing a concordat that granted political and fiscal autonomy to Vatican City. It also made Roman Catholicism the official state religion of Italy; that designation was removed in 1978 through a revision of the concordat.

WORLD WAR II & THE AXIS   During the Spanish Civil War (1936–39), Mussolini's support of the Falangists, under Francisco Franco, helped encourage the formation of the "Axis" alliance between Italy and Nazi Germany. Despite its outdated military equipment, Italy added to the general horror of the era by invading Abyssinia (Ethiopia) in 1935, supposedly to protect Italian colonial interests there. In 1940, Italy invaded Greece through Albania, and in 1942 sent thousands of Italian troops to assist Hitler in his disastrous campaign along the Russian front. In 1943, Allied forces, under the command of U.S. Gen. George Patton and British Gen. Bernard Montgomery, landed in Sicily and quickly secured the island as they prepared to move north, toward Rome.

In the face of likely defeat and humiliation, Mussolini was overthrown by his own cabinet (Grand Council). The Allies made a separate deal with Italy's king, Victor Emmanuel III, who had more or less gracefully collaborated with the Fascists during the previous two decades, and who now shifted allegiances without too much visible fuss. A politically divided Italy watched as battalions of fanatical German Nazis released Mussolini from his Italian jail cell to establish the short-lived Republic of Salò, headquartered on the edge of Lake Garda, hoping for a groundswell of popular opinion in favor of Italian Fascism. Events quickly proved this nothing more than a futile dream.

In April 1945, with almost half a million Italians rising in a mass demonstration against him and the German war machine, Mussolini was captured by Italian partisans as he fled to Switzerland. With his mistress, Claretta Petacci, and several others of his intimates, he was shot and strung upside-down from the roof of a gasoline station in Milan.

POSTWAR ITALY   Disaffected with the monarchy and its identification with the fallen Fascist dictatorship, Italian voters in 1946 voted for the establishment of a republic. The major political party that emerged in the aftermath of World War II was the Christian Democrats, a right-of-center group whose leader, Alcide De Gasperi (1881–1954), served as premier until 1953. The second largest party was the Communists, who, however, by the mid-1970s had abandoned their revolutionary program in favor of a democratic form of "Eurocommunism" (in 1991 the Communists even changed their name, to Democratic Party of the Left).

Although, after the war, Italy was stripped of all its overseas colonies, it quickly succeeded, in part because of U.S. aid under the Marshall Plan (1948–52), in rebuilding its economy, both agriculturally and industrially. By the 1960s, as a member of the European Community (founded in Rome in 1957), Italy had become one of the leading industrialized nations of the world, prominent in the manufacture of automobiles and office equipment.

But the country continued to be plagued by economic inequities between the prosperous, industrialized north and the economically depressed south. It suffered an unprecedented flight of capital (frequently aided by Swiss banks only too willing to accept discreet deposits from wealthy Italians) and an increase in bankruptcies, inflation (almost 20% during much of the 1970s), and unemployment.

During the late 1970s and early 1980s, Italy was rocked by the rise of terrorism, instigated both by neo-Fascists and by left-wing intellectuals from the Socialist-controlled universities of the north. In the early 1990s Italians were stunned as many leading politicians were accused of wholesale corruption. As a result, a newly formed right-wing grouping, led by media magnate Silvio Berlusconi, swept to

Impressions

Their smiles and laughter are due to their habit of thinking pleasurably aloud about the pleasures of life. They have humanity rather than humour, and the real significance of the distinction is seldom understood.

—Peter Nichols, *Italia, Italia,* 1973

victory in general elections in 1994. Berlusconi became prime minister at the head of a coalition government.

In December of 1994, Berlusconi resigned as prime minister after the federalist Northern League party defected from his coalition. That meant a loss of parliamentary majority for him. Treasury Minister, Lamberto Dini, a nonpolitical banker with international financial credentials, was named to replace Berlusconi. Dini's government is viewed only as transitional until national elections can be held.

IL SORPASSO

Besides soccer (*calcio*), the family, and affairs of the heart, the national obsession of Italy today is *il sorpasso*, a term that describes Italy's surpassing of its archrivals France and Britain in economic indicators. Economists disagree about whether or not *il sorpasso* has happened, and statistics (complicated by the presence of Italy's vast underground economy) vary widely from source to source. All levels of Italian society are actively engaged to some degree in withholding funds from the government. Today, Italy's underground economy (*economia sommersa*) competes on a monumental scale with the official economy, with participation by all sorts of otherwise respectable businesses and individuals. Complicating Italy's problems for economists, the police, and politicians is the constant interference of the Mafia, whose methods—despite numerous more or less heartfelt crackdowns—continue today even more ruthlessly than ever.

Despite these burdensome problems, Italy today is well entrenched as one of Europe's superpowers, eager to play a role in an increasingly complicated global economy.

3 The Italians

La famiglia still looms large in Italian life, with mamma mia at gravity center. That sense of family also extends to distant cousins—even those who left decades ago for Boston or wherever. "They make some money," one old peasant woman in Cefalù said, "then they come back home to show off their fancy clothes and their fancy rented cars. They've got more money than us, but they also buy the sauce for their pasta in jars, and I make my own with vegetables and herbs from my own garden. So, who's got the better life?"

Whether *la famiglia* always stands by you is another matter, but in theory family members are supposed to lend you money when you're about to be made homeless, they're supposed to nurse you back to health when you're sick, and they're supposed to get you a job in the family business should you need one. They're also supposed to provide a roof over your head even if that means allowing you to sleep for months at a time in the living room. After all, Italians don't have a word for privacy.

In truth, although the family remains strong in the Italy of the 90s, it has also eroded greatly. In spite of the teachings of the Catholic church and an arch-conservative pope not known for his toleration of alternative lifestyles, divorce and abortion are commonplace in Italy. That holds true even for some families to which either divorce or abortion only a decade or so ago would have been considered an abomination.

Many old people grew up in a culture that encouraged them to have lots of children who presumably would provide for them in their old age. Many of those elderly now live alone and poor, waiting for the son who went off to Rome to come home for a visit. Often they wait in vain.

The pivotal axis in the Italian family remains mother and son, a virtual cult known as *mammismo*. There is an old joke in Italy that goes: "Jesus Christ—an Italian, of course—was raised at home for 30 or so years. He believed that his mamma was a virgin and he was the son of God." Although incredibly strict with her daughters, that mamma could be overly indulgent with her son. She could even forgive him for his roving eye and philandering, as she once had to forgive papa. Sometimes, when mamma would eventually emerge from that eternal kitchen, she might give her daughter-in-law some advice. Inevitably that would be to overlook the latest sexual indiscretion of her son. "It is just what men do," she'd advise. Eventually, she would assure the daughter-in-law, her husband would come back home to his wife, family, and most definitely his mamma. If for no other reason because mamma cooked better than the wife. Mammas always did and they always will, at least in the view of some Italian men.

In spite of all this talk about sexual exploits in the café during male-bonding sessions, the Italian male often remains a mamma's boy throughout his life. Mamma keeps the family together, regardless of how extended it may be and how unworthy the in-laws are.

In reality, it is almost impossible to provide a national stereotype for the Italians, as they are so widely diverse. Those in the Alto Adige might fit in more comfortably in Germany or Austria. They certainly don't like being ruled from Rome, a city they hold with lots of justification in great mistrust. The blue-eyed Sicilians of Norman descent in Palermo call themselves Sicilians, never Italians, as if Sicily were its own separate nation, which perhaps it is. The arrogant Florentine, speaking a perfect Tuscan dialect in this land of Dante, can with some justification appear snobbish and condescending to the wildly gesticulating and semi-articulate countryman in the south. The Roman often has a certain sharpness and abrasiveness in contrast to the more courtly manners of the Venetian. The Piedmontese are sometimes more comfortable speaking French than Italian.

If Italy can be discussed as a single nation (and there are those who say after all these years it still can't be viewed that way), there is one instinct that stands out above all others—and that is the instinct for survival. Sharpened over the ages, that instinct has gotten the Italians through hordes of foreign invasions and political upheavals. Providing we're not discussing *la famiglia*, Italians are notorious for shifting loyalties. As an old bar owner in Naples once told me: "For me, the war was no problem. When the Germans were here, I displayed the swastika and a portrait of Hitler. About ten minutes before the first Americans arrived, those were down and up went the Stars and Stripes." Could you imagine a German changing political sides as rapidly? Certainly not overnight.

Sometimes the sheer inefficiency of Italians will drive you mad, especially if you make an appointment with someone for 2:30pm and the party shows up at four o'clock. Yet there is something to admire in the free spirit of all that. In Italy, we were once told, always invite people an hour or so earlier than when you actually want them to show up.

Italy today has been called a soap opera. Beset with scandal, corruption, and political chaos at every turn, Italy is in transition today. But it's always been in transition. Some elements are new and different. A feminist movement, for example, is sweeping across the north. I've actually seen Italian women, not necessarily those born and bred in a convent, whistle at men in those tight-fitting Italian pants, instead of the other way around. That would have been unthinkable in Mussolini's day. This fascist dictator known for his flamboyant braggadocio once raped a woman journalist when he didn't like the question she put to him in his presidential office.

A lot of people believed in Mussolini. Even today Il Duce portraits hang in many an Italian home, especially low-cost slums around Rome and in the south. Few Italians get passionate over their politicians any more, although traditionally the nation votes in larger turnouts on election day than any other country of Europe. "We must be realistic, however," said one political commentator, "and we must not lose our sense of humor. How could it be otherwise when half of the people you voted for only a year ago are either in jail, under investigation, on trial, or hiding out in Tunisia?"

As one voter said, "When I go into a voting booth, I know both of the leading candidates are already corrupt. Political power will only make them more so. I vote for the candidate I perceive to be less corrupt."

Ever since the days of Machiavelli, there has existed something known as *clientelismo*, a "kickback," so to speak. In other words, "I'll vote you into power where you might be able to turn the office into profit for yourself if you perhaps provide my son with a job, especially a bureaucratic one in government."

This is not to suggest that the old system of graft and corruption that has characterized Italian politics since the post-war era isn't changing. In the 1990s there were just too many government scandals, reaching up to the highest levels. Misappropriation of billions of Italian lire seemed among the least serious of offenses. Murder might top the list. For the first time ever, a party called La Rete, or "the network," organized in the south of Italy to campaign against the political corruption of the Mafia. That would have been unthinkable a few years ago. Or the organizers of La Rete would have ended up dead.

One cynical political observer noted, "These current political upheavals about getting rid of corruption in government will die down. As they are inclined to do, Italians will grow bored with the process. As we approach the millennium, Italians will return to the old way of doing politics Italian style—that is, greed, corruption, bribery, blackmail, and, well, *clientelismo*."

A visitor to today's Italy might never encounter Italian politics at any level, and might even be unaware of who's running the government. It is the people of Italy, certainly not their government, that are likely to impress the visitor. That passion for sports, especially soccer, is unlikely to be shared by a visitor from America. But the Italian love of café life can be infectious.

Exposure to the people of Italy, those same people who gave us Leonardo da Vinci and Michelangelo, will be reason enough to go. If for no other reason, you can share their great style for life and fashion and perhaps some of their spontaneity will rub off.

There is no better place to observe the Italian in action than in the beloved institution of the café.

It is here that the Italian-style *joie de vivre* is best lived out. Many Italians live in overcrowded apartments, and the café is the only place at which to meet and entertain their friends. The café becomes like an extended living room of Italian life.

Italians use the café as a combination club/tavern/snack bar, and certainly as a rendezvous point. There are spots where you can read your newspaper, magazine, or guidebook; meet a friend or make a new one; do your homework; write your memoirs; order a Cinzano, eat a hard-boiled egg; pick up a stranger; and even drink yourself into oblivion on fine Italian wine if that is your desire.

At cafés you meet your dates to go to a show or a night club or else you'll sit there and talk, promising to be forever faithful and not meaning to keep such a commitment at all. Above all, cafés are for people-watching.

In Italy, it's always back to the people who make up this country, perhaps the single most fascinating one on earth. Italians will tell you their country is the most fascinating one without qualification.

POLITICS *La politica e una cosa sporca* (politics are dirty) is an expression often heard in Italy. The charge is certainly justified. Corruption, scandal, and political chaos are parts of everyday life on the Italian landscape. The word *politician* is almost always preceded by the word *corrupt*. It is virtually assumed that anyone entering politics is doing so for personal gain.

Italy is a young republic and it's had a troubled democracy. It has had 52 governments since World War II, and the words *embattled*, *shaky*, and *fractious* could be used for all of them.

In recent years charges of major corruption in government have made headlines not only in Italy but also throughout the world. The breaking point came in the early 1990s when millions of dollars began to disappear from the coffers of state-run industries.

In the elections in March of 1994, the voters of Italy rejected the long-ruling Christian Democrats and the Socialists, as both parties were tainted by scandal. Emerging triumphant was Silvio Berlusconi, a billionare businessman and media czar. Many Italian voters perceived Berlusconi as "too rich to bribe." In his few short months in office, Berlusconi was revealed to have betrayed the voters' trust. A Milan magistrate ordered an investigation into the prime minister's earlier role in payoffs by Fininvest, his media conglomerate. Rather than face a vote of no confidence in Parliament, Berlusconi resigned. He is hardly out of the political picture, however, as national elections loom as of this writing. Berlusconi has alleged that Italian democracy has been "hijacked by Communists and their allies who are preparing an all-out war" against his center-right alliance.

Prime minister Lamberto Dini is heading up an interim government that faces monumental problems, including the lack of confidence in the lire on world financial markets and a massively rising deficit. Dini seems to hold out little hope for Italy's political future. He said that it seems "Italy's political forces are unable to see why they should all pull together to confront a dramatic emergency."

Local critics of the social and political scene tie the corruption of politics to the circumvention of the law that exists in private life.

Michael Mewshaw, author of *Playing Away*, a book about Italy, writes: "In fact, Italy suffers from both a glut of laws, many of them contradictory, and a bloated bureaucracy. Something as simple as cashing a check or paying a bill can devour half a day. To escape the brambles of red tape, Italians have become marvelous improvisers and corner-cutters. Whenever possible they bypass the sclerotic public sector and negotiate private deals *fra amici*—among friends."

There is talk today of a symbolic passage from a corrupt First Republic to a new Second Republic.

LANGUAGE   Italian, of course, is the official language, and it's spoken all over the country, with many regional dialects. The purest form of Italian is said to be spoken in Tuscany. Italian is probably more directly derived from Latin than many of the other romance languages, which also include French, Spanish, Portuguese, and Romanian.

In the 14th century the dialect of Tuscany became the literary language of Italy. Dante did more than anyone else to promulgate the language, although he was aided by such other Tuscan writers as Petrarch and Boccaccio.

Linguists consider Italian the most "musical" and mellifluous language in the West. In fact, it has always been a puzzle why Casanova chose to write his racy memoirs in French instead of Italian, as he was born in Venice. Some critics have suggested that the memoirs would have had even more of an effect had they been written in Italian.

The Italian language easily lent itself to librettos and operas. Many English-speaking people have to draw upon Italian words, especially musical terms, such as *basso profundo*, to describe various items. *Prima donna, la dolce vita* (aided in part by the Fellini film), and *inamorata* are just a few Italian words widely used around the world.

The language is a phonetic one. That means you pronounce a word the way it is written, unlike many languages, including English. It has been said that if an Italian sentence sounds "off key," it is because the grammar is incorrect.

The Italian alphabet is not as extensive as the one in English in that it doesn't use such letters as *J, K, W, X,* and *Y*. Italians discovered the *J* with the advent of jeans in the postwar era, although they often pronounce the word "yeans."

Since the coming of television—mainly in the 1950s—more and more Italians speak the language similarly. Even in World War II many Italian soldiers couldn't understand each other, as some men spoke only in dialect.

A lot of so-called Americanisms have now infiltrated the Italian language, largely because of the success of U.S.-made films in Italy. The films also did much to popularize a Sicilian word now known around the world: *Mafia*. Although it evokes a menacing international crime organization, some linguists claim it means "I'll beat you so hard you'll dance with pain."

SOCCER   In Italy, a sportsperson is anyone who enjoys watching sports, and not necessarily playing them, and practically no other nation throws itself so whole-heartedly into occasionally fanatical allegiance to favorite **calcio (soccer)** teams. Originally imported from England, soccer first came to Italy in 1898, when about a hundred spectators on a ragged field near Turin came to blows over the much disputed outcome of the country's first match. The combined contributions by that historic match's spectators totaled 197 lire, an insignificant amount compared to the trillions of lire amassed in the name of Italian soccer ever since. Today the sport attracts millions of Italian devotees, and is taken so seriously that heart attacks by spectators (both in stadiums or in front of television sets), major riots that have often led to multiple deaths, and endless traffic jams and car accidents have occurred because of it.

Soccer is a fast game played by two teams of 11 men for 90 minutes (two halves of 45 minutes). They are allowed to use only their feet and their heads to move the ball, and score goals by kicking it between two fixed goal posts. At least part of the popularity of soccer was encouraged by Mussolini and the Fascists, who used it to increase the patriotic feelings of Italians, especially by stressing Italy's sports victories over other nations. Today, in a game that seems to renew its modernity with every match, intense competition (and staggeringly large betting pools) accompany matches between Italian villages, Italian cities, and Italian districts. Many famous Italian architects have based their reputations on their designs for sports stadiums. On Sunday afternoon in Italy (the traditional time for the beginning of a match is 2:30pm), all traffic seems to lead in or out of stadium parking lots, all televisions seem to be tuned in to the televised match, and even the most outwardly staid citizens become enmeshed in what has been defined as a regularly scheduled manifestation of national hysteria.

4 Art & Architecture

The mysterious Etruscans, whose earliest origins lay probably somewhere in Mesopotamia, brought the first truly impressive art and architecture to mainland Italy. Little remains of their architecture, but historical writings by the Romans themselves record their powerful walls, bridges, and aqueducts, which were very similar to the Mycenaean architecture of Crete. The handful of remaining Etruscan murals was discovered in tombs. More numerous are the finely sculpted sarcophagi, many of which rest today in Italian museums. The best collection is at the National Museum of the Villa Giulia in Rome. Several of the most frequently visited of these tombs can be visited on day trips from Rome (see "Easy Excursions" in Chapter 6).

As Rome asserted its own identity and overpowered its Etruscan masters, it borrowed heavily from themes already established by Etruscan artists and architects. In time, however, the Romans discovered Greek art, fell in love with that country's statuary, and looted much of it. Partly because of the admiration of the Romans, the Hellenistic tradition, launched so bravely in the eastern Mediterranean, continued in somewhat altered (some say corrupted) form in the West.

It was in architecture, however, that Rome flourished magnificently, advancing in size and majesty far beyond the architectural examples set by the Greeks. Part of this was because of the development of a primitive form of concrete, but even more important was the fine-tuning of the arch, which was used with a logic, rhythm, and ease never before seen. Monumental buildings were erected, each an embodiment of the strength, power, and careful organization of the empire itself. Examples include forums and baths scattered across the Mediterranean world (the greatest of which were Trajan's Forum and Caracalla's Baths, both in Rome). Equally magnificent were the Colosseum and a building that later greatly influenced the Palladians during the Renaissance, Hadrian's Pantheon, both erected in Rome.

Of course, these immense achievements were made possible by two major resources: almost limitless funds pouring in from all regions of the empire, and an unending supply of slaves captured during military campaigns abroad.

The aesthetic and engineering concepts of the Roman Empire eventually evolved into early Christian and Byzantine art. More concerned with moral and spiritual values than with the physical beauty of the human form or the celebration of political grandeur, early Christian artists turned to the supernatural and spiritual world for their inspiration. Basilicas and churches were lavishly decorated with mosaics and colored marble, while painting depicted the earthly suffering (and heavenly rewards) of martyrs and saints. Unlike the Etruscans, the Christians depicted death as a beginning (of either salvation or damnation), and God as all-powerful, omniscient, and (according to the artist's depiction) either loving or wrathful.

The art and architecture in the centuries that followed the collapse of Rome became known as early medieval or romanesque. In its many variations, it flourished between A.D. 1000 and 1200, although in isolated pockets away from Europe's commercial mainstreams it continued for several centuries later. Supported by monasteries or churches, it was almost wholly concerned with ecclesiastical subjects, often with the intention of educating the worshipers who studied it. Biblical parables were carved in stone or painted into frescoes, often useful teaching aids for a church eager to spread its messages.

As the appeal of the romanesque faded, the gothic or late-medieval style encouraged a vast increase in both the quantities and preconceptions of Italian art and architecture. The Italians interpreted gothic into their own particular style, which was much different from the version manifested by the French. Although the gothic age continued to be profoundly religious, many secular buildings, including an array of palaces intended to show off the increasing prestige and wealth of Italy's ruling families, were erected. Artists such as Cimabue and Giotto blazed new trails and brought emotional realism into their work in what were later seen as complete breaks from Byzantine gloom and rigidity, and early harbingers of the Renaissance.

The Italian Renaissance was born in Florence during the 15th century, where members of the powerful Medici family emerged as some of the greatest art patrons in history. The Renaissance began with great artistic events: Ghiberti defeated Brunelleschi in a contest to design bronze doors for the Baptistery of the Cathedral of Florence. (The original doors were recently removed to the Duomo Museum for safekeeping and replaced by copies.) But Brunelleschi designed a dome for the cathedral that has been hailed ever since as "a miracle of design." In Rome, Urbino-born Donato Bramante worked with others on St. Peter's Basilica, the most significant and imposing building of the High Renaissance. (Venice during this period grew prosperous, but differed from Florence in that its architecture adhered steadfastly to gothic features and influences from Byzantium.)

Sculpture took on a renewed importance during the Renaissance as many great artists, including Michelangelo, dazzled the world with new and uniquely individual versions of *pietàs* and Davids. Perhaps it was in painting, however, that the Renaissance excelled. Leonardo da Vinci, whose all-encompassing skill in everything from painting to engineering has defined him as "the epitome of the Renaissance man," gave the world such works as *The Last Supper* and *Mona Lisa*. Urbino-born Raffaello Santi was another giant of the Renaissance. In Rome, he was commissioned to fresco the apartments of Pope Julius II. Simultaneously, Michelangelo painted the ceiling frescoes of the Sistine Chapel, an assignment that took four back-breaking years of his life to complete.

The period known as the High Renaissance was said to last for only about 25 years, beginning in the early 16th century. Despite the subtle differences between the stages of the Renaissance, Italy remained Europe's artistic leader for nearly 200 years.

The transitional period between the Renaissance and the baroque came to be called "Mannerism." Out of this period emerged such great artists as Tintoretto, whose major work was the cycle of frescoes for the Scuola di San Rocco in Venice (it took 23 years to finish); Verona-born Paolo Veronese; and perhaps the most sensitive, and some say the finest, of the Mannerists, Parmigianino.

In the early 17th century and into the 18th century, the Baroque (meaning absurd or irregular) movement swept Europe, including Italy. The development of the Baroque movement was linked to the much-needed reforms and restructuring of the Catholic Church that followed the upheavals of the Protestant Reformation. Many great Italian churches and palazzi were constructed during this period. Great artists emerged, including Bernini, who became renowned both as a sculptor and as a painter, and Borromini, one of the great architects of his age. The two painters who best represented the movement were Carracci, who decorated the Roman palace of Cardinal Farnese, and Caravaggio, one of the pioneers of baroque painting. The even more flamboyant rococo grew out of the baroque style.

In the 19th century the great light had gone out of art in Italy. (The beacon was picked up instead by France.) Neoclassicism—a return to the aesthetic ideals of ancient Greece and Rome, whose ideals of patriotism were resonant with the growing sense of pan-Italian patriotism—swept through almost every aspect of the Italian arts.

The 20th century witnessed the birth of several major Italian artists whose works once again captured the imagination of the world. De Chirico and Modigliani (the latter's greatest contribution lay in a new concept of portraiture) were only two among many. The Bolognese painter of bottles and jugs, Morandi, also became known around the world. The greatest Italian sculptor of the 20th century was Medardo Rosso, who died in 1928, and the leading figure in Italian architecture was Pier Luigi Nervi, born in 1891 in Milan. His best-known commission is probably the Palazzo della Sport in Rome, which he designed for the 1960 Olympics.

Since then Italy has been a European leader in sophisticated and witty interpretations of buildings, paintings, fashion, industrial design, and decor. Many modern Italian artists have infused Italian flair into the lines of workaday and utilitarian objects whose quality, humor, and usefulness have become legendary.

5 Literature & Music

LITERATURE The Italian writer most familiar to readers today is probably Umberto Eco, whose fascinating novel *The Name of the Rose* was translated in 1983; the English version became a runaway bestseller. Eco follows in the train of a long, long line of literary figures of note who use the Tuscan dialect-based Italian language with outstanding effect.

Since the institution of the Nobel Prize for Literature in 1901, five Italians have been recipients of the coveted prize: Giosuè Carducci, poet and professor of Italian literature at the University of Bologna, in 1906; Grazia Deledda, Sardinia-born writer who used her native island as the subject of her work, in 1926; Luigi Pirandello, Sicily-born dramatist, in 1934; Salvadore Quasimodo, a poet, also a native of Sicily, in 1959; and Eugenio Montale, poet, in 1975.

In the days of Rome's glory—shortly before and after the birth of Christ—mighty men of letters included Cicero, Julius Caesar, Virgil, Horace, Ovid, and Livy. When the people's thoughts turned heavenward, which was inevitable when the Christian faith became accepted by the majority of Romans and other Italians, Christian Latin literature became the order of the day. Such writers as St. Augustine, St. Ambrose, and St. Jerome gained repute for their writings and are remembered as among the few voices heard during the Dark Ages.

Arguably the greatest period in Italian literature was ushered in during the 14th century, with world-acclaimed works that made the Tuscan dialect the literary language of Italy. Immortals such as Dante, Petrarch, and Boccaccio flourished in this era. *The Divine Comedy* by Dante is called the first masterpiece of the then-modern national language. Petrarch is hailed as the forerunner of humanism, and scholars say that Boccaccio, best known for the *Decameron*, did for Italian prose what Dante did for its poetry.

The term "Renaissance man" is applied to those who excelled in many fields of endeavor in that era. Among these, shining examples are Michelangelo, who wrote sonnets in addition to all his other talents; Leonardo da Vinci, writer, inventor, artist, astronomer, whatever; and even Lorenzo de' Medici (Lorenzo the Magnificent), who is credited with establishing the Tuscan dialect as the national speech of Italy. Machiavelli in the 16th century, Goldoni in the 18th century, and D'Annunzio in the early 20th century are other names connected with Italian literary achievement. We have mentioned a few. You perhaps have other names to remember in the long annals of Roman and Italian literature.

MUSIC Though the ultimate expression of Italian musicality would not reveal itself until the operatic tradition of the 18th and 19th centuries, music has always been a part of Italian life.

Late in the 900s, a Benedictine monk from Arezzo named Guido Monaco invented a musical scale that was used within monasteries for the notation of single-melody, unharmonized religious chanting known as Gregorian chants.

Many of these medieval traditions were reformed by Palestrina during the 1500s, but a truly idiosyncratic version of Italian music only began to be defined in the late 1600s. At that time, Corelli (1653–1713) originated a musical form known as the *concerto grosso* and founded a particular and highly colorful style of violin playing. Scarlatti (1660–1725) refined thematic development of musical scores, popularized the concept of chromatic harmonies, and helped to define the makeup of the operatic orchestra. A few generations later, Boccherini (1743–1805) contributed greatly to sophisticated applications of the chamber orchestra, defining appropriate musical contexts for string quartets at some of the most influential gatherings of Europe.

Especially important was Vivaldi (1678–1741), the Venice-born composer (and ordained priest) who was considered one of the most influential European composers of his day. An innovator in form and orchestration (and composer of more than 700 musical works), he developed techniques that greatly influenced the compositions of Bach.

As mentioned earlier, however, most musicologists best remember Italy for its opera (a drama or comedy in which music is the essential factor, with showcases for both instruments and individual voices). Italy and opera are linked by marriage, and, in fact, many visitors to Italy consider it one of the country's prime touristic attractions. (The opera season in Italy begins in early December and continues through mid-April.)

Jacopo Peri's *Dafne* (first performed in 1597, inspired by the recitative style of ancient Greek dramas and commissioned by the Medicis) is now regarded as the world's first opera. Claudio Monteverdi (1567–1643), however, is viewed as the father of modern opera. Developing new styles of operatic oratorios, his masterpiece was *L'Incoronazione di Poppea* (1642). From its origins in Florence, opera moved to Venice before catching on, around 1650, with the audiences of Naples. Even the previously mentioned Vivaldi, although best remembered for his orchestral works, composed 43 different operas, the most famous of which is *Armida al campo d'Egitto* (1718).

From this rich musical tradition arose the *bel canto* (beautiful singing) method of the 18th and early 19th centuries. The movement's most famous adherent was Vincenzo Bellini (1801–35), whose masterpiece, *Norma* (composed just four years before his early death), is considered a *tour de force* of the melodic line, and with dozens of famous and challenging arias for coloratura soprano. Opera, particularly its Neapolitan versions, spread around the world. Bellini was followed in the bel canto tradition by Gioacchino Rossini (1792–1868). He moved to Paris in 1823 and remained there for most of the rest of his life. His operas retain the Italian-inspired opera buffa comedic tradition (he's considered the last of the masters of that particular form) as well as a series of brilliant crescendos that express great emotional power. Rossini is best known for his sparkling and witty *The Barber of Seville*.

Romantic opera also flowered, particularly in the works of Donizetti, best known for his *Lucia di Lammermoor*, which many years later brought Joan Sutherland fame at New York's Metropolitan Opera.

It was Giuseppe Verdi (1813–1901) who became the greatest Italian operatic composer, credited (with Richard Wagner) with developing opera into a fully integrated art that combined many different disciplines into a coherent whole. In all, Verdi produced 26 operas, many of which are widely performed today, including *Il Trovatore, La Traviata, Rigoletto, Un Ballo in Maschera,* and *Aïda.*

Verdi's musical heir was Giacomo Puccini (1858–1924), who trained in what had become the operatic headquarters of Italy (Milan). Greatly influenced by Wagner, his music was melodious and romantic, revolving around plots based on tragic love themes. Set in deliberately exotic settings, his most popular operas included *Madama Butterfly, La Bohème, Tosca,* and the incomplete *Turandot* (completed after Puccini's death by his musical disciple, Franco Alfano).

Enrico Caruso (1873–1921), one of the most famous operatic tenors of all time, based his career on his interpretations of Puccini operas, performing some of them for the first time in concert halls from Buenos Aires to San Francisco. Since Verdi and Puccini, however, no Italian composer has entered this exclusive pantheon of the musical greats.

Despite its potency and influence on formal musical compositions around the world, none of the above-mentioned composers or works gives credit to the richness and diversity of Italian popular song. In the early 1900s Italy had one of the wealthiest traditions of folk music in the world, with strongly defined differences among the country's various districts. (Naples, in particular, produced such globally popular songs as "O Sole Mio" and "Funiculè Funiculà.")

The effect of television, radio, and cultural inroads from the rest of the world has obliterated at least some of these musical traditions, although musical output in one form or another is still one of Italy's greatest exports to the world. (You're

A Star Is Born

She's young, she's beautiful, and the quality of Cecilia Bartoli's mezzo-soprano voice (which *Newsweek* has referred to as "a rich, dark miracle of expressiveness") has thrilled audiences on at least three continents. Rich with sounds that portray both an ingenue and a sophisticated woman of the world, it is perfectly suited, according to opera directors, for roles by Rossini and Mozart. Scholars call her a "coloratura mezzo"; audiences refer to her as sensational, with a voice that winds its way through a libretto rather than crushing the nuances of the orchestra like a bulldozer.

The great publicity which she's earned comes at a time when audiences and impresarios were fed up with the histrionic public behavior of other opera stars. Reared in Rome, she used to sing around her family's apartment ("very loud"), and trained first in flamenco dancing, then in piano and voice. At least part of the credit for her discovery lies with Daniel Barenboim, musical director of the Chicago Symphony Orchestra, and the late Herbert von Karajan.

Today, Ms. Bartoli, after Pavarotti, is the most famous opera star in Italy. (The wizards who manage the train which navigates through the Channel Tunnel recently named one of their locomotives the "Cecilia Bartoli" in her honor.)

Where can you find Italy's newest diva in your musical peregrinations through the peninsula? Probably not at La Scala, and probably not to an excessive degree in Italy at all. In her words, "I don't sing much at La Scala, because it's Verdi, Verdi, Puccini, and Verdi, and I don't do that." (Her coaches say that she doesn't have the vocal projection for those roles.) But to even her own surprise, and despite the fact her greatest successes have been outside of Italy, the Italians are suddenly referring to her with a territorial pride as "*la nostra Bartoli.*"

far more likely to hear someone break into spontaneous song in Italy than in almost any other country in Europe.) In the 1950s and early 1960s, Ornella Vanoni and Gino Paoli, Domenico Modugno ("Volaré"), Mina, and Peppino di Capri provided much of the music for the sybaritic but fleeting moment known ever after as *la dolce vita.* Italy seemed carefree, stylish, and romantic as it enjoyed an economic boom and the devoted patronage of the world's most beautiful people. During this era there developed a greater consciousness of what such singers as Frank Sinatra and Peggy Lee were doing (musically) in America, and an increased awareness of musical trends in both the United States and Britain.

Today, jazz, rock, blues, folk music, and (to a lesser degree) heavy metal flourish in Italy in patterns that frequently parallel similar developments in the United States and the rest of Europe. But Italy, which has always appreciated showmanship, manages to infuse the barrage of outside influences with its own particular expression of style and wit.

6 Italian Cuisine

Many North American visitors erroneously think of Italian cuisine as limited. Of course, everybody has heard of minestrone, spaghetti, chicken cacciatore, and spumoni. But Italian chefs hardly confine themselves to such a limited repertoire. Incidentally, except in the south, Italians don't use as much garlic in their food as many foreigners seem to believe. Most Italian dishes, especially those in the north, are butter based. Spaghetti and meatballs, by the way, is not an Italian dish, although certain restaurants throughout the country have taken to serving it "for homesick Americans."

THE CUISINE

Rome might be the best place to introduce yourself to the cookery of Italy, as it has specialty restaurants that represent all the culinary centers such as Bologna and Genoa. Throughout your Roman holiday, you'll encounter such savory viands as *zuppa di pesce* (a soup or stew of various fish, cooked in white wine and herb-flavored), *cannelloni* (tube-shaped pasta baked with any number of stuffings), *riso col gamberi* (rice with shrimp, peas, and mushrooms, flavored with white wine and garlic), *scampi alla griglia* (grilled prawns, one of the best-tasting, albeit expensive, dishes in the city), *quaglie col risotto e tartufi* (quail with rice and truffles), *lepre alla cacciatore* (hare flavored with tomato sauce and herbs), *zabaglione* (a cream made with sugar, egg yolks, and marsala), *gnocchi alla romana* (potato-flour dumplings with a sauce made with meat and covered with grated cheese), *abbacchio* (baby spring lamb, often roasted over an open fire), *saltimbocca alla romana* (literally "jump-in-your-mouth"—thin slices of veal with sage, ham, and cheese), *fritto alla romana* (a mixed fry that's likely to include everything from brains to artichokes), *carciofi alla romana* (tender artichokes cooked with such herbs as mint and garlic, and flavored with white wine), *fettuccine all'uovo* (egg noodles served with butter and cheese), *zuppa di cozze* (a hearty bowl of mussels cooked in broth), *fritti di scampi e calamaretti* (baby squid and prawns fast-fried), *fragoline* (wild strawberries, in this case from the Alban Hills), and *finocchio* (fennel, a celery-like raw vegetable with the flavor of anisette, often eaten as a dessert or in a salad).

From Rome, it's on to **Florence** and **Siena,** where you'll encounter the hearty, rich cuisine of the Tuscan hills (for comments on that cuisine, refer to the introduction to the dining section of Chapter 7).

The next major city to visit is **Venice,** where the cookery is typical of the Venetia district. It has been called "tasty, straightforward, and homely" by one long-ago food critic, and I concur. One of the most typical dishes is *fegato alla veneziana* (liver and onions), as well as *risi e bisi* (rice and fresh peas). Seafood figures heavily in the Venetian diet, and grilled fish is often served with the bitter red radicchio, a lettuce that comes from Treviso.

In **Lombardy,** of which Milan is the center, the cookery is more refined and tasty, in my opinion. No dish here is more famous that *cotoletta alla milanese* (cutlets of tender veal, dipped in egg and breadcrumbs, and fried in olive oil until they're a golden brown)—the Viennese called it Wiener Schnitzel. *Osso buco* is the other great dish of Lombardy; this is cooked with the shinbone of veal in a ragoût sauce and served on a bed of rice and peas. *Risotto alla milanese* is also a classic Lombard dish. This is rice that can be dressed in almost any way, depending on the chef's imagination. It's often flavored with saffron and butter, to which chicken

Impressions

The more I see of them the more struck I am with their having no sense of the ridiculous.
—Henry James, Letter to Ms. Fanny Kemble, March 24, 1881

It is not impossible to govern Italians. It is merely useless.

—Benito Mussolini

giblets have been added. It's always served, seemingly, with heaps of parmesan cheese. *Polenta*, a cornmeal mush that's "more than mush," is the staff of life in some parts of northeastern Italy and is eaten in lieu of pasta.

The cooking in **Piedmont,** of which Turin is the capital, and the Aosta Valley is different from that in the rest of Italy. Its victuals are said to appeal to strong-hearted men returning from a hard day's work in the mountains. You get such dishes as *bagna cauda*, which is a sauce made with olive oil, garlic, butter, and anchovies in which you dip uncooked fresh vegetables. *Fonduta* is celebrated: It's made with melted Fontina cheese, butter, milk, egg yolks, and, for an elegant touch, white truffles.

In the **Trentino–Alto Adige area,** whose chief towns are Bolzano, Merano, and Trent, the cooking is naturally influenced by the traditions of the Austrian and Germanic kitchens. South Tyrol, of course, used to belong to Austria, and here you get such tasty pastries as strudel.

Liguria, whose chief town is Genoa, turns to the sea for a great deal of its cuisine, as reflected by its version of bouillabaisse, a *buridda* flavored with spices. But its most famous food item is *pesto*, a sauce made with fresh basil, garlic, cheese, and walnuts. It not only dresses pasta or fish, but many dishes such as *gnocchi* (little dumplings).

Emilia-Romagna, with such towns as Modena, Parma, Bologna, Ravenna, and Ferrara, is one of the great gastronomic centers of Italy. Rich in produce, its school of cooking produces many notable pastas that are now common around Italy. They include *tagliatelle, tortellini,* and *cappelletti* (larger than tortellini and made in the form of "little hats"). Tagliatelle, of course, are long strips of macaroni, and tortellini are little squares of dough that have been stuffed with chopped pork, veal, or whatever. Equally as popular is *lasagne*, which by now nearly everybody has heard of. In Bologna it's often made by adding finely shredded spinach to the dough. The best-known sausage of the area is *mortadella*, and equally famous is a *cotoletta alla bolognese* (veal cutlet fried with a slice of ham or bacon). The distinctive and famous cheese, *parmigiana*, is a product of Parma and also Reggio Emilia. *Zampone* (stuffed pig's foot) is a specialty of Modena.

Much of the cookery of **Naples**—spaghetti with clam sauce, pizzas, and so forth—is already familiar to North Americans because so many Neapolitans moved to the New World and opened restaurants there. *Mozzarella*, or buffalo cheese, is the classic cheese of this area. Mixed fish fries, done a golden brown, are a staple feature of nearly every table.

Sicily has a distinctive cuisine, with good strong flavors and aromatic sauces. A staple of the diet is *maccheroni con le sarde* (spaghetti with pine seeds, fennel, spices, chopped sardines, and olive oil). Fish is good and fresh in Sicily (try swordfish). Among meat dishes, you'll see *involtini siciliani* on the menu (rolled meat with a stuffing of egg, ham, and cheese cooked in breadcrumbs). A *caponata* is a special way of cooking eggplant in a flavor-rich tomato sauce. The desserts and homemade pastries are excellent. The *cannoli* are cylindrical pastry cases stuffed with ricotta and candied fruit (often chocolate). Their ice creams, called *gelati*, are among the best in Italy.

Sardinia is a land unto itself. Game such as wild boar often appears on the Sardinian table, as does *porceddi* (roast suckling pig prepared using methods a thousand years old); it's cooked in an open-air pit under myrtle branches. *Malloreddus* are little dumplings of corn flour flavored with saffron and served in a spicy sauce (everything sprinkled with goat cheese), and *cassola* is a highly spiced fish stew.

ITALIAN WINE

Italy is the largest wine-producing country in the world; as far back as 800 B.C. the Etruscans were vintners. It is said that more soil is used in Italy for the cultivation of grapes than for food. Many Italian farmers produce wine just for their own consumption or for their relatives in a big city. However, it wasn't until 1965 that laws were enacted to guarantee regular consistency in winemaking. Wines regulated by the government are labeled DOC (*Denominazione di Origine Controllata*). If you see DOCG on a label (the "G" means *guarantita*), that means even better quality control.

THE VINEYARDS OF ITALY   Based on traditions and priorities established by the ancient Greeks, Italy produces more wine than any other nation on earth. More than four million acres of Italian soil are cultivated as vineyards, and in recent years, there's been an increased emphasis on recognizing vintages from lesser-known growers who may or may not be designated as working within a zone of controlled origin and name. (It's considered an honor, and usually a source of profit, to own vines within a DOC—*Denominazione di Origine Controllata*. Vintners who are presently limited to marketing their products as unpretentious table wines (*vino di tavola*) often expend great efforts lobbying for an elevated status as a DOC)

Italy's wine growers range from among the most automated and technologically sophisticated in Europe to low-tech, labor-intensive family plots turning out just a few hundred bottles of wine a year. You can sometimes save costs by buying direct from a grower (the signs beside the highway of any wine-growing district will advertise "venditta dretta"). Not only will you avoid paying the retailer's markup, but also you might get a glimpse of the vines that produced the vintage you carry home with you.

Useful vocabulary words for such endeavors include *bottiglierie* (a simple wine shop with almost no pretentions) and *enoteca* (a more upscale shop where many different vintages, from several different growers, are displayed and sold like magazines in a bookstore). In some cases, you can buy a glass of the product before you buy the bottle, and in some cases, platters of coldcuts and/or cheeses are available to offset the tang (and alcoholic effects) of the wine.

REGIONAL WINES   Coming from the volcanic soil of Vesuvius, the wines of **Campania (Naples)** have been extolled for 2,000 years. Homer praised the glory of Falerno, which is straw yellow in color. Neapolitans are fond of ordering a wine known as Lacrima Christi, or "tears of Christ," to accompany many seafood dishes. It comes in amber, red, or pink. With meat dishes, try the dark mulberry-colored Gragnano, which has a faint bouquet of faded violets. Also, the red and white wines of Ischia and Capri are justly renowned.

The heel of the Italian boot, **Apulia (Puglia),** produces more wine than any other part of Italy. Try Castel del Monte, which comes in shades of pink, white, and red.

Latium (Rome) is a major wine-producing region of Italy. Many of the local wines come from the Castelli Romani, the hill towns around Rome. Horace and Juvenal sang the praises of Latium wines even in imperial times. These wines, experts agree, are best drunk when young, and they are most often white, mellow, and dry (or else "demi-sec"). There are seven different types, including Falerno (yellowish straw in color) and Cecubo (often served with roast meat). Try also Colli Albani (strawyellow with amber tints and served with both fish and meat). The golden-yellow wines of Frascati are famous, produced both in a demi-sec and sweet variety, the latter served with dessert.

The wines of **Tuscany (Florence and Siena)** are famous, and they rank with some of the finest reds in France. Chianti is the best known, and it comes in several varieties. The most highly regarded is Chianti Classico, a lively ruby-red wine mellow in flavor with a bouquet of violets. A good label is Antinori. A less known but remarkably fine Tuscan wine is Brunello di Montalcino, a brilliant garnet red that's served with roasts and game. The ruby-red, almost-purple Vino Nobile di Montepulciano has a rich, rugged body; it's a noble wine that is aged for four years.

The sparkling Lambrusco of **Emilia-Romagna** is by now best known by Americans, but this wine can be of widely varying quality. Most of it is a brilliant ruby red. Be more experimental and try such wines as the dark ruby-red Sanglovese (with a delicate bouquet) and the golden-yellow Albana, which is somewhat sweet. Trebbiano, generally dry, is best served with fish.

From the **Marches** (capital: Ancona) comes one major wine, Verdicchio dei Castelli di Jesi, which is amber-straw in color, clear, and brilliant. Some have said that it's the best wine in Europe "to marry with fish."

From **Venetia** (Venice and Verona) in northeastern Italy, a rich breadbasket of the country, come such world-famous wines as Bardolino (a light ruby-red wine often served with poultry), Valpolicella (produced in "ordinary quality" and "superior dry," and best served with meats), and Soave, so beloved by W. Somerset Maugham, which has a pale amber-yellow color with a light aroma and a velvety flavor. Also try one of the Cabernets, either the ruby-red Cabernet di Treviso (ideal with roasts and game) or the even deeper ruby-red Cabernet Franc, which has a marked herbal bouquet and is also served with roasts.

The **Friuli–Venezia Giulia area,** whose chief towns are Trieste and Udine, attract those who enjoy a "brut" wine with a trace of flint. From classic grapes comes Merlot, deep ruby in color, and several varieties of Pinot, including Pinot Grigio, whose color ranges from straw yellow to gray-pink (good with fish). Also served with fish, the Sauvignon has a straw-yellow color and a delicate bouquet.

The **Trentino–Alto Adige area,** whose chief towns are Bolzano and Trent, produces wine influenced by Austria. Known for its vineyards, the region has some 20 varieties of wine. The straw yellow, slightly pale-green Riesling is served with fish, as is the pale greenish yellow Terlano. Santa Maddalena, a cross between a garnet and a ruby in color, is served with wild fowl and red meats, and Traminer, straw yellow in color, has a distinctive aroma and is served with fish. A Pinot Bianco, straw yellow with greenish glints, has a light bouquet and a noble history, and is also served with fish.

The wines of **Lombardy (Milan)** are justly renowned, and if you don't believe me, would you then take the advice of Leonardo da Vinci, Pliny, and Virgil? These great men have sung the praise of this wine-rich region bordered by the Alps to the north and the Po River to the south. To go with the tasty, refined cuisine of the Lombard kitchen, add such wines as Frecciarossa (a pale straw yellow in color with a delicate bouquet; order with fish), Sassella (bright ruby red in color; order with game, red meat, and roasts), and the amusingly named Inferno (a deep ruby red in color with a penetrating bouquet; order with meats).

The finest wines in Italy, mostly red, are said to be produced on the vine-clad slopes of the **Piedmont** district (Turin), the word translated literally as "at the foot of the mountain." Of course, Asti Spumante, the color of straw with an abundant champagne-like foam, is considered the prototype of Italian sparkling wines. While traveling through this area of northwestern Italy, you'll want to sample Barbaresco (brilliant ruby red with a delicate flavor; order with red meats), Barolo (also brilliant ruby red, best when it mellows into a velvety old age), Cortese (pale straw-yellow with green glints; order with fish), and Gattinara (an intense ruby-red beauty in youth that changes with age). Piedmont is also the home of Vermouth, a white wine to which aromatic herbs and spices, among other ingredients, have been added. It's served as an apéritif.

Liguria, which includes Genoa and the Italian Riviera, doesn't have as many wine-growing regions as other parts of Italy, yet produces dozens of different grapes. These are made into such wines as Dolceacqua (lightish ruby red, served with hearty food) and Vermentino Ligure (a pale yellow in color with a good bouquet; often served with fish).

The wines of **Sardinia** are usually heavy, but many find them satisfying. They include Canonau, a light garnet-red color, served with desserts; Vermentino di Gallura, straw yellow in color, produced in both dry and sweet varieties; and one of the several versions of Torbato, classified as extra, passito, and secco.

The wines of **Sicily,** called a "paradise of the grape," were extolled by the ancient poets, including Martial. Caesar himself lavished praise on Mamertine when it was served at a banquet honoring his third consulship. Marsala, of course, an amber-yellow wine served with desserts, is the most famous wine of Sicily; it's velvety and fruity and is sometimes used in cooking, as in veal marsala. The wines made from grapes grown in the volcanic soil of Etna come in both red and white varieties. Also try the Corvo Bianco di Casteldaccia (straw yellow in color, with a distinctive bouquet) and the Corvo Rosso di Casteldaccia (ruby red in color, almost garnet in tone, full-bodied and fruity).

I've only cited a few popular wines. Rest assured that there are hundreds more you may want to discover for yourself.

OTHER DRINKS Italians drink other libations as well. Perhaps their most famous drink is **Campari,** bright red in color and herb flavored, with a quinine bitterness to it. It's customary to serve it with ice cubes and soda.

Beer is also made in Italy and, in general, it is lighter than that served in Germany. If you order beer in a bar or restaurant, chances are it will be an imported beer, for which you will be charged accordingly unless you specify otherwise. Some famous names in European beer-making now operate plants in Italy where the brew has been "adjusted" to Italian taste.

High-proof **Grappa** is made from the "leftovers" after the grapes have been pressed. Many Italians drink this before or after dinner (some put it into their coffee). To an untrained foreign palate, it often appears rough and harsh. Some say it's an acquired taste.

Italy has many **brandies** (according to an agreement with France, Italians are not supposed to use the word "cognac" in labeling them). A popular one is Vecchia Romagna.

Other popular drinks include several **liqueurs,** to which the Italians are addicted. Try herb-flavored Strega, or perhaps an Amaretto tasting of almonds. One of the best known is Maraschino, taking its name from a type of cherry used in its preparation. Galliano is also herb flavored, and Sambucca (anisette) is made of aniseed and is often served with a "fly" (coffee bean) in it. On a hot day, an Italian orders a vermouth, Cinzano, with a twist of lemon, ice cubes, and a squirt of soda water.

7 Recommended Books & Films

BOOKS

GENERAL & HISTORY   Luigi Barzini's *The Italians* (Macmillan, 1964) should almost be required reading for anyone contemplating a trip to Italy. The section on Sicily alone is worth the price of the book. Critics have hailed it as the liveliest analysis yet of the Italian character.

Edward Gibbon's *The History of the Decline and Fall of the Roman Empire* is published in six volumes, but Penguin issues a passable abridgement. Gibbon issued the first volume in 1776. It has been hailed as a masterpiece and considered one of the greatest histories ever written. No one has ever recaptured the saga of the glory that was Rome the way that Gibbon did.

Giuliano Procacci surveys the spectrum in his *History of the Italian People* (Harper & Row, 1973), which provides an encompassing look at how Italy became a nation.

If you like your history short, readable, and condensed, try *A Short History of Italy,* edited by H. Hearder and D. P. Waley (Cambridge University Press, 1963).

One of the best books on the long history of the papacy—detailing its excesses, its triumphs and its defeats, and its most vivid characters—is Michael Walsh's *An Illustrated History of the Popes: Saint Peter to John Paul II* (St. Martin's Press, 1980).

The roots of modern Italy are explored in Christopher Hibbert's *Garibaldi and His Enemies: The Clash of Arms and Personalities in the Making of Italy* (Penguin, 1989).

In the 20th century, the most fascinating period in Italian history was the rise and fall of Fascism, as detailed in countless works. Try Vittorio De Fiori's *Mussolini, The Man of Destiny: Studies in Fascism, Ideology and Practice* (AMS Press, 1982). One of the best and most recent biographies of Il Duce is Denis M. Smith's *Mussolini: A Biography* (Random House, 1983). Eugen Weber writes of *Varieties of Fascism: Doctrines of Revolution in the Twentieth Century* (Krieger, 1982). Stein Larsen edited *Who Were the Fascists? Social Roots of European Fascism* (Oxford University Press, 1981).

One subject that's always engrossing is the Mafia, and that sinister organization is detailed in Pino Arlacchi's *Mafia Business: The Mafia Ethic and the Spirit of Capitalism* (Routledge, Chapman, & Hall, 1987). The Mafia from yet another point of view is described in Norman Lewis's *The Honoured Society: The Sicilian Mafia Observed* (Hippocrene Books, 1985).

William Murray's *The Last Italian: Portrait of a People* (Prentice Hall, 1991) is the writer's second volume of essays on his favorite subject—Italy, its people and civilization. The *New York Times* called it "partly a lover's keen, observant diary of his affair."

Amzat and His Brothers: Three Italian Tales Remembered, by Floriano Vecchi, retold by Paula Fox (Orchard/Jackson, 1993), is a rare book of folktales told to the author (Fox) by a friend (Vecchi), who grew up near Bologna. One story, although set in Italy, evokes *The Bremen Town Musicians*. This is a tour de force of transferring the spoken word to the printed page.

Once Upon a Time in Italy: The Vita Italiana of an American Journalist, by Jack Casserly (Roberts Rinehart, 1995), is the entertaining and affectionate memoir of a former bureau chief in Rome from 1957 to 1964. He captures the spirit of *Italian sparita* (bygone Italy) with such celebrity cameos as those of Maria Callas and the American expatriate singer, Bricktop.

ART & ARCHITECTURE   Michael Baxandall provides a primer in the social history of the pictorial style in *Painting & Experience in Fifteenth Century Italy* (Oxford University Press, 1988).

In art, the Renaissance period in Italy seems to capture the public's imagination more than any other time, and one of the best accounts is provided in Peter Murray's *The Architecture of the Italian Renaissance* (Schocken, 1986). The same subject is covered by Frederick N. Hartt in his *History of Italian Renaissance Painting* (Abrams, 1987).

Giorgio Vasari's *The Lives of the Most Eminent Italian Architects, Painters, and Sculptors* was originally published in 1550 and was enlarged in 1568. In spite of some fanciful inventions, it remains the definitive work on Renaissance artists, from Cimabue to Michelangelo. Penguin Classics issues a paperback abridged version, called *Lives of the Artists* (1985).

Michael Levey has produced two engrossing books: *Early Renaissance* (Penguin, 1967) and *High Renaissance* (Penguin, 1975), both available in paperback. From a somewhat scholarly point of view, J. R. Hale edited the *Concise Encyclopedia of the Italian Renaissance* (Thames & Hudson, 1981), an exemplary reference book.

The Sistine Chapel: A Glorious Restoration, by Michael Hirst et al. (Abrams, 1994), tells of the lengthy and painstaking restoration of Michelangelo's 16th-century frescoes in the Vatican. It features nearly 300 color photographs. Hirst is an art history professor at the University of London.

FICTION & BIOGRAPHY   Both foreign and domestic writers have tried to capture the peculiar nature of Italy—each seen from a completely different angle—in such notable works as Thomas Mann's *Death in Venice* (Random House, 1965); E. M. Forster's *Room with a View* (Random House, 1923), the subject of a famous movie in the 1980s; and Ernest Hemingway's *A Farewell to Arms* (Macmillan, 1929), which remains one of the most enduring novels of World War I. Fred M. Stewart's books are so popular they're sold in supermarkets, and he spins a lively tale in his *Century* (NAL, 1981), tracing the saga of several generations of an Italian family.

John Hersey's Pulitzer Prize–winner *A Bell for Adano* (Knopf, 1944) has now entered the realm of a classic and is frequently reprinted. It is a well-written and disturbing story of the American invasion of Italy.

Benvenuto Cellini's *Autobiography,* also available in Penguin Classics, was first printed in Italy in 1728, although Cellini lived from 1500 to 1571. It's a Renaissance romp, filled with gossip and interesting details, so much so that it has been compared to a novel. It launched the tide of the romantic movement.

Giorgio Bassani, born in 1916, provides the bourgeois milieu of a Ferrara Jewish community under Mussolini in *The Garden of the Finzi-Continis* (Harcourt Brace Jovanovich, 1977).

The novels of Alberto Moravia, born in 1907, are classified as neo-Realism. Moravia is one of the best-known Italian writers read in English. Notable works include *Roman Tales* (Farrar, Straus, and Cudahy, 1957), *The Woman of Rome* (Penguin, 1957; also available in the Playboy paperback series), and *The Conformist* (Greenwood Press, 1975).

Maria Meneghini Callas, by Michael Scott (Northeastern University, 1992), is written by the same author who published *The Great Caruso*. Here he turns his attention to the controversial diva (1923–77), documenting the prima donna at her prime but also describing the deterioration of her voice, which began in the 1950s and lasted until her death.

Donatello, one of the supreme artists of the western world, known for such sculptures as *Mary Magdalene* in the 1450s, was the subject of at least two books in 1994: *Donatello Sculptor*, by John Pope-Hennessy (Abbeville Press, 1994), and *Donatello and His World: Sculpture of the Italian Renaissance*, by Joachim Poeschke (Harry N. Abrams, 1994).

Verdi: A Biography, by Mary Jane Phillips-Matz (Oxford University Press, 1994), is a towering work by an author who spent more than 30 years in research. Many new details about Verdi have been revealed and some myths exploded—namely that Verdi had a poverty-stricken childhood (his father actually had substantial land holdings).

TRAVEL H. V. Morton's *A Traveler in Italy* (Methuen, 1964) is a towering work by one of the world's most widely read travel writers, who has a rare sense of history and is at his best in describing great centers of culture such as Florence and Venice.

Many great writers—when faced with the challenge of Italy—decided to become travel writers. These have included Charles Dickens, who wrote *Pictures from Italy* (Ecco Press, 1988), a classic 19th-century account of the Grand Tour, going from Tuscany to Naples via Rome. Wolfgang Goethe's *Italian Journey* (Penguin, 1982) devotes more attention to Roman antiquities, and Henry James's *Italian Hours* (1909) is young James at his best, capturing the special atmosphere of Italy. It is currently issued by Ecco Press.

D. H. Lawrence and Italy (Viking Press, 1972) is three classic Italian travelogues collected in a single volume that includes *Sea and Sardinia* and *Twilight in Italy*. It also includes *Etruscan Places*, which was published posthumously. Lawrence writes of a way of life that was disappearing even as he wrote the work.

Mary McCarthy gave Italian travel literature two distinguished works, *The Stones of Florence* (Harcourt Brace Jovanovich, 1959) and *Venice Observed* (Penguin, 1972). "The lady of the barbs" pulls no punches in observing these two famed tourist meccas with a sharp eye for detail. These two works were definitely researched on the streets and not in some library.

Kate Simon's *Italy: The Places in Between* (Harper & Row, 1960) explores many of the towns overlooked as one races between Rome, Florence, and Venice, including Ferrara, Gubbio, Spoleto, and Padua.

Within Tuscany: Reflections on a Time and Place, by Matthew Spender (Viking, 1992), is the work of a London-born sculptor who's lived in Tuscany for a quarter of a century. He spins a lively account of the cultural, artistic, and literary soul of the region.

About Florence The city of the Renaissance is one of the most written-about in the world—from many points of view. Peter Burke's *Culture and Society in Renaissance Italy 1420–1540* received acclaim (published in London by Batsford, 1972, it's often available in libraries). Florence is a backdrop for much of

R. Couglan's *The Life and Times of Michelangelo 1475–1564* (Time-Life International, 1975).

J. H. Phumb wrote *The Penguin Book of the Renaissance* (Penguin, 1964), which offers a lively account of the era, as does B. Pullan's *A History of Early Renaissance Art* (St. Martin's Press, 1972). N. Rubinstein also provides an interesting portrait of those patrons of the arts, the Medicis, in *The Government of Florence Under the Medici 1434–1494* (Oxford University Press, 1966). *Florence: The Biography of a City*, by Christopher Hibbert (W. W. Norton, 1993), was hailed as a "lavish celebration" of an extraordinary city.

The City of Florence: Historical Vistas and Personal Sightings, by R.W.B. Lewis (Farrar, Straus & Giroux, 1995), the author of a Pulitzer Prize–winning biography of Edith Wharton, writes of the city where he lived for some half a century. One reviewer called the guide "treasurable."

About Venice   John Ruskin wrote a definitive account of this city in his *The Stones of Venice,* first published in 1853 and in print by Little, Brown (1981). Although Ruskin may have come to Venice to debunk (he, for example, found San Giorgio Maggiore "contemptible"), his work has many notable sections, including "The Nature of Gothic."

Peter Lauritzen published *Venice, a Thousand Years of Culture and Civilization* (Atheneum, 1978), and John J. Norwich traces a *History of Venice* (Knopf, 1982). Oliver Logan's *Culture and Society in Venice 1470–1790* is a well-researched work, often available in libraries (London: Batsford, 1972).

A more recent work is George Bull's *Venice, the Most Triumphant City* (St. Martin's, 1982).

A guide to Venice's sights is *Frommer's Walking Tours: Venice,* by Robert Ullian (Macmillan, 1994).

FILMS

Italian films have never regained the glory enjoyed in the postwar era. Roberto Rossellini's *Rome, Open City* (1946) influenced Hollywood's *films noirs* of the late 1940s. Set in a poor section of occupied Rome, the film tells the story of a partisan priest and a Communist who aid the resistance.

Vittorio de Sica's *Bicycle Thief* (1948) achieved world renown. Also set in one of Rome's poor districts, it tells of the destruction of a child's illusions and the solitude of a steel worker.

The Leopard (1963), set in Sicily, gained a world audience for Luchino Visconti and was the first major Italian film made in color. Visconti first came to the attention of cinema audiences with his 1942 *Ossessione* (Obsession).

Federico Fellini burst into Italian cinema with his highly individual style, beginning with *La Strada* (1954) and going on to such classics as *Juliet of the Spirits* (1965), *Amarcord* (1974), *Roma,* and *The City of Women* (1980). *La Dolce Vita* (1961) helped to define an era.

Marxist, homosexual, and practicing Catholic Pier Paolo Pasolini was the most controversial of Italian filmmakers until his mysterious murder in 1975. Explicit sex scenes in *Decameron* (1971) helped make it a world box-office hit.

Bernardo Bertolucci, once an assistant to Pasolini, achieved fame with such films as *The Conformist* (1970), based on the novel by Moravia. His *1900* is an epic spanning 20th-century Italian history and politics. One of his biggest international films was *Last Tango in Paris* (1971), starring Marlon Brando.

Michelangelo Antonioni swept across the screens of the world with his films of psychological anguish, including *La Notta* (1961), *L'Avventura* (1964), and *The Red Desert* (1964).

A Neapolitan director, Francesco Rosi became known for semidocumentary films, exploring such subjects as the Mafia in *Salvatore Giuliano* (1962) and the army in *Just Another War* (1970). His *Three Brothers* (1980) examines three different political attitudes, as the brothers have a reunion at their mother's funeral in Apulia.

Current Italian directors include the Taviani brothers, Paolo and Vittorio. Their *Padre Padrone* (1977) takes place in Sardinia and their *Kaos* (1984) is set in Sicily and is an adaptation of a Pirandello story. Their late 1980s film, *Good Morning, Babylon,* brought them worldwide acclaim. The Taviani brothers created a stir in 1994 with the release of their film *Fiorile.* Set in their native Tuscany, it supposedly was a local folktale passed on by their mother. The film is a multigenerational saga.

Although directors more than stars have dominated Italian cinema, three actors have emerged to gain worldwide fame, including Marcello Mastroianni, star of such hits as *La Dolce Vita* (1961), and Sophia Loren, whose best film is considered *Two Women* (1961). Mastroianni was Fellini's favorite male actor and he starred him once again in *$8^{1}/_{2}$*.

Anna Magnani not only starred in Italian films but made many American films as well, including *The Rose Tattoo* (1955), with Burt Lancaster, and *The Fugitive Kind* (1960), with Marlon Brando.

Several Italian films in the late 1980s and the 1990s have captured an international audience. *Cinema Paradiso,* directed by Giuseppe Tornatore, won the Academy Award for Best Foreign Language Film of 1989. *Fellini's Intervista* (1992) is a film within a film, with the director, who died in 1993, discussing his movies and the actors who starred in them.

Caro Diario (1994), starring and directed by Nanni Moretti, is a three-part traipse through modern-day Italy. Moretti, a cult figure in Italy, began to make an impression in America with this film. The actor-director is noted for his prickly personality, quirky sense of humor, and deadpan tone.

3 Planning a Trip to Italy

This chapter is devoted to the where, when, and how of your trip—the advance-planning issues required to get it together and take it on the road.

After deciding where to go, most people have two fundamental questions: "What will it cost?" and "How do I get there?" This chapter will answer both these questions and also resolve other important issues, such as when to go, what pretrip preparations are needed, where to obtain more information about Italy, and much more.

1 Information, Entry Requirements & Money

INFORMATION

For information before you go, contact the **Italian National Tourist Office.** In the United States branches are located at 630 Fifth Ave., Suite 1565, **New York,** NY 10111 (☎ 212/245-4822); 500 N. Michigan Ave., **Chicago,** IL 60611 (☎ 312/644-0990); and 12400 Wilshire Blvd., Suite 550, **Los Angeles,** CA 90025 (☎ 310/820-0098). In Canada, contact the Italian National Tourist Office at 1 Place Ville Marie, **Montréal,** Québec ☎ 514/866-7667); and in England at 1 Princes St., **London** W1R 8AY (☎ 071/408-1254).

You can also write directly (in English or Italian) to the provincial or local tourist boards of areas you plan to visit. These provincial tourist boards (known as **Ente Provinciale per il Turismo**) operate in the principal towns of the provinces. The local tourist boards (known as **Azienda Autonoma Soggiorno**) operate in all places of tourist interest, and a list can be obtained from the Italian government tourist offices.

Other useful sources are, of course, **newspapers and magazines.** To find the latest articles that have been published on the destination, go to your library and consult the *Reader's Guide to Periodical Literature* and look under the city/country for listings.

You may also want to obtain **U.S. State Department** background bulletins. Contact the Superintendent of Documents, U.S. Government Printing Office, Washington, D.C. 20402 (☎ 202/783-3238).

A good travel agent can also be a source of information. Make sure that the agent is a member of the **American Society of Travel**

Agents (ASTA). If you get poor service, write to ASTA Consumer Affairs Department, 1101 King St., Alexandria, VA 23314, or you can call their direct line at 703/739-2851.

And, finally, we come to the best source of all—friends and other travelers who have just returned from Italy.

ENTRY REQUIREMENTS

United States, Canadian, British, Australian, New Zealand, and Irish citizens with a valid passport do not need a visa to enter Italy if they do not expect to stay more than 90 days and do not expect to work there. Those who, after entering Italy, find that they would like to stay more than 90 days can apply for a permit for an additional stay of 90 days, which as a rule is granted immediately.

MONEY

There are no restrictions as to how much foreign currency you can bring into Italy, although visitors should declare the amount brought in. This proves to the Italian Customs office that the currency came from outside the country and therefore the same amount or less can be taken out. Italian currency taken into or out of Italy may not exceed 200,000 lire in denominations of 50,000 lire or lower.

The basic unit of Italian currency is the **lira** (plural: **lire**). Coins are issued in denominations of 10, 20, 100, 200, and 500 lire, and bills come in denominations of 1,000 lire; 5,000 lire; 10,000 lire; 50,000 lire; 100,000 lire; and 500,000 lire.

The Italian Lira, the U.S. Dollar & the U.K. Pound

At this writing, US$1 = approximately 1,600 Italian lire, and this was the rate of exchange used to calculate the dollar values given throughout the book. The rate fluctuates from day to day and may not be the same when you travel to Italy.

Likewise, the ratio of the British pound to the lira fluctuates constantly. At press time, £1 = approximately 2,745 lire, an exchange rate reflected in the table below.

Lira	U.S.$	U.K.£	Lira	U.S.$	U.K.£
50	0.03	0.02	20,000	12.50	7.28
100	0.06	0.04	25,000	15.63	9.10
300	0.19	0.11	30,000	18.75	10.92
500	0.31	0.18	35,000	21.88	12.74
700	0.44	0.25	40,000	25.00	14.56
1,000	0.63	0.36	45,000	28.13	16.38
1,500	0.94	0.55	50,000	31.25	18.20
2,000	1.25	0.73	100,000	62.50	36.40
3,000	1.88	1.09	125,000	78.13	45.50
4,000	2.50	1.46	150,000	93.75	54.60
5,000	3.13	1.82	200,000	125.00	72.80
7,500	4.69	2.73	250,000	156.25	91.00
10,000	6.25	3.64	500,000	312.50	182.00
15,000	9.38	5.46	1,000,000	625.00	364.00

What Things Cost in Rome	U.S.$
Taxi (central rail station to piazza di Spagna)	8.80
Subway or public bus (to any destination)	0.75
Local telephone call	0.14
Double room at the Hassler (very expensive)	387.50–562.50
Double room at Hotel Columbus (moderate)	153.00
Double room at Hotel Corot (inexpensive)	93.75–112.57
Continental breakfast (cappuccino and croissant at most cafés and bars)	3.00
Lunch for one at Ristorante da Pancrazio (moderate)	27.00
Dinner for one, without wine, at Relais Le Jardin (expensive)	75.00
Dinner for one, without wine, at L'Eau Vive (moderate)	32.00
Dinner for one, without wine, at Otello alla Concordi (inexpensive)	23.00
Pint of beer	3.75
Glass of wine	2.00
Coca-Cola	1.50
Cup of coffee	1.30
Roll of color film, 36 exposures	5.90
Admission to the Vatican museums and Sistine Chapel	7.80
Movie ticket	7.95
Theater ticket at the Terme di Caracalla	15.00–39.00

For the best exchange rate, go to a bank, not to hotels or shops. Currency and traveler's checks (for which you'll receive a better rate than cash) can be changed at the airport and some travel agencies, such as American Express and Thomas Cook. Note the rates; it can sometimes pay to shop around.

TRAVELER'S CHECKS   Before leaving home, purchase traveler's checks and arrange to carry some ready cash (usually about $250, depending on your needs). In the event of theft, the value of your checks will be refunded if properly documented. Most large banks sell traveler's checks, charging fees that average between 1% and 2% of the value of the checks you buy, although some out-of-the-way banks, in rare instances, have charged as much as 7%. If your bank wants more than a 2% commission, it sometimes pays to call the traveler's check issuers directly for the address of outlets where this commission will cost less.

Issuers sometimes have agreements with groups to sell checks commission free. For example, Automobile Association of America (AAA) clubs sell American Express checks in several currencies without commission.

American Express (☎ 800/221-7282 in the U.S. and Canada) is one of the largest and most immediately recognized issuers of traveler's checks. No commission is charged to holders of certain types of American Express credit cards. The company issues checks denominated in U.S. dollars, Canadian dollars, British pounds sterling, Swiss francs, French francs, German marks, Japanese yen, and

What Things Cost in Naples	U.S.$
Taxi from rail station to the port	8.50
Subway (to any destination)	0.90
Local telephone call	0.14
Double room at Grande Albergo Vesuvio (expensive)	243.75
Double room at Hotel Rex (inexpensive)	100.00
Continental breakfast (cappuccino and croissant)	2.25
Lunch for one at Giuseppone a Mare (moderate)	21.00
Lunch for one at Brandi (historic pizzeria)	15.00
Dinner for one, without wine, at La Sacrestia (moderate)	36.00
Dinner for one, without wine, at Rosolino (inexpensive)	22.00
Dinner for one, without wine, at Dante e Beatrice	18.00
Pint of beer	3.60
Glass of wine	1.50
Coca-Cola	1.50
Cappuccino	0.85
Roll of color film, 36 exposures	5.95
Admission to the Museo Archeologico Nazionale	4.80
Movie ticket	5.00

Dutch guilders. The vast majority of checks sold in North America are denominated in U.S. dollars. For questions or problems that arise outside the U.S. or Canada, contact any of the company's many regional representatives.

Citicorp (☎ 800/645-6556 in the U.S. and Canada, or 813/623-1709, collect, from anywhere else in the world) issues checks in U.S. dollars, British pounds, German marks, Japanese yen, and Australian dollars.

Thomas Cook (☎ 800/223-7373 in the U.S. and Canada; otherwise call 609/987-7300 collect from other parts of the world) issues MasterCard traveler's checks denominated in U.S. dollars, Canadian dollars, French francs, British pounds, German marks, Dutch guilders, Spanish pesetas, Australian dollars, and Japanese yen. Depending on individual banking laws in each of the various states, some of the above-mentioned currencies might not be available at every outlet.

Interpayment Services (☎ 800/221-2426 in the U.S. or Canada; call 212/858-8500 collect from other parts of the world) sells VISA checks which are issued by a consortium of member banks and the Thomas Cook organization. Traveler's checks are denominated in U.S. or Canadian dollars, British pounds, and German marks.

CURRENCY EXCHANGE   Many hotels in Italy will not accept a dollar-denominated check, and if they do, they'll certainly charge for the conversion. In some cases they'll accept countersigned traveler's checks, or a credit card, but if you're prepaying a deposit on hotel reservations, it's cheaper and easier to pay with a check drawn upon an Italian bank.

This can be arranged by a large commercial bank or by a currency specialist such as **Ruesch International,** 825 14th St. NW, Washington, DC 20005 (☎ 202/408-1200, or toll free 800/424-2923), which can perform a wide variety of conversion-related financial transactions for individual travelers. To place an order, call them and tell them the type and amount of the check you need. Ruesch will quote a U.S. dollar equivalent, adding a $2 fee per check as their service fee. After receiving your dollar-denominated personal check for the agreed-upon amount, Ruesch will mail you a lire-denominated bank draft, drawn at an Italian bank and payable to whichever party you specified. Ruesch will also convert checks expressed in foreign currency into U.S. dollars, provide foreign currencies in cash from more than 120 countries, and sell traveler's checks payable in either dollars or any of six foreign currencies, but not in Italian lire. (Most Italian banks and bureaux de change prefer traveler's checks denominated in either U.S. dollars or Swiss francs. Ruesch can provide either.) In addition to its Washington, D.C., office, Ruesch maintains offices in New York, Los Angeles, Chicago, Atlanta, and Boston, although the Washington, D.C., office can supply, through phone orders, any of the bank draft and traveler's check services mentioned above. Ruesch will mail brochures and information packets upon request.

2 When to Go—Climate, Holidays & Events

CLIMATE

It's warm all over Italy in summer. The high temperatures (measured in Italy in degrees Celsius) begin in Rome in May, often lasting until some time in October. Winters in the north of Italy are cold with rain and snow, but in the south the weather is warm all year, averaging 50°F in winter (summers tend to be very hot, especially inland).

For the most part, it's drier in Italy than in North America. High temperatures, therefore, don't seem as bad since the humidity is lower. In Rome, Naples, and the south, temperatures can stay in the 90s for days, but nights are most often comfortably cooler.

Italy's Average Daily Temperature & Monthly Rainfall

FLORENCE	Jan	Feb	Mar	Apr	May	June	July	Aug	Sept	Oct	Nov	Dec
Temp.(°F)	45	47	50	60	67	75	77	70	64	63	55	46
Rainfall"	3	3.3	3.7	2.7	2.2	1.4	1.4	2.7	3.2	4.9	3.8	2.9

NAPLES	Jan	Feb	Mar	Apr	May	June	July	Aug	Sept	Oct	Nov	Dec
Temp.(°F)	50	54	58	63	70	75	83	79	74	66	60	52
Rainfall"	4.7	4	3	3.8	2.4	.8	.8	2.6	3.5	5.8	5.1	3.7

ROME	Jan	Feb	Mar	Apr	May	June	July	Aug	Sept	Oct	Nov	Dec
Temp.(°F)	49	52	57	62	70	77	82	78	73	65	56	47
Rainfall"	2.3	1.5	2.9	3.0	2.8	2.9	1.5	1.9	2.8	2.6	3.0	2.1

VENICE	Jan	Feb	Mar	Apr	May	June	July	Aug	Sept	Oct	Nov	Dec
Temp.(°F)	43	48	53	60	67	72	77	74	68	60	54	44
Rainfall"	2.3	1.5	2.9	3.0	2.8	2.9	1.5	1.9	2.8	2.6	3.0	2.1

HOLIDAYS

Offices and shops in Italy are closed on the following dates: January 1 (New Year's Day), Easter Monday, April 25 (Liberation Day), May 1 (Labor Day), August 15 (Assumption of the Virgin), November 1 (All Saints' Day), December 8 (Feast of the Immaculate Conception), December 25 (Christmas Day), and December 26 (Santo Stefano).

Closings are also observed in the following cities on feast days honoring their patron saints: Venice, April 25 (St. Mark); Florence, Genoa, and Turin, June 24 (St. John the Baptist); Rome, June 29 (Sts. Peter and Paul); Palermo, July 15 (Santa Rosalia); Naples, September 19 (St. Gennaro); Bologna, October 4 (St. Petronio); Cagliari, October 30 (St. Saturnino); Trieste, November 3 (San Giusto); Bari, December 6 (St. Nicola); and Milan, December 7 (St. Ambrose).

ITALY CALENDAR OF EVENTS

For more information about these and other events, contact the various tourist offices throughout Italy. Dates often vary from year to year.

January

- **Viareggio Carnival,** on the Tuscan Riviera. Fireworks, pageants, parades, and a flower show. Dates vary.
- **Epiphany Celebrations.** All cities, towns, and villages in Italy stage Roman Catholic Epiphany observances. One of the most festive celebrations is the Epiphany Fair at Rome's piazza Navona. Usually January 5–6.
- **Festival of Italian Popular Song,** San Remo (the Italian Riviera). A three-day festival when major artists perform the latest Italian song releases. Late January.
- **Foire de Saint Ours,** Aosta, Valle d'Aosta. Observing a tradition that's existed for 10 centuries, artisans from the mountain valleys come together to display their wares—often made of wood, lace, wool, or wrought iron—created during the long winter months. Late January.

February

✪ **Carnevale in Venice.** Carnevale is a riotous time in Venice. Theatrical presentations and masked balls cap the festivities.

Where: Throughout Venice and on the islands in the lagoon. **When:** The week before Lent. **How:** The balls are by invitation, but the street events and fireworks are open to everyone. More information is available from the Venice Tourist Office, San Marco Ascensione 71C (☎ 041/522-6356).

March

- **Good Friday Processions.** Held throughout Italy. The most notable one is in Rome. Usually the end of March.

April

- **Easter Week** observances, throughout Italy. Processions and age-old ceremonies—some from pagan days, some from the Middle Ages—are staged. The best are in Sicily. Begin four days before Easter Sunday.
- **Scoppio del Carro** (Explosion of the Cart), in Florence. An ancient observance: A cart laden with flowers and fireworks is drawn by three white oxen to the Duomo, where at noon mass a mechanical dove detonates it from the altar. Easter Sunday.

May

⭐ **Maggio Musicale Fiorentino ("Musical May Florentine").** Italy's oldest and most prestigious festival takes place in Florence, the venue for opera, ballet performances, and concerts.

   Where: Teatro Comunale, via Solferino 16; Teatro della Pergola, via della Pergola 18; and various other venues, including piazza della Signoria and the courtyard of the Pitti Palace. **When:** Late April into July. **How:** Schedule and ticket information available from Maggio Musicale Fiorentino/Teatro Comunale, via Solferino 16, 50123 Firenze (☎ 055/2779-1). Tickets cost 20,000–250,000 lire ($12.50–$156.25).

June

• **L'Infiorata,** Genzano, Lazio, is a religious procession along streets carpeted with flowers in splendid designs, often copies of famous artworks. Details available from Azienda Autonoma di Soggiorno e Turismo dei Laghi e Castelli Romani, via Risorgimento 1, 00041 Albano Laziale (☎ 06/938-4081).

• **San Ranieri e Gioco del Ponte,** Pisa. Pisa honors its own saint, with candlelit parades followed the next day by eight-rower teams in 16th-century costumes competing. June 16.

⭐ **Festival dei Due Mondi.** Dating from 1958, this was the creation of Maestro Gian Carlo Menotti. International performers convene for three weeks of dance, drama, opera, concerts, and art exhibits.

   Where: Spoleto, an Umbrian hill town north of Rome. **When:** June 24–July 16. **How:** Tickets and information available from Festival dei Due Mondi, via Cesare Beccaria 18, 00196 Roma (☎ 06/321-0288). Information is also available from The Festival Office, c/o Teatro Nuovo, 06049 Spoleto, Italy (☎ 0743/44097).

July

⭐ **Il Palio.** Palio fever grips the Tuscan hill town of Siena for a wild and exciting horse race from the Middle Ages. Pageantry, costumes, and the celebrations of the victorious *contrada* mark the well-attended spectacle. It's a "no rules" event: Even a horse without a rider can win the race.

   Where: The piazza del Campo at Siena. **When:** July 2 and August 16. **How:** Details available by writing Azienda di Promozione Turistica, Piazza del Campo 56, 53100 Siena (☎ 0577/280551).

• **Arena Outdoor Opera Season, Verona.** Brings culture buffs to the 20,000-seat Roman amphitheater. Season lasts from early July to mid-August.

• **La Festa del Redentore** (The Feast of the Redeemer), in Venice. Marks the lifting of the plague in July of 1578, with fireworks, pilgrimages, and boating on the lagoon. Third Saturday and Sunday in July.

• **Festival Internazionale di Musica Antica,** Urbino. A cultural extravaganza, as international performers converge on Raphael's birthplace. It is the most important Renaissance and baroque music festival in Italy. Details available from Urbino Tourist Information, via Puccinotti 35 (☎ 0722/2613).

August

⭐ **Venice International Film Festival.** Ranking after Cannes, this film festival at Venice brings together stars, directors, producers, and filmmakers from all over the world. Films are shown both day and night to an international jury.

Where: Palazzo del Cinema, on the Lido. **When:** Late August to early September. **How:** Contact the Venice Tourist Office, San Marco Ascensione 71C, 30100 Venezia (☎ 041/522-6356), for exact dates in 1996.

September

- **Regatta Storica,** on the Grand Canal in Venice. All seaworthy gondolas in Venice participate in this maritime spectacular. First Sunday in September.

October

- **Sagra del Tartufo,** Alba, Piedmont. Honors the expensive truffle in Alba, the truffle capital of Italy, with contests, truffle-hound competitions, and tastings of this ugly but very expensive fungus. For details, contact the Azienda di Promozione Turistica, piazza Medford, 12051 Alba (☎ 0173/35833).

ROME CALENDAR OF EVENTS

January

- **Carnival,** in piazza Navona. Marks the last day of the children's market and lasts until dawn of the following day. Usually January 5.
- **Festa di Sant'Agnese,** at Sant' Agnese Fuori le Mura. An ancient ceremony in which two lambs are blessed and shorn. Their wool is then used later for palliums. Usually January 17.

March

- **Festa di Santa Francesca Romana,** at piazzale del Colosseo near the Church of Santa Francesco Romana in the Roman Forum. A blessing of cars. Usually March 9.
- **Festa di San Giuseppe,** in the Trionfale Quarter, north of the Vatican. The heavily decorated statue of the saint is brought out at a fair with food stalls, concerts, and sporting events. Usually March 19.

April

- **Festa della Primavera.** The Spanish Steps are decked out with banks of flowers, and later orchestral and choral concerts are presented in Trinità dei Monti. Dates vary.
- **Holy Week.** The most notable procession is led by the pope, passing the Colosseum and the Roman Forum up to Palatine Hill. A torchlit parade caps the observance. Sometimes at the end of March, but often in April.
- **Easter Sunday,** piazza di San Pietro. In an event broadcast around the world, the pope gives his blessing from a balcony of St. Peter's.

May

- **International Horse Show,** at the piazza di Siena in the Villa Borghese. Usually May 1–10 but dates can vary.

June

- **Son et Lumière,** at the Roman Forum and Tivoli. These areas are dramatically lit at night. Early June until the end of September.
- **Festa di San Pietro,** St. Peter's Basilica. The most significant Roman religious festival, observed with solemn rites in St. Peter's. Usually around June 29.

July

- ✪ **La Festa di Nolantri.** Trastevere, the most colorful quarter of Old Rome, becomes a gigantic outdoor restaurant, as tons of food and drink are consumed at tables lining the streets. Merrymakers and musicians provide the entertainment.

Where: Trastevere. **When:** Mid-July. **How:** After reaching the quarter, find the first empty table and try to get a waiter. But guard your valuables. Details available from Ente Provinciale per il Turismo, via Parigi 11, 00185 Roma (☎ 06/488-99-200).

August

- **Festa delle Catene,** in the Church of San Pietro in Vincoli. The relics of St. Peter's captivity go on display. August 1.

September

- **Sagra dell'Uva,** a harvest festival in the Basilica of Maxentius in the Roman Forum. Musicians in ancient costumes entertain, and grapes are sold at reduced prices. Dates vary, usually early September.

December

- **Christmas Blessing of the Pope,** piazza di San Pietro. Delivered at noon from a balcony of St. Peter's Basilica. It's broadcast around the world. December 25.

3 Health & Insurance

HEALTH   You will encounter few health problems traveling in Italy. The tap water is generally safe to drink, the milk pasteurized, and health services good. Occasionally the change in diet may cause some minor diarrhea so you may want to take some antidiarrhea medicine along.

Carry all your vital medicine in your carry-on luggage and bring enough prescribed medicines to last you during your stay. Bring along copies of your prescriptions that are written in the generic—not brand-name—form. If you need a doctor, your hotel can recommend one or you can contact your embassy or consulate. You can also obtain a list of English-speaking doctors before you leave from the **International Association for Medical Assistance to Travelers (IAMAT),** in the United States at 417 Center St., Lewiston, NY 14092 (☎ 716/754-4883); in Canada, at 40 Regal Rd., Guelph, ON N1K 1B5 (☎ 519/836-0102).

If you suffer from a chronic illness or special medical condition, talk to your doctor before taking the trip. For conditions such as epilepsy, diabetes, or heart condition, wear a Medic Alert identification bracelet or necklace, which will immediately alert any doctor to your condition and will provide Medic Alert's 24-hour hotline phone number so that foreign doctors can obtain medical information on you. A lifetime membership costs $35, $45, or $60, depending on your choice of identification. In addition, there is a $15 fee. Contact the **Medic Alert Foundation,** P.O. Box 1009, Turlock, CA 95381-1009 (☎ 800/432-5378).

INSURANCE   Before purchasing any additional insurance, check your homeowner's, automobile, and medical insurance policies, as well as the insurance provided by your credit card companies and auto and travel clubs. You may have adequate off-premises theft coverage or your credit card company may even provide cancellation coverage if the ticket is paid for with a credit card.

Remember, Medicare only covers U.S. citizens traveling in Mexico and Canada.

Also note that to submit any claim you must always have thorough documentation, including all receipts, police reports, medical records, and such.

If you are prepaying for your vacation or are taking a charter or any other flight that has cancellation penalties, look into cancellation insurance.

Travel Guard International, 1145 Clark Street, Stevens Point, WI 54481 (☎ 800/826-1300), features comprehensive insurance programs starting as low as $44. The program covers basically everything: trip cancellation and interruption—including bankruptcy and financial default, lost luggage, medical coverage abroad, emergency assistance, accidental death, and 24-hour worldwide emergency hotline.

Travel Insured International, Inc., P.O. Box 280568, East Hartford, CT 06128-0568 (☎ 800/243-3174 in the U.S., 203/528-7663 outside the U.S. between 7:45am and 7pm EST). Trip cancellation and emergency evacuation costs $5.50 for each $100 of coverage. Travel accident and illness insurance goes for $10 for 6 to 10 days, and $500 of insurance for lost, damage, or delayed luggage is $20 for 10 days. The insurance is underwritten by The Travelers.

Mutual of Omaha (Tele-Trip), Mutual of Omaha Plaza, Omaha, NE 68175, offers insurance packages priced from $115 per couple for a three-week trip. Included in the packages are travel-assistance services, and financial protection against trip cancellation, trip interruption, flight and baggage delays, accident-related medical costs, accidental death and dismemberment, and medical evacuation coverages. A deluxe package costing $213 per couple offers double the coverage of the standard policy mentioned above. Application for insurance can be made over the phone for major credit card holders (☎ 800/228-9792).

Healthcare Abroad (MEDEX), c/o Wallach & Co., 107 W. Federal St. (P.O. Box 480), Middleburg, VA 22117-0480 (☎ 703/687-3166, or 237-6615), offers coverage for between 10 and 120 days at $3 per day; this policy includes accident and sickness coverage to the tune of $100,000. Medical evacuation is also included, along with a $25,000 accidental death and dismemberment compensation. Provisions for trip cancellation and lost or stolen luggage can also be written into this policy at a nominal cost.

Access America, 6600 W. Broad St., Richmond, VA 23230 (☎ 800/284-8300), offers comprehensive travel insurance and assistance packages, including medical expenses, on-the-spot hospital payments, medical transportation, baggage insurance, trip cancellation-interruption insurance, and collision-damage insurance for a car rental. Their 24-hour hotline connects you to multilingual coordinators who can offer advice and help on medical, legal, and travel problems. Varying coverage levels are available.

Insurance for British Travelers   Most big travel agents offer their own insurance, and will probably try to sell you their package when you book a holiday. Think before you sign. Britain's Consumers' Association recommends that you insist on seeing the policy and reading the fine print before buying travel insurance.

You should also shop around for better deals. You might contact Columbus Travel Insurance Ltd. (☎ 0171/375-0011 in London), or, for students, Campus Travel (☎ 0171/730-3402 in London). Columbus Travel will sell travel insurance only to people who have been official residents of Britain for at least a year.

4 Tips for Special Travelers

FOR PEOPLE WITH DISABILITIES   Before you go, there are several agencies that can provide advance-planning information. One is the Travel Information Service, MossRehab Hospital, 1200 W. Tabor Rd., Philadelphia, PA 19141, which provides information to telephone callers only: Call 215/456-9603 for assistance with your travel needs.

You may also want to consider joining a tour for visitors with disabilities. Names and addresses of such tour operators can be obtained by writing to the **Society for the Advancement of Travel for the Handicapped,** 347 Fifth Ave., New York, NY 10016 (☎ 212/447-7248). Annual membership dues are $45, or $25 for senior citizens and students. Send a stamped, self-addressed envelope.

FEDCAP Rehabilitation Services (formerly known as the Federation of the Handicapped), 154 W. 14th St., New York, NY 10011 (☎ 212/727-4200), operates summer tours to Europe and elsewhere for its members. Membership costs $4 yearly.

You can also obtain a copy of **"Air Transportation of Handicapped Persons,"** published by the U.S. Department of Transportation. The copy is sent free by writing for Free Advisory Circular No. AC12032, Distribution Unit, U.S. Department of Transportation, Publications Division, M-4332, Washington, DC 20590.

For the blind or visually impaired, the best source is the American Foundation for the Blind, 15 W. 16th Street, New York, NY 10011 (☎ 212/620-2147, or toll free 800/232-5463 for ordering of information kits and supplies). It offers information on travel and various requirements for the transport and border formalities for seeing-eye dogs. It also issues identification cards to those who are legally blind.

The Information Center for Individuals with Disabilities, Fort Point Place, 27-43 Wormwood Street, Boston, MA 02210 (☎ 617/727-5540), is another good source. It has lists of travel agents who specialize in tours for the disabled.

One of the best organizations serving the needs of the disabled (wheelchairs and walkers) is Flying Wheels Travel, 143 West Bridge, P.O. Box 382, Owatoona, MN 55060 (☎ 800/535-6790, or 507/451-5005), offering various escorted tours and cruises internationally.

For a $20 annual fee, consider joining Mobility International USA, P.O. Box 10767, Eugene, OR 97440 (☎ 503/343-1284). It answers questions on various destinations and also offers discounts on videos, publications, and programs it sponsors.

Finally, a bimonthly publication, Handicapped Travel Newsletter, keeps you current on accessible sights worldwide for the disabled. To order an annual subscription for $15 call 903/677-1260.

Tips for British Travelers with Disabilities   **RADAR** (the Royal Association for Disability and Rehabilitation), Unit 12, City Forum, 250 City Rd., London EC1V 8AF (☎ 0171/250-3222), publishes two annual holiday guides for the disabled. "Holidays and Travel Abroad" costs £5, while "Holidays in the British Isles" goes for £7. RADAR (whose patroness is Elizabeth, the Queen Mother) also provides a number of holiday fact sheets on such subjects as sports and outdoor holidays, insurance, financial arrangements for the disabled, and accommodations within nursing care units for groups or for the elderly. Each of these fact sheets is available for 75p. Fact sheets or the above-mentioned holiday guides can be mailed outside the U.K. for a nominal mailing fee.

Another good service is the Holiday Care Service, 2 Old Bank Chambers, Station Road, Horley, Surrey RH6 9HW (☎ 01293/774-535; fax 01293/784-647), a national charity that advises on accessible accommodations for elderly and disabled people. Annual membership costs £25. Once someone is a member, he or she can receive a newsletter and access to a free reservations network for hotels throughout Britain and—to a lesser degree—Europe and the rest of the world.

If you're flying around Europe, the airlines and ground staff will help you on and off planes, and reserve seats for you with sufficient leg room, but it is essential to arrange for this assistance in advance by contacting your airline.

FOR SENIORS   Many senior discounts are available, but note that some may require membership in a particular association.

For information before you go, obtain a free booklet, **"101 Tips for the Mature Traveler,"** from **Grand Circle Travel,** 347 Congress St., Suite 3A, Boston, MA 02210 (☎ 617/350-7500, or toll free 800/221-2610).

SAGA International Holidays, 222 Berkeley St., Boston, MA 02116 (☎ 800/ 343-0273), runs all-inclusive tours for seniors, preferably for those 50 years old or older. Insurance is included in the net price of their tours.

AARP (American Association of Retired Persons) is the best organization in the United States for seniors. It offers discounts on car rentals and hotels. For more information, contact AARP at 601 E. St., NW, Washington, DC 20049 (☎ 202/434-AARP).

Information is also available from the **National Council of Senior Citizens,** 1331 F St. NW, Washington, DC 20005-1171 (☎ 202/347-8800), which charges $12 per person or per couple, for which you receive a monthly newsletter, part of which is devoted to travel tips. Reduced discounts on hotel and auto rentals are available.

If you're between 45 and 89 and need a travel companion, **Golden Companions,** P.O. Box 754, Pullman, WA 99163 (☎ 208/858-2183), might provide the answer. A research economist, Joanne R. Buteau, founded this helpful service and is quick to point out that it's not a dating service. Travelers meet potential companions through a confidential mail network. Members, once they have "connected," make their own travel arrangements. Created in 1987, this organization draws members from many walks of life. Members also receive a bimonthly travel newsletter, *The Golden Gateways.* Membership for a full year costs $85 per person.

Mature Outlook, 6001 North Clark Street, Chicago, IL 60660 (☎ 800/336-6330), is a travel organization for people over 50 years of age. Members are offered discounts at ITC-member hotels and will receive a bi-monthly magazine. Annual membership is $9.95, which entitles its members to discounts and in some cases free coupons for discounted merchandise from Sears Roebuck Co. Savings are also offered on selected auto rentals and restaurants.

Tips for British Seniors   **Wasteels,** Victoria Station, opposite platform 2, London SW1V 1JY (☎ 071/836-7066), will sell a Rail Europe Senior Pass to bona fide residents of the U.K. for £5. With it, a British resident more than 60 years of age can buy discounted rail tickets on many of the rail lines of Europe. To qualify, British residents must present a valid British Senior Citizen rail card, which is available for £16 at any BritRail office if proof age and British residency is presented. Wasteel's main office lies just around the corner from Victoria Station, at 122A Wilton Road, London SW1 V1J (☎ 0171/834-6744).

FOR SINGLES   Unfortunately for the 85 million or so single Americans, the travel industry is far more geared toward couples, and so singles often wind up paying the penalty. It pays to travel with someone, and one company that resolves this problem is **Travel Companion,** which matches single travelers with like-minded companions. It's headed by Jens Jurgen, who charges $99 for a six-month listing in his well-publicized records. People seeking travel companions fill out forms stating their preferences and needs and receive a listing of potential travel partners. Companions of the same or opposite sex can be requested. A bimonthly newsletter averaging 46 large pages also gives numerous money-saving travel tips of special interest to solo travelers. A sample copy is available for $5. For an application and more information, contact Jens Jurgen at Travel Companion, P.O. Box P-833, Amityville, NY 11701 (☎ 516/454-0880).

Another agency to check is **Grand Circle Travel,** 347 Congress St., Suite 3A, Boston, MA 02210 (☎ 617/350-7500, or toll free 800/221-2610), which offers escorted tours and cruises for retired people, including singles.

Since single supplements on tours carry a hefty price tag, some tour companies will arrange for you to share a room with another single traveler of the same gender. One such company that offers a "guaranteed-share plan" is Cosmos Tourama, with offices at 5310 South Federal Circle, Littleton, CO 80123 (☎ 800/221-0090).

Tips for British Singles   Single people sometimes feel comfortable traveling with groups which contain a significant number of other singles. One tour operator whose groups are usually composed of at least 50% of unattached travelers is Explore World-wide, Ltd. 1 Frederick St., Aldershot, Hampshire GU11 1LQ (☎ 01252/344-161). Established in the late 1970s, they specialize in compiling small groups of travelers (i.e., with from 12 to 20 participants) who embark on offbeat tours of parts of Europe, Africa, Asia, and the Middle East. Children are not encouraged to participate, and because the company prefers to sell land packages as entities separate from airline tickets, clients from around the world tend to participate. The company's U.S.-based sales agent is Adventure Center, 1311 63rd Street, Suite 200, Emeryville, CA 94608 (☎ 510/654-1879).

Dedicated independent travelers may want to check out The Globetrotters Club, BCM/Roving, London, WC1N 3XX (no phone), which enables members to exchange information and generally assist each other in traveling as cheaply as possible. Persons wishing to join in the U.K. pay £12 for the first year, and £9 for each year's renewal.

FOR FAMILIES   *Family Travel Times* is published 10 times a year by TWYCH, **Travel with Your Children,** and includes a weekly call-in service for subscribers. Subscriptions cost $55 a year and can be ordered by writing to TWYCH, 45 W. 18th St., 7th Floor, New York, NY 10011 (☎ 212/206-0688). TWYCH also publishes two nitty-gritty information guides, *Skiing with Children* and *Cruising with Children*, which sell for $29 and $22, respectively, and a description of TWYCH's publications that includes a recent sample issue is available by sending $3.50 to the above address.

Families Welcome!, 21 West Colony Place, Suite 140, Durham, NC 27705 (☎ 919/489-2555, or toll free 800/326-0724), a travel company specializing in worry-free vacations for families, offers "City Kids" packages to Rome, featuring accommodations in family-friendly hotels or apartments. Some hotels include a second room for children at a reduced rate during certain time periods. Packages can include car rentals, train and ferry passes, and special air prices, and are individually designed for each family. A welcome kit is distributed, containing "insider's information" for families traveling in Rome—reliable babysitters, where to buy diapers, and other such information. Also a list of restaurants suitable for visiting with children is included.

You may find that it's worth a detour to visit the tiny town of **Collodi,** 22 miles northeast of Pisa. Collodi was the hometown of the author of the famous

Pinocchio story, Carlo Lorenzini. Today the people of the town operate Pinocchio Park, which is "dedicated to the happiness of children everywhere," to honor the memory of the author. The park, with many attractions, is dominated by a statue of Pinocchio with the "Blue Fairy."

Tips for British Families   The best deals for families are often package tours put together by some of the giants of the British travel industry. Foremost among these is **Thomsons Tour Operators.** Through its subsidiary, **Skytours** (☎ 0171/ 387-9321), it offers dozens of air/land packages to continental Europe where a designated number of airline seats are reserved for the free use of children under 18 who accompany their parents. To qualify, parents must book airfare and hotel accommodations lasting two weeks or more, and book as far in advance as possible. Savings for families with children can be substantial.

FOR STUDENTS   Council Travel (a subsidiary of the Council on International Educational Exchange) is America's largest student, youth, and budget travel group, with more than 60 offices worldwide. The main office is at 205 E. 42nd St., New York, NY 10017 (☎ 212/661-1450). Council Travel's London Centre is conveniently located at 28A Poland St., W1V 3DB, just off Oxford Circus (☎ 0171/287-3337 for European destinations, 0171/437-7767 for other destinations). International Student Identity Cards, issued to all bona fide students for $16, entitle holders to generous travel and other discounts. Discounted international and domestic air tickets are available.

Eurotrain rail passes, YHA passes, weekend packages, overland safaris, and hostel/hotel accommodations are also bookable. Council Travel sells a number of publications for young people, including *Work, Study, Travel Abroad: The Whole World Handbook; Volunteer: The Comprehensive Guide to Voluntary Service in the U.S. and Abroad;* and *Going Places: The High School Student's Guide to Study, Travel, and Adventure Abroad.*

For real budget travelers it's worth joining **Hostelling/International/IYHF** (International Youth Hostel Federation). For information write Hostelling Information/American Youth Hostels (HI-AYH), 733 15th St., NW, No. 840, Washington, DC 20005 (☎ 202/783-6161). Membership costs $25 annually, but those under age 18 pay $10 and those over 54 pay $15.

Tips for British Students   Campus Travel, 52 Grosvenor Gardens, London SW1W OAG (☎ 0171/730-3402), opposite Victoria Station, open seven days a week, is Britain's leading specialist in student and youth travel worldwide. Founded to meet the needs of students and young people, it provides a comprehensive travel service specializing in low-cost rail, sea, and airfares, holiday breaks, and travel insurance, plus student discount cards. Whether you're booking a visit to Vienna, a skiing trip to Norway, or a round-the-world trip, the experienced staff at Campus Travel can help you.

The International Student Identity Card (ISIC) is an internationally recognized proof of student status that will entitle you to savings on flights, sightseeing, food and accommodation. It sells for £5 and is well worth the cost. Always show your ISIC when booking a trip—you may not get a discount without it.

Youth hostels are the place to stay if you're a student or, in some cases, if you're traveling on an ultra-tight budget. You'll need an International Youth Hostels Association card, which you can purchase from either of London's youth hostel retail outlets. Housed near Covent Garden at 14 Southampton St., London WC23 7HY (☎ 0171/836-4739) or within the same building as the previously recommended Campus Travel, 52 Grosvenor Gardens, London SW1W OAG (☎ 0171/823-4739), they sell rucksacks, hiking boots, maps, and all the paraphernalia a camper, hiker, or shoestring traveler might need. To apply for a membership card, take both your passport and some passport-sized photos of yourself, plus a membership fee of £9. For membership by mail from outside of London, call the IYHA membership offices at 0171/730-5769.

The Youth Hostel Association puts together a YHA Budget Accommodations Guide (Volumes 1 and 2), which lists the address, phone number, and admissions policy for every youth hostel in the world. (Volume 1 covers Europe and the Mediterranean; volume 2 covers the rest of the globe.) Their cost is £6.99 each, and either of them can be purchased at the retail outlets listed above. If ordering by mail, add 61p for postage if either volume is mailed to any point within the U.K.

If you're traveling in summer, many youth hostels will be full. To avoid disappointment, it's best to book ahead.

5 Special Interest, Educational & Active Vacations

SPECIAL INTEREST CHOICES

There has emerged a demand for specialized travel experiences whose goals and objectives are clearly defined. There is also an increased demand for organizations that can provide like-minded companions to share and participate in increasingly esoteric travel plans.

Caveat: Under no circumstances is the inclusion of an organization in this section a guarantee either of its creditworthiness or of its competency. Information about the organizations is presented only as a preliminary preview, to be followed by your own investigation should you be interested.

PROMOTING INTERNATIONAL UNDERSTANDING   About the only thing the following organizations have in common is reflected in that heading. They not only promote trips to increase international understanding, but they also often encourage and advocate what might be called "intelligent travel."

The Friendship Force, 57 Forsyth St., NW, Suite 900, Atlanta, GA 30303 (☎ 404/522-9490), is a nonprofit organization existing to foster friendship among disparate peoples around the world. Dozens of branch offices exist throughout North America and can arrange for en masse visits, usually once a year. Because of group bookings, the price of air transportation to the host country is usually less than what volunteers would pay if they bought APEX tickets individually. Each participant is required to spend two weeks in the host country. One stringent requirement is that a participant must spend one full week in the home of a family as a guest. Most volunteers spend the second week traveling in the host country.

Servas (an Esperanto word meaning "to serve"), 11 John St., Room 407, New York, NY 10038 (☎ 212/267-0252), is a nonprofit, nongovernmental, international, interfaith network of travelers and hosts whose goal is to help build world peace, goodwill, and understanding. They do this by providing opportunities for deeper, more personal contacts among people of diverse cultural and political communities worldwide through home visits of two days. Travelers pay a $55 annual fee, a $25 list deposit, fill out an application, and are interviewed for suitability. Hosts also are interviewed, make a voluntary contribution of $25, and are contacted by travelers who arrange for a two-night visit.

HOME EXCHANGES   Italy doesn't have an established "Meet the Italians" program, but cities and most towns have an official tourist office (called either Ente Provinciale per il Turismo or Azienda Autonoma di Soffiorno e Turismo) that might arrange for you to stay with or just meet an Italian family. Such arrangements are usually made for those staying for several weeks or more in an Italian city, not for brief visits. Requests for such attention should be sent several months before your trip to Italy by writing to the official tourist office of the town.

Intervac U.S. is part of the largest worldwide exchange network. It publishes four catalogues a year, containing more than 9,400 homes in more than 36 countries. Members contact each other directly. The cost is $65 plus postage, which includes the purchase of three of the company's catalogs, which will be mailed to you, plus the inclusion of your own listing in whichever one of the three catalogs you select. A fourth catalog costs an extra $19. If you want to publish a photograph of your home, there is an additional charge of $11. The organization can be contacted at P.O. Box 590504, San Francisco, CA 94119 (☎ 415/435-3497, or toll free 800/756-HOME).

The Invented City, 41 Sutter St., Suite 1090, San Francisco, CA 94104 (☎ 415/673-0347), is another international home-exchange agency. Home-exchange listings are published three times a year, in February, May, and November. A membership fee of $50 allows you to list your home, and you can also give your preferred time to travel, your occupation, and your hobbies.

TOURS   For Senior Citizens   One company that has a reputation based exclusively on its quality tours for senior citizens is SAGA International Holidays, 222 Berkeley St., Boston, MA 02116 (☎ 800/343-0273). Established in the 1950s, they prefer that participants be at least 50 years of age or older. Insurance and airfare are included in the net price of any of their tours, all of which encompass dozens of locations in Europe and usually last for an average of 17 nights.

SAGA's grand tour of Italy takes participants by deluxe motorcoach (leaving the driving and parking hassles to professionals), staying at four-star hotels in about eight different cities on the peninsula over a duration of 15 nights.

Opera Tours   Dailey-Thorp, 330 W. 58th St., Suite 610, New York, NY 10019-1817 (☎ 212/307-1555), in business since 1971, is probably the best regarded organizer of music and opera tours operating in the United States. Because of its "favored" relations with European box offices, it's often able to purchase blocks of otherwise unavailable tickets to such events as the Salzburg Festival; the Vienna, Milan, Paris, and London operas; and the Bayreuth Festival in Germany. Tours range from 7 to 21 days and include first-class or deluxe accommodations and meals in top-rated European restaurants.

For British Travelers   The oldest travel agency in Britain, Cox & Kings (☎ 0171/873-5006) was established in 1758 as the paymasters and transport directors for the British armed forces in India. The company continues to send large numbers of travelers from Britain throughout the rest of the world, specializing in unusual, if pricey, holidays. Their offerings in Italy include organized tours through the country's gardens and sites of historic or aesthetic interest; opera tours; pilgrimage-style visits to sites of religious interest; and food- and wine-tasting tours. The company's staff is noted for their focus on tours of ecological and environmental interest.

There is one final possibility, if your interests are more varied than those items mentioned in this brief list. A phone call to the London headquarters of **IATA (International Association of Travel Agencies)** (☎ 0181/744-9280) can provide names and addresses of tour operators who specialize in travel relating to your particular interest.

EDUCATIONAL/STUDY TRAVEL

LEARNING THE LANGUAGE Courses in Italian language, fine arts, history, literature, and Italian culture for foreign students are available at several centers throughout the Italian peninsula, with the best-recommended usually headquartered in what most Italians refer to as their nation's intellectual and cultural capital, Florence. You can write to any of the following addresses for information: The British Institute of Florence, Courses on Italian Language and Culture, Palazzo Lanfredini, lungarno Guicciardini 9, 50125 Firenze (☎ 055/284031; fax 055/289557); the Centro di Lingua e Cultura Italiana per Stranieri, Piazza Santo Spirito 4; 50134 Firenze (☎ 055/239-6966; fax 055/28-08-00); and the Centro Linguistico Italiano Dante Alighieri, via de' Bardi 12, 50125 Firenze (☎ 055/234-2984; fax 055/234-2985). Additional insights are sometimes offered regarding these matters from the Italian Cultural Institute in New York (☎ 212/879-4242).

FOR SENIOR-CITIZENS One of the most dynamic organizations for senior citizens is **Elderhostel,** 75 Federal St., Boston, MA 02110 (☎ 617/426-7788), established in 1975. Elderhostel maintains an array of programs throughout Europe, including Italy. Most courses last for around three weeks and represent good value, considering that airfare, hotel accommodations in student dormitories or modest inns, all meals, and tuition are included. Courses involve no homework, are ungraded, and are especially focused in the liberal arts. This is not a luxury vacation, but rather an academic fulfillment of a type never possible for senior citizens until several years ago. Participants must be older than 55. Elderhostel offers Italian experiences that include a historic and artistic overview of Sicily from headquarters in the fishing village of Mondello (near Palermo), and an introduction to the art and architecture of Umbria and Tuscany, with detailed overviews of the attractions of Assisi, Perugia, and Siena. Anyone interested in participating in one of Elderhostel's programs should write for the free catalog and a list of upcoming courses and destinations. Programs, of course, are subject to change.

ACTIVE VACATIONS

The Italian countryside has always been legendary for its beauty and architectural richness. Several companies specialize in exposing their clients to its wonders, usually through participation in hill treks and mountain climbing. One of the most recommended of these companies is **Mountain Travel–Sobek,** 6420 Fairmount Ave., El Cerrito, CA 94350 (☎ 510/527-8100, or toll free 800/227-2384 in the U.S.), which is a wilderness specialist formed by a 1991 union between two of California's largest adventure-tour operators.

Mountain Travel–Sobek offers at least three different hill-climbing itineraries through the hills and valleys of Italy. In order of difficulty, the least strenuous (and most historically rewarding) is a 12-day trip through the fields and vineyards of Tuscany. Traversing most of the width of the district, the tours explore a region dotted with centuries of architectural monuments. With five departures every year, during spring and autumn when the temperature is most comfortable, the price of $2,490 per person, double occupancy, includes most meals, transfers, guide services, and overnight accommodations in a renovated farmhouse, country inns, and an occasional monastery.

A similar trek through harsher terrain is the Sicily Adventure, a 10-day hiking adventure which includes overnight stays in the historic town of Cefalu, and hiking along the northern slopes of Mount Etna. Also included are day trips for hiking across the rocky and sunscorched terrains of the offshore islands of Lipari and Vulcano. Rates cost $1,950 per person, double occupancy. Departures are twice a year, usually in springtime. Airfare is not included.

The company also offers high-altitude explorations of the rocky (glacier-free) Dolomites. Varying from year to year based on demand and the availability of guides, they're designed only for experienced mountaineers in excellent physical condition. These tours are usually sited around high-altitude base camps of extraordinary natural beauty, and tend to last for around 12 days.

Some travelers prefer to visit Tuscany in a style popularized by everyone from the Etruscans to the soldiers and *condottieri* of the Renaissance: on horseback. One company that can help you combine a trek through the Italian countryside with equestrian panache is **Equitour,** P.O. Box 807, Dubois, WY 82513 (☎ 800/545-0019 in the U.S. and Canada). Established in 1983 from a base in northwestern Wyoming, this company markets highly organized horseback-riding holidays throughout the world, including tours to such faraway places as Botswana, Iceland, and the Kazakhstan region of formerly Soviet Asia. In Italy, Equitour represents an outfit that specializes in equestrian treks through Tuscany. Only English tack is used for tours that are limited to four to seven participants, which last for eight days and usually include six days of riding through the region around Siena. The tour involves traversing most of the breadth of Tuscany, spending nights in a series of farmhouses and inns. The trek costs around $1,250 per person, double occupancy, and includes all meals and accommodations, all horseback riding, and guide fees.

Active Specialists in the U.K.   Cycling tours are a good way to see Italy at your own pace. Some of the best are featured by the Cyclists' Touring Club, 69 Meadrow, Godalming, Surrey GU7 3HS (☎ 01483/417-217). It charges £25 a year for membership, part of which includes information and suggested cycling routes through most European countries.

The appeal of hill-climbing and hiking, especially in areas of scenic or historic interest, is almost universal. Waymark Holidays, 44 Windsor Rd., Slough, Berkshire SL1 2EJ (☎ 01753/516-477), owned by avid naturalists and mountaineers, offers walking tours of Europe. Sherpa Expeditions, 131A Heston Rd., Hounslow, Middlesex TW5 ORD (☎ 0181/577-7187), offers treks through off-the-beaten-track regions of the world.

You may have read a lot about archaeology tours—but most let you look, not dig. A notable and much-respected exception is Earthwatch Europe, 57 Woodstock Rd., Delsyre Court, Oxford OX2 6HU (☎ 01865/311-600), whose more than 150 programs are designed and supervised by well-qualified academic and ecological authorities. At any time, at least 50 of these welcome lay participants in hands-on experience to preserve or document historical, archaeological, or ecological phenomena of interest to the global community.

6 Getting There

BY PLANE

"All roads lead to Rome" in ways the emperors never dreamed of—by super-fast *autostrade*, by cruise ships, by freighters, and last but certainly not least, by jet plane. Indeed, of all the various ways of reaching Italy, the airplane is the best—and for the United States–Italy run, the cheapest.

If you're already in Europe, visiting some other capital such as Paris or London, and then planning to fly on to Rome, you'll have relatively little problem making a suitable airline connection. Both Rome and Milan are considered lucrative and essential destinations by the dozens of European carriers that service them. Alitalia flies to all the major capitals of Europe while each of the national carriers of the various countries (such as Air France, British Airways, and Lufthansa) fly to Rome and/or Milan. The only problem is that it's sometimes extremely expensive to book these flights once you're in Europe. It's better to have Rome or Milan written into your ticket when you first book your flight to Europe from North America, a process that will eventually save you a lot of money.

THE MAJOR AIRLINES

Specific upheavals that shook the airline industry during the early 1990s had subsided a bit as of this writing. Despite the relative calm, the industry may still undergo some changes during the life of this edition. For last-minute conditions, including even a run-down on carriers flying into Italy, check with a travel agent or the individual airlines. Here is the current status:

FROM NORTH AMERICA   American Airlines (☎ 800/433-7300) was among the first North American-based newcomers to fly into Italy. From Chicago's O'Hare Airport, American flies nonstop every evening to Milan. Flights from all parts of American's vast network fly regularly into Chicago.

TWA (☎ 800/221-2000) offers daily nonstop flights from New York's JFK to both Rome and Milan. In summer, the airline steps up its service, with two daily flights from New York to Rome, and maintains its daily nonstop flight to Milan. Because of the frequency of flights, it's often convenient and cost-effective to fly into Rome, and depart from Milan, or vice versa, depending on your travel plans.

Delta (☎ 800/241-4141) flies from New York's JFK to both Milan and Rome. Separate flights depart every evening for both destinations, with fine links to the rest of Delta's rapidly growing network of domestic and international destinations. For a few months in midwinter, service to one or both of these destinations might be reduced to six flights a week.

For anyone interested in combining a trip to Italy with a stopover in, say, Britain or Germany along the way, there are sometimes attractive deals offered by **British Airways** (☎ 800/AIRWAYS) and **Lufthansa** (☎ 800/645-3880). Flights from either London or Frankfurt, for example, sometimes fly nonstop to secondary cities of Italy (such as Genoa, Turin, or Venice) which would require a change of aircraft for anyone whose flight originated within North America. Because of the need to change flights anyway (say, in either Rome or Milan, if your flight originated in, say, New York), you might want to fly from North America nonstop to a major airport in Britain or Germany, explore either of those countries for a while, then re-embark upon a nonstop flight to the specific Italian city of your choice.

Canada's second largest airline, Calgary-based **Canadian Airlines International** (☎ 800/426-7000), flies every day of the week during summer, and a bit less frequently in winter, from Toronto to Rome. Two of the flights are nonstop, while the others touch down en route in Montreal depending on the schedule. Many other Canadians opt for transfers from their nearest international airport through such hubs as New York, Chicago, London, or Paris on such other carriers as Delta, British Airways, or American.

One well-known Italian specialist, **Alitalia** (☎ 800/223-5730), flies nonstop to both Rome and Milan from different North American cities. These include New York's JFK, Newark, Boston, Chicago, Miami, and Los Angeles. Schedules are carefully designed to facilitate easy air transfers on to all the major cities. The airline also offers periodic promotions, with details changing frequently, but sometimes featuring bargains. For example, one recent promotion involved a free round-trip ticket from Rome or Milan to many of the European cities serviced by Alitalia. To qualify, passengers needed to fly transatlantic on Alitalia before an agreed-upon date in early spring, but usually were able to include a short visit to Paris, London, or Berlin as an unexpected add-on to their holiday in Italy. Other promotions involved two-for-the-price-of-one tickets (or free upgrades to business or first class) during predesignated periods if passage was charged to an American Express credit card. Alitalia, incidentally, participates in the frequent-flyer programs of other airlines, including Continental and USAir.

Be aware that Alitalia's (and most other airlines') most economical tickets are nonrefundable. Alitalia's sole exception to this rule is in the event of your hospitalization or the death of someone in your immediate family. Air travel between Monday and Thursday will save you money; fares for Friday to Sunday are higher.

FROM GREAT BRITAIN   Both **British Airways** (☎ 0181/897-4000) and **Alitalia** (☎ 0181/745-8200) have frequent flights from London's Heathrow Airport to Rome, Milan, Venice, Pisa (the gateway to Florence), and Naples. Flying time from London to these cities is anywhere from 2 to 3 hours. BA also has one direct flight a day from Manchester to Rome, which is convenient for passengers who live in the Midlands.

REGULAR FARES

Most of the major airlines that fly to Rome charge approximately the same fare, but if a price war should break out over the Atlantic (and these are almost always brewing over the most popular routes), fares could change overnight, usually in the consumer's favor. Specific fares and restrictions, of course, should be carefully understood before you make your final plans.

If seeking a budget fare is uppermost in your mind, the key to getting one is "advance booking"—you must be willing to make your travel plans and purchase your tickets as far ahead as possible. Moreover, since the number of seats allocated to low-cost "advance-purchase" fares is severely limited (sometimes to less than 25% of the capacity of a particular plane), it will often be the early bird who obtains the low-cost seat, although this may not always be the case. If your travel plans can possibly permit it, many discounts are available for passengers who can travel either midweek or midwinter in either direction.

High season on most airlines' routes to Rome usually stretches from June 1 until September 6 (this could vary), and it is both the most expensive and most crowded time to travel. If your schedule will permit it, you should try to plan your departure for the low or shoulder season. Shoulder season is from April through May and September 7 through October and December 15 through 24. Low season is November 1 through December 14 and December 25 through March 31.

All the major carriers offer an **APEX ticket,** which is generally their cheapest transatlantic option. Usually such a ticket must be purchased 14 to 21 days in advance, and a stay in Italy must last at least 7 days but not more than 30. Changing the date of departure from North America within 21 days of departure will sometimes entail a penalty of around $150 with some APEX tickets, while with others, no changes of any kind are permitted. Many travelers who opt for the enhanced savings associated with APEX tickets find that sticking to their predetermined dates usually doesn't present any real hardship.

A more flexible (but more expensive) option, which most casual visitors might want to avoid, is the **regular economy fare.** This ticket offers the same seating and the same services received by passengers using an excursion ticket, but is usually purchased by those who need to return to North America before spending their obligatory seven days in Europe, the number usually required for an APEX ticket. One of the most attractive side benefits of a regular economy-class ticket is the absolute freedom granted to a passenger (if space is available) regarding last-minute changes in flight dates and unrestricted stopovers.

If comfort is your primary objective, you might want the more luxurious services offered by the major carriers. **Business class** and **first class,** although substantially more expensive, are especially useful for anyone who needs to be as rested and alert as possible upon arrival in Italy.

Good-Value Choices

Alitalia clusters the price of tickets for promotional fares to its destinations in Italy into four different zones, each centered around the cities of Milan, Rome, Naples, and Palermo. If you intend to fly from North America to local airports at, say, Genoa, Venice, Rimini, or any of the towns of Sardinia or Sicily, you can add on a connecting flight from the main airport of that region to a secondary airport within the same region without any additional charge. (Alitalia calls these **"common-rated" fares,** meaning that it costs no more to fly to Venice from New York than it would have cost to fly to Rome from New York.) Considering the distance between Rome and Venice, or the distance from Rome to Pisa or Florence, and the extra expense you'd have encountered on the train or highway, it's an attractive offer.

And for students, or anyone aged 12 to 24, special extensions are granted on the length of time a passenger can stay abroad. Alitalia's **youth fare** permits a stay abroad for up to one year. The round-trip high-season fare from New York to Rome is currently $938. With the year-long validity of the return half of the ticket, a North American student could, say, complete two full semesters at the University of Bologna and still fly home at a substantial savings over equivalent fares on some other airlines.

BUCKET SHOPS   The name originated in the 1960s in Britain, where mainstream airlines gave that (then-pejorative) name to resalers of blocks of unsold tickets consigned to them by major transatlantic carriers. "Bucket shop" has stuck as a label, but it might be more polite to refer to them as "consolidators." They exist in many shapes and forms. In its purest sense, a bucket shop acts as a clearinghouse for blocks of tickets that airlines discount and consign during normally slow periods of air travel.

Charter operators (see below) and bucket shops used to perform separate functions, but their offerings in many cases have been blurred in recent times. Many outfits perform both functions.

Tickets are sometimes—but not always—priced at up to 35% less than the full fare. Perhaps your reduced fare will be no more than 20% off the regular fare. Terms of payment can vary—say, anywhere from 45 days prior to departure to last-minute sales offered in a final attempt by an airline to fill an empty aircraft.

Since dealing with unknown bucket shops might be a little risky, it's wise to call the Better Business Bureau in your area to see if complaints have been filed against the company from which you plan to purchase a ticket.

One of the biggest U.S. consolidators is Travac, 989 Sixth Ave., New York, NY 10018 (☎ 212/563-3303 or 800/TRAV-800), which offers discounted seats throughout the U.S. to most cities in Europe on airlines that include TWA, United, and Delta. Another branch office is at 2601 East Jefferson St., Orlando, FL 32803 (☎ 407/896-0014).

In New York try TFI Tours International, 34 W. 32nd St., 12th Floor, New York, NY 10001 (☎ 212/736-1140 in New York State, or 800/745-8000 elsewhere in the U.S.) This tour company offers services to 177 cities worldwide.

For the Middle West, explore the possibilities of Travel Avenue, 10 S. Riverside Plaza, Suite 1404, Chicago, IL 60606 (☎ in the U.S. 800/333-3335), a national agency whose headquarters are here. Its tickets are often cheaper than those of most shops, and it charges the customer only a $25 fee on international tickets, rather than taking the usual $10 commission from an airline. Travel Avenue rebates most of that back to the customers—hence, the lower fares.

In New England, a possibility is TMI (Travel Management International), 39 JFK St. (Harvard Square), 3rd Floor, Cambridge, MA 02138 (☎ 800/245-3672), which offers a wide variety of discounts, including youth fares, student fares, and access to other kinds of air-related discounts as well.

UniTravel, 1177 North Warson Rd., St. Louis, MO 63132 (☎ 800/325-2222), offers tickets to Europe at prices which may or may not be reduced from the price a client would get if he or she had phoned the airlines directly. UniTravel is best suited to providing discounts for passengers who decide (or need) to get to Europe on short notice.

One final option suitable for clients with flexible travel plans is available through Airhitch, 2472 Broadway, Suite 20, New York, NY 10025 (☎ 212/864-2000). Prospective travelers inform Airhitch of any five consecutive days in which they're available to fly to Europe. Airhitch agrees to fly its passengers within those five days from any of three regions of the U.S. Attempts will be made to fly passengers to and from the cities of their choice, but there are no guarantees. Most passengers are booked within their first or second day. Typical fares from the northeast to Europe (all one way) are $169; midwest or southeast to Europe, $229; west coast or northwest to Europe, $269.

CHARTER FLIGHTS   Strictly for reasons of economy (and never for convenience), some travelers are willing to accept the possible uncertainties of a charter flight to Italy.

In a strict sense, a charter flight occurs on an aircraft reserved months in advance for a one-time-only transit to some predetermined point. Before paying for a charter, check the restrictions on your ticket or contract. You may be asked to purchase a tour package and pay far in advance. You'll pay a stiff penalty (or forfeit the ticket entirely) if you cancel. Charters are sometimes canceled when the plane doesn't fill up. In some cases, the charter-ticket seller will offer you an insurance policy for your own legitimate cancellation (hospitalization, death in the family, whatever).

There is no way to predict whether a proposed flight to Rome will cost less on a charter or less through a bucket shop. You'll have to investigate at the time of your trip. Some charter companies have proved unreliable in the past.

One reliable charter-flight operator is Council Charter, run by the Council on International Educational Exchange, 205 E. 42nd St., New York, NY 10017 (☎ 212/661-0311, or 800/800-8222), which arranges charter seats on regularly scheduled aircraft.

One of the biggest New York charter operators is Travac, 989 Sixth Ave., New York, NY 10018 (☎ 212/563-3303, or toll free in the U.S. 800/TRAV-800).

REBATORS To confuse the situation even more, rebators also compete in the low-cost airfare market. These outfits pass along to the passenger part of their commission, although many of them assess a fee for their services. Most rebators offer discounts that range from 10% to 25% (but this could vary from place to place), plus a $25 handling charge. They are not travel agents, although they sometimes offer similar services, including land arrangements and car rentals.

Specializing in clients within the Middle East, Travel Avenue, 10 South Riverside Plaza, Suite 1404, Chicago, IL 60606 (☎ 312/876-1116 or 800/333-3335), is said to be one of the oldest agencies of its kind. It offers up-front cash rebates on every airfare over $300 it sells. In a style similar to a discount brokerage firm, they pride themselves on NOT offering travel counseling. Instead, they sell airline tickets to independent travelers who have already worked out their travel plans. Also available are tour and cruise fares, plus hotel reservations, usually at prices less expensive than if you have pre-reserved them on your own.

Another major rebater is The Smart Traveller, 3111 SW 27th Ave. (P.O. Box 330010), Miami, FL 33133 (☎ 305/448-3338, or 800/448-3338). The agency also offers discounts on packaged tours.

GOING AS A COURIER This cost-cutting technique may not be for everybody. You travel as a passenger and courier, and for this service you'll secure a greatly discounted airfare or sometimes even a free ticket.

You're allowed one piece of carry-on luggage only; your baggage allowance is used by the courier firm to transport its cargo (all of which, by the way, is perfectly legal). As a courier, you don't actually handle the merchandise you're "transporting" to Europe—you just carry a manifest to present to Customs.

Upon arrival, an employee of the courier service will reclaim the company's cargo. Incidentally, you fly alone, so don't plan to travel with anybody. (A friend may be able to arrange a flight as a courier on a consecutive day.) Most courier services operate from Los Angeles or New York, but some operate out of other cities, such as Chicago or Miami.

Courier services are often listed in the *Yellow Pages* or in advertisements in travel sections of newspapers.

For a start, check **Halbart Express,** 147-05 176th St., Jamaica, NY 11434 (☎ 718/656-8189 from 10am to 3pm daily); or **Now Voyager,** 74 Varick St., Suite 307, New York, NY 10013 (☎ 212/431-1616 from 10am to 6pm daily; at other times you'll get a recorded message announcing last-minute special round-trip fares).

The **International Association of Air Travel Couriers,** P.O. Box 1349, Lake Worth, FL 33460 (☎ 407/582-8320), for an annual membership of $35, will send you six issues of its newsletter, *Shoestring Traveler,* and about half a dozen issues of *Air Courier Bulletin,* a directory of air-courier bargains around the world. Other advantages of membership are photo identification cards, and the organization acts as a troubleshooter if a courier runs into difficulties. The fee also includes access to their 24-hour fax-on-demand system, and a computer bulletin board which is updated daily with last-minute flights.

TRAVEL CLUBS   Another possibility for low-cost air travel is the travel club, which supplies an unsold inventory of tickets offering discounts in the usual range of 20% to 60%.

After you pay an annual fee, you are given a hotline number to call to find out what discounts are available. Many of these discounts become available several days in advance of actual departure, sometimes as long as a week and sometimes as much as a month. It all depends. Of course, you're limited to what's available, so you have to be fairly flexible.

Discount Travel International, 25 East Athens Avenue, Ardmore, PA 19003 (☎ 610-645-9532), charges $45 membership dues each year, and offers its members discounts of between 50% and 60% on selected hotels and tour packages around the world.

Moment's Notice, 425 Madison Ave., New York, NY 10017 (☎ 212/486-0500), charges $25 per year for membership, which allows spur-of-the-moment participation in dozens of tours. Each is geared for impulse purchases and last-minute getaways, and each offers air and land packages which sometimes represent substantial savings over what you'd have paid through more conventional channels. Although membership is required for participation in the tours, anyone can call the company's hotline (☎ 212/750-9111) to learn what options are available. Most of the company's best-valued tours depart from New Jersey's Newark airport.

Sears Discount Travel Club, 3033 South Parker Rd., Suite 900, Aurora, CO 80014 (☎ in the U.S. 800/255-1487), offers members, for $50, a catalog (issued four times a year), maps, discounts at select hotels, and a limited guarantee that equivalent packages will not be undersold by any other travel organization. It also offers a 5% rebate on the value of all airline tickets, tours, hotels, and car rentals which are purchased through them. (To collect this rebate, participants are required to fill out some forms and photocopy their respective receipts and itineraries.)

FOR BRITISH TRAVELERS   A regular fare from the U.K. to Italy is considered extremely high, so savvy Brits usually call a travel agent for a "deal"—either a charter flight or some special air travel promotion. These so-called deals are always available because of great interest in Italy as a tourist destination. If one is not possible for you, then an APEX ticket might be the way to keep costs trimmed. These tickets must be reserved in advance. However, an APEX ticket offers a discount without the usual booking restrictions. You might also ask the airlines about a "Eurobudget ticket," which imposes restrictions or length-of-stay requirements.

British newspapers are always full of classified advertisements touting "slashed" fares to Italy. One good source is *Time Out,* a magazine published in London.

London's *Evening Standard* has a daily travel section, and the Sunday editions of almost any newspaper will run many ads. Although competition is fierce, one well-recommended company which consolidates bulk ticket purchases, and then passes the savings on to its consumers, is Trailfinders (☎ 0171/937-5400 in London). It offers access to tickets on such carriers as SAS, British Airways, and KLM. You can fly to such cities as Lisbon, Paris, Geneva, Milan, Zurich, or Rome, or on to the capitals of Scandinavia if you wish.

In London, there are many bucket shops around Victoria and Earls Court that offer cheap fares. Make sure that the company you deal with is a member of the IATA, ABTA, or ATOL. These umbrella organizations will help you out if anything goes wrong.

CEEFAX, a British television information service included on many home and hotel TVs, runs details of package holidays and flights to Europe and beyond. Just switch to your CEEFAX channel and you'll find a menu of listings that includes travel information.

Make sure you understand the bottom line on any special deal you purchase—that is, ask if all surcharges, including airport taxes and other hidden costs—are cited before committing yourself to purchase. Upon investigation, some of these "deals" are not as attractive as advertised. Also, make sure you understand what the penalties are if you're forced to cancel at the last minute.

BY TRAIN

If you plan to travel heavily on the European and/or British railroads, you'll do well to secure the latest copy of the **Thomas Cook European Timetable of Railroads.** This comprehensive, 500+-page timetable documents all of Europe's mainline passenger rail services with detail and accuracy. It is available exclusively in North America from **Forsyth Travel Library,** P.O. Box 2975, Shawnee Mission, KS 66201 (☎ 800/367-7984), at a cost of $25.95 plus $4 postage (priority airmail to the U.S. and U.S. $5 for shipments to Canada).

EURAILPASS   Many travelers to Europe take advantage of one of its greatest travel bargains, the Eurailpass, which permits unlimited first-class rail travel in any country in Western Europe except the British Isles, and also includes Hungary in Eastern Europe. Oddly, it does *not* include travel on the rail lines of Sardinia, which are organized independently of the rail lines of the rest of Italy. Passes are purchased for periods as short as 15 days or as long as three months.

Here's how it works: The pass is sold only in North America. Vacationers in Europe for 15 days can purchase a Eurailpass for $498; a pass for 21 days costs $648, and a one-month pass costs $798. A two-month pass goes for $1,098, a three-month pass for $1,398. Children under 4 travel free providing they don't occupy a seat (otherwise, they are charged half fare); children under 12 pay half fare. If you're under 26, you can purchase a **Eurail Youthpass,** which entitles you to unlimited second-class travel for 15 days for $398, or for one or two months, costing $578 and $768, respectively.

The advantages are tempting: No tickets; simply show the pass to the ticket collector, then settle back to enjoy the scenery. Seat reservations are required on some trains. Many of the trains have couchettes (sleeping cars), for which an additional fee is charged. Obviously, the two- or three-month traveler gets the greatest economic advantages; the Eurailpass is ideal for such extensive trips. Passholders can visit all of Italy's major sights, from the Alps to Sicily, then end the vacation in Norway, for example.

Fourteen-day or one-month voyagers have to estimate rail distance before determining if such a pass is to their benefit. To obtain full advantage of the ticket for 15 days or one month, you'd have to spend a great deal of time on the train.

Eurailpass holders are entitled to considerable reductions on certain buses and ferries. You'll get a 20% reduction on second-class accommodations from certain companies operating ferries between Naples and Palermo, or for crossings to Sardinia and Malta.

Travel agents in all towns, and railway agents in such major cities as New York, Montréal, or Los Angeles, sell all these tickets. A Eurailpass is available at the North American offices of CIT Travel Service, the French National Railroads, the German Federal Railroads, and the Swiss Federal Railways.

Eurail Saverpass is a money-saving ticket that offers discounted 15-day travel, but only if groups of three people travel constantly and continuously together between April and September, or if two people travel constantly and continuously together between October and March. The price of a Saverpass, valid all over Europe, good for first class only, is $430 for 15 days, $550 for 21 days, and $678 for one month.

Eurail Flexipass allows passengers to visit Europe with more flexibility. It's valid in first class and offers the same privileges as the Eurailpass. However, it provides a number of individual travel days that can be used over a much longer period of consecutive days. That makes it possible to stay in one city and yet not lose a single day of travel. There are three passes: 5 days of travel within 2 months, $348; 10 days of travel within 2 months, $560; and 15 days of travel within 2 months, $740.

With many of the same qualifications and restrictions as the previously described Flexipass is a Eurail Youth Flexipass. Sold only to travelers under age 26, it allows 5 days of travel within 2 months for $255; 10 days of travel within 2 months for $398; and 15 days of travel within 2 months for $540.

FROM THE U.K.   Many different rail passes are available in the U.K. for travel in Europe. Stop in at the **International Rail Centre,** Victoria Station, London SW1V 1JY (☎ 0171/834-2345), or **Wasteels,** 121 Wilton Rd., London SW1V 1JZ (☎ 0171/834-7066). They can help you find the best option for the trip you're planning. Some of the most popular passes, including Inter-Rail and EuroYouth, are offered only to travelers under 26 years of age, entitling them to unlimited second-class travel in 26 European countries.

Eurotrain "Explorer" tickets are another worthwhile option for travelers who can show proof that they are under age 26. They allow passengers to move in a leisurely fashion from London to Rome, with as many stopovers en route as their holders want, and a different route southbound (through Belgium, Luxembourg, and Switzerland) than the return route northbound (exclusively through France). All travel must be completed within two months of the date of departure. Such a ticket sells for £205 round-trip.

Persons under 26 (with proof of age) who want to travel from London to Rome as quickly and directly as possible pay £165 round trip for a ticket allowing no stopovers, and which retraces an identical route (exclusively through France) in both directions of travel. The cost of either of these tickets includes ferryboat transport across the Channel. Campus Travel, 52 Grosvenor Gardens, London SW1W OAG (☎ 0171/730-3402), can give you prices and help you book tickets.

Eurolines is the leading operator of scheduled coach services across Europe. Its comprehensive network of services includes regular departures to destinations throughout Italy, including Turin, Milan, Bologna, Florence, and Rome; plus summer services to Verona, Vicenza, Padua, and Venice.

Eurolines' services to Italy depart from London's Victoria Coach Station and are operated by modern coach, with reclining seats and a choice of smoking or nonsmoking areas. Return tickets are valid for up to six months, and for added flexibility passengers may also leave their return date open.

Information and credit card reservations can be obtained by telephoning 01582/404511. Alternatively, passengers may book in person at Eurolines, 52 Grosvenor Gardens, Victoria, London SW1 (opposite Victoria Rail Station). A round-trip ticket from London to Rome using as direct a route as possible costs between £129 and £139, and from £85 to £90 one way, depending on the season. Persons under 26 pay £5 less, each way, than the prices listed above. Departures in either direction are daily, and transit requires around 37 hours each way. Passengers can interrupt their journey, pending available space on subsequent legs of their trip, in Paris or Milan en route.

BY CAR

If you're already on the Continent, particularly in a neighboring country such as France or Austria, you may want to drive to Italy. However, arrangements should be made in advance with your car-rental company.

It is also possible to drive from London to Rome, a distance of 1,124 miles, via Calais/Boulogne/Dunkirk, or 1,085 miles via Oostende/Zeebrugge, not counting Channel crossings either by Hovercraft ferry or the Chunnel. Milan is some 400 miles closer to Britain than Rome. If you cross over from England and arrive at one of the continental ports, you still face a 24-hour drive. Most drivers play it safe and budget three days for the journey.

Most of the roads from Western Europe leading into Italy are toll free, with some notable exceptions. If you use the Swiss superhighway network, you'll have to purchase a special tax sticker at the frontier. You'll also pay to go through the St. Gotthard Tunnel into Italy. Crossings from France can be through the Mont Blanc Tunnel, for which you'll pay, or you can leave the French Riviera at Menton (France) and drive directly into Italy along the Italian Riviera in the direction of San Remo.

If you don't want to drive such distances, ask a travel agent to book you on a Motorail arrangement where the train carries your car. This service, however, is good only to Milan, as there are no car and sleeper expresses running the approximately 390 miles south to Rome.

BY ORGANIZED TOUR

With all the features provided by a good tour group, you can know ahead of time just what your visit will cost. Perhaps best of all, you won't be bothered with having to arrange your own transportation in places where language might be a problem, looking after your own luggage, coping with reservations and payment at individual hotels, and facing other "nuts and bolts" requirements of travel that can make or break your enjoyment of a European journey. Although a sampling of two of the best-rated tour companies follows, you should consider consulting a good travel agent for the latest offerings and advice.

There are many different tour operators eager for a share of your business, but one that seems to meet with consistent approval from its participants has been a family-operated company for three generations named **Perillo Tours,** 577 Chest-nut Ridge Rd., Woodcliff Lake, NJ 07675-9888 (☎ 201/307-1234, or 800/431-1515 in the U.S.). Since it was established in 1945, it has sent more than a million travelers to Italy in comfortable and well-informed circumstances. As one of the world's largest Italy tour operators, it uses more first-class hotel rooms in Italy than any other company in America. Known and well respected for the value they offer, Perillo tours cost much less than the assembled elements of each tour if each component had been arranged separately. Accommodations are in first-class hotels, and guides tend to be well qualified, well informed, and sensitive to the needs of tour participants.

Perillo operates hundreds of departures year-round. Between April and October, eight different itineraries are offered, ranging from 8 to 14 days each, covering broadly different regions of the peninsula. Between November and April, the "Off-Season Italy" tour covers three of Italy's premier cities during a season when they're likely to be less densely crowded with other visitors. All tours include airfare from North America (usually on Alitalia), overnight accommodations in first-class hotels, breakfast and (in all but a few cases) dinner daily, and all baggage handling and taxes. Also included are all sightseeing fees, transfers, and in many cases tours by train or deluxe motorcoach (most buses contain their own lavatory). Tours range from around $1,499 per person for one of the 10-day off-season short tours to around $3,159 for a deluxe tour (by rail) of Venice, Florence, Capri, and Rome in what some visitors consider the ideal season, September. (Dinners are not included on this particular tour.)

Incidentally, if you loathe the idea of touring by motorcoach and want to focus exclusively on the charms of one of Europe's greatest cities—Rome—Perillo offers a midwinter bargain which includes airfare from any of seven North American cities, and six nights' hotel accommodations in Rome, with breakfast and some guided tours included, for a very reasonable $899 per person.

Another contender for package-tour business in Italy is **Italiatour,** a company of the Alitalia Group (☎ 212/765-2183, or 800/845-3365), which offers a widely varied selection of tours through all parts of the peninsula. The company appeals to the free-at-heart (i.e., clients who don't want any semblance of a tour at all). Catering to the reluctance of many travelers to commit themselves too rigidly to group travel in a bus, the company specializes in tours for independent travelers who ride from one destination to another by train or by rental car. They offer a wide choice of loosely structured itineraries to Italy's classical cities. In most cases, the company sells pre-reserved hotel accommodations which, because of their volume purchases, are usually less expensive than if you had reserved the accommodations yourself. A choice of accommodations in several different price ranges is available, to the urban centers of Italy as well as to such less-often visited cities as Orvieto, Lucca, Viterbo, Mantua, and Perugia. With any of these tours, there is a strong incentive to book air passage from North America at the same time as the hotel nights, and because of the company's close link with Alitalia, the prices quoted for air passage are sometimes among the most reasonable on the retail market. Repeat travelers to Italy sometimes opt for one of the Fly-Drive programs, where discounted prices on rental cars are combined with airfare from North America.

Italiatour's longest offering is a loosely supervised 8-night jaunt through the major art cities of Italy, with accommodations in luxury hotels. Prices begin at

$1,625 per person. Airfare is extra, but the price includes hotel accommodations (double occupancy), breakfasts, transfers between cities, some city tours, and a gondola ride in Venice. An especially noteworthy experience is a 9-day/7-night fully escorted tour called "Treasures of Sicily," which includes hotel accommodations, all meals, guide fees, and the safety and convenience of a tour guide, an air-conditioned bus, and a driver to negotiate the island's roads. Prices begin at around $700 per person, double occupancy. Airfare is extra.

7 Getting Around

BY PLANE

Italy's domestic air network on **Alitalia** is one of the largest and most complete in Europe. There are some 40 airports serviced regularly from Rome, and most flights are under an hour. Fares vary, but some discounts are available. For those passengers 2 to 12 years old, all tickets are discounted 50%; for passengers 12 to 22 years old, there's a youth fare. And anyone can get a 30% reduction by taking domestic flights that depart at night.

BY TRAIN

Trains can provide a medium-priced means of transportation, even if you don't buy the Eurailpass or one of the special Italian Railway tickets (see below). A typical one-way fare on Intercity, Diretto, or EuroCity (the terms are interchangeable) between Rome and Florence costs $24 in second class, $39 in first class. Between Rome and Venice, the one-way fare is $44 in second class, $71 in first class. Between Rome and Naples, the one-way fare is $16 in second class, $27 in first class. As a rule of thumb, second-class travel regardless of the destination usually costs about two-thirds the price of an equivalent trip in first class. When available, the rental of a couchette (a private fold-down bed in a communal cabin) requires a supplement above the price of first-class travel. In a land where mamma and bambini are highly valued, children aged 4 to 11 receive a discount of 50% off the adult fare, while children under 4 travel free with their parents.

Senior citizens traveling on Italy's rails get a break, too. A **Senior Citizen's Silver Card (Carta d'Argento)** can be bought by anyone 60 and over, but must be purchased in Italy (it is not sold in North America) upon presentation of proof of age at any railway station. It will allow a 30% discount off the price of any ticket between points on the Italian rail network. It's good for one year and costs 40,000 lire ($25). It's not valid on Friday, Saturday, or Sunday between late June and late August or anytime during Christmas week. The Italian railway system also offers a *cartaverde*, good for anyone under 26. Valid for three years, the card costs 40,000 lire ($25) and entitles a passenger to a 20% reduction off any state train fare. This pass can only be purchased in Italy.

An **Italian Railpass** (known within Italy as a BTLC Pass) allows non–Italian citizens to ride as much as they like on the entire rail network of Italy. Buy the pass in the United States, have it validated the first time you use it at any railway station in Italy, and ride as frequently as you like within the time validity of your pass. An 8-day pass costs $226 in first class and $152 in second class, a 15-day pass is $284 in first class and $190 in second, a 21-day pass runs $330 in first class and $220 in second, and a 30-day pass costs $396 in first class and $264 in second.

The rail systems of Sardinia are administered by a separate entity and are not included in this or any of the other passes mentioned. In the rest of Italy, however, with the Italian Railpass and each of the other special passes, a supplement must be paid to ride on certain very rapid trains. These are designated ETR-450 trains. (Also known as "Pendolino" trains, their high-speed technology is based on the principle of a pendulum, enabling trains to safely negotiate the sharp curves of Italy's railway tracks at high speeds. Some readers have mentioned the surprisingly high quality of meals served in the dining cars of these trains.)

Especially flexible and adaptable to the individual schedule of a traveler is the **Italian Flexirail Card,** which entitles its holder to a predetermined number of days of travel on any rail line of Italy within a certain period of validity. It's ideal for passengers who plan in advance to spend several days sightseeing before boarding a train for another city. A pass giving 4 possible travel days out of a block of 9 days costs $176 in first class and $120 in second class, a pass for 8 travel days stretched over a 21-day period costs $258 in first class and $168 in second, and a pass for 12 travel days within a time frame of 30 days costs $324 in first class and $216 in second class.

In addition, the **Kilometric Ticket** is valid for two months' worth of travel on regular trains. However, it can also be used on special train rides if you pay a supplement. The ticket is valid for 20 trips, providing that your total riding distance does not exceed 1,875 miles (3,000 kilometers). The price is $264 in first class, dropping to $156 in second class.

In previous years, Italian Railway authorities maintained strict rules requiring that many of the above-mentioned passes needed to be purchased outside of Europe. These rules have relaxed considerably in recent years, and at press time, many of the above-mentioned passes could be purchased within Italy. (Check carefully before your departure, as this might change at any time.) The notable exception to this rule is the Italian Flexirail Card, which requires purchase in North America. With the exception of the Carta d'Argento, which requires purchase in Italy, the place to purchase any of these passes is CIT Tours, the official representative of Italian State Railway, 342 Madison Ave., New York, NY 10173 (☎ 212/697-2100, or 800/223-7987), or from a travel agent. If you phone CIT, be prepared to wait, as the phones are notoriously busy. Clients west of Colorado might fare better by calling the organization's Los Angeles office at 310/338-8616, or toll free 800/248-7245. You can also fax the New York office at 212/697-1394, or Los Angeles at 310/670-4269. CIT also offers excellent rail tours, coach tours, hotel accommodations, spa bookings, and cruises, including Sicily and the Aeolian Islands.

A warning: Many irate readers have complained about train service in Italy—they have found the railroads dirty, overcrowded, unreliable, and with little regard for schedules. As you may have heard, strikes plague the country, and you never know as you board a train when it will reach your hoped-for destination. A sense of humor (and a flexible itinerary) might be your best defense against aggravation and irritating delays.

BY BUS

Italy has an extensive and intricate bus network, covering all regions of the country. Because most Italians regard rail travel as inexpensive, the bus is not the preferred method of travel.

SITA, viale dei Cadorna 105, in Florence (☎ 055/214721) blankets the country with air-conditioned coaches. Its schedule is available at the address cited in

Florence. Sometimes tourist offices also have schedules of bus companies if you prefer to travel by bus.

ANAC, piazza Esquilino 29, in Rome (☎ 06/463383), like SITA, also blankets the country with air-conditioned coaches. You can pick up a copy of the company's timetable at the address above.

Other companies operating buses are Autostradale, piazzale Castello in Milan (☎ 02/801161), which serves a large chunk of North Italy, and Lazzi, via Mercadante 2 in Florence (☎ 055/363041), which goes through Tuscany, including Siena, and much of central Italy.

Where these nationwide services leave off, local bus companies operate in most regions, particularly in the hill sections and in the alpine regions where travel by rail is not possible. For more information about these services, refer to the "By Bus" sections, listed under "Getting There" in the various city, town, and village headings.

BY TAXI

Taxi service is readily available throughout Italy, in all towns and tourist resorts. Generally, cabs wait in special taxi stands at railway stations and main parts of a city, but one can always be called by phone. Meters are provided and fares are displayed. Fares vary considerably from place to place. Find out the starting rate that is legal in the city or town you visit, and be sure that that's the amount showing on the meter when you embark, or you might find yourself paying for someone else's ride. Taxi trips outside the town area will have a supplemental charge.

BY CAR

U.S. and Canadian drivers must carry an International Driver's License when touring Italy unless they obtain from the Automobile Club d'Italia a declaration entitling them to drive on Italian roads upon presentation of a valid U.S. or Canadian driver's license. The declaration is available from any ACI frontier or provincial office. U.S. and Canadian licenses are valid in Italy if accompanied by an official translation.

For an international driver's license, apply at a branch of the **American Automobile Association (AAA)**. You must be at least 18 years old and have 2 two-by-two-inch photographs, a $10 fee, and a photcopy of your U.S. driver's license with an AAA application form. AAA's nearest office will probably be listed in the local telephone directory, or you can contact AAA's national headquarters at 1000 AAA Dr., Heathrow, FL 32746-5063 (☎ 407/444-4300). Remember that an international driver's license is valid only if physically accompanied by your original driver's license. In Canada, you can get the address of the Canadian Automobile Club closest to you by calling its national office at 613/226-7631.

The **Automobile Club d'Italia (ACI)** is the equivalent of the AAA (American Automobile Association). It has offices throughout Italy, including the head office, via Marsala 8, 00185 Rome (☎ 06/499-8389), open Monday through Saturday from 8:30am to 1:30pm. The Information and Assistance Center (CAT) of the ACI is at via Magenta 5, 00185 Roma (☎ 06/4477), and is open around the clock. Both offices are easily accessible by public transpiration, lying close to the main railway station (Stazione Termini).

RENTALS   Many say that the best way to see the country is by car, and I heartily agree with them. Many of the most charming landscapes lie away from the main cities, far away from the train stations. For that, and for the sheer convenience that train travel will never match, you'll find that renting a car is usually the best way to travel if you plan to explore part of the country.

Despite the pleasures afforded by having your own car, the legalities and contractual obligations of renting one in Italy (where accident and theft rates are very high) are more complicated than in almost any other country in Europe.

All drivers in Italy must have nerves of steel, a sense of humor, a valid driver's license, a valid passport, and in most cases, must be over age 25. (In some rare instances, a 21-year-old can rent a car, but only if he or she already has a credit history with the rental company.) In all cases, payment and paperwork are simpler if you present a valid credit card with your completed rental contract. If that isn't possible, the payment of a substantial deposit will almost certainly be required, sometimes in cash, in advance.

Insurance on all vehicles is compulsory in Italy, although any reputable car-rental firm will arrange it in advance before you're even given the keys. (If you bring your own car in from another country, you'll need a *Carta Verde,* or "green card," which is valid for 15, 30, or 45 days and should be issued by an insurance agent or automobile salesperson before the vehicle crosses the border into Italy. Beyond 45 days, you must have a regular Italian insurance policy.)

You'll find a bewildering assortment of car-rental kiosks at the airports and railway stations of many Italian cities, including the airports of Rome and Milan when you arrive. Especially prominent are the facilities of **Avis** (☎ 800/ 331-2112), **Budget Rent a Car** (☎ 800/472-3325), and **Hertz** (☎ 800/ 654-3001), as well as several local car-rental companies. Although there are several reputable European-based car-rental companies, including the Italy-based Maggiore, we have usually found that billing errors are more easily resolved if you stick to an affiliate of one of North America's larger companies. If you do want to try **Maggiore,** they have offices at the Rome and Milan airports, as well as Roman headquarters at piazza della Repubblica 57 (☎ 06/854-1620). Another attractive option might be to contact **Kemwell,** 106 Calvert St., Harrison, NY 10528 (☎ 800/678-0678). Because of the high volume of cars rented from Italian car-rental companies (including Maggiore), Kemwell can reserve your vehicle more easily (and probably less expensively) than if you had done it yourself.

All three of the major car-rental companies charge approximately the same for their least expensive vehicles, although each holds out the possibility of offering seasonal promotions. Cars rented in one Italian city can be dropped off at other Italian cities at all three of the car companies, either for free or for an additional fee of around $25. Dropoffs at many other cities of Europe (such as Vienna) can be arranged for between $100 and $400, depending on the city and the distance from the Italian border.

Each of the major companies quotes two tiers of rental prices that either do or do not include collision-damage insurance. Each of the companies, for an additional cost of between $12 and $20 a day (the amount varies according to the value of the car), issues a collision-damage waiver (CDW). This extra protection will cover all or part of the repair-related costs if there's an accident. (In some cases, even if you agree to purchase the CDW, you'll still pay between $200 and $300 per accident. Asking a few pertinent questions before you rent might save a lot of anxiety later.) Know in advance that if you *don't* purchase the waiver, you're likely to be responsible for up to the full value of the car.

Also, if you opt not to buy the CDW, the renting company will impose a temporary charge on your credit card of up to $6,000 as a form of security deposit. (This charge, or "credit hold" as they call it, is removed as soon as you return the car in an undamaged condition.)

That's not all. Because of the rising theft rate in Italy, all three of the major U.S.-based companies offer theft and break-in protection policies. (At Avis and Budget, purchase of this theft policy is mandatory; at Hertz, it is strongly encouraged.) Such policies are usually priced at around $11 per day, and even if there is a break-in (or if the car is stolen), you might still have to pay a deductible of between $100 and $200.

Realizing the prevalence of car and luggage theft, many travelers consider the best insurance against such an incident is *never* to leave luggage visible through the windows of a parked car.

Some companies include CDWs in the prices they quote; others do not. In some, but not all, cases, slight discounts are offered to members of the American Automobile Association (AAA) or the American Association of Retired Persons (AARP). For a weeklong midsummer rental of a cramped but peppy Peugeot 205 or Volkswagon Polo, each of the companies charges between $240 and $350, depending on the season and the circumstances. In many cases, the rentals at Budget tend to be among the most economical, although the exact promotions and price ratios vary according to the car and the season. For pickups at most airports in Italy, all three of the companies are obligated to impose a 10% government tax. To avoid that charge, consider pickup of your car at any of the inner-city locations that each of the companies maintains throughout Italy.

As the size and comfort level of cars increase, so do the rental costs, although at the midsized level all three of the companies tend to charge roughly equivalent rates. Special promotions, which come and go frequently, tend to favor one or another company over its competitors. As always, it pays to phone around before committing yourself. The smallest available cars at all three of the companies tend to be small, very cramped, and not suitable for large or long-legged renters, or for clients with lots of luggage.

To each of these rates is added the unavoidable 19% government tax, plus the cost of any optional medical insurance you arrange at the time of rental. Depending on the fine print and the benefits, such policies cost between $5 and $7 extra per day. Bear in mind that these figures do not include the costs of the above-mentioned CDW and theft insurance policies.

As mentioned previously, special promotions might apply when you rent, so it pays to make separate calls to each of the companies before your trip.

Despite the appeal of extra insurance, many renters nonetheless decline it and save themselves the equivalent of $85 to $150 per week. Even for drivers who always select the most comprehensive policies, declining this extra insurance is not as foolish as it sounds. Certain credit-card and charge-card companies, including American Express, offer to pay the cost of any deductible damage to a rented car in certain countries *if the imprint of the credit or charge card is made on the original rental contract.* The details of this arrangement with the credit card companies, however, change frequently, so you must check with them before you decide to handle your coverage in this way. If you rely on the guarantee of your credit card company to reimburse you for the value of the deductible damages to your car, be fully aware that you will first have to pay out a cash or credit card settlement for the value of the damage to your car. (In some cases, this might be equivalent to the vehicle's entire replacement cost.) You'll have to file multiple copies of detailed forms with the credit card company, then wait for some time before the money is reimbursed or until the extra charges on your credit card are voided.

Some visitors only want a car for a two- or three-day visit to the countryside using Rome or perhaps Milan as their base. If you want just a short holiday in the countryside, try to plan your visit for a weekend, when some companies, most notably Hertz, and in some cases Budget, offer values for short-term weekend rentals. Some companies might advertise certain weekend specials directly from their countertops in Italy, bypassing their North American reservations network completely.

The best prices are almost always available at any company for clients who reserve their car well in advance from a telephone in North America.

GASOLINE Gasoline is expensive in Italy, as are autostrade tolls. Carry enough cash if you're going to do extensive motoring. Depending on market conditions and the octane level, gasoline (known as *benzina*) costs around 1,740 lire ($1.10) per liter, a price which translates into around 6,600 lire ($4.15) per gallon for the blend whose octane rating is appropriate for most of the cars you'll be able to rent. Filling the tank of a medium-sized car will usually cost around 60,000 lire ($37.50), a potent drain on your finances, and a cost to be reckoned with.

Gas stations on autostrade are open 24 hours a day, but on regular roads gas stations are rarely open on Sunday, many close between noon and 2pm for lunch, and most of them shut down after 7pm. Make sure the pump registers zero before an attendant starts refilling your tank. A popular scam, particularly in the south, is to fill your tank before resetting the meter so that you pay not only your bill but the charges run up by the previous motorist who'd already paid them.

DRIVING RULES The Italian Highway Code follows the Geneva Convention, and Italy uses international road signs. Driving is on the right, passing on the left. Violators of the highway code are fined; serious violations may also be punished by imprisonment. In cities and towns, the speed limit is 50 kilometers per hour (kmph) or 31.25 miles per hour (mph). For all cars and motor vehicles on main roads and local roads, the limit is 90kmph or 56.25mph. For the autostrade (national express highways), the limit is 130kmph or 81.25mph. Use of seat belts is compulsory.

ROAD MAPS The best touring maps are published by the **Automobile Club d'Italia (ACI)** and the **Italian Touring Club,** or you can purchase the maps of the **Carta Automobilistica d'Italia,** covering Italy in two maps on the scale of 1:800,000 (1cm = 8km). These two maps should fulfill the needs of most motorists. If you plan to explore one region of Italy in depth, then consider one of 15 regional maps (1:200,000; 1cm = 2km), published by **Grande Carta Stradale d'Italia.**

All maps mentioned above are sold at certain newsstands and at all major bookstores in Italy, especially those with travel departments. Many travel bookstores in the United States also carry them. If U.S. outlets don't have these maps, they often offer Michelin's red map (no. 988) of Italy, which is on a scale of 1:1,000,000 (1cm = 10km). This map covers all of Italy in some detail.

BREAKDOWNS/ASSISTANCE In case of car breakdown and for any tourist information, foreign motorists can call 116 (nationwide telephone service). For road information, itineraries, and all sorts of travel assistance, call 06/499-8389 (ACI's information center). Both services operate 24 hours a day.

BY FERRY

Ferries are used primarily in the south. Driving time from **Naples to Sicily** is cut considerably by taking one of the vessels operated by Tirrenia Lines, Molo Angioino, Stazione Maritime, in Naples (☎ 081/761-36-88). Departures are daily at 8pm for the 11-hour trip to Palermo. Frequent ferry services and hydrofoils also depart from Naples for the offshore islands of Capri and Ischia.

HITCHHIKING

It is extremely risky to hitchhike anywhere in the world today and *Frommer's Italy* does not recommend it, although recognizing that hundreds of people will hitchhike regardless of the risks.

In Italy, it is illegal to hitch a ride on the autostrade, mainly because it's dangerous for a car to stop to take on a passenger. Savvy hitchhikers take the primary road systems instead. The less you're burdened by luggage and possessions, of course, the better your chances of getting a ride. Write your destination on a sign with large letters—it helps. Use the Italian name for a city, not the English one (Firenze instead of Florence, for example). Women should hitch in pairs, if at all, because sexual harassment—or worse—is commonly reported. One Italian male driver confided that he considered any woman hitching a ride "fair game," and such attitudes are prevalent. Of course, young men traveling alone are also subject to propositions, and should take precautions. For example, don't let your baggage be stored in a locked truck in case you should decide to make a hasty departure from the vehicle.

SUGGESTED ITINERARIES

If You Have 1 Week

Days 1–3   Fly to Rome and spend most of the day recovering. If it's summer, view the floodlit Roman Forum at sunset from the balcony of the Campidoglio. Have a drink and dinner near the Spanish Steps and turn in early for a big day of sightseeing tomorrow. Your second day, take in the Colosseum and Forum and visit St. Peter's. On the morning of the third day, explore some of the highlights of the Vatican before going outside Rome to see the gardens at Tivoli and Hadrian's Villa.

Days 4–5   Transfer to Florence and soak up as much of the city of the Renaissance as time allows.

Days 6–7   Transfer to Venice, where so many attractions await you that you'll promise yourself a return visit when you have more time.

If You Have Another Week

Day 1   Leave Venice in the morning and head for the attractions of Padua (Padova) in the west. Visit at least the Capella degli Scrovegni and the Basilica di Sant' Antonio. Have lunch at Belle Parti-Toulà and continue northwest to Vicenza for the night. See as many sights in the city of Andrea Palladio as you can before nightfall.

Day 2   In the morning continue west to Verona, city of Romeo and Juliet, which will consume at least a day for only the most superficial of visits. See such attractions as Arena di Verona, Castelvecchio, Il Duomo, and the Church of San Zeno Maggiore.

Day 3   Leave Verona in the morning and stop for a morning in Brescia to visit its piazza della Loggia, piazza del Duomo, and Tosio-Martinengo Civic Picture Gallery. After lunch there, continue for the night to Bergamo (see Chapter 18).

Days 4–5   Milan, Milan, and more Milan (see Chapter 18), and if time remains on the fifth day visit the Certosa of Pavia on the outskirts.

Day 6   Head west for the city of Turin (see Chapter 19) to visit its Egyptian Museum, Galleria Sabauda, Capella della Santa Sindone, and other attractions.

Day 7   For a final day of sightseeing, go southeast to the ancient seaport of Genova (see Chapter 20) for an action-packed day. Tour the harbor by boat and dine in a typical seaport restaurant at night.

If You Have 2 Weeks

One of the most interesting trips in Italy is along its western coast.

Day 1   Begin at the Italian Riviera near the French border, heading first for an overnight stay in San Remo, capital of the Riviera. Visit its old city, its flower market (most famous in Italy), and drop in at its casino at night.

Day 2   Leave San Remo in the morning and drive along the coast, stopping at random at such towns as Albenga or Savona before reaching Genoa. Spend the night here if you haven't visited it previously (see above).

Day 3   Leave Genova in the morning and continue in the general direction of Rome, favoring one of three resorts as previewed in Chapter 20. Take your choice: Portofino (the most chic), Rapallo, or Santa Margherita Ligure.

Day 4   Continue along the coast and schedule a luncheon stopover in La Spezia. In the afternoon visit the art city of Lucca and see its cathedral, dating from 1060, and its Churches of San Michele and San Frediano. For the night, go to Pisa to view its Leaning Tower and other attractions.

Days 5–6   Head southeast from Pisa and plan to be in San Gimignano for lunch. Called the "Manhattan of Tuscany" because of its noble brick towers, it is one of the most interesting of the hill towns of Italy. Continue southeast for the night, arriving in Siena. On Day 6, explore history-rich Siena, which is filled with attractions that can hardly be viewed in one day.

Day 7   From Siena head out in the morning to another hill town, Arezzo, to the east. See at least the frescoes of Piero della Francesca in St. Francis' Church and perhaps the romanesque church of Santa Maria della Pieve. Continue southeast to the ancient university city of Perugia for the night.

Day 8   You'll need most of the following day to see the attractions of Perugia, especially its Galleria Nazionale dell'Umbria, with one of the world's greatest collections of Umbrian art.

Day 9   From Perugia drive through the Umbrian countryside until you reach Assisi, hometown of native son, St. Francis. This is one of the most popular destinations in Italy, and you'll want to spend at least a day and a night there.

Day 10   Leave Assisi and head south to Spoleto for a morning visit and lunch. After Spoleto, drive southwest to Viterbo, which is still girdled by its walls and is definitely medieval looking with its piazza San Lorenzo and its Papal Palace. After a visit head south for Rome.

Days 11–14 Explore the riches and architectural treasures of Rome, the former seat of one of the world's greatest empires.

If You Have Another 2 Weeks

Days 1–2 To save time take a domestic flight to Naples. You can explore once-buried Roman towns and ancient centers of Magna Græcia. You can be in Naples for lunch and afternoon sightseeing. The next morning, catch the hydrofoil to Capri and spend the day there, to visit the Blue Grotto and many other attractions, before returning to Naples for the night.

Days 3–4 Leave Naples in the morning, and head south to Sorrento or one of the other resorts along the Amalfi Drive, including Amalfi itself or, better yet, Positano. Spend the rest of the day enjoying one of these resorts and get to bed early so you'll be prepared for a strenuous day of sightseeing. Either on your own or via an organized tour, make the traditional visits to the two towns that Vesuvius destroyed, Herculaneum and Pompeii. If time remains in your day, you can even go up to Mount Vesuvius itself to see the crater from which came the violent eruption. Return to Sorrento or one of the other towns for the night.

Day 5 Head down the coast to Paestum to see its three Doric temples before returning to Naples in the early evening to board a boat for Palermo, the capital of Sicily. If you don't have time for Sicily, you can break the tour here, returning to Rome for your flight back home. If you're going on to Sicily, you'll spend the night aboard the boat in a rented cabin, arriving in Palermo in the early hours of morning.

Day 6 Spend the day in Palermo, exploring its monuments and museums, and save time to visit the Church of Monreale in the hills. Overnight in Palermo.

Day 7 Drive west from Palermo and stop over in Erice, Trapani, or Marsala for lunch. However, don't linger too long in any place, as your major goal should be the ruins of Selinunte on the southern coast. Arrive in Agrigento for an overnight stop and drive through the "Valley of the Temples" at night (the ruins are floodlit).

Days 8–9 Spend a leisurely day driving from Agrigento along the southeastern coast of Sicily. Arrive in Siracusa by the late afternoon. Spend two nights here, as it will take all of the following day to see its many archaeological treasures.

Day 10 From Siracusa drive north along the eastern coast, stopping for the night in the resort of Taormina, one of the most idyllic in Italy.

Day 11 Begin the long drive back to Rome, but get a taste of southern Italy by heading north to Taranto for the night. The seaport of Taranto lies 44 miles west of Brindisi and 331 miles south of Rome. Visit its Museum Nazionale di Taranto in the afternoon, with its priceless array of Magna Grecian art. Overnight in Tarot.

Day 12 Continue west to Brindisi the following morning. Then head northwest for 45 miles to Alberobello, a colony of beehive houses called *trulli*. Unique in Europe, the houses are whitewashed and characterized by their conical roofs of earth-colored stones. Overnight there.

Day 13 Drive north to the seaport of Bari, along Italy's Adriatic coastline. This is often called the country's "doorway to the Orient." It was through here that Crusaders passed on their way to the Holy Land. Bari is the capital of Apulia. Instead of overnighting there you can drive along the autostrada across Italy to Naples in the west. Overnight there.

Day 14 After seeing some of the most important sights of Naples in the morning, head north to Rome (see Chapters 4–6). Overnight there and promise a return visit to Italy.

8   Tips on Accommodations

A Note on Prices: In this guide hotels rated **very expensive** generally cost 450,000 lire ($281.25) and up for a double room. Accommodations judged **expensive** typically charge 300,000 to 450,000 lire ($187.50 to $281.25) for a double room; those in the **moderate** category usually ask 210,000–300,000 lire ($131.25–$187.50) for a double. Anything from 80,000 lire ($50) all the way up to 210,000 lire ($131.25) is judged **inexpensive.** A double room—most often without bath—that rents for under about 80,000 lire ($50) is definitely in the **budget** classification.

Note that all rooms have **private bath** unless specified otherwise. Most hotels in Italy do not have **parking garages**; in those that do, we have indicated charges (which can vary widely from place to place). If you're driving into a congested Italian city, you can usually park in front of the hotel long enough to unload your baggage. Someone from the hotel staff will direct you to the nearest available parking—usually a neighborhood garage.

HOTELS   The Italians are never simple. If you aren't aware of that now, you soon will be as you find yourself coping with the myriad Italian hotel prices and classifications.

Cardinal rule: If you want to enjoy average, "middle-class" comfort while keeping your wallet fairly intact, patronize the top-rated second-class hotels and their equivalents, the first-class pensiones. Many travelers frequent unheralded small establishments in Italy not because of financial need but because of the charm and atmosphere they find there.

Italy controls the prices of its hotels, designating a minimum and a maximum rate. The difference between the two may depend on the season, the location of the room, or even its size. Hotels are classified by stars in Italy, indicating their category of comfort: five stars for deluxe, four stars for first class, three stars for second class, two stars for third class, and one star for fourth class. Government ratings do not depend on sensitivity of decoration or on frescoed ceilings, but rather on such facilities as elevators and the like. Many of the finest hostelries in Italy are rated second class because they serve only breakfast (a blessing really, for those seeking to escape the board requirements).

Hotels in Italy today are divided on the question of whether breakfast is included in the room price. Usually the more expensive establishments charge extra for this meal. If you're really watching your lire, and if breakfast is included in the room price, always determine exactly what is included and what is extra. For example, mineral water, if ordered at breakfast, is nearly always à la carte.

Reservations are advised, even in the so-called slow hotel-booking months from November to March. Tourist travel to Italy peaks from May to October, when moderate and budget hotels are full. Only the most adventurous show up without a reservation. It's easiest to reserve with a chain via their representatives in North America (and 800 numbers), but they might not be the type of accommodations you're seeking.

For hotels without representatives in North America, write, fax, or call. If you write, send an International Reply Coupon, available at post offices. Give alternative dates if possible. You may be asked to send one night's deposit. At small places in Italy, many readers reported great difficulty or even complete failure in getting their deposit returned if they were forced to cancel their reservations suddenly.

If you call a hotel right before your arrival, you may be lucky enough to secure a room because of a last-minute cancellation.

Like airlines, hotels traditionally overbook, counting on last-minute cancellations. When everybody shows up, however, they face irate customers shouting at the desk, waving a confirmed reservation. To avoid this, give the hotel a credit card number to hold your reservation even if you arrive late.

PENSIONES The pensione is generally more intimate and personal than a hotel—in a pensione, the nature and quality of the welcome depend largely on the host or hostess, who might also be the cook and chief maid. As a general rule, a first-class pensione in Rome is the equivalent of a second-class hotel, and a second-class pensione is the equivalent of a third-class hotel. In many of these pensiones, you'll be asked to take half-board arrangements, although not always. A vast number serve only breakfast.

ALPINE LIVING The Club Alpino Italia, via Silvio Pellico 6, 20121 Milan (☎ 02/805-6971), owns and operates hundreds of huts in mountain districts, and annually publishes a mini-guide with a map and information on access, equipment, and tariffs for lodgings within them. Membership in the club costs 50,000 lire ($31.25), and provides a copy of this mini-guide plus the availability of advice and information about skiing and climbing throughout northern Italy. You can write or call for information.

HOME EXCHANGES An increasingly popular and economical way to travel is to exchange your home with that of an Italian family, often with a car included, provided you extend the same privilege. Several U.S.-based organizations specialize in this unique form of vacationing. For specific recommendations, refer to "Home Exchanges" in Section 5 of this chapter.

RELAIS & CHATEAUX Most member hotels of this association are in France, but many of these prestigious (and invariably expensive) hotels also exist in Italy, 23 in all. If you travel the Relais & Châteaux route, it will invariably be deluxe. But instead of sterile modern hotels, you'll frequently get places steeped in atmosphere and quality, often palaces or ancient castles, abbeys, or convents converted to receive guests.

Prices for a double room in these places can range anywhere from $150 (usually from $200) to as much as $1,000 a night. To qualify for membership in the organization, all participating hotels must satisfy a demanding set of criteria for food, accommodations, and service.

For an illustrated catalogue of these establishments worldwide, send $10 to Relais & Châteaux, 11 East 44th St., Suite 704, New York, NY 10017 (☎ 212/856-0115). For reservations, each individual hotel or inn must be contacted directly.

RELIGIOUS INSTITUTIONS Convents, monasteries, and other religious institutions in Italy offer accommodations, generally of the fourth-class hotel or *pensioni* category. Some are just for men; others are for women only. Many, however, accept married couples. Italian tourist offices generally have abbreviated listings of these accommodations, or you can write directly to the archdiocese (Archidiocesi di Roma, for example) in cities in which you desire such an accommodation.

VILLAS & APARTMENTS For information on renting villas or apartments, you may write directly to the local tourist board or the provincial tourist office in the city or town where you expect to stay. For addresses, refer to "Essentials" in the individual city or town listings. In Italy, information on villas and apartments is also available in daily newspapers or through local real-estate agents. The following organizations deal in the rental of villas or apartments in Italy.

Hideaways International, 767 Islington St. (P.O. Box 4433), Portsmouth, NH 03801 (☎ 603/430-4433 or 800/843-4433), represents an Italian-based real-estate management company that makes available several hundred villas scattered throughout Italy. A catalogue listing color photos of each property is available upon request for $15. Most villas are in Tuscany and Umbria.

At Home Abroad, Inc., 405 E. 56th St., #6H, New York, NY 10022-2466 (☎ 212/421-9165; fax 212/752-1591), represents about 150 villas, primarily inland, as well as coastal Tuscany and Umbria (plus a scattering of other homes throughout Italy). Except for Florence, these properties are rarely available in major cities such as Rome. They can arrange a rental for time periods of between one week to two months. Their real estate ranges from solidly traditional houses to sumptuous bastions of chic. Payment of a $25 registration fee (which is applied toward any eventual rental) prompts the company to send color photographs and descriptions of a wide selection of properties.

Rent a Vacation Everywhere, Inc. (RAVE), 135 Meigs Street, Rochester, NY 14607 (☎ 716/256-0760; fax 716/256-2676), was established in 1981 and grew out of the personal travels and experiences of its partners, Gloria Gioia and Annette Waldman. They have, for the most part, personally visited the villas they represent. They offer moderately priced to deluxe apartments and villas throughout Italy, in Veneto, Tuscany, Liguria, Umbria, and along the Amalfi Coast, plus apartments in Florence and Rome. The minimum rental is one week. Prices range from around $825 a week for their least expensive studio, suitable for two, to monthly rentals going all the way up to $40,000 a month for something really luxurious.

Another reputable company renting privately owned Italian houses, farmhouses, apartments, and villas is **Hometours International, Inc.,** P. O. Box 11503, 5412 Kingston Pike, Knoxville, TN 37919 (☎ 800/367-4568). The company offers rentable dwellings in Umbria, along the Amalfi coast, in Tuscany, and in or around such cities as Livorno, Lucca, and Grosseto. There are also apartments in central Rome, Siena, Venice, and Florence, and a handful of large and echoing baroque palaces suitable for up to a dozen occupants at a time. Units are rented for a minimum of seven days. Unlike many other travel outfits, Hometours can also arrange accommodations in simple, family-run one-, two-, and three-star hotels throughout Italy. To obtain their 260-page color catalogue with descriptions and pictures, send $8 for postage and handling, $3 for their bed-and-breakfast catalogue of small, family-run hotels, or $2 for descriptive literature about any other locations.

Grand Luxe International, Inc., 165 Chestnut St., Allendale, NJ 07401 (☎ 201/327-2333), rents Italian villas, castles, farmhouses, and apartments, and is especially known for its customized weddings, often in historic castles. The services are wide-ranging, including honeymoons at romantic hideaways or family reunions at five-star hotels. Rentals are always for a minimum of one week, run from Saturday to Saturday, and are scattered throughout the Italian peninsula, with a dense concentration in Tuscany, Umbria, and the Veneto.

Suzanne T. Pidduck operates **Rentals in Italy**, 1742 Calle Corva, Camarillo, CA 93010 (☎ 805/987-5278, or toll free 800/726-6702; fax 805/482-7976), giving each client personal attention. In business since 1979, it is the largest vacation home rental in Italy, issuing a main catalog of about 275 pages with some 1,200 rental properties in Tuscany, Umbria, Veneto, Rome, Calabria, Puglia, and Sicily, among other places, including Sardinia. Car rentals at Maggiore can also be arranged.

FARMHOUSE ACCOMMODATIONS   Some visitors find the price of lodgings in the major tourist cities of Italy almost overwhelmingly expensive. One cost-conscious alternative is a stay in a house, an apartment, or bedroom on an Italian farm as part of a program known as *agriturismo*. The farms that participate produce wine, jams, olive oil, honey, grains, liqueurs, meat, or dairy products, or they breed horses; most lie in rural areas outside the main touristic centers. Some visitors, however, relish the contact with the Italian earth, and appreciate the agricultural bounty and country traditions for which Italy is famous.

A company that specializes in arranging stays in these farmhouses is **Italy Farm Holidays,** 547 Martling Ave., Tarrytown, NY 10591 (☎ 914/631-7880; fax 914/631-8831). The company is owned and operated by the Levey family, avid travelers in Italy who began pursuing their interest in this field more than 20 years ago. (Since then, they have purchased a farmhouse of their own in Tuscany.) Today, they represent about 50 working farms scattered for the most part within Piedmont, Tuscany, Umbria, Veneto, and Paula, any of which would be suitable as a base for touring the art cities of the region.

Each farm or cooperative has successfully passed a personal inspection, and some of the most desirable ones lie just a few miles from the heart of Florence and Siena. Most properties require minimum stays of three to seven days, and require payment in full in advance. Many offer meals (usually breakfast) as part of the arrangement; others provide such amenities as free use of bicycles or optional horseback-riding packages. Only a few of the establishments contain more than seven rentable accommodations, most have private bathrooms, and many contain kitchens of their own.

Because the company imposes penalties of between 50% and 100% of the agreed-upon price for cancellations, trip-cancellation insurance is strongly recommended. Depending on the season and the category of accommodation, weekly rates for two persons begin at around $600 per week in low season in a modest accommodation, rising to around $3,500 per week in high season for rental of a historic and elegant villa suitable for up to 10 occupants.

House cleaning or maid service is not provided during your occupancy unless it's specifically arranged as a supplement, or when a client stays for more than one week in an apartment or house.

YOUTH HOSTELS   The Italian Youth Hostel Association operates more than 50 hostels throughout Italy, and they are likely to be overcrowded in summer, particularly at popular tourist meccas. Reservations can be made by writing directly to the individual youth hostel. The headquarters, **Associazione Italiana Alberghi per la Gioventu,** via Cavour 44, 00184 Roma (☎ 06/487-1152; fax 06/ 488-0492), provides details. You must be a member. In the United States you can join before you go by contacting **Hostelling International/American Youth Hostels (HI-AYH),** 733 15th St. NW, #840, Washington, DC 20005 (☎ 202/ 783-6161). Membership is $25; if you're under 18 the charge is $10, and if you're over 54, it's $15.

9 Tips on Dining

In this guide meals rated **very expensive** usually cost more than 120,000 lire ($75); **expensive,** 65,000 to 120,000 lire ($40.65 to $75); **moderate,** 40,000 to 65,000 lire ($25 to $40.65); and anything under 40,000 lire ($25) is considered **inexpensive.**

Some restaurants offer a tourist menu, or *menu turistico,* at an inclusive price. The tourist menu includes soup (nearly always minestrone) or pasta, followed by a meat dish with vegetables, topped off by dessert (fresh fruit or cheese), as well as a quarter liter of wine or mineral water, along with the bread, cover charge, and service (you'll still be expected to tip something extra).

If you order from the tourist menu, you'll avoid the array of added charges that the restaurateur likes to tack on. You won't get the choicest cuts of meat, nor will you always be able to order the specialties of the house, but you'll probably get a quite good, filling repast if you pick and choose your restaurants carefully. But be warned. Even though a restaurant owner offers such a menu, the staff is often reluctant to serve it, since it is their least profitable item. Often the owner will advertise a tourist menu in the window, but it won't be featured on the menu you're shown by the waiter. You'll have to ask for it in most cases, and you won't win any "most beloved patron" contests when you do.

What about the *prezzo fisso* (fixed price)? A confused picture. A fixed-price meal might even undercut the tourist menu. On the other hand, it might not include wine, service, bread, or cover charge—for which you'll be billed extra. If you're on the most limited of budgets, make sure you understand what the prezzo fisso entails to avoid misunderstandings when you settle the tab.

The distinction between expensive and moderate restaurants in Italy is often blurred. For example, if you order a pasta, a fresh salad, and perhaps a selection of fresh fruit, along with a carafe of the house wine, the restaurant is likely to be a less expensive choice. However, should you prefer a heaping plate of antipasti, a separate pasta course, followed by bottled wine and a Florentine beefsteak, perhaps topped off by dessert, then your bill is likely to be in the more expensive category. So it depends a great deal on how much you want to eat. In many places, most vegetable courses are priced separately.

Most restaurants will impose a *pane e coperto* (bread and cover) charge for the privilege of your patronizing their establishment. This charge often ranges from about 1,000 to 3,000 lire (65¢ to $1.90) per person, and it's unavoidable. A tip (*servizio*), ranging from 10% to 15%, is usually added to your bill, but it is customary to leave some small change as an extra reward, especially if the service has been good.

Here's how to order a full meal in Italy. Begin with a *primo piatto,* or first course, which is usually a pasta dish. It is also possible to order *antipasti* (hors d'oeuvres) as a first course. The *secondo piatto* (second course) consists of fish, meat, or poultry, often with a side dish of vegetables or a salad. The main course is called *contorno.* If you're still hungry, you can ask for a *dolce* (dessert). Restaurants almost insist that diners order at least a first and second course. Owners highly disapprove of foreign visitors who come in and order pasta as a main course, perhaps a salad, and then leave. Pressure, subtle or otherwise, is often applied for one to order both a first and a second plate of food. Otherwise, the restaurant figures it loses money on your patronage.

Restaurant owners have a ready response to those visitors who protest they don't want "so much food." If you want only a plate of spaghetti or something light, you need not reserve a table in a proper restaurant, but can patronize any number of cafeterias, *rosticcerias*, or *tavola caldas*. Regardless of what name they come under, these are usually low-priced establishments serving fast-food orders. Often their offerings are behind glass display cases. You don't pay a cover charge, and you can order as much or as little as you wish. You can also go to one of hundreds of pizzerias if you want only a light meal or snack. Many bars or café-bars, as the case may be, also offer both hot and cold food throughout the day. If you're lunching light in the heat, ask for a variety of sandwiches. Called *panini*, they are usually rolls stuffed with meat. *Tramezzini* are white-bread sandwiches with the crust trimmed. It's also possible to go into one of hundreds of general food stores throughout the country (called *alimentari*) and have sandwiches prepared on the spot, or else purchase the makings for a picnic lunch to be enjoyed in a park.

As a final caveat, phone numbers of restaurants often aren't valid for more than a year or two. For reasons known only to the restaurateurs themselves, opening hours, even days of closing, are changed frequently. So, if possible, always check the specific details with the restaurant of your choice before heading there. If the staff doesn't speak English and you need a confirmed reservation (always a good idea), ask someone at your hotel reception desk to make a reservation for you.

10 Tips on Shopping

BEST BUYS   Because of the Italians' consummate skill as manufacturers and designers, it's no surprise that consumers from all over the world flock to Italy's shops, trade fairs, and design studios to see what's new, hot, and saleable back home.

Most obvious is **fashion,** which since World War II has played a major part in the economy of Milan, whose entrepreneurs view Rome as a principal distribution center. There are literally hundreds of famous designers for both men and women, most of whom make eminently stylish garments. Materials include silks, leathers, cottons, synthetics, and wools, often of the finest quality.

Italian design influences everything from typewriter keyboards to kitchen appliances to furniture. The Italian studios of Memphis-Milano and Studio Alchimia are two of the leaders in this field, and many of their products (and many copies of their products) are now highly visible in machines and furnishings throughout the world. Many of Italy's new products and designs can be previewed by reading a copy of *Domus*, a monthly magazine that reports, with photographs, on many different aspects of the country's design scene.

Food and wine never go out of style, and many gourmets import to North America the gastronomic entities that somehow always taste better in Italy. Many shops sell chocolates, pastries, liqueurs, wines, and limited-edition olive oils. Be alert to restrictions in North America against importing certain food products. Italian wines, of course, include many excellent vintages, and bottles of liqueurs (which are sometimes distilled from herbs and flowers) make charming and unusual gifts.

The **glassware** of Italy (and especially of Venice) is famous throughout the world. Elegant homes from Florida to California benefit greatly from the addition of a glass chandelier from Murano, for example, or a set of wine goblets. Shipping is a problem, but for a price, any object—no matter how fragile or elaborate—can be packed, shipped, and insured.

The **porcelain** of Italy is elegant and sought-after, but we personally prefer the hand-painted rustic plates and bowls of thick-edged **stoneware.** Done in strong and clear glazes, and influenced by their rural origins, the bowls and plates are both charming and humorous, and are often used at the most formal dinners for their originality and style. The **tiles and mosaics** of Italy are also charming, whether used individually as drink coasters or decorative ornaments, or in groups set into masonry walls.

Lace was, for many years, made in convents by nuns in cloisters. Venice became the country's headquarters. Handmade Italian lace is beautiful and justifiably expensive, crafted into an amazing array of tablecloths, napkins, clothing, and bridal veils. Beware of machine-made imitations, although with a bit of practice you'll soon be able to recognize the shoddy copies.

Paper goods, writing stationery, and beautifully bound books, prints, and engravings are specialties of Italy. The engraving you find amid stacks of dozens of others will invariably look beautiful when hanging—framed—on a wall back home.

Fabrics, especially silk, are made near Lake Como, in the foothills of the Italian Alps. Known for their supple beauty and their ability to hold color for years (the thicker the silk, the more desirable), these silks are rivaled only by the finest of India, Thailand, and China. Their history in Italy goes back to the era of Marco Polo, and possibly much earlier.

Finally, ranging from inspirational to grossly tasteless, Rome is the home to a **religious objects** industry that supplies virtually everything a conservative Catholic might want as a religious aid. Centered in Rome around the streets near the Church of Santa Maria Sopra Minerva are dozens of shops selling pictures, statues, and reliefs of most of the important saints, the Madonna, Jesus, and—a perennial favorite—John the Baptist.

TAX REBATES   Visitors to Italy are often appalled at the high taxes and the "add-ons" that influence so many bottom-line costs of a trip. A value-added tax (called IVA) is imposed on all consumer goods and services. The average tax is 19%, but it could be as high as 35% on certain luxury items. If you spend more than 300,000 lire ($187.50) at any one store, regardless of how many individual items are involved, you are entitled to a refund.

At the time of your purchase (of the antique, vase, or garment you couldn't live without), collect a formal receipt from the vendor. When you leave Italy, find an Italian Customs agent at the airport (or at the point of your exit from the country if you're traveling by train, bus, or car). The agent will want to see the item you've bought, confirm that it is physically leaving Italy, and stamp the vendor's receipt.

You should then mail the stamped receipt (keeping a photocopy for your records) back to the original vendor. The vendor will, sooner or later, send you a refund of the tax you paid at the time of your original purchase. Reputable stores view this as a matter of ordinary paperwork and are very businesslike about it. Less honorable stores might lose your dossier. It pays to deal with established vendors on purchases of this size.

FAST FACTS: Italy

American Express Offices are found in Rome at piazza di Spagna 38 (☎ 06/67641), in Florence at via Dante Alighieri (☎ 055/50981), in Venice at San Marco 1471 (☎ 041/520-0844), and in Milan at via Brera 3 (☎ 02/72-85571).

Business Hours Regular business hours are Monday through Friday from 9am (sometimes 9:30am) to 1pm and 3:30 (sometimes 4) to 7 or 7:30pm. In July or August, offices may not open in the afternoon until 4:30 or 5pm. **Banks** in Italy are open Monday through Friday from 8:30am to 1 or 1:30pm, and 2 or 2:30 to 4pm; and are closed all day Saturday, Sunday, and national holidays. This siesta (*riposo*) closing is often observed in Rome, Naples, and most cities of southern Italy; however, in Milan and other northern and central cities the custom has been completely abolished by some merchants. Most shops are closed on Sunday, except for certain barbershops that are open on Sunday morning. However, hairdressers are closed on Sunday and Monday. If you're traveling in Italy in summer and the heat is intense, we suggest that you learn the custom of the riposo, too.

Camera/Film U.S.-brand film is available in Italy but it's expensive. Take in as much as Customs will allow if you plan to take a lot of pictures.

Cigarettes Seek out stores called *tabacchi*. Some bars also sell cigarettes. American and British contraband cigarettes are sold freely on the streets for much less than you'll pay in the shops. Although purchasing them is illegal, it seems to be the custom.

Climate See "When to Go," earlier in this chapter.

Crime See "Safety," below.

Currency See "Information, Entry Requirements & Money," earlier in this chapter.

Customs Overseas visitors to Italy can bring along most items for personal use duty free. This includes fishing tackle, a sporting gun and 200 cartridges, a pair of skis, two tennis racquets, a portable typewriter, a record player with 10 records, a tape recorder, a baby carriage, two ordinary hand cameras with 10 rolls of film, a movie camera with 10 rolls of film, a portable radio set (subject to a small license fee), and 400 cigarettes (two cartons) or a quantity of cigars or pipe tobacco not exceeding 500 grams (1.1 lb). There are strict limits on importing alcoholic beverages. However, limits are much more liberal for alcohol bought tax-paid in other countries of the European Union.

Upon leaving Italy, citizens of the United States who have been outside the country for 48 hours or more are allowed to bring back to their home country $400 worth of merchandise duty free—that is, if they have claimed no similar exemption within the past 30 days. If you make purchases in Italy, it is important to keep your receipts.

Driving Rules See "Getting Around," earlier in this chapter.

Drug Laws Penalties are severe and could lead to either imprisonment or deportation. Selling drugs to minors is dealt with particularly harshly.

Drugstores At every drugstore (*farmacia*), there is a list of those that are open at night and on Sunday. This list rotates.

Electricity   The electricity in Italy varies considerably. It's usually alternating current (A.C.), varying from 42 to 50 cycles. The voltage can be anywhere from 115 to 220. It is recommended that any visitor carrying electrical appliances obtain a transformer. Check the exact local current with the hotel where you are staying. Plugs have prongs that are round, not flat; therefore, an adapter plug is also needed.

Embassies/Consulates   The Embassy of the **United States** is in Rome at via Vittorio Veneto 121 (☎ 06/46741). The consular and passport services, however, are located at via Torrorio Veneto 121 (☎ 06/47741). Other U.S. consulates are in Florence at lungarno Amerigo Vespucci 46 (☎ 055/2398276); and in Milan at largo Donegani 1 (☎ 02/290-018-41). These offices are open Monday through Friday from 8:30am to 12:30pm and 2 to 4:30pm. There is also a consulate in Naples at piazza della Republicca (☎ 081/5838-111), which is open Monday through Friday from 8am to noon and 2 to 5pm. The consulate in Genoa is closed; however, there is an office of the U.S. Foreign Commercial Service, via Dante 2-43 (Palazzo Borsaz) (☎ 010/543-877), which is open Monday through Friday from 8:30am to 12:30pm and 2 to 4:30pm.

Consulate and passport services for **Canada** are in Rome at via Zara 30 (☎ 06/445981), which is open Monday through Friday from 10am to noon and 2 to 4pm. The office of the **United Kingdom** is in Rome at via XX Settembre 80A (☎ 06/4825441), open in summer, Monday through Friday, from 8am to 1:30pm, and in off-season, Monday through Friday, from 9am to 12:30pm and from 2 to 4:30pm. The **Australian** Embassy is in Rome at via Alessandria 215 (☎ 06/85272-1), which is open Monday through Thursday from 8:30am to 12:30pm and from 1:30 to 5:30pm, and on Friday from 8:30am to 1:15pm. The consular services for Australia are in Rome at Corso Trieste 25 (☎ 06/852-272-1), open Monday through Thursday from 8:30am to noon and 2 to 4pm, and on Friday from 9am to noon. For **New Zealand,** the office in Rome is at via Zara 28 (☎ 06/440-2928), and hours are Monday through Friday from 8:30am to 12:45pm and 1:45 to 5pm. In case of emergency, embassies have a 24-hour referral service.

Emergencies   Dial **113** for an ambulance, police, or fire. In case of a breakdown on an Italian road, dial 116 at the nearest telephone box; the nearest Automobile Club of Italy (ACI) will be notified to come to your aid.

Etiquette   Women in sleeveless dresses and men with bare chests are not welcome in the best bars and restaurants of Italy and may be refused service. Also, persons so attired are ordered to cover up when they visit museums and churches.

Gasoline   See "Getting Around," earlier in this chapter.

Hitchhiking   See "Getting Around," earlier in this chapter.

Holidays   See "When to Go," earlier in this chapter.

Information   See "Information, Entry Requirements & Money," earlier in this chapter, and specific cities for local information offices.

Laundry   All deluxe and first- and second-class hotels have laundry and dry-cleaning facilities. Prices are usually moderate, and a small service charge is added to the actual cost. If a hotel doesn't provide these services, the desk clerk can direct you to the nearest *tintoria* (shop), or you can look in the classified telephone directory under *tintorie* (cleaning and pressing) and *lavanderie* (laundry).

Legal Aid   The consulate of your country is the place to turn, although offices cannot interfere in the Italian legal process. They can, however, inform you of your rights and provide a list of attorneys. You'll have to pay for the attorney out of your pocket, however, as there is no free legal assistance. If you're arrested for a drug offense, about all the consulate will do is notify a lawyer about your case and perhaps inform your family.

Liquor Laws   Wine with meals has been considered a normal part of family life for hundreds of years in Italy. Children are exposed to wine at an early age, and alcoholic consumption is not considered anything out of the ordinary. There is no legal drinking age for buying or ordering alcohol. Alcohol is sold day and night throughout the year, as there is almost no restriction on the sale of wine or liquor in Italy.

Lost Property   Report the loss to the nearest police station. For large cities, such as Rome, refer to "Fast Facts" in the individual city listings.

Mail   At post offices, General Delivery service is available in Italy. Correspondence can be addressed c/o the post office by adding *Fermo Posta* to the name of the locality. Delivery will be made at the local central post office upon identification of the addressee by passport. In addition to all post offices, you can purchase stamps at little *tabacchi* (tobacco) stores throughout the city.

Mail delivery in Italy is notoriously bad. One letter from a soldier, postmarked in 1945, arrived in his home village in 1982. Letters sent from New York, say, in November, are often delivered (if at all) the following year. If you're writing for hotel reservations, it can cause much confusion on both sides. Many visitors arrive in Italy long before their hotel deposits. Fax machines speed up the process tremendously.

Maps   See "Getting Around," earlier in this chapter. Also see certain map recommendations in the city listings for such cities as Rome, Florence, and Venice.

Newspapers/Magazines   In major cities, it is possible to find the *International Herald Tribune* or *USA Today* as well as other English-language newspapers and magazines at hotels and news kiosks, including *Time* and *Newsweek.*

Pets   A veterinarian's certificate of good health is required for dogs and cats, and should be obtained by owners before entering Italy. Dogs must be on a leash or muzzled at all times. Other animals must undergo examination at the border or port of entry. Certificates for parrots or other birds subject to psittacosis must state that the country of origin is free of disease. All documents must be certified first by a notary public, then by the nearest Italian consulate.

Police   Dial **113,** the all-purpose number for police emergency assistance in Italy.

Radio/TV   Most radio and television broadcasts are on RAI, the Italian state radio and television network. Occasionally, especially during the tourist season, the network will broadcast special programs in English. Announcements are made in the radio and TV guide sections of local newspapers. Vatican Radio also carries foreign-language religious news programs, often in English. Shortwave transistor radios pick up broadcasts from the BBC (British), Voice of America (United States), and CBC (Canadian). RAI television and private channels broadcast only in Italian. More expensive hotels often have TV sets in the bedrooms with cable subscriptions to the CNN news network.

Restrooms All airport and railway stations have restrooms, often with attendants, who expect to be tipped. Bars, nightclubs, restaurants, cafés, and all hotels have facilities as well. Public toilets are also found near many of the major sights.

Usually they are designated as W.C. (water closet) or as DONNE (women) or UOMINI (men). The most confusing designation is SIGNORI (gentlemen) and SIGNORE (ladies), so watch those final I's and E's!

Safety The most common menace, especially in large cities, particular Rome, is the plague of pickpockets and roving gangs of gypsy children who virtually surround you, distract you in all the confusion, and steal your purse or wallet. Never leave valuables in a car, and never travel with your car unlocked. A U.S. State Department travel advisory warns that every car—whether parked, stopped at a traffic light, or even moving—can be a potential target for armed robbery.

Taxes As a member of the European Union, Italy imposes a tax on most goods and services. It is a "value-added tax," called IVA in Italy. For example, the tax affecting most visitors is that imposed at hotels, which ranges from 9% in first- and second-class hotels and pensions to 19% in deluxe hotels.

Telegrams/Telephone/Telex/Fax For **telegrams,** ITALCABLE operates services abroad, transmitting messages by cable or satellite. Both internal and foreign telegrams may be dictated over the phone (dial 186).

A **public telephone** is always near at hand in Italy, especially if you're near a bar. Local calls cost 200 lire. You can use 100, 200, or 500 lire coins or the old, grooved telephone tokens—called *gettone*—which are equivalent to 200 lire. Most phones, especially in the cities, now accept a multiple-use phone card called CartaSIP, which can be purchased at all *tabacchi* and bars in increments of 2,000, 5,000, 10,000, or 20,000 lire. To use this card, insert it into the slot in the phone and then dial. A digital display will keep track of how many lire you use up during your call. The card is good until it runs out of lire, so don't forget to take it with you when you hang up.

Thanks to ITALCABLE, **international calls** to the United States and Canada can be dialed directly. Dial 00 (the international code from Italy), then the country code (1 for the United States and Canada), the area code, and the number you're calling. Calls dialed directly are billed on the basis of the call's duration only. A reduced rate is applied from 11pm to 8am Monday through Saturday and all day Sunday.

If you wish to make a **collect call** from a pay phone, simply deposit 200 lire (don't worry—you get it back when you are done), dial 170, and an ITALCABLE operator will come on and will speak English. For **calling card calls**, drop in the refundable 200 lire, then dial the appropriate number for your card's company to be connected with an operator in the U.S.: for AT&T, 172-1011; for MCI, 172-1022; and for Sprint, 172-1877.

If you make a long-distance call from a public telephone, there is no surcharge. *However, hotels have been known to double or triple the cost of the call, so be duly warned.*

Chances are your hotel will send or receive a **telex** or **fax** for you.

Television Government-sponsored RAI is the chief Italian television authority, operating three channels. RAI-1 and, to a lesser degree, RAI-2 are known for their family-oriented entertainment and news broadcasts, whereas RAI-3 features programs relating to cultural, sociological, and artistic issues. Independent broadcasters include channels 4 and 5.

Time   In terms of standard time zones, Italy is six hours ahead of eastern standard time in the United States. Daylight saving time goes into effect in Italy each year from May 22 to September 24.

Tipping   This custom is practiced with flair in Italy—many people depend on tips for their livelihoods. In hotels, the service charge of 15% to 19% is already added to a bill. In addition, it's customary to tip the chambermaid 1,000 lire (65¢) per day; the doorman (for calling a cab), 1,000 lire (65¢); and the bellhop or porter 2,000 lire ($1.25) per bag. A concierge expects 3,000 lire ($1.90) per day, as well as tips for extra services performed, which could include help with long-distance calls, newspaper, or stamps. In expensive hotels these lire amounts are often doubled.

In restaurants, 15% is added to your bill to cover most charges. An additional tip for good service is almost always expected. Know that it is customary in certain fashionable restaurants in Rome, Florence, Venice, and Milan to leave an additional 10%, which, combined with the assessed service charge, is a very high tip indeed. The sommelier expects 10% of the cost of the wine. Checkroom attendants now expect 1,500 lire (95¢), although in simple places Italians still hand washroom attendants 200 to 300 lire (15¢ to 20¢), more in deluxe and first-class establishments. Restaurants are required by law to give customers official receipts.

In cafés and bars, tip 15% of the bill, and give a theater usher 1,500 lire (95¢). Taxi drivers expect at least 15% of the fare.

Tourist Offices   See "Information, Entry Requirements & Money," earlier in this chapter, and also specific city chapters.

Visas   See "Information, Entry Requirements & Money," earlier in this chapter.

Water   It is generally considered safe to drink. However, if you venture into the south of Italy, particularly the Naples region, it's best to stick to bottled water.

Introducing Rome

4

The population of Rome is composed of Romans and visitors, in varying numbers, depending on the season. In this city of easy amiability, however, residents and visitors mingle so freely that sometimes you can hardly tell them apart. Indeed, during the summer months especially, Rome seems to become one big host for the countless sightseers who converge upon it, guidebook and camera in hand, from points east and west; to all of them—Americans, Europeans, Japanese—it extends a warm and friendly welcome, wining them, dining them, and entertaining them in its inimitable fashion.

Rome gives to its visitors as much as it receives from them. A mixture of sophisticated world capital and provincial Italian town, it is alive with reminders of the past, which it preserves and cherishes all the more because they inspire so many foreigners to come here and by their presence—in museums and galleries, in piazzas and churches, amid ancient and medieval ruins and monuments—to reaffirm the city's importance as a center of Western civilization.

Rome is a city of images, vivid and unforgettable. One of the most striking may be seen at dawn—ideally from Janiculum Hill—as the city's silhouette, with its bell towers and cupolas, comes gradually into view. Rome is also a city of sounds, beginning, early in the morning, with the peal of church bells calling the faithful to Mass. As the city awakens and comes to life, the sounds multiply and merge into a kind of *sinfonia urbana*. The streets fill with cars, taxis, and motor scooters, blaring their horns as they weave in and out of traffic; the sidewalks become overrun with bleary-eyed office workers rushing off to their desks, but not before stealing into crowded cafés for their first cappuccino of the day; the shops lining the streets open for business by raising their protective metal grilles as loudly as possible, seeming to delight in their contribution to the general din; even the many fruit-and-vegetable stands are abuzz with activity, as housewives, maids, widowers, cooks, and others arrive to purchase their day's supply of fresh produce, haggling over price and caviling over quality.

By 10am the tourists themselves are on the street, battling the crowds and traffic as they wend their way from Renaissance palaces and baroque buildings to the famous ruins of antiquity—the Colosseum and the Forum, symbols of a once great empire whose heart was Rome, the Eternal City.

What's Special About Rome

Ancient Monuments
- The Foro Romano (Roman Forum), ringed by the Palatine and Capitoline hills, hub of a great imperial city.
- The Colosseum, symbol of Imperial Rome, built in A.D. 80 by 20,000 slaves—Byron called it the "gladiator's bloody circus."
- Ostia Antica, the long-buried city at the mouth of the Tiber, seaport and naval base of ancient Rome.
- The Pantheon, the best-preserved monument of ancient Rome, constructed by order of Emperor Hadrian around A.D. 120.

Religious Shrines
- St. Peter's, the world's greatest basilica, spiritual home for millions of Roman Catholics.
- Basilica of San Giovanni in Laterano, the cathedral of Rome, seat of the archbishop of Rome.
- The Vatican, a sovereign state, papal residence for 600 years and site of some 4$^{1}/_{2}$ miles of priceless art, including Michelangelo's Sistine Chapel.

Parks and Gardens
- Villa Borghese, a public park with open-air cafés and the Borghese Gallery.
- Villa d'Este, at Tivoli outside Rome, with its wonderfully imaginative 16th-century fountains.

Ace Attractions
- Spanish Steps, perennial favorite of ordinary tourists and famous expatriates, among them John Keats and Richard Wagner.
- Piazza Navona, the finest of Rome's squares, a former stadium of Domitian now filled with visitors ringing Bernini's *Fountain of the Four Rivers*.

Film Locations
- Home of Cinecittà, the hub of Italy's movie industry since the 1930s. In the postwar period, three famous films helped put Rome on the tourist map: *Roman Holiday* (1953); *Three Coins in the Fountain* (1954), which inspired the tradition of tourists' tossing coins over their shoulders to make sure they'll come back to Rome; and Federico Fellini's *La Dolce Vita* (1960).

In Chapter 6, "What to See & Do in Rome," we'll take you on fascinating walks through the major historical and architectural sites of Rome. But important though the sites may be to an appreciation of this centuries-old city, they represent only one aspect of Rome—the past. Rome is also a vibrant, exciting *modern* metropolis, pulsing with all kinds of daytime and nighttime activities. As you take part in them, you'll find yourself embracing the city's life with intensity, like a Roman. As the saying goes, "When in Rome. . . . "

1 Orientation

ARRIVING

BY PLANE Chances are that you'll arrive in Italy at Rome's **Leonardo da Vinci International Airport** (☎ 06/659-51), popularly known as Fiumicino, from the town located adjacent to the airport, 18^1/$_2$ miles from the center of the capital. Domestic flights arrive at one terminal, international ones at the other. (If you're flying by charter, you might arrive at Ciampino Airport.)

After leaving Passport Control, two tourist information desks—one for Rome, one for all of Italy—come into view. At the Rome desk you can pick up a general (not a detailed) map and some pamphlets. Hours are Monday through Saturday from 8:30am to 7pm. A bureau de change operates daily from 7:30am to 11pm. Following your next stopover at Customs, you can enter the main arrivals building with a luggage store office open daily and charging 5,000 lire ($3.15) per bag.

To get into the city, Rome operates a shuttle service directly from Fiumicino to the main station Termini. Upon leaving Customs, follow the signs marked TRENO. Trains go back and forth between the airport and the rail station daily from 7am to 10pm. A one-way ticket costs 12,000 lire ($7.50).

Trains arrive at Track 22 at Termini. A local train, costing 7,000 lire ($4.40), also runs between the airport and Tiburtina Station, from which passengers can go the rest of the way to Rome's Termini by subway line B, costing another 1,000 lire (65¢).

Should you arrive on a charter flight at Ciampino (☎ 06/7934-0297), take a COTRAL bus, departing every 30 minutes or so, which will deliver you to the Anagnina stop of Metropolitana Line A. At Anagnina you can take Linea A to the Stazione Termini, the rail station in the heart of Rome, where your final connections can be made. Trip time is about 45 minutes, and the cost is 2,000 lire ($1.25).

Taxis from Fiumicino are expensive—70,000 lire ($43.75) and up—and therefore not recommended for the trip from the airport.

If you arrive at Ciampino, you're nearer the city. Because of the shorter distance, you pay the amount shown on the meter if you go by taxi (not double, as some drivers may insist).

BY TRAIN   Trains arrive in the center of old Rome at the **Stazione Termini,** piazza dei Cinquecento (☎ 4775), the train and subway transportation hub for all of Rome. Many hotels lie near the station, and you can walk to your hotel if you don't have too much luggage. Otherwise, an array of taxi, bus, and subway lines awaits you.

If you're taking the Metropolitana (Rome's subway network), follow the illuminated M sign in red that points the way. To catch a bus, go straight through the outer hall of the Termini and enter the sprawling bus lot of the piazza dei Cinquecento. Taxis are also found here.

The Termini is filled with services. At a branch of the Banca Nazionale delle Communicazioni (between Tracks 8–11 and Tracks 12–15) you can exchange money. Information on rail travel to other parts of Italy is dispensed at Informazioni Ferroviarie, in the larger outer hallway. There is also a tourist information booth here, along with baggage services, barbershops, day hotels, gift shops, restaurants, and bars. But beware of pickpockets, perhaps quick-fingered young children.

BY BUS   Arrivals are at the **Stazione Termini** (see above), where all the same facilities awaiting train passengers are also available to bus passengers. Information on buses is dispensed at a booth operated by ATAC, the city bus company, at piazza dei Cinquecento (☎ 469-51), which is open daily from 7:30am to 7:30pm.

BY CAR From the north the main access route is the **A1 (Autostrada del Sole),** cutting through Milan and Florence, or you can take the coastal route, SSI Aurelia, from Genoa. If you're driving north from Naples, you take the southern lap of the **Autostrada del Sole (A2).** All these autostrade join with the **Grande Raccordo Anulare,** a ring road that encircles Rome, channeling traffic into the congested city. Long before you reach this ring road, you should study a map carefully to see what part of Rome you plan to enter and mark your route accordingly. Route markings along the ring road tend to be confusing.

VISITOR INFORMATION

Tourist information is available at the **Ente Provinciale per il Turismo,** via Parigi 5, 00185 Roma (☎ 06/488-99-200), open Monday through Saturday from 8:15am to 7:15pm. The information dispensed here is meager. There's another information bureau at the Stazione Termini (☎ 06/487-1270), open daily from 8:15am to 7:30pm.

CITY LAYOUT

Your feet will probably first touch Roman soil at **Leonardo da Vinci International Airport,** near the mouth of the Tiber River, $18^1/_2$ miles from the center of Rome. The drive into the city is rather uneventful until you pass through the city wall, the still remarkably intact **Great Aurelian Wall,** started in A.D. 271 to calm Rome's barbarian jitters. Suddenly, ruins of imperial baths loom on one side, and great monuments can be seen in the middle of blocks. Inside the walls you'll find a city designed for a population that walked to get where it was going. Parts of Rome actually feel more like an oversized village than the former imperial capital of the Western world.

The Stazione Termini faces a huge piazza, **piazza dei Cinquecento,** named after 500 Italians who died heroically in a 19th-century battle in Africa. There are certainly many more attractive sites in Rome, but this piazza has several noteworthy aspects. First, it's next to the modern railroad station. Immediately next to the sculptured concrete cantilevered roof of the station facade is a remnant of the Servian Wall, built nearly six centuries before the birth of Christ by an ancient Roman king. If that isn't enough, the far side of the piazza is bordered by the ruins of the Baths of Diocletian, a former bastion of imperial luxury whose crumbling brick walls were once covered with the rarest of colored marbles and even now enclose marble and bronze statuary.

Most of the old city and its monuments lie on the east side of the **Tiber River (Fiume Tevere),** which meanders through town between 19th-century stone embankments. However, several important monuments are on the other side: **St. Peter's Basilica** and the **Vatican;** the **Castel Sant' Angelo** (formerly the tomb of the Emperor Hadrian), and the colorful section of town known as **Trastevere.** The bulk of ancient, Renaissance, and baroque Rome lies across the Tiber from St. Peter's on the same side as the Stazione Termini. The various quarters of the city are linked by large boulevards (large at least in some places) that have mostly been laid out since the late 19th century.

Starting from the **Victor Emmanuel monument,** a highly controversial pile of snow-white Brescian marble, there's a street running practically due north to the **piazza del Popolo** and the city wall. This is **via del Corso,** one of the main streets of Rome—noisy, congested, always crowded with buses and shoppers, called simply "Corso." Again from the Victor Emmanuel monument, the major artery going west (and ultimately across the Tiber to St. Peter's) is **corso Vittorio Emanuele.** To go in the other direction, toward the Colosseum, you take **via del Fori Imperiali,** named for the excavated ruins of the imperial forums that flank this avenue. This road was laid out in the 1930s by Mussolini, who was responsible for much of the fine archaeological work in Rome, if perhaps for the wrong reasons. Yet another central conduit is **via Nazionale,** running from piazza della Repubblica (also called piazza Esedra), and ending again right near the Victor Emmanuel monument at **piazza Venezia,** which lies in front of it. The final lap of via Nazionale is called via Quattro Novembre.

For the $2^1/_2$ millennia before these boulevards were built, the citizens had to make their way through narrow byways and curves that defeated all but the best senses of direction. These streets—among the most charming aspects of the city—still exist in large quantities, mostly unspoiled by the advances of modern construction. However, this tangled street plan has one troublesome element: automobiles. The traffic in Rome is awful! When the claustrophobic street plans of the Dark Ages open unexpectedly onto a vast piazza, every driver accelerates full throttle for the distant horizon, while pedestrians flatten themselves against marble fountains for protection or stride with firm jaws right into the thick of the howling traffic.

The traffic problem in Rome is nothing new. Julius Caesar was so exasperated by it that he banned all vehicular traffic during daylight hours. Sometimes it's actually faster to walk than to take a bus, especially during any of Rome's four daily rush hours (that's right, *four*: to work, home for lunch/siesta, back to work, home in the evening). The hectic crush of urban Rome is considerably less during August, when many Romans are out of town on holiday. If you visit at any other time of year, however, be prepared for the general frenzy that characterizes your average Roman street.

FINDING AN ADDRESS Finding an address in Rome can be a problem because of the narrow, often cobbled streets of old Rome and the little, sometimes "hidden" piazzas or squares. Numbers usually run consecutively, with odd numbers on one side of the street and even numbers on the other side. However, in the old districts a different system is sometimes followed, although it is rare. These ancient streets begin their numbering on one side, running in order until the end, then running back in the opposite direction on the other side. Therefore, no. 50 could be opposite no. 308.

STREET MAPS Arm yourself with a detailed street map, not the general overview often handed out free at tourist offices. Even if you plan to see only the major monuments, you'll still need a detailed street map to find such attractions as the Trevi Fountain. The best ones are published by **Falk,** and they're available at most newsstands and kiosks in Rome. The best selections of maps are sold in the travel departments of various bookstores. See "Shopping" in Chapter 6.

NEIGHBORHOODS IN BRIEF

Here are the main districts of interest, and some of their more important attractions. Often a district will be named for a major square or monument, such as the piazza di Spagna or the piazza Navona district.

Ancient Rome This is the district that most visitors come to Rome to explore, taking in the Colosseum, Palatine Hill, the Roman Forum, the Fori Imperiali (Imperial Forums), and Circus Maximus.

Appian Way   Via Appia Antica is a 2,300-year-old road that has witnessed much of the history of the ancient world. By 190 B.C. it extended from Rome to Brindisi, and its most famous sights today are the catacombs, the graveyards of patrician families.

Città del Vaticano (Vatican City)   Vatican City is a small "city-state," but its influence extends around the world. The Vatican museums and St. Peter's take up most of the land area, and the popes have lived here for six centuries.

Medieval Rome (piazza Navona and the Pantheon)   One of the most alluring areas of Rome, the district is a maze of narrow streets and alleys from the Middle Ages and is filled with churches and palaces built during the Renaissance era, often with materials stripped from Ancient Rome, including rare marbles. The only way to explore it is on foot.

Monte Mario   On the northwestern precincts of Rome, this residential area offers panoramic views over the Eternal City especially from Villa Madama, which was launched by Raphael but is closed to the public. Monte Mario is the site of the deluxe Cavalieri Hilton, where you can stop in for a drink.

Parioli   This is the most elegant residential section of Rome, framed by the green spaces of Villa Borghese to the south and Villa Glori and Villa Ada to the north. It's a setting for some of the city's finest restaurants, hotels, and nightclubs.

Piazza di Spagna   Ever since the 17th century these steps—former site of the Spanish ambassador's residence—have been the center of tourist Rome. Keats lived in a house opening onto the steps, and some of Rome's most prestigious shopping streets fan out from it, including via Condotti.

Prati   Known only to the connoisseurs of Rome, this district is really a middle-class suburb, lying north of Castel Sant'Angelo and Vatican City. It's becoming increasingly patronized by budget travelers because of its low-cost *pensioni* (boarding houses). The flower market in the Trionfale Quarter to the west is worth the trip.

Renaissance Rome   South of corso Vittorio Emanuele, many buildings in this district were constructed in Renaissance times as private homes. Much of the section centers around the Palazzo Farnese. Walk on via Giulia with its antiques stores, interesting hotels, and modern art galleries.

Stazione Termini   The station adjoins the piazza della Repubblica, and, for many, this is their introduction to Rome. Much of the area is seedy and filled with gas fumes from all the buses and cars, but there's still much here to interest the visitor, including the Basilica da Santa Maria Maggiore and the Baths of Diocletian. Many good hotels remain.

Trastevere   This is the most authentic district of Rome, lying "across the Tiber," and its people are of mixed ancestry, including Jewish, Roman, and Greek, and speak their own dialect. The area centers around the ancient churches of Santa Cecilia in Trastevere and Santa Maria in Trastevere.

Via Vittorio Veneto   In the 1950s and early 1960s this was the haunt of the *dolce vita* set, as the likes of King Farouk and Swedish actress Anita Ekberg paraded up and down the boulevard to the delight of the *paparazzi*. The street is still there, still the site of luxury hotels and elegant cafés and restaurants, although it no longer has the allure it did in its heyday. Rome city authorities would like to restore this legendary street to some of its former glory. Frank Sinatra and Elizabeth Taylor may never stroll it again, but Rome is trying to spruce up the via Veneto by banning vehicular traffic on the top half of the street.

2 Getting Around

BY PUBLIC TRANSPORTATION

SUBWAY   The **Metropolitana,** or **Metro** for short, is the fastest means of transportation in Rome. It has two underground lines: Line A goes from via Ottaviano, near St. Peter's, to Anagnina, stopping at piazzale Flaminio (near piazza del Popolo), piazza Vittorio Emanuele, and piazza San Giovanni in Laterano. Line B connects the Rebibbia district with via Laurentina, stopping at via Cavour, piazza Bologna, Stazione Termini, the Colosseum, Circus Maximus, the Pyramid of C. Cestius, St. Paul's Outside the Walls, the Magliana, and the E.U.R. A big red letter M indicates the entrance to the subway. The price is 1,200 lire (75¢). A booklet of 10 tickets costs 9,000 lire ($5.65).

Tickets are available from vending machines at all stations. These machines accept 50-lira, 100-lira, and 200-lira coins. Some stations have managers, but they will not make change. Booklets of tickets are available at tabacchi (tobacco) shops and in some terminals. Some machines change 1,000 lire (65¢) notes into coins.

Building an underground system for Rome has not been easy, since every time workers start digging, they discover an old temple or other archaeological treasure and heavy earth-moving has to cease for a while.

BUS/TRAM   Roman buses are operated by an organization known as **ATAC** or **Azienda Tramvie e Autobus del Commune di Roma,** via Volturno 65 (☎ 46951 for information).

For only 1,200 lire (75¢) you can ride to most parts of Rome on quite good bus service. The ticket is valid for 1^1/$_2$ hours, and you can get on many buses during that time period, using the same ticket. At the Stazione Termini, you can purchase a special tourist bus pass, costing 5,000 lire ($3.15) for one day or 18,000 lire ($11.25) for a week. This allows you to ride on the ATAC network without bothering to purchase individual tickets. The tourist pass is also valid on the subway—but never ride the trains when the Romans are going to or from work or you'll be mashed flatter than fettuccine. On the first bus you board, you place your ticket in a small machine that prints the day and hour you boarded. And you do the same on the last bus you take during the validity period of the ticket.

Buses and trams stop at areas marked FERMATA, and in general they are in service from 6am to midnight daily. After that and until dawn, service, on main-line stations only, is very marginal. It's best to take a taxi in the wee hours—if you can find one.

At the bus information booth at the piazza dei Cinquecento, in front of the Stazione Termini, you can purchase a directory complete with maps summarizing the particular routes. Ask there about where to purchase bus tickets, or buy them in a tobacco shop or at a bus terminal. You must have your ticket before boarding the bus, as there are no ticket-issuing machines on the vehicles.

Take extreme caution riding the overcrowded buses of Rome—pickpockets abound! This is particularly true on bus no. 64, a favorite of tourists because of its route through Rome's historic districts and also a favorite of Rome's vast pickpocketing community. Bus 64 has earned various nicknames: "The Pickpocket Express" or "The Wallet Eater."

BY TAXI

If you're accustomed to hopping a cab in New York or London, then do so in Rome. If not, take less expensive means of transport. Avoid paying your fare with large bills—invariably, taxi drivers claim they don't have change, hoping for a bigger tip. The driver will also expect a 10% tip. Don't count on hailing a taxi on the street or even getting one at a stand. If you're going out, have your hotel call one. At a restaurant, ask the waiter or cashier to dial for you. If you want to phone yourself, try one of these numbers: 6645, 3570, or 4994.

The meter begins at 7,500 lire ($4.70) for the first 3 kilometers, then 1,500 lire (95¢) per kilometer. On Sunday a 1,000 lire (65¢) supplement is assessed, plus another 3,000 lire ($1.90) supplement from 10pm to 7am. There's yet another 500 lire (30¢) supplement for every suitcase.

BY CAR

For general information, see "Getting Around," in Chapter 3.

Hertz has its main office near the parking lot of the Villa Borghese, via Vittorio Veneto 156 (☎ 321-68-31). The **Budget** headquarters are at via Boncompagni 14C (☎ 48-4810). The downtown **Avis** office is at piazza Isquilino 1C (☎ 470-1216). **Maggiore,** an Italian company, has an office at via di Tor Cervara 225 (☎ 06/229-351).

DRIVING & PARKING   All roads may lead to Rome if you're driving, but don't count on much driving once you get there. Since reception desks of most Roman hotels have at least one English-speaking person, it's wise to call ahead to find out the best route into Rome from wherever you're starting out.

Find out if the hotel has a garage. If not, you are usually allowed to park your car in front of the hotel long enough to unload your luggage. Someone at the hotel—a doorman, if there is one—will direct you to the nearest garage or place to park.

To the neophyte, Roman driving will appear like the chariot race in *Ben Hur*. When the light turns green, go forth with caution. Many Roman drivers are still going through the light even though it has turned red. Roman drivers in traffic gridlock move bravely on, fighting for every inch of the road until they can free themselves from the tangled mess.

To complicate matters, many zones, such as that around the piazza di Spagna, are traffic-free, and other traffic-free zones are being tried out in various parts of Rome.

In other words, try to get your car into Rome as safely as possible, park it, and proceed on foot or by public transportation from then on.

BY BICYCLE, MOTORSCOOTER & MOTORCYCLE

St. Peter Moto Renting & Selling, via di Porto Castello 43 (☎ 687-4909), open Monday through Saturday from 9am to 1pm and 3:30 to 7pm, rents Mopeds. Rates range from 50,000 lire ($31.25) per day. For motorcycles, the minimum age for a renter is 18, and a valid driver's license is required. Only the most experienced drivers should rent a motorcycle—it's dangerous riding in the city's traffic. Take the Metro to Ottaviano.

Bicycles are rented at many places throughout Rome. Ask at your hotel for the nearest rental location, or else go to **I Bike Rome,** via Vittorio Veneto 156 (☎ 322-5240), which rents bicycles from the underground parking garage at the

Villa Borghese. Most rentals cost 5,000 lire ($3.15) per hour, or 15,000 lire ($9.40) per day. It's open daily from 9am to 8pm.

BY FOOT

Much of the inner core of Rome is traffic-free—so you'll need to walk whether you like it or not. Walking is the perfect way to see the ancient narrow cobbled streets of Old Rome. However, walking in many parts of the city is hazardous and uncomfortable, because of overcrowded streets, heavy traffic, and very narrow sidewalks. Sometimes sidewalks don't exist at all, and it becomes a sort of free-for-all with pedestrians competing for space against vehicular traffic, with the traffic always seeming to win. If your hotel is outside Old Rome, you can take the bus or Metro. For such a large city, Rome can be covered on foot, because so much of what will interest a visitor lies in various clusters.

FAST FACTS: Rome

American Express The offices of American Express are at piazza di Spagna 38 (☎ 67641). The travel service is open Monday through Friday from 9am to 5:30pm and on Saturday from 9am to 12:30pm. Hours for the financial and mail services are Monday through Friday from 9am to 5pm and on Saturday from 9am to noon. The tour desk is open during the same hours as those for travel services and also on Saturday afternoon from 2 to 2:30pm only from May through October.

Area Code The telephone area code for Rome and its environs is 06.

Babysitters Most hotel desks in Rome will help you secure a babysitter. You should ask for an English-speaking sitter if available. Or you can call a local agency, Centro Bimbi (☎ 687-3508). Also available for bambino watching is ARCI, via dei Mille 23 (☎ 446-5455).

Bookstores See "Shopping," in Chapter 6.

Business Hours In general, **banks** are open Monday through Friday from 8:30am to 1:30pm and 3 to 4pm. Some banks keep afternoon hours ranging from 2:45 to 3:45pm. Two U.S. banks in Rome include Chase Manhattan Bank, via Michele Mercati 39 (☎ 06/809-76), and Citibank, via de Bruxelles 61 (☎ 06/85-45-61). **Shopping** hours are governed by the siesta. Most stores are open year round Monday through Saturday from 9am to 1pm and then 3:30 or 4pm to 7:30 or 8pm. Most shops are closed on Sunday, except for some barbershops that are open Sunday morning. Hairdressers are closed Sunday and Monday.

Car Rentals See "Getting Around," earlier in this chapter.

Climate See "When to Go," earlier in this chapter.

Crime See "Safety," below.

Currency Exchange This is possible at all major rail and airline terminals in Rome, including the Stazione Termini, where the *cambi* (exchange booth) beside the rail information booth is open daily from 8am to 8pm. At some cambi you'll have to pay commissions, often 1 1/2%. Banks, likewise, often charge commissions. Many so-called money changers will approach you on the street, but often they're pushing counterfeit lire, and they offer very good rates for their fake money!

Dentist   To secure a dentist who speaks English, call the U.S. Embassy in Rome, via Vittorio Veneto (☎ 46741). You may have to call around in order to get an appointment. There is also the 24-hour G. Eastman Dental Hospital, viale Regina Elena 287 (☎ 49-00-42).

Doctor   Call the U.S. Embassy (see "Dentist," above), which will provide a list of doctors who speak English. All big hospitals in Rome have a 24-hour first-aid service (go to the emergency room). You'll find English-speaking doctors at the privately run Salvator Mundi International Hospital, viale delle Mura Gianicolensi (☎ 58-60-41). For medical assistance, the International Medical Center is on 24-hour duty at via Giovanni Amendola 7 (☎ 488-23-71).

Drugstores   A reliable pharmacy is Farmacia Internazionale, piazza Barberini 49 (☎ 482-5456), open day and night. Most pharmacies are open from 8:30am to 1pm and 4 to 7:30pm. In general, pharmacies follow a rotation system so that several are always open on Sunday.

Embassies/Consulates   See "Fast Facts: Italy" in Chapter 3.

Emergencies   The police "hotline" number is 212121. Usually, however, dial 112 for the police, to report a fire, or summon an ambulance.

Eyeglasses   Try Vasari, piazza della Repubblica 22 (☎ 48-82-240), which lies adjacent to the Grand Hotel, and is a very large shop with lots of choices and a central location.

Hairdressers/Barbers   Romans are considered great hair stylists for both men and women. Sometimes large hotels have these services on the premises, and all neighborhoods have them. Just ask at the reception desk of your hotel for a good one. Otherwise, women can patronize Gracia, via Frattina 75 (☎ 679-2046). Handling both men and women, Sergio Valente, at via Condotti 11 (☎ 679-4515), is an elegant choice. Both these establishments are in the center of Rome.

Hospitals   An expensive private clinic with English-speaking doctors is Salvator Mundi International Hospital, viale delle Mura Gianicolensi 67 (☎ 58-60-41). You might also prefer the services of the Rome American Hospital, via Emilio Longoni 69 (☎ 22-55-71).

Hotlines   Dial 113, which is a general SOS, to report any kind of danger, such as rape. You can also dial 112, the police emergency number. For an ambulance call 5100; for personal crises, call Samaritans, via San Giovanni in Laterno 250 (☎ 70-45-44-44), daily from to 1 to 10pm.

Laundry/Dry Cleaning   First-class and deluxe hotels provide this service, often on the same day, but you'll pay for the extra convenience. All neighborhoods in Rome have laundries (not self-service) and dry-cleaning establishments. Most laundries have minimum-load requirements ranging from 3 to 4kg (6.6 to 8.8 lbs.). A central laundry is found at Sarti, via di Ripetta (☎ 321-9409). It also does dry cleaning.

Libraries   There's the British Council Library, via Quattro Fontane 20 (☎ 4826641), open Monday, Wednesday, and Friday from noon to 1pm and Tuesday and Thursday from 2:30 to 7:30pm.

Lost Property   Usually lost property is gone forever. But you might try checking at Ogetti Rinvenuti, via Nicolò Bettoni (☎ 581-6040), which is open Monday through Saturday from 9am to noon. A branch at the Stazione Termini off Track 1 (☎ 473-0602) is open daily from 7am to midnight.

Luggage Storage/Lockers   These are available at the Stazione Termini, piazza dei Cinquecento, along Tracks 1 and 22 daily from 5am to 1am, costing 1,500 lire (95¢) daily per piece of luggage.

Mail   Post office boxes in Italy are red and are attached to walls. One slot is for letters intended just for the city (on the left). On the right is a slot for letters for all other destinations. Vatican post office boxes are blue, and you can buy special stamps at the Vatican City Post Office. Letters mailed at Vatican City reach North America far more quickly than does mail sent from within Rome.

The Vatican City Post Office is adjacent to the information office in St. Peter's Square. It's open Monday through Friday from 8:30am to 7pm and on Saturday from 8:30am to 6pm.

Packages weighing more than 1 kilo (2.2 lb.) must be firmly wrapped and taken to one of the larger post offices that takes packages (some of the smaller post offices don't accept them). The main post office of Rome is at piazza San Silvestro 19, 00186 Roma (☎ 6771), lying between via Corso and piazza di Spagna. Hours are Monday through Friday from 8:25am to 7:40pm and Saturday from 8:20 to 11:50pm. A currency exchange office here is open Monday through Friday from 8:25am to 5:30pm and Saturday from 8:20 to 11:50am. Stamps (*francobolli*) can be purchased at tabacchi (tobacconists). But before posting stamps on your letters, ask at your hotel for current rates, as they are constantly rising. See also "Post Office," below.

Newspapers/Magazines   The English-language daily published in Rome is the *International Daily News,* and in addition to its news coverage (with an emphasis on Europe, of course), it also provides several lists of local events and services that the foreign visitor should find helpful.

Police   See "Emergencies," above.

Post Office   The central post office is on piazza San Silvestro, behind the Rinascente department store on piazza Colonna (☎ 672225). It's open Monday through Friday from 8:30am to 7:50pm for mail service, to 1:50pm for money service. Both are open from 8:30am to noon on Saturday. Mail addressed to you c/o that central office, with *fermo posta* written after the name and address of the post office, will be given to you upon identification by passport.

Radio/Television   In both radio and television, RAI, the Italian state radio and television network, dominates the broadcast waves. RAI has three radio stations broadcasting from Rome, and the Vatican Radio has its own station, often carrying religious news in English. RAI also has three national television channels broadcasting from Rome. There are also several private TV channels which have more liberal telecasts.

Religious Services   Catholic churches abound in Rome and throughout Italy. Several of these conduct services in English, including San Silvestro, piazza San Silvestro 1 (☎ 679775), and Santa Susanna, via XX Settembre 14 (☎ 488-2748). The American Episcopal Church is St. Paul's, via Napoli 58 at via Nazionale (☎ 488-3339). The Jewish temple, Sinagoga Ebraica, is at lungotevere dei Cenci (☎ 656-4648). "Pro Unione" Ecumenical Gatherings, conducted by the Franciscan Friars of the Atonement for non–Roman Catholics visiting Rome, include background briefings, slide presentations, and excursions to some of the most important places of ecumenical interest in Rome, including St. Peter's Basilica, Santa Sabina, San Clemente, the Colosseum, the Roman Forum, the

Vatican Gardens, and the Catacombs (where eucharistic liturgies and prayer services can be arranged for groups). Through these services, the Centro Pro Unione hopes to offer an opportunity for encounter and dialogue. All services are free, but a voluntary contribution is requested. "Pro Unione" Ecumenical Gatherings take place at the Centro Pro Unione located on the first floor of the Palazzo Doria Pamphilj, via Santa Maria dell'Anima 30 (piazza Navona). For information, call 06/687-9552.

Restrooms   Facilities are found near many of the major sights, often with attendants, as are those at bars, nightclubs, restaurants, cafés, and hotels, plus the airports and the railway station. You're expected to leave 200–500 lire (10¢–30¢) for the attendant. If you're not checking into a hotel in Rome but going on by train elsewhere, you can patronize the Albergo Diurno (☎ 48-48-19), a hotel without beds at the Stazione Termini. It has baths, showers, and well-kept toilet facilities.

Safety   Purse-snatching is commonplace in Rome. Young men on Vespas or whatever ride through the city looking for victims. To avoid trouble stay away from the curb and hold on tightly to your purse. Don't lay anything valuable on tables or chairs where it can be grabbed up easily. Gypsy children are a particular menace. You'll often virtually have to fight them off, if they completely surround you. They'll often approach you with pieces of cardboard hiding their stealing hands.

Shoe Repair   Many department stores have these services, and each Rome neighborhood has its favorite shoe-repair place. Ask at your hotel reception desk, or go to Leotta, via del Boschetto 20 (☎ 481-9177).

Taxes   A value-added tax (called IVA in Italy) is added to all consumer products and most services, including restaurants and hotels.

Taxis   See "Getting Around," earlier in this chapter.

Telegrams/Telex/Fax   You can send telegrams from all post offices during the day and from the telegraph office at the central post office in San Silvestro, off via della Mercede, at night. Your hotel will probably send a telex or fax for you. If your hotel doesn't have a fax, go to Capitalexpress, via Bresadola 55 (☎ 258-5404), Monday through Friday from 8:30am to 6:30pm. See also "Fast Facts: Italy," in Chapter 3.

Transit Information   For airport information at Leonardo da Vinci International Airport, phone 06/659-51; for Ciampino Airport, phone 7934-0297. For bus information, phone 469-51, and for rail information, call 4775.

Water   Rome is famed for its drinking water, which is generally safe, even from its outdoor fountains. If it isn't, there's a sign reading ACQUA NON POTABILE. Nevertheless, Romans traditionally order bottled mineral water in restaurants, but mostly they prefer wine with their meals.

3 Networks & Resources

FOR STUDENTS   The Rome center for budget student travel is **Centro Turistico Studentesco e Giovanile (CTS),** via Genova 16 (☎ 467-91). Air, sea, train, and bus discounts are available here, and you can pick up a helpful brochure, "Young Rome." An accommodation-booking service is also available that can help you find low-cost hotels in other Italian cities. On the bulletin board young people post notices offering or seeking rides (which is a better arrangement than hitch-hiking). The office is open Monday through Friday from 9am to 1pm and 4 to 7pm, and on Saturday from 9am to 1pm.

FOR GAY MEN & LESBIANS   Before going to Italy, men can order *Spartacus,* the international gay guide ($29.95), from Giovanni's Room, 1145 Pine St., Phila-delphia, PA 19107 (☎ 215/923-2960). Both lesbians and gay men might want to pick up a copy of *Ferrari's Places of Interest* ($15) at the same outlet. In Rome information about gay and lesbian life is available at the local branch of ARCI-gay, the national gay organization of Italy, at via dei Mille 23 (☎ 446-58-39), lying 3 blocks up from via Marsala and also north of Termini. Another gay organiza-tion, this one much older, is OMPO Gay House, via Ghiberti (☎ 93-54-7567), in Testaccio. This outfit also publishes a trio of magazines on gay life in Italy, and has a weekly open house Thursday from 8 to 10pm.

FOR WOMEN   A feminist bookstore and a clearinghouse for "what's happen-ing" is **Al Tempo Ritrovato,** piazza Farnese 103 (☎ 68-80-37-49). Here you'll find an array of international publications appealing to women's interests. It is open Monday from 3 to 8pm and Tuesday through Saturday from 10am to 8pm (it closes at 7:30pm in winter).

FOR SENIORS   Every city of Italy, including Rome, has slightly different guide-lines for senior citizen discounts, so it's a good idea to visit the tourist office in Rome (see "Tourist Information" in "Orientation," earlier in this chapter). Ask about any special discounts that might be available on transportation, hotels, cul-tural events, and museums for older travelers. Many senior citizen discounts are available in Italy, although it's often not convenient or possible for short-term trav-elers to take full advantage of them. Nevertheless, it always pays to ask if there are special rates for senior citizens at various cultural events and national monuments.

5 Where to Stay & Dine in Rome

There have been no exciting breakthroughs on the hotel front in Rome. A few small hostelries have recently opened but many of these are in remote if not undesirable areas, since all the central locations in the heart of monumental Rome have long ago been grabbed up.

By the mid-1900s the major change in Rome hotels concerns not the opening of new hotels but reservations. Time was, you could almost always get a room off-season (roughly from November until early March). Because of Rome's importance as a religious center, some groups book hundreds of rooms in the low season because of better discounts. That and other factors have combined to make Rome a year-round tourist destination. There is no longer any time of the year when there are numerous rooms to fill.

Rome has more than 500 hotels. Decisions on which to recommend were based on whether they offered good value—regardless of their price range—and special considerations, such as charm, comfort, and convenience of location.

All the hotels recommended serve breakfast, and many of them, as will be noted, also have good restaurants. Some of the deluxe hotels have among the finest restaurants in Rome.

Most well-recommended hotels in Rome have private baths, although some of the inexpensive or budget choices do not. If you don't mind the inconvenience of sharing a bath with other visitors, these will be your best bets for economy.

Nearly all hotels are heated in the cooler months; but not all hotels are air-conditioned. The deluxe and first-class ones are, but after that it's a toss-up. Air conditioning could be vitally important to you if you're planning to visit Rome during July and August. Many hotels will grant winter discounts—usually no more than 10%. These discounts are not necessarily published, but some negotiation on your part at the reception desk may get you an off-season discount.

Hotels are divided on the question of whether breakfast is included in the room rate or is extra. Always determine this when checking in—it can make a difference on your final bill. If breakfast is included, it's one of the continental variety—that is, cappuccino and croissants, along with jam and butter. American-type breakfasts of bacon and eggs always cost extra.

Nearly all hotels today quote an inclusive rate, including service and value-added taxes. Again, to be perfectly certain and to avoid any misunderstanding when the time comes to pay the bill, ask when checking in if service and tax are included in the rate you are being quoted, or if they will be added to your final bill. It's rare for Roman hotels to have private garages. Hotel reception desks will advise about nearby garages, where fees usually range from 5,000–60,000 lire ($3.15–$37.50).

Rome is one of the world's great capitals for dining. From elegant, deluxe palaces with lavish trappings to little trattorias opening onto hidden piazzas deep in the heart of Old Rome, the city abounds with good restaurants in all price ranges.

1 Accommodations

NEAR STAZIONE TERMINI
VERY EXPENSIVE

H.R. Hotel Reservation is a free telematic hotel reservation service, representing some 200 hotels in the Rome area, with a constant updating of availability. Call 06/699-1000 any time to book a hotel of your choice; it usually takes one minute. The reservation is offered by Roman hotelkeepers themselves daily from 7am to 10pm. The service is also available at welcome desks at Leonardo da Vinci airport and at the Termini (in front of platform 10).

✪ Le Grand Hotel

Via Vittorio Emanuele Orlando 3, 00185 Roma. ☎ **06/4709,** 800/221-2340 in the U.S., or 800/955-2442 in Canada. Fax 06/474-7307. 134 rms, 36 suites. A/C MINIBAR TV TEL. 530,000–580,000 lire ($331.25–$362.50) double; 900,000–1,600,000 lire ($562.50–$1,000) suite. Breakfast 28,000 lire ($17.50) extra. 10% IVA tax extra. AE, DC, MC, V. Parking 40,000–60,000 lire ($25–$37.50). Metro: Piazza della Repubblica.

When it was inaugurated by its creator, Cesar Ritz, in 1894, Le Grand struck a note of grandeur it has tried to maintain ever since. Located just off piazza della Repubblica, and considered one of the great hotels of Italy, it has welcomed an impressive roster of guests, including Henry Ford, J. P. Morgan, a long list of royal titles, and its share of well-heeled travelers from around the world. Only a few minutes from via Vittorio Veneto, the Grand looks like a large late-Renaissance palace, its five-floor facade covered with carved loggias, lintels, quoins, and cornices. Inside, the floors are covered with marble and Oriental rugs; the walls are a riot of baroque plasterwork; and crystal chandeliers, Louis XVI furniture, potted palms, antique clocks, and wall sconces complete the picture.

The spacious bedrooms are conservatively decorated with matching curtains and carpets, and equipped with dressing room and fully tiled bath. Every accommodation is different. While most are traditional, with antique headboards and Venetian chandeliers, some are modern. Every room is soundproof.

Dining/Entertainment: The hotel's Le Grand Bar is an elegant meeting place where tea is served every afternoon in winter, accompanied by harp music. At the Salad Bar, you can enjoy quick meals or else try Le Restaurant, the hotel's more formal dining room. Dietetic and kosher foods can be arranged with advance notice. Service is first-rate.

Services: 24-hour room service, babysitting, laundry and valet service.
Facilities: Beauty salon.

MODERATE

Britannia Hotel

Via Napoli 64, 00184 Roma. ☎ **06/488-3153.** Fax 06/488-2343. 32 rms. A/C MINIBAR TV TEL. 280,000 lire ($175) double. Rates include buffet breakfast. AE, DC, MC, V. Free parking. Bus: 57, 64, 75, or 170.

Britannia Hotel takes its name from its location next to an Anglican church on a street right off via Nazionale, within walking distance of the main railroad station. Its elaborately detailed Victor Emmanuel facade is graced with plant-filled upper terraces, each of which adds a note much like that of a private garden. Inside is one of the neighborhood's most stylish renovations. The bar is in the English country club style, with Chesterfield leather armchairs. The restored breakfast room has walls decorated with art work. Upstairs, the bedrooms are outfitted in monochromatic schemes of gray, blue, or pink, and filled with carpeting and modern paintings. Each unit has a TV, radio, personal safe, fire alarm, and a bath with radio, hairdryer, scales, and a sun lamp. Some of the rooms have wide private terraces.

Medici

Via Flavia 96, 00187 Roma. ☎ **06/482-7319.** Fax 06/474-0767. 68 rms. MINIBAR TV TEL. 220,000 lire ($137.50) double. Rates include breakfast. AE, DC, MC, V. Parking 25,000–35,000 lire ($15.65–$21.90). Metro: Piazza della Repubblica.

Medici, built in 1906, is a substantial hotel that has easy access to the railway terminal and the shops along via XX Settembre. Many of its better rooms overlook an inner patio garden, with Roman columns and benches, and posts holding up greenery and climbing ivy. The patio is often filled with Vespas and hotel deliveries, so breakfast is served downstairs below the bar. The lounge, with its white-coved ceiling, has many nooks, all connected by wide white arches. Furnishings are traditional, with lots of antiques. Likewise, the generous-size bedrooms are attractively furnished. The few rooms that are air-conditioned carry a 20,000 lire ($12.50) supplement to the rates quoted above.

Nord Nuova Roma

Via Giovanni Amendola 3, 00185 Roma. ☎ **06/488-5441** or 800/223-9832 in the U.S. 159 rms. A/C MINIBAR TV TEL. 275,000 lire ($171.90) double. Rates include breakfast. AE, DC, MC, V. Parking 35,000–45,000 lire ($21.90–$28.15). Metro: Stazione Termini.

Nord Nuova Roma, near the railway station, is the best bargain in the family-run Bettoja chain. It has garage parking for 100 cars, and a small, intimate bar. Its well-maintained and most comfortable rooms are standard and modernized, making the hotel a good family choice. A most satisfying table d'hôte lunch or dinner can be arranged at the nearby Massimo d'Azeglio Restaurant, beginning at 32,000 lire ($20).

San Giorgio

Via Giovanni Amendola 61, 00185 Roma. ☎ **06/482-7341** or 800/223-9832 in the U.S. Fax 06/488-3191. 186 rms, 5 suites. A/C MINIBAR TV TEL. 340,000 lire ($212.50) double; from 465,000 lire ($290.65) suite. Rates include breakfast. AE, DC, MC, V. Parking 35,000–45,000 lire ($21.90–$28.15). Metro: Stazione Termini.

A four-star first-class hotel built in 1940, San Giorgio is constantly being improved by its founders, the Bettoja family (in 1950 it became the first air-conditioned hotel in Rome, and is now also soundproof). The San Giorgio is connected to the Massimo d'Azeglio, so guests can patronize that establishment's fine restaurant without having to walk out on the street. The hotel is ideal for families, as many of its corner rooms can be converted into larger quarters. Each bedroom has a radio, along with other amenities that often lie behind wood-veneer doors. Breakfast is served in a light and airy room. The staff is most helpful in easing your adjustment into the Italian capital.

INEXPENSIVE

Aberdeen Hotel

Via Firenze 48, 00184 Roma. ☎ **06/482-3920.** Fax 06/482-1092. 26 rms (all with bath or shower). MINIBAR TV TEL. 230,000 lire ($143.75) double. Rates include breakfast. AE, DC, MC, V. Parking 25,000 lire ($15.65). Metro: Stazione Termini.

This is a completely renovated 26-room hotel near the Rome Opera House, and centrally located for most of the landmarks and for rail and bus connections at the main station. It's in a quiet and safe area of Rome, as it lies in front of the Ministry of Defense. Rooms are furnished with sleek modern styling, and with such amenities as color TV, hairdryer, and radio. Air conditioning is available for 20,000 lire ($12.50). Only a breakfast buffet is served, although many inexpensively priced *trattorie* lie nearby.

Fiamma

Via Gaeta 61, 00185 Roma. ☎ **06/481-84-36.** Fax 06/488-3511. 79 rms (all with bath or shower). TV TEL. 170,000–210,000 lire ($106.25–$131.25) double. Rates include breakfast. AE, DC, MC, V. Parking 10,000 lire ($6.25). Metro: Stazione Termini.

The Fiamma, on the far side of the Baths of Diocletian, is a renovated old building, with five floors of shuttered windows and a ground floor faced with marble and plate-glass windows. The lobby is long and bright, filled to the brim with a varied collection of furnishings, including overstuffed chairs, blue enamel railings, and indirect lighting. On the same floor (made of marble, no less) is a monklike breakfast room. Air conditioning is available in some of the comfortably furnished bedrooms.

Hotel Corot

Via Marghera 15–17, 00185 Roma. ☎ **06/4470-0900.** Fax 06/4470-0905. 20 rms. A/C MINIBAR TV TEL. 150,000–180,000 lire ($93.75–$112.50) double; 170,000–205,000 lire ($106.25–$128.10) triple; 190,000–220,000 lire ($118.75–$137.50) quad. Rates include breakfast. 15% discounts to clients staying two nights anytime from Fri to Sun. AE, DC, MC, V. Parking 20,000–25,000 lire ($12.50–$15.65). Metro: Stazione Termini.

Modernized and comfortable, this hotel occupies the second and third floors of a turn-of-the-century building that contains a handful of private apartments as well as another somewhat less well-accessorized hotel. Guests register within a small, paneled area on the building's street level, then take an elevator to their respective floors. Bedrooms are airy, high-ceilinged, and filled with simple but traditional furniture and soothing colors. Bathrooms are modern and contain hairdryers. There's a residents' bar near one of the sun-flooded windows in one of the public rooms.

Hotel Pavia

Via Gaeta 83, 00185 Roma. ☎ **06/483801.** Fax 06/481-9090. 50 rms (all with bath or shower). A/C MINIBAR TV TEL. 130,000–190,000 lire ($81.25–$118.75) double. Rates include breakfast. AE, DC, MC, V. Parking 12,000–20,000 lire ($7.50–$12.50). Metro: Stazione Termini.

Hotel Pavia is a popular choice on this quiet street near the gardens of the Baths of Diocletian and the railway station. Established in the 1980s, it occupies a much-renovated century-old building. You'll pass through a wisteria-covered passageway

Rome Accommodations

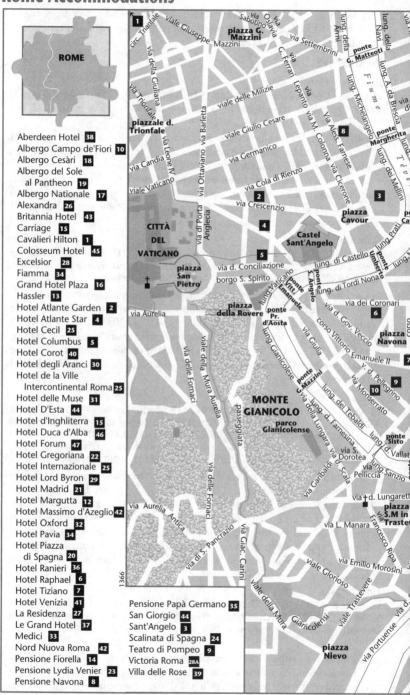

1366

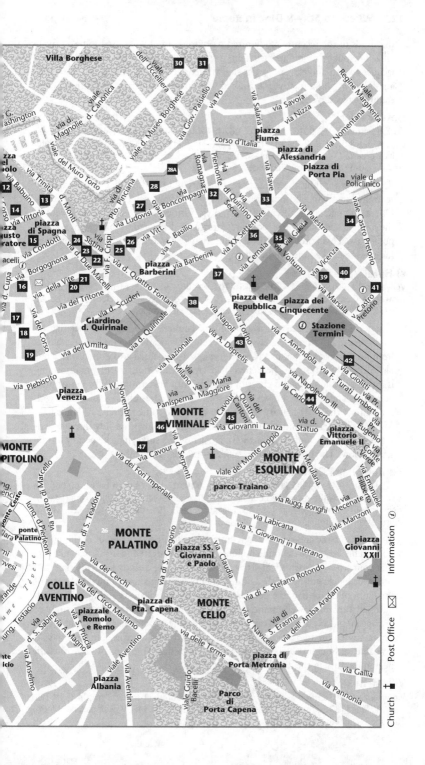

Church   +■   Post Office   ⊠   Information ⓘ

that leads to the recently modernized reception area of what used to be a private villa. The public rooms are tastefully covered in light-grained paneling with white lacquer accents and carpeting. The staff is attentive. Each room is quiet, often with a good view, and attractively furnished with simple, modern wood furniture and calming colors.

Hotel Ranieri

Via XX Settembre 43, 00187 Roma. ☎ **06/481-4467.** Fax 06/481-8834. 40 rms (all with bath or shower). A/C MINIBAR TV TEL. 160,000–215,000 lire ($100–$134.40) double. Rates include breakfast. Weekend discounts sometimes granted. AE, MC, V. Parking 20,000–30,000 lire ($12.50–$18.75). Metro: Piazza della Repubblica.

Ranieri is a winning three-star hotel in a very old building that was completely renovated in 1990. The location is good; from the hotel you can stroll to the Rome Opera, the piazza della Repubblica, and via Vittorio Veneto. The public rooms, the lounge, and the dining room are attractively decorated, in part with contemporary art. This hotel offers good, comfortable bedrooms. Residents can arrange for a home-cooked meal in the dining room.

⑤ Hotel Venezia

Via Varese 18, 00185 Roma. ☎ **06/445-7101.** Fax 06/49-57-687. 61 rms (all with bath or shower). A/C MINIBAR TV TEL. 230,000 lire ($143.75) double. Rates include breakfast. AE, DC, MC, V. Parking 30,000 lire ($18.75). Metro: Stazione Termini.

Hotel Venezia, near the intersection of via Marghera, is the type of place that restores one's faith in moderately priced hotels. The location is good—three blocks from the railroad station, in a part-business, part-residential area dotted with a few old villas and palm trees. The Venezia had a total renovation in 1991, transforming it into a good-looking and cheerful hostelry, with a charming collection of public rooms. The floors are brown marble. Bedrooms are furnished in some cases with furniture in the 17th-century style. Other pieces are contemporary. All units have Murano chandeliers, and all are air-conditioned, but only from July through September. Some accommodations have a balcony for surveying the action on the street below. The housekeeping is superb—the management really cares.

Pensione Papà Germano

Via Calatafimi 14A, 00185 Roma. ☎ **06/486-919.** 13 rms (2 with bath). 60,000 lire ($37.50) double without bath; 75,000 lire ($46.90) double with bath; 70,000 lire ($43.75) triple without bath; 85,000 lire ($53.15) triple with bath. 10% discounts Nov–Feb. MC, V. Metro: Stazione Termini.

It's about as basic and simple as anything you're likely to read about in this guidebook. This 1892 belle époque building was last renovated in 1987. Chances are that your fellow residents will arrive, backpack in tow, directly from the train station four blocks to the south. Located on a block-long street immediately east of the Baths of Diocletian, the pension offers simple but clean accommodations with battered furniture, well-maintained showers, and a high-turnover clientele of European and North American students. The energetic owner, Gino Germano, offers advice on sightseeing attractions to anyone who asks. No breakfast is available, although dozens of cafés nearby serve steaming cups of *caffè con latte* beginning early in the day. English is spoken.

Villa delle Rose

Via Vicenza 5, 00185 Roma. ☎ **06/44-51-788.** Fax 06/44-51-639. 38 rms. A/C TV TEL. 220,000 lire ($137.50) double. Rates include breakfast. AE, DC, MC, V. Free parking. Metro: Stazione Termini or Castro Pretorio.

Set less than two blocks north of the railway station, behind a dignified cut-stone facade inspired by the Renaissance, this hotel was originally built as a private home in the late 1800s. Despite many renovations, the ornate trappings of the wealthy family who built the place are still visible, including a set of Corinthian-capped marble columns in the lobby and a flagstone-covered terrace that fills part of a verdant garden in back. Much of the interior, however, has been stripped down to a functionally modern 1960s kind of minimalism, with comfortable but boxy furniture and not a great deal of charm. Morning breakfasts in the garden, however, where rows of pink and red roses bloom (and give the hotel its name) do a lot to add country flavor to an otherwise very urban location. The English-speaking staff is helpful and tactful.

NEAR THE PARIOLI DISTRICT, VIA VENETO & VILLA BORGHESE
VERY EXPENSIVE

Excelsior
Via Vittorio Veneto 125, 00187 Roma. ☎ **06/4708**, 800/221-2340 in the U.S., or 800/955-2442 in Canada. Fax 06/482-6205. 327 rms, 45 suites. A/C MINIBAR TV TEL. 480,000–540,000 lire ($300–$337.50) double; 1,200,000–1,500,000 lire ($750–$937.50) suite. Breakfast 28,000 lire ($17.50) extra. 10% IVA extra. AE, DC, MC, V. Parking 30,000 lire ($18.75). Metro: Piazza Barberini.

The Excelsior (pronounced Ess-*shell*-see-or) is a limestone palace whose baroque corner tower, which looks right over the U.S. Embassy, is a landmark in Rome. Guests enter a string of cavernous reception rooms of the same design as the Grand Hotel a few blocks away. That means thick rugs, marble floors, gilded garlands and pilasters decorating the walls, and Empire furniture (supported by winged lions and the like).

The rooms come in two basic varieties: new (the result of a major renovation) and traditional. Doubles are spacious and elegantly furnished, often with antiques and silk curtains. The furnishings in singles are also of high quality. Most of the bedrooms are different, many with a sumptuous Hollywood-style bath—marble-walled with separate bath and shower, sinks, bidet, and a mountain of fresh towels.

The palatial hotel once attracted some of the stellar lights of the "Hollywood on the Tiber" era—notably Shelley Winters, Elizabeth Taylor, Ingrid Bergman, and Roberto Rossellini. Nowadays, you're more likely to bump into international financiers and Arab princesses.

Dining/Entertainment: The Excelsior Bar, open daily from 10:30am to 1am, is perhaps the most famous on via Vittorio Veneto, and La Cupola is known for its national and regional cuisine, with dietetic and kosher food prepared on request.

Services: Room service, babysitting, laundry and valet service.

Facilities: Beauty salon, barbershop.

✪ Hotel Lord Byron
Via G. de Notaris 5, 00197 Roma. ☎ **06/322-0404.** Fax 06/322-0405. 28 rms, 9 suites. A/C MINIBAR TV TEL. Apr–July and Sept–Oct, 430,000–540,000 lire ($268.75–$337.50) double; 800,000–1,200,000 lire ($500–$750) suite. Nov–Mar and July–Aug, 350,000–420,000 lire ($218.75–$262.50) double; 600,000–800,000 lire ($375–$500) suite. Rates include breakfast. AE, DC, MC, V. Metro: Piazzale Flaminio. Bus: 52.

Hotel Lord Byron is an art deco villa set on a residential hilltop in Parioli, an area of embassies and exclusive town houses at the edge of the Villa Borghese. From the curving entrance steps off the staffed parking lot in front, you'll notice design accessories that attract the most sophisticated clientele in Italy. In a niche in the reception area is an oval Renaissance urn in chiseled marble. Flowers are everywhere, the lighting is discreet, and everything is on a cultivated small scale that makes it seem more like a well-staffed (and extremely expensive) private home than a hotel. Each of the guest rooms is different, most often with lots of mirrors, upholstered walls, spacious bathroom with gray marble accessories, big dressing room/closet, and all the amenities.

Dining/Entertainment: On the premises is one of Rome's best restaurants, recommended separately in the dining section.

Services: 24-hour room service, laundry and valet service, concierge desk.

Facilities: Car-rental desk.

EXPENSIVE

Victoria Roma

Via Campania 41, 00187 Roma. ☎ **06/473931.** Fax 06/487-1890. 108 rms, 4 suites. A/C MINIBAR TV TEL. 320,000 lire ($200) double; 350,000 lire ($218.75) suite. Rates include breakfast. AE, DC, MC, V. Parking 30,000–40,000 lire ($18.75–$25). Metro: Piazza Barberini. Bus: 910.

Victoria Roma will fool you. As you sit on wrought-iron chairs in its roof garden, drinking your apéritif in a forest of palms and potted plants—all overlooking the Borghese Gardens—you'll think you're at a country villa. But via Vittorio Veneto's just across the way. Even the lounges and living rooms retain that country-house decor, with soft touches that include high-backed chairs, large oil paintings, bowls of freshly cut flowers, provincial tables, and Oriental rugs. The Swiss owner, Alberto H. Wirth, has set unusual requirements of innkeeping (no groups), and has attracted a fine clientele over the years—diplomats, executives, artists. The bedrooms are well furnished and maintained. Meals can be taken à la carte in the elegant grill room, which serves the best of Italian and French cuisine. A fixed-price menu costs 40,000 lire ($25).

MODERATE

Alexandra

Via Vittorio Veneto 18, 00187 Roma. ☎ **06/488-1943.** Fax 06/487-1804. 39 rms, 6 suites. A/C MINIBAR TV TEL. 260,000 lire ($162.50) double; 350,000 lire ($218.75) suite. Rates include breakfast. AE, DC, MC, V. Parking 35,000 lire ($21). Metro: Piazza Barberini.

Set behind the dignified stone facade of what was originally a 19th-century private mansion, this hotel offers clean, comfortable accommodations filled with antique furniture and modern convenience. Rooms facing the front are exposed to the roaring traffic and animated street life of the via Veneto; those in back are quieter but with less of a view. No meals are served other than breakfast, although the hall porter or a member of the staff can carry drinks to clients seated in the reception area. The breakfast room is especially appealing: Inspired by an Italian garden, it was designed by the noted architect Paolo Portoghesi.

Hotel degli Aranci

Via Barnaba Oriani 9–11, 00197 Roma. ☎ **06/808-5250.** Fax 06/807-0202. 54 rms (all with bath or shower), 3 suites. A/C MINIBAR TV TEL. 220,000 lire ($137.50) double; 350,000 lire

($218.75) suite. Rates include breakfast. AE, MC, V. Free parking. Bus: 3 from Stazione Termini.

Hotel degli Aranci is a former private villa on a tree-lined residential street in Parioli, surrounded by similar villas now used, in part, as consulates and ambassadorial town houses. Most of the accommodations have tall windows opening onto city views, and are filled with provincial furnishings or English-style reproductions. The public rooms have memorabilia of ancient Rome scattered about, including bisque-colored medallions of soldiers in profile, old engravings of ruins, and classical vases highlighted against the light-grained paneling. A marble-top bar in an alcove off the sitting room adds a relaxed touch. From the glass-walled breakfast room, at the rear of the house, you can see the tops of orange trees.

Hotel Oxford

Via Boncompagni 89, 00187 Roma. ☎ **06/482-8952.** Fax 06/481-5349. 57 rms, 2 suites. A/C MINIBAR TV TEL. 250,000 lire ($156.25) double; 290,000 lire ($181.25) triple; 350,000 lire ($218.75) suite. Rates include breakfast. 15% reductions Jan–Mar 15. AE, DC, MC, V. Parking 30,000–35,000 lire ($18.75–$21.90). Bus: 3, 56, 58, or 62.

The centrally located Hotel Oxford, off via Vittorio Veneto, is adjacent to the Borghese Gardens. Recently renovated, the Oxford is now air-conditioned, centrally heated, and fully carpeted throughout. There is a pleasant lounge and a cozy bar (which serves snacks), plus a dining room offering a good Italian cuisine. The hotel is on the U.S. Embassy's preferred list of moderately priced hotels in Rome that can be confidently recommended to U.S. visitors.

La Residenza

Via Emilia 22-24, 00187 Roma ☎ **06/488-0789.** Fax 06/485721. 27 rms (all with bath or shower), 6 suites. A/C MINIBAR TV TEL. 248,000 lire ($155) double; 280,000 lire ($175) suite. Rates include buffet breakfast. MC, V. Parking 5,000 lire ($3.15). Metro: Piazza Barberini.

La Residenza successfully combines the intimacy of a generously sized town house with the elegant appointments of a well-decorated hotel. The location is superb—in the neighborhood of via Vittorio Veneto, the U.S. Embassy, and the Villa Borghese. The converted villa has an ocher-colored facade, an ivy-covered courtyard, a quiet location, and a labyrinthine series of plushly upholstered public rooms. These contain Oriental rugs, Empire divans, oil portraits, and warmly accommodating groupings of rattan chairs with cushions. Each bedroom has a radio in addition to other amenities. A series of terraces is scattered strategically throughout the hotel, which combines to make this one a favorite stopover in the city for many international visitors.

INEXPENSIVE

⑤ Hotel delle Muse

Via Tommaso Salvini 18, 00197 Roma. ☎ **06/808-8333.** Fax 06/808-5749. 61 rms (all with bath or shower). TV TEL. 147,000 lire ($91.90) double; 160,000–180,000 lire ($100–$112.50) triple. Rates include buffet breakfast. AE, DC, MC, V. Bus: 4.

Hotel delle Muse is a three-star establishment, one half mile north of Villa Borghese. It's run by the efficient, English-speaking Giorgio Lazar. Furnishings are modern and come in a wide range of splashy colors. In the summer Mr. Lazar operates a restaurant in the garden, where you can enjoy a complete meal for 25,000 lire ($15.65). A bar is open 24 hours a day in case you get thirsty at 5am. There's also a TV room, plus a writing room and a dining room.

NEAR THE SPANISH STEPS & PIAZZA DEL POPOLO
VERY EXPENSIVE

Hassler

Piazza Trinità dei Monti 6, 00187 Roma. ☎ **06/678-2651** or 800/223-6800 in the U.S. Fax 06/678-9991. 85 rms, 15 suites. A/C MINIBAR TV TEL. 620,000–900,000 lire ($387.50–$562.50) double; 1,470,000 lire ($918.75) suite. Breakfast 30,000–45,000 lire ($18.75–$28.15) extra. AE, DC, MC, V. Parking 40,000 lire ($25). Metro: Piazza di Spagna. Bus: 497 from Stazione Termini.

The Hassler, the only deluxe hotel in this old part of Rome, uses the Spanish Steps as its grand entrance. The original 1885 Hassler was rebuilt in 1944, and used as headquarters of the American Air Transport Command for the last year of World War II. In 1947 the hotel reopened its doors and became an immediate success, regaining its original glory. Through the years its reputation has become almost legendary. This lush hotel, with its ornate decor, has been favored by such Americans as the Kennedys, Eisenhowers, and Nixons—and by titled Europeans and movie stars. The brightly colored rooms, the lounges with a mixture of modern and traditional furnishings, and the bedrooms with their "Italian Park Avenue" trappings all strike a 1930s note.

The bedrooms have a personalized look—Oriental rugs, tasteful draperies at the French windows, brocade furnishings, comfortable beds, and (the nicest touch of all) bowls of fresh flowers. Some rooms have balconies with views of the city. Each accommodation contains a private bath, usually with two sinks and a bidet.

Dining/Entertainment: The Hassler Roof Restaurant, on the top floor, is a favorite with visitors and Romans alike for its fine cuisine and view. Its Sunday brunch is a popular rendezvous time in Rome. The Hassler Bar is ideal for an apéritif or a drink; in the evening, it has piano music. In summer, breakfast and lunch are served in a flower-bedecked courtyard. The recently renovated Salone Eva is an elegant and cozy tea room.

Services: Room service, telex and fax, limousine, in-room massages, in-house laundry.

Facilities: Nearby garage, tennis court in summer, free bicycles available.

Hotel de la Ville Inter-Continental Roma

Via Sistina 67–69, 00187 Roma. ☎ **06/67331** or 800/327-0200 in the U.S. or Canada. Fax 06/678-4213. 192 rms, 23 suites. A/C MINIBAR TV TEL. 510,000–645,000 lire ($318.75–$403.15) double; from 845,000 lire ($528.10) suite. Rates include breakfast. AE, DC, MC, V. Parking 35,000 lire ($21.90). Metro: Piazza di Spagna or Barberini.

Hotel de la Ville Inter-Continental Roma looks deluxe (even though it's officially rated first class) from the minute you walk through the revolving door, which is attended by a smartly uniformed doorman. Once inside this palace, built in the 19th century on the site of the ancient Lucullus's Gardens, you'll see Oriental rugs, marble tables, brocade-covered furniture, and a staff who speak English. There are endless corridors leading to what at first seems a maze of ornamental lounges, all elegantly upholstered and hung with their quota of crystal lighting fixtures. Some of the public rooms have a sort of 1930s elegance. Others are strictly baroque, and in the middle of it all is an open courtyard.

The bedrooms and the public areas have been completely renovated in a beautifully classic and yet up-to-date way. The higher rooms with balconies have the most panoramic views of Rome to be found anywhere, and all guests are free to use the roof terrace with the same view.

Dining/Entertainment: La Piazzetta de la Ville Restaurant, on the second floor overlooking the garden, serves an Italian and international cuisine. Meals begin at 65,000 lire ($40.65). The hotel also has an American bar with a pianist during cocktail hours.

Services: 24-hour room service, babysitting, laundry and valet service.

Facilities: Roof terrace.

EXPENSIVE

Hotel d'Inghliterra

Via Bocca di Leone 14, 00187 Roma. ☎ **06/69-981.** Fax 06/699-22-243. 102 rms. 12 suites A/C MINIBAR TV TEL. 370,000–440,000 lire ($231.25–$275) double; 486,000 lire ($303.75) triple; 646,000–846,000 lire ($403.75–$528.75) suite. Rates include breakfast. 10% IVA extra. AE, DC, MC, V. Metro: Piazza di Spagna.

Hotel d'Inghliterra nostalgically holds onto its traditions and heritage, even though it has been completely renovated. Considered the most fashionable small hotel in Rome, it has been the favorite of many a discriminating "personage"—Anatole France, Ernest Hemingway, Alec Guinness. (In the 19th century, the king of Portugal met here with the pope.) The bedrooms have mostly old pieces—gilt and much marble, along with mahogany chests and glittery mirrors, as well as modern conveniences. The hotel's restaurant, the Roman Garden, serves excellent Roman dishes. The main salon of the hotel is dominated by an impressive gilt mirror and console, surrounded by Victorian furniture. The preferred bedrooms are higher up, opening onto a tile terrace, with a balustrade and a railing covered with flowering vines and plants. The English-style bar is a favorite gathering spot in the evening, with its paneled walls, tip-top tables, and old lamps casting soft light. The Roman Garden Lounge offers light lunches and snacks.

✪ Scalinata di Spagna

Piazza Trinità dei Monti 17, 00187 Roma. ☎ **06/679-3006.** Fax 06/699-40-598. 15 rms (all with bath or shower), 1 suite. A/C MINIBAR TV TEL. 350,000–380,000 lire ($218.75–$237.50) double; 480,000 lire ($300) triple; 650,000 lire ($406.25) suite. AE, MC, V. Parking 35,000 lire ($21.90). Metro: Piazza di Spagna.

This was the most appealing pension near the Spanish Steps before its conversion in 1988 into a three-star hotel. It's right at the top of the steps, directly across the small piazza from the deluxe Hassler. This is a delightful little building—only two floors are visible from the outside—done up in mustard-yellow and burgundy-red paint and nestled between much larger structures. You'll recognize the four relief columns across the facade and the window boxes with their bright blossoms. The interior is like an old inn—the public rooms are small with bright print slipcovers, old clocks, and low ceilings.

The decorations vary radically from one room to the next; some have low, beamed ceilings and ancient-looking wood furniture, while others have loftier ceilings and more average appointments. Everything is spotless and most pleasing to the eye. In season, breakfast is served on the roof garden terrace with its sweeping view of the dome of St. Peter's across the Tiber. Reserve well in advance.

MODERATE

Carriage

Via della Carrozze 36, 00187 Roma. ☎ **06/699-0124.** Fax 06/678-8279. 24 rms, 2 suites. A/C MINIBAR TV TEL. 270,000 lire ($168.75) double; 330,000 lire ($206.25) triple; 450,000 lire ($281.25) suite. Rates include breakfast. AE, DC, MC, V. Metro: Piazza di Spagna.

The aptly named Carriage caters to the "carriage trade," which in today's sense means staff members of the British and French embassies, plus an occasional movie star or film director. The 18th-century facade covers some charming, although small, accommodations (if you reserve, ask for one of the two rooftop bedrooms). Antiques have been used tastefully, creating a personal aura, even in the bedrooms with their matching bedcovers and draperies. Each bedroom has a radio and other amenities. To meet your fellow guests, head for the Renaissance-style salon that is called an American bar or the roof garden. There is no dining room in the hotel.

Hotel Gregoriana

Via Gregoriana 18, 00187 Roma. ☎ **06/679-4269.** Fax 06/678-4258. 19 rms (all with bath or shower). A/C TV TEL. 280,000 lire ($175) double. Rates include breakfast. No credit cards. Parking 25,000 lire ($15.65). Metro: Piazza di Spagna.

Hotel Gregoriana is a small, elite hotel favored by members of the Italian fashion industry who book rooms here for visiting friends from out of town. The ruling matriarch of an aristocratic family left the building to an order of nuns in the 19th century, but they eventually retreated to other quarters. Today there might be a slightly more elevated spirituality in Room C than in the rest of the hotel, as it used to be a chapel. Throughout the establishment, however, the smallish rooms provide comfort and Italian design. The elevator cage is a black-and-gold art deco fantasy, and the door to each accommodation has a reproduction of an Erté print whose fanciful characters indicate the letter designating that particular room. You'll pay the bill in the tiny, rattan-covered lobby.

Hotel Internazionale

Via Sistina 79, 00187 Roma. ☎ **06/699-41-823.** Fax 06/678-4764. 42 rms, 2 suites. A/C MINIBAR TV TEL. 285,000 lire ($178.15) double; from 550,000 lire ($343.75) suite. Rates include breakfast. AE, MC, V. Parking 40,000 lire ($25). Bus: 492 from Stazione Termini.

Hotel Internazionale emerged from the combination of several old palaces, and traces of their past splendor can be seen in a few of the public rooms. Just half a block from the top of the Spanish Steps, the Internazionale has been a favorite of knowledgeable travelers since the 1920s. The atmosphere is like that of a small inn, and service is efficient. The rooms are furnished with old wooden pieces that couldn't really be called antiques, yet are substantial and comfortable. Accommodations facing the narrow and often-noisy via Sistina now have double windows. Bits and pieces of former elegance remain, especially in the dining room or Sala de Pranzo, whose ceiling is paneled.

Hotel Madrid

Via Mario de' Fiori 94–95, 00187 Roma. ☎ **06/699-1511**. Fax 06/679-1653. 26 rms, 7 suites. A/C MINIBAR TV TEL. 242,300 lire ($151.45) double; from 282,600 lire ($176.65) suite for 3; 302,800 lire ($189.25) suite for 4. Rates include breakfast. AE, DC, MC, V. Metro: Piazza di Spagna.

Hotel Madrid evokes fin-de-siècle Roma. The interior has been redone, and many modern comforts have been added. The hotel appeals to the individual traveler who wants a good standard of service. Guests often take their breakfast amid ivy and blossoming plants on the roof terrace. The view of the rooftops and the distant dome of St. Peter's is beautiful. Some of the doubles are really quite large, equipped with small scatter rugs, veneer armoires, and shuttered windows. All accommodations contain radios. The hotel is an ocher building with a shuttered facade on a narrow street practically in the heart of the boutique area centering around via Frattina, near the Spanish Steps.

Hotel Piazza di Spagna

Via Mario de' Fiori 61, 00187 Roma. ☎ **06/679-6412.** Fax 06/679-0654. 16 rms. A/C MINIBAR TV TEL. 250,000 lire ($156.25) double. Rates include breakfast. AE, MC, V. Metro: Piazza di Spagna. Bus: 61, 71, 81, or 85.

Set about a block from the downhill side of the Spanish Steps, this hotel was a run-down pensione until members of the Giocondi family radically renovated it in 1991. Originally built in the early 1800s, the building enjoys a favorable position. Scattered over three floors, you'll find well-scrubbed, simply furnished bedrooms with views of the street, high ceilings, and cool terrazzo floors. There's no elevator, but an ornate wrought-iron balustrade flanks the staircase leading upstairs. Although there's no bar and no restaurant inside, the neighborhood is filled with options for drinking and dining.

INEXPENSIVE

Hotel Margutta

Via Laurina 34, 00187 Roma. ☎ **06/322-3674.** Fax 06/32-00-395. 21 rms. 140,000 lire ($87.50) single or double; 180,000 lire ($112.50) triple. Rates include breakfast. AE, DC, MC, V. Metro: Flaminio.

Hotel Margutta, on a cobblestone street, offers attractively decorated rooms and a helpful staff. The hotel is housed in a two-century-old building that was transformed into a small hotel in 1961. Located off the paneled lobby with a black stone floor is a simple breakfast room with framed lithographs. The best rooms are on the top floor, each with a view. Two of these three rooms share a terrace, and another larger bedroom has a private terrace. Management always reserves the right to charge a 20% to 35% supplement for these accommodations.

Pensione Fiorella

Via del Babuino 196, 00187 Roma. ☎ **06/361-0597.** 7 rms (none with bath). 82,000 lire ($51.25) double. Rates include breakfast. No credit cards. Metro: Flaminio.

A few steps from the piazza del Popolo is the utterly basic Pensione Fiorella. Antonio Albano and his family are one of the best reasons to visit this unstylish but comfortable pensione. They speak little English, but their humor and warm welcome make renting one of their well-scrubbed bedrooms a lot like visiting a light-hearted relative. The bedrooms open onto a high-ceilinged hallway. The doors of the Fiorella shut at 1am. Reservations can be made only a day before you check in.

Pensione Lydia Venier

Via Sistina 42, 00187 Roma. ☎ **06/679-1744.** Fax 06/679-72-63. 30 rms (10 with bath, 10 with shower but no toilet). 115,000 lire ($71.90) double without shower or toilet; 170,000 lire ($106.25) double with shower but no toilet; 200,000 lire ($125) double with bath. Rates include breakfast. AE, MC, V. Metro: Piazza Barberini.

This respectable but cost-conscious pensione is set on one of the upper floors of a gracefully proportioned apartment building on a street that radiates out from the top of the Spanish Steps. Bedrooms are a simple but dignified combination of slightly battered modern and antique, with understated furnishings and an occasional reminder (such as a ceiling fresco) of an earlier era.

NEAR PIAZZA COLONNA
EXPENSIVE

Albergo Nazionale

Piazza Montecitorio 131, 00186 Roma. ☎ **06/678-9251.** Fax 06/678-6677. 87 rms. 15 suites. TV TEL. 380,000 lire ($237.50) double; 800,000 lire ($500) suite. Rates include breakfast. AE, DC, MC, V. Bus: 95.

Albergo Nazionale faces one of Rome's most historic squares, piazza Colonna, with its Column of Marcus Aurelius, the Palazzo di Montecitorio, and the Palazzo Chigi. Because of its location next to the Parliament buildings, the *albergo* is frequently used by government officials and members of diplomatic staffs. In fact, it maintains the atmosphere of a gentlemen's club, although women are welcome, too. There are many nooks conducive to conversation in the public lounges. The lobbies are wood-paneled, and there are many antiques throughout the hotel. Rooms are usually spacious and decorated in a traditional style, either carpeted or floored with marble.

MODERATE

Hotel Cecil

Via Francesco Crispi 55A, 00187 Roma. ☎ **06/679-7998.** Fax 06/679-7996. 41 rms (all with bath or shower). TV TEL. 270,000–290,000 lire ($168.75–$181.25) double. Rates include breakfast. AE, MC, V. Parking 25,000–30,000 lire ($15.65–$18.75). Metro: Piazza Barberini.

This hotel in a 17th-century building lies in the heart of Rome near such monuments as the piazza di Spagna and the Fontana di Trevi. It has entertained everybody from Casanova to Henrik Ibsen, who wrote *Brandt* and conceived *Peer Gynt* here. Today it's attractively streamlined, with comfortable bedrooms, each with private bath, satellite TV, and radio. There's a panoramic terrace for viewing "monumental Rome."

INEXPENSIVE

Albergo Cesàri

Via di Pietra 89A, 00186 Roma. ☎ **06/679-2386.** Fax 06/679-0882. 50 rms (40 with bath). A/C TV TEL. 130,000 lire ($81.25) double without bath; 170,000 lire ($106.25) double with bath; 195,000 lire ($121.90) triple with bath; 215,000 lire ($134.40) quad with bath. Breakfast 15,000 lire ($9.40) extra. AE, DC, MC, V. Parking 45,000 lire ($28.15). Bus: 492 from Stazione Termini.

Albergo Cesàri, on a quiet street in the old quarter of Rome, has been around since 1787. Its overnight guests have included Garibaldi and Stendhal. Its well-preserved exterior harmonizes with the Temple of Neptune and many little antiques shops nearby. The completely renovated interior has mostly functional modern pieces in the bedrooms, although there are a few traditional trappings as well to maintain character. Breakfast (which costs extra) is the only meal available.

NEAR THE PANTHEON, PIAZZA NAVONA & PIAZZA CAMPO DE' FIORI
EXPENSIVE

✪ Albergo del Sole al Pantheon

Piazza della Rotonda 63, 00186 Roma. ☎ **06/678-0441.** Fax 06/699-40-689. 26 rms, 4 suites. A/C MINIBAR TV TEL. 450,000 lire ($281.25) double; 530,000 lire ($331.25) suite.

Rates include breakfast. AE, DC, MC, V. Parking 25,000–30,000 lire ($15.65–$18.75). Bus: 56, 62, 64, or 70.

The Albergo del Sole al Pantheon, overlooking the Pantheon, is an absolute gem. The present-day Albergo is one of the oldest hotels in the world; the first records of it as a hostelry appear in 1467. Long known as a retreat for emperors and sorcerers, the hotel has hosted such guests as Frederick III of the Hapsburg family. Mascagni celebrated the premiere of *Cavalleria Rusticana* here. Later, it drew such distinguished company as Jean-Paul Sartre and his companion, Simone de Beauvoir. Today the rooms are exquisitely furnished and decorated with period pieces and stylized reproductions. The hotel staff will direct you to a nearby garage.

Grand Hotel Plaza

Via del Corso 126, 00186 Roma. ☎ **06/699-21-111.** Fax 06/699-41-575. 207 rms, 5 suites. A/C TV TEL. 360,000–450,000 lire ($225–$281.25) double; 700,000–1,500,000 lire ($437.50–$937.50) suite. Breakfast 19,000 lire ($11.90) extra. AE, DC, MC, V. Parking 30,000 lire ($18.75). Bus: 2, 81, 90, or 115.

Empress Carlotta of Mexico received Pope Pius IX here in 1866, and in 1933 Pietro Mascagni composed his *Nerone* in one of its bedrooms. Vincent Price always stayed here while making "all those bad movies," and when you see the very grand decor, you'll understand why. The hotel was partially renovated in 1993. The public rooms are vintage 19th century and contain stained-glass skylights, massive crystal chandeliers, potted palms, inlaid marble floors, and a life-size stone lion guarding the entrance to the ornate stairway leading upstairs. The bar seems an interminable distance across the parquet floor of the opulent ballroom.

The hotel contains well-furnished bedrooms, many quite spacious; some have been modernized and others are old-fashioned. Many rooms have minibars. The Mascagni Restaurant serves an Italian cuisine.

Hotel Raphael

Largo Febo 2, 00186 Roma. ☎ **06/68-28-31.** Fax 06/687-8993. 45 rms, 10 suites. A/C MINIBAR TV TEL. 450,000–475,000 lire ($281.25–$296.90) double; 580,000–605,000 lire ($362.50–$378.15) suite. Breakfast 24,000 lire ($15) extra. AE, DC, MC, V. Parking 35,000 lire ($21) nearby. Bus: 64, 70, or 492.

In the heart of ancient Rome adjacent to the piazza Novonna with Bernini's Four Rivers Fountain, this hotel lies within easy distance of the Vatican Museums, St. Peter's Cathedral, and the Pantheon, among other attractions. Its rooftop garden terrace boasts a panorama of the ancient city. The charming ivy-covered facade invites one to enter the lobby decorated with antiques that might rival a museum in Rome. Some of the suites have private terraces, and all the well-appointed bedrooms are air conditioned, with direct-dial phone, minibar, and satellite TV.

Dining/Entertainment: The elegant restaurant and bar, Café Picasso, serves an international cuisine.

Services: Room service, babysitting, laundry, currency exchange.

Facilities: Fitness room.

MODERATE

Hotel Tiziano

Corso Vittorio Emanuele 110, 00186 Roma. ☎ **06/686-5019.** Fax 06/686-5019. 46 rms, 4 suites. A/C MINIBAR TV TEL. 270,000 lire ($168.75) double; 300,000 lire ($187.50) triple; 320,000 lire ($200) suite. Rates include buffet breakfast. Discounts of 15% offered Fri–Sun. AE, DC, MC, V. Parking 28,000 lire ($17.50). Bus: 64, 65, 75, or 170.

This hotel occupies the central section of the Pacelli Palace, a 16th-century structure best known as the family home of Pope Pius XII. (Those sections of the palace to the left and right of the Tiziano are occupied by another hotel and by offices of the Italian government, respectively.) Despite many improvements and modernizations, the hotel retains its neoclassical allure and some of the dignity of the original structure. It enjoys a prominent position on a main thoroughfare between piazza Venezia and St. Peter's. It maintains a restaurant, open for lunch and dinner Monday to Friday, which charges from around 40,000 lire ($25) for a full meal and is popular with the neighborhood's business and government community. The hotel also maintains its own garage, set within a three-minute walk, where patrons may park their cars for a supplemental charge.

Teatro di Pompeo

Largo del Pallaro 8, 00186 Roma. ☎ **06/683-00-170.** Fax 06/688-05-531. 12 rms (all with shower). A/C TV TEL. 260,000 lire ($162.50) double. Rates include breakfast. AE, DC, MC, V. Bus: 64.

Built on the top of the ruins of the Theater of Pompey, which dates from about 55 B.C., this small charmer lies near the spot where Julius Caesar met his final fate. It's on a quiet piazzetta near the Palazzo Farnese and the campo de' Fiori. The bedrooms, all doubles, are decorated in an old-fashioned Italian style with beamed ceilings and hand-painted tiles. There's no restaurant, but breakfast is served. It's possible to exchange foreign currency here, and English is spoken.

INEXPENSIVE

⑤ Albergo Campo de' Fiori

Via del Biscione 6, 00186 Roma. ☎ **06/688-06-865.** Fax 06/687-6003. 27 rms (9 with bath and sink), 1 honeymoon suite. 100,000 lire ($62.50) double without bath; 115,000 lire ($71.90) double with shower; 170,000 lire ($106.25) double with bath; 135,000 lire ($84.40) triple without bath; 145,000 lire ($90.65) triple with shower; 210,000 lire ($131.25) triple with bath. Rates include breakfast. MC, V. Bus: 64 from Stazione Termini to Museo di Roma; then arm yourself with a good map for the walk to this place.

This seems to be everybody's favorite budget hideaway. Lying in the historic center of Rome at a market area that has existed since the 1500s, this cozy, narrow six-story hotel offers rustic rooms, many quite tiny and sparsely adorned, others with a lot of character. The best of them have been restored and are on the first floor. Yours might have a ceiling of clouds and blue skies along with mirrored walls. The best accommodation is the honeymoon retreat on the sixth floor, with a canopied king-size bed. Honeymooners beware: there's no elevator.

Guests can enjoy the panorama from the terrace overlooking the fruits and vegetables below, and, in the distance, St. Peter's. There is no restaurant or bar.

Pensione Navona

Via dei Sediari 8, 00186 Roma. ☎ **06/686-4203.** Fax 06/68-80-38-02. 22 rms (10 with shower). 105,000 lire ($65.65) double without bath; 115,000 lire ($71.90) double with bath. Rates include breakfast. AE. Bus: 64.

Although the individual accommodations inside are not as glamorous as the exterior of this palace, the Pensione Navona offers clean and decent accommodations, some of which are open to views of the building's central (and quiet) courtyard. Run by an Australian-born family of Italian descent, the place has tiled bathrooms, ceilings high enough to relieve the midsummer heat, and an array of architectural oddities that remain the legacy of the continual construction this palace has endured since its foundation was first laid in 1360. The pensione lies on a small street that radiates out from the southeastern tip of the piazza Navona.

NEAR PIAZZA CAVOUR
INEXPENSIVE

Sant'Angelo
Via Mariana Dionigi 16, 00193 Roma. ☎ **06/32-20-758**. Fax 06/32-04-451. 15 rms. TV TEL. 125,000 lire ($78.15) double. AE, DC, MC, V. Parking 35,000 lire ($21.90). Bus: 23, 62, 64, 70, or 87.

Lying across the Tiber, right off the piazza Cavour and northeast of Castel Sant'Angelo (from which it takes its name), this hotel stands in a relatively untouristy area. Maintained and operated by several members of the Torre family, the hotel occupies the third floor of an imposing 200-year-old building whose other floors are devoted to office and private apartments. Bedrooms are simple, modern, clean, and uncomplicated, with wooden furniture and views of either the street or of a rather bleak courtyard in back. (Views over the back are quieter.) No meals are served other than breakfast, although the neighborhood around the hotel offers many acceptable choices.

NEAR ST. PETER'S
EXPENSIVE

✪ Hotel Atlante Star
Via Vitelleschi 34, 00193 Roma. ☎ **06/687-32-33**. Fax 06/687-2300. 80 rms, 10 suites. A/C MINIBAR TV TEL. 445,000 lire ($278.15) double; 550,000 lire ($343.75) suite. Rates include breakfast. AE, DC, MC, V. Parking 40,000 lire ($25). Metro: Ottaviano. Bus: 64, 81, or 492.

Atlante Star is a first-class hotel a short distance from St. Peter's Basilica and the Vatican. The tastefully renovated lobby is covered with dark marble, chrome trim, and lots of exposed wood, while the upper floors somehow give the impression of being inside a luxuriously appointed ocean liner. This stems partly from the lavish use of curved and lacquered surfaces, walls upholstered in freshly colored

---

🅐 Family-Friendly Hotels

Cavalieri Hilton *(see p. 134)* This hotel is like a resort at Monte Mario, with a swimming pool, gardens, and plenty of grounds for children to run and play, yet it's only 15 minutes from the center of Rome, reached by the hotel shuttle bus.

Hotel Massimo d'Azeglio, Via Cavour 18. *(see p. 135)* Near the Stazione Termini, this has long been a family favorite. Rooms are large, well kept, and comfortable, and the well-trained staff is solicitous of children.

Hotel Ranieri *(see p. 120)* This hotel offers a family-style atmosphere in rooms that are air-conditioned with private bath. Many are large enough to house families of three or four, and baby cots are on hand as well.

Hotel Venezia *(see p. 120)* At this good, moderately priced family hotel near the Stazione Termini, rooms are renovated and most are large enough for extra beds for children.

printed fabrics, modern bathrooms, and wall-to-wall carpeting. Even the door handles are art deco–inspired. These doors open into small but posh accommodations outfitted with all the modern comforts. There's also a royal suite with a Jacuzzi. The hotel has the most striking views of St. Peter's of any hotel in Rome. If there is no room at this inn, the owner will try to get you a room at his nearby Atlante Garden.

Dining/Entertainment: The restaurant, Les Etoiles, is an elegant roof-garden choice at night, overlooking a 360° panoramic view of Rome, with an illuminated St. Peter's in the background. A flavorful cuisine—inspired in part by Venice—is served. A meal here begins at 100,000 lire ($62.50).

Services: 24-hour room service, laundry/valet, babysitting, express checkout.

Facilities: Roof garden, foreign-currency exchange, secretarial services in English, translation services.

MODERATE

✪ Hotel Atlante Garden

Via Crescenzio 78, 00193 Roma. ☎ **06/687-2361.** Fax 06/687-2315. 43 rms. A/C MINIBAR TV TEL. 305,000 lire ($190.65) double. Rates include breakfast. AE, DC, MC, V. Parking 40,000 lire ($25). Metro: Ottaviano.

Atlante Garden stands on a tree-lined street near the Vatican. The entrance takes you through a garden tunnel lined with potted palms, which eventually leads into a series of handsomely decorated public rooms. More classical in its decor than the Hotel Atlante Star, its neighbor under the same management, the Atlante Garden offers 19th-century bedrooms, which have been freshly papered and painted, and contain tastefully conservative furniture and all the modern accessories. The renovated baths are tiled.

Hotel Columbus

Via Della Conciliazione 33, 00193 Roma. ☎ **06/686-5435.** Fax 06/686-4874. 105 rms (all with bath or shower), 4 suites. A/C MINIBAR TV TEL. 245,000 lire ($153.15) double; 350,000 lire ($218.75) suite. Rates include breakfast. AE, DC, MC, V. Free parking. Bus: 64.

In an impressive 15th-century palace, built some 12 years before its namesake set off for America, the Hotel Columbus is a few minutes' walk from St. Peter's. It was once the private home of a wealthy cardinal who later became Pope Julius II, who tormented Michelangelo into painting the Sistine Chapel. The building looks much as it must have those long centuries ago—a severe, time-stained facade, small windows, and heavy wooden doors leading from the street to the colonnades and arches of the inner courtyard. The cobbled entranceway leads to a reception hall with castlelike furniture, then on to a series of baronial public rooms. Note especially the main salon with its walk-in fireplace, oil portraits, battle scenes, and Oriental rugs. The hotel is conveniently located on the triumphal boulevard built by Mussolini in the 1930s to "open up" the Vatican after the Lateran Treaty of 1929, which created the Vatican State.

The bedrooms are considerably simpler than the tiled and tapestried salons, done in soft beiges and furnished with comfortable and serviceable modern pieces. All accommodations are spacious, but a few are enormous and still have such original details as decorated wood ceilings and frescoed walls. The hotel also contains a restaurant, serving lunch or dinner for 55,000 lire ($34.40).

NEAR THE CIRCUS MAXIMUS, THE FORUM & THE COLOSSEUM

EXPENSIVE

Hotel Forum

Via Tor de Conti 25-30, 00184 Roma. ☎ **06/679-2446.** Fax 06/678-6479. 80 rms, 6 suites. A/C TV TEL. 400,000–565,000 lire ($250–$353.15) double; 400,000–565,000 lire ($250–$353.15) triple; 700,000 lire ($437.50) suite. Rates include breakfast. AE, DC, MC, V. Parking 40,000 lire ($25). Bus: 27, 81, 85, or 87.

Hotel Forum, built around a medieval bell tower off the Fori Imperiali, offers an elegance that savors the drama of Old Rome, as well as tasteful, sometimes opulent accommodations. At the peak of the *dolce vita* heyday of the 1950s, this former convent was converted into a hotel. The bedrooms, which look out on the sights of the ancient city, are well appointed with antiques, mirrors, marquetry, and Oriental rugs. The hotel's lounges are conservatively conceived as a country estate, with paneled walls and furnishings that combine Italian and French provincial styles. Dining is an event in the roof-garden restaurant. During the season, you can enjoy an *aperitivo* at the hotel's bar on the roof, surveying the timeless Roman Forum. Reserve well in advance.

INEXPENSIVE

Colosseum Hotel

Via Sforza 10, 00184 Roma. ☎ **06/482-7228.** Fax 06/482-7285. 50 rms. TEL. 190,000 lire ($118.75) double. Rates include breakfast. AE, DC, MC, V. Parking 30,000 lire ($18.75). Metro: Cavour.

Not far from the Santa Maria Maggiore Basilica, the Colosseum Hotel offers baronial living on a miniature scale. Someone with insight and lira notes designed this hotel, which opened in 1965, in excellent taste, a reflection of the best in Italy's design heritage. The bedrooms are furnished with well-conceived antique reproductions (beds of heavy carved wood, dark-paneled wardrobes, leatherwood chairs)—and all with monklike white walls. Air conditioning is available on request for 20,000 lire ($12.50). TV is also available for 10,000 lire ($6.25). The drawing room, with its long refectory table, white walls, red tiles, and provincial armchairs, invites lingering. The reception room, with its parquet floors, arched ceilings, and Savonarola chair, makes a good impression.

Hotel Duca d'Alba

Via Leonina 14, 00184 Roma. ☎ **06/484471.** Fax 06/488-4840. 26 rms. MINIBAR TV TEL. 170,000–230,000 lire ($106.25–$143.75) double. Rates include breakfast. AE, DC, MC, V. Parking 30,000 lire ($18.75). Metro: Cavour.

Close to the Roman Forum and the Colosseum, this hotel has been restored but maintains an aura of the 19th century, when it was built. Although it looks old from the outside, it has been renovated inside with modern yet classic styling. This is a well-run hotel, with comfortably furnished bedrooms, each with a personal safe and hairdryer. The hotel has both a breakfast room and a bar. If no room is available at the Duca d'Alba, the management will book you into their other hotel, the Britannia.

MONTE MARIO
EXPENSIVE

Cavalieri Hilton

Via Cadiolo 101, 00136 Roma. ☎ **06/35-091** or 800/445-8667 in the U.S. or Canada. Fax 06/3509-2241. 359 rms, 17 suites. A/C MINIBAR TV TEL. 450,000–620,000 lire ($281.25–$387.50) double; from 1,000,000 lire ($625) suite. Breakfast 30,000–40,000 lire ($18.75–$25) extra. AE, DC, MC, V. Parking 5,000 lire ($3.15). Transportation: Free hotel shuttle bus goes back and forth to the city center.

Cavalieri Hilton combines all the advantages of a resort hotel with the convenience of being a 15-minute drive from the center of Rome. Overlooking Rome and the Alban Hills from its perch on top of Monte Mario, it is set in 15 acres of trees, flowering shrubs, and stonework. Its facilities are so complete that many visitors (obviously not first-timers to Rome) never leave the hotel grounds. The entrance leads into a marble lobby, whose sculpture, 17th-century art, and winding staircases are usually flooded with sunlight from the massive windows.

The guest rooms and suites, many with panoramic views, are designed to fit contemporary standards of comfort, quality, and style. Soft furnishings in pastel colors are paired with Italian furniture in warm-tone woods. Each unit has a keyless electronic lock, independent heating and air conditioning, color TV with in-house movies, radio, and bedside control for all electric apparatus in the room, as well as a spacious balcony. The bathrooms, sheathed in Italian marble, are

---

J. Paul Getty's Former Villa

La Posta Vecchia, in Palo Laziale, just south of Ladispoli (☎ 06/994-9501; fax 06/994-9507), lies 22 miles northwest of Rome and about 14 miles up the coast from Leonardo da Vinci airport at Fiumicino. Set on foundations of villas which were possibly built by Tiberius, this palatial villa was owned between 1960 and 1976 by one of the world's richest men, J. Paul Getty. In 1654 it was a guesthouse for the nearby Castello Oldescalchi. Set behind iron gates, the stucco-sided building stands amid formal gardens in an eight-acre park.

The villa retains many antiques collected by Getty, as well as many carefully disguised steel doors, escape routes, and security devices installed to protect Getty from intruders. Following the tragic kidnapping of his son in the early 1970s, Getty declared that the building's access to the sea was an unacceptable security risk. The house was sold and became a private home until 1990, when it was transformed into an exceptionally elegant hotel.

From March 11 to January 9, guests are housed in 14 sumptuously decorated suites, which range in price from 770,000 to 2,140,000 lire ($462 to $1,284) a night.

Lunch and dinner, featuring an international cuisine, are served in a richly formal dining room where staff members serve with discretion and politeness. Meals cost from 140,000 lire ($84).

Extensive renovations initiated during Getty's ownership revealed hundreds of ancient Roman artifacts, many of which are on display in a mini-museum. On the premises is an indoor pool, plus a staff (some of whom used to work for Getty) adept at maintaining the illusion that clients have arrived as friends of the long-departed billionaire.

equipped with large mirrors, hairdryer, international electric sockets, vanity mirror, piped-in music, and phone.

Dining/Entertainment: The hotel's stellar restaurant, La Pergola, is regarded as one of the finest in Rome. In summer, a garden restaurant, Il Giardino dell'Uliveto, with a pool veranda, is an ideal choice.

Services: 24-hour concierge, room service, laundry/valet, hotel bus to city center.

Facilities: Tennis courts, jogging paths, health center, indoor arcade of shops, outdoor swimming pool, facilities for the disabled.

2 Dining

A difficult task confronting guidebook writers is compiling a list of the best restaurants in such cities as Rome and Paris. Everybody—locals, expatriates, even those who have chalked up only one visit—has favorites ("What . . . you don't know about that little trattoria three doors down from piazza Navona?").

What follows is not a list of all the best restaurants of Rome, but simply a running commentary on a number of personal favorites. For the most part, we've chosen not to document every deluxe spot known to all big spenders. Rather, we've tried to seek out equally fine (or better) establishments often patronized by some of the finest palates in Rome (but not necessarily by the fattest wallets).

Rome's cooking is not subtle, but its kitchen rivals anything the chefs of Florence or Venice can turn out. A feature of Roman restaurants is skill at borrowing—and sometimes improving upon—the cuisine of other regions. Throughout the capital you'll come across Neapolitan, Bolognese, Florentine, even Sicilian specialties. These dishes carry such designations as *alla genovese, alla milanese, alla napolitana, alla fiorentina,* and *alla bolognese,* to cite only a few. And if you don't like the food, you may enjoy the view—of piazza Navona, the Spanish Steps, or via Vittorio Veneto.

One of the oldest sections of the city, Trastevere is a gold mine of colorful streets and, for our purposes, restaurants with inspired cuisine. Although across the Tiber, it's rather far from St. Peter's. It's adjacent to the old ghetto, whose synagogue can be seen across the river between the spires of the island called Tibertina.

In general, lunch is served from 1 to 3pm and dinner from 8 to around 10:30pm. August, when the most tourists are in town, is the most popular month for closing.

NEAR STAZIONE TERMINI
MODERATE

Massimo d'Azeglio

Via Cavour 18. ☎ **481-4101.** Reservations recommended. Main courses 22,000–32,000 lire ($13.75–$20); fixed-price menu 32,000–42,000 lire ($20–$26.25). AE, DC, MC, V. Mon–Sat 12:30–3pm and 7–11pm. Metro: Stazione Termini. ROMAN.

Massimo d'Azeglio, in a hotel but with a separate entrance, has dispensed Roman cuisine since 1875. Built near the Stazione Termini, which was a fashionable address in the 19th century, it was named after a famous Savoy-born statesman who helped Garibaldi unify Italy. The premises have remained as they were in the 19th century. Wood covers the walls and floors, and paintings of heroes of the Risorgimento hang on all the restaurant's walls. The cuisine is classic and traditional Italian with some innovation. The bollito (boiled meats and vegetables served with a fruity mustard sauce) has reigned supreme since the opening of the restaurant. The wine cellar has a wide selection, some bottles dating back to the 1800s. Begin with Parma ham or melon or else a selection of antipasti. Many habitués prefer to open with a pasta dish, or else risotto with mushrooms and salad. Try such main dishes as grilled squid with turnip tops and lemon sauce or a mixed grill of Tyrrhenian fish. Grilled lamb chops tempt, as do the grilled spring chicken or filet steak tartare.

Ⓢ Scoglio di Frisio

Via Merulana 256. ☎ **487-2765.** Reservations recommended. Main courses 16,000–28,000 lire ($10–$17.50); fixed-price menu 60,000–90,000 lire ($37.50–$56.25). AE, DC, MC, V. Mon–Fri 12:30–3pm; daily 7:30–11pm. Bus: 93 from Stazione Termini. NEAPOLITAN.

Scoglio di Frisio is the choice *suprême* to introduce yourself to the Neapolitan kitchen. While here, you should get reacquainted with pizza ("pizza pie" is redundant) by abandoning your Yankee concepts so you can begin to appreciate the genuine article. At night, you can begin with a plate-size Neapolitan pizza (crunchy, oozy, and excellent) with clams and mussels. After a medley of stuffed vegetables and antipasti, you may then settle for chicken cacciatore or hunter's style, or veal scaloppine. Scoglio di Frisio also has entertainment—so it makes for an inexpensive night on the town. All the fun, cornball "O Sole Mio" and Neapolitan bel canto elements, springs forth in the evening—a guitar, mandolin, and a strolling tenor who is like Mario Lanza reincarnate. The nautical decor is in honor of the top-notch fish dishes—complete with a high-ceilinged grotto with craggy walls, fisher's nets, crustaceans, and a miniature three-masted schooner hanging overhead. It lies on a broad street, south of the Stazione Termini.

Taverna Flavia di Mimmo

Via Flavia 9. ☎ **474-5214.** Reservations recommended. Main courses 16,000–28,000 lire ($10–$17.50). AE, DC, MC, V. Mon–Fri 12:30–3pm; daily 7:30–11pm. Metro: Piazza della Repubblica. ROMAN/INTERNATIONAL.

Taverna Flavia di Mimmo, just a block from via XX Settembre, is a robustly Roman restaurant where during the heyday of *la dolce vita,* movie people used to meet over tasty dishes. The restaurant still serves the same food that used to delight Frank Sinatra and the "Hollywood on the Tiber" crowd, especially Elizabeth Taylor. Specialties include a risotto with scampi and spaghetti al whisky. A different regional dish is featured daily, which might be Roman-style tripe. Exceptional dishes include *osso buco* with peas, a seafood salad, and fondue with truffles.

INEXPENSIVE

Monte Arci

Via Castelfidardo 33. ☎ **494-1220.** Reservations recommended. Main courses 13,000–20,000 lire ($8.15–$12.50). AE, V. Mon–Fri 12:30–3pm; Mon–Sat 7–11:30pm. Bus: 36 from Stazione Termini. ROMAN/SARDINIAN.

Monte Arci, on a cobblestone street not far from the railway station, is set behind a sienna-colored facade that also shelters a stately but faded apartment building. The restaurant features low-cost Roman and Sardinian specialties (you'll spend less money if you have pizza). Typical dishes include *nialoreddus* (a regional form of gnocchetti), pasta with clams or lobster, green and white spaghetti with bacon, spinach, cream, and cheese; pasta with pesto, pasta with those delectable porcini mushrooms, *saltimbocca* (veal and ham), and lamb sausage flavored with herbs and pecorino cheese. The restaurant lies near the piazza Indipendenza.

Trimani Wine Bar

Via Cernaia 37b. ☎ **06/446-9630.** Reservations not necessary. Salads and platters of light food 12,000–19,000 lire ($7.50–$11.90); glasses of wine 3,000–12,000 lire ($1.90–$7.50) depending on the vintage. AE, DC, MC, V. Mon–Sat 11:30am–3pm and 5:30pm–midnight. Closed three weeks in August and Dec 25–Jan 1. Metro: Piazza della Repubblica or Castro Pretorio. CONTINENTAL.

Specifically conceived as a tasting center for French and Italian wines, spumantis, and liqueurs, this elegant wine bar lies at the edge of a historic district whose vehicular traffic is partially restricted. Amid a postmodern, award-winning interior decor inspired by classical Rome, you'll find comfortable seating, occasional live music, and a staff devoted to pressurizing half-full bottles of wine between pours. Menu items are inspired by the cuisine of stylish bistros in Paris, and might include vegetarian pastas (in summertime only), salades niçoises, herb-laden bean (*fagiole*) soups, slices of quiche, Hungarian goulash, gazpacho, and platters of French and Italian cheeses and pâtés.

Trimani, a family of wine brokers whose company was established in 1821, maintains a well-stocked shop about 40 yards from its wine bar, at via Goito 20 (☎ 446-9661), where an astonishing array of the oenological bounty of Italy is for sale.

NEAR THE PARIOLI DISTRICT, VIA VENETO & VILLA BORGHESE
EXPENSIVE

George's

Via Marche 7. ☎ **484575.** Reservations required. Main courses 30,000–42,000 lire ($18.75–$26.25). AE, DC, MC, V. Mon–Sat 12:30–3pm and 7:30pm–midnight. Closed Aug. Metro: Piazza Barberini. INTERNATIONAL.

George's has been a favorite of ours ever since Romulus and Remus were being tended by the she-wolf. Right off via Vittorio Veneto, in a dignified 18th-century building, it's not run by George, but by Michele Pavia, *maître d' hôtel* for a quarter of a century before becoming its owner. Many guests drop in for a before-dinner drink, enjoying the music in the piano bar. They then proceed to an elegantly decorated and raised dining room with a tented ceiling. There is a relaxed clublike atmosphere, and English is spoken, of course. Specialties include pappardelle with rabbit and risotto with squid ink, or with braised radiccio; linguini with porcini, mushrooms, and all kinds of veal dishes (including a savory version of *vitello tonnato*). The kitchen has an uncompromising dedication to quality, as reflected by such dishes as marinated mussels, smoked Scottish salmon, and sole Georges; many veal and steak dishes are offered as well. From June to October, depending on the weather, the action shifts to the garden, suitably undisturbed because it's in the garden of a papal villa.

✪ Relais Le Jardin

In the Hotel Lord Byron, via G. de Notaris 5. ☎ **361-3041.** Reservations required. Main courses 45,000–53,000 lire ($28.15–$33.15). AE, DC, MC, V. Mon–Sat 1–3pm and 8–10:30pm. Closed Aug. Bus: 52. ITALIAN.

Relais Le Jardin is one of the best places to go in Rome for both a traditional and a creative cuisine. Inside one of the most elite small hotels of the capital (see my hotel recommendation in "Accommodations," earlier in this chapter), the restaurant sports a decor that's almost aggressively lighthearted, combining white lattice with bold colors and flowers. Many of the cooks and service personnel were trained

Rome Dining

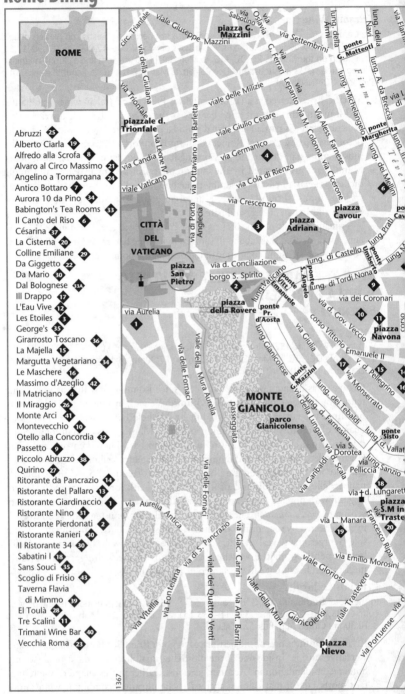

1367

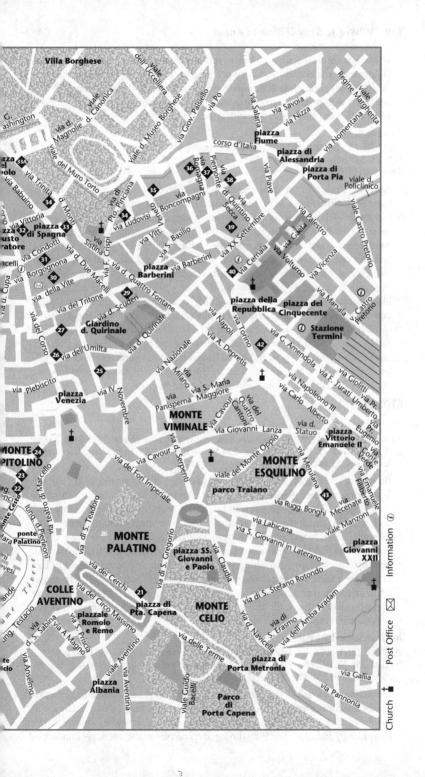

Church †   Post Office ⊠   Information ⓘ

at foreign embassies or diplomatic residences abroad. Classified as a Relais Gourmands, the establishment serves a frequently changing array of dishes that might include grilled swordfish with capers; prosciutto of wild boar, with pork liver and olives with pasta; a soup of artichoke hearts and octopus with braised chicory; and a coffee and chocolate torte with anise.

✪ Sans Souci

Via Sicilia 20. ☎ **482-1814.** Reservations required. Main courses 54,000–60,000 lire ($33.75–$37.50). AE, DC, MC, V. Tues–Sun 8pm–1am. Closed Aug 10–30. Metro: Piazza Barberini. FRENCH.

Sans Souci is one of the most elegant dining choices in Rome, and it also serves some of the finest food. With this unbeatable combination, it's no wonder that it has a chic—and frequently famous—clientele. To begin your evening, you'll enter the dimly lit small lounge/bar to the right at the bottom of the steps. Here, amid tapestries and glittering mirrors, the *maître d'* will present you with the menu, and you can leisurely make selections while sipping a drink. The menu is ever changing, as "new creations" are devised. You might begin with a terrine of goose liver with truffles, a special creation of the chef, or else escalopes of foie gras and black truffles in salad. Fish soup is, according to one Rome restaurant critic, "a legend to experience." Soufflés are also popular, including artichoke, asparagus, or spinach, and risottos are also prepared for two. One of the most popular pasta dishes is large fettuccine with wild mushrooms and black truffles. Beef filet en croûte comes with foie gras, and if you have fish on your mind try the chef's medley of fresh fish with a sauce provençale. Dessert soufflés, also prepared for two, are also a specialty, including chocolate or Grand Marnier.

MODERATE

Al Ceppo

Via Panama 2. ☎ **841-9696.** Reservations recommended. Main courses 18,000–45,000 lire ($11.25–$28.15). AE, DC, MC, V. Tues–Sun 12:30–3pm and 8–11pm. Closed last 3 weeks of Aug. Bus: 4, 52 or 53. ROMAN.

Because of its somewhat hidden location (although it's only two blocks from the Villa Borghese, near piazza Ungheria), the clientele is likely to be Roman rather than foreign. "The Log" (its name in English) features an open fireplace that's fed with wood on which the chef does lamb chops, liver, and bacon, to charcoal perfection. The beefsteak, which hails from Tuscany, is also succulent. Other dishes on the menu include *linguine monteconero* (made with clams and fresh tomatoes); a savory version of spaghetti with pepperoni, fresh basil, and pecorini cheese; a filet of swordfish filled with grapefruit, parmesan cheese, pine nuts, and dry grapes; and a fish carpaccio (raw sea bass) with a green salad, onions, and green pepper. Save room for dessert, especially the apple cobbler, the pear and almond tart, or the chocolate meringue hazelnut cake.

Ambasciata d'Abruzzo

Via Pietro Tacchini 26. ☎ **807-8256.** Reservations recommended. All-you-can-eat 50,000 lire ($31.25). AE, DC, MC, V. Mon–Sat 1–3:30pm and 7pm–midnight. Closed Aug. Bus: 26, 52, 53, 168, or 910. ABRUZZI.

If you like generous, all-you-can-eat portions and tasty, well-cooked food that's a good value for the money, then strike out for this little, hard-to-find restaurant in the Parioli district. It's both superb value and great fun, providing you are ravenously hungry and enjoy bountiful dining. It accomplishes the seemingly impossible, not skimping on quality or quantity. The atmosphere is exceedingly informal, and you may have to stand in line if you didn't reserve a table. It's in the true tavern style, with strings of sausages, peppers, and garlic hung about. The culinary parade commences with a basket overflowing with assorted sausages placed on your table; even an herb-flavored baked ham is presented, resting on a cutting board with a knife. Help yourself—but go easy, as there's more to come. Another wicker basket holds moist, crunchy peasant-style bread. Next, a hearty mass of *spaghetti vongole* (with baby clams) is placed before you. Then proceed to an overloaded antipasto table with selections including marinated artichokes, salads, whatever. Later, those still at the table are served a main dish such as grilled fish. Then comes the large salad bowl, mixed to your liking, followed by an assortment of country cheeses, plus a basket brimming with fresh fruit. You're even given your choice of a dessert. A pitcher of the house wine is at your disposal, and the price not only includes coffee but a chaser of Sambuca as well.

Aurora 10 da Pino il Sommelier
Via Aurora 10. ☎ **474-2779.** Reservations recommended. Main courses 20,000–30,000 lire ($12.50–$18.75). AE, DC, MC, V. Tues–Sun noon–3pm and 7–11:15pm. Closed three weeks in August. Metro: Piazza Barberini. ROMAN/SICILIAN.

Established in 1981 a few paces from the top of via Vittorio Veneto, this restaurant lies within the vaulted interior of what was originally a Maronite convent. Its manager (and namesake) is a Sicilian, Pino Salvatore, whose high-energy direction and staff have attracted some of the capital's most influential diplomats and a sprinkling of film stars.

The place is especially noted for its awesome array of more than 250 kinds of wine, collectively representing every province of Italy. Unusual for Rome, the restaurant features a large soup menu, along with a tempting array of freshly made antipasti. You can begin with a selection of your favorite pasta or risotto, then follow with perhaps a salade "Aurora," linguine with lobster, a Sicilian-style fish fry, swordfish in herb sauce, filet of beef with porcini mushrooms, risotto with asparagus, beef stew flambé, and fish, either grilled or baked, in the Sicilian style, with tomatoes and herbs.

INEXPENSIVE

Césarina
Via Piemonte 109. ☎ **488-08-28.** Reservations recommended. Main courses 15,000–25,000 lire ($9.40–$15.65). AE, DC, MC, V. Mon–Sat 12:30–3pm and 7:30–11pm. Bus: 56. EMILIANA-ROMAGNOLA/ROMAN.

Specializing in the cuisine of Rome and the region around Bologna (Emilia-Romagna), this restaurant has grown since it was originally established by a well-meaning matriarch, Césarina Masi, around 1960. (Many tourist veterans of Rome remember Ms. Masi fondly because of her strict supervision of the kitchens, and because of the way she would lecture regular clients who didn't finish their tagliatelle.) Although she died in the mid-1980s, the restaurant perpetuates her culinary traditions in a newer manifestation of the original corner-in-the-wall. Today, with three dining rooms and more than 200 seats, the restaurant serves excellent versions of *bollito misto* (an array of well-seasoned boiled meats), which is rolled from table to table on a trolley; and a misto Césarina—three kinds of pasta, each handmade and served with a different sauce. Equally appealing is the saltimbocca and the *cotoletta alla bolognese*, a veal cutlet baked with ham and cheese. A dessert specialty is semifreddo Césarina served with hot chocolate. The staff is tactful and polite, the food is excellent, and the selection of antipasti is freshly made and very appealing.

Girarrosto Toscano

Via Campania 29. ☎ **482-3835.** Reservations required. Main courses 18,000–50,000 lire ($11.25–$31.25). AE, DC, MC, V. Thurs–Tues 12:30–3pm and 7:30–11:30pm. Bus: 90B, 95, 490, or 495. TUSCAN.

Girarrosto Toscano, facing the walls of the Borghese Gardens, draws a coterie of guests from via Vittorio Veneto haunts, which means that you may have to wait. Under vaulted ceilings in a cellar setting, some of the finest Tuscan specialties in Rome are served. Begin by enjoying an enormous selection of antipasti, which the waiters bring around: succulent little meatballs, vine-ripened melon with prosciutto, an omelet, mozzarella, and especially delicious Tuscan salami. You're then given a choice of pasta, such as fettuccine in a cream sauce. Priced according to weight, the *bistecca alla fiorentina* is the best item to order, although it's expensive. This is a grilled steak seasoned with oil, salt, and pepper. Oysters and fresh fish from the Adriatic are served every day. Of course, the beefsteak, fresh fish, or fresh oysters—all based on weight by the gram and also on daily market quotations—will be much more expensive than the prices indicated above. So order with care if you're on a strict budget. For dessert, I'd recommend what everybody has—an assortment of different flavors of ice cream, called gelato misto.

Piccolo Abruzzo

Via Sicilia 237. ☎ **482-0176.** Reservations recommended. Main courses 15,000–25,000 lire ($9.40–$15.65). AE, DC, MC, V. Mon–Sat 12:30–3pm and 7pm–midnight. Bus: 490, 495, 580, and 590. ABRUZZI.

An imaginative array of antipasti and copious portions make Piccolo Abruzzo—a good stroll from via Vittorio Veneto—one of the most popular restaurants in its neighborhood. The antipasti buffet contains at least 20 kinds of offerings. Many habitués plan a meal either early or late to avoid the jam, as the place is small and popular. Full meals are priced according to what you take from the groaning antipasti buffet. You can follow with a pasta course, which might be samples of three different versions, followed by a meat course, then cheese and dessert. A meat specialty is agnello d'Abruzzi, regional roast lamb. All this lively scene takes place in a brick- and stucco-sheathed room perfumed with hanging cloves of garlic, salt-cured hams, and beribboned bunches of Mediterranean herbs.

NEAR THE SPANISH STEPS & PIAZZA DEL POPOLO
EXPENSIVE

✪ El Toulà

Via della Lupa 29B. ☎ **687-3498.** Reservations required for dinner. Main courses 35,000–48,000 lire ($21.90–$30); fixed-price menu 90,000 lire ($56.25). AE, DC, MC, V. Tues–Fri 1–3pm; Mon–Sat 8–11pm. Closed Aug. Bus: 90, 913, or 926. ROMAN/VENETIAN.

El Toulà offers the quintessence of the Roman haute cuisine with a creative flair. The restaurant is the glamorous flagship of what is now an upscale chain with eight restaurants in Italy and overseas branches in Tokyo and Beijing. (Its name is derived from a word which translates from the alpine dialect of Cortina d'Ampezzo as "Hayloft.") The elegant setting, attracting the international set, is one of vaulted ceilings and large archways that divide the rooms. Guests stop in the charming bar to order a drink while deciding on their food selections from the impressive menu.

The menu changes every month. In honor of the restaurant's Venetian origins, one section of the menu is devoted exclusively to culinary specialties of that city in the lagoons. Items include *fegago* (liver) *alla Veneziana*, the most classic dish of Venice, along with calamari stuffed with vegetables, bigoli pasta in squid ink, *baccala* (codfish mousse served with polenta), and another Venetian classic, *broetto*, a fish soup made with monkfish and clams. The selection of sherbets depends on the availability of fruits—the cantaloupe and fresh strawberry sherbets are celestial concoctions. You can request a mixed plate if you'd like to sample several of them. El Toulà usually isn't crowded at lunchtime.

MODERATE

Dal Bolognese

Piazza del Popolo 1–2. ☎ **361-1426.** Reservations required. Main courses 18,000–26,000 lire ($11.25–$16.25). AE, DC, V. Tues–Sun 12:45–3pm and 8:15–11pm. Closed Aug 5–20. Metro: Flaminio. BOLOGNESE.

If *La Dolce Vita* were being filmed now, this restaurant would probably be used as a backdrop. It is one of those rare dining spots that's not only chic, but noted for its food as well. Young actors, shapely models, artists from nearby via Margutta, even industrialists on an off-the-record evening on the town show up here, quickly booking the limited sidewalk tables. To begin your repast, we suggest a *misto de pasta*, four forms of pasta, each flavored with a different sauce, arranged on the same plate. A worthy substitute would be thin, savory slices of Parma ham or perhaps the melon and prosciutto if you're feeling extravagant (try a little freshly ground pepper on the latter). For your main course, specialties include lasagne verde, tagliatelle alla bolognese, and a most recommendable cotolette alla bolognese. Instead of lingering in the restaurant, you may want to cap your evening by calling on the Rosati next door (or its competitor, the Canova, across the street), and enjoying one of the tempting pastries.

INEXPENSIVE

Da Mario

Via della Vite 55–56. ☎ **678-3818.** Reservations recommended. Main courses 13,000–19,000 lire ($8.15–$11.90). AE, DC, MC, V. Mon–Sat 12:30–3pm and 7:30–11pm. Closed Aug. Metro: Piazza di Spagna. ROMAN/FLORENTINE.

Da Mario is noted for its moderately priced game specialties. Mario also does excellent Florentine dishes, although the typical beefsteak is too costly these days for most budgets. You can dine in air-conditioned comfort on the street level or descend to the cellars. A good beginning is a wide-noodle dish, pappardelle, best when served with a game sauce (*caccia*) or with chunks of rabbit (*lepre*) which is available only in winter. *Capretto* (kid) and beefsteaks are served in the Florentine fashion, although you may prefer two roasted quail with polenta. I heartily recommend the gelato misto, a selection of mixed ice cream.

Il Ristorante 34 (also A1 34)

Via Mario de' Fiori 34. ☎ **679-5091.** Reservations required. Main courses 15,000–28,000 lire ($9.40–$17.50). AE, DC, MC, V. Tues–Sun 12:30–3pm; Tues–Sat 7:30–10:30pm. Closed 3 weeks in Aug, one week at Easter. Metro: Piazza di Spagna. ROMAN.

Il Ristorante 34 is a very good and increasingly popular restaurant close to the most famous shopping district of Rome. Its long and narrow interior is sheathed in scarlet wallpaper, ringed with modern paintings, and capped with a vaulted ceiling.

In the rear, stop to admire a display of antipasti proudly exhibited near the entrance to the bustling kitchen. Your meal might include noodles with caviar and salmon, risotto with chunks of lobster, pasta-and-lentil soup, meatballs in a sauce with fat mushrooms, two kinds of entrecôte, or pasta in a pumpkin-flavored cream sauce. The spaghetti with clams is among the best in Rome.

Otello alla Concordia

Via della Croce 81. ☎ **679-1178.** Reservations not necessary. Main courses 13,000–25,000 lire ($8.15–$15.65). AE, DC, MC, V. Mon–Sat 12:30–3pm and 7:30–11pm. Metro: Piazza di Spagna. ROMAN.

Set on a side street amid the glamorous boutiques near the northern edge of the Spanish Steps, this is one of the most popular and consistently reliable restaurants of Rome. Diners enter from a stone corridor that leads into a dignified building, the Palazzo Povero, from the street, choosing a table (space permitting) in either an arbor-covered courtyard or within a cramped but convivial series of inner dining rooms. Banks of fruit from the Roman countryside and displays of Italian bounty decorate an interior well known to many of the district's shopkeepers from the surrounding fashion district. The *spaghetti alle vongole veraci* (spaghetti with clams) is excellent, as well as breast of turkey with mushrooms, Roman-style saltimbocca *abbacchio arrosto* (roasted baby lamb), eggplant parmigiana, a selection of grilled or sautéed fish dishes (including swordfish), and several different preparations of veal.

Ristorante Nino

Via Borgognona 11. ☎ **679-5676.** Reservations recommended. Main courses 15,000–25,000 lire ($9.40–$15.65). AE, DC, MC, V. Mon–Sat 12:30–3pm and 7:30–11pm. Closed Aug. Metro: Piazza di Spagna. TUSCAN.

Ristorante Nino, off via Condotti a short walk from the Spanish Steps, is a tavern mecca for writers, artists, and an occasional model from one of the nearby high-fashion houses. Nino's enjoys deserved acclaim for its Tuscan dishes. The cooking is hearty and completely unpretentious. The restaurant is particularly known for its steaks shipped in from Florence and charcoal broiled—and these are priced according to weight and change daily. A plate of *cannelloni nino* is one of the chef's specialties. Other good dishes include grilled veal liver, *fagioli cotti al fiasco*, codfish *alla livornese*, and *zampone*. For dessert, I suggest the Florentine cake called *castagnaccio*.

Ristorante Ranieri

Via Mario de' Fiori 26. ☎ **679-1592.** Reservations required. Main courses 22,000–32,000 lire ($13.75–$20). AE, DC, MC, V. Mon–Sat 12:30–3pm and 7:30–11pm. Metro: Piazza di Spagna. Bus: 52, 53, 56, 81, or 90. INTERNATIONAL.

Ristorante Ranieri, off via Condotti, is well into its second century (it was founded in 1843). Neapolitan-born Giuseppe Ranieri, for whom the restaurant is named, was the chef to Queen Victoria. Long a favorite dining place of the cognoscenti, Ranieri still maintains its Victorian trappings. Nothing ever seems to change here. Many of the dishes on the good menu reflect the restaurant's ties with royalty; veal cutlet l'Impériale, mignonettes of veal à la Regina Victoria, and tournedos Enrico IV. A suitable starter might be crêpes Ranieri, stuffed with eight kinds of cheese. The imperial veal cutlet dish—served with asparagus and mushrooms—was actually created some time in the 19th century for the queen herself. Most of the dishes are French and Italian, although overall the cookery is international.

NEAR PIAZZA COLONNA, THE TREVI FOUNTAIN & THE QUIRINALE HILL

INEXPENSIVE

Colline Emiliane

Via Avignonesi 22. ☎ **481-7538.** Reservations required. Main courses 16,000–25,000 lire ($10–$15.65). No credit cards. Sat–Thurs 12:30–2:45pm and 7:30–10:45pm. Closed Aug. Metro: Piazza Barberini. EMILIANA-ROMAGNOLA.

Colline Emiliane, established in 1936, is a small restaurant right off piazza Barberini, serving the *classica cucina bolognese.* It's a family-run place where everybody helps out. The owner is the cook, and his wife makes the pasta, which, incidentally, is about the best you'll encounter in Rome. The house specialty is an inspired tortellini *alla panna* (cream sauce) with truffles. You might prefer one of the less expensive pastas, however, and all of them are excellent and handmade— *maccheroncini al funghetto* and tagliatelle alla bolognese. As an opener for your meal, I suggest *culatello di Zibello,* a delicacy from a small town near Parma that's known for having the finest prosciutto in the world. Main courses include *braciola di maiale,* boneless rolled port cutlets that have been stuffed with ham and cheese, breaded, and sautéed. *Bollito misto* (mixed boiled meats) is another specialty, as is *ciambonnetto* (roast veal Emilian style with roast potatoes. To finish your meal, we'd recommend *budino al cioccolato,* a chocolate pudding that's baked like flan.

Il Miraggio

Vicolo Sciarra 59. ☎ **678-0226.** Reservations recommended. Main courses 10,000–18,000 lire ($6.25–$11.25). AE, V. Mon–Sat 12:30–3:30pm and 7:30–10:30pm. Bus: 60, 85, 87, or 90B. ROMAN/SARDINIAN.

While shopping near piazza Colonna, you may want to escape the roar of traffic along the Corso by dining at this informal, hidden-away "mirage" in a charming location on a crooked street. It's a cozy, neighborhood setting with good food. The decor in the dining room includes a wine keg set in the wall. A specialty of the house is tortellini *alla papalina.* You might want to try filet of beef with truffles, *rosetta di vitello modo nostro* (veal "our style"), or *spiedino alla siciliana* (rolls of veal with ham and cheese inside, onions and bay leaves outside, grilled on a skewer). There is also an array of fresh fish.

Quirino

Via delle Muratte 84. ☎ **679-4108.** Reservations not necessary. Main courses 20,000–32,000 lire ($12.50–$20). AE, MC, V. Mon–Sat 12:30–3:30pm and 7:30–10:30pm. Closed three weeks in Aug. Metro: Piazza Barberini. ROMAN/SICILIAN.

Quirino is a good place to dine right after you've tossed your coin into the Trevi Fountain. The atmosphere inside is typically Italian, with hanging chianti bottles, a beamed ceiling, and muraled walls. The food is strictly in the "home-cooking" style of Roman trattorie. We are also fond of a mixed fry of tiny shrimp and squid rings that resemble onion rings. For an opening course, we recommend risotto, Milanese style, or spaghetti with clams. The classic Sicilian pasta dish, pasta *alla Norma,* is served here—tomatoes, eggplant, and salata (a salted ricotta). You can also order *involtini alla Messinese,* a roulade of either fish or meat, filled with cheese, grilled, and served with salad greens in the Sicilian style. For dessert, a basket of fresh fruit will be placed on your table.

NEAR THE PANTHEON, PIAZZA NAVONA & PIAZZA DE' FIORI
EXPENSIVE

Il Drappo

Vicolo del Malpasso 9. ☎ **687-7365.** Reservations required. Fixed-price menu 70,000 lire ($43.75) including Sardinian wine. AE, MC, V. Mon–Sat 8pm–midnight. Closed Aug 12–27. Bus: 46, 62, or 64. SARDINIAN.

Il Drappo, on a hard-to-find, narrow street off a square near the Tiber, is operated by a woman known to her habitués only as "Valentina." The facade is graced with a modernized *trompe-l'oeil* painting above the stone entrance, which is flanked with potted plants. Inside, you'll have your choice of two tastefully decorated dining rooms festooned with yards of patterned cotton draped from supports on the ceiling. Flowers and candles are everywhere. Fixed-price dinners may include a wafer-thin appetizer called *carte di musica* (sheet-music paper), which is topped with tomatoes, green peppers, parsley, and olive oil, followed by fresh spring lamb in season, a fish stew made with tuna caviar, or a changing selection of strongly flavored regional specialties that are otherwise difficult to find in Rome. Service is first rate.

MODERATE

Alfredo alla Scrofa

Via della Scrofa 104. ☎ **688-06-163.** Reservations recommended. Main courses 18,000–26,000 lire ($11.25–$16.25). AE, DC, MC, V. Wed–Mon 12:30–3pm and 7:30–11:30pm. Metro: Piazza di Spagna. ROMAN/INTERNATIONAL.

Established in 1925 in a 400-year-old building, this restaurant maintains a visitors' autograph book that reads like a detailed retrospective of 20th-century history. Famous clients have included everyone from Mussolini to Ava Gardner, Arthur Miller (who arrived with Marilyn Monroe in 1960), and, in 1993, Tony Curtis. Gold-framed photographs of many of the visitors hang against oak paneling on the walls, adding a distinct memory of Rome's glamorous years of *dolce vita*. Many first-time visitors order the *maestose fettuccine al triplo burro*, where waiters make choreography out of whipping butter and cheese on rolling carts at tableside. The main-course specialties include *filetto di tacchino dorato* (breast of turkey, sautéed in batter and covered with thin slices of Piedmontese white truffles), filet mignon Casanova (prepared with red wine, pepper, and foie gras); roasted lamb with potatoes in the Roman style; and saltimbocca.

La Carbonara

Piazza Campo de' Fiori 23. ☎ **06/6864783.** Reservations recommended. Main courses 18,000–25,000 lire ($11.25–$15.65). AE, MC, V. Wed–Mon noon–2:30pm and 6:30–10:30pm. Closed 3 weeks Aug. Bus: 64. ROMAN.

Contained within an antique palazzetto, at the edge of a square dominated with the severe-looking statue of one of Italy's political patriarchs, this amicable trattoria claims to be the home of the original version of spaghetti carbonara. (According to legend, the forebears of the present owners devised the recipe in the final days of World War II, when American G.I.s donated their K-rations of powdered eggs and salted bacon to the chef. The result—which is much disputed in other parts of Italy—is the egg yolk, cheese, and bacon-enriched pasta dish that is famous throughout the world.) The dining room features succulent antipasti, grilled meats, fresh and intelligently prepared seasonal vegetables, and—in addition to its famous version of carbonara—several other kinds of pasta, including tagliolini with porcini mushrooms. Another specialty is *bucatini alla matriciana,* a well-flavored chef's version of roast veal with potatoes and vegetables.

Montevecchio

Piazza di Montevecchio 22. ☎ **686-1319.** Reservations required. Main courses 24,000–30,000 lire ($15–$18.75). AE, MC, V. Tues–Sun 1–3pm and 8–11:30pm. Closed Aug 10–25. Bus: 70 or 492. ROMAN/ITALIAN.

To visit, you must negotiate the winding streets of one of Rome's most confusing neighborhoods, near piazza Navona. The heavily curtained restaurant on this Renaissance piazza is where both Raphael and Bramante created many of their masterpieces and where Lucrezia Borgia spun many of her intrigues. The entrance opens onto a high-ceilinged, not particularly large room filled with rural mementos and bottles of wine. Your meal might begin with a strudel of fungi porcini (mushrooms) followed by the invariably good pasta of the day, perhaps a bombolotti stuffed with prosciutto and spinach. Then select roebuck with polenta, roast Sardinian goat, or one of several veal dishes (on one occasion, served with salmon mousse).

Passetto

Via Zanardelli 14. ☎ **68-80-3696.** Reservations recommended. Main courses 15,000–35,000 lire ($9.40–$21.90). AE, DC, MC, V. Daily 12:30–3:30pm and 7–11:30pm. Bus: 70, 87, or 492. ROMAN/INTERNATIONAL.

Passetto, dramatically positioned at the north end of the landmark piazza Navona, draws patrons with its reputation for excellent Italian food. The surroundings are stylish—three rooms, one containing frosted-glass cylinder chandeliers, which maintains the tradition of the past. In summer, however, it's better to try one of the outside tables on the big terrace looking out on piazza Sant'Apollinare. Formally dressed waiters, crisp white linen, and heavy silverware add a touch of luxury. Pastas are exceptional, including penne alla Norma. One recommended main dish is *orata* (sea bass) *al cartoccio* (baked in a paper bag with tomatoes, mushrooms, capers, and white wine). Another house specialty is *rombo passetto* (a fish similar to sole) cooked in a cognac and pine-nut sauce. Fresh fish is often priced by its weight and tabs can soar quickly—be careful! Meals can be accompanied by a selection of fresh varied salads personally chosen from a service trolley. Fresh vegetables are abundant in summer, and a favorite dessert is seasonal fruits, such as lingonberries, raspberries, or blackberries, with fresh thick cream.

Ristorante da Pancrazio

Piazza del Biscione 92. ☎ **686-1246.** Reservations recommended. Main courses 15,000–30,000 lire ($9.40–$18.75); set menu 40,000 lire ($25). AE, DC, MC, V. Thurs–Tues noon–3pm and 7:30–11:15pm. Closed two weeks in Aug (dates vary). Bus: 46 or 62. ROMAN.

Ristorante da Pancrazio is a dining oddity visited as much for its archaeological interest as for its culinary allure. One of its two dining rooms is gracefully and authentically decorated in the style of an 18th-century tavern. Another occupies the premises of Pompey's ancient theater, and as such is lined with marble columns, carved capitals, and bas-reliefs that would be the envy of many museums. Classified as a national monument, it's probably the only such establishment that feeds the body as well as a visitor's sense of history. Menu items include the full range of traditional Roman dishes, such as risotto alla pescatora (with an assortment of seafood), mixed fish fry, several preparations of scampi, saltimbocca, and a Roman specialty, *abbacchio al forno*, a special preparation of roast baby lamb with potatoes. You might also order ravioli stuffed with pulverized hearts of artichokes, and filet of turbot or brill (depending on availability) served with a green peppercorn sauce.

Tre Scalini

Piazza Navona 30. ☎ **06/687-9148.** Reservations recommended. Main courses 20,000–29,000 lire ($12.50–$18.15). AE, DC, MC, V. Thurs–Tues 12:15–3:30pm and 7:15–11:15pm. Closed Dec–Feb. ROMAN.

Established in 1882, this is probably the most famous and most respected restaurant on the piazza Navona—a landmark for ice creams as well as more substantial meals. Although there's a cozy bar on the upper floor, outfitted with simple furniture with a view over the piazza, most visitors opt for a seat either on the ground-floor café or restaurant. Both areas expand their premises during warm weather with chairs and tables on the piazza. Both are serviced by efficient waiters serving portions of ice creams and more substantial meals as well. Inform whomever greets you of your dining intentions, and you'll be seated in the appropriate section.

House specialties include *canfallo in passitte* (butterfly-shaped pasta in an herb and cheese sauce); *risotto con porcini*; risotto with pesto; spaghetti with clams; roast duck with prosciutto; many choices of fish, including a carpaccio of sea bass; saltimbocca; and roast lamb in the Roman style. No one will object if you order just a pasta and salad, unlike other restaurants nearby, which oblige visitors to order several different courses. *Tartufi* (ice cream disguised with a coating of bittersweet chocolate, cherries, and whipped cream) and simpler versions of ice creams range from 5,000 lire ($3.15) to 10,000 lire ($6.25) each; whisky with soda costs from 10,000 to 12,000 lire ($6.25 to $7.50).

INEXPENSIVE

⑤ La Majella

Piazza del Teatro di Pompeo 18. ☎ **686-4174.** Reservations recommended for dinner. Main courses 18,000–30,000 lire ($11.25–$18.75). AE, DC, MC, V. Mon–Sat 12:30–3pm and 8pm–midnight. Closed three weeks in Aug. Bus: 62 or 64. ABRUZZI.

For many years, La Majella served well-prepared food to a clientele that included Polish Cardinal Karol Wojtyla before his elevation to the papal throne. In 1993, the restaurant moved out of its premises in a small palazzo into new premises nearby because of the encroachment of a nearby museum. Its latest venue lies with a trio of old-fashioned dining rooms in an old building a block northeast of the Campo de' Fiori, about a block south of the corso Vittorio Emanuele.

Despite the move, the cuisine changed hardly at all, and includes such Abruzzi mountain food as partridge and venison with polenta, suckling pig, an array of pastas (including pappardelle with rabbit), and roasted lamb with herbs. Fish includes grilled or fried versions of sea bass, flounder, lobster, and shrimp. Two especially recommendable dishes include risotto with zucchini flowers and wild mushrooms or else oven-baked pork served with roast potatoes.

L'Eau Vive

Via Monterone 85. ☎☎ **68-80-10-95.** Reservations recommended. Main courses 18,000–25,000 lire ($11.25–$15.65); fixed-price menus 15,000 lire ($9.40), 20,000 lire ($12.50), and 30,000 lire ($18.75). AE, MC, V. Mon–Sat noon–4pm and 8pm–midnight. Closed Aug 1–20. Bus: 64 or 78. FRENCH/INTERNATIONAL.

Dining at L'Eau Vive qualifies as an offbeat adventure, an unusual experience for many people. It is run by lay missionaries who wear the dress or costumes of their native countries. The restaurant fills the cellar and the ground floor of a 17th-century palace, the Palazzo Lantante della Rovere, and is filled with monumental paintings. In this formal atmosphere, at 10 o'clock each evening, the waitresses sing religious hymns and *Ave Marias*. Your gratuity for service will be turned over for religious purposes. Pope John Paul II used to dine here when he was still archbishop of Cracow.

Specialties include hors d'oeuvres and frogs' legs. An international dish is featured daily. The restaurant's cellar is well stocked with French wines. Main dishes range from guinea hen with onions and grapes in a wine sauce to couscous. Other selections include platters of charcuterie, several kinds of homemade pâté, salad niçoise, and beefsteaks in wine sauce. A smooth finish is the chocolate mousse. Under vaulted ceilings, the atmosphere is deliberately kept subdued, and the place settings—with fresh flowers and good glassware—are tasteful. However, some of the most flamboyant members of international society have adopted L'Eau Vive as their favorite spot. Located on a narrow street in Old Rome, it's hard to find, but it's near the Pantheon.

Le Maschere

Via Monte della Farina 29. ☎ **687-9444.** Reservations recommended. Main courses 12,000–30,000 lire ($7.50–$18.75). AE, DC, MC, V. Tues–Sun 7:30pm–midnight. Bus: 26, 44, 60, 70, or 75. CALABRIAN.

Le Maschere, near largo Argentina, and within walking distance of piazza Navona, specializes in the fragrant, often fiery cookery of Calabria's Costa Viola. That means lots of fresh garlic and wake-up-your-mouth red peppers. The restaurant, decorated with regional artifacts of Calabria, occupies a cellar from the 1600s with small outside tables in summer overlooking a tiny little piazza deep in the heart of Rome. Begin with a selection of antipasti calabresi. There are many different preparations of eggplant. Others prefer the pasta dishes, one made with broccoli, and one flavored with devilish red peppers, garlic, breadcrumbs, and more than a touch of anchovy. The chef also grills meats and fresh swordfish caught off the Calabrian coast. For dessert, finish with a sheep cheese of Calabria or a fresh fruit salad. If you don't want a full meal, you can just visit for pizza and beer.

⑤ Ristorante del Pallaro

Largo del Pallaro 15. ☎ **6880-1488.** Reservations recommended for dinner on weekends. Fixed-price menu 30,000 lire ($18.75). No credit cards. Tues–Sun 1–3pm and Tues–Sun 7:30–12:30pm. Bus: 46, 62, 64, or 70. ROMAN.

The cheerful and kind-hearted woman in white who emerges with clouds of steam from this establishment's bustling kitchen is the owner, Paola Fazi. She maintains a simple duet of very clean dining rooms where price-conscious Romans go for good food at bargain prices. The owners of the restaurant claim that the assassination of Julius Caesar occurred on the site of this house with its ancient foundations. No à la carte meals are served, but the fixed-price menu has made the place famous. As you sit down, the first of eight courses will appear, one following the other, until you've had more than your fill. You begin with antipasti, then go on to such dishes as the pasta of the day, which might be spaghetti, rigatoni, or pappardelle. The meat courses include roast veal, white meatballs, or (only on Friday) dried cod. Potatoes and eggplant are offered. For your final courses, you're served mozzarella cheese, cake with custard, and fruit in season. The meal also includes bread, a liter of mineral water, and half a liter of the house wine.

NEAR ST. PETER'S
MODERATE

Il Matriciano

Via dei Gracchi 55. ☎ **321-2327.** Reservations required, especially for dinner. Main courses 16,000–30,000 lire ($10–$18.75). AE, DC, MC, V. Daily 12:30–3pm and 8–11:30pm. Closed Aug 2–29 and Wed (Nov–Apr) and Sat (May–Oct). Metro: Lepanto. ROMAN.

Il Matriciano is a family restaurant with a devoted following. Its location near St. Peter's makes it all the more distinguished. The food is good, but it's only country fare—nothing fancy. The decor, likewise, is kept to a minimum. In summer, try to get one of the sidewalk tables behind a green hedge and under a shady canopy. The luncheon clientele seems to linger a long time, perhaps out of reluctance to get back to their offices. For openers, you might prefer a *zuppa di verdura* or *ravioli di ricotta*. The preferred choice, however, is tagliolini *con tartufi*. From many dishes, I recommend *scaloppa alla valdostana*, *abbacchio* (baby lamb) *al forno*, and *trippa* (tripe) *alla romano*. The most obvious specialty of the house is derived from what some experts say is the favorite sauce in the Roman repertoire of cuisine, matriciana sauce. Here, it's prepared with bucatini pasta, and richly flavored with bacon, tomatoes, and basil. Dining at the home-like convivial tables, you're likely to see an array of modern-day Romans who include everything from a scattering of prelates and cardinals, escaping from the confines of the nearby Vatican for a while, to such stars of the Italian cinema as Francesco Nunti, Carlo Verdone, and Marcello Mastroiani.

Les Etoiles

In the Hotel Atlante Star, via Vitelleschi 34. ☎ **68-93-434.** Reservations required. Main courses 80,000–120,000 lire ($50–$75). AE, DC, MC, V. Daily 12:30–2:30pm and 7:30–11pm. Metro: Ottaviano. Bus: 64, 81, or 492. MEDITERRANEAN.

Les Etoiles, which means "The Stars," deserves all the stars it receives—both for its cuisine and for its spectacular view of Rome. The restaurant in this previously recommended hotel has been called "the most beautiful rooftop in Italy." At this garden in the sky you'll have an open window over the rooftops of Rome—a 360° view of landmarks, especially the floodlit dome of St. Peter's. A flower terrace contains a trio of little towers, named Michelangelo, Campidoglio, and Ottavo Colle.

In summer everyone wants a table outside if the weather's right, but in winter almost the same view is possible from tables near picture windows. The color and fragrance of a refined Mediterranean cuisine is served here. Food items include quail cooked either with radicchio or in a casserole with mushrooms and herbs, artichokes stuffed with ricotta and pecorino cheese, and Venetian-style risotto with squid ink, roast suckling lamb with mint, and preparations of fish identified as being prepared either in the style of the Tyrrhenian or the Adriatic Sea. The creative chef is rightly proud of his many regional dishes, and the service is deluxe, with a wine list some Roman food critics have labeled "exciting."

Ristorante Pierdonati

Via della Conciliazione 39. ☎ **6880-3557.** Reservations not necessary. Main courses 12,000–25,000 lire ($7.50–$15.65); set menu 25,000 lire ($15.65). AE, MC, V. Fri–Wed noon–3:30pm and 7–10:30pm. Closed Aug. Bus: 64 from Stazione Termini. ROMAN.

Ristorante Pierdonati has been serving wayfarers to the Vatican since 1868. In the same building as the Hotel Columbus (see my hotel recommendation in "Accommodations," earlier in this chapter), this restaurant was the former home of Cardinal della Rovere. Today it's the headquarters of the Knights of the Holy Sepulchre of Jerusalem, and the best restaurant in the gastronomic wasteland of the Vatican area. Its severely classical facade is relieved inside by a gargoyle fountain spewing water into a basin. You'll dine beneath a vaulted ceiling. Try the calves' liver Venetian style, the stewed veal with tomato sauce, or ravioli bolognese. To get really Roman, order the tripe. It can get rather crowded here on days that see thousands upon thousands flocking to St. Peter's.

INEXPENSIVE

Ristorante Giardinaccio

Via Aurelia 53. ☎ **631367.** Reservations recommended, especially on weekends. Main courses 11,000–32,000 lire ($6.90–$20). AE, DC, MC, V. Wed–Mon 12:15–3:30pm and 7:15–11pm. Bus: 46, 62, or 98. MOLISIAN.

This popular restaurant, operated by Nicolino Mancini, is only 200 yards from St. Peter's; unusual for Rome, it offers Molisian specialties (from one of the provincial regions of southeastern Italy). It's rustically decorated in the country-tavern style with dark wood and exposed stone. Flaming grills provide succulent versions of perfectly done quail, goat, and other dishes, but perhaps the mutton goulash would be more adventurous. Many versions of pasta are featured, including taconelle, a homemade pasta with lamb sauce. Vegetarians and others will like the large self-service selection of antipasti.

TRASTEVERE
EXPENSIVE

Alberto Ciarla

Piazza San Cosimato 40. ☎ **581-8668.** Reservations required, especially on weekends. Main courses 30,000–60,000 lire ($18.75–$37.50); fixed-price menus 70,000–95,000 lire ($43.75–$59.40). AE, DC, MC, V. Mon–Sat 8:30pm–12:30am. Closed one week in Aug and one week in Jan. Bus: 44, 75, or 170. SEAFOOD.

Alberto Ciarla is one of the best and most expensive restaurants in Trastevere. Some critics consider it one of the finest restaurants in all of Rome. Contained in an 1890 building set into an obscure corner of an enormous square, it serves some of the most elegant fish dishes in the city. You'll be greeted at the door with a cordial reception and a lavish display of seafood on ice. A dramatically modern decor plays shades of brilliant light against patches of shadow for a result that a Renaissance artist might have called chiaroscuro. Specialties include a handful of ancient recipes subtly improved by Signor Ciarla (an example is the soup of pasta and beans with seafood). Original dishes include a delectable salmon Marcel Trompier with lobster sauce, and other delicacies feature a well-flavored sushi, spaghetti with clams, and a full array of shellfish. The filet of sea bass is prepared in at least three different ways, including an award-winning version with almonds.

MODERATE

La Cisterna

Via della Cisterna 13. ☎ **581-2543.** Reservations recommended. Main courses 10,000–30,000 lire ($6.25–$18.75). AE, DC, MC, V. Mon–Sat 7pm–midnight. Bus: 44, 75, or 170. ROMAN.

La Cisterna lies deep in the heart of Trastevere. For more than half a century it has been run by the Simmi family, who are genuinely interested in serving only the best as well as providing a good time for all guests. The cistern in the name comes from an ancient well discovered in the cellar, dating from Imperial Rome. When the weather's good, you can dine outside at sidewalk tables. If it's rainy or cold, you can select from one of a series of inside rooms decorated with murals, including the *Rape of the Sabine Women*. In summer you can inspect the anti-pasti—a mixed selection of hors d'oeuvres—right out on the street before going in. Specialties of the house include Roman-style suckling lamb (abbacchio); rigatoni a *l'amatriciana* (with diced bacon, olive oil, garlic, tomatoes, red peppers, and onions); pappallini Romana (wide noodles flavored with prosciutto, cheese, and eggs); shrimp; and fresh fish—especially sea bass baked with herbs.

Sabatini

Piazza Santa Maria in Trastevere 13. ☎ **581-2026.** Reservations recommended. Main courses 18,000–55,000 lire ($11.25–$34.40). AE, DC, MC, V. Daily noon–3pm and 8pm–midnight. Closed two weeks in Aug (dates vary). Bus: 44, 75, or 170. ROMAN/SEAFOOD.

Owned by the Sabatini brothers, this is one of the most popular dining spots in Rome. At night, piazza Santa Maria—one of the settings used in Fellini's *Roma*—is the center of the liveliest action in Trastevere. The place is very tied to the hustle-bustle of the Trastevere landscape and its memories of *la dolce vita* and the celebrities it used to attract. In summer, tables are placed outside on this charming square, and you can look across at the floodlit golden mosaics of the church on the piazza. If you can't get a table outside, you may be assigned to a room inside under beamed ceilings, with stenciled walls, lots of paneling, and framed oil paintings. So popular is this place that you may have to wait for a table even if you have a reservation. You can choose from a large table of antipasti. Fresh fish and shellfish, especially grilled scampi, may tempt you. The spaghetti with seafood is excellent. For a savory treat, try *pollo con pepperoni*, chicken cooked with red and green peppers. The meal price will rise if you order grilled fish or the Florentine steaks. For wine, if it goes with what you ordered, try a white Frascati or an Antinori chianti in a hand-painted pitcher.

THE OLD GHETTO
MODERATE

Vecchia Roma

Via della Tribuna di Campitelli 18. ☎ **686-4604.** Reservations recommended. Main courses 15,000–22,000 lire ($9.40–$13.75). AE, DC. Thurs–Tues 1–3:30pm and 8–11:30pm. Closed 10 days in Aug. Bus: 64. ITALIAN.

Vecchia Roma is a charming, moderately priced trattoria in the heart of the ghetto (a short walk from Michelangelo's Campidoglio). Head toward the Theater of Marcellus, but turn right at the synagogue. Movie stars have frequented the place, sitting at the crowded tables in one of the four small dining rooms. The room in the back, with a bas-relief, is more popular. The owners are known for their "fruits of the sea," or a selection of fresh seafood. The minestrone of the day is made with fresh vegetables or else you may want to begin with an order of vegetables, such as spinach. An interesting selection of antipasti is always presented, including salmon or else a vegetable antipasto. The pastas and risottos are also excellent, including linguine alla marinara with scampi. A "green" risotto with porcini mushrooms is invariably good. Excellent cuts of meat are served, including lamb, a specialty of the chef.

INEXPENSIVE

Angelino a Tormargana

Piazza Margana 37. ☎ **678-3328.** Reservations not necessary. Main courses 13,000–21,000 lire ($8.15–$13.15). MC, V. Mon–Sat noon–3:30pm and 7:30–11pm. Bus: 64, 70, 170, or 710. ROMAN.

Angelino a Tormargana, about three blocks from piazza Venezia, is housed in Goethe's historic inn. The German writer frequented the tavern between 1786 and 1788. In the years to come, it would draw a long list of celebrities, including Anna Magnani, Jean-Paul Sartre, Simone de Beavoir, even Richard Nixon. For years, the tavern had gone out of fashion, but it's now been around for so long that once again it attracts the chic crowds. Everything—from atmosphere to the food—has remained unchanged, and that's why Romans like it so. In this setting of old palazzi and ancient cobblestone squares, you can dine al fresco at tables hedged with greenery. At night the colored lanterns are turned on. The food is very much in the typical Roman trattoria style—not exceptionally imaginative, but good for what it is. I'd recommend the cold seafood risotto or else the peppery *penne all'arrabbiata* (pasta with a spicy tomato and chili pepper sauce). For a main course, you might select kidneys with mushrooms or else veal scaloppine flavored with lemon juice. Other main dish selections are *pollo alla diavola*, grilled deviled chicken, and tripe.

Da Giggetto

Via del Portico d'Ottavia 21–22. ☎ **686-1105.** Reservations recommended. Main courses 15,000–22,000 lire ($9.40–$13.75). AE, DC, MC, V. Tues–Sun 12:30–3pm and 7:30–11pm. Closed Aug 1–15. Bus: 62, 64, 75, or 170. ROMAN.

Da Giggetto, in the old ghetto, is a short walk from the Theater of Marcellus. Not only is it right next to these ruins, but old Roman columns extend practically to its doorway. The Romans flock to this bustling trattoria for their special traditional dishes. None is more typical than *carciofi alla giudia*, the baby-tender fried artichokes—thistles to make you whistle with delight. This is a true delicacy! The cheese concoction, mozzarella in carrozza, is another delight. Yet another specialty is zucchini flowers stuffed with mozzarella and anchovies. Or else sample fettuccine alla matriciana, shrimp sautéed in garlic and olive oil, tripe, saltimbocca, or codfish.

NEAR THE CIRCUS MAXIMUS, THE FORUM & THE COLOSSEUM
MODERATE

Alvaro al Circo Massimo

Via dei Cerchi 53. ☎ **678-6112.** Reservations required. Main courses 40,000–60,000 lire ($25–$37.50). AE, MC, V. Tues–Sun 1–3pm; Tues–Sat 7–11pm. Closed Aug. Metro: Circo Massimo. Bus: 15, 90, or 160. ITALIAN.

Alvaro al Circo Massimo is the closest thing in Rome to a genuine provincial inn. It's at the edge of the Circus Maximus, which brings back memories of *Ben Hur*. Here is all the decor associated with Italian taverns, including corn on the cob hanging from the ceiling and rolls of fat sausages. You can begin with the antipasti or one of the fine pasta dishes, such as fettuccine. Meat courses are well prepared, and there is an array of fresh fish. Other specialties include risotto with seafood; tagliolini with mushrooms and black truffles; roasted turbot with potatoes; and many other kinds of seafood. They are especially well stocked with seafood, exotic seasonal mushrooms, and black truffles. A basket of fresh fruit rounds out the repast. Try to linger longer and make an evening of it—the atmosphere is mellow.

INEXPENSIVE

ⓢ Abruzzi

Via de Vaccaro 1. ☎ **679-3897.** Reservations recommended. Main courses 12,000–18,000 lire ($7.50–$11.25). DC, MC, V. Sun–Fri 12:30–3pm and 7:30–10:30pm. Closed two weeks in Aug (dates vary). Bus: 64, 70, or 75. ABRUZZI.

Abruzzi takes its name from a little-explored region east of Rome known for its haunting beauty and curious superstitions. The restaurant is located at one side of piazza SS. Apostoli, just a short walk from piazza Venezia. Many young people have selected this restaurant as their enduring favorite—probably because they get good food here at reasonable prices. The chef is justly praised for his satisfying assortment of cold antipasti. You can make your own selection from the trolley cart. With your beginning, we suggest a liter of garnet-red wine; we once had one whose bouquet was suggestive of the wildflowers of Abruzzi. If you'd like a soup as well, you'll find a good stracciatella (made with a thin batter of eggs and grated parmesan cheese poured into a boiling chicken broth). A typical main dish is saltimbocca, the amusing name ("jump-in-the-mouth") for tender slices of veal that have been skewered with slices of ham, sautéed in butter, and seasoned with marsala.

ALONG THE TIBER

Il Canto del Riso

Moored in the Tiber, in front of no. 7 lungotevere dei Mellini. ☎ **32-20-859.** Reservations required. Main courses 15,000–28,000 lire ($9.40–$17.50). No credit cards. Daily 12:30–3pm and 7:30pm–midnight. Closed Sun night and Mon in winter. Metro: Piazza Cavour. ITALIAN.

This barge and passenger ship is permanently moored beside one of the quays of the Tiber, a short walk north of Ponte Cavour. The barge which contains this restaurant was originally designed as a floating swimming pool, offering midsummer recreation for thousands of Roman teenagers between 1960 and 1990. Eventually declared obsolete, it has functioned since 1990 as a floating restaurant you'll see today. Below decks, you'll find a cozy dining room outfitted with nautical accessories. Many diners prefer to eat here during warm weather, when management expands its premises by setting up tables on the riverside quay. Then, strings of colored lights and potted plants add a festive note, despite the nearby traffic that races along parallel to the edges of the Tiber.

Menu items include veal, lamb, beef, and lots of fish and seafood, especially shrimp, mussels, and clams in tomato-garlic sauce, served as dressings for pastas or as main courses. Also featured are many kinds of risotto, including varieties made with asparagus, artichokes, spinach, and other ingredients favored by vegetarians.

MONTE TESTACCIO

Checchino dal 1887

Via di Monte Testaccio 30. ☎ **574-6318.** Reservations recommended. Main courses 12,000–26,000 lire ($7.50–$16.25). AE, DC, MC, V. Tues–Sun 12:30–3pm; Tues–Sat 8–11pm.

🏵 Family-Friendly Restaurants

Ambasciata d'Abruzzo (see p. 140)   This all-you-can-eat place is recommended for its lively excitement as much as for its hearty cuisine. Your children can pick and choose what they want from a wide assortment of food.

Il Matriciano (see p. 150)   This is a safe, clean, and reasonably priced family restaurant near St. Peter's. It's good country fare—nothing fancy.

Closed Aug, one week around Christmas, and Sun for lunch between June and Sept. Bus: 27. ROMAN.

In A.D. 55, Nero ordered that Rome's thousands of broken amphoras and terra-cotta roof tiles be stacked in a carefully designated pile to the east of the Tiber, just west of Pyramide and today's Ostia Railway Station. Over the centuries, the mound grew to a height of around 200 feet, then compacted to form the center-piece for one of the city's most unusual neighborhoods. Eventually, houses were built on the terra-cotta mound, and caves were dug into its mass for the storage of wine and foodstuffs. (A constant temperature of 50°F was maintained, thanks to the porosity of the terra cotta, throughout the winter and summer.)

During the 1800s, a local wine shop flourished by selling drinks to the corps of butchers working in the neighborhood's many slaughterhouses. In 1887, the ancestors of the present owners obtained a license to sell food, thus giving birth to the restaurant you'll find on these premises today. Slaughterhouse workers in those days were paid part of their meager salaries with the *quinto quarto* (fifth quarter) of each day's slaughter (i.e., the tail, the feet, the intestines, and the offal), which otherwise had no commercial value. Following many centuries of Roman traditions, Ferminia, the wine shop's cook, somehow transformed these products into the tripe and oxtail dishes that form an integral part of the Roman working-class diet to this day.

Many Italian diners come here to relish these dishes, which admittedly might not be to every foreign visitor's taste. They include *rigatone con pajata* (pasta with small intestines), *coda alla vaccinara* (oxtail stew), *fagiole e cotiche* (beans with intestinal fat), and other examples of *la cocina povera* (food of the poor). Less adventurous, and probably more appealing to readers of this guide, are the restaurant's array of well-prepared salads, soups, pastas, steaks, cutlets, grills, and ice creams, which the kitchens produce in abundance. The English-speaking staff is helpful and kind, tactfully proposing well-flavored alternatives to a cuisine which, at least in Rome, is by now a well-established legend.

APPIAN WAY

Hostaria l'Archeologia
Va Appia Antica 139. ☎ **788-0494.** Reservations recommended, especially on weekends. Main courses 18,000–22,000 lire ($11.25–$13.75). AE, DC, MC, V. Fri–Wed 12:30–3:30pm and 8–10:30pm. Bus: 60. ROMAN/ITALIAN.

Hostaria l'Archeologia, on the historic Appian Way, is only a short walk from the catacombs of St. Sebastian. The family-run restaurant is like an 18th-century vil-lage tavern with lots of atmosphere, strings of garlic and corn, oddments of cop-per hanging from the ceiling, earth-brown beams, and sienna-washed walls. In summer, guests dine in the garden out back, sitting under the spreading wisteria.

For the chilly months, there are two separate dining rooms on either side of a gravel walkway. The Roman victuals are first-rate; you can glimpse the kitchen from behind a partition from the exterior garden parking lot. Many Roman families visit on the weekend, sometimes as many as 30 diners in a group.

Of special interest is the wine cellar, excavated in an ancient Roman tomb. Wines dating back to 1800 are kept there. You go through an iron gate, down some stairs, and into the underground cavern. Along the way, you can still see the holes once occupied by funeral urns.

AN ENGLISH TEA ROOM

Babington's Tea Rooms

Piazza di Spagna 23. ☎ **678-6027.** Reservations not necessary. Main courses 19,000–36,000 lire ($11.90–$22.50); brunch 45,000 lire ($28.15). AE, MC, DC, V. Wed–Mon 9am–8pm. Metro: Piazza di Spagna. ENGLISH/MEDITERRANEAN.

When Victoria was on the English throne in 1893, an Englishwoman named Anne Mary Babington arrived in Rome and couldn't find a place for "a good cuppa." With stubborn determination, she opened her own tea rooms near the foot of the Spanish Steps, and the rooms are still going strong. You can order everything from Scottish scones to a club sandwich to Ceylon tea to American coffee. Brunch is served at all hours. Pastries cost from 4,000 to 13,000 lire ($2.50 to $8.15), while a pot of tea (dozens of varieties available) goes for 12,000 lire ($7.50). Popular menu items include English muffins, pancakes, and waffles.

FOR VEGETARIANS

Antico Bottaro

Passeggiata di Ripetta 15. ☎ **32-40-200.** Reservations recommended. Main courses 17,000–26,000 lire ($10.65–$16.25). AE, DC, MC, V. Tues–Sun 8–11:30pm. Metro: Flaminio. VEGETARIAN.

Established in the early 1990s, this is the second vegetarian restaurant opened by Rome's most prominent vegetarian guru, Claudio Vannini. (His older, better-known, and somewhat less expensive vegetarian restaurant, Margutta Vegetariano, is recommended separately below.) Set within a Renaissance building on a narrow street near piazza del Popolo, Antico Bottaro offers a consciously formal setting, a sense of grandeur, and food items that reflect the agrarian bounty of Italy. Menu items include a seasonally changing selection of risotto and pasta, garnished with asparagus, exotic mushrooms, truffles, and/or a lavish array of herbs; soufflés made with spinach, wild mushrooms, potatoes, and whatever happens to be fresh at the market that day; meatless goulash; carefully prepared crudités; and eggplant parmigiana. The restaurant carries a wide selection of ciders and wines.

Margutta Vegetariano

Via Margutta 119. ☎ **678-6033.** Reservations recommended. Main courses 9,000–19,000 lire ($5.65–$11.90). AE, DC, MC, V. Mon–Sat 1–3pm and 7:30–10:30pm. Closed two weeks in August. Metro: Piazza di Spagna. VEGETARIAN.

Established in 1980 by Claudio Vannini, an enthusiast of new-wave thinking and Indian philosophy, and a former friend and neighbor of Federico Fellini, this functioned for many years as one of Rome's only vegetarian restaurants. Partly because of the patronage of Mr. Fellini and his entourage, and partly because of its excellent cuisine, the restaurant quickly became a stylish favorite of Italian film stars and TV personalities. Recent visitors have included Michael Bolton (in 1993), Marcello Mastroianni, and hundreds of less celebrated clients who ignore the traditional riches of Italian cuisine in favor of the high-fiber specials served within. In an 18th-century building, you can order from a sophisticated list of risotto and pasta, herb-enriched soups, mixed salads, a mélange of fried vegetables, meatless goulash, soyburgers, and a selection of soufflés made with potatoes, spinach, or wild mushrooms. Eggplant parmigiana is a perennial favorite. There's also a large selection of wines and ciders. In 1993, Vannini established a second vegetarian restaurant, Antico Bottaro (recommended separately above).

6

What to See & Do in Rome

Rome is studded with ancient monuments that silently evoke its history as one of the greatest centers of Western civilization. In the millennium of the Eternal City's influence, all roads led to Rome with good reason. It became one of the first cosmopolitan cities in the world, importing slaves, gladiators, great art—even citizens—from the far corners of the Empire. With all its carnage and mismanagement, it left a legacy of law and an uncanny lesson in how to conquer enemies by absorbing their cultures.

But ancient Rome is only part of the spectacle. The Vatican has had a major effect in making the city a center of world tourism. Although Vatican architects stripped down much of the glory of the past, they created great Renaissance treasures, occasionally incorporating the old—as Michelangelo did in turning the Baths of Diocletian into a church.

In the years that followed, Bernini adorned the city with the wonders of the baroque, especially the fountains. The modern sightseer even owes a debt (as reluctant as one may be to acknowledge it) to Mussolini, who did much to dig out the past, particularly at the Imperial Forum. Today, besides being the Italian capital, Rome, in a larger sense, belongs to the world.

SUGGESTED ITINERARIES

These itineraries obviously are designed for the first-time visitor; the more seasoned traveler will want to seek out other treasures. However, such sights as the Vatican Museum can be visited virtually every day of the year, and something new and artistically different will be waiting.

If You Have 1 Day

Far too brief—after all, Rome wasn't built in a day and you aren't likely to see it in a day either, but make the most of your limited time. You'll basically have to decide on the legacy of imperial Rome—mainly the Roman Forum, the Imperial Forum, and the Colosseum, or else St. Peter's and the Vatican. Walk along the Spanish Steps at sunset. At night go to the piazza del Campidoglio for a fantastic view of the Forum below. Have a nightcap on the via

Veneto which, although past its prime, is still a lure for the first-time visitor. Toss a coin in the Trevi fountain and promise a return visit to Rome.

If You Have 2 Days

If you elected to see the Roman Forum and the Colosseum, then spend the second day exploring St. Peter's and the Vatican Museum (or vice versa). Have dinner that night in a restaurant in Trastevere.

If You Have 3 Days

Spend your first two days as above. Go in the morning to the Pantheon in the heart of Old Rome, then try to explore two museums after lunch: Castel Sant'Angelo and the Etruscan Museum. Have dinner at a restaurant on piazza Navona.

If You Have 5 Days

Spend your first three days as above. On Day 4 head for the environs, notably Tivoli, where you can see the Villa d'Este and Hadrian's Villa. On Day 5 explore the ruins of Ostia Antica, return to Rome for lunch, and visit the Galeria Borghese and Basilica di San Giovanni in Laterano in the afternoon. If available in the evening, try to attend an opera at the Baths of Caracalla.

1 Attractions

THE TOP ATTRACTIONS

In addition to the top attractions in the city itself, there are several places in the environs of Rome worth visiting before leaving this part of the country. It would be a shame to strike out for Naples or Florence without having at least visited Hadrian's Villa and the Villa d'Este, not to mention Palestrina and Ostia Antica (see "Easy Excursions," later in this chapter).

✪ ST. PETER'S BASILICA

As you stand in Bernini's **piazza di San Pietro** (St. Peter's Square), you'll be in the arms of an ellipse dominated by St. Peter's (☎ 698-4466). Like a loving parent, the Doric-pillared colonnade reaches out to embrace the faithful. Holding 300,000 is no problem for this square. To reach it, take bus no. 23, 30, 32, 49, 51, or 64.

In the center of the square is an Egyptian obelisk, brought from the ancient city of Heliopolis on the Nile Delta, and used to adorn Nero's Circus, which was nearby. Flanking the obelisk are two 17th-century fountains—the one on the right (facing the basilica) by Carlo Maderno, who designed the facade of St. Peter's, was placed there by Bernini himself; the other is by Carlo Fontana.

Inside, the size of this famous church (open daily from 7am to 7pm April through August, daily from 7am to 6pm September through March) is

Impressions

Turn all the pages of history, but Fortune never produced a greater example of her own fickleness than the city of Rome, once the most beautiful and magnificent of all that ever were or will be . . . not a city in truth, but a certain part of heaven.
                                                                —Poggio Bracciolini (1380–1459)

> **? Did You Know?**
>
> • Along with miles of headless statues and acres of paintings, Rome has 913 churches.
>
> • Some Mongol khans and Turkish chieftains pushed westward to conquer the Roman Empire after it had ceased to exist.
>
> • At the time of Julius Caesar and Augustus, Rome's population reached the million mark, the largest city in the Western world. Some historians claim that by the year A.D. 500 only 10,000 inhabitants were left.
>
> • Pope Leo III sneaked up on Charlemagne and set an imperial crown on his head, a surprise coronation that launched a precedent of Holy Roman Emperors being crowned by popes in Rome.
>
> • More than 90% of Romans live in private apartments, some rising 10 floors without elevators.
>
> • The bronze of Marcus Aurelius, one of the world's greatest equestrian statues, escaped being melted down because the early Christians thought the statue was of Constantine.
>
> • The Theater of Marcellus incorporated a gory realism in some of its stage plays: condemned prisoners were often butchered before audiences as part of the plot.
>
> • Christians were not fed to the lions at the Colosseum, but in one day 5,000 animals were slaughtered (one about every 10 seconds). North Africa's native lions and elephants were rendered extinct.

awe-inspiring—although its dimensions are not apparent at first. Guides like to point out to Americans that the basilica is like two football fields joined together. St. Peter's is said to have been built over the tomb of the crucified saint. Originally, it was erected on the order of Constantine, but the present structure is essentially Renaissance and baroque; it showcases the talents of some of Italy's greatest artists: Bramante, Raphael, Michelangelo, and Maderno.

In a church of such grandeur—overwhelming in its detail of gilt, marble, and mosaic—don't expect subtlety. But the basilica is rich in art. The truly devout are prone to kiss the feet of the 13th-century bronze of St. Peter, attributed to Arnolfo di Cambio (at the far reaches of the nave, against a corner pillar on the right). Under Michelangelo's dome is the celebrated *baldacchino* by Bernini, resting over the papal altar. The canopy was created in the 17th century—in part, so it is said, from bronze stripped from the Pantheon. However, analysis of the bronze seems to contradict that.

In the nave on the right (the first chapel) is the best-known piece of sculpture, the *Pietà* that Michelangelo sculpted while still in his early 20s. In one of the worst acts of vandalism on record, a madman screaming "I am Jesus Christ" attacked the *Pietà*, battering the Madonna's stone arm, the folded veil, her left eyelid, and nose. Now restored, the *Pietà* is protected by a wall of reinforced glass.

Much farther on, in the right wing of the transept near the Chapel of St. Michael, rests Canova's neoclassic sculptural tribute to Pope Clement XIII.

In addition, you can visit the sacristy and treasury, filled with jewel-studded chalices, reliquaries, and copes. One robe worn by Pius XII strikes a simple note in these halls of elegance. Later you can make a visit underground to the **Vatican**

Impressions

As a whole St. Peter's is fit for nothing but a ballroom, and it is a little too gaudy even for that.

—John Ruskin, Letter to the Rev. Thomas Dale, December 1840.

grottoes, with their tombs, both ancient and modern (Pope John XXII gets the most adulation). The grottoes are open daily from 7am to 6pm April through September, daily from 7am to 5pm October through March.

To go even farther down, to the area around St. Peter's tomb, you must apply several days beforehand to the excavations office beneath Arco della Campana to the left of the basilica. You can make your applications Monday through Saturday from 9am to noon and 2 to 5pm. It is reached by passing under the arch to the left of the facade of St. Peter's. For 10,000 lire ($6.25), you'll take a guided tour of the tombs that were excavated in the 1940s, 23 feet beneath the floor of the church.

The grandest sight is yet to come: the climb to Michelangelo's dome, which towers about 375 feet high. Although you can walk up the steps for 5,000 lire ($3.15), we recommend the elevator for as far as it'll carry you; the cost is 6,000 lire ($3.75).

The dome is open daily from 8am to 6:15pm March through September, and daily from 8am to 4:30pm October through February. You can walk along the roof, for which you'll be rewarded with a panoramic view of Rome and the Vatican.

Note: To be admitted to St. Peter's women are advised to wear longer skirts or pants—anything that covers the knees. Men in shorts are not allowed in. Sleeveless tops are not allowed for either gender.

Papal Audiences Private audiences with the pope are not normally a possibility and procedures would in any case begin at local ecclesiastical or nunciature levels. Public audiences with the pope are given each Wednesday morning except when the pope is absent from Rome. The audience begins at 11am, but sometimes in the summer period, because of the heat, it begins at 10am. The general audience takes place in the Paul VI Hall of Audiences, although to accommodate very large attendances, the Basilica of St. Peter's and St. Peter's Square may also be used. Anyone is welcome.

To attend a general audience, you can obtain a free ticket from the office of the Prefecture of Papal Household, accessible from St. Peter's Square by the Bronze Door, situated where the right-hand colonnade begins, as one looks toward the basilica. The office is open Monday through Saturday from 9am to 1pm. On Monday and Tuesday the entrance cards for the audience are immediately available; often on the Wednesday before the audience the office is not accessible, although if there is space one can go to the audience even without a ticket.

Prospective visitors should write to the Prefecture of the Papal Household, 00120 Città del Vaticano (☎ 6982), indicating their language, the dates of their visit, the number of people in the party, and, if possible, the hotel in Rome to which the cards should be sent by hand on the afternoon preceding the audience. American Catholics, armed with a letter of introduction from their parish priest, should apply to the North American College, via Dell'Umiltà 30, 00187 Rome (☎ 678-91-84).

Rome Attractions

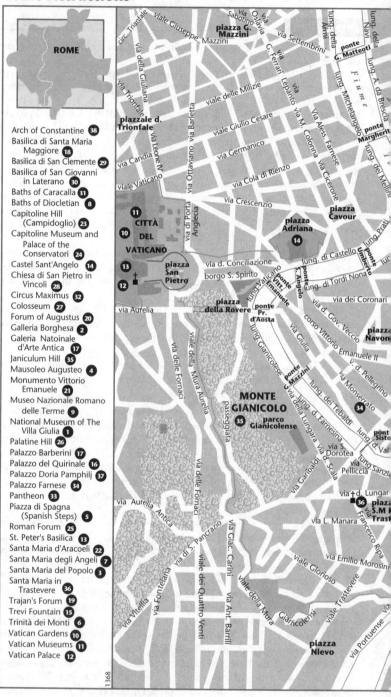

1368

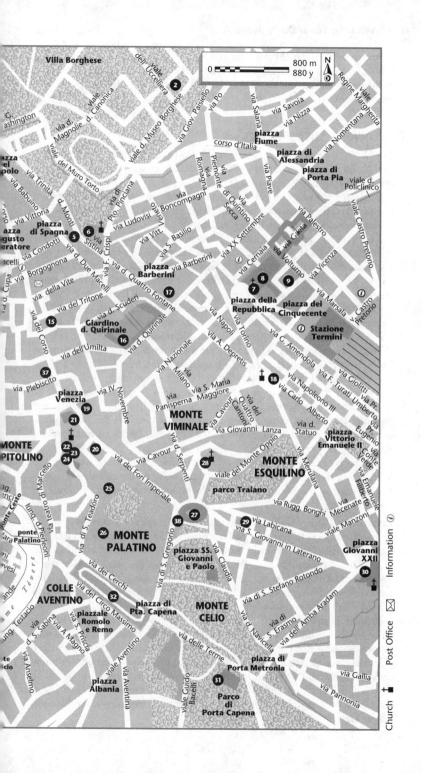

Church   ✝ ■   Post Office ⊠   Information ⓘ

At noon on Sunday the pope speaks briefly from his study window and gives his blessing to the visitors and pilgrims gathered in St. Peter's Square. From about mid-July to mid-September the Angelus and blessing take place at the summer residence at Castelgandolfo, some 16 miles out of Rome and accessible by Metro and bus.

✪ VATICAN & SISTINE CHAPEL

In 1929 the Lateran Treaty between Pope Pius XI and the Italian government created Vatican City, viale Vaticano (☎ 6988-4466), the world's smallest independent state, located in Rome.

This state may be small, but it contains a gigantic repository of treasures from antiquity and the Renaissance housed in labyrinthine galleries. The Vatican's art collection reaches its apex in the Sistine Chapel.

The Vatican museums (a house of museums) comprise a series of lavishly adorned palaces and galleries built over the centuries. The entrance is on viale Vaticano, a long walk around from St. Peter's Square. Take bus no. 19, 23, 32, 34, 49, 51, or 64; or the Metro to the Ottaviano station; or a taxi. The museums are open Monday through Saturday (except religious holidays) from 8:45am to 1:45pm (8:45am to 4:45pm from July to the end of September and the week before and after Easter). Ticket sales stop one hour before closing time. The admission price may seem high—13,000 lire ($8.15) for adults and 8,000 lire ($5) for children—but it's reasonable when you see what's inside. Entrance is free on the last Sunday of each month. A cafeteria is open to visitors from 8:45am to 2:30pm (to 4:30pm from July to the end of September and during Easter week).

Visitors to the Vatican museums can follow one of four itineraries—A, B, C, or D—according to the time they have at their disposal (from 1.5 to 5 hours) and their special interests. Determine your choice by consulting large-size panels placed at the entrance; then follow the letter and color of the itinerary chosen. Facilities for disabled visitors are available.

Obviously, 1, 2, or even 20 trips will not be enough to see the wealth of the Vatican, much less digest it. With that in mind, we've previewed only a representative sampling of masterpieces. A dozen museums and galleries should be inspected.

Pinacoteca (Picture Gallery)   After climbing the spiral stairway, keep to the right; the path will take you to the Pinacoteca, which houses paintings and tapestries from the 11th to the 19th centuries. For a break with the Byzantine, see one of the Vatican's finest artworks—the *Stefaneschi Triptych* (six panels) by Giotto and his assistants. You'll also see the works of Fra Angelico, the 15th-century Dominican monk who distinguished himself as a miniaturist (his *Virgin with Child* is justly praised—look for the microscopic eyes of the Madonna).

In the Raphael salon you'll find three paintings by that giant of the Renaissance—including the *Coronation of the Virgin,* the *Virgin of Foligno* and *The Transfiguration* (completed by Raphael shortly before his death). There are also eight tapestries made by Flemish weavers from cartoons by Raphael. Seek out Leonardo da Vinci's masterful—but uncompleted—*St. Jerome with the Lion,* as well as Giovanni Bellini's *Pietà.* One of Titian's greatest works, the *Virgin of Frari,* is also displayed. Finally, feast your eyes on one of the masterpieces of the Baroque period, Carvaggio's *Deposition from the Cross.*

Egyptian-Gregorian Museum   Review the grandeur of the Pharaohs by studying sarcophagi, mummies, statues of goddesses, vases, jewelry, sculptured pink-granite statues, and hieroglyphics.

Estruscan-Gregorian Museum   With sarcophagi, a chariot, bronzes, urns, jewelry, and terra-cotta vases, this gallery affords remarkable insights into an ancient civilization. One of the most acclaimed exhibits is the Regolini-Galassi tomb, unearthed at Cerveteri (see "Easy Excursions," later in this chapter) in the 19th century. It shares top honors with the *Mars of Todi,* a bronze sculpture that probably dates from the 5th century B.C.

Pius Clementinus Museum   Here you'll find Greek and Roman sculptures, many of which are immediately recognizable masterpieces. In the rotunda is a large gilded bronze of Hercules that dates from the late 2nd century A.D. Other major works of sculpture are under porticoes in cabinets that open onto the Belvedere courtyard. Dating from the 1st century B.C., one sculpture shows Laocoön and his two sons locked in an eternal struggle with the serpents. The incomparable *Apollo of Belvedere* (a late Roman reproduction of an authentic Greek work from the 4th century B.C.) has become the symbol of classic male beauty. The rippling muscles of the *Torso of Belvedere,* a partially preserved Greek statue (1st century B.C.) that was much admired by the artists of the Renaissance, especially Michelangelo, reveal an intricate knowledge of the human body.

Chiaramonti Museum   You'll find a dazzling array of Roman sculpture and copies of Greek originals in these galleries. In the following section, called Braccio Nuovo, you can admire *The Nile,* a magnificent reproduction of a long-lost Hellenistic original, and one of the most remarkable pieces of sculpture from antiquity. The imposing statue of Augustus of Prima Porta presents him as a regal commander.

Vatican Library   The Library is richly decorated and frescoed, representing the work of a team of Mannerist painters commissioned by Sixtus V.

Stanze of Raphael   While still a young man, Raphael was given one of the greatest assignments of his short life: the decoration of a series of rooms in the apartments of Pope Julius II. The decoration was carried out by Raphael and his workshop between 1508 and 1524. In these works, Raphael achieves the Renaissance aim of blending classic beauty with realism. In the first chamber, the Stanza dell'Incendio, you'll see much of the work of Raphael's pupils, but little of the master—except in the fresco across from the window. The figure of the partially draped man rescuing an older comrade (to the left of the fresco) is generally attributed to Raphael.

Raphael reigns supreme in the next and most important salon, the Stanza della Segnatura, the first room decorated by the artist, where you'll find the majestic *School of Athens,* one of the artist's best-known works, which depicts such figures as Aristotle and Plato (and even Raphael himself). Another well-known masterpiece, the *Disputà del Sacramento,* is across from it. The Stanza d'Eliodoro, also by the master, manages to flatter Raphael's papal patrons (Julius II and Leo X) without compromising his art (although one rather fanciful fresco depicts the pope driving Attila from Rome). Finally, there's the Sala di Constantino, which was completed by his students after Raphael's death. And the loggia, frescoed with more than 50 scenes from the Bible, was designed by Raphael, although the actual work was done by his loyal students.

Collection of Modern Religious Art   This museum represents the American artists' first invasion of the Vatican. Before this museum opened in 1973, the church limited its purchases to European art, and usually did not exhibit any works created after the 18th century. But Pope Paul VI's hobby changed all that. Of the 55 rooms in the new museum complex, at least 12 are devoted solely to American artists. All the works chosen for the museum were judged on the basis of their "spiritual and religious values," but religious groups outside the Vatican are represented as well. Among the American works is Leonard Baskin's five-foot bronze sculpture of *Isaac.* Modern Italian artists such as de Chirico and Manzù are also displayed, and there's a special room for the paintings of the French artist Georges Rouault.

Borgia Apartments   These apartments, frescoed with biblical scenes by Pinturicchio of Umbria and his assistants, were designed for Pope Alexander VI (the famous Borgia pope). The rooms, although generally badly lit, have great splendor and style. At the end of The Stanze of Raphael is the Chapel of Nicholas V, an intimate interlude within this field of museums. The chapel was frescoed by the Dominican monk Fra Angelico, probably the most saintly of all Italian painters.

Sistine Chapel   Michelangelo, of course, considered himself a sculptor, not a painter. While in his 30s, he was virtually commanded by Julius II to stop work on the pope's own tomb and to devote his considerable talents to painting ceiling frescoes—an art form of which the Florentine master was contemptuous.

Michelangelo labored for four years (1508–12) over this epic project, which was so physically taxing that it permanently damaged his eyesight. All during the task, he had to contend with the pope's incessant urgings to hurry up; at one point, Julius threatened to topple Michelangelo from the scaffolding—or so Vasari relates.

It is ironic that a project undertaken against the artist's wishes would form his most enduring legend. Glorifying the human body as only a sculptor could, Michelangelo painted nine panels, taken from the pages Genesis, the panels surrounded by prophets and sibyls. The most notable panels detail the expulsion of Adam and Eve from the Garden of Eden, and the creation of man—where God's outstretched hand imbues Adam with spirit.

The Florentine master was in his 60s when he began to paint the masterly *Last Judgment* on the altar wall. Again working against his wishes, Michelangelo presents a more jaundiced view of people and their fate; God sits in judgment, and sinners are plunged into the mouth of hell.

A master of ceremonies under Paul III, Monsignor Biagio da Cesena, protested to the pope against the "shameless nudes" painted by Michelangelo. Michelangelo showed he wasn't above petty revenge by painting the prude with the ears of a jackass in hell. When Biagio complained to the pope, Paul III maintained that he had no jurisdiction in hell. However, Daniele de Volterra was summoned to drape clothing over some of the bare figures—thus earning for himself a dubious distinction as a haberdasher.

On the side walls are frescoes by other Renaissance masters such as Botticelli, Perugino, Luca Signorelli, Pinturicchio, Cosimo Roselli, and Ghirlandaio. We'd guess that if these paintings had been displayed by themselves in other chapels, they would be the object of special pilgrimages. But since they have to compete unfairly with the artistry of Michelangelo, they're virtually ignored by the average visitor.

The restoration of the Sistine Chapel in the 1990s touched off a worldwide debate among art historians. The Sistine Chapel was on the verge of collapse, both from its age and the weather, and restoration has taken years, as restorers used advanced computer analyses in their painstaking and controversial work. They reattached the fresco and repaired the ceiling. No longer dark and shadowy, Michelangelo's frescoes are now bright and pastel. Critics claim that in addition to removing centuries of dirt and grime, a vital second layer of paint was removed as well. Purists argue that many of the restored figures seem flat compared to the original which had more shadow and detail. Others in the media have hailed the project for having saved Michelangelo's masterpiece for future generations to appreciate.

The History Museum   This museum, founded by Pope Paul VI, was established to tell the history of the Vatican. It exhibits arms, uniforms, and armor, some of which dates back to the early days of the Renaissance. The carriages on display are those used by the popes and cardinals in religious processions. Among the showcases of dress uniforms are the colorful outfits worn by the Pontifical Army Corps, which was discontinued by Pope Paul VI.

The Ethnological Museum   The Ethnological Museum is an assemblage of works of art and objects of cultural significance from all over the world. The principal route is a half-mile walk through 25 geographical sections, which display thousands of objects covering 3,000 years of world history. The section devoted to China is especially interesting and worthwhile.

The Vatican Gardens   Separating the Vatican from the secular world on the north and west are 58 acres of lush, carefully tended gardens filled with winding paths, brilliantly colored flowers, groves of massive oaks, and ancient fountains and pools. In the midst of this pastoral setting is a small summer house, the Villa Pia, built for Pope Pius IV in 1560 by Pirro Ligorio.

On the left side of piazza San Pietro, near the Arco delle Campane, is the **Vatican Tourist Office** (☎ 6988-4466), open Monday through Saturday from 8:30am to 7pm. Here you can buy a map of the Vatican and have your questions answered about St. Peter's or the Vatican museums. Tours of the Vatican gardens, which must be arranged in advance, run from March to October, Monday through Saturday at 10am; November to February, tours are conducted only on Saturday at 10am. Tickets, which cost 16,000 lire ($10) per person, are available here at the Vatican Tourist Office. In summer, arrange tours as far in advance of departure as your schedule permits; the size of the tour group is limited to 33 people, and no reservations are taken on the phone.

✪ ROMAN FORUM

When it came to cremating Caesar, raping Sabine women, purchasing a harlot for the night, or sacrificing a naked victim, the Roman Forum (Foro Romano), via dei Fori Imperiali (☎ 699-0110), was where the action was hot. Traversed by via Sacra, it was built in the marshy land between the Palatine and the Capitoline hills. It flourished as the center of Roman life in the days of the Republic, before it gradually lost prestige to the Imperial Forum.

Be warned: Expect only fragmented monuments, an arch or two, and lots of overturned boulders. That any semblance of the Forum remains today is miraculous, as it was used for years, like the Colosseum, as a quarry. Eventually it reverted to what the Italians call *campo vaccino* (cow pasture). But excavations in the 19th century began to bring to light one of the world's most historic spots.

By day, the columns of now-vanished temples and the stones from which long-forgotten orators spoke are mere shells. Bits of grass and weed grow where a triumphant Caesar was once lionized. But at night, when the Forum is silent in the moonlight, it isn't difficult to imagine that Vestal Virgins still guard the sacred temple fire. (Historical footnote: The function of the maidens was to keep the temple's sacred fire burning—but their own flame under control. Failure to do the latter sent them to an early grave . . . alive!)

You can spend at least a morning wandering alone through the ruins of the Forum. If you're content with just looking at the ruins, you can do so at your leisure. But if you want the stones to have some meaning, you'll have to purchase a detailed plan, as the temples are hard to locate otherwise.

Some of the ruins are more important than others, of course. The best of the lot is the handsomely adorned Temple of Castor and Pollux, erected in the 5th century B.C. in honor of a battle triumph. The Temple of Faustina, with its lovely columns and frieze (griffins and candelabra), was converted into the San Lorenzo in Miranda Church.

The senators used to meet and walk on the Curia's marble floors. Diocletian reconstructed the Senate, and it was later transformed into a medieval church. Across from the curia is the "Lapis Niger," a black marble slab said to be the tomb of Romulus, legendary founder of the city (you can go downstairs).

The Temple of the Vestal Virgins is a popular attraction. Some of the statuary, mostly headless, remains. The Temple of Saturn was rebuilt in the days of the Republic in the 1st century B.C.

The Temple of Julius Caesar was ordered constructed by Octavian, in honor of the place where Caesar's body was cremated following his assassination. Rather oddly placed is the Church of Santa Maria Antiqua, with Christian frescoes that go back to the 7th century A.D.

Finally, the two arches are memorable: the Arch of Septimius Severus, erected in A.D. 203 with bas-reliefs, and the Arch of Titus, with much better carving commemorating a victory in Jerusalem.

The Roman Forum can be reached by taking bus no. 27, 30, 85, 87, or 88, or the Metro to the Colosseo station. The Forum is open on Sunday and Tuesday year round from 9am to 2pm. It is open Monday and Wednesday through Saturday on the following dates: June 1 to July 15, 9am to 7pm; May and July 16 to August 15, 9am to 6:30pm; April 16 to April 30 and August 16 to August 31, 9am to 6pm; March 16 to April 15, 9am to 5:30pm; February 16 to March 15 and October, 9am to 5pm; and November through January 15, 9am to 4:30pm. It is closed from January 16 to February 15. Last admission is always one hour before it closes. Admission costs 10,000 lire ($6.25) for adults, free for children under 12 if accompanied by adults.

PALATINE HILL

A long walk up from the Roman Forum leads to the Palatine Hill, one of the seven hills of Rome. Your ticket from the Forum will admit you to this attraction (it's open the same hours). The Palatine, tradition tells us, was the spot on which the first settlers built their huts, under the direction of Romulus. In later years the hill became a patrican residential district that attracted such citizens as Cicero. In time, however, the area was gobbled up by imperial palaces, and it drew a famous and infamous roster of tenants, such as Caligula (who was murdered here), Nero, Tiberius, and Domitian.

Only the ruins of its former grandeur remain today, and you really need to be an archaeologist to make sense of them, as they are more difficult to understand than those in the Forum. But even if you're not interested in the past, it's worth the climb for the panoramic, sweeping view of both the Roman and Imperial forums, as well as the Capitoline Hill and the Colosseum.

Of all the ruins to inspect, none is finer than the so-called **House of Livia** (the "abominable grandmother" of Robert Graves's *I, Claudius*). Actually, archaeological research indicates that the house was in fact that of her husband, Augustus. Livia used to slip him maidens noted for their discretion. A guard who controls the gate will show you the mythological frescoes reminiscent of those discovered at Herculaneum and Pompeii.

Domitian lived in the Imperial Palace—the **Domus Augustana**—which is an easy walk away, in the virtual heart of the Palatine. In the middle of the once-lavish estate—now stripped to the brick—is a large peristyle with a fountain. Domitian also ordered the building of the Palatine Stadium or **Hippodrome,** below, as well as a once-remarkable structure, the **Palace of Flavii,** which has a triclinium, or great hall. When not overseeing real estate construction, Domitian was ensuring that his name became immortal in the history of vice.

When the glory that was Rome has completely overwhelmed you, you can enjoy a respite in the cooling **Farnese Gardens,** laid out in the 16th century, which incorporate some of the designs of Michelangelo.

✪ COLOSSEUM

In spite of the fact that it's a mere shell, the Colosseum (Colosseo), piazzale del Colosseo, via dei Fori Imperiali (☎ 700-4261), remains the greatest architectural inheritance from ancient Rome. Take the Metro to Colosseo. Vespasian ordered the construction of the elliptically shaped bowl, called the Amphitheatrum Flavium, in A.D. 72; it was inaugurated by Titus in A.D. 80 with a many-weeks-long bloody combat between gladiators and wild beasts. At its peak, under the cruel Domitian, the Colosseum could seat 50,000 spectators. The vestal virgins from the temple screamed for blood, as more and more exotic animals were shipped in from the far corners of the empire to satisfy jaded tastes (lion vs. bear, two humans vs. hippopotamus). Not-so-mock naval battles were staged (the canopied Colosseum could be flooded), in which the defeated combatants might have their lives spared if they put up a good fight. One of the most enduring legends linked to the Colosseum—that Christians were fed to the lions here—is considered to be without foundation by some historians.

Long after it ceased to be an arena to amuse sadistic Romans, the Colosseum was struck by an earthquake. Centuries later it was used as a quarry, and its rich marble facing was stripped away to build palaces and churches.

On one side, part of the original four tiers remain; the first three levels were constructed in Doric, Ionic, and Corinthian styles to lend it variety.

Admission to the Colosseum at the street level is free; it costs 6,000 lire ($3.75) to visit the upper levels. It is open on Wednesday and holidays from 9am to 2pm. It is also open Monday, Tuesday, and Thursday through Saturday on the following dates: June 1 to July 15, 9am to 7pm; May and July 16 to August 15, 9am to 6:30pm; April 16 to April 30 and August 16 to August 31, 9am to 6pm; March 16 to April 15 and September, 9am to 5:30pm; February 16 to March 16 and

October, 9am to 5pm; and November to January 15, 9am to 4:30pm. It is closed from January 16 to February 15.

A highly photogenic memorial (next to the Colosseum on piazzale del Colosseo), the **Arch of Constantine** was erected in honor of Constantine's defeat of the pagan Maxentius (A.D. 306). It's a landmark in every way, physically and historically. Physically it's beautiful, perhaps marred by the aggravating traffic that zooms around it at all hours, but so intricately carved and well preserved that you almost forget the racket of the cars and buses. Many of the reliefs have nothing whatsoever to do with Constantine or his works, but tell of the victories of earlier Antonine rulers—they were apparently lifted from other, long-forgotten memorials.

Historically, the arch marks a period of great change in the history of Rome and therefore the history of the world. Rome, which had been pagan since the beginning, now had a Christian emperor, Constantine. Converted by a vision on the battlefield, he led his forces to victory, and officially ended the centuries-long persecution of the Christians. By Constantine's time many devout followers of the new religion had been put to death (oftentimes horribly) for the sake of their religion, and the new emperor put an end to it. While he did not ban paganism (which survived officially until the closing of the temples more than half a century later), he interceded on an imperial level to stop the persecutions. And by espousing Christianity himself, he began the inevitable development that culminated in the conquest of Rome by the Christian religion. The arch is a tribute to the emperor erected by the Senate in A.D. 315.

After visiting the Colosseum, it is also convenient to look at the site of the **Domus Aurea,** or the Golden House of Nero, on via Labicana on the Esquiline Hill; it faces the Colosseum and is adjacent to the Forum. The Domus Aurea was one of the most sumptuous palaces of all time, and constructed by Nero after disastrous fire swept over Rome in A.D. 64. Not much remains of its former glory, but once the floors were made of mother-of-pearl and the furniture of gold. The area that is the Colosseum today was an ornamental lake, which reflected the grandeur and glitter of the Golden House. The hollow ruins—long stripped of their lavish decorations—lie near the entrance of the Oppius Park.

During the Renaissance, painters such as Raphael chopped holes in the long-buried ceilings of the Domus Aurea to gain admittance. Once there, they were inspired by the frescoes and the small "grotesques" of cornucopia and cherubs. The word *grotto* came from this palace, as it was believed to have been built underground. Remnants of these original, almost-2,000-year-old frescoes and fragments of mosaics remain. All interiors have been closed for years.

CAPITOLINE HILL (CAMPIDOGLIO)

Of the Seven Hills of Rome, the Campidoglio, piazza del Campidoglio, is considered the most sacred—its origins stretch way back into antiquity (an Etruscan temple to Jupiter once stood on this spot). The most dramatic approach to the Capitoline Hill is to walk from piazza Venezia, the center of Rome, to via di Teatro Marcello.

On your left, you can climb the steps designed by Michelangelo. At the top of the approach is the perfectly proportioned square, piazza del Campidoglio, also laid out by the Florentine artist.

Michelangelo positioned the bronze equestrian statue of Marcus Aurelius in the center, but it has now been moved inside to be protected from pollution.

One side of the piazza is open; the others are bounded by the **Senatorium** (Town Council), the statuary-filled **Palazza dei Conservatori,** and the **Capitoline Museum** (see "Museums and Galleries" in "More Attractions," below). The Campidoglio is dramatic at night (walk around to the back for a regal view of the floodlit Roman Forum). On your return, head down the small steps on your right. If you care to climb the other steps adjoining Michelangelo's approach, they'll take you to Santa Maria d'Aracoeli (see "Churches" in "More Attractions," below). Take bus no. 46, 89, or 92.

CASTEL SANT'ANGELO

This overpowering structure, in a landmark position on the Tiber, at lungotevere Castello 50 (☎ 687-5036), was originally built in the 2nd century A.D. as a tomb for the Emperor Hadrian; it continued as an imperial mausoleum until the time of Caracalla. It is an imposing and grim castle with thick walls and cylindrical shape. If it looks like a fortress, it should, as that was its function in the Middle Ages (it was built over the Roman walls and linked by an underground passageway to the Vatican which was much used by the fleeing papacy, who escaped from unwanted visitors like Charles V, during his sack of the city in 1527).

In the 14th century it became a papal residence, enjoying various connections with Boniface IX, Nicholas V, even Julius II, patron of Michelangelo and Raphael. But its legend rests largely on its link with Pope Alexander VI, whose mistress bore him two children—Cesare and Lucrezia Borgia.

Of all the women of the Italian Renaissance, Lucrezia is the only one who commands universal recognition in the Western world; her name is a virtual synonym for black deeds such as poisoning. But popular legend is highly unreliable: Many of the charges biographers have made against her (such as incestuous involvements with her brother and father) may have been only successful attempts to blacken her name. In addition to being part of an infamous family, she was a patron of the arts and a devoted charity worker, especially after she moved to Ferrara. Her brother, Cesare, of course, is without defense—he was a Machiavellian figure who is remembered accurately as a symbol of villainy and cruel spite.

Today the highlight of the castle is a trip through the Renaissance apartments with their coffered ceilings and lush decoration. Their walls have witnessed plots and intrigues that make up some of the arch-treachery of the High Renaissance. Later, you can go through the dank cells that once rang with the screams of Cesare's victims of torture, such as Astorre Manfredi of Faenza, who was finally relieved of his pain by being murdered.

Perhaps the most famous figure imprisoned here was Benvenuto Cellini, the eminent sculptor and goldsmith, remembered chiefly for his classic, candid *Autobiography.* Cellini kept getting into trouble—murdering people, whatever—but was jailed here on a charge of "peculation" (embezzlement of public funds). He escaped, was hauled back to jail, but was finally freed.

Now an art museum, the castle halls display the history of the Roman mausoleum, along with a wide-ranging selection of ancient arms and armor. Don't fail to climb to the top terrace for another one of those dazzling views of the Eternal City. The museum, which can be visited on your way to St. Peter's, is open on Monday from 2 to 6:30pm, Tuesday through Saturday from 9am to 1pm, and on Sunday from 9am to noon. Admission is 8,000 lire ($5) per person. Take bus no. 23, 46, 49, 62, 64, 87, 98, 280, or 910. Metro: Ottaviano.

APPIAN WAY & CATACOMBS

Of all the roads that led to Rome, the **Appia Antica**—built in 312 B.C.—was the reigning leader. It eventually stretched all the way from Rome to the seaport of Brindisi, through which trade with the colonies in Greece and the East was funneled. According to the Christian tradition, it was on the Appian Way that an escaping Peter encountered the vision of Christ, which caused him to go back into the city to face subsequent martyrdom.

Along the Appian Way the patrician Romans built great monuments above the ground, while Christians met in the catacombs beneath the earth. The remains of both can be visited today. In some dank, dark grottoes (never stray too far from either your party or one of the exposed lightbulbs), you can still discover the remains of early Christian art.

Only someone wanting to write a sequel to *Quo Vadis?* would visit all the catacombs. Of those open to the public, the Catacombs of St. Callixtus and those of St. Sebastian are the most important. Both can be reached by taking bus no. 118, which leaves from near the Colosseum close to the Metro station.

The **Tomb of St. Sebastian,** called the Catacombe di San Sebastiano, is at via Appia Antica 136 (☎ 788-7035). Today the tomb of the martyr is in the basilica (church), but his original tomb was in the catacomb under the basilica. From the reign of Emperor Valerian to the reign of Emperor Constantine, the bodies of Saint Peter and Saint Paul were hidden in the catacomb. The big church was built here in the 4th century. None of the catacombs, incidentally, is a grotto; all are dug from tufo, a soft volcanic rock. This is the only Christian catacomb in Rome that is always open.

The tunnels here, if stretched out, would reach a length of seven miles. In the tunnels and mausoleums are mosaics and graffiti, along with many other pagan and Christian objects from centuries even before the time of Constantine. Visiting hours are Wednesday through Monday from 9am to noon and 2:30 to 5:30pm, and admission is 8,000 lire ($5); children under 10 are admitted free.

The **Catacombs of St. Callixtus,** via Appia Antica 110 (☎ 51-36-725), are "the most venerable and most renowned of Rome," according to Pope John XXIII. The founder of Christian archaeology, Giovanni Battista de Rossi (1822–94), called them "catacombs par excellence." They are the first cemetery of the Christian community of Rome, burial place of 16 popes in the 3rd century. They bear the name of St. Callixtus, the deacon whom the pope St. Zephyrinus put in charge of them. Callixtus himself was later elected pope (217–22). The cemeterial complex is made up of a network of galleries, stretching for nearly 15 miles. It is structured in five different levels, reaching a depth of about 30 meters. There are many sepulchral chambers and some 10,000 tombs. Paintings, sculptures, and epigraphs (with such symbols as the fish, the anchor, and the dove) provide invaluable material for the study of the life and customs of the ancient Christians and the story of their persecutions.

Entering the catacombs, one sees at once the most important crypt, that of the nine popes (three of whom were martyrs). Some of the original marble tablets of their tombs are still preserved. The next crypt is that of St. Cecilia, the patron of sacred music. This early Christian martyr received three ax strokes on her neck, the maximum allowed by Roman law, which failed to kill her outright. Further on, the famous Cubicula of the Sacraments can be reached, with 3rd-century frescoes. The catacombs were dug in the middle of the 2nd century up until the middle of the 5th century. They were cemeteries and places of prayers—never private dwellings.

Access for visitors has been improved by well-lighted galleries, providing an underground route through the maze. Admission is 8,000 lire ($5) for adults, 4,000 lire ($2.50) for children. Hours are Thursday through Tuesday from 8:30am to noon and 2:30 to 5:30pm in summer, and Thursday through Tuesday from 8:30am to noon and 2:30 to 5pm in the off-season. Take bus no. 218 from San Giovanni in Laterano to Fosse Ardeatine. Ask the driver to let you off at the Catacombs of St. Callixtus.

Of the Roman monuments, the most impressive is the **Tomb of Cecilia Metella,** on via Appia Antica, within walking distance of the catacombs. The cylindrical tomb honors the wife of one of Julius Caesar's military commanders from the Republican era. Why such an elaborate tomb for such an unimportant person in history? Cecilia Metella happened to be singled out for enduring fame because her tomb remained and the others decayed.

PANTHEON

Of all the great buildings of ancient Rome, only the Pantheon ("All the Gods"), at piazza della Rotunda (☎ 369831) remains intact today. It was built in 27 B.C. by Marcus Agrippa, and later reconstructed by Emperor Hadrian in the first part of the 2nd century A.D. This remarkable building is among the architectural wonders of the world because of its dome and its concept of space. Byron described the temple as "simple, erect, austere, severe, sublime."

The Pantheon was once ringed with white marble statues of pagan gods, such as Jupiter and Minerva, in its niches. Animals were sacrificed and burned in the center, and the smoke escaped through the only means of light, an opening at the top 27 feet in diameter. The Pantheon is 142 feet wide and 142 feet high. Michelangelo came here to study the dome before designing the cupola of St. Peter's (whose dome is 2 feet smaller than the Pantheon's).

Other statistics are equally impressive. The walls are 25 feet thick, and the bronze doors leading into the building weigh 20 tons each. The temple was converted into a church in the early 7th century.

About 125 years ago, the tomb of Raphael was discovered in the Pantheon (fans still bring him flowers). Victor Emmanuel II, king of Italy, was interred here.

The Pantheon can be reached by bus no. 64, 170, or 175 to largo di Torre Argentina. It's open (admission is free) July through September, daily from 9am to 6pm; and October through June, Monday through Saturday from 9am to 4pm, and Sunday from 9am to 1pm.

PIAZZA DI SPAGNA (SPANISH STEPS)

The Spanish Steps were the last part of the outside world that Keats saw before he died in a house at the foot of the stairs (see the "Keats-Shelley Memorial" in "Special-Interest Sightseeing," below). The steps—filled, in season, with flower vendors, jewelry dealers, and photographers snapping pictures of tourists—and the square take their names from the Spanish Embassy, which used to have its headquarters here.

At the foot of the steps is a nautically shaped fountain that was designed by Pietro Bernini (papa is not to be confused with his son, Giovanni Lorenzo Bernini, who proved to be a far greater sculptor of fountains). About two centuries ago, when the foreign art colony was in its ascendancy, the 136 steps were covered with young men and women who wanted to pose for the painter—men with their shirts unbuttoned to show off what they hoped was a Davidesque physique, and women consistently draped like Madonnas.

At the top of the steps is a good view and the 16th-century church of Trinità dei Monti, built by the French, with twin towers. Take the Metro to piazza di Spagna.

FOUNTAINS OF ROME

Rome is a city of fountains—a number of which are so exceptionally beautiful that they're worth a special pilgrimage. Some of the more famous ones are the Four Seasons and Bernini's Triton Fountain at piazza Barberini, but the two that hold the most enduring interest are the Fountain of Trevi and the waterworks at piazza Navona.

Piazza Navona, surely one of the most beautifully baroque sites in all of Rome, is like an ocher-colored gem, unspoiled by new buildings or even by traffic. The shape results from the ruins of the Stadium of Domitian, which lie underneath the present constructions. Great chariot races, some of which were rather unusual, were once held here. In one, for instance, the head of the winning horse was lopped off as he crossed the finish line and carried by runners to be offered as a sacrifice by Vestal Virgins on top of the Capitoline Hill. Historians note that in medieval times the popes used to flood the piazza to stage mock navel encounters. Today the most strenuous activities are performed by occasional fire-eaters, who go through their evening paces before an interested crowd of Romans and visitors.

Beside the twin-towered facade of the Church of Saint Agnes (17th century), the piazza boasts several other baroque masterpieces. Perhaps the best known, in the center, is Bernini's **Fountain of the Four Rivers,** whose four stone personifications symbolize the world's greatest rivers—the Ganges, Danube, della Plata, and Nile. It's fun to try to figure out which (hint: the figure with the shroud on its head is the Nile, so represented because the river's source was unknown at the time the fountain was constructed). The fountain at the south end, the **Fountain of the Moor,** is also by Bernini and dates from the same period as the church and the Fountain of the Four Rivers. The **Fountain of Neptune,** which balances that of the Moor, is a 19th-century addition. During the summer there are outdoor art shows in the evening, but visit during the day—it's the best time to inspect the fragments of the original stadium under a building on the north side of the piazza. If you're interested, walk out at the northern exit and turn left for a block. It's astonishing how much the level of the ground has risen since ancient times.

As you elbow your way through the summertime crowds around the **Fontana di Trevi (Trevi Fountain)** at piazza di Trevi, you'll find it hard to believe that this little piazza was nearly always deserted before *Three Coins in the Fountain* brought

Simple, erect, severe, austere, sublime—shrine of all saints and temple of all gods, from Jove to Jesus—spared and blest by time; looking tranquility, while falls or nods arch, empire, each thing round thee, and man plods his way through thorns to ashes— glorious dome! Shalt thou not last?—Time's scythe and tyrant's rods shiver upon thee— sanctuary upon thee—sanctuary and home of art and piety—Pantheon prime of Rome.
—Byron, *Childe Harold's Pilgrimage*

the tour buses. Today it's a must on everybody's itinerary. To do it properly, hold your lira coin in the right hand, turn your back to the fountain, and toss the coin over your shoulder (being careful not to bean anyone behind you). Then the spirit of the fountain will see to it that you return to Rome one day—or that's the tradition, at least. Actually, this is an evolution of an even older tradition of drinking from the fountain. Nathaniel Hawthorne (1804–64), in the novel *The Marble Faun,* wrote that anyone drinking from this fountain's water "has not looked upon Rome for the last time." Because of pollution, no one drank from it for years. Since the fountain has been restored in 1994 and is running again, the water is supposedly pure, owing to an electronic device that keeps the pigeons at bay. I'd still suggest you skip the "Trevi cocktail" and have a mineral water at a café instead.

Pope Urban VIII (1623–44), à Barberini, asked artists of his day to design the fountain and they did, emerging with a triumphant figure of Neptunus Rex. The figure occupies the main niche of a palace wall, and stands on a shell chariot drawn by winged steeds and led by a pair of tritons. Two allegorical figures in the side niches represent good health and fertility.

Piazza Barberini lies at the foot of several Roman streets, among them via Barberini, via Sistina, and via Vittorio Veneto. It would be a far more more pleasant spot were it not for the considerable amount of traffic swarming around its principal feature, Bernini's **Fountain of the Triton.** For more than three centuries the strange figure sitting in a vast open clam has been blowing water from his triton. Off to one side of the piazza is the clean, aristocratic side facade of the Palazzo Barberini, named for one of Rome's powerful families. The Renaissance Barberini reached their peak when a son was elected pope (Urban VIII). This Barberini pope encouraged Bernini and gave him great patronage.

As you go up via Vittorio Veneto, look for the small fountain on the right-hand corner of piazza Barberini, which is another of Bernini's works, the small **Fountain of the Bees.** At first they look more like flies, but they are the bees of the Barberini, the crest of that powerful family complete with the crossed keys of St. Peter above them (the keys were always added to a family crest when a son was elected pope).

MORE ATTRACTIONS
✪ BATHS OF CARACALLA

Named for the Emperor Caracalla, the Terme di Caracalla (☎ 575-8302) were completed in the early part of the 3rd century. The richness of decoration has faded and the lushness can only be judged from the shell of brick ruins that remain. These imperial baths at via delle Terme di Caracalla 52 can be visited for an admission fee of 6,000 lire ($3.75); children under 12 enter free. Visiting hours are April through September, Tuesday through Saturday from 9am to 6pm, and on Sunday and Monday from 9am to 1pm; and October through March, Tuesday through Saturday from 9am to 3pm, and on Sunday and Monday from 9am to 1pm.

Viewing the baths during the day is one experience. Even more fascinating, however, is to attend an opera here, perhaps a spectacular version of Verdi's *Aida* (see "Evening Entertainment," later in this chapter). Take bus no. 90 or 118.

CEMETERIES

For details of the Protestant Cemetery, refer to "Special-Interest Sightseeing," below.

Pyramid of Caius Cestius
Piazzale Ostiense. Bus 30.

Dating from the 1st century B.C., the Pyramid of Caius Cestius, about 120 feet high, looks as if it belongs to the Egyptian landscape. It was constructed during the "Cleopatra craze" in architecture that swept across Rome. The pyramid can't be entered, but it's fun to circle and photograph. Who was Caius Cestius? A rich magistrate in Imperial Rome whose tomb is more impressive than his achievements. It can be visited at any time.

Cimitero Monumentale dei Padri Cappucini
In the Church of the Immaculate Conception, via Vittorio Veneto 27. Admission 1,000 lire (65¢). Apr–Sept daily 9am–noon and 3–6:30pm; Oct–May daily 9am–noon and 3–6pm. Metro: Piazza Barberini.

This cemetery, Rome's most macabre sight, is a short walk from piazza Barberini. You enter from the first staircase on the right of the church, at the entrance to the friary. Guidebooks of old used to rank this sight along with the Forum and the Colosseum as one of the city's top attractions. Qualifying as one of the most horrifying sights in all Christendom, it is a cemetery of skulls and crossbones woven into "works of art." To make this allegorical dance of death, the bones of more than 4,000 Capuchin brothers were used. Some of the skeletons are intact, draped with Franciscan habits. The creator of this chamber of horrors? The tradition of the friars is that it was the work of a French Capuchin. Their literature suggests that the cemetery should be visited keeping in mind the historical moment of its origins, when Christians had a rich and creative cult for their dead, when great spiritual masters mediated and preached with a skull in hand. Those who have

---

★ Frommer's Favorite Rome Experiences

Fountain Hopping. Rome abounds in Renaissance and baroque fountains—lavish, theatrical, spectacular—none more so than the Trevi Fountain. They're fed by an abundant freshwater supply. A tour of them will lock in your memory. See "Fountains of Rome" in "The Top Attractions," above.

The Campidoglio at Night. Climb steps designed by Michelangelo to the back of the square to see a sound-and-light summer spectacle. Suddenly, you hear marching legions, blaring trumpets, rumbling drums—all the sounds needed to convince you you're back in the days of ancient Rome, with soldiers, soothsayers, and Vestal Virgins.

Opera at the Baths of Caracalla. In the gigantic ruins of a former Roman bath house, open-air opera is presented, none more spectacular than *Aïda*. An army of extras people the stage, and elephants or braces of horses come charging in near curtain time.

Flea-Market Shopping. Every Sunday morning (until 1pm) make your way to the flea market of Rome, stretching for two miles from Porta Portese to the Trastevere rail station. Barter, bargain, buy, or "window shop"—this array of merchandise, everything from fake antiques to illegally cut tapes, from "oddities" from the attic to portraits of Mussolini, will equal one of the shopping adventures of a lifetime.

lived through the days of crematoriums and other such massacres may view the graveyard differently, but to many who pause to think, this macabre sight of death has a message. It's not for the squeamish.

CHURCHES

St. Peter's is not the only church you should see in Rome. The city's hundreds of churches—some built with marble stripped from ancient monuments—form a major sightseeing treasure. We've highlighted the best of the lot, including four patriarchal churches of Rome that belong to the Vatican. Others are equally worth viewing, especially one designed by Michelangelo.

Basilica di San Clemente

Piazza di San Clemente, via Labicana 95. ☎ **731-5723.** Admission to church, free; grottoes, 2,000 lire ($1.25). Mon–Sat 9am–12:30pm and 3:30–6:30pm, Sun 10am–noon and 3:30–6:30pm. Metro: Colosseo.

From the Colosseum, head up via di San Giovanni in Laterano, which leads to the Basilica of Saint Clement. This isn't just another Roman church—far from it! In this church-upon-a-church, centuries of history peel away. In the 4th century a church was built over a secular house of the 1st century A.D., beside which stood a pagan temple dedicated to Mithras (god of the sun). Down in the eerie grottoes (which you can explore on your own—unlike the catacombs on the Appian Way), you'll discover well-preserved frescoes from the 1st through 3rd century A.D. After the Normans destroyed the lower church, a new one was built in the 12th century. Its chief attraction is its bronze-orange mosaic (from that period) that adorns the apse, as well as a chapel honoring St. Catherine of Alexandria (murals are by Masolino de Panicale, who decorated the Branaccaci Chapel in the Church of Carmine in Florence in the 15th century).

Basilica di San Giovanni in Laterano

Piazza di San Giovanni in Laterano 4. ☎ **698-6433.** Admission is free; cloisters, 2,000 lire ($1.25). Daily 7am–6pm. Metro: San Giovanni.

This church—not St. Peter's—is the cathedral of the diocese of Rome. Catholics all over the world refer to it as their "mother church." Originally built in A.D. 314 by Constantine, the cathedral has suffered the vicissitudes of Rome, and was badly sacked and forced to rebuild many times. Only fragmented parts of the baptistery remain from the original structure.

The present building is characterized by its 18th-century facade by Alessandro Galilei (statues of Christ and the Apostles ring the top). A terrorist bomb in 1993 caused severe damage, especially to the facade. Borromini gets the credit (some say blame) for the interior, built for Innocent X. It is said that in the misguided attempt to redecorate, frescoes by Giotto were destroyed (remains believed to have been painted by Giotto were discovered in 1952 and are now displayed). In addition, look for the unusual ceiling and the sumptuous transept, and explore the 13th-century cloisters with their twisted double columns.

The popes used to live next door at the **Lateran Palace** before the move to Avignon in the 14th century. But the most unusual sight is across the street at the "Palace of the Holy Steps," called the **Santuario della Scala Sancta,** piazza San Giovanni in Laterano (☎ 759-4619). It is alleged that these were the actual steps that Christ climbed when he was brought before Pilate. These steps are supposed to be climbed only on your knees, which you're likely to see the faithful doing throughout the day.

Basilica di Santa Maria Maggiore (Saint Mary Major)

Piazza di Santa Maria Maggiore. ☎ **483195**. Admission is free. Daily 7am–7pm. Metro: Stazione Termini.

This great church, one of the four major basilicas of Rome, was originally founded by Pope Liberius in A.D. 358 but rebuilt by Pope Sixtus III in 432–440. Its campanile, erected in the 14th century, is the loftiest in the city. Much doctored in the 18th century, the church's facade is not an accurate reflection of the treasures inside. The basilica is especially noted for the 5th-century Roman mosaics in its nave, as well as for its coffered ceiling, said to have been gilded with gold brought from the New World. In the 16th century Domenico Fontana built a now-restored "Sistine Chapel." In the following century Flaminio Ponzo designed the Pauline (Borghese) Chapel in the baroque style. The church contains the tomb of Bernini, Italy's most important architect during the flowering of the baroque in the 17th century. Ironically, the man who changed the face of Rome with his elaborate fountains was buried in a tomb so simple it takes a sleuth to track it down (to the right near the altar).

San Paolo Fuori le Mura (St. Paul Outside the Walls)

Via Ostiense. ☎ **541-0341**. Admission is free. Cloisters, Mon–Sat 9–11:45am; basilica, Mon–Sat 9am–1pm and 3–6pm. Metro: San Paolo Basilica. Bus: 23, 170, or 673.

The Basilica of St. Paul, whose origins go back to the time of Constantine, is the fourth great patriarchal church of Rome. It burned in 1823 and was subsequently rebuilt. This basilica is believed to have been erected over the tomb of St. Paul (St. Peter's was built over the tomb of that saint). From the inside, its windows may appear at first to be stained glass, but they are alabaster—the effect of glass is created by the brilliant light shining through. With its forest of single-file columns and its mosaic medallions (portraits of the various popes), it is one of the most streamlined and elegantly decorated churches in Rome. Its single most important treasure is a 12th-century candelabrum designed by Vassalletto, who is also responsible for the remarkable cloisters—in themselves worth the trip "outside the walls." They contain twisted pairs of columns enclosing a rose garden. The Benedictine monks and students sell a fine collection of souvenirs, rosaries, and bottles of Benedictine. The gift shop is open every day except Sunday and religious holidays.

Chiesa di San Pietro in Vincoli (Saint Peter in Chains)

Piazza di San Pietro in Vincoli 4A, off via degli Annibaldi. ☎ **488-2865**. Admission is free. Mon–Sat 7am–12:30pm and 3:30–6pm, Sun 7–11:45am and 3–7pm. Metro: Piazza Cavour. Bus: 11, 27, or 81.

From the Colosseum, head up a "spoke" street, via degli Annibaldi, to a church founded in the 5th century A.D. to house the chains that bound St. Peter in Palestine. The chains are preserved under glass. But the drawing card is the tomb of Julius II, with one of the world's most famous pieces of sculpture, *Moses* by Michelangelo. As readers of Irving Stone's *The Agony and the Ecstasy* know, Michelangelo was to have carved 44 magnificent figures for Julius's tomb. That didn't happen, of course, but the pope was given one of the greatest consolation prizes—a figure intended to be "minor" that is now numbered among Michelangelo's masterpieces. Of the stern father symbol of Michelangelo's *Moses*, Vasari, in his *Lives of the Artists*, wrote: "No modern work will ever equal it in beauty, no, nor ancient either."

Santa Maria degli Angeli

Piazza della Repubblica 12. ☎ **488-0812.** Admission is free. Daily 7:30am–noon and 4–6:30pm. Metro: Piazza della Repubblica.

On this site, which adjoins the National Roman Museum near the railway station, once stood the "tepidarium" of the 3rd-century Baths of Diocletian. But in the 16th century, Michelangelo—nearing the end of his life—converted the grand hall into one of the most splendid churches in Rome. Surely the artist wasn't responsible for "gilding the lily"—that is, putting *trompe-l'oeil* columns in the midst of the genuine pillars. The church is filled with tombs and paintings, but its crowning treasure is the genuine statue of St. Bruno by the great French sculptor Jean-Antoine Houdon. His sculpture is larger than life and about as real.

Santa Maria in Cosmedin

Piazza della Bocca della Verità 18. ☎ **678-1419.** Admission is free. Daily 9am–noon and 3–5pm. Bus: 57, 95, or 716.

This little church was founded in the 6th century, but subsequently rebuilt—and a campanile was added in the 12th century in the romanesque style. The church is ever popular with pilgrims drawn not by its great art treasures but by its "Mouth of Truth," a large disk under the portico. It is supposed to chomp down on the hand of liars who insert their paws. According to local legend, a former priest used to keep a scorpion in back to bite the fingers of anyone he felt was lying. In the movie *Roman Holiday,* Gregory Peck put his hand in the *bocca.* But when he pulled it out, his hand had disappeared up his sleeve, causing Audrey Hepburn to scream in shock, fearing he'd lost his hand. On one of our visits to the church, a little woman, her head draped in black, sat begging a few feet from the medallion. A scene typical enough—except this woman's right hand was covered with bandages.

Santa Maria D'Aracoeli

Piazza d'Aracoeli. Admission is free. Daily 7am–noon and 4–7pm. Bus: 46, 89, or 92.

Sharing a spot on Capitoline Hill, this landmark church was built for the Franciscans in the 13th century. According to legend, Augustus once ordered a temple erected on this spot, where a sibyl, with her gift of prophecy, forecast the coming of Christ. In the interior of the present building, you'll find a nave and two aisles, two rows with 11 pillars each, a Renaissance ceiling, and a mosaic of the Virgin over the altar in the Byzantine style. If you're sleuth enough, you'll also find a tombstone carved by the great Renaissance sculptor Donatello. The church is known for its Bufalini Chapel, a masterpiece of Pinturicchio, who frescoed it with scenes illustrating the life and death of St. Bernardino of Siena. He also depicted St. Francis receiving the stigmata. These frescoes are considered a highpoint in early Renaissance Roman painting. The church is reached by a long flight of steep steps. However, if you're on the piazza del Campidoglio, you can reach it by crossing the piazza and climbing steps on the far side of the Museo Capitolino.

Janiculum Hill (Gianicolo)

From many vantage points in the Eternal City the views are panoramic. Scenic gulpers, however, have traditionally preferred the outlook from the Janiculum Hill (across the Tiber), not one of the "Seven Hills" but certainly one of the most visited (and a stopover on many bus tours). The view is seen at its best at sundown, or at dawn when the skies are often fringed with mauve. The Janiculum was the site of a battle between Guiseppe Garibaldi and the forces of Pope Pius IX in

1870—an event commemorated today with statuary. To reach "Gianicolo" without a private car, take bus no. 41 from Ponte Sant'Angelo.

MUSEUMS & GALLERIES

✪ Capitoline Museum and Palace of the Conservatori

Piazza del Campidoglio. ☎ **6710-2475.** Admission for museum and palace 10,000 lire ($6.25). Apr–Sept, Tues 9am–1:30pm and 5–8pm, Wed–Fri 9am–1:30pm, Sat 9am–1:30pm and 8–11pm, Sun 9am–1pm. Oct–Mar, Tues and Sat 9am–1:30pm and 5–8pm, Wed–Fri 9am–1:30pm, Sun 9am–1pm. Bus: 46, 89, or 92.

These two museums house some of the greatest pieces of classical sculpture in the world. The **Capitoline Museum,** or Musei Capitolini, was built in the 17th century, based on an architectural sketch by Michelangelo. It originally housed a papal collection which was founded by Sixtus IV in the 15th century.

In the first room is *The Dying Gaul,* a work of majestic skill that brings worldwide instant recognition. It's a copy of a Greek original that dates from the 3rd century B.C. And in a special gallery all her own is *The Capitoline Venus,* who demurely covers herself; this statue was the symbol of feminine beauty and charm down through the centuries (this one is a Roman copy of the Greek original from the 3rd century B.C.). Finally *Amore* (Cupid) and *Psyche* are up to their old tricks.

The famous equestrian statue of *Marcus Aurelius* that stood for years in the middle of the piazza was unveiled after a restoration; it had been a victim of pollution. Now it is located in the museum for greater protection. This is the only bronze statue to have survived from ancient Rome, and it survived only because it had been tossed into the Tiber by marauding barbarians. For centuries after its discovery it was thought to be a statue of Constantine the Great; this mistake protected it further, since Papal Rome respected the memory of the first Christian emperor. It's a beautiful statue even though the perspective is rather odd—it was originally designed to sit on top of a column, hence the foreshortened effect. The emperor's stirrups, by the way, are not missing—they were simply unknown in classical times, and Roman horsemen never used them. The statue is found in a glassed-in room on the street level called Cortile di Marforio; it's a kind of Renaissance greenhouse, surrounded by windows.

The **Palace of the Conservatori,** across the way, was also based on an architectural plan by Michelangelo. It is rich in classical sculpture and paintings. One of the most notable bronzes—a work of incomparable beauty—is the *Spinario* (the little boy picking a thorn from his foot), a Greek classic that dates from the 1st century B.C. In addition, you'll find *Lupa Capitolina* (the Capitoline Wolf), a rare Etruscan bronze that may go back to the 6th century B.C. (Romulus and Remus, the legendary twins that the wolf suckled, were added at a later date). The palace also contains a "Pinacoteca"—mostly paintings from the 16th and 17th centuries. Notable canvases include Caravaggio's *Fortune-Teller* and his curious *John the Baptist,* the *Holy Family* by Dosso Dossi, *Romulus and Remus* by Rubens, and Titian's *Baptism of Christ.*

✪ Galleria Borghese

Piazzale del Museo Borghese, off via Pinciano. ☎ **8548577.** Admission 4,000 lire ($2.50). Tues–Sat 9am–2pm, Sun 9am–1pm. Bus: 910 from Stazione Termini or 56 from piazza Barberini.

The gallery, housed in a handsome villa, contains some of the finest paintings in Rome; there's a representative collection of Renaissance and baroque masters, along with important Bernini sculpture. Among these is the so-called *Conquering Venus* by Antonio Canova, Italy's greatest neoclassic sculptor. Actually, this early 19th-century work created a sensation in its day, because its model was Pauline Bonaparte Borghese, sister of Napoleon (if the French dictator didn't like to see his sister naked, he was even more horrified at Canova's totally nude version of himself). In the rooms that follow are three of Bernini's most widely acclaimed works: *David, Apollo and Daphne* (his finest piece), and finally *The Rape of Persephone.*

The second floor, which normally houses the collection of Renaissance and baroque paintings, is closed for restoration. The paintings are temporarily on display at San Michele a Ripa, via di San Michele 22 (☎ 58-431) in the Trastevere district. Admission is included in your Galleria Borghese ticket, and it's open Monday to Friday from 9:30 am to 1 pm and 4 to 8 pm; Saturday from 9:30 am to 1 pm.

After visiting the gallery, you many want to join the Italians in their strolls through the Villa Borghese, replete with zoological gardens and small bodies of water. Horse shows are staged at piazza di Siena.

Galleria Nazionale D'Arte Antica

Via delle Quattro Fontane 13. ☎ **481-4430.** Admission 6,000 lire ($3.75) adults, free for children under 18. Tues–Sun 9am–2pm, Thurs and Sat 9am–7pm. Metro: Piazza Barberini.

The Palazzo Barberini, right off piazza Barberini, is one of the most magnificent baroque palaces in Rome. It was begun by Carlo Maderno in 1627 and completed in 1633 by Bernini, whose lavishly decorated rococo apartments, called the Gallery of Decorative Art, are on view. The palace houses the Galleria Nazionale.

The bedroom of Princess Cornelia Costanza Barberini and Prince Giulio Cesare Colonna di Sciarra still stands just as it was on their wedding night, and many household objects are displayed in the decorative art gallery. In the chambers, which have frescoes and hand-painted silk linings, you can see porcelain from Japan and Bavaria, canopied beds, and a baby carriage made of wood.

On the first floor of the palace, a splendid array of paintings includes works that date back to the 13th and 14th centuries, most notably the *Mother and Child* by Simone Martini. Also praiseworthy are paintings by Florentine artists from the 15th century, including art by Filippo Lippi. Some salons display 15th- and 16th-century paintings by such artists as Andrea Solario and Francesco Francia. Il Sodoma (Giovanni Antonio Bazzi) has some brilliant pictures here, including *The Rape of the Sabines* and *The Marriage of St. Catherine.* One of the best-known paintings is Raphael's beloved *La Fornarina,* of the baker's daughter who was his mistress and who posed for his Madonna portraits. Titian is represented by *Venus and Adonis.* Other artists exhibited include Tintoretto, El Greco, and Holbein the Younger. Many visitors come here just to see the magnificent Caravaggios, including *Narcissus.*

Galleria Nazionale D'Arte Moderna

Viale delle Belle Arti 131. ☎ **322-4151.** Admission 8,000 lire ($5) adults, free for children 17 and under. Tues–Sat 9am–2pm, Sun 9am–1pm. Bus: 19 or 30.

The National Gallery of Modern Art is in the Villa Borghese Gardens, a short walk from the Etruscan Museum. With its neoclassic and romantic paintings and sculpture, it's a dramatic change from the glories of the Renaissance and the Romans. Its 75 rooms house the largest collection in Italy of 19th- and 20th-century artists, including a comprehensive collection of modern Italian paintings.

Also included are important works of Balla, Boccioni, de Chirico, Morandi, Manzù, Marini, Burri, Capogrossi, and Fontana, and a large collection of Italian optical and pop art.

Look for Modigliani's *La Signora dal Collaretto* and the large *Nudo*. Several important sculptures, including one by Canova, are on display in the museum's gardens. The gallery also houses a large collection of foreign artists, including French impressionists Degas, Cézanne, and Monet, and the post-impressionist van Gogh. Surrealism and expressionism are well represented in works by Klee, Ernst, Braque, Miró, Kandinsky, Mondrian, and Pollock. You'll also find sculpture by Rodin. The collection of graphics, the storage rooms, and the department of restoration can be visited by appointment Tuesday through Friday.

Museo Nazionale del Palazzo di Venezia

Via del Plebiscito 118. ☎ **679-8865.** Admission 8,000 lire ($5) adults, free for children under 18. Tues–Sat 9am–2pm, Sun 9am–1pm. Bus: 64, 75, 85, or 170.

The Museum of the Palazzo Venezia, in the geographic heart of Rome, is the building that served until the end of World War I as the seat of the Embassy of Austria. During the Fascist regime (1928–43), it was the seat of the Italian government. The balcony from which Mussolini used to speak to the Italian people was built in the 15th century. Standing on part of the Capitoline Hill and overlooking the piazza is the 20th-century monument of Victor Emmanuel II, king of Italy, a lush work that has often been compared to a wedding cake. Here you'll find the Tomb of the Unknown Soldier that was created in World War I. Less known is the museum, founded in 1916 in the former papal residence that dates back to the 15th century. You can now visit the rooms and halls containing oil paintings, porcelain, tapestries, ivories, and ceramics. No one particular exhibit stands out—it's the sum total that adds up to a major attraction.

Museo Nazionale Romano (National Roman Museum)

Via Enrico De Nicola 79. ☎ **482-4181.** Admission 3,000 lire ($1.90). Tues–Sat 9am–2pm, Sun and holidays 9am–1pm. Metro: Piazza della Repubblica.

Located near piazza dei Cinquecento, which fronts the railway station, this museum occupies part of the 3rd-century A.D. Baths of Diocletian and a section of a convent that may have been designed by Michelangelo. It houses one of Europe's finest collections of Greek and Roman sculpture and early Christian sarcophagi.

The Ludovisi Collection is the apex of the museum, particularly the statuary of the Gaul slaying himself after he has done in his wife (a brilliant copy of a Greek original from the 3rd century B.C.).

Another prize is a one-armed Greek *Apollo.* A galaxy of other sculptured treasures includes *The Discus Thrower of Castel Porziano* (an exquisite copy), *Aphrodite of Cirene* (a Greek original), and the so-called *Hellenistic Ruler,* a Greek original of an athlete with a lance. A master of Greek sculpture, *The Birth of Venus,* is in the Ludovisi Throne room. *The Sleeping Hermaphrodite* (Ermafrodito Dormiente) is an original Hellenistic statue. Don't fail to stroll through the cloister, filled with statuary and fragments of antiquity, including a fantastic mosaic.

Museo Nazionale di Villa Giulia (Etruscan)

Piazzale di Villa Giulia 9. ☎ **3226571.** Admission 8,000 lire ($5) adults, free for children under 18 and adults over 60 years old. June–Sept Tues–Sat 9am–7pm, Sun 9am–1pm; Oct–May Tues–Sun 9am–2pm, Wed 9am–7pm. Bus: 19, 30, 225, or 926.

A 16th-century papal palace in the Villa Borghese Gardens shelters this priceless collection of art and artifacts of the mysterious Etruscans, who predated the Romans. Known for their sophisticated art and design, the Etruscans left a legacy of sarcophagi, bronze sculptures, terra-cotta vases, and jewelry, among other items.

If you have time only for the masterpieces, head for Sala 7, which has a remarkable *Apollo* from Veio from the end of the 6th century B.C. (clothed, for a change). The other two widely acclaimed pieces of statuary in this gallery are *Dea con Bambino* (a goddess with a baby) and a greatly mutilated, but still powerful, *Hercules* with a stag. In the adjoining room, Sala 8, you'll see the lions' sarcophagus from the mid-6th century B.C. which was excavated at Cerveteri, north of Rome.

Finally, one of the world's most important Etruscan art treasures is the bride and bridegroom coffin from the 6th century B.C., also dug out of the tombs of Cerveteri (in Sala 9). Near the end of your tour, another masterpiece of Etruscan art awaits you in Sala 33: the *Cista Ficoroni*, a bronze urn with paw feet, mounted by three figures, which dates from the 4th century B.C.

Palazzo Doria Pamphilj

Piazza dei Collegio Romano 1A. ☎ **679-4365.** Admission to gallery, 10,000 lire ($6.25) per person; apartments 5,000 lire ($3.15) per person. Tues and Fri–Sun 10am–1pm. Metro: Flaminio.

Located off via del Corso, the museum offers visitors a look at what it's really like to live in an 18th-century palace. Like many Roman palaces of the period, the mansion is partly leased to tenants (on the upper levels), and there are even shops on the street level, but all this is easily overlooked after you enter the grand apartments of the historic princely Doria Pamphilj family, which traces its lines to before the great 15th-century Genoese admiral Andrea Doria. The regal apartments surround the central court and gallery of the palace. The 18th-century decor pervades the magnificent ballroom, drawing rooms, dining rooms, and even the family chapel. Gilded furniture, crystal chandeliers, Renaissance tapestries, and portraits of family members are everywhere. The Green Room is especially rich in treasures, with a 15th-century Tournay tapestry, paintings by Memling and Filippo Lippi, and a semi-nude portrait of Andrea Doria by Sebastiano del Piombo. The Andrea Doria Room is dedicated to the admiral and to the ship of the same name. It contains a glass case with mementos of the great maritime disaster of the 1950s.

Skirting the central court is a picture gallery with a memorable collection of frescoes, paintings, and sculpture. Most important among a number of great works are the portrait of *Innocent X* by Velázquez, called one of the three or four best portraits ever painted; *Salome* by Titian; and works by Rubens and Caravaggio. Notable also are *Bay of Naples* by Pieter Brueghel the Elder and a copy of Raphael's portrait of Principessa Giovanna d' Aragona de Colonna (who looks remarkably like Leonardo's *Mona Lisa*). Most of the sculpture came from the Doria country estates. It includes marble busts of Roman emperors, bucolic nymphs, and satyrs. Even without the paintings and sculptures, that gallery would be worth a visit— just for its fresco-covered walls and ceilings.

PARKS & GARDENS

The **Villa Borghese** in the heart of Rome covers a landmass of 3.5 miles in circumference. One of the most elegant parks in Europe, it was created by Cardinal Scipione Borghese in the 1600s. Umberto I, king of Italy, acquired it in 1092 and presented it to the city of Rome, renaming it Villa Umberto I. However, Romans preferred their old name, which has stuck. A park of landscape vistas and wide-open "green lungs," the greenbelt is crisscrossed by roads. But you can escape from the traffic and seek a shaded area—usually pine or oak—where you can enjoy the makings of a picnic. In the northeast of the park is a small zoo, and the park is also host to the Galleria Borghese, one of the finest museums of Rome, with many masterpieces by Renaissance and baroque artists.

ESPECIALLY FOR KIDS

Rome has lots of other amusements for children when they tire of ancient monuments, although they're usually fond of wandering around the **Colosseum** and the **Roman Forum** (see "The Top Attractions," above). Many children also enjoy the climb to the top of **St. Peter's.** The **Fun Fair (Luna Park),** along via delle Tre Fontane (☎ 592-5933), at E.U.R., is one of the largest in Europe. It's known for its "big wheel" at the entrance, and there are merry-go-rounds, miniature railways, and shooting galleries, among other attractions. Admission is free, but you pay for each ride. It is closed Tuesday.

Teatro delle Marionette degli Accettella, performing at the Teatro Mongiovino, via Giovanni Genocchi 16 (☎ 5139405), has performances for children on Saturday and Sunday (except in August), at 4:30pm. Both adults and children pay 10,000 lire ($6.25) for tickets.

The **Puppet Theater** on Pincio Square in the Villa Borghese gardens has "Punch and Judy" performances nearly every day. While there, you might also like to take your children through the park (it's closed to traffic). Children enjoy the fountain displays and the lake, and there are many wide spaces in which they can play. Boats can be hired at the **Giardino del Lago.** A trip to the **zoo** in Rome is also possible, as it lies in the Villa Borghese, at viale del Giardino Zoologico 10 (☎ 321-65-64). It's open Monday through Friday from 8:30am to 4pm and Saturday and Sunday from 8:30am to 5pm; admission is 10,000 lire ($6.25) for adults, free for children. Take bus no. 19 or 30.

At 4pm every day, you can take your child to the Quirinale Palace, piazza del Quirinale, the residence of the president of Italy. There's a military band and a parade at that time, as the guards change shifts.

SPECIAL-INTEREST SIGHTSEEING
FOR THE LITERARY ENTHUSIAST

Keats-Shelley Memorial
Piazza di Spagna 26. ☎ **678-4235.** Admission 5,000 lire ($3.15). June–Sept, Mon–Fri 9am–1pm and 3–6pm; Oct–May, Mon–Fri 9am–1pm and 2:30–5:30pm. Metro: Piazza di Spagna.

At the foot of the Spanish Steps is this 18th-century house where Keats died of consumption on February 23, 1821. "It is like living in a violin," wrote Italian author Alberto Savinio. The apartment where Keats spent his last months, carefully tended by his close friend Joseph Severn, shelters a museum and research library, with a strange death mask of Keats as well as the "deadly sweat" drawing by Severn and many other mementoes of Keats, Shelley, and Byron. For those interested in the full story of the involvement of Keats and Shelley in Italy, books are sold on the premises.

Protestant Cemetery

Via Caio Cestio 6. ☎ **574-1900.** Admission is free, but a 1,000 lire (65¢) offering is customary, more if you feel generous. Apr 1–Sept 30, 9am–6pm; Oct 1–Mar 31, 9am–5pm. Closed Mondays. Metro: St. Paul's. Bus: 13, 27, or 30.

Near St. Paul's Station, in the midst of a setting of cypress trees, lies the old cemetery where John Keats was buried. In a grave nearby, Joseph Severn, his "deathbed" companion, was interred beside him six decades later. Dejected, and feeling his reputation as a poet diminished by the rising vehemence of his critics, Keats asked that the following epitaph be written on his tombstone: "Here lies one whose name was writ in water." A great romantic poet Keats certainly was, but a prophet, thankfully not.

Shelley, author of *Prometheus Unbound*, drowned off the Italian Riviera in 1822, before his 30th birthday. His ashes rest alongside those of Edward John Trelawny, fellow romantic and man of the sea. Trelawny maintained—but this was not proved—that Shelley may have been murdered, perhaps by petty pirates bent on robbery. While you're here, you may want to drop in at the neighboring Pyramid of Caius Cestius (see "Cemeteries," above).

WALKING TOUR
Imperial Rome

Start: Colosseum.
Finish: Circus Maximus.
Time: 2 hours.
Best Time: Any sunny day.
Worst Times: Morning or early-evening rush hours.

Even in the days of the Republic, the population explosion was a problem. Julius Caesar saw the overcrowding and began to expand, starting what were known as the Imperial Forums in the days of the empire. After the collapse of Rome and during the Dark Ages, the Forums were lost to history, buried beneath layers of debris, until Mussolini set out to restore the grandeur of Rome by reminding his compatriots of their glorious past.

Take the Metro to the Colosseo stop for the:

1. Colosseum, a good starting point, as you get your bearings with the traffic at the piazza del Colosseo. The Colosseum is the greatest monument of ancient Rome, and visitors are impressed with its size and majesty. Either visit it now or return later.

With your back to the Colosseum, begin your walk up:

2. via dei Fori Imperiali, keeping to the right side of the street. It was Mussolini who ordered Roman workers to cut through the years of debris and junky buildings to carve out this boulevard, linking the Colosseum to piazza Venezia. Excavations began at once, and much was revealed. Today the boulevard makes for one of the most fascinating walks in Rome. All the Imperial Forums can be seen from street level.

The ruins across the street are what's left of the colonnade that once surrounded the Temple of Venus and Roma. Next to it, you'll see the back wall of the Basilica of Constantine. Shortly, you'll come to a large outdoor restaurant, where via Cavour joins the boulevard you're on. Just beyond the small park across via Cavour are the remains of the:

3. **Forum of Nerva,** built by the emperor whose two-year reign (A.D. 96–98) followed that of the paranoid Domitian. The Forum of Nerva is best observed from the railing that skirts it on via dei Fori Imperiali. You'll be struck by just how much the ground level has risen in 19 centuries. The only really recognizable remnant is a wall of the Temple of Minerva with two fine Corinthian columns. This forum was once flanked by that of Vespasian, which is now, however, completely gone. It's possible to enter the Forum of Nerva from the other side, but you can see it just as well from the railing.

☕ **TAKE A BREAK**   **Bar Martini,** piazza del Colosseo 3A (☎ 700-4431), stands on a hill in back of the landmark Colosseum. Have your coffee or cool drink outside at one of the tables and absorb one of the world's greatest architectural views: that of the Colosseum itself. A pasta dish costs 8,000 lire ($5), a sandwich 2,000 lire ($1.25). Service is daily from 8:30am to midnight.

The next forum you approach is the:

4. **Forum of Augustus,** built before the birth of Christ to commemorate the emperor's victory over the assassins Cassius and Brutus in the Battle of Philippi (42 B.C.). Fittingly, the temple that once dominated this forum—and whose remains can still be seen—was that of Mars Ultor, or Mars the Avenger. In the temple once stood a mammoth statue of Augustus, which has unfortunately completely vanished. Like the Forum of Nerva, you can enter the Forum of Augustus from the other side (cut across the wee footbridge).

Continuing along the railing, you'll see next the vast semicircle of:

5. **Trajan's Market,** via Quattro Novembre 95 (☎ 67-10-20-70), whose teeming arcades stocked with merchandise from the far corners of the Roman world long ago collapsed, leaving only a few ubiquitous cats to watch after things. The shops once covered a multitude of levels, and you can still wander around many of them. In front of the perfectly proportioned semicircular facade—designed by Apollodorus of Damascus at the beginning of the 2nd century—are the remains of a great library, and fragments of delicately colored marble floors still shine in the sunlight between stretches of rubble and tall grass. While the view from the railing is of interest, Trajan's Market is worth the descent below street level. To get there, follow the service road you're on until you reach the monumental Trajan's Column on your left, where you turn right and go up the steep flight of stairs that leads to via Nazionale. At the top of the stairs, about half a block farther on the right, you'll see the entrance to the market. From April to September it is open Tuesday through Saturday from 9am to 1:30pm, and also in the afternoon from 4 to 7pm; Sunday hours are 9am to 1pm. From October to March, it operates Tuesday through Saturday from 9am to 1:30pm and on Sunday from 9am to 1pm. Admission is 3,750 lire ($2.35) for adults; half price for children.

Before you head down through the labyrinthine passageways, you might like to climb the:

6. **Tower of the Milizie,** a 12th-century structure that was part of the medieval headquarters of the Knights of Rhodes. The view from the top (if it's open) is well worth the climb. From the tower, you can wander where you will through

the ruins of the market, and admire the sophistication of the layout and the sad beauty of the bits of decoration that still remain. When you've examined the brick and travertine corridors, head out in front of the semicircle to the site of the former library; from here, scan the retaining wall that supports the modern road and look for the entrance to the tunnel that leads to the:

7. Forum of Trajan (Foro Traiano), entered on via Quattro Novembre near the steps of via Magnanapoli. Once through the tunnel, you'll emerge in the newest and most beautiful of the Imperial Forums, designed by the same man who laid out the adjoining market. There are many statue fragments, and pedestals that bear still-legible inscriptions, but more interesting is the great Basilica Ulpia, whose gray marble columns rise roofless into the sky. You wouldn't know it to judge from what's left, but the Forum of Trajan was once regarded as one of the architectural wonders of the world. Constructed between 107 and 113, it was designed by the Greek architect Apollodorus of Damascus.

Beyond the Basilica Ulpia is:

8. Trajan's Column, already mentioned, which is in magnificent condition, with intricate bas-relief sculpture depicting Trajan's victorious campaign (although from your vantage point you'll only be able to see the earliest stages). The emperor's ashes were kept in a golden urn at the base of the column. If you're fortunate, someone on duty at the stairs next to the column will let you out there. Otherwise, you'll have to walk back the way you came.

The next stop is the:

9. Forum of Julius Caesar, the first of the Imperial Forums. It lies on the opposite side of via dei Fori Imperial, the last set of sunken ruins before the Victor Emmanuel Monument. While it's possible to go right down into the ruins, you can see everything just as well from the railing. This was the site of the Roman stock exchange, as well as of the Temple of Venus, a few of whose restored columns stand cinematically in the middle of the excavations.

From here, retrace your last steps until you're in front of the white Brescian marble monument around the corner on piazza Venezia, where the:

10. Vittorio Emanuele Monument dominates the piazza. The most flamboyant landmark in Italy, it was constructed in the late 1800s to honor the first king of Italy. It has been compared to everything from a frosty birthday cake to a Victorian typewriter. An eternal flame burns at the Tomb of the Unknown Soldier. The interior of the monument has been closed to the public for many years.

Keep close to the monument and walk to your left, in the opposite direction from via dei Fori Imperiali. You might like to pause at the fountain that flanks one of the monument's great white walls and splash some icy water on your face. There is another fountain just like this one on the other side of the monument, and they're both favorite spots for tired visitors. Stay on the same side of the street, and just keep walking around the monument. You'll be on via del Teatro Marcello, which takes you past the twin lions that guard the sloping stairs and on along the base of the Capitoline Hill.

Keep walking along this boulevard until you come to the:

11. Teatro di Marcello, on your right. You'll recognize the two rows of gaping arches, which are said to be the models for the Colosseum. Julius Caesar is credited with starting the construction of this theater, but it was finished many years after his death (in 11 B.C.) by Augustus, who dedicated it to his favorite nephew,

Marcellus. You can look around the 2,000-year-old arcade, a small corner of which has been restored to what presumably was the original condition. Here, as everywhere, there are numerous cats stalking around the broken marble.

The bowl of the theater and the stage were adapted many centuries ago as the foundation for the Renaissance palace of the Orsini family. The other ruins belong to old temples. To the right is the Porticus of Octavia, dating from the 2nd century B.C. Note how later cultures used part of the Roman structure without destroying its original character. There's another good example of this on the other side of the theater. There you'll see a church with a wall that completely incorporates part of an ancient colonnade.

Returning to via del Teatro Marcello, keep walking away from piazza Venezia for two more long blocks, until you come to piazza della Bocca della Verità. The first item to notice in the attractive piazza is the rectangular:

12. **Temple of Fortuna Virile.** You'll see it on the right, a little off the road. Built a century before the birth of Christ, it's still in a magnificent condition. Behind it is another temple, dedicated to Vesta. Like the one in the forum, it is round, symbolic of the prehistoric huts where continuity of the hearthfire was a matter of survival.

About a block to the south, you'll pass the facade of the Church of Santa Maria in Cosmedin, set on the piazza della Bocca della Verità. Even more noteworthy, a short walk to the east, is the:

13. **Circus Maximus,** whose elongated oval proportions and ruined tiers of benches might remind visitors of the setting for *Ben Hur.* Today a formless ruin, the victim of countless raids upon its stonework by medieval and Renaissance builders, the remains of the once-great arena lie directly behind the church. At one time 250,000 Romans could assemble on the marble seats, while the emperor observed the games from his box high on the Palatine Hill.

The circus lies in a valley formed by the Palatine Hill on the left and the Aventine Hill on the right. Next to the Colosseum, it was the most impressive structure in ancient Rome, located certainly in one of the most exclusive neighborhoods. Emperors lived on the Palatine, while the great palaces of patricians sprawled across the Aventine, which is still a rather nice neighborhood. For centuries the pomp and ceremony of imperial chariot races filled this valley with the cheers of thousands.

When the dark days of the 5th and 6th centuries fell on the city, the Circus Maximus seemed a symbol of the complete ruination of Rome. The last games were held in 549 on the orders of Totilla the Goth, who had seized Rome in 547 and established himself as emperor. He lived in the still-glittering ruins on the Palatine and apparently thought that the chariot races in the Circus Maximus would lend credence to his charade of empire. It must have been a pretty miserable show, since the decimated population numbered something like 500 when Totilla had recaptured the city. The Romans of these times were caught between Belisarius, the imperial general from Constantinople, and Totilla the Goth, both of whom fought bloodily for control of Rome. After the travesty of 549, the Circus Maximus was never used again, and the demand for building materials reduced it, like so much of Rome, to a great dusty field.

To return to other parts of town, head for the bus stop adjacent to the Santa Maria in Cosmedin Church, or walk the length of the Circus Maximus to its far end and pick up the Metro to Stazione Termini.

Walking Tour—Imperial Rome

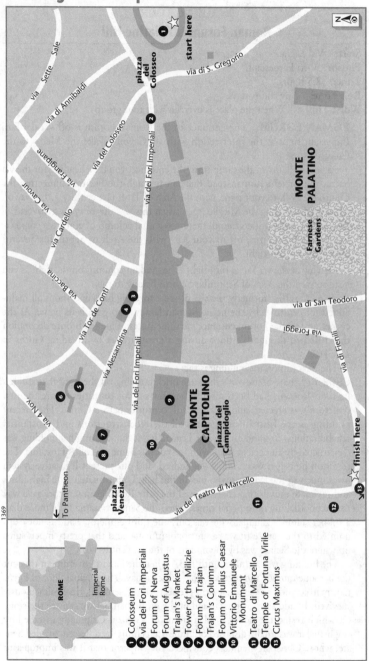

1369

ROME

Imperial
Rome

1. Colosseum
2. via dei Fori Imperiali
3. Forum of Nerva
4. Forum of Augustus
5. Trajan's Market
6. Tower of the Milizie
7. Forum of Trajan
8. Trajan's Column
9. Forum of Julius Caesar
10. Vittorio Emanuele Monument
11. Teatro di Marcello
12. Temple of Fortuna Virile
13. Circus Maximus

WALKING TOUR
Roman Forum & Palatine Hill

Start: Via Sacra.
Finish: Orti Farnesiani.
Time: 2.5 hours.
Best Time: Any sunny day.
Worst Times: When the place is overrun with tour groups.

ROMAN FORUM   The entrance to the Roman Forum is off via dei Fori Imperiali, right at the intersection with via Cavour. Take the Metro to the Colosseo stop.

As you walk down the ramp from the entrance, you'll be heading for the via Sacra, the ancient Roman road that ran through the Forum connecting the Capitoline Hill, to your right, with the Arch of Titus (1st century A.D.), way off to your left. During the Middle Ages, when this was the *campo vaccino* and all these stones were underground, there was a dual column of elm trees connecting the Arch of Titus, off to your left, with the Arch of Septimius Severus (A.D. 200) to your right.

Arriving at the via Sacra, turn right. The random columns on the right as you head toward the Arch of Septimius Severus belong to the:

1. **Basilica Aemilia,** formerly the site of great meeting halls and shops all maintained for centuries by the noble Roman family who gave it its name. At the corner nearest the Forum entrance are some traces of melted bronze decoration that fused to the marble floor during a great fire set by invading Goths in A.D. 410.

The next important building is the:

2. **Curia,** or Senate house—it's the large brick building on the right that still has its roof. Romans had been meeting on this site for centuries before the first structure was erected, and that was still centuries before Christ. The present building is the fifth (if one counts all the reconstructions and substantial rehabilitations) to stand on the site. Legend has it that the original building was constructed by an ancient king, with the curious name of Tullus Hostilius. The tradition he began was a noble one indeed, and our present legislative system owes much to the Romans who met in this hall. Unfortunately, the high ideals and inviolate morals that characterized the early Republican senators gave way to the bootlicking of imperial times, when the Senate became little more than a rubber stamp. Caligula, who was only the third emperor, had his horse appointed to the Senate (it was a life appointment), and that pretty much sums up where the Senate was by the middle of the 1st century A.D.

The building was a church until 1937, when the Fascist government tore out the baroque interior and revealed what we see today. The original floor of Egyptian marble and the tiers that held the seats of the senators have miraculously survived. In addition, at the far end of the great chamber we can see the stone on which rested the fabled golden statue of Victory. Originally installed by Augustus, it was finally disposed of in the 4th century by a fiercely divided Senate, whose Christian members convinced the emperor that it was improper to have a pagan statue in such a revered place.

Outside, head down the Curia stairs to the:

3. **Lapis Niger,** the remains of black marble that reputedly mark the tomb of Romulus. They bask today under a corrugated roof. Go downstairs for a look at the excavated tomb. There's a stone here with the oldest Latin inscription in existence, which unfortunately is nearly unintelligible. All that can be safely assumed is that it genuinely dates from the Rome of the kings. Remember, they disappeared in a revolution in 510 B.C.

Across from the Curia, the:

4. **Arch of Septimius Severus** was dedicated at the dawn of the troubled 3rd century to the last decent emperor who was to govern Rome for some time. The friezes on the arch depict victories over Arabs and Parthians by the cold but upright Severus and his two dissolute sons, Geta and Caracalla. Severus died on a campaign to subdue the unruly natives of Scotland and at the end of the first decade of the 3rd century, Rome unhappily fell into the hands of young Caracalla, chiefly remembered today for his baths.

Walk around to the back of the Severus arch, face it, and look to your right. There amid the rubble can be discerned a semicircular stair that led to the famous:

5. **Rostra,** the podium from which dictators and caesars addressed the throngs of the Forum below. One can just imagine the emperor, shining in his white toga surrounded by imperial guards and distinguished senators, gesticulating grandly like one of the statues on a Roman roofline. The motley crowd falls silent, the elegant senators pause and listen, the merchants put down their measures, even the harlots and unruly soldiers lower their voices in such an august presence. Later emperors didn't have much cause to use the Rostra, making their policies known through edict and assassination instead.

Now, facing the colonnade of the Temple of Saturn, once the public treasury, and going to the left, you'll come to the ruins of the:

6. **Basilica Julia,** again little more than a foundation. The basilica gets its name from Julius Caesar, who dedicated the first structure in 46 B.C. Like many buildings in the Forum, the basilica was burned and rebuilt several times, and the last structure dated from those shaky days after the Gothic invasion of 410. Throughout its history, it was used for the hearing of civil court cases, which were conducted in the pandemonium of the crowded Forum, open to anyone who happened to pass by. The building was also reputed to be particularly hot in the summer, and it was under these sweaty and unpromising circumstances that Roman justice, the standard of the world for a millennium, was meted out.

Walking back down the ruined stairs of the Basilica Julia and into the broad area whose far side is bounded by the Curia, you'll see the:

7. **Column of Phocas.** Probably lifted from an early structure in the near vicinity, this was the last monument to be erected in the Roman Forum, and it commemorates the Byzantine emperor Phoca's generous donation of the Pantheon to the pope of Rome, who almost immediately transformed it into a church.

Now make your way down the middle of the Forum nearly back to the ramp from which you entered. The pile of brick with the semicircular indentation that stands in the middle of things was the:

8. **Temple of Julius Caesar,** erected some time after the dictator was deified. Judging from the reconstruction, it was quite an elegant building. As you stand facing the ruins, with the entrance to the Forum on your left, you'll see on your right three columns belonging originally to the:

9. Temple of the Castors. This temple perpetuated the legend of Castor and Pollux, who appeared out of this air in the Roman Forum and were observed watering their horses at the fountain of Juturna (still visible today), just as a major battle against the Etruscans turned in favor of Rome. Castor and Pollux, the heavenly twins—and the symbol of the astrological sign Gemini—seem a favorite of Rome.

The next major monument is the circular:

10. Temple of Vesta, wherein dwelt the sacred flame of Rome, and the Atrium of the Vestal Virgins. A vestal virgin was usually a girl of good family who signed a contract for 30 years. During that time, she lived in the ruin we're standing in right now. Of course, back then it was an unimaginably rich marble building with two floors. There were only six vestal virgins during the imperial period, and even though they had the option of going back out into the world at the end of their 30 years, few did. The cult of Vesta came to an end in 394, when a Christian Rome secularized all its pagan temples. A man standing on this site before then would have been put to death immediately.

Stand in the atrium with your back to the Palatine and look beyond those fragmented statues of former vestals to the:

11. Temple of Antoninus and Faustina. It's the building with the freestanding colonnade just to the right of the ramp where you first entered the Forum. Actually, just the colonnade dates from imperial times; the building behind is a much later church dedicated to San Lorenzo.

After you inspect the beautifully proportioned Antoninus and Faustina temple, head up via Sacra away from the entrance ramp in the direction of the Arch of Titus. Pretty soon, on your left, you'll see the twin bronze doors of the:

12. Temple of Romulus. It's the doors themselves that are really of note here— they're the original Roman doors, and swing on the same massive hinges they were originally mounted on in A.D. 306. In this case, the temple is not dedicated to the legendary cofounder of Rome, but to the son of its builder, the emperor Maxentius, who gave Romulus his name in a fit of antiquarian patriotism. Unfortunately for both father and son, they competed with a general who deprived them of their empire and lives. That man was Constantine, who, while camped outside Rome during preparations for one of his battles against Maxentius, saw the sign of the Cross in the heavens with the insignia IN HOC SIGNO VINCES (in this sign shall you conquer). Raising the standard of Christianity above his legions, he defeated the (pagan) Emperor Maxentius and later became the first Christian emperor.

At the time of Constantine's victory (A.D. 306) the great:

13. Basilica of Constantine (marked by those three gaping arches up ahead on your left) was only half finished, having been started by the unfortunate Maxentius. However, Constantine finished the job and affixed his name to this, the largest and most impressive building in the Forum. To my taste, the more delicate, Greek-influenced temples are more attractive, but you have to admire the scale and the engineering skill that erected this monument. The fact that portions of the original coffered ceiling are still intact is amazing. The basilica once held a statue of Constantine so large that his little toe was as wide as an average man's waist. You can see a few fragments from this colossal thing—the remnants were found in 1490—in the courtyard of the Conservatory Museum on the Capitoline Hill. As far as Roman emperors went, Christian or otherwise, ego knew no bounds.

Walking Tour
Roman Forum & Palatine Hill

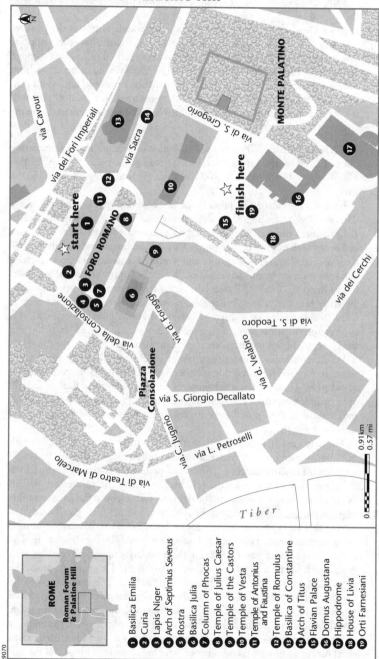

1. Basilica Emilia
2. Curia
3. Lapis Niger
4. Arch of Septimius Severus
5. Rostra
6. Basilica Julia
7. Column of Phocas
8. Temple of Julius Caesar
9. Temple of the Castors
10. Temple of Vesta
11. Temple of Antonius and Faustina
12. Temple of Romulus
13. Basilica of Constantine
14. Arch of Titus
15. Flavian Palace
16. Domus Augustana
17. Hippodrome
18. House of Livia
19. Orti Farnesiani

ROME
Roman Forum & Palatine Hill

9070

From Constantine's basilica, follow the Roman paving stones of via Sacra to the:

14. Arch of Titus, clearly visible on a low hill just ahead. Titus was the emperor who sacked the great Jewish temple in Jerusalem, and the bas-relief sculpture inside the arch shows the booty of the Jews being carried in triumph through the streets of Rome, while Titus is crowned by Victory, who comes down from heaven for the occasion. You'll notice in particular the candelabrum, for centuries one of the most famous pieces of the treasure of Rome. In all probability, it lies at the bottom of the Busento River in the secret tomb of Alaric the Goth.

PALATINE HILL   When you've gathered your strength in the shimmering hot sun, head up the Clivus Palatinus, the road to the palaces of the Palatine Hill. With your back to the Arch of Titus, it's the road going up the hill to the left.

It was on the Palatine Hill that Rome first became a city. Legend tells us the date was 753 B.C. The new city originally consisted of nothing more than the Palatine, which was soon enclosed by a surprisingly sophisticated wall, remains of which can still be seen on the Circus Maximus side of the hill. As time went on and Rome grew in power and wealth, the boundaries were extended and later enclosed by the Servian Wall. When the last of the ancient kings was overthrown (510 B.C.), Rome had already extended onto several of the adjoining hills and valleys. As Republican times progressed, the Palatine became a fashionable residential district. So it remained until Tiberius—who, like his predecessor, Augustus, was a bit too modest to really call himself "emperor" out loud—began the first of the monumental palaces that were to cover the entire hill.

It's difficult today to make sense out of the Palatine. The first-time viewer might be forgiven for suspecting it to be an entirely artificial structure built on brick arches. Those arches, which are visible on practically every flank of the hill, are actually supports that once held imperial structures. Having run out of building sites, the emperors, in their fever, simply enlarged the hill by building new sides on it.

The road goes on only a short way, through a small sort of valley filled with lush, untrimmed greenery. After about five minutes (for slow walkers), you'll see the ruins of a monumental stairway just to the right of the road. The Clivus Palatinus turns sharply to the left here, skirting the monastery of San Bonaventura, but we'll detour to the right and take a look at the remains of the:

15. Flavian Palace. As you walk off the road and into the ruins, you'll be able to discern that there were once three rooms here. But it's impossible for anyone but an archaeologist to comprehend quite how splendid these rooms were. The entire Flavian Palace was decorated in the most lavish of colored marbles, with gold. Much of the decoration survived as late as the 18th century, when the greedy Duke of Parma removed most of what was left. The room closest to the Clivus Palatinus was called the Lararium, and held statues of the divinities that protected the imperial family. The middle room was the grandest of the three. It was the imperial throne room, where sat the ruler of the world, the emperor of Rome. The far room was a basilica, and as such was used for miscellaneous court functions, among them audiences with the emperor. This part of the palace was used entirely for ceremonial functions. Adjoining these three rooms are the remains of a spectacularly luxurious peristyle. You'll recognize it by the hexagonal remains of a fountain in the middle. Try, if you can, to imagine this fountain surrounded by marble arcades, planted with mazes, and equipped with mica-covered walls. On the opposite side of the peristyle from the throne rooms are several other great reception and entertainment rooms. The banquet hall was here, and beyond it, looking over the Circus Maximus, are a few ruins of former libraries. Although practically nothing remains except the foundations, every now and again you'll catch sight of a fragment of colored marble floor, in a subtle, sophisticated pattern.

The imperial family lived in the:

16. Domus Augustana, the remains of which lie toward the Circus Maximus, and slightly to the left of the Flavian Palace. The new building that stands here—it looks old to us, but in Rome it qualifies as a new building—is a museum (usually closed). It stands in the absolute center of the Domus Augustana. In the field adjacent to the stadium well into the present century stood the Villa Mills, a gingerbread Gothic villa of the 19th century. It was quite a famous place. Owned by a rich Englishman who came to Rome from the West Indies, Villa Mills was the scene of many fashionable entertainments in Victorian times, and it's interesting to note, as H. V. Morton pointed out, that the last dinner parties that took place on the Palatine Hill were given by an Englishman.

Heading across the field parallel to the Clivus Palatinus you come to the north end of the:

17. Hippodrome, or Stadium of Domitian. The field was apparently occupied by parts of the Domus Augustana, which in turn adjoined the enormous stadium. The stadium itself is worth examination, although sometimes it's difficult to get down inside it. The perfectly proportioned area was usually used for private games, staged for the amusement of the imperial family. As you look down the stadium from the north end, you can see, on the left side, the semicircular remains of a structure identified as Domitian's private box. We'll note at this point that some archaeologists claim the "stadium" was actually an elaborate sunken garden, and perhaps we'll never know exactly what it was.

The aqueduct that comes up the wooded hill used to supply water for the Baths of Septimius Severus, whose difficult-to-understand ruins lie in monumental poles of arched brick at the far end of the stadium.

Returning to the Flavian Palace, leave the peristyle on the opposite side from Domus Augustana and follow the signs for the:

18. House of Livia. They take you down a dusty path to your left, from which entrance to the house is made. Although legend says that this was the house of Augustus's consorts, it actually was Augustus's all along. The place is notable for some rather well-preserved murals showing mythological scenes. But more interesting is the aspect of the house itself—it's smallish, and there never were any great baths or impressive marble arcades. Augustus, even though he was the first emperor, lived simply compared to his successors. His wife, Livia, was a fiercely ambitious aristocrat who divorced her own husband to marry the emperor (the ex-husband was made to attend the wedding, incidentally) and according to some historians was the true power behind Roman policy between the death of Julius Caesar and the ascension of Tiberius. She even controlled Tiberius, her son, since she had engineered his rise to power through a long string of intrigues and poisonings.

After you've examined the frescoes in Livia's parlor, head up the steps that lead to the top of the embankment to the north. Once on top, you'll be in the:

19. **Orti Farnesiani,** the 16th-century addition of a Farnese cardinal. They are built on the top of the Palace of Tiberius, which, you'll remember, was the first of the great imperial palaces to be put up. It's impossible to see any of it, but the gardens are cool and nicely laid out. You might stroll up to the promontory above the Forum and admire the view of the ancient temples and the Capitoline heights off to the left.

When you've seen this much, you've seen the best of the Forum and the Palatine. To leave the archaeological area, you should now continue through the Orti Farnesiani, keeping the Forum on your left. Soon you'll come to a stairway that leads to the path from the Arch of Titus. There is an exit just behind the arch, but since it's usually closed, you'll probably have to exit up the ramp you entered by.

WALKING TOUR
Spanish Steps to Quirinale

Start: Piazza di Spagna.
Finish: Palazzo del Quirinale.
Time: 2 hours.
Best Time: Sunday morning.
Worst Times: Morning and afternoon rush hours.

1. **Piazza di Spagna (Spanish Steps)** and the adjoining piazza di Spagna both take their name from the Spanish Embassy, which was in a palace here during the 19th century. The Spanish, however, had nothing to do with the construction of the steps. They were built by the French, and lead to the French church in Rome, Trinità dei Monti, and that's why they're called "Scala della Trinità dei Monti." There is nothing Spanish in their real Italian name. "Spanish Steps" is just an easy way of referring to them in English. The twin-towered church behind the obelisk at the top of the steps is early 16th century. The steps themselves are early 18th century. The French are in the church to this day, and the adjoining Villa Medici is now a French school.

The Spanish Steps are at their best in spring, when the many flights are filled with flowers. You'll see a wide variety of types of people, most of them young, sitting around here any time of the year. In the fall and winter the population is much sparser, with only an occasional Roman soaking up a few of the sun's warming rays. It is a rare visitor who hasn't sat for a while on one of the landings—there's one every 12 steps—perhaps to read a letter from home or observe the other sitters. It's interesting to note that in the early 19th century the steps were famous for the sleek young men and women who lined the travertine steps flexing muscles and exposing ankles in hopes of attracting an artist and being hired as a model. The Barcaccia fountain at the foot was designed by Bernini's father at the end of the 16th century.

There are two nearly identical houses at the foot of the steps on either side. One is the home of Babington's Tea Rooms (our "Take a Break," below); the other is the house where the English romantic poet John Keats lived—and died. The:

2. **Keats-Shelley Memorial,** at piazza di Spagna 26, has been bought by English and American contributors and turned into a museum. The rooms where Keats lived are chock-full of mementos of the poet.

☕ **TAKE A BREAK** **Babington's Tea Rooms,** piazza di Spagna 23 (☎ 678-6027), was opened in 1893 by Miss Anna Maria Babington, and it has been serving homemade scones and muffins—along with a "good cuppa"—ever since, based on her original recipes. Celebrities and thousands upon thousands of tourists have stopped off here. Prices are high, however.

In the past the piazza di Spagna area was a favorite of English lords, who rented palaces hereabouts and parked their coaches on the street. Americans predominate in the 20th century, especially since the main office of American Express is right on piazza di Spagna and dispenses all those letters (and money) from home. There's a street called:

3. **via della Croce** that intersects the northern end of piazza di Spagna perpendicularly from the left. Follow this street for four blocks, passing vendors selling the choicest and most expensive fruit in town between parked cars, and small workrooms filled with dust, where old men are repairing 16th-century gilt frames, until you come to via del Corso. Continue straight across the Corso, where the street takes a sharp turn to the left. At the first intersection, turn right, and across the piazza is your next stop, the:

4. **Mausoleo Augusteo (Augustus Mausoleum).** This seemingly indestructible pile of bricks along via di Ripetta has been here for 2,000 years, and will probably remain for another 2,000. Like the larger tomb of Hadrian across the river, this was once a circular, marble-covered affair with tall cypress trees on the earth-covered dome. Many of the emperors of the 1st century had their ashes deposited in golden urns inside this building, and it was probably due to the resultant crowding that Hadrian decided to construct an entirely new tomb for himself. The imperial remains stayed intact until the 5th century, when invading barbarians smashed the bronze gates and stole the golden urns, probably emptying the ashes on the ground outside. The tomb was restored in the 1930s. You cannot enter, but you can walk around looking inside.

Across via di Ripetta, the main street on the far side of the tomb, is an airy glass-and-concrete building right on the banks of the Tiber at Ponte Cavour. Within it is one of the treasures of antiquity, the:

5. **Ara Pacis (Altar of Peace),** built by the Senate during the reign of Augustus as a tribute to that emperor and the peace he had brought to the Roman world. On the marble walls can be seen portraits of the imperial family—Augustus, Livia (his wife), Tiberius (Livia's son and the successor to the empire), even Julia (the unfortunate daughter of Augustus, exiled by her father for her sexual excesses). The altar was reconstructed from literally hundreds of fragments scattered in museums for centuries. A major portion came from the foundations of a Renaissance palace on the Corso. The reconstruction—quite an archaeological adventure story in itself—was executed by the Fascists during the 1930s. The Ara Pacis (☎ 710-2071) is open on Tuesday and Wednesday and Friday through Sunday from 9am to 1:30pm. From April through September, it is also open in the afternoon on Tuesday and Saturday from 4 to 7pm. Admission is 3,750 lire ($2.35).

Continuing south, take via del Corso, a shopping artery leading to piazza Colonna, and its Marcus Aurelius Column, which dominates the piazza. Here is the Palazzo Chigi, official residence of the Italian prime minister, and the Bernini-designed Palazzo di Montecitorio east of the Italian legislature, the Chamber of Deputies (closed to the public).

From via del Corso, walk up the right side of via del Tritone and then follow the signs to the:

6. **Fontana di Trevi.** At piazza di Trevi, the Trevi Fountain is the most famous one in all of Rome. Tourists come here and toss a coin in the fountain, which according to legend ensures their return. Supplied by water from the Acqua Vergine aqueduct, it was based on the design of Nicolo Salvi and completed in 1762.

On one corner of the piazza you'll see an ancient church with a strange claim to fame. In it are contained the hearts and viscera of several centuries of popes. This was the parish church of the popes when they resided at the Quirinal Palace on the hill above, and for many years each pontiff willed those parts of his body to the church.

To reach the Quirinal, take via Lucchesi from the church for two blocks, where it intersects with via Doloria. Turn left and straight ahead you'll see the steps to the:

7. **Palazzo del Quirinale.** At the top of the stairs, you'll be in a wide, pink piazza, piazza del Quirinale, with the palace of the president of Italy on your left. Until the end of World War II the palace was the home of the king of Italy, and before that it was the residence of the pope. In antiquity this was the site of Augustus's Temple of the Sun. The steep marble steps that lead to Santa Maria d'Aracoeli on the Capitoline Hill once led to that temple. The great baths of Constantine also stood nearby, and that's the origin of some of the fountain statuary. The palace is open to the public Sunday between 9am and 1pm. Admission is free but a passport or similar identification is required for entrance.

From here, your closest public transportation is on via Nazionale, reached by taking via della Consulta between the Palazzo Consulta and the little park.

ORGANIZED TOURS

Because of the sheer volume of artistic riches, some visitors prefer to begin their stay in Rome with an organized tour. While few things can really be covered in any depth on these "overview tours," they are sometimes useful for getting the feel and geography of a complicated city. One of the leading tour operators (among the zillions of possibilities) is **American Express,** piazza di Spagna 38 (☎ 67641). It's open Monday to Friday from 9am to 5:30pm and Saturday from 9am to noon. Of the many tour operators functioning within Rome, American Express is the one whose tours are the most closely geared to the American language and American visitors. All tours are conducted strictly in English.

One of the most popular tours is a four-hour orientation tour of Rome and the Vatican, which departs most mornings at 9:30am and costs 60,000 lire ($37.50) per person. Another four-hour tour which focuses on the Rome of antiquity (including visits to the Colosseum, the Roman Forum, the ruins of the Imperial Palace, and the Church of San Pietro in Vincola) costs 50,000 lire ($31.25). Of the many excursions offered to sites outside the city limits of Rome, the most popular is a five-hour bus tour to Tivoli, where visits are conducted of the Villa d'Este and its spectacular gardens and the ruins of the Villa Adriana, all for the price of 63,000 lire ($39.40) per person.

If your time in Italy is rigidly limited, you might opt for one-day excursions to points farther afield on tours which are marketed by (but not conducted by)

Walking Tour
The Spanish Steps To Quirinale

1. Piazza di Spagna (Spanish Steps)
2. The Keats-Shelley Memorial
3. Via della Croce
4. Mausoleo Augusteo (Augustus' Tomb)
5. Ara Pacis (Altar of Peace)
6. Fontana di Trevi
7. Palazzo del Quirinale

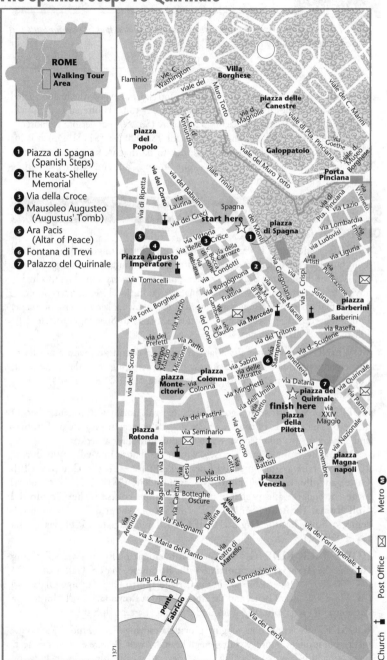

Church ✚■   Post Office ✉   Metro Ⓜ

One of those miserable ruins which refused to disintegrate, a spot fit only for lame cats to seek refuge from small boys.

—H.V. Morton, *A Traveller in Rome*

American Express. Although rushed and far too short to expose the many-layered majesty of these destinations, a series of one-day tours is offered to Pompeii, Naples, and Sorrento for a price of 132,000 lire ($82.50) per person; to Florence for 162,000 lire ($101.25); and to Capri for 184,000 lire ($115). Lunch is included on each of these full-day trips, but to participate you'll need a lot of stamina, as each tour departs from Rome around 7am and returns sometime after 9 or 10pm to your hotel.

2 Sports & Outdoor Activities

OUTDOOR ACTIVITIES

BIKING The traffic is murderous, and the pollution might make your head spin, but there are quiet times (early mornings and Sunday) when a spin beside the Tiber or through the Borghese gardens might prove very appealing. It's highly advisable to wear a helmet when bicycling, even if the local Vespa riders don't.

Bike-rental concession stands are found at the following Metro stops: piazza del Popolo, largo San Silvestro, largo Argentina, piazza di Spagna, and viale della Pineto in the Villa Borghese.

BOWLING One of the city's largest bowling complexes, whose hordes of participants provide a spectacle almost more interesting than the game itself, lies at Bowling Roma, viale Regina Margherita 181 (☎ 855-11-84), off via Nomentana.

GOLF Rome boasts several golf courses that will usually welcome members of other golf clubs. Each, of course, will be under the greatest pressure on Saturday and Sunday, so as a nonmember try to schedule arrival for a weekday.

One of the capital's best courses, with a clubhouse in a villa built during 1600s and fairways designed by Robert Trent Jones, is the **Country Club Castelgandolfo,** via Santo Spirito 13, Castelgandolfo (☎ 931-2301). An older, more entrenched, and probably more prestigious course is the **Circolo del Golf Roma,** via Acqua Santa 3 (☎ 780-3407). About 8.5 miles from the center of town lies the **Olgiata Golf Club,** largo Olgiata 15, off via Cassia (☎ 378-9141).

HORSEBACK RIDING The most convenient of Rome's several riding clubs is the **Associazione Sportiva Villa Borghese,** via del Galoppatoio 23 (☎ 360-6797). Other stables are in the **Circolo Ippico Olgiata,** largo Olgiata 15 (☎ 378-8792), near Cassia, and the **Società Ippica Romana,** via del Monti della Farnesina 18 (☎ 396-6214). Tack and equipment are English style.

JOGGING Not only does jogging provide a moving view of the city's monuments, but it might improve your general health as well. Beware of the city's heat, however, and be alert to speeding traffic. Several possible itineraries include the park of the **Villa Borghese,** where the series of roads and pathways, some of them beside statuary, provide a verdant oasis within the city's congestion. The best places to enter the park are at piazza del Popolo or at the top of via Vittorio Veneto. The **Cavalieri Hilton,** via Cadlolo 101, Monte Maria (☎ 35-091), offers a jogging path (measuring a third of a mile) through the trees and flowering shrubs of its landscaping. The grounds that surround the **Villa Pamphilj** contain three running tracks, although they might either be locked or in use by local sports teams for runners during your exercise. A final possibility, not recommended for jogging after dark, is the rounded premises of the Circus Maximus. Built by the ancient Romans, it contains a footpath inside its ruined walls, and an outward perimeter (ringed with roaring traffic) that measures about half a mile.

SOCCER   Soccer is one of the three or four all-consuming passions of thousands of Italians, richly intertwined with their image of the country. Rome boasts two intensely competitive teams, Lazio and Roma, which tend to play either against each other or against visiting teams from other parts of the world every Sunday afternoon. Matches are held at the **Stadio Olimpico,** Foro Italico dei Gladiatori (☎ 3336316), originally built by Mussolini as a nationalistic (Fascist) statement. Thousands of tickets are sold during the two or three hours before each game. The players usually take a break during June, July, and August, beginning the season with something approaching pandemonium in September.

SWIMMING   One of the busiest all-year pools is the **Roman Sport Center,** via del Galoppatoio 33 (☎ 320-1667), which lies adjacent to the parking lot on the grounds of the Villa Borghese. Open to the public, it contains two large swimming pools, squash courts, a gym, and saunas. In another part of town, the **Piscina della Rose**, viale America (☎ 592-67-17), is an Olympic-size pool open to the public (and crowded with teenagers and *bambini*) between June and September. More sedate, set in lushly landscaped gardens, and open to nonresidents, is the pool in the resort-inspired premises of the **Cavalieri Hilton,** via Cadlolo 101 (☎ 35-091).

TENNIS   The best tennis courts are at private clubs, many of which are within a handful of suburbs. Players are highly conscious of proper tennis attire, so be prepared to don your most sparkling whites and your best manners. One of the city's best-known clubs is the **Tennis Club Parioli,** largo Umberto de Morpurgo 2, via Salaria (☎ 862-00-882), open daily from 8am to noon only.

3 Shopping

Rome offers temptations of every kind, but this section will try to focus on the urge to shop that sometimes overcomes even the most stalwart of visitors. You might find hidden oases of charm and value in hitherto unpublicized streets and districts, but what follows is a listing and description of certain streets known throughout Italy for the desirability of their shops. The monthly rental of floor space on these famous streets is very high, and those costs will almost certainly be passed on to the consumer. Nonetheless, a stroll down some of these streets usually presents a cross section of the most desirable wares in Italy.

Cramped urban spaces and a well-defined sense of taste has encouraged most Italian stores to elevate the boutique philosophy to its highest levels. A boutique, at least in theory, is a smallish space filled with a well-defined congregation of specifically chosen merchandise for a specific type of client. The theory is that if you like what you see in a shop window, you'll find it duplicated, in spirit and style, inside. Lack of space, and definition of a merchandising program, usually restrict an establishment's merchandise to one particular style, degree of formality, or mood. Therefore, browse at will, and let the allure of the shop window communicate the mood and style of what you're likely to find inside.

Caveat: We won't pretend that Rome is Italy's finest shopping center (Florence and Venice are), or that its shops are unusually inexpensive—many of them aren't. But even on the most elegant of Rome's thoroughfares, there are values mixed in with the costly boutiques.

THE SHOPPING SCENE

I don't know who numbered Rome's streets—doubtless it was done centuries ago—but many times you'll find that numbers start on one side of the street, run all the way down that side in sequence to the far end of the street, then change sides and run all the way back. Therefore, no. 500 is sometimes across the street from no. 1. Thus warned, you're ready to begin strolling.

Via Borgognona   Beginning near piazza di Spagna, both the rents and the merchandise are chic and very, very expensive. Like its neighbor, via Condotti, it's a mecca for wealthy, well-dressed women from around the world. Its architecture, and its storefronts, have retained their baroque or neoclassical facades.

Via Condotti   Easy to find because it begins at the base of the Spanish Steps, this is probably the poshest and the most visible upper-bracket shopping street in Rome, and probably the best example in Europe of a certain kind of avidly elegant consumerism. Even the recent incursion of some less elegant stores hasn't diminished the allure of this street as a consumer's playground for the rich and the very, very rich.

Via del Corso   Not attempting the stratospheric image (or prices) of via Condotti or Borgognona, the styles here tend to be aimed at younger consumers. There are, however, some gems scattered amid the shops selling jeans and sporting equipment. These you'll identify according to your particular tastes. This street had most of its automobile traffic diverted for some of its length, a lucky change that improved merchandising considerably. The most interesting shops are the section nearest the fashionable café of piazza del Popolo.

Via Francesco Crispi   Most shoppers reach this street by following via Sistina (see below) one long block from the top of the Spanish Steps. Near the intersection of these streets are several shops well suited for unusual and less expensive gifts.

Via Frattina   Running parallel to via Condotti, it begins, like its more famous sibling, at piazza di Spagna. Part of its length is closed to traffic. Here, the concentration of shops is denser, although some aficionados claim that its image—and its prices—are slightly less chic and slightly less expensive than its counterparts on via Condotti. It's usually thronged with shoppers who appreciate the lack of motor traffic.

Via Nazionale   The layout here recalls 19th-century grandeur and ostentatious beauty, but the traffic is horrendous; crossing via Nazionale requires a good sense of timing and a strong understanding of Italian driving patterns. It begins at piazza della Repubblica (with its great Fountain of the Naiads in front of the Baths of Diocletian) and runs down almost to the 19th-century monuments of piazza Venezia. There is an abundance of leather stores—more reasonable than in many other parts of Rome—many different apartment buildings, and a welcome handful of stylish boutiques.

Via Sistina   Beginning at the top of the Spanish Steps, via Sistina runs from that point (the Trinità dei Monti) into piazza Barberini. Shops are small, stylish, and based on the personalities of their owners. Pedestrian traffic is less dense than on other major streets. It's convenient to combine a visit to this street with the afore-mentioned via Francesco Crispi.

Via Vittorio Veneto and via piazza Barberini   Evocative of *La Dolce Vita* fame, via Vittorio Veneto is filled these days with expensive hotels and cafés and an array of relatively expensive stores selling shoes, gloves, and leather goods.

SHOPPING A TO Z
ANTIQUES

Some visitors to Italy consider the trove of salable antiques the country's greatest treasure. But long gone are the days when you could find priceless treasures for pocket change. The value of almost any antique has risen to alarming levels as increasingly wealthy Europeans have outbid one another in frenzies of acquisitive lust. You might remember that any antiques dealer who risks the high rents of central Rome to open an antiques store is probably acutely aware of the value of almost everything ever made, and will probably recognize anything of value long before his or her clients. Beware of fakes, remember to insure anything you have shipped home, and for larger purchases—anything more than 300,000 lire ($180) at any one store—keep your paperwork in order to obtain your eventual tax refund. (See "What to Buy" in Chapter 3.)

If you love to shop for antiques, one street that you should not miss is **via dei Coronari.** Buried in a colorful section of the Campus Martius (Renaissance Rome), via dei Coronari is an antiquer's dream, literally lined with magnificent vases, urns, chandeliers, breakfronts, chaises, refectory tables, candelabra—you name it. You'll find the entrance to the street just north of piazza Navona. Turn left outside the piazza, past the excavated ruins of Domitian's Stadium, and the street will be just ahead of you. There are more than 40 antiques stores in the next four blocks, and on our last trip we saw in the windows inlaid secretaries, marble pedestals, claw and ball tables, gilded consoles, and enamel clocks, among countless other treasures. Bring your pocket calculator with you (and know how to use it), and keep in mind that stores are frequently closed between 1 and 4pm.

Galleria Coronari
Via dei Coronari 59. ☎ **686-9917.**

Galleria Coronari is a desirable shop that might be used as a starting point to many other shops nearby. Many of its antiques are nostalgia-laden bric-a-brac small enough to fit into a suitcase, including jewelry, dolls, paintings, and elaborately ornate picture frames from the 19th century. Also represented is furniture from the 18th, 19th, and early 20th centuries, and such oddities as a completely

---

Impressions

A place where people scrutinized and jostled one another. It was open-air promiscuity, all Rome gathered together in the smallest possible space. . . . Its pleasure lay . . . in the forced elbowings which facilitated not only desired meetings but the satisfaction of curiosity, the display of vanity, and the garnering of endless tittle-tattle.
                                                                —Emile Zola on the via del Corso

furnished dollhouse, accurate even down to the miniature champagne bottles in the miniature pantry. Open Monday from 3:30 to 7:30pm and Tuesday through Saturday from 10am to 1pm and 3:30 to 7:30pm.

ART

Aldo di Castro
Via del Babuino 71. ☎ **679-4900.**

Aldo di Castro is one of the largest dealers of antique prints and engravings in Rome. You'll find rack after rack of depictions of everything from the Colosseum to the Pantheon, each evocative of the best architecture in the Mediterranean world, priced between $25 and $1,000 depending on the age and rarity of the engraving. Open Monday from 3:30 to 7:30pm and Tuesday through Saturday from 10am to 1pm and 3:30 to 7:30pm.

Galleria d'Arte Schneider
Rampa Mignanelli 10. ☎ **678-4019.**

Located a few steps from one of the ramps leading into the side of the Spanish Steps near the Hassler Hotel, this is one of the most enduring art galleries in Rome. Established in 1953 by Robert Schneider, an American-born professor of languages and art connoisseur, it specializes in lesser-known sculpture and paintings by Italians or foreign residents of Rome. Among the artists whose work has been promoted early in their careers by this gallery are Dimitre Hadzi, George d'Almeida, Paolo Buggiani, and Mirko Balsedella. Surprisingly, within the world of Italian art galleries, the frequently changing inventories here are considered relatively affordable, ranging in price from 1,000,000 to 10,000,000 lire ($625–$6,250). The building that contains the gallery, incidentally, was designed in the 19th century by a Danish sculptor with the intention that it serve as a refuge for artists ever after. The day-to-day operations of the gallery are conducted by Mr. Schneider's charming wife, Dolores. Open Monday through Saturday from 4:30 to 7:30pm (closed for part of August).

Giovanni B. Panatta Fine Art Shop
Via Francesco Crispi 117. ☎ **679-5948.**

Giovanni B. Panatta Fine Art Shop, in business since 1890, is up the hill toward the Borghese gardens. Here you'll find excellent prints in color and black and white covering a variety of subjects from 18th-century Roman street scenes to astrological charts. There is also a good selection of reproductions of medieval and Renaissance art that are attractive and reasonably priced. Open Monday from 3:30 to 7:30pm and Tuesday through Saturday from 9:15am to 1pm and 3:30 to 7:30pm.

BOOKSTORES

Economy Book and Video Center
Via Torino 136. ☎ **474-6877.**

Catering to the expatriate English-speaking communities of Rome, this bookstore sells only English-language books (both new and used, paperback and hardcover), greeting cards, and videos. Staffed by British, Australian, or American workers, it lies about a block from the piazza della Repubblica Metro station, and bus lines no. 64 and 70. In summer, it's open Monday through Friday from 9am to 8pm and Saturday from 9am to 2pm. In winter, it's open Monday from 3 to 8pm and Tuesday through Saturday from 9am to 8pm.

The Lion Bookshop
Via del Babuino 181. ☎ **322-58-37.**

The Lion Bookshop is the oldest English-language bookshop in town, specializing in literature, both American and English. It also sells children's books and photographic volumes on both Rome and Italy. A vast choice of English-language videos is for sale or rent. The store is open Monday through Saturday from 9:30am to 1:30pm and 3:30 to 7:30pm (closed in August).

Rizzoli
Largo Chigi 15. ☎ **679-6641.**

Rizzoli's collection of Italian-language books is one of the largest in Rome, but if your native language is French, English, German, or Spanish, the interminable shelves of this very large bookstore have a section to amuse, enlighten, and entertain you. Open Monday through Saturday from 9am to 2pm and 2:30 to 7:30pm and Sunday 10:30am to 1:30pm and 4 to 8pm.

DEPARTMENT STORES

La Rinascente
Piazza Colonna, via del Corso 189. ☎ **679-7691.**

The upscale department store La Rinascente offers clothing, hosiery, perfume, cosmetics, housewares, and furniture. It also has its own line of clothing (Ellerre) for men, women, and children. This is the largest of the Italian department-store chains; its name is seen frequently on billboards and in newspaper ads throughout the country. Open Monday from 2 to 7:30pm and Tuesday through Saturday from 9:30am to 7:30pm.

Standa
Corso Francia 124. ☎ **333-8719.**

Rome's six Standa branches could not be considered stylish by any stretch of the imagination, but some visitors find it enlightening to wander—just once—through the racks of department-store staples to see what an average Italian household might accumulate. Other branches are at corso Trieste 200, via Trionfale, via Cola di Rienzo 173, viale Regina Margherita, and viale Trastevere 60. Open Monday from 3:30 to 7:30pm and Tuesday through Saturday from 9am to 1pm and 2:30 to 7:30pm.

DISCOUNT SHOPPING

Certain stores that can't move their merchandise at any price often consign their unwanted goods to discounters. In Italy, the original labels are usually still inside the garment (and you'll find some very chic labels strewn in with mounds of other garments). Know in advance, however, that these garments couldn't be sold at higher prices in more glamorous shops, and some garments are either the wrong size, the wrong "look," or a stylistic mistake that the original designer wishes had never been produced.

Discount System
Via del Viminale 35. ☎ **474-6545.**

Discount System sells men's and women's wear by many of the big names (Armani, Valentino, Nino Cerruti, Fendi, and Krizia). Even if an item isn't from a famous designer, it often belongs to a factory that produces some of the best qual-ity of Italian fashion. However, don't give up hope: if you find something you like, know that it will be priced at around 50% of its original price tag in its original boutique, and it just might be a cut-rate gem well worth your effort. Open Mon-day from 3:30 to 7:30pm and Tuesday through Saturday from 9:30am to 1pm and 3:30 to 7:30pm.

EYEGLASSES

La Barbera
Via Barberini 74. ☎ **483628.**

La Barbera, in business since 1837, has built a substantial reputation in the field of optical equipment. The store also carries a full spectrum of related wares: cam-eras, films, binoculars, opera glasses, and microscopes. You can have prescription glasses reproduced in 48 hours. For those hangouts on via Vittorio Veneto and piazza del Popolo, take a look at Barbera's collection of sunglass frames—more than 5,000 varieties. Open Monday from 3:30 to 7:30pm and Tuesday through Saturday from 9am to 7:30pm.

FASHION

For Men

Angelo
Via Bissolati 34. ☎ **474-1796.**

This exclusive store is a custom tailor for discerning men. It has been featured in such publications as *Esquire* and *Gentleman's Quarterly.* Angelo employs the best cutters and craftspeople, and his taste in style and design is impeccable. Custom shirts, dinner jackets, even casual wear, can be made on short notice. If you don't have time to wait, Angelo will ship anywhere in the world. The outlet also sells ready-made items such as cardigans, cashmere pullovers, evening shirts, suits, and overcoats. Open Monday through Friday from 9:30am to 1pm and 3:30 to 7:30pm and Saturday 3:30 to 7:30pm.

Emporio Armani
Via del Babuino 119. ☎ **679-6898.**

This store stocks relatively inexpensive men's wear crafted by the couturier who has dressed perhaps more stage and screen stars than any other designer in Italy. The designer's more expensive line—sold at sometimes staggering prices that are nonetheless sometimes 30% less expensive than what you'd pay in the United States—lies a short walk away, at Giorgio Armani, via Condotti 77 (☎ 699-1460). Hours of both branches are Monday from 3 to 7pm, Tuesday through Friday from 10am to 7pm, and Saturday from 9am to 7pm.

Valentino
Via Mario de' Fiori 22. ☎ **678-3656.**

Behind all the chrome mirrors at via Mario de' Fiori is this swank emporium, which sells the men's clothing of this acclaimed designer. Here you can become the most fashionable man in town (if you can afford the high prices). Valentino's women's haute couture is sold around the corner, in an even bigger showroom at via Bocce di Leone 15 (☎ 679-5862). Open Monday from 3 to 7pm and Tues-day through Saturday from 10am to 7pm.

For Women

Benetton

Via Condotti 18. ☎ **679-7982.**

Prices at this branch of the worldwide sportswear distributor are about the same as at branches at less glamorous addresses. Famous for woolen sweaters, tennis wear, blazers, and the kind of outfits you'd want to wear on a private yacht, this company has suffered (like every other clothier) from inexpensive Asian copies of its designs. The original, however, is still the greatest. Open Monday from 3:30 to 7:30pm and Tuesday through Saturday from 10am to 7:30pm.

Gianfranco Ferre

Via Borgognona 42B. ☎ **679-0050.**

Here you can find the women's line of this famous designer whose clothes have been called "adventurous." Open Monday from 3:30 to 7:30pm and Tuesday through Saturday from 9:30am to 1:30pm and 3:30 to 7:30pm.

Givenchy

Via Borgognona 21. ☎ **678-4058.**

This is the Roman headquarters of one of the great designer names of France, Givenchy, a company known since World War I for its couture. In its Roman branch, the company emphasizes ready-to-wear garments for stylish women with warm Italian weather in mind. Open Monday from 3 to 7pm and Tuesday through Saturday from 10am to 7pm.

Max Mara

Via Frattina 28, at largo Goldoni. ☎ **679-3638.**

Max Mara is one of the best outlets in Rome for women's clothing if you like to look chic and witty. The fabrics are appealing and the alterations are free. Open Monday from 3:30 to 7:30pm and Tuesday through Saturday from 10am to 2pm and 3:30 to 7:30pm.

Renato Balestra

Via Sistina 67. ☎ **679-5424.**

Rapidly approaching the stratospheric upper levels of Italian fashion is Renato Balestra, whose women's clothing attains standards of lighthearted elegance at its best when designed and worn in Italy. This branch carries a complete line of the latest Balestra ready-to-wear designs for women. The company's administrative headquarters and the center of its couture department is nearby, at via Ludovici 35 (☎ 482-1723), although advance appointments are recommended there. It's probably advisable to stop into the via Sistina branch for an idea of the designer's style before launching yourself into a dialogue with Balestra's couture department, if only to save costs. Both outlets are open Monday from 3 to 7pm, Tuesday through Friday from 10am to 7:30pm, and Saturday from 9am to 7pm.

For Children

Baby House

Via Cola di Rienzo 117. ☎ **321-4291.**

Baby House offers what might be the most label-conscious collection of children's and young people's clothing in Italy. With an inventory of clothes suitable for children and adolescents to age 15, they sell clothing by Valentino, Bussardi, and Laura

Biagiotti, whose threads are usually reserved for adult, rather than juvenile, playtime. Open Monday from 3:30 to 7:30pm and Tuesday through Saturday from 9am to 1pm and 3:30 to 7:30pm.

Benetton
Via Condotti 19. ☎ **679-7982.**

Despite its elegant address (see above), Benetton isn't as expensive as you might expect. This store is an outlet for children's clothes (from infants to age 12) of the famous sportswear manufacturer. You can find rugby shirts, corduroys and jeans, and accessories for junior or your favorite nephews and nieces in a wide selection of colors and styles. Open Monday from 3:30 to 7:30pm and Tuesday through Saturday from 10am to 7:30pm.

The College
Via Vittoria 52. ☎ **678-4073.**

The College has everything you'll need to make adorable children more adorable, and less-adorable children at least presentable. Part of the inventory of this place is reserved for adult men and women, but the majority is intended for the infant and early adolescent offspring of the store's older clients. Open Monday from 3:30 to 7:30pm and Tuesday through Saturday from 9:30am to 1pm and 3:30 to 7:30pm. This establishment maintains another branch at via Condotti 47 (☎ 678-7737), which sells only clothes for women, not for children or men. Both branches maintain the same hours.

Sportswear

Oliver
Via del Babuino 61. ☎ **67-98-314.**

Specializing exclusively in sportswear for men and for women, this is the least expensive line of clothing offered by the otherwise chillingly expensive designer, Valentino. Clothing is easy to wear and casually stylish, with warm-weather climates in mind. Open Monday from 3 to 7pm, and Tuesday through Saturday from 10am to 7:30pm.

FOOD

Castroni
Via Cola di Rienzo 196. ☎ **687-4383.**

Castroni carries an amazing array of unusual foodstuffs from throughout the Mediterranean. If you want herbs from Apulia, pepperoncino oil, cheese from the Valle d'Aosta, or that strange brand of balsamic vinegar whose name you can never remember, Castroni will probably have it. Large, old-fashioned, and filled to the rafters with the abundance of agrarian Italy, it also carries certain foods that are considered exotic in Italy but commonplace in North America, such as taco shells and corn curls. Open Monday through Saturday from 8am to 2pm and 3:30 to 8pm.

GIFTS

Anatriello del Regalo
Via Frattina 123. ☎ **678-9601.**

This store is known for stocking an inventory of new and antique silver, some of it among the most unusual in Italy. All of the new items are made by Italian silversmiths, in designs ranging from the whimsical to the severely formal and dignified. Also on display are antique pieces of silver from England, Germany, and Switzerland. Open Monday from 3:30 to 7:30pm and Tuesday through Saturday from 9am to 1pm and 3:30 to 7:30pm.

A. Grispigni

Via Francesco Crispi 59. ☎ **679-0290.**

At the corner of via Sistina is A. Grispigni, which has a large assortment of leather-covered boxes, women's purses, compacts, desk sets, and cigarette cases. Many items, like Venetian wallets and Florentine boxes, are inlaid with gold. Open Monday from 3:30 to 7pm and Tuesday through Saturday from 9:30am to 1pm and 3:30 to 7pm.

JEWELRY

Federico Buccellati

Via Condotti 31. ☎ **679-0329.**

Federico Buccellati, one of the best gold- and silversmiths in Italy, sells neo-Renaissance creations that will change your thinking about the way gold and silver are designed. Here you will discover the tradition and beauty of handmade jewelry and holloware with designs that recall those of Renaissance goldmaster Benvenuto Cellini. Open Tuesday through Saturday from 10am to 1:30pm and 3 to 7pm.

Bulgari

Via Condotti 10. ☎ **679-3876.**

Bulgari is Rome's most prestigious jeweler and has been for more than a century. The shop window, on a conspicuously affluent stretch of the via Condotti, is a bit of a visual attraction in its own right. Bulgari designs combine classical Greek aesthetics with Italian taste. Over the years Bulgari has followed changes in style, yet clings to tradition as well. Prices range from "affordable" to the "sky is the limit." Open Monday from 3 to 7pm and Tuesday through Saturday from 10am to 7pm.

E. Fiore

Via Ludovisi 31. ☎ **481-9296.**

At E. Fiore, near via Vittorio Veneto, you can choose a jewel and have it set according to your specifications. Or you can make your selection from a rich assortment of charms, bracelets, necklaces, rings, brooches, corals, pearls, and cameos. Also featured are elegant watches, silverware, and goldware. Fiore also does expert repair work on jewelry and watches. Open Monday from 3:30 to 7pm and Tuesday through Saturday from 9am to 1pm and 3:30 to 7pm (closed August).

LEATHER

Italian leather is among the very best in the world; it can attain butter-soft textures more pliable than cloth. You'll find hundreds of leather stores in Rome, many of them excellent.

Cesare Diomedi Leather Goods

Via Vittorio Emanuele Orlando 96–97. ☎ **488-4822.**

Cesare Diomedi Leather Goods, located in front of the Grand Hotel, offers one of the most outstanding collections of leather goods in Rome. And leather isn't all you'll find in this small, two-story shop with an attractive winding staircase.

There are many other distinctive gift items—small gold cigarette cases, jeweled umbrellas—that make this a good stopping-off point for that last important item. Upstairs is a wide assortment of elegant leather luggage and accessories. Open Monday from 3:30 to 7:30pm and Tuesday through Saturday from 9am to 1pm and 3:30 to 7:30pm.

Fendi
Via Borgognona 36A–39. ☎ **679-7641.**

Fendi is mainly known for its avant-garde leather goods, but it also has furs, stylish purses, ready-to-wear clothing, and a new men's line of clothing and accessories. Gift items, home furnishings, and sports accessories are also sold in Fendi's, which is designated by an "F." Open Monday from 3:30 to 7:30pm and Tuesday through Saturday from 9:30am to 7:30pm (closed Saturday afternoon from July to September).

Gucci
Via Condotti 8. ☎ **679-0405.**

Gucci, of course, is a legend. An established firm since 1900, its merchandise consists of high-class leather goods, such as suitcases, handbags, wallets, shoes, and desk accessories. It also has departments of elegant men's and women's wear, including beautiful shirts, blouses, and dresses, as well as ties and neck scarves of numerous designs. *La bella figura* is alive and well at Gucci, and prices have never been higher. Among the many temptations is Gucci's own perfume. Open Monday from 3 to 7pm and Tuesday through Saturday from 10am to 7pm.

Pappagallo
Via Francesco Crispi 115. ☎ **678-3011.**

At Pappagallo ("Parrot"), a suede-and-leather factory, the staff make all manner of leather goods, including bags, wallets, and suede coats. The quality is fine, too, and the prices are reasonable. Open Monday from 3:30 to 7pm and Tuesday through Saturday from 9am to 1pm and 3:30 to 7pm.

LINGERIE

Brighenti
Via Frattina 7–8. ☎ **679-1484.**

At Brighenti, amid several famous neighbors on via Frattina, you might run across a "seductive fantasy." It is strictly *lingerie di lusso,* or perhaps better phrased, *haute corseterie.* Open Monday from 3:30 to 7:30pm and Tuesday through Saturday from 9am to 1pm and 3:30 to 7:30pm (closed August).

Tomassini di Luisa Romagnoli
Via Sistina 119. ☎ **488-1909.**

Tomassini di Luisa Romagnoli offers delicately beautiful lingerie and negligees, all of which are original designs of Luisa Romagnoli. Most of the merchandise sold here is of shimmery Italian silk; other items, to a lesser degree, are of fluffy cotton or frothy nylon. Highly revealing, garments are sold either ready-to-wear or are custom-made. Open Monday from 3:30 to 7:30pm and Tuesday through Sunday from 9am to 1pm and 3:30 to 7:30pm.

LIQUORS

Ai Monasteri
Piazza delle Cinque Lune 76. ☎ **68-80-2783.**

Ai Monasteri has one of the city's best selections; there's a treasure trove of liquors (including liqueurs and wines), honey, and herbal teas made in monasteries and convents all over Italy. You can buy excellent chocolates and other candies here as well. You make your selections in a quiet atmosphere that is reminiscent of a monastery, just two blocks from Bernini's Fountain of the Four Rivers in piazza Navona. The shop will ship some items home for you. Open Monday through Wednesday and Friday and Saturday from 9am to 1pm and 4:30 to 7:30pm, and on Thursday from 9am to 1pm.

MARKETS

At the sprawling **Porta Portese** open-air flea market of Rome held every Sunday morning, every peddler from Trastevere and the surrounding Castelli Romani sets up a temporary shop. The vendors are likely to sell merchandise ranging from secondhand paintings of madonnas to termite-eaten Il Duce wooden medallions, to pseudo-Etruscan hairpins, to bushels of rosaries, to 1947 TV sets, to books printed in 1835. Serious shoppers can often ferret out a good buy. If you've ever been impressed with the bargaining power of the Spaniard, you haven't seen anything till you've viewed an Italian.

Go to the flea market in Trastevere, near the end of viale Trastevere (bus no. 75 to Porta Portese), then a short walk away to via Portuense, to catch the workday Roman in an unguarded moment. By 10:30am the market is full of people. Some of the vendors get there as early as midnight to get their choice space. As you would at any street market, beware of pickpockets. Open Sunday from 7am to 1pm.

MOSAICS

Savelli

Via Paolo VI no. 27. ☎ **683-07-017.**

This company specializes in the manufacture and sale of mosaics, an art form as old as the Roman Empire itself. Many of the objects displayed in the company's gallery were inspired by ancient originals discovered in thousands of excavations throughout the Italian peninsula, including those at Pompeii and Ostia. Others, especially the floral designs, depend on the whim and creativity of the artists. Objects include tabletops, boxes, and vessels for holding flowers or whatever. The cheapest mosaic objects begin at around $125, and are unsigned products crafted by students at a school for artists that is partially funded by the Vatican. Objects made in the Savelli workshops that are signed by the individual artists (and that tend to be larger and more elaborate) range from $500 to as much as $25,000. The outlet also contains a collection of small souvenir items such as keychains and carved statues. Open Monday through Saturday from 9am to 6:30pm and Sunday from 9:30am to 1:30pm.

RELIGIOUS ART

Anna Maria Gaudenzi

Piazza delle Minerva 69A. ☎ **679-0431.**

Set in a neighborhood loaded with purveyors of religious art and icons, this shop claims to be the oldest of its type in Rome. If you collect depictions of the Mother of Jesus, paintings of the saints, exotic rosaries, chalices, small statues, or medals, you can feel secure knowing that thousands of pilgrims have spent their money here before you. Whether you view its merchandise as a devotional aid or as bizarre kitsch, this shop has it all. Open Monday from 3:30 to 7:30pm and Tuesday through Saturday from 9am to 1pm and 3:30 to 7:30pm (closed August 10–20).

SHOES

Dominici
Via del Corso 14. ☎ **361-0591.**

Dominici, located behind an understated facade a few steps from piazza del Popolo, shelters an amusing and lighthearted collection of men's and women's shoes in a pleasing variety of vivid colors. The style is aggressively young at heart and the quality is good. Open Monday from 3:30 to 8pm and Tuesday through Saturday from 9:30am to 1pm and 3:30pm.

Salvatore Ferragamo
Via Condotti 73–74. ☎ **679-8402.**

Salvatore Ferragamo sells elegant and fabled footwear, plus women's clothing and accessories, and ties, in an atmosphere full of Italian style. The name became famous in America when such screen stars as Pola Negri and Greta Garbo began appearing in Ferragamo shoes. The shop is open Monday through Saturday from 10am to 7pm. There are always many customers waiting to enter the shop. Management allows them in in small groups. Figure on a 30-minute wait outside.

Fragiacomo
Via Condotti 35. ☎ **679-8780.**

Fragiacomo sells shoes for men and women in a champagne-colored showroom with gilt-painted chairs and big display cases. Open Monday from 3:30 to 7:30pm and Tuesday through Saturday from 9:30am to 1:30pm and 3:30 to 7:30pm.

Lily of Florence
Via Lombardia 38 (off via Vittorio Veneto). ☎ **474-0262.**

This famous Florentine shoemaker now has a shop in Rome, with the same merchandise that made the outlet so well known in the Tuscan capital. Colors come in a wide range, the designs are stylish, and leather texture is of good quality. Shoes for both men and women are sold here, and American sizes are a feature. Open Monday through Saturday from 9:30am to 8pm.

WINE

Buccone
Via Ripetta. ☎ **361-2154.**

This is a historic wine shop, right near piazza del Popolo. Its selection of wines and gastronomic specialties is considered among the finest in Rome. Open Monday through Saturday from 9am to 1:30pm and 4 to 8:30pm.

Enoteca Rocchi
Via Alessandro Scarlatti 7. ☎ **855-1022.**

Rocchi carries one of Rome's largest selections of wines and liqueurs; they'll ship your purchase anywhere. Open Monday through Saturday from 8:30am to 2pm and 4:30 to 8pm (closed August).

Trimani il Wine Bar
Via Goito 20. ☎ **446-9661.**

Trimani, established in 1821, sells wines and spirits from Italy, among other offerings. Purchases can be shipped to your home. Trimani collaborates with the
Italian wine magazine *Gambero Rosso,* organizing some lectures about wine where
devotees can improve their knowledge and educate their tastebuds. Open Monday through Saturday from 8:30am to 1:30pm and 3:30 to 8pm.

Offbeat Shopping

- **Galleria 2 RC**, via dei Delfini 16 (☎ 6792811), has the best print studio in
  Rome, a collection of beautifully reproduced works from famous artists. It's
  almost as good as owning the real thing.

- **Avignonese,** via Margutta 16 (☎ 361-4004), can be counted on to come up
  with unusual and tasteful objects for the home. Each object from lamps to
  terra-cotta boxes appears unique and unusual.

- **Alinari,** via d'Albert 16A (☎ 6792923), takes its name from the famed
  Florentine photographer of the 19th century. Original prints of Alinari are
  almost as prized as paintings in national galleries. Photographs by him are sold
  here, a record of how Rome looked a century ago.

- **Olivi,** via del Babuino 136 (☎ 6798682), might be called "The Old Curiosity Shop of Rome." Professor Olivi is a whiz when it comes to knowing
  Roman history and collecting a treasure trove of old prints.

- **Fava,** via del Babuino 180 (☎ 3610807), recaptures the era when Neapolitans sold 17th- and 18th-century pictures of the eruptions of Vesuvius, once
  highly sought by collectors. Many of these "volcanic paintings" of yesterday—
  so eagerly sought by Britishers in particular—can still cause a conflagration
  today. Really unusual art from the attics of yesterday.

- **Livio di Simone,** via San Giacomo 23 (☎ 6783906). Unusual suitcases (in
  many shapes and sizes) in which hand-painted canvas has been sewn into the
  bags are sold here. Every one is chic and lovely.

- **Papirus,** via di Capo le Case 55A (☎ 6780418), is for the paper aficionado.
  All paper sold here is colored by hand. Especially enticing is marblized paper
  that first came from France in the days of Louis XIII. Beautiful diary covers
  are sold for the budding Anaïs Nin of the future.

- **Battistoni,** via Condotti 61A (☎ 6786241). The finest men's shirts in the
  world. After having said that, as Marlene Dietrich once noted, you don't need
  to sell the shop anymore. In addition, they also hawk a men's cologne, called
  Marte, or Mars, for the "man who likes to conquer."

- **Apollodoro,** piazza Mignanelli 17 (☎ 6787557), is one of the most spectacular design outlets and art galleries in Italy. The gallery was designed by
  Paolo Portoghesi, one of Italy's leading architects, who was inspired by the
  1st century A.D. Trajan's Forum. Some of the most avant garde paintings and
  sculpture in town are on sale here.

- **Siragusa,** via delle Carrozze 64 (☎ 6797085), is more like a museum than a
  shop, specializing in unusual jewelry, based on ancient carved stones or archaeological pieces. Handmade chains, for example, often hold coins and beads
  discovered in Asia Minor that date from the 3rd to the 4th century B.C.

4 Rome After Dark

When the sun goes down across the city, palaces, ruins, fountains, and monuments are bathed in a theatrical white light. There are actually few evening occupations quite as pleasurable as a stroll past the solemn pillars of old temples or the cascading torrents of Renaissance fountains glowing under the blue-black sky. Of the **fountains,** the Naiads (piazza della Repubblica), the Tortoises (piazza Mattei), and, of course, the Trevi are particularly beautiful at night. The **Capitoline Hill** is magnificently lit after dark, with its measured Renaissance facades glowing like jewel boxes. Behind the Senatorial Palace is a fine view of the **Roman Forum.** If you're staying across the Tiber, **piazza di San Pietro** (in front of St. Peter's Basilica) is particularly impressive at night without tour buses and crowds. And a combination of illuminated architecture, Renaissance fountains, and, frequently, sidewalk shows and art expositions is at **piazza Navona.** If you're ambitious and have a good sense of direction, try exploring the streets to the west of piazza Navona, which look like a stage set when they're lit at night.

There are no inexpensive nightclubs in Rome, so be duly warned. Another important warning: During the peak of the summer visiting days, usually in August, all nightclub proprietors seem to lock their doors and head for the seashore. Many of them seem to operate alternate clubs at coastal resorts. Some of them close at different times each year, so it's hard to keep up-to-date. Always have your hotel check to see if a club is operating before you make a trek to it. Many of the legitimate nightclubs, besides being expensive, are highlighted by hookers plying their trade. Younger people fare better than some more sedate folk, as the discos open and close with freewheeling abandon.

But remember that for many Romans, a night on the town means dining late at a trattoria. The local denizens like to drink wine and talk after their meal, even when the waiters are putting chairs on top of empty tables.

Even if you don't speak Italian, you can generally follow the listings of special events and evening entertainment featured in *La Repubblica,* one of the leading Italian newspapers. *TrovaRoma,* a special weekly entertainment supplement—good for the coming week—is published in this paper on Thursday.

THE PERFORMING ARTS
CLASSICAL MUSIC

Academy of St. Cecelia
Via della Conciliazione 4. ☎ **678-0742.** Tickets 25,000–55,000 lire ($15.65–$34.40).

Concerts given by the orchestra of the Academy of St. Cecilia usually take place at piazza di Villa Giulia, site of the Etruscan Museum, from the end of June to the end of July (take bus no. 30); in winter they are held in the Academy's concert hall on via della Conciliazione. Depending on circumstances, the organization sometimes selects other addresses in Rome for its concerts, including a handful of historic churches, when available. Performance nights are Saturday, Sunday, and Monday.

Teatro Olimpico
Piazza Gentile da Fabriano. ☎ **323-4890.** Tickets 20,000–80,000 lire ($12.50–$50), depending on the event.

Large and well-publicized, this echoing stage hosts a widely divergent collection of singers, both classical and pop, who perform according to a schedule that sometimes changes at the last minute. Occasionally, the space is devoted to chamber orchestras or orchestral visits from foreign countries.

OPERA

Teatro dell'opera

Piazza Beniamino Gigli 1. ☎ **481601.** Tickets 20,000–260,000 lire ($12.50–$162.50).

If you're in the capital for the opera season, usually from the end of December until June, you may want to attend the historic Rome Opera House, located off via Nazionale. Nothing is presented here in August. In the summer the venue switches to the Terme di Caracalla.

Terme di Caracalla

Via delle Terme di Caracalla. ☎ **488-3641.** Tickets, 30,000–65,000 lire ($18.75–$40.65) opera; 25,000–50,000 lire ($15.65–$31.25) ballet.

When the Romans stage an event, they like it to be of epic quality. At the Imperial Baths of Caracalla, you can attend summer performances of grand opera, usually from the first of July to the middle of August. Ballet troupes also perform. Sponsored by the Teatro dell'Opera, the season is likely to include Verdi's *Aïda,* the best selection to employ the grandeur of the setting. The ending of *Aïda* is a smash—the celebrated "double scene," the floodlit upper part representing the Temple of Vulcan and the part underneath, the tomb. And for sheer unrivaled Cecil B. de Mille, it's worth seeing the phalanx of trumpeters enter in the second act, playing the "Grand March." They are followed by Egyptian troops, with banners, chariots, Ethiopian slaves, dancing girls—a spectacular crescendo.

Tickets are on sale at the Teatro dell'Opera (see above). If you don't mind taking along a pair of binoculars, try an unreserved seat.

BALLET & DANCE

Performances of the **Rome Opera Ballet** are given at the Teatro dell'Opera (see above). The regular repertoire of classical ballet is supplemented by performances of internationally acclaimed guest artists, and Rome is on the major agenda for troupes from around the world, ranging from the United States to Russia. Major performances are at the Teatro dell'Opera, but watch for announcements in the weekly entertainment guides to Rome about other venues, including Teatro Olimpico or even open-air ballet performances. Both modern (such as the Alvin Ailey dancers) or classical dance troupes appear frequently in Rome. Check the entertainment guides to see what's happening at the time of your visit.

DINNER THEATER

Fantasie di Trastevere

Via di Santa Dorotea 6. ☎ **588-1671.**

Roman rusticity is combined with theatrical flair at Fantasie di Trastevere, the "people's theater" where the famous actor Petrolini made his debut. Dressed in regional garb of Italian provinces, the waiters serve with drama. The cuisine isn't subtle, but it's bountiful. Such dishes as the classic saltimbocca (ham with veal) are prepared, preceded by tasty pasta (including one with sauce made with red peppers), and everything is aided by the wines from the Castelli Romani.

Accompanying the main dishes is a big basket of warm, country-coarse herb bread (you'll tear off hunks). Expect to pay 75,000–85,000 lire ($46.90–$53.15) for a full meal. If you visit for a drink, the first one will cost 35,000 lire ($21.90). Some two dozen folk singers and musicians in regional costumes perform, making it a festive affair. Meals are served daily beginning at 8pm, and piano bar music is offered from 8:30 to 9:30pm, followed by the show, lasting from 9:30 to 10:30pm.

THE CLUB & MUSIC SCENE
NIGHTCLUBS
Arciliuto

Piazza Monte Vecchio 5. ☎ **687-9419.** Cover (including one drink) 35,000 lire ($21.90); subsequent drinks are 10,000 lire ($6.25). Closed July 20–Sept 3.

Arciliuto is one of the most romantic candlelit spots in Rome. It was reputedly the former studio of Raphael. From 10pm to 2am Monday through Saturday guests enjoy a musical salon ambience, listening to both a guitarist and flutist. The evening's presentation also includes live Neapolitan songs, and new Italian madrigals, even current hits from Broadway or the London's West End. The setting and atmosphere are intimate. This highly recommended establishment is hard to find, but it's within walking distance of piazza Navona. Closed Sunday.

La Cabala/The Blue Bar/Hostaria dell'Orso

Via dei Soldati 25. ☎ **686-4221.** Cover in Blue Bar, first drink 35,000 lire ($21.90); subsequent drinks 25,000 lire ($15.65). In La Cabala, first drink 35,000 lire ($21.90); subsequent drinks 25,000 lire ($15.65).

During the heyday of *la dolce vita*, these premises were the most talked-about evening venue of Rome, attracting elegant Italians and well-heeled foreigners throughout the 1950s and 1960s. Today, the spotlight of glamor has shifted to other venues, although many Romans continue to view the place with affection and nostalgia. The setting is a 14th-century palazzo, near piazza Navona, which began its life as a simple inn. Clients who used its dining and/or overnight facilities through the ages have included St. Francis of Assisi, Dante, Rabelais, Montaigne, Goethe, and thousands of other, less well-documented scholars and pilgrims.

Today, the establishment contains three separate areas. In the cellar, The Blue Bar is a moody but mellow enclave featuring cocktails and the music from two pianists and guitarists. On the street level is a formal restaurant serving international cuisine, the Hostaria dell'Orso. Appetizers range from 25,000–35,000 lire ($15.65–$21.90), with main courses costing 50,000–70,000 lire ($31.25–$43.75). Menu items include *spigolo in cartoccio con frutti di mar* (sea bass cooked in a paper bag, garnished with shellfish), turbot with sliced and herbed potatoes, *spaghetti in cartoccio* with lobster and risotto served with scampi and radiccio. One floor above street level is La Cabala, a disco that attracts a well-dressed, over-25-year-old crowd who tend to know their way around. Some clients merge time in all three areas during a night on the town, although no one will mind if you decide to visit only the disco or only the bar. The restaurant serves dinner only, Monday through Saturday from 7:30pm to midnight. The Blue Bar and La Cabala are open Monday through Saturday from 10:30pm to 3 or 4am, depending on business. All three floors are closed on Sunday. If you plan to dine here, reservations are recommended.

Divina

Via Romagnosi 11A. ☎ **361-1348.** Cover (including one drink) Tues–Thurs 30,000 lire ($18.75), Fri–Sat 35,000 lire ($21.90).

The aptly named Divina is a chic rendezvous, a relaxing piano bar where you just might end up spending the evening. Many people still come here looking for Gil's, a famous club that once stood on this spot, which has gone down in Roman nightlife history. What you get today is a romantic evening in one of several small rooms lined with mirrors. It's open Tuesday through Saturday from 11pm to either 4 or 5am. *Note:* It's important to call for a reservation, as some nights are by invitation only, at which time you can't get in unless you're a "friend of the club" (frequent patron).

Da Ciceruacchio

Via del Porto 1. ☎ **580-6046.**

Located on piazza dei Mercanti, this restaurant was once a sunken jail—the ancient vine-covered walls date from the days of the Roman Empire. Folkloric groups are presented throughout the evening, especially singers of Neapolitan songs, accompanied by guitars and harmonicas—a rich repertoire of oldtime favorites, some of them with bawdy lyrics. Featured here are charcoal-broiled steaks and chops, along with lots of local wine. Bean soup is a specialty. The grilled mushrooms are another good opening, as is the spaghetti with clams. For a main course, I'd recommend scampi with curry or charcoal-broiled meats. You can dine here Tuesday through Sunday from 8pm to midnight for 50,000–60,000 lire ($31.25–$37.50).

Da Meo Patacca

Piazza dei Mercanti 30. ☎ **5833-1086.**

Da Meo Patacca, in Trastevere, would certainly have pleased Barnum and Bailey. On a gaslit piazza from the Middle Ages, it serves bountiful self-styled "Roman country" meals to flocks of tourists. The atmosphere is one of extravaganza— primitive, colorful, theatrical in a carnival sense—good fun if you're in the mood. From the huge open spit and the charcoal grill, many platters are served. Downstairs is a vast cellar with strolling musicians and singers. Utilizing a tavern theme, the restaurant is decked out with wagon wheels, along with garlands of pepper and garlic. And many offerings are as adventurous as the decor: wild boar, wild hare, and quail; but there are also corn on the cob, pork and beans, thick-cut sirloins, and chicken on a spit. Come here if you desire general fun and entertainment—not refined cuisine. Expect to spend 60,000 lire ($37.50) and up for a meal here. In summer, you can dine at outdoor tables. It's open daily from 8 to 11:30pm.

JAZZ, SOUL & FUNK

Alexanderplatz

Via Ostia 9. ☎ **372-9398.**

At Alexanderplatz, at this leading club, you can hear jazz (not rock) every night except Sunday from 9pm to 2am, with live music beginning at 10:15pm. Entrance costs 12,000 lire ($7.50). A whisky costs from 10,000 lire ($6.25). There's also a restaurant, with a good Italian kitchen, that serves everything from pesto alla genovese to gnocchi alla romana. Full meals cost 35,000–40,000 lire ($21.90–$25).

Big Mama

Vicolo San Francesco a Ripa 18. ☎ **581-2551.** Cover 20,000 lire ($12.50) one-time membership card, plus 20,000–30,000 lire ($12.50–$18.75) cover for big acts; free for minor shows.

Big Mama is a hangout for jazz and blues musicians where you're likely to meet the up-and-coming jazz stars of tomorrow. But sometimes the big names do appear as well. The entrance fee, therefore, depends on what's being presented. The club is open Monday through Saturday from 9pm to 1:30am. Drinks range from 8,000–10,000 lire ($5–$6.25). Closed July through September.

Fonclea

Via Crescenzio 82A. ☎ **689-6302.** Cover 10,000 lire ($6.25) except Sunday through Thursday, when it's free, but only between 8pm and 9pm.

Fonclea offers live music every night—dixieland, rock, rhythm and blues. This is basically a cellar jazz establishment and crowded pub that attracts patrons from all walks of Roman life. The music starts at 10:30pm and usually lasts until 12:30pm. The club is open nightly from 8pm to 2:30am (on Friday and Saturday it stays open until 3:30am). There's also a restaurant that features grilled meats, salads, and crêpes. A meal starts at 35,000 lire ($21.90), but if you want dinner it's best to reserve a table, as the club becomes crowded after 10:30pm. Drinks run 8,000–12,000 lire ($5–$7.50). Closed July and August.

Gilda

Via Mario dei Fiori 97. ☎ **678-4838.** Cover (including one drink) Sun–Thurs 35,000 lire ($21.90), Fri–Sat 40,000 lire ($25).

Gilda is an adventurous combination of nightclub, disco, and restaurant known for the glamorous acts it books. In the past it has hosted Diana Ross and splashy, Paris-type revues, often with young women from England and the United States. The artistic direction assures first-class shows, a well-run restaurant, and disco music played between the live musical acts. Former patrons have included everybody from Sylvester Stallone to Vanessa Redgrave. The restaurant opens at 9:30pm and occasionally presents shows. An international cuisine is featured, with meals costing from 85,000 lire ($53.15). The nightclub, opening at midnight, presents music of the 1960s as well as modern recordings. The club stays open Tuesday through Sunday until 3 or 3:30am. There is also an attractive piano bar within the premises called Swing, featuring Italian and Latino-American music.

Music Inn

Largo dei Fiorentini 3. ☎ **688-02-220.** Cover 15,000 lire ($9.40).

The Music Inn is considered among the leading jazz clubs of Rome. Some of the biggest names in jazz, both European and American, have performed here. Open Tuesday through Sunday from 8pm to 2am. Closed in July and August.

Notorious

Via San Nicola de Tolentino 22. ☎ **474-6888.** Cover (including one drink) 35,000 lire ($21.90).

Notorious really isn't. It's one of the most popular discos of Rome, open Tuesday through Sunday from 11pm to 4am. The music is always recorded. Some of the most beautiful people of Rome show up in these crowded confines, often in their best disco finery. But show up late—it's more fashionable.

Saint Louis Music City

Via del Cardello 13A. ☎ **474-5076.** Cover 10,000 lire ($6.25), which includes club membership.

Saint Louis Music City is another leading jazz venue. With large, contemporary surroundings, it doesn't necessarily attract the big names in jazz. What you get instead are young and sometimes very talented groups beginning their careers. Many celebrities have been known to patronize the place. Soul and funk music are also performed on occasion. You can also dine at a restaurant on the premises, where meals cost 35,000 lire ($21.90) and up. Drinks range from 8,000–12,000 lire ($5–$7.50). Open Tuesday through Sunday from 9pm to 2am.

Veleno

Via Sardegna 27. ☎ **493583.** Cover (including one drink): Tues–Thurs 22,000 lire ($13.75), Fri–Sat 32,000 lire ($20).

Veleno is a Roman nightlife oddity, off via Vittorio Veneto and north of piazza Barberini. Many Romans often show up here in their fashionable finery to enjoy rap, soul, and funk music. It has also been a favorite on the celebrity circuit. Open Tuesday through Saturday from 10pm to 4am.

GAY CLUBS

Angelo Azzuro

Via Cardinal Merry del Val 13. ☎ **580-0472.** Cover (including an obligatory first drink) Fri and Sun, 10,000 lire ($6.25); Sat 20,000 lire ($12.50).

Angelo Azzuro is a gay "hot spot," deep in the heart of Trastevere, which is open Friday, Saturday, and Sunday from 11pm to 4am. No food is served, nor is live music presented. Men dance with men to recorded music, and women are also invited to patronize the club. Friday is for women only. Saturday and Sunday nights are reserved for gay men only. After the drink requirement is met (see below), subsequent libations cost 8,000 lire ($5) each.

L'Alibi

Via Monte Testaccio 44. ☎ **574-34-48.** Cover Wed–Thurs and Sun 10,000 lire ($6.25); Fri–Sat, 15,000 lire ($9.40).

L'Alibi, in the Testaccio sector, away from the heart of Rome, is a year-round venue on many a gay man's agenda. The crowd, however, tends to be mixed, both Roman and international, straight and gay, male and female. One room is devoted to dancing. It's open Wednesday through Sunday from 11pm to 5am. Take bus no. 20N or 30N from largo Argentina near the Piramide. Drinks run 10,000 lire ($6.25).

The Hangar

Via in Selci 69. ☎ **488-13-97.** No cover.

Established in 1984 by an expatriate, Louisiana-born American, John, and his Italian partner Gianni, this is probably the premier gay bar in Rome. It's set on one of Rome's oldest streets, adjacent to the Roman Forum, in the house on the site of the palace inhabited by Emperor Nero's deranged wife, Messalina. (Her ghost is rumored to still inhabit the premises.) Each of the establishment's two bars contains its own independent sound system. Women are welcome any night except Monday, when videos and entertainment for gay men are featured. The busiest nights are Saturday, Sunday, and Monday, when as many as 500 clients cram inside. Beer costs from 6,000 lire ($3.75); whisky from 10,000 lire ($6.25). It's open Wednesday through Monday from 10:30pm to 2am. The Hangar is closed for three weeks in August.

Joli Coeur

Via Sirte 5. ☎ **8393523. Cover** (including the first drink) 15,000 lire ($9.40).

Open only on Saturday and Sunday nights, from 10:30pm to 2am, this bar caters only to gay women. A fixture upon the city's lesbian nighttime scene, it attracts women from around Europe during its very limited hours. Information about Joli Coeur (which translates as "Pretty Heart") is offered at the Hangar (see above), because of the difficulties in reaching Joli Coeur directly. After the obligatory first drink (see below), subsequent libations cost from 8,000 lire ($5).

THE BAR & CAFE SCENE

Unless you're dead set on making the Roman nightclub circuit, try what might be a far livelier and less expensive scene—sitting late at night on via Vittorio Veneto or piazza del Popolo (see below)—all for the cost of an espresso.

ON VIA VITTORIO VENETO

Back in the 1950s—a decade that *Time* magazine gave to Rome, in the way it conceded the 1960s to London—via Vittorio Veneto rose in fame and influence as the choicest street in Rome, crowded with aspirant and actual movie stars, their directors, and a fast-rising group who were card-carrying members of the so-called jet set. Fashions, of course, are one of the most fickle elements in social culture. Today the *belle gente* (beautiful people), movie stars, and directors wouldn't be caught dead on via Vittorio Veneto—even with night-owl sunglasses. In the course of time, via Vittorio Veneto has moved into the mainstream of world tourism. It's about as "in" and undiscovered today as pretzels. But you may want to spend some time there.

Caffè de Paris

Via Vittorio Veneto 90. ☎ **488-5284.**

Caffè de Paris rises and falls in popularity depending on the decade. In the 1950s it was a haven for the fashionable, and now it's a popular restaurant in summer where you can occupy a counter seat along a bar or select a table inside. However, if the weather's right, the tables spill right out onto the sidewalk, and the passing crowd walks through the maze. A cup of coffee costs 5,000 lire ($3.15) if you sit outside but only 1,200 lire (75¢) if you stand at the bar. A whisky with soda costs 13,000 lire ($8.15). Open Thursday through Tuesday from 8am to 1am.

Harry's Bar

Via Vittorio Veneto 50. ☎ **484-643.**

Harry's Bar is a perennial favorite. Every major Italian city (Florence and Venice, for example) seems to have one, and Rome is no exception, although the one here has no connection with the others. The haunt of the IBF—International Bar Flies—at the top of Vittorio Veneto is elegant, chic, and sophisticated. In summer, sidewalk tables are placed outside, but off-season the ambience is more intimate, with walls of tapestry, ornate wood paneling, carved plastering, and Florentine sconces. In back is a small dining room, which serves some of the finest food in central Rome; meals go for 90,000–100,000 lire ($56.25–$62.50).

A whisky costs 9,000–12,000 lire ($5.65–$7.50). The bar is open from 11:30am to 1:30am; closed Sunday and August 1–10.

PIAZZA DEL POPOLO

The piazza is haunted with memories. According to legend, the ashes of Nero were enshrined here, until 11th-century residents began complaining to the pope about his imperial ghost. The Egyptian obelisk seen here today dates from the 13th century B.C., removed from Heliopolis to Rome during the reign of Augustus (it originally stood at the Circus Maximus). The present piazza was designed in the early 19th century by Valadier, Napoleon's architect. The twin baroque churches also stand on the square, overseeing the never-ending traffic.

Café Rosati

Piazza del Popolo 4–5. ☎ **361-1418.**

Café Rosati, which has been around since 1923, attracts guys and dolls of all persuasions who drive up in Maseratis and Porsches. It's really a sidewalk café/ice-cream parlor/candy store/confectionery that has been swept up in the fickle world of fashion. The later you go, the more interesting the action. Whisky at the table begins at 12,000 lire ($7.50). Open daily from 7:30am to 1am (closed Tuesday from November through March).

Canova Café

Piazza del Popolo. ☎ **361-2231.**

Although management has filled the interior with boutiques that sell expensive gift items, including luggage and cigarette lighters, many Romans still consider this the place to be on piazza del Popolo. The Canova has a sidewalk terrace for pedestrian-watching, plus a snack bar, a restaurant, and a wine shop inside. In summer you'll have access to a courtyard whose walls are covered with ivy and where flowers grow in terra-cotta planters. Expect to spend 1,200 lire (75¢) for coffee at the stand-up bar. If ordered at a table, coffee costs 6,000 lire ($3.75). A meal is offered for 38,000 lire ($23.75) and up. Food is served daily from noon to 3:30pm and 7 to 11pm, but the bar is open from 7am to midnight or 1am. It's closed Monday from November to April.

NEAR THE PANTHEON

Many visitors to the Eternal City now view piazza della Rotonda, located across from the Pantheon, and reconstructed by the Emperor Hadrian in the first part of the 2nd century A.D., as the "living room" of Rome. This is especially true on a summer night.

Di Rienzo

Piazza della Rotonda 8–9. ☎ **686-9097.**

Di Rienzo, the most desirable café here, is open Wednesday through Monday from 7am to either 1 or 2am. In fair weather you can sit at one of the sidewalk tables (if you can find one free) and contemplate life on the square and the Pantheon. In cooler weather you can retreat inside, where the walls are inlaid with the type of marble found on the Pantheon's floor. You can order a coffee for 4,000 lire ($2.50) at a table or 1,200 lire (75¢) at the bar. Many types of pastas appear on the menu, as does risotto alla pescatora (fisherman's rice) and several meat courses such as roast veal. You can also order pizzas.

Caffè Sant'Eustachio
Piazza Sant'Eustachio 82. ☎ **686-1309.**

Strongly brewed coffee might be considered one of the elixirs of Italy, and many Romans will walk many blocks for what they consider a superior brew. Caffè Sant'Eustachio, one of the most celebrated espresso shops, is on a small square near the Pantheon, where the water supply comes from a source outside Rome, which the Emperor Augustus funneled into the city with an aqueduct in 19 B.C. Rome's most experienced espresso judges claim that the water plays an important part in the coffee's flavor, although steam forced through ground Brazilian coffee roasted on the premises has an important effect as well. Stand-up coffee at this well-known place costs 1,200 lire (75¢); if you sit, you'll pay 4,000 lire ($2.50). Purchase a ticket from the cashier for as many cups as you want, and leave a small tip—about 1,200 lire (75¢)—for the counterperson when you present your receipt. Open from 8:30am to 1am every day except Monday; open until 1:30am on Saturday.

IN TRASTEVERE

Piazza del Popolo lured the chic and sophisticated from via Vittorio Veneto, and now several cafés in the district of Trastevere, across the Tiber, threaten to attract the same from Popolo. Fans who saw Fellini's *Roma* know what **piazza di Santa Maria in Trastevere** looks like. The square—filled with milling throngs in summer—is graced with an octagonal fountain and a church that dates from the 12th century. On the piazza, despite a certain amount of traffic, children run and play, and occasional spontaneous guitar fests are heard when the weather's good.

Café-Bar di Marzio
Piazza di Santa Maria in Trastevere 18B. ☎ **581-6095.**

This warmly inviting place, which is strictly a café (not a restaurant), has both indoor and outdoor tables at the edge of the square with the best view of its famous fountain. Whisky begins at 12,000 lire ($7.50), and a coffee goes for 3,000 lire ($1.90). Open Tuesday through Saturday from 7am to 2:30am.

ON THE CORSO

Café Alemagna
Via del Corso 181. ☎ **678-9135.**

The monumental Café Alemagna is usually filled with busy shoppers. You'll find just about every kind of dining facility a hurried resident of Rome could want, including a stand-up sandwich bar with dozens of selections from behind a glass case, a cafeteria, and a sit-down area with waiter service. The decor includes high coffered ceilings, baroque wall stencils, globe lights, crystal chandeliers, and black stone floors. Pastries start at 1,600 lire ($1), coffee at 1,200–1,500 lire (75¢–95¢). Open daily from 7am to 10pm.

NEAR THE SPANISH STEPS

Antico Caffè Greco
Via Condotti 86. ☎ **679-1700.**

Since 1760 the Antico Caffè Greco has been the poshest and most fashionable coffee bar in Rome. Attired in the trappings of the turn of the century, it has for years enjoyed a reputation as the gathering place of the literati. Previous sippers included Stendhal, Goethe, even D'Annunzio. Keats would also sit here and write. Today, however, you're more likely to see dowagers on a shopping binge and

American tourists, but there's plenty of atmosphere here. In the front is a wooden bar, and beyond that a series of small salons, decorated in the 19th-century style with oil paintings in gilded frames. You sit at marble-top tables of Napoleonic design, against a backdrop of gold or red damask, romantic paintings, and antique mirrors. Waiters are attired in black tailcoats. A cup of cappuccino costs 8,000 lire ($5) if you're seated. The house specialty is paradiso, made with lemon and orange, costing 10,000 lire ($6.25). The café is open Monday through Saturday from 8am to 9pm, but closed for 10 days in August (days vary).

Enoteca Fratelli Roffi Isabelli
Via della Croce 76B. ☎ **679-0896.**

The fermented fruits of the vine have played a prominent role in Roman life since the word *bacchanalian* was first invented (and that was very early indeed), and one of the best places to taste the wines of Italy is at the Enoteca Fratelli Roffi Isabelli. A stand-up drink within its darkly antique confines might be the perfect ending to a visit to the nearby Spanish Steps. Set behind an unflashy facade in a chic shopping district, this is the best repository for Italian wines, brandies, and grappa. You can opt for a postage-stamp table in back, if you desire, or stay at the bar with its impressive display of wines that lie stacked on shelves in every available corner. Open Monday through Saturday from 11am to 12:30am. A glass of wine costs 4,000–10,000 lire ($2.50–$6.25), depending on its quality. Grappa costs 5,500 lire ($3.45) and up.

NEAR PIAZZA COLONNA

Giolitti
Via Uffici del Vicario 40. ☎ **699-1243.**

For devotees of *gelato* (addictively tasty ice cream), Giolitti is one of the city's most popular nighttime gathering spots; in the evening it's thronged with strollers with a sweet tooth. To satisfy that craving, try a whipped-cream–topped Giolitti cup of gelato. The ice cream costs 3,500 lire ($2.20) and up. Some of the sundaes look like Vesuvius about to erupt. If you sit at a table and order one, the cost is from 8,000 lire ($5). During the day, good-tasting snacks are also served. Many people take gelato out to eat on the streets; others enjoy it in the post-Empire splendor of the salon inside. You can have your "coppa" from 7am to 2am every day except Monday. There are many excellent, smaller *gelateria* throughout Rome, wherever you see the cool concoction advertized as PRODUZIONE PROPRIA (homemade).

NEAR PIAZZA NAVONA

Bar della Pace
Via della Pace 3–5. ☎ **686-1216.**

Bar della Pace, located near piazza Navona, has elegant neighbors, such as Santa Maria della Pace, a church with sybils by Raphael and a cloister designed by Bramante. The bar dates from the beginning of this century, with wood, marble, and mirrors forming its decor. Open Tuesday through Sunday from 3pm to 2:30am. A whisky begins at 12,000 lire ($7.50).

Hemingway
Piazza delle Coppelle 10. ☎ **6880-41-35.**

Hemingway's discreet door is located off one of the most obscure piazzas in Rome. Inside, the owners have re-created a 19th-century decor beneath soaring vaulted ceilings that shimmer from the reflection of various glass chandeliers. An interior room repeats in scarlet what the first room did with shades of emerald. Evocations of a Liberty-style salon are strengthened by the sylvan murals and voluptuous portraits of reclining odalisques. Assorted painters, writers, and creative dilettantes occupy the clusters of overstuffed armchairs, listening to conversation or classical music. The establishment is open Monday through Saturday from 9am to 3am. Drinks cost 18,000 lire ($11.25) and up. Closed August 9–19.

IRISH PUBS

It's an indication of the diversity of their tastes that young Italians are drawn in large numbers to Irish-style pubs. The two most popular ones are previewed below.

Druid's Den
Via San Martino ai Monti 28. ☎ **488-0258.**

The popular Druid's Den is open daily from 6pm to 12:30am. Here, while enjoying a pint of beer at 7,000 lire ($4.40), you can listen to recorded Irish music and dream of Eire. A group of young Irishmen one night even did the Irish jig in front of the delighted Roman spectators. Live music, Irish style, is usually presented on Wednesday. The "den" is near piazza Santa Maria Maggiore and the train station.

Fiddler's Elbow
Via dell'Olmata 43. ☎ **487-2110.**

Fiddler's Elbow, near piazza Santa Maria Maggiore and the railway station, is reputedly the oldest pub in the capital. It's open daily from 4:30pm to 12:15am; a pint of Guinness is 7,000 lire ($4.40). Sometimes, however, the place is so packed you can't find room to drink it.

MOVIES

Pasquino Cinema
Vicolo del Piede 19 Piazza Santa Maria in Trastevere. ☎ **580-3622.**

In the Trastevere neighborhood, across the Tiber, just off the corner of the piazza Santa Maria in Trastevere, alongside the church, the little Pasquino draws a faithful coterie of English-speaking fans, including Italians and expatriates. The average film—usually of recent vintage—costs 10,000–12,000 lire ($6.25–$7.50). There are usually four screenings daily between 4 and 11pm. Take bus no. 56 or 60 from via Vittorio Veneto or no. 170 from Stazione Termini.

5 Easy Excursions

Most European capitals are ringed with a number of scenic attractions, and as far as sheer variety, Rome tops all of them. Just a few miles away, you can walk across the cemetery of U.S., Canadian, and British servicemen killed on the beaches of Anzio in World War II, or go back to the dawn of Italian history and explore the dank tombs the Etruscans left as their legacy.

You can wander around the ruins of Hadrian's Villa, the "queen of villas of the ancient world," or be lulled by the music of baroque fountains in the Villa d'Este. You can drink the golden wine of the Alban hill towns (Castelli Romani), or turn yourself bronze on the beaches of Ostia di Lido—or even explore the ruins of Ostia Antica, the ancient seaport of Rome.

Unless you're rushed beyond reason, allow at least three days for taking a look at the attractions in the environs. We've highlighted the best of the lot below.

TIVOLI

GETTING THERE   The town of Tivoli is 20 miles east of Rome on via Tiburtina—about an hour's drive with traffic. Even if you don't have a car, you won't have to take a guided tour but can use public transportation. Take Metro Linea B to the end of the line, the Rebibbia station. After exiting the station, take an Acotral bus the rest of the way to Tivoli. Generally, buses depart about every 20 minutes during the day.

WHAT TO SEE & DO

Tivoli, known as Tibur to the ancient Romans, was the playground of emperors. Today its reputation continues unabated: it's the most popular half-day jaunt from Rome.

The ruins of Hadrian's Villa as well as the Villa d'Este, with their fabulous fountains and gardens, remain the two chief attractions of Tivoli—and both should be seen, even if you must curtail your sightseeing in Rome.

Right inside the town, you can look at two villas before heading to the environs of Tivoli and the ruins of Hadrian's Villa.

✪ Villa d'Este

Piazza Trento, viale delle Centro Fontane. ☎ **0774/22070.** Admission 10,000 lire ($6.25) when the water jets are set at full power; 5,000 lire ($3.15) otherwise. Feb–Oct daily 9am– 6:30pm; Nov–Jan daily 9am–4pm. Transportation: The bus from Rome stops right near the entrance (see "Getting There," above).

Like Hadrian centuries before, Cardinal Ippolito d'Este of Ferrara believed in heaven on earth. In the mid-16th century he ordered this villa built on a hillside. The dank Renaissance structure, with its second-rate paintings, is hardly worth the trek from Rome, but the gardens below—designed by Pirro Ligorio—dim the luster of Versailles.

Visitors descend the cypress-studded slope to the bottom, and on their way are rewarded with everything from lilies to gargoyles spouting water, torrential streams, and waterfalls. The loveliest fountain—on this there is some agreement—is the Fontana del'Ovato, designed by Ligorio. But nearby is the most spectacular achievement—the hydraulic organ fountain, dazzling visitors with its water jets in front of a baroque chapel, with four maidens who look tipsy. The work represents the genius of Frenchman Claude Veanard.

Don't miss the moss-covered, slime-green Fountain of Dragons, also by Ligorio, and the so-called Fountain of Glass by Bernini. The best walk is along the promenade, which has 100 spraying fountains. The garden, filled with rhododendron, is worth hours of exploration but you'll need frequent rest periods after those steep climbs.

Villa Gregoriana

Largo Sant'Angelo. ☎ **0774/21249.** Admission 3,000 lire ($1.90). Daily 9am to one hour before sunset. Transportation: The bus from Rome stops near the entrance (see "Getting There," above).

Whereas the Villa d'Este dazzles with artificial glamour, the Villa Gregoriana relies more on nature. The gardens were built by Pope Gregory XVI in the 19th century. At one point on the circuitous walk carved along a slope, visitors stand and look out onto the most panoramic waterfall (Aniene) at Tivoli. The trek to the bottom on the banks of the Anio is studded with grottoes and balconies that open onto the chasm. The only problem is that if you do make the full journey, you may need a helicopter to pull you up again (the climb back is fierce). From one of the belvederes there's an exciting view of the Temple of Vesta on the hill.

○ Villa Adriana (Hadrian's Villa)

Via di Villa Adriana. ☎ **0774/530203.** Admission 8,000 lire ($5) adults, free for children. Daily 9am–sunset (about 7:30pm in summer, 4pm Nov–Mar). Bus: 2 or 4 from Tivoli to the villa gateway.

Of all the Roman emperors dedicated to *la dolce vita*, the globe-trotting Hadrian spent the last three years of his life in the grandest style. Less than four miles from Tivoli he built one of the greatest estates ever erected in the world, and filled acre after acre with some of the architectural wonders he'd seen on his many trips.

Perhaps as a preview of what he envisioned in store for himself, the emperor even created a representation of hell centuries before Dante got around to recording its horrors in a poem. A patron of the arts, a lover of beauty, and even something of an architect, Hadrian directed the staggering feat of constructing much more than a villa—a self-contained world for a vast royal entourage and the hundreds of servants and guards they required to protect them, feed them, bathe them, and satisfy their libidos.

On the estate were erected theaters, baths, temples, fountains, gardens, and canals bordered with statuary. Hadrian filled the palaces and temples with sculpture, some of which now rests in the museums of Rome. In later centuries, barbarians, popes, and cardinals, as well as anyone who needed a slab of marble, carted off much that made the villa so spectacular. But enough of the fragmented ruins remain for us to piece together the story.

For a glimpse of what the villa used to be, see the plastic reconstruction at the entrance. Then, following the arrows around, look in particular for the Marine Theater (ruins of the round structure with Ionic pillars); the Great Baths, with some intact mosaics; and the Canopus, with a group of caryatids whose images are reflected in the pond, as well as a statue of Mars. For a closer look at some of the items excavated, you can visit the museum on the premises and a museum and visitor center near the villa parking area.

WHERE TO DINE

Albergo Ristorante Adriano

Via di Villa Adriana 194. ☎ **0774/535028.** Reservations not required. Main courses 18,000–40,000 lire ($11.25–$25); fixed-price menu 65,000–80,000 lire ($40.65–$50). AE, DC, MC, V. Daily 12:30–2:30pm; Mon–Sat 8–10pm. Bus: 2 or 4 from Tivoli. ITALIAN.

Albergo Ristorante Adriano might be the perfect stopover point either before or after you visit Hadrian's Villa. At the bottom of the villa's hill, in a stucco-sided villa a few steps from the ticket office, it offers terrace dining under plane trees or indoor dining in a high-ceilinged room with terra-cotta walls, neoclassical moldings, and Corinthian pilasters painted white. Menu items—everything homemade—include roast lamb, saltimbocca, a variety of veal dishes, deviled chicken, a selection of salads and cheeses, and simple desserts. They are especially proud of their homemade pasta dishes.

Le Cinque Statue

Via Quintillio Varo 8. ☎ **0774/20366.** Reservations recommended. Main courses 10,000–20,000 lire ($6.25–$12.50). AE, DC, MC, V. Sat–Thurs 12:30–3pm and 7:30–10pm. Closed Aug 15–Sept 7. Transportation: The bus from Rome stops nearby. ROMAN.

Easy Excursions From Rome

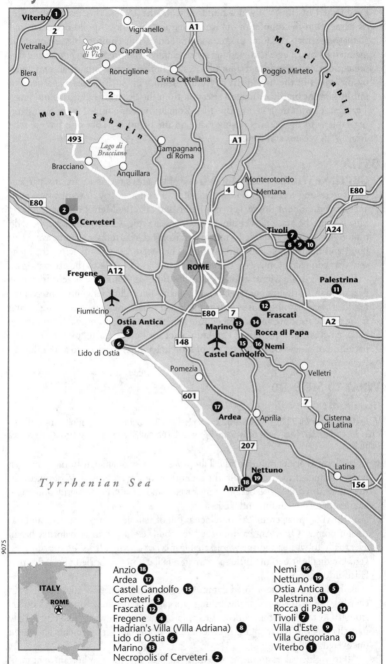

N 0 ▮▮▮▮▮ 9 mi / 15 km

Viterbo ①
Vignanello
Vetralla
Caprarola
Lago di Vico
Blera
Ronciglione
Cívita Castellana
A1
Monti Sabini
Poggio Mirteto

Monti Sabatin
493
Lago di Bracciano
Campagnano di Roma
A1
Monterotondo
Mentana
E80

Bracciano
Anquillara
4

E80
Cerveteri ②③
Tivoli ⑦
⑧⑨⑩
A24

Fregene ④
A12
ROME
Palestrina ⑪

Fiumicino
E80 7
Frascati ⑫
A2
Ostia Antica ⑤
Marino ⑬⑭
Rocca di Papa
Lido di Ostia ⑥
148
⑮⑯ Nemi
Castel Gandolfo
Pomezia
Velletri

601
Ardea ⑰
Aprília
7
Cisterna di Latina

207
Nettuno ⑲
Latina
156
Tyrrhenian Sea
Anzio ⑱

9075

ITALY
ROME

Anzio ⑱
Ardea ⑰
Castel Gandolfo ⑮
Cerveteri ③
Frascati ⑫
Fregene ④
Hadrian's Villa (Villa Adriana) ⑧
Lido di Ostia ⑥
Marino ⑬
Necropolis of Cerveteri ②

Nemi ⑯
Nettuno ⑲
Ostia Antica ⑤
Palestrina ⑪
Rocca di Papa ⑭
Tivoli ⑦
Villa d'Este ⑨
Villa Gregoriana ⑩
Viterbo ①

Established in the 1950s in a building from the 1920s, this restaurant takes its name from the quintet of old carved statues, including Apollo Belvedere and gladiators, which decorate the restaurant. Today, this comfortable restaurant is maintained by a single hardworking Italian family, who prepare an honest and unpretentious cuisine without a lot of fuss and bother. Everything is accompanied by the wines of the hill towns of Rome. Begin with such dishes as pastiche of mushrooms or brains, or make a selection from their excellent antipasti offerings. Try rigatoni with fresh herbs, tripe fried Roman style, or a mixed fry of brains and vegetables. All the pasta is freshly made on the premises. They also have a wide array of ice creams and fruits.

OSTIA

GETTING THERE   Ostia Antica is one of the area's major attractions, particularly interesting to those who can't make it to Pompeii. If you want to see both ancient and modern Rome, get your bikini and take the Metropolitana (subway) Line B from the Stazione Termini to the Magliana stop. Change there for the Lido train to Ostia Antica, about 16 miles from Rome. Departures are about every half hour, and the trip takes only 20 minutes. The Metro lets you off across the highway that connects Rome with the coast. It's just a short walk to the excavations.

Later, board the Metro again to visit the **Lido di Ostia,** the beach. Italy may be a strongly Catholic country, but the Romans don't allow religious conservatism to affect their bathing attire. This is the beach where the denizens of the capital frolic on the seashore and at times create a merry carnival atmosphere, with dance halls, cinemas, and pizzerias. The Lido is set off best at Castelfusano, against a backdrop of pinewoods. This stretch of shoreline is often referred to as the Roman Riviera.

WHAT TO SEE & DO

Ostia Antica

Viale dei Romagnoli 717. ☎ **565-0022.** Admission 10,000 lire ($6.25) adults, free for children 17 and under. Mar–Sept daily 9am–7pm; Oct–Feb daily 9am–5pm. Metro: Ostia Antica (Line B).

Ostia, located at the mouth of the Tiber, was the port of ancient Rome. Through it were funneled the riches from the far corners of the empire. It was founded in the 4th century B.C., and became a major port and naval base primarily under two later emperors: Claudius and Trajan.

A thriving, prosperous city developed, full of temples, baths, theaters, and patrician homes. Ostia Antica flourished for about eight centuries before it began eventually to wither and the wholesale business of carting off its art treasures began. Gradually it became little more than a malaria bed, a buried ghost city that faded into history.

Although a papal-sponsored commission launched a series of digs in the 19th century, the major work of unearthing was carried out under Mussolini's orders from 1938 to 1942 (the work had to stop because of the war). The city is only partially dug out today, but it is believed that all the chief monuments have been uncovered.

All the principal monuments are clearly labeled. The most important spot in all the ruins is piazzale delle Corporazioni, an early version of Wall Street. Near the theater, this square contained nearly 75 corporations; the nature of their businesses was identified by the patterns of preserved mosaics.

Greek dramas were performed at the ancient theater that was built sometime in the early days of the Empire. The classics are still aired here in summer (check with the tourist office for specific listings), but the theater as it looks today is the result of much rebuilding. Every town the size of Ostia had a forum, and during the excavations a number of pillars of the ancient Ostia Forum were uncovered. At one end is a 2nd-century B.C. temple honoring a trio of gods—Minerva, Jupiter, and Juno (little more than the basic foundation remains). In addition, there is a well-lit museum within the enclave that displays Roman statuary along with some Pompeii-like frescoes. There are perfect picnic spots beside fallen columns or near old temple walls.

CASTELLI ROMANI

For the Roman emperor, and the wealthy cardinal in the heyday of the Renaissance, the Castelli Romani (Roman Castles) exerted a powerful lure, and they still do. Of course, the Castelli are not castles, but hill towns—many of them with an ancient history. The wines from the Alban Hills will add a little *feu de joie* to your life. The ideal way to explore the hill towns is by car. But you can get a limited review by taking one of the buses that leaves every 20 minutes from Rome from the Subaugusta stop of the Metro system (Line A). Our selection of the most interesting towns follows.

CASTELGANDOLFO

Since the early 17th century this resort on Lake Albano, 16 miles from Rome, has been the summer retreat of the popes. As such, it attracts thousands of pilgrims yearly, although the papal residence, Villa Barberini, and its surrounding gardens, are private and open only on special occasions. Interestingly, the pope's summer place incorporates part of Domitian's imperial palace (but the pastimes have changed). Domitian (A.D. 51–96) was one of the most notorious of Roman emperors, reigning from A.D. 81. As he grew more and more despotic, he viciously persecuted his opponents until stabbed to death by a freed man (the instigation came from his wife, Domitia).

On days that the pope grants a mass audience, thousands of visitors—many of whom arrive on foot—stream into the audience hall. Pope Pius XII, worried about the thousands of people who waited out in the rain to see him, built this now air-conditioned structure to protect the faithful from the elements. On a summer Sunday, the pope usually appears on a small balcony in the palace courtyard, reciting with the crowd the noon Angelus prayers.

The seat of the papacy opens onto a little square in the center of the town, where holiday-markers sip their wine—nothing pontifical here. A chair lift transports visitors from the hillside town to the lake, where some of the aquatic competitions were held in the 1960 Olympics. The Church of St. Thomas of Villanova, on the principal square, as well as the fountain, reveal Bernini's hand. If you need to be sold more on visiting Castelgandolfo, remember that it was praised by the eminent guidebook writer Goethe.

NEMI

The Romans flock to Nemi in droves, particularly from April through June for the succulent strawberry of the district—acclaimed by some gourmets as the finest in Europe. (In May, there's a strawberry festival.) Nemi was also known to the ancients. A temple to the huntress Diana was erected on Lake Nemi, which was said to be her "looking glass."

In A.D. 37 Caligula built luxurious barges to float on the lake. Mussolini, much later, drained Nemi to find the barges, but it was a dangerous time to excavate them from the lake's bottom. They were senselessly destroyed by the Nazis during the infamous retreat.

What to See & Do

While at Nemi, you can visit the Roman Ship Museum, or **Museo delle Navi,** via di Diana (☎ 06/936-8140). The ships destroyed by the Nazis have been replaced by two scale models. The major artifacts on display are mainly copies, as the originals now rest in world-class museums. The museum is open Tuesday through Sunday from 9am to 2pm, and admission is 4,000 lire ($2.50) for adults, free for children under 18, and free for those over 60. To reach the museum, unless you're driving, you have to walk from the center of Nemi toward the lake.

The 15th-century **Palazzo Ruspoli,** a baronial estate, is the focal point of Nemi, but the hill town itself invites exploration—particularly the alleyways the local denizens call streets and the houses with balconies jutting out over the slopes. While darting like Diana through the Castelli Romani, try to time your schedule for lunch in Nemi.

Where to Dine

La Taverna

Via Nemorense 13. ☎ **06/936-8135.** Reservations required. Main courses 16,000–21,000 lire ($10–$13.15). AE, DC, MC, V. Thurs–Tues 12:30–2pm and 8–10pm. INTERNATIONAL.

Offering a large array of regional dishes and a rustic atmosphere, La Taverna is worth the trouble it takes to get there. In April the FRAGOLE (wild strawberries) signs go out. Try fettuccine with mushrooms. For a main dish, I suggest the chef's specialty, *arrosto di abbacchio e maiale* (it consists of both a pork chop and grilled lamb). Fresh fish is also featured. If you want to have a Roman feast, accompany your main dish with large roasted mushrooms, priced according to size, and a small fennel salad. To top off the galaxy of goodies, it's traditional to order Sambucca, a clear white drink like anisette, "with a fly in it." The "fly," of course, is a coffee bean, which you suck on for added flavor.

FRASCATI

Located about 13 miles from Rome out via Tuscolana, and some 1,073 feet above sea level, Frascati is one of the most beautiful of the hill towns—known for the wine to which it lends its name and its villas. The town bounced back from the severe destruction caused by bombers in World War II.

To get there, take one of the Cotral buses leaving from the Subaugusta stop of the Metro system (Line A). You can also take a small train that leaves from the Ferrorie Laziali section of the central Stazione Termini in Rome. This train runs only to Frascati.

WHAT TO SEE & DO

Although bottles of Frascati wine are exported—and served in many of the restaurants and trattorie of Rome—tradition holds that the wine is best near the golden vineyards from which it came. Romans drive up on Sunday just to drink *vino.* To sample some of that golden white wine yourself, head for **Cantina Comandini,** via E. Filiberto 1 (☎ 06/942-0915), right off piazza Roma. The Comandini family welcomes you to the wine cellar, a regional tavern in which they sell Frascati wine from their own vineyards. You can stop and drink the wine on the spot for 5,500 lire ($3.45) if you sit at a table, or 3,000 lire ($1.90) if you stand at the bar. This is not a restaurant, but they sell sandwiches to go with your wine for 4,000 lire ($2.50). The tavern is open daily from 3:30 to 7:30pm.

For your other sightseeing, stand in the heart of Frascati, at piazza Marconi, to see the most important of the estates: **Villa Aldobrandini,** via Massala (☎ 942-0331). The finishing touches to this 16th-century villa were applied by Maderno, who designed the facade of St. Peter's. Only its gardens may be visited. With its grottoes, yew hedges, statuary, and splashing fountains, it makes for an exciting outing. To visit the gardens, which are open only in the morning, go to Azienda di Soggiorno e Turismo, piazza Marconi 1 (☎ 06/942-0331), and ask for a free pass. The office is open Monday through Friday from 9am to 1pm and 4 to 7pm and on Saturday from 9am to 1pm.

If you have a car, you can continue past the Villa Aldobrandini to **Tuscolo,** about three miles beyond the villa. An ancient spot with the ruins of an amphitheater dating from about the 1st century B.C., Tuscolo offers what may be one of Italy's most panoramic views.

You may also want to go to the bombed-out **Villa Torlonia.** Its grounds have been converted into a public park whose chief treasure is the "Theater of the Fountains," also designed by Maderno.

WHERE TO DINE

Cacciani Restaurant
Via Armando Diaz 13. ☎ **06/942-0378**. Reservations required on weekends. Main courses 18,000–28,000 lire ($11.25–$17.50). AE, DC, MC, V. Tues–Sun 12:30–3pm and 7:30–10:30pm. Closed Jan 6–16 and Aug 15–25. ROMAN.

Cacciani is the choicest restaurant in Frascati, where the competition has always been tough (Frascati foodstuffs once attracted Lucullus, the epicurean). A large, modern restaurant in the center of town, with a terrace commanding a view of the valley, Cacciani has drawn such long-departed celebrities as Clark Gable. The kitchen is exposed to the public, and it's fun just to watch the women wash the sand off the spinach. To get you started, we recommend the pasta specialties, such as fettuccine (thin noodles) or rigatoni alla vaccinara (oxtail in tomato sauce). For a main course, the baby lamb with a special sauce of white wine and vinegar is always reliable. There is a large choice of wines, which are kept in a cave under the restaurant.

The owners, the Cacciani family, will arrange a combined visit to several of the wine-producing villas of Frascati along with a memorable meal at their elegant restaurant, on terms that can be arranged before your arrival if you call.

PALESTRINA

If you go out via Prenestina for about 24 miles, you'll eventually come to Palestrina, a medieval hillside town which overlooks a wide valley.

WHAT TO SEE & DO

When U.S. airmen flew over in World War II and bombed part of the town, they scarcely realized their actions would launch Palestrina as an important tourist attraction. After the debris was cleared, a pagan temple—once one of the greatest in the world—emerged: the **Fortuna Primigenia,** rebuilt in the days of the empire but dating from centuries before.

Palestrina antedates the founding of Rome by several hundred years. It resisted conquest by the early Romans, and later took the wrong side in the civil war between Marius and Sulla. When Sulla won, he razed every stone in the city except the Temple of Fortune, and then built a military barracks on the site. Later, as a favorite vacation spot for the emperors and their entourages, it sheltered some of the most luxurious villas of the Roman Empire.

In medieval feuds, the city was repeatedly destroyed. Its most famous child was Pier Luigi da Palestrina, who is recognized as the father of polyphonic harmony.

The **Barberini Palace** (☎ 06/955-8100), high on a hill overlooking the valley, today houses Roman statuary found in the ruins, plus Etruscan artifacts, such as urns the equal of those in the Villa Giulia Museum in Rome. But the most famous work—worth the trip itself—is the "Nile Mosaic," a well-preserved ancient Roman work, the most remarkable one ever uncovered. The mosaic details the flooding of the Nile, a shepherd's hunt, mummies, ibises, and Roman warriors, among other things. The museum is open November through February, Tuesday through Sunday from 9am to 4pm; in March, from 9am to 5pm; in April, from 9am to 6pm; in May, from 9am to 6:30pm; June through August, from 9am to 7:30pm; in September, from 9am to 5:30pm; and in October, from 9am to 5pm. Admission is 8,000 lire ($5).

You'll also find a cathedral here that dates from 1100, with a mostly intact bell tower. It rests on the foundation of a much earlier pagan temple.

WHERE TO STAY & DINE

Albergo Ristorante Stella (Restaurant Coccia)
Piazza della Liberazione 3, Palestrina, 00036 Roma. ☎ **06/953-8172.** Fax 06/957-3360. 27 rms (all with bath), 1 suite. AC TV TEL. 85,000 lire ($53.15) double; 140,000 lire ($87.50). Breakfast 7,000 lire ($4.40) extra. AE, DC, V.

Albergo Ristorante Stella, a buff-colored hotel set in the commercial center of town, is located on a cobblestone square filled with parked cars, trees, and a small fountain. It was renovated in 1995. The simple lobby is filled with warm colors, curved leather couches, and autographed photos of local sports heroes. The restaurant is sunny. There is a small bar where you might have an apéritif before lunch. Meals begin at 45,000 lire ($28.15). The restaurant is open daily from noon to 3pm and 7 to 9pm.

ANZIO & NETTUNO

Motorists can visit Ostia Antica in the morning, then Anzio and Nettuno in the afternoon. Go out via Ostiense until you reach Route 8, which you take to the coast. Once at Lido di Ostia, you can head south along Route 41 to Anzio.

The two towns of Anzio and Nettuno are peaceful seaside resorts today, but to many Americans and English they conjure up bitter memories. On January 22, 1944, an Allied amphibious task force landed the U.S. VI Corps at both towns, as a prelude to the liberation of Rome. Fighting terrific odds, the Allies lost many lives.

The Italian government presented 77 acres in **Nettuno** to the United States for a cemetery. The graves are visited today by those who lost relatives in the campaign. The cemetery contains graves not only of those who died on the beaches of Anzio and Nettuno (where holiday-makers now revel), but also of those who were killed in the Sicilian campaign.

The fields of Nettuno contain 7,862 American dead—39% of those originally buried (the others have been returned home by their relatives). In Nettuno, a Graves Registry office helps visitors locate the markers of particular servicemen. The neatly manicured fields are peppered with crosses and stars of David, plus the saddest sight of all: 488 headstones that mark the graves of the unknowns. The cemetery is open daily from 8am to 6pm.

In **Anzio,** you can visit the British cemetery filled with war dead. One memorial to B. J. Pownell, a gunner in the Royal Artillery, seems to symbolize the plight of all the young men who died on either side. "He Gave the Greatest Gift of All: His Unfinished Life." Gunner Pownell was struck down on January 29, 1944, at age 20.

Anzio was the birthplace of both Nero and Caligula. Many wealthy Romans once erected villas here at the port said to have been founded by Antias, the son of Circe and Odysseus. In the ruins of Nero's fabulous villa, the world-famous statue of *Apollo Belvedere* was discovered.

FREGENE

The fame of this coastal city north of the Tiber—24 miles from Rome—dates back to the 1600s when the land belonged to the Rospigliosi, a powerful Roman family. Pope Clement IX, a member of the wealthy family, planted a forest of pine that extends along the shoreline for 2.5 miles and half a mile deep to protect the land from the strong winds of the Mediterranean. Today the wall of pines makes a dramatic backdrop for the golden sands and luxurious villas of the resort. You can take a Civitavecchia-bound train from the Stazione Termini in Rome to Fregene, the first stop.

WHERE TO STAY & DINE

La Conchiglia

Lungomare di Ponente 4, Fregene, 00050 Roma. ☎ **06/668-5385**. Fax 06/668-5385. 36 rms (all with bath). A/C TV TEL. 150,000 lire ($93.75) double. Rates include breakfast. AE, DC, MC, V. Free parking. Bus: The bus from Rome leaves from the Lepanto Metro stop and takes passengers to the center of Fregene.

Built in 1934, La Conchiglia means "the shellfish" in Italian—an appropriate name for this hotel and restaurant right on the beach, which offers views of the water and of the pine trees. Its circular lounge is painted white, with built-in curving wall banquettes that face a cylindrical fireplace with a raised hearth. It seems like a setting for one of those modern Italian films. A resort aura, however, is created by the large green plants. The bar in the cocktail lounge, which faces the terrace, is also circular. The rooms are comfortable and well furnished. Some contain a minibar.

It's also possible to stop by for a meal, and the food is good. Try, for example, spaghetti with lobster and grilled fish. Many excellent meat dishes are offered. Meals start at 45,000 lire ($28.15). The restaurant is set within the garden, shaded by bamboo. Oleander flutters in the sea breezes. The restaurant is open daily from 1 to 3pm and 8 to 10pm.

ETRUSCAN HISTORICAL SIGHTS

CERVETERI (CAERE)

As you walk through the Etruscan Museum in Rome (Villa Giulia), you'll often see the word *Caere* written under a figure vase or a sarcophagus. This is a reference to the nearby town known today as Cerveteri. Caere was one of the great Etruscan cities of Italy, whose origins may go as far back as the 9th century B.C. Of course, the Etruscan town has long since faded, but not the **Necropolis of Cerveteri.** The effect is eerie; Cerveteri is often called a "city of the dead."

When you go beneath some of the mounds, you'll discover the most striking feature of the necropolis—the tombs are like rooms in Etruscan homes. The main burial ground is called the Necropolis of Banditacca. Of the graves thus far uncovered, none is finer than the Tomba Bella (sometimes called the Reliefs' Tomb), the burial ground of the Matuna family. Articles such as utensils and even house pets were painted in stucco relief. Presumably these paintings were representations of items the dead family would need in the world beyond. The necropolis is open May through September, Tuesday through Sunday from 9am to 6pm; October through April, Tuesday through Sunday from 11am to 4pm. Admission is 8,000 lire ($5).

Relics from the necropolis are displayed at the **Museo Nazionale Cerite,** piazza Santa Maria Maggiore (☎ 955-0003). The museum is housed in Ruspoldi Castle, with its ancient walls and crenellations. It is open May through September, Tuesday through Sunday from 9am to 4pm; off-season, Tuesday through Sunday from 9am to 2pm. Admission is free.

Cerveteri can be reached by bus or car. If you're driving, head out via Aurelia, northwest of Rome, for a distance of 28 miles. By public transportation, take Metro Line A in Rome to the Lepanto stop. From via Lepanto you can take an Cotral coach to Cerveteri; the trip takes about an hour and costs 3,800 lire ($2.40). Once at Cerveteri, it's a 1.25-mile walk to the necropolis. Just follow the signs that point the way.

TARQUINIA

If you wish to see tombs even more striking and more recently excavated than those at Cerveteri, go to Tarquinia. The medieval turrets and fortifications atop the rocky cliffs overlooking the sea seem to contradict the Etruscan name of Tarquinia. Actually, Tarquinia is the adopted name of the old medieval community of Corneto, in honor of the major Etruscan city that once stood nearby. The main attraction within the town is the **Tarquinia National Museum,** piazza Cavour (☎ 0766/856036), which is devoted to Etruscan exhibits and sarcophagi excavated from the necropolis a few miles away. The museum is housed in the Palazzo Vitelleschi, a gothic palace that dates from the mid-15th century. Among the exhibits are gold jewelry, black vases with carved and painted bucolic scenes, and sarcophagi decorated with carvings of animals and relief figures of priests and military leaders. But the biggest attraction is in itself worth the ride from Rome—the almost life-size pair of winged horses from the pediment of a Tarquinian temple. The finish is worn here and there, and the terra-cotta color shows through, but the relief stands as one of the greatest Etruscan masterpieces ever discovered. The museum is open May through October, Tuesday through Sunday from 9am to 7pm, and 9am to 2pm in the off-season, and charges 8,000 lire ($5) admission.

The same ticket also admits you to the **Etruscan Necropolis** (☎ 0766/856308), which covers more than 2.5 miles of rough terrain near where the ancient Etruscan city once stood. Thousands of tombs have been discovered here, some of which have not been explored even today. Others, of course, were discovered by looters, but many treasures remain even though countless pieces were removed to museums and private collections. The paintings on the walls of the tombs have helped historians reconstruct the life of the Etruscans—a heretofore impossible feat without a written history. The paintings depict feasting couples in vivid colors mixed from iron oxide, lapis lazuli dust, and charcoal. One of the oldest tombs (from the 6th century B.C.) depicts young men fishing while dolphins play and colorful birds fly high above. Many of the paintings convey an earthy, vigorous, sex-oriented life among the wealthy Etruscans. The tombs are generally open Tuesday through Sunday from 9am to 6pm (until 2pm November through March). You can reach the grave sites by taking a bus from the Barriera San Guisto to the Cimitero stop. Or try the 20-minute walk from the museum. Inquire at the museum for directions.

To reach Tarquinia by car, take via Aurelia outside Rome, and continue on the autostrada toward Civitavecchia. Bypass Civitavecchia and continue another 13 miles north until you see the exit signs for Tarquinia. As for public transportation, going by train is the preferred choice: a *diretto* train from Roma Ostiense station takes 50 minutes. Also, eight buses a day leave from the via Lepanto stop in Rome for the two-hour trip to the neighboring town, Barriera San Giusto, which is 1.5 miles from Tarquinia. Bus schedules are available at the tourist office in Barriera San Giusto (☎ 856384), which is open Monday through Saturday from 8am to 2pm and 5 to 7pm.

7

Introducing Florence (Firenze)

On the banks of the Arno, Florence became a Roman stronghold in the 1st century B.C.; it was not until after A.D. 1200 that it began to come into its own as a commercial and cultural center. During the 13th century, merchants and tradesmen organized the guilds that controlled the city's economy and government for nearly 150 years. These guilds, with their newfound wealth, commissioned works of art to adorn the churches and palaces.

This revival of interest in art and architecture brought about the Italian Renaissance, an amazing outburst of activity between the 14th and the 16th centuries that completely changed the face of the Tuscan town. During its heyday under the benevolent eye (and purse) of the Medicis, the city became the world's greatest repository of art treasures. The list of geniuses who lived or worked here reads like a "who's who" in the world of art and literature: Dante, Boccaccio, Fra Angelico, Brunelleschi, Donatello, da Vinci, Raphael, Cellini, Michelangelo, Ghiberti, and Giotto.

When the last Renaissance artist capitulated to the baroque and pundits began to evaluate the era, the question was asked, "Why was Florence the city chosen for the 'rebirth'?" Some long-forgotten individual concluded that the Renaissance didn't choose Florence, but Florence chose the Renaissance.

The Florentines are a unique lot. A Genoese sailor could persuade Isabella to finance his expedition to the Americas, but it took a Florentine by the name of Amerigo Vespucci to get the country named after himself. The Florentines are the champions of the vigorous life. To adapt another saying, they believe in taking the dilemma by the horns. Thus the Florentine Dante wrote *The Divine Comedy* in the vernacular—and not only persuaded his readers to accept such a "vulgar" work but helped make the Tuscan dialect and language *the* tongue of Italy.

1 Orientation

ARRIVING

BY PLANE If you're flying from New York, the best air connection is Rome, where you can board a domestic flight to the **Galileo Galilei Airport** at Pisa (☎ 050/50-07-07), 58 miles west of Florence. You can then take an express train to Florence in an hour.

What's Special About Florence

Museums
- Uffizi Galleries, one of the world's great art museums, and repository of masterpieces of the Renaissance.
- Pitti Palace, a complex of museums whose Galleria Palatina is second only to the Uffizi in art.
- Il Bargello, a treasure house of Renaissance sculpture, including works by Michelangelo, Donatello, and the della Robbias.

Religious Shrines
- Duomo, one of the largest cathedrals in the Christian world, begun in 1296 and consecrated in 1436, with the dome by Brunelleschi.
- Battistero di San Giovanni, famed for Lorenzo Ghiberti's pair of bronze exterior doors known as the *Gates of Paradise.*

Ace Attractions
- Piazza della Signoria, set against the background of the Palazzo Vecchio and the statue-filled Loggia della Signoria.
- Galleria dell'Accademia, proud home of the world's most famous statue: Michelangelo's majestic *David.*
- Medici Chapels, in the Basilica di San Lorenzo, containing Michelangelo's tomb for Lorenzo de Medici, with the figures of *Dawn* and *Dusk.*

Shopping
- Some of the most elegant merchandise in Europe is for sale in this chic, fashion-conscious city, especially Florentine leather goods.

There is also a small domestic airport, **Amerigo Vespucci,** on via del Termine, near the A11 (☎ 37-3498), which lies 3¹/₂ miles northwest of Florence, a 15-minute ride. This airport not only receives domestic flights from such cities as Rome and Milan but also planes from international destinations, notably Brussels, Frankfurt, London, Lugano, Munich, and Nice. This airport can be reached by city bus service available on the ATAF line (no. 23C), departing from the main Santa Maria Novella rail terminal. Domestic air service is provided by **Alitalia,** lungarno degli Acciaiuoli 10–12 in Florence (☎ 27889).

BY TRAIN A major stopover in Europe for holders of the Eurailpass, Florence lies in the heart of Italy. If you're coming north from Rome, count on a two- to three-hour trip, depending on your connection. Bologna is just an hour away by train, and if you decide to see Venice first, it's only four hours' traveling distance by train. The **Santa Maria Novella rail station,** in piazza della Stazione, adjoins piazza di Santa Maria Novella, which has one of the great churches of Florence. From here, most of the major hotels are within easy reach, either on foot or by taxi or bus. For railway information, phone 28-8785.

In the station is a bank in the outer hall that exchanges money Monday through Saturday from 8:20am to 6:30pm. There is also a day hotel, Albergo Diurno, where you can take a shower after a long train ride and rest up. At the top of Track 16 is a place where you can store your luggage.

Some trains into Florence stop at the **Stazione Campo di Marte,** on the eastern side of Florence. A 24-hour bus service (no. 91) runs between the two rail terminals.

The **Alitalia Airport Train** by FS (the Italian State Railways) links Florence with Rome's Leonardo da Vinci International Airport without intermediate stops. Twice a day, seven days a week, trains depart from Florence's Santa Maria Novella station at times that have been scheduled to connect with Alitalia's most important international and intercontinental flights. All that is needed to travel on the train is an Alitalia airline ticket. Passengers check in at the Disco Verde railway lounge in Florence, where they are given a boarding card for the train and also the plane connection.

BY BUS   Long-distance buses service Florence, run by **SITA,** via Santa Caterina de Siena 15R (☎ 48-36-51), and **Lazzi Eurolines,** piazza Stazione 4–6 (☎ 215154). SITA connects Florence with such Tuscan hill towns as Siena, Arezzo, Pisa, and San Gimignano, and Lazzi Eurolines provides service from such cities as Rome and Naples.

BY CAR   If you're driving, you'll find that Florence, because of its central location, enjoys good autostrada connections with the rest of Italy, especially Rome and Bologna.

Autostrada A1 connects Florence with both the north and south of Italy. Drivers need about an hour to reach Bologna and about three hours to reach Rome in the south (or vice versa). The Tyrrhenian coast is only an hour from Florence on the A11 heading west.

Florence lies 172 miles north of Rome, 65 miles west of Bologna, and 185 miles south of Milan.

Use a car only to get to Florence. Don't even comtemplate its use once there, as most of the monumental belt of central Florence is closed to all vehicles except those of local residents.

VISITOR INFORMATION

Contact the **Azienda Promozione Turistica,** via A. Manzoni 16 (☎ 055/2346284). Offices are open Monday through Saturday from 8:30am to 1:30pm. Another helpful office handling data about Florence and Tuscany as well is at via Cavour 1R (☎ 055/290832), open Monday through Saturday from 8am to 7:30pm.

CITY LAYOUT

Florence is a city seemingly designed for walking. It's amazing how nearly all major sights can be discovered on foot. The only problem is that the sidewalks in summer are so crowded that we can only hope you don't suffer from claustrophobia.

The city is split by the **Arno River,** which usually looks serene and peaceful, but can turn ferocious with flood waters on rare occasions. The major part of Florence, certainly its monumental and historical core, lies on the north or "right" side of the river. But the "left" side is not devoid of attractions. Many long-time visitors frequent the left bank for its tantalizing trattoria meals; they also maintain that the shopping here is less expensive. Even the most hurried visitor will want to cross over to the left bank to see the Pitti Palace with its many art treasures and walk through the Giardini di Boboli, a series of formal gardens, the most impressive in Florence. In addition, you'll also want to cross over to the left bank heading for the belvedere piazzale Michelangelo for one of the most panoramic vistas of this city of the Renaissance. To reach it, follow viale Michelangelo up the flank of the hill (one easy way to go is to take bus no. 13 from the train station).

The Arno is spanned by eight bridges, of which the **Ponte Vecchio,** with jewelry stores on either side, is the most celebrated and most central. Many of these bridges were ancient structures until the Nazis, in a hopeless and last-ditch effort, senselessly destroyed them in their "defense" of Florence in 1944. With tenacity, Florence rebuilt its bridges, using, whenever possible, pieces from the destroyed structures. The Ponte S. Trinità is the second most important bridge spanning the Arno. After crossing it you can continue along **via dei Tornabuoni,** which is the most important right-bank shopping street (don't look for bargains, however). At the Ponte Vecchio you can walk, again on the right bank, along via Por Santa Maria, which will become Calimala. This will lead you into the heartbeat **piazza della Repubblica,** a commercial district known for its cafés such as the Caffè Gilli.

From there, you can take via Roma, which leads directly into **piazza di San Giovanni.** There you'll find the baptistery and its neighboring sibling, the larger **piazza Duomo,** with a world-famous cathedral and bell tower by Giotto. From the far western edge of piazza Duomo, you can take via del Proconsolo south to **piazza della Signoria,** to see the landmark Palazzo Vecchio and its sculpture-filled Loggia della Signoria.

High in the hills overlooking Florence is the ancient town of **Fiesole,** with Roman ruins and a splendid cathedral.

NEIGHBORHOODS IN BRIEF

Florence isn't divided into neighborhoods the way many cities are. Most locals refer to either the left bank or the right bank of the Arno—and that's about it, unless they head out of town for the immediate environs, such as Fiesole. The following selection of "neighborhoods"—most of them grouped around a monumental palace, church, or square—is therefore rather arbitrary.

Centro Called simply that by the Florentines, the Centro could, in effect, be all the historic heart of Florence, but mostly the term is used to describe the area southwest of the Duomo. Most of it has a 19th-century overlay, and its focal point is piazza della Repubblica. On the western part of this old town is via dei Tornabuoni, flanked with palazzi and quality shops selling expensive merchandise.

Piazza della Signorla The ancient center of city life, this busy square was once the forum of the Republic. It's overlooked by the Palazzo Vecchio, Florence's massive, fortresslike town hall. To the south of the Palazzo Vecchio are the Uffizi Galleries.

Piazza del Duomo In the center of Florence, this square is dominated by the Duomo Santa Maria del Fiore, and immediately adjoins piazza San Giovanni, site of the Baptistery, a domed structure on an octagonal plan. The square bell tower was begun in 1334 by Giotto.

Impressions

[When in Florence] it's very popular to admire the Arno. It is a great historical creek with four feet in the channel and some scows floating around. It would be a very plausible river if they could pump some water into it. They all call it a river, and they honestly think it is a river do these dark and bloody Florentines. They even help out the delusion by building bridges over it. I do not see why they are too good to wade.
                                                —Mark Twain, *The Innocents Abroad,* 1869

Santa Maria Novella   On the northwestern edge of central Florence is the large piazza di Santa Maria Novella with its church of the same name. Northwest of Santa Maria Novella lies piazza della Stazione, the main railway terminal of Florence. Southwest of Santa Maria Novella, via del Melarancio goes a short distance east to San Lorenzo, the first cathedral of Florence. Beyond San Lorenzo is piazza Madonna degli Aldobrandini, the entrance to the Medici Chapels.

Piazza San Marco   Piazza San Marco is dominated by its church, now the Museo di San Marco. To the south is the Accademia di Belle Arti, with the Galleria dell'Accademia, at via Ricasoli 52, containing Michelangelo's *David*.

Santa Croce   This section is in the southeastern part of the old town of Florence, near the Arno, dominated by its Gothic Santa Croce or Holy Cross Church, completed in 1442. A little distance to the north of Santa Croce is Casa Buonarroti, at via Ghibellina 70, which Michelangelo acquired for his nephew.

Ponte Vecchio   Southwest of piazza della Signoria is the Ponte Vecchio (Old Bridge) area. This is the oldest of the bridges of Florence, and it is flanked by jewelry stores. The bridge will carry you across the Arno onto the left bank.

The Palazzo Pitti   This area lies to the southwest of Ponte Vecchio, on the slopes of the Colle di Boboli. This fortresslike palace—filled with museums—faces the Giardino di Boboli (Boboli Gardens) to the south, an 11-acre site laid out in 1560.

Fiesole   Although a town in its own right, Fiesole is treated by some as a neighborhood or suburb of Florence. An ancient town on a hill overlooking Florence, it has panoramic views of the city of the Renaissance and the Arno Valley. It was founded by the Etruscans, perhaps as early as the 7th century B.C. Its center is the large piazza Mino da Fiesole.

2 Getting Around

BY PUBLIC TRANSPORTATION   The major sights in the small city of Florence are within walking distance of most hotels, but you might prefer to use the public transportation provided by **buses.** If you do, you must purchase your bus ticket before boarding one of the public vehicles. For 1,200 lire (75¢), you can ride on any public bus in the city for a total of 70 minutes. A 24-hour pass costs 6,000 lire ($3.75). Bus tickets can be purchased from tobacconists and news vendors. The local bus station (which serves as the terminal for ATAF city buses) is at piazza del Duomo 57F (☎ 580528). Bus routes are posted at bus stops, but for a comprehensive map of the Florentine bus network, go to the ATAF booth at the rail station. If you're caught riding a bus without a ticket, you'll be fined 34,000 lire ($21.25).

BY TAXI   Taxis can be found at stands at nearly all the major squares in Florence. If you need a radio taxi, call 4390 or 4798.

BY CAR   As mentioned, driving a car in Florence is a hopeless undertaking—not only because of the snarled traffic, but because much of the district you've come to see is a pedestrian zone. If your hotel doesn't have a garage, someone on the staff will direct you to the nearest garage after you've parked long enough to unload your luggage. Garage fees for the night average from 25,000–50,000 lire ($15.65–$31.25).

You'll need a car to explore the surrounding countryside of Tuscany in any depth, and these are available at **Avis,** borgo Ognissanti 128R (☎ 21-36-29);

Budget, borgo Ognissanti 134R (☎ 287161); and **Eurodollar,** borgo Ognissanti 133R (☎ 21-86-65).

BY BICYCLE   Bicycles are a practical means of transport in Florence. You can rent one from **Ciao & Basta,** whose headquarters are on via Alamanni (☎ 21-33-07), near the Central Station. The average rental is 15,000 lire ($9.40) per day.

BY FOOT   Because Florence is so compact, getting around on foot is the ideal way to do it—at times, the only way because of so many pedestrian zones. In theory at least, pedestrians have the right of way at uncontrolled zebra crossings, but don't count on that should you encounter a speeding Vespa.

MAPS   Arm yourself with a map from the tourist office (see "Orientation," earlier in this chapter). But if you'd like to see Florence in any depth—particularly those little side streets, ask for a **Falk** map (indexes are included), which gives all the streets. These are available at all bookstores and at most newsstands.

FAST FACTS: Florence

American Express   Amex is at via Dante Alighieri 20-22R. (☎ 50981). It's open Monday through Friday from 9am to 5:30pm and on Saturday from 9am to 12:30pm.

Area Code   The telephone area code for Florence and Fiesole is 055.

Babysitters   Most hotel desks will make arrangements for you to have a babysitter. If you need an English-speaking sitter, try to make arrangements as far in advance as possible.

Bookstores   See "Savvy Shopping," in Chapter 9.

Business Hours   From mid-June to mid-September most shops and business offices are open Monday through Friday from 9am to 1pm and 4 to 8pm. Off-season hours, in general, are Monday from 3:30 to 7:30pm and Tuesday through Saturday from 9am to 1pm and 3:30 to 7:30pm.

Car Rentals   See "Getting Around," earlier in this chapter.

Climate   See "When to Go," in Chapter 3.

Consulates   The U.S. Consulate is at lungarno Amerigo Vespucci 46 (☎ 2398726), open Monday through Friday from 8:30am to 12:30pm and 2 to 4:30pm. The British Consulate is at lungarno Corsini 2 (☎ 284133), near the piazza Santa Trinità, open Monday through Friday from 9:30am to 12:30pm and 2:30 to 4:30pm.

Citizens of other English-speaking countries, including Canada, Australia, and New Zealand, should contact their diplomatic representatives in Rome.

Currency   See "Information, Entry Requirements & Money," in Chapter 3.

Currency Exchange   Local banks in Florence grant the best rates. Most banks are open Monday through Friday from 8:30am to 1:30pm and 2:45 to 3:45pm. The tourist office (see "Orientation," earlier in this chapter) exchanges money at official rates when banks are closed and on holidays, but a commission is often charged. You can also go to the Ufficio Informazione booth at the rail station, which is open daily from 7:30am to 7:40pm. The American Express office (see above) also exchanges money.

One of the best places to exchange currency is the post office (see below).

Dentist   For a list of English-speaking dentists, consult your consulate if possible or contact Tourist Medical Service, via Lorenzo il Magnifico 59 (☎ 475411). Visits are possible only Monday through Friday from 11am to noon and 5 to 6pm and on Saturday from 11am to noon.

Doctor   Night service is available by calling 474891. Otherwise, contact your national consulate for a list of English-speaking physicians. You can also contact Tourist Medical Service, via Lorenzo il Magnifico 59 (☎ 475411).

Drugstores   Pharmacy service is available at Farmacia Molteni, via Calzaiuoli 7R (☎ 588565), which is open daily, including Sunday, from 8am to 1am. If you need an all-night pharmacy, the name of one is posted every evening in all of the city's pharmacy windows, in a kind of rotating system.

Emergencies   For fire, call 115; for an ambulance, call 212222; for the police, 113; and for road service, 116.

Eyeglasses   Two well-accessorized and centrally located possibilities include Salmoiraghi, via Panzani 42 (☎ 215941), and the Centro Ottico Optometrico, via Cavour 94R (☎ 287210).

Hairdressers/Barbers   Both women and men are fond of Big Art, piazza della Repubblica 3 (☎ 212016), right in the center of Florence. Call for an appointment. It is on the floor above street level.

Holidays   See "When to Go," in Chapter 3.

Hospitals   Call the General Hospital of Santa Maria Nuova, piazza Santa Maria Nuova 1 (☎ 27581).

Hotlines   Call the police at 113.

Information   See "Tourist Information" under "Orientation," earlier in this chapter, and also "Information, Entry Requirements & Money," in Chapter 3.

Laundry/Dry Cleaning   Lavanderia Superlava Splendid, via del Sole 29R (☎ 21-88-36), is a good choice because of its central location off piazza Santa Maria Novella. Hours for this self-service laundry are Monday through Friday from 8:30am to 7:30pm. Most hotels can arrange for dry cleaning, although you'll pay extra for the convenience. You can also ask at your hotel reception desk for the nearest dry-cleaning establishment in your neighborhood.

Libraries   An American studies library of the University of Florence, the Biblioteca di Storia e Letteratura Nordamericana (American Library), is at via San Gallo 10 (☎ 275-7940), open Monday through Friday from 9am to 1pm.

Lost Property   The lost-and-found office, Oggetti Smarrito, is at via Circondaria 19 (☎ 367943), near the rail terminal.

Luggage Storage/Lockers   These are available at Santa Maria Novella Stazione, in the center of the city at piazza della Stazione (☎ 278785). It's open daily from 7am to 9pm.

Newspaper/Magazines   Copies of the *International Herald Tribune* or *USA Today* are sold at many first-class and deluxe hotels and at most newsstands, especially in the summer. You can also obtain copies of *Time* and *Newsweek*.

Photographic Needs   One of the best places to patronize is Bottega della Fotto, piazza del Duomo 17 (☎ 283006), across from the cathedral in the center of Florence.

Police   Dial 113 in an emergency. English-speaking foreigners who want to see and talk to the police should go to the Ufficio Stranieri station at via Zara 2 (☎ 49771), where English-speaking personnel are available daily from 9am to 2pm.

Post Office   The Central Post Office is at via Pellicceria 3, off piazza della Repubblica (☎ 21-11-27), open Monday through Friday from 8:15am to 7pm and Saturday from 8:15am to 12:30pm. Stamps are purchased in the main post office at windows 21–22. If you want your mail sent to Italy general delivery (*fermo postal*), have it sent in care of this post office (use the 50100 Firenze zip code). Mail can be picked up at windows 23–24. A telegram, telex, and fax office on the second floor is open daily from 8:15am to 10pm (you can also send telegrams by phoning 186 during the same hours). A foreign exchange office is open Monday through Friday from 8:15am to 6pm; you can also exchange money at automatic tellers on the second floor daily from 7am to 10pm. If you want to send packages, go to the rear of the building and enter at piazza Davantzi 4; opening hours are the same as the main post office.

Radio   Although there are some private channels, the air waves are dominated by RAI, the national radio network. In the summer months, RAI broadcasts some news in English. Vatican Radio's foreign news broadcasts (in English) also reach Florence. Shortwave radio reception is also possible, and you can pick up American (VOA), British (BBC), and Canadian (CBC) radio broadcasts. The American Southern European Broadcast Network (SEB) from Vicenza can also be heard on regular AM radio (middle or medium wave).

Religious Services   There is a Baptist church at via Borgognissanti 6 (☎ 210537), and a Jewish synagogue at via Farini 4 (☎ 245252). Florence also has a Lutheran church at via dei Bardi 20 (☎ 234-2775). If you're Catholic, you can walk into virtually any church in the city. The American Episcopalian church is St. James, at via Bernardo Rucellai 9 (☎ 294417).

Restrooms   Public toilets are found in most galleries, museums, bars and cafés, and restaurants, as well as bus, train, and air terminals. Usually they are designated as W.C. (water closet) or DONNE (women) or UOMINI (men). The most confusing designation is SIGNORI (gentlemen) and SIGNORE (ladies), so watch those final I's and E's!

Safety   The most violent crimes are rare in Florence, where crime consists mainly of pickpockets who frequent crowded tourist centers, such as corridors of the Uffizi Galleries. Members of group tours who cluster together are often singled out as victims. Car thefts are relatively common: Don't leave your luggage in an unguarded car, even if it's locked in the trunk. Women should be especially careful in avoiding purse snatchers, some of whom grab a woman's purse while whizzing by on a Vespa, often knocking the woman down. Documents such as passports and extra money are better stored in safes at your hotel if available.

Shoe Repairs   Try Riparazioni Scarpe Il Ciabattino, via del Moro 88R, near piazza Santa Maria Novella, a short walk from the main rail terminal. It's open Monday through Friday from 8:30am to noon and 2:30 to 7:30pm, and on Saturday from 8:30am to noon.

Taxes   A value-added tax (IVA) is added to all consumer products and most services, including those at hotels and restaurants. The tax is refundable if you spend more than 300,000 lire ($187.50) at any one store.

Taxis   See "Getting Around," earlier in this chapter.

Telegrams/Telex/Fax   Most of these can be sent at your hotel, or you can go to the post office.

Television   The RAI is the chief television network broadcasting in Italy. Every TV in the country receives these highly politicized channels: RAI-1 for Christian Democrats, RAI-2 for Italian Socialists, and RAI-3 for the Democratic Party of the Left.

Transit Information   For international flights from Galileo Galilei Airport, dial 050/50-07-07; for domestic flights at Peretola, call 306-15; for railway information, dial 278785; for long-distance bus information, call 215154; and for city buses, dial 580528.

Weather   May and September are the ideal times to visit. The worst times to go are the week before and including Easter and from June until the first week of September. Florence is literally overrun with tourists, and the city streets, or anything else, weren't designed for mass tourism. Temperatures in July and August hover in the 70s, dropping to a low of 45° or 46° Fahrenheit in December and January, the coldest months.

3 Networks & Resources

FOR STUDENTS   The **University of Florence** lies between piazza San Marco and the Mercato Centrale. Most of the student activity takes place in and around piazza San Marco. For information about discounted bus, air, and train tickets, go to **S.T.S. Student Travel Service,** via Zanetti 18R (☎ 28-41-83), which is open Monday through Friday from 9:30am to 12:30pm and 3:30 to 6:30pm, and on Saturday from 9:30am to 12:30pm.

FOR GAY MEN & LESBIANS   The local headquarters of gay liberation in Tuscany is **Arci Gay,** via de Leone 5 (☎ 288126 or 2398772), which holds official meetings at regular intervals which change according to the circumstances. Linked to an organization with other branches at large cities throughout Italy, its offices are open for advice and information about local gay-related activities and organizations for both men and women every Monday, Tuesday, and Thursday from 4 to 8pm, and every Wednesday from 3:30 to 5:30pm. AIDS counseling and education plays an important part in this organization's agenda. Female staffers offer advice specifically geared to women, and sponsor frequent meetings of their own. Call them for current information, and look for the gay and lesbian magazine, *QUIR*, published monthly by Arci Gay.

FOR WOMEN   The city's leading feminist bookstore is **La Libreria delle Donne,** via Fiesolana 2B (☎ 240384), which sells books and magazines pertaining to women's issues in politics, sociology, and the arts. Most of the material is in Italian; some is in English and, to a lesser degree, French. The organization is proud of its membership in LILITH, a computerized network of women's organizations with branches throughout Italy. The bookstore is open Tuesday through Saturday from 9am to 1pm and Monday through Saturday from 3:30 to 7:30pm.

FOR SENIORS   Go to the **tourist office** (see "Orientation," earlier in this chapter) and inquire about any discounts—such as on transportation and museum entrances—that pertain to senior citizens. These data are always changing, so it's best to get the latest information.

Where to Stay & Dine in Florence

8

The days when Aldous Huxley called Florence "under-bathroomed and over-monumented" are past. The monuments are still there, but bathrooms today are plentiful. Even some of the monuments that Huxley obviously referred to have been turned into hotels, with bathrooms installed.

A vast array of hotels—sometimes not enough in the peak tourist months from spring to fall—await today's visitor. They range from deluxe to fourth class, and they are supplemented by an array of *pensioni* (boarding houses) of varying standards, ranked P1 (the best) to P3 (the most modest). Many students and young people from all over the world—especially those interested in art—fill up these pensioni, often for weeks at a time.

The Florentine table has always been set with the abundance provided by the Tuscan countryside. That means the best of olive oil and wine, such as chianti, succulent fruits and vegetables, fresh fish from the coast, and the best of game in season. Meat-lovers all over Italy sing the praise of *bistecca alla fiorentina,* a thick and juicy steak on the bone often served with white Tuscan beans. It is said that you can gauge the cost of a meal in the restaurant before you go in by the price charged per kilo (2.2 lb.) for the Florentine beefsteak printed on the menu outside. It isn't considered impolite to order one steak for two diners.

1 Accommodations

Florence was always a leader in architecture. Consequently, with the decline and fall of the great aristocratic families of Tuscany, many of the city's grand old villas and palaces have been converted into hotels. For sheer charm and luxury, the hotels of Florence are among the finest in Europe. There are not too many tourist cities where you can find a 15th- or 16th-century palace—tastefully decorated and most comfortable—rated as a second-class pensione (boarding house). Florence is equipped with hotels in virtually all price ranges and of widely varying standards, comfort, service, and efficiency.

However, during the summer there simply aren't enough rooms to meet the demand, and if you arrive without a reservation you may not find a place for the night and will have to drive to nearby Montecatini, where you'll always stand a good chance of securing accommodations.

If you should arrive without a reservation and don't want to wander around town on your own looking for a room, go in person (instead of calling) to the **Consorizio ITA office** in the rail terminal at piazza della Stazione (☎ 282893). The office is open daily from 9am to 8:30pm.

NEAR PIAZZA OGNISSANTI
VERY EXPENSIVE

Grand Hotel

Piazza Ognissanti 1, 50123 Firenze. ☎ **055/288781,** or 800/325-3589 in the U.S. and Canada. Fax 055/217400. 90 rms, 17 suites. A/C MINIBAR TV TEL. 510,000–580,000 lire ($318.75–$362.50) double; from 900,000 lire ($562.50) suite. Breakfast 26,000 lire ($16.25) extra per person. 10% IVA tax extra. AE, DC, MC, V. Parking from 45,000 lire ($28.15). Bus: 8 or 16.

The Grand Hotel is a bastion of luxury, fronting a little Renaissance piazza across from the Excelsior. A hotel of history and tradition, the Grand is known for its halls and salons. Its legend grew under its name as the Continental Royal de la Paix. In both the 19th and 20th centuries it has attracted many famous people. Its rooms and suites have a refined elegance, and the most desirable overlook the Arno. Each bedroom contains all the silks, brocades, and real or reproduction antiques you'd expect from such a highly regarded establishment.

Dining/Entertainment: A highlight of the hotel is the Winter Garden, an enclosed court lined with arches, which has been restored. Here regional and seasonal specialities are served along with an array of international dishes. Guests gather at night in the Fiorino Bar to listen to piano music.

Services: Room service, babysitting, laundry, valet.

Facilities: Foreign currency exchange.

EXPENSIVE

✪ Hotel Excelsior

Piazza Ognissanti 3, 50123 Firenze. ☎ **055/264201,** or 800/325-3589 in the U.S. and Canada. Fax 055/210278. 177 rms, 15 suites. A/C MINIBAR TV TEL. 420,000–490,000 lire ($262.50–$306.25) double; from 800,000 lire ($500) suite. Breakfast 26,000 lire ($16.25) extra per person. 10% IVA tax extra. AE, DC, MC, V. Parking 50,000 lire ($31.25). Bus: 6 or 16.

Hotel Excelsior, set on a Renaissance square in a neo-Renaissance palace, is the ultimate in well-ordered luxury during a stopover in Florence. Demand for the elegant bedrooms is so great that during peak season most of the accommodations are reserved many weeks in advance. Once part of the hotel was owned by Carolina Bonaparte, sister of Napoleon. The present hotel was formed in 1937 by the combination of two other hotels, the De la Ville and the Italie. Several of the bedrooms have terraces, and many open onto views of the Arno. The rooms offer lots of comfortable chairs, well-appointed space, and baths with heated racks, thick towels, and high-ceilinged comfort.

Dining/Entertainment: Il Cestello, the hotel's deluxe restaurant, attracts an upper-crust clientele. The hotel also operates one of the most important rendezvous spots in Florence, the Donatello Bar (see Section 5, "Evening Entertainment," in the following chapter).

Services: Room service, babysitting, laundry, valet, express checkout, translation services.

Facilities: Foreign currency exchange.

NEAR PIAZZA MASSIMO D'AZEGLIO
EXPENSIVE

✪ Hotel Regency

Piazza Massimo D'Azeglio 3, 50121 Firenze. ☎ **055/245247.** Fax 055/2346735. 29 rms, 5 suites. A/C MINIBAR TV TEL. 350,000–550,000 lire ($218.75–$343.75) double; from 750,000 lire ($468.75) suite. Rates include breakfast. AE, DC, MC, V. Parking 45,000 lire ($28.15). Bus: 6.

Hotel Regency lies a bit apart from the shopping and sightseeing center of Florence, but it's only a 15-minute stroll to the cathedral. And although its location isn't central (a blessing for tranquility seekers), it is conveniently and quickly reached by taxi or bus. This well-built, old-style villa, a member of Relais & Châteaux, has its own garden across from a park in a residential area of the city. This luxurious hideaway, filled with stained glass, paneled walls, and reproduction antiques, offers exquisitely furnished rooms. There are some special rooms on the top floor with walk-out terraces. The owner, who also has the prestigious Lord Byron in Rome, has a capable staff at the Regency.

Dining/Entertainment: The attractive dining room, Relais le Jardin, is renowned for its haute cuisine. You can also take your meals in the well-lit winter garden.

Services: Room service, babysitting, laundry, valet.

Facilities: Garden.

INEXPENSIVE

Albergo Losanna

Via Vittorio Alfieri 9, 50121 Firenze. ☎ **and fax 055/245840.** 10 rms (4 with bath), 1 suite. TEL. 88,000 lire ($55) double without bath; 99,000 lire ($61.90) double with bath; 180,000 lire ($112.50) suite. Rates include breakfast. MC, V. Parking 30,000–35,000 lire ($18.75–$21.90). Bus: 6.

A good, inexpensive choice, Albergo Losanna is a tiny, family-run place off viale Antonio Gramsci, between piazzale Donatello and piazza Massimo d'Azeglio. It offers utter simplicity and cleanliness. The bus stops a block and a half away. The bedrooms, all doubles, are homey and well kept.

🏨 Family-Friendly Hotels

Hotel Casci *(see p. 252)*   This hotel is not only inexpensive but it's well located in the historic district. Many of its bedrooms are rented as triples and quads.

Nuova Italia *(see p. 252)*   This 17th-century building near the rail station offers some very large rooms suitable for families, for whom management offers special discounts.

Relais Certosa *(see p. 264)*   For families wanting to escape the congestion of overcrowded Florence, this relais hotel—a former monastery—is set on five acres of land. Motorists like its wide-open spaces and inviting, family-type atmosphere.

Florence Accommodations

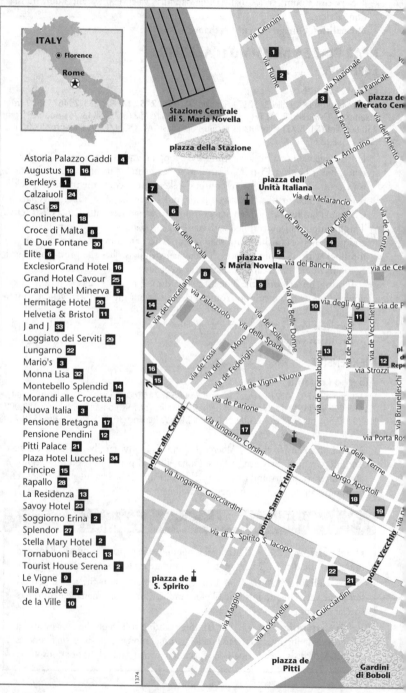

via S. Reparata

via San Gallo

28

27

via de Ginobi

26

via Cavour

via C. Battisti

via Gino Capponi

via G. Giosti

29

via Laura

30

via della Colonna

31

via Guelfa

via Ricasoli

via del Servi

via del Castellaccio

via degli Alfani

via de Pucci

piazza Brunelleschi

via de Martelli

via Bufalini

via della Pergola

borgo Pinti

via dei Pilastri

piazza S.M. Nuova

32

via Fiesolana

via S. Egidio

via de' Pepi

piazza del Duomo

via de Oriuolo

33

via de Mezzo

ghi

via d. Oche

via d. Studio

via del Proconsolo

25

via del Corso Borgo degli Albizi

via Pietrapiana

via de Calzaiuoli

via de Cerchi

24

via de Pandolfini

via dell'Ulivo

via Palmieri

via M. Buonarroti

via Condotta

via G. Verdi

via del Pepi

via Ghibellina

piazza della Signoria

via dell' Anguillara

via Torta

Elco

borgo Allegri

borgo del Greci

piazza S. Croce

via de Leoni

via del Neri

via de Rustici

borgo S. Croce

sca

piazzale degli Uffizi

corso dei Tintori

via Tripoli

Fiume Arno

lungarno Genevale Diaz

cia dei Benci

lungarno delle Grazie

lungarno d. Zecca Vecchia

34

ponte alle Grazie

via lungarno Torrigiani

Church

Post Office

Information

NEAR THE RAILWAY STATION
EXPENSIVE

Hotel Astoria Palazzo Gaddi

Via del Giglio 9, 50123 Firenze. ☎ **055/239-8095**. Fax 055/214632. 90 rms, 5 suites. A/C MINIBAR TV TEL. 270,000–360,000 lire ($168.75–$225) double; 460,000 lire ($287.50) suite. Rates include buffet breakfast. AE, DC, MC, V. Parking 40,000 lire ($25) nearby. Bus: 19.

Hotel Astoria at one time housed the office of a now-defunct newspaper. In the 17th century John Milton wrote parts of *Paradise Lost* in one of the bedrooms. This 16th-century palace has been renovated and turned into one of the most unusual hotels in the historic district. From the bedrooms on the upper floors, you'll have a view over the terra-cotta rooftops of Florence. If you choose to stay in one of the stylishly comfortable bedrooms of this hotel, be sure to inspect the conference rooms of what used to be the adjoining Palazzo Gaddi, whose frescoes are filled with chubby cherubs.

Dining/Entertainment: On the premises is a garden-style restaurant, Palazzo Gaddi, with wall murals, beamed ceilings, and Empire lyre-backed chairs. It serves an international cuisine, with meals starting at 55,000 lire ($34.40).

Services: Room service, laundry, babysitting.

Facilities: Car-rental desk, shopping boutique, money exchange.

Hotel Kraft Spa

Via Solferino 2, 50123 Firenze. ☎ **055/284273**. Fax 055/2398267. 76 rms, 2 suites. A/C MINIBAR TV TEL. 390,000 lire ($243.75) double; 420,000 lire ($262.50) suite. Rates include breakfast. AE, DC, MC, V. Parking 20,000–45,000 lire ($12.50–$28.15). Bus: 3, 6, 11, 16, 31, or 32.

Hotel Kraft was created in the 1960s by the son of one of Italy's greatest hoteliers (the father, Herman Kraft, of Berne, Switzerland, founded the Excelsior in the 19th century). The present-day Kraft is far removed from the baroque—instead, it meets the requirements of today quite beautifully. It's at the side of a square, close by the railroad station and almost next to the Arno and the U.S. Consulate. Fine antiques or reproductions are used in the comfortable bedrooms. Many have little terraces, perfect for morning coffee. Several terraces above the dining room is an open-air swimming pool. Imagine swimming with a view of the Duomo, piazzale Michelangelo, and Fiesole. Being so near the opera house, the Kraft is popular with maestros and singing stars.

Dining/Entertainment: The Kraft is crowned with a rooftop dining room that opens onto a covered terrace. An Italian/international cuisine is served, with meals costing 40,000 lire ($25) to 60,000 lire ($37.50).

Services: Room service, babysitting, laundry, valet.

Facilities: Swimming pool in summer, gymnasium.

Hotel Montebello Splendid

Via Montebello 60. 50123 Firenze. ☎ **055/2398051**. Fax 055/211867. 51 rms, 3 suites. A/C MINIBAR TV TEL. 385,000 lire ($240.65) double; 444,000 lire ($277.50) suite. Rates include breakfast. AE, DC, MC, V. Bus: 3, 6, 11, 31, or 32.

Midway between the railway station and the Arno, this historic and elegant hotel was built as a private villa during the 19th century, and later wound up as a run-down pensione during the 1960s and 1970s. Around 1985 the owners spent large sums of money to restore it to its former grandeur, polished the marble sheathing of the public rooms, restored the neoclassical bas-reliefs adorning the curving staircase, and upgraded the plantings within the villa's rear garden. Today, the hotel is charming and intimate, a restful oasis from the congestion of the city that surrounds it. Bedrooms contain conservatively modern furniture, deep cove moldings, white marble bathrooms, and many contemporary comforts.

Dining/Entertainment: The hotel's stylishly elegant restaurant, Capriccio, contains an adjacent bar decorated like a private club, and serves fixed-price lunches and dinners priced at 45,000 lire ($28.15) each.

Services: Room service, laundry, valet, concierge.

Facilities: Conference facilities in a lavishly restored neo-Palladian villa (the Palazzetto Concordia) in the rear of the garden.

Villa Medici

Via il Prato 42, 50123 Firenze. ☎ **055/238-1331**. Fax 055/238-1336. 93 rms, 14 suites. A/C MINIBAR TV TEL. 470,000 lire ($293.75) double; 800,000 lire ($500) suite. Breakfast 25,000 lire ($15.65) extra. 10% IVA tax extra. Parking from 25,000 lire ($15.65). Bus: 3, 6, 11, 31, or 32.

Villa Medici, centrally located between the railway station and Arno, creates its own world once you walk through its glass doorways. This 1962 luxury hotel has all the trappings and extra services needed to attract the famous and glamorous, even kings and princesses. The super-size, handsomely maintained bedrooms (each with radio) combine both traditional and modern features in decor. The big draw at the Medici is its private garden, with its open-air, onion-shaped swimming pool. On the rooftop terrace you can enjoy a view of Brunelleschi's dome and Giotto's bell tower. In summer, meals are served by the pool.

Dining/Entertainment: Dining is in the Lorenzo de' Medici Restaurant, which offers both international and Florentine cuisine. Meals begin at 70,000 lire ($43.75).

Services: Room service, babysitting, laundry, valet.

Facilities: Cleaning and pressing facilities, swimming pool.

MODERATE

Hotel Croce di Malta

Via della Scala 7, 50123 Firenze. ☎ **055/282600**, or 800/528-1234 in the U.S. and Canada. Fax 055/287121. 82 rms, 15 duplex suites. A/C MINIBAR TV TEL. 240,000–320,000 lire ($150–$200) double; 350,000–430,000 lire ($218.75–$268.75) suite. Rates include breakfast. One child 12 or under free in parents' room. AC, DC, MC, V. Parking 25,000–45,000 lire ($15.65–$28.15). Bus: 31, 32, 36, or 37.

Hotel Croce di Malta is housed in a stately palace whose soaring interior was modernized in the early 1970s. It's one of the few hotels in Florence with its own swimming pool, whose curved edges are partially shaded by the rear garden's 100-year-old magnolia. The stylish lobby has massive stone columns between which the architects placed rounded doorways. The bedrooms are classically elegant, filled with Florentine furniture and frescoed headboards showing landscapes that might have been done by an artist of the early Renaissance. Some of the more expensive accommodations are duplexes with their own sleeping lofts set midway between the floors and high ceilings.

Dining/Entertainment: There's a whimsically decorated restaurant, Il Coccodrillo, which serves well-prepared meals ranging from 40,000 lire ($25) to 60,000 lire ($37.50).

Services: 24-hour room service, babysitting, laundry, valet.

Facilities: Swimming pool open June through September.

INEXPENSIVE

Hotel Berkleys

Via Fiume 11, 50123 Firenze. ☎ **or Fax 055/212302**. 9 rms. TV TEL. 109,000 lire ($68.15) double; 145,000 lire ($90.65) triple; 160,000 lire ($100) quad. Rates include breakfast. MC, V.

This pleasant but modest hotel occupies the top floor of a 19th-century apartment building whose lower floors contain two roughly equivalent two-star hotels. It lies about a block east of the railway station, and offers a polite but friendly greeting from its owners, the Andreoli family. There's an employee on duty throughout the day and night, and a simple lobby that leads into a breakfast nook and a bar area, where drinks are served on request. Bedrooms are simple but clean.

⊛ Hotel Casci

Via Cavour 13, 50129 Firenze. ☎ **055/211686**. Fax 055/239-6461. 25 rms. TV TEL. 90,000–130,000 lire ($56.25–$81.25) double; 120,000–175,000 lire ($75–$109.40) triple; 150,000–220,000 lire ($93.75–$137.50) quad. Rates include breakfast. AE, DC, MC, V. Parking 35,000–40,000 lire ($21.90–$25). Bus: 1, 6, 7, 11, or 17.

Casci is a well-run little hotel in the historic district, 200 yards from the main railway station and 100 yards from piazza del Duomo. The building dates from the 14th century, and some of the public rooms feature the original frescoes. Gioacchio Rossini, the famous composer of *The Barber of Seville* and *William Tell*, lived in the building between 1851 and 1855 before moving to Paris, where he died. The hotel is both traditional and modern, and the English-speaking reception staff looks after guests very well. The bedrooms are comfortably furnished, and each contains a hairdryer.

⊛ Hotel Elite

Via della Scala 12, 50123 Firenze. ☎ **055/215395**. 8 rms (all with shower; 5 with toilet and shower). TV TEL. 120,000 lire ($75) double with shower and toilet. Rates include breakfast. No credit cards. Parking from 25,000 lire ($15.65). Bus: 7, 31, or 32.

The Elite is a little pensione worthy of being better known, lying two floors above street level in a 19th-century apartment building. Attractive in scale and appointments, it's about a two-block walk from the main railway station. It's also convenient for exploring most of the major monuments. The owner, Maurizio Maccarini, speaks English and he's a helpful, welcoming host. The small hotel rents light and airy bedrooms, divided equally between singles and doubles.

Hotel Mario's

Via Faenza 89, 50123 Firenze. ☎ **055/216801**. Fax 055/212039. 16 rms, 1 suite. TV TEL. 120,000–185,000 lire ($75–$115.65) double; 210,000 lire ($131.25) suite. Rates include breakfast. AE, DC, MC, V. Parking 30,000 lire ($18.75). Bus: 31 or 32.

The spotless Hotel Mario's has been completely restored and refurnished in 16th-century Florentine style. Mario Noce is a gracious host, and he and his staff speak English. Although you'll find cheaper inns in Florence, the service, hospitality, and good level of innkeeping make Mario's worth your lire. The bedrooms contain direct-dial phones and hairdryers, and laundry service is provided upon request.

Nuova Italia

Via Faenza 26, 50123 Firenze. ☎ **055/287508**. Fax 055/210941. 20 rms. TEL. 110,000–140,000 lire ($68.75–$87.50) double; 185,000 lire ($115.65) triple. Rates include breakfast. AE, DC, MC, V. Parking 35,000–40,000 lire ($21.90–$25) nearby. Bus: 31 or 32.

Nuova Italia is a renovated hotel in a 17th-century building in the center of Florence. All the bedrooms have private bath, direct-dial phones, soundproof windows, and are pleasantly furnished and decorated with paintings and posters. Some large rooms are suitable for families, to whom the management—the Viti family—grants special reductions. The family helps guests face the problems of getting around Florence, giving them tips on where to shop and itinerary suggestions. The little hotel has been welcoming Frommer readers since 1958 and the pioneering budget guide, *Europe on $5 a Day*. The location is only one block from the railway station, near the San Lorenzo Market and the Medici Chapels.

Soggiorno Erina

Via Fiume 17, 50123 Firenze. ☎ **055/284343**. 7 rms. TEL. 100,000 lire ($62.50) double; 130,000 lire ($81.25) triple. Rates include breakfast. AE, MC, V. Bus: 14, 28, or 31.

Soggiorno Erina is convenient to the railway station, along a street lined with residential buildings. It sits on the third floor of a 19th-century building whose facade is ornamented with sculpted faces peering from above the windows. The wrought-iron elevator requires a coin before it will take you to the hotel's third-floor reception areas, or else you can take the stairs. The double bedrooms stretch off a wide central hallway. The place is basic and simple, but newcomers are made to feel welcome.

Stella Mary Hotel

Via Fiume 17, 50123 Firenze. ☎ **055/215694**. Fax 055/264206. 7 rms (all with bath or shower). TV TEL. 60,000–110,000 lire ($37.50–$68.75) double; 90,000–130,000 lire ($56.25–$81.25) triple. Breakfast 10,000 lire ($6.25) extra. MC, V. Parking 20,000 lire ($12.50). Bus: 14, 28, or 31.

Stella Mary Hotel is a small pensione lying 12 blocks from the train station and around the corner from a bus station that gets a lot of traffic 24 hours a day. The owners operate a clean and comfortable "home in Firenze." Rooms are cozy and full of light. Breakfast is extra. A sitting room with a TV set is reserved for guests. Born in Florence, Mrs. Vittoria and her son speak English and run the hotel personally. The hotel has an arrangement with some restaurants and trattorias, which will provide hotel guests with a Tuscan dinner, costing from 25,000–30,000 lire ($15.65–$18.75) per person. The hotel, in a classic Florentine-style building with an elevator, is only a short walk from the San Lorenzo Church and the San Lorenzo Market.

Tourist House Serena

Via Fiume 20, 50123 Firenze. ☎ **055/213643**. 7 rms (1 with shower). 85,000 lire ($53.15) single or double without shower; 100,000 lire ($62.50) single or double with shower. Rates include breakfast. V. Bus: 14, 28, or 31.

The building that houses Tourist House Serena was erected in 1905 as an apartment house. Today it still contains a scattering of stained-glass doors and ornate plaster ceilings, but the furnishings are considerably simpler than they were in the building's heyday. The owner makes guests feel comfortable and welcome as soon as they walk in. All rooms are doubles, and single guests are accepted at the double rate. After riding the elevator to the first floor, guests register in the wide hallway and are taken to high-ceilinged but dimly illuminated bedrooms. The house lies 30 yards from the railway station.

Villa Azalée

Viale Fratelli Rosselli 44, 50123 Firenze. ☎ **055/214242**. Fax 055/268264. 24 rms (all with bath or shower). A/C MINIBAR TV TEL. 204,000 lire ($127.50) double; 283,000 lire ($176.90) triple. Rates include buffet breakfast. AE, DC, MC, V. Parking from 25,000 lire ($15.65). Bus: 17.

Little Known Hotel Lore

Jennings-Riccioli, Corso Tintori 7, is the pensione that was featured in *A Room With a View,* the Merchant-Ivory film based on the novel by E.M. Forster. The film was shot, however, at Quisisana e Ponte Vecchio, which was damaged by terrorists in a 1993 bombing and has never reopened.

Hotel Brunelleschi, piazza Santa Elisabetta, took over part of what had been a church in the Middle Ages, containing a half-moon shaped Byzantine tower. For a time it was a prison for women.

Hotel Savoy was once known as the Hotel Savoia. It changed its name after the royal family of Italy was politely asked to abdicate.

Annalena, via Romana 34, is a pensione in a 15th-century stucco palazzo. Cosimo de'Medici presented the building to a Florentine woman named Annalena. After losing her husband and son, she became a nun and turned the building into a convent. In World War II it was a hideaway for political refugees.

Villa San Michele, via Doccia 4, at Fiesole, above Florence, claims that Michelangelo designed its facade and loggia. The great artist wasn't responsible for the Jacuzzi, however. Brigitte Bardot once honeymooned here (the staff doesn't remember which husband it was).

Hotel Helvetia & Birstol, via dei Pescioni 2, was a favorite address for Giorgio di Chirico, Luigi Pirandello, Igor Stravinsky, and Gabriele D'Annunzio.

Villa Azalée, a handsome structure set on a street corner with a big garden, is a re-make of a gracious private home originally built in the 1860s and transformed into a hotel in 1964. The owners have provided a personal touch in both atmosphere and decor. The decorating is tasteful: tall, white-paneled doors with ornate brass fittings, parquet floors, crystal chandeliers, and antiques intermixed with credible reproductions. The lounge is a private home, and the bedrooms have distinction (one, in particular, boasts a flouncy canopy bed). The hotel is a five-minute walk from the rail station. Clients can rent bicycles at the hotel for 5,000 lire ($3.15) per day.

AT PIAZZA S. MARIA NOVELLA
INEXPENSIVE

Hotel Le Vigne
Piazza S. Maria Novella 24, 50123 Firenze. ☎ **055/294449.** Fax 055/230-2263. 19 rms (16 with bath), 2 suites. A/C TEL. 130,000 lire ($81.25) double with bath; 180,000 lire ($112.50) triple with bath; 240,000 lire ($150) suite for four. Rates include breakfast. AE, DC, MC, V. Parking 20,000–30,000 lire ($12.50–$18.75). Bus: 11, 36, or 37.

Hotel Le Vigne, which offers comfortably furnished bedrooms, enjoys a prime location on one of the most central squares of Florence. Its sitting room overlooks the square. An Italian family took over this ancient building and restored it, preserving the old features, including frescoes, whenever possible. Some of the rooms, those containing three to six beds, are suitable for families. This small hotel is on the first floor (second to Americans) of this old-fashioned building. Five of the units are air-conditioned. Breakfast is the only meal served and it's a generous self-service one. Take your problems to English-speaking Giovanna Ciatta.

ON OR NEAR VIA TORNABUONI
MODERATE

Hotel De La Ville
Piazza Antinori 1, 50123 Firenze. ☎ **055/238-1805.** Fax 055/2381809. 75 rms, 4 suites. A/C MINIBAR TV TEL. 280,000–412,000 lire ($175–$257.50) double; 600,000 lire ($375) suite. Rates include buffet breakfast. AE, DC, MC, V. Parking 40,000 lire ($25). Bus: 22, 31, 32, 36, or 37.

Established in the 1960s, on the most elegant street of the historic center, close to the Arno and the railway station, this hotel has a loyal following among Italian business travelers. It has a conservatively contemporary appearance, with a decor that includes flowering plants, mirror-bright marble floors, and many sitting areas. Bedrooms are soundproof, with contemporary decors in muted colors and cable-TV reception. There's an American-style bar, a breakfast room, and a parking area reserved for guests. Laundry and babysitting are available.

Tornabuoni Beacci
Via Tornabuoni 3, 50123 Firenze. ☎ **055/212645.** Fax 055/283594. 29 rms. A/C MINIBAR TV TEL. 200,000–240,000 lire ($125–$150) double. Rates include breakfast. AE, DC, MC, V. Parking 30,000 lire ($18.75). Bus: 14, 31, or 32.

Near the Arno and piazza S. Trinità, on the city's principal shopping street, is the Tornabuoni Beacci. The pensione occupies the three top floors of a 14th-century palazzo. All its living rooms have been furnished in a tatty provincial style, with bowls of flowers, parquet floors, a formal fireplace, old paintings, murals, and rugs. The hotel was completely renovated recently, but it still bears an air of gentility. The roof terrace, surrounded by potted plants and flowers, is for late-afternoon drinks or breakfast. Dinner is served here in summer. Typically Florence and Italian dishes are served, costing 35,000 lire ($21.90) per person. The view of the nearby churches, towers, and rooftops is worth experiencing. The names in the guest book are numerous, including, in days of yore, many personalities such as John Steinbeck, the Gish sisters, and Fredric March. The bedrooms are moderately well furnished. It offers good value, and there are three elevators and a bar.

INEXPENSIVE

La Residenza
Via Tornabuoni 8, 50123 Firenze. ☎ **055/218684.** Fax 055/284197. 25 rms (all with bath or shower). A/C TEL. 215,000 lire ($134.40) double. Rates include breakfast. AE, DC, MC, V. Parking 30,000–35,000 lire ($18.75–$21.90). Bus: 4.

La Residenza, right in the hub of Florence, is on an elegant shopping street of fashion houses, boutiques, and palaces. It occupies the top floors of a 16th-century Renaissance building, just a few blocks from American Express and the Arno, right next door to the Palazzo Strozzi. The palace housing the hotel belongs to the descendents of the Tornabuoni, the family of Lorenzo de Medici's mother. The hotel offers freshness, comfort, and style. The elevator is a mahogany-and-glass jewel rising up the interior of the stone stairwell, whose entrance is graced by a statue of a bashful Venus. The dining room is elegant with high ceilings, and antiques are extensively used. The rooms have been redecorated with reproductions and color-coordinated pieces, and some have private balconies. You can have morning coffee in the roof garden, enjoying the wisteria, pots of flowering plants. The bathrooms have been recently renovated.

PIAZZA DELLA REPUBBLICA
VERY EXPENSIVE

Savoy Hotel

Piazza della Repubblica 7, 50123 Firenze. ☎ **055/283313.** Fax 055/284840. 97 rms, 4 suites. A/C MINIBAR TV TEL. 390,000–530,000 lire ($243.75–$331.25) double; from 550,000 lire ($343.75) suite. Rates include breakfast. AE, DC, MC, V. Parking 40,000–50,000 lire ($25–$31.25). Bus: 31 or 32.

The dignified Savoy Hotel has a buff-colored facade with neoclassical trim that was carved from gray stone in 1900, when it was built at the height of the belle époque era. It sits in what might be called the commercial center of Florence (also the historic district), an area filled with fine stores, a few blocks from the Duomo and a five-minute walk from the railway station. The predictably upper-class interior includes potted plants, patterned carpeting, and coffered ceilings. Bedrooms have traditional Italian styling.

Dining/Entertainment: The hotel offers an elegant Tuscan restaurant with formal service, featuring both a regional and international cuisine, with meals ranging from 80,000–105,000 lire ($50–$65.65). An accommodating bar area has frescoed walls reminiscent of a *trompe l'oeil* view from an 18th-century balcony, with jardinières and depictions of fluttering parrots.

Services: Room service, babysitting, laundry, valet.

Facilities: Limited facilities for the disabled.

INEXPENSIVE

Pensione Pendini

Via Strozzi 2, 50123. ☎ **055/211170.** Fax 055/281807. 42 rms. TEL. Bus: 22 or 4. 200,000 lire ($125) double. Rates include breakfast. AE, DC, MC, V. Parking 30,000–43,000 lire ($18.75–$26.90).

Founded in 1879, the family-owned and -run Pensione Pendini offers an old-fashioned environment in a distinguished setting. Your room may overlook the active piazza or front an inner courtyard (more peaceful). One of the oldest pensioni in Florence, it's located on the fourth floor of an arcaded building. The all-purpose lounge is furnished family style with a piano and card tables. The breakfast room, located in a redecorated large room inside one of the arcades, offers a view of the whole via Strozzi. Some of the bedrooms have quite a lot of character, with reproduction antiques. The bar lounge is open 24 hours. The Pendini is not for everyone, but it's one of the long-enduring favorites among pensione devotees visiting Florence. Only breakfast is served.

NEAR THE DUOMO
VERY EXPENSIVE

✪ Hotel Helvetia & Bristol

Via dei Pescioni 2, 50123 Firenze. ☎ **055/287814.** Fax 055/88353. 52 rms, 15 suites. A/C MINIBAR TV TEL. 425,000–530,000 lire ($264.65–$331.25) double; 671,000–1,320,000 lire ($419.40–$825) suite. Breakfast 28,600 lire ($17.90) extra. AE, DC, MC, V. Parking 35,000 lire ($21.90). Bus: 31 or 32.

Hotel Helvetia & Bristol is located in the most elegant part of Florence, just a few steps from the Duomo between via Tornabuoni and via degli Strozzi. Constructed in the late 19th century, and reopened in 1989 after a massive restoration, it was once considered the most exclusive hotel in Florence, frequented by noble

Florentines and British aristocrats. It has now been restored to its former pedestal. Strict attention was devoted to preserving its original architectural features. Period decoration and furnishings include a famous set of 17th-century paintings representing the five senses. The bedrooms are attractively decorated and comfortable.

Dining/Entertainment: The Giardino d'Inverno (Winter Garden) is a first-class restaurant, and what was a gathering for Florentine intellectuals in the 1920s is now a cocktail bar serving light food. The main dining room, "The Bristol," serves a deluxe cuisine, with meals costing from 85,000 lire ($53.15) and up.

Services: Room service, babysitting, laundry, valet.

Facilities: Car-rental desk.

MODERATE

Grand Hotel Cavour

Via del Proconsolo 3, 50122 Firenze. ☎ **055/282461**. Fax 055/218955. 89 rms. A/C MINIBAR TV TEL. 225,000 lire ($140.65) double. Rates include breakfast. AE, DC, MC, V. Parking 30,000–50,000 lire ($18.75–$31.25). Bus: 14, 19, or 23.

Opposite the Bargello Museum, between via del Proconsolo and via Dante Alighieri, is the Grand Hotel Cavour, an elaborate palace built in the 13th century and now standing on one of the busiest streets in Florence. The hotel is located on an important corner of the city, near the Badia Church, between the houses of the Cerchi and Pazzi families. It once belonged to the Cerchis, and in the lounge you can see where the old courtyard was laid out. In the basement, a historic well is called Beatrice's Well. The Portinaris, family of Dante's beloved Beatrice, lived nearby, and it's possible that the young woman actually drew water from the well. Such a chore was at least certainly done by Beatrice's nurse, Monna Tessa. The Hotel Cavour came into being when Florence was the capital of Italy (1860–65), and it was nicknamed "The Senators' Hotel" because it was frequented by the members of the highest assembly of the new state.

The Cavour maintains its architectural splendor. The coved main lounge, with its frescoed ceiling and crystal chandelier, is of special interest, as is the old chapel, now used as a dining room. The altar and confessional are still there. The ornate ceiling and stained-glass windows reflect superb crafting. The Cavour attained a curious supremacy in Florence in 1905, when it gained the first elevator in town. Elevators now take you to the traditionally styled and comfortably furnished bedrooms. Each unit has a hairdryer.

Hotel J and J

Via di Mezzo 20, 50121 Firenze. ☎ **055/2345005**. Fax 055/240282. 15 rms, 5 suites. A/C MINIBAR TV TEL. 270,000–330,000 lire ($168.75–$206.25) double; 420,000 lire ($262.50) suite. Rates include breakfast. AE, DC, MC, V. Parking 35,000 lire ($21.90). Bus: 15.

This charming hotel was originally built in the 16th century as a monastery. Set within a five-minute walk of the church of Santa Croce, it underwent a massive restoration in 1990, and was soon after transformed into the hotel you'll see today. Developed and managed by the Cavagnari family, the hotel is named after the initials of their two children, James and Jacqueline. You'll find many sitting areas throughout the property, including a flagstone-covered courtyard with stone columns, and a salon with vaulted ceilings and several carefully preserved ceiling frescoes. Bedrooms combine an unusual mixture of modern furniture, some of it built in, with the monastery's original beamed ceilings. Suites usually contain sleeping lofts and, in some cases, rooftop balconies overlooking Florence's historic core. There's a bar on the premises, but other than breakfast, no meals are served.

Hotel Monna Lisa

Borgo Pinti 27, 50121 Firenze. ☎ **055/247-9751.** Fax 055/247-9755. 30 rms. A/C MINIBAR TV TEL. 350,000 lire ($218.75) double; 420,000 lire ($262.50) triple. Rates include breakfast. AE, DC, MC, V. Parking 30,000 lire ($18.75). Bus: 6 or 14.

Hotel Monna Lisa (yes, that's the right spelling), a well-preserved structure, is a privately owned Renaissance palazzo. Located on a narrow street where carts were once driven, the palace facade is forbiddingly severe, in keeping with the style of its day. But when one enters the reception rooms, the atmosphere is inviting. Most of the great old rooms overlook either an inner patio or the garden in the rear. Each of the salons is handsomely furnished in a restrained way, utilizing many fine antiques and oil paintings. The bedrooms vary greatly.

NEAR THE OPERA HOUSE
EXPENSIVE

Anglo-American Regina Hotel

Via Garibaldi 9, 50123 Firenze. ☎ **055/282114.** Fax 055/268513. 107 rms, 12 suites. A/C MINIBAR TV TEL. 370,000 lire ($231.25) double; 450,000 lire ($281.25) suite. Rates include breakfast. AE, DC, MC, V. Bus: 6.

Anglo-American Regina Hotel occupies an old Florentine palace near Cascine Park. The hotel is well placed near the Arno, close to the opera house and the U.S. Consulate. Its streetside buildings enclose a covered garden room, lounge, and loggia—springlike all year. The older parts of the hostelry have exquisite architectural features, as does the dining room, with ornate plaster designs on the walls in pink, red, and white. Crystal chandeliers and towering gilt mirrors grace the public salons. The lobby has draperies covering the sloping skylights. Each room has a radio, and a garage for your car is available nearby.

Dining/Entertainment: There's an elegant dining room with Victorian chairs and an English club-style bar. Piano music is provided every night except Sunday.

Services: Room service, babysitting, laundry, valet.

Facilities: Inside garden and loggia.

INEXPENSIVE

Ariele

Via Magenta 11, 50123 Firenze. ☎ **055/211509.** Fax 055/268521. 40 rms (all with bath or shower). AC TV TEL. 170,000 lire ($106.25) double; 200,000 lire ($125) triple. Rates include breakfast. AE, DC, MC, V. Parking 15,000 lire ($9.40). Bus: 1 or 13.

Just a block from the Arno is the Ariele, which calls itself "Your Home in Florence." It's an old corner villa that has been converted into a roomy pensione. The building is architecturally impressive, with large salons and lofty ceilings. The furnishings, however, combine antique with functional. The bedrooms are a grabbag of comfort.

Pensione Bretagna

Lungarno Corsini 6, 50123 Firenze. ☎ **055/289618.** Fax 055/289619. 18 rms (10 with bath). 100,000 lire ($62.50) double without bath; 135,000 lire ($84.40) double with bath. Rates include breakfast. AE, MC, V. Parking 25,000 lire ($15.65). Bus: 13, 14, 15, 23, 31, or 32.

Pensione Bretagna is in a palace that was the residence of Louis Napoleon in the 1820s. It's run by a helpful staff, most of whom speak English. Offering bed and breakfast only, the pensione is centrally located. Rates depend on the plumbing, as some rooms don't have private bath or shower. Accommodations are furnished in a basic style, but the public rooms of this early Renaissance palace impress with their gilded stucco work, painted ceilings, fireplaces, and a balcony overlooking the Arno.

NEAR PIAZZA SS. ANNUNZIATA
MODERATE

Hotel Le Due Fontane

Piazza SS. Annunziata 14, 50122 Firenze. ☎ **055/210185.** Fax 055/294461. 53 rms, 3 suites. A/C MINIBAR TV TEL. 240,000 lire ($150) double; 250,000 lire ($156.25) suite for two; 330,000 lire ($206.25) suite for four. Rates include breakfast. AE, DC, MC, V. Free parking. Bus: 17.

Hotel Le Due Fontane is a small palace on the best-known Renaissance square in Florence, right in the heart of the artistic center of the city, within an easy walk of the Duomo. In spite of its antique origins in the 14th century, the hotel has been completely renovated and modernized. Today it offers simply but tastefully furnished bedrooms. The upper-floor rooms are preferred for those desiring the most tranquil sleep. Services and facilities include laundry, personal hotel bus service, car-rental facilities, shopping boutiques, a concierge, a business center, babysitting, and a bar.

✪ Loggiato dei Serviti

Piazza SS. Annunziata 3, 50122 Firenze. ☎ **055/219165.** Fax 055/289595. 29 rms, 4 suites. A/C MINIBAR TV TEL. 255,000 lire ($159.40) double; 320,000–490,000 lire ($200–$306.25) duplex suite for four. Rates include breakfast. AE, DC, MC, V. Parking 32,000–42,000 lire ($20–$26.25). Bus: 1 or 17.

In the historical center of Florence, you'll find the Loggiato dei Serviti. Built in the early 1500s as a monastery, it has served as a hotel since the turn of this century. Its entrance lies beneath soaring arcades that face the Renaissance Hospital of the Innocents and an imposing equestrian statue. More than any other hotel in the neighborhood, its bedrooms evoke the aura of an austerely elegant monastery, with vaulted or beamed ceilings, some of which are painted with Renaissance-inspired designs.

INEXPENSIVE

⑤ Hotel Morandi alla Crocetta

Via Laura 50, 50121 Firenze. ☎ **055/234-4747.** Fax 055/248-0954. 10 rms. A/C MINIBAR TV TEL. 179,000 lire ($111.90) double; 215,000 lire ($134.40) triple. Breakfast 18,000 lire ($11.25) extra. AE, DC, MC, V. Bus: 1, 7, 10, 11, or 17.

The small, charming Hotel Morandi alle Crocetta is administered by one of the most experienced hoteliers in Florence, a sprightly matriarch, Katherine Doyle, who came to Florence from her native Ireland when she was 12. It contains all the elements needed for a Florence pensione, lying on a little-visited backstreet near a university building. The structure was built in the 1500s as a convent. The bedrooms have been tastefully and gracefully restored, filled with framed examples of 19th-century needlework, beamed ceilings, and antiques. In the best Tuscan tradition, the tall windows are sheltered from the summer sunlight with heavy draperies. You register in a high-ceilinged and gracefully austere salon filled with Persian carpets. The hotel lies right behind the Archaeological Museum and two blocks from the Accademia (which displays Michelangelo's *David*).

OFF PIAZZA DELL'INDIPENDENZA
MODERATE

Rapallo

Via Santa Caterina d'Alessandria 7, 50129 Firenze. ☎ **055/472412.** Fax 055/470385. 30 rms. MINIBAR TV TEL. 192,000 lire ($120) double. Rates include breakfast. AE, DC, MC, V. Parking 25,000 lire ($15). Bus: 12.

An "E" for effort is due Rapallo, which has attempted to make its rooms liveable and comfortable. Without succeeding in being typical of Florence, it is, nevertheless, completely revamped and inviting. The lounge, ingeniously using small space, is brightened by planters, Oriental rugs, and barrel stools set in the corners for drinking and conversation. The bedrooms are furnished mostly with blond-wood suites, quite pleasant, and all have a private safe and, upon request, a TV. The hotel is within walking distance of the railway station.

INEXPENSIVE

Hotel Splendor

Via S. Gallo 30, 50129 Firenze. ☎ **055/483427.** Fax 055/461276. 31 rms (25 with bath or shower). TV TEL. 120,000 lire ($75) double without bath; 180,000 lire ($112.50) double with bath; 240,000 lire ($150) triple with bath. Rates include buffet breakfast. AE, MC, V. Parking 30,000 lire ($18.75). Bus: 1, 7, 10, 17, or 25.

Although the Hotel Splendor is within a 10-minute walk from the Duomo, the residential neighborhood it occupies is a world away from the milling hordes of the tourist district. The hotel has three high-ceiling floors of a 19th-century apartment building. Its elegantly faded public rooms evoke the kind of family-run pensione which, early in the century, attracted genteel visitors from northern Europe for prolonged art-related visits. This is the domain of the Masoero family, whose rooms contain an eclectic array of semi-antique furniture and much of the ambience of bedrooms in a private house. All the singles have baths. There is no restaurant, but room service is available.

ON THE ARNO
EXPENSIVE

Hotel Principe

Lungarno Vespucci 34, 50123 Firenze. ☎ **055/284848.** Fax 055/283458. 18 rms, 2 suites. A/C MINIBAR TV TEL. 230,000–380,000 lire ($143.75–$237.50) double; 485,000 lire ($303.15) suite. Rates include breakfast. AE, DC, MC, V. Parking 40,000 lire ($25). Bus: 6 or 16.

Hotel Principe is a real "find," occupying a villa dating from 1860. Its facade is dignified, like an old embassy town house, and its bedrooms have been well adapted. Each bedroom is treated differently, reflecting the taste of the owner, who blends antique and modern. Ask for one of the terrace rooms, where tables and chairs are set out for breakfast facing the Arno. Double glass doors protect the bedrooms from street noises. One of the nicest features of the hotel is its little walled garden in back where drinks are served. The hotel serves breakfast only.

Lungarno

Borgo San Jacopo 14, 50125 Firenze. ☎ **055/264211.** Fax 055/268437. 66 rms (all with bath or shower), 12 suites. A/C MINIBAR TV TEL. 390,000 lire ($243.75) double; 540,000 lire ($337.50) suite. Rates include breakfast. AE, DC, MC, V. Parking 25,000–35,000 lire ($15.65–$21.90). Bus: 36 or 37.

As you stand on the banks of the Arno, looking at the facade of the 10 floors of the Lungarno, you'll find it difficult to believe that the hotel was built entirely in the 1960s. It's proof that a modern, comfortable hotel can be created in the old style without sacrificing conveniences of the 20th century. Imagine sitting in a stone tower suite, enjoying a room-long view through a picture window of the rooftops of Florence, including the Duomo and campanile. Throughout the hotel is a collection of contemporary watercolors and oils. Around the fireplace is a "clutter wall" of framed art. On sunny days guests congregate on the upper terrace, enjoying the drinks and a view of the bridges spanning the Arno. The bedrooms are consistently well designed and attractive, each with its own color theme. Singles have showers and doubles have baths. The hotel lies near the Ponte Vecchio on the Palazzo Pitti side. The hotel has no restaurant but does offer a snack bar. Laundry, babysitting, and 24-hour room service are available.

Plaza Hotel Lucchesi

Lungarno della Zecca Vecchia 38, 50122 Firenze. ☎ **055/26236,** or 800/223-9832 in the U.S. Fax 055/248-0921. 97 rms, 10 suites. A/C MINIBAR TV TEL. 400,000 lire ($250) double; 520,000 lire ($325) suite. Rates include breakfast. AE, DC, MC, V. Parking 18,000–36,000 lire ($11.25–$22.50). Bus: 19, 31, or 32.

Plaza Hotel Lucchesi, one of the most charming and best-managed hotels in Florence, offers many of the facilities and services of the city's famous five-star hotels, but at about half the price. Originally built in 1860, and renovated many times since then, it lies along the banks of the Arno, a 10-minute walk from the Duomo and a few paces from the imposing Church of Santa Maria della Croce. Its interior decor includes lots of glossy mahogany, acres of marble, and masses of fresh flowers. Each of the handsomely furnished and beautifully kept bedrooms contains all the modern equipment and comfort you'd expect from such a stellar property. About 20 accommodations open onto private terraces or balconies, some with enviable views over the heart of historic Florence.

Dining/Entertainment: In the sunny lobby-level restaurant, La Serra, the site of copious morning breakfast buffets and elegant dinners, diners often enjoy the melodies of a resident pianist/singer. The comfortably appointed bar reigns supreme as the hotel's social center.

Services: 24-hour room service, babysitting, laundry, valet.

Facilities: Car-rental desk.

MODERATE

Hotel Augustus

Vicolo del'Oro 5, 50123 Firenze. ☎ **055/283054.** Fax 055/268557. 62 rms (all with bath or shower), 8 suites. A/C MINIBAR TV TEL. 180,000–360,000 lire ($112.50–$225.00) double; 500,000 lire ($312.50) suite. Breakfast 25,000 lire ($15.65) extra. AE, DC, MC, V. Parking 25,000–35,000 lire ($15.65–$21.90). Bus: 14 or 23.

Hotel Augustus is for those who require modern comforts in a setting of historical and monumental Florence. The Ponte Vecchio is just a short stroll away, as is the Uffizi Gallery. The exterior is rather pillbox modern, but the interior seems light, bright, and comfortable. The expansive lounge and drinking area is like an illuminated cave, with a curving ceiling and built-in conversational areas interlocked on several levels. Some of the bedrooms open onto little private balconies with garden furniture. Laundry, babysitting, and 24-hour room service are provided.

INEXPENSIVE

Hotel Columbus

Lungarno Cristofore Colombo 22A, 50136 Firenze. ☎ **055/669100.** Fax 055/669100. 96 rms (all with bath or shower). A/C TV TEL. 144,000 lire ($90) double. Rates include breakfast. AE, DC, MC, V. Free parking, but limited. Bus: 14.

This 1956 hotel is built and furnished with good taste. Although set quite a distance from the city's major attractions, it's still only a 20-minute walk from the Ponte Vecchio and can also be reached by bus. The air-conditioned public rooms, with light-inviting windows, have informal furnishings. The dining room has round tables, with ladder-back chairs, potted greenery, and a sense of space. The bedrooms (each with a private balcony) are compact, in the motel fashion, with everything built in: bedside table, lights, and all. There's no fussy decor—instead, the tone is severe but restful.

NEAR THE PONTE VECCHIO
EXPENSIVE

Hotel Continental

Lungarno Acciaiuoli 2, 50123 Firenze. ☎ **055/282392.** Fax 055/283139. 48 rms (all with bath or shower), 6 suites. A/C MINIBAR TV TEL. 290,000–410,000 lire ($181.25–$256.25) double; 460,000–680,000 lire ($287.50–$425) suite. AE, DC, MC, V. Parking 25,000–35,000 lire ($15.65–$21.90). Bus: 14 or 23.

Located at the entrance of the Ponte Vecchio, the Hotel Continental occupies some choice real estate. Through the lounge windows and from some of the bedrooms you can see the little jewelry and leather shops that flank the much-painted bridge over the Arno. Despite its perch in the center of historic Florence, the hotel was created in the 1960s, so its style of accommodation is utilitarian, with functional furniture that's softened by the placement of decorative accessories. The hotel was overhauled in 1992. You reach your bedroom by the elevator or by climbing a wrought-iron staircase (note that parts of the old stone structure have been retained). The management likes to put up North Americans, knowing they'll be attracted to the roof terrace, a vantage point for viewing piazzale Michelangelo, the Pitti Palace, the Duomo, the campanile, and Fiesole. Artists fight to get the penthouse suite up in the tower ("Torre Guelfa dei Consorti"). Laundry, babysitting, and 24-hour room service are available.

MODERATE

Hermitage Hotel

Vicolo Marzio 1, piazza del Pesce I, 50122 Firenze. ☎ **055/287216**. Fax 055/212208. 22 rms (all with bath or shower). AC TV TEL. 210,000–260,000 lire ($131.25–$162.50) double. Rates include breakfast. MC, V. Bus: 3 or 23.

The offbeat, intimate Hermitage Hotel is a charming place to stay right on the Arno, with a sun terrace on the roof providing a view of much of Florence, including the nearby Uffizi. You can take your breakfast under a leafy arbor surrounded by potted roses and geraniums. The success of the small hotel has much to do with its English-speaking owner, Vincenzo Scarcelli, who has made the Hermitage an extension of his home, furnishing it in part with antiques and well-chosen reproductions. Best of all is his warmth toward guests, many of whom keep coming back to enjoy the gatherings in the top-floor living room around the wood-burning fireplace on nippy nights.

The bedrooms are pleasantly furnished, many with Tuscan antiques, rich brocades, and good beds. The tiled baths are superb and contain lots of gadgets. Breakfast is served in a dignified, beam-ceilinged dining room. Rooms overlooking the Arno have the most scenic view, and they've been fitted with double-glass windows, which reduces the traffic noise by 40%.

Hotel Pitti Palace

Via Barbadori 2, 50125 Firenze. ☎ **055/23-98-711.** Fax 055/23-98-867. 72 rms. A/C MINIBAR TV TEL. 260,000 lire ($162.50) double. Rates include breakfast. AE, DC, MC, V.

This is a recent overhaul of a 19th-century building set within 100 yards of the Uffizi Gallery and close to the Ponte Vecchio. Maintained today by a chain of hotels with other representatives throughout Florence, the hotel contains six floors of comfortable, green-toned rooms, each of which has a modern white-tiled bathroom and double-paned windows to reduce noise from the nearby quays of the Arno. Rooms on the fifth floor have the finest views over Florence, while a panoramic bar and breakfast terrace occupy part of the sixth floor.

INEXPENSIVE

Hotel Calzaiuoli

Via dei Calzaiuoli, 50122 Firenze. ☎ **055/212456.** Fax 055/268310. 48 rms (all with bath or shower). A/C MINIBAR TV TEL. 209,000 lire ($130.65) double. Rates include breakfast. AE, DC, MC, V. Bus: 1, 14, 19, or 23.

This hotel occupies the premises of what was originally built in the 1800s as the prosperous private home of a wealthy Tuscan family. It's set on the pedestrian walkway that was known long ago as the headquarters of Florence's many shoemakers (*calzaiuoli*), on a well-located street interconnecting the piazza del Signoria with the Duomo. The location is one of the city's most desirable in terms of sightseeing, as the major attractions lie virtually on the hotel's doorstep. Although the building is old and the location historic, the interior has been completely modernized in a rather severe contemporary style. Rooms are simple but comfortable, each furnished with functional and efficient pieces. Guests register in a marble-and-teakwood lobby.

ON THE LEFT BANK
INEXPENSIVE

Pensione Annalena

Via Romana 34, 50125 Firenze. ☎ **055/222403.** Fax 055/222403. 20 rms. TV TEL. 220,000 lire ($137.50) double; 300,000 lire ($187.50) triple. Rates include breakfast. AE, DC, MC, V. Parking 30,000 lire ($18.75). Bus: 36 or 37.

In existence since the 15th century, Pensione Annalena has had many owners, including the Medici. Once a convent, in the past three-quarters of a century it has been a haven for artists, poets, sculptors, and writers (Mary McCarthy once wrote of its importance as a cultural center). During a great deal of that period it was the domain of the late sculptor Olinto Calastri. Now it's owned by Claudio Salvestrini, who attracts paying guests sympathetic to the pensione's special qualities. Most of the accommodations overlook a garden. During the war, the Annalena was the center of much of the underground, as many Jews and rebel Italians found safety hidden away in an underground room behind a secret door. The pensione is about a 5-minute walk from the Pitti Palace, 10 minutes from the Ponte Vecchio.

AT GALLUZZO
EXPENSIVE

Relais Certosa
Via di Colle Ramole 2, 50124 Firenze. ☎ **055/204-7171,** or 800/223-9832 in the U.S. Fax 055/268575. 69 rms, 6 suites. A/C MINIBAR TV TEL. 340,000 lire ($212.50) double; 495,000 lire ($309.40) suite. Rates include breakfast. AE, DC, MC, V. Free parking. Take the Rome–Milan expressway to exit A1, "Firenze/Certosa"; go 300 yards and turn left on a signposted road leading to the hotel. Bus: 37 from the center of Florence to Certosa.

Relais Certosa, a four-star hotel of exceptional merit, is set on five acres of land with tennis courts. The Relais was originally a guesthouse for the monastery near here, but during the Renaissance it became the villa that stands today. In the 19th century it was a farm. After centuries of use in private hands, it became a hotel in the 1970s, which today could easily become your home in Florence. Convenient for motorists who want to avoid the hysterical city center, it's only 10 minutes from the monumental district and 5 minutes from the Rome–Milan expressway. Its rooms are well furnished, and each has individual climate control. Somehow the owners, the Bettoja family, have managed to blend Renaissance charm and style with today's comfort. The atmosphere is a special Florentine one. All rooms face a park with views of the Tuscan hills and the Certosa monastery. There's parking space for 200 cars.

Dining/Entertainment: For some of the best Tuscan dining in the area, you can patronize the Greenhouse Restaurant even if you're not a guest of the hotel. It offers regional specialities as well as continental dishes. Guests also enjoy a garden and terrace for drinks and snacks and a bar and a piano bar.

Services: Room service, laundry, valet.

Facilities: Tennis courts, sauna, solarium, parking.

NEAR PIAZZALE MICHELANGELO
MODERATE

Hotel Villa Carlotta
Via Michele di Lando 3, 50125 Firenze. ☎ **055/220530.** Fax 055/233-6147. 27 rms. A/C MINIBAR TV TEL. 320,000–350,000 lire ($200–$218.75) double. Rates include breakfast. AE, DC, MC, V. Free parking. Bus: 11, 36, or 37.

The lavish renovations that the owner poured into her distinguished establishment transformed it into one of the most charming smaller hotels in Florence. It was built during the Edwardian age as a private villa and acquired in the 1950s by Carlotta Buchholz, who named it after herself. The aura here is still very much like that of a private villa. It's in a residential section of the city, behind a neoclassical facade whose entrance columns are capped with stone lions and flanked with venerable cypresses. In 1985 all bedrooms were upgraded with the addition of a sheathing of pink or blue silk wallpaper, reproduction antiques, silk bedspreads, private safety-deposit boxes, and crystal chandeliers; each also has a view of the surrounding garden. The hotel lies only 10 pedestrian minutes from the Ponte Vecchio; by taxi, it's a 5-minute ride.

Dining/Entertainment: The dining room, Il Bobolino, serves meals ranging from fresh salads to full culinary regalias, always accompanied by top-notch service and personal touches.

Services: Room service, babysitting, laundry, valet.

Facilities: Garden, car-rental desk.

2   Dining

After checking into your hotel you'll begin an even more interesting search—this time for a restaurant that may represent your introduction to Florentine cuisine.

The Tuscan cuisine (except for some of its hair-raising specialities) should please most North Americans, as it's simply flavored, without rich spices, and based on the hearty, bountiful produce brought in from the hills. Florentine restaurants are not generally as acclaimed by gourmets as those of Rome, but many dishes are prepared so well that the Tuscan kitchen is considered among the finest in Italy. Florentines often assert that the cooking in the other regions of Italy "offends the palate."

The case was stated most critically by Mary McCarthy, who wrote: "The food in the restaurants is bad, for the most part, monotonous, and rather expensive. Many of the Florentine specialties—tripe, paunch, rabbit, and a mixture of the combs, livers, hearts, and testicles of roosters—do not appeal to the foreign palate." The statement is funnier than it is true, although I concede the point about some of the specialties. And although I don't know where Ms. McCarthy dined, it's true that Florence has many expensive spots that dispense viands at "Grand Duke" prices. On the other hand, the city often stuns visitors with the sheer preponderance of good, moderately priced eating establishments. And one of the most typical platters, the Florentine beefsteak, is savored by foreigners and locals alike, although this is a very expensive item.

The one Italian wine all foreigners recognize, the ruby-red chianti, usually in a straw bottle, comes from Tuscany. Although shunned by some wine snobs, it's a fit complement to many a local repast.

Armed with a knife and fork, we'll eat our way down through the pick of the restaurants. We hasten to point out that the reference to "down" is in price only. Many of our most memorable and top-level dinners have been in some of the completely unheralded trattorie and *buca* (cellar) restaurants of the city.

NEAR THE RAILWAY STATION
MODERATE

Don Chisciotte

Via Ridolfi 4R. ☎ **47-54-30.** Reservations recommended. Main courses 21,000–40,000 lire ($13.15–$25). AE, DC, MC, V. Mon–Sat 1–2:30pm and 8–10:30pm. ITALIAN/SEAFOOD.

Set one floor above the street level, within a venerable Florentine *palazzo* near the railway station, this restaurant is known for its creative cuisine and its changing array of very fresh fish. The dining room, outfitted in soft tones of pink, green, and ivory, reflects the colors of the menu items, which are produced with a flourish from the kitchens. The cuisine is creative (i.e., eclectic, and imbued with the

Florence Dining

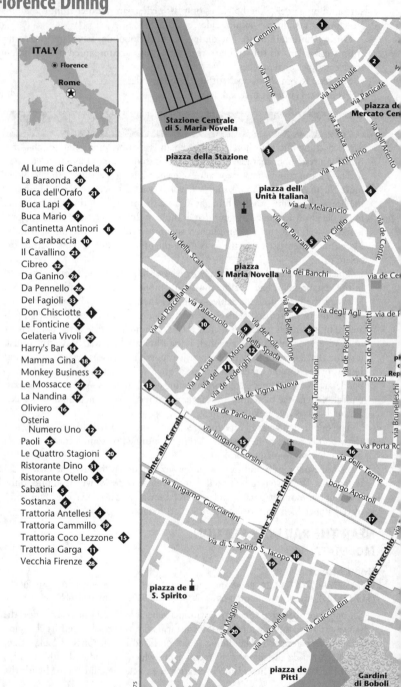

Al Lume di Candela 16
La Baraonda 30
Buca dell'Orafo 21
Buca Lapi 7
Buca Mario 9
Cantinetta Antinori 8
La Carabaccia 10
Il Cavallino 23
Cibreo 32
Da Ganino 24
Da Pennello 26
Del Fagioli 33
Don Chisciotte 1
Le Fonticine 2
Gelateria Vivoli 29
Harry's Bar 14
Mamma Gina 18
Monkey Business 22
Le Mossacce 27
La Nandina 17
Oliviero 16
Osteria
  Numero Uno 12
Paoli 25
Le Quattro Stagioni 20
Ristorante Dino 31
Ristorante Otello 3
Sabatini 5
Sostanza 6
Trattoria Antellesi 4
Trattoria Cammillo 19
Trattoria Coco Lezzone 15
Trattoria Garga 11
Vecchia Firenze 28

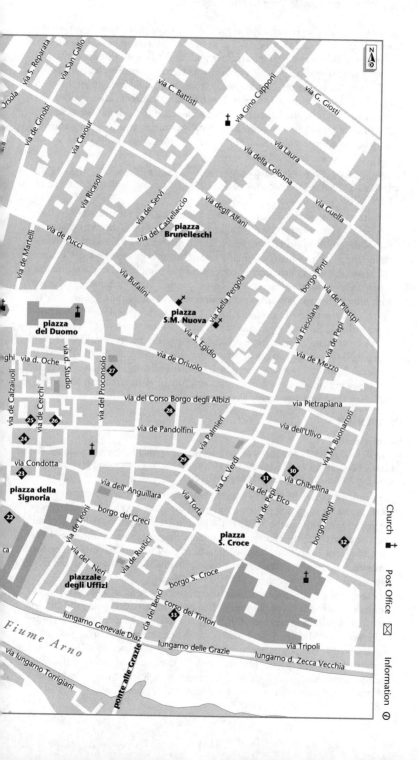

Church ■ †

Post Office ⊠

Information ⊙

wisdom, training, and inspiration of the chef), based on flavors that are often enhanced with the boiled-down essence of an unusual assortment of fresh herbs, vegetables, and fish stocks. Examples include pink tagliatelle with shrimp, herbs, and cream sauce; risotto of broccoli and baby squid; red taglierini with clams, pesto, and a sprinkling of cheese; black ravioli colored with squid ink and stuffed with a purée of shrimp and crayfish; filet of turbot with a radicchio sauce; grilled filet of sea bass with baby artichokes, herbs, and wine sauce; and a classic sole meunière. The price of meals can vary with the seasonally changing cost of the ingredients, but tends to average around 65,000 lire ($40.65) per person, without wine.

Sabatini

Via de'Panzani 9A. ☎ **211559.** Reservations recommended. Main courses 27,000–28,000 lire ($16.90–$17.50). AE, DC, MC, V. Tues–Sun 12:30–2:30pm and 7:30–10:30pm. Bus: 19. FLORENTINE.

Despite its less than chic location near the railway station, Sabatini has long been extolled by Florentines and visitors alike as the finest of the restaurants characteristic of the city. To celebrate my return visit to this restaurant, I ordered the same main course I had when I originally researched this guide—boiled Valdarno chicken with a savory green sauce. Back then I had complained to the waiter that the chicken was tough. He'd replied, "But, of course!" The Florentine likes chicken with muscle, not the hot-house variety so favored by Americans. Having eaten a lot of Valdarno chicken since those long-ago days back in the 1960s, I was more appreciative of Sabatini's dish this time. But on a subsequent visit I found some of the other main courses more delectable, especially the veal scaloppine with artichokes. Of course, you can always order a good sole meunière and the classic beefsteak Florentine. Another specialty is spaghetti Sabatini, a cousin of spaghetti carbonara but enhanced with fresh tomatoes. American-style coffee is also served, following the Florentine cake, called *zuccotto*.

INEXPENSIVE

Le Fonticine

Via Nazionale 79R. ☎ **282106.** Reservations recommended for dinner. Main courses 14,000–25,000 lire ($8.75–$15.65). AE, DC, MC, V. Tues–Sat noon–3pm and 7:30–10:30pm. Closed July 25–Aug 25. Bus: 19. TUSCAN/BOLOGNESE.

Le Fonticine used to be part of a convent until the owner, Silvano Bruci, converted both it and its adjoining garden into one of the most hospitable restaurants in Florence, lying close to the San Lorenzo food market. Today the richly decorated interior contains all the abundance of an Italian harvest, as well as the second passion of Signor Bruci's life, his collection of original modern paintings. The first passion, as a meal here reveals, is the cuisine that he and his wife produced from recipes she collected from her childhood in Bologna.

Proceed to the larger of the establishment's two dining areas, and along the way you can admire dozens of portions of freshly made pasta decorating the table of an exposed grill. At the far end of the room, a wrought-iron gate shelters the wine collection that Mr. Bruci has amassed, like his paintings, over many years. The food, served in copious portions, is both traditional and delectable. Begin with a platter of fresh antipasti, then follow with samplings of three of the most excellent pasta dishes of the day. This might be followed by fegatina di pollo (chicken), veal scaloppine, or one of the other main dishes.

PIAZZA SANTA MARIA NOVELLA
MODERATE

I Quattro Amici

Via degli Orti Oricellari 29. ☎ **21-54-13**. Reservations recommended. Main courses 23,000–30,000 lire ($14.40–$18.75). AE, DC, MC, V. Thurs–Tues 12:20–2:30pm and 7–10:30pm. Closed Aug and Sun in June–Sept. Bus: 31 or 32. SEAFOOD.

Established in 1990 by four Tuscan entrepreneurs who had known one another since childhood, this restaurant occupies the street level of a modern building near the railway station. Inside, amid a vaguely neoclassical decor, the place serves endless quantities of fish to a landlocked clientele eager for memories of the sea. Specialties include such dishes as pasta with fish sauce and fragments of sausage, fish soup, fried shrimp and squid in the style of Livorno, and grilled, stewed, or baked versions of all the bounty of the Mediterranean. The roast sea bass and roast snapper, flavored with Mediterranean herbs, are among the finest dishes. Vegetables are fresh and flavorful, an appropriate foil for the seafood being featured.

Osteria Numero Uno

Via del Moro 22. ☎ **284897**. Reservations recommended. Main courses 18,000–35,000 lire ($11.25–$21.90). AE, DC, MC, V. Tues–Sat 12:30–3:30pm; Mon–Sat 7:30–11:30pm. Closed Aug. Bus: 13. ITALIAN/INTERNATIONAL.

This restaurant derives its name from its position since 1959 at number one ("numero uno") on a street near its present location on the via del Moro. In 1985, the restaurant moved to its new premises in a 15th-century palazzo within a three-minute walk from the railway station. Its cuisine is a well-prepared, well-presented blend of international foods and dishes derived from throughout the Italian peninsula.

Many diners prefer a seat in the main dining room, with its vaulted ceiling and oversized fireplace, although two adjacent dining rooms contain part of the spillover. Menu choices include taglierini with mushrooms (with or without the optional truffles); ravioli stuffed either with ricotta and basil or with fresh artichokes; risotto with asparagus or sweet peppers; carpaccio of beef or salmon; the classic Florentine tripe; chicken with marsala or with parmesan; turbot baked with artichokes, herbs, and potatoes; and Florentine-style beefsteak, which is usually prepared for two diners. Dessert might be succulent *torta della nonna*.

Ristorante Otello

Via degli Orti Oricellari 36R. ☎ **216517**. Reservations recommended. Main courses 10,000–27,000 lire ($6.25–$16.90). AE, DC, MC, V. Wed–Mon noon–3pm and 7:30–11pm. Bus: 14, 17, 23, 28, 35, or 62. FLORENTINE.

Beside the train station, Ristorante Otello is a long-established Florentine dining room that serves an animated clientele in comfortably renovated surroundings. Its antipasto Toscano is considered one of the best in town, an array of appetizing hors d'oeuvres that practically becomes a meal in itself. The waiter urges you to "Mangi, mangi, mangi!" ("Eat, eat, eat!") and that's what diners do here, as the victuals at Otello have been known to stir the most lethargic of appetites. The true trencherperson goes on to order one of the succulent pasta dishes, such as spaghetti with small baby clams or pappardelle with garlic sauce. The meat and poultry dishes are equally delectable, including sole meunière or veal pizzaiola with lots of garlic.

🐙 Family-Friendly Restaurants

Da Pennello *(see p. 272)*　This family-style trattoria near Dante's house offers filling, tasty, and inexpensive dishes.

Gelateria Vivoli *(see p. 281)*　After tasting the ice cream here—in virtually every known flavor—your child might agree that this place was worth the trip to Florence.

La Nandina *(see p. 275)*　Florentine families frequent this place off the Arno, a four-mile walk from the Uffizi.

INEXPENSIVE

La Carabaccia

Via Palazzuolo 190R. ☎ **214782.** Reservations not required. Main courses 16,000–35,000 lire ($10–$21.90). AE, MC, V. Tues–Sat 12:30–2:30pm; Mon–Sat 7:30–10:30pm. Closed Aug. Bus: 19. FLORENTINE.

Two hundred years ago a *carabaccia* was a workaday boat, shaped like a hollowed-out half onion and used on the Arno to dredge silt and sand from the river bottom. The favorite onion soup of the Medici was zuppa carabaccia, which this restaurant still features today. It's a creamy white onion soup served with croûtons (and not in the French style, the chef rushes to tell you). Carabaccia is a style of Florentine cuisine that still presents a meat, such as boar, with stewed onions on the side. You can, of course, eat more than onions here. The menu changes every day and is based on the use of fresh local ingredients. There is always one soup, followed by four or five pastas, including crespelle (crêpe) of such fresh vegetables as asparagus or artichokes. The restaurant was established in the 1970s within a building two centuries old.

⑤ Le Mossacce

Via del Proconsolo 55R. ☎ **294361.** Reservations not necessary. Main courses 8,000–10,000 lire ($5–$6.25). AE, MC, V. Mon–Fri noon–2:30pm and 7–9:30pm. Closed Aug. TUSCAN.

Le Mossacce, patronized by a long list of faithful Tuscan devotees, is conveniently located midway between two of the city's most famous monuments, the Bargello and the Duomo. This small 35-seat restaurant was established at the turn of the century. Within its 300-year-old walls, a team of hardworking waiters serve excellent meals, offering selections from a wide range of Florentine and Italian specialties, including *ribollita* (a thick regional vegetable soup), cannelloni, heavily seasoned baked pork, and involtini. Bistecca alla fiorentina is also a preferred selection.

⑤ Sostanza

Via del Porcellana 25R. ☎ **212691.** Reservations recommended. Main courses 14,000–27,000 lire ($8.75–$16.90). No credit cards. Mon–Fri noon–2:10pm and Mon–Fri 7:30–9:30pm. Closed Aug and 2 weeks at Christmas. Bus: 31 or 32. FLORENTINE.

Sostanza is a tucked-away little trattoria where working people have gone for years to get excellent, moderately priced food. But in more recent times the invading sophisticates have been pouring in to share tables with them. Florentines call the place Troia, which means "hog," but also suggests a woman of easy virtue. It is the city's oldest and most revered trattoria. The small dining room has crowded family tables. The rear kitchen is open, its secrets exposed to diners. When you taste what comes out of that kitchen, you'll know that fancy decor would be superfluous. Specialties include breaded chicken breast and a succulent T-bone steak. You might also want to try tripe here the Florentine way—that is, cut into strips, then baked in a casserole with tomatoes, onions, and parmesan cheese. A fine beginning is the tortellini and a fit ending is Florentine cake. A daily fish dish is also featured. Run by a trio of Florentine friends, the restaurant features white walls decorated with ceramic and copper objects.

⑤ Trattoria Antellesi

Via Faenza 9R. ☎ **216990.** Reservations recommended. Main courses 12,000–24,000 lire ($7.50–$15). AE, MC, V. Mon–Sat noon–3pm and 7–10:30pm. Bus: 13. TUSCAN.

Set on the ground floor of a 15th-century historic monument, a few steps from the Medici Chapel, this restaurant is devoted almost exclusively to well-prepared versions of Tuscan recipes that have stood the test of time. Owned by the Italian-American team of Enrico Verrecchia and his Arizona-born wife, Janice, the restaurant prepares at least seven *piatti del giorno* that change according to the availability and seasonality of the ingredients. Menu items might include tagliatelle with porcini mushrooms or with braised arugula; penne arrabiata; *crespelle alla Fiorentina* (a Tuscan Renaissance cheesy Spinach crêpe introduced to France by Catherine de Medici's kitchen staff); pappardelle with wild boar; market-fresh fish (generally on Fridays); delicious Valdostana chicken; and properly grilled bistecca alla Fiorentina. The array of quality Italian wines (with an emphasis on Tuscany) has for the most part been selected by Janice herself (a third-year sommelier).

NEAR THE DUOMO
MODERATE

Trattoria Coco Lezzone

Via del Parioncino 26R. ☎ **287178.** Reservations accepted only for groups of 10 or more. Main courses 15,000–50,000 lire ($9.40–$31.25). No credit cards. Mon–Sat noon–3pm; Wed–Mon 7:30–10:30pm. Closed last week of July through Aug. Bus: 27 or 31. FLORENTINE.

In Florentine dialect, the establishment's name refers to the sauce-stained apron of the extroverted chef who established this place more than a century ago. Today, some of the heartiness of the Tuscan countryside can be purchased for the price of a meal at this duet of tile-covered rooms on a backstreet a short walk from the Duomo. Florentine "blue bloods" wait with workers crowding in on their lunch hours for a seat at one of the long tables. Go early before the rush begins if you want a seat in this crowded, bustling trattoria. The fare includes generous portions of boiled meats with a green sauce, pasta fagiole (beans), osso buco, tripe, or beefsteak Florentine, which is the most expensive item on the menu and must be ordered on the phone in advance of your coming to the restaurant.

INEXPENSIVE

⑤ Vecchia Firenze

Borgo degli Albizi 18. ☎ **234-0361.** Reservations not necessary. Main courses 10,000–20,000 lire ($6.25–$12.50). AE, DC, MC, V. Daily noon–2pm and 7–10pm. FLORENTINE.

Established in the 1950s, Vecchia Firenze combines atmosphere and budget meals. Near the Duomo, it's housed in an old palace with an elegant entrance, through high doors. Some of the tables are in the courtyard; others are inside the vaulted dining rooms. The restaurant is lit by a wrought-iron chandelier. It's not elaborately voguish—in fact, it caters to students and the working people of Florence, who eat here regularly and never seem to tire of its offerings. You might begin with a tagliatelle Vecchia Firenze, then follow with a quarter of a roast chicken or sole in butter.

NEAR PIAZZA DELLA SIGNORIA
MODERATE

Monkey Business
Chiasso dei Baroncelli. ☎ **28-82-19.** Reservations recommended. Main courses 27,000–35,000 lire ($16.90–$21.90). AE, DC, MC, V. Mon–Fri 12:30–3:30pm; Mon–Sat 8–10:30pm. Closed Aug. Bus: 31 or 32. TUSCAN.

Stylish and innovative, this restaurant, affectionately called "Monkey," is attuned to new ideas and trends in Tuscan cuisine. Opened in 1990, it's set within four well-staffed dining rooms in a 500-year-old building on an alleyway leading south from the piazza della Signoria. It was named for the 1950s film that starred, among others, Cary Grant and Marilyn Monroe. Its decor was inspired partly by medieval Florence and partly by India and Nepal, with a scattering of hunting trophies and souvenirs of a turn-of-the-century safari.

The menu changes daily, but might include such modern interpretations of Tuscan recipes as a light soufflé of cheese with a cream sauce, a limited but succulent array of light-textured pastas, fresh shrimp served with white beans (*fagiole*) and arugula, grilled Florentine beefsteak marinated in young wine and crushed peppercorns, a flan of zucchini flowers served with a creamy truffle sauce, and sea bass cooked in paper (*en papillotte*) with aromatic herbs. Desserts are appropriately delicious, and include a vanilla mousse served with chocolate sauce and a *bavaroise* of wild strawberries, and a thin, flat tart of bitter chocolate and fresh cream.

INEXPENSIVE

⑤ Il Cavallino
Via della Farine 6R. ☎ **215818.** Reservations recommended. Main courses 12,000–25,000 lire ($7.50–$15.65). AE, DC, MC, V. Thurs–Tues noon–2:30pm and 7–10pm. Bus: 31 or 32. TUSCAN/ITALIAN.

Il Cavallino is the kind of discreetly famous restaurant where Florentines invariably go just to be with one another. The place has been a local favorite since the 1930s. It's on a tiny street (which probably won't even be on your map) that leads into piazza della Signoria at its northern end, not far from the equestrian statue. There's usually a gracious reception at the door, especially if you called ahead for a reservation. The walls are dotted with unusual art, and seating is divided into three rooms, two of which have vaulted ceilings and peach-colored marble floors. The main room looks out over the piazza right in the heart of Florence. Menu items are typical Tuscan fare, including an assortment of boiled meats in a green herb sauce, grilled filet of steak, breast of chicken Medici style, a mixed fish fry, grilled sole, and the inevitable Florentine spinach.

Da Ganino
Piazza dei Cimatori 4R. ☎ **214125.** Reservations recommended. Main courses 18,000–25,000 lire ($11.25–$15.65). AE, DC, MC, V. Mon–Sat 1–3pm and 8–11pm. Bus: 31 or 32. FLORENTINE/TUSCAN.

The well-established Da Ganino is staffed with the kind of waiters who take the quality of your meal as their personal responsibility. This little-known restaurant has vaulted ceilings, glazed walls, and an array of paintings by Florentine artists. Someone will recite to you the frequently changing specialties of the day, including, perhaps, well-seasoned versions of Tuscan beans, spinach risotto, grilled veal liver, grilled veal chops, and Florentine beefsteak on the bone. Other dishes to delight are tagliatelle con tartufo, the most expensive appetizer because of the truffles used. Also worthwhile is filet of chicken with a lemon cream sauce and a *fritto misto* of meats, including brains, kidneys, beef filets, lamb chops, and a selection of grilled vegetables. The cost of your gastronomic sins will be figured on the paper tablecloth. Small and intimate, it lies on a square in the center of town near piazza della Signoria.

⑤ Da Pennello

Via Dante Alighieri 4R. ☎ **294848.** Reservations accepted but not necessary. Main courses 12,000–20,000 lire ($7.50–$12.50). No credit cards. Tues–Sun noon–3pm; Tues–Sat 7–10pm. Closed Aug 1–30 and Dec 25–Jan 3. FLORENTINE/ITALIAN.

At the family-style Da Pennello the waiters speak some English. The food is top-notch, produced with skill by the women in the kitchen. The informally operated trattoria offers many Florentine specialties on its à la carte menu. A filling and good-tasting dish is spaghetti alla carbonara. Da Pennello is known for its wide selection of antipasti; you can make a meal out of these delectable hors d'oeuvres. The ravioli is homemade and one pasta specialty—beloved of locals—is spaghetti carretiera, made with tomatoes and pepperoni. To follow, you can have deviled roast chicken. Typically Italian dishes include a plate of mixed roast and a Florentine beefsteak. The chief posts daily specials, and sometimes it's best to order one of these, as the food offered was bought fresh that day at the market. A Florentine cake, zuccotto, rounds out the meal. The restaurant is on a narrow street, near Dante's house, about a five-minute walk from the Duomo toward the Uffizi.

Paoli

Via dei Tavolini 12R. ☎ **216215.** Reservations required. Main courses 15,000–28,000 lire ($9.40–$17.50); fixed-price menu 34,000 lire ($21.25). AE, DC, MC, V. Wed–Mon noon–2:30pm and 7–10:30pm. Closed 3 weeks in Aug. Bus: 14, 19, or 23. TUSCAN/ITALIAN.

Paoli, between the Duomo and piazza della Signoria, is one of the finest restaurants in Florence. Established in 1824 by the Paoli brothers in a building that dated in part from the 13th century, the restaurant has retained the name ever since. It turns out a host of specialties but it could be recommended almost solely for its medieval-tavern atmosphere, with arches and ceramics stuck into the walls like medallions. The walls are adorned with frescoes. Its pastas are homemade, and the fettuccine alla Paoli is served piping hot. The chef also does a superb *rognoncino* (kidney) *trifolato* and a sole meunière. A recommendable side dish is *piselli* (garden peas) *alla fiorentina*.

ON THE ARNO
EXPENSIVE

La Campannina di Sante

Piazza Ravenna, adjacent to the Ponte Giovanni da Verrazzano. ☎ **688345.** Reservations recommended. Main dishes 20,000–40,000 lire ($12.50–$25). AE, DC, MC, V. Mon–Sat 8pm–midnight. Closed 2 weeks in Aug. Bus: 23. SEAFOOD.

Set on the banks of the Arno, with a river-view terrace available for outdoor seating, this simple and unpretentious restaurant has functioned in more or less the same way on and off since 1935. Its specialty is fish, which is prepared simply and healthfully, usually with olive oil or butter and Mediterranean seasonings. Examples include filets of sea bass or turbot, mixed seafood grills, and an occasional portion of veal or steak for anyone who doesn't care for fish. The most expensive item on the menu is beluga caviar, but you might more happily and economically settle for the antipasti. Wines are simple and straightforward, and the greeting is warm and friendly, but know in advance that fish is considered a (relatively expensive) delicacy in landlocked Florence, and you'll pay accordingly for the pleasures of sampling it.

Harry's Bar

Lungarno Vespucci 22R. ☎ **239-6700**. Reservations required. Main courses 22,000–33,000 lire ($13.75–$20.65). AE, MC, V. Mon–Sat noon–3pm and 7–11pm. Closed mid-Dec to Jan 10. Bus: 9. ITALIAN.

Harry's Bar, in a prime position on the Arno, is an enclave of expatriate and well-heeled visiting Yankees that deserves its well-earned reputation, a position it has enjoyed since its opening in 1953 in an 18th-century building. You'll be welcomed at the bar and in the dining room, and you'll soon find that Harry's is the easiest place in Florence to meet your fellow Americans and (at least for a while) escape from some of the glory of the Renaissance. On a recent visit I heard three words of Italian from a frustrated woman from Alabama who was kindly assured by the Tuscan waiter (in English) that she need struggle no more. As if by inner radar, patrons know they'll be able to order from an international menu—small but select, and beautifully prepared. A specialty is either risotto or tagliestelle with ham, onions, and cheese. The *gamberetti* (crayfish) cocktail is very tempting. Harry has created his own tortellini (stuffed pasta), but Harry's hamburger and his club sandwich are the most popular items. The chef also prepares about a dozen specialties every day: breast of chicken "our way," grilled giant-size scampi, and a lean broiled sirloin steak. An apple tart with cream nicely finishes off a meal.

NEAR THE PONTE VECCHIO
INEXPENSIVE

⑤ Buca dell'Orafo

Via Volta dei Girolami 28R. ☎ **213619**. Reservations not necessary. Main courses 18,000–22,000 lire ($11.25–$13.75). No credit cards. Tues–Sat 12:30–2:30pm and 7:30–10:30pm. Closed Aug. Bus: 3, 31, or 32. FLORENTINE.

Established in the 1940s, Buca dell'Orafo is a little dive (one of the many cellars or *buca*-type establishments beloved by Florentines). An *orafo* is a goldsmith, and it was in this part of Florence that the goldsmith trade grew up. The buca, once part of an old goldsmith shop, stands near the Ponte Vecchio, reached via a street under a vaulted arcade right off piazza del Pesce. The trattoria is usually stuffed with its regulars, so if you want a seat, go early. Over the years the chef has made little concession to the foreign palate, turning out instead genuine Florentine specialties, including tripe and mixed boiled meats with a green sauce and *stracotto e fagioli* (beef braised in a sauce of chopped vegetables and red wine), served with beans in a tomato sauce. For a savory beginning, try the fennel-flavored salami or asparagus in the spring. In season you can order fresh peas flavored with fresh ham or asparagus. Florentine beefsteak is the most expensive item on the menu. There's a feeling of camaraderie among the diners here.

La Nandina

Borgo SS. Apostoli 64R. ☎ **213024**. Reservations recommended. Main courses 20,000–25,000 lire ($12.50–$15.65). AE, DC, MC, V. Tues–Sat noon–3pm; Mon–Sat 7–10:30pm. Closed Aug. Bus: 3, 31, or 32. TUSCAN/INTERNATIONAL.

The elegant La Nandina is an old favorite with both Florentine and visitors alike. One of the oldest restaurants in Florence, this place was established in 1924 and has had only two continuous owners during this period. A family-run restaurant, it's just off the Arno, about a four-minute walk from the Uffizi (in fact, it's an excellent choice for lunch if you're viewing the galleries). Fresh flowers are placed on the tables under vaulted ceilings and iron chandeliers. If you arrive early, you can have an apéritif in the intimate and plushy upholstered cocktail lounge near the entrance. There is also a 14th-century cellar for dining. The cuisine consists of dishes from the provinces and such cities as Rome, Tuscany, and Venice, and might include ravioli with flap mushrooms, spinach crêpes, curried breast of capon, veal piccatina, several kinds of beefsteak, and a changing array of daily specials.

NEAR SANTA CROCE
MODERATE

La Baraonda

Via Ghibellina 67R. ☎ **23-41-171**. Reservations recommended. Main courses 20,000–24,000 lire ($12.50–$15). AE, DC. Tues–Sat 12:30–2:30pm; Mon–Sat 7:30–9:30pm. Bus: 14. TUSCAN.

About 80% of the clientele of this bustling trattoria comes from local residents, many of them merchants and hotel employees from the surrounding neighborhood. Small, gregarious, and well choreographed—with a name that translates as "hubhub" or "disorder"—the restaurant serves Tuscan cuisine flavored with seasonally available local ingredients. Some members of the staff speak fluent English, and in many cases will propose carefully assembled fixed-price meals concocted from strictly fresh local ingredients. The menu changes every week, although some featured dishes change daily. Examples include a changing array of *sformato di verdure* (vegetable soufflés made from, among other ingredients, artichokes or whatever else is in season at the moment), risotto with fresh greens, pennette with broccoli, and a savory version of meatloaf (*polpettone in umido*) made with veal and fresh tomatoes. Other dishes might include baby squid in lemon sauce, sea bass with herbs, and tagliatelle with pine nuts and fresh herbs.

⊛ Cibreo

Via dei Macci 118R. ☎ **234-1100**. Reservations recommended in the restaurant, not accepted in the trattoria. In the restaurant, main courses 35,000 lire ($21.90). In the trattoria, main courses 13,000 lire ($8.15). AE, DC, MC, V accepted, but only in the restaurant. Tues–Sat 12:30pm and 8–11pm. Closed late July–early Sept. Bus: 14 or 49. MEDITERRANEAN.

Despite its lack of pretentions, Cibreo is one of the largest eateries in the neighborhood. From a small and impossibly old-fashioned kitchen, it prepares food for a restaurant, a less formal tavern-style trattoria, and a café-bar across the surging traffic of the street outside. The kitchens are noteworthy for not containing a grill, and for not serving pastas. Instead, they specialize in foodstuffs cooked within a wood-burning oven, and cold marinated dishes (especially vegetables) that presumably taste better when prepared a day or several hours in advance.

The owners are Fabio and Benedetta Picchi, some of whose staff includes expatriate New Yorkers who excel at explaining the restaurant's culinary themes. The restaurant takes its name from (and serves) an old Tuscan dish (Cibreo) that was allegedly so delectable it nearly killed Catherine de' Medici. (She consumed so much that she was overcome with near-fatal indigestion.) At nighttime, the restaurant sets up tables on a square in back of the restaurant; trattoria diners remain inside.

Menu items include a *sformato* (a soufflé made from potatoes and ricotta, served with parmesan cheese and tomato sauce); *inzimmino* (Tuscan-style squid stewed with spinach); a flan of parmesan cheese, veal tongue, and artichokes; several kinds of roasted (but not fried) meats; and such soups as potato with chickpea, or pumpkin.

Also on the premises under the same management is a food store selling local foodstuffs you're not likely to find in North America.

⊛ Del Fagioli

Corso dei Tintori 47R. ☎ **244-285**. Reservations recommended. Main courses 15,000–45,000 lire ($9.40–$28.15). No credit cards. Mon–Fri 12:30–2:30pm and 7:30–10:30pm. Closed Aug. Bus: 19, 31, or 32. TUSCAN.

Devoted to the pleasures of country-style Tuscan cuisine, this restaurant (whose name translates as "beans") was established in 1966 within a pair of dining rooms lined with old engravings of the monuments of Florence. Set near the church of Santa Croce, it serves a choice of locally made *affettati toscani* (sausages, pâtés, and dried or salted meats); a hearty *ribollita* (cabbage and bread soup); several types of spaghetti and tagliatelle; sliced breast of turkey; Florentine beefsteak; and such game dishes as partridge, whenever it's in season. Fish might include oven-roasted sea bass or monkfish with herbs. *Fagioli,* incidentally, was also a traditional name for the buffoons (clowns and humorists) who performed throughout the Renaissance for the political rulers of Florence.

INEXPENSIVE

Ristorante Dino

Via Ghibellina 51. ☎ **241452**. Reservations recommended. Main courses 16,000–23,000 lire ($10–$14.40). AE, DC, MC, V. Tues–Sun noon–3pm; Tues–Sat 7:30–10:30pm. AE, DC, MC, V. Bus: 14. TUSCAN.

Set within a trio of dining rooms in a 14th-century building near the Casa Buonarroti, this restaurant has vaulted ceilings and a cuisine inspired by members of the Casini family. Its most visible personalities include Dino and his wife Renza (each of whom have dishes of their invention named in their honor). Specialties include *spaghetti alla Dino* flavored with carrots, celery, chile peppers, and aromatic herbs; *risotto della Renza,* rich with aromatic herbs and fresh tomatoes; *ribollita,* the cabbage, bean, and bread soup of Tuscany; a fragrant *inizimino* of squid; and thick Florentine beefsteaks. Tuscan purists are often jolted with memories of their childhood at the mention of one of the restaurant's ever-present dishes, *garetto Ghibellino,* a historic recipe made from pork shanks with celery and sage. The establishment is especially known for its wine list, which includes a bountiful choice of vintages from throughout Italy, especially Tuscany.

NEAR THE STRAW MARKET
MODERATE

Al Lume di Candela

Via delle Terme 23R. ☎ **294566**. Reservations required. Main courses 20,000–35,000 lire ($12.50–$21.90). AE, MC, V. Mon–Sat 7:30–11pm. Closed Aug 10–30. Bus: 22. TUSCAN/INTERNATIONAL.

Established in 1948, Al Lume di Candela is uniquely located in a 13th-century tower that was partially leveled when its patrician family fell from grace (the prestige of Tuscan families was once reflected in how high their family towers soared). With a tavern decor, the restaurant offers a typically Florentine cuisine, under the deft guiding hand of the padrone in the kitchen. The candelit atmosphere makes for a romantic dining place and has drawn celebrities in the past. Both Tuscan and international specialties are served, including such dishes as taglierini with sage and porcini mushrooms; a very light version of house-smoked salmon; veal chops stuffed with white beans (cannellini) and arugula; entrecôte (sirloin) of beef grilled with pepper, olive oil, and Tuscan herbs; and *maccheroncini* served with thyme and calamari seared in sherry with pecorino cheese. A suitable accompaniment for any of these might be a chicory salad garnished with carrots, parmesan cheese, and—in season—artichoke hearts. The bistro lies off the major shopping artery, via Porta Santa Maria, near the straw market.

Oliviero

Via delle Terme 51R. ☎ **287643**. Reservations required. All main courses 22,000 lire ($13.75). AE, DC, MC, V. Mon–Sat 7:30–11:30pm. Closed Aug. Bus: 11, 31, or 32. TUSCAN.

This is a small but smart, luxurious dining room. You can arrive here any time after 7:30pm except Sunday and enjoy a drink. From 8pm on, live music entertains guests in the piano bar. The service is elegantly courteous. The finest traditions of Tuscan cookery are maintained here, with highly select, fresh ingredients. Therefore, the menu is frequently changed to keep abreast of what is the best at any time in any given season. You might, for example, begin with such appetizers as octopus salad with basil, string beans, and tomatoes; fried mussels and squash blossoms; or Tuscan ham with figs and bread coated with virgin olive oil. Main courses usually include fresh fish; grilled, boned rabbit and young cock with shell beans; or ravioli stuffed with chopped liver and served with a delicate sauce of white onions. Desserts are often quite special, as exemplified by the green fig mousse with almonds and chocolate.

NEAR PIAZZA GOLDONI
MODERATE

§ Trattoria Garga

Via del Moro 48-52. ☎ **239-8898**. Reservations required. Main courses 22,000–28,000 lire ($13.75–$17.50). AE, DC, MC, V. Tues–Sun 7:30pm–12:30am. Closed Aug 3–16. Bus: 6, 13, or 26. TUSCAN.

Some of the most creative cuisine in Florence is served here. The establishment is run by Giuliano Gargani and his Canadian wife, Sharon, a combination of personalities that began when a strawberry blond met "Signor Right." The building's thick Renaissance walls contain paintings by both Florentine and American artists, including those painted by the owners themselves. Operatic arias emerge along with heavenly odors from a postage-stamp-size kitchen. Many of the Tuscan menu items are so unusual that Sharon's bilingual skills are put to good use. You can enjoy a fine array of salads, including a well-dressed combination of artichokes, hearts of palm, fresh lettuce, and parmigiana cheese. Other dishes include tagliatelle with garlic, tomatoes, anchovies, and smoked salmon, along with octopus with peppers and garlic, boar with juniper berries, grilled marinated quail, and "whatever strikes the mood" of Giuliano. One dish, created in 1992, has earned a lot of publicity—it's *tagliarini magnifico*, made with angel-hair pasta, orange and lemon rind, mint-flavored cream, and parmesan. Call ahead for a table. The location is in the monumental center of Florence, between the Ponte Vecchio and Santa Maria Novella.

AT PIAZZA ANTINORI
MODERATE

Buca Lapi

Via del Trebbio 1R. ☎ **213768**. Reservations required for dinner. Main courses 11,000–22,000 lire ($6.90–$13.75). AE, DC, MC, V. Tues–Sat 12:30–2:30pm; Mon–Sat 7:30–10:30pm. Closed 2 weeks in Aug. Bus: 31 or 32. TUSCAN.

Buca Lapi, a cellar restaurant founded in 1880, is big on glamor, good food, and the enthusiasm of fellow diners. Its decor alone—under the Palazzo Antinori—makes it fun: vaulted ceilings are covered with travel posters from all over the world. There's a long table of interesting fruits, desserts, and vegetables. The cooks know how to turn out the most classic dishes of the Tuscan kitchen with superb finesse. Specialties include pâté; cannelloni; *scampi giganti alla girglia*, a super-size shrimp; and bistecca alla fiorentina (local beefsteak). In season, the fagioli toscani all'olio—Tuscan beans in the native olive oil—are considered a delicacy by many palates. For dessert, you can order the international favorite, crêpes Suzette, or the local choice, zuccotto, a Florentine cake that's *delicato*. Evenings can be quite festive, as the singing becomes contagious.

INEXPENSIVE

Buca Mario

Piazza Ottaviani 16R. ☎ **214179**. Reservations required. Main courses 18,000–28,000 lire ($11.25–$17.50). AE, DC, MC, V. Thurs–Tues 12:15–2:30pm; Fri–Tues 7:15–10:30pm. Closed Aug. Bus: 6, 9, 17, or 19. FLORENTINE.

Buca Mario, in business for a century, is one of the most famous cellar restaurants of Florence. It's located right in the monumental historic center in the 1886 Palazzo Niccolini. Tables are placed beneath vaulted ceilings, and you'll often find that some of the waiters have worked in the States. They might suggest an array of Florentine pastas, beefsteak (the most expensive item on the menu), Dover sole, or beef carpaccio, followed by a tempting selection of desserts.

Cantinetta Antinori

Piazza Antinori 3. ☎ **292234**. Reservations recommended. Main courses 20,000–28,000 lire ($12.50–$17.50). AE, DC, MC, V. Mon–Fri 12:30–2:30pm and 7–10:30pm. Closed Aug and Dec 24–Jan 6. Bus: 1, 14, 23, 31, or 32. ITALIAN.

Hidden behind the severe stone facade of the 15th-century Palazzo Antinori is the Catinetta Antinori, one of Florence's most popular restaurants and one of the city's few top-notch wine bars. Small wonder that the cellars should be supremely well stocked since the restaurant is one of the city's showplaces for the vintages of the oldest and most distinguished wine company in Tuscany, Umbria, and Piedmont. It has become the preferred rendezvous point for wine lovers who appreciate an overview of the assembled wines of the region, readily available and cheerfully served. Vintages can be consumed by the glass at the stand-up bar or by the bottle as an accompaniment for the Italian meals served at wooden tables. The room is not especially large, and the decorative statement is from the floor-to-ceiling racks of aged and undusted wine bottles set on their sides in wooden racks. The overflow from the ground floor goes up to the overhanging balcony. You can eat a full meal or sample only such snacks as salads, sandwiches, and other light dishes.

NEAR PIAZZA TADDEO GADDI
MODERATE

⑤ Trattoria Vittoria

Via della Fonderia 52R. ☎ **225657**. Reservations recommended. Main courses 21,000–30,000 lire ($13.15–$18.75). AE, DC, MC, V. Thurs–Tues noon–3:30pm and 7:30–10:30pm. Bus: 6. SEAFOOD.

Trattoria Vittoria is unheralded and untouristy, but it serves some of the finest fish dishes in Florence. This big, bustling trattoria offers you three dining rooms. Service is frenetic. Most of the fresh fish dishes of the day are priced according to weight, making a main dish considerably higher than stated above. Sole is the most expensive, although you can also order equally tempting lower-priced dishes. Two outstanding choices to begin your meal include risotto alla marinara and spaghetti alla vongole (clams). The mixed fish fry gives you a little bit of everything. Desserts are homemade and extremely rich.

INEXPENSIVE

Pierot

Piazza Tadeo Gaddi 25R. ☎ **702100**. Reservations recommended. Main courses 12,000–20,000 lire ($7.50–$12.50). AE, DC, MC, V. Mon–Sat noon–3pm and 7–11:30pm. Closed July 15–Aug 7. Bus: 1, 2, 9, or 27. SEAFOOD/TUSCAN.

Pierot is housed in a 19th-century building constructed during the reign of Vittorio Emmanuel. Before World War II a food store was here, but since 1955 Pierot has been a restaurant fixture of Florence. The restaurant is unusual in that it specializes in seafood, and therefore is considered a bit of an oddity in landlocked Florence. The seasonal menu varies with the availability of ingredients, but might include linguini with frutti di mare, pasta with lobster sauce, and an array of traditional Tuscan steaks, soups, and vegetables. Seafood risotto is a perennial favorite.

ON THE LEFT BANK
INEXPENSIVE

Mamma Gina

Borgo Sant'Jacopo 37R. ☎ **239-6009**. Reservations required for dinner. Main courses 16,000–24,000 lire ($10–$15). AE, DC, MC, V. Mon–Sat noon–2:30pm and 7–10pm. Closed Aug 7–21. Bus: 6. TUSCAN.

Mamma Gina is a rustic left-bank restaurant that's a winner for fine foods prepared in the traditional manner. Although it's run by a corporation with other restaurants scattered throughout Tuscany, this restaurant is named after its founding matriarch (Mamma Gina), whose legend has continued despite her death in the 1980s. This exceptional trattoria, well worth the trek across the Ponte Vecchio, is a center for hearty Tuscan fare. Menu items are rich, savory, and tied to the seasons, and include such dishes as cannelloni Mamma Gina (stuffed with a purée of minced meats, spices, and vegetables); tagliolini with artichoke hearts or mushrooms, and whatever else is in season at the time; pasta fagiole; chicken breast "Mamma Gina," baked in the northern Italian style with prosciutto and Emmenthaler cheese; and grilled Florentine beefsteaks served with braised arugula and rosemary-infused olive oil. Mamma Gina is ideal for lunch after visiting the Pitti Palace.

Le Quattro Stagioni

Via Maggio 61R. ☎ **21-89-06**. Reservations recommended. Main courses 16,000–26,000 lire ($10–$16.25). AE, DC, MC, V. Mon–Sat 12:15–2:30pm and 7:30–10:30pm. Closed Aug. Bus: 11, 15, or 36. TUSCAN/SEAFOOD.

Set within a historic building near the Pitti Palace, this charming and old-fashioned restaurant specializes in both seafood and classic preparations of Tuscan recipes. Within one of a pair of dining rooms, an efficient and professional staff serves such dishes as gnocchi, crostinis, pasta with squid in its own ink, roast lamb with artichokes, sea bass roasted with fennel, a succulent array of fresh vegetables, beefsteak, several different preparations of veal, and homemade desserts. As the establishment's name (The Four Seasons) implies, the menu changes according to the seasonal availability of the ingredients.

Trattoria Cammillo

Borgo Sant' Jacopo 57. ☎ **212427**. Reservations required. Main courses 18,000–35,000 lire ($11.25–$21.90). AE, DC, MC, V. Fri–Tues noon–2:30pm and 7:30–10:30pm. Closed Dec 7–Jan 7 and July 27–Aug 19. Bus: 1, 3, 6, 11, or 36. TUSCAN.

Trattoria Cammillo is one of the most popular—and perhaps the finest—of the left-bank dining spots, housed on the ground floor of a former Medici palace. It's good enough to lure the snobbish owners of the boutiques, who cross the Arno regularly to feast here. They know they'll get such specialties as tagliatelle flavored with fresh peas and truffles; excellent assortments of fried vegetables, often presented as antipasti; super-fresh scampi and sole; fried, de-boned pigeon served with artichokes; and breast of chicken with truffles and parmesan. The owners pride themselves on serving an all-Italian array of meats, derived only from within the borders of Italy, and served in generous portions. In modest but attractive surroundings, the trattoria is between the Ponte Vecchio and the Ponte S. Trinità. Because of increased business, you're likely to be rushed through a meal.

FOR VEGETARIANS

Inexpensive

⊖ Il Vegetariano

Via della Rote 30R. ☎ **475030**. Reservations not accepted. Main courses 9,000–11,000 lire ($5.65–$6.90). No credit cards. Tues–Fri 12:30–2:30pm; Tues–Sun 7:30–10:30pm. Closed August. Bus: 31 or 32. VEGETARIAN.

This all-vegetarian restaurant began its life as a semiprivate club for vegetarians and counterculture activists working to change Italian society from within. (Membership fees were imposed before a newcomer could dine, a policy that baffled many foreign visitors.) In recent years, however, the establishment is less politically active and much more concerned with providing wholesome, all-vegetarian food to a growing corps of enthusiasts throughout Florence. (Thankfully, membership fees are no longer collected at the door.) Within an environment accented with terra-cotta floors and white plaster walls, scarred wooden tables, and basket-shaped lamps, an employee ladles vegetarian food onto platters served to clients who pass through a cafeteria-style lineup. Menu items, whose names are chalked onto a plastic whiteboard, vary with the seasonality of Italy's produce, but might include vegetarian pastas and risottos, eggplant parmigiana, country-derived pizza with thick crusts and vegetable toppings, meatless Mexican tortillas, vegetable curries in the style of India, and pita bread served with salad, olives, and hummus in the style of Lebanon. Wine is served, some of it produced from organically grown grapes.

GELATO

✪ Gelateria Vivoli

Via Isola delle Stinche 7R. ☎ **292334**. Gelati 2,500–14,000 lire ($1.55–$8.75). No credit cards. Tues–Sun 8am–1am. Closed 3 weeks in Aug (dates vary). Bus: 14 or 23. ICE CREAM.

Established in the 1930s, and today run by the third generation of the Vivoli family, this establishment produces some of the finest ice cream in Italy. They provide the *gelati* for many of the restaurants of Florence, which sometimes serve it as their own "homemade" variety. Buy your ticket first and select your flavor from among such delights as blueberry, fig, melon, and other fruits in season, as well as chocolate mousse, or even coffee ice cream flavored with espresso. A special ice cream is made from rice. The establishment offers a number of semifreddi concoctions—an Italian ice cream using cream as a base instead of milk. Semifreddi are hardly obtainable outside Italy, and the most popular flavors are almond, marengo (a type of meringue), and zabaglione (eggnog). Other flavors include *limoncini alla crema* (candied lemon peels with vanilla-flavored ice cream) and *aranciotti al cioccolate* (candied orange peels with chocolate ice cream). On a back street near the church and cloisters of Santa Croce, the establishment has a white marble and chrome interior, spotlights, and palm trees.

9

What to See & Do in Florence

Florence was the fountainhead of the Renaissance, the city of Dante and Boccaccio. Characteristically, it was the city of Machiavelli and uncharacteristically, of Savonarola. For three centuries it was dominated by the Medici family, patrons of the arts, masters of assassination. But it is chiefly through its artists that we know of the apogee of the Renaissance: Ghiberti, Fra Angelico, Donatello, Brunelleschi, Botticelli, and the incomparable Leonardo da Vinci and Michelangelo.

In Florence we can trace the change from medievalism to an age of "rebirth." For example, all modern painters owe a debt to an ugly, awkward, unkempt man who died at age 27. His name was Masaccio (Vasari's "Slipshod Tom"). Modern painting began with his frescoes in the Brancacci Chapel in the Church of Santa Maria del Carmine, which you can go see today. Years later Michelangelo painted a more celebrated Adam and Eve in the Sistine Chapel, but even this great artist never realized the raw humanity of Masaccio's Adam and Eve fleeing from the Garden of Eden.

In *The Man of the Renaissance* (1930), Ralph Roeder wrote: "In the broadest sense the Renaissance might be described as one of those recurring crises in the annals of the race when a ferment of a new life, like a rising sap, bursts the accepted codes of morality and men revert to Nature and the free play of instinct and experience in its conduct."

SUGGESTED ITINERARIES

These itineraries were obviously designed for the first-time visitor. Those calling on Florence for the second or third time might want to discover more esoteric treasures in this city of the Renaissance. However, one could wander every day of the year through the Uffizi, always finding something new and different to look at.

If You Have 1 Day

You will have to accept the inevitable—you can see only a small fraction of Florence's three-star attractions. Go to the Uffizi Galleries as soon as they open and concentrate only on some of the masterpieces. Before 1:30pm, visit the Accademia to see Michelangelo's *David* . . . at least that.

❷ Did You Know?

- In 1503 both Michelangelo and Leonardo da Vinci won commissions to fresco the walls of the council chamber of the republic. Neither work has survived.
- Some 500 sculptures and 1,000 paintings—considered priceless in the art world—were destroyed in the disastrous flood of 1966.
- In 1865, Florence—not Rome—became the capital of Italy.
- The word *renaissance* to describe the historic and artistic period that swept across Florence did not come into vogue until the publication in 1855 of Jules Michelet's *La Renaissance.*
- Mark Twain, working on *Pudd'nhead Wilson* in the 1890s, claimed that he could write more in four months in the Tuscan countryside than he could produce in two years at home.
- No dome since antiquity had been raised more than 180 feet above the ground until Brunelleschi created the dome for the Duomo of Florence.
- The oldest bridge in Florence, the Ponte Vecchio, was the only bridge over the Arno spared in August 1944 by the retreating Nazis.

Have lunch on piazza della Signoria, dominated by the Palazzo Vecchio, and admire the statues in the Loggia della Signoria. After lunch, visit the Duomo and Baptistery, then pay a late-afternoon visit to the open-air straw market, Mercanto San Lorenzo, before crossing the Ponte Vecchio at sunset. Finish a very busy day with a hearty Tuscan dinner in one of Florence's many *bucas,* or cellar restaurants.

If You Have 2 Days

Spend your first day in Florence as suggested above.

On Day 2, return to the Uffizi Galleries for a more thorough look at this museum—the most important in Italy. Then in the afternoon visit the Pitti Palace, on the other side of the Arno, and wander through the Galleria Palatina, with its 16th- and 17th-century masterpieces, including 11 works by Raphael alone. After a visit, stroll through the adjoining Boboli Gardens. At sunset, go again to the Duomo and the Baptistery for a much better look.

If You Have 3 Days

Spend your first two days as suggested above.

In the morning of Day 3, visit the Palazzo Vecchio on piazza della Signoria, then walk nearby to the Palazzo del Bargello, which contains the most important works of Tuscan and Florentine sculpture from the Renaissance era. After lunch, visit the Museo dell'Opera del Duomo, with its sculptural masterpieces from the Duomo, including Donatello's *Mary Magdalene.*

If You Have 5 Days

Spend Days 1–3 as suggested above.

On Day 4, continue your exploration of Renaissance masterpieces by visiting the Medici Chapels, with Michelangelo's tomb for Lorenzo de Medici, including the figures of *Dawn* and *Dusk.* Later in the morning, go to the Museo di San

Marco, a small museum that is a monument to the work of Fra Angelico. Before it closes at 6:30pm, call at the Basilica di Santa Croce, with its two restored chapels by Giotto.

On Day 5, leave Florence, as fascinating as it is, and head south to yet another fascinating art city, Siena, most important of the Tuscan hill towns.

1 Attractions

Readers traveling to Florence on limited time (two or three days) should be there toward the middle or end of the week if possible. Most museums close at 12:30 or 1pm on Sunday and are closed all day Monday, so it's wise to plan your visit accordingly.

THE TOP ATTRACTIONS

In the heart of Florence, at piazza del Duomo and piazza S. Giovanni (named after John the Baptist), is a complex of ecclesiastical buildings that form a triumvirate of top sightseeing attractions.

In addition to the sights listed below, consider visiting **piazza della Signoria.** This square, although never completed, is one of the most beautiful in Italy; it was the center of secular life in the days of the Medici. Through it pranced church robbers, connoisseurs of entrails, hired assassins seeking employment, chicken farmers from Valdarno, book burners, and many great men—including Machiavelli on a secret mission to the Palazzo Vecchio, and Leonardo da Vinci, trailed by his inevitable entourage.

On the square is the Fountain of Neptune, the sea god surrounded by creatures from the deep, as well as frisky satyrs and nymphs. It was designed by Ammannati, who later repented for chiseling Neptune in the nude. But Michelangelo, to whom Ammannati owes a great debt, judged the fountain inferior.

Near the fountain is a spot where Savonarola walked his last mile. This zealous monk was a fire-and-brimstone reformer who rivaled Dante in conjuring up the punishment hell would inflict on sinners. Two of his chief targets were Lorenzo the Magnificent and the Borgia pope, Alexander VI, who excommunicated him. Savonarola whipped the Florentine faithful into an orgy of religious fanaticism, but eventually fell from favor. Along with two other friars, he was hanged in the square in 1498. Afterward, as the crowds threw stones, the pyre underneath the men consumed their bodies. It is said that the reformer's heart was found whole and grabbed up by souvenir collectors. His ashes were tossed into the Arno.

For centuries Michelangelo's *David* stood in piazza della Signoria, but it was moved to the Academy Gallery in the 19th century. The work you see on the square today is an inferior copy, commonly assumed by many first-time visitors to be Michelangelo's original.

In the 14th-century **Loggia della Signoria** (sometimes called the Loggia dei Lanzi) is a gallery of sculpture that often depicts fierce, violent scenes. The most famous and the best piece is a rare work by Benvenuto Cellini, the goldsmith and

Impressions

Florence is the home of those who cultivate with an equal ardour Mah-jongg and a passion for Fra Angelico.

—Aldous Huxley

tell-all autobiographer. Critics have said that his exquisite but ungentlemanly *Perseus*, who holds the severed head of Medusa, is the most significant Florentine sculpture since Michelangelo's *Night* and *Day*. Two other well-known, although less skillfully created, pieces are Giambologna's *Rape of the Sabines* and his *Hercules with Nessus the Centaur*. For those on the mad rush, We suggest saving the interior of the Palazzo Vecchio (see "More Attractions," below) for another day.

✪ Campanile (Giotto's Bell Tower)

Piazza del Duomo. ☎ **230-2885.** Admission 8,000 lire ($5). Mid-Mar to Sept daily 9am–7:30pm; Oct to mid–Mar daily 9am–5:30pm. Bus: 1, 6, 11, 17, 19, or 23.

If we can believe the accounts of his contemporaries, Giotto was the ugliest man ever to walk the streets of Florence. Ironically, then, he left to posterity the most beautiful bell tower, or campanile, in Europe, rhythmic in line and form. That Giotto was given the position of "capomastro" and grand architect (and pensioned for 100 gold florins for his service) is remarkable in itself, for he is famous for freeing painting from the confinements of Byzantium. He designed the campanile in the last two or three years of his life, and he died before its completion.

The final work was admirably carried out by Andrea Pisano, one of the greatest gothic sculptors in Italy (see his bronze doors on the nearby Baptistery). The 274-foot tower, a "Tuscanized" Gothic, with bands of colored marble, can be scaled for a panorama of the sienna-colored city. The view will surely rank among your most memorable—it encompasses the enveloping hills and Medici villas. If a medieval pageant happens to be passing underneath (a likely possibility in spring), so much the better. After Giotto's death, Pisano and Luca della Robbia did some fine bas-relief and sculptural work, now in the Duomo Museum, behind the cathedral.

✪ Battistero San Giovanni (Baptistery)

Piazza S. Giovanni. ☎ **2302885.** Admission is free. Mon–Sat 1–6pm, Sun 9am–1pm. Bus: 1, 6, 11, 17, 19, or 23.

Named after the city's patron saint, Giovanni (John the Baptist), the present octagonal Battistero dates from the 11th and 12th centuries. The oldest structure in Florence, the baptistery is a highly original interpretation of the Romanesque style, with its bands of pink, white, and green marble. Visitors from all over the world come to gape at its three sets of bronze doors. The east door is a copy; the other two are originals. In his work on two sets of doors, Lorenzo Ghiberti reached the pinnacle of his artistry in "quattrocento" Florence. To win his first commission on the north door, the then 23-year-old sculptor had to compete against such formidable opposition as Donatello, Brunelleschi (architect of the dome crowning the cathedral), and Siena, born Jacopo della Quercia. Upon seeing Ghiberti's work, Donatello and Brunelleschi conceded defeat. By the time he completed the work, Ghiberti was around 44 years old. The gilt-covered panels—representing scenes from the New Testament, including the *Annunciation*, the *Adoration*, and Christ debating the elders in the temple—make up a flowing rhythmic narration in bronze.

After his long labor, the Florentines gratefully gave Ghiberti the task of sculpting the east door (directly opposite the entrance to the Duomo). Upon seeing the doors, Michelangelo is said to have exclaimed, "The Gateway to Paradise!" Given carte blanche, Ghiberti designed his masterpiece, choosing as his subject familiar scenes from the Old Testament, including Adam and Eve at the creation. This

Florence Attractions

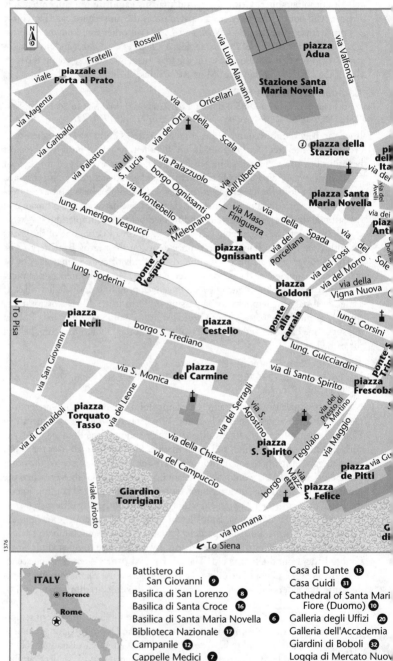

N

piazzale di
Porta al Prato

Fratelli
Rosselli
via Luigi Alamanni
piazza
Adua
via Valfonda

Stazione Santa
Maria Novella

via Oricellari

via Magenta
viale
via Garibaldi
via Palestro
via di S. Lucia
via dei Orti della
Scala
via dell'Alberto

(i) piazza della
Stazione

via Palazzuolo
borgo Ognissanti
via Montebello
via Maso
Finiguerra

piazza Santa
Maria Novella

lung. Amerigo Vespucci
via Melegnano
via della Spada
via dei Porcellana

piazza
Ognissanti

lung. Soderini
Ponte A. Vespucci

via dei Fossi
via del Morro
via della
Vigna Nuova

piazza
Goldoni

← To Pisa

piazza
dei Nerli
borgo S. Frediano
piazza
Cestello
ponte alla Carraia
lung. Guicciardini
lung. Corsini

via S. Monica
piazza
del Carmine
via di Santo Spirito
piazza
Frescoba

via San Giovanni
via del Leone
via dei Serragli
via S. Agostino
via dei Presto di S. Martino

piazza
Torquato
Tasso
via della Chiesa
piazza
S. Spirito
Tegolaio
via Maggio

via di Camaldoli
via del Campuccio
borgo
via Mazzetta

piazza
de Pitti

Giardino
Torrigiani

viale Ariosto
piazza
S. Felice

via Romana

← To Siena

G
di

1376

ITALY

● Florence

Rome
⊛

Battistero di
San Giovanni ❾

Basilica di San Lorenzo ❽

Basilica di Santa Croce ⓰

Basilica di Santa Maria Novella ❻

Biblioteca Nazionale ⓱

Campanile ⓬

Cappelle Medici ❼

Casa Buonarroti ⓯

Casa di Dante ⓭

Casa Guidi ㉛

Cathedral of Santa Mari
Fiore (Duomo) ❿

Galleria degli Uffizi ⓴

Galleria dell'Accademia

Giardini di Boboli ㉜

Loggia di Mercato Nuov

Museo Archeologico ❹

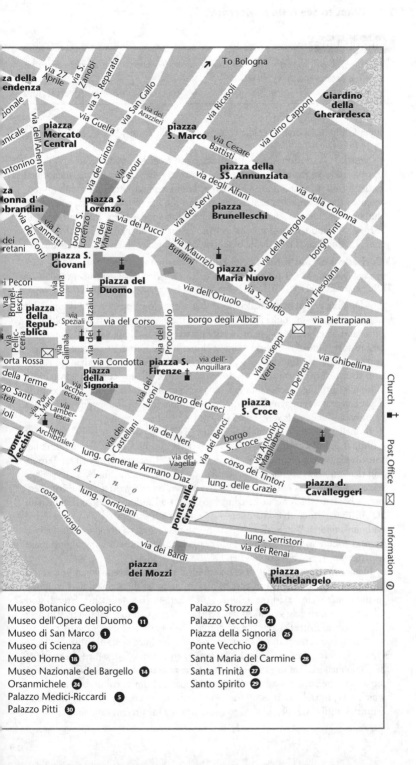

Church ✝

Post Office ⊠

Information ⊖

Impressions

Florence! One of the only places in Europe where I understood that underneath my revolt, a consent was lying dormant.

—Albert Camus

time, Ghiberti labored over the rectangular panels from 1425 to 1452 (he died in 1455).

Shuttled off to adorn the south entrance and to make way for Ghiberti's "gate" to paradise were the oldest doors of the baptistery, by Andrea Pisano, mentioned earlier for his work on Giotto's bell tower. For his subject, the Gothic sculptor represented the "Virtues" as well as scenes from the life of John the Baptist, whom the baptistery honors. The door was completed in 1336. On the interior (just walk through Pisano's door—no charge) the dome is adorned with 13th-century mosaics, dominated by a figure of Christ. Mornings are reserved for worship.

✪ Cathedral of Santa Maria del Fiore (Duomo)

Piazza del Duomo. ☎ **23-02-885.** Admission to cathedral, free; excavations 3,000 lire ($1.90); cupola 8,000 lire ($5). Daily 10am–5:40pm (excavations and cupola closed Sun).

The Duomo, graced by Brunelleschi's dome, is the crowning glory of Florence. But don't rush inside too quickly, as the view of the exterior, with its bands of white, pink, and green marble—geometrically patterned—is, along with the dome, the best feature. One of the world's largest churches, the Duomo represents the flowering of the "Florentine gothic" style. Typical of the history of cathedrals, construction stretched over centuries. Begun in 1296, it was finally consecrated in 1436, although finishing touches on the facade were applied as late as the 19th century. The cathedral was designed by Arnolfo di Cambio in the closing years of the 13th century, and the funds were raised in part by a poll tax.

Brunelleschi's efforts to build the dome (1420–36) would make the subject of a film, as did Michelangelo's vexations over the Sistine Chapel. At one time before his plans were eventually accepted, the architect was tossed out on his derrière and denounced as an idiot. He eventually won the commission by a clever "egg trick," as related in Giorgio Vasari's *Lives of the Painters,* written in the 16th century, a book to which we are here indebted (as are all authors of books dealing with Italian Renaissance art). His dome—a "monument for posterity"—was erected without supports. When Michelangelo began to construct a dome over St. Peter's, he paid tribute to Brunelleschi's earlier cupola in Florence: "I am going to make its sister larger, yes, but not lovelier."

Inside, the overall effect of the cathedral is bleak, except when you stand under the cupola, frescoed in part by Vasari. Some of the stained-glass windows in the dome were based on designs by Donatello (Brunelleschi's friend) and Ghiberti (Brunelleschi's rival). If you resisted scaling Giotto's bell tower, you may want to climb Brunelleschi's ribbed dome. The view is well worth the trek.

Also in the cathedral are some terra-cottas by Luca della Robbia. In 1432 Ghiberti, taking time out from his "Gateway to Paradise," designed the tomb of St. Zenobius. Excavations in the depths of the cathedral have brought to light the remains of the ancient Cathedral of Santa Reparata (tombs, columns, and floors), which was probably founded in the 5th century and transformed in the following centuries until it was demolished to make way for the present cathedral.

Incidentally, during some 1972 excavations the tomb of Brunelleschi was discovered, and new discoveries indicate the existence of a second tomb nearby. Giotto's tomb, which has never been found, may be in the right nave of the cathedral, beneath the campanile that bears his name.

✪ Galleria dell'Accademia
Via Ricasoll 60. ☎ **2388609.** Admission 10,000 lire ($6.25). Tues–Sat 9am–7pm, Sun 9am–2pm. Bus: 1, 4, 6, 10, 11, 15, 17, 20, or 25.

After coming out of the entrance to the Duomo, turn right, then head down via Ricasoll to the Academy Gallery. This museum contains paintings and sculpture, but it is completely overshadowed by one work, Michelangelo's colossal *David*, unveiled in 1504. One of the most sensitive accounts I've ever read of how Michelangelo turned the 17-foot "Duccio marble" into *David* is related in "The Giant" chapter of Irving Stone's *The Agony and the Ecstasy*. Stone describes a Michelangelo "burning with marble fever" who set out to create a *David* who "would be Apollo, but considerably more; Hercules, but considerably more; Adam, but considerably more; the most fully realized man the world had yet seen, functioning in a rational and humane world." How well he succeeded is much in evidence today.

David once stood in piazza della Signoria but was removed in 1873 to the Academy (a copy was substituted). Apart from containing the masterwork, the sculpture gallery is also graced with Michelangelo's unfinished quartet of slaves, carved around 1520 and intended for the ill-fated tomb of Julius II, and his *St. Matthew*, which he worked on (shortly after completing *David*) for the Duomo. His unfinished *Palestrina Pietà* displayed here is a much later work, dating from 1550.

In the connecting picture gallery is a collection of Tuscan masters, such as Botticelli, and Umbrian works by Perugino (teacher of Raphael).

✪ Cappelle Medici
Piazza Madonna degli Aldobrandini 6. ☎ **213206.** Admission 9,000 lire ($5.65). Tues–Sat 9am–2pm, Sun 9am–1pm. Bus: 1, 6, 11, 17, 19, or 23.

A mecca for all pilgrims, the Medici tombs are sheltered adjacent to the Basilica of San Lorenzo (see "Churches" in "More Attractions," below). The tombs, housing the "blue-blooded" Medici, are actually entered in back of the church by going around to piazza di Madonna degli Aldobrandini. First, you'll pass through the octagonal, baroque "Chapel of the Princes," which has colored marble but a cold decoration. In back of the altar is a collection of Italian reliquaries.

The real reason the chapels are visited en masse, however, is the "New Sacristy," designed by Michelangelo. Working from 1521 to 1534, he created the Medici tomb in a style that foreshadowed the coming of the baroque. Lorenzo the Magnificent—a ruler who seemed to embody the qualities of the Renaissance itself, and one of the greatest names in the history of the Medici family—was buried near Michelangelo's uncompleted *Madonna and Child* group, a simple monument that evokes a promise unfulfilled.

Impressions

"Michelangelo's David . . . The Florentine! The Tuscan pose—half self-conscious all the time."

—D. H. Lawrence

Great Art & High Camp

The world's most reproduced statue—Michelangelo's *David*—has spawned controversy down through the centuries. When it was exposed out in the open at the piazza della Signoria, it was the subject of cruel jeers and was frequently targeted for rotten egg attacks. In his grand tour of Italy, a 19th-century visitor, William Hazlitt, recorded his impression and called the masterpiece an "awkward overgrown actor at one of our minor theatres, without his clothes."

In 1873, to protect the statue from the elements, *David* was rolled on logs to the Galleria dell'Accademia, where it stands inside today. The statue on the piazza della Signoria is a copy, although many visitors rushing through Florence assume it to be Michelangelo's original.

Many critics consider the sculpture (1501–1504) the world's greatest, although some art historians cite other works. The artist's study of the male anatomy has been hailed as "flawless," even though Michelangelo had hardly turned 26 when he began the four-year project. Michelangelo worked from a towering, columnlike stone which the Tuscans had nicknamed *il Gigante.* Another artist, Agostino di Duccio, had attempted to work on the marble but had abandoned it.

This controversial statue of David brought Michelangelo the recognition he wanted as the leading sculptor of the Renaissance, earning for him sponsors such as the pope, who brought commissions including the Sistine Chapel. The artist's depiction of this biblical figure in the nude caused a scandal in its day, and to some extent it still does. Note all those horrible reproductions of the statue sold all over Florence with and without the fig leaf.

In 1991 a frustrated artist with a hammer attacked the statue, but succeeded only in making a few minor nicks on its toes.

Over the years *David* has also become a virtual symbol of homosexual camp, its reproductions adorning gay venues such as restaurants, bars, hotels, and certainly apartments all over the world. There's even a restaurant in Las Vegas where the statue's rhinestone-studded figleaf is raised and lowered every five minutes.

In spite of all the tawdry reproductions, in spite of all the hype and camp surrounding the figure, it remains in Florence to welcome new generations, an enduring legacy of the ideals of the High Renaissance in art. A true Goliath. Or, as one visitor put it, "So alive!"

Ironically, the finest, world-renowned groups of sculpture were reserved for two Medici "clan" members, who (in the words of Mary McCarthy) "would better have been forgotten." Both are represented by Michelangelo as armored, regal, idealized princes of the Renaissance. In fact, Lorenzo II, Duke of Urbino, depicted as "the thinker," was a deranged young man (just out of his teens before he died). Clearly, Michelangelo was not working to glorify these two Medici dukes. Rather, he was chiseling for posterity. The other two figures on Lorenzo's tomb are most often called *Dawn* and *Dusk,* with morning represented as woman and evening as man.

The two best-known figures—Michelangelo at his most powerful—are *Night* and *Day* at the feet of Giuliano, the Duke of Nemours. *Night* is chiseled as a woman in troubled sleep; *Day* is a man of strength awakening to a foreboding world. These two figures were not the sculptural works of Michelangelo's innocence.

Discovered in a sepulchral chamber beneath the Medici Chapel was Michelangelo's only group of mural sketches. Access is through a trap door and a winding staircase. The walls apparently had been used by the great artist as a giant doodling sheet. Drawings include a sketch of the legs of Duke Giuliano, Christ risen, and a depiction of the Laocoön, the Hellenistic figure group. Fifty drawings, done in charcoal on plaster walls, were found. The public can sometimes view these sketches in the choir.

✪ Galleria degli Uffizi

Piazzale degli Uffizi 6. ☎ **23885.** Admission 12,000 lire ($7.50). Tues–Sat 9am–7pm, Sun and holidays 9am–2pm (last entrance 45 minutes before closing time). Bus: 14 or 15.

When the last grand duchess of the Medici family died, she bequeathed to the people of Tuscany a wealth of Renaissance, even classical, art. The paintings and sculpture had been accumulated by the powerful grand dukes in three centuries of rule that witnessed the height of the Renaissance. Vasari designed the palace in the 16th century for Cosimo I.

The Uffizi, with the finest collection of art in Italy, ranks along with the Prado and would fill a very thick volume, and to see and have time to absorb all the Uffizi paintings would take at least two weeks. We'll present only the sketchy highlights to get the first-timer through a citadel of madonnas and bambini, mythological figures, and Christian martyrs. The Uffizi is nicely grouped into periods or schools to show the development and progress of Italian and European art.

The first room begins with classical sculpture. You'll then meet up with those rebels from Byzantium, Cimabue and his pupil Giotto, with their madonnas and bambini. Since the Virgin and Child seem to be the overriding theme of the earlier of the Uffizi artists, it's enlightening just to follow the different styles over the centuries, from the ugly, almost midget-faced babies of the post-Byzantine works to the chubby, red-cheeked cherubs that glorified the baroque.

Look for Simone Martini's *Annunciation*, a collaborative venture. The halo around the head of the Virgin doesn't conceal her pouty mouth. Fra Angelico of Fiesole, a 15th-century painter, lost in a world peopled with saints and angels, makes his Uffizi debut with (naturally) a *Madonna and Bambino*. A special treasure is a work by Masaccio, who died at an early age, but is credited as the father of modern painting. In his madonnas and bambini we see the beginnings of the use of perspective in painting. Two important portraits are by Piero della Francesca, the 15th-century painter. Fra Angelico's *Coronation of the Virgin* is also in this salon.

In another room you'll find Friar Filippo Lippi's far-superior *Coronation*, as well as a galaxy of charming madonnas. He was a rebel among the brethren.

The Botticelli rooms, which contain his finest works, are popular, especially with visitors who contemplate what is commonly referred to as "Venus on the Half-Shell." This supreme conception of life—the *Birth of Venus*—really packs them in. Flora tries to cover the nude goddess, while the gods of the wind puff up a storm. But before being captured by Venus, don't miss *Minerva Subduing the Centaur*, an important painting that brought about a resurgence of interest in mythological subjects. Botticelli's *Allegory of Spring* or *Primavera* is a gem; it's often called a symphony because you can listen to it. Set in a citrus grove, the painting depicts Venus with Cupid hovering over her head. "The Wind" tries to capture a nymph; but the three graces, in a lyrical composition, form the painting's chief claim to greatness. Mercury looks out of the canvas to the left. Before leaving the room, look for Botticelli's *Adoration of the Magi*, in which we find portraits of the Medici (the vain man at the far right is Botticelli). Also here is Botticelli's small, allegorical *Calumny.*

The *Adoration of the Shepherds* is a superbly detailed triptych, commissioned for a once-important Tuscan family and painted by Hugo van der Goes, a 15th-century artist. In another room we come across one of Leonardo da Vinci's unfinished paintings, the brilliant *Adoration of the Magi,* and Verrocchio's *Baptism of Christ,* not a very important painting, but noted because da Vinci painted one of the angels when he was 14 years old. Also in this salon hangs da Vinci's *Annunciation,* which reflects the early years of his genius with its twilight atmosphere and each leaf painstakingly in place. Proof that Leonardo was an architect? The splendid Renaissance palace he designed is part of the background.

The most beautiful room in the gallery with its dome of pearl shells contains the *Venus of the Medici* at center stage; it's one of the most reproduced of all Greek sculptural works. Also displayed are *Apollo* and *The Wrestlers,* from Greek originals of the 3rd and 4th centuries B.C.

In the rooms to follow are works by Perugino, Dürer, Mantegna, Giovanni Bellini, Giorgione, and Correggio. Finally, don't miss Michelangelo's *Holy Family,* as well as Raphael's *Madonna of the Goldfinch,* plus his portraits of Julius II and Leo X. There is also what might be dubbed the Titian salon, which has two of his interpretations of Venus (one depicted with Cupid). When it came to representing voluptuous females on canvas, Titian had no rival. In other rooms are important Mannerists: Parmigianino, Veronese, and Tintoretto (*Leda and the Swan*). In the rooms nearing the end are works by Rubens, Caravaggio (*Bacchus*), and Rembrandt.

On May 27, 1993, a terrorist bomb—presumably planted by the Mafia—blasted through a section of the gallery. Although paintings were destroyed, many of the Uffizi's masterpieces, including works by Botticelli and Michelangelo, were spared, some because they were protected by shatter-proof glass. Early in 1994, the world press headlined the news: "The Uffizi reborn." Today, most of what one goes to see at the Uffizi is proudly exhibited, although a lot of important masterpieces may not be in their usual positions. In all, 200 works of art were damaged, but only three of these paintings were completely destroyed.

✪ Palazzo Pitti

Piazza de'Pitti. ☎ **213440.** Admission to Palatina, 12,000 lire ($7.50); Modern Art Gallery, 6,000 lire ($3.75); Argenti, 8,000 lire ($5). Tues–Sat 9am–2pm. Bus: 3.

The Palatine Gallery, on the left bank (a five-minute walk from the Ponte Vecchio), houses one of Europe's great art collections, with masterpieces hung one on top of the other, as in the days of the Enlightenment. If for no other reason, it should be visited for its Raphaels alone. The Pitti, built in the mid-15th century (Brunelleschi was the original architect), was once the residence of the powerful Medici family.

There are actually several museums in this complex, including the most important, the **Galleria Palatine,** a repository of old masters. Other museums include

---

Impressions

"He apparently never received an impression of evil; and his conception of human life was a perpetual sense of sacredly loving and being loved. . . ."

—Henry James on Fra Angelico

⭐ Frommer's Favorite Florence Experiences

Standing in Awe in front of Michelangelo's David. Some one million visitors a year can't be wrong: In spite of countless copies, there is nothing as majestic as seeing the original statue of "The Giant"—carved from a single block of Carrara marble.

A Shopping Spree. Florence, Italy's most fashionable city, dazzles with its merchandise—everything from gold jewelry to leather and fashion. Stroll the Ponte Vecchio, via Tornabuoni, via della Vigna Nova, and via Roma.

Having a Campari at piazza della Signoria. In the "living room" of Florence, at an open-air café, enjoy a refreshing drink while surrounded by some of the world's most famous statues—everything from Cellini's *Perseus* to Giambologna's *Rape of the Sabines*.

Wandering in the Uffizi Galleries. There are those who come to Florence every year with good reason: to explore gallery after gallery of Italy's most important museum, treasure trove of Renaissance masterpieces.

the **Appartamenti Reali,** which the Medici family once called home, and the **Museo degli Argenti,** 16 rooms devoted to displays of the "loot" acquired by the Medici dukes. Others are the **Coach and Carriage Museum** and the **Galleria d'Arte Moderna,** as well as the **Museo della Porcellane** (porcelain) and the **Galleria del Costume.**

After passing through the main door, proceed to the Sala di Venere (Room of Venus). In it are Titian's *La Bella*, of rich and illuminating color (entrance wall), and his portrait of Pietro Aretino, one of his most distinguished works. On the opposite wall are Titian's *Concert of Music*, often attributed to Giorgione, and his portrait of Julius II.

In the Sala di Apollo (on the opposite side of the entrance door) are Titian's *Man with Gray Eyes*—an aristocratic, handsome romanticist—and his *Mary Magdalene*, covered only with her long hair. On the opposite wall are Van Dyck portraits of Charles I of England and Henrietta of France.

In the Sala di Marte (entrance wall) is an important *Madonna and Child* by Murillo of Spain, as well as the Pitti's best-known work by Rubens: *The Four Philosophers*. On the left wall is one of Ruben's most tragic and moving paintings, depicting the *Consequences of War*—an early *Guernica*.

In the Sala di Giove (entrance wall) are Andrea del Sarto's idealized John the Baptist in his youth, Fra Bartolomeo's *Descent from the Cross,* and one of Rubens's most exciting paintings (even for those who don't like art), which depicts a romp of nymphs and satyrs. On the third wall (opposite the entrance wall) is the Pitti's second famous Raphael, the woman under the veil, known as *La Fornarina*, his bakery-girl mistress.

In the following gallery, the Sala di Saturno, look to the left on the entrance wall to see Raphael's *Madonna of the Canopy*. On the third wall near the doorway is the greatest Pitti prize, Raphael's *Madonna of the Chair*, his best-known interpretation of the Virgin, and what is in fact probably one of the six most celebrated paintings in all of Europe.

In the Sala dell'Iliade (to your left on the entrance wall) is a work of delicate beauty, Raphael's rendition of a pregnant woman. On the left wall is Titian's

Portrait of a Gentleman, which he was indeed. (Titian is the second big star in the Palatine Gallery.) Finally, as you're leaving, look to the right of the doorway to see one of Velázquez's representations of the many faces of Philip IV of Spain.

In the rooms that follow, the drama of the salons remains vivid—enhanced by portraits by Justus Sustermans, who could be almost as devastating as Velázquez.

Major works in the Sala di Prometeo include Filippo Lippi's *Madonna and Child,* and two Botticelli portraits. In the Sala dell'Educazione di Giove hangs Caravaggio's *Sleeping Cupid,* and in the Sala della Giustizia you'll find Tintoretto's *Virgin and Child,* a vintage work by that Venetian master.

✪ Museo Nazionale del Bargello

Via del Proconsolo 4. ☎ **23-88-606.** Admission 8,000 lire ($5). Tues–Sun 9am–2pm. Bus: 14.

The National Museum, a short walk from piazza della Signoria, is a 13th-century fortress palace whose dark underground chambers once resounded with the echoing cries of the tortured. Today it's a vast repository of some of the most important sculpture of the Renaissance, including works by Michelangelo and Donatello.

Here you'll see another Michelangelo *David* (referred to in the past as *Apollo*), chiseled perhaps 25 to 30 years after the statuesque figure in the Academy Gallery. The Bargello *David* is totaly different—even effete when compared to its stronger brother. The gallery also displays Michelangelo's grape-capped *Bacchus* (one of his earlier works), who is tempted by a satyr. Among the more significant sculptures is Giambologna's *Winged Mercury.*

The Bargello displays two versions of Donatello's John the Baptist—one emaciated, the other a younger and much kinder edition. Donatello, of course, was one of the outstanding and original talents of the early Renaissance. In this gallery you'll learn why. His *St. George* is a work of heroic magnitude. According to an oft-repeated story, Michelangelo, upon seeing it for the first time, commanded it to "March!" Donatello's bronze *David* in this salon is one of the most remarkable figures of all Renaissance sculpture—it was the first "freestanding" nude since the Romans stopped chiseling. As depicted, *David* is narcissistic (a stunning contrast to Michelangelo's latter-day virile interpretation). For the last word, however, I'll have to call back our lady of the barbs, Mary McCarthy, who wrote: "His David . . . wearing nothing but a pair of fancy polished boots and a girlish bonnet, is a transvestite's and fetishist's dream of alluring ambiguity."

Look for at least one more notable work, another *David*—this one by Andrea del Verrocchio, one of the finest of the 15th-century sculptors. The Bargello contains a large number of terra-cottas by the della Robbia clan.

Museo di San Marco

Piazza San Marco 1. ☎ **238-8608.** Admission 6,000 lire ($3.75). Tues–Sat 9am–2pm, Sun 9am–2pm. Bus: 1, 6, 7, 11, 15, 17, or 20.

Museo di San Marco, a state museum, is a handsome Renaissance palace whose cell walls are decorated with frescoes by the mystical Fra Angelico, one of Europe's greatest 15th-century painters. In the days of Cosimo dei Medici, San Marco was built by Michelozzo as a Dominican convent. It originally contained bleak, bare cells, which Angelico and his students then brightened considerably with some of the most important works of this pious artist of Fiesole, who portrayed recognizable landscapes in strong, vivid colors.

One of his better-known paintings found here is *The Last Judgment,* which depicts people with angels on the left dancing in a circle, and lordly saints towering overhead. Hell, as it is depicted on the right, is naive—Dante-esque—infested with demons, reptiles, and sinners boiling in a stew. Much of hell was created by his students; Angelico's brush was inspired only by the Crucifixion, madonnas, and bambini—or landscapes, of course. Here, also, are his *Descent from the Cross* and an especially refined interpretation, a panel of scenes from the life of Christ, including the *Flight into Egypt*.

In one room are frescoes by Fra Bartolomeo, who lived from 1475 to 1517 and worked with Raphael. Note his *Madonna and Child with Saints*. In the Capitolo is a powerful *Crucifixion* by Angelico.

Turn right at the next door and you'll enter a refectory devoted to the artistic triumph of Domenico Ghirlandaio, who taught Michelangelo how to fresco. Ghirlandaio's own *Last Supper* in this room is rather realistic; his saints have tragic faces and silently evoke a feeling of impending doom.

Upstairs on the second floor—at the top of the hallway—is Angelico's masterpiece, *The Annunciation*, a perfect gem of a painting. From here, you can walk down the left corridor to explore the cells of the Dominicans, which are enhanced by frescoes by Angelico and his pupils. Most of the frescoes depict scenes from the Crucifixion.

After turning to the right, you may want to skip the remaining frescoes, which appear to be uninspired student exercises. But at the end of the corridor is the cell of Savonarola, which was the scene of his arrest. The cell contains portraits of the reformer by Bartolomeo, who was plunged into acute melancholy by the jailing and torturing of his beloved teacher. Pictures of the reformer on the pyre at piazza della Signoria are on display.

If you retrace your steps to the entrance, then head down still another corridor, you'll see more frescoes, past a library with Ionic columns designed by Michelozzo. Finally, you'll come to the cell of Cosimo dei Medici, with a fresco by Gozzoli, who worked with Angelico.

MORE ATTRACTIONS

PIAZZALE MICHELANGELO

For a view of the wonders of Florence below and Fiesole above, climb aboard bus no. 13 from the central station and head for piazzale Michelangelo, a 19th-century belvedere overlooking a view seen in many a Renaissance painting. It's best at dusk, when the purple-fringed Tuscan hills form a frame for Giotto's bell tower, Brunelleschi's dome, and the towering hunk of stones that stick up from the Palazzo Vecchio. Another copy of Michelangelo's *David* dominates the square.

Warning: At certain times during the day the square is so crowded with tour buses and peddlers selling trinkets and claptrap souvenirs that the balcony is drained of its chief drama. If you go at these times, often midday in summer, you'll find that the view of Florence is still intact—but you may be run down by a Vespa if you try to enjoy it.

PONTE VECCHIO

Spared by the Nazis in their bitter retreat from the Allied advance in 1944, "The Old Bridge" is the last remaining medieval *ponte* spanning the Arno (the Germans blew up the rest). The bridge was again threatened in the flood of 1966 when the waters of the Arno swept over it and washed away a fortune in jewelry from the goldsmiths' shops that flank the bridge.

Today the restored Ponte Vecchio is closed to traffic except for the *pedoni* (pedestrian) type. The little shops continue to sell everything from the most expensive of Florentine gold to something simple—say, a Lucrezia Borgia poison ring. Florentine hog butchers once peddled their wares on this bridge.

OSPEDALE DEGLI INNOCENTI

At piazza SS. Annunziata 12 is the Hospital of the Innocents (☎ 243670), the oldest of its kind in Europe. The building, and the loggia, with its Corinthian columns, was conceived by Brunelleschi and marked the first architectural bloom of the Renaissance in Florence. In the cortile are terra-cotta medallions done in blues and opaque whites by Andrea della Robbia that depict babes in swaddling clothes.

Still used as a hospital, the building also contains an art gallery. Notable among its treasures is a terra-cotta *Madonna and Child* by Luca della Robbia, plus works by Andrea del Sarto and Filippo Lippi. One of the gallery's most important paintings is an *Adoration of the Magi* by Domenico Ghirlandaio (the chubby Bambino looks a bit pompously at the Wise Man kissing his foot). The gallery is open Monday and Tuesday and Thursday through Saturday from 9am to 1pm and Sunday from 8am to noon. Admission is 3,000 lire ($1.90).

CHURCHES

The wealth of architecture, art, and treasures of Florence's churches is hardly secondary, but if you want to see even a sampling of the best, you'll have to schedule an extra day or more in the City of the Renaissance.

Basilica di Santa Croce

Piazza Santa Croce 16. ☎ **244619.** Admission to church, free; cloisters and church museum, 3,000 lire ($1.90) adults, 1,000 lire (65¢) children. Church, daily 8am–12.30pm and 3–6:30pm; museum and cloisters, Mar–Sept Thurs–Tues 10am–12:30pm and 2:30–6:30pm; Oct–Feb daily 10am–12:30pm and 3–5pm. Bus: 13, 14, or 19.

The Pantheon of Florence, this church shelters the tombs of everyone from Michelangelo to Machiavelli, from Dante (he was actually buried at Ravenna) to an astronomer (Galileo) who—at the hands of the Inquisition—"recanted" his concept that the earth revolves around the sun. Just as Santa Maria Novella was the church of the Dominicans, Santa Croce was the church of the Franciscans, said to have been designed by Arnolfo di Cambio.

In the right nave (first tomb) is the Vasari-executed monument to Michelangelo, whose body was smuggled back to his native Florence from its original burial place in Rome. Along with a bust of the artist are three allegorical figures who represent the arts. In the next memorial a prune-faced Dante, a poet honored belatedly in the city that exiled him, looks down. Farther on, still on the right, is the tomb of Machiavelli, whose *The Prince* became a virtual textbook in the art of wielding power. Nearby is a lyrical bas-relief, *The Annunciation* by Donatello.

The "Trecento" frescoes are reason enough for visiting Santa Croce—especially those by Giotto to the right of the main chapel. Once whitewashed, the Bardi and Peruzzi chapels were "uncovered" in the mid-19th century in such a clumsy fashion that they have had to be drastically restored. Although badly preserved, the frescoes in the Bardi Chapel are most memorable, especially the deathbed scene of St. Francis. The cycles in the Peruzzi Chapel are of John the Baptist and St. John. In the left transept is Donatello's once-controversial wooden *Crucifix*—too gruesome for some Renaissance tastes, including that of Brunelleschi, who is claimed to have said: "You (Donatello) have put a rustic upon the cross." (For Brunelleschi's "answer," go to Santa Maria Novella.) Incidentally, the Pazzi Chapel, entered through the cloisters, was designed by Brunelleschi, with terra-cottas by Luca della Robbia.

Additionally, inside the monastery of this church the Franciscan fathers established the **Leather School** at the end of World War II. The purpose of the school was to prepare young boys technically to specialize in Florentine leather work. The school has flourished and produced many fine artisans who continue their careers here. Stop in and see the work when you visit the church.

Basilica di San Lorenzo

Piazza San Lorenzo. ☎ **2342731.** Admission is free. Library, Mon–Sat 9am–1pm; study room, Mon–Sat 8am–2pm. Bus: 1, 6, 11, 17, 19, or 23.

This is Brunelleschi's 15th-century Renaissance church, where the Medici used to attend services from their nearby palace on via Larga, now via Camillo Cavour. Most visitors flock to see Michelangelo's "New Sacristy" with his *Night* and *Day* (see the Medici Chapels under "The Top Attractions," above), but Brunelleschi's handiwork deserves some time, too.

Built in the style of a Latin cross, the church is distinguished by harmonious grays and rows of Corinthian columns. The Old Sacristy (walk up the nave, then turn left) was designed by Brunelleschi and decorated, in part, by Donatello (see his terra-cotta bust of St. Lawrence).

After exploring the Old Sacristy, go through the first door (unmarked) on your right, then turn right again and climb the steps.

The **Biblioteca Medicea Laurenziana** (☎ 210760) is entered separately at piazza San Lorenzo 9 and was designed by Michelangelo to shelter the expanding library of the Medici. Beautiful in design and concept, and approached by exquisite stairs, the library is filled with some of Italy's greatest manuscripts—many of which are handsomely illustrated.

After a visit here, you may want to wander through the cloisters of San Lorenzo and study their Ionic columns.

Basilica di Santa Maria Novella

Piazza Santa Maria Novella. ☎ **215918.** Admission to church, free; Spanish Chapel and cloisters 4,000 lire ($2.50). Church, Mon–Fri 7–11:30am and 3:30–6pm, Sat 10–11:30am and 3:30–5pm, Sun 3:30–5pm; Spanish Chapel and cloisters, Mon–Thurs and Sat 9am–2pm, Sun 8am–1pm. Bus: 1, 6, 7, 14, 17, 19, 22, or 23.

Near the railway station is one of Florence's most distinguished churches, begun in 1278 for the Dominicans. Its geometric facade, with bands of white and green marble, was designed in the late 15th century by Leon Battista Alberti, an aristocrat and true Renaissance man (philosopher, painter, architect, poet). The church borrows from and harmonizes the Romanesque, Gothic, and Renaissance styles.

In the left nave as you enter (the third large painting) is the great Masaccio's *Trinity*, a curious work that has the architectural form of a Renaissance stage setting, but whose figures—in perfect perspective—are like actors in a Greek tragedy. If you view the church at dusk you'll see the stained-glass windows in the fading light cast kaleidoscope fantasies on the opposite wall.

Head straight up the left nave to the Gondi Chapel for a look at Brunelleschi's wooden *Christ on the Cross*, which is said to have been carved to compete with Donatello's same subject in Santa Croce (see above). According to Vasari, when Donatello saw Brunelleschi's completed Crucifix, he dropped his apron full of eggs intended for their lunch. "You have symbolized the Christ," Donatello is alleged to have said. "Mine is an ordinary man." (Some art historians reject this story.)

In the late 15th century Ghirlandaio contracted with a Tornabuoni banker to adorn the choir with frescoes that illustrate scenes from the lives of Mary and John the Baptist. Michelangelo, only a teenager at the time, is known to have studied under Ghirlandaio (perhaps he even worked on this cycle).

If time remains, you may want to visit the cloisters, going first to the "Green Cloister," and then the splendid Spanish Chapel frescoed by Andrea di Bonaiuto in the 14th century (one panel depicts the Dominicans in triumph over heretical wolves).

Santa Maria del Carmine

Piazza Santa Maria del Carmine. Admission 5,000 lire ($3.15). Mon and Wed–Sat 10am–4:30pm; Sun 1–4:30pm. Bus: 3.

A long walk from the Pitti Palace on the left bank is this baroque church, a result of rebuilding after a fire in the 18th century. Miraculously, the renowned Brancacci Chapel was spared—miraculous because it contains frescoes by Masaccio, who ushered in the great century of "Quattrocento" Renaissance painting. Forsaking the ideal, Masaccio depicted man and woman in their weakness and their glory.

His technique is seen at its most powerful in the expulsion of Adam and Eve from the Garden of Eden. The artist peopled his chapel, a masterpiece of early perspective, with scenes from the life of St. Peter (the work was originally begun by his master, Masolino). Note especially the fresco, *Tribute Money*, and the baptism scene with the nude youth freezing in the cold waters.

No less an authority than Leonardo da Vinci commented on Masaccio's work: "Masaccio showed by his perfect works how those who take for their ideal anything but nature—mistress of all masters—tire themselves in vain." Masaccio did the upper frescoes, but because of his early death, the lower ones were completed by Filippino Lippi (not to be confused with his father, Filippo Lippi, a greater artist).

La Sinagoga di Firenze

Via Farini 4. ☎ **245252.** Admission 5,000 lire ($3.15) adults, 4,000 lire ($2.50) children. Apr–Sept Sun–Thurs 10am–1pm and 2–5pm, Fri 10am–1pm; Oct–Mar Mon–Thurs 11am–1pm and 2–5pm; Fri and Sun 10am–1pm. Closed Jewish holidays. Bus: 6.

The synagogue is in the Moorish style, inspired by Constantine's Byzantine church of Hagia Sophia. Completed in 1882, it was badly damaged by the Nazis in 1944 but has been restored to its original splendor. A museum is upstairs.

PALACES

Palazzo Medici-Riccardi

Via Camillo Cavour 1. ☎ **2760340.** Admission 6,000 lire ($3.75). Mon–Tues and Thurs–Sat 9am–1pm and 3–6pm, Sun 9am–1pm. Bus: 1, 6, 11, 14, or 23.

This palace, a short walk from the Duomo, was the home of Cosimo dei Medici before he took his household to the Palazzo della Signoria. Built by palace architect Michelozzo in the mid-15th century, the brown stone building was also the scene, at times, of the court of Lorenzo the Magnificent. Art lovers visit today chiefly to see the mid-15th-century frescoes by Benozzo Gozzoli in the Medici Chapel.

Gozzoli's frescoes, which depict the *Journey of the Magi,* form his masterpiece—in fact, they are considered a hallmark in Renaissance painting in that they abandoned ecclesiastical themes to celebrate emerging man (he peopled his work with the Medici, the artist's master Fra Angelico, and even himself). Gozzoli's ability as a landscape artist and a distinguished portraitist (each man in the procession is a distinctly identifiable individual—often elaborately coifed and clothed) is seen at its finest here.

Another gallery, which has to be entered by a separate stairway, was frescoed by Luca Giordano in the 18th century, but his work seems merely decorative. The apartments, where the prefect lodges, are not open to the public. The gallery, incidentally, may also be viewed free.

Palazzo Vecchio

Piazza della Signoria. ☎ **276-8465**. Admission 8,000 lire ($5). Mon–Wed and Fri–Sat 9am–7pm, Sun 8am–1pm. Bus: 14.

The secular "Old Palace" is without doubt the most famous and imposing palace in Florence. It dates from the closing years of the 13th century. Its remarkable architectural feature is its 308-foot tower, an engineering feat that required supreme skill. Once home to the Medici, the Palazzo Vecchio (also called the Palazzo della Signoria) is occupied today by city employees, but much of it is open to the public.

The 16th-century "Hall of the 500" ("Dei Cinquecento"), the most outstanding part of the palace, is filled with Vasari & Co. frescoes as well as sculpture. As you enter the hall, look for Michelangelo's *Victory*. It depicts an insipid-looking young man treading on a bearded older man (it has been suggested that Michelangelo put his own face on that of the trampled man).

Later you can stroll through the rest of the palace, through its apartments and main halls. You can also visit the private apartments of Eleanor of Toledo, wife of Cosimo I, and a chapel that was begun in 1540 and frescoed by Bronzino. The palace displays the original of Verrocchio's bronze putto (from 1476) from the courtyard fountain. This work is called both *Winged Cherub Clutching a Fish* and *Boy with a Dolphin*. The palace also shelters a 16th-century *Portrait of Machiavelli* that is attributed to Santi di Tito. Donatello's famous bronze group, *Judith Slaying Holofernes*, once stood on piazza della Signoria, but it was brought inside.

The salons, such as a fleur-de-lis apartment, have their own richness and beauty. Following his arrest, Savonarola was taken to the Palazzo Vecchio for more than a dozen torture sessions, including "twists" on the rack. The torturer pronounced him his "best" customer.

MUSEUMS & GALLERIES

Museo Archeologico

Via della Colonna 38. ☎ **23575**. Admission 6,000 lire ($3.75). Tues–Sat 9am–2pm, Sun 9am–1pm. Bus: 1, 6, 7, 11, 15, 17, or 20.

The Archaeological Museum, a short walk from piazza della SS. Annunziata, houses one of the most outstanding Egyptian and Etruscan collections in Europe. Its Egyptian mummies and sarcophagi are on the first floor, along with some of the better-known Etruscan works. Pause to look at the lid to the coffin of a fat Etruscan (unlike the blank faces staring back from many of these tombs, this overeater's countenance is quite expressive).

One room is graced with three bronze Etruscan masterpieces, among the rarest objects d'art of these relatively unknown people. They include the *Chimera*, a lion with a goat sticking out of its back. The lion's tail—in the form of a venomous reptile—lunges at the trapped beast. The others are a statue of *Minerva* and one of an *Orator*. These pieces of sculpture range from the 5th to the 1st century B.C. Another rare find is a Roman bronze of a young man, the so-called *Idolino from Pesaro*. The François vase on the ground floor, from the year 570 B.C., is celebrated.

Museo dell'Opera del Duomo

Piazza del Duomo 9. ☎ **2302885**. Admission 8,000 lire ($5). Mar–Oct Mon–Sat 9am– 7:30pm; Nov–Feb Mon–Sat 9am–6pm. Bus: 1, 6, 11, 14, 19, or 23.

Museo dell'Opera del Duomo, across the street but facing the apse of Santa Maria del Fiore, is beloved by connoisseurs of Renaissance sculptural works. It shelters the sculpture removed from the campanile and the Duomo—not only to protect the pieces from the weather, but from visitors who want samples. A major attraction of this museum is the unfinished *Pietà* by Michelangelo, which is in the middle of the stairs. It was carved between 1548 and 1555 when the artist was in his 70s. In this vintage work, a figure representing Nicodemus (but said to have Michelangelo's face) is holding Christ. The great Florentine intended it for his own tomb, but he is believed to have grown disenchanted with it and to have attempted to destroy it. The museum has a Brunelleschi bust, as well as della Robbia terra-cottas. The museum's premier attraction is four restored panels of Ghiberti's "Doors to Paradise" removed from the Baptistery.

You'll see bits and pieces from what was the old Gothic-Romanesque fronting of the cathedral, with ornamental statues, as conceived by the original architect, Arnolfo di Cambio. One of Donatello's early works, *St. John the Evangelist*, is here—not his finest hour certainly, but anything by Donatello is worth looking at, including one of his most celebrated works, the *Magdalene*, which is in the room with the *cantorie* (see below). This wooden statue once stood in the Baptistery, and had to be restored after the flood of 1966. Dating from 1454–55, it is stark and penitent.

A good reason for visiting the museum is to see the marble choirs—*cantorie*— of Donatello and Luca della Robbia (the works face each other, and are in the first room you enter after climbing the stairs). The Luca della Robbia choir is more restrained, but it still "Praises the Lord" in marble—with clashing cymbals and sounding brass that constitute a reaffirmation of life. In contrast, all restraint breaks loose in the *cantoria* of dancing cherubs in Donatello's choir. It's a romp of chubby bambini. Of all of Donatello's works, this one is perhaps the most lighthearted. But, in total contrast, don't miss Donatello's *Zuccone*, which some consider to be one of his greatest masterpieces; it was done for Giotto's Bell Tower.

GARDENS

Giardini di Boboli (Boboli Gardens)

Piazza de'Pitti 1. ☎ **213-440**. Admission 5,000 lire ($3.15). Apr–Oct daily 9am–6:30pm; Nov–Mar daily 9am–4:30pm. Bus: 3 or 15.

Behind the Pitti Palace are the Giardini di Boboli, through which the Medici romped. The gardens were originally laid out by Triboli, a great landscape artist, in the 16th century. The Boboli is ever-popular for a promenade or an idyllic interlude in a pleasant setting. The gardens are filled with fountains and statuary, such as a *Venus* by Giambologna in the "Grotto" of Buontalenti. You can climb to the top of the Fortezza di Belvedere for a dazzling view of the city.

SPECIAL-INTEREST SIGHTSEEING

FOR THE LITERARY ENTHUSIAST

Casa di Dante

Via Santa Margherita 1. ☎ **283343**. Admission is free. Mon–Tues and Thurs–Sat 9:30am–12:30pm and 3:30–6:30pm, Sun 9:30am–12:30pm. Closed approximately three weeks during July–Aug (dates vary). Bus: 14, 15, 18, 19, or 23.

For those of us who were spoon-fed hell but spared purgatory, a pilgrimage to this rebuilt medieval house may be of passing interest, although it contains few specific exhibits of note. Dante was exiled from his native Florence in 1302 for his political involvements. He never returned, and thus wrote his *Divine Comedy* in exile, conjuring up fit punishment in the *Inferno* for his Florentine enemies. Dante certainly had the last word. The house is reached by walking down via Dante Alighieri.

FOR THE ART ENTHUSIAST

Casa Buonarroti

Via Ghibellina 70. ☎ **241752**. Admission 8,000 lire ($5) adults, 6,000 lire ($3.75) children. Wed–Mon 9:30am–1:30pm. Bus: 14

Only a short walk from Santa Croce stands the house that Michelangelo managed to buy for his nephew. Turned into a museum by his descendants, the house was restored in 1964. It contains some fledgling work by the great artist, as well as some models by him. Here you can see his *Madonna of the Stairs*, which he did when he was 16 years old, as well as a bas-relief he did later, depicting the *Battle of the Centaurs*. The casa is enriched by many of Michelangelo's drawings, shown to the public in periodic exhibitions.

FOR VISITING AMERICANS

Florence American Cemetery and Memorial

Via Cassia, 50023 Impruneta. ☎ **055/202-0020**. Admission is free. May 15–Sept 15 daily 8am–6pm; Sept 16–May 14 daily 8am–5pm. The SITA city bus stops at the cemetery entrance every two hours, except on holidays, when there is usually no bus service. The bus follows via Cassia.

The Florence American Cemetery and Memorial is on a 70-acre site about $7^1/_2$ miles south of the city on the west side of via Cassia, the main highway connecting Florence with Siena and Rome. One of 14 permanent American World War II military cemetery memorials built on foreign soil by the American Battle Monuments Commission, the memorial is on a site that was liberated on August 3, 1944, and later became part of the zone of the U.S. Fifth Army. It is adjacent to the Greve River and framed by wooded hills. Most of the 4,402 servicemen and women interred here died in the fighting that occurred after the capture of Rome in June 1944.

WALKING TOUR
Heart of Florence

Start: Piazza de' Pitti.
Finish: Ponte Trinità.
Time: 2 hours.
Best Times: Any sunny day.
Worst Times: From 8 to 9:30am and 5 to 7:30pm Monday through Saturday (rush hours).

This tour begins at piazza de' Pitti, where you may or may not elect to visit the art treasures of the:

1. Pitti Palace, or walk through the Boboli Gardens in back of the palace. Head up via di Guicciardini until you reach the ancient, shop-flanked:

2. Ponte Vecchio, which spans the river. Pause at the top of the bridge, where a vista from the double-sided belvedere offers views of the Arno on both sides. The calm waters you see today belie the unpredictable torrents that are capable of sweeping over sections of the bridge, as they did in 1966.

After crossing the bridge, turn right and walk alongside the Arno, passing beneath a riverside arcade pierced both longitudinally and latitudinally by a series of arches that open from four directions like a Renaissance study in perspectives. Traffic whizzes beside you, funneling into the tiny piazza del Pesce. The riverside promenade that supports you now changes its name to the lungarno degli Archibusieri, which, a few steps later, gives way to lungarno Anna Maria Luisa de' Medici, just at the end of your sheltering arcade. Note the almost-medieval view of the Ponte Vecchio from this spot.

In about 40 paces you'll come to a soaring canopy of one of the most impressive arcades in Florence. This closes off the Arno side of the three-sided colonnades of the:

3. Uffizi Gallery, Italy's greatest museum. Walk between the rhythmically spaced arches of the arcades onto flagstones, which in sunny weather support dozens of hawkers and vendors. The Tower of the Signoria opens to your sight as you approach it. At:

4. Piazza della Signoria, stop to admire the sculpture-filled Loggia della Signoria and the Palazzo Vecchio. Pass the Fountain of Neptune and turn right just before the equestrian statue. Head to the far corner of the square and take the small street at the side of the Palazzo Vecchio. This street, via de'Gondi, takes you to piazza di San Firenze in one block. Cross this street, climb seven stone steps of the baroque palace in front of you, and turn to contemplate your first view of the very top of Brunelleschi's dome on the Duomo.

☕ **TAKE A BREAK**   At the west end of piazza della Signoria, the most famous square in Florence, **Rivoire** is known for its chocolate, either served hot or else packaged to take with you. A seat at one of its outdoor tables is considered the ideal way to observe the glory of the Renaissance in the sculpture-filled square.

Proceed down a narrow alley, borgo de'Greci, where a yellow-and-black sign points the way to the:

5. **Basilica of Santa Croce.** You emerge onto piazza Santa Croce, for a view of the pink, green, and white bands that ornament the facade of the Basilica of Santa Croce.

    After visiting the church, take a small street in front of it, called via Torta. Continue along to the first intersection, going along via della Burella, a narrow, flagstone-covered street. At the end, you'll come to via dell'Acqua. Turn right and walk a short distance until the foreboding brown stone bulk of the:

6. **Palazzo Bargello** now soars above you. Turn left on via della Vigna Vecchia, which parallels the side of the Bargello. At the end of this narrow street, your sightlines will expand into piazza di San Firenze. Go right onto via del Proconsolo. The sidewalk is very narrow, often crowded, and somewhat a threat because of traffic. But, suddenly, there explodes the intricately patterned facade of what might be Italy's most obvious symbol of the Renaissance, the red-tile dome of the:

7. **Duomo.** Head across the crosswalk and continue more or less in a straight line along the periphery of shops and buildings that ring the edges of the rear side of the Duomo. Stop at piazza del Duomo 9, if you have time, and visit the:

8. **Museo del Duomo.** As you leave the museum, continue to ring the periphery of the piazza until you reach a pedestrian crosswalk, which leads you to a point between the cathedral's entrance and the doors of the:

9. **Baptistery,** which actually sits on its own satellite square, piazza San Giovanni. After visiting the Duomo and the Baptistery, cross the same street you approached them from. Turn left as soon as you reach via Martelli and walk 1½ blocks until you turn right at borgo San Lorenzo. Walk a short distance until you reach piazza San Lorenzo. Pass to the right of the roughly textured facade of the:

10. **Basilica of San Lorenzo** and go along the side of this building. Continue in a crescent-shaped arc, always following the periphery of this huge church. You'll reach the wooden doors leading to the:

11. **Medici chapels,** containing sculpture by Michelangelo. At this point, you'll be on piazza di Madonna degli Aldobrandini.

    Take via del Giglio, and walk straight across the busy traffic of via Panzani. Continue straight along via del Giglio until its end, via de Banchi, where you turn right. This will take you to the:

12. **Piazza della Santa Maria Novella** and its famous church of the same name. After visiting the church, take via delle Belle Donne and follow it past a granite column. Cross via del Moro, taking via del Trebbio. Follow this narrow street, past the Buca Lapi restaurant, until you come to piazza degli Antinori. Turn right onto the most famous shopping street of Florence:

13. **Via dei Tornabuoni.** Walk along this street, checking out its many elegant shops, until you pass the soaring column of piazza Trinità, up to the banks of the Arno again. At a point between the pair of statues that flank the entrance to the:

14. **Ponte Trinità,** your tour has ended.

Walking Tour—Heart of Florence

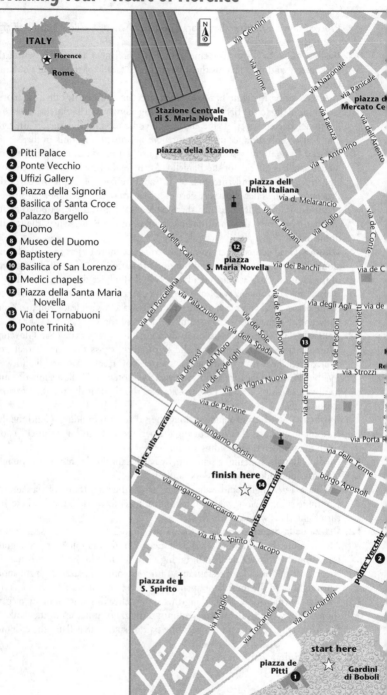

ITALY

Rome

★ Florence

1. Pitti Palace
2. Ponte Vecchio
3. Uffizi Gallery
4. Piazza della Signoria
5. Basilica of Santa Croce
6. Palazzo Bargello
7. Duomo
8. Museo del Duomo
9. Baptistery
10. Basilica of San Lorenzo
11. Medici chapels
12. Piazza della Santa Maria Novella
13. Via dei Tornabuoni
14. Ponte Trinità

Stazione Centrale di S. Maria Novella

piazza della Stazione

piazza dell' Unità Italiana

piazza S. Maria Novella

piazza d. Mercato Ce

via Gennini

via Flume

via Nazionale

via Panicale

via Faenza

via dell'Ariento

via S. Antonino

via d. Melarancio

via de Panzani

via Giglio

via de Conte

via dei Banchi

via de C

via della Scala

via della Porcellana

via Palazzuolo

via del Sole

via della Spada

via de Belle Donne

via degli Agli

via de Pescioni

via de Vecchietti

via de

via de Fossi

via del Moro

via de Federighi

via de Vigna Nuova

via de Tornabuoni

via Strozzi

via de Pariane

via lungarno Corsini

ponte alla Carraia

finish here ☆

via lungarno Guicciardini

ponte santa Trinità

via Porta R

via delle Terme

borgo Apostoli

ponte Vecchio

via di S. Spirito S. Iacopo

piazza de S. Spirito

via Maggio

via Toscanella

via Guicciardini

start here ☆

piazza de Pitti

Gardini di Boboli

Re

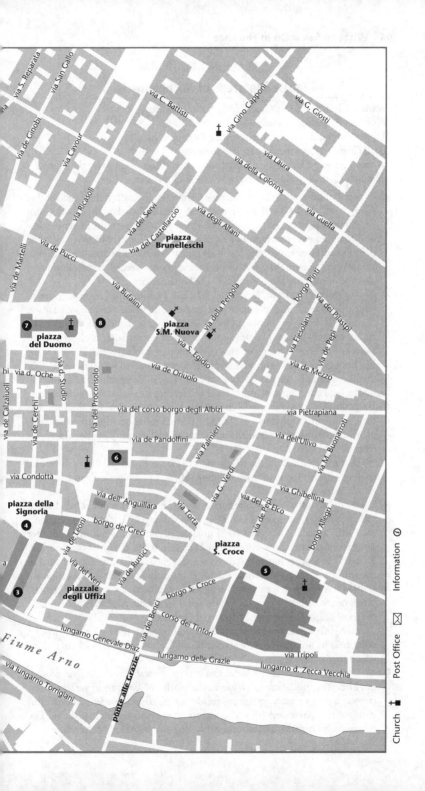

Church ✝ ▪ Post Office ⊠ Information ⊘

WALKING TOUR
In the Footsteps of Michelangelo

Start: Church of Santa Croce. *Note:* See map on page 308–9.
Finish: Piazzale Michelangelo.
Time: About 2^1/$_2$ hours, not counting interior visits.
Best Times: Early morning or late afternoon.
Worst Times: During the midafternoon heat. If you plan to visit the museums that dot this tour, avoid Monday, when most of them are closed.

Begin in front of the elegant marble geometrics that adorn the facade of the:

1. **Church of Santa Croce,** whose confines contain Michelangelo's tomb. After paying your respects, and admiring the design of what might be Florence's second most famous church, head west along borgo de'Greci, which begins at the piazza's southwestern corner. It will eventually narrow to become via de'Gondi before opening onto the piazza whose buildings once housed the administration of some of the most famous rulers of the Renaissance:

2. **Piazza della Signoria.** Notice the elaborate Fountain of Neptune, close to which lies a brass plaque commemorating the site where the religious fanatic Savonarola's body was burned in 1498. (Michelangelo at the time was 23.) The square contains a series of dramatically displayed statues, some of them beneath soaring loggias. The most instantly recognizable statue is a copy of Michelangelo's *David,* the original of which was removed for safekeeping. Exit the piazza from its northeastern corner (take via dei Maggazzini) and follow the signs to the once-fortified walls of one of Florence's most famous galleries, the:

3. **Bargello Museum** (Palazzo del Bargello). Originally built during the 13th century, it contains depiction's of David by both Donatello and Verrocchio (both of which Michelangelo studied intensely), as well as many of the greatest art treasures of Florence.

Continue north along the clearly marked via del Proconsolo for four blocks, passing between the solid stone buildings of one of Florence's oldest neighborhoods, until you arrive at:

4. **Piazza del Duomo.** The architectural ensemble contained within it has changed little (apart from the roaring traffic) since Michelangelo first saw it. The cupola atop the cathedral, designed by Brunelleschi and completed in 1436 after 16 years of construction, inspired Michelangelo in his design of St. Peter's in Rome. (The soaring square bell tower was designed by Giotto.) Constructed of the same pink, green, and white marble as the cathedral itself is the octagonal:

5. **Baptistery,** whose eastern doors (designed by Ghiberti) are considered masterpieces of the metalworker's art. (What you'll see on the Baptistery are excellent copies of originals now in the Museo del Duomo.)

After your exploration of the famous buildings on the piazza, exit from a point near its northwestern corner, via Ricasoli, and walk 2^1/$_2$ blocks to no. 60, which marks the site of:

6. **The Academy** (Galleria dell'Accademia). Its premises shelter the original of what might be the most famous statue in the world, Michelangelo's *David.* Less famous but immensely intriguing are the artist's *Four Prisoners,* whose forms struggle to be released from the marble that seems to enslave them. The museum also contains a *Pietà,* and Michelangelo's figures of St. Matthew.

Retrace your path south, walking toward piazza del Duomo, but turn right before you reach it at via dei Pucci. Within one block, at the corner of via Cavour, you'll reach the:

7. Medici Palace (Palazzo Medici-Riccardi). Originally constructed by the founder of the legendary dynasty (Cosimo dei Medici) as the ancestral home for his off-spring, it was the birthplace of Lorenzo the Magnificent and the home of young Michelangelo during his art studies with Bertoldo.

One block to the Medici Palace's southwest, along the continuation of via dei Pucci (which changes its name to via Canto de Nelli), you'll arrive at the:

8. Church of San Lorenzo, parish church of the Medici family. Within its massive confines lie the Laurentian Library (piazza San Lorenzo 9), which is sometimes more easily accessible via the church's cloisters. Designed by Michelangelo to shelter the Medici family's impressive collection of original manuscripts, it contains what might be the most photographed staircase (also designed by Michelangelo) in Florence. At the rear of the church, accessible from the small and sun-flooded piazza di Madonna dei Aldobrandini, lies the:

9. New Sacristy, designed by Michelangelo and adorned with some of his most evocative sculptures. These include *Dawn, Dusk, Day,* and *Night.* (In the same church is another chapel known as the Old Sacristy, designed by Brunelleschi, and partly decorated by Donatello.)

☕ **TAKE A BREAK** An ideal place for a lunch after all that walking, **La Loggia,** overlooking piazzale Michelangelo, has outdoor tables in summer and serves Florentine classic dishes such as bistecca alla fiorentina. Dress is casual.

After your visit, walk west from the Church of San Lorenzo along via del Melarancio to the city bus station in:

10. Piazza Stazione. From there, as part of an optional excursion, take bus no. 13 (or a cab) to the opposite side of the Arno, to the much-visited but nonetheless charming:

11. Piazzale Michelangelo. From its panorama, you'll have a view over the city like the one that fed the creative juices of Michelangelo. Appropriately, the piazzale's crowning feature is yet another copy of Michelangelo's *David,* which overlooks from afar most of the monuments you've already examined close at hand.

2 Special & Free Events

The architectural setting of Florence is so richly evocative that many visitors consider it amply rewarding without the added theatricality of seasonal events. Despite the appeal of "everyday Florence," there are, however, several annual events which—depending on your interests—might heighten even further the city's legendary allure.

Much of the innate religiosity of Florence is especially visible during **Holy Week.** Two days after the sobriety of Good Friday, Easter is an extroverted religious event whose highlight is the Scoppio del Carro (Explosion of the Cart). A two-wheeled cart filled with fireworks and flowers is drawn to the historic piazza in front of Florence's cathedral by six white oxen. Then, during the Easter Sunday High Mass, a small rocket attached to a facsimile of a white dove is lit at the

Walking Tour—In The Footsteps of Michelangelo

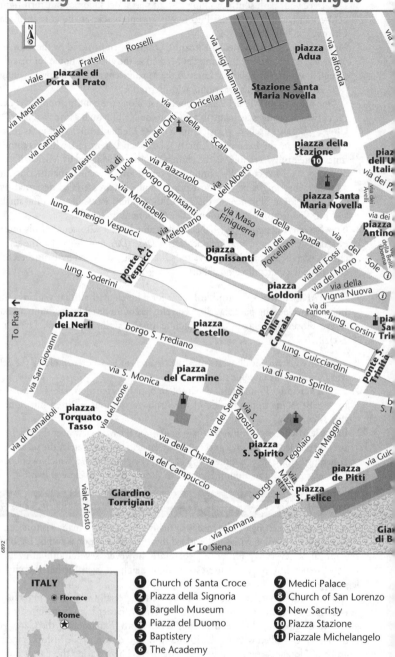

ITALY

- Florence
- Rome ★

1. Church of Santa Croce
2. Piazza della Signoria
3. Bargello Museum
4. Piazza del Duomo
5. Baptistery
6. The Academy
7. Medici Palace
8. Church of San Lorenzo
9. New Sacristy
10. Piazza Stazione
11. Piazzale Michelangelo

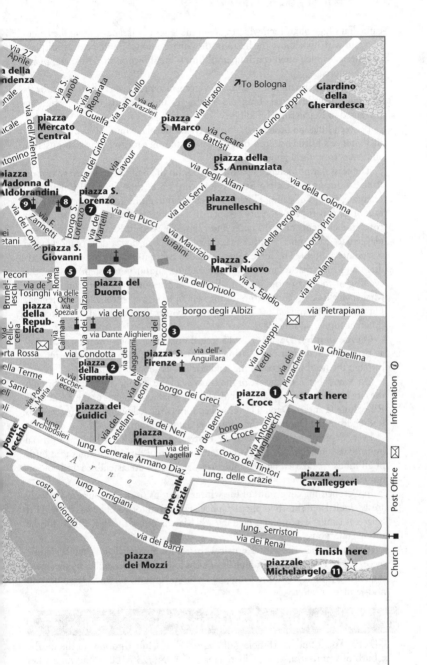

cathedral's high altar, then whizzes down the length of the nave along the length of a taut wire high above the heads of the congregation. Simultaneously, displays of flowers—which often continue until June—are shown in the Uffizi and piazza della Signoria.

Throughout the month of May, the city welcomes classical musicians for its **Maggio Musicale** festival of cantatas, madrigals, and concertos, many of which are presented in Renaissance buildings.

Between June and September, don't overlook the many musical events presented in Florence's hillside suburb of **Fiesole.** Its summer festival draws enthusiastic audiences from throughout Italy.

The feast day of Florence's patron saint, John the Baptist, occurs every year on June 24 during the **Calcio Storico** (also known as the Gioco del Calcio). To celebrate, groups of young Florentine men organized into teams representing the four original parishes of the city compete in a reenactment of a medieval sport that combines elements of both soccer and rugby. Dressed in Renaissance costumes, players face each other at either piazza Santa Croce or piazza della Signoria (and sometimes at both). The contest uses a wooden ball, a minimum of protective padding, and rules that to an observer appear fluid and/or nonexistent. During the evening of the day of the contest, displays of fireworks are shot from piazzale Michelangelo out over the Arno for the benefit of viewers throughout the region. For anyone who missed the first one, these contests are repeated, in somewhat different forms, on June 28.

On **Assumption Day,** August 15, caged crickets are sold throughout the city as part of a modern interpretation of a medieval custom where children ran through the nearby fields catching wild crickets as good-luck charms.

On September 7, on the eve of the Nativity of the Virgin, children run through the city's medieval streets carrying colorful paper lanterns as part of the **Festa delle Rificolone (Lantern Day).** The festival continues the following day in processions leading from the Duomo to the Church of Santa Annunziata.

Every September 28, the eve of the **Festival of St. Michael,** Tuscany's official hunting season begins. At the Porta Romana, hunting equipment and caged birds of all kinds (parakeets, falcons, bluebirds, and owls) are assembled and sold to hunters and bird lovers alike.

In October, the collections of the **winter fashions** from the couturiers of Italy are assembled and shown to photographers, fashion editors, and buyers in the Pitti Palace. A similar exposition is held in early March, also in the Pitti Palace, for the spring collections.

Also in October, the **winter musical season** for orchestral and chamber music pieces begins at the Teatro Comunale. This is followed in November by the opening of the **opera season.** These musical divisions continue till mid-December and mid-January, respectively.

3 Sports & Outdoor Activities

GOLF You'll find an 18-hole golf course, **Golf Club Ugolino,** in the nearby suburb of Impruneta, at via Chiatigiana 3 (☎ 055/230-1009). Impruneta lies about nine miles south of the center.

JOGGING One of the city's finest stretches of uninterrupted pedestrian footpaths is in **La Cascine Park,** west of the center on the north bank of the Arno. Its eastern end begins beside the Ponte della Vittoria, and it includes tennis courts, a racetrack, a public swimming pool, and miles of pedestrian walkways. (You can jog there by following the river to piazza Vittorio Veneto, although bus no. 17 will carry you there from the cathedral.) Another possibility is to jog amid the ornamental walkways of the **Boboli Gardens,** behind the Pitti Palace, although there you might find greater crowds of art lovers. If none of this appeals to you, you might jog along any of the city's **riverside quays** (the best time is early morning, if you're up to it), although you'll have to pay close attention to breakneck traffic feeding onto the Arno bridges.

SOCCER   Florence's hometown team is Fiorentina and the city's residents take their games very seriously indeed. To watch them, head for the **Stadio Comunale,** viale Manfredi Fanti 4-6 (☎ 572625), near the Campo di Marte, about 1 1/2 miles northeast of the town's historic center. Games are usually held on Sunday afternoon between September and May, and tickets go on sale at the stadium two or three hours before the scheduled beginning. Any hotel receptionist in Florence can give you details for the upcoming week.

If you're interested in practicing your dribble, and perhaps practicing with local enthusiasts, head for the previously mentioned La Cascine Park, beside the river west of town, or to the Campo di Marte, the soccer headquarters of Florence, where a handful of youths will likely be practicing.

SQUASH   The city's squash headquarters lies at the **Centro Squash Firenze,** viale Piombino 24–29 (☎ 710055), about 1.5 miles due west of the center.

SWIMMING   There's a public pool at the eastern edge of La Cascine, the **Piscine Le Pavoniere,** viale degli Olmi (☎ 367506). Another possibility is the **Piscina Bellariva,** lungarno Colombo 6 (☎ 677521). These pools are crowded, however, with lots of *bambini,* and visitors might prefer the more secluded premises of the pools (if one exists) in their hotels.

TENNIS   Although technically classified as semiprivate clubs, you'll often find an available court at one of a handful of Florentine tennis venues. Be aware of dress codes which might strongly encourage you to dress in tennis court whites with appropriate shoes. Possibilities include **Tennis Club Rifredi,** via Facibeni (☎ 432-552); **Il Poggetto,** via Michele Mercati 24B (☎ 460127); and the **Circolo Tennis alle Cascine,** viale Visarno 1 (☎ 356651).

4 Shopping

Skilled craftsmanship and traditional design unchanged since the days of the Medici have made Florence a destination for the serious shopper. Florence is noted for its hand-tooled **leather goods** and its various **straw merchandise,** as well as superbly crafted **silver jewelry.** Its reputation for fashionable custom-made clothes is no longer what it was, having lost its position of supremacy to Milan.

The whole city of Florence strikes many visitors as a gigantic department store. Entire neighborhoods on both sides of the Arno offer good shops, although those along the medieval Ponte Vecchio (with some exceptions) strike most people as too touristy.

Florence's Fifth Avenue is **via dei Tornabuoni,** with its flagship Gucci stores for leather and Ferragamo for stylish but costly shoes.

The better shops are for the most part along Tornabuoni, but there are many on **via Vigna Nuova, via Porta Rossa,** and **via degli Strozzi.** You might also stroll on the lungarno along the Arno.

ANTIQUES

There are many outlets for antiques in Florence (but those high prices!). If you're in the market for such expensive purchases, or even if you like to browse, try the following:

Bottega San Felice

Via Maggio 39R. ☎ **215479.**

Bottega San Felice offers many intriguing items from the 19th century, sometimes in the style known as "Charles X," but also sells more modern pieces (those made in this century). Many art deco items are for sale, as are many Biedermeier pieces. Open Monday from 4 to 7:30pm and Tuesday through Saturday from 9am to 1pm and 4 to 7:30pm.

Gallori Turchi

Via Maggio 14R. ☎ **282279.**

Gallori Turchi is one of the best antiques stores in Florence for the serious collector—that is, the serious well-heeled collector. Some of its rare items go back to the 15th century. Each item seems well chosen, ranging from polychrome figures to gilded Tuscan pieces. Open Monday from 4 to 7:30pm and Tuesday through Saturday from 10am to 1pm and 4 to 7:30pm (closed July 20–August 20).

ART

Galleria Masini

Piazza Goldoni 6R. ☎ **294000.**

Established in 1870, the oldest art gallery in Florence, Galleria Masini lies a few minutes' walk from the Hotel Excelsior and other leading hotels. The selection of modern and contemporary paintings by top artists is extensive, representing the work of more than 5,000 Italian painters and sculptors. Even if you're not a collector, this is a good place to select a picture that will be a lasting reminder of your visit to Italy—you can take it home duty-free. Open Monday from 3 to 7pm and Tuesday through Saturday from 9am to 1pm and 3 to 7pm. Closed in August.

BOOKS

Bm Bookshop

Borgo Ognissanti 4R. ☎ **294575.**

A vast array of books is carried here at one of the finest such stores in Europe. It is the oldest English bookstore in Florence devoted to American and British books and carries a large and excellent selection of paperbacks, travel guides, art and architecture books, history, Italian interest, fashion, design, and children's books, plus the largest collection of Italian cookbooks in English to be found in the city. Books are chosen by an expert staff and can be shipped anywhere in the world at nominal rates. The bookshop is near the Excelsior Hotel. Open Monday through Saturday from 9am to 1pm and 3:30 to 7:30pm.

Libreria il Viaggio

Borgo degli Albizi 41R. ☎ **240489.**

In the center of Florence is a specialty bookstore selling maps and guidebooks from all over the world, in a wide variety of languages, including English, of course. It's one of the finest bookstores of its type in Italy, with a tempting variety of titles and merchandise. Open Monday through Saturday from 9am to 1pm and 3:30 to 7:30pm.

DEPARTMENT STORES

Standa
Via Panzani 31R. ☎ **239-8963.**

Here you'll find general merchandise, including moderately priced clothing, household goods, and other items. Open on Monday from 2 to 7:30pm and Tuesday through Saturday from 9am to 7:30pm.

Upim
Piazza della Repubblica 1. ☎ **210317.**

Upim is a nationwide chain of stores similar to Standa. Open June to September, Monday through Friday from 8:45am to 7:45pm and on Saturday from 8:45am to 7pm; October to May, on Monday from 2 to 7:45pm and Tuesday through Saturday from 8:45am to 7:45pm.

FABRIC

Casa di Tessuti
Via de' Pecori 20. ☎ **215961.**

In business for more than half a century, Casa di Tessuti is a shop for connoisseurs, those seeking one of the largest and highest-quality selections of materials in linen, silk, wool, and cotton. The Romoli family, longtime proprietors, are proud of their assortment of fabrics, and rightly so, and are known for their selections of design and colors. Open Monday from 3:30 to 7:30pm and Tuesday through Saturday from 9am to 1pm and 3:30 to 7:30pm.

FASHION (MEN & WOMEN)

Mariposa
Lungarno Corsini 1B-20R. ☎ **284259.**

Mariposa offers women's fashions with such famous design labels as Krizia, Fendi, Rocco Barocco, Missoni, and Mimmina. Foreign customers are often granted a 10% discount. Open Monday through Saturday from 9:30am to 7:30pm.

Romano
Piazza della Repubblica. ☎ **239-6890.**

In the commercial center of town near the Duomo is Romano, a glamorous clothing store for both women and men. The owners commissioned a curving stairwell to be constructed under the high ornate ceiling. But even more exciting are their well-stocked leather and suede goods, along with an assortment of dresses, shoes, and handbags, many at very high prices if you're willing to pay for quality. Open Monday from 3:30 to 7:30pm and Tuesday through Saturday from 9:30am to 1pm and 3:30 to 7:30pm.

GIFTS

Balatresi Gift Shop
Lungarno Acciaiuoli 22R. ☎ **287851.**

The Balatresi Gift Shop is presided over by Umberto and Giovanna Balatresi, who have stocked their shop full of treasures. Among them are Florentine mosaics created for them by Maestro Metello Montelatici, who is arguably one of the greatest mosaicists alive today. The store also sells original ceramic figurines by the sculptor Giannitrapani, and a fine selection of hand-carved alabaster, enamel ware and tuscan glass. Many Americans come into this store every year to do their Christmas shopping. Open Monday through Saturday from 9:30am to 1pm and 3:30 to 7:30pm.

Menegatti
Piazza del Pesce–Ponte Vecchio. ☎ **215202.**

You'll find a wide selection of items at Menegatti, including pottery from Florence, Faenza, and Deruta. There are also della Robbia reproductions made in red clay like the originals. Items can be sent home if you arrange it at the time of your purchase. Open Tuesday through Saturday from 10am to 6pm.

HANDCRAFTS

S.E.L.A.N.
Via Porta Rossa 113R. ☎ **212995.**

S.E.L.A.N., off piazza S. Trinità, is a star choice for traditional designs in Italian ceramics. A wide assortment of merchandise, all made by hand in Italy, is offered. Open Monday from 3:30 to 7:30pm and Tuesday through Saturday from 9am to 1pm and 3:30 to 7:30pm.

JEWELRY

Buying jewelry is almost an art in itself, so proceed with caution. Florence, of course, is known for its jewelry. You'll find some stunning antique pieces, and if you know how to buy, much good value.

Aurum
Lungarno Corsini 16R. ☎ **284259.**

Aurum sells contemporary 18-karat gold jewelry. Many pieces of the selection are modern, based on designs created exclusively for this store. Others are reproductions of Etruscan designs. Open Monday through Saturday from 9:30am to 7:30pm.

Befani E Tai
Via Vacchereccia 13R. ☎ **287825.**

Befani E Tai is one of the most unusual jewelry stores in Florence—some of its pieces date back from the 19th century. The store was established right after World War II by expert goldsmiths who were childhood friends. Some of their clients even design their own jewelry for special orders. Artisans are skilled at working in gold and platinum. Open mid-June to mid-September, Monday through Friday from 9am to 1pm and 3:30 to 7:30pm; off-season, Tuesday through Saturday from 9am to 1pm and 3:30 to 7:30pm (closed August).

Faraone-Settepassi
Via Tornabuoni 25R. ☎ **215506.**

Faraone-Settepassi, one of the most distinguished jewelers of the Renaissance city, draws a well-heeled patronage. Open Monday from 3:30 to 7:30pm and Tuesday through Saturday from 9:45am to 1pm and 3:30 to 7:30pm (closed August 8–21).

Mario Buccellati
Via Tornabuoni 69-71R. ☎ **239-6579.**

Away from the Ponte Vecchio, Mario Buccellati specializes in exquisite handcrafted jewelry and silver. A large selection of intriguing pieces at high prices is offered. Open June 15 to September 15, Monday through Friday from 9am to 1pm and

3:30 to 7:30pm; off-season, on Monday from 3:30 to 7:30pm, Tuesday through Friday from 9am to 1pm and 3:30 to 7pm, and on Saturday from 9am to 1pm (closed August).

LEATHER

Universally acclaimed, Florentine leather is still the fine product it always was—smooth, well shaped, and vivid in such colors as green and red.

Bojola

Via dei Rondinelli 25R. ☎ **211155.**

Bojola is a leading name in leather. Sergio Bojola has distinguished himself in Florence by his selections for many types and tastes, in both synthetic materials and beautiful leathers. Hundreds of customers are always enthusiastic about the variety of items found here, which reflect first-class quality and craftsmanship. Open Monday through Saturday 9:30am to 7:30pm.

John F.

Lungarno Corsini 2. ☎ **239-8985.**

John F., located near the S. Trinità Bridge, is a high-fashion house of leather in a Florentine palace. The leather clothing is of exclusive design, and the salon shows models from the *crème de la crème* of its collection. Although foreign patronage is high, the shop also dresses some of the most chic Florentine women. Accessories, including handbags and leather articles, made here are well crafted and beautifully styled. There is also a vast selection of Missoni sports sweaters. Open Monday through Saturday from 9:30am to 7:30pm. Closes Monday in winter.

Leonardo Leather Works

Borgo dei Greci 16A. ☎ **292202.**

Leonardo Leather Works concentrates on two of the oldest major crafts of Florence: leather and jewelry. Leather goods include wallets, bags, shoes, boots, briefcases, clothing, travel bags, belts, and gift items, with products by famous designers. No imitations are permitted here. The jewelry department has a large assortment of gold chains, bracelets, rings, earrings, and charms. Open Monday through Saturday from 9am to 6:30pm. Closes Monday in winter.

Pollini

Via Calimala 12R. ☎ **214738.**

Pollini, one of the leading leather-goods stores of Florence, offers a wide array of stylized merchandise, including shoes, suitcases, clothing, belts, and virtually anything made of leather. It's located in the monumental heart of Florence, near the Ponte Vecchio. Open Monday from 3:30 to 7:30pm, Tuesday through Friday from 9:30am to 1pm and 5:30 to 7:30pm, and on Saturday from 9:30am to 7:30pm.

MARKETS

After checking into a hotel, the most intrepid shoppers head for **piazza del Mercato Nuovo (the Straw Market),** called Il Porcellino by the Italians because of the bronze statue of a reclining wild boar there (it's a copy of the one in the Uffizi). Tourists pet its snout (which is well worn) for good luck. The market stands in the monumental heart of Florence, an easy stroll from the Palazzo Vecchio. It sells not only straw items but leather goods as well, along with an array of typically Florentine merchandise—frames, trays, hand-embroidery, table

Offbeat Shopping

Fratelli Favilli, piazza del Duomo 13R (☎ 211846), is considered the finest engraver in the city, with a specialty in signet rings. Virtually any design you bring to them can be crafted here.

Il Papiro, via Cavour 55R (☎ 215262), was said to have launched the revival of marbelized paper. From wrapping paper to desk sets, the craze continues.

Store, via dell'Oche, 9-11R (☎ 287009), is something new for Florence: a close-out discount store for designer label shopping. Discontinued designs or else fashion from some of Italy's most prestigious houses that bombed with the public are sold here. The prices aren't as low as they should be, but savvy fashion hunters will find much to clothe themselves in at a fraction of the price charged by the elegant Florentine boutiques.

Taddei, via Santa Margherita 11 (☎ 2398960), is THE place for exquisitely made leather boxes and desk accessories. This family owned and run business has been turning out quality items now into its third generation of owners.

I Maschereri, via dei Tavo Tavolini 13R (☎ 213823), is the best shop for masks which after a long sleep has become a fad again. Some of the masks are based on Florentine Renaissance patterns; others are in the Venetian commedia dell'arte style.

Alessandro Bizzarri, via della Condotta 32R (☎ 211580), is one of those musty old stores found only in Europe. It's been in business since 1842, dispensing spices and minerals, the only store of its kind in Florence. Some of its extracts and essences are based on formulas in use in the Middle Ages or Renaissance era.

Antica Farmacia del Cinghiale, piazza del Mercato Nuovo 4R (☎ 282128), in business for some three centuries, is an erboristeria, dispensing herbal teas and fragrances, along with herbal potpourris. A pharmacy is also situated here.

Cirri, via Por Santa Maria 38-40R (☎ 2396593), continues to market Florentine embroidery known for its delicacy and design. Although perhaps once considered a dying art, Cirri keeps the art of embroidery alive, with literally hundreds of beautiful designs in linen, cotton, or silk.

linens, and hand-sprayed and painted boxes in traditional designs. Open Monday through Saturday from 9am to 7pm.

However, even better bargains await those who make their way through pushcarts to the stalls of the open-air **Mercato Centrale,** in and around borgo San Lorenzo, near the railway station. If you don't mind bargaining, which is imperative here, you'll find an array of merchandise that includes raffia bags, Florentine leather purses, salt-and-pepper shakers, straw handbags, and art reproductions.

Warning: In some of these markets you may think you've found Puccis, Guccis, and Louis Vuittons selling for peanuts. You can be sure that such low-priced merchandise is imitation. Most often it is easily recognized as fake.

MOSAICS

Arte Musiva

Largo Bargellini 2–4. ☎ **241647**.

Florentine mosaics are universally recognized for their distinction. Bruno Lastrucci, the director of Arte Musiva, located in the old quarter of Santa Croce, is one of the most renowned living exponents of this art form. In the workshop you can see artisans plying their craft; some of the major mosaicists of Italy are here. In addition to traditional Florentine, modern mosaic has developed. A selection of the most significant works is permanently displayed in the gallery. These include decorative panels and tiles. Open Tuesday through Saturday from 9am to 1pm and 3 to 7pm.

PAPER & STATIONERY

Giulio Giannini & Figlio

Piazza Pitti 36–37R. ☎ **212621**.

Giulio Giannini & Figlio is the leading stationery store in Florence. Much of its merchandise is so exquisite that it's snapped up by foreigners for gift-giving later in the year. The English-speaking staff is helpful. This has been a family business for more than 140 years. Open Monday through Saturday from 9am to 7:30pm. Closes Monday in winter.

A PHARMACY

Officina Profumo Farmaceutica di Santa Maria Novella

Via della Scala 16N. ☎ **216276**.

This is perhaps the most fascinating pharmacy in Italy. Northwest of the Church of Santa Maria Novella, it opened its doors to the public in 1612, offering a selection of herbal remedies that were created by friars of the Dominican order. Those closely guarded secrets have been retained, and many of the same elixirs are still sold today. You've heard of papaya as an aid to digestion, but what about elixir of rhubarb? A wide selection of perfumes, scented soaps, shampoos, and of course potpourris, along with creams and lotions, is handsomely presented in these old-fashioned precincts, which qualify as a sightseeing attraction. Open Monday from 3:30 to 7:30pm and Tuesday through Saturday from 9:30am to 1pm and 3:30 to 7:30pm. It is also closed on Saturday afternoon in July and August.

PRINTS & ENGRAVINGS

Giovanni Baccani

Via della Vigna Nuova 75R. ☎ **214467**.

Giovanni Baccani has long been a specialist in this field. Everything it sells is old—nothing new here. "The Blue Shop," as it is called, offers a huge array of prints and engravings, often of Florentine scenes. These are found in bins, and you're free to look as long as you want. Tuscan paper goods are also sold. Open Monday from 3:30 to 7:30pm and Tuesday through Saturday from 8:30am to 1pm and 3:30 to 7:30pm (closed August).

SHOES

Salvatore Ferragamo
Via Tornabuoni 16R. ☎ **292123.**

Salvatore Ferragamo has long been one of the most famous names in shoes. Although he started in Hollywood just before the outbreak of World War I, the headquarters of this famed manufacturer were installed here in the Palazzo Ferroni, on the most fashionable shopping street of Florence, before World War II broke out. Ferragamo sells shoes for both men and women, along with some of the most elegant boutique items in the city, including scarves, handbags, and other merchandise. But chances are you'll want to visit it for its stunning shoes, known for their durability and style. Hours are Monday from 3:30 to 7:30pm and Tuesday through Saturday from 9:30am to 7:30pm.

Lily of Florence
Via Guicciardini 2R. ☎ **294748.**

Both men and women can buy shoes in American sizes at Lily of Florence. For women, Lily distributes both her own designs and other well-known names in shoes. Color comes in a wide range, the designs are stylish, and leather texture is of good quality. Open Monday through Saturday from 9:30am to 7:30pm. Closes Monday in winter.

SILVER

Pampaloni
Borgo Santi Apostoli, 47R. ☎ **289094.**

This shop is headed by Gianfranco Pampaloni, the third generation silversmith in his family. An inspired artist, he often bases designs on past achievements, for example a 1604 drinking goblet by the Roman artist Giovanni Maggi. The business was launched in 1902, and some of those classic designs turned out back then are still being made. Gianfranco doesn't live in the past, however, as he designs his own adventurous pieces and sells them to such prestigious outlets as the Rome-based jeweler Bulgari or Tiffany & Co. Open Tuesday through Saturday from 9:30am to 1pm and 3:30 to 7:30pm.

5 Florence After Dark

Evening entertainment in Florence is not an exciting prospect unless you simply like to walk through the narrow streets or head up toward Fiesole for a view of the city at night (truly spectacular). The typical Florentine begins an evening early, perhaps at one of the cafés listed below.

For theatrical and concert listings pick up a free copy of **Welcome to Florence,** available at the tourist office. This helpful publication contains information on recitals, concerts, theatrical productions, and other cultural presentations that are offered at Florence at the time of your visit.

Many cultural presentations are performed in churches. These might include open-air concerts in the cloisters of the Badia Fiesolana in Fiesole (the hill town above Florence), or at the Ospedale degli Innocenti, the foundling "hospital of the innocents" on summer evenings only.

Orchestral offerings—performed by the Regional Tuscan Orchestra—are often presented at the Church of Santo Stefano al Ponte Vecchio.

THE PERFORMING ARTS

Teatro Comunale

Corso Italia 16. ☎ **211158.** Opera tickets, 22,000–150,000 lire ($13.75–$93.75); concerts 16,000–90,000 lire ($10–$56.25).

This is the main theater in Florence, with an opera, concert, and ballet season presented from September through April. The short Florence opera season usually lasts from mid-December to mid-January only. This theater is also the major venue for the Maggio Musicale, or musical May festival of opera, ballet, concerts, and recitals, lasting from late April until July. The box office is open Tuesday through Saturday 1 to 7:30pm and one hour before the curtain.

Teatro della Pergola

Via della Pergola 18. ☎ **2479651.** Tickets 20,000–80,000 lire ($12.50–$50).

This is the major legitimate theater of Florence, but you'll have to understand Italian to appreciate most of its plays, except for opera, which is universal. Plays are performed year round except during the Maggio Musicale, when the theater becomes the setting for the many musical presentations of the festival. Performances are Tuesday through Saturday at 8:45pm.

THE CLUB & MUSIC SCENE
NIGHTCLUBS

Full-Up

Via della Vigna Vecchia 23-25R. ☎ **293006.** Cover (including one drink) 15,000–25,000 lire ($9.40–$15.65).

Contained within the cellar of an antique building in the historic heart of town, this well-known establishment attracts college students from the city's many universities, who appreciate the establishment's two-in-one format. One section contains a smallish dance floor and recorded dance music; another is devoted to the somewhat more restrained ambience of a piano bar. The place can be fun, and even older clients usually feel at ease here. Drinks cost from 10,000 lire ($6.25) to 15,000 lire ($9.40). Open Wednesday through Monday from 11pm to 4am.

ROCK

The Red Garter

Via de' Benci 33R. ☎ **234-4904.** No cover.

Perhaps nothing could be more unexpected in this city of Donatello and Michelangelo than a club called the Red Garter, right off piazza Santa Croce. The American Prohibition era lives on—in fact, it has been exported. Visitors to the Red Garter can hear a variety of music, from rock to bluegrass. The club attracts young people from all over the world. A mug of Heineken lager on tap goes for 7,000 lire ($4.40), and most tall drinks, made from "hijacked hootch," as it's known here, begin at 10,000 lire ($6.25). The club is open Monday through Thursday from 8:30pm to 1am and Friday through Sunday from 9pm to 1:30am. "Happy Hour" is every evening until 9:30pm.

Space Electronic

Via Palazzuolo 37. ☎ **293082.** Cover (including one drink) 20,000 lire ($12.50).

This club is the only disco in Florence with karaoke. On the ground floor, you can have a quiet drink singing or listening to karaoke. The decor consists of gigantic carnival heads, wall-to-wall mirrors, and an imitation space capsule that goes back and forth across the dance floor. On the upper level is a large dance floor with a wide choice of music, and the best sound-and-light show in town. This place attracts a lot of foreign women who want to hook up with Florentine men on the prowl. The disco opens nightly at 10pm (usually going until 2:30am or later, depending on business).

Yab

Via dei Sassetti 5R. ☎ **282018.** Cover Tues–Thurs 10,000 lire ($6.25); Fri–Sat 20,000 lire ($12.50).

American, British, and Italian music, live or recorded, is often presented at this long-enduring club that has a minimalist decor. Beer goes for 8,000 lire ($5), with drinks costing from 10,000 lire ($6.25). Near piazza della Repubblica, the club is open Tuesday through Saturday from 10pm to 4am.

THE BAR & CAFE SCENE
BARS & PUBS

Donatello Bar

In the Hotel Excelsior, piazza Ognissanti 3. ☎ **264201.**

The Donatello Bar, on the ground floor of this previously recommended deluxe hotel, is the city's most elegant watering hole. Named in honor of the great Renaissance artist, this bar and its adjoining restaurant, Il Cestello (see Section 2, "Dining," in the previous chapter) attracts well-heeled international visitors along with the Florentine elite from the world of culture and business. The ambience is enlivened by a marble fountain and works of art. The decor is elegant, with leather armchairs, brocaded sofas, antique polychrome works, tapestries, Chinese vases, and an abundance of fresh flowers. Piano music is featured daily from 7pm to 1am and the bar is open daily from 11am to 1:30am. Drinks cost from 10,000 lire ($6.25).

Fiddler's Elbow

Piazza Santa Maria Novella 7R. ☎ **797-514.**

After an initial success in Rome, this Irish pub has now invaded the city of Donatello and Michelangelo. It quickly became one of the most popular watering holes in Florence. An authentic pint of Guinness is the most popular item to order. The location is in the vicinity of the rail station. You can order a pint of beer for 7,000 lire ($4.40). The pub is open daily from 3pm to 1am.

CAFES

Café Rivoire

Piazza della Signoria 4R. ☎ **214412.**

Café Rivoire offers a classy and amusing old-world ambience with a direct view of the statues of one of our favorite squares in the world. You can sit at one of the metal tables set up on the flagstones outside, or at one of the tables in a choice of inner rooms filled with marble detailing and unusual oil renderings of the piazza outside. If you don't want to sit at all, try the mahogany and green-marble bar, where many of the more colorful characters making the Grand Tour of Europe talk, flirt, or gossip. A member of the staff will serve you espresso for 4,000 lire ($2.50) at a table or a long drink for 13,000 lire ($8.10). There is also a selection of small sandwiches, omelets, and ice creams. The café is noted for its hot chocolate as well. It's open Tuesday through Sunday from 8am to midnight.

Giacosa
Via Tornabuoni 83R. ☎ **239-6226.**

Giacosa is a deceptively simple-looking café whose stand-up bar occupies more space than its limited number of sit-down tables. Set behind three Tuscan arches on a fashionable shopping street in the center of the old city, it has a warmly paneled interior, a lavish display of pastries and sandwiches, and a reputation as the birthplace of the Negroni. That drink, as you probably know, is a combination of gin, Campari, and red vermouth. Other drinks served here include Singapore slings, Italian and American coffee, and a range of apéritifs. Ice cream, for which the café is famous, ranges from 6,000 lire ($3.75) to 10,000 lire ($6.25). A Negroni costs 7,000 lire ($4.40) at a counter or 12,000 lire ($7.50) at a table, with such light meals as an omelet costing 10,000 lire ($6.25) to 12,000 lire ($7.50). The café is open Monday through Saturday from 7:30am to 8:30pm.

Gilli
Piazza della Repubblica 39R. ☎ **213896.**

Gilli, said to be the oldest and most beautiful café in Florence, occupies a desirable position in the center of the city, a few minutes' walk from the Duomo. It was founded in 1733, when piazza della Repubblica had a different name. You can sit at a small, brightly lit table near the bar, or retreat to an intricately paneled pair of rooms to the side and enjoy the flattering light from the Venetian-glass chandeliers. A cappuccino costs 5,000 lire ($3.15) at a table or 1,700 lire ($1.05) if you stand at the bar. Daily specials, sandwiches, toasts, and hard drinks are sold, along with an array of "tropical" libations. Open Wednesday through Monday from 8am to midnight.

Giubbe Rosse
Piazza della Repubblica 13R. ☎ **212280.**

The waiters of this place still wear the red coats as they did when the establishment was founded in 1888. Originally a beer hall, it is today an elegantly paneled café, bar, and restaurant filled with turn-of-the-century chandeliers and polished granite floors. You can enjoy a drink or cup of coffee, which costs 4,000 lire ($2.50) at one of the small tables near the zinc-top bar. An inner dining room has a soaring vaulted ceiling of reddish brick, and an Italian menu where meals begin at 35,000 lire ($21.90). Light lunches are a specialty, as well as full American breakfasts. Open Thursday through Tuesday from 7:30am to 2am.

FILMS

Cinema Astro
Piazza San Simone, near Santa Croce. ☎ **222388.** Tickets, 8,000 lire ($5).

Across from the famous ice-cream emporium, Gelateria Vivoli, this cinema shows English-language films. The schedule changes about twice a week. It's closed Monday and in August.

GAY NIGHTLIFE

Crisco

Via S. Egidio 43R. ☎ **248-0580.** Cover 12,000–16,000 lire ($7.50–$10), depending on the night of the week.

Florence's leading gay bar caters only to men from premises within an 18th-century building that contains a bar and dance floor. Drinks cost from 8,000 lire ($5) each. Classified as a *club privato*, it's open Wednesday, Thursday, Sunday, and Monday from 10:30pm to 3:30am, Friday and Saturday from 10:30pm to 5 or 6am.

Alcatraz

Via del Pandolfini. ☎ **243356.** Cover (including the first drink) 20,000–25,000 lire ($12.50–$15.65).

Catering to gay and straight clients of both genders, this bar probably attracts the greatest percentage of lesbians of any nightclub in Florence. In summertime, the crowd gets very international, looking like a cross-section of all the nations of Europe. A beer costs 5,000 lire ($3.15). The club is open Tuesday and Thursday through Sunday from 9:30pm to 2:30am (perhaps later).

Tabasco

Piazza Santa Cecelia 3. ☎ **213000.** Cover (including one drink) 15,000–20,000 lire ($9.40–$12.50).

One of the leading gay bars of Florence, Tabasco stands near piazza della Signoria in the heart of the city. Renewed in 1989, it is open Tuesday through Sunday from 10pm to at least 3am or later on weekends. The club offers a bar, along with video games and X-rated male-action movies. You must be 18 to be admitted.

6 Easy Excursion to Fiesole

For more extensive day trips, you can refer to the next chapter. But Fiesole is a virtual suburb of Florence.

When the sun shines too hot on piazza della Signoria and tourists try to prance bare-backed into the Uffizi, Florentines are likely to head for the hills—usually to Fiesole. But they will probably encounter more tourists, as this town—once an Etruscan settlement—is the most popular outing from the city. Bus no. 7, which leaves from piazza San Marco, will take you there in 25 minutes and give you a panoramic view along the way. You'll pass fountains, statuary, and gardens strung out over the hills like a scrambled jigsaw puzzle.

WHAT TO SEE & DO

When you arrive at Fiesole, by all means don't sit with the throngs all afternoon in the central square sipping Campari (although that isn't a bad pastime). Explore some of Fiesole's attractions. You won't find anything as dazzling as the Renaissance treasures of Florence, however—the charms of Fiesole are more subtle. Fortunately, all major sights branch out within walking distance of the main piazza, beginning with the **Cattedrale di San Romolo.** At first this cathedral may seem austere, with its concrete-gray Corinthian columns and Romanesque arches. But it has its own beauty. Dating from A.D. 1000, it was much altered during the Renaissance. In the Salutati Chapel are important sculptural works by Mino da Fiesole. Hours are daily 7:30am to noon and 4 to 7pm.

Bandini Museum

Via Dupre. ☎ **59061.** Admission 3,000 lire ($1.90). Apr–Sept daily 9:30am–1pm and 3–7pm; Oct–Mar, Wed–Mon 10am–1pm and 3–6pm. Bus: 7.

This ecclesiastical museum, around to the side of the Duomo, belongs to the Fiesole Cathedral Chapter, established in 1913. On the ground floor are della Robbia terra-cotta works, as well as art by Michelangelo and Nino Pisano. On the top floors are paintings by the best Giotto students, which reflect ecclesiastical and worldly themes, most of them the work of Tuscan artists of the 14th century.

Museo Missionario Frances Cano Fiesole

Via San Francesco 13. ☎ **59175.** Admission is free (donation expected). Apr–Sept daily 10am–noon and 3–6pm; Oct–Mar daily 10am–noon and 3–5pm. Bus: 7.

The hardest task you'll have in Fiesole is to take the steep goat-climb up to the Convent of San Francesco. You can visit the Franciscan church, in the gothic style, which was built in the first years of the 1400s. The church was consecrated in 1516. Inside are many paintings by well-known Florentine artists. In the basement of the church is the ethnological museum, which is situated in six rooms. Begun in 1906, the collection has a large section of Chinese artifacts, including ancient bronzes. An Etruscan-Roman section contains some 330 archaeological pieces, and an Egyptian section also has numerous objects.

Teatro Romano e Museo Civico

Via Portigiani 1. ☎ **59477.** Admission 6,000 lire ($3.75). Apr–Sept daily 9am–7pm; Oct and Mar, Tues–Sun 9am–6pm; Nov–Feb, Wed–Mon 9am–5pm. Bus: 7.

On this site is the major surviving evidence that Fiesole was an Etruscan city six centuries before Christ, and later a Roman town. In the 1st century B.C. a theater was built, the restored remains of which you can see today. Near the theater are the skeletonlike ruins of the baths, which may have been built at the same time. Try to visit the Etruscan-Roman museum, with its many interesting finds that date from the days when Fiesole—not Florence—was supreme (a guide is on hand to show you through).

WHERE TO STAY
VERY EXPENSIVE

Villa San Michele

Via Doccia 4, Fiesole, 50014 Firenze. ☎ **055/59451.** Fax 055/598734. 26 rms, 10 suites. A/C TEL. 920,000–1,140,000 lire ($575–$712.50) double; 1,580,000–1,850,000 lire ($987.50–$1,156.25) suite. Rates include half-board. AE, DC, MC, V. Free parking. Closed mid-Nov to mid-Mar. Bus: 7.

Villa San Michele is an ancient monastery of unsurpassed beauty—the setting is memorable, even breathtaking. On a hill just below Fiesole, a 15-minute walk south of the center, and complete with gardens, the monastery was built in the 15th century on a wide ledge. After being damaged in World War II, the villa was carefully restored. It is said that the facade and the loggia were designed by Michelangelo. A curving driveway, lined with blossoming trees and flowers, leads to the entrance. A 10-arch covered loggia continues around the view side of the building to the Italian gardens at the rear. On the loggia, chairs are set out for drinks and moonlight dinners. Most of the bedrooms open onto the view, or the inner courtyard. Each room is unique, all with private baths, some with iron or wooden canopy beds, antique chests, Savonarola chairs, formal draperies, old ecclesiastical paintings, candelabra, and statues—in other words, a stunning tour de force of rich but restrained design. TV and minibar are available upon request. Poets and artists have stayed at the San Michele and sung its praise.

MODERATE

Hotel Aurora

Piazza Mino da Fiesole 39, Fiesole, 50014 Firenze. ☎ **055/59100.** Fax 055/59587. 26 rms. A/C MINIBAR TV TEL. 265,000–326,000 lire ($165.65–$203.75) double. Rates include breakfast. AE, DC, MC, V. Free parking. Bus: 7.

Set on the Fiesole's main square, behind a facade of green shutters and ochre-colored stucco, Aurora occupies a structure built in the 18th century as a private house. In 1890, it became a hotel that catered almost exclusively to arts-conscious English people making their grand tour through the historic cities of Italy. The hotel continues to rent rooms, which have been modernized and simplified to meet today's needs. Views over faraway Florence are visible from the hotel's back bedrooms, which cost more than those overlooking the piazza in front. On the premises is a back terrace with hanging vines, a pergola, and views of the city. There's also a high, beamed reception area, a restaurant, and functional furniture throughout. Interconnecting doors can be opened between some rooms to create a pair of suites, which cost around 650,000 lire ($406.25) each.

INEXPENSIVE

Pensione Bencista

Via Benedetto de Maiano 4, Fiesole, 50014 Firenze. ☎ **055/59163.** Fax 055/59163. 44 rms (32 with bath). TEL. 105,000 lire ($65.65) per person without bath; 125,000 lire ($78.15) per person with bath. Rates include half-board. No credit cards. Free parking. Bus: 7.

Pensione Bencista has been the family villa of the Simoni family for years. It was built around 1300, with an addition made to the existing building about every 100 years after that. In 1925 Paolo Simoni opened the villa to paying guests. Today it is run by his son, Simone Simoni. Its position, high up on the road to Fiesole, is commanding, with an unmarred view of the city and the hillside villas. The driveway to the formal entrance, with its circular fountain, winds through olive trees. The widely spread-out villa has many lofty old rooms—unspoiled and furnished with family antiques. The bedrooms vary in size and interest; many are without bath and have hot and cold running water only. In chilly weather, guests meet each other in the evening in front of a huge fireplace. The Bencista is suitable for parents who might want to leave their children in the country while they take jaunts into the city. It's a 10-minute bus ride from the heart of Florence.

WHERE TO DINE

Trattoria le Cave di Maiano

Via delle Cave 16. ☎ **59133.** Reservations required. Main courses 20,000–24,000 lire ($12.50–$15). AE, DC, MC, V. Fri–Wed noon–3pm; Mon–Wed and Fri–Sat 7:30–10pm. Closed Aug 10–20. Bus: 7. TUSCAN.

This restaurant, at Maiano, is a 15-minute ride east from the heart of Florence and just a short distance south of Fiesole. It's a family-run establishment, which since the 17th century has been an esoteric address to discerning Florentines. It's imperative, incidentally, that you reserve a table before heading here. The rustically decorated trattoria is a garden restaurant, with stone tables and large sheltering trees, which create a setting for the excellent cooking. Inside, the restaurant is in the tavern style, with a beamed ceiling. I recommend highly the antipasto and the homemade green tortellini. For a main course, there is a golden grilled chicken or perhaps a savory herb-flavored roast lamb. For side dishes, I suggest fried polenta, Tuscan beans, and fried potatoes. As a final treat, the waiter will bring you homemade ice cream with fresh raspberries.

10 Siena, Pisa & the Hill Towns

The hill towns of Tuscany and Umbria are prized not only for their essential beauty (for example, the unspoiled medieval severity in the heart of Siena and San Gimignano)—but for their spectacular art treasures, created by such "hometown boys" as Leonardo da Vinci. From Florence, you can explore numerous nearby cities, including Pisa and Siena, as well as San Gimignano with its medieval towers.

And if you're traveling between Rome and Florence, why not veer off the autostrada and visit a string of other hill towns, such as Spoleto and Perugia, that preserve the past? The joy of Tuscany is that almost any corner of its varied and beautiful landscape harbors some natural or man-made treasure.

A DRIVING TOUR

Day 1   From Florence head west to the sea for a visit to Pisa, with its famous Leaning Tower and Duomo. Even though you can no longer climb the tower, Pisa with its many attractions merits an overnight stopover. If your wallet's full, dine at Sergio on the banks of the Arno.

Day 2   Travel southeast for a visit to San Gimignano, ringed by three sets of historic walls and known for its medieval towers. No cars are allowed within the city walls. Most of the sights can be covered in a day, and San Gimignano is one of the most romantic stopovers in the province.

☕ **TAKE A BREAK**   Pizzeria Perucà, via XX Settembre 4 (☎ 941845), in San Gimignano has only three tables, although you can order take-out slices to go for 2,000 lire ($1.25) and up. A specialty is calzone alla casa, which is covered with mushrooms, mozzarella, fresh vegetables, and prosciutto. Hours are Friday through Wednesday from noon to 3pm and 4 to 9:30pm.

Day 3   Go in the direction of Poggibonsi and cut south to Sienna, the highlight of the driving tour, one of the world's best preserved medieval cities. For a view of the city (before exploring it) go to the top of the Toree del Mangia, next to the Palazzo Comunale. Visit the Duomo, the Battistero, and the Cathedral Museum, and most definitely the Pinacoteca Nazionale. Siena is rich in many other

What's Special About Siena, Pisa & the Hill Towns

Great Towns/Villages
- Siena, which after the incomparable Florence contains the richest artistic heritage in Italy.
- Assisi, the birthplace of St. Francis of Assisi in 1182.
- Pisa, a once-great maritime port on the Arno—now visited for its leaning tower, Duomo, and Baptistery.
- San Gimignano, called the "Manhattan of Tuscany," containing some one dozen of its original 72 medieval towers.

Museums
- The Pinacoteca Nazionale, Siena, containing the collection of the Sienese school of painting that once rivaled that of Florence.
- The National Gallery of Umbria, Perugia, housing the more comprehensive collection of Umbrian art from the 13th up to the 18th century.

Religious Shrine
- Il Duomo, Siena, dating from the 13th century, with a zebralike interior of black and white stripes.

Ace Attraction
- The Leaning Tower of Pisa, dangerously tilting as the world waits for what may be inevitable.

Festival
- July's Palio della Contrade, at Siena, a historical pageant and horse-racing tournament.

sights, and you may not have time for everything if you're limited to only one night.

☕ **TAKE A BREAK** Victoria Caffè Tea Room, 130 via di Città (☎ 46720), in Siena is the city's finest tea room. But it's more than that, in that you can order meals, ice cream, various snacks, even champagne. The ambience is cozy and comfortable, with wicker furnishings.

Day 4 Head southeast along E78 crossing the autostrada between Florence and Rome and follow the signs to the ancient city of Perugia, where you'll want to stay overnight. The regional capital of Umbria is rich in sights—notably its piazza IV Novembre and its Galleria Nazionale dell'Umbria.

Day 5 Head southeast to Assisi to see some of its major attractions, including the Temple of Minerva and the Basilica di San Francesco. However, instead of anchoring there for the night, as most visitors do, head south to Spoleto for the night. Have a good dinner (with truffles) and wander at leisure that night around this too often neglected art city (except at festival time).

FOOD & WINE

Tuscan grain and olive oil are said to be the finest in Italy, and centuries of stock-breeding have created Tuscan beef from which comes the fabled Florentine steak, praised by gourmets as among the finest in the world. Although Tuscan cuisine has its detractors, many food critics claim that local chefs take the ordinary dish and make it sublime by the use of such basic materials as incomparable olive oil, the tenderest of meat, and excellent wines.

One early visitor said all the Florentines "eat is tripe and entrails." Tripe remains a favorite dish (it's most often stewed in a meat sauce with spices and tomatoes). The Tuscan steak is a thick cut of tender beef grilled over coal and soft-wood embers and seasoned with olive oil, salt and pepper. Other notable dishes include *fagioli al fiasco* (beans boiled in a flash so that none of their substance might be lost, and then dressed with uncooked olive oil, salt and pepper). Game dishes are often featured, including *pappardella alla lepre*, pasta with a strong ragoût of hare giblets. First and foremost among the wines is Chianti classico, with its lively ruby color and mellow flavor, with a bouquet of violets. The most notable Chiantis are from Coltibono and Brolio.

A wine that has no rivals with roasts *is vino nobile di Montepulciano*, so ruby red it's almost purple, with a rich rugged body. Like certain Chiantis, it has a perfume of violets as it ages. Tuscany also produces white wines, including Ugolino, a pale straw-yellow in color, with a refined bouquet and pleasing flavor, which is served with fish.

1 Siena

21 miles S of Florence, 143 miles NW of Rome

After visiting Florence, it's altogether fitting, certainly bipartisan, to call on what has been labeled in the past its natural enemy. In Rome we saw classicism and the baroque; in Florence, the Renaissance; but in the walled city of Siena we stand solidly planted back in the Middle Ages. On three sienna-colored hills in the center of Tuscany, "Sena Vetus" lies in chianti country. Perhaps preserving its original character more markedly than any other city in Italy, it is a showplace of the Italian Gothic.

William Dean Howells, the American novelist (*The Rise of Silas Lapham*), called Siena "not a monument but a light." Regrettably too often visited on a quick day's excursion, Siena is a city of contemplation and profound exploration. It is characterized by gothic palaces, almond-eyed madonnas, aristocratic mansions, letter-writing St. Catherine (patron saint of Italy), narrow streets, and medieval gates, walls, and towers.

Although such a point of view may be heretical, one can almost be grateful that Siena lost its battle with Florence. Had it continued to expand and change after reaching the zenith of its power in the 14th century, chances are it would be markedly different now, influenced by the rising tides of the Renaissance and the baroque (represented today only in a small degree). But Siena retained its uniqueness (certain Sienese painters were still showing the influence of Byzantium in the late 15th century).

ESSENTIALS

GETTING THERE   By Plane   Fly either to Florence's Peretola Airport or Pisa's Galileo Galilei Airport.

By Train   Trains arrive hourly from both Florence and Pisa.

By Bus   TRA-IN, piazza San Domenico 1 (☎ 0577/204201), in Siena, offers bus service to all of Tuscany, with air-conditioned coaches. The one-way cost between Florence and Siena is 10,000 lire ($6.25) per person.

Siena, Pisa & The Hill Towns

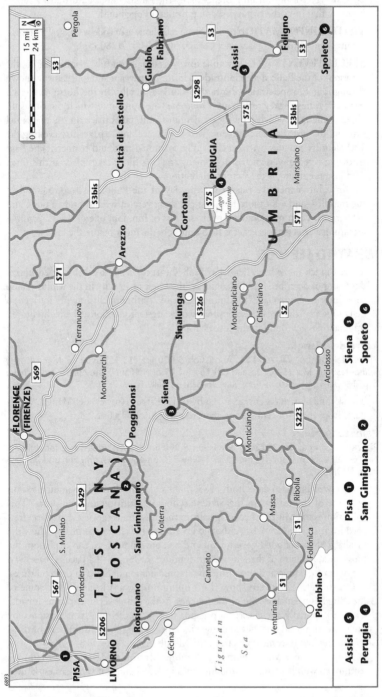

Pisa **1**
San Gimignano **2**
Siena **3**
Spoleto **6**

Assisi **5**
Perugia **4**

By Car   Head south from Florence along the Firenze-Siena autostrada, a super-highway that links the two cities, going through Poggibonsi.

VISITOR INFORMATION   The Siena telephone area code is 0577. The tourist information office is at piazza del Campo 56 (☎ 0577/280551).

SPECIAL EVENTS   The best time to visit is usually on July 2 or August 16, the occasions of the **Palio delle Contrade,** a historical pageant and tournament known throughout Europe, which draws thousands annually. In the horse race, each bareback-riding jockey represents a *contrada* (the wards into which the city is divided). The race, which requires tremendous skill, takes place on the piazza del Campo, the historic heart of Siena. Before the race, much pageantry evoking the 15th century parades by, with colorfully costumed men and banners. The flag-throwing ceremony, depicted in so many travelog films, takes place at this time. And just as enticing is the victory celebration.

Don't buy expensive tickets for the day of the Palio. It's free to stand in the middle—and a lot more fun. Just get there very early, and bring a book and a Thermos. For a memorable dinner and lots of fun, join one of the 17 *contrade* attending a *cena* (supper) that is held outdoors the night before the race.

WHAT TO SEE & DO

There's much to see here. Let's start in the heart of Siena, the shell-shaped **piazza del Campo,** described by Montaigne as "the finest of any city in the world." Pause to enjoy the *Fonte Gaia,* the fountain of joy, with embellishments by Jacopo della Quercia (the present sculptured works are reproductions; the badly beaten original ones are found in the town hall).

Torre del Mangia

Piazza del Campo. ☎ **292111.** Admission 5,000 lire ($3.15). Nov 15–Mar 14 daily 10am–1:30pm; Mar 15–Apr 15 and Oct 16–Nov 15 daily 10am–5pm; Apr 16–June 15 and Sept 16–Oct 15 daily 10am–6pm; June 16–Sept 15 daily 10am–7pm.

The skyline of Siena is characterized by its lithe Torre (tower) del Mangia, which dates from the 14th century and soars to a height of 335 feet.

Palazzo Pubblico

Piazza del Campo. ☎ **292263.** Admission 6,000 lire ($3.75) adults, free for children. Nov 6–Feb daily 9:30am–1:30pm; Mar 1–Nov 5, Mon–Sat 9am–7pm, Sun and holidays 9am–1:30pm.

The Palazzo Pubblico dates from 1288–1309 and is filled with important artworks by some of the leaders in the Sienese school of painting and sculpture. This collection is the Museo Civico. Upstairs in the museum is the Sala della Pace, frescoed from 1337 to 1339 by Ambrogio Lorenzetti; the allegorical frescoes show the idealized effects of good government and bad government. In this depiction, the most notable figure of the Virtues surrounding the king is "La Pace" (Peace). To the right of the king and the Virtues is a representation of Siena in peaceful times.

On the left, Lorenzetti showed his opinion of "ward heelers," but some of the sting has been taken out of the frescoes, as the evil-government scene is badly damaged. Actually, these were propaganda frescoes in their day, commissioned by the party in power, but they are now viewed as among the most important of all secular frescoes to come down from the Middle Ages.

In the Sala del Mappomondo is Simone Martini's *Majesty,* the Madonna enthroned with her Child, surrounded by angels and saints. It is his earliest-known documented work (ca. 1315). The other remarkable Martini fresco (on the opposite wall) is the equestrian portrait of Guidoriccio da Fogliano, general of the Sienese Republic, in ceremonial dress.

✪ Il Duomo

Piazza del Duomo. ☎ **283048.** Admission is free. Nov–Mar 16 daily 7:30am–1:30pm and 2:30pm–sunset; Mar 17–Oct daily 7:30am–7:30pm.

At piazza del Duomo, directly southeast of piazza del Campo, stands an architectural fantasy. With its colored bands of marble, the Sienese cathedral is an original and exciting building, erected in the romanesque and Italian gothic styles and dating from the 12th century. The dramatic facade—designed in part by Giovanni Pisano—dates from the 13th century, as does the romanesque bell tower.

The zebralike interior, with its black-and-white stripes, is equally stunning. The floor consists of various embedded works of art, many of which are roped off to preserve the richness in design, which depict both biblical and mythological subjects. Numerous artists worked on the floor, notably Domenico Beccafumi. For most of the year, a large part of the cathedral floor is covered to protect it.

The octagonal 13th-century pulpit is by Niccolo Pisano (Giovanni's father), who was one of the most significant Italian sculptors before the dawn of the Renaissance (see his pulpit in the Baptistery at Pisa). The Siena pulpit is considered his masterpiece; it reveals in relief such scenes as the slaughter of the innocents and the Crucifixion. The elder Pisano finished the pulpit in 1268, aided by his son and other artists. Its pillars are supported by four marble lions, again reminiscent of the Pisano pulpit at Pisa.

In the chapel of the left transept (near the library) is a glass-enclosed box with an arm that tradition maintains is John the Baptist's, used to baptize Christ, and Donatello's bronze of John the Baptist. To see another Donatello work in bronze—a bishop's gravemarker—look at the floor in the chapel to the left of the pulpit's stairway. Some of the designs for the inlaid wooden stalls in the apse were by Riccio. A representational blue starry sky twinkles overhead.

Libreria Piccolomini

Inside Il Duomo, piazza del Duomo. ☎ **283048.** Admission 2,000 lire ($1.25). Mar 16–Oct 31 daily 9am–7:30pm; Nov–Mar 15 daily 10am–1pm and 2:30–5pm. Closed Dec 25 and Jan 1.

Founded by Cardinal Francesco Piccolomini (later Pius III) to honor his uncle (Pius II), the library inside Il Duomo is renowned for its cycle of frescoes by the Umbrian master Pinturicchio. His frescoes are well preserved, even though they date from the early 16th century. In Vasari's words, the panels illustrate "the history of Pope Pius II from birth to the minute of his death." Raphael's alleged connection with the frescoes, if any, is undocumented. In the center is an exquisite *Three Graces*, a Roman copy of a 3rd-century B.C. Greek work from the school of Praxiteles.

Museo Dell'Opera Metropolitana

Piazza del Duomo 8. ☎ **283048.** Admission 5,000 lire ($3.15). Mar 16–Sept daily 9am–7:30pm; Oct daily 9am–6pm; Nov–Mar 15 daily 9am–1:30pm. Closed Dec 25–Jan 1.

This museum housing paintings and sculptures originally created for the cathedral deserves some attention. On the ground floor you'll find much interesting sculpture, including works by Giovanni Pisano and his assistants. But the real draw hangs on the next floor in the Sala di Duccio: his fragmented *La Maestà*, a

Madonna enthroned, painted from 1308 to 1311. The panel was originally an altarpiece by Duccio di Buoninsegna for the cathedral, filled with dramatic moments that illustrate the story of Christ and the Madonna. A student of Cimabue's, Duccio was the first great name in the school of Sienese painting. In the rooms upstairs are the collections of the treasury, and on the very top floor is a display of paintings from the early Sienese school.

Battistero

Piazza San Giovanni. ☎ **283048.** Admission 3,000 lire ($1.90). Mar 16–Sept daily 9am–7:30pm; Oct daily 9am–6pm; Nov–Mar 15 daily 10am–1pm and 2:30–5pm. Closed Dec 25 and Jan 1.

The facade of the Baptistery dates from the 14th century. In the center of the interior is the baptismal font by Jacopo della Quercia, which contains some bas-reliefs by Donatello and Ghiberti.

Pinacoteca Nazionale (Picture Gallery)

In the Palazzo Buonsignori, via San Pietro 29. ☎ **281161.** Admission 8,000 lire ($5) adults, free for children. Mon 8:30am–1:30pm; Tues–Sat 9am–7pm; Sun 8am–1pm. Bus: 3.

Housed in the 14th-century palazzo near piazza del Campo is the national gallery's collection of the Sienese school of painting, which once rivaled that of Florence. Displayed here are some of the giants of the pre-Renaissance. Most of the paintings cover the period from the late 12th century to the mid-16th century.

The principal treasures are on the second floor, where you'll contemplate the artistry of Duccio in the early salons. The gallery is rich in the art of the two Lorenzetti brothers, Ambrogio and Pietro, who painted in the 14th century. Ambrogio is represented by an *Annunciation* and a *Crucifix*, but one of his most celebrated works, carried out with consummate skill, is an almond-eyed *Madonna and Bambino* surrounded by saints and angels. Pietro's most important entry here is an altarpiece—*The Madonna of the Carmine*—made for a church in Siena in 1329. Simone Martini's *Madonna and Child* is damaged but one of the best-known paintings here.

In the salons to follow are works by Giovanni di Paolo (*Presentation at the Temple*) and Sano di Pietro, who seemed to have had an eternal fixation on the Madonna and Child. In one room is a masterpiece of Giovanni Antonio Bazzi (called "Il Sodoma," allegedly because of his sexual interests). It's a picture of Christ at a column, a work of such plastic quality it almost qualified for publication in a body-beautiful magazine.

Santuario e Casa di Santa Caterina (St. Catherine's Sanctuary)

Costa di S. Antonio. ☎ **280330.** Admission is free, but an offering is expected. Mon–Sat and holidays 9am–12:30pm and 3:30–6pm.

Of all the personalities associated with Siena, the most enduring legend surrounds that of St. Catherine, acknowledged by Pius XII in 1939 as the patron saint of Italy. The mystic, who was the daughter of a dyer, was born in 1347 in Siena. She was instrumental in persuading the papacy to return to Rome from Avignon. The house where she lived, between piazza del Campo and San Domenico, has now been turned into a sanctuary—it's really a church and oratory, with many works of art, located where her father had his dyeworks. Nearby at the 13th-century Basilica of St. Domenico is a chapel dedicated to St. Catherine, frescoed by Il Sodoma.

Enoteca Italica Permanente

Fortezza Medicea, viale Maccari. ☎ **288497.** Admission is free. Daily noon–midnight.

Owned and operated by the Italian government, Enoteca Italica Permanente, which serves as a showcase for the finest wines of Italy, would whet the palate of even the most demanding wine devotee. An unusual architectural setting is designed to show bottles to their best advantage. The establishment lies just outside the entrance to an old fortress, at the bottom of an inclined ramp, behind a massive arched doorway. Marble bas-reliefs and wrought-iron sconces, along with regional ceramics, are set into the high brick walls of the labyrinthine corridors, the vaults of which were built by Cosimo dei Medici in 1560. On the premises are several sunny terraces for outdoor wine tasting, an indoor stand-up bar, and voluminous lists of available vintages, which are for sale either by the glass, from 2,500 lire ($1.55), or by the bottle. Count yourself lucky if the bartender will agree to open an iron gate for access to the subterranean wine exposition. There, in the lowest part of the fortress, carpenters have built illuminated display racks containing bottles of recent vintages.

Spectacle of Violence

Like the Spanish bullfight, Siena's major event of the year, its Palio della Contrade (see Calendar of Events, Chapter 3) is coming under increasing fire for its brutality. For the event, the temperature in town rises higher than the blistering Tuscan sun. All the pomp and ritual of the Middle Ages live again, as heralds, child drummers, flag-bearers, and Renaissance costumes evoke the pomp of the festival.

Three days before the big race, trial races are held, the final trial on the morning of the event. Siena is divided into 17 *contrade,* or wards, and each district—identified by its characteristic colors—competes. However, because the site of the event, Il Campo, will hold only 10 contrade, wards are chosen by lot. Young partisans, flaunting the colors of their contrade, race through the medieval streets of Siena in packs. Food and wine are bountifully served on the streets of each contrada on the eve of the race.

The event could easily be considered all in good fun, except some partisans take it too seriously. There have been kidnappings of the most skilled jockeys before the race. Bribery has been reported as commonplace. So fiercely competitive is the race that all that seems to remain taboo is the sabotaging of the horse's reins.

During the race jockeys have been known to unseat the competition, although a horse without a rider is allowed to win. The event has been cited for its cruelty to animals, as horses are sometimes impaled by guardrails along the track. TV cameras move in on the gore, capturing live the spurting blood as a horse collides with the rail. Jockeys have been caught on camera kicking the horses. In theory, riders are supposed to alternate whip strokes between their mounts and the competitors.

The crowd screams with an excitment unheard in Italy since gladiators battled lions in the Roman Colosseum.

One local Siennese who has attended 30 different Palios said, "winning, not sportsmanship, is the only thing that's important. There are rules, but we Italians never bother to worry about rules. Instead of a horse race, you might call the event a rat race."

WHERE TO STAY

You'll *definitely* need hotel reservations if you're here in summer for the Palio. Make them far in advance, and secure your room with a deposit.

VERY EXPENSIVE

✪ Certosa di Maggiano

Strada di Certosa 82, 53100 Siena. ☎ **0577/288180.** Fax 0577/288189. 5 rms, 12 suites. A/C MINIBAR TV TEL. 500,000 lire ($312.50) double; 640,000–820,000 lire ($400–$512.50) suite. Breakfast 35,000 lire ($21.90) extra. AE, DC, MC, V. Free parking outside, garage 40,000 lire ($25). Bus: Pollicino 6.

Certosa di Maggiano had been lying in dusty disrepair until 1975, when Anna Grossi Recordati renovated it and began attracting some of the world's social luminaries into its 700-year-old interior. It was built as a monastery by Certosinian monks in the early 13th century, and they maintained their vegetable gardens in an area just beyond the stone walls. These have been transformed into elegant gardens dotted with old masonry, flowering shrubs, and arcaded terraces. The public rooms fill the spaces between what used to be the ambulatory of the central courtyard, and include a stylish and plush collection of intimately proportioned gathering places (including a re-creation of a Renaissance library), filled with antiques and old masonry. A medieval church with a separate entrance adjoins the hotel and still holds mass on Sunday. The entire hotel contains only 17 accommodations, one of which has a private walled garden. It's filled with lighthearted summer furniture, and has attracted such guests as the late Richard Burton, the prime minister of Austria, and the president of Italy. On warm days, breakfast is served in the courtyard, within sight of the ancient well, which adds a decorative note to the otherwise severe stonework. The hotel is not easy to find; it's set away from the center of town on a narrow road barely wide enough for two cars. You might phone for directions before you set out, although the city has made efforts to post signs for general directions.

Dining/Entertainment: The vaulted dining room contains seven tables, a marble fireplace, and entire walls of modern ceramics. It's open to nonresidents who make a reservation. Lunch costs 80,000–110,000 lire ($50–$68.75); dinner 100,000–160,000 lire ($62.50–$100). Beverages are extra.

Services: Room service, guide service, massages, babysitting.

Facilities: Heliport, tennis courts, swimming pool.

EXPENSIVE

Park Hotel Siena

Via di Marciano 18, 53100 Siena. ☎ **0577/44803.** Fax 0577/49020. 63 rms, 6 suites. A/C MINIBAR TV TEL. 380,000 lire ($237.50) double; from 750,000 lire ($468.75) suite. Breakfast 23,000 lire ($14.40) extra. AE, DC, MC, V. Free parking. Bus: Hotel shuttle bus to center.

This is a luxurious hotel whose physical plant was originally commissioned in 1530 by one of Siena's most famous Renaissance architects. The building was transformed into a hotel around the turn of the century by a scion of one of Siena's wealthiest families, and has remained a leading hotel ever since. A difficult access road leads around a series of hairpin turns (watch the signs carefully) to a buff-colored villa set with a view over green trees and suburbanite houses about a 12-minute drive (1¹/₂ miles) southwest of the city center. The landscaped swimming pool, double-glazed windows, upholstered walls, and plush carpeting have set new standards around here. The hotel is well tended, with stylish modern decoration, and a comfortably furnished series of public salons.

Dining/Entertainment: Meals in the hotel restaurant might include wild mushroom salad with black truffles, tortellini with spinach and ricotta, and a regularly featured series of regional dishes from Tuscany, Umbria, or Emilia-Romagna. Prices begin at 65,000 lire ($40.65).

Services: Room service, laundry, valet.

Facilities: Swimming pool, public salons, two tennis courts.

MODERATE

Jolly Hotel Excelsior

Piazza La Lizza, 53100 Siena. ☎ **0577/288448.** Fax 0577/41272. 123 rms, 3 suites. A/C MINIBAR TV TEL. 252,300 lire ($157.70) double; 454,200 lire ($283.90) suite. Rates include breakfast. AE, DC, MC, V. Parking 35,000 lire ($21.90).

Set in the commercial center of the newer section of Siena, near the sports stadium, this hotel is a distinguished member of a nationwide chain. Originally built as the Excelsior Hotel in the 1880s, and completely renovated about a century later, the hotel is sheltered behind an imposing red-brick facade set with neoclassical stone trim. The high-ceilinged lobby is stylishly Italian, with terra-cotta accents and white columns, plus an illuminated bar set up at the far end. The bedrooms offer modern furniture, a trim monochromatic color scheme, and many conveniences.

Dining/Entertainment: A restaurant is on the premises, serving both regional and international dishes. Decorated in a modern style, it serves meals that begin at 52,000 lire ($32.50).

Services: Room service, laundry, valet, babysitting.

Villa Scacciapensieri

Via di Scacciapensieri 10, 53100 Siena. ☎ **0577/41441.** Fax 0577/270854. 26 rms, 5 suites. A/C MINIBAR TV TEL. 260,000–310,000 lire ($162.50–$193.75) double; 380,000 lire ($237.50) suite. Rates include breakfast. AE, DC, MC, V. Free parking. Closed Jan–Feb. Bus: 8 or 12 into Siena (an 8-minute ride) every 15 minutes.

This is one of the lovely old villas of Tuscany, where you can stay in a personal atmosphere. The hostess, Mrs. Emma Nardi, opened her hotel in the summer of 1934, and it is still run by her family. Standing on the crest of a hill, about two miles from Siena, the villa is approached by a private driveway under shade trees. The bedrooms vary widely in style and comfort, and your opinion of this hotel may depend on your room assignment.

Dining/Entertainment: A Tuscan and Italian cuisine is served in the informal restaurant, Altri Tempi. You can dine here Thursday through Tuesday for 55,000 lire ($34.40), but it's advisable to call and make a reservation.

Services: Room service, laundry, valet, babysitting.

Facilities: A handsomely landscaped swimming pool, tennis court.

INEXPENSIVE

Albergo Chiusarelli

Via Curtatone 15, 53100 Siena. ☎ **0577/280562.** Fax 0577/27177. 50 rms (472 with bath). TV TEL. 111,000 lire ($69.40) double with bath; 149,300 lire ($93.30) triple with bath. Breakfast 12,000 lire ($7.50) extra. MC, V. Bus: 3.

Albergo Chiusarelli is housed in an ochre-colored building with Ionic columns and Roman caryatids supporting a second-floor loggia. It looks much older, but the building was constructed in 1870. The interior has been almost completely renovated into a functional format that includes a modern bath and electric hairdryer in each room. The hotel is just at the edge of the old city, and is convenient to the parking areas at the sports stadium a five-minute walk away. A bar and restaurant on the basement level serve full meals for around 30,000 lire ($18.75) and up.

⑤ Castagneto Hotel

Via del Cappuccini 39, 53100 Siena. ☎ **0577/45103.** 11 rms (all with bath or shower). TV TEL. 140,000 lire ($87.50) double. Breakfast 15,000 lire ($9.40) extra. No credit cards. Free parking. Closed Dec 10–Dec 23 and Jan 10–Mar 15. Bus: 1.

Set on a low hill commanding a view over Siena, about a mile northwest of the center, this modestly proportioned brick villa was built in the 1700s as a farmhouse for a family of local landowners. Today, it's a hotel maintained by the Franchoni brothers, and is set behind a gravel-covered parking lot near a garden with birds, vines, and trees. It was renovated into a hotel in 1973, and contains simple, unpretentious rooms in clean and functional working order. Only doubles are available, although single travelers are often accepted at the rate quoted above.

Garden Hotel

Via Custoza 2, 53100 Siena. ☎ **0577/47056.** Fax 0577/46050. 136 rms (all with bath or shower). TV TEL. 88,000–168,000 lire ($55–$105) single; 120,000–230,000 lire ($75–$143.75) double. Rates include breakfast. AE, DC, MC, V. Free parking. Bus: 6.

The Garden Hotel is a well-styled country house, built by a Sienese aristocrat in the 16th century. On the edge of the city, high up on the ledge of a hill, it commands a view of Siena and the surrounding countryside that has been the subject of many a painting. The hotel stands formal and serene, with an entrance on the garden side and a long avenue of clipped hedges. There's a luxurious sense of space and an aura of freshness. Some of the rooms are in the old villa, and the others in adjoining buildings. One hundred rooms contain a minibar and 60 are air-conditioned. An enjoyable spot for morning coffee is the breakfast room, with its flagstone floor, decorated ceiling, and view of the hills. You can take your other meals in an open-air restaurant on the premises. There's also a swimming pool open June through September.

⑤ Palazzo Ravizza

Pian dei Mantellini 34, 53100 Siena. ☎ **0577/280462.** Fax 0577/271370. 30 rms (21 with bath), 3 suites. TEL. 132,000–160,000 lire ($82.50–$100) per person. Rates include half-board. AE, DC, MC, V. Parking 35,000 lire ($21.90). Bus: 3.

Palazzo Ravizza is an old-fashioned place that appeals to some traditionalists. A first-class pensione in Siena, it's really a palace, within walking distance of the major attractions. In the front is a formal facade, in the rear a terraced garden with shade trees and benches for viewing the sweeping countryside. For years the home of great Tuscan families, it's owned and managed by people who have not allowed modernization, except for the installation of water basins and a few private baths. The bedrooms, each with a different personality, utilize old furniture. The living room and drawing rooms of the second floor are furnished with antiques, including a grand piano. The pensione accepts guests only on the half-board plan.

NEARBY PLACES TO STAY

✪ Relais la Suvera

Pievescola, Val d'Elsa, 53030 Siena. ☎ **0577/960300.** Fax 0577/960220. 11 rms, 10 junior suites, 13 suites. A/C MINIBAR TV TEL. 300,000 lire ($187.50) double; 400,000–500,000 lire ($250–$312.50) suite. Rates include breakfast. AE, DC, MC, V. Free parking. Closed Nov 1–Mar 30.

One of the most talked about and glamorous hideaways in Italy, with links to some of the pivotal characters in medieval and Renaissance history, La Suvera opened its doors to the hotel-going public in 1989. Surrounded by fields and its own vine-yards, and named after the region (La Suvera) it occupies, the compound lies about 17 miles northwest of Siena and 36 miles south of Florence, near the village of Pievescola.

It was mentioned in a document during the 1100s as one of northern Italy's most important strongholds. In 1507, the Republic of Siena raised enough money to buy the fortress and its extensive acreage from two intensely competitive local families as a gift for the then-pope, Julius II delle Rovere. Julius II, best known as the on-again, off-again patron of Michelangelo, retained the original medieval fortress as a core, but transformed its design into that of a Renaissance villa with the help of Sienese architect Baldassare Peruzzi.

The bedrooms are scattered among three different buildings, which include a converted horse stable and a medieval olive press. Each contains a remark-able sprinkling of antiques, contemporary bathrooms, and all the modern con-veniences.

Dining/Entertainment: The establishment's restaurant, L'Oliviera, serves simple lunches (outdoors, if possible) and elegantly formal dinners every evening from 8 to 10:30pm for 60,000 to 70,000 lire ($37.50 to $43.75) and up, per person. (The resident chefs, both of them highly creative women, are both gradu-ates of Paris's Cordon Bleu, and mingle classic Tuscan recipes with modern Italian cuisine.) There's also an elegant in-house bar with a billiard table and furnishings suitable for entertaining a pope.

Services: Room service, valet, laundry, and a tactful concierge staff well-versed in the art of obtaining almost anything.

Facilities: Prefaced with an antique wrought-iron aviary, the grounds contain a private baroque chapel for weddings; tiers of terraced gardens with ample statuary and a swimming pool; tennis court, sauna, and Turkish bath. The on-site confer-ence facilities are among the most elegant in the region.

Villa Belvedere

Belvedere, 53034 Colle di Val d'Elsa Siena. ☎ **0577/920966.** Fax 0577/924128. 15 rms. TEL. 240,000 lire ($150) double. Rates include half-board. AE, DC, MC, V. Free parking. Exit the autostrada from Florence at Colle di Val d'Elsa and follow the signs.

Villa Belvedere, about 7^1/$_2$ miles from Siena and halfway to San Gimignano, occupies a structure built in 1795. In 1820 it was the residence of Ferdinand III, Archduke of Austria and Grand Duke of Tuscany, and in 1845 of Grand Duke Leopold II. Surrounded by a large park, with a swimming pool, the hotel has bar service, a garden with a panorama, and elegant dining rooms, where typical Tuscan and classic Italian dishes are served. The bedrooms, furnished in part with antiques, all have central heating, and overlook the park. Each room is a double. There is also a tennis court.

WHERE TO DINE

Even those on a brief excursion sometimes find themselves in Siena for lunch, and that's a happy prospect, as the Sienese are good cooks, in the best of the Tuscan tradition.

MODERATE

Al Mangia

Piazza del Campo 42. ☎ **281121**. Reservations recommended. Main courses 16,000–24,000 lire ($10–$15). AE, DC, MC, V. Daily noon–3pm and 7–10pm. Closed Mon Nov–Mar. TUSCAN.

Al Mangia, one of the finest restaurants in the heart of the city, dates from 1937 and has outside tables that overlook the town hall. The food is not only well cooked but appetizingly presented. To begin with, the house specialty is cannoli alla Mangia. If you then crave a savory Tuscan main dish, try a *bollito di manzo con salsa verde* (boiled beef with green sauce). Another excellent course is the osso buco with artichokes, and in season roast boar hunter's style is featured. This is also a good place at which to order beefsteak *fiorentino*. For dessert, there's one specialty that transcends identification with its hometown and is known all over Europe: *panforte*, made of spicy delights, including almonds and candied fruits.

INEXPENSIVE

Al Marsili (Ristorante Enoteca Gallo Nero)

Via del Castors 3. ☎ **47154**. Reservations recommended. Main courses 14,000–22,000 lire ($8.75–$13.75). AE, DC, MC, V. Tues–Sun 12:30–2:30pm and 7:30–10:30pm. Bus: 2, 3, 4, 9, 10. SIENESE/ITALIAN.

This beautiful restaurant, the best in Siena, stands between the Duomo and via di Città in a neighborhood packed with medieval and Renaissance buildings. You dine beneath crisscrossed ceiling vaults whose russet-colored brickwork was designed centuries ago. Specialties of the chef include roast boar with tomatoes and herbs, *ribollita* (a savory vegetable soup in the Sienese style), spaghetti covered with a sauce of seasonal mushrooms, and veal scaloppine with tarragon and tomato sauce. There is also *una cantina* of wines (the *enoteca* part of its name), where glasses begin at 3,000 lire ($1.90) if you'd like to indulge in a little wine tasting.

Da Guido

Vicolo Pier Pettinaio 7. ☎ **280042**. Reservations required. Main courses 20,000–25,000 lire ($12.50–$15.65). AE, MC, V. Thurs–Tues 12:30–2:30pm and 7:30–10pm. Closed 2 weeks in Jan and 2 weeks in July. Bus: 2, 3, 4, 9, 10. SIENESE/INTERNATIONAL.

Da Guido is a medieval Tuscan restaurant about 100 feet off the promenade street near piazza del Campo. It's decked out with crusty old beams, time-aged brick walls, arched ceilings, and iron chandeliers. My approval is backed up by the public testimony of more than 300 prominent people, who have left autographed photographs to adorn the walls of three dining rooms—film stars, diplomats, opera singers, and car-racing champions, even popes and presidents. There's a grill for steaks, chickens, and roasts. You may want to order some of the specialties on the à la carte list. That way, you can have assorted antipasti, which are most rewarding. For a main dish, you may want to stick to the roasts, or try a pasta, tagliata alla Guido. Their signature appetizer is *fiocchi di neve alla tartufo*, a gnocchi-like object made with wheat flour, filled with ricotta, eggs, basil, and spices—everything topped with a black truffle. Desserts are good, too.

Grotta Santa Caterina–da Bagoga

Via della Galluzza 26. ☎ **282208**. Reservations recommended. Main courses 11,000–20,000 lire ($6.90–$12.50). AE, MC, V. Tues–Sun 12:30–3pm; Tues–Sat 7–10pm. Closed July 21–July 30, Nov, and Sun night and Mon Dec–Mar. Bus: 10. TUSCAN/INTERNATIONAL.

In the heart of historic Siena, this building dates from the 1400s, although the restaurant wasn't established until 1953. Midway up a narrow, steeply inclined cobblestone street, the restaurant is an unpretentious gathering place popular with local residents. Inside are brick arches, lots of rustic detailing, plants, and wooden chairs. You are served such specialties as eight kinds of scaloppine, beef or gnocchi with truffles, or chicken cooked in beer. Rabbit in champagne is a favorite, and the kitchen will also prepare a wide variety of mixed roast meats, including veal, pork, and lamb. Many dishes are based on 16th-century recipes—which means no tomatoes and no potatoes, since these vegetables were not in use at the time.

Nello la Taverna

Via del Porrione 28–30. ☎ **289043.** Reservations required. Main courses 10,000–25,000 lire ($6.25–$15.65). AE, DC, MC, V. Tues–Sun noon–3pm; Tues–Sat 7–10pm. Closed 3 weeks in Feb. Bus: Pollicino 6. TUSCAN.

Established in the 1930s, Nello La Taverna offers an ambience that's about as typical of the Sienese region as anything you'll find. On a narrow stone-covered street about half a block from piazza del Campo, the establishment, as its name implies, offers a tavern decor that includes brick walls, hanging lanterns, racks of wine bottles, and sheaves of corn hanging from the ceiling. Best of all, you can view the forgelike kitchen with its crew of uniformed cooks busily preparing your dinner from behind a row of hanging copper utensils. Specialties include a salad of fresh radicchio, green lasagne ragoût style, and lamb cacciatore with beans. Other popular dishes include tagliatelle with mushroom sauce, roast wild boar cacciatore, and pappardelle with rabbit. The best wines, according to the owner, come from the region. Your waiter will gladly suggest a local vintage for you.

2 San Gimignano

23 miles NW of Siena, 34 miles SW of Florence

A golden lily of the Middle Ages! Called the Manhattan of Tuscany, the town preserves 13 of its noble brick towers, which give it a skyscraper skyline. The approach to the walled town today is dramatic, but once it must have been fantastic, as San Gimignano in the heyday of the Guelph and Ghibelline conflict had as many as 72 towers. Today its fortresslike severity is softened by the subtlety of its quiet, harmonious squares, and many of its palaces and churches are enhanced by Renaissance frescoes, as San Gimignano could afford to patronize major painters.

ESSENTIALS

GETTING THERE   By Bus   TRA-IN buses service San Gimignano from Florence with a change at Poggibonsi (trip time: 75 minutes); the one-way fare is 8,800 lire ($5.50). The same company also operates service from Siena, with a change at Poggibonsi (trip time: 50 minutes); the one-way fare is 6,700 lire ($4.20).

By Car   From Florence, take the Firenze–Siena autostrada south to Poggibonsi, where you'll need to cut west along a secondary route (no. 324). From Siena, head northwest along the Firenze–Siena autostrada until you reach Poggibonsi, where Route 324 leads west to San Gimignano.

VISITOR INFORMATION   The telephone area code is 0577. Information is available from Associazione Pro Loco, piazza del Duomo 1 (☎ 940008).

WHAT TO SEE & DO

In the center of town is the palazzo-flanked **piazza della Cisterna** (see our hotel recommendations)—so named because of the 13th-century cistern in its heart. Connected with the irregularly shaped square is its satellite, **piazza del Duomo.** The square's medieval architecture—towers and palaces—is almost unchanged, and it's the most beautiful spot in town. One ticket, available at any of the sites, below, allows admission to all of them, costing 16,000 lire ($10) for adults or 12,000 lire ($7.50) for students and children.

The **Palazzo del Popolo** is a palace designed by Arnolfo di Cambio in the 13th century, with a tower built a few years later that's believed to have been the tallest "skyscraper" (about 178 feet high), and a symbol of the *podesta,* or mayor. You can scale this tower, the Torre Grossa (the tallest in town), and be rewarded with a bird's-eye view of this most remarkable town. Hours and admission charges are the same as for the Museo Civico (see below).

Duomo Collegiata o Basilica di Santa Maria Assunta

Piazza del Duomo. No phone. Admission to church free; chapel 3,000 lire ($1.90) adults; 2,000 lire ($1.25) students. Apr–Sept daily 9am–12:30pm and 3–6:30pm; off-season daily 9am–12:30pm and 3–6pm.

The present Duomo dates essentially from the 12th century. Inside, the church is richly frescoed. In the right aisle, panels trace scenes from the life of Christ—the kiss of Judas, the Last Supper, the flagellation, and the Crucifixion. In the left are frescoes by Bartolo di Fredi; this mid-14th-century cycle represents scenes from the Old Testament, including the massacre of Job's servants.

The chief attraction of the basilica is the Chapel of Santa Fina, designed by Giuliano and da Maiano. It was frescoed in about 1475 by Domenico Ghirlandaio, who depicted scenes from the life of Saint Fina, as in the memorable deathbed panel. Ghirlandaio, you may recall, was Michelangelo's fresco teacher.

Museo Civico

In the Palazzo del Popolo, piazza del Duomo 1. ☎ **940340.** Admission 7,000 lire ($4.40) adults, 5,000 lire ($3.15) students; 3,500 lire ($2.20) children. Apr–Sept daily 9:30am–7:30pm; Oct and Mar daily 9:30am–5:30pm; Nov–Feb daily 9:30am–1:30pm and 2:30–4pm.

Installed upstairs in the Palazzo del Popolo (Comune, or town hall) is the Museo Civico, notably the Sala di Dante, where the Guelph-supporting poet spoke out for his cause in 1300. Look for one of the masterpieces of San Gimignano—the *Maestà,* or Madonna enthroned, by Lippo Memmi (later "touched up" by Gozzoli).

The first large room you enter upstairs contains the other masterpieces of the museum—a *Madonna in Glory,* with Saints Gregory and Benedict, painted by Pinturicchio when perspective was flowering. On the other side of it are two different depictions of the *Annunciation* by Filippino Lippi. On the opposite wall, note the magnificent primitive *Crucifix* by Coppo di Marcovaldo.

Around to the left of the cathedral on a little square (piazza Luigi Pecori) is the **Museum of Sacred Art,** an unheralded museum of at least passing interest for its medieval tombstones and wooden sculpture. It also has an illustrated-manuscript section and an Etruscan section.

WHERE TO STAY
INEXPENSIVE
Bel Soggiorno

Via San Giovanni 91, 53037 San Gimignano. ☎ **and fax 0577/940375.** 18 rms, 4 suites. TV TEL. 125,000 lire ($78.15) double; from 170,000 lire ($106.25) suite. Breakfast 10,000 lire ($6.25) per person extra. AE, DC, MC, V. Parking 15,000 lire ($9.40).

Bel Soggiorno's rear bedrooms and dining room open on the lower pastureland and the bottom of the village, providing a splendid view of the Val d'Elsa. The front is in the unspoiled Tuscan style, with an entryway and arched windows. Although rated only three stars by the government, the lodgings offered are far superior to what you might expect. The rooms are small and pleasantly revamped, and they offer excellent views (some have antiques and terraces). All of them were designed in the High Tuscan style by an architect from Milan; eight contain air conditioning and four offer minibars.

In summer you'll be asked to have your meals here—which is no great hardship as the cuisine is excellent. The dining room opens onto picture-window views. Done in the medieval style, it contains murals depicting the hunting of wild boar. There's a country fireplace with rustic chairs. Nonresidents are welcome to come in for meals Tuesday through Sunday. Meals begin at 45,000 lire ($28.15).

La Cisterna

Piazza della Cisterna 24, 53037 San Gimignano. ☎ **0577/940328.** Fax 0577/942080. 50 rms (all with bath or shower), 1 suite. TV TEL. 124,000–159,000 lire ($77.50–$99.40) double; 184,000 lire ($115) suite. Rates include breakfast. AE, DC, MC, V. Parking 18,000 lire ($11.25). Closed Jan 8–Mar 8.

A second-class hotel, La Cisterna is modernized but still retains its medieval lines (it was built at the base of some 14th-century patrician towers). In its heyday La Cisterna was the palazzo of a Tuscan family of nobility. Many tourists visit it just for the day, and to patronize Le Terrazze restaurant (see "Where to Dine," below). The bedrooms are generally large; some of the more superior lodgings open onto terraces with views of the Val d'Elsa (the hotel rests on a hilltop). Within two minutes after leaving the front door, you'll be at all the major sightseeing attractions.

Pescille

Località Pescille, 53037 San Gimignano. ☎ **0577/940186.** Fax 0577/940186. 33 rms, 7 suites. TEL. 125,000 lire ($78.15) double; 175,000 lire ($109.40) suite. Breakfast 15,000 lire ($9.40) extra. AE, DC, MC, V. Free parking. Closed Nov 6–Mar 10.

This is the most tranquil hotel in the San Gimignano area. A castle stood on this site as early as A.D. 1000, and later the property was a monastery. Napoleon came this way in 1812 and chased out the monks. Later in its career the building became a winery, and, finally, in 1971, was turned into a hotel in a setting of olive groves and vineyards. Rooms are furnished in traditional taste. The most desirable accommodation is the two-level Tower Room, opening onto a framed picture view of San Gimignano. Since it costs the same as the other accommodations, this "room with a view" is naturally every guest's first choice. The Pescille lies 2¹/₂ miles north of the center of town heading toward Volterra, and therefore is best for motorists.

Relais Santa Chiara

15 via Matteotti, 53037 San Gimignano. ☎ **0577/940701.** Fax 0577/942096. 39 rms, 2 suites. A/C MINIBAR TV TEL. 195,000–295,000 lire ($121.90–$184.40) double; 225,000–335,000 lire ($140.65–$209.40) suite. Rates include buffet breakfast. AE, DC, MC, V. Free parking.

Originally built in the 1960s as a lingerie factory, this solid and comfortable brick-sided building lies in a residential neighborhood about a 10-minute walk south of the medieval ramparts of San Gimignano. Surrounded with elegant gardens and a swimming pool, the hotel is considered the finest and most comfortable in town. Its spacious public rooms contain Florentine terra-cotta floors and mosaics. Bedrooms, furnished in precious brierwood and walnut, are well furnished and comfortable. Although the hotel is relatively new, furnishings and ambience blend in harmoniously with the Tuscan countryside. The hotel does not have a restaurant, but serves a buffet breakfast along with snacks at lunch in summer.

WHERE TO DINE
INEXPENSIVE

Ristorante le Terrazze

In La Cisterna hotel, piazza della Cisterna 24. ☎ **940328.** Reservations required. Main courses 19,000–35,000 lire ($11.90–$21.90). AE, DC, MC, V. Thurs–Mon 12:30–2:30pm; Wed–Mon 7:30–10pm. Closed Nov 1–Mar 9. TUSCAN.

Set in the center of San Gimignano, this restaurant offers a pair of dining rooms, one of which boasts stones originally laid in the 1300s. The newer dining room, which was added in 1969, has lots of rustic accessories, and large windows which overlook the old town and the fertile fields of the Val d'Elsa beyond. The setting is one of a country inn, with food comprised of an assortment of produce from the surrounding farms of Tuscany. Many soups and pastas make for fine beginnings, and specialties of the house include sliced filet of wild boar prepared with polenta and Chianti, breast of goose with walnut sauce and roasted potatoes; vitello alla Cisterna, served with buttered beans; and breaded lamb cutlets with fried artichokes.

3 Pisa

47 miles W of Florence, 207 miles NW of Rome

One of Katherine Anne Porter's best short stories is called "The Leaning Tower." A memorable scene in that story deals with a German landlady's sentimental attachment to a five-inch plaster replica of the Leaning Tower of Pisa, a souvenir whose ribs caved in at the touch of a prospective tenant. "'It cannot be replaced,' said the landlady, with a severe, stricken dignity. 'It was a souvenir of the Italian journey.'" Ironically the year (1944) Miss Porter published her "Leaning Tower," a bomb fell near the real campanile, but, fortunately, it wasn't damaged.

Few buildings in the world have captured imaginations as much as the Leaning Tower of Pisa. It's probably the single most instantly recognizable building in all the Western world. Perhaps visitors are drawn to it as a symbol of the fragility of people or at least the fragility of their work.

The Leaning Tower is a landmark powerful enough to entice visitors to call, and once there, they usually find other sights to explore as well. We'll survey the top attractions first, as most visitors pass through just for the day.

ESSENTIALS

GETTING THERE **By Plane** Both domestic and international flights arrive at Pisa's Galileo Galilei Airport (☎ 28088 for information). Trains into the center of Pisa make the five-minute trip for 1,000 lire (65¢) per person.

By Train Trains link Pisa and Florence every 30 minutes. Trip time is one hour, and a one-way fare is 6,700 lire ($4.20). Coastal trains also link Pisa and Rome.

By Bus There is frequent bus service to Florence operated by APT (☎ 23384 in Pisa for more information and schedules).

By Car From Florence, take the autostrada west (A11) to the intersection (A12) going south to Pisa.

VISITOR INFORMATION The telephone area code is 050. The tourist information office is on piazza del Duomo (☎ 560464).

WHAT TO SEE & DO

In the Middle Ages, Pisa reached the apex of its power as a maritime republic before it eventually fell to its rivals, Florence and Genoa. As is true of most cities at the zenith, Pisa turned to the arts, and made contributions in sculpture and architecture. Its greatest legacy remains at **piazza del Duomo,** which D'Annunzio labeled "Piazza dei Miracoli" (miracles). Here you'll find an ensemble of the top three attractions—original "Pisan-Romanesque" buildings, including the Duomo, the Baptistery, and the Leaning Tower itself. Nikolaus Pevsner, in his classic *An Outline of European Architecture*, wrote: "Pisa strikes one altogether as of rather an alien character—Oriental more than Tuscan."

Construction of the ✪ **Leaning Tower,** an eight-story campanile, began in 1174 by Bonanno, and a persistent legend is that the architect deliberately intended the bell tower to lean (but that claim is undocumented). Another legend is that Galileo let objects of different weights fall from the tower, then timed their descent to prove his theories on bodies in motion.

Unfortunately, the tower is in serious danger of collapse. The government is taking various measures to keep the tower from falling, including clamping five rings of half-inch steel cable around its lower stones and pouring tons of lead around its base to keep it stabilized. The tower is said to be floating on a sandy base of water-soaked clay; it leans at least 14 feet from perpendicular. If it stood up straight, the tower would measure about 180 feet tall.

In 1990 the government suspended visits inside the tower. In years gone by, one of the major attractions in Europe was to climb the Tower of Pisa—taking all 294 steps. But that's considered too dangerous today, and visitors must be content to observe the tower from the outside—but at a safe distance, of course.

✪ Il Duomo

Piazza del Duomo 17. ☎ **560547.** Admission is free. May–Oct daily 7:45am–12:45pm and 3–6:45pm; Nov–Apr daily 7:45am–12:45pm and 3–4pm. Bus: 1.

The cathedral, which dates from 1063, was designed by Buschetto, although Rainaldo in the 13th century erected the unusual facade with its four layers of open-air arches that diminish in size as they ascend. The cathedral is marked by three bronze doors—rhythmic in line—which replaced those destroyed in a disastrous fire in 1596. The south door, considered the most notable, was designed by Bonanno in 1180.

In the restored interior, the chief art treasure is the pulpit by Giovanni Pisano, which was finished in 1310. The pulpit, damaged in the cathedral fire, was finally rebuilt (with bits and pieces of the original) in 1926. The polygonal pulpit is held up by porphyry pillars and column statues that symbolize the Virtues (two posts are supported on the backs of lions). The relief panels depict scenes from the Bible. The pulpit is similar to an earlier one by Giovanni's father, Niccolò Pisano, which is in the Baptistery across the way.

There are other treasures, too—Galileo's lamp (according to unreliable tradition, the Pisa-born astronomer used the chandelier to formulate his laws of the pendulum), mosaics in the apse said to have been designed by Cimabue, the tomb of Henry VII of Luxembourg, a *St. Agnes* by Andrea del Sarto, a *Descent from the Cross* by Il Sodoma, and a *Crucifix* by Giambologna.

Battistero

Piazza del Duomo. ☎ **560547**. Admission (including entry to the Museo dell'Opera) 5,000 lire ($3.15). May–Oct daily 8am–7:40pm; Nov–Apr daily 9am–4:40pm. Bus: 1.

Begun in 1153, the Baptistery is like a romanesque crown capped by gothic. Although it's most beautiful on the exterior, with its arches and columns, it should be visited inside to see the hexagonal pulpit made by Niccolò Pisano in 1260. Supported by pillars that rest on the backs of a trio of marble lions, the pulpit contains bas-reliefs of the Crucifixion, the Adoration of the Magi, the presentation of the Christ child at the temple, and the Last Judgment (many angels have lost their heads over the years). Column statues represent the Virtues. At the baptismal font is a contemporary John the Baptist by a local sculptor. The echo inside the Baptistery shell has enthralled visitors for years.

Museo dell'Opera

Piazza Arcivescovado. ☎ **560547**. Admission included in admission price to the Battistero (see above). May–Oct daily 8am–7:30pm; Nov–Apr daily 9am–12:30pm and 3–4:30pm. Bus: 1, 3, or 4.

Opened in 1986, this museum exhibits works of art removed from the monumental buildings on the piazza. The heart of the collection, on the ground floor, consists of sculptures spanning the 11th to the 13th century. The most famous exhibit is an ivory *Madonna* and the *Crucifix* by Giovanni Pisano. Also exhibited is the work of French goldsmiths, which was presented by Maria de'Medici to Archbishop Bonciani in 1616. Upstairs are paintings from the 16th to the 18th centuries. Some of the textiles and embroideries date from the 15th century. Another section of the museum is devoted to Egyptian, Etruscan, and Roman works of art.

Camposanto

Campo dei Miracoli. ☎ **560547**. Admission 5,000 lire ($3.15). May–Oct daily 8am–7:40pm; Nov–Apr daily 9am–4:40pm. Closed Dec 15–Jan 1. Bus: 1.

This cemetery was originally designed by Giovanni di Simone in 1278, but a bomb hit it in 1944. Recently it has been partially restored. It is said that earth from Calvary was shipped here by the Crusaders on Pisan ships (the city was a great port before its water receded). The cemetery is of interest because of its sarcophagi, statuary, and frescoes. Notable frescoes, badly damaged, were by Benozzo Gozzoli, who illustrated scenes from the Old Testament; he paid special attention to architectural details. One room contains three of the most famous frescoes from the 14th century: the *Triumph of Death*, the *Last Judgment*, and the *Inferno*, with the usual assortment of monsters, reptiles, and boiling caldrons. The *Triumph of Death* is the most interesting, with its flying angels and devils—superb in composition. In addition, you'll find lots of white-marble bas-reliefs, including Roman funerary sculpture.

Museo Nazionale di San Matteo

Piazzetta San Matteo 1. ☎ **541865.** Admission 8,000 lire ($5). Tues–Sat 9am–7:30pm (until sunset in winter); Sun 9am–2pm. Bus: 5 or 7.

The well-planned Museo Nazionale di San Matteo, near piazza Mazzini, contains a good assortment of paintings and sculpture, many of which date from the 13th through the 16th centuries. In the museum are statues by Giovanni Pisano; Simone Martini's *Madonna and Child with Saints*, a polyptych, as well as Nino Pisano's *Madonna de Latte* (milk), a marble sculpture; Masaccio's *St. Paul,* painted in 1426; Domenico Ghirlandaio's two *Madonna and Saints* depictions; works by Strozzi and Alessandro Magnasco; and very old copies of works by Jan and Pieter Brueghel. You enter from piazza San Matteo.

WHERE TO STAY
MODERATE

Grand Hotel Duomo

Via Santa Maria 94, 56126 Pisa. ☎ **050/561894.** Fax 050/560418. 94 rms, 2 suites. A/C MINIBAR TV TEL. 250,000 lire ($156.25) double; 300,000 lire ($187.50) suite. Rates include breakfast. AE, DC, MC, V. Parking 30,000 lire ($18.75). Bus: 1, 3, or 4.

Grand Hotel Duomo, dating from the 1940s, lies in the heart of Pisa, a short walk from the Leaning Tower. In a buff-colored stucco building, it has a covered roof garden for uninterrupted views. Inside, there's a liberal use of marble, crystal chandeliers, even tall murals in the dining room, one of which is an artist's rendering of a verdant, blooming Pisa. A garage is on the premises. The bedrooms are well furnished, with parquet floors, big windows, built-in headrests, and individual lights. Laundry service is provided, as is 24-hour room service. Babysitting can be arranged.

Jolly Hotel Cavalieri

Piazza della Stazione 2, 56125 Pisa. ☎ **050/43290.** Fax 050/502242. 100 rms. A/C MINIBAR TV TEL. 265,000–360,000 lire ($165.65–$225) double. Rates include breakfast. AE, DC, MC, V. Parking 25,000 lire ($15.65). Bus: 1, 3, or 4.

This is the best hotel in Pisa, with a view over the monumental train station and the piazza in front of it, just miles from Pisa's international airport. It was built in 1948, in a design that emphasizes strong angles and postwar modernity. Since then it has been practically rebuilt from the inside out. Today the rooms are filled with plush furniture, paneling, and large expanses of glass; each one has a radio and a TV. The hotel has been visited by such personalities as former British Prime Minister Edward Heath, Actor Eduardo de Filippo, and Actor Vittorio Gassman. The hotel also hosts dozens of business travelers, who appreciate the serenity of the bar and restaurant for their meetings. On the premises is the Restaurant Cavalieri, one of Pisa's best restaurants, which is open daily for lunch and dinner, charging from 46,000 lire ($28.75) for a meal. Modern, elegant, and romantically illuminated at night with candles, the restaurant has a piano bar adjacent to it and a menu of Italian and international cuisine. Parking is often possible in the square in front of the station or, for better security, in a nearby garage.

INEXPENSIVE

Hotel D'Azeglio

Piazza Vittorio Emanuele II 18B, 56125 Pisa. ☎ **050/500310.** Fax 050/28017. 29 rms. A/C MINIBAR TV TEL. 190,000 lire ($118.75) double. Breakfast 13,000 lire ($8.15) extra. AE, DC, MC, V. Parking 15,000 lire ($9.40). Bus: 1, 3, or 4.

This is a well-run hotel in the vicinity of the railway station and the air terminal, in the historic and commercial center of Pisa. On the premises is an American bar and roof garden with a view of the city. A garage is adjacent to the hotel. The rooms are well furnished and comfortable.

Royal Victoria

Lungarno Pacinotti 12, 56126 Pisa. ☎ **050/940111.** Fax 050/940180. 48 rms (42 with bath or shower). TEL. 80,000 lire ($50) double without bath; 130,000 lire ($81.25) double with bath; 141,000 lire ($88.15) triple with bath; 150,000 lire ($93.75) quad with bath. Rates include breakfast. AE, DC, MC, V. Parking 30,000 lire ($18.75). Bus: 7 from Central Station.

Royal Victoria is conveniently located on the Arno, within walking distance of most of the jewels in Pisa's crown. The oldest hotel in Pisa, it was launched in 1839 and is still under the same family management today. Its tastefully decorated lounge sets the hospitable scene. Most rooms are devoted to the past only through painted ceilings, spaciousness, and the warmth of antiques suitable to contemporary comfort.

WHERE TO DINE

MODERATE

✪ Al Ristoro dei Vecchi Macelli

Via Volturno 49. ☎ **20424.** Reservations required. Main courses 16,000–28,000 lire ($10–$17.50). AE, DC. Mon–Tues and Thurs–Sat noon–3pm and 8–10:30pm. Closed Aug 3–18. Bus: 1, 3, or 4. INTERNATIONAL/TUSCAN.

This is one of the best restaurants in Pisa, set in a comfortably rustic 1930s building near piazzetta di Vecchi Macelli. Residents of Pisa claim that the cuisine is prepared with something akin to love, and they prove their devotion by returning frequently. After selecting from a choice of two dozen varieties of seafood antipasti, you can enjoy a homemade pasta with scallops and zucchini or fish-stuffed ravioli in a shrimp sauce. Other dishes include gnocchi with pesto and shrimp and roast veal with a truffle-flavored cream sauce.

✪ Ristorante Sergio

Lungarno Pacinotti 1. ☎ **580580.** Reservations required. Main courses 25,000–45,000 lire ($15.65–$28.15). AE, DC, MC, V. Tues–Sat 12:30–3pm; Mon–Sat 7:30–10pm. Closed Jan 10–30. Bus: 1 or 3. TUSCAN.

The locals flock to the Ristorante Sergio, which sits on the banks of the Arno in a building whose walls are 1,000 years old. In days of yore, when it was an inn, the building sheltered such illustrious guests as Montaigne, Shelley, and Garibaldi. A long bar area is near the entrance, flanked by a massive stone wall that's dotted with medieval wrought-iron keys, wood carvings, and rare wines. Dining is on two levels, on comfortably rustic chairs pulled up to beautifully set tables. The service is impeccable, with help offered at the proper moments by Sergio Lorenzi's gracious wife and daughter. The bouquets, as well as many of the herbs and vegetables, come from the family garden.

All the finest ingredients combine with Sergio's talents to form a unique *cucina Toscana* that has been presented by him on cooking lectures throughout Europe and North America. Dishes might include a rich salad with truffles, a re-creation of an ancient Tuscan recipe for vegetable-and-meat soup, and a range of delicacies that make this the best-rated restaurant in Pisa. These include red mullet in the style of Livorno (with tomatoes, garlic, pepper, white wine, and parsley); taglioline with baby squid and artichokes; and a dessert, *millefeuille,* with strawberries. The collection of wines is superb, and the waiter will be pleased to help you in selecting one.

INEXPENSIVE

Da Bruno

Via Luigi Bianchi 12. ☎ **560818.** Reservations recommended for dinner. Main courses 18,000–21,000 lire ($11.25–$13.15). AE, DC, MC, V. Wed–Mon noon–2:30pm; Wed–Sun 7:30–10pm. Closed 10 days in Aug. PISAN.

For around half a century, Da Bruno has survived in its location some 400 yards from the Leaning Tower of Pisa. One of Pisa's finest restaurants, although charging moderate tabs, the restaurant is decorated like a Tuscan inn under beamed ceilings. Locals are particularly fond of this place, which lies outside Pisa's old walls, but still within walking distance of the Duomo. Many in-the-know diners prefer the old-fashioned dishes of the Tuscan kitchen, including hare with pappardelle (a wide noodle), a thick regional vegetable soup (*zuppa all pisana)*, and codfish with leeks (*bacalà con porri*). Service is professional, and clients show up in rather casual wear.

Emilio

Via del Cammeo 44. ☎ **562141**. Reservations recommended. Main courses 13,500–25,000 lire ($8.45–$15.65). AE, DC, MC, V. Sat–Thurs noon–3:15pm and 7–11pm. Bus: 1, 3, or 4. PISAN/ITALIAN.

Partly because of its well-prepared food, and partly because of its nearness to the piazza dei Miracoli (site of the Leaning Tower), this restaurant attracts more foreign tourists than almost any other restaurant in Pisa. Built in the 1960s, and renovated in 1991 in a style that some visitors compare to a South American hacienda, it contains a large, high window similar to what you might expect in a church, which filters light down on the interior brick walls. The menu features a very fresh assortment of antipasti, spaghetti with clams, risotto with mushrooms, such fish dishes as *branzini a l'Isolana* oven-baked with tomatoes and vegetables, and Florentine-style beefsteaks. The owners are the Virgili family, whose son, Andreas, speaks English.

4 Perugia

50 miles SE of Arezzo, 117 miles N of Rome, 96 miles SE of Florence

For one of the greatest cities, the Etruscans chose a setting of remarkable beauty— much like Rome, with a group of hills overlooking the Tiber River Valley. In Perugia we can peel away the epochs. For example, one of the town gates is called the **Arco di Augusto,** or Arch of Augustus. The loggia spanning the arch dates from the Renaissance, but the central part is Roman. Builders from both periods used the reliable Etruscan foundation, which was the work of architects who laid stones to last. Perugia was one of a dozen major cities in the mysterious Etruscan galaxy.

Today the city is the uncrowned capital of Umbria; it has retained much of its Gothic and Renaissance charm, although it has been plagued with wars and swept up in disastrous events. To capture the essence of the Umbrian city, you must head for piazza IV Novembre in the heart of Perugia. During the day the square is over-run, so try to go to the piazza late at night when the old town is sleeping. That's when the ghosts come out to play.

ESSENTIALS

GETTING THERE　By Train　Perugia enjoys excellent rail connections with central Italy. Daily trains arrive from Rome (trip time: 3 hours), a one-way ticket costing 23,000 lire ($14.40). Daily trains also arrive from Florence (trip time: 2½ hours, at 15,800 lire ($9.90) for a one-way ticket.

By Bus　Frequent ASP buses arrive from Rome and Florence.

By Car　From either Florence (coming from the north) or Rome (coming from the south) use the A1 autostrada until you reach the junction signposted to Perugia, at which point you head east.

VISITOR INFORMATION　The telephone area code is 075. The tourist infor-mation office is at piazza IV Novembre 3 (☎ 5723327).

WHAT TO SEE & DO

As the villages of England compete for the title of most picturesque, so the cities of Italy vie for the honor of having the most beautiful square. As you stand on the central ✪ **piazza IV Novembre,** you'll know that Perugia is among the top con-tenders for that honor.

In the heart of the piazza is the **Fontana Maggiore** (Grand Fountain), built some time in the late 1270s by a local architect, a monk named Bevignate. The fountain's artistic triumph stems from the sculptural work by Niccolò Pisano and his son, Giovanni. Along the lower basin of the fountain—which is the last major work of the elder Pisano—is statuary that symbolizes the arts and sciences, Aesop's fables, the months of the year, signs of the zodiac, and scenes from the Old Testament and Roman history. On the upper basin (mostly the work of Giovanni) is allegorical sculpture, such as one figure representing Perugia, as well as saints, biblical characters, even local officials of the city in the 13th century.

After viewing the marvels of the fountain, you'll find that most of the other ma jor attractions either open onto piazza IV Novembre or lie only a short distance away.

The exterior of the **Cathedral of San Lorenzo,** piazza IV Novembre, is rather raw-looking, as if the builders were suddenly called away and never returned. The basilica is built in the Gothic style, and dates from the 14th and 15th centuries. Inside, you'll find the *Deposition* of Frederico Barocci. In the museum, Luca Signorelli's *Virgin Enthroned* with saints is displayed. Signorelli was a pupil of della Francesca. It's open daily from 8am to 1pm and 4 to 7:30pm.

On the opposite side of piazza IV Novembre is the **Palazzo dei Priori (Palace of the Priors),** on corso Vannucci. The town hall, considered one of the finest secular buildings in Italy, dates from the 13th century. Its facade is characterized by a striking row of mullioned windows. Over the main door is a Guelph (mem-ber of the papal party) lion and a griffin of Perugia, which hold chains once looted from a defeated Siena. You can walk up the stairway—the Vaccara—to the pulpit. By all means explore the interior, especially the vaulted Hall of the Nota-ries, frescoed with stories of the Old Testament and from Aesop.

An escalator has been installed to take passengers from the older part of Perugia at the top of the hill and the upper slopes to the lower city. During construction of the escalator the old fortress, **Rocco Paolina,** via Marzia, was rediscovered, along with buried streets. The fortress had been covered over to make the gardens and viewing area at the end of corso Vannucci in the last century. The old streets and street names have been cleaned up, and the area is well lighted, with an old wall exposed and modern sculpture added. The fortress was built in the 1500s by Sangallo. The Etruscan gate, *Porta Marzia*, is buried in the old city walls and can be viewed from via Bagliona Sotterranea. This street lies within the fortress and is lined with houses, some of which date from the 1400s and were buried at one time when gardens were constructed above them. The Etruscan gate is open Tuesday through Saturday from 8am to 2pm and Sunday from 9am to 1pm. The escalator to the Rocca operates daily from 6am to 1am.

✪ Galleria Nazionale dell'Umbria

Upstairs in the Palazzo dei Priori, piazza IV Novembre. ☎ **5720316.** Admission 8,000 lire ($5) adults, free for children (under 18) and seniors. Mon–Sat 9am–1:45pm and 3–7pm; Sun 9am–1pm. Bus: 11, 12, 33, or 36.

Upstairs in the Palace of the Priors is the National Gallery of Umbria, which houses the most comprehensive collection of Umbrian art from the 13th to the 19th century. Among the earliest paintings of interest is a *Virgin and Child* by Duccio di Buoninsegna, the first important master of the Sienese school. You'll see statuary by the Pisano family, who designed the Grand Fountain out front, and by Arnolfo di Cambio, the architect of the Palazzo Vecchio in Florence.

Tuscan artists are well represented—the pious Fra Angelico's *Virgin and Child* with saints and angels is there, as well as the same subject treated differently by Piero della Francesca and Benozzo Gozzoli.

You'll also see works of native-son Perugino, among them his *Adoration of the Magi*. Perugino, of course, was the master of Raphael. Often accused of sentimentality, Perugino does not enjoy the popularity today that he did at the peak of his career, but he remains a key painter of the Renaissance, who is noted especially for his landscapes.

The gallery also displays art by Pinturicchio, who studied under Perugino, and whose most notable work was the library of the Duomo of Siena. Vasari had few kind words for Pinturicchio: "It seems that fortune's favorites are those who must depend on her alone, unaided by any ability, and of this we have an instance in Pinturicchio of Perugia, whose reputation was far greater than he deserves." In this salon, you can decide for yourself.

Collegio del Cambio

Corso Vannucci 25. ☎ **5728599.** Admission 5,000 lire ($3.15). Mar–Oct Mon–Sat 9am–12:30pm and 2:30–5:30pm; Nov–Feb Tues–Sat 8am–2pm. Bus: 26, 27, 29, 32, or 36.

Right off piazza IV Novembre, this medieval exchange building—part of the Palazzo dei Priori—opens onto the main street of Perugia, corso Vannucci (Vannucci was the real name of Perugino). The collegio is visited chiefly by those seeking to view the Hall of the Audience, frescoed by Perugino and his assistants, including a teenage Raphael. On the ceiling Perugino represented the planets allegorically. The Renaissance master peopled his frescoes with the Virtues, sybils, and such biblical figures as Solomon. But his masterpiece is his own countenance. It seems rather ironic that—at least for once—Perugino could be realistic. Another room of interest is the Chapel of S. J. Battista, which contains many frescoes painted by a pupil of Perugino, G. Nicola di Paolo.

WHERE TO STAY

Suitable accommodations in most price ranges can be found in Perugia. It's best to arrive with a reservation.

EXPENSIVE

Hotel Brufani

Piazza Italia 12, 06121 Perugia. ☎ **075/5732541.** Fax 075/5720210. 21 rms, 3 suites. A/C MINIBAR TV TEL. 250,000–435,000 lire ($156.25–$271.90) double; 450,000–600,000 lire ($281.25–$375) suite. Rates include breakfast. AE, DC, MC, V. Parking 25,000 lire ($15.65). Bus: 27.

This hotel, at the top of the city, was built by Giacomo Brufani in 1884 on the ruins of the ancient Rocca Paolina, a site known to the ancient Romans that later served as the home of one of the Renaissance popes. It is placed on a cliff edge, only a few yards from the main street of Perugia, corso Vannucci. A view of the Umbrian landscape so beloved by painters is offered in most of the rooms and suites of this five-star hostelry, which was completely renovated in 1984. All rooms are equipped with radio and color TV (with news broadcasts from the United States). The hotel has a good café-restaurant, Collins, named for the great-grandfather of Mr. Bottelli, who succeeded the original owner, Mr. Brufani, nearly a century ago.

MODERATE

Hotel la Rosetta

Piazza Italia 19, 06121 Perugia. ☎ **075/5720841.** Fax 075/7220841. 95 rms, 1 suite. MINIBAR TV TEL. 195,000 lire ($121.90) double; 275,000 lire ($171.90) suite. Rates include breakfast. AE, DC. Parking 25,000–35,000 lire ($15.65–$21.90). Bus: 26, 27, 28, 29, or 36.

Since 1927 when this Perugian landmark was established, it has expanded from a seven-room pensione to a labyrinthine complex. With its frescoed ceiling, Room 55 has been declared a national treasure. (The bullet holes that papal mercenaries shot into the ceiling in 1848 have been artfully preserved.) The other, less grandiose accommodations include decors ranging from slickly contemporary to Victorian to the 1960s era. Each unit is peaceful, clean, and comfortable, regardless of decor. The in-house restaurant is recommended separately (see "Where to Dine," below).

Locanda della Posta

Corso Vannucci 97, 06121 Perugia. ☎ **075/5728925.** Fax 075/5722413. 40 rms (all with bath or shower), 1 suite. A/C MINIBAR TV TEL. 295,000 lire ($184.40) double; 350,000 lire ($218.75) suite. Rates include breakfast. AE, DC, MC, V. Parking 25,000–30,000 lire ($15.65–$18.75) in nearby garage. Bus: 26, 27, or 36.

Goethe slept here. So did Hans Christian Andersen. The hotel sits on the main street of the oldest part of Perugia, behind an impressively ornate facade that was originally sculpted in the 1700s. The hotel lies in the center of town, 15 yards from piazza Italia. All buses coming to the center stop at piazza Italia, so it's very convenient if you're depending on public transportation. The hotel, which used to be the only hotel in Perugia, is at the beginning of a pedestrian zone.

WHERE TO DINE
MODERATE

La Rosetta

In the Hotel La Rosetta, piazza Italia 19. ☎ **5720841.** Reservations recommended, especially in summer. Main courses 18,000–27,000 lire ($11.25–$16.90). AE, DC, MC, V. Tues–Sun 12:30–3pm and 7:30–10pm. Bus: 26, 27, 29, 32, or 36. UMBRIAN.

La Rosetta has gained more fame than the hotel in which it's lodged. This is not the best-rated hotel in Perugia (the Brugani has five stars, but not the Rosetta), but the political and jazz life of the city revolves around the hotel and its restaurant.

For example, Silvio Berlusconi came here even before his elevation to president in 1994. Every politician from the region uses the restaurant, and during the Perugia jazz festival (10 days in midsummer), virtually every jazz star (Miles Davis, Dizzy Gillespie, and members of the Wynton Marsalis Troupe) always stay and dine here. Food-smart Italian travelers manage to arrive here at mealtime—it's that good and reasonable. You'll find three areas in which to dine: an intimate wood-paneled salon, a main dining area divided by Roman arches and lit by brass chandeliers, and a courtyard enclosed by the walls of the villa-style hotel. Under shady palm trees you can have a leisurely meal. The menu choice is vast, but a few specialties stand out over the rest. To begin, the finest dishes are either spaghetti alla Norcina (with a truffle sauce) or vol-au-vent di tortellini Rosetta. Among the main dishes, the outstanding entry is scaloppine alla Perugina. The vegetable choices are fresh and tasty, and several desserts, such as fresh fruit and ice cream, are the pick of the after-dinner choices.

✪ Osteria del Bartolo

Via Bartolo 30. ☎ **5731561.** Reservations recommended. Main courses 22,000–30,000 lire ($13.75–$18.75); fixed-price all Umbrian menu 40,000 lire ($25); 75,000 lire ($46.90) *menu degustazione.* AE, DC, MC, V. Mon–Sat 1–2:45pm and 8–10:30pm. Closed two weeks in January and for two weeks in midsummer. Bus: 33, 36. UMBRIAN.

Set in the historic center of town in a palazzo whose foundations date from the 14th century, this family-run restaurant is known for its fresh ingredients, culinary flair, and elegant presentations. In one of two charming dining rooms, you can feast on an Umbrian cuisine; many dishes are quite traditional. Straight from the cookbooks of the 1600s, *botaccio* is made with farmer's bread stuffed with sausage, vegetables, and a sharp pecorino cheese that is baked in the oven. Also tempting are fresh tortelli with porcini (flap mushrooms), ricotta de pecoro, steamed tomatoes, and olive oil. Other menu specialties change with the seasons, but are likely to include pâté with essence of fresh tomato, veal with morels, sea bass with tarragon and celeriac sauce, and a tempting array of antipasti. The restaurant makes its own butter twice a day, its own bread once a day, and its own pasta fresh with every order. The chef also makes his own desserts. There's enough distance between tables to allow discreet conversations.

Trattoria Ricciotto

Piazza Danti 19. ☎ **5721956.** Reservations recommended. Main courses 40,000–50,000 lire ($25–$31.25). AE, DC, MC, V. Mon–Sat 12:30–2:30pm and 7:30–9:30pm. Bus: 33, 36. UMBRIAN.

Since 1888 this rustically elegant restaurant has been owned and operated by members of the Betti family, who cook, serve the food, uncork the wine, and welcome visitors to Perugia. In a building that dates in part from the 14th century, the restaurant offers a variety of well-prepared specialties. These include, for example, fettuccine with artichokes or with green olives and capers; maccheroni with cream and mushrooms; suckling pig, *arrosto morto*, a typical Perugian roast; *giardino ricciotto*, a full array of grilled meats with seasonal vegetables; or *kartocci kaiser*, a combination of beef with Emmenthal, smoked ham, and pork sausage.

INEXPENSIVE

✪ Il Falchetto

Via Bartolo 20. ☎ **5731675**. Reservations not required. Main courses 14,000–22,000 lire ($8.75–$13.75). AE, DC, MC, V. Bus: 26, 27, 29, 32, or 36. UMBRIAN/ITALIAN.

Many of the dishes here adhere to traditional themes and have a certain zest that has won critical approval for this medieval-style restaurant the owner works so hard to maintain. Menu items include tagliatelle with truffles, grilled trout from the Nera River, prosciutto several different ways, pasta with chickpeas, and grilled filet of goat. One special dish, of which the chef is justly proud, is falchetti (gnocchi with ricotta and spinach). The restaurant is a short walk from piazza Piccinino (where you'll be able to park).

La Taverna

Via delle Streghe 8. ☎ **5724128**. Reservations recommended. Main courses 15,000–25,000 lire ($9.40–$15.65). Bus: 26, 27, 29, 32, or 36. UMBRIAN.

Considered one of the finest and most innovative restaurants in Umbria, La Taverna lies within a medieval house originally built around 700 years ago. Its entrance is at the bottom of one of the narrowest alleyways in town, in the heart of Perugia's historic center. (Prominent illustrated signs indicate its position off corso Vannucci at the bottom of a flight of stairs.) You'll enter a high-ceilinged vestibule. Three dining rooms radiate out from there, each filled with exposed masonry, oil paintings, and a polite staff. Cuisine is inspired by Claudio Brugaloss, Umbrian chef who spent part of his career in Tampa, Florida, working for the Hyatt chain. Your meal might include such dishes as ravioli filled with rapini and ricotta; a soup of lima beans and artichokes; half-moon-shaped ravioli filled with salmon and saffron; and a creative array of fish, polentas, risottos, and fresh meats whose makeup depends on the inspiration of the chef and the seasonal availability of the ingredients. Note that the optional presentation of black or white truffles on any dish will add about 12,000 lire ($7.50) to its price.

5 Assisi

110 miles N of Rome, 15 miles SE of Perugia

Ideally placed on the rise to Mount Subasio, watched over by the medieval Rocco Maggiore, this purple-fringed Umbrian hill town retains a mystical air. The site of many a pilgrimage, Assisi is forever linked in legend with its native son, St. Francis. The gentle saint founded the Franciscan order and shares honors with St. Catherine of Siena as the patron saint of Italy. But he is remembered by many, even non-Christians, as a lover of nature (his preaching to an audience of birds is one of the legends of his life).

ESSENTIALS

GETTING THERE   By Train   Assisi lies on the Foligno-Teròntola train line, a 30-minute ride from the terminal at Foligno. The one-way fare from Perugia is 2,500 lire ($1.55). At Teròntola connections are made for Florence and at Foligno for Rome.

By Bus   One bus a day arrives from Rome and two from Florence. Local buses also run back and forth between Assisi and Perugia.

By Car   From Perugia (see earlier in this chapter), continue east on Route 3, continuing east toward Assisi at the junction of Route 147.

VISITOR INFORMATION   The telephone area code is 075. The tourist information office is at piazza del Comune 12 (☎ 812534).

WHAT TO SEE & DO

In addition to the sights listed below, you might also visit the **Cattedrale di San Rufino** (☎ 812285). Built in the mid-12th century at piazza San Rufino, the Duomo of Assisi is graced with a Romanesque facade, greatly enhanced by rose windows. It's one of the finest churches in the hill towns, as important as the one at Spoleto. Adjoining the cathedral is a bell tower or campanile. Inside, the church has been baroqued, an unfortunate decision that lost the purity that the front suggests. St. Francis and St. Clare were both baptized here. It's open daily from 7am to noon and 2 to 7pm. It costs 2,000 lire ($1.25) to visit the crypt.

The **Basilica of Santa Chiara** (Clare), on piazza Santa Chiara (☎ 812282), is dedicated to "the little plant of Blessed Francis," as St. Clare liked to describe herself. Born in 1193 into one of the richest and noblest families of Assisi, Clare was to give all her wealth to the poor and to found, together with St. Francis, the Order of the Poor Clares. She was canonized by Pope Alexander IV in 1255. Pope Pius XII declared her Patroness of Television in 1958. It was decided to entrust to her this new means of social communication on the basis of a vision that she related she had on Christmas Eve in 1252 in which she saw the manger and heard the friars sing in the Basilica of St. Francis while she was bedridden in the Monastery of San Damiano.

Although many of the frescoes which once adorned the basilica have been either completely or partially restored, much remains that is worthy of note. On entering, one's attention is caught by the striking Crucifix behind the main altar, a painting on wood dating from the time of the church itself (circa 1260). The work is by "the Master of St. Clare," who is also responsible for the beautiful icons on either side of the transept. An oft-reproduced fresco of the Nativity from the 14th century can be admired in the left transept.

The closest bus stop to the Basilica of Santa Chiara (Clare) is to be found near Porta Nuova, the eastern gate to the city at the beginning of viale Umberto I. The bus in question does not bear a number; it departs from the depot in piazza Matteotti for its first run to the train station at 5:40am and concludes its final run at 9:40pm. Buses arrive at half-hour intervals. Admittance to the basilica is free; however, the custodian turns away visitors in shorts, miniskirts, plunging necklines, and backless attire. It's open November through March, daily from 6:30am to noon and 2 to 6pm; April through October, daily from 6:30am to 12:15pm and 2 to 7pm.

The **Temple of Minerva** opens onto piazza del Comune, the heart of Assisi. The square is a dream for a lover of architecture from the 12th through the 14th century. A pagan structure, with six Corinthian columns, the Temple of Minerva dates from the 1st century B.C. With Minerva-like wisdom, the people of Assisi let it stand, and turned it into a baroque church inside so as not to offend the devout. Adjoining the temple is the 13th-century Tower of the People, built by Ghibelline supporters.

✪ Basilica di San Francesco

Piazza di San Francesco. ☎ **812238.** Admission is free. Apr–Oct daily 6:30am–7pm; Nov–Mar daily 6:30am–noon and 2–6pm. Bus: 2.

This important church, which consists of both an upper and lower church, houses some of the most important cycles of frescoes in Italy, including works by such pre-Renaissance giants as Cimabue and Giotto. Both churches were built in the first part of the 13th century. The basilica and its paintings form the most significant monument to St. Francis.

Upon entering the upper church through the principal doorway, look to your immediate left to see one of Giotto's most celebrated frescoes, that of St. Francis preaching to the birds. In the nave of the upper church you'll find the rest of the cycle of 27 additional frescoes, some of which are by Giotto, although the authorship of the entire cycle is a subject of controversy. Many of the frescoes are almost surrealistic—in architectural frameworks—like a stage setting that strips away the walls and allows us to see the actors inside. In the cycle we see pictorial evidence of the rise of humanism that led to Giotto's and Italy's split from the rigidity of Byzantium.

Proceed up the nave to the transept and turn left to find a masterpiece of Cimabue's, the *Crucifixion*. Time has robbed the fresco of its former radiance, but its power and ghostlike drama remain. The cycle of badly damaged frescoes in the transept and apse are other works by Cimabue and his paint-smeared helpers.

From the transept, proceed down the stairs through the two-tiered cloisters to the lower church, which will put you in the south transept. Look for Cimabue's faded but masterly *Virgin and Child* with four angels and St. Francis looking on from the far right. The fresco is often reproduced in detail as one of Cimabue's greatest works. On the other side of the transept is the *Deposition from the Cross*, a masterpiece by that Sienese artist Pietro Lorenzetti, plus a *Madonna and Child* with St. John and St. Francis (stigmata showing). In a chapel honoring St. Martin of Tours, Simone Martini of Siena painted a cycle of frescoes, with great skill and imagination, which depicts the life and times of that saint. Finally, under the lower church is the crypt of St. Francis.

Eremo delle Carceri

Via Eremo delle Carceri. ☎ **812301.** Admission is free (donations accepted). Daily 6:30am–sunset. Transportation: By car, taxi, or foot.

Eremo delle Carceri (Prisons' Hermitage), in a setting 2¹/₂ miles east of Assisi (out via Eremo delle Carceri), is from the 14th and 15th centuries. The "prison" is not a penal institution but rather a spiritual retreat. It is believed that St. Francis retired to this spot for meditation and prayer. Out back is a gnarled, moss-covered ilex (or live oak) tree, more than 1,000 years old, where St. Francis is believed to have blessed the birds, after which they are said to have flown in the four major directions of the compass to symbolize that Franciscans, in coming centuries, would spread out from Assisi all over the world. The friary contains some faded frescoes. One of the handful of friars who still inhabit the retreat will show you through. Donations are gratefully accepted to defray the cost of maintenance. In keeping with the Franciscan tradition, the friars at Le Carceri are completely dependent on alms for their support.

Rocca Maggiore

Reached by an unmarked stepped street opposite the basilica. Admission 3,000 lire ($1.90). Apr–Oct daily 9am–8pm; Nov–Mar daily 10am–4pm.

The Rocca Maggiore (Great Fortress) sits astride a hill overlooking Assisi. It should be visited if for no other reason than for the view of the Umbrian countryside from its ramparts. The present building—now in ruins—dates from the 14th century, and the origins of the structure go back beyond time.

WHERE TO STAY

Space in Assisi tends to be tight—so reservations are important. Still, for such a small town, Assisi has a good number of accommodations.

MODERATE

Hotel Giotto

Via Fontebella 41, 06082 Assisi. ☎ **075/812209.** Fax 075/816479. 70 rms, 2 suites. MINIBAR TV TEL. 195,000 lire ($121.90) double; 325,000 lire ($203.15) suite. Rates include breakfast. AE, DC, MC, V. Free parking. Bus: 2.

Hotel Giotto is an up-to-date and well-run hotel, built at the edge of town on several levels. Near the Basilica of St. Francis, and opening onto panoramic views, the Giotto offers little formal gardens and terraces for meals or sunbathing. It has spacious modern public rooms and an elevator, which leads to the well-furnished and comfortable rooms. Bright colors predominate, and there's a Parmeggiani (a modern artist from Bologna) mural over the bar. The hotel is open all year.

Hotel Subasio

Via Frate Elia 2, 06082 Assisi. ☎ **075/812206.** Fax 075/816691. 66 rms. MINIBAR TV TEL. 250,000 lire ($156.25) double. Rates include breakfast. AE, DC, MC, V. Bus: 2.

This is a first-class hotel with a decidedly old-fashioned aura. The Subasio has been the unquestioned choice of many a famous visitor—the king and queen of Belgium as well as the queen of the Netherlands, plus such old-time movie legends as Charlie Chaplin, Merle Oberon, Marlene Dietrich, and James Stewart. The hotel is linked to the Church of St. Francis by a covered stone arched colonnade, and its dining terrace (with extremely good food) is perhaps the most dramatic in Assisi. Your table will be shaded by a sprawling vine. Dining is also an event on the vaulted medieval loggia. The bedrooms at the front open onto balconies with a good view. The rooms are furnished with Italian flair.

INEXPENSIVE

Umbra

Via degli Archi 6, 06081 Assisi. ☎ **075/812240.** Fax 075/813653. 25 rms (all with bath or shower). 5 suites. TEL. 115,000–130,000 lire ($71.90–$81.25) double; 140,000–160,000 lire ($87.50–$100) suite. Rates include breakfast. AE, DC, MC, V. Parking 10,000 lire ($6.25). Closed Jan–Feb. Bus: 2.

Umbra is the most centrally located accommodation in Assisi, in a position right off piazza del Comune with its Temple of Minerva. The outdoor terraced dining room forms an important part of the hotel's entryway. You enter through old stone walls covered with vines and walk under a leafy pergola. The lobby is compact and functional. The bedrooms offer comfortable beds; some have a tiny balcony overlooking the crusty old rooftops and the Umbrian countryside. Five rooms are air-conditioned.

⑤ St. Anthony's Guest House

Via Galeazzo Alessi 10, 06081 Assisi. ☎ **075/812542.** Fax 075/812542. 20 rms. 70,000 lire ($43.75) double. Rates include breakfast. No credit cards. Parking available (fee left to discretion of client). Bus: 2.

This special hotel provides economical and comfortable accommodations in a medieval villa turned guesthouse. Operated by the Franciscan Sisters of the Atonement (an order that originated in Graymoor, New York), the guesthouse offers the pilgrim/traveler hospitality and a peaceful atmosphere. Located on the upper ledges of Assisi, St. Anthony's Guest House contains its own terraced garden and panoramic view. In all, 35 people can be accommodated. For an additional 20,000 lire ($12.50) a midday meal is served at 1pm. Meals and companionship are enjoyed in a restored 12th-century dining room. The sisters and their co-workers welcome you, showing you their library with English-language books.

A NEARBY PLACE TO STAY

Hotel Palazzo Bocci

Via Cavour 17, 06038 Spello. ☎ **0742/301021.** Fax 0742/301464. 17 rms, 6 suites. A/C MINIBAR TV TEL. 180,000–220,000 lire ($112.50–$137.50) double; 260,000–320,000 lire ($162.50–$200) suite. Rates include breakfast. AE, DC, MC, V. Free parking. Head 6$^1/2$ miles SE of Assisi along S147.

In the historical center of town, this palace dates from the second half of the 18th century. The owner of the hotel purchased the palace in 1989, renovated it, and opened it as a hotel in 1992. Inside is a courtyard with a view of the valley, a beautiful fountain, and two age-old palms. Taste and restraint went into designing both the public and private rooms, some of which open onto panoramic views. Bedrooms have such equipment as hydromassage, safes, a writing desk with two chairs, hairdryer, and soundproofing.

Dining/Entertainment: For hotel guests there is a nice bar and a large open garden with a panoramic view where drinks are served. A buffet breakfast is served, and a well-known restaurant, Il Molino, is just in front of the hotel.

Services: Laundry, room service, babysitting.

Facilities: Riding school, tennis courts, golf courses, and swimming pool—nearby.

WHERE TO DINE
MODERATE

Umbra

Via degli Archi 6. ☎ **812240.** Reservations recommended. Main courses 14,000–21,000 lire ($8.75–$13.15). AE, DC, MC, V. Wed–Mon noon–2pm and 7:30pm–9pm. Closed Jan 15–Mar. Bus: 2. UMBRIAN.

Although most of the building which contains this venerable restaurant dates from the Middle Ages, the walls of the laundry and the kitchens (which occupy the basement) are from the final days of the Roman Empire. The restaurant was originally established as an inn in either 1926 or 1928 (the owners can't remember exactly which), and its shaded garden is charming enough to have pleased even St. Francis. On a warm day you'll probably hear birds chirping. In the heart of the old city, not far from the basilica, the establishment is the personal statement of the owner and his staff of capable helpers. Umbrian menu items include dishes that range from the fanciful to the classically popular. In any event, ample use is made of truffles. The best cuts of meat are generally used, along with very fresh vegetables. Two specialties include *crespelle* and roasted lamb infused with Umbrian herbs.

INEXPENSIVE

Il Medio Evo

Via dell'Arco dei Priori 4B. ☎ **813068.** Reservations recommended. Main courses 18,000–26,000 lire ($11.25–$16.25). AE, DC, MC, V. Thurs–Tues noon–2:30pm and 7:30–9:45pm. Closed January and three weeks in July. Bus: 2. UMBRIAN/INTERNATIONAL.

Assisi's best restaurant is Il Medio Evo, one of the architectural oddities of the town's historic center. The foundations on which the restaurant rests are at least 1,000 years old. During the Middle Ages and again in Renaissance times it was successively enlarged and modified until today it is considered an authentic medieval gem of heavy stonework. Fresh ingredients and skill go into the genuine Umbrian cooking served here. Alberto Falsinotti and his family prepare superb versions of Umbrian recipes whose origins are as old as Assisi itself. Specialties include tortelloni stuffed with minced turkey, veal, and beef, served simply but flavorfully with butter and parmesan; gnocchi stuffed with ricotta and spinach, and served with parmesan; roasted duck; roasted rabbit with red wine sauce and truffles; and roast lamb with rosemary, potatoes, and herbs.

Ristorante Buca di San Francesco

Via Brizi 1. ☎ **812204.** Reservations recommended. Main courses 15,000–25,000 lire ($9.40–$15.65). AE, DC, MC, V. Tues–Sun 12:30–3pm; Tues–Sat 7:30–9:30pm. Closed Jan 7–Feb 28 and July 1–28. Bus: 2. UMBRIAN/ITALIAN.

This restaurant, set in a medieval palace, is outfitted with stone walls. The menu changes frequently, according to the availability of ingredients. One of the specialties is spaghetti alla buca, as well as onion soup. Grilled meats are always featured, and sometimes they are served with truffles, which are so popular in the Umbrian countryside. In summer, guests can dine outside on a terrace.

6 Spoleto

80 miles N of Rome, 30 miles SE of Assisi

Hannibal couldn't conquer it, but Gian-Carlo Menotti did—and how! Before Maestro Menotti put Spoleto on the tourist map in 1958, it was known mostly to art lovers, teachers, and students. Today the chic and fashionable, artistic, and arty flood the Umbrian hill town to attend performances of the world-famous **Festival dei Due Mondi (Festival of Two Worlds),** most often held in June and July. Menotti searched and traveled through many hill towns of Tuscany and Umbria before making a final choice. When he saw Spoleto, he fell in love with it. And quite understandably.

Long before Tennessee Williams arrived to premiere a new play, Thomas Schippers to conduct the opera *Macbeth,* or Shelley Winters to do three one-act plays by Saul Bellow, Spoleto was known to St. Francis and to Lucrezia Borgia (she occupied the 14th-century castle that towers over the town, the Rocca Dell'Albornoz). The town is filled with palaces of Spoletan aristocracy, medieval streets, and towers for protection from a time when visitors weren't as friendly as they are today. There are churches, churches, and more churches—some of which, such as **San Gregorio Maggiore,** were built in the romanesque style in the 11th century.

But the tourist center is **piazza del Duomo,** with its cathedral and **Teatro Caio Melisso (Chamber Theater).** The cathedral is a hodgepodge of romanesque and medieval architecture, with a 12th-century campanile. Its facade is of exceptional beauty, renowned especially for its mosaic by Salsterno. The interior should be visited if for no other reason than to see the cycle of frescoes in the chancel by Filippo Lippi. His son, Filippino, also an artist, designed the tomb for his father. The keeper of the apse will be happy to unlock it for you. These frescoes, believed to have been carried out largely by students, were the elder Lippi's last work; he died in Spoleto in 1469. Vasari writes, "Some said he was poisoned by certain persons related to the object of his love." As friars went in those days, Lippi was a bit of a swinger; he ran off with a nun, Lucrezia Buti, who later posed as the Madonna in several of his paintings.

Spoleto should be visited even when the festival isn't taking place, as it's a most interesting town. It has a number of worthwhile sights, including the remains of a **Roman theater** off piazza della Libertà (entrance via S. agata). Motorists wanting a view can continue up the hill from Spoleto around a winding road (about five miles) to **Monteluco,** an ancient spot 2,500 feet above sea level. Monteluco is peppered with summer villas.

ESSENTIALS

GETTING THERE   By Train   Daily trains arrive from Rome (trip time: 2 hours), with a one-way fare of 11,700 lire ($7.30). Ten trains arrive from Perugia (trip time: 1 hour), with a one-way ticket costing 5,000 lire ($3.15).

By Bus   Spoleto is served by daily buses from Rome. Two buses a day arrive from Perugia and Assisi.

By Car   From Perugia, continue south along Route 3.

VISITOR INFORMATION   The telephone area code is 0743. The tourist information office is at piazza della Libertà 7 (☎ 220311).

SPECIAL EVENTS   Dates, programs, and ticket prices change yearly for the Festival dei Due Mondi (Festival of Two Worlds), discussed below. In Spoleto, the general offices of the festival are at piazza del Duomo 7.

WHERE TO STAY

Spoleto offers an attractive range of hotels, but when the "two worlds" crowd in at festival time, the going's rough (one year a group of students bedded down on piazza del Duomo). In an emergency, the tourist office at piazza della Libertà 7 (☎ 0743/220311) can probably arrange for you to stay in a private home—at a moderate price. The office is open only during regular business hours, but it's imperative to telephone in advance for a reservation. Many of the private rooms are often rented well in advance to artists appearing at the festival. Innkeepers are likely to raise all the prices listed below to whatever the market will bear.

INEXPENSIVE

Albornoz Palace Hotel

Viale Matteotti (without number), 06049 Spoleto. ☎ **0743/221221.** Fax 0743/221600. 92 rms, 4 suites. A/C MINIBAR TV TEL. 160,000–190,000 lire ($100–$118.75) double;

from 350,000 lire ($218.75) suite. Rates include breakfast. AE, DC, MC, V. Free parking.
Bus: A, B, or C.

Starkly modern, and perched within a residential neighborhood half a mile south
of the town center, this five-story building is the largest and newest (circa 1990)
hotel in Spoleto. A small garden in back contains a swimming pool. On the premises are two restaurants, serving meals that average around 50,000 lire ($31.25)
each; a bar; and a marble-trimmed lobby decorated with large modern paintings
created by American-born artist Sol Lewitt. Bedrooms are painted in cool tones
of blue-gray, and contain modern bathrooms and views over either Spoleto, Monte
Luco, or the surrounding hills. The hotel, incidentally, is named after the
14th-century cardinal-soldier (Albornoz) who built parts of Spoleto.

Dei Duchi

Viale Giacomo Matteotti 4, 06049 Spoleto. ☎ **0743/44541.** Fax 0743/44543. 51 rms (all
with bath or shower). MINIBAR TV TEL. 200,000 lire ($125) double. Rates include breakfast.
Half-board 155,000–160,000 lire ($96.90–$100) per person. AE, DC, MC, V. Free parking.
Bus: A, B, or C.

This well-designed, modern hotel is within walking distance of the major sights—
yet it perches on a hillside with views and terraces. Near the Roman theater, Dei
Duchi is graced with walls of natural brick, open-to-the-view glass, and lounges
with modern furnishings and original paintings. Some bedrooms have their own
balconies, plus brightly colored bed coverings, wood-grained furniture, and
built-in cupboards—quite a good layout. In high season, half-board is required.
In summer you have a choice of two dining rooms, each airy, light, and roomy.

✪ Gattapone

Via del Ponte 6, 06049 Spoleto. ☎ **0743/223447.** Fax 0743/223448. 7 rms, 7 junior suites.
MINIBAR TV TEL. 180,000 lire ($112.50) double; from 280,000 lire ($175.00) suite. Breakfast 15,000 lire ($9.40) extra. AE, DC, MC, V. Free parking. Bus: A, B, or C.

The Gattapone is more a spectacle than a hotel. Probably the only 14-room
hotel in Italy to be rated first class, it's among the clouds, high on a twisting road
leading to the ancient castle and the 13th-century Ponte delle Torri, a bridge 250
feet high. The hotel occupies two separate stone cottages, which are side by side.
The buildings cling closely to the road, and each descends the precipice overlooking the gorge. The hotel's view side is equipped with a two-story picture window
and an open spiral stairway that leads from the intimate lounge to the bedrooms.
Each of the rooms is individually furnished, with comfortable beds, antiques, and
plenty of space. Only breakfast is served.

Hotel Charleston

Piazza Collicola 10, 06049 Spoleto. ☎ **0743/220052.** Fax 0743/222010. 18 rms (all with
bath or shower). MINIBAR TV TEL. 130,000 lire ($81.25) double. Rates include breakfast.
AE, DC, MC, V. Parking 15,000 lire ($9.40). Bus: A, B, or C.

This tile-roofed, sienna-fronted building was originally built in the 17th century.
Today it serves as a pleasantly accessorized hotel, conveniently located in the
historic center. Each of the bedrooms has a ceiling accented with beams of honey-
colored planking, and comfortable mattresses. On the premises is a sauna, as well
as a bar, library, and a sitting room with sofas and a writing table.

✪ Hotel Clarici

Piazza della Vittoria 32, 06049 Spoleto. ☎ **0743/223311.** Fax 0743/222010. 24 rms (all
with bath or shower). A/C MINIBAR TV TEL. 130,000 lire ($81.25) double. Rates include
breakfast. AE, DC, MC, V. Parking 5,000 lire ($3.15). Bus: A, B, or C.

The Clarici is rated only third class, but it's airy and modern. Each accommodation has a private balcony, which opens onto a view. The hotel doesn't emphasize style, but rather the creature comforts: soft low beds, built-in wardrobes, steam heat, an elevator. There's a large terrace for sunbathing or sipping drinks.

WHERE TO DINE
MODERATE

Il Tartufo

Piazza Garibaldi 24. ☎ **40236.** Reservations required. Main courses 16,000–36,000 lire ($10–$22.50). AE, DC, MC, V. Thurs–Tues noon–3pm and Thurs–Tues 7:30–10:30pm. Closed July 15–31. Bus: A, B, or C. UMBRIAN.

At Il Tartufo, outside the heart of town near the amphitheater, you may be introduced to the Umbrian *tartufo* (truffle) if you can afford it. It is served in the most expensive appetizers and main courses (see above). This immaculately kept, excellent tavern serves at least nine regional specialties that use the black tartufo of Spoleto. But you'll pay a hefty supplement, depending on market conditions. An ever-popular dish—and a good introduction for neophyte palates who may never have tried truffles—is strengozzi al tartufo, a pasta dish with truffles. Alternatively, you may want to start your meal with an omelet—for instance, frittata al tartufo. Main dishes of veal and beef are also excellently prepared. For such a small restaurant, the menu is large.

Inexpensive

Tric-Trac da Giustino

Piazza del Duomo, via dell'Arringo 10. ☎ **44592.** Reservations recommended. Main courses 18,000–30,000 lire ($11.25–$18.75). AE, DC, MC, V. Thurs–Tues 9am–2am. Bus: A, B, or C. UMBRIAN/INTERNATIONAL.

This restaurant is frequented by an international clientele at the Festival of Two Worlds. The setting on this landmark square evokes the 16th century. The restaurant, established in 1970 in a 17th-century building, shares its locale with Giustino's American Bar. The food is well prepared and the service excellent. Try the risotto with truffles or carpaccio with a veloute sauce.

Bologna & Emilia-Romagna

Lying in the northern reaches of central Italy, Emilia-Romagna is known for gastronomy and for its art cities, Modena and Parma. Once-great families, including the Renaissance dukes of Ferrara, rose in power and influence, creating courts that attracted painters and poets, notably Tasso and Ariosto.

Bologna, the capital, stands at the crossroads between Venice and Florence, and is linked by express highways to Milan and Tuscany. By basing yourself in this ancient university city, you can branch out in all directions: north for 32 miles to Ferrara, southeast for 31 miles to the ceramics-making town of Faenza, northwest for 25 miles to Modena with its Romanesque cathedral, or 34 miles farther northwest to Parma, the legendary capital of the Farnese family duchy in the 16th century. Ravenna, famed for its mosaics, lies 46 miles east of Bologna on the Adriatic Sea.

Most of our sightseeing destinations lie on the ancient Roman road, via Emilia, that began in Rimini and stretched all the way to Piacenza, a Roman colony that often attracted invading barbarians.

This ancient land (known to the Romans as "Æmilia" and to the Etruscans before them) is rich in attractions—the cathedral and baptistery of Parma, for instance—and in scenic beauty (the green plains and the slopes of the Apennines). Emilia is one of the most bountiful farming districts in Italy, and sets a table highly praised in Europe—both for its wines and for its imaginatively prepared pasta dishes.

A DRIVING TOUR

There is much to see and do in Emilia-Romagna, but those on the tightest schedules may want to confine themselves to the following route.

Day 1 Begin in Bologna, sampling its excellent cuisine and viewing its major sights, all in the city center. These include Basilica di San Petronius and Fontana del Nettuno.

Day 2 Take the autostrada A13 northwest to Ferrara, a distance of only 32 miles but a world apart. The former seat of the Este dynasty is filled with many palaces and castles from that era.

Emilia-Romagna

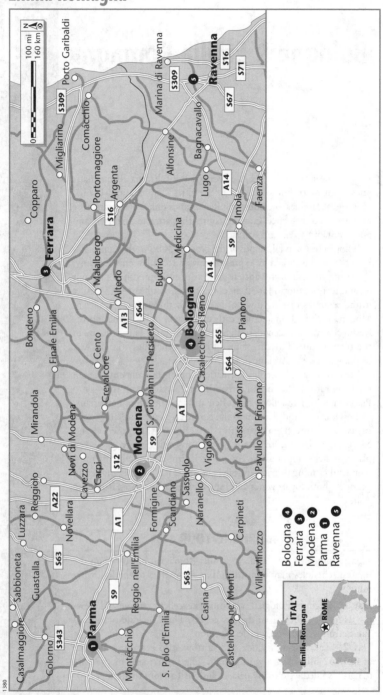

What's Special About Bologna & Emilia-Romagna

Great Towns/Villages

- Bologna, gastronomic capital of Italy, a historical city that reached its artistic peak in the 16th century.
- Parma, home of Correggio, Il Parmigianino, Bodoni (of type fame), Toscanini, and Parmesan cheese.
- Ravenna, a city of faded glory, once the capital of the Roman Empire.

Museums

- Pinacoteca Nazionale, in Bologna, containing major works from the 14th century to the advent of the baroque.
- Galleria Estense, in Modena, with a collection of Emilian works from the 14th through the 18th century.

Religious Shrines

- Duomo at Modena, one of the glories of the Romanesque in northern Italy.
- St. Petronius Basilica, in Bologna, begun in 1390, but never fully completed.
- Tomb of Galla Placidia, at Ravenna, offering mosaics famous for their range of color, in the city's oldest structure.

Ace Attraction

- San Domenico, a restaurant in Imola, outside Bologna, considered by many food critics to be the greatest in Italy.

☕ **TAKE A BREAK**   Osteria Al Brindisi, via G. degli Adelandi 9B (☎ 0532/37015), is the oldest *osteria* in Italy, known to such former habitués as Cellini and Copernicus. It is said to make the best sandwiches in town, costing from 4,500 lire ($2.80), and it also serves some 600 varieties of wine, beginning at 1,000 lire (65¢) per glass. Hours are Monday through Saturday from 10am to 11pm.

Day 3   From Ferrara drive south until you link up with the highway to the Adriatic, cutting southeast toward Ravenna. As you near the coast continue south along Route E55 until you approach Ravenna, a former imperial city, the Byzantium of the West. Consider at least an overnight stopover, more if you have the time. There is much to see here (see below).

Day 4   Connect with the autostrada west going to Bologna, but this time bypass the city and head for Modena for the night. In Modena visit its Duomo and Galleria Estense, two of the major attractions of Emilia-Romagna. At one of the many local restaurants, sample such regional dishes as *zampone* (stuffed pig's feet), everything washed down with Lambrusco.

☕ **TAKE A BREAK**   Forno San Giogo, via Taglio 6 (☎ 059/223514), is the town's leading baker. You can purchase bread for a picnic, as well as some of the town's best pizzas and pastries.

Day 5   For a final look at the province, continue northwest along the autostrade 9 (A1) to Parma, where you can overnight, visiting at least the Duomo and Baptistry before wandering through the city's National Gallery.

FOOD & WINE

Emilia-Romagna, whose chief towns are Bologna, Modena, Parma, and Ravenna, is acclaimed for having the best cuisine in Italy. In his definitive *La scienza in cucina* (The Science of Cooking), Pellegrino Artusi writes: "When you hear mention made of Bolognese cooking drop a little curtsy, for it deserves it. It is a rather heavy cuisine, if you like, because the climate requires it; but how succulent it is, and what good taste it displays! It is wholesome too and, in fact, octogenarians and nonagenarians abound there as nowhere else."

A land rich in agricultural resources, Emilia-Romagna prepares a bountiful table. In the field of gastronomy "well-fed Bologna" is known for its tagliatelle, which exists all over Italy but is at its best in Emilia-Romagna. These long strips of macaroni are boiled and served with a ragoût. Tortellini is the second most fabled pasta dish—little squares of dough stuffed with chopped veal, turkey, pork, egg, beef marrow, spices, and cheese and served in consommé or with ragoût. Cappelletti is rather larger than tortellini, really "little hats" made of dough and filled with such items as minced turkey and Parmesan cheese. Zampone is the specialty of Modena—a pig's foot deboned and stuffed with minced and spicy pork, then boiled for several hours. Cotechino is a highly spiced pork sausage renowned locally, and Parmesan cheese from Parma now is sprinkled on dishes around the world. Ragoût à la Bolonaise is actually a bolognese sauce (meat and tomato sauce), and it's gone on to become the world's most famous spaghetti meat sauce.

The list of foodstuff in the province is endless, ranging from *involtini* (stuffed veal rolls) to fragrant smoked meats. *Cotoletta alla bolognese* is veal prepared with slices of ham and fondant cheese (often called veal Cordon Bleu around the world). It is the most famous meat dish of the area. Mortadella is a large, tasty sausage made with highly spiced pork and cut into paper-thin slices.

Among wines, the limpid Albana, with its golden yellow color, has a mellow flavor and an enticing bouquet; the sparkling, incomparable Lambrusco is ruby red in color, with a bouquet of violets and is perfect with tortellini or tagliatelle. Sanglovese is a dark ruby-red "brut" wine with a trace of flint in the flavor and a tartish aftertaste, again evoking the bouquet of violets.

1 Bologna

32 miles S of Ferrara, 94 miles SW of Venice, 227 miles N of Rome

The manager of a hotel in Bologna laments: "The Americans! They spend a week in Florence, a week in Venice. Why not six days in Florence, six days in Venice, and two days in Bologna?" That's a good question. Bologna is one of the most sadly overlooked Italian cities—we've found cavernous accommodation space here in July and August, when the hotels in Venice and Florence were packed as tightly as a can of Progresso clam sauce.

"But what is there to see in Bologna?" is also a common question. True, it boasts no Uffizi or Doges' Palace. However, it does offer a beautiful city considered by some to be the most architecturally unified in Europe—a panorama of marbled sidewalks and porticos that, if spread out, would surely stretch all the way to the border.

Filled with sienna-colored buildings, Bologna is the leading city of Emilia. Its rise as a commercial power was almost assured by its strategic location as the geographic center between Florence and Venice. Its university, the oldest in Europe, has for years generated a lively interest in art and culture.

Bologna is also considered the gastronomic capital of Italy. Gourmets flock here just to sample the food—the pasta dishes (tortellini, tagliatelle, lasagne verde), the meat and poultry specialties (zampone, veal cutlet bolognese, tender breasts of turkey in sauce supreme), and, finally, mortadella, the incomparable sausage of Bologna, as distant a cousin to baloney as porterhouse is to the hot dog.

The city seems to take a vacation in August, becoming virtually dead. Everywhere you see the sign proclaiming CHIUSO ("closed").

ESSENTIALS

GETTING THERE   By Plane   The international airport, the **Aeroporto Guglielmo Marconi,** is 4 miles north of the center of town and serviced by such domestic carriers as Aermediterranea and ATI. All the main European airlines have connections through this airport. For information about flights, phone 311578. A frequent bus runs from the airport to the air terminal at the rail station in the center of Bologna.

By Train   There is one rail station in Bologna at piazza Medaglie d'Oro (☎ 246490). Trains arrive from Rome every hour (trip time: 3$^1/_2$ hours). Trains arrive from Milan every hour (trip time: 2 hours).

By Bus   ATC buses serve the area from their terminal at piazza XX Settembre (☎ 248374 for information). Buses to and from Florence run at the rate of one every hour (trip time: 1$^1/_2$ hours). Buses from Venice also arrive every hour (trip time: 2 hours), and from Milan, also every hour (trip time: 3 hours).

By Car   From Florence, continue north along autostrada A1 until you reach the outskirts of Bologna where signs direct you to the center of the city. Coming over the Apennines, the Autostrada del Sole (A1) runs northwest to Milan just before reaching the outskirts of Bologna. The A13 superhighway cuts northeast to Ferrara and Venice and the A14 dashes east to Rimini, Ravenna, and the towns along the Adriatic.

VISITOR INFORMATION   The telephone area code for Bologna is 051. The tourist information office is at piazza Maggiore 6 (☎ 239660).

GETTING AROUND   Bologna is easy to cover on foot, as most of the major sights are in and around piazza Maggiore, the heart of the city. However, if you don't want to walk, **city buses** leave for most points from either piazza Nettuno or piazza Maggiore. Free maps are available at the storefront office of the A.T.C. in the Palazzo del Podesta, right between piazza Nettuno and piazza Maggiore in the heart of town. Tickets can be purchased at one of many booths throughout Bologna. Once on board, however, you must have your ticket validated.

Taxis are on radio call (☎ 372727).

WHAT TO SEE & DO

Basilica di San Petronius
Piazza Maggiore. ☎ **225442.** Admission is free. Daily 7:30am–7pm. Bus: 25 or 30.

Sadly, the facade of this enormous Gothic basilica honoring the patron saint of Bologna was never completed. Although the builders went to work in 1390, after three centuries the church was still not completed (even though Charles V was crowned emperor here in 1530). However, Jacopo della Quercia of Siena did grace the central door with Renaissance sculpture, which is considered a masterpiece. Inside, the church could accommodate the traffic of Grand Central

Bologna

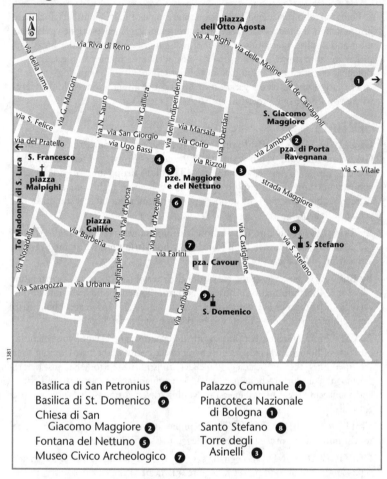

Basilica di San Petronius **6**

Basilica di St. Domenico **9**

Chiesa di San
   Giacomo Maggiore **2**

Fontana del Nettuno **5**

Museo Civico Archeologico **7**

Palazzo Comunale **4**

Pinacoteca Nazionale
   di Bologna **1**

Santo Stefano **8**

Torre degli
   Asinelli **3**

Terminal. The central nave is separated from the aisles by pilasters shooting upward to the flying arches of the ceiling. Of the 22 art-filled chapels, the most interesting is the Bolognini Chapel, the fourth chapel on the left as you enter. It is embellished with frescoes representing heaven and hell. The purity and simplicity of line represent some of the best of the Gothic in Italy.

✪ Fontana del Nettuno
Piazza del Nettono. Bus: 25 or 30.

Characteristic of the pride and independence of Bologna, this fountain has gradually become a symbol of the city, but it was in fact designed in 1566 by a Frenchman named Giambologna by the Italians (his fame rests largely on the work he did in Florence). Considered irreverent by some, vulgar by others, and magnificent by more liberal appraisers, this 16th-century fountain depicts Neptune with rippling muscles, a trident in one arm, and a heavy foot on the head of a dolphin. Around his feet are four cherubs, also with dolphins. At the base of the fountain are four very erotic sirens, each spouting five different streams of water from her breasts.

Palazzo Comunale

Piazza Maggiore 6. ☎ **203526**. Admission 5,000 lire ($3.15) each museum; 8,000 lire ($5) combined ticket to both museums. Tues–Sat 9am–2pm, Sun 9:30am–12:30pm. Closed holidays. Bus: 25 or 30.

Built in the 14th century, this town hall has seen major restorations, but happily retains its splendor. Enter through the courtyard, then proceed up the steps on the right to the **Comunal Collection of Fine Arts,** which includes many paintings from the 14th- and 19th-century Emilian school. Another section includes the Museum of Giorgio Morandi, an entire section devoted to the works of this famed Italian artist.

Basilica di St. Domenico

Piazza San Domenico 13. ☎ **6400411**. Admission is free. Daily 7:30am–7pm. Bus: 30.

The basilica dates from the 13th century, but it has seen many alterations and restorations. The church houses the tomb of St. Domenico, in front of the Capella della Madonna. The sculptured tomb—known as an *area*—is a Renaissance masterpiece, a joint enterprise of Niccolò Pisano, Guglielmo (a friar), Niccolò dell'Arca, Alfonso Lombardi, and the young Michelangelo. The choir stalls, the second major artistic work in the basilica, were carved by Damiano da Bergamo, another friar, in the 16th century.

Torre degli Asinelli

Piazza di Porta Ravegnanna. Admission 3,000 lire ($1.90). May–Sept daily 9am–6pm; Oct–Apr daily 9am–5pm. Bus: 25 or 30.

These leaning towers keep defying gravity year after year. The Due Torri were built by patricians in the 12th century. In the Middle Ages, Bologna had dozens of these skyscraper towers, anticipating Manhattan by several centuries. They were status symbols: the more powerful the family, the taller the tower. The smaller one, the **Garisenda,** is only 162 feet tall, leaning approximately $10^1/_2$ feet from the perpendicular. The taller one, the **Asinelli** (334 feet tall, a walk up of nearly 500 steps), inclines almost $7^1/_2$ feet. Those who scale the Asinelli should be awarded a medal, but instead they're presented with a panoramic view of the tile roofs of Bologna and the hills beyond.

After visiting the towers, take a walk up what must be the most architecturally elegant street in Bologna, strada Maggiore, with its colonnades and mansions.

Santo Stefano

Via Santo Stefano. ☎ **223256**. Admission is free. Apr–Sept daily 9am–noon and 3:30–6:30pm; off-season 9am–noon and 3:30–5:30pm. Bus: 25 or 30.

From the leaning towers, head up via Santo Stefano to see a virtual community of churches, linked together like Siamese twins. The first church you enter is the Church of the Crucifix, relatively simple with only one nave and a crypt. It dates from the 11th century. To the left is the entrance to the Church of Santo Sepolcro, its present structure dating principally from the 12th century. Under the altar is the tomb of patron saint Petronius. Continuing left, you enter another rebuilt church, this one honoring Saints Vitale and Agricola. The present building, graced with three apses, also dates from the 11th century. Reentering Sepolcro, take the back entrance this time into the Courtyard of Pilate, onto which several more chapels open. Through the courtyard entrance to the right, proceed into the Romanesque cloisters, dating from the 11th and 12th centuries. The names on the wall of the lapidary honor Bolognese war dead.

Chiesa di San Giacomo Maggiore

Piazza Rossini via Zamboni 15. ☎ **225970.** Admission is free. Daily 7am–noon and 3:30–6:30pm. Bus: 14, 25, or 50.

Located on piazza Rossini, the Church of St. James was originally a Gothic structure in the 13th century. But, like so many others, it has been altered and restored at the expense of its original design. Still, it's one of Bologna's most interesting churches, filled with art treasures. The Bentivoglio Chapel is the most sacred haunt, even though time has dimmed the luster of its frescoes. Near the altar, seek out a Madonna and Child enthroned, one of the most outstanding works of the artist Francesco Erancia. The holy pair are surrounded by angels and saints, as well as a half-naked Sebastian to the right. Nearby is a sepulchre of Antonio Bentivoglio, designed by Jacopo della Quercia, who labored so long over the doors to the Basilica of San Petronio. In the Chapel of Santa Cecilia you'll discover important frescoes by Francia and Lorenzo Costa.

Museo Civico Archeologico

Via dell'Archiginnasio 2. ☎ **233849.** Admission 5,000 lire ($3.15) adults, 2,500 lire ($1.55) children 15–18, free for children under 14. Tues–Fri 9am–2pm, Sat–Sun 9am–1pm and 3:30–7pm. Bus: Any bus to piazza Maggiore.

Housed in this museum is one of the major Egyptian collections in Italy, as well as important discoveries dug up in Emilia. As you enter, look to the right in the atrium to see a decapitated marble torso, said to be that of Nero. Opened in 1994, on the lower floor, a modern new Egyptian section presents a notable array of mummies and sarcophagi. The chief attraction in this collection is a cycle of bas-reliefs from Horemheb's tomb. On the ground floor a new wing contains a gallery of casts, displaying copies of famous Greek and Roman sculptures. On the first floor, reached through a gallery of casts, two exceptional burial items from Verucchio (Rimini) are exhibited. Note the wood furnishings, footrests, and the throne of tomb 89 which is decorated with scenes from everyday life and ceremonial parades.

Upstairs are cases of prehistoric objects, tools, and artifacts. The relics of the Etruscans comprise the best part of the museum, especially the highly stylized Askos Benacci, depicting a man on a horse that is perched on yet another animal. Also displayed are terro-cotta urns, a vase depicting fighting Greeks and Amazons, and a bronze Certosa jar dating from the 6th century B.C. The museum's greatest single treasure is Phidias's head of Athena Lemnia, a copy of a Greek work dating from the 5th century B.C.

Pinacoteca Nazionale di Bologna

Via delle Belle Arti 56. ☎ **243222.** Admission 8,000 lire ($5). Tues–Sat 9am–2pm, Sun 9am–1pm. Closed holidays. Bus: 36, 37, or 50.

The most significant works of the school of painting that flourished in Bologna from the 14th century to the heyday of the baroque have been assembled under one roof in this second-floor pinacoteca. In addition, the gallery houses works by other major Italian artists, such as Raphael's *St. Cecilia in Estasi.* Guido Reni (1575–1642) of Bologna steals the scene with his *St. Sebastian* and his *Pietà,* along with his equally penetrating *St. Andrea Corsini, The Slaying of the Innocents,* and his idealized *Samson the Victorious.* Other Reni works at the National include *The Flagellation of Christ, The Crucifixion,* and his masterpiece—*Ritratto della Madre*—a revealing portrait of his mother that must surely have inspired Whistler. Then, don't miss Vitale de Bologna's (1330–61) rendition of St. George slaying the

The World's Greatest China Shop

Faenza lent its name to a form of ceramics known as faïence which had originated on the Balearic island of Majorca, off the east coast of Spain. The town of Faenza, lying only 36 miles southeast of Bologna, became the Italian center of this industry. Faenza potters found inspiration in the work coming out of Majorca, and began to produce their own designs—characterized by brilliant, rich colors and floral decorations—in the 12th century. The art reached its pinnacle in the 16th century when the "hot-fire" process was perfected, during which ceramics were baked at a temperature of 1,742°F.

The legacy of this fabled industry is preserved today at the International Museum of Ceramics (Museo Internazionale delle Ceramiche), 2 via Campidoro (☎ 0546/21240), called "the world's greatest china shop." Housed here are works not only from the artisans of Faenza, but from throughout the world including pre-Columbian pottery from Peru. Of exceptional interest are Etruscan and Egyptian ceramics, as well as a wide-ranging collection from the Orient, even from the days of the Roman Empire.

Deserving special attention is the section devoted to modern ceramic art, including works by Matisse and Picasso. Displayed are Picasso vases including a platter with his dove of peace, a platter in rich colors by Chagall, a "surprise" from Matisse, and a framed ceramic plaque of the crucifixion by Georges Rouault. Another excellent work, the inspiration of a lesser-known artist, is a ceramic woman by Dante Morozzi. Even the great Léger tried his hand at ceramics.

The museum, attracting not only ceramic makers but interested visitors worldwide, is open June through September, Tuesday through Sunday from 9:30am to 1pm and 3:30 to 6:30pm (closes at 5:30pm off-season). Admission is 8,000 lire ($5).

dragon—a theme in European art that parallels Moby Dick in America. Also displayed are works by Francesco Francia, and especially noteworthy is a polyptych attributed to Giotto.

WHERE TO STAY

Bologna has four to six trade fairs a year, when prices of hotel rooms rise dramatically. Some hotels announce their prices in advance to clients; others prefer to wait until bookings are actually being accepted, perhaps to see what the market will bear. Be duly warned: At trade fair times (dates vary yearly) business clients from throughout Europe book the best rooms and you—as a tourist—will be paying a lot of money to visit Bologna. When inquiring about a good time to visit, try to avoid trade fairs if you're not there on business. The tourist office has dates of trade fairs as they are announced.

VERY EXPENSIVE

Grand Hotel Baglioni

Via dell'Indipendenza 8, 40121 Bologna. ☎ **051/225445.** Fax 051/234840. 117 rms, 8 suites. A/C MINIBAR TV TEL. 495,000–535,000 lire ($309.40–$334.40) double; from 800,000 lire ($500) suite. Rates include breakfast. AE, DC, MC, V. Parking 40,000 lire ($25). Bus: 27 or 11.

The Grand Hotel boasts a desirable location in the center of Bologna, near the main square and Neptune's fountain. Its facade is crafted of the same reddish brick that distinguishes many of the city's older buildings. The interior is noted for its wealth of wall and ceiling frescoes, many of which were painted by two of Bologna's most famous 17th-century artists, the Carracci brothers. Each room contains reproductions of antique furniture as well as all the modern conveniences that one would expect in a grand hotel.

Dining/Entertainment: Good-tasting Bolognese cooking is served in the elegant à la carte restaurant, I Carracci. See "Where to Dine" below.

Services: Room service, babysitting, laundry, valet.

Facilities: Hairdresser.

EXPENSIVE

Royal Hotel Carlton
Montebello 8, 40121 Bologna. ☎ **051/249361.** Fax 051/249724. 251 rms, 22 suites. A/C MINIBAR TV TEL. 395,000 lire ($246.90) double; from 500,000 lire ($312.50) suite. Rates include breakfast. AE, DC, MC, V. Parking 30,000 lire ($18.75). Bus: 25 or 30.

Royal Hotel Carlton, only a few minutes' walk from the railway station and many of the national monuments, is L-shaped, rises six stories high, and has a triangular garden. It's in the modern style, with a balcony and picture window for each bedroom. Inside, the decorator infused the establishment with warmth.

Dining/Entertainment: One of the most dramatic staircases in Bologna sweeps from the second floor in an elegant crescent to a point near the comfortable American Bar. The grill restaurant serves good regional and international food in an ambience of style and comfort.

Services: Room service, babysitting, laundry, valet.

Facilities: Limited facilities for the disabled.

MODERATE

Grand Hotel Elite
Via Aurelio Saffi 36, 40131 Bologna. ☎ **051/6498222.** Fax. 051/6492426. 153 rms, 20 suites. A/C MINIBAR TV TEL. 195,000 lire ($121.90) double; 245,000 lire ($153.15) suite. During trade fairs 320,000 lire ($200) double; 380,000 lire ($237.50) suite. Rates include breakfast. AE, DC, MC, V. Parking 20,000–27,000 lire ($12.50–$16.90). Closed Aug. Bus: 13 or 23.

Rising eight floors from a position on the city's northwestern edge, a 12-minute walk to the center, this establishment was originally built in the 1970s as a combination of private apartments and hotel rooms. In 1993, its administration transformed the entire structure into hotel rooms, thereby greatly enlarging its capacity to hold short-term visitors. Bedrooms are comfortable. Even if you're not staying at the hotel, you may want to patronize the hotel's restaurant, Cordon Bleu, which features international food and the classic cuisine of Emilia-Romagna. Also popular is a bar with comfortable banquettes and a good selection of whisky and regional wines.

Hotel Milano Excelsior
Viale Pietramellara 51, 40121 Bologna. ☎ **051/246178.** Fax 051/249448. 72 rms. A/C MINIBAR TV TEL. 250,000 lire ($156.25) double. During trade fairs 360,000 lire ($225) double. Rates include breakfast. AE, DC, MC, V. Free parking. Bus: 25 or 30.

Hotel Milano Excelsior, built in the 1950s, is a first-class hotel near piazza Medaglie d'Oro. It has all the trappings and fringe benefits associated with its class: a private bath in every soundproof room, an American bar, and a restaurant decorated with crystal chandeliers. Frequented largely by a commercial clientele, the Milano Excelsior has a completely modern decor, although a number of its bedrooms have been filled with the traditional designs of the past. The hotel offers excellent service and an attentive staff. The hotel dining room, the Ristorante Felsineo, serves tasty Emilian cookery.

Tre Vecchi

Via dell'Indipendenza 47, 40121 Bologna. ☎ **051/231991.** Fax 051/224143. 96 rms. A/C MINIBAR TV TEL. 190,000 lire ($118.75) double. Breakfast 18,000 lire ($11.25) extra. During trade fairs (including breakfast) 290,000 lire ($181.25) double. AE, DC, MC, V. Parking 30,000 lire ($18.75). Bus: 25 or 30.

This hotel was established in the 1970s within a century-old building on a much-traveled street in the center of town. Despite the traffic, bedrooms are clean, bright, and relatively quiet, thanks to the insulated windows and soundproofing. The gentle humor within the establishment's name ("Three Geriatrics") was conceived by the trio of aging entrepreneurs who originally founded it. The hotel contains two elevators, four stories, and several lounges where guests can relax and watch TV. The hotel lies a 5-minute walk from the railway station, from which many buses depart for all parts of Bologna. No meals are served other than breakfast.

INEXPENSIVE

Alexander

Viale Pietramellara 47, 40121 Bologna. ☎ **051/247118.** Fax 051/247248. 108 rms. A/C MINIBAR TV TEL. 195,000 lire ($121.90) double. During trade fairs 240,000 lire ($150) double. Rates include breakfast. AE, DC, MC, V. Parking 10,000 lire ($6.25) outside. Closed Aug. Bus: 25 or 30.

Built in the early 1960s, the Alexander, perhaps the best hotel buy near the main hub of automotive and rail traffic, piazza Medaglie d'Oro, is for the wayfarer who wants comfort at a moderate price. Perched near the more expensive Hotel Milano Excelsior, the Alexander tempts with its quite-good monochromatic bedrooms, which contain brightly painted foyers, compact furnishings, and neat, tidy baths. The thickness of the double glass in the windows helps to blot out street noises. The main lounge is crisply and warmly paneled in wood, with lounge chairs placed on Turkish rugs.

✪ Regina Hotel

Via dell'Indipendenza 51, 40121 Bologna. ☎ **051/248878.** Fax 051/224143. 61 rms (all with bath). A/C MINIBAR TV TEL. 160,000 lire ($100) double. Breakfast 20,000 lire ($12.50) extra. During trade fairs (with breakfast) 200,000 lire ($125) double. AE, DC, MC, V. Parking 20,000 lire ($12.50). Bus: 25 or 30.

Regina Hotel, located right off piazza dell'Otto Agosta, was originally built in the 1800s, then modernized in the 1970s. Its functional bedrooms are small and without many frills, but they're attractive and comfortably furnished. The personnel who run the place are helpful, and the maids keep everything clean. The hotel has no restaurant, but there is a pleasant bar and a modern lounge dotted with sofas.

WHERE TO DINE
EXPENSIVE

Nuovi Notai

Via de'Pignattari 1. ☎ **228694**. Reservations required. Main courses 15,000–25,000 lire ($9.40–$15.65); fixed-price menus 45,000–60,000 lire ($28.15–$37.50). AE, DC, MC, V. Mon–Sat 12:30–2:30pm and 8–10:30pm. INTERNATIONAL.

Hidden behind a lattice- and ivy-covered façade next to the cathedral, within view of one of the most beautiful squares in Italy, this popular restaurant draws from a loyal clientele of local residents. In summer, sidewalk tables are placed outside. Music lovers and relaxing businesspeople appreciate the piano bar. The decor combines belle époque with Italian flair and includes artwork, hanging Victorian lamps, and clutches of beautifully arranged flowers on each table, all in a subdued color scheme. The building dates from 1382.

The Notai, has been praised by a variety of Italian food critics for having some of the best food in a town distinguished for its fine restaurants. Menu items include a flan of cheese fondue; gratin of gnocchi with truffles; a filet of beef cooked in *cartoccio* (a paper bag), and garnished with porcini mushrooms; or else a breast of deboned wild goose. Dessert might be a suprême of almonds served with ricotta cheese and coffee sauce.

MODERATE

Antica Osteria Romagnola

Via Rialto 13. ☎ **263699**. Reservations recommended for dinner. Main courses 22,000–30,000 lire ($13.75–$18.75). AE, DC, MC, V. Wed–Sun 12:30–2:30pm, Tues–Sat 7:30–11pm. Closed Aug and Jan 1–15. Bus: 25 or 30. ITALIAN.

Unlike many of its competitors in Bologna, this establishment offers cuisine from throughout Italy, including the distant south, instead of focusing exclusively on the dishes of Emilia-Romagna. Unusual and well-flavored risottos might launch many a repast. Or you can make a selection of antipasti, as the kitchen puts much effort into a savory selection of dishes. The array of pastas is also impressive, including ravioli with essence of truffles, garganelli pasta with zucchini, or pasta whipped with asparagus tips. You might also select a terrine of ricotta and arugula, the latter considered an aphrodisiac by the ancient Romans. For your main course you might try a springtime specialty of cabretto (roast goat) with artichokes and potatoes, or filet mignon prepared with basil.

Grassilli

Via del Luzzo 3. ☎ **237938**. Reservations required. Main courses 18,000–36,000 lire ($11.25–$22.50). AE, MC, V. Thurs–Tues 12:30–2:30pm and 8–10:15pm. Closed July 15–Aug 15 and Dec 23–Jan 1. Bus: 14, 23, 27, or 45. BOLOGNESE.

Grassilli is a good bet for conservative regional cooking with few deviations from the time-tested formulas that have made Bolognese cuisine famous. It's located in a 1750s building across from an antique store, on a narrow cobblestone alleyway a short block from the two leaning towers. The restaurant also has a summertime streetside canopy for outdoor dining. At night it can be festive, and your good time will probably be enhanced if you order such specialties as tortellini in a mushroom-cream sauce, the chef's special tournedos, maccheroni with fresh peas and prosciutto, a range of grilled and roasted meats, and many tasty desserts.

I Carracci

In the Grand Hotel Baglioni, via dell'Indipendenza 8. ☎ **225445.** Reservations required. Main courses 20,000–30,000 lire ($12.50–$18.75). AE, DC, MC, V. Mon–Sat noon–2:30pm and 7:30–10:30pm. Closed Aug 1–25. Bus: 27 or 11. ITALIAN/INTERNATIONAL.

The most fashionable restaurant in Bologna—and arguably the best—this restaurant is named after a family of artists who decorated the premises with frescoes depicting the four seasons. The elegant dining room dates from the 16th century. The frescoes on the ceiling were painted in the 1700s by the Carracci brothers, and their interpretation of the four seasons is richly allegorical and mythical. Table linen and fabrics are color coordinated into one of the most harmonious dining rooms in the city. The service is impeccable. In air-conditioned comfort, you can peruse a menu that is seasonally adjusted to secure only the freshest produce and the most high-quality meat, poultry, and fish. Dishes that have proven reliable in the past include tortellini in brodo, tagliatelle in ragú de Bologna, lasagne Emiliana, veal scallop alla Bolognese, wild boar cacciatore, and grilled filet of salmon. The wine list is among the finest of any restaurant in the province.

Montegrappa da Nello

Via Montegrappa 2. ☎ **236331.** Reservations recommended for dinner. Main courses 15,000–25,000 lire ($9.40–$15.65). AE, DC, MC, V. Tues–Sun noon–3pm and 7–11:30pm. Closed Aug. Bus: 25 or 30. BOLOGNESE/INTERNATIONAL.

Montegrappa da Nello has a faithful following that swears by its pasta dishes. It's one of the few restaurants that still does the old-fashioned and classic Bolognese cuisine. Franco and Ezio Bolini are your hosts, and they insist that all produce be fresh. The restaurant, just a short walk from piazza Maggiore, offers tortellina Montegrappa, a pasta favorite served in a cream-and-meat sauce. Another fine spaghetti pasta dish is *graminia*, a very fine white spaghetti served with a medley of mushrooms, cream, and pepper. The restaurant is also known for its fresh white truffles and mushrooms. You can try these in an unusual salad with porcini, the large wild mushrooms. Another salad I like is made with truffles, mushrooms, parmesan cheese, and artichokes. For a main course, I suggest misto del cuoco—a mixed platter from the chef, featuring a selection of his specialties, including zampone, cotoletta bolognese, and scaloppine with fresh mushrooms.

Ristorante al Pappagallo

Piazza della Mercanzia 3C. ☎ **232807.** Reservations required. Main courses 30,000–35,000 lire ($18.75–$21.90). AE, DC, MC, V. Tues–Sat 12:30–2:30pm, Mon–Sat 8–10:20pm. Bus: 25 or 30. BOLOGNESE.

This restaurant draws a faithful coterie of gastronomes. Long-ago diners have included Einstein, Hitchcock, and Toscanini. It's still going strong, with memories of a glorious past, but competition long ago buried its former reputation as the finest restaurant in Italy. "The Parrot" is housed on the ground floor of a Gothic mansion, across the street from the landmark 14th-century Merchants' Loggia (a short walk from the leaning towers). Under a beamed ceiling and crystal chandeliers, diners from many lands are introduced to the Bolognese cuisine.

For the best possible introduction, begin your meal with lasagne verde al forno (baked lasagne that gets its green color from minced spinach). And then, for the main course, the specialty of the house: filetti di tacchino, superb turkey breasts baked with white wine, parmigiano cheese, and truffles. With your meal, the restaurant serves the amber-colored Albana wine and the sparkling red Lambrusco, two of the best-known wines from the vineyards of Emilia.

INEXPENSIVE

☺ Diana

Via Indipendenza 24. ☎ **231302.** Reservations recommended. Main courses 18,000–26,000 lire ($11.25–$16.25). AE, DC, MC, V. Tues–Sun noon–2:30pm and 7–10:30pm. Closed Aug 1–20 and Jan 1–10. Bus: 25 or 27. REGIONAL/INTERNATIONAL.

Set within a late medieval building in the heart of town, this well-recommended restaurant has been a popular fixture in Bologna since around 1920. It offers three gracefully decorated dining rooms (one large one lined with murals and two small ones) and a verdant terrace for outdoor dining during clement weather. This restaurant was named in honor of the goddess of the hunt, because of the many game and seasonal dishes it served when it was first established. In recent years, although game is still featured in season, it opts for a staple of regional and international cuisine, not all of it game, but all of it competently prepared. Examples include tortellini in brodo; roasted or boiled meats of all kinds; veal cutlet bolognese; grilled turbot, grilled sole, or grilled scampi.

Rosteria da Luciano

Via Nazario Sauro 19. ☎ **231249.** Reservations recommended. Main courses 18,000–26,000 lire ($11.25–$16.25). AE, DC, MC, V. Thurs–Tues noon–2pm and 7:30–10:30pm. Closed Aug and Dec 24–Jan 1. Bus: 25 or 30. BOLOGNESE.

Rosteria da Luciano is seriously challenging the competition for supremacy. It serves some of the best food in Bologna. On a side street, within walking distance of the city center, it has an art deco style and contains three large rooms with a real Bolognese atmosphere. The front room, opening onto the kitchen, is preferred. As a novelty, there's a see-through window on the street, looking directly into the kitchen.

The chefs not only can't keep any secrets from you, but you get an appetizing preview of what awaits you before you step inside. To begin your gargantuan repast, request the tortellini Petroniani. Well-recommended main dishes include the fritto misto all'Italiana and the scaloppe con porcini (mushrooms). One savory offering is cotoletta alla bolognese, layered with ham and Parmesan, then baked. A dramatic dessert is crêpes flambés.

A NEARBY PLACE TO DINE

✪ San Domenico

Via Gaspara Sacchi 1, Imola. ☎ **0542/29000.** Reservations required. Main courses 42,000–50,000 lire ($26.25–$31.25); fixed-price lunch (Tues–Sat) 55,000 lire ($34.40); fixed-price Sun lunch or fixed-price dinner 80,000 lire ($50) including wine. AE, DC, MC, V. Tues–Sun 12:30–2:30pm and 8–10:30pm. Closed first two weeks of Jan; Aug 1–24 and Sun–Mon June–Aug. ITALIAN.

To an increasing degree, gastronomes from all over Europe and America are traveling to the unlikely village of Imola, which lies 21 miles southeast of Bologna, to savor the cuisine of what some food critics consider the best restaurant in Italy. The restaurant can also be easily reached from Ravenna as well.

The cuisine here is sometimes compared to modern cuisine creations in France. However, owner Gian Luigi Morini claims that his delectable offerings are nothing more than adaptations of festive regional dishes rendered lighter and subtler, then served in more manageable portions. He was born in this rambling stone building whose simple facade faces the courtyard of a neighboring church.

For 25 years Signor Morini worked at a local bank, returning home every night to administer his restaurant. Now his establishment is among the primary attractions of Emilia-Romagna.

A tuxedo-clad member of his talented young staff will escort you to a table near the tufted leather banquettes whose dark colors offset the candles, baroque silver, and hanging lamps whose fabric matches that of the tented ceilings. Meals include heavenly concoctions made with the freshest ingredients. You might select goose-liver pâté studded with white truffles, fresh shrimp in a creamy sweet bell-pepper sauce, roast rack of lamb with fresh rosemary, stuffed suprême of chicken wrapped in lettuce leaves, or fresh handmade spaghetti with shellfish. Signor Morini has collected some of the best vintages in Europe for the past 30 years. Men are required to wear a jacket and tie.

2 Ferrara

259 miles N of Rome, 32 miles N of Bologna, 62 miles SW of Venice

When Papa Borgia, also known as Pope Alexander VI, was shopping around for a third husband for the apple of his eye, darling Lucrezia, his gaze fell on the influential house of Este. From the 13th century, this great Italian family had dominated Ferrara, building up a powerful duchy and a reputation as builders of palaces and patrons of the arts. Alfonse d'Este, son of the shrewd but villainous Ercole I, who was the ruling duke of Ferrara, was an attractive, virile candidate for Lucrezia's much-used hand (her second husband had already been murdered, perhaps by her brother, Cesare, who was the apple of nobody's eye—with the possible exception of Machiavelli).

Although the Este family may have had private reservations (after all, it was common gossip that the pope "knew" his daughter in the biblical sense), they finally consented to the marriage. As the Duchess of Ferrara, a position she held until her death, Lucrezia was to have seven children. But one of her grandchildren, Alfonso II, wasn't as prolific as his forebear, although he had a reputation as a roué. He left the family without a male heir. The greedy eye of Pope Clement VIII took quick action on this, gobbling up the city as his fief in the waning months of the 16th century. The great house of Este went down in history, and Ferrara sadly declined under the papacy.

Incidentally, Alfonso II was a dubious patron of Torquato Tasso (1544–95), author of the epic *Jerusalem Delivered,* a work that was to make him the most celebrated poet of the late Renaissance. The legend of Tasso—who is thought to have been insane, paranoid, or at least tormented—has steadily grown over the centuries. It didn't need any more boosting, but Goethe fanned the legend through the Teutonic lands with his late 18th-century drama *Torquato Tasso.* It is said that Alfonso II at one time made Tasso his prisoner.

Ferrara today is still relatively undiscovered, especially by the globe-trotting North American. The city is richly blessed, with much of its legacy intact. Among the historic treasures remaining are a great cathedral and the Este Castle, along with enough ducal palaces to make for a fast-paced day of sightseeing. Its palaces, for the most part, have long been robbed of their lavish furnishings, but the faded frescoes, the paintings not carted off, and the palatial rooms are reminders of the vicissitudes of power.

ESSENTIALS

GETTING THERE **By Train** Getting there by train is fast and efficient, as Ferrara lies on the main train line between Bologna and Venice. A total of 33 trains a day pass through here, originating in Bologna. Trip time is 40 minutes, and the cost is 4,000 lire ($2.50) one way. Some 24 trains arrive from Venice (trip time: 1¹/₂ hours). A one-way fare is 8,800 lire ($5.50).

By Bus From most destinations the train is best, but if you're in Modena (see below) you'll find 11 bus departures a day for Ferrara. Trip time is between 1¹/₂ and 2 hours, and a one-way ticket costs 8,200 lire ($5.15). In Ferrara, bus information for the surrounding area is available by calling 205235.

By Car From Bologna, take A13 north. From Venice, take A4 southwest to Padua and continue on A13 south to Ferrara.

VISITOR INFORMATION The telephone area code for Ferrara is 0532. The tourist information office is at corso Giovecca 21 (☎ 209370).

WHAT TO SEE & DO

Castello Estense

Piazza della Repubblica. ☎ **299279.** Admission 6,000 lire ($3.75). Tues–Sat 9:30am–12:30pm and 1:30–6:30pm, Sun 10am–6pm. Bus: 1, 2, or 9.

A moated, four-towered castle (lit at night), this proud fortress began as a bricklayer's dream near the end of the 14th century, although its face has been lifted and wrenched around for centuries. It was home to the powerful Este family. Here the dukes went about their daily chores: murdering their wives' lovers, beheading or imprisoning potential enemies, whatever. Today it's used for the provincial and prefectural administration offices, and many of its once-lavish rooms may be inspected—notably the Salon of Games, the Room of Games, and the Room of Dawn, as well as a chapel that once belonged to Renata di Francia, daughter of Louis XII.

Il Duomo

Piazza Cattedrale. ☎ **207449.** Admission is free. Apr–Sept daily 10am–noon and 4–6pm; Oct–Mar daily 10am–noon and 3–5pm. Bus: 1, 2, or 9.

Located only a short stroll from the Este castle, the Duomo weds the delicate Gothic with the more virile Romanesque. The offspring: an exciting marble facade. Behind the cathedral is a typically Renaissance campanile (bell tower). Inside, the massive structure is heavily baroqued, as the artisans of still another era festooned it with trompe l'oeil. The entrance to the **Museo del Duomo** lies to the left of the atrium as you enter. It's worth a visit just to see works by Ferrara's most outstanding painter of the 15th century, Cosmé Tura. Aesthetically controversial, the big attraction here is Tura's St. George slaying the dragon to save a red-stockinged damsel in distress. Opposite is a work by Jacopo della Quercia depicting a sweet, regal Madonna with a pomegranate in one hand and the Child in the other. This is one of della Quercia's first masterpieces. Also from the Renaissance heyday of Ferrara are some bas-reliefs, notably a "Giano bifronte," a mythological figure looking at the past and the future, along with some 16th-century *arazzi*, or tapestries, woven by hand.

Palazzo Schifanoia

Via Scandiana 23. ☎ **64178.** Admission 6,000 lire ($3.75) adults, free for children under 18. Daily 9am–7pm. Closed major holidays. Bus: 1, 2, or 9.

Housing the **Museo Civico d'Arte Antica,** the first part of the Schifanoia Palace was built in 1385 for Albert V d'Este, and later enlarged by Borso d'Este (1450–71). The museum was founded in 1758 and was transferred to its present site in 1898. The first part of the collection then exhibited, which consisted of coins and medals, was enhanced by donations of archaeological finds, antique bronzes, small Renaissance plates and pottery, and other collections.

Art lovers are lured to its Salon of the Months to see the astrological cycle. The humanist Pellegrino Prisciani at court conceived the subjects of the cycle, though Cosmé Tura, the official court painter for the Estes, was probably the organizer of the works. Tura was founder of the Ferrarese School, to which belonged, among others, Ercole de'Roberti and Francesco del Cossa, who painted the March, April, and May scenes. In the wall cycle, which represents the 12 months of the year, each month is subdivided into three horizontal bands: the lower band shows scenes from the daily life of courtiers and people, the middle one the relative sign of the zodiac, and the upper one presents the triumph of the classical divinity for that particular myth. The frescoes form a complex presentation, leading to varying interpretations as to the meaning.

The Este Tomb
At the Monastery of Corpus Domini, via Pergolato 4. ☎ **207825.** Admission is free (donations accepted). Mon–Fri 9:30am–noon and 4–5:30pm. Bus: 1 or 9.

Lucrezia Borgia, the most famous woman of the Renaissance, lies here buried with her secrets. The much-married duchess gave up her wicked ways in Rome when she became the wife of Alfonso I (except for, perhaps, a discreet love affair with the handsome, romantic Venetian poet Bembo). The woman whose very name has become synonymous with evil lies under a flat slab, a simple tomb. Frankly, it's not much of a sight, but it would be heretical to come all this way and not pay your respects to the seductive enchantress who, dressed in crimson velvet, died on a warm Emilian morning on June 24, 1519, having only days before given birth to a daughter.

Palazzo Ludovico il Moro
Via XX Settembre no. 124. ☎ **66299.** Admission is free. Tues–Sun 9am–2pm. Closed at presstime; check status locally. Bus: 1, 2, or 9.

This ducal Renaissance palace makes a handsome background for the priceless collection of Etruscan works discovered in the necropolis at Spina (in the environs of Comechio). The **National Archeological Museum,** which is housed in the building, contains the booty unearthed from the Etruscan tomb. Downstairs is a salon with admirable frescoes by Garofalo. In another room are two hand-hewn trees (pirogues) that date from late Roman years. Afterward, you may want to stroll through the gardens behind the palace.

Palazzo dei Diamanti
Corso Ercole d'Este 21. ☎ **205844.** Admission 6,000 lire ($3.75). Tues–Sat 9am–2pm, Sun 9am–1pm. Bus: 1, 2, or 9.

Palazzo dei Diamanti, another sparkler to d'Este splendor, is so named because of the diamond-shaped stones on its facade. Of the handful of museums sheltered here, the **National Picture Gallery (Pinacoteca Nazionale)** is the most important, holding the works of the Ferrarese artists—notably the trio of old masters, Tura, del Cossa, and Roberti. The collection covers the chief period of artistic expression in Ferrara from the 14th to the 18th century. The palace also houses

the Municipal Gallery of Modern Art, which sponsors the most important contemporary exhibitions of modern art in town.

Casa Romei

Via Savonarola 30. ☎ **40341**. Admission 4,000 lire ($2.50). Daily 10am–5pm. Bus: 1, 2,
or 9.

This 15th-century palace, Casa Romei, was the property of a rich man, John
Romei, a friend and confidant of the fleshy Duke Borso d'Este, who made the Este
realm a duchy. John (or Giovanni) was later to marry one of the Este princesses,
although we don't know if it was for love or power or both. In later years, Lucrezia
and her gossipy coterie—the ducal carriage drawn by handsome white horses—
used to descend upon the Romei house, perhaps to receive Borgia messengers from
Rome. The house is near the Este tomb. Its once-elegant furnishings have been
carted off, but the chambers—many with terra-cotta fireplaces—remain, and the
casa has been filled with frescoes and sculpture.

WHERE TO STAY
EXPENSIVE

Hotel-Restaurante Duchessa Isabella

Via Palestro 70, 44100 Ferrara. ☎ **0532/202121.** Fax 0532/202638. 22 rms (all with bath),
6 suites. A/C MINIBAR TV TEL. 430,000 lire ($268.75) double; from 550,000 lire ($343.75)
suite. Rates include breakfast. MC, V. Free parking. Bus: 1, 2, or 9.

Originally this hotel was the private home of the head of one of the region's most
respected Jewish organizations until the late 1980s. In 1990, it reopened as a five-
star hotel with a spectacular decor. Named in honor of the d'Este family's most
famous ancestor, Isabella, the hotel maintains a lavish garden—which adjoins
several other gardens to appear larger than it is—and many of the building's
original frescoes. Bedrooms are each decorated in a different color scheme, and are
identified by the names of the flowers whose colors they most closely resemble.
Each imbues a sense of history, is outfitted with all the electronic amenities a visitor
might want, and is very, very comfortable.

Dining/Entertainment: The hotel operates an elegant restaurant that is set beneath lavishly gilded and painted ceilings. (In summer, the venue moves outside
into the garden.) Cuisine is based on the traditional recipes of Emilia-Romagna,
with meals ranging from 75,000 to 95,000 lire ($46.90 to $59.40) per person.
Care has been taken to research and revive some very old regional recipes that
might not be readily available in other restaurants, although a wide choice of less
esoteric dishes is also available.

Services: A horse-drawn landau, decorated with the image of Isabella d'Este, will
take guests on excursions around Ferrara's historic center. There's also room
service, conference facilities, laundry and valet service, and free use of bicycles.

Facilities: A private garden blooming with flowers, vines, and venerable trees.

MODERATE

Ripagrande Hotel

Via Ripagrande 21, 44100 Ferrara. ☎ **0532/765250.** Fax 0532/764377. 20 rms,
20 junior suites. A/C MINIBAR TV TEL. 270,000–290,000 lire ($168.75–$181.25) double;
from 330,000 lire ($206.25) junior suite. Rates include breakfast. AE, DC, MC, V. Parking
20,000 lire ($12.50). Bus: 1, 2, or 9.

Ripagrande Hotel, one of the most unusual hotels in town, occupies one of the
city's Renaissance palaces. Rich coffered ceilings, walls in Ferrarese brickwork,

16th-century columns, and a wide stairway with a floral cast-iron handrail characterize the broad entrance hall. On the inside are two Renaissance courtyards decorated with columns and capitals. The hotel has 40 rooms, half of which are junior suites with sleeping areas connected to an internal stairway. The furnishings are modern and in good taste. Laundry and room service are provided.

WHERE TO DINE
INEXPENSIVE

Grotta Azzurra
Piazza Sacrati 43. ☎ **209152.** Reservations recommended. Main courses 13,500–35,000 lire ($8.45–$21.90). AE, DC, MC, V. Thurs–Tues 12:30pm–2:30pm, Mon–Tues and Thurs–Sat 7:30–9:30pm. Closed Jan 2–10 and Aug 1–15. Bus: 3, 6, 9, or 11. BOLOGNESE/EMILIANA.

Behind a classic brick facade on a busy square, Grotta Azzurra seems like a restaurant you might encounter on the sunny isle of Capri, not in Ferrara. It was established back in the halcyon La Dolce Vita days of the 1950s. However, the cuisine is firmly entrenched in the northern Italian kitchen. It's best to visit in the autumn when favorite dishes include wild boar and pheasant. Usually these dishes are served with the characteristic polenta. Many sausages, served as antipasti, are made with game as well. The chef also prepares esoteric dishes such as a boiled calf's head and tongue. A local favorite is stuffed pork leg, which is also boiled. He's also an expert at grilled meats, especially pork, veal, and beef. If you're rushed, a number of dishes can be prepared in just 15 minutes. You might begin with a tasty helping of creamy lasagne.

La Provvidenza
Corso Ercole I d'Este 92. ☎ **205187.** Reservations required. Main courses 18,000–22,000 lire ($11.25–$13.75). AE, DC, MC, V. Tues–Sun noon–2:30pm and 8–10pm. Closed Aug 11–17. Bus: 5. ITALIAN.

La Provvidenza stands on the same street as the Palazzo dei Diamanti, a sightseeing attraction already mentioned. The building itself is from around 1750, and there's been a restaurant here for at least a century, although present management dates only from the 1970s. It has a farm-style interior, with a little garden where its regulars request tables in fair weather. The antipasti table spread before you is the finest I have seen—or sampled—in Ferrara. It includes fresh anchovies, mozzarella with sweet yellow peppers, fresh asparagus in spring and several kinds of shellfish. Really hearty eaters should order a pasta, such as fettuccine with smoked salmon, before tackling the main course, perhaps perfectly grilled and seasoned veal chops. Other specialties include pasticchio alla Ferrarese (macaroni mixed with a mushroom and meat sauce laced with a creamy white sauce), or baked lasagne. A *fritto misto di carne* or mixed grill is also served. The dessert choice is wide and luscious. Take a large appetite to this local favorite.

3 Modena

25 miles NW of Bologna, 250 miles NW of Rome, 81 miles N of Florence

After Ferrara fell to Pope Clement VIII, the duchy of the Este family was established at Modena in the closing years of the 16th century. Lying in the Po Valley, the provincial and commercial city possesses a great many art treasures that evoke its more glorious past. And, too, the chefs of Modena enjoy an outstanding reputation in hard-to-please gastronomic circles. Traversed by the ancient

Roman road, via Emilia, Modena (pronounced *Mo*-den-ah) is often visited by European art connoisseurs, less frequently by overseas travelers.

Many visitors who care little about antiquities come to Modena just to visit the plants that make the sports cars of Ferrari and Maserati. Ask at the tourist office (see above) for details and a map. Those who can veer from northern Italy's main-line attractions for a few hours will be richly rewarded by a visit to Modena.

ESSENTIALS

GETTING THERE **By Train** There are good connections to and from Bologna (one train every 30 minutes); trip time is 20 minutes, and a one-way fare is 3,200 lire ($2). Trains arrive from Parma once per hour (trip time: 40 minutes); the one-way fare is 4,300 lire ($2.70).

By Bus The train is better. However, if you're in Ferrara (see above), one local ATCM bus (no. 7) leaves Ferrara for Modena every hour; trip time is an hour and a half, and a one-way fare runs 5,400 lire ($3.40). In Modena, telephone 308801 for bus information, including local connections.

By Car From Bologna, take Autostrada A1 northeast until you see the turnoff for Modena.

VISITOR INFORMATION Modena's telephone area code is 059. The tourist information office is at via Scudari 30 (☎ 222482).

WHAT TO SEE & DO

✪ Il Duomo

Piazza del Duomo. ☎ **216078.** Admission is free. Daily 7am–1pm and 3:30–7pm. Bus: 7 or 11.

One of the glories of the Romanesque in northern Italy, the Duomo of Modena was built in a style that will be familiar to those who've been to Lombardy. It was founded in the summer of the closing year of the 11th century, and designed by an architect named Lanfranco, with Viligelmo serving as decorator.

The work was carried out by Campionesi masons from Lake Lugano. The cathedral, consecrated in 1184, was dedicated to St. Geminiano, the patron saint of Modena, a 4th-century Christian and defender of the faith. Towering from the rear is the "Ghirlandina," a 12th- to 14th-century campanile, 285 feet tall. Leaning slightly, the bell tower guards the replica of the "Secchia Rapita" (stolen bucket), which was garnered as booty from a defeated Bolognese.

The facade of the Duomo features a 13th-century rose window by Anselmo da Campione. It also features Viligelmo's main entryway, with pillars supported by lions, as well as Viligelmo bas-reliefs depicting scenes from Genesis. But don't confine your look to the front. The south door, the so-called Princes' Door, was designed by Viligelmo in the 12th century, and is framed by bas-reliefs that illustrate scenes in the saga of the patron saint. You'll find an outside pulpit from the 15th century, with emblems of Matthew, Mark, Luke, and John.

Inside, there's a vaulted ceiling, and the overall effect is gravely impressive. It was all wisely and prudently restored by the Modenese during the first part of the 20th century, so that its present look resembles the original design. The gallery above the crypt is an outstanding piece of sculpture, supported by four lions. The pulpit, also intriguing, is held up by two hunchbacks. The crypt, where the body of the patron saint was finally taken, is a forest of columns. In it, you'll find Guido Mazzoni's *Holy Family* group in terra-cotta, which was completed in 1480.

After visiting the crypt, head up the stairs on the left, where the custodian (tip expected) will lead you to the Museum of the Cathedral. In many ways the most intriguing of the Duomo's art, the metropes displayed here used to adorn the architecture. Like gargoyles, these profane bas-reliefs are a marvelous change of pace from solemn ecclesiastical art. One, for example, is part bird and part man—with one hoof. But that's not all: He's eating a fish whole.

✪ Galleria Estense

Palazzo del Musei, largo Sant'Agostino 48, off via Emilia. ☎ **235004.** Admission to gallery, 8,000 lire ($5) adults, free for children under 18; library, free. Gallery, Tues–Wed and Fri 9am–2pm, Thurs and Sat 9am–7pm, Sun 9am–2pm. Library, Apr–Oct Mon–Sat 9am–2pm; Nov–Mar Mon–Fri 9am–8pm, Sat 9am–2pm. Bus: 7 or 11.

The Estense Gallery is noted for its paintings from the Emilian or Bolognese schools from the 14th to the 18th century. The nucleus of it was created by the Este family in Ferrara's, and afterward, Modena's heyday as duchies. Some of the finest work is by Spanish artists, including a miniature triptych by El Greco of Toledo and a portrait of Francesco I d'Este by Velázquez. Other works of art include Bernini's bust of Francesco I, plus paintings by Cosmé Tura, Correggio, Veronese, Tintoretto, Carracci, Reni, and Guercino.

Considered one of the greatest libraries in southern Europe, the Biblioteca Estense (☎ 222248), contains around 500,000 printed works and 13,000 manuscripts. An assortment of the most interesting volumes are kept under glass for visitors to inspect. Of these, the most celebrated is the 1,200-page Bible of Borso d'Este, bordered with stunning miniatures.

WHERE TO STAY
MODERATE

Canalgrande Hotel

Corso Canalgrande 6, 41100 Modena. ☎ **059/217160.** Fax 059/221674. 68 rms, 4 suites. A/C MINIBAR TV TEL. 262,000 lire ($163.75) double; from 400,000 lire ($250) suite. Rates include breakfast. AE, DC, MC, V. Parking 15,000 lire ($9.40). Bus: 7 or 11.

Located in the old town, the Canalgrande Hotel is housed in a stucco 300-year-old palace. It has elaborate mosaic floors, Victorian-era furniture, carved and frescoed ceilings, and chandeliers. There's a garden behind the hotel whose central flowering tree seems filled with every kind of bird in Modena. Some visitors find the monumental oil paintings of the salons like a museum. Under the basement's vaulted ceiling is a tavern, La Secchia Rapita (the stolen bucket).

INEXPENSIVE

☉Hotel Roma

Via Farini 44, 41100 Modena. ☎ **059/222218.** Fax 059/223747. 53 rms. MINIBAR TV TEL. 155,000 lire ($96.90) double. Rates include breakfast. AE, DC, MC, V. Parking 15,000 lire ($9.40). Bus: 7 or 11.

Hotel Roma, which became a hotel circa 1950, is a buff-and-white neoclassical building about two blocks from the cathedral. The building dates from the 17th century, when it belonged to the Duke of Este. It's one of my favorite hotels in its category in Modena, and is preferred above many others by opera stars who gravitate to Pavarotti's hometown for concerts and auditions. The windows and doors are soundproof, presumably so anyone can imitate his or her favorite diva while practicing an aria. The guest rooms have high ceilings, tasteful colors, and comfortable and attractive furnishings. The lobby is a long skylit room with an arched ceiling and a bar and a snack bar at the far end.

WHERE TO DINE
MODERATE

✪ Fini

Rue Frati Minori 54. ☎ **223314.** Reservations recommended. Main courses 30,000–50,000 lire ($18.75–$31.25). AE, DC, MC, V. Wed–Sun 12:30–2:30pm and 7:30–10pm. Closed Aug. Bus: 7 or 11. MODENESE/INTERNATIONAL.

A visit to this restaurant alone is well worth making the trip to Modena. Proudly maintaining the high reputation of the city's kitchens, Fini is one of the best restaurants you're likely to encounter in Emilia-Romagna. In spite of its modernized art nouveau decor, the restaurant was founded in 1912. This is a favorite restaurant of Pavarotti when he visits Modena.

For an appetizer, try the green lasagne or the tortellini (prepared in six different ways here—for example, with truffles). Caviar is the most expensive appetizer. For a main dish, the gran bollito misto reigns supreme. A king's feast of boiled meats, accompanied by a selection of four different sauces, is wheeled to your table. Included on this board of meats is zampone, the specialty of Modena. As prepared at Fini's it is stuffed pigs' trotters boiled with beef, a calf's head, ox tongue, chicken, and ham. After all this rich fare, you may settle for the fruit salad for dessert. For wines, Lambrusco is the local choice, and it's superb. The Fini is splashed with Picasso-esque murals and equipped with banquettes.

INEXPENSIVE

Ristorante Da Enzo

Via Coltellini 17. ☎ **225177.** Reservations recommended. Main courses 14,000–20,000 lire ($8.75–$12.50). AE, DC, MC, V. Tues–Sun noon–3pm and 7–10:30pm. Bus: 7 or 11. MODENESE.

Clean, conservative, and well-known within Modena, this restaurant lies one floor above street level in an old building a few steps from the piazza Mazzini and a prominent synagogue, within the historic center's pedestrian zone. Specialties of the dignified dining room include all the classic dishes of Modena, including pappardelle (wide noodles) with rabbit meat, lasagne verde, several kinds of tortellini, and an array of grilled meats liberally seasoned with herbs and balsamic vinegar. *Zampone* (stuffed pigs' trotters) is another specialty.

4 Parma

284 miles NW of Rome, 60 miles NW of Bologna

Straddling via Emilia, Parma was the home of Correggio, Il Parmigianino, Bodoni (of type fame), Toscanini, and Parmesan cheese. It rose in influence and power in the 16th century as the seat of the Farnese duchy, then in the 18th century came under Bourbon rule. For years Parma has been a favorite of art lovers.

It has also been a mecca for opera lovers such as Verdi, the great Italian composer. Verdi, whose works included *Il trovatore* and *Aïda*, was born in the small village of Roncole, north of Parma, in 1813. In time, his operas echoed through the opera house, the Teatro Regio, which was ordered constructed by Queen Marie Louise. Because of Verdi, Parma became a center of music, and even today the opera house is jam-packed in season. It's said that the Teatro Regio is the most "critical Verdi house" in Italy.

ESSENTIALS

GETTING THERE **By Train** Parma is conveniently served by the Milan-Bologna rail line, with 20 trains a day arriving from Milan (trip time: 80 minutes); the one-way fare is 10,500 lire ($6.55). From Bologna, 34 trains per day arrive in Parma (trip time: 1 hour); the one-way fare is 6,500 lire ($4.05). There are also seven connections a day from Florence, with a one-way fare of 13,800 lire ($8.65).

By Bus From major towns or cities in Italy, it's best to go by train because of faster connections. The bus comes into play only if you're planning to visit provincial towns in the Parma area. Information and schedules are available at the terminal at viale Toschi right before the Ponte Verdi (☎ 233813).

By Car From Bologna, head northwest along autostrada A1.

VISITOR INFORMATION The telephone area code for Parma is 0521. The tourist information center is at piazza del Duomo 5 (☎ 234735).

WHAT TO SEE & DO
THE TOP ATTRACTIONS

✪ **Il Duomo**
Piazza del Duomo. ☎ **235886.** Admission is free. Daily 9am–12:30pm and 3–7pm. Bus: 6 or 7.

Built in the Romanesque style in the 11th century, with 13th-century Lombard lions guarding its main porch, the dusty-pink Duomo stands side by side with a campanile (bell tower)—in the Gothic-Romanesque style—completed in 1294. The facade of the cathedral is highlighted by three open-air loggias. Inside, two darkly elegant aisles flank the central nave. The octagonal cupola was frescoed by the "divine" Correggio. Master of light and color, Correggio (1494–1534) was one of Italy's greatest painters of the High Renaissance. His fresco here, *Assumption of the Virgin,* foreshadows the baroque. The frescoes were painted from 1522 to 1534. In the transept to the right of the main altar is a Romanesque bas-relief, *The Deposition from the Cross* by Benedetto Antelami, which is somber, with each face bathed in tragedy. Made in 1178, the bas-relief is the best-known work of the 12th-century artist, who is considered the most important sculptor of the Romanesque in northern Italy.

✪ **Battistero**
Piazza del Duomo 7. ☎ **235886**. Admission 3,000 lire ($1.90). Daily 9am–12:30pm and 3–8pm.

Among the greatest Romanesque buildings in northern Italy, the Baptistery was the work of Antelami. The project was begun in 1196, although the date it was actually completed is in doubt. Made of salmon-colored marble, it's spanned by four open tiers (the fifth one is closed off). Inside, the Baptistery is richly frescoed with biblical scenes: a *Madonna Enthroned* and a *Crucifixion*. But it is the sculpture by Antelami that forms the most worthy treasure and provides the basis for that artist's claim to enduring fame.

Abbey of St. John (San Giovanni Evangelista)

Piazzale San Giovanni 1. ☎ **235592.** Admission is free. Daily 6:30am–noon and 3:30–8pm. Bus: 6 or 7.

Behind the Duomo is this church of unusual interest. After admiring the baroque front, pass into the interior to see yet another cupola by Correggio. Working from 1520 to 1524, the High Renaissance master depicted the *Vision of San Giovanni.* Vasari liked it so much that he became completely carried away in his praise, suggesting the "impossibility" of an artist's conjuring up such a divine work and marveling that it could actually have been painted "with human hands." Correggio also painted a St. John with pen in hand, in the transept (over the doorway to the left of the main altar). Il Parmigianino, the second Parmesan master, also did some frescoes in the chapel at the left of the entrance.

Casa Natale E Museo di Arturo Toscanini

Via Rodolfo Tanzi 13. ☎ **285499.** Admission is free. Tues–Sun 10am–1pm, Tues–Sat 3–6pm. Bus: 1, 7, or 11.

This is the house where the great musician and conductor was born in 1867. The Italian orchestral conductor was unquestionably the greatest of the first half of the 20th century, and one of the most astonishing musical interpreters of all time. He spent his childhood and youth in this house, which has been turned into a museum with interesting relics and a record library, containing all the recorded works that he conducted.

More Attractions

After viewing Parma's ecclesiastical buildings, you'll find its second batch of attractions conveniently sheltered under one roof at the **Palazzo della Pilotta,** via della Pilotta 5. This palazzo once housed the Farnese family in Parma's heyday as a duchy in the 16th century. Badly damaged by bombs in World War II, it has been restored and turned into a palace of museums.

✪ Galleria Nazionale

In the Palazzo della Pilotta, piazza della Pace, via della Pilotta 5. ☎ **233309.** Admission 10,000 lire ($6.25) adults, free for children under 18 and seniors over 60. Daily 9am–1:45pm. Bus: 1, 2, 8, or 13.

The most important component of the Palazzo della Pilotta is the National Gallery. Filled with the works of Parmesan artists from the late 15th century to the 19th century—notably paintings by Correggio and Parmigianino—the National Gallery offers a limited but well-chosen selection of art. In one room is an unfinished head of a young woman attributed to da Vinci. Correggio's *Madonna dell Scala* (of the stairs), the remains of a fresco, is also displayed. But his masterpiece—one of the celebrated paintings of northern Italy—is *St. Jerome with the Madonna and Child.* Imbued with a delicate quality, it represents age, youth, love—a gentle ode to tenderness. In the next room is Correggio's *Madonna della Scodella* (with a bowl), with its agonized faces. You'll also see Correggio's *Coronation,* a golden fresco and a work of great beauty, and his less successful *Annunciation.* One of Parmigianino's best-known paintings is here, *St. Catherine's Marriage,* with its rippling movement and subdued colors.

You can also view **St. Paul's Chamber,** which Correggio frescoed with mythological scenes, including one of Diana. The chamber lies on via Macedonio Melloni. On the same floor as the National Gallery is the **Farnese Theater,** evocative of Palladio's theater at Vicenza. Originally built in 1618, the structure was bombed in 1944 and has been restored.

Museo Archeologico Nazionale

In the Palazzo della Pilotta, piazza della Pace. ☎ **233718.** Admission 4,000 lire ($2.50) adults, free for children under 18. Tues–Sun 9am–1:30pm. Bus: 1, 2, 8, 13.

This most interesting museum houses Egyptian sarcophagi, Etruscan vases, Roman- and Greek-inspired torsos, Bronze Age relics, and its best-known exhibition called "Tabula Alimentaria," a bronze-engraved tablet dating from the reign of Trajan and excavated at Velleia in the province of Piacenza.

WHERE TO STAY
EXPENSIVE

Palace Hotel Maria Luigia

Viale Mentana 140, 43100 Parma. ☎ **0521/281032.** Fax 0521/231126. 101 rms. A/C MINIBAR TV TEL. 345,000 lire ($215.65) double. Rates include breakfast. AE, DC, MC, V. Parking 20,000 lire ($12.50). Bus: 1, 7, or 11.

This hotel, built in 1974 and located near the station, was and still is a welcome addition to the Parma hotel scene. Bold colors and molded plastic built-ins set the up-to-date mood, and bedrooms are made particularly comfortable by soundproof walls and other amenities. There's a very Italian-looking American bar on the premises. The hotel has one of the best restaurants in Parma, Maxim's, which serves excellent Italian and international specialties daily except in August. Dinners range from 60,000 lire ($37.50) and up.

MODERATE

Park Hotel Stendhal

Piazzetta Bodini 3, 43100 Parma. ☎ **0521/208057.** Fax 0521/285655. 60 rms. A/C MINIBAR TV TEL. 252,000 lire ($157.50) double. Breakfast 18,000 lire ($11.25) extra. AE, DC, MC, V. Parking 15,000 lire ($9.40). Bus: 2, 8, 9, or 13.

Park Hotel Stendhal sits on a square near the opera house, a few minutes' walk from many of the city's important sights. The bedrooms are well maintained and furnished with contemporary pieces. There's a traditional American bar and lounge, with comfortable armchairs for before- and after-dinner drinks. La Pilotta, the hotel restaurant, serves a cuisine typical of Parma, with a medley of international dishes; meals begin at 38,000 lire ($23.75). Laundry service and room service are also provided.

INEXPENSIVE

Farnese International

Via Reggio 51A, 43100 Parma. ☎ **0521/994247.** Fax 0521/992317. 76 rms. A/C MINIBAR TV TEL. 150,000 lire ($93.75) double. Rates include breakfast. AE, DC, MC, V. Free parking outdoors, 10,000 lire ($6.25) indoors. Bus: 11.

Farnese International is one of the best choices. It's located in a quiet area but convenient from the town center, airport, and fairs. Parma specialties are served in the hotel restaurant, Il Farnese. Bedrooms are comfortably furnished in Italian marble. Laundry and room service are provided.

⑤ Hotel Button

Strada San Vitale 7, 43100 Parma. ☎ **0521/208039.** Fax 0521/238783. 41 rms. TV TEL. 115,000 lire ($71.90) double. Breakfast 10,000 lire ($6.25) extra. AE, DC, MC, V. Closed July 8–31. Bus: 1, 7, or 11.

Hotel Button is a local favorite, one of the best bargains in the town center. This is a family-owned and -run hotel, and you're made to feel welcome. Rooms are simply but comfortably furnished. It stands just off the heartbeat piazza Garibaldi. The hotel doesn't have a restaurant—in Parma this is no problem at all—but will serve you a continental breakfast for an extra charge.

WHERE TO DINE

The chefs of Parma are known throughout Italy for the quality of their cuisine. Of course, Parmesan cheese has added just the right touch to millions of Italian meals, and the word *parmigiana* is quite familiar to American diners.

MODERATE

✪ La Greppia

Strada Garibaldi 39A. ☎ **233686.** Reservations required. Main courses 24,000–45,000 lire ($15–$28.15). AE, DC, MC, V. Wed–Sun 12:30–2:30pm and 7:30–10:30pm. Closed July 5–Aug 2. Bus: 8 or 68. PARMIGIANA.

La Greppia has an unpretentious decor yet it's near the top of every gourmet's list of the finest dining rooms of Parma. Through a plate-glass window at one end of the dining room, you can see the chefs at work. Making a creative statement about food, *cucina feminina* style, is the all-woman staff in the kitchen. Leading the team is the co-owner Paola Cavassini and her good-natured husband, Maurizio Rossi, who presides over the dining room. The women adjust their menus depending on the season. You are likely to have, for example, veal kidneys sautéed with *fines herbes* and a demi-glacé sauce, breast of chicken with orange sauce, *pappardella alla greppia* (prepared with cream and dried flap mushrooms), or roast rack of rabbit flavored with thyme. Many dishes are flavored, in season, with fresh thyme or mushrooms, even cherries. All of this good food is served in a building dating from the 17th century. The tarts made with fresh fruit are succulent desserts. Even better, the kitchen is known for its compelling chocolate cake, which one reviewer claimed was much better than the famed Sachertorte served at the Hotel Sacher in Vienna.

INEXPENSIVE

Croce di Malta

Borgo Palmia 8. ☎ **235643.** Reservations recommended. Main courses 15,000–25,000 lire ($9.40–$15.65). AE, DC, MC, V. Tues–Sun 12:30–2:30pm and 7:30–10:30pm. Closed 2 weeks in Aug. Bus: 3, 4, 5, or 8. PARMIGIANA.

Local legend has it that angry citizens plotted to assassinate the last Duke of Parma while drowning in *vino* at this tavern.

All the dishes for which Parma is famous are served here, even some esoteric ones, such as *cappellotti*, a pasta turned magenta in color because of its use of beets, or else *tortelli* made a golden amber with the addition of pumpkin, although another version is made with potatoes. *Tagliatelle* is served here almost in any style. Other dishes include roast veal stuffed with cheese or chicken flavored with wine and gorgonzola cheese.

Parizzi

Strada della Repubblica 71. ☎ **285952**. Reservations required. Main courses 16,000–29,000 lire ($10–$18.15). Mon–Sat noon–2:30pm and 7–9:30pm. AE, DC, MC, V. Bus: 3, 4, 5, or 8. PARMIGIANA.

In the historic core of Palma, this building has a history going back to 1551, when it was first established as an inn. At Parizzi, under a skylit patio, the people of Parma, known for their exacting tastes and demanding palates, enjoy the rich cuisine for which their town is celebrated. There are those who say that this restaurant serves the best food in town. After you're shown to a table in one of the good-size dining rooms, a trolley cart filled with antipasti is wheeled before you, containing shellfish and salmon among its many delectable offerings. The stuffed vegetables are especially good (try the zucchini). You might begin with the chef's specialty, crêpes alla parmigiana—that is, crêpes stuffed with fontina, Parma ham, and ricotta, or with truffles in September. In May you'll want to try the asparagus fresh from the fields. A good main course is the veal scaloppine with fontina and ham. Desserts include zabaglione laced with marsala.

5 Ravenna

46 miles E of Bologna, 90 miles S of Venice, 227 miles N of Rome

Ravenna is one of the most unusual towns in Emilia-Romagna. It is famous for its Early Christian and Byzantine mosaics, the most splendid outside Istanbul, many of them dating from the 6th century. In turn, the capital of the Western Roman Empire (from 402 A.D.), the Visigoth Empire (from 473 A.D.), and the Byzantine Empire under the Emperor Justinian and the Empress Theodora (540–752), Ravenna became one of the greatest cities on the Mediterranean. Though today it looks much like any other Italian city, the low Byzantine domes of its churches still evoke its eastern past.

ESSENTIALS

GETTING THERE **By Train** Ravenna can be visited on a day trip from Bologna as there is frequent service; a one-way fare is 6,700 lire ($4.20). There is also frequent service to Ferrara, costing 6,000 lire ($3.75) for a one-way ticket. At Ferrara, you can make connections to Venice, for 17,800 lire ($11.15) each way.

By Bus Trains are better. Once at Ravenna, however, you'll find both a regional (ATR) system and a municipal (ATM) bus network serving the area. Buses depart from outside the train station. The tourist office (see below) will have bus schedules and more details, depending on where you want to go, or call 35288 for information.

By Car From Bologna, head east along Autostrada A14.

VISITOR INFORMATION Ravenna's telephone area code is 0544. The tourist information center is at piazza Mameli 4 (☎ 37333). At the tourist office you can purchase a ticket to visit six monuments for a single cost of 7,000 lire ($4.40). These sights include the Battistero Neoniano, Archepiscopal Museum and Church of St. Andrea, Church of San Vitale, Mausoleum of Galla Placidia, the Adrian Baptistery, and Basilica of St. Apollinare Nuovo.

WHAT TO SEE & DO

Battistero Neoniano

Piazza del Duomo. ☎ **33696.** Admission 3,000 lire ($1.90). Daily 9am–7pm. Bus: 1 or 11.

The octagonal Baptistery was built in the 5th century. In the center of the cupola is a tablet showing John the Baptist baptizing Christ. The circle around the tablet depicts in mosaics the 12 crown-carrying Apostles, dramatic in deep violet-blues and sparkling golds. The Baptistery originally serviced a cathedral that no longer stands. (The present-day Duomo of Ravenna was built around the mid-18th century and is of little interest except for some unusual pews.) Beside it is a campanile from the 11th century, perhaps earlier.

Museo Arcivescovile and Church of St. Andrea

Piazza Arcivescovado. ☎ **33696**. Admission 4,000 lire ($2.50). Tues–Sat 9am–7pm; closes 4:30pm in winter; Sun 9am–1pm. Bus: 1 or 11.

This twofold attraction is housed in the Archbishop's Palace, which dates from the 6th century. In the museum, the major exhibit is a throne carved out of ivory for Archbishop Maximian, which dates from around the mid-6th century.

In the chapel or oratory dedicated to St. Andrea are brilliant mosaics. Pause a while in the antechamber and look over the entrance for a most intriguing mosaic. Here is an unusual representation of Christ as a warrior, stepping on the head of a lion and a snake. Although haloed, he wears partial armor, evoking "Onward, Christian Soldiers." The chapel—built in the shape of a cross—contains other mosaics that are "angelic," both figuratively and literally. Busts of saints and apostles stare down at you with the ox-eyed look of Byzantine art.

Basilica di San Vitale

Via San Vitale 17. ☎ **33696**. Admission 5,000 lire ($3.15). Daily 9am–7pm; closes 4:30pm in winter. Bus: 1 or 11.

On via San Vitale sits an octagonal domed church that dates from the mid-6th century. Inside, the mosaics—in brilliant greens and golds, lit by poetic light from translucent panels—are among the most celebrated in the Western world. Covering the apse is a mosaic rendition of a clean-shaven Christ, astride the world, flanked by saints and angels. To the right is a mosaic of Empress Theodora and her court, and to the left, the man who married the courtesan-actress, Emperor Justinian, and his entourage. If you can tear yourself away from the mosaics long enough, you might admire the church with its marble decoration. Seven large arches span the temple, but the frescoes of the cupola are unimaginative.

✪ Mausoleum of Galla Placidia

Via San Vitale. ☎ **34266**. Entrance included with admission to Basilica di San Vitale (see above). Daily 9am–7pm. Bus: 1 or 11.

This 5th-century chapel is so unpretentious that you'll think you're at the wrong place. But inside it contains mosaics of exceptional merit—dripping with antiquity, but not looking it. Translucent panels bring the mosaics alive in all their grace and harmony—rich and vivid with peacock-blue, moss-green, Roman gold, eggplant, and burnt orange. The mosaics in the cupola literally glitter with stars. Popular tradition has it that the cross-shaped structure houses the tomb of Galla Placidia, sister of Honorius, but there is evidence that this claim may be false.

Museo Nazionale di Ravenna

Via Fiandrini. ☎ **34424**. Admission 8,000 lire ($5) adults, free for children under 18. Tues–Sun 8:30am–7:30pm. Bus: 1 or 11.

This museum, adjacent to San Vitale, contains archaeological objects from the early Christian and Byzantine periods—icons, fragments of tapestries, medieval armaments and armory, sarcophagi, ivories, ceramics, and bits of broken pieces from the stained-glass windows of St. Vitale.

Basilica of St. Apollinare in Classe

Località Classe. ☎ **527004**. Admission is free. Mon–Fri 9am–12:30pm and 2–7pm, Sat–Sun 2–5pm. Bus: 4 or 44 from the railroad station (every 20 minutes).

About 3¹/₂ miles south of the city (it can be visited on the way to Ravenna if you're heading north from Rimini), this church dates from the 6th century, having been consecrated by Archbishop Maximian. Before the waters receded, Classe was a seaport of Rome's Adriatic fleet. Dedicated to St. Apollinare, the bishop of Ravenna, the early basilica stands side-by-side with a campanile—both symbols of faded glory now resting in a lonely low-lying area. Inside is a central nave flanked by two aisles, the latter containing tombs of ecclesiastical figures in the Ravenna hierarchy. The floor—once carpeted with mosaics—has been rebuilt. Along the central nave are frescoed tablets. Two dozen marble columns line the approach to the apse, where you find the major reason for visiting the basilica. The mosaics are exceptional, rich in gold and turquoise, set against a background of top-heavy birds nesting in shrubbery. St. Apollinare stands in the center, with a row of lambs on either side lined up as in a processional, the 12 lambs symbolizing the Apostles, of course.

WHERE TO STAY
MODERATE
Jolly Hotel

Piazza Mameli 1, 48100 Ravenna. ☎ **0544/35762.** Fax 0544/216055. 75 rms, 3 suites. A/C MINIBAR TV TEL. 230,000 lire ($143.75) double; from 300,000 lire ($187.50) suite. Rates include breakfast. AE, DC, MC, V. Parking 20,000–25,000 lire ($12.50–$15.65). Bus: 1 or 11.

This four-story hotel, built in 1950, contains two elevators and a conservative decor that includes a bunkerlike facade, stone floors, and lots of paneling. The Jolly is usually preferred by traveling businesspeople. The hotel lies 50 yards from the railway station. Its La Veranda restaurant serves a local and international cuisine. Services include babysitting, laundry, and room service from 7am to 11pm.

INEXPENSIVE
⊖ Bisanzio

Via Salara 30, 48100 Ravenna. ☎ **0544/217111.** Fax 0544/32539. 38 rms. A/C MINIBAR TV TEL. 155,000–200,000 lire ($96.90–$125) double. Rates include breakfast. AE, DC, MC, V. Bus: 1 or 11.

Bisanzio stands in the heart of town, just a few minutes' walk from many of Ravenna's treasures, such as the Basilica of St. Vitale and the Mausoleum of Galla Placida. This is a pleasantly coordinated and completely renovated modern hotel with guest rooms that have attractive Italian styling. It's ideal for those who want the comfort of a well-organized hotel, with good bedrooms, offering simplicity and compactness. Other amenities include an uncluttered breakfast room with softly draped windows and all the other modern conveniences that travelers have come to expect. Guests also have use of a garden.

⊖ Hotel Centrale Byron

Via IV Novembre no. 14, 48100 Ravenna. ☎ **0544/212225.** 54 rms. A/C TV TEL. 105,000–120,000 lire ($65.65–$75) double. Breakfast 7,200 lire ($4.50) extra. AE, DC, MC, V. Bus: 1 or 11.

Hotel Central Byron is an art deco–inspired hotel a few steps from piazza del Popolo. The lobby is an elegantly simple combination of white marble and brass detailing. The public rooms stretch "railroad style" in a long narrow format past a reception desk, an alcove sitting room, a long hallway, and a combination TV room, bar, and snacking and breakfast-room area. Rooms are simply but comfortably furnished.

WHERE TO DINE
INEXPENSIVE

Bella Venezia

Via IV Novembre no. 16. ☎ **212746**. Reservations required. Main courses 13,000–22,000 lire ($8.15–$13.75). AE, DC, MC, V. Mon–Sat noon–2:30pm and 7–10pm. Closed Dec 24–Jan 16. Bus: 1 or 11. EMILIA-ROMAGNA.

Bella Venezia, a few steps from piazza del Popolo, is the kind of well-known restaurant that many of the city's hotel managers recommend to their clients. Located next to the Hotel Centrale Byron, the restaurant offers well-prepared food. Despite this restaurant's name, the only dish from the repertoire of Venice prepared here is *fegato (liver) alla veneziana*, which is admittedly, delicious. Other than that, the repertoire is almost exclusively regional, with such dishes as risotto, cappelletti alla romagnola (round, cap-shaped pasta stuffed with a mixture of ricotta, roasted pork loin, chicken breast, and nutmeg, served with a meat sauce), and garganelli pasta served with whatever happens to be in season (baby asparagus, mushrooms, or peas) at the time. All pastas are made by hand, and the place is very family-run, very warm, very old Italy.

✪ Ristorante La Gardèla

Via Ponte Marino 3. ☎ **217147**. Reservations recommended. Main courses 20,000–30,000 lire ($12.50–$18.75). AE, DC, MC, V. Fri–Wed noon–1:45pm and 7–10pm. Closed Aug 10–25. Bus: 1 or 11. EMILIA-ROMAGNA.

Ristorante La Gardèla, which is located a few steps from one of Ravenna's most startling leaning towers, is spread out over two levels with paneled walls lined with racks of wine bottles. The waiters bring out an array of typical but savory dishes. Specialties include tortelloni della casa (made with ricotta, cream, spinach, tomatoes, and herbs), and spezzatino alla contadina (roasted veal served with potatoes, tomatoes, and herbs).

Ristorante Tre Spade

Via Faentina 136. ☎ **500522**. Reservations recommended. Main courses 16,000–30,000 lire ($10–$18.75). AE, DC, MC, V. Tues–Sun 12:30–2:30pm, Tues–Sat 7:30–10:30pm. Closed first 3 weeks of Aug. Bus: 1 or 11. INTERNATIONAL/EMILIAN.

Ristorante Tre Spade is an appealing spot with a good cuisine, which it has served since 1980. Specialties include an asparagus parfait accompanied by a zesty sauce of bits of green peppers and black olives, and an appetizing assortment of carpaccio (thinly sliced raw meat covered with sliced sheets of Parmesan cheese with raw artichoke hearts in olive oil). This might be followed by taglioni with smoked salmon sauce, veal cooked with sage, spaghetti with fruits of the sea (which includes clams in their shells), green gnocchi in Gorgonzola sauce, or roast game in season, plus a good collection of wines. The menu changes frequently, and daily specials are offered according to the market.

Introducing Venice | 12

One rainy morning as I was leaving my hotel—a converted palazzo—a decorative stone fell from the lunette, narrowly missing me. For a second it looked as if I was a candidate for the gondola funeral cortège to the island of marble tombs, San Michele. In dismay, I looked back at the owner, a woman straight from a Modigliani portrait. From the doorway, she leaned like the Tower of Pisa, mocking the buildings of her city. Throwing up her hands, she sighed: "Venezia, Venezia," then turned and went inside.

Stoically, she had long ago surrendered to the inevitable decay that embraces Venice like moss at the base of the pilings. Venice is a preposterous monument to both the folly and the obstinacy of humankind. It shouldn't exist . . . but it does, much to the delight of thousands upon thousands of tourists, gondoliers, lacemakers, hoteliers, restaurateurs, and glassblowers.

Fleeing the barbarians, centuries ago Venetians left drydock and drifted out to a flotilla of "uninhabitable" islands in the lagoon. Survival was difficult enough, but no Venetian has ever settled for mere survival. The remote ancestors of the present inhabitants created the world's most beautiful city.

However, to your children or their children, Venice may be a legend from the past. It is sinking at a rate of about 2.5 inches per decade. It's estimated that one-third of the city's art will have deteriorated hopelessly within the next decade or so, if action is not taken to save it. Clearly, Venice is in peril. One headline recently read, "The Enemy's at the Gates."

Working on a campaign to save Venice, John R. McDermott put the case this way: "Venice is under assault by uncontrolled tides, pollution, and old age. Atmospheric acid is eating away its art treasures—stone, bronze, and pigment—and the walls of its buildings are being eroded by floods; industrial waste is polluting its water. Unless these conditions are alleviated and repairs made, some of the loveliest art in the world will be lost forever, and eventually the city itself could cease to exist as we know it now."

1 Orientation

ARRIVING

All roads lead not necessarily to Rome but, in this case, to the docks on the mainland of Venice. The arrival scene at the unattractive

What's Special About Venice

Museums

- Palazzo Ducale, with its Bridge of Sighs, the home of the doges who ruled Venice with an iron fist.
- Accademia, a treasure trove of Venetian painting from the 13th through the 18th centuries.
- Collezione Peggy Guggenheim, one of Italy's most outstanding modern-art museums, created by the late American heiress.

Religious Shrine

- Basilica di San Marco, a sumptuous Byzantine confection with glorious mosaics and several bulbed domes.

Ace Attractions

- Scuola Grande di San Rocco, a vast monument to the work of Tintoretto, the largest collection anywhere.
- A gondola ride, symbol of romance and passion—something to try at least once in a lifetime.

Shopping

- Venetian glass—known around the world; it's sold on virtually every street or you can buy it on the island of Murano where it's made.

Fun for Kids

- Many kids consider "fantasy, fairytale" Venice an Italian extension of Disneyland, and they love those boat rides across the canals.

Events/Festivals

- Carnevale, during the week and a half before Ash Wednesday, a bacchanalian affair when revelers take over the streets.
- The Venice International Film Festival, in August, second in Europe after the French Riviera's fête at Cannes.

Beaches

- The Lido, the most fashionable beachfront in Italy, former stomping ground of everybody from Goethe to Byron to Thomas Mann.

piazzale Roma is filled with nervous expectation, and even the most veteran traveler can become confused. Whether you arrive by train, bus, car, or airport limousine, there is one common denominator—everyone walks to the nearby docks to select a method of transport to his or her hotel. The cheapest way is by vaporetto, the more expensive by gondola or motor launch (see "Getting Around," later in this chapter).

If your hotel lies near one of the public vaporetto stops, you can sometimes struggle with your own luggage until you reach the hostelry's reception area. In any event, the one time-tested rule for Venice-bound travelers is that excess baggage is bad news, unless you're willing to pay dearly to have it carried for you. Porters cannot accompany you and your baggage on the vaporetto.

BY PLANE   You can now fly from North America to Venice via Rome on Alitalia. You'll land at Mestre, with its Marco Polo Aeroporto. Boats depart directly from the airport, taking visitors to a terminal near piazza San Marco.

Impressions

She (Venice) is the Shakespeare of cities—unchallenged, incomparable, and beyond envy.
—John Addington Symonds

It's less expensive to take a bus from the airport, a trip of less than 5 miles. Cross the Ponte della Libertà to the Stanzione di Santa Lucia, the railway station of Venice. You will be at piazzale Roma, where you can make transportation connections to most parts of Venice, including the Lido. It is at this point that first-time visitors encounter the Canal Grande or Grand Canal, a channel leading to the Canale di San Marco, which itself heads directly to the Adriatic.

If you need to find out about flight arrivals or departures at Marco Polo Airport, call 5415491.

BY TRAIN   Trains pull into the **Stazione de Santa Lucia,** at piazzale Roma. Travel time by train from Rome is about $5^1/_4$ hours; from Milan, $3^1/_2$ hours; from Florence, 4 hours; and from Bologna, 2 hours. For information about rail connections, dial 715555. The best—and the least expensive—way to get from the station to the rest of town is to take a vaporetto, which departs near the main entrance to the station.

BY BUS   Buses arrive from the points on the mainland of Italy at piazzale Roma. For information about schedules, call the office of ACTV at piazzale Roma (☎ 5287886). If you're coming from a distant city in Italy, it's better to take the train. But Venice has good bus connections with such nearby cities as Padua. A one-way fare from Padua to Venice (or vice versa) is 4,200 lire ($2.65). After disembarking from the bus in Venice, the nearby vaporetto is the cheapest way to reach the heart of Venice.

BY CAR   Venice has autostrada links with the rest of Italy, with direct routes from such cities as Trieste (driving time: $1^1/_2$ hours), Milan (driving time: 3 hours), and Bologna (driving time: 2 hours). Bologna is 94 miles southwest of Venice; Milan, 165 miles west of Venice; and Trieste, 97 miles east. Rome is 327 miles to the southwest.

If you arrive in Venice by car, there are several multitiered parking areas at the terminus where the roads end and the canals begin. One of the most visible is the **Garage San Marco,** piazzale Roma (☎ 5235101), near the vaporetto, gondola, and motorlaunch docks. You'll be charged 30,000 to 45,000 lire ($18.75 to $28.15) per day, maybe more, depending on the size of your car. However, I must warn you that from spring to fall this municipal car park is nearly always filled, and often people have to park great distances away at Mestre. It's open 24 hours daily. You are more likely to find parking on the **Isola del Tronchetto** (☎ 5207555), which costs 32,000 to 35,000 lire ($20 to $21.90) per day. From Tronchetto take vaporetto 82 to the piazza San Marco. If you have heavy luggage, you'll need a water taxi.

VISITOR INFORMATION

Visitors can get information at the **Azienda di Promozione Turistica,** piazza San Marco 71C (☎ 5226356). It's open Monday through Saturday from 8:30am to 6:45pm. However, these hours are not always consistent.

CITY LAYOUT

MAIN ARTERIES & STREETS   Venice, lying $2^1/_2$ miles from the Italian mainland and $1^1/_4$ miles from the open seas of the Adriatic, is an archipelago of some 117 islands. Most visitors, however, concern themselves only with piazza San Marco and its vicinity. In fact, the entire city has only one "piazza," which is San Marco. Venice is divided into six quarters that local residents call **sestieri.** These include the most frequented, San Marco, but also Santa Croce, San Paolo, Castello, Cannaregio, and Dorsoduro, the last of which has been compared to New York's Greenwich Village.

Many of the so-called streets of Venice are actually **canals,** 150 in all. A canal is called a *rio,* and a total of 400 bridges span these canals. If Venice has a main street, it's the **Grand Canal,** which is spanned by three bridges: the Rialto, the Academy Bridge, and the stone Railway Bridge (the last dates from the 20th century). The canal splits Venice into two unequal parts.

Get used to a lot of unfamiliar street designations. A street running alongside a canal is called a *fondamenta,* and major thoroughfares are known as *salizzada, ruga,* or a *calle larga.* But what is a *sottoportego?* That's a passageway beneath buildings. You'll often encounter the word *campo* when you come to an open-air area. That's a reference to the fact that such a place was once grassy, and in days of yore cattle grazed there.

South of the section called Dorsoduro, which is south of the Grand Canal, is **Canale della Guidecca,** a major channel separating Dorsoduro from the large island of La Guidecca. At the point where Canale della Guidecca meets the Canale di San Marco, you'll spot the little **Isola di San Giorgio Maggiore,** with a church by Palladio. The most visited islands in the lagoon, aside from the **Lido,** are **Murano, Burano, and Torcello,** each of which we'll visit in due course.

Once you land and explore piazza San Marco and its satellite, piazzetta San Marco, you can head down **Riva degli Schiavoni,** with its deluxe and first-class hotels, or follow the signs along the **Mercerie,** the major shopping artery of Venice, which leads to the Rialto, site of the market area.

But with all the directions in the world and with all the signposts and maps, the best thing for an explorer in Venice is to get lost, which you'll invariably do anyway.

FINDING AN ADDRESS   A maniac must have numbered the buildings of Venice at least six centuries ago. There seems to be no numbering system. Numbers are completely illogical. Therefore, before you set out on your journey to a specific place, get detailed instructions and have the establishment marked on your map. Instead of depending on street numbers, try to locate the nearest cross street instead and, once there, look for signs posted outside instead of searching out a number, many of which have decayed over the ages until they are no longer legible.

STREET MAPS   If you really want to tour Venice and find that little hidden trattoria on a nearly forgotten street, you might as well abandon any map that

Impressions

When I went to Venice—my dream became my address.
                    —Marcel Proust, letter to Madame Strauss, May 1906

doesn't detail every street and have an index in the back so you can find what you're looking for. The best of the lot is the **Falk** map of Venice. It details everything and is sold at many news kiosks and at all bookstores. Since it's pocket size, you can open it in the Adriatic winds without having it blow away from you as do many larger maps.

NEIGHBORHOODS IN BRIEF

SAN MARCO   Everybody goes here: It's the center of Venice. The main square is piazza San Marco, or St. Mark's Square, dominated by St. Mark's Basilica. Just outside the basilica is the campanile, or bell tower, a reconstruction of one that collapsed in 1902. Around the corner is the Palazzo Ducale or doge's palace. In and around San Marco lie expensive hotels, restaurants, cafés, and shops.

CANNAREGIO   This section basically runs from the Rialto to the Jewish Ghetto and contains much of sightseeing interest, including Ca' d'Oro, housing the Galleria Giorgio Franchetti. Beyond the train station lies the old Jewish Ghetto, the first one established on the continent.

SAN POLO   This commercial district of Venice is reached by crossing the Ponte Rialto (Rialto Bridge) spanning the Grand Canal. Its open-air market is called Erberia, and its center is the Church of San Giacomo di Rialto, oldest in the city. The district also encloses the Scuola Grande di San Rocco, a repository of the works of Tintoretto.

CASTELLO   The San Marco district is bordered on its east by Castello, the most amorphous Venetian district. One of its major attractions is the Gothic church of Santa Giovanni e Paolo, or Zanipolo. This was the Pantheon of the doges of Venice. Its most popular boulevard is Riva degli Schiavoni, bordering the Grand Canal.

SANTA CROCE   Taking its name from an old church that was long ago destroyed, Santa Croce generally follows the snakelike curve of the Grand Canal from piazzale Roma to a point just short of the Ponte Rialto. At this point it flows into the district of San Polo.

DORSODURO   This district is compared variously to New York's Greenwich Village or London's Chelsea, although in truth it doesn't resemble either section very much. The least populated of the sestieri, it's filled with old homes and half-forgotten churches. It is the southernmost section of the historic district, and its major attraction is the Gallerie dell'Accademia.

THE LIDO   This slim, sandy island cradles the Venetian lagoon, offering protection against the Adriatic Sea. Italy's most fashionable bathing resort, it's $7^1/_2$ miles long and about half a mile wide. It was the setting for many famous books, including Thomas Mann's *Death in Venice* and Evelyn Waugh's *Brideshead Revisited.*

TORCELLO   Lying $6^1/_2$ miles northeast of Venice, Torcello is called "the mother of Venice," having been settled between the 9th and 17th centuries. Once

Impressions

Wonderful city, streets full of water, please advise.

—Robert Benchley

it was the most populous of the islands in the lagoon, but since the 18th century it has been nearly deserted. Tourists visit it today to see its cathedral.

BURANO Perched 5½ miles northeast of Venice, Burano is the most populous of the lagoon islands. In the 16th century it produced the finest lace in Europe. Today lace is still made here, although nothing like the production of centuries ago.

MURANO This island three-quarters of a mile northeast of Venice has been famed since 1291 for its glassmakers. At its apex in the 16th century, the island had 37 glass factories and a thriving population of 30,000 people. Once a closely guarded secret, Murano glassmaking is now clearly visible to any tourist who wants to visit the island and observe the technique on a guided tour.

2 Getting Around

Since you can't hail a taxi, at least not on land, what you do in Venice is walk and walk and walk. Of course, such walks can be broken up by vaporetto or boat rides.

It may seem that excessive attention is devoted in this chapter to porters, water taxis, vaporetti, and gondoliers, but I've seen too many visits to Venice marred by a hassle that dampens the tourist's enthusiasm for the city at the outset. Providing you can overcome the problem of getting yourself and your luggage transported safely—and without fisticuffs—to your hotel, you'll probably be set to embark on one of the grandest experiences of a lifetime: the exploration of Venice.

BY PUBLIC TRANSPORTATION Much to the chagrin of the once-ubiquitous gondolier, the motorboats, or **vaporetti,** of Venice provide inexpensive and frequent, if not always fast, transportation in this canal-riddled city. An *accelerato* is a vessel that makes every stop and a *diretto* makes only express stops. The average fare is 3,000 lire ($1.90). In summer, the vaporetti are often fiercely crowded. Pick up a map of the system from the tourist office. Rarely will you have to wait more than 15 minutes for the approach of a vaporetto. Service is daily from 7am to midnight, then hourly between midnight and 7am.

Discount Passes Visitors to Venice may avail themselves of a 24-hour, 17,000 lire ($10.65) *biglietto turistico,* or tourist ticket, which allows them to travel all day long on any of the many routes of the city's boat services. This all-inclusive ticket is a bargain, as is the three-day ticket allowing travel for 20,000 lire ($12.50).

BY WATER TAXI/MOTOR LAUNCH It costs more than the public vaporetto, but you won't be hassled as much when you arrive with your luggage if you hire one of the city's many private motor launches, called **taxi acquei.** You may or may not have the cabin of one of these sleek vessels to yourself, since the captains fill their boats with as many passengers as the law allows before taking off. Your porter's uncanny radar will guide you to one of the inconspicuous piers where a water taxi waits.

The price of a transit by water taxi from the Piazzale Roma (road terminus and rail terminus) to the piazza San Marco costs from 80,000 lire ($50) for between 1 to 6 passengers. The sailors seem to follow in the footsteps of the most cunning of doges. To their credit, the captains of Venice's motor launches are usually adroit about depositing you, with your luggage, at the canalside entrance to your hotel or on one of the city's smaller waterways within a short walking distance of your

The Gondola

In *Death in Venice*, Thomas Mann wrote: "Is there anyone but must repress a secret thrill, on arriving in Venice for the first time—or returning thither after long absence—and stepping into a Venetian gondola? That singular conveyance, come down unchanged from ballad times, black as nothing else on earth except a coffin—what pictures it calls up of lawless, silent adventures in the plashing night; or even more, what visions of death itself, the bier and solemn rites and last soundless voyage!"

In the 12th century the word *gondola* referred to the canal boats with flat bottoms traversing the canals of Venice. But it wasn't until the latter 18th century that the gondola became "the taxi of Venice." The building of gondolas became a thriving and highly individualized craft, calling forth great artistry.

When gondolas once got too ostentatious and the Doge in 1562 thought too much money was being spent on them, he decreed that henceforth all gondolas would be painted black. Gondolas—at least the best of them—became known for their precision at maneuvering through the canals of the city.

It is estimated that in the heyday of the Renaissance, long before the age of the vaporetto, there were some 15,000 gondolas afloat in Venice, and what a sight it must have been, like a giant festive regatta. Nowadays, there are only about 350 gondolas, mostly serving tourists wanting a ride for the thrill of it as opposed to using it as a taxi.

There are only about three gondola-makers still left in Venice, although at one time there were dozens. In former days, a gondola workshop might turn out 35 gondolas a year. Nowadays, a gondola-maker makes perhaps only four vessels, selling each craft for some $25,000 apiece, although the price could be much higher depending on elaborate ornamentation.

You can still visit a gondola workshop. Dating from the 17th century, Squèro di San Trovaso is considered the oldest boatyard in Venice. The kings of Italy used to have gondolas constructed for themselves at this workshop in sleepy Dorsoduro. The address is Dorsoduro 1097 (☎ 5229146). Once this boatyard was the official one sanctioned by the city to make its gondolas. To show how times have changed, today's official municipal water vehicle is a speedboat.

destination. You can also call for a taxi acquei—try **Cooperation Ducale** (☎ 5238835).

BY GONDOLA   When riding in a gondola, two major agreements have to be reached: (1) the price of the ride and (2) the length of the trip. If you even vaguely suggest in any way one of Barnum's suckers, you're likely to be taken on both counts. It's a common sight in Venice to see a gondolier huffing and puffing to take his passengers on a "quickie," often reducing the hour to 15 minutes. The gondolier, with his eye on his watch, is anxious to dump his load and pick up the next batch of passengers. Consequently, his watch almost invariably runs fast.

There is an accepted official rate schedule for gondoliers, but we've never known anyone to honor it. The actual fare depends on how effective you are in standing up to the gondolier's attempt to get more money out of you. The official rate is 80,000 lire ($50) but virtually no one pays that amount. Prices begin at 100,000 lire ($62.50) for up to 50 minutes, maybe a lot more. One gondolier confided to us he settled for that amount in 1972. Today, most gondoliers will ask *at least* double the official rate, and will reduce your time aboard to 30 to 40 minutes, or even less. Prices go up after 9pm. In fairness to the gondoliers, it must be said that they have an awful job, which is romanticized out of perspective by the world. They row boatloads of tourists across hot, smelly canals with such endearments screamed at them as "No sing! No pay!" And these fellows must make plenty of lire while the sun shines, as their work ends when the first cold winds blow in from the Adriatic.

Two major stations at which you can hire gondolas include piazza San Marco (☎ 5200685) and Ponte Rialto (☎ 5224904).

ON FOOT   This is the only way to explore Venice unless you plan to see it from a boat on the Grand Canal. Everybody walks in Venice: There's no other way. The streets are too crowded for bicycles or much else. In summer, the overcrowding is so severe you'll often have a hard time finding room for your feet on the street.

FAST FACTS: Venice

American Express   The office of American Express in Venice is at San Marco 1471 (☎ 5200844), in the San Marco area. City tours and mail handling can be obtained here. The office is open May through October, Monday through Saturday, from 8am to 8pm. Off-season hours are Monday through Friday from 9am to 5:30pm and Saturday from 9am to 12:30pm.

Area Code   The telephone area code is 041.

Babysitters   In lieu of a central booking agency, arrangements have to be made individually at various hotels. Obviously, the more advanced your notice the better your chances of getting a sitter who speaks English.

Bookstores   One of the best stocked, with titles in both English and Italian, is Serenissima, Salizzada San Julian 739 (☎ 5223050).

Car Rentals   Obviously you won't need a car in Venice. But you may need one upon departure. You can make arrangements at Europcar, piazzale Roma 496H (☎ 5238616), or at Avis, piazzale Roma 496G (☎ 5225825). Offices are open Monday through Friday from 8:30am to 12:30pm and 2:30 to 6pm and on Saturday from 8:30am to noon.

Climate   See "When to Go" in Chapter 3.

Consulates   There is no U.S. Consulate in Venice; the closest is in Milan, at largo Donegani 1 (☎ 29001841). The British Consulate is at Dorsoduro 1051 (☎ 5227207), open Monday through Friday from 9am to noon and 2 to 4pm.

Crime   See "Safety" in this section.

Currency Exchange   There are many banks in Venice where you can exchange money. For example, try the Banca d'America e d'Italia, San Marco 2216 (☎ 5200766). Many travelers find that Guetta Viaggi, San Marco 1289 (☎ 5208711), offers the best rates in Venice.

Dentist   Your best bet is to have your hotel call and set up an appointment with an English-speaking dentist. The American Express office and the British Consulate also have a list.

Doctors   See "Hospitals" below. The suggestion given for a dentist in Venice (see above) also pertains to English-speaking doctors.

Drugstores   If you need a drugstore in the middle of the night, call 192 for information about which one is open. Pharmacies take turns staying open late. A well-recommended centrally located pharmacy is International Pharmacy, via XXII Marzo 2067 (☎ 5222311).

Emergencies   Phone numbers are 113 for police, 523-0000 for an ambulance, and 522-2222 to report a fire.

Eyeglasses   This service is available at Querzola, Cannaregio 5902 (☎ 5228366).

Hairdressers/Barbers   Women or men can patronize Bruno, Cannaregio 3924 (☎ 5285833). Bruno should be called for an appointment.

Holidays   See "When to Go" in Chapter 3.

Hospitals   Get in touch with the Civili Riuniti di Venezia, campo Santi Giovanni e Paolo (☎ 5294517).

Information   See "Visitor Information" in "Orientation" earlier in this chapter.

Laundry/Dry Cleaning   Go to Lavaget, Cannaregio 1269 (☎ 715976), on fondamenta Pescaria off rio Tera San Leonardo. It is open Monday through Friday from 8:15am to 12:30pm and 3 to 7pm. This is the most convenient self-service laundry to the rail station, only a 5-minute walk away. It also does dry cleaning.

Libraries   The biggest library is Biblioteca Nazionale Marciana, piazetta San Marco 7 (☎ 5208788). Hours are Monday through Friday from 9am to 6:45pm and Saturday from 9am to 1:30pm.

Lost Property   The central office for recovering lost property is the Ufficio Oggetti Rinvenuti, an annex to the Municipio (town hall) at San Marco 4134 (☎ 788225), on calle Piscopia o Loredan, lying off rive del Carbon on the Grand Canal. Open Monday, Wednesday, and Friday from 9:30am to 12:30pm.

Luggage Storage/Lockers   These services are available at the main rail station, Stazione di Santa Lucia, at piazzale Roma (☎ 715555).

Newspapers/Magazines   The *International Herald Tribune* and *USA Today* are sold at most newsstands and in many first-class and deluxe hotels, as are the European editions (in English) of *Time* and *Newsweek.*

Police   See "Emergencies" in this section.

Post Office   The main post office is at Fondaco dei Tedeschi (☎ 5286212), in the vicinity of the Rialto Bridge. It's open Monday through Saturday from 8:15am to 7pm.

Radio   The main station is run by RAI, the Italian state radio and TV network, and broadcasts in Italian only (at least you can listen to the music even if you don't speak the tongue). Vatican Radio is received in Venice and often carries English-language news broadcasts. Throughout the night and for part of the day, shortwave radio reception in Venice is excellent, including British (BBC), American (VOA), and Canadian (CBC). At night, the American Armed Forces Network (AFN) from Munich or Frankfurt can be heard on regular AM radio (middle or medium wave).

Religious Services   If you're Catholic, you'll find churches all over Venice. There is a Jewish synagogue in the Ghetto Vecchio (☎ 715012). A Methodist church is at Santa Maria Formosa 5170 (☎ 5227549), and there's an Anglican Episcopal church, St. George's, in Dorsoduro at campo San Vio 870 (☎ 5200571).

Restrooms   These are available at piazzale Roma and various other places in Venice, but not as plentiful as they should be. Often you'll have to rely on the facilities of a café, although you should purchase something, perhaps a light coffee, as in theory, commercial establishments reserve their toilets for customers only. Most museums and galleries have public toilets. You can also use the public toilets at the Albergo Diurno, on via Ascensione, just behind piazza San Marco. Remember, *Signori* means men and *Signore* is for women.

Safety   The curse of Venice is the pickpocket artist. Violent crime is rare. But because of the overcrowding in vaporetti and even on the small narrow streets, it's easy to pick pockets. Purse snatchers are commonplace as well. A purse snatcher seemingly darts out of nowhere, grabs a purse, and in seconds seems to have disappeared down some narrow alleyway. Secure your valuables, and if your hotel has such amenities, keep them locked in a safe there when not needed.

Shoe Repairs   A shoe-repair shop that never bothered to name itself is found at Dorsoduro 871, Tel. 5231163 on calle Nuova Sant'Agnese. This is the route most visitors travel between the Accademia and the Collezione Peggy Guggenheim.

Taxes   A 19% value-added tax (called IVA) is added to the price of all consumer goods and products and most services, such as those in hotels and restaurants.

Taxis   See "Getting Around" earlier in this chapter.

Telegrams/Telex/Fax   The post office maintains a telegram and fax service 24 hours a day. You can also call Italcable at 170 if you wish to send an international telegram; otherwise, call 186.

Television   The RAI is the chief television network broadcasting in Italy. Every TV in Venice has these highly politicized channels: RAI-1 for Christian Democrats, RAI-2 for Italian Socialists, and RAI-3 for the Democratic Party of the Left.

Transit Information   For flights, call 5415491; for rail information, 715555; and for bus schedules, 5287886.

Useful Telephone Numbers   To check on the time, call 161; for the weather, 191.

3 Networks & Resources

FOR STUDENTS   The center for budget student travel is **Centro Turistico Studentesco (CTS),** Dorsoduro 3252, on fondamenta Tagliapietra (☎ 5205660). The office is near campiello Squellini, lying to the west of campo Santa Margherita, and is reached by going to vaporetto stop San Toma. Cheap transportation and low-cost lodgings can be arranged here. Hours are Monday through Friday from 9am to 12:30pm and 3:30 to 7pm.

The tourist office distributes a free **"Youth Card,"** which entitles holders to various discounts throughout the city. But takers must be between the ages of 16 and 26 and have a photo ID to prove it. The cost of the card is 15,000 lire ($9.40).

FOR GAY MEN & LESBIANS   There are no gay liberation headquarters or club centers in Venice. There are also no gay bars as such, although this condition could change at any minute. Lesbians have bars, bookstores, and women's centers in some parts of Italy, but not in Venice.

FOR WOMEN   The **Instituto Suore Canossiane,** fondamenta del Ponte Piccolo, Guidecca 428 (☎ 5222157), is a 35-bed, private Catholic hotel for women (usually young women). Guests must vacate the premises by 9am, however. Rooms reopen at 4pm. The cost is 17,000 lire ($10.65) per person per night. A 10:30pm curfew is imposed.

FOR SENIORS   Go to the tourist office and inquire about any discounts—such as on transportation and museum admissions—that pertain to senior citizens. These data are always changing, so it's best to get the latest information. Also, for some good travel discounts, go to the Centro Turistico Studentesco (see "For Students" above) which, although essentially a student budget travel agency, may also help you with discounts on senior-citizen travel within Italy.

13

Where to Stay & Dine in Venice

Venice has some of the most expensive hotels in the world within its borders, including the Gritti Palace and the Cipriani. These pockets of posh cosset their guests in complete luxury and comfort, but there are also dozens of unheralded and moderately priced places to stay, often on narrow, hard-to-find streets. Venice has never been known, however, as an inexpensive destination. Everything, even a cup of coffee, costs a lot of money here. To combat high prices, many travelers—much to the chagrin of local merchants—have taken to visiting Venice on a day trip (along with their packed lunches).

The cheapest way to visit Venice is to book in a locanda, which means a small inn, carrying an even lower rating than the three categories of pensioni (boarding houses). Standards are highly variable in these places, many of which are dank, damp, and dark. Rooms even in many second- or first-class hotels are often cramped, as space has always been a problem in Venice.

It is estimated that in this "City of Light," at least half the bedrooms in any category are dark, so be duly warned. Rooms with lots of light opening onto the Grand Canal cost a hefty price. While single rooms are almost always available (call and ask about rates), they are often a horror in Venice. One frequent traveler who goes to Venice at least once a month on business confides that he rents a double room in a third- or fourth-class hotel and finds it a better value than a single room in a second- or first-class establishment.

Likewise, restaurants, even the so-called cheap ones, may appear expensive to you. For example, if you come from the state of Missouri, where you can find all-you-can-eat buffets for $6.95, you may be horrified to find yourself paying that for a cappuccino in certain Venetian cafés.

Seafood is the specialty of Venice, but it's very expensive, especially fish priced by weight.

Dining hours tend to be short, lunch starting at either 12:30 or 1pm and ending at 2:30pm. Most restaurants reopen at 8pm and close by 10 or 11pm. A service charge of 15% to 20% will almost certainly appear on your final bill, and it isn't necessary to tip extra. You've paid enough.

1 Accommodations

The most difficult times to find rooms are the busy seasons: the February Carnevale, Easter, and anytime from June through September. Because of the tight hotel situation, reservations as far in advance as possible are highly recommended. After those peak times, you can virtually have your pick of rooms, as many travelers avoid the damp, cold, and windy months of winter.

Hotel breakfasts are generally disappointing. Unless your breakfast is included in the rates, you may want to avoid breakfast at your hotel and retreat to a bar or café.

Be very careful about making long-distance phone calls from your hotel room in Venice: Many hoteliers impose a 40% phone surcharge. Go to the post office or use public phones instead.

Most hotels, if you ask at the reception desk, will grant you a 10% to 15% discount in winter (that is, from November until March 15). But getting this discount may require a little negotiation at the desk. A few hotels close in January if there's no prospect of business.

If an elevator is essential for you, always inquire in advance when booking a room. Many do not have public lounges.

Often facilities normally associated with first-class and deluxe hotels don't exist in Venetian hotels, many of which have floor plans laid out centuries ago. Unless otherwise specified, room service is only from 7am to midnight in Venetian hotels.

Even though Venice doesn't have cars making noise, it does have a lot of boat traffic and the streets are often filled with chattering, noisy people until late at night. If you like to turn in early, a set of earplugs is always helpful.

Should you arrive without a reservation, go to the AVA (Hotel Association) reservations booth at the train station, at the municipal parking garage at piazzale Roma, at the airport, or at the information point on the mainland where the highway comes to an end. The main office is at piazzale Roma (☎ 5228640). You're required to post a deposit to secure a room, which is then rebated on your final hotel bill. Depending on the classification of hotel, deposits range from 15,000 to 60,000 lire ($9.40 to $37.50) per person. All hotel booths mentioned above are open daily from 9am to 9pm.

Because of their age and lack of uniformity, hotels in Venice offer widely varying rooms. For example, it's entirely possible to stay in a hotel generally considered "expensive," while paying only a "moderate" rate—that is, if you'll settle for the less desirable accommodations. Many so-called inexpensive hotels and boarding houses have two or three rooms considered "expensive." Usually these accommodations are more spacious and open to a view. Therefore, the following price guidelines are only a rough idea of costs. Note that each category of hotels often has many exceptions to these general price rules.

Impressions

. . . a dying glory smiles/O'er the far times when many a subject land/Looked to the winged Lion's marble piles/Where Venice sat in state, throned on her hundred isles!
—Lord Byron

ISOLA DELLA GIUDECCA
VERY EXPENSIVE

✪ Cipriani
Isola della Guidecca 10, 30133 Venezia. ☎ **041/5207744.** Fax 041/5203930. 76 rms, 28 suites. A/C MINIBAR TV TEL. 850,000–1,200,000 lire ($531.25–$750) double; from 1,850,000 lire ($1,156.25) suite. AE, DC, MC, V. Breakfast from 35,000 lire ($21.90) extra. Closed Nov–Mar. Vaporetto: Zitelle.

Isolated, security-conscious, and elegant, Cipriani is a resort hotel set within a 16th-century cloister on the residential island of Giudecca. The hotel was established in 1958 by the late Giuseppe Cipriani, the founder of Harry's Bar and the one real-life character in Hemingway's Venetian novel. Clients in the past have included everyone from Margaret Thatcher to Barbra Streisand. The Cipriani, incidentally, is the only hotel on the island, which otherwise has a refreshing sense of calm and quiet. Today, the hotel is owned and operated by Orient Express Hotels.

Guest rooms have different amenities but all have splendid views.

Dining/Entertainment: Lunch is served at Il Gabbiano, either indoors or on terraces overlooking the water. More formal meals are served at night in The Restaurant.

Services: A private launch service ferries guests, at any hour, to and from the hotel's own pier near the piazza San Marco. Room service, babysitting, laundry, and valet are available.

Facilities: Olympic-size swimming pool, tennis courts, sauna.

NEAR PIAZZA SAN MARCO
VERY EXPENSIVE

Hotel Luna Baglioni
Calle Vallaresso 1243, 30124 Venezia. ☎ **041/5289840.** Fax 041/5287160. 118 rms, 7 suites. A/C MINIBAR TV TEL. 320,000–570,000 lire ($200–$356.25) double; from 800,000 lire ($500) suite. Rates include breakfast. AE, DC, MC, V. Vaporetto: San Marco.

Hotel Luna is "the oldest hotel in Venice," although it was long ago modernized in an international style. In spite of modernization, it still retains traces of its gracefully Napoleonic look. Founded in 1474 as a monastery by the Congrega di Fratti della Luna, it took in traveling pilgrims on their way through Venice. The tradition of hospitality remains for the thousands of visitors who have found a room at this deluxe hotel near piazza San Marco. Some of the rooms look over the Grand Canal, and most of them have high ceilings, renovated interiors, and marble and parquet floors. Floral bouquets are in the hallways of the upper floors, which can be reached by elevator or by a wide marble staircase.

Dining/Entertainment: The hotel serves a refined Venetian and international cuisine in its Ristorante Canova.

Services: Room service, babysitting, laundry, valet.

Hotel Monaco & Grand Canal
Calle Vallaresso 1325, 30124 Venezia. ☎ **041/5200211.** Fax 041/5200501. 65 rms, 5 suites. A/C MINIBAR TV TEL. 460,000–540,000 lire ($287.50–$337.50) double; 700,000–950,000 lire ($437.50–$593.75) suite. Rates include breakfast. AE, DC, MC, V. Vaporetto: San Marco.

The intimate and refined Hotel Monaco & Grand Canal captures the essence of Venice with its panoramic view of the Grand Canal. Harry's Bar is right across the way. It has been a hotel for more than 100 years; the structure dates from the 18th century when it was built as a private villa. This five-star hostelry is a favorite with discriminating Italians, particularly in the fall and winter seasons. It was the choice place in Venice of Simone de Beauvoir and Jean-Paul Sartre. More recently, Prince Ranier stayed here.

Dining/Entertainment: The hotel harbors one of the city's leading restaurants, named for the Grand Canal, where you can partake of Venetian specialties of the highest quality, coupled with impeccable service and a panorama. In season, meals are also served on the terrace along the canal.

Services: Room service, babysitting, laundry, valet.

EXPENSIVE

Gabrielli-Sandwirth

Riva degli Schiavoni 4110, 30122 Venezia. ☎ **041/523-1580.** Fax 041/520-9455. 100 rms. A/C TV TEL. 420,000–470,000 lire ($262.50–$293.75) double. Rates include breakfast. AE, DC, MC, V. Closed Dec–Jan. Vaporetto: Arsenale.

Gabrielli-Sandwirth was originally built in 1238 as a Venetian-Gothic palace; today its peach-colored stone-and-stucco facade stands a few paces from some of the most expensive and glamorous hotels in Venice. Two medieval houses have been joined to its high-ceilinged core to form a labyrinth of interior courtyards, rambling hallways, and a number of tastefully conservative bedrooms.

This is the only hotel on riva degli Schiavoni with its own garden, an idyllic enclave banked on one side by a canal. The panoramic rooftop sun terrace affords views of the Grand Canal and the Venetian lagoon such as Guardi might have painted. Public rooms in the hotel have beamed ceilings and a marble-covered charm.

Dining/Entertainment: The dining room, outfitted in a turn-of-the-century art nouveau, contains three of the most beautiful Murano chandeliers in Venice.

Services: Concierge, room service, babysitting, laundry, valet.

Facilities: Solarium.

Hotel Cavaletto e Doge Orseolo

Calle del Cavaletto 1107, 30124 Venezia. ☎ **041/5200955.** Fax 041/5238184. 96 rms. A/C MINIBAR TV. 440,000 lire ($275) double. Rates include breakfast. AE, DC, MC, V. Vaporetto: San Marco.

Filled with the accumulated charm of its 800-year history, the elegant Hotel Cavaletto e Doge Orseolo occupies a prime position on a narrow cobblestone street a few paces from St. Mark's Square. The hotel was created when three buildings were unified into one well-managed unit in the early 1900s. In the 1100s the oldest of the three was the private home of Doge Orseolo.

Today the Cavaletto is best viewed from its sinuously curved rear, where a flotilla of gondolas are moored within a stone-sided harbor, one of only two such basins in Venice. Each of the hotel's bedrooms is comfortably outfitted with glass chandeliers from nearby Murano, hardwood floors, and elegant Italian-inspired furniture. Many have views of canals and ancient stones.

Dining/Entertainment: The hotel has a big-windowed restaurant, with reflected sunlight from the lagoon dappling the high ceiling. There's also a kind of *dolce vita* bar where a relaxing cocktail might be the perfect end to a day.

Hotel Concordia

Calle larga San Marco 367, 30124 Venezia. ☎ **041/5206866.** Fax 041/5206775. 55 rms. A/C MINIBAR TV TEL. 210,000–410,000 lire ($131.25–$256.25) double. Rates include breakfast. AE, DC, MC, V. Vaporetto: San Marco.

Venice Accommodations

American Hotel **6**
Bonvecchiati **22**
Boston Hotel **10A**
La Calcina **7**
Caneva **21**
Cipriani **33**
Danieli Royal Exclesior **32**
Doni Pensione **31**
Gabrielli-Sandwirth **30**
Giorgione **2**
Gritti Palace **8**
Hotel Bisanzio **28**
Hotel Carpaccio **3**
Hotel Casanova **18**
Hotel Cavaletto
  e Doge Orseolo **20**
Hotel Concordia **25**
Hotel di Pozzi **16**
Hotel Europa & Regina **9**
Hotel La Fenice
  et des Artistes **17**
Hotel Luna Baglioni **19**
Hotel Metropole **31**
Hotel Monaco
  & Grand Canal **10**
Hotel Montecarlo **24**
Hotel Panada **24**
Hotel Rialto **23**
Hotel San Cassiano
  Ca'Favretto **1**
Hotel Scandinavia **27**
La Residenza **29**
Locanda Montin **4**
Londra Palace **31**
Marconi **31**
Pensione Accademia **5**
Pensione Seguso **7**
Saturnia-International **9**
Savoia & Jolanda **31**

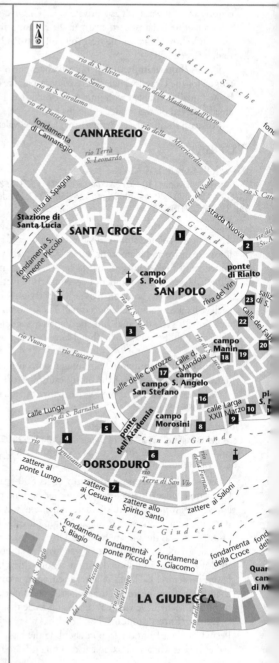

1382

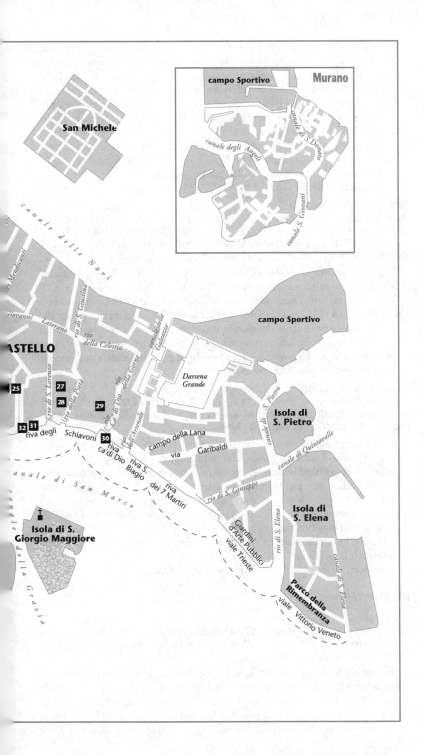

campo Sportivo   **Murano**

canale di S. Donato

canale degli Angeli

canale S. Giovanni

San Michele

canale delle Navi

a Mendicanti

Giovanni   Laterano

rio di S. Giustina

rio della Celestia

ASTELLO

rio di S. Lorenzo

rio della Pietà

rio di Ca' di Dio - della Gorne

canale delle Galeazze

campo Sportivo

*Darsena
Grande*

canale di S. Pietro

**Isola di
S. Pietro**

25   **27**
        28

29

32 **31**

riva degli   Schiavoni

30

rio dell'Arsenale

riva
ca'di Dio

riva S.
Biagio

rio di Ca' di Dio

campo della Lana

via   Garibaldi

canale di Quintavalle

canale di San Marco

riva
dei 7 Martiri

rio di S. Giuseppe

rio di S. Elena

**Isola di
S. Elena**

canale della Grazia

**Isola di S.
Giorgio Maggiore**

Giardini
d'Arte Pubblici
viale Trieste

canale di S. Elena

**Parco della
Rimembranza**

viale Vittorio Veneto

The Concordia is the only hotel in Venice containing rooms that look out over St. Mark's Square. Completely renovated, the century-old hotel, now a four-star choice, is housed in a five-story russet-colored building with stone-trimmed windows. The name of the hotel is spelled out in mosaics just below your feet as you enter. A series of gold-plated marble steps takes you to the lobby where you'll find a comfortable bar area, good service, and elevators to whisk you to the labyrinthine corridors upstairs. All bedrooms are decorated in a Venetian antique style and contain an electronic safe and hairdryer in addition to other amenities. Light meals and Italian snacks are available in the bar. Otherwise only breakfast is served.

Services: 24-hour room service, babysitting, laundry valet.

Facilities: Business center.

Hotel Europa & Regina

Via XXII Marzo no. 2159, 30124 Venezia. ☎ **041/5200477** or 800/221-2340 in the U.S., 800/955-2442 in Canada. Fax 041/5231533. 189 rms. A/C MINIBAR TV TEL. 385,000–440,000 lire ($240.65–$275) double. Breakfast 24,000 lire ($15) extra. AE, DC, MC, V. Vaporetto: San Marco.

A longtime favorite on the Grand Canal is the Hotel Europa & Regina, which can be reached by motorboat at its canal side or through a courtyard on via XXII Marzo. The hotel was formed by combining two Venetian palaces, both of which face the Grand Canal and the Church of La Salute, with a restaurant terrace and a café terrace between them. The accommodations in this five-star deluxe hotel are beautifully furnished, with varying decor. Most rooms have canal views, with the most expensive opening onto a view of the lagoon. Both Venetian and international food is served in the hotel restaurant.

Saturnia-International

Calle larga XXII Marzo no. 2398, 30124 Venezia. ☎ **041/5208377**. Fax 041/5207131. 95 rms. A/C MINIBAR TV TEL. 280,000–494,000 lire ($175–$308) double. Rates include breakfast. AE, DC, MC, V. Vaporetto: San Marco.

Saturnia-International is a 14th-century Venetian palazzo near piazza San Marco, part and parcel of old Venice. Wherever you wander throughout this palace, you'll find richly embellished beauty—the grand hallway with its wooden staircase, heavy iron chandeliers, fine paintings, and beamed ceilings. The bedrooms are spacious and furnished with chandeliers and Venetian antiques and enriched with tapestry rugs, gilt mirrors, and ornately carved ceilings. Many of these bedrooms overlook the quiet and dignified courtyard in the back.

Dining/Entertainment: Its restaurant, La Caravella, merits a separate recommendation (see "Dining," below).

Services: Room service, babysitting, laundry, valet.

MODERATE

Bonvecchiati

Calle Goldoni 4488, 30124 Venezia. ☎ **041/5285017**. Fax 041/5285230. 86 rms. TEL. 230,000–310,000 lire ($143.75–$193.75) double. Rates include breakfast. AE, DC, MC, V. Vaporetto: San Marco.

Looking much like the private villa of a titled Venetian family, Bonvecchiati near piazza San Marco stands proudly on its little square. A favorite spot is the outside canopied terrace, which borders the canal and is decorated with potted plants, lanterns, and garden furniture. The lounges are more like personalized living rooms. This three-star hotel was completely renovated in 1992, and the bedrooms are well furnished with a number of amenities, including a private safe deposit. Many of the accommodations contain air conditioning, minibar, and satellite color TV.

Hotel Bisanzio

Calle della Pietà 3651, 30122 Venezia. ☎ **041/5203100** or 800/528-1234 in the U.S. Fax 041/5204114. 40 rms. A/C MINIBAR TV TEL. 270,000 lire ($168.75) double. Rates include buffet breakfast. AE, DC, MC, V. Vaporetto: San Zaccaria.

Lying a few steps from St. Mark's Square, in one of the oldest parts of Venice, this hotel offers hospitality and a good standard of service. A fine restored 16th-century building, the hotel occupies the former home of sculptor Alessandro Vittoria. It has an elevator and terraces, plus a private little bar and also a mooring for gondolas and motorboats. The bedrooms are generally quiet, each decorated in a Venetian antique style. Amenities available are 24-hour room service, babysitting, and laundry. The lounge opens onto a traditional old Venetian courtyard.

Hotel Carpaccio

San Tomà 2765, 30125 Venezia. ☎ **041/5235946.** Fax 041/5242134. 18 rms. MINIBAR TEL. 250,000 lire ($156.25) double. Rates include breakfast. MC, V. Closed mid-Nov–Feb. Vaporetto: San Tomà.

Don't be put off by the narrow, winding alleyways leading up to the wrought-iron entrance of this second-class hotel—the building was meant to be approached by gondola. Once you're inside, you'll realize that your location in the heart of the oldest part of the city justifies your confusing arrival. This building used to be the Palazzo Barbarigo della Terrazza, and part of it is still reserved for private apartments. The hotel maintains tasteful and spacious rooms filled with serviceable furniture. The salon is decorated with gracious pieces, marble floors, and a big arched window whose exterior is crowned with a bearded head of stone looking, along with you, over the Grand Canal. Breakfast is the only meal served.

Hotel Casanova

Frezzeria 1284, 30124 Venezia. ☎ **041/5206855.** Fax 041/5206413. 43 rms, 3 suites. A/C MINIBAR TV TEL. 320,000 lire ($200) double; 360,000 lire ($225) suite. Rates include breakfast. AE, DC, MC, V. Vaporetto: San Marco.

Hotel Casanova, located a few steps from piazza San Marco, was formerly a private home. Today transformed into a hotel, it contains an elegant collection of church art and benches from old monasteries. These sit on flagstone floors near oil portraits. The reception manager will give you a key to a modernized bedroom with comfortably contemporary furnishings.

Hotel la Fenice et Des Artistes

Campiello de la Fenice 1936. 30124 Venezia. ☎ **041/5232333.** Fax 041/5203721. 65 rms, 4 suites. TV TEL. 280,000 lire ($175) double; 390,000 lire ($243.75) suite. Rates include breakfast. MC, V. Vaporetto: San Marco.

This hotel offers widely varying accommodations in two connected buildings, each at least 100 years old. One building is rather romantic in decor, with an architecturally rich staircase leading to beautifully decorated bedrooms (one accommodation was once described as "straight out of the last act of *La Traviata*, enhanced by small gardens and terraces"). Your satin-lined room may have an inlaid desk and a wardrobe painted in the Venetian manner to match a baroque bed frame. Capping the decor are velvet bedcovers, gilt mirrors, and crystal chandeliers. Chambers in the other building are far less glamorous. The older of the two has no elevator, and while the newer has an elevator, its modern bedrooms have conservative, rather sterile furniture. All but about three of the rooms are air-conditioned. This hotel, one of the most famous in Venice, occupies a location behind the opera house.

Hotel Montecarlo

Calle dei Specchieri 463, 30124 Venezia. ☎ **041/5207144.** Fax 041/5207789. 48 rms. A/C TV TEL. 300,000 lire ($187.50) double. Rates include breakfast. AE, DC, MC, V. Vaporetto: San Marco.

Hotel Montecarlo, located only a 2-minute walk from St. Mark's Square, was established some years ago in a 17th-century building. It was recently renovated to include modern baths. Your walk to your bedroom leads through upper hallways lined with paintings by Venetian artists. The double rooms are comfortably proportioned and decorated with Venetian-style furniture. However, the handful of singles are very small. Venetian-glass chandeliers in the rooms add a festive note. The hotel's restaurant, Antico Pignolo, serves lunch and dinner from an à la carte menu that embraces both the Venetian and the international kitchen. It is closed Tuesdays in winter.

Hotel Do Pozzi

Corte do Pozzi 2373, 30124 Venezia. ☎ **041/5207855.** Fax 041/5229413. 35 rms. MINIBAR TV TEL. 222,000 lire ($138.75) double. Rates include breakfast. AE, DC, MC, V. Vaporetto: San Marco.

Hotel Do Pozzi is small, modernized, and centrally located just a short stroll from the Grand Canal and St. Mark's Square. Its original structure is 200 years old. More a little country tavern than a hotel, it opens onto a paved front courtyard with potted greenery. You can arrive via water-taxi, boat, gondola, or vaporetto. The sitting and dining rooms are furnished with antiques (and near antiques), all intermixed with utilitarian modern decor. Baths have been added, and a major refurbishing has given everything a fresh touch. Laundry and babysitting are available.

Hotel San Cassiano Ca'Favretto

Calle della Rosa 2232, 30135 Venezia. ☎ **041/5241768.** Fax 041/721033. 36 rms. A/C MINIBAR TV TEL. 150,000–311,000 lire ($93.75–$194.40) double. Rates include breakfast. AE, DC, MC, V. Vaporetto: San Stae.

Hotel San Cassiano Ca'Favretto used to be the studio of the 19th-century painter Giacomo Favretto. The views from the hotel's gondola pier and from the four-arched porch of the dining room encompass the lacy facade of the Ca' d'Oro, sometimes considered the most beautiful building in Venice. The hotel was constructed in the 14th century as a palace. The present owner has worked closely with Venetian authorities to preserve the original details, which include a 20-foot beamed ceiling in the entrance area. Today, the architectural plans from the many renovations hang in gilt frames above the antiques in the lobby. Patrons have included George McGovern and guests of the U.S. Embassy. Fifteen of the conservatively decorated rooms overlook one of two canals, and many of them are filled with antiques or high-quality reproductions.

Savoia & Jolanda

Riva degli Schiavoni 4187, 30122 Venezia. ☎ **041/5206644.** Fax 041/5207494. 78 rms, 3 suites. TEL. 260,000 lire ($162.50) double; 350,000 lire ($218.75) suite. Rates include breakfast. AE, MC, V. Vaporetto: San Zaccaria.

Savoia & Jolanda is in a prize position on Venice's main street, with a lagoon at its front yard. The hotel was established at the turn of the century as one of the most prominent along riva degli Schiavoni, transformed from an old Venetian palazzo. Most of the bedrooms have a view of the boats and the Lido. While its exterior reflects much of old Venice, the interior is somewhat spiritless. However, the staff makes life here comfortable and relaxed. The bedrooms are neutral modern, with plenty of space for daytime living (desk and armchairs). An addition to the hotel contains 20 rooms, each with air conditioning, minibar, and TV.

INEXPENSIVE

Boston Hotel

Ponte dei Dai 848, 30124 Venezia. ☎ **041/5287665.** Fax 041/5226628. 42 rms. TEL. 240,000 lire ($150) double. Rates include buffet breakfast. AE, DC, MC, V. Closed Nov–Feb. Vaporetto: San Marco.

Boston Hotel, built in 1962, is just a whisper away from St. Mark's. It's run by Mario and Adriana Bernardi. The hotel was named after an uncle who left to seek his fortune in Boston . . . and never returned. The little living rooms combine the old and the new, containing many antiques and Venetian ceilings. For the skinny guest, there's a tiny, self-operated elevator and a postage-stamp-size street entrance. Most of the bedrooms with parquet floors have built-in features, snugly designed beds, chests, and wardrobes. Fortunately, several have tiny balconies that open onto canals. Some rooms are air-conditioned, and a TV is available upon request.

Doni Pensione

Calle de Vin 4656, 30122 Venezia. ☎ **041/5224267.** 13 rms (none with bath). 90,000 lire ($56.25) double. Rates include breakfast. No credit cards. Vaporetto: Zaccaria.

Doni Pensione sits in a private position, about a 3-minute walk from St. Mark's. Most of its rooms either overlook a little canal, where four or five gondolas are usually tied up, or a garden with a tall fig tree. Simplicity prevails, especially in the pristine and down-to-earth bedrooms, but the level of cleanliness is high.

Giorgione

SS. Apostoli 4586, 30131 Venezia. ☎ **041/5225810.** Fax 041/5239092. 70 rms, 8 suites. A/C MINIBAR TV TEL. 165,000–300,000 lire ($103.15–$187.50) double; 215,000–390,000 lire ($134.40–$243.75) suite. Rates include buffet breakfast. AE, MC, V. Vaporetto: Ca' d'Oro.

Giorgione is a glamorous little hotel. In spite of its modernization, its decor is traditionally Venetian. The lounges and public rooms are equipped with fine furnishings and decorative accessories. Likewise, the comfortable as well as stylish bedrooms are designed to coddle guests. The hotel also has a typical Venetian garden. It's rated second class by the government, but the Giorgione maintains higher standards than many of the first-class establishments. Only breakfast is served.

ON THE LIDO

VERY EXPENSIVE

✪ Excelsior Palace

Lungomare Marconi 41, 30126. Venezia Lido. ☎ **041/5260201** or 800/325-3535 in the U.S. and Canada. Fax 041/5267276. 196 rms, 18 suites. A/C MINIBAR TV TEL. 473,000–572,000 lire ($295.65–$357.50) double; from 1,430,000 lire ($893.75) suite. Breakfast 29,700 lire ($18.55) extra. AE, DC, MC, V. Parking 30,000 lire ($18.75). Closed end of Oct–Apr 1. Vaporetto: Lido; then bus A, B, or C.

When the mammoth Excelsior Palace was built, it was the biggest resort hotel of its kind in the world. The Excelsior is a monument to *la dolce vita* and did much to make the Lido fashionable. Its rooms range in style and amenities from cozy singles to suites. Most of the social life here takes place around the angular swimming pool or on the flowered terraces leading up to the cabañas on the sandy beach.

All guest rooms—some of them big enough for tennis games—have been modernized, often with vivid colors that look like reminders of summer, regardless of the season.

Dining/Entertainment: On the premises is one of the most elegant dining rooms of the Adriatic, the Tropicana. The Blue Bar on the ground floor has piano music and views of the beach.

Services: 24-hour room service, babysitting, laundry, valet.

Facilities: Six tennis courts, a swimming pool, and a private pier with boat rental. A private launch makes hourly runs to the other CIGA hotels on the Grand Canal.

EXPENSIVE

✪ Hotel des Bains

Lungomare Marconi 17, 30126 Venezia Lido. ☎ **041/5265921** or 800/325-3535 in the U.S. and Canada. Fax 041/5260113. 191 rms, 19 suites. A/C MINIBAR TV TEL. 352,000–495,000 lire ($220–$309.40) double; from 726,000 lire ($453.75) suite. Rates include breakfast. AE, DC, MC, V. Free parking. Closed Nov–Mar. Vaporetto: Lido; then bus A, B, or C.

Hotel des Bains was built in the grand era of European resort hotels. It has its own wooded park and private beach with individual cabañas along with a kind of confectionary facade from the turn of the century. Thomas Mann stayed here several times before making it the setting for his novella *Death in Venice,* and later it was used as a set for the film of the same name. The renovated interior exudes the flavor of the leisurely life of the Belle Epoque era. The hotel, which overlooks the sea, has well-furnished, fairly large rooms.

Dining/Entertainment: Guests can dine in a large veranda room cooled by Adriatic sea breezes. The food is top-rate and the service is superior.

Services: A motorboat shuttles back and forth between Venice and the Lido, room service, babysitting, laundry, valet.

Facilities: Many resort-type amenities at Golf Club Alberoni (tennis courts, a large swimming pool, a private pier, and a park).

🏔 Family-Friendly Hotels

American Hotel *(see p. 413)*   Secluded away from the tourist hordes across the Grand Canal, this is a moderately priced choice where many rooms are rented as triples.

Pensione Accademia *(see p. 414)*   Considered the best of the pensioni of Venice, this villa has a garden and large rooms. The former Russian Embassy was the fictional home of Katharine Hepburn in the film *Summertime.*

Pensione Seguso *(see p. 417)*   An antique-filled palace dating from the 15th century, this is a relatively secluded family-type place where the half-board rates are good value.

Quattro Fontane *(see p. 413)*   Long a Lido family favorite, this hotel guarantees summertime fun. It's somewhat like staying in the big chalet of a Venetian family. There's a private beach too.

MODERATE

Hotel Belvedere

Piazzale Santa Maria Elisabetta 4, 30126 Lido di Venezia. ☎ **041/5265773.** Fax 041/5261486. 30 rms (all with shower). A/C TV TEL. 180,000 lire ($112.50) double. Rates include breakfast. AE, DC, MC, V. Free parking. Vaporetto: Lido.

Built in 1857, Hotel Belvedere is still run by the same family. Restored and modernized, it also offers a popular restaurant (recommended in "Dining" later in this chapter). The hotel is open all year, which is unusual for the Lido. It offers simply furnished double rooms. All have air conditioning or a view of the St. Mark lagoon. For the Lido, prices are reasonable. The hotel has parking in its garden, and it's located right across from the vaporetto stop. As an added courtesy, the hotel offers guests free entrance to the casino, and in summer guests can use the hotel's bathing huts that have been reserved on the Venetian Lido.

Hotel Helvetia

Gran Viale 4–6, 30126 Lido di Venezia. ☎ **041/5260105.** Fax 041/5268903. 56 rms. TEL. 120,000–250,000 lire ($75–$156.25) double. Rates include breakfast. MC, V. Parking 10,000 lire ($6.25). Closed Nov–Mar. Vaporetto: Lido; then bus A, B, or C.

Hotel Helvetia is a four-story, russet-colored, 19th-century building with stone detailing on a side street near the lagoon side of the island, an easy walk from the vaporetto stop. The quieter rooms face away from the street and rooms in the older wing have belle époque high ceilings and attractively comfortable furniture. The newer wing, dating from around 1950, is more streamlined, and has been renovated in a more conservative style. Breakfast is served, weather permitting, in a flagstone-covered wall garden behind the hotel. Babysitting, laundry, and 24-hour room service are available.

○ Quattro Fontane

Via Quattro Fontane 16, 30126 Lido di Venezia. ☎ **041/5260227.** Fax 041/5260726. 57 rms. A/C TV TEL. 290,000–320,000 lire ($181.25–$200) double. Rates include breakfast. AE, DC, MC, V. Free parking. Closed Nov–Mar. Vaporetto: Lido; then bus A, B, or C.

In its price bracket, Quattro Fontane is one of the most charming hotels on the Lido. The trouble is, a lot of people know that, so it's likely to be booked. Like a chalet from the Dolomites, this former summer home of a 19th-century Venetian family is most popular with the discriminating British. They seem to appreciate the homelike atmosphere, the garden, the helpful staff, the rooms with superior amenities, and the good food served at tables set under shade trees. Many of the rooms are furnished with antiques. The hotel has a private beach and a tennis court.

NEAR THE ACCADEMIA
MODERATE

American Hotel

Campo San Vio 628, 30123 Venezia. ☎ **041/5204733.** Fax 041/5204048. 29 rms. A/C MINIBAR TV TEL. 290,000 lire ($181.25) double; 350,000 lire ($218.75) triple. Rates include breakfast. AE, DC, MC, V. Vaporetto: Accademia.

Set on a small waterway, the American Hotel lies in an ochre building across the Grand Canal from the most heavily touristed areas. The lobby is filled with murals, warm colors, and antiques, and the location is perfect for anyone wanting to avoid the crowds that descend on Venice in summer. Bedrooms are comfortably furnished in a Venetian style. On the second floor is a beautiful terrace where guests relax over drinks. Many rooms with their own private terrace face the canal.

INEXPENSIVE

⑤ Locanda Montin

Fondamenta di Borgo 1147, in Dorsoduro, 31000 Venezia. ☎ **041/5227151.** Fax 041/5200255. 7 rms (none with bath). 70,000–80,000 lire ($43.75–$50) double. Breakfast 7,000 lire ($4.40). AE, DC, MC, V. Vaporetto: Accademia.

The well-recommended Locanda Montini is an old-fashioned Venetian inn whose adjoining restaurant is one of the most loved and frequented in the area. The hotel is located in the Dorsoduro section, an area across the Grand Canal from the most popular tourist zones. The establishment is officially listed as a fourth-class hotel, but its accommodations are considerably larger and better than that rating would suggest. Reservations are virtually mandatory, because of the reputation of this locanda. Marked only by a small carriage lamp etched with the name of the establishment extending over the pavement, the inn is a little difficult to locate, but worth the search.

⑤ Pensione Accademia

Fondamenta Bollani 1058, in Dorsoduro, 30123 Venezia. ☎ **041/5237846.** Fax 041/5239152. 29 rms (22 with bath). 160,000 lire ($100) double without bath; 210,000 lire ($131.25) double with bath. Rates include breakfast. AE, DC, MC, V. Vaporetto: Accademia.

Pensione Accademia is the most patrician of the pensioni. It's in a villa whose garden extends into the angle created by the junction of two canals. Iron fences, twisting vines, and neoclassical sculpture are a part of the setting, as are Gothic-style paneling, Venetian chandeliers, and Victorian-era furniture. The building served as the Russian Embassy before World War II, and as a private house before that. There's an upstairs sitting room flanked with two large windows and a formal rose garden, which is visible from the breakfast room. The bedrooms are spacious and decorated with original furniture from the 19th century. Some of the rooms are air-conditioned. The Pensione Accademia was the fictional residence of Katharine Hepburn's character in the film *Summertime*. Incidentally, it was when Hepburn was in Venice for the film that she fell into a canal and got a permanent eye infection.

NEAR THE RIALTO
MODERATE

Hotel Rialto

Riva del Ferro 5149, 30124 Venezia. ☎ **041/5209166.** Fax 041/5238958. 77 rms. A/C MINIBAR TV TEL. 290,000–320,000 lire ($181.25–$200) double. Rates include breakfast. AE, DC, MC, V. Vaporetto: Rialto.

Hotel Rialto opens right onto the Grand Canal at the foot of the Ponte di Rialto, the famous bridge flanked with shops. Its bedrooms are quite satisfactory, combining modern or Venetian furniture with the complexities of ornate Venetian ceilings and wall decorations. The hotel has been considerably upgraded to second class, and private baths or showers have been installed in each unit. The most desirable and expensive double rooms overlook the Grand Canal, and these go first.

Marconi

Riva del Vin 729, 30125 Venezia. ☎ **041/5222068.** Fax 041/5229700. 26 rms (all with bath or shower). A/C MINIBAR TV TEL. 150,000–310,000 lire ($93.75–$193.75) double. Rates include breakfast. AE, MC, V. Vaporetto: Rialto.

Marconi was built in 1500 when Venice was at the height of its naval supremacy. It incorporates a later addition. The drawing-room furnishings would be appropriate for visiting archbishops. The hotel lies less than 50 feet from the much portraited Rialto Bridge. The Maschietto family operates everything efficiently. Only four of the lovely old bedrooms open onto the Grand Canal, and these, of course, are the most eagerly sought after. Meals are usually taken in an L-shaped room with Gothic chairs. In fair weather, the sidewalk tables facing on the Grand Canal are preferred by many.

RIVA DEGLI SCHIAVONI
VERY EXPENSIVE

☼ Danieli Royal Excelsior
Riva degli Schiavoni 4196, 30122 Venezia. ☎ **041/5226480,** or 800/325-3535 in the U.S. and Canada. Fax 041/5200208. 231 rms, 9 suites. A/C MINIBAR TV TEL. 567,000–632,000 lire ($354.40–$395) double; from 1,052,000 lire ($657.50) suite. Rates include breakfast. AE, DC, MC, V. Vaporetto: San Zaccaria.

Danieli Royal Excelsior was built as a grand showcase by the Doge Dandolo in the 14th century. In 1822 it was transformed into a deluxe "hotel for kings." Placed in a most spectacular position, right on the Grand Canal, it has sheltered not only kings, but princes, cardinals, ambassadors, and such literary figures as George Sand and Charles Dickens. The palace fronts the canal with the New Danieli Excelsior, a modern wing. Another palace has been incorporated into this *serenissima* ensemble.

You enter into a four-story-high stairwell, with Venetian arches and balustrades. The atmosphere is luxurious throughout—even the balconies opening off the main lounge have been illuminated by stained-glass skylights. The bedrooms range widely in price, dimension, decor, and vistas, and those opening onto the lagoon cost more.

Dining/Entertainment: The hotel has a rooftop dining room, Terrazza Danieli, giving you an undisturbed view of the canals and "crowns" of Venice, as well as an intimate cocktail lounge and a bar offering piano music.

Services: Room service, babysitting, laundry, valet.

Facilities: Hotel launch to the Lido.

EXPENSIVE

Hotel Metropole
Riva degli Schiavoni 4149, 30122 Venezia. ☎ **041/5205044.** Fax 041/5223679. 70 rms, 3 junior suites. A/C MINIBAR TV TEL. 480,000 lire ($300) double; 530,000 lire ($331.25) junior suite. Rates include buffet breakfast. AE, DC, MC, V. Vaporetto: San Zaccaria.

At the widest part of the Grand Canal, an easy walk from Piazzo San Marco, is the Hotel Metropole. This was once a house with a small musical chapel where Antonio Vivaldi taught and composed music from 1703 to 1740.

This is a good hotel, dotted with unusual detailing and craftsmanship, and filled with lots of antiques and personal touches. The Trattoria al Buffet, a buffet-style restaurant, is unique in Venice, patronized by Venetians as well as visitors. The hotel has an attractive sitting room and even a boat landing on a side canal for water-taxi and gondola embarkations. Built at the beginning of the 17th century, the premises were used as a private residence, then as a military hospital, and finally, in 1909, as a hotel. Totally renovated in 1985, the bedrooms, many with views, are filled with elegantly conservative furniture, Venetian-glass chandeliers, painted headboards, and marble baths.

✪ Londra Palace

Riva degli Schiavoni 4171, 30122 Venezia. ☎ **041/5200533.** Fax 041/5225032. 61 rms, 6 junior suites. A/C MINIBAR TV TEL. 280,000–510,000 lire ($175–$318.75) double; 390,000–750,000 lire ($243.75–$468.75) suite. Rates include breakfast. AE, DC, MC, V.

Londra Palace is an elegant hotel with 100 windows on the Venetian lagoon, a few yards from piazza San Marco. It was formed by two palaces that were joined together about 80 years ago. The hotel's most famous patron was arguably Tchaikovsky, who wrote his Fourth Symphony in Room 108 in December 1877. He also composed several other works here. The cozy reading room off the main lobby is decorated like a section of an English club, with leaded windows and blow-ups of some of Tchaikovsky's sheet music set into frames along the paneled walls. Other public rooms contain modern paintings, some showing an apocalyptic end of Venice by flooding. Bedrooms are luxuriously furnished.

Dining/Entertainment: The hotel has a popular piano bar and an excellent restaurant, Do Leoni.

Services: Room service, babysitting, laundry, valet.

Facilities: Conference hall.

INEXPENSIVE

Hotel Scandinavia

Campo Santa Maria Formosa 5240, 30122 Venezia. ☎ **041/5223507.** Fax 041/5235232. 34 rms (30 with bath). A/C MINIBAR TV TEL. 180,000 lire ($112.50) double without bath; 250,000 lire ($156.25) double with bath. Rates include breakfast. AE, MC, V. Vaporetto: San Zaccaria.

A radical overhaul in 1992 added a third star to this hotel's rating. The entrance to the Hotel Scandinavia is set behind a dark-pink facade just off one of the most colorful squares in Venice. The public rooms are filled with copies of 18th-century Italian chairs, Venetian-glass chandeliers, and a re-created rococo decor. The decoration of the bedrooms is in the Venetian style, but modern comforts have been added. There is also a bar, and room service is available for drinks 24 hours a day. A lobby lounge overlooks campo Santa Maria Formosa.

CAMPO MARIA DEL GIGLIO
VERY EXPENSIVE

✪ Gritti Palace

Campo Santa Maria del Giglio 2467, 30124 Venezia. ☎ **041/794611,** or 800/221-2340 in the U.S., 800/955-2442 in Canada. Fax 041/5200942. 96 rms, 10 suites. A/C MINIBAR TV TEL. 671,000–836,000 lire ($419.40–$522.50) double; from 1,760,000 lire ($1,100) suite. Breakfast 35,000 lire ($21.90) extra. AE, DC, MC, V. Vaporetto: Santa Maria del Giglio.

Gritti Palace, in a stately setting on the Grand Canal, is a renovated palazzo of the 15th-century doge Andrea Gritti. "Our home in Venice" to Ernest Hemingway, it has for years drawn a select clientele of some of the world's greatest theatrical, literary, political, and royal figures—Queen Elizabeth and Prince Philip, Greta Garbo, Herbert von Karajan, and Winston Churchill. The range and variety of the rooms seem almost limitless, from elaborate suites to relatively small singles. But in every case, the stamp of glamor is evident. Antiques are often used in both the bedrooms and the public rooms. For a splurge, ask for Hemingway's old suite or the Doge Suite, once occupied by W. Somerset Maugham.

Dining/Entertainment: The cuisine served at the hotel's Ristorante Club del Doge is among the best in Venice.

Services: 24-hour room service, babysitting, laundry, valet.

Facilities: Use of Hotel Excelsior facilities on the Lido.

NEAR THE SALUTE
INEXPENSIVE

⑤ La Calcina

Zattere al Gesuati 780, 30123 Venezia. ☎ **041/5206466.** Fax 041/5227045. 40 rms (20 with bath or shower). TEL. 90,000–105,000 lire ($56.25–$65.65) double without bath or shower; 135,000–165,000 lire ($84.40–$103.15) double with bath or shower. Rates include breakfast. AE, MC, V. Closed Jan 9–Feb 4. Vaporetto: Accademia.

La Calcina lies in a less-trampled, secluded, and dignified district of Venice. This used to be the English enclave before the area developed a broader base of tourism. John Ruskin, who wrote *The Stones of Venice*, stayed here in 1877, and he charted the ground for his latter-day compatriots. This pensione is absolutely clean, and the furnishings are deliberately simple and unpretentious. The rooms are comfortable.

Pensione Seguso

Zattere al Gesuati 779, 30123 Venezia. ☎ **041/5286858.** Fax 041/5222340. 40 rms (30 with bath or shower). TEL. 260,000 lire ($162.50) double without bath or shower, 270,000 lire ($168.75) double with bath or shower. Rates include half-board. AE, DC, MC, V. Closed Dec–Feb. Vaporetto: Accademia.

Pensione Seguso is a terra-cotta colored house whose foundation dates from the 15th century. Set at the junction of two canals, this hotel is located on a less-traveled side of Venice across the Grand Canal from piazza San Marco. Its relative isolation made it attractive to such tenants as Ezra Pound and John Julius Norwich and his mother, Lady Diana Cooper. The interior is furnished with the family antiques of the Seguso family, who have maintained the hotel for more than 80 years. Small tables are set up near the hotel entrance, where breakfast is served on sunny days. Half-board, obligatory, is served in the elegantly upper-crust dining room, where antique reproductions, real heirlooms, and family cats vie for the attention of the many satisfied guests.

NEAR THE ARSENALE
INEXPENSIVE

⑤ La Residenza

Castello 3608, campo Bandiera e Moro, 30122 Venezia. ☎ **041/5285315.** Fax 041/5238859. 15 rms. MINIBAR TV TEL. 185,000 lire ($115.65) double. Rates include breakfast. AE, DC, MC, V. Closed Nov and Jan. Vaporetto: Arsenale.

La Residenza is in a pleasingly proportioned 14th-century building that looks a lot like a miniature version of the Doge's Palace. It's on a residential square where children play soccer and older people feed the pigeons. After gaining access (just press the button outside the entrance), you'll pass through a stone vestibule lined with ancient Roman columns before ringing another bell at the bottom of a flight of stairs. First an iron gate and then a door will open into an enormous salon with elegant antiques, 300-year-old paintings, and some of the most marvelously preserved walls in Venice.

The bedrooms are far less opulent than the public salons, and are furnished with contemporary pieces and functional accessories. The choice ones are usually booked far in advance, especially for carnival season.

SECRETS OF VENICE

In addition to the establishments listed above, there are a couple of relatively undiscovered places that deserve special mention. **Hotel Agli Alboretti,** Rio Terra Antonio Foscarini 882884 (☎ 5210158), is a secret address in Dorsoduro, former stamping grounds of the poet Ezra Pound, although also home to Susanna Agnelli, sister of FIAT president Gianni. In this old and fascinating part of town, this hotel is cheap and comfortable, offering you a little private room in a pleasant setting. They don't advertise and they're not too fond of publicity, but it's worth reserving well in advance for a chance to stay here. **Casa Dè Stefani,** Calle del Traghetto 2786 (☎ 5223337), lies only a few steps from the Ca'Rezzonico vaporetto stop. In an overpriced city, it defiantly still charged reasonable prices. The proprietor will give you the key to the front door, and after that you're pretty much on your own. The hotel—really, guest house—is like wandering back into Venice of yesterday. The floors are wavy, like the waters on the Grand Canal, as the building has shifted and sagged with time. Some rooms are without private bath.

2 Dining

Although Venice doesn't grow much foodstuff, and is hardly a victory garden, it's bounded by a rich agricultural district and plentiful vineyards in the hinterlands. The city gets the choicest items on its menu from the Adriatic, although the fish dishes, such as scampi, are very expensive. The many rich and varied specialties prepared in the Venetian kitchen will be surveyed in the restaurant recommendations to follow. For Italy, the restaurants of Venice are high priced, though there are many trattorie that cater to moderate budgets.

NEAR PIAZZA SAN MARCO & LA FENICE
EXPENSIVE

○ **Antico Martini**
San Marco 1983, campo San Fantin. ☎ **5224121.** Reservations required. Main courses 32,000–50,000 lire ($20–$31.25); fixed-price lunch 40,000–55,000 lire ($25–$34.40); fixed-price dinner 85,000–98,000 lire ($53.15–$61.25). AE, DC, MC, V. Thurs–Mon noon–2:30pm; Wed–Mon 7–11:30pm. Vaporetto: San Marco. VENETIAN.

As the city's leading restaurant, Antico Martini elevates Venetian cuisine to its highest level. Inside, the walls are paneled; elaborate chandeliers glitter overhead and gilt-framed oil paintings adorn the walls. Outside, the courtyard is favored in summer. It was founded in 1720 as a coffeehouse. A wine grower from Tuscany acquired the coffeehouse as a bad debt in 1921. That long-ago proprietor was the father of the present owner, Emilio Baldi, who runs the present Antico Martini with just the right amount of dash and flair.

An excellent beginning is the risotto di frutti di mare, creamy Venetian style with plenty of fresh seafood. For a main dish, try the fegato alla veneziana, which is tender liver fried with onions and served with a helping of polenta, a yellow cornmeal mush praised by Goldoni. The yellow Tocai is an interesting local wine and especially good with fish dishes.

Venice is like eating an entire box of chocolate liqueurs at one go.

—Truman Capote

✪ La Caravella

Calle larga XXII Marzo no. 2398. ☎ **5208901.** Reservations required. Main courses 37,000–52,000 lire ($23.15–$32.50). AE, DC, MC, V. Daily noon–3pm and 7pm–midnight. Vaporetto: San Marco. VENETIAN/INTERNATIONAL.

La Caravella, next door to the Hotel Saturnia International, offers with its gracious ambience an elegant nautical atmosphere with time-mellowed paneling. The decor is inspired by the interior of an 18th-century clipper ship, *una caravella*. The restaurant contains four different dining rooms and the option of overflowing its tables into a garden. The decor is rustically elegant, with frescoed ceilings, bouquets of flowers, and wrought-iron lighting fixtures. Many of the specialties are featured nowhere else in town. You might begin with an *antipasti misto de pesce* (fish) with olive oil and lemon juice, or perhaps prawns with avocado. Two specialties of the house include *granceola* (Adriatic sea crab on a bed of carpaccio) or else chateaubriand for two. The best item to order, however, is one of the poached-fish dishes, such as bass—all priced according to weight and served with a tempting sauce. After all that, the ice cream in champagne is welcome.

Harry's Bar

Calle Vallaresso 1323. ☎ **5285777.** Reservations required. Main courses 73,000–78,000 lire ($45.60–$48.75). AE, DC, MC, V. Tues–Sun noon–3pm and 7 –11pm. Vaporetto: San Marco. VENETIAN.

Harry's Bar serves the best food in Venice. Its fame was spread by Ernest Hemingway. A. E. Hotchner, in his *Papa Hemingway*, quoted the writer as saying, "We can't eat straight hamburger in a Renaissance palazzo on the Grand Canal." So he ordered a 5-pound "tin of beluga caviar" to, as he said, "take the curse off it." Harry, by the way, is an Italian named Arrigo, son of the late Commendatore Cipriani. Like his father, Arrigo is an entrepreneur extraordinaire known for the standard of his cuisine. His bar is a watering spot for martini-thirsty Americans—the vodka martini is dry and well chilled, but Hemingway and Hotchner always ordered Bloody Marys. You can have your choice of dining in the bar downstairs or the room with a view upstairs. We recommend the Venetian fish soup, followed by the scampi Thermidor with rice pilaf, and topped off by a chocolate mousse.

Quadri

Piazza San Marco 120–124. ☎ **5289299.** Reservations required. Main courses 33,000–55,000 lire ($20.65–$34.40). AE, DC, MC, V. Tues–Sun noon–2:30pm and Tues–Sun 7–10:30pm. Vaporetto: San Marco. INTERNATIONAL.

One of the most famous restaurants of Europe, Quadri is even better known as a café (see "Venice After Dark " in Chapter 14). This deluxe restaurant, with its elegant decor and clientele, is on the second floor, overlooking the "living room" of Venice. Many diners come here just for the view, and are often surprised when they are treated not only to a memorable setting, but a high-quality cuisine and impeccable service. The place is often packed with celebrities during art and film festivals, the world glitterati taking delight in this throwback to the days of La Serenissima. The Venetian cuisine has been acclaimed—at least by one food

Venice Dining

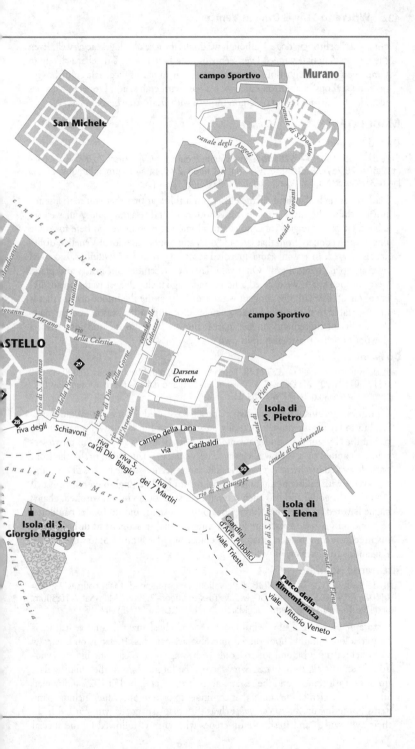

critic—as "befitting a doge," although we doubt if those old doges ate as well. Even the classic Venetian sautéed liver seems to taste better here. The chef is likely to tempt you with such dishes as octopus in fresh tomato sauce, salt codfish with polenta, scallops in a saffron sauce, or sea bass with crab sauce. Dessert specialties include "baked" ice cream or lemon mousse with fresh strawberry sauce.

MODERATE

Da Ivo

Calle dei Fuseri 1809. ☎ **5285004.** Reservations required. Main courses 20,000–42,000 lire ($12.50–$26.25). AE, DC, MC, V. Mon–Sat noon–2:40pm and 7pm–midnight. Closed Jan 6–31. Vaporetto: San Marco. TUSCAN/VENETIAN.

Da Ivo has such a faithful clientele that you'll think at first that you're in a semi-private club. The rustic atmosphere is both cozy and relaxing, and your well-set table flickers to the glow of candlelight. Homesick Florentines go here for some fine Tuscan cookery from that land of "milk and honey." Regional Venetian dishes are also served. In season, game, prepared according to ancient traditions, is cooked over an open charcoal grill. On a cold day one December our hearts and plates were warmed when we ordered a homemade tagliatelli. Over it were spread slivers of tartufi bianchi, the pungent white truffle from the Piedmont district that is unforgettable to the palate. Dishes change according to the season and the daily availability of ingredients on the market but are likely to include anglerfish, a stewpot of fish, or cuttlefish in its own ink.

Do Forni

Calle dei Specchieri 468. ☎ **5232148.** Reservations required. Main courses 20,000–35,000 lire ($12.50–$21.90). AE, DC, MC, V. Daily noon–3pm and daily 6–11pm. Closed Nov–Dec. Vaporetto: San Marco. INTERNATIONAL.

Centuries ago, this was the site where bread was baked for some local monasteries, but today it's the most frenetically busy restaurant in Venice—even when the rest of the city slumbers under a wintertime Adriatic fog. It's divided into two sections, separated by a narrow alleyway. The Venetian cognoscenti prefer the front part, decorated in *Orient Express* style. The larger section at the back is like a country tavern, with ceiling beams and original paintings. The English menu is entitled "food for the gods" and lists such specialties as spider crab in its own shell, champagne flavored risotto, calves' kidney in a bitter mustard, and sea bass in papillotte, to name only a few items. The food is international in scope, and dishes appear inspired not only by the cuisine of Venice, but the United States, Morocco, England, and Germany as well.

Ristorante Noemi

Calle dei Fabbri 912. ☎ **5225238.** Reservations recommended. Main courses 23,000–30,000 lire ($14.40–$18.75). AE, DC, MC, V. Tues–Sat noon–2:30pm; Mon–Sat 7–10:30pm. Closed Dec 15–Feb 1. Vaporetto: San Marco. INTERNATIONAL/VENETIAN.

Ristorante Noemi is a simple but tasteful room whose main decorative feature is a multicolored marble floor pieced into abstract patterns. It stands on a narrow street behind a marble and stucco facade with swag curtains covering big glass windows, a short walk from piazza San Marco. The foundations of the building date from the 14th century and the restaurant itself was established in 1927 and named after the matriarch of the family that continues to own it. Specialties include many items bordering on *nuova cucina,* such as thin black spaghetti with cuttlefish "in their own sauce" and fresh salmon crêpes with cheese, followed by the special lemon sorbet of the house, made with sparkling wine and fresh mint. More recent dishes include filet of salmon with white raisins, served with a sauce made from white wine and laurel leaves, and a filet of sole "Casanova," concocted with a velouté of white wine, shrimps, and mushrooms.

Ristorante à la Vecia Cavana

Rio Terà SS. Apostoli 4624. ☎ **5287106.** Reservations not required. Main courses 20,000–32,000 lire ($12.50–$20). AE, DC, MC, V. Fri–Wed noon–2:30pm and 7:30–10:30pm. Vaporetto: Ca' d'Oro. SEAFOOD.

Ristorante à la Vecia Cavana is off the tourist circuit and well worth the trek through the winding streets to find it. A *cavana* is a place where gondolas are parked, a sort of liquid garage, and the site of this restaurant used to be such a place in the Middle Ages. When you enter, you'll be greeted with brick arches, stone columns, terra-cotta floors, framed modern paintings, and a photograph of 19th-century fishermen relaxing after a day's work. It's an appropriate introduction to a menu that specializes in seafood including a mixed grill from the Adriatic, fried scampi, fresh sole, squid, three different types of risotto (each prepared with seafood), and a spicy zuppa di pesce (fish soup). Another specialty of the house is antipasti di pesce Cavana, which includes an assortment of just about every sea creature.

Taverna la Fenice

Campiello de la Fenice 1938. ☎ **5223856.** Reservations required. Main courses 20,000–40,000 lire ($12.50–$25). AE, DC, MC, V. Tues–Sat noon–2:30pm; Mon–Sat 7–10:30pm. Closed last 2 weeks in Jan. Vaporetto: San Marco. ITALIAN/VENETIAN.

Established in 1907, when Venetians were flocking in record numbers to hear the *bel canto* performances in the opera house nearby, this restaurant is one of the most romantic dining spots in Venice. The interior is suitably elegant, but the preferred spot during clement weather is outdoors beneath a canopy, a few steps from the Teatro La Fenice, where Stravinski introduced works that included *The Rake's Progress.* The service is smooth and efficient. The most appetizing beginning is the selection of seafood antipasti. Fish is fresh from the Mediterranean. You might enjoy the risotto con scampi e arugula; the freshly made tagliatelle with cream and exotic mushrooms; John Dory filets with artichokes; turbot roasted with olive oil and broccoli; scampi with tomatoes and rice; and carpaccio alla Fenice.

Trattoria alla Columba

San Marco-Piscina-Frezzeria 1665. ☎ **5221175.** Reservations recommended. Main courses 25,000–40,000 lire ($15.65–$25). AE, DC, MC, V. Thurs–Tues noon–3pm and Thurs–Tues 7–11pm. In May–June and Sept–Oct, the restaurant is open daily. Vaporetto: San Marco. VENETIAN/INTERNATIONAL.

This is one of the most distinctive and popular *trattorie* in town, with a history going back for at least a century and a by-now legendary association with some of the leading painters of Venice. In 1985, a $2-million restoration improved the infrastructure, making it a more attractive foil for the dozens of modern paintings that hang upon its walls. These collections change seasonally and are discreetly available for sale. Menu items are likely to include at least five daily specials based exclusively on the time-honored cuisine of Venice. Otherwise, you can order such specialties as *risotto di funghi del Montello* (risotto with mushrooms from the local hills of Montello) or *baccalà alla vicentina* (milk-simmered dry cod seasoned with onions, anchovies, and cinnamon, and served with polenta). Fruits and vegetables used within the dishes are for the most part produced locally on the islands near Venice.

INEXPENSIVE

Alfredo, Alfredo

Campo San Felipe e Giacomi, Castello 4294. ☎ **5225331.** Main courses 8,000–22,000 lire ($5–$13.75). Fixed-price menu 20,000 to 30,000 lire ($12.50 to $18.75). No credit cards. Thurs–Tues 11am–2am. Vaporetto: San Zaccaria. VENETIAN.

Alfredo, Alfredo might be classified as a coffee shop. Here you can order any number of items, prepared in short order. These include pasta dishes such as spaghetti with a number of sauces, freshly made salads, crêpes, various grilled meats, and omelets. Its long hours make it convenient to have a light meal at almost any time of the day.

Le Chat Qui Rit

San Marco 1131. ☎ **5229086.** Full meals begin at 20,000 lire ($12.50). No credit cards. Daily 11am–9:30pm. Closed Sat Oct–May. Vaporetto: San Marco. VENETIAN/PIZZA.

This is a self-service cafeteria and pizzeria that offers Venetian dishes prepared "just like mama made." These might include cuttlefish simmered in stock and served on a bed of yellow polenta or various fried fish. You can also order a steak grilled very simply, flavored with oil, salt, and pepper, perhaps a little garlic and herbs if you prefer. Main-dish platters, are served rather quickly after you order them.

ⓢ Nuova Rivetta

Castello 4625, campo San Filippo. ☎ **5287302.** Reservations required. Main courses 14,000–24,000 lire ($8.75–$15). No credit cards. Tues–Sun 10am–10pm. Closed July 23–Aug 20. Vaporetto: San Zaccaria. SEAFOOD.

Nuova Rivetta is an old-fashioned Venetian trattoria where you eat well without having to pay a lot. The restaurant stands in the monumental heart of the old city. Many find it best for lunch during a stroll around Venice. The most representative dish to order is frittura di pesce, a mixed fish fry from the Adriatic, which includes squid or various other "sea creatures" that turned up at the market on that day. Other specialties include gnocchi stuffed with Adriatic spider crab, pasticcho of fish (a main course), and spaghetti flavored with squid ink. The most typical wine of the house is Prosecco, whose bouquet is refreshing and fruity with a slightly sharp flavor. This is one of the most celebrated wines of the Veneto region, and that's been true for centuries.

Ristorante al Mondo Novo

Salizzada di San Lio, Castello 5409. ☎ **5200698.** Reservations recommended. Main courses 16,000–28,000 lire ($10–$17.50); fixed-price meals 22,000–60,000 lire ($13.75–$37.50). AE, MC, V. Tues–Sun 11am–3pm and 7pm–midnight (last order). Vaporetto: Rialto. VENETIAN.

Set within a very old Venetian building originally built during the Renaissance, amid a dining room outfitted in a regional style, this well-established restaurant offers professional service, a kindly staff, and a willingness to remain open later than many of its nearby competitors. Menu items include a wide array of seafood, prepared succulently as frittura misto à l'Adriatico, or else charcoal grilled. Other items include an array of such pastas as maccaroni alla verdura (with fresh vegetables and greens), an antipasti of fresh fish, and filets of beef with pepper sauce and rissole potatoes. Locals who frequent the place always order the fresh fish, knowing that the owner of the restaurant is a wholesaler in the Rialto fish market.

Ristorante da Raffaele

Calle larga XXII Marzo no. 2347 (fondamenta delle Ostreghe). ☎ **5232317.** Reservations recommended. Main courses 16,000–38,000 lire ($10–$23.75); fixed-price menu 36,000 lire

($22.50). AE, DC, MC, V. Fri–Wed noon–3pm and Fri–Wed 7–10:30pm. Closed Dec 15–Feb 15. Vaporetto: San Marco. ITALIAN/VENETIAN.

Ristorante da Raffaele, a 5-minute walk from piazza San Marco and a minute from the Grand Canal, has long been a favorite canalside restaurant in Venice. Dating from 1953 the restaurant offers the kind of charm and special atmosphere that are unique to the city. However, the inner rooms are popular with Venetians and visitors alike. The huge inner sanctum has a high-beamed ceiling, 17th- to 19th-century pistols and sabers, exposed brick, wrought-iron chandeliers, a massive fireplace, and copper pots (hundreds of them), all of which contribute to the rustic ambience. The food is excellent, beginning with a choice of tasty antipasti or well-prepared pastas. Seafood specialties include scampi, squid, or a platter of deep-fried fish from the Adriatic. The grilled meats are also succulent and can be followed by rich, tempting desserts. The crowded conviviality is part of the experience.

Vini da Arturo

Calle degli Assassini 3656. ☎ **5286974.** Reservations recommended. Main courses 22,000–36,000 lire ($13.75–$22.50). No credit cards. Mon–Sat noon–2:30pm and 7–10:30pm. Vaporetto: San Marco. VENETIAN.

Vini Da Arturo attracts many devoted regulars, including artists and writers. Here you get some of the most delectable of the local cooking—and not just the standard cliché Venetian dishes. One local restaurant owner, who likes to dine here occasionally instead of at his own place, explained, "The subtle difference between good and bad food is often nothing more than the amount of butter and cream used." Instead of ordering plain pasta, one might try a tantalizing dish called spaghetti alla Gorgonzola. The beef is also good, especially when prepared with a cream sauce flavored with mustard and freshly ground pepper. Salads are made with crisp, fresh ingredients, often in unusual combinations. The place is small and contains only seven tables; it's located between the Fenice Opera House and St. Mark's Square.

EAST OF PIAZZA SAN MARCO
MODERATE

Arcimboldo

Castello, calle dei Furiani 3219. ☎ 528-6569. Reservations recommended. Main courses 18,000–20,000 lire ($11.25–$12.50). AE, DC, MC, V. Wed–Mon 7:30pm–midnight. Vaporetto: Arsenale or San Zaccaria. VENETIAN/ITALIAN.

At the corner on which sits the Scuola di San Giorgio degli Schiavoni (containing Carpaccio's celebrated cycle of paintings), turn into a little street and follow a narrow footpath leading deep into Venice's oldest quarter. At the end of the

---

🏛 Family-Friendly Restaurants

Alfredo, Alfredo *(p. 424)*   For the family on a sightseeing run. Short-order items are served quickly, including spaghetti with a number of sauces and freshly made salads.

Le Chat Qui Rit *(p. 424)*   This is a self-service cafeteria where children are allowed to select what they want. Lots of pasta dishes.

Tiziano Snack *(p. 428)*   You can order hot pasta dishes and sandwiches, consumed standing at the counter or seated on one of the high stools.

street, you'll stumble upon Arcimboldo, one of the city's most charming restaurants. It overlooks a canal and is named for Giuseppe Arcimboldo, a famous 16th-century painter who worked at the Hapsburg court. Reproductions of his work line the walls.

The intimate and romantic decor is a fitting backdrop for the traditional Venetian fare served here. Both old and modern dishes are prepared with the excellent fruit and vegetables grown on the neighboring islands. Diners can enjoy Venetian-style antipasti, excellent pasta dishes, fish, risotto, and the pick of poultry and meat. Everything is washed down with quality wines. In spring and summer tables are placed outside along the canal.

Hostaria da Franz

Fondamenta San Iseppo 754. ☎ **5220861.** Reservations required. Main courses 23,000–45,000 lire ($14.40–$28.15). DC, MC, V. Wed–Mon 12:30–3pm and 7:30pm–midnight. Closed Jan. Vaporetto: Giardini. SEAFOOD.

Much of the experience of this place derives from the promenade along a narrow canal required to visit it. Its original founder was an Austrian ex-soldier named Franz who married a Venetian woman and together they built the place to house, feed, and entertain Austrian troops. Despite the establishment's subsequent ownership by several other families, the original name has remained intact. Today you'll find a bar, a dining room spanned with weathered beams, and an ebullient reception. In summer, elegant candlelit tables are placed along the river. Your meal might include a pasticcio of fresh fish, fish-flavored gnocchi, and a satisfying choice of fresh seafood, including lobster flown in from the waters off North America. The maître d' will recommend one of the local vintages to accompany your meal. Most maps spell this establishment's street name as "rio di S. Giuseppe," although local street signs refer to it as "rio di S. Iseppo."

ON THE LIDO
MODERATE

Ristorante Belvedere

Piazzale Santa Maria Elisabetta 4, Lido di Venezia. ☎ **5265773.** Reservations required. Main courses 25,000–40,000 lire ($15.65–$25). AE, DC, MC, V. Tues–Sun noon–2:30pm and 7–9:30pm. Closed Oct 31–Easter. Vaporetto: Lido. VENETIAN.

Outside the big hotels, the best food on the Lido is served at the Ristorante Belvedere. Don't be put off by its location, across from where the vaporetto from Venice stops. In such a location, one might expect a touristy establishment. Actually, the Belvedere attracts some of the finest people of Venice. They often come here as an excursion, knowing that they can get some of the best fish dishes along the Adriatic. Sidewalk tables are placed outside, and there is a glass-enclosed portion for windy days. The main dining room is attractive, with cane-backed bentwood chairs and big windows. In back, reached through a separate entrance, is a busy café. Main dishes include the chef's special sea bass, along with grilled dorade (or sole), fried scampi, and other selections. You might begin with the special fish antipasti or spaghetti en papillote.

INEXPENSIVE

⑤ Da Ciccio

Via San Gallo 241, Lido di Venezia. ☎ **5265489.** Reservations recommended. Main courses 14,000–25,000 lire ($8.75–$15.65). MC, V. Wed–Mon noon–3:30pm and 7:30–11pm. Transportation: See below. VENETIAN/SEAFOOD.

Diners (or drinkers) here can sit either indoors or outside beneath a lovely pergola. This restaurant is located on the main street of the Lido. The atmosphere is decidedly informal. Most guests opt for a platter of fish, often fried, from the Adriatic, washed down with a simple wine from the Veneto area.

To reach the place, take the vaporetto to piazzale Santa Maria Elisabetta. From there, take bus D or G and ask the driver to let you off near the trattoria.

NEAR THE RIALTO
MODERATE

"Al graspo de ua"

Calle dei Bombaseri 5093. ☎ **5200150.** Reservations required. Main courses 23,000–35,000 lire ($14.40–$21.90). AE, DC, MC, V. Wed–Sun noon–3pm and 8–11pm. Closed Dec 20–Jan 5. Vaporetto: Rialto. SEAFOOD.

"Al graspo de ua" is one bunch of grapes you'll want to pluck. For that special meal, it's a winner. Decorated in the old taverna style, it offers several air-conditioned dining rooms. One has a beamed ceiling, hung with garlic and copper bric-a-brac. Considered among the best fish restaurants in Venice, "al graspo de ua" has been patronized by such celebs as Elizabeth Taylor, Jeanne Moreau, Rossano Brazzi, even Giorgio de Chirico. You can help yourself to all the hors d'oeuvres you want—known on the menu as "self-service mammoth." You can order the gran fritto dell'Adriatico, a mixed treat of deep-fried fish from the Adriatic. Desserts are good, especially the peach Melba.

Poste Vechie

Pescheria Rialto 1608. ☎ **721822.** Reservations recommended. Main courses 22,000–35,000 lire ($13.75–$21.90). AE, DC, MC, V. Wed–Mon noon–3:30pm and 7–10:30pm. Vaporetto: Rialto. SEAFOOD.

This is one of the most charming restaurants of Venice, set near the Rialto fish market and connected to the rest of the city with a small, privately owned bridge. It was established in the early 1500s as the local post office—food was served to the mail carriers to fortify them for their deliveries. Today, it claims to be one of the oldest restaurants in Venice, with a pair of intimate dining rooms (both graced with paneling, murals, and 16th-century mantelpieces) and a verdant outdoor courtyard that evokes the countryside northwest of Venice.

Menu items include a super-fresh array of fish from the nearby markets; a salad of shellfish and exotic mushrooms; a spicy soup of Adriatic fish; tagliolini flavored with squid ink, crabmeat, and fish sauce; aad the restaurant's *pièce de résistance*, seppie (cuttlefish) à la veneziana con polenta. If you don't like fish, calf's liver or veal shank with ham and cheese are also well prepared. Desserts come rolling to your table on a trolley and are usually delicious.

INEXPENSIVE

Fiachetteria Toscana

San Giovanni Crisostomo 5719. ☎ **5285281.** Reservations recommended. Main courses 18,000–30,000 lire ($11.25–$18.75). AE, DC, MC, V. Wed–Mon 12:30pm–2:30pm and 7:30–10:30pm. Closed July. Vaporetto: Rialto. VENETIAN.

A century ago, this stone-fronted building stored the wine and olive oil of a Tuscan-born merchant. Today, despite the establishment's association with Tuscany, it serves pure Venetian cuisine in a style that's changed very little since the restaurant was established more than 30 years ago. A street-level dining room spanned by old ceiling beams contains amusing modern art and an impressive display of the day's catch. A country-style wooden staircase leads past marble columns to an upper room and additional tables. Menu specialties mainly consist of different varieties of fish, including an octopus-and-celery salad, spider crab in its own shell, grilled razor clams, seafood risotto with champagne, and baked eel. A red-chicory salad from Treviso is the perfect accompaniment.

Restaurant da Bruno

Castello, calle del Paradiso 5731. ☎ **5221480.** Reservations not necessary. Main courses 16,000–24,000 lire ($10–$15); fixed-price menus 24,000–35,000 lire ($15–$21.90). Wed–Mon noon–3pm and 7–11pm. Closed Jan 15–31. Vaporetto: San Marco. VENETIAN.

Restaurant de Bruno is like a country taverna in the center of Venice. On a narrow street about halfway between the Rialto Bridge and piazza San Marco, the restaurant attracts its crowds by grilling meats on an open-hearth fire. Get your antipasti at the counter and watch your prosciutto order being prepared—paper-thin slices of spicy flavored ham wrapped around breadsticks (grissini). In the right season, da Bruno does some of the finest game specialty dishes in Venice. If featured, try in particular its capriolo (roebuck) and its fagiano (pheasant). A typical Venetian specialty—prepared well here—is the zuppa di pesce (fish soup). Other specialties include filet of beef with pepper sauce, veal scallopini with wild mushrooms, scampi and calamari, grilled John Dory with herbs, and a local favorite, squid with polenta. After that rich fare, you may settle for a macedonia of mixed fruit for dessert.

Ⓢ Rosticceria San Bartolomeo

Calle della Bissa, San Marco 5424. ☎ **5223569.** Reservations not necessary. Main courses 20,000–36,000 lire ($12.50–$22.50); fixed-price menu 20,000–36,000 lire ($12.50–$22.50). AE, MC, V. Tues–Sun 10am–2:30pm and Tues–Sun 5–9pm. Vaporetto: Rialto. VENETIAN.

Rosticceria San Bartolomeo is the most frequented fast-food eatery in Venice and has long been a haven for budget travelers. Downstairs is a *tavola calda* where you can eat standing up, but upstairs is a budget-level restaurant with waiter service. Typical dishes include *baccalà alla vicentina* (codfish simmered in herbs and milk), deep-fried mozzarella (which the Italians call *in carrozza),* and *seppie con polenta* (squid in its own ink sauce, served with a cornmeal mush). Everything is washed down with typical Veneto wine.

Once you leave the vaporetto, take an underpass on your left (that is, with your back facing the bridge). This passageway is labeled "sottoportego della Bissa." The restaurant will be at the first corner, off campo San Bartolomeo.

Ⓢ Tiziano Snack

Cannaregio 5747. ☎ **5235544.** Most dishes 9,000–13,000 lire ($5.65–$8.15). Sun–Fri 8am–10:30pm. Vaporetto: Rialto. SANDWICHES/PIZZA.

Tiziano Snack is a *tavola calda* (literally "hot table"). There is no waiter service. You eat standing at a counter or on one of the high stools. The place is known in Venice for selling pizza by the yard. From noon to 3pm, they serve hot pastas such as rigatoni and cannelloni. But throughout the day you can order sandwiches or perhaps a plate of mozzarella.

Ⓢ Trattoria Madonna

Calle de la Madonna 594. ☎ **5223824.** Reservations recommended but not always accepted. Main courses 14,000–20,000 lire ($8.75–$12.50). AE, MC, V. Thurs–Tues noon–3pm and 7:15–10pm. Closed Aug 1–15 and Dec 8–Jan 31. Vaporetto: Rialto. VENETIAN.

Despite the similarity of its name with that of a popular American singer (and many local jokes to that effect), this restaurant was established in 1954 within a

300-year-old building of historical distinction. Named after *another* famous Madonna, it's one of the most popular and characteristic trattorie of Venice, specializing in traditional Venetian recipes and an array of grilled fresh fish. A suitable beginning might be the *antipasto frutti mare* (fruits of the sea). Pastas, polentas, risottos, meats (including *fegato alla veneziana,* liver with onions), and many kinds of fresh fish are widely available. Many creatures of the sea are displayed in a refrigerated case near the entrance. The mixed fish fry of the Adriatic is a preferred dish, when available.

RIVA DEGLI SCIAVONI

Do Leoni

In the Londra Palace Hotel, riva degli Schiavoni 4171. ☎ **5200533.** Reservations recommended. Lunch 39,000 lire (24.40) without drinks or dessert; dinner main courses 60,000–70,000 lire ($37.50–$43.75). Residents of the Londra Palace Hotel receive a 20% discount on dinner, but not on lunch. AE, DC, MC, V. Daily 11:30am–3pm; Wed–Mon 7:30–11pm. Vaporetto: San Zaccaria. VENETIAN/INTERNATIONAL.

For years, this restaurant preferred the French version of its name (Les Deux Lions), until a recent management change decided to express its name in Venetian dialect. Set within the street level of an elegant and well-recommended hotel, the restaurant offers a view of a panoramic 19th-century equestrian statue ringed with heroic women taming—you guessed it—lions. The restaurant is filled with scarlet and gold, a motif of lions patterned into the carpeting, and reproductions of English furniture.

Lunches are brief, buffet-style affairs, where clients serve themselves from a long choice of cold and hot Italian and international food. Dinners are candlelit, more formal, and very appealing, with emphasis on Venetian cuisine. Examples include a chilled fish terrine, baked salmon with truffles, or baby rooster with green pepper sauce. At both lunch and dinner, the restaurant, depending on the weather, offers the option of dining outside on the piazza, overlooking the bronze lions and their masters.

NEAR THE ARSENALE

Ristorante Corte Sconta

Calle del Pestrin 3886. ☎ **5227024.** Reservations required. Main courses 22,000–36,000 lire ($13.75–$22.50); fixed price menu 70,000 lire ($43.75). AE, MC, V. Tues–Sat 12:30–2:30pm and 7:30–9:30pm. Closed Jan 7–Feb 7 and July 15–Aug 15. Vaporetto: Arsenale. SEAFOOD.

Ristorante Corte Sconta is located behind a narrow storefront that you'd probably ignore if you didn't know about this place. On a narrow alley whose name is shared by at least three other streets in Venice (this particular one is near campo Bandiere Moro and San Giovanni in Bragora), the restaurant has a multicolored marble floor, plain wooden tables, hanging metallic lights, and no serious attempt at decoration. It has become well known, however, as a sophisticated gathering place. As the depiction of the satyr chasing the mermaid above the entrance implies, this is a fish restaurant, serving a variety of grilled creatures (much of the "catch" is largely unknown in North America). If you don't like fish, a tender filet of beef is available. A good selection of wines adds to the enjoyment of your meal. There's a big stand-up bar in an adjoining room that seems to be almost a private fraternity of the locals.

IN THE DORSODURO
INEXPENSIVE

La Furatola

Calle lunga San Barnaba 2870A. ☎ **5208594.** Reservations recommended for dinner. Main courses 24,000–28,000 lire ($15–$17.50). No credit cards. Fri–Tues noon–2:30pm and 7–9:30pm. Closed July–Aug. Vaporetto: Ca' Rezzonico or Accademia. SEAFOOD.

La Furatola (an old Venetian word meaning "restaurant") is very much a neighborhood hangout, but it has captured the imagination of restaurant aficionados. It's located in a 300-year-old building in the Dorsoduro section, along a narrow flagstone-paved street that you'll need a good map and a lot of patience to find. Perhaps you'll have lunch here after a visit to the Church of San Rocco, which is located only a short distance away. You'll push past double glass doors and enter a simple dining room. The specialty is fish brought to your table in a wicker basket so that you can judge its size and freshness. A display of seafood antipasti is set out near the entrance.

✪ Locanda Montin

Fondamenta di Borgo 1147. ☎ **5227151.** Reservations recommended. Main courses 15,000–26,000 lire ($9.40–$16.25). AE, DC, MC, V. Thurs–Tues 12:30–2:30pm; Thurs–Mon 7:30–9:30pm. Vaporetto: Accademia. INTERNATIONAL/ITALIAN.

Locanda Montin is the kind of rapidly disappearing Venetian inn that virtually every literary and artistic figure in Venice has visited since it opened just after World War II. Famous clients have included Ezra Pound, Jackson Pollock, Mark Rothko, and many of the assorted artist friends of the late Peggy Guggenheim. The inn is owned and run by the Carretins, who have covered the walls with paintings donated by or purchased from their many friends and clients.

Today the arbor-covered garden courtyard of this 17th-century building is filled with regular clients, many of whom allow their favorite waiter to select most of the items for their meal. The frequently changing menu includes a variety of salads, grilled meats, and fish caught in the Adriatic. Dessert might be a semifreddo di fragoline, a tempting chilled liqueur-soaked cake, capped with whipped cream and wild strawberries. The Locanda lies in one of the least-trampled sections of Venice, the Dorsoduro, across the Grand Canal from piazza San Marco.

AT SAN POLO
MODERATE

Osteria da Fiore

Calle del Scaleter 2202. ☎ **721308.** Reservations required. Main courses 24,000–32,000 lire ($15–$20). AE, DC, MC, V. Tues–Sat 12:30–2:30pm and 8–9:30pm. Closed Aug and Dec 25–Jan 14. Vaporetto: Silvestro. SEAFOOD.

The breath of the Adriatic seems to blow through this place, although how the wind finds this little restaurant tucked away in a labyrinth is a mystery. The restaurant serves only fish. An imaginative and changing fare is offered, depending on the availability of fresh fish and produce. If you have a love of maritime foods, you'll find them here—everything from scampi (a sweet Adriatic prawn, cooked in as many different ways as there are chefs) to granzeola, a type of spider crab. In days gone by, we've sampled everything from fried calamari (cuttlefish) to bottarga (dried mullet roe eaten with olive oil and lemon). For your wine, we suggest Prosecco, which has a distinctive golden-yellow color and a bouquet that's refreshing and fruity. The proprietors extend a hearty welcome to match their fare.

INEXPENSIVE

Trattoria Antica Besseta

Calle Savio 1395. ☎ **721687.** Reservations required. Main courses 15,000–20,000 lire ($9.40–$12.50). No credit cards. Thurs–Mon 12:30–2:30pm and Thurs–Mon 7:30–9:30pm. Closed July 15–Aug 31. Vaporetto: Rive Biasio. VENETIAN.

If you manage to find this place (go armed with a good map), you'll be rewarded with true Venetian cuisine at its most unpretentious. Head for campo San Giacomo dell'Orio, then negotiate your way across infrequently visited piazzas and winding alleys. Push through saloon doors into a bar area filled with African masks and modern art. The dining room in back is ringed with paintings and illuminated with wagon-wheel chandeliers. Nereo Volpe, his wife, Mariuccia, and one of their sons are the guiding force, the chefs, the buyers, and even the "talking menus." The food depends on what looked good in the market that morning. The menu could include roast chicken, fried scampi, fritto misto, spaghetti in a sardine sauce, various roasts, and a selection from the day's catch. The Volpe family produces two kinds of their own wine, a pinot blanc and a cabernet.

LA GIUDECCA

Harry's Dolci

Fondamenta San Biago, Isola della Giudecca. ☎ **5224844.** Reservations recommended, especially Sat–Sun. Main courses 28,200–47,000 lire ($17.60–$29.40); fixed-price menu 46,000 lire ($28.75). AE, MC, V. Wed–Mon 12:30–3:30pm and 7:30–10pm. Closed Nov–Easter. Vaporetto: S. Eufemia. INTERNATIONAL.

The people at the famed Harry's Bar have established their latest enclave far from the maddening crowds of St. Mark's Square on this little-visited island. From the quayside windows of this chic place, you can watch seagoing vessels, including everything from yachts to lagoon-based barges. White napery and uniformed waiters grace a modern room, where no one minds if you order only coffee and ice cream or perhaps a selection from the large pastry menu (the zabaglione cake is divine). Popular items include carpaccio Cipriani, chicken salad, club sandwiches, gnocchi, and house-style cannelloni. Dishes are deliberately kept simple, but each is well prepared.

SECRETS OF VENICE

If you'd like to escape the throngs of visitors that overrun Venice and eat where the natives eat, here are a few suggestions. **Pasticceria Marchini,** Calle del Piovan 2769 (☎ 5229109), is where your Venetian friend (if you had one) would take you for the most delectable pastries served in Venice. Their small pastries are made according to old recipes—ask for their *bigna* or *cannolo.* Closed Tuesday. **Al Bacareto,** Salizzada San Samuele 3447 (☎ 5289336). If you had a Venetian mamma, she probably served food similar to the cuisine dished up here. Don't expect fancy viands. Just good honest cooking. Venetians like to keep this place to themselves. **Il Guanotto,** Ponte del Lovo 4819 (☎ 5208439), is a *gelateria/ pasticceria/bar.* It is said to have virtually invented the *spritzer,* a combination of soda water, bitters, and white wine, a drink whose popularity has spread around the world. Its drinks and cocktails are renowned, and you can also cheer up a rainy day in Venice by going here and ordering a cappuccino.

14

What to See & Do in Venice

Venice appears to have been created specifically to entertain its legions of callers. Ever since the body of St. Mark was smuggled out of Alexandria and entombed in the basilica, Venice has been host to a never-ending stream of visitors—famous, infamous, and otherwise—from all over the world.

Venice has perpetually captured the imagination of poets, artists, and travelers. Wordsworth, Byron, and Shelley addressed poems to the city, and it has been written about or used as a setting by many contemporary writers.

In the pages ahead, we'll explore the city's great art and architecture. But, unlike Florence, Venice would reward its guests with treasures even if they never ducked inside a museum or church. In the city on the islands, the frame eternally competes with the picture inside.

"For all its vanity and villainy," wrote Lewis Mumford, "life touched some of its highest moments in Venice."

SUGGESTED ITINERARIES

These itineraries are designed for the first-time visitor. Those visiting Venice for the second or third time may want to seek out the city's other mysteries and treasures.

If You Have 1 Day

Get up early in the morning and watch the sun rise over piazza San Marco, as the city wakes up. The pigeons will already be there to greet you. Have an early-morning cappuccino on the square, then visit the Basilica of San Marco and the Palazzo Ducale later. Ride the Grand Canal in a gondola 2 hours before sunset, and spend the rest of the evening wandering the narrow streets of this strangely unreal and most fascinating of the cities of Europe. Apologize to yourself for such a short visit and promise to return.

If You Have 2 Days

Spend your first day as suggested above. On Day 2 it's time for more concentrated sightseeing. Begin at piazza San Marco (viewing it should be a daily ritual regardless of how many days you have in Venice), then head for the major museum, the Accademia, in the

Impressions

A city for beavers.

—Ralph Waldo Emerson, on Venice, in his journal, June 1833

morning. In the afternoon, visit the Collezione Peggy Guggenheim (modern art) and perhaps the Ca' d'Oro and Ca' Rezzonico.

If You Have 3 Days

Spend your first two days as above. Begin the morning of Day 3 by having a cappuccino on the piazza San Marco, then ride the elevator to the top of the Campanile di San Marco. Later in the morning visit the Museo Correr. In the afternoon, go to the Scuola Grande di San Rocco to see the works of Tintoretto. Spend the rest of the day strolling the streets of Venice and ducking into shops that capture your imagination. Even if you get lost, you'll eventually return to a familiar landmark, and you can't help but see the signs pointing you back to piazza San Marco. Have dinner in one of the most typical of Venetian trattorias, such as Locanda Montin.

If You Have 5 Days

Spend Days 1–3 as outlined above. On Day 4 plan to visit the islands of the lagoon, including Murano, Burano, and Torcello. All three can be covered—at least briefly—on one busy day. On Day 5, take an excursion to Verona (see Chapter 15).

1 Attractions

THE TOP ATTRACTIONS
✪ ST. MARK'S SQUARE

Piazza San Marco was the heartbeat of the Serenissima in the heyday of Venice's glory as a seafaring republic, the crystallization of the city's dreams and aspirations. If you have only one day for Venice, you need not leave the square, as the city's major attractions, such as the Basilica of St. Mark and the Doges' Palace, are centered here or nearby.

The traffic-free square, frequented by tourists and pigeons, and sometimes by Venetians, is a constant source of bewilderment and interest. If you rise at dawn, you can almost have the piazza to yourself as you watch the sun come up—the sheen of gold mosaics glisten into a mystic effect of incomparable beauty. At midmorning (9am) the overstuffed pigeons are fed by the city (if you're caught under the whir, you'll think you're witnessing a remake of Hitchcock's *The Birds*). At midafternoon the tourists reign supreme, and it's not suprising in July to witness fisticuffing over a camera angle. At sunset, when the two Moors in the Clock Tower strike the end of another day, lonely sailors begin a usually frustrated search for those hot spots that characterized the Venice of yore but not of today. Deep in the evening the strollers parade by or stop for espresso at the fashionable Florian Caffè and sip while listening to a band concert.

Thanks to Napoleon, the square was unified architecturally. The emperor added the Fabbrica Nuova, thus bridging the Old and New Procuratie. Flanked with medieval-looking palaces, Sansovinos Library, elegant shops and colonnades, the square is now finished—unlike piazza della Signoria at Florence.

❍ Basilica di San Marco

Piazza San Marco. ☎ **5225205.** Admission to the basilica is free. Apr–Sept, Mon–Sat 9:30am–5:30pm, Sun 2–5:30pm; Oct–Mar, Mon–Sat 9:30am–4:30pm, Sun 1:30–4:30pm. Vaporetto: San Marco.

The so-called Church of Gold dominates piazza San Marco. This is one of the world's greatest and most richly embellished churches. In fact, it looks as if it had been moved intact from Istanbul. The basilica is a conglomeration of styles, although it's particularly indebted to Byzantium. It incorporates other schools of design, such as Romanesque and Gothic, with freewheeling abandon. Like Venice, it is adorned with booty from every corner of the city's once far-flung mercantile empire—capitals from Sicily, columns from Alexandria, porphyry from Syria, sculpture from old Constantinople.

The basilica is capped by a dome that—like a spider plant—sends off shoots, in this case a quartet of smaller-scale cupolas. Spanning the facade is a loggia, surmounted by replicas of the four famous St. Mark's horses—the *Triumphal Quadriga.*

On the facade are rich marble slabs and mosaics that depict scenes from the lives of Christ and St. Mark. One of the mosaics re-creates the entry of the evangelist's body into Venice, transported on a boat. St. Mark's body, hidden in a pork barrel, was smuggled out of Alexandria in 828 and shipped to Venice. The evangelist dethroned Theodore, the Greek saint who up until then had been the patron of the city that had outgrown him.

In the atrium are six cupolas filled with mosaics illustrating scenes from the Old Testament, including the story of the Tower of Babel. Once the private chapel and pantheon of the doges, the interior of the basilica is a stunning wonderland of marbles, alabaster, porphyry, and pillars. Visitors walk in awe across the undulating multicolored ocean floor, which is patterned with mosaics.

To the right is the **baptistery** (no admission charge), dominated by the Sansovino-inspired baptismal font, upon which John the Baptist is ready to pour water. If you look back at the aperture over the entryway, you can see a mosaic, the dance of Salome in front of Herod and his court. Wearing a star-studded russet-red dress and three white fox tails, Salome dances under a platter holding John's head. Her glassy face is that of a Madonna, not an enchantress.

After touring the baptistery, proceed up the right nave to the doorway to the **treasury** (*tesoro*), open Monday through Saturday from 9:30am to 5:30pm and Sunday from 2 to 5pm, and charging 3,000 lire ($1.90) for admission. The oft-looted treasury contains the inevitable skulls and bones under glass, plus goblets, chalices, and Gothic candelabra.

The entrance to the **presbytery** is nearby, and admission is 3,000 lire ($1.90). In it, on the high altar, the alleged sarcophagus of St. Mark rests under a green marble blanket and is held up by four sculptured, Corinthian-style alabaster columns. The Byzantine-style **Pala d'Oro,** from Constantinople, is the rarest treasure at St. Mark's—made of gold and studded with precious stones.

On leaving the basilica, head up the stairs in the atrium for the **Marciano Museum** and the Loggia dei Cavalli. The star attraction of the museum is the world-famous Quadriga, four horses looted from Constantinople by Venetian crusaders in the sack of that city in 1204. These horses once surmounted the basilica, but were removed because of damage by pollution. They were subsequently restored. This is the only quadriga (which means a quartet of horses yoked together) to have survived from the classical era. They are believed to have been cast in the

4th century. Napoleon once carted these much-traveled horses off to Paris for the Arc du Carousel, but they were returned to Venice in 1815. The museum is open Monday through Saturday from 10am to 5:30pm and Sunday from 2 to 4:30pm; off-season, it closes at 4:45pm Monday through Saturday. Admission is 3,000 lire ($1.80). The museum, with its mosaics and tapestries, is especially interesting, but walk out onto the loggia for a view of piazza San Marco.

✪ Palazzo Ducale

Piazzetta San Marco. ☎ **5224951**. Admission 10,000 lire ($6.25). Easter–Oct, daily 8:30am–7pm; Nov–Easter, daily 9am–4pm. Vaporetto: San Marco.

The Palace of the Doges is entered through the magnificent 15th-century Porta della Carta at the piazzetta. This palace is part of the legend and lore of Venice. It's somewhat like a frosty birthday cake in pinkish-red marble and white Istrian stone. The Venetian-Gothic palazzo—with all the architectural intricacies of a paper doily—gleams in the tremulous Venetian light. Considered by many to be the grandest civic structure in Italy, it dates back to 1309, although a fire in 1577 destroyed much of the original building.

If you enter from the piazzetta, past the four porphyry Moors, you'll be right in the middle of the splendid Renaissance courtyard, one of the most recent additions to a palace that has experienced the work of many different architects with widely varying tastes. You can take the "giants' stairway" to the upper loggia—so called because of the two Sansovino statues of mythological figures.

The fire made ashes of many of the palace's greatest masterpieces, and almost spelled doom for the building itself, as the new architectural fervor of the post-Renaissance was in the air. However, fortunately, sanity prevailed. Many of the greatest Venetian painters of the 16th century contributed to the restored palace, replacing the canvases or frescoes of the old masters.

After climbing the Sansovino stairway of gold you'll enter some get-acquainted rooms. Proceed to the Anti-Collegio salon, which houses the palace's greatest artworks—notably Veronese's *Rape of Europa*, to the far left on the right-hand wall. One critic called the work delicious. Tintoretto is well represented with his *Three Graces* and his *Bacchus and Ariadne*. Some critics consider the latter his supreme achievement. In the adjoining Sala del Collegio, you'll find allegorical paintings by Veronese on the ceiling. As you proceed to the right, you'll enter the Sala del Senato o Pregadi, with its allegorical painting by Tintoretto in the center of the ceiling.

In the Sala del Consiglio dei Dieci, with its gloomy paintings, the dreaded Council of Ten (often called The Terrible Ten for good reason) used to assemble to decide who was in need of decapitation. In the antechamber, bills of accusation were dropped in the lion's mouth.

Now trek downstairs through the once-private apartments of the doges to the grand Maggior Consiglio, with its allegorical *Triumph of Venice* on the ceiling, painted by Veronese. What makes the room outstanding, however, is Tintoretto's *Paradise*, over the Grand Council chamber—said to be the largest oil painting in the world. Paradise seems to have an overpopulation problem, perhaps a too-optimistic point of view on Tintoretto's part. Tintoretto was in his 70s when he began this monumental work (he died only six years later). The second grandiose hall, entered from the grand chamber, is the Sala dello Scrutinio, with paintings that tell of the past glories of Venice.

Reentering the Maggior Consiglio, follow the arrows on their trail across the **Bridge of Sighs,** linking the Doges' Palace with the Palazzo delle Prigioni, where

Venice Attractions

 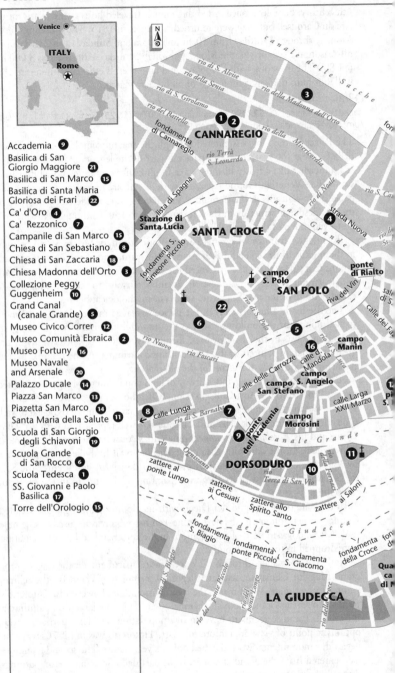

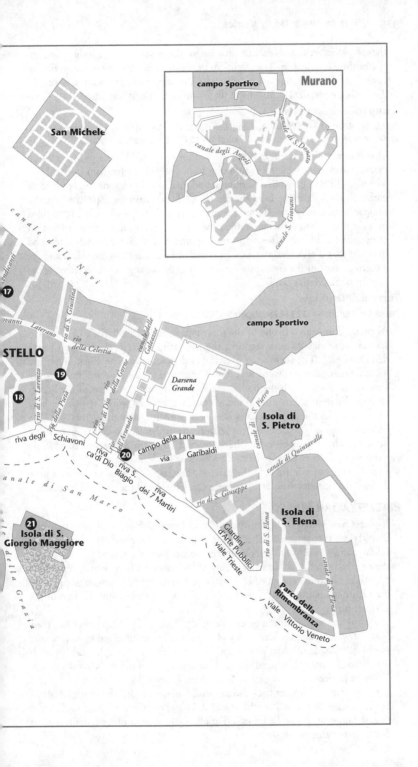

the cell blocks are found, the ones that lodged the prisoners who felt the quick justice of the Terrible Ten. The "sighs" in the bridge's name stemmed from the sad laments of the numerous victims led across it to certain torture and possible death. The cells are just dank remnants of the horror of medieval justice.

Campanile di San Marco

Piazza San Marco. ☎ **5224064.** Admission 5,000 lire ($3.15). May–Oct, daily 9:15am–8:30pm; Nov–Apr, daily 10am–4pm. Closed Jan 15–31. Vaporetto: San Marco.

One summer night back in 1902, the bell tower of the Basilica of St. Mark on piazza San Marco, which was suffering from years of rheumatism in the damp Venetian climate, gave out a warning sound that sent the elegant and fashionable coffee drinkers scurrying from the Florian Caffè in a dash for their lives. But the campanile gracefully waited until the next morning—July 14—before it tumbled into the piazza. The Venetians rebuilt their belfry, and it's now safe to ascend. In campanile-crazed Italy, where visitors must often ascend circuitous stairs, its good to report that the Venetian version has a modern elevator. You can ride it and get a pigeon's view of the city. It's a particularly good vantage point for viewing the cupolas of St. Mark's Basilica.

Torre dell'Orologio

Piazza San Marco. ☎ **5231879.** Vaporetto: San Marco.

At piazza San Marco is one of the most typical and characteristic of Venetian scenes—the two Moors striking the bell atop the Clock Tower (Torre dell'Orologio). The torre soars over the Old Procuratie. The clock under the winged lion not only tells the time, but is a boon to the astrologer: it matches the signs of the zodiac with the position of the sun. If the movement of the Moors striking the hour seems slow in today's fast, mechanized world, remember how many centuries the poor wretches have been at their task without time off. The "Moors" originally represented two European shepherds. However, after having been reproduced in bronze, they have grown darker with the passing of time. As a consequence, they came to be called Moors by the Venetians.

Sightseers can admire only the exterior, however. Venetian authorities have decided that interior visits are dangerous and have closed the tower indefinitely.

PIAZZETTA SAN MARCO

If piazza San Marco is the drawing room of Europe, then its satellite, piazzetta San Marco, is the antechamber. Hedged in by the Doges' Palace, Sansovinos Library, and a side of St. Mark's, the tiny square faces the Grand Canal. One of the two tall granite columns is mounted by a winged lion, which represents St. Mark. The other is topped by a statue of a man taming a dragon, supposedly the dethroned patron saint Theodore. Both columns came from the East in the 12th century.

During the heyday of the Serene Republic, dozens of victims either lost their heads or were strung up here, many of them first being subjected to torture that would have made the Marquis de Sade flinch. One, for example, had his teeth hammered in, his eyes gouged out, and his hands cut off before being strung up. Venetian justice became notorious throughout Europe.

If you stand with your back to the canal, looking toward the south facade of St. Mark's Basilica, you'll see the so-called *Virgin and Child* of the poor baker, a mosaic honoring Pietro Fasiol (also Faziol), a young man unjustly sentenced to death on a charge of murder.

To the left of the entrance to the Doges' Palace are four porphyry figures, which, for want of a better description, the Venetians called "Moors." These puce-colored fellows are huddled close together, as if afraid. Considering the decapitations and torture that have occurred on the piazzetta, I shouldn't wonder. Vaporetto: San Marco.

LIDO

Along the white sands of the Lido strolled a hand-holding Eleonora Duse and Gabriele d'Annunzio (*Flame of Life*), Goethe in Faustian gloom, a clubfooted Byron trying to decide with whom he was in love that day, de Musset pondering the fickle ways of George Sand, and Thomas Mann's Gustave von Aschenbach with his eye on Tadzio in *Death in Venice*. But gone is the relative isolation of yore. The de Mussets of today aren't mooning over lost loves—they're out chasing bikini-clad new ones.

Near the turn of the century the Lido began to blossom into a fashionable beachfront resort, complete with deluxe hotels and its Casino Municipale (see "Venice After Dark" later in this chapter). Lido prices are usually stratospheric. It is not a haven for the budget-minded tourists.

Even if you aren't lodging at the Lido, you may still want to come over for a swim in the Adriatic. And if you don't want to cross the thresholds of the rarefied citadels of hotel beachfront property—with huts lining the beach like those of some tropical paradise—you can try the Lungomare G. d'Annunzio Public Bathing Beach at the end of the Gran Viale (piazzale Ettore Sorger), a long stroll from the vaporetto stop. You can book cabins—called *camerini*—and enjoy the sand. Rates change seasonally.

To reach the Lido, take vaporetto no. 6 (the ride takes about 15 minutes). The boat departs from a landing stage near the Doges' Palace.

GRAND CANAL

Peoria may have its Main Street, Paris its Champs-Elysées—but Venice, for uniqueness, tops them all with its Canal Grande. Lined with palazzi—many in the elegant Venetian-Gothic style—this great road of water is today filled with vaporetti, motorboats, and gondolas. Along the canal the boat moorings are like peppermint sticks. It begins at piazzetta San Marco on one side and Longhenas Salute Church on the opposite bank. At midpoint, it is spanned by the Rialto Bridge. Eventually, the canal winds its serpentine course to the railway station. I can guarantee that there's not a dull sight en route.

Of course, the gloriously coiffured ladies Longhi painted have faded with the high tide. Many of the lavish furnishings and tapestries that adorned the interiors of the palaces were hauled off to museums or ended up in the homes of the heirs of the rising mercantile class of two centuries ago. In the sad decline of their city, the Venetian nobility didn't become less noble; they only went broke.

Some of the major and most impressive buildings along the Grand Canal have been converted into galleries and museums. Others have been turned into cooperative apartments. Venetian housewives aren't as incurably romantic as foreign visitors. A practical lot, these women can be seen stringing up their laundry in front of thousands upon thousands of tourists.

Along this canal one foggy day came Madame Amandine Lucile Aurore Dudevant, née Dupin (otherwise known as George Sand), with her effete, poetic young lover, Alfred de Musset. John Ruskin came this way to debunk and expose

Frommer's Favorite Venice Experiences

Riding the Grand Canal on a Gondola. Just before sunset, order some delectable sandwiches from Harry's Bar and a bottle of chilled Prosecco, then take someone you love on a gondola ride along the Grand Canal for the boat trip of a lifetime.

Sitting on piazza San Marco. Select a choice spot on one of the world's most famous and photographed squares, order a cup of cappuccino, listen to the classical music, and absorb the special atmosphere of Venice.

A Day at the Lido. The world has seen better beaches, but few sights equal the parade of flesh and humanity of this fashionable beach on a hot summer day. Everybody from Thomas Mann's fictional von Aschenbach to a horseback-riding Byron have romped here.

Contemplate Giorgione's Tempest. If you have time to see only one painting, make it this one at the Accademia. The artist's haunting sense of oncoming menace superimposed over a bucolic setting will become a memory page for you.

in his *The Stones of Venice.* Robert Browning, burnt out from the loss of his beloved Elizabeth and his later rejection at the hands of Lady Ashburton, came here to settle down in a palazzo where he eventually died. More recently, Eleonora Duse came this way with the young poet to whom she had given her heart, Gabriele d'Annunzio. Even Shakespeare came here in his fantasies. Intrepid guides will point out the "Palazzo de Desdemona."

MUSEUMS & GALLERIES

Venice is a city of art. Decorating its palazzi and adorning its canvases were artists such as Giovanni Bellini, Carpaccio, Giorgione, Titian, Lotto, Tintoretto, Veronese, Tiepolo, Guardi, Canaletto, and Longhi, to name just the more important ones. In the museums and galleries to follow, important works by all these artists are exhibited, as well as a number of modern surprises, such as those in the Guggenheim Collection.

Open hours are often subject to major variations, so keep this in mind as you go sightseeing. Many visitors who have budgeted only two or three days for Venice often express disappointment when, for some unknown reason, a major attraction closes abruptly.

✪ Accademia

Campo della Carità, Dorsoduro. ☎ **5222247.** Admission 10,000 lire ($6.25). July–Sept, Mon–Sat 9am–7pm, Sun 9am–1pm; Oct–June Mon–Sat 9am–2pm, Sun 9am–1pm. Vaporetto: Accademia.

The pomp and circumstance, the glory that was Venice, lives on in this remarkable collection of paintings which span the 14th to the 18th century. The hallmark of the Venetian school is color and more color. From Giorgione to Veronese, from Titian to Tintoretto, with a Carpaccio cycle thrown in, the Accademia has samples—often their best—of its most famous sons. I'll highlight only some of the most-renowned masterpieces for the first-timer in a rush.

You'll first see works by such 14th-century artists as Paolo and Lorenzo Veneziano, who bridged the gap from Byzantine art to Gothic (see the latter's *Annunciation*). Next, you'll view Giovanni Bellini's *Madonna and Saint* (poor

Sebastian, not another arrow), and Carpaccio's fascinating, although gruesome, work of mass crucifixion. As you move on, head for the painting on the easel by the window, attributed to the great Venetian artist Giorgione. On this canvas he depicted the *Madonna and Child*, along with the mystic St. Catherine of Siena and John the Baptist (a neat trick for Catherine, who seems to have perfected transmigration to join the cast of characters).

Two of the most important works with secular themes are Mantegna's armored *St. George*, with the dragon slain at his feet, and Hans Memling's 15th-century portrait of a young man. A most unusual *Madonna and Child* is by Cosmé Tura, the master of Ferrara, who could always be counted on to give a new twist to an old subject.

The madonnas and bambini of Giovanni Bellini, an expert in the harmonious blending of colors, are the focus of another room. None but the major artists could stand the test of a salon filled with the same subjects, but under Bellini's brush each Virgin achieves her individual spirituality. Giorgione's *Tempest*, displayed here, is the single most famous painting at the Accademia. It depicts a baby suckling from the breast of its mother, while a man with a staff looks on. What might have emerged as a simple pastoral scene on the easel of a lesser artist comes forth as a picture of rare and exceptional beauty. Summer lightning pierces the sky, but the tempest seems to be in the background—far away from the figures in the foreground, who are menaced without knowing it.

The masterpiece of Lorenzo Lorto, a melancholy portrait of a young man, can be seen before you come to a room dominated by Paolo Veronese's *The Banquet in the House of Levi*. This is, in reality, a "Last Supper" that was considered a sacrilege in its day and Veronese was forced to change its name to indicate a secular work. Impish Veronese caught the hot fire of the Inquisition by including in the mammoth canvas dogs, a cat, midgets, blackamoors, Huns, and drunken revelers. Four large paintings by Tintoretto—noted for their swirling action and powerful drama—depict scenes from the life of St. Mark. Finally, painted in his declining years (some have suggested in his 99th year before he died from the plague), is Titian's majestic *Pietà*.

After a long and unimpressive walk, you can search out Canaletto's *Porticato*. Yet another room is heightened by Gentile Bellini's stunning portrait of St. Mark's Square, back in the days (1496) when the houses glistened with gold in the sunlight. All the works in this salon are intriguing, especially the re-creation of the *Ponte de Rialto*, and a covered wood bridge, by Carpaccio.

The cycle of narrative paintings that Vittore Carpaccio did of St. Ursula for the Scuola (School) of Santa Orsola is displayed. The most famous is no. 578, which shows Ursula asleep on her elongated bed, with a dog nestled on the floor nearby, as the angels come for a visitation. Finally, on the way out, look for Titian's *Presentation of the Virgin*, a fit farewell to this galaxy of great Venetian art.

Museo Civico Correr

In the Procuratie Nuove, piazza San Marco. ☎ **5525625**. Admission 8,000 lire ($5) adults, 5,000 lire ($3.15) children 12–18, free for children under 11. Thurs–Tues 10am–4pm. Vaporetto: San Marco.

This museum traces the development of Venetian painting from the 14th to the 16th century. On the second floor are the red and maroon robes once worn by the doges, plus some fabulous street lanterns. There is also an illustrated copy of *Marco Polo in Tartaria*. You can see Cosmé Tura's *La Pietà*, a miniature of renown from the genius in the Ferrara School. This is one of his more gruesome works. It depicts a bony, gnarled Christ sprawled on the lap of the Madonna. Farther on, search out a Schiavone *Madonna and Child* (no. 545), our candidate for ugliest bambino ever depicted on canvas (no wonder the mother looks askance).

One of the most important rooms at the Correr is filled with three masterpieces: *La Pietà* by Antonello da Messina, a *Crucifixion* by the Flemish painter Hugo van der Goes, and a *Madonna and Child* by Dieric Bouts, who depicted the baby suckling his mother in a sensual manner. The star attraction of the Correr is the Bellini salon, which includes works by founding padre Jacopo and his son, Gentile. But the real master of the household was the other son, Giovanni, the major painter of the 15th-century Venetian school (see his *Crucifixion* and compare it with his father's treatment of the same subject).

A small but celebrated portrait of St. Anthony of Padua by Alvise Vivarini is here, plus works by Bartolomeo Montagna. The most important work in the gallery, however, is Vittore Carpaccio's *Two Venetian Ladies*, popularly known as "The Courtesans." A lesser work, *St. Peter*, depicts the saint with the daggers in him, and hangs in the same room.

The entrance is under the arcades of Ala Napoleonica at the western end of the square.

Ca' d'Oro

Cannaregio 3931-3932, Ca' d'Oro. ☎ **5238790.** Admission 4,000 lire ($2.50). Mon–Sat 9am–1:30pm, Sun and holidays 9am–12:30pm. Vaporetto: Ca' d'Oro.

This is one of the grandest and most handsomely embellished palaces along the Grand Canal. Although it contains the important Galleria Giorgio Franchetti, the House of Gold (so named because its facade was once gilded) competes with its own paintings. Built in the first part of the 15th century in the ogival style, it has a lacy Gothic look. Baron Franchetti, who restored the palace and filled it with his own collection of paintings, sculpture, and furniture, presented it to Italy during World War I.

You enter into a stunning courtyard, 50 yards from the vaporetto stop, which has a multicolored patterned marble floor and is filled with statuary. Then proceed upstairs to the lavishly appointed palazzo. One of the gallery's major paintings is Titian's voluptuous *Venus*. She coyly covers one breast, but what about the other?

In a special niche reserved for the masterpiece of the Franchetti collection is Andrea Mantegna's icy-cold *St. Sebastian*, the central figure of which is riddled with what must be a record number of arrows. You'll also find works by Carpaccio. Dont fail to walk out onto the loggia for a view of the Grand Canal.

Ca' Rezzonico

Fondamenta Rezzonico, Dorsoduro. ☎ **5224543.** Admission 8,000 lire ($5) adults, 5,000 lire ($3.15) children 12–18, free for children 11 and under. Sat–Thurs 10am–4pm. Vaporetto: Ca' Rezzonico.

This 17th and 18th-century palace along the Grand Canal is where Robert Browning set up his bachelor headquarters. Pope Clement XIII also stayed here. It's a virtual treasure house, known for both its baroque paintings and furniture. First, you enter the Grand Ballroom with its allegorical ceiling, then proceed through lavishly embellished rooms with Venetian chandeliers, brocaded walls, portraits of patricians, tapestries, gilded furnishings, and touches of chinoiserie. At the end of the first walk is the Throne Room, with its allegorical ceilings by Giovanni Battista Tiepolo.

On the first floor you can walk out onto a balcony for a view of the Grand Canal as the aristocratic tenants of the 18th century saw it. After this, another group of rooms follow, including the library. In these salons, look for a bizarre collection of paintings. One, for example, depicts half-clothed women beating up a defenseless naked man (one Amazon is about to stick a pitchfork into his neck, another to crown him with a violin). In the adjoining room another woman is hammering a spike through a man's skull—enough torture performed by the ladies to please even the most fervent masochist.

Upstairs you'll find a survey of 18th-century Venetian art. As you enter the main room from downstairs, head for the first salon on your right (facing the canal), which contains the best works of all, paintings from the brush of Pietro Longhi. His most famous work, *The Lady and the Hairdresser*, is the first canvas to the right on the entrance wall. Others depict the life of the idle Venetian rich. On the rest of the floor are bedchambers, a chapel, and salons—some with badly damaged frescoes, including a romp of satyrs.

✪ Collezione Peggy Guggenheim

Ca' Venier dei Leoni, Dorsoduro 701, calle San Cristoforo. ☎ **5206288**. Admission 10,000 lire ($6.25) adults, 5,000 lire ($3.15) students and children under 17. Wed–Mon 11am–6pm. Vaporetto: Accademia.

This is one of the most comprehensive and brilliant modern-art collections in the Western world, and it reveals both the foresight and critical judgment of its founder. The collection is housed in an unfinished palazzo, the former Venetian home of Peggy Guggenheim, who died in 1979. In the tradition of her family, Peggy Guggenheim was a lifelong patron of contemporary painters and sculptors. Founder of the Art of This Century Gallery in New York in the 1940s, she created one of the most avant-garde galleries for the works of contemporary artists. Critics were impressed not only by the high quality of the artists she sponsored, but by her methods of displaying them.

As her private collection increased, she decided to find a larger showcase and selected Venice, steeped in a long tradition as a haven for artists. While the Solomon Guggenheim Museum was going up in New York according to Frank Lloyd Wright's specifications, she was creating her own gallery in Venice. Guests can wander through and enjoy art in an informal and relaxed way. Max Ernst was one of Peggy Guggenheim's early favorites, as was Jackson Pollock (she provided a farmhouse where he could develop his painting technique). Displayed here are works not only by Pollock and Ernst, but also by Picasso (see his cubist *The Poet* of 1911), Duchamp, Chagall, Mondrian, Brancusi, Delvaux, and Dalí, and a garden of modern sculpture that includes works by Giacometti. Temporary modern-art shows may be presented during the winter months. Since Peggy Guggenheim's death, the collection has been administered by the Solomon R. Guggenheim Foundation, which also operates the Solomon R. Guggenheim Museum in New York. Visitors can also enjoy a museum shop and café in the new wing of the museum, overlooking the sculpture garden.

Museo Navale & Arsenale

Campo San Biasio, Castello 2148. ☎ **5200276**. Admission 2,000 lire ($1.25). Mon–Sat 9am–1pm. Closed holidays. Vaporetto: Arsenale.

The Naval Museum of Campo San Biasio (**Museo Storico Navale**) is filled with cannons, ships' models, and fragments of old vessels that date back to the days when Venice was supreme in the Adriatic. The prize exhibit is a gilded model of the *Bucintoro*, the great ship of the doge that surely would have made Cleopatra's barge look like an oil tanker in comparison. In addition, you'll find models of historic and modern fighting ships, of local fishing and rowing craft, and a collection of 24 Chinese junks, as well as a number of maritime *ex voto* from churches of Naples.

If you walk along the canal as it branches off from the museum, you come first (about 270 yards from the museum and before the wooden bridge) to the **Ships' Pavilion** where historic vessels are displayed. Proceeding on along the canal, you soon reach the **Arsenale,** campo del'Arsenale, guarded by stone lions, Neptune with a trident, and other assorted ferocities. You'll spot it readily enough because of its two towers which flank each side of the canal. In its day the Arsenale turned out galley after galley at speeds usually associated with wartime production.

Museo Fortuny

Campo San Benedetto 3780. ☎ **5200995**. Admission 5,000 lire ($3.15) adults, 3,000 lire ($1.90) children. Tues–Sun 9am–7pm. Vaporetto: San Angelo.

The 15th-century Palazzo Pesaro degli Orfoi is now the Museo Fortuny. Here you can see the home and work surroundings of Mariano Fortuny, who lived here for almost 50 years. The Spanish-born Fortuny was known for his fabric and dress designs, especially his pleated silk Grecian gowns popular around the turn of the century. However, he was also engaged in theater set design, painting, and photography. In his fabric designs, he used motifs of Islam, France, Greece, Africa, and Italy, as well as pre-Columbian civilizations. In the museum and the artist's former living quarters, you can see murals, fabrics (including a fine Oriental rug simulated on velvet), portraits, his own copies of old masters, and other interesting decorative pieces.

MORE ATTRACTIONS
SCHOOLS & CHURCHES

Much of the great art of Venice lies in its churches and *scuole* (schools). The latter weren't schools in the usual sense, but fraternities or guilds. Most of their members were drawn from the rising bourgeoisie of Venice. Through male bonding, fraternity members were said to have had both their material and spiritual needs fulfilled by these guilds. The members of the scuole, such as that of San Rocco, often engaged in charitable works in honor of the saint for whom their fraternity was named. Many of the greatest artists of Venice, including Tintoretto, were commissioned to decorate these schools with art. Some of the artists created masterpieces that can still be viewed today. Often the lives of the patron saints of the schools were commemorated. Narrative canvases that depicted the lives of the saints were called *teleri*.

✪ Scuola di San Rocco

Campo San Rocco, San Polo. ☎ **5234864**. Admission 8,000 lire ($5) adults, 2,500 lire ($1.55) children. Mar 28–Nov 2, daily 9am–5:30pm; Nov 3–Mar 27, Mon–Fri 10am–1pm, Sat–Sun 10am–4pm. Closed Dec 25–Jan 1 and Easter. Vaporetto: San Tomà; from the station, walk straight onto ramo Mondoler, which becomes larga Prima; then take salizzada San Rocco, which opens into campo San Rocco.

Of the scuole of Venice, none is as richly embellished as the Scuola di San Rocco, which is filled with epic canvases by Tintoretto. By clever trick, he won the competition to decorate the darkly illuminated early 16th-century building. He began painting in 1564, and the work stretched on till his powers as an artist waned. The paintings sweep across the upper and lower halls, mesmerizing the viewer with a kind of passion play. In the grand hallway, they depict New Testament scenes, devoted largely to episodes in the life of Mary (the *Flight into Egypt* is among the best). In the top gallery are works that illustrate scenes from both the Old and New Testaments, the most renowned being those devoted to the life of Christ. In a separate room is what is considered Tintoretto's masterpiece—his mammoth *Crucifixion*, one of the world's most celebrated paintings. In it he showed his dramatic scope and sense of grandeur as an artist, creating a deeply felt scene that virtually comes alive—filling the viewer with the horror of systematic execution, thus transcending its original subject matter.

Basilica di Santa Maria Gloriosa del Frari

Campo dei Frari, San Polo. ☎ **5222637.** Admission 1,500 lire (90¢). Mon–Sat 9–11:45am and 2:30–6pm, Sun 3–5:30pm. Vaporetto: San Tomà.

Known simply as the Frari, this Venetian-Gothic church is only a short walk from the Scuola di San Rocco (Vaporetto: San Tomà). The church is filled with some great art. First, the best—Titian's *Assumption* over the main altar is a masterpiece of soaring beauty that depicts the ascension of the Madonna on a cloud puffed up by floating cherubs. In her robe, but especially in the robe of one of the gaping saints below, "Titian red" dazzles as never before.

On the first altar to the right as you enter is Titian's second major work here— a *Madonna Enthroned*, painted for the Pesaro family in 1526. Although lacking the power and drama of the *Assumption*, it nevertheless is brilliant in its use of color and light effects. But Titian surely would turn redder than his madonna's robes if he could see the latter-day neoclassical tomb built for him on the opposite wall. The kindest word for it: large.

Facing the tomb is a memorial to Canova, the Italian sculptor who led the revival of classicism. To return to more enduring art, head to the sacristy for a Giovanni Bellini triptych on wood, painted in 1488. The Madonna is cool and serene, one of Bellini's finest portraits of the Virgin. Also see the almost primitive-looking wood carving by Donatello of *St. John the Baptist*.

Scuola di San Giorgio degli Schiavoni

Calle Furiani, Castello. ☎ **5228828.** Admission 5,000 lire ($3.15). Apr–Oct, Tues–Sat 9:30am–12:30pm and 3:30–6:30pm, Sun 9:30am–12:30pm; Nov–Mar, Tues–Sat 10am–12:30pm and 3–6pm, Sun 10am–12:30pm. Vaporetto: San Zaccaria.

At the St. Antonino Bridge (fondamenta dei Furlani) is the second important school to visit in Venice. Between 1502 and 1509, Vittore Carpaccio painted a pictorial cycle here of exceptional merit and interest. Of enduring fame are his works of St. George and the dragon—these are my favorite art in all of Venice and certainly the most delightful. For example, in one frame St. George charges the dragon on a field littered with half-eaten bodies and skulls. Gruesome? Not at all. Any moment you expect the director to call "Cut!" The pictures relating to St. Jerome are appealing but don't compete with St. George and his ferocious dragon.

Chiesa Madonna dell'Orto

Campo dell'Orto, Cannaregio 3512. ☎ **719933.** Admission is free. May–Oct, daily 9:30am–noon and 3:30–5:30pm; Nov–Apr, daily 9:30am–noon and 3–4:30pm. Vaporetto: Madonna dell'Orto.

This church provides a good reason to walk to this fairly remote northern district of Venice. At the church on the lagoon you'll be paying your final respects to Tintoretto. The brick structure with a Gothic front is famed not only because of its paintings by that artist, but because the great master is buried in the chapel to the right of the main altar. At the high altar are Tintoretto's *Last Judgment* (on the right) and his *Sacrifice of the Golden Calf* (left)—two monumental paintings that curve at the top like a Gothic arch. Over the doorway to the right of the altar is Tintoretto's superb portrayal of the presentation of Mary as a little girl at the temple. The composition is unusual in that Mary is not the focal point—rather, a pointing woman bystander dominates the scene. The first chapel to the right of the main altar contains a masterly work by Cima de Conegliano, showing the presentation of a sacrificial lamb to the saints (the plasticity of St. John's body evokes Michelangelo). Finally, the first chapel on the left (as you enter) is graced with an exquisite Giovanni Bellini *Madonna and Child*. Note the eyes and mouth of both the mother and child—they constitute a work of consummate skill. Two other pictures in the apse are *The Presentation of the Cross to St. Peter* and *The Beheading of St. Christopher* (1551–55). Besides the five paintings in the apse are works by Tintoretto and his school. Two paintings are by Palma the Younger: *The Annunciation* and *The Crucifixion* (where the influence of his master, Tintoretto, can be seen).

Chiesa di San Zaccaria

Campo San Zaccaria, Castello. ☎ **5221257.** Admission is free. Daily 10am–noon and 4–6pm. Vaporetto: San Zaccaria.

Behind St. Mark's Basilica is a Gothic church with a Renaissance facade. The church is filled with works of art, notably Giovanni Bellini's *Madonna Enthroned*, painted with saints (second altar to the left). Many have found this to be one of Bellini's finest madonnas, and it does have beautifully subdued coloring, although it appears rather static. Apply to the sacristan to see the Sisters' Choir, with works by Tintoretto, Titian, Il Vecchio, Anthony van Dyck, and Bassano. The paintings aren't labeled, but the sacristan will point out the names of the artists. In the Sisters' Choir are five armchairs in which the Venetian doges of yore sat. Also, if you save the best for last, you can see the faded frescoes of Andrea del Castagno in the shrine that honors San Tarasio.

Basilica di San Giorgio Maggiore

San Giorgio Maggiore, across from piazzetta San Marco. ☎ **5289900.** Admission 3,000 lire ($1.90) adults, 2,000 lire ($1.25) children. June–Sept, daily 9:30am–12:30pm and 2:30–6:30pm; Oct–May, daily 10am–12:30pm and 2:30–4:30pm. Transportation: Take the Giudecca-bound vaporetto (no. 82) on riva degli Schiavoni and get off at the first stop, right in the courtyard of the church.

This church sits on the little island of San Giorgio Maggiore. The building was designed by Palladio, the great Renaissance architect of the 16th century—perhaps as a consolation prize since he was not chosen to rebuild the burnt-out Doges' Palace. The logical rhythm of the Vicenza architect is played here on a grand scale. But inside it's almost too stark since Palladio was not much on gilded adornment. The chief art hangs on the main altar—two epic paintings by Tintoretto, one to the left, the *Fall of Manna*, and then the far more successful *Last Supper* to the right. It's interesting to compare Tintoretto's *Cena* with that of Veronese at the Academy. Afterward, you may want to take the elevator—for 2,000 lire ($1.25)—to the top of the belfry for a view of the greenery of the island itself, the lagoon, and the Doges' Palace across the way. In a word, it's unforgettable.

Santa Maria della Salute

Campo della Salute, Dorsoduro. ☎ **5225558.** Admission to church, free; sacristy 1,000 lire (65¢). Daily 9am–noon and 3–6:30pm. Vaporetto: Salute.

Like the proud landmark that it is, this church—the pinnacle of the baroque movement in Venice—stands at the mouth of the Grand Canal overlooking piazzetta San Marco. It opens onto campo della Salute, Dorsoduro. One of the most historic churches in Venice, it was built by Longhena in the 17th century as an offering to the Virgin for delivering the city from the grip of the plague. It was erected on enough pilings to support the Empire State Building (well, almost). Surmounted by a great cupola, the octagonal basilica makes for an interesting visit, as it houses a small art gallery in its sacristy (tip the custodian)—a marriage feast of Cana by Tintoretto, allegorical paintings on the ceiling by Titian, a mounted St. Mark, and poor St. Sebastian with his inevitable arrow. The latter works, however, did not earn for Titian the title of "Il Divino."

SS. Giovanni e Paolo Basilica

Campo SS. Giovanni e Paolo, Castello 6363. ☎ **5237510.** Admission is free. Daily 7:30am–12:30pm and 3–7:15pm. Vaporetto: Rialto or fondamenta Nuove.

This church, also known as Zanipolo, is often called the pantheon of Venice since it houses the tombs of many doges. One of the great Gothic churches of Venice, the building was erected between the 13th and 14th centuries. Inside, it contains artwork by many of the most noted Venetian painters. As you enter (right aisle), you'll find a retable by Giovanni Bellini (which includes a St. Sebastian filled with arrows). In the Rosary Chapel are ceilings by Veronese, depicting New Testament scenes, including *The Assumption of the Madonna.* To the right of the church is one of the world's best-known equestrian statues—that of Bartolomeo Colleoni (paid for by the condottiere), sculpted in the 15th century by Andrea del Verrochio. The bronze has long been acclaimed as his masterpiece, although it was completed by another artist. The horse is far more beautiful than the armored military hero, who looks as if he had just stumbled upon a three-headed crocodile.

To the left of the pantheon is the Scuola di San Marco, with its stunning Renaissance facade (it's now run as a civic hospital).

THE GHETTO

The Ghetto of Venice, called the Ghetto Nuovo, was instituted in 1516 by the Venetian Republic in the Cannaregio district. It is considered to be the first ghetto in the world, and also the best kept. The word *geto* comes from the Venetian dialect, meaning foundry, because originally there were two iron foundries here where metals were fused. The Ghetto stands in what is now the northwestern corner of Venice. Once Venetian Jews were confined to a walled area and obliged to wear distinctive red or yellow marks (cloth circles or hats). The walls were torn down long ago, but much remains of the past.

One of the most beautiful synagogues, the **Scola Tedesca,** has been restored with funds from Germany. This is the German Scola, one of five synagogues: The others are Spanish (the oldest continuously functioning synagogue in Europe), the Italian, the Levantine-Oriental, and the Scola Canton. All the synagogues were built between the beginning and the end of the 16th century. Three of them can be visited Sunday through Friday from 10am to 4:30pm in winter (until 7pm in summer). Tours leave between 10:30am and 3:30pm (until 5:30pm in summer), depending on demand. Call 715359 to book tours. Tours include three synagogues, with the museum and tourist service run by a partnership providing tourists with multilingual guides.

The tiny **Museo Comunità Ebraica,** campo di Ghetto Nuovo 2902B (☎ 715359), is open from 10am to 4:30pm Sunday through Friday from October

---

❓ Did You Know?

- The Gritti Palace, the most famous hotel of Venice, is named for the notorious womanizer, Doge Andrea Gritti.
- John Ruskin once wrote that nothing could have been more childish in conception, more servile in plagiarism than Palladios Church of San Giorgio Maggiore.
- Many famous foreigners have asked to be buried on the cemetery island of San Michele: Lord Byron, John Ruskin, and Ezra Pound among them.
- The Lido, the bathing beach of Venice, was the original Lido, lending its name to innumerable bathing spots and cinemas the world over.
- In the 16th century, any master glassblower escaping Murano with the secrets of the trade was tracked down by the Venetian republic. For punishment, his hands were cut off or he was murdered.
- The idea of encasing a Jewish settlement into a ghetto is of Venetian origin.
- When Paolo Veronese's *The Last Supper*—filled with buffoons, drunkards, Germans, dwarfs, and similar indecencies—brought down the wrath of the Inquisition, he simply retitled it *The Banquet in the House of Levi*.
- The dogeship of Venice was the monopoly of old men because a ruler in his 70s would have fewer chances to abuse his position.

---

to the end of May. From June through September, it is open Sunday through Friday from 10am to 7pm. Closed on Saturday and Jewish holidays. Admission is 4,000 lire ($2.50).

While in the area, you can explore on your own, seeing houses huddled close together along narrow streets. In all, it represents a complex that is unique in the world. Vaporetto: San Marcuola.

ESPECIALLY FOR KIDS

Unlike any other European city, Venice seems made for kids. Providing you don't mind issuing a lot of warnings about avoiding the edge of every canal you see (and you'll see plenty); Venice is like wandering around in a Disneyland fantasy for a child, complete with vaporetto rides to yet-unexplored islands. After a day of wandering endless alleyways and crossing dozens of footbridges, most children tire early and few have to be coaxed to turn in.

The most exciting activity for children is a **gondola ride.** Gondoliers are usually very patient with children, explaining (in Italian) the intricacies of their craft, although their actual demonstrations are more effective in getting the point across. Later in the day you can take your child to the **glass-manufacturing works** at **Murano** (see "Easy Excursions," below), where the intricacies of the craft of blowing glass will be demonstrated.

The one museum that seems to fascinate children the most is the **Naval Museum and Arsenale** (see above), where the glorious remnants of Venice's maritime past are presented.

To cap the day, you can always purchase a bag of corn from a street vendor so your child can feed the fat pigeons at **piazza San Marco.**

WALKING TOUR
Piazza San Marco to the Grand Canal

Start: Piazza San Marco.
Finish: Grand Canal at the Ponte Rialto.
Time: 2 hours, not including stops.
Best Times: Any sunny day.
Worst Times: Holidays and festivals (streets are too crowded).

There are hundreds of byways, alleyways, and canals stretching across the faded splendor of Venice. This 2-hour walking tour will give you at least an exterior view plus a general orientation to the layout of parts of the city, often showing lesser-known sights, which can best be seen from the outside, on foot. Later, you can pick and choose at your leisure the sights you most want to revisit, especially those requiring interior inspections.

Our tour begins, appropriately enough, at the heart of the city:

1. **Piazza San Marco,** or St. Mark's Square, perhaps the most famous in Italy. Here and on its satellite square, piazzetta San Marco, you can explore the major attractions of the city. These include the:

2. **Basilica di San Marco,** named for St. Mark, whose body was allegedly stolen from his tomb in Alexandria in 828 and brought to Venice. This basilica was built to enshrine the body of the man who became the city's patron saint. Next door is the:

3. **Palazzo Ducale,** with its adjoining Ponte dei Sospiri (Bridge of Sighs), a pink confection that was the home of the doges (dukes) who ruled Venice for years. In front of the palace is the:

4. **Campanile di San Marco,** the bell tower of Venice, which visitors climb for a spectacular view of the city and lagoon.

   The Renaissance mariners who supplied the lifelines that led to their Adriatic capital realized that the most impressive view of the city was, and perhaps still is, visible only from the water. To better see this unforgettable view, take a brief vaporetto ride across the Grand Canal to the baroque white walls of:

5. **Santa Maria della Salute.** Buy your ticket at either of two vaporetto stops: no 16 (San Zaccaria), just east of St. Mark's Square or no. 15 (San Marco), which lies just west of the square along the Grand Canal. Enjoy the short water ride and the view before getting off on the opposite canal at the pier marked "Salute." There you can look back across the Grand Canal at the rows of palazzi, many of which have been turned into glamorous hotels.

   Walk to the right side of the church along campo della Salute, past a pair of wooden bridges, and continue until you reach the third bridge, the only one of the three that's made of stone. Cross this bridge and head onto rio Terradei Catecumeni. After one block, turn left onto calle Constantina. Now walk toward the water, along a wide flagstone-covered walkway divided by a single row of trees which must struggle to survive in the salt air of Venice. The waterway you'll soon reach separates this section of Venice from the rarely visited:

6. **Island of Giudecca,** which lies across the broad Canale di Giudecca. Though you won't visit it as part of this walking tour, you might decide to return to explore its untrammeled streets later during your visit. From this vantage point, you can also gaze upon the cranes of the industrialized mainland town of Mestre, to the north.

Turn right along the waterfront of a district known to Venetians as Dorsoduro. Much more of a residential neighborhood than the area around piazza San Marco, it has often been compared to New York's Greenwich Village because artists and writers have traditionally been attracted to it. Many, of course, came to avoid the stratospheric prices charged on the opposite side of the Grand Canal. With water to your left and a changing panorama of brick and stone buildings to your right, you'll cross over the high arches of several bridges, always continuing along the canalside walkway which, in characteristically Venetian fashion, will change its name at least three times.

At the third and last bridge, the Ponte della Calcina, at campiello della Calcina, you will notice two of the most famous pensiones of Venice—La Calcina, where John Ruskin stayed, and the Pensione Seguso. The name of the pavement that supports you here is zattere ai Gesuati. You'll notice a pair of wooden platforms, managed by local cafés and separated from one another by drydocked steel-hulled ships. After, perhaps, a coffee, you reach the acanthus–inspired pilasters of the baroque:

7. Chiesa dei Gesuiti. After visiting the church, take the street to its right, which is referred to variously as rio Terrà Antonio Foscarini, the rio Terrà Marco Foscarini, or simply rio Terrà Foscarini, and walk northwest. At the side of the church, admire campo Santa Agnese, where tolling bells call the neighborhood to mass.

Now continue north along rio Foscarini until you reach the Grand Canal and the:

8. Gallerie dell'Accademia. You can either visit this great gallery of art or save it for another day. Cross the bridge, and you may notice the German consulate beside the elegant garden to the left. When you step off the bridge, you'll be on campo San Vidal. At this point, the city of Venice has graciously mapped out one of the most logical walking tours in the city by posting prominent yellow signs with black lettering on dozens of appropriate street corners.

Your walk, if you follow the signs, will take you back to St. Mark's Square through dozens of claustrophobic alleys, which are crumbling from exposure to the Adriatic winds, and into gloriously proportioned squares whose boundaries are often ornamented with exquisite detailing. From this point on, follow the signs that say PER S. MARCO. You can afford to ignore your map and lose yourself in the Renaissance splendor in this most unusual city.

At campo San Vidal, the pavement will funnel you in only one possible direction. After several twists and turns, you'll be in the huge expanse of:

9. Campo San Stefano (whose southern end is referred to on some maps as campo Francesco Morosini). Keep walking across the square, past a wood-and-iron flagpole capped with the Lion of St. Mark. Midway along the right side of the square, follow the PER S. MARCO sign down a tiny alleyway called calle del Spezier. The alley funnels across a bridge and then changes its name to calle del Piovan. This will open to the wide expanses of:

10. Campo San Maurizio. Walk directly across the square, looking for yet another PER S. MARCO sign, which should direct you over another set of bridges.

This square funnels into the narrow calle Zaguri. Cross another canal's arched bridge and enter campiello de la Feltrina. Keep following the signs to San Marco. Soon you'll come to one of the most famous Venetian squares, which is shaped roughly like a crucifix. One end opens onto the Grand Canal, near

Walking Tour—Piazza San Marco
To The Grand Canal

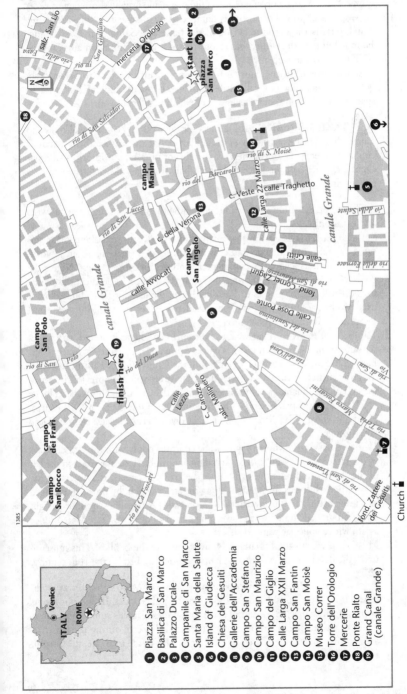

1. Piazza San Marco
2. Basilica di San Marco
3. Palazzo Ducale
4. Campanile di San Marco
5. Santa Maria della Salute
6. Island of Giudecca
7. Chiesa dei Gesuiti
8. Gallerie dell'Accademia
9. Campo San Stefano
10. Campo San Maurizio
11. Campo del Giglio
12. Calle Larga XXII Marzo
13. Campo San Fantin
14. Campo San Moisè
15. Museo Correr
16. Torre dell'Orologio
17. Mercerie
18. Ponte Rialto
19. Grand Canal (canale Grande)

the famous hotel in Venice, the Gritti Palace. The full name of the square is campo Santa Maria Zobenigo O del Giglio, a name usually shortened to:

11. Campo del Giglio. The square is dominated by a larger-than-life-size statue, which guards the baroque facade of the Chiesa di Santa Maria del Giglio. Founded in the 9th century, but reconstructed in the 17th, it contains canvases by Tintoretto and Rubens.

As you exit from the church, follow once again the signs to San Marco, going down an alleyway, calle delle Ostreghe. Cross the high arch of a canal-spanning bridge, on the opposite side of which you'll spot your:

☕ **TAKE A BREAK** Bar Ducale, calle delle Ostreghe, offers cocktails and sandwiches. The owner once worked at Harry's Bar and learned the restaurant's culinary secrets. The only difference here is not in taste, but in price—the Bar Ducale charges half the price of Harry's Bar. If not a sandwich, then enjoy a cappuccino.

When you exit from the Bar Ducale, follow the street through several twists and turns onto:

12. Calle Larga XXII Marzo, whose many shops, cafés, and restaurants make this one of the most-frequented and crowded streets of Venice. In about a block, midway down its length, I recommend a short detour off to the left. Notice the gold, white, and red sign pointing to "al teatro la Fenice." The street this points to is calle del Sartor da Veste. Turn neither to the left nor right, but follow it over two bridges, into what is often considered one of the most intimate summertime "living rooms" of Venice:

13. Campo San Fantin. In fair weather, the enclosed square is dotted with tables set out by the best restaurant in Venice, Antico Martini, and its lesser rivals. Here you'll find the Teatro La Fenice and the Church of St. Fantin. After visiting the church, retrace your steps along the street you took previously. From the end of the square, its name appears as calle del Cafetier. This walk will take you back over the pair of bridges leading once again to calle larga XXII Marzo. Head left, toward San Moisè Church. By now the PER S. MARCO signs will lead you through:

14. Campo San Moisè, whose ornate facade contrasts oddly with the modern bulk of the Hotel Bauer Grünwald & Grand on your right. Take the street to the left of the church, and note the sign PER S. MARCO as you pass by the American Express office while heading straight along the street which, by now, has changed its name once again, this time to calle Seconda de l'Ascension. Continue straight under an arched tunnel to the sweeping expanses of piazza San Marco, once again, where you may want to visit the:

15. Museo Correr, in the Procuratie Nuove, opposite the basilica. This museum traces the development of Venetian painting from the 14th to the 16th century.

☕ **TAKE A BREAK** Since Florian, piazza San Marco 56-59, was established, it has been considered the most Venetian of all cafés. Its interior rooms drip with a nostalgic 18th-century decor, but if the weather's sunny most guests prefer to sit outside. The Venetians patronized this café during the Austrian occupation, whereas the occupying army brass went to the rival café, the Quadri, across the square.

Later, walk through the square and pass to the left of the Basilica of St. Mark, stopping perhaps to admire a pair of lions carved from red porphyry. As you gaze with the lions back across the wide expanse of the square, notice the arched tunnel that pierces the base of the:

16. **Torre dell'Orologio.** Pass beneath the Moorish bellringers and the zodiac representations of the clock face. Here you will be on the major shopping street of Venice, the:

17. **Mercerie.** Of course, this is the popular name of the street. It actually has many longer names, preceded by the word *merceria*. From now on, your guiding light will be the signs that say PER RIALTO. They will be either formally positioned at strategic corners in yellow or black or scrawled sometimes graffiti-style on the sides of buildings.

Soon you'll reach the:

18. **Ponte Rialto,** from the Latin *rivo alto*, meaning high bank. The Istrian-stone bridge dates from 1588. The architect, Antonio da Ponte, actually won in a competition against Michelangelo, Palladio, and Sansovino, among others, to design this bridge. Until 1854 the bridge was the only pedestrian crossing on the Grand Canal.

Once at this point, you can board a vaporetto to take you back to piazza San Marco. Along the way you can enjoy the:

19. **Grand Canal.** A ride along the palazzo-flanked banks of this highly touted waterway is not only one of the grandest experiences in all of Italy, but the entire world. It is the one experience visitors are likely to remember when their memories of other monuments have gone hazy.

2 Organized Tours

Tours through the streets and canals of Venice are distinctly different from tours through other cities of Italy because of the complete absence of traffic. You can always wander at will through the labyrinth of streets, but many visitors opt for a guided tour to at least familiarize themselves with the geography of the city.

American Express, San Marco 1471 (☎ 5200844), which operates from a historic building a few steps from St. Mark's Square, offers an array of guided city tours. Some of the most popular offerings include the following:

Every morning at 9:10am a 2-hour guided tour of the city departs from in front of the American Express building for a cost of 33,000 lire ($20.65). Sights include St. Mark's Square, the basilica, the Doges' Palace, the prison, the bell tower, and a demonstration of the art of Venetian glassblowing.

Every afternoon, between 3 and 5pm a 2-hour guided tour incorporates visits to the exteriors of several palaces along campo San Benetto, and other sights of the city. Clients eventually cross the Grand Canal to visit the Church of Santa Maria dei Frari (which contains the *Assumption* by Titian). The tour continues by gondola down the canal to visit the Ca' d'Oro and eventually ends at the Rialto Bridge. Cost of the afternoon tour is 35,000 lire ($21.90)). A combined purchase of the morning and afternoon tour is just 60,000 lire ($37.50).

The "Evening Serenade Tour," priced at 40,000 lire ($25) per person, allows a nocturnal view of Venice accompanied by the sound of singing musicians in gondolas. From May to October there are two daily departures, one at 7:30 and another at 8:30pm, which leaves from campo Santa Maria del Giglio. Four to five occupants fit in each gondola as a singer and a handful of musicians sing throughout the Venetian evening.

A "Tour of the Islands of the Venetian Lagoon," priced at 25,000 lire ($15.65), departs twice daily, at 9:30am and again at 2:30pm, and lasts 3 hours. You'll pass the islands of San Giorgio and San Francesco del Deserto, and eventually land at Burano, Murano, and Torcello for brief tours of their churches and landmarks. This trip departs from and returns to the pier at riva del Schiavoni.

If you'd like more personalized tours than those offered by American Express, contact *Venice Travel Advisory Service*, 22 Riverside Dr., New York, NY 10023; tel. and fax 212/873-1964. The number to call for help in Venice is 5232379. Born in New York City, Samantha Durell is a professional photographer, and has lived and worked in Venice as a private tour guide for more than five years. Some locals claim she knows Venice far better than they do, even though they've lived here all their lives.

She arranges tours, conducts orientation sessions, and aids in any advance-planning service, such as securing a hotel during Carnevale or getting a ticket to La Fenice. She also advises about seeking out that little trattoria—far removed from the tourist circuit—serving a typical Venetian cuisine. In addition, she also has a wealth of information about shopping purchases, Venetian sightseeing, art and history, dining, and entertainment. Her private guided tours are individually tailored to your needs. She's also known for taking you through what she calls tiny winding back streets and timeless neighborhoods.

Morning or afternoon tours, for a maximum of six people, lasting about 4 hours, cost $175 for two people, and $50 for each additional person.

For do-it-yourself walking tours of Venice's major sights, try *Frommer's Walking Tours: Venice.*

3 Special & Free Events

Although cities from New Orleans to Rio celebrate their own respective carnivals with their own kinds of panache, the **Carnavale of Venice** might be the oldest, most historic, and most eerily evocative. Continuing a tradition established during the Renaissance, it occupies 10 days in February with sometimes-raucous parties that seem to anticipate the upcoming sobriety of Lent, Good Friday, and Easter. Declared an official holiday by the mayor of Venice in the 1970s, it includes around-the-clock street theater, highly electrified pop concerts, and the presence of thousands of non-Venetians who pour into the city for a series of private and public masked balls. The festival's most famous garb includes three-cornered hats, elaborate wigs, costumes inspired by something out of an opera by Mozart, and blandly enigmatic porcelain masks whose contours and nuances are considered a well-established art form in their own right.

In springtime, on the first Sunday after Ascension Day, Venetians observe **La Vogalonga** ("The Long Row"). Established as late as 1975, it's now one of the best-attended events in the Venetian calendar year. More of an oarsman's marathon than a race, it includes all kinds of oar-powered seacraft whose 20-mile course takes them from the base of St. Mark's Square around Saint-Elena, to points as far away as San Francesco del Deserto and Burano before returning to Venice via the Cannaregio Canal and the Grand Canal. Boats depart around 9:30am, returning (with very tired oarsmen) anytime between 11am and into the early evening.

Unlike many other nautical events in Venice's calendar of events, this one is open to any foreigner with a safely outfitted oar-driven craft.

At midsummer, during the crush of the tourist season's third weekend in July, illuminated gondolas, fireworks above the lagoon, and roaming musicians floating on barges contribute to a holiday known as **the Feast of the Redeemer (Festa del Redentore).** A bridge of boats is erected across the Guidecca Canal near the base of the Church of the Redentore, commemorating the end of the plague of 1576, and many Venetians spend most of the festival picnicking from the gunnels of their boats. Many end the festival early the next morning, perhaps on the beaches of Lido.

In September, one of Italy's most famous nautical events is the **Historic Regatta (Regatta Storica).** Then, richly decorated gondolas, staffed by boatmen in Renaissance costumes, race one another along the Grand Canal. Floating barges and historically important boats carry the music and parties out into the open lagoons in an event that perhaps better than any other evokes the nautical traditions of imperial Venice.

Late in August and early in September, the **International Film Festival** is hosted on the Lido, during which the stars, starlets, producers, directors, salespeople, artists, charlatans, and wannabees of the film industry congregate in a frenzy of exhibitionistic and voyeuristic yearning to promote, titillate, or whatever the emissaries of the viewing public. Hundreds of films are shown almost around the clock. Ticket costs spiral as the festival progresses.

During alternate (even-numbered) years, between June and October, the **International Exposition of Modern Art,** better known as the **Biennale d'Arte,** adds a modern note to the antique charm of Venice with some of the largest imported collections of contemporary paintings and sculptures in the world. These are displayed in a series of around 35 different exposition spaces, both indoor and outdoor, whose locations are announced as part of each (alternate) year's events. (Most are centered around the vaporetto stop of La Giardini.) Originally established in 1895, the Biennale is one of the most famous art events in Europe.

In November, during a wet and rainy season that attracts what might be the fewest numbers of international visitors, the **opera season** at the theaters of Malibran and Fenice begins, continuing through till mid-May. On November 21, a **religious procession,** ending within the imperious white walls of Santa Maria della Salute (considered the most important baroque building in Venice), remembers the end of the plague of 1630. To commemorate the event, a pair of floating bridges are devised, spanning the Grand Canal for the benefit of the faithful and/or nostalgic.

4 Sports & Outdoor Activities

Venice is so full of architectural and artistic riches that few visitors will look for opportunities for sport and conventional recreations. In a city without cars, the labyrinth of pedestrian walkways and steeply inclined bridges offers ample opportunities for walking, with never a dull expanse between landmarks. The densely populated labyrinth of the city itself offers almost no sports facilities within its historic or residential core; if you insist on diversions you'll have to head out to the flat and sandy expanses of Venice's playground, the Lido.

GOLF With the salt air whipping in from the Adriatic, a brisk 18 holes of golf might be especially invigorating. At the extreme western end of the Lido you'll find the **Golf Club Lido di Venezia,** via del Forte (☎ 731333). To reach it, take vaporetto no. 11 from riva degli Schiavoni or the C bus from the Lido's main dock at Santa Maria Elisabetta.

JOGGING The broad thoroughfares of central Venice's riva degli Schiavoni, just east of piazza San Marco, are usually suitable for jogging, except in midsummer when they tend to be jammed with slowly meandering pedestrians. Another possibility includes the lengthy and often less-crowded expanse of paved-over shoreline beside the Giudecca Canal. More suitable in any season is the beach of the Lido.

SAILING Sailing boats, with or without skippers, can be rented, and sailing lessons are given at the **Ciga Yacht Club,** based beside the Excelsior Hotel (☎ 5260201), the most prominent hotel on the Lido.

SOCCER The season for spectator soccer (by far the best-attended sports event in Venice) lasts from September to May. The city's soccer team, Venezia, welcomes visiting teams from throughout the rest of Europe for games that are usually held on Sunday afternoon at the **Stadio Comunale P.L. Pezo,** San Elena (☎ 5225770). Tickets go on sale at the stadium's box office several hours before play begins. If you want to actually play soccer, you'll have to content yourself with joining a scrimmage or spontaneous pickup game in one of the city's residential squares.

SWIMMING Because the waters of Venice itself are polluted, all swimming should be confined to the tide-scoured beaches of the Lido, and even then it probably isn't such a great idea. Most of the city's public beaches lie along the Lido's northern end, while beaches fronting the island's southern and central end tends to be reserved for clients of the various hotels that line its shores. There's a public pool, the **Piscina Gandini,** on the Isola di San Giorgio (☎ 5285430), where waters might be somewhat healthier.

TENNIS The **Tennis Club,** lungomare Marconi 41D (☎ 5267194) offers a handful of courts which, if not being used by members, can be rented by the hour to players appropriately dressed in tennis whites. You can also try the **Tennis Club Lido,** via Sandra Gallo 163 (☎ 5260954). Because of the frequent winter rainfall, all of these tend to close down in winter.

5 Shopping

THE SHOPPING SCENE

Venetian **glass** and **lace** are known throughout the world. However, selecting quality products in either craft requires a shrewd eye. There is much that is tawdry and shoddily crafted in Venetian shops. Some of the glassware hawked isn't worth the cost of shipping it home. Yet other pieces represent some of the world's finest artistic and ornamental glass. Murano is the island where glass is made, and the women of Burano put in painstaking hours turning out lace. If you're interested in some little glass souvenir of your stay, perhaps an animal or a bird, you'll find such items sold in shops all over Venice.

SHOPPING A TO Z
ANTIQUES

Antichita Santomanco
Frezzeria 1504, San Marco. ☎ **5236643.** Vaporetto: San Marco.

This store is for the specialist only—especially the well-heeled specialist. It specializes in antique furniture, books, prints, and coins. Of course, the merchandise is ever-changing, but you're likely to pick up some little heirloom item in the midst of the clutter. Many of the items date from the Venetian heyday of the 1600s. Open Monday through Saturday from 10am to 1pm and 3:30 to 7:30pm, and sometimes on Sunday from 10am to 1pm. Call about Sunday openings.

BRASS OBJECTS

Valese Fonditore
Calle Fiubera 793, San Marco. ☎ **5227282.** Vaporetto: San Marco.

Founded in 1913, Valese Fonditore is located only a short walk away from piazza San Marco. It serves as a showcase outlet for one of the most famous of the several foundries that make their headquarters in Venice. Many of the brass copies of 18th-century chandeliers produced by this company grace fine homes in the United States. Many visitors to Venice invest in these brass castings, which eventually become family heirlooms. If you're looking for a brass replica of the sea horses decorating the sides of gondolas, this shop stocks them in five or six different styles and sizes. Open Monday from 2 to 7:30pm and Tuesday through Saturday from 10:30am to 7:30pm.

CARNIVAL MASKS

Laboratorio Artigiano Maschere
Castello 6657, Barbaria delle Tole. ☎ **5223110.** Vaporetto: Rialto.

This shop is one of the best places to purchase carnival masks hand-crafted in papier-mâché or leather. The masks carry names and symbols, the best known being the birdlike luck bringer, called *Buonaventura* in Italian. Masks are sold all over Venice, but this well-established store has a particularly good selection, including masks that depict characters of the Commedia dell'Arte. Since the late 1980s a variety of hand-crafted items for interior decoration (picture and mirror frames, pots, consoles, boxes in the shape of pets) are also made in papier mâché. Such articles are standard or custom made in Renaissance (fruit, leaf, and animal garlands and triumphs), baroque, and neoclassical styles. Hours are Monday from 10 to 11:30am, Tuesday through Friday from 10am to 1pm and 3 to 7pm, and Saturday from 10am to 1pm.

FASHIONS
Men's

La Bottega di Nino
San Marco 223, Mercerie dell'Orologio. ☎ **5225608.** Vaporetto: San Marco.

This is one of the leading Venetian retail outlets for the elegantly attired male. It features the work of many European designers, even some from England, but it shines brightest in its Italian names, such as Nino Cerruti, Valentino, and Zenia.

The prices are also better for Italian wear. Styling is first-rate. April through October, it's open daily from 9:30am to 7:30pm; off-season, Monday 9:30am to 12:30pm and Tuesday through Saturday 9:30am to 12:30pm and 3:30 to 5:30pm.

La Fenice

Calle larga XXII Marzo no. 2255, San Marco. ☎ **5231273.** Vaporetto: San Marco.

Despite the similarity of its name with one of Venice's most visible theaters, this is a large and well-stocked outlet for some of the most visible clothing manufacturers of Italy. One of four outlets of a city-wide chain, La Fenice sells clothing for men and women from designers who include Ferré, Dior, Montana, Mügler, and several others. Open Monday from 4 to 7:30pm, Tuesday through Saturday from 9:30am to 7:30pm.

See also Belvest Boutique, below.

Women's

Belvest Boutique

Calle Vallaresso 1305, San Marco. ☎ **5287933.** Vaporetto: San Marco, near Harry's Bar.

This is one of the finest boutiques of Venice, specializing in clothing for women and men, both handmade and ready to wear. Fabrics used in the apparel are from some of the world's leading clothmakers. Linked with Vogini, the famous purveyor of leatherwork, the boutique displays top-quality craftsmanship and high-fashion style.

Open April to October, Monday through Saturday from 9am to 7:30pm; November through March, Monday from 3 to 7:30pm and Tuesday through Saturday from 9am to 12:30pm and 3 to 7:30pm.

GIFTS

Il Papiro

Campo San Maurizio 2764. ☎ **5223055.** Vaporetto: Accademia.

Il Papiro is mainly noted for its stationery supplies, but it also carries and sells many different textures and colors of writing paper and cards. In addition to hand-printed paper, it sells any number of easy-to-pack gift items, which include wooden animals and copybooks. It's a good bet for those who want to take back small, inexpensive gifts. Open Monday from 3:30 to 7:30pm, Tuesday through Saturday from 9:30am to 7:30pm, and Sunday from 10am to 6pm.

GLASS

Pauly & Co.

San Marco, Ponte Consorzi. ☎ **5209899.** Vaporetto: San Zaccaria.

This award-winning house exports its products all over the world. You can wander through its 21 salons, enjoy an exhibition of artistic glassware, and later see a furnace in full action. There is no catalog offered; Pauly's production, which is mainly made to order, consists of continually renewed patterns, subject to change and alteration based on customer desire. Open Easter through October, daily from 10am to 7pm; off-season, Monday through Saturday from 10am to 1pm and 3 to 7pm.

Venini

Piazzetta Leoncini 314, San Marco. ☎ **5224045.** Vaporetto: San Zaccaria.

Venini has won collector fans all over the globe for its Venetian art glass. They sell lamps, bottles, and vases, but not ordinary ones. Many are considered works of art, representing the best of Venetian craftsmanship in design and manufacture. Along with the previously recommended Pauly & Co., Venini represents the big triumvirate of Venetian glassmakers. Their best-known glass has a distinctive swirl pattern in several colors, which is called a venature. This shop is known for the refined taste of its glass, some of which appears almost transparent. Much of it is very fragile, but they long ago learned how to ship it anywhere safely. Open Monday from 3:30 to 7:30pm and Tuesday through Saturday from 9am to 7:30pm.

GRAPHICS

Bac Art Studio

Campo San Maurizio 2663, San Marco. ☎ **5228171.** Vaporetto: Santa Maria del Giglio.

This studio sells paper goods, but it's mainly a graphics gallery, noted for its selection of engravings, posters, and lithographs, which represent Venice at carnival time. Many views of Venice parade before you. Items for the most part are reasonably priced as well, and care and selection obviously went into the gallery's choice of its merchandise. Open Monday through Saturday from 10am to 1pm and 3 to 7pm.

Osvaldo Böhm

San Moisè 1349–1350. ☎ **5222255.** Vaporetto: San Marco.

For the right—and light—souvenir of Venice. Osvaldo Böhm has a rich collection of photographic archives specializing in Venetian art as well as original engravings and maps, lithographs, watercolors, and Venetian masks. Also you can see modern serigraphies by local artists and some fine hand-crafted bronzes. Open Monday through Saturday from 9am to 7:30pm and sometimes on Sunday from 10am to 5pm.

JEWELRY

Missiaglia

Piazza San Marco 125. ☎ **5224464.** Vaporetto: San Marco.

Since 1864 Missiaglia has been the private supplier to rich Venetians and savvy shoppers from around the world seeking the best in gold and jewelry. Go here for that special, often classic piece. However, the family also keeps its attennae trained on the latest developments in jewelry design worldwide so that it can stay abreast of the times.

LACE

Jesurum

Mercerie Del Capitello, S. Marco N. 4857. ☎ **5206177.** Vaporetto: San Zaccaria.

For serious purchases, Jesurum is the best place. This elegant shop, a center of noted lacemakers and fashion creators, has been located in a 12th-century church since 1868. You'll find Venetian handmade or machine lace and embroidery on table, bed, and bath linens; and hand-printed bathing suits. Quality and originality are guaranteed, and special orders are accepted. The exclusive linens created here are expensive, but the inventory is large enough to accommodate any kind of budget. Open Monday through Saturday from 9:30am to 7:30pm and (April to November) on Sunday from 10am to 1pm and 2 to 7pm.

LEATHER

Bottega Veneta

Calle Vallaresso 1337, San Marco. ☎ **5228489.** Vaporetto: San Marco.

Bottega Veneta is primarily known for its woven leather bags. These bags are sold elsewhere too, but the cost is said to be less at the company's flagship outlet in Venice. In addition, the shop sells shoes for men and women, suitcases, belts, and everything made of leather. There is also an array of high-fashion accessories. Both men and women will find this store a delight. Men will enjoy the assortment of leather wallets, for example. Open Monday from 3 to 6:30pm and Tuesday through Saturday from 9:30am to 1pm and 3 to 6:30pm; from June to September, also on Sunday from 11am to 1pm and 2 to 6pm.

Furla

San Marco 4954, Mercerie del Capitello. ☎ **5230611.** Vaporetto: Rialto.

Furla is a specialist in women's leather bags. It also sells belts and gloves for women. Many of the bags are stamped with molds, making them appear to be alligator, lizard, or some other exotic creature. These bags come in a varied choice of colors, including what the Austrians call "Maria Theresa ocher." Furla also displays a varied selection of costume jewelry. Open October to May, on Monday from 3 to 7:30pm, Tuesday through Saturday from 9:15am to 12:30pm and 3 to 7:30pm, and Sunday from 10:30am to 1:15pm and 2:15 to 6:30pm; June to September, daily from 9:15am to 7:30pm.

Marforio

Campo San Salvador 5033, San Marco. ☎ **5225734.** Vaporetto: Rialto.

Marforio is located in the heart of the city. Founded in 1875, it is probably the oldest and largest leather-goods retail outlet in Italy. The company has been run by the same family for five generations. It is known for the quality of its leather products, and the outlet here has an enormous assortment, including all the famous European labels such as Valentino, Giorgio Armani, Cerruti, and Pierre Cardin among others. Open Monday from 9am to 12:30pm and Tuesday through Saturday from 9am to 7:30pm.

Vogini

San Marco Ascensione 1291, 1292, and 1301. ☎ **5222573.** Vaporetto: San Marco, near Harry's Bar.

Every kind of leatherwork is offered at Vogini, especially women's handbags, which are exclusive models. There's also a large assortment of handbags in petit-point, plus men's and women's wear and shoes. The collection of artistic Venetian leather is of the highest quality. The travel-equipment department contains a large assortment of trunks and wardrobe suitcases as well as dressing cases—many of the latest models in luggage. Open April to October, Monday through Saturday from 9am to 7:30pm; November to March, on Monday from 3 to 7:30pm and Tuesday through Saturday from 9am to 12:30pm and 3 to 7:30pm.

MARKETS

If you're seeking some bargain-basement buys, head not for any basement but to one of the little shops that line the **Rialto Bridge.** The shops there branch out to encompass fruit and vegetable markets as well. The Rialto isn't the Ponte Vecchio in Florence, but, for what it offers, it isn't bad, particularly if your lire are running short. You'll find a wide assortment of merchandise here, from angora sweaters to leather gloves. Quality is likely to vary widely, so plunge in with the utmost discrimination. Vaporetto: Rialto.

PAPER

Antica Legatoria Piazzesi

Santa Maria del Giglio 2511. ☎ **049/8718621.** Vaporetto: San Marco.

You can browse or buy at Legatoria Piazzesi, among the displays of patterned, hand-painted paper. You can select paper-covered objects in bright colors as souvenirs of Venice. *Legatoria* means bookbindery, and some of this work is still done on special order, but the shop mainly offers such objects as scrapbooks, address books, diaries, Venetian carnival statues, and paperweights. Of course you can also find writing paper and decorative pieces. Open Monday through Saturday from 9:30am to 12:30pm and 4 to 7pm; closed January 15 to 30.

6 Venice After Dark

For such a fabled city, Venice has some of the most meager nightlife of any of the tourist meccas of Europe. Few patrons seem to want to patronize nightclubs when walking about the city at night is more interesting than any spectacle staged inside. Cafés and bars, however, are well-recommended places to enjoy a brief interlude before you continue your walk of exploration. Venice, although it offers gambling and a few other diversions, is pretty much an early-to-bed town. Most restaurants close at midnight.

The tourist office distributes a free pamphlet (part in English, part in Italian), called *"Un Ospite di Venezia."* A section of this useful publication lists events, including any music and opera or theatrical presentations, along with art exhibitions and local special events. It's the best guide to "what's happening" at the time of your visit to Venice.

In addition, classical concerts are often featured using various churches, such as the Chiesa di Vivaldi, as a venue. To see if any church concerts are being presented at the time of your visit, call 5208722 for information.

THE PERFORMING ARTS

Teatro la Fenice

Campo San Fantin, San Marco 2549. ☎ **5210161.** Tickets 34,800–240,000 lire ($21.75–$150). Vaporetto: San Marco.

One of the most famous theaters in Europe, Teatro la Fenice has existed in its present incarnation from the 19th century (an earlier structure was gutted by fire). To cap the perfect visit, try to attend either a concert or an opera at this theater should it be open at the time of your visit. The box office is open Monday through Saturday from 9:30am to 12:30pm and 4 to 6pm, and also 30 minutes before curtain time. If a Sunday performance is given, the box office will be open, closing on Monday instead. Performances are usually presented Tuesday through Saturday at 8pm; sometimes 4pm matinees are offered (check at the box office). The Venetian opera season runs from December to May. The opera theater, however, presents a year-round repertoire of concerts and ballets—except in August when everybody is on vacation.

Teatro Goldoni

Calle Goldoni, near campo San Luca. ☎ **5207583**. Tickets 20,000–40,000 lire ($12.50–$25).

This theater, close to the Ponte Rialto in the San Marco district, honors Carlo Goldoni (1707–93), the most prolific—critics say the best—of Italian playwrights. The theater presents a changing repertoire of productions, often plays in Italian, but musical presentations as well. The box office is open Monday through Saturday from 10am to 1pm and 4:30 to 7pm.

THE CLUB & MUSIC SCENE

El Souk

Calle Contarini Corfu 1056A. ☎ **5200371**. Cover (including first drink) Thurs–Fri and Sun–Tues 15,000 lire ($9.40); Sat 18,000 lire ($11.25). Vaporetto: Accademia.

Near the Accademia, this kasbahlike nightclub continues year after year to swim in the otherwise shallow sea of Venetian nightlife. It's run somewhat like a private club, but everybody is welcome, provided they're dressed properly. The crowd is often young, and disco music prevails. It's open Thursday through Tuesday from 10pm to 4am, but the action usually doesn't begin until after midnight.

THE BAR SCENE

Want more in the way of nightlife? All right, but be warned: The Venetian nightclub owners may sock it to you when they present the bill.

Bar ai Speci

In the Hotel Panada, calle dei Specchieri 646. ☎ **5209088**. Vaporetto: San Marco.

Bar ai Speci is a charming corner bar located only a short walk from St. Mark's Basilica. Its richly grained paneling is offset by dozens of antique mirrors, each different, whose glittering surfaces reflect the rows of champagne and scotch bottles and the clustered groups of Biedermeier chairs. The bar is open to the public Tuesday through Sunday from 4:30pm to midnight; on Monday only hotel guests may use it. Drinks cost 7,000 to 9,000 lire ($4.40 to $5.65).

Bar Ducale

San Marco 2354, calle delle Ostreghe. ☎ **5210002**. Vaporetto: San Marco.

Bar Ducale occupies a tiny corner of a building near a bridge over a narrow canal. Customers stand at the zinc bar facing the carved 19th-century Gothic-reproduction shelves. A specialty is the mimosa cocktail, but the sandwiches are also one of the bar's attractions. The ebullient owner learned his craft at Harry's Bar before going into business for himself. Today his small establishment is usually mobbed every day of the week. It's ideal for an early-evening apéritif as you stroll about. Open daily from 7am to 11pm (closed Tuesday in winter). Whisky begins at 5,500 lire ($3.45); beer, at 3,000 lire ($1.90).

Do Leoni

In the Londra Palace Hotel, riva degli Schiavoni 4171. ☎ **5200533**. Vaporetto: San Zaccaria.

The hotel's exclusive restaurant has already been recommended (see "Dining" in Chapter 13). Here, the interior is a rich blend of scarlet-and-gold carpeting with a motif of lions, English pub–style furniture, and Louis XVI–style chairs, along with plenty of exposed mahogany. The view is of a 19th-century bronze statue, the lagoon, and the foot traffic along the Grand Canal. Hours are daily from 9am to 1am. A whisky starts at 8,000 lire ($5).

Fiddler's Elbow

Cannaregio 3847. ☎ **5239930.** Vaporetto: Ca' d'Oro.

Five minutes from the Rialto Bridge, this pub—called Irish pub by the Venetians—is run by the same people who also operate the equally popular Fiddler's Elbow in both Florence and Rome. Since its opening late in 1992, it has become one of Venice's most popular watering holes. A half-pint of Guinness costs 3,500 lire ($2.20), a full pint going for 6,000 lire ($3.75). Hours are daily from 5pm to 12:30am.

Harry's Bar

Calle Vallaresso 1323. ☎ **5285777.** Vaporetto: San Marco.

The single most famous of all the watering holes of Ernest Hemingway, Harry's Bar is known for inventing its own drinks and exporting them around the world. It is also said that carpaccio, the delicate raw-beef dish, was also invented here. Devotees say that Harry's makes the best Bellini (champagne and peach juice) of any bar in the world. A libation costs 15,300 lire ($9.60), although many oldtime visitors still prefer a vodka martini at 11,600 lire ($7.25). Harry's Bar is now found around the world, from Munich to Los Angeles, from Paris to Rome, but this is the original bar carrying this moniker. Except for a restaurant, Harry Cipriani, in New York City, the other bars are unauthorized copies of the Venetian bar. In Venice, the bar is a Venetian tradition and landmark, not quite as famous as the Basilica di San Marco, but almost. Celebrities frequent the place during the various film and art festivals. Hours are Tuesday through Sunday from noon to 11pm.

Linea d'Ombra

Fondamenta delle Zattere, Dorsoduro 19. ☎ **5285259.** Vaporetto: Salute.

Venice, to the surprise of many of its visitors, has few real nightclubs. However, a good piano bar with a restaurant is found at Linea d'Ombra. It has a terrace that overlooks the Canale della Giudecca. A pianist sings international songs, and if the night is right, it can make for one of the more romantic evenings in Venice. Drinkers and diners are treated to a view of the island of San Giorgio. You should reserve a table if you want to dine. The restaurant is open Monday, Tuesday, and Thursday through Saturday from 12:30 to 2:30pm and 8 to 10:30pm, and Sunday from 12:30 to 2:30pm; the bar is open daily from 8am to 2am. Meals run 50,000–70,000 lire ($31.25–$43.75); drinks are 7,000–12,000 lire ($4.40–$7.50).

Martini Scala Club

Campo San Fantin 1980. ☎ **5224121.** Vaporetto: San Marco.

Martini Scala Club is an elegant restaurant with a piano bar and has functioned as some kind of an inn, in one manifestation or another, since 1724. You can enjoy its food and wine until 2am—it's the only kitchen in Venice that stays open late. You can order such dishes as smoked goose breast with grapefruit and arugula, fresh salmon with black butter and olives, or gnocchi (dumplings) with butter and sage.

Impressions

I'm glad to find that you dislike Venice because I thought it detestable when we were there both times—once it might be due to insanity but not twice, so I thought it must be my fault.

—Virginia Woolf, letter to Vanessa Bell, April 25, 1913

After 10pm, you can come here to enjoy the piano bar. It's possible to order drinks without having food. The restaurant is open year round, daily except Tuesday from 7pm to 2am. Meals average 100,000 lire ($62.50) each. The bar is open daily except Tuesday from 10pm to 3am. Whisky soda costs 12,000 lire ($7.50).

WINE BARS

Cantina Do Spade
San Polo 860. ☎ **5210574.** Vaporetto: Rialto.

This historic wine bar beneath an arcade near the main fish and fruit market of Venice dates from 1475, and was once frequented by Casanova. Venetians call it a *bacaro* instead of a wine bar. The place is completely rustic and barebone, but has its devotees who come here to order the equivalent of Spanish tapas, which the Italians call *chicchetti.* Although there's no menu, the kitchen will occasionally turn out typical Venetian fare. Many diners prefer to order one of 250 different sandwiches the kitchen is usually willing to prepare. Often in-season game dishes, including boar, deer, or reindeer are served, but don't count on this. Venetians delight in the 220 different types of wine, costing from 1,000 to 4,000 lire (65¢ to $2.50) per glass. The place is really a local favorite, and has been for centuries, and unless you appreciate this particular type of Venice institution, you'll find far more glamorous spots elsewhere, such as Harry's Bar. Meals cost from 20,000 lire ($12.50). Hours are Monday through Saturday from 9am to 3pm and 5 to 11pm.

✪ Mascarete
Calle Lunga Santa Maria Formosa 5138, Castello. ☎ **5230744.** Vaporetto: Rialto.

This wine bar was established in 1995. The focus is on dozens of bottles of Italian wines, many from the Veneto region, which sell for between 1,500 lire (95¢) and 4,000 lire ($2.50) a glass, depending on the vintage. There's only room for 20 persons, seated at cramped tables in an old Venetian building, but if you're hungry, you can order simple platters of snack-style food (prosciutto, cheese plates, and other dishes) priced at from 6,000 to 10,000 lire ($3.75 to $6.25), depending on what's available that day.

✪ Vino Vino
Calle del Cafetier 2007A. ☎ **5237027.** Vaporetto: San Marco.

This wine bar has a selection of more than 250 Italian and imported wines. Vino Vino attracts a varied clientele. It wouldn't be unusual to see a Venetian countess sipping Prosecco near a gondolier eating a meal. This place is loved by everyone from snobs to young people to tourists with little money left. It offers wines by the bottle or glass, including Italian grappas. Dishes of Venetian popular cuisine are served, including pastas, beans, baccalà (codfish), and polenta. The two rooms are always jammed like a vaporetto in rush hour, and there's take-away service if you can't find a place. The bar is open daily from 10am to 7pm, with glasses of wine costing from 1,200–8,000 lire (75¢–$5). The restaurant serves lunch Thursday through Monday from noon to 2:30pm and dinner nightly from 7 to 11:30pm. Main courses range from 14,000 to 21,000 lire ($8.75 to $13.15).

CAFES

Florian

Piazza San Marco 56–59. ☎ **5285338.** Vaporetto: San Marco.

The most famous café is the Florian. The Florian was built in 1720 and it remains romantically and elegantly decorated—pure Venetian salons with red plush banquettes, intricate and elaborate murals under glass, and art nouveau lighting and lamps. It's considered the most fashionable and aristocratic rendezvous in Venice: The Florian roster of customers has included such figures as Casanova, Lord Byron, Goethe, Canova, de Musset, and Madame de Stael. Special cocktails include a Bellini or a mimosa. It's possible to have a light lunch at Florian daily from noon to 3pm, costing from 30,000 to 60,000 lire ($18.75 to $37.50), or an English tea from 3 to 6pm, when you can select from a choice of pastries, ice creams, and cakes. Open Thursday through Tuesday from 9am to midnight. An espresso is 6,000 lire ($3.75); long drinks cost 19,000 lire ($11.90), plus 5,000 lire ($3.15) extra if you drink on the square when music is playing, from April to October only.

Gran Caffè Lavena

Piazza San Marco 133–134. ☎ **5224070.**

Gran Caffè Lavena is a popular but intimate café under the arcades of piazza San Marco. The establishment was frequented by Richard Wagner during his stay in Venice; he composed some of his greatest operas here. It has one of the most beautifully ornate glass chandeliers in town—the kind you'll love even if you hate Venetian glass. They hang from the ceiling between the iron rails of an upper-level balcony. The most interesting tables are near the plate-glass window in front, although there's plenty of room at the stand-up bar as well. Open daily from 9am to midnight. Coffee costs 1,400 lire (90¢) if you're standing, 5,500 lire ($3.45) if you're sitting at a table. And there's a music surcharge of 4,000 lire ($2.50).

Quadri

Piazza San Marco 120–124. ☎ **5289299.** Vaporetto: San Marco.

Quadri, previously recommended as a restaurant, stands on the opposite side of the square from the Florian. It, too, is elegantly decorated in antique style. It should be, as it was founded in 1638. Wagner used to drop in for a drink when he was working on *Tristan und Isolde*. Its prices are virtually the same as at the Florian, and it, too, imposes that surcharge on drinks ordered during concert periods. The bar was a favorite with the Austrians during their long-ago occupation. Open October to June, Tuesday through Sunday from 9am to midnight; July to September, daily from 9am to midnight. A whisky costs 15,000 lire ($9.40); coffee 5,500 lire ($3.45). There's a music surcharge of 4,000 lire ($2.50).

ICE CREAM

Gelateria Paolin

Campo San Stefano 2962A. ☎ **5225576.**

For many, strolling to Gelateria Paolin (set in a large colorful square), and ordering some of the tastiest ice cream (gelato) in Venice is nightlife enough. That's the way many a Venetian spends the evening in the summer. This ice-cream parlor (gelateria) stands on the corner of the busy square. You can order your ice cream to go or eat it at one of the sidewalk tables. Many interesting flavors are offered, including pistachio. However, you may want to be adventurous and try something known as Malaga. Open spring through fall, Tuesday through Sunday from 7:30am to 11:30pm; in winter, Tuesday through Sunday from 7:30am to 8:30pm (closed Dec 15–Jan 30). Ice cream costs 2,000 to 13,000 lire ($1.25 to $8.15).

GAMBLING

Casino Municipale

Lungomare G. Marconi 4, Lido. ☎ **5297111.** Admission 18,000 lire ($11.25).

If you want to risk your luck and your lire, you can take a vaporetto ride on the Casino Express, which leaves from the stops at the railway station, piazzale Roma, and piazzetta San Marco, and delivers you to the landing dock of the Casino Municipale. The Italian government wisely forbids its nationals to cross the threshold unless they work here, so bring your passport. The building itself is foreboding, almost as if it could have been inspired by Mussolini-era architects. However, the action gets hotter once you step inside. At the casino, you can play blackjack, roulette, baccarat, or whatever. You can also dine, drink at the bar, or enjoy a floor show. Open June through September, daily from 4pm to 2:30am.

Vendramin-Calergi Palace

Cannaregio 2040, Strada Nuova. ☎ **5297111.** Admission 18,000 lire ($11.25). Vaporetto: San Marcuola.

From October to May, the casino action moves to the Vendramin-Calergi Palace. Incidentally, in 1883 Wagner died in this house, which opens onto the Grand Canal. Open daily from 3pm to 2:30am.

7 Easy Excursions

MURANO

On this island **glassblowers** have for centuries performed oral gymnastics to turn out those fantastic chandeliers that Victorian ladies used to prize so highly. They also produce heavily ornamented glasses so ruby-red or so indigo-blue you can't tell if you're drinking blackberry juice or pure wood-grain. Happily, the glassblowers are still plying their trade, although increasing competition—notably from Sweden—has compelled a greater degree of sophistication in design.

Murano remains the chief expedition from Venice, but it's not the most beautiful nearby island. (Burano and Torcello are far more attractive.)

You can combine a tour of Murano with a trip along the lagoon. To reach it, take vaporetto no. 5 at riva degli Schiavoni, a short walk from piazzetta San Marco. The boat docks at the landing platform at Murano where—lo and behold—the first furnace awaits conveniently. It's best to go Monday through Friday from 10am to noon if you want to see some glassblowing action.

WHAT TO SEE & DO

As you stroll through Murano, you'll find that the factory owners are only too glad to let you come in and see their age-old crafts. These managers aren't altogether altruistic, of course. While browsing through the showrooms, you'll need stiff resistance to keep the salespeople at bay. And it's possible to bargain down the initial price quoted. Don't—repeat *don't*—pay the marked price on any item. That's merely the figure at which to open negotiations.

An exception to that is made-on-the-spot souvenirs, which are turned out at Murano. For example, you might want to purchase a horse streaked with blue. The artisan takes a piece of incandescent glass, huffs, puffs, rolls it, shapes it, snips it, and behold—he has shaped a horse. The showrooms of Murano also contain a fine assortment of Venetian crystal beads, available in every hue of the rainbow. You may find some of the best work to be the experiments of apprentices.

While on the island, you can visit the Renaissance palazzo that houses the **Museo Vetrario di Murano,** fondamenta Giustinian (☎ 739586). From April through October, it's open Monday, Tuesday, and Thursday through Saturday from 10am to 5pm. Off-season, it's open Monday, Tuesday, and Thursday through Saturday from 10am to 4pm. Admission costs 5,000 lire ($3.15) for adults and 3,000 lire ($1.90) for children. Inside is a spectacular collection of Venetian glass.

The **Church of San Pietro Martire** dates from the 1300s but was rebuilt in 1511. Richly decorated, with paintings by Tintoretto and Veronese, it offers a respite from the glass factories. Its proud possession is a *Madonna and Child Enthroned* by Giovanni Bellini, plus two superb altarpieces by the same master. The church lies right before the junction with Murano's Grand Canal, about 250 yards from the vaporetto landing stage. It opens daily from 8am to noon and 4 to 7pm.

Even more notable is **Santi Maria e Donato,** campo San Donato, which is open daily from 8am to noon and 4 to 7pm. This building is a stellar example of the Venetian Byzantine style, in spite of its 19th-century restoration. It dates from the 7th century but was reconstructed in the 1100s. The interior is known for its mosaic floor—a parade of peacocks and eagles, as well as other creatures—and a 15th-century ship's-keel ceiling. Over the apse is an outstanding mosaic of the Virgin against a gold background, which dates from the early 1200s.

You can take the same ferry back, but why not get off at fondamenta Nuove, then slowly stroll through an unheralded section of the city that will bring you closer to the quiet charm and serene beauty of Venice?

WHERE TO DINE

Inexpensive

Ai Vetrai

Fondamenta Manin 29. ☎ **739293.** Reservations recommended. Main courses 14,000–28,000 lire ($8.75–$17.50). AE, DC, MC, V. Fri–Wed 11am–4pm. Vaporetto: 5 to Murano. VENETIAN.

Ai Vetrai entertains and nourishes its guests in a large room not far from the Canale dei Vetrai. If you're looking for fish prepared in the local style, with what might be called the widest selection in Murano, this is it. Most varieties of crustaceans and gilled creatures are available on the spot. However, if you phone ahead and order food for a large party, as the Venetians sometimes do, the owners will prepare what they call "a noble fish" on special command. You might begin with spaghetti in a green clam sauce.

Al Corallo

Fondamenta dei Vetrai 73. ☎ **739080.** Reservations not necessary. Main courses 8,000–25,000 lire ($5–$15.65). AE, DC, MC, V. Wed–Mon noon–3pm and 7–8:30pm. Closed mid-Dec to mid-Jan (dates vary). Vaporetto: 5 to Murano. VENETIAN.

Small and intimate, and somewhat isolated from the bustle and hurry of the larger islands of Venice, this family-run restaurant is one of the most well-established of the eateries on the island of Murano. Very little English is spoken, but it's usually filled with a wide variety of clients from all walks of life. Specialties are typically Venetian, and the service is polite. Locals, many of them workers at the nearby glass factories, choose this place for a well-deserved meal after a morning of hard physical labor, and blend with the tourists. The menu changes daily, according to whatever's available in the local markets.

BURANO

Burano became world famous as a center of **lacemaking,** a craft that reached its pinnacle in the 18th century (recall Venetian point?). The visitor who can spare a morning to visit this island will be rewarded with a charming little fishing village far removed in spirit from the grandeur of Venice, but lying half an hour away by ferry. Boats leave from fondamente Nuove, which overlooks the Venetian graveyard (which is well worth the trip all on its own). To reach fondamente Nuove, take vaporetto no. 5 from riva degli Schiavoni. Get off at fondamente Nuove and catch a separate boat, Line 12, marked Burano.

WHAT TO SEE & DO

Once at Burano, you'll discover that the houses of the islanders come in varied colors—sienna, robin's-egg or cobalt blue, barn-red, butterscotch, grass green. If you need a focal point for your excursion, it should be the **Scuola Merietti** in the center of the fishing village at piazza Baldassare Galuppi. The Burano School of Lace was founded in 1872 as part of a resurgence movement aimed at restoring the age-old craft that had earlier declined, giving way to such other lacemaking centers as Chantilly and Bruges. By going up to the second floor you can see the lacemakers, mostly young women, at painstaking work, and can purchase hand-embroidered or handmade-lace items.

After visiting the lace school, you can walk across the square to the **Duomo** and its leaning campanile (inside, look for the *Crucifixion* by Tiepolo). However, do so at once, because the bell tower is leaning so precariously it looks as if it may topple at any moment.

WHERE TO DINE

Inexpensive

Ostaria ai Pescatori

Piazza Baldassare Galuppi 371. ☎ **730650.** Reservations recommended. Main courses 17,000–35,000 lire ($10.65–$21.90). AE, MC, V. Thurs–Tues noon–3pm and 6–9:30pm. Closed Jan. Vaporetto: Line 12 from Murano. SEAFOOD.

The family that pools its efforts to run this well-known restaurant maintains strong friendships with the local fishers, who often reserve the best parts of their daily catch for preparation in the kitchen here. The cooking is performed by the matriarch of an extended family. The place has gained a reputation as the preserver of a type of simple and unpretentious restaurant unique to Burano. Locals in

---

Impressions

An overcrowded little island where the women make splendid lace and the men make children.

—Ernest Hemingway on Burano

Easy Excursions from Venice

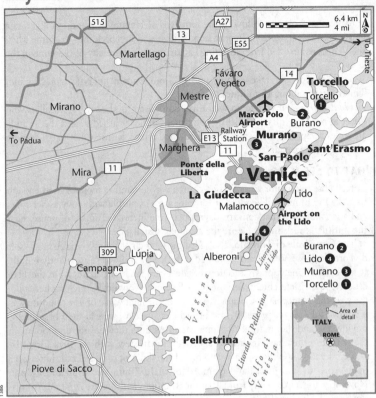

dialect call it a *buranello*. Clients often take the vaporetto from other sections of Venice (the restaurant lies close to the boat landing) to eat at the plain wooden tables set up either indoors or on the small square in front. Specialties feature all the staples of the Venetian seaside diet, including fish soup, risotto di pesce, pasta seafarer's style, tagliolini in squid ink, and a wide range of crustaceans, plus grilled, fried, or baked fish. Your meal might also include a bottle of fruity wine from the region.

Trattoria de Romano

Via Baldassare Galuppi 223. ☎ **730030**. Reservations recommended. Main courses 14,000–24,000 lire ($8.75–$15). AE, MC, V. Wed–Mon noon–2:30pm and 7–8:30pm. Closed Dec 15–Feb 15. Vaporetto: Line 12 from Murano. VENETIAN.

If you're on the island at mealtime, you may want to join a long line of people who have patronized the rather simple-looking *caratteristico* Trattoria de Romano, which is around the corner from the lace school. You can enjoy a superb dinner here, which might consist of risotto di pesce (the Italian version of the Valencian paella), followed by fritto misto di pesce, a mixed fish fry from the Adriatic, with savory bits of mullet, squid, and shrimp. The tab might also include refreshing wine, fresh fruit, and service.

TORCELLO

Of all the islands of the lagoon, Torcello—the so-called Mother of Venice—offers the most charm. If Burano is behind the times, Torcello is positively antediluvian. You can follow in the footsteps of Hemingway and stroll across a grassy meadow, traverse an ancient stone bridge, and step back into that time when the Venetians first fled from invading barbarians to create a city of Neptune in the lagoon.

To reach Torcello, take vaporetto no. 12 from fondamenta Nuova on Murano. The trip takes about 45 minutes.

Final Warning: If you go on your own, don't listen to the savvy gondoliers who hover at the ferry quay. They'll tell you that both the cathedral and the locanda are miles away. Actually, they're both reached after a leisurely 12- to 15-minute stroll along the canal.

WHAT TO SEE & DO

Torcello has two major attractions: a church with Byzantine mosaics good enough to make the Empress Theodora at Ravenna turn as purple with envy as her robe, and a *locanda* (inn) that converts daytrippers into inebriated angels of praise. First the spiritual nourishment before the alcoholic sustenance.

The **Cattedrale di Torcello,** also called the Church of Santa Maria Assunta Isola di Torçello (☎ 730084), was founded in A.D. 639 and was subsequently rebuilt. It stands in a lonely, grassy meadow beside a campanile that dates from the 11th century. It is visited chiefly because of its Byzantine mosaics. Clutching her child, the weeping Madonna in the apse is a magnificent sight while on the opposite wall is a powerful *Last Judgment.* Byzantine artisans, it seems, were at their best in portraying hell and damnation. At Santa Maria Assunta they do not disappoint. In their Inferno they have re-created a virtual human stew with the fires stirred by wicked demons. Reptiles slide in and out of the skulls of cannibalized sinners. It's open April to October, daily from 10am to 12:30pm and 2:30 to 6:30pm; November to March, daily from 10am to 12:30pm and 2:30 to 5:30pm. Admission costs 1,500 lire (95¢).

WHERE TO DINE
Moderate

Locanda Cipriani
Piazza S. Fosca 29. ☎ **730150.** Reservations recommended. Main courses 28,000–45,000 lire ($17.50–$28.15). AE, DC, MC, V. Wed–Mon noon–3pm and 7–10pm. Closed Dec 1–Feb 28. VENETIAN.

Locanda Cipriani, located just across from the church, is an inn extraordinaire. The term *locanda* usually denotes an inexpensive lodging, rated under the lowliest pensione. However, that's not the case at Cipriani. This country inn is well appointed, with an open-air dining loggia. The chef features a number of high-priced dishes. Specialties include cannelloni, a most savory fish soup, and a rice pilaf. For an appetizer, try the gnocchi, a Roman-inspired dish made with a semolina base. Most guests prefer the fresh fish from the Adriatic. The place, originally a 19th-century house, was bought by members of the Cipriani family (famous for Harry's Bar) in 1938. The place is run by Carla Cipriani, sister of Arrigo, of Harry's Bar.

15

Verona, Padua (Padova) & Vicenza

Tearing yourself away from the piazza San Marco in Venice is a task for those of iron will. However, Venice doesn't have a regional monopoly on art or tourist treasures. Of the cities of interest easily reached from Venice, three tower above the rest. They are Verona, the home of the eternal lovers, Romeo and Juliet; Padua, the city of Mantegna, with frescoes by Giotto; and Vicenza, city of Palladio, with streets of Renaissance palazzi and villa-studded hills. The miracle of all these cities is that Venice did not siphon off their creative drive completely, although the Serene Republic dominated them for centuries.

A DRIVING TOUR

Day 1   Leave Venice (as hard as that is to do) and drive west along autostrada A4 to Padua, a distance of 25 miles. In Padua visit at least Cappella degli Scrovegni and Basilica di'Sant'Antonio

☕ **TAKE A BREAK**   Caffè Pedrocchi, piazzetta Pedrocchi 15 (☎ 8752020), is the most famous 19th-century monument in Padua. Designed by Giuseppe Jappelli in 1831, it stands in the precincts of the university just off piazza Cavour. This coffeehouse is considered "the living room" of Padua.

At the end of the afternoon, you can take Autostrada A4 northwest to the turnoff north to Vicenza, city of Palladio. Overnight there.

Day 2   There are a number of attractions to see in this city, including Teatro Olimpico. A visit will consume most of your day. In the late afternoon you can connect with the autostrada going west to Verona where you'll want to spend at least two nights.

Day 3   While still based in Verona set out to explore its rich architectural and artistic legacy, visiting the Arena, Castellvecchio, Teatro Romano, and Giardino Giusti. You might want to skip such artificially created tourist attractions as the "tomb" or "house" of Juliet, however.

FOOD & WINE

In the northeastern part of the agriculturally rich Po Valley, the Veneto section of Italy is rich in fruit and vegetables. The cuisine is

What's Special About Verona, Padua & Vicenza

Great Towns/Villages

- Verona, one of the most romantic and beautiful of all northern Italian cities, forever associated with the legend of Romeo and Juliet.
- Padua, an art-filled city with Italy's second-oldest university.
- Vicenza, the home of Palladianism, the most influential building style in the history of Western architecture.

Architectural Highlights

- Piazza dei Signori, at Vicenza, a classical square partially designed by Palladia, the open-air "living room" of the city.
- Piazza delle Erbe, Verona, the "square of herbs," a former Roman forum, lined with old houses and towers.

Ancient Monuments

- The Tombs of the Scaligere, Verona, an artistic treasure, mostly 14th century.
- The Roman Arena, Verona, completed in A.D. 30, the third-largest and one of the best-preserved Roman amphitheaters extant.

Church

- The Cappella degli Scrovegni, Padua, visited by art lovers from all over the world who come to see its remarkable cycle of 35 frescoes by Giotto, begun around 1305.

considered tasty but straightforward. Three of the region's most famous dishes are *risi e bisi* (rice and peas); *fegato alla veneziana* (liver and onions), and *baccalà alla vicentina* (codfish) cooked with milk and flavored with anchovies, garlic, and onion to which cinnamon and other spices are added. Radicchio, dark red in color with white markings, is the chief salad of the region, in spite of its slightly bitter taste. *Pasta e fagioli* (made with beans and pasta) is the ideal dish for a cold winter's day.

Some of the most famous wines of the area include Bardolino, a light ruby red color, which is generally dry. With a medium alcohol content, it is one fo the most popular wines of the area, often served with rabbit, chicken, and young pigeon. Soave, W. Somerset Maugham's favorite, is a pale amber yellow wine, with a delicate bouquet and light aroma. It has a velvety flavor. Valpolicella is the third famous wine of the region, and is usually served with all meals, especially roasts. Two varieties of this wine, ordinary quality and superior dry, are bottled. The first is ruby red with a delicate and characteristic bouquet, and the second is an even darker ruby in color, with a light bouquet of bitter almonds.

1 Verona

71 Miles W of Venice, 312 miles NW of Rome

The home of a pair of star-cross'd lovers, Verona was the setting for the most famous love story in the English language, Shakespeare's *Romeo and Juliet*. A long-forgotten editor of an old volume of the bard's plays once wrote: "Verona, so rich in the associations of real history, has even a greater charm for those who would live in the poetry of the past." It's not known if a Romeo or a Juliet ever existed,

Verona, Padua & Vicenza

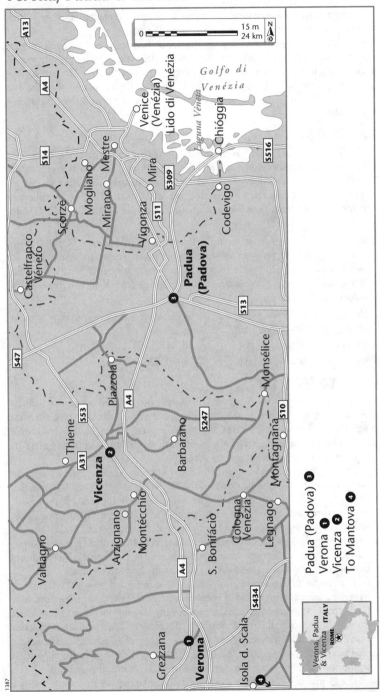

Padua (Padova) ❸
Verona ❶
Vicenza ❷
To Mantova ❹

but the remains of Verona's recorded past are much in evidence today. Its Roman antiquities, for example, are unequaled north of Rome.

In the city's medieval golden age under the despotic, cruel Scaligeri princes, Verona reached the pinnacle of its influence and prestige, developing into a town that, even today, is considered among the great cities of Italy. The best-known member of the ruling Della Scala family, Cangrande I, was a patron of Dante. His sway over Verona has often been compared to that of Lorenzo the Magnificent over Florence.

ESSENTIALS

GETTING THERE   By Train   A total of 37 trains a day make the 2-hour run between Venice and Verona, at 8,800 lire ($5.50) for a one-way ticket. If you're in the west—say, at Milan—there are even more connections, some 40 trains a day, taking 2 hours to reach Verona at a cost of 10,500 lire ($6.55) for a one-way ticket. Six trains arrive from Rome, a 6-hour trip, costing 30,800 lire ($19.25) one-way.

By Bus   APT buses depart from the Porta Nuova FS Station (☎ 8004129) in Verona, serving the province and fanning out to such cities as Brescia, Mantua, and Riva del Garda. If you're coming from Venice, it's better to take the train. From mid-June to mid-September, it's possible to go from Venice to Verona without a change of bus.

By Car   From Venice, take the autostrada (A4) west all the way until you see the signposted cutoff for Verona.

VISITOR INFORMATION   The telephone area code is 045. The tourist information office is at piazza delle Erbe (☎ 8030086).

WHAT TO SEE & DO

Verona lies alongside the Adige River. It's most often visited on a quick half-day excursion (easily reached on the autostrada), but Verona deserves more time. It's meant for wandering and for contemplation. If you're rushed, head first to the old city to begin your explorations. In addition to the sights listed below, there are other attractions that might merit a visit.

Opening onto piazza dei Signori, the handsomest in Verona, is the **Palazzo del Governo,** where Cangrande extended the shelter of his hearth and home to that fleeing Ghibelline, Dante Alighieri. The marble statue in the center of the square, whose expression is as cold as a Dolomite icicle, is of the "divine poet," but unintimidated pigeons perch on his pious head. Facing Dante's back is the late 15th-century **Loggia del Consiglio,** surmounted by five statues. The most attractive building on the square, the loggia is frescoed. Five different arches lead into **piazza dei Signori,** the innermost chamber of the heart of Verona.

The **Arche Scaligere** are outdoor tombs surrounded by highly decorative wrought iron that form a kind of open-air pantheon of the Scaligeri princes. One tomb, that of Cangrande della Scala, rests directly over the door of the Santa Maria Antica Church, which dates from the 12th century. The mausoleum contains many Romanesque features. It's crowned by a copy of an equestrian statue (the original is now at the Castelvecchio). The tomb nearest the door is that of Mastino II; the one behind it—and the most lavish of all—that of Cansignorio.

The ✪ **piazza delle Erbe** is a lively, palace-flanked square that was formerly a Roman forum. Today it's the setting of the fruit and vegetable market as well as milling Veronese, both shoppers and vendors. In the center of the square is a fountain dating from the 14th century and a Roman statue dubbed *The Virgin of Verona*. The pillar at one end of the square, crowned by a chimera, symbolizes the many years that Verona was dominated by the Serenissima. Important buildings and towers include the **House of Merchants,** which dates from the early years of the 14th century. Other interesting structures include the **Gardello Tower,** built by one of the Della Scala princes; the restored former city hall and the **Lamberti Tower,** soaring about 260 feet; the **Maffei Palace,** in the baroque style; and finally, the **Casa Mazzanti.**

From the vegetable market, you can walk down **via Mazzini,** the most fashionable street in Verona, to **piazza Brà,** with its neoclassical town hall and the Renaissance palazzo, the Gran Guardia.

Arena di Verona

Piazza Brà. ☎ **8003204.** Admission 6,000 lire ($3.75). Tues–Sun 8am–6:30pm. Bus: 11, 12, or 21.

The elliptical amphitheater on piazza Brà, which resembles the Colosseum in Rome, dates from the 1st century A.D. Standing today are four arches of the "outer circle" and a complete "inner ring." It is the setting of a summer opera house, usually from mid-July to mid-August. More than 20,000 people are treated to Verdi or Mascagni, for example.

Reservations can be made and tickets purchased at the box office of the arena daily from 9am to 12:30pm and 3 to 5:30pm. Reservations can also be made by letter: enclose a bank draft or money order and indicate the date of performance, the section, and the number of tickets desired. Tickets cost from 35,000 lire ($21.90). Write to Ente Lirico Arena di Verona, piazza Brà 28, 37100 Verona—phone orders are not accepted.

Castelvecchio

Corso Castelvecchio 2. ☎ **594734.** Admission 5,000 lire ($3.15) adults, 3,000 lire ($1.90) students, free for children under 11. Tues–Sun 8am–6:45pm. Bus: 21, 22, 23, 24, 41, or 61.

Built on the order of Cangrande II in the 14th century, the Old Castle is alongside the Adige River (reached by heading out via Roma). It stands near the Ponte Scaligero, the bridge bombed by the Nazis in World War II and subsequently reconstructed. The former seat of the Della Scala family, the restored castle has been turned into an art museum, with important paintings from the Veronese school and works by other masters of northern Italy. On the ground floor are displays of 14th- and 15th-century sculpture, and on the upper floor you'll see masterpieces of painting from the 15th to the 18th century.

In the Sala Monga is Jacopo Bellini's *St. Jerome,* in the desert with his lion and crucifix. Two sisterlike portraits of Saint Catherina and Veneranda by Vittore Carpaccio grace the Sala Rizzardi Allegri. The Bellini family is also represented here by a lyrical *Madonna con Bambino* painted by Giovanni, the master of that subject.

Between the buildings is the most charming equestrian statue I've ever seen, that of Cangrande I, grinning like a buffoon, with a dragon sticking out of his back like a projectile. In the Sala Murari dalla Corte Brà is one of the most beguiling portraits in the castle—Giovanni Francesco Caroto's smiling red-haired boy. In the Sala di Canossa are paintings by Tintoretto, a *Madonna Nursing the Child* and a *Nativity,* and by Veronese, a *Deposition from the Cross* and the *Pala Bevilacqua Lazise.*

In the Sala Bolognese Trevenzuoli is a rare self-portrait of Bernardo Strozzi, and in the Sala Avena, among paintings by the most famous Venetian masters such as Gianbattista and Giandomenico Tiepolo and Guardi, hangs an almost satirical portrait of an 18th-century patrician family by Longhi.

Church of San Zeno Maggiore

Piazza San Zeno. ☎ **8006120.** Admission is free. Daily 8:30am–noon and 3–8pm. Bus: 11, 12, or 21.

This near-perfect Romanesque church and campanile is graced with a stunning entrance—two pillars supported by puce-colored marble lions and surmounted with a rose window. On either side of the portal are bas-reliefs depicting scenes from the Old and New Testaments, as well as a mythological story portraying Theodoric as a huntsman lured to hell (the king of the Goths defeated Odoacer in Verona). The panels on the bronze doors, nearly 50 in all, are a remarkable achievement of primitive art, sculpted perhaps in the 12th century. They reflect, of course, a naive handling of their subject matter—see John the Baptist's head resting on a platter. The artists express themselves with such candor that they achieve the power of a child's storybook. Inside, the church is divided into a central nave and two aisles. Somber and severe, it contains a major Renaissance work at the main altar, a triptych by Andrea Mantegna, which shows the Madonna and Child enthroned with saints. Although not remarkable in its characterization, it reveals the artist's genius for perspective.

Basilica of Sant'Anastasia

Piazza Sant'Anastasia. ☎ **8004325.** Admission is free. Apr–Oct daily 8am–12:30pm and 4–7pm; Nov–Mar daily 9am–noon and 3–5:30pm. Bus: 70 or 72.

This church dates from the 13th century. Its facade isn't complete, yet nevertheless it is considered the finest representation of Gothic design in Verona. Many artists in the 15th and 16th centuries decorated the interior, and few of the works seem worthy of being singled out for special mention. The exception, however, is the Pellegrini Chapel, with the reliefs in terra-cotta by the Tuscan artist Michele, and the Giusti Chapel, with a fresco by Pisanello representing St. George preparing to face his inevitable dragon. The interior consists of one nave flanked by two aisles, and the overall effect is impressive, especially the patterned floor. As you enter, look for two hunchbacks.

Il Duomo

Piazza del Duomo. ☎ **595627.** Admission is free. Apr–Oct daily 9am–noon and 3–6pm; Nov–Mar daily 9am–noon and 3–5:30pm. Bus: 11, 12, or 21.

The cathedral of Verona is less interesting than San Zeno Maggiore, but it still merits a visit. A blend of the Romanesque and Gothic styles, its facade contains (lower level) 12th-century sculptured reliefs by Nicolaus that depict scenes of Roland and Oliver, two of the legendary dozen knights attending Charlemagne. In the left aisle (first chapel) is an *Assumption* by Titian. The other major work of art is the rood screen in front of the presbytery, with Ionic pillars, designed by Samicheli.

Chiesa di San Fermo

Piazza San Fermo. ☎ **8007287.** Admission is free. Apr–Oct daily 9am–noon and 3–6pm; Nov–Mar daily 9am–noon and 3–5:30pm. Bus: 11, 12 or 21.

This Romanesque church, which dates from the 11th century, forms the foundation of the 14th-century Gothic building that surmounts it. Through time it has been used by both the Benedictines and the Franciscans. The interior is unusual, with a single nave and a splendid roof constructed of wood and exquisitely paneled. The most important work inside is Pisanello's frescoed *Annunciation*, to the left of the main entrance (at the Brenzoni tomb). Delicate and graceful, the work reveals the artist's keen eye for architectural detail and his bizarre animals.

✪ Teatro Romano (Roman Theater) and Museum

Via Rigaste Redentore 2A. ☎ **8000360.** Admission to theater and museum 5,000 lire ($3.15). Theater and museum, Tues–Sun 8:30am–1:30pm. Bus: 31, 32, 33.

The **Teatro Romano,** originally built in the 1st century A.D., now stands in ruins at the foot of St. Peter's Hill. For nearly a quarter of a century a Shakespearean festival has been staged here on certain dates in July and August, and, of course, a unique theater-going experience is to see *Romeo and Juliet* or *Two Gentlemen of Verona* in this setting. The theater is across from the Adige River (take the Ponte di Pietra).

After seeing the remains of the theater, you can take a rickety elevator to the 10th-century Santa Libera Church towering over it. In the cloister of St. Jerome is the **Roman Archeological Museum** (same phone), which has interesting mosaics and Etruscan bronzes.

Giardino Giusti

Via Giardino Giusti. ☎ **8034029.** Admission 5,000 lire ($3.15) adults, 2,000 lire ($1.25) children. Daily 9am–sunset. Bus: 11, 12, or 21.

One of the oldest and most famous gardens in Italy, the Giardino Giusti was created at the end of the 14th century. These well-manicured Italian gardens, studded with cypress trees, form one of the most relaxing and coolest spots in all of Verona for strolls. You can climb all the way to the "monster balcony" for an incomparable view of the city. The romantic Arcadians of the 18th century met here in a setting appropriate to their idealized beliefs.

What we see today is the layout given the gardens by Agostino Giusti. All of its 16th-century characteristics—the grottoes, the statues, the fountains, the mascarons, the box-enclosed flower garden, and the maze—have remained intact. In addition to the flower displays, you can admire the statues by Lorenzo Muttoni and Alessandro Vittoria, interesting Roman remains, and the great cypress mentioned by Goethe.

These gardens have been visited by the illustrious over the centuries, including Addison, de Brosses, Mozart, Goethe, and Emperor Joseph II. The gardens, with their adjacent 16th-century palazzo, form one of Italy's most interesting urban complexes. The maze, constructed with myrtle hedges, faithfully reproduces the 1786 plan of the architect Trezza. Its complicated pattern and small size make it one of the most unusual in Europe.

The gardens lie near the Roman Theater, only a few minutes' walk from the heart of the city.

Tomba di Giulietta

Via Luigi da Porto 5. ☎ **8000361.** Admission 5,000 lire ($3.15). Tues–Sun 8am–1:30pm. Bus: 70.

The so-called Juliet's Tomb is sheltered in a Franciscan monastery entered on via Luigi da Porto, off via del Pontiere. "A grave? O, no, a lantern . . . For here lies Juliet, and her beauty makes this vault a feasting presence full of light." Don't you believe it! Still, the cloisters, near the Adige River, are graceful. Adjoining the tomb is a museum of frescoes, dedicated to G. B. Cavalcaselle.

Casa Giulietta

Via Cappello 23.☎ **8034303.** Admission 5,000 lire ($3.15). Tues–Sun 8am–6:30pm. Bus: 11, 12, 70, 71, 72, or 73.

Juliet's house is a small home with a balcony and a courtyard. With a little bit of imagination, it's not difficult to hear Romeo say: "But, soft! what light through yonder window breaks? It is the east, and Juliet is the sun!"

WHERE TO STAY

Hotel rooms tend to be scarce during the County Fair in March and the opera and theater season in July and August.

VERY EXPENSIVE

✪ Due Torri Hotel Baglioni

Piazza Sant'Anastasia 4, 37121 Verona. ☎ **045/595044.** Fax 045/800130. 81 rms, 10 suites. A/C MINIBAR TV TEL. 530,000 lire ($331.25) double; 1,000,000 lire ($625) suite. Rates include breakfast. AE, DC, MC, V. Parking 35,000 lire ($21.90). Bus: 11, 12, or 21.

Owned and operated by a nationwide chain of upscale hotels (Cogeta Palace Hotels), this establishment was originally built in the 1400s as the private home of the Scaligeri dynasty, a family noted for their hospitality. During the 18th and 19th centuries, the palace hosted many of the VIPs who stopped in Verona during their peregrinations through classical Europe, including Mozart, Goethe, and Tsar Alexander I of Russia. Set in the monumental heart of Verona, the palace was (and still is) among the most visible institutions in town.

Late in the 1950s, a legendary hotelier, the late Enrico Wallner, transformed the palace into a hotel, filling it with a stunning collection of antique furniture. Despite the takeover in 1990 by Cogeta, which richly renovated and restored the entire hotel over a four-year period, many of these antiques remain in both the public areas and bedrooms. They include a splendid range of Directoire, Empire, Louis XVIII, and Biedermeier. Also on the premises are many old oil paintings, a very large lobby sited in what was originally conceived as the palace's courtyard, and a series of well-upholstered salons permeated with charm and serviced by a discreet staff.

Dining/Entertainment: If you order dinner, expect to pay from 65,000 to 110,000 lire ($40.60–$68.75) for a gourmet meal served in the hotel's restaurant, All'Aquila. Menus are based on typical local and light cuisine. This is one of the most distinguished restaurants of Verona, and even if you're not registered as a guest of the hotel, you can visit for a meal. Food is served daily from 12:30 to 2:30pm and 7:30pm to 10pm. The hotel also contains an elegant bar.

Services: 24-hour room service, babysitting, laundry, valet.

✪ Hotel Gabbia d'Oro

Corso Porta Borsari 4A, 37121 Verona. ☎ **045/8003060.** Fax 045/590293. 8 double rms, 19 suite. A/C MINIBAR TV TEL. 210,000–400,000 lire ($131.25–$250) double; from 410,000–908,000 lire ($256.25–$612.50) suite. Buffet breakfast 40,000 lire ($25) per person. AE, DC, MC, V. Parking 25,000 lire ($15.65). Bus: 11, 12, or 21.

One of the newest upscale hotels in town was inaugurated in 1990 within the premises of a historic 18th-century palazzo in Verona's monumental center. Small, discreet, and devoted to the privacy of its guests, it contains many of the building's original grandiose frescoes, its beamed ceiling, and (in the cozy bar area) much of the original carved paneling. Since opening, its clients have included Rita Levi-Montalchino (Italy's winner of the Nobel prize for medicine) and such

Italian actors and singers as Pippo Franco and Francesco di Gregori. They all seem to appreciate the protection and glamour of the hotel's policy of allowing only residents of the hotel within its bar and restaurant, where meals cost from 75,000 lire ($46.90) per person, and where advance reservations are strictly required. Even the hotel's name (which translates as "Golden Cage") seems to enhance its exclusivity. Although there's no garden, the hotel's interior courtyard contains potted plants, flowering shrubs, and tables devoted to drinking and dining facilities during clement weather. Bedrooms contain framed engravings, antique furniture, and—in some cases—narrow balconies with wrought-iron detailing overlooking either the street or the courtyard below.

EXPENSIVE

Hotel Accademia

Via Scala 12, 37121 Verona. ☎ **045/596222.** Fax 045/596222. 92 rms, 5 suites. A/C MINIBAR TV TEL. 375,000 lire ($234.40) double; 500,000 lire ($312.50) suite. Rates include breakfast. AE, DC, MC, V. Parking 25,000 lire ($15.65). Bus: 11, 12, 21.

This is one of the few older hotels of Verona that was custom built as a hotel, rather than being transformed from the premises of a monastery, palazzo, or whatever. Dating from the late 1800s, when it welcomed a goodly percentage of English visitors on their grand tour of Italy, it contains Oriental carpets, a medieval tapestry, and a pair of grandiose marble columns flanking the polished stone stairwell leading to the three floors of bedrooms. Accommodations are conservatively traditional and high-ceilinged. On the premises is a paneled, modern bar at the lobby's far end, a parking garage, and a restaurant (The Accademia) that operates under a separate management. Residents of the hotel receive a 10% discount on meals served within.

MODERATE

Colomba d'Oro

Via C. Cattaneo 10, 37121 Verona. ☎ **045/595300.** Fax 045/594974. 52 rms, 2 suites. A/C MINIBAR TV TEL. 282,000 lire ($176.25) double; 340,000 lire ($212.50) suite. Rates include breakfast. AE, DC, MC, V. Parking 23,000 lire ($14.40). Bus: 11, 12, or 21.

Venerable and historic, the Colomba d'Oro was originally built as a private villa during the 1600s, and was later transformed into a monastery. During the 18th and 19th centuries, it served as a coaching inn for travelers and employees of the postal services, and eventually grew into the large and much-renovated hotel you'll see today. Inside, the building is efficiently organized to accommodate voyagers in an atmosphere somewhere between semitraditional and contemporary. Bedrooms are nicely furnished with matching fabrics and comfortable furniture. Other than breakfast, no meals are served, although because of its central location near the piazza Brà, many restaurants lie nearby.

INEXPENSIVE

Hotel De' Capuleti

Via del Pontiere 26, 37122 Verona. ☎ **045/8000154.** Fax 045/8032970. 42 rms (all with shower). A/C MINIBAR TV TEL. 185,000 lire ($115.65) double. Breakfast 16,000 lire ($10) extra. AE, DC, MC, V. Free parking. Closed Dec 24–Jan 10. Bus: 51 or 70.

Hotel de' Capuleti is an attractively pristine little hotel, conveniently located a few steps from Juliet's (supposed) Tomb and the chapel where she is said to have been married. The reception area has stone floors and leather-covered couches, along with a tastefully renovated decor that's reflected upstairs in the comfortable bedrooms.

WHERE TO DINE
EXPENSIVE

✪ Arche

Via Arche Scaligere 6. ☎ **8007415**. Reservations required. Main courses 32,000–45,000 lire ($20–$28.15). AE, DC, MC, V. Tues–Sat 12:30–2:30pm; Mon–Sat 7:30–9:30pm. Closed Jan. Bus: 11, 12, or 21. ITALIAN.

Classic and elegant, this restaurant in the heart of old Verona is acclaimed by some as the finest in Verona. It's certainly a major rival of Il Desco (see below), which also has its admirers. Giancarlo and Paola Gioco, the owners, insist on market-fresh fish from nearby Chioggia. In a building dating from 1420, this has operated as a restaurant since 1879. Giancarlo is the great-grandson of the creator of the restaurant. Traditional recipes passed down from generation to generation, including some hard-to-find ones discovered in ancient cookbooks, are used in the preparation of the seafood dishes. Steamed, baked, or "however," your fish dish can often be done to your specifications. Many locals begin with antipasti, a soup, pasta, or risotto, before going on to the main dish of the day, perhaps sea bass cooked with those delectable porcini mushrooms. Sole and scampi are among the eternal favorites here. Baked "sea scorpion" with black olives is one of the chef's finest specialties, as is his ravioli stuffed with sea bass and served with a clam sauce. The furnishings are in the Liberty style, the setting enhanced by candlelight and fresh flowers.

MODERATE

Nuovo Marconi

Via Fogge 4. ☎ **591910**. Reservations required. Main courses 28,000–40,000 lire ($17.50–$25); fixed-price menu 55,000 lire ($34.40). AE, DC, MC, V. Mon–Sat 12:30–2:45pm and 8–11:30pm. Bus: 11, 12, or 21. ITALIAN.

Nuovo Marconi is one of the most glamorous restaurants in Verona. It's in an ochre-colored villa with canopies on a narrow street just around the corner from piazza dei Signori. The exterior doors are covered with an art nouveau wrought-iron grill, and the interior has stone columns, silk-shaded lamps, lots of framed paintings, and some of the best food in Verona. The menu reflects the best of traditional and regional dishes, many of which change daily, depending on the availability of ingredients at the market. The kitchen uses only fresh products, whether it be pasta, fish, or meat. In season, the chef likes to specialize in game dishes and the fish antipasti is reason enough to visit. The wine list is updated every six months. Dining is on two levels, and the service is agreeable.

✪ Ristorante il Desco

Via Dietro San Sebastiano 7. ☎ **595358**. Reservations recommended. Main courses 34,000–38,000 lire ($21.25–$23.75); menu dégustation 110,000 lire ($68.75). AE, DC, MC, V. Mon–Sat 12:30–2pm and 7–10pm. Closed Dec 25–26, Jan 1–7. Bus: 11, 12, or 21. ITALIAN.

Ristorante il Desco is a handsome restaurant, among the top two in Verona. It's located in the city's historic center, inside a tastefully renovated palazzo that's one of the civic prides of the city. The restaurant is ably directed by Elia Rizzo. The menu steers closer to the philosophy of nouvelle cuisine than anything else in town.

Specialties make use of the freshest ingredients, including a purée of shrimp, potato pie with mushrooms and black truffles, calamari salad with shallots, tortellini with sea bass, risotto with radicchio and truffles, and tagliolini with fresh mint, lemon, and oranges. The wine cellar is superb, and your sommelier will help you with a choice if you're unfamiliar with regional vintages. The cheese selection is wide ranging, featuring choices from France.

Ristorante 12 Apostoli

Vicolo Corticella San Marco 3. ☎ **596999.** Reservations recommended. Main courses 28,000–36,000 lire ($17.50–$22.50). AE, DC, MC, V. Tues–Sun 12:30–2:30pm and Tues–Sat 7:30–10pm. Closed Jan 2–8 and June 15–July 5. Bus: 2 or 5. ITALIAN.

This is the oldest restaurant in Verona, in business for 250 years. It's a festive place, steeped in tradition, with frescoed walls and two dining rooms separated by brick arches. It's operated by the two Gioco brothers. Giorgio, the artist of the kitchen, changes his menu daily in the best tradition of great chefs, while Franco directs the dining room.

Just consider some of these delicacies: salmon baked in a pastry shell (the fish is marinated the day before, seasoned with garlic and stuffed with scallops); or chicken stuffed with shredded vegetables and cooked in four layers of paper. To begin, I recommend the tempting antipasti alla Scaligera. Another specialty is cotoletta 12 Apostoli. Even the spaghetti alla salmi d'olive is superb. For dessert, try the homemade cake.

INEXPENSIVE

Ristorante Re Teodorico

Piazzale di Castel San Pietro 1. ☎ **8349990.** Reservations required. Main courses 25,000–30,000 lire ($15.65–$18.75). AE, DC, MC, V. Thurs–Tues noon–3pm and 7–10pm. Closed Jan. Bus: 11, 12, or 21. ITALIAN/INTERNATIONAL.

Ristorante Re Teodorico is perched in a choice scenic position, high on a hill at the edge of town, with a panoramic view of Verona and the Adige River. From its entrance, you descend a cypress-lined road to a ledge-hanging restaurant, which is somewhat suggestive of a lavish villa. Tables are set out on a wide flagstone terrace edged with a row of classical columns and an arbor of red, pink, and yellow vines. Specialties include homemade pasta; swordfish with tomatoes, capers, and fresh basil; and chateaubriand with a Béarnaise sauce. The dessert specialty is crêpes suzette.

✪ VeronAntica

Via Sottoriva 10. ☎ **8004124.** Reservations recommended. Main courses 12,000–23,000 lire ($7.50–$14.40). MC, V. Wed–Mon 12:30–2:30pm and 7–10:45pm; July–Aug, 6–10:45pm. Bus: 72 or 73. INTERNATIONAL.

VeronAntica is a distinguished local restaurant housed on the ground floor of a five-story town house. It lies a short block from the river, across from a cobblestone arcade similar to the ones used in the film *Romeo and Juliet*. This place attracts the locals—not just tourists. It's made even more romantic at night by a hanging lantern that dimly illuminates the street. The chef knows how to prepare all the classic Italian dishes as well as some innovative ones too. Try his seafood risotto or turbot with thyme. He also prepares excellent veal escalopes with wild mushrooms. From June through September you can dine on an open-air terrace.

2 Padua (Padova)

25 miles W of Venice, 50 miles E of Verona, 145 miles E of Milan

Padua no longer looks as it did when Burton tamed shrew Taylor in the Zeffirelli adaptation of Shakespeare's *The Taming of the Shrew,* which was set in old Padua. However, it remains a major art center of Venetia. Shakespeare called Padua a "nursery of arts."

Padua is sometimes known as "La Città del Santo" (the city of the saint), a reference to St. Anthony of Padua, who is buried at a basilica that the city dedicated to him. "Il Santo" was an itinerant Franciscan monk who should not be confused with St. Anthony of Egypt, the monastic hermit who could resist all the temptations of the Devil.

ESSENTIALS

GETTING THERE   By Train   The train is best if you're coming from such major transportation hubs as Venice and Milan. Padua lies on the main rail lines between Venice and Milan and Venice and Bologna. Trains depart for or arrive from Venice once very 30 minutes (trip time: 30 minutes), at a one-way cost of 3,200 lire ($2). Trains from Milan arrive or depart every hour (trip time: $2^1/_2$ hours), charging 17,800 lire ($11.15) one way.

By Bus   Buses from Venice arrive every 30 minutes (trip time: 45 minutes), a one-way fare is 4,300 lire ($2.70). There are also connections to Vicenza every 30 minutes (trip time: 30 minutes), charging 4,800 lire ($3).

The local bus station in Padua is at via Trieste 40 (☎ 8206833), near piazza Boschetti, five minutes from the rail station.

By Car   Take the autostrada (A4) west from Venice.

VISITOR INFORMATION   The telephone area code for Padua is 049. The tourist information center is at Stazione Ferrovie Stato (☎ 8752077).

WHAT TO SEE & DO

A university that grew to fame throughout Europe was founded here as early as 1222 (Galileo and the poet Tasso attended). Petrarch also lectured here, and the University of Padua has remained one of the great centers for learning in Italy. Today its buildings are scattered throughout the city. The historic main building of the university is called **Il Bo,** which was the name of an inn with an ox as its sign. The chief entrance to Palazzo Bo is on via Otto Febbraio (☎ 651400). Incidentally, Il Bo was the major font of learning in the heyday of the Venetian Republic. Of particular interest is an anatomy theater, which dates from 1594 and was the first of its kind in Europe. Guided tours of the university are conducted Monday through Friday from 9am to noon and 3 to 5pm, and on Saturday from 9am to noon.

If you're on a tight schedule when you visit Padua, concentrate on the Cappella degli Scrovegni (Giotto frescoes) and the Basilica di San Antonio.

✪ Cappella degli Scrovegni (also Arena Chapel)

In the public gardens off corso Garibaldi. ☎ **650845.** Admission 10,000 lire ($6.25) adults, 7,000 lire ($4.40) children 6–17. Free children 5 and under. Feb–Oct daily 9am–7pm; Nov–Jan daily 9am–6pm. Bus: 3, 8, or 18.

This modest (on the outside) chapel is the best reason for visiting Padua. Sometime around 1305 and 1306 Giotto did a cycle of more than 35 (remarkably well-preserved) frescoes inside, which, along with those at Assisi, form the basis of his claim to fame. Like an illustrated storybook, the frescoes unfold biblical scenes. The third bottom panel (lower level on the right) depicts Judas kissing a most skeptical Christ and is perhaps the most reproduced and widely known panel in the cycle. On the entrance wall is Giotto's *Last Judgment*, in which hell wins out in sheer fascination. The master's representation of the *Vices and Virtues* is bizarre; it reveals the depth of his imagination in personifying the nebulous evil or the elusive good. One of the most dramatic of the panels depicts the raising of Lazarus from the dead. This is a masterfully balanced scene, rhythmically ingenious for its day. The swathed and cadaverous Lazarus, however, looks indecisive as to whether or not he'll rejoin the living.

Chiesa degli Eremitani

Piazza Eremitani 9. ☎ **8750905.** Admission is free (donations accepted). Apr–Sept Mon–Sat 8:15am–noon and 3:30–6:30pm, Sun and religious holidays 9am–noon and 3:30–5:30pm; Oct–Mar Mon–Sat 8:15am–noon and 3:30–5:30pm, Sun and religious holidays 9am–noon and 3:30–5:30pm. Bus: 3, 8, 11, 13, 14, 16, 17, 18, or 22.

One of the tragedies of Padua is that this church was bombed during World War II. Before that time it housed one of the greatest treasures in Italy, the Ovetari Chapel frescoed by Andrea Mantegna. The cycle of frescoes was the first significant work by Mantegna (1431–1506). The church was rebuilt, but, unfortunately, one can't resurrect 15th-century frescoes. Inside, to the right of the main altar, are fragments left after the bombing, a glimpse of what we lost of Mantegna's work. The most interesting fresco saved is a panel depicting the dragging of St. Christopher's body through the streets. Note also the *Assumption of the Virgin*. Mantegna is recommended even to those who don't like "religious painting." Like da Vinci, the artist had a keen eye for architectural detail.

✪ Basilica di Sant'Antonio

Piazza del Santo 11. ☎ **8225000.** Admission is free. Apr–Sept, daily 6:30am–7:45pm; Oct–Mar daily 6:30am–7pm. Bus: 8, 12, 18, or 22.

This building was constructed in the 13th century and dedicated to St. Anthony of Padua, who is interred within. The basilica is a synthesis of styles, with mainly Romanesque and Gothic features. It has eight cupolas. Campanili and minarets combine to give it an Eastern appearance. Inside, it is richly frescoed and decorated, and usually filled with pilgrims devoutly touching the saint's marble tomb. One of the more unusual relics is in the treasury—the seven-centuries-old, still-uncorrupt tongue of St. Anthony.

The great art treasurers are the Donatello bronzes at the main altar, with a realistic *Crucifix* towering over the rest. Seek out, too, the Donatello relief depicting the removal of Christ from the cross (at the back of the high altar), a unified composition that expresses in simple lines and with an unromantic approach, the tragedy of Christ and the sadness of the mourners.

In front of the basilica is one of Italy's best-known statues—this one by Donatello. Donatello broke with the regimentation and rigidity of medievalism in the 15th century by sculpting an undraped *David*. Likewise, in the work in front of the basilica, he restored the lost art of the equestrian statue. Though the man it honors—called Gattamelata—is of little interest to art lovers, the statue is of prime importance. The large horse is realistic, as Donatello was a master of detail. He cleverly directs the eye to the forceful, commanding face of the Venetian military hero. Gattamelata was a dead ringer for the late Laurence Olivier.

Musei Civici di Padova

Piazza Eremitani 8. ☎ **8751153.** Admission included with admission to Cappella degli Scrovegni (see above). Tues–Sun 9am–7pm. Bus: 3, 8, or 18.

This picture gallery is important. It's filled with minor works by major Venetian artists, some of which date from the 14th century. Look for a wooden *Crucifix* by Giotto and two miniatures by Giorgione (Leda and her amorous swan, and a mother and child in a bucolic setting). Other works include Giovanni Bellini's *Portrait of a Young Man* and Jacopo Bellini's miniature *Descent into Limbo*, with its childlike devils. The 15th-century Arras tapestry is also on display. Other works are Veronese's *Martyrdom of St. Primo and St. Feliciano*, plus Tintoretto's *Supper in Simone's House* and his *Crucifixion* (the latter is probably the finest single painting in the gallery).

Palazzo della Ragione

Via 8 Febbraio, between piazza delle Erbe and piazza dell Frutta. ☎ **820-5006.** Admission 7,000 lire ($4.40) adults, 4,000 lire ($2.50) children under 12. Daily 9am–7pm. Bus: 3, 8, or 18.

This "Palace of Law," which dates from the early 13th century, is among the remarkable buildings of northern Italy. Ringed with loggias, and with a roof shaped like the hull of a sailing vessel, it sits in the marketplace of Padua. Climb the steps and enter the grandiose Salone, an assembly hall that's about 270 feet long. In the hall is a gigantic wooden horse that dates from the 15th century. The walls are richly frescoed with symbolic paintings in place of the frescoes by Giotto and his assistants that were destroyed in a fire in 1420.

WHERE TO STAY
MODERATE

Hotel Donatello

Piazza del Santo 102-104, 35123 Padova. ☎ **049/8750634.** Fax 049/8750829. 49 rms, 4 suites. A/C MINIBAR TV TEL. 206,000 lire ($128.75) double; from 326,000 lire ($203.75) suite. Breakfast 17,000 lire ($10.65) extra. AE, DC, MC, V. Parking 28,000 lire ($17.50). Closed Dec 15–Jan 15. Bus: 8, 16, or 18.

Donatello is a renovated hotel with an ideal location near the Basilica of St. Anthony. Its buff-colored facade is pierced by an arched arcade, and the oversize chandeliers of its lobby combine with the checkerboard marble floor for a hospitable ambience. To prepare you for the eventual sight of Padua's famed wooden horse, the management has placed a big illuminated photo of it in the lobby. The rooms are well furnished.

INEXPENSIVE

ⓢ Europa-Zaramella

Largo Europa 9, 35137 Padova. ☎ **049/661200.** Fax 049/661508. 59 rms. A/C MINIBAR TV TEL. 158,000 lire ($98.75) double. Rates include breakfast. AE, DC, MC, V. Parking 20,000 lire ($12.50). Bus: 7, 8, 16, or 18.

Europa-Zaramella was built in the 1960s and remains inviting today. It's located near the Padua post office. The tasteful bedrooms are compact and serviceable and have pastel walls and built-in furnishings. The rooms open onto small balconies.

Public rooms are enhanced by cubist murals, free-form ceramic plaques, and furniture placed in conversational groupings. The American bar is popular, as is the dining room. The Zaramella Restaurant features a good Paduan cuisine, with an emphasis on seafood dishes from the Adriatic. Meals begin at 30,000 lire ($18.75).

Hotel Plaza

Corso Milano 40, 35139 Padova. ☎ **049/656822.** Fax 049/661117. 142 rms, 5 suites. A/C MINIBAR TV TEL. 240,000 lire ($150) double; from 350,000 lire ($218.75) suite. Rates include breakfast. AE, DC, MC, V. Parking 15,000 lire ($9.40). Bus: 3, 8, or 18.

The Plaza is a business hotel with brown ceramic tiles and concrete-trimmed square windows in pairs. Constructed in the 1970s, it was last renovated in 1992. The entrance is under a modern concrete arcade, which leads into a contemporary lobby. Its angular lines are softened with an unusual Oriental needlework tapestry, brown leather couches, and a pair of gilded baroque cherubs. The rooms are comfortable and well decorated. The bar, which you can reach through a stairwell and an upper balcony dotted with modern paintings, is a relaxing place for a drink. There is also a restaurant on the premises, plus a parking garage.

Majestic Hotel Toscanelli

Piazzetta dell'Arco 2, 35122 Padova. ☎ **049/663244.** Fax 049/8760025. 29 rms, 3 suites. A/C MINIBAR TV TEL. 215,000 lire ($134.40) double; from 280,000 lire ($175) suite. Rates include breakfast. AE, DC, MC, V. Parking 22,000 lire ($13.75). Bus: 5, 7, 8, 16, or 18.

Majestic Hotel Toscanelli is in a pastel-pink building on a cobblestone square in the heart of town. Wrought-iron balconies protect the French windows, whose edges are trimmed with stone. There's even a Renaissance well and dozens of potted shrubs in front. Inside, you'll find a breakfast room surrounded by a garden of green plants. The lobby has white marble floors, Oriental rugs, an upper balcony, and a mishmash of old and new. There's also a restaurant in the basement called the Toscanelli. In 1992 a complete overhaul of the bedrooms was completed. Elegant furniture crafted by Tuscan artisans was added, along with mahogany and white marble. Pastel colors predominate in the bedrooms, with traditional Louis XV or Louis XVI decorating styles.

WHERE TO DINE
MODERATE

✪ Belle Parti-Toulà

Via Belle Parti 11. ☎ **8751822.** Reservations required. Main courses 25,000–30,000 lire ($15.65–$18.75). AE, MC, V. Tues–Sat 12:30–2:30pm and 8–10:30pm. Closed Aug. Bus: 6, 7, or 10. INTERNATIONAL/ITALIAN.

Toulà was established in 1982 in a building that had housed an earlier restaurant for over 200 years, under ceiling beams that are at least 500 years old. The age of the physical plant, however, did not stop a team of designers from creating a sensual decor that showcases Italian style at its best. The ground-floor level includes a slick black bar. The main dining area offers the kind of excellent service that this most sophisticated of nationwide restaurant chains is eager to provide.

The palate-pleasing menu items change monthly, but might on any given day include crayfish salad with artichokes; scampi salad with fennel, orange slices, and olives; a salad of radicchio with bacon; a savory salad composed of *bottargha* fish, beans, and celery; filet of beef with a sauce of rosemary and balsamic vinegar; pan-fried filet of veal with black olives; or fresh sea bass baked in a salt crust.

INEXPENSIVE

Ristorante Dotto

Via Squarcione 23. ☎ **8751490.** Reservations not necessary. Main courses 16,000–30,000 lire ($10–$18.75); fixed-price menu 50,000 lire ($31.25). AE, DC, MC, V. Tues–Sun noon–2pm; Tues–Sat 8–10:15pm. Closed Aug 8–20. Bus: 6, 7, or 10. PADUAN.

Ristorante Dotto takes its name from the *dottori* (doctors) of the university for which Padua is famous. The discreet, elegant restaurant is in the heart of the city, suitable not only for an academic or business meal but also for an intimate tête-à-tête dinner. Try their pasta e fagioli, grilled sole, risotto made with fresh asparagus, or the chef's pâté. You could top all this off with a feathery dessert soufflé, the most elaborate of which must be ordered at the beginning of a meal.

A FAMOUS COFFEEHOUSE

✪ Caffè Pedrocchi

Piazzetta Pedrocchi 15. ☎ **8762576.**

Caffè Pedrocchi, located off piazza Cavour, is a neoclassical landmark. It was opened by Antonio Pedrocchi in 1831 and was hailed at the time as the most elegant coffeehouse in Europe. Its green, white, and red rooms reflect the national colors of Italy. On sunny days you might want to sit under one of the two stone porches, architectural oddities in themselves, and in winter you'll have plenty to distract you inside. There, the sprawling bathtub-shaped travertine bar has a brass top and brass lion's feet. The velvet banquettes have maroon upholstery, red-veined marble tables, and Egyptian Revival chairs. And if you tire of all this 19th-century outrageousness, you can retreat to a more conservatively decorated English-style pub on the premises, whose entrance is under a covered arcade a few steps away. Coffee costs 1,400 lire (90¢) at the stand-up bar, 2,600 lire ($1.65) at a table. Drinks begin at 5,500 lire ($3.45) at the bar, 10,000 lire ($6.25) at a table. Although drinks cost more than they would in a lesser café, you haven't heard the heartbeat of Padua until you've been at the Pedrocchi. It's open Tuesday through Sunday from 7:30am to 1am.

3 Vicenza

126 miles E of Milan, 32 miles NE of Verona

In the 16th century, Vicenza was transformed into a virtual laboratory for the architectural experiments of Andrea Palladio, a Paduan who arrived there in 1523. One of the greatest architects of the High Renaissance, he was inspired by the classical art and architecture of ancient Greece and Rome. Palladio peppered the city with palazzi and basilicas, and the surrounding hills with villas for patrician families.

The architect was particularly important to England and America. In the 18th century Robert Adam was especially inspired by him, as reflected by many country homes in England today. Then, through the influence of Adam and others even earlier, the spirit of Palladio was imported across the waves to America (examples include Jefferson's Monticello or plantation homes in the antebellum South). Palladio even lent his name to this style of architecture—"Palladianism"—identified by regularity of form, massive, often imposing size, and an adherence to lines established in ancient Greece and Rome.

ESSENTIALS

GETTING THERE   **By Train**   Most visitors arrive from Venice (trip time: 50 minutes); a one-way ticket costs 5,200 lire ($3.25). Trains also arrive frequently from Padua (trip time: 25 minutes) charging 3,300 lire ($2.05) one way. There are also frequent connections from Milan (trip time: 2 1/2 hours), at 14,100 lire ($8.80) one way.

By Bus   It's best to arrive by train. Once at Vicenza, however, you'll find good bus connections for the province of Vicenza if you'd like to tour the environs. The service is operated by FTV, viale Milano 7 (☎ 223111), to the left as you exit from the rail station.

By Car   From Venice, take the autostrada (A4) west toward Verona, bypassing Padua.

VISITOR INFORMATION   The telephone area code is 0444. The tourist information center is at piazza Matteotti 5 (☎ 320854).

WHAT TO SEE & DO

To introduce yourself to the "world of Palladio," head for ✪ **piazza dei Signori.** In this classical square stands the **Basilica Palladiana**, partially designed by Palladio. The loggias consist of two levels, the lower tier with Doric pillars, the upper with Ionic. In its heyday, this building was much frequented by the aristo-crats among the Vicentinos, who lavishly spent their gold on villas in the neigh-boring hills. They met here in a kind of social fraternity, perhaps to talk about the excessive sums being spent on Palladio-designed or -inspired projects. Originally, the basilica was in the Gothic style, and served as the Palazzo della Ragione (jus-tice). The roof collapsed following a 1945 bombing, but has been subsequently rebuilt. To the side is the Tower of the Piazza, which dates from the 13th century and soars approximately 270 feet high. Across from the basilica is the **Loggia del Capitanio** (guard), designed by Palladio in his waning years. On the square are two pillars, one supporting a chimera, another a saint.

✪ Teatro Olimpico (Olympic Theater)

Piazza Matteotti. ☎ **323781.** Admission 5,000 lire ($3.15) adults, 3,000 lire ($1.90) stu-dents, 1,000 lire (65¢) children. Mar 16–Oct 15, Mon–Sat 9:30am–12:20pm and 3–5:30pm, Sun 9:30am–12:30pm; Oct 16–Mar 15, Mon–Sat 9:30am–12:20pm and 2–4:30pm, Sun 9:30am–12:20pm. Bus: 1 or 7.

The masterpiece and last work of Palladio—ideal for performances of classical plays—is one of the world's greatest theaters still in use. It was completed in 1585, five years after Palladio's death, by Vincenzo Scamozzi, and the curtain went up on the Vicenza première of Sophocles' *Oedipus Rex*. The arena seating area, in the shape of a half moon, is encircled by Corinthian columns and balustrades. The simple proscenium is abutted by the arena. What is ordinarily the curtain in a con-ventional theater is here a permanent facade, U-shaped, with a large central arch and a pair of smaller ones flanking it. The permanent stage setting represents the ancient streets of Thebes, combining architectural detail with trompe l'oeil. Above the arches (to the left and right) are rows of additional classic statuary on pedes-tals or in niches. Over the area is a dome, with trompe-l'oeil clouds and sky, giving the illusion of an outdoor Roman amphitheater.

Museo Civico (City Museum)

In Palazzo Chiericati, piazza Matteotti 37–39. ☎ **321348.** Admission 3,000 lire ($1.90) adults, 2,000 lire ($1.25) children. Tues–Sat 9am–12:30 and 2:15–5pm, Sun 9am–12:30pm. Bus: 1 or 7.

This museum is housed in one of the most outstanding buildings by Palladio. Begun in the mid-16th century, it was not finished until the late 17th century, during the baroque period. Today the palazzo is visited chiefly for its excellent collection of Venetian paintings on the second floor. Works by lesser-known artists—Paolo Veneziano, Bartolomeo Montagna, and Jacopo Bassano—are displayed alongside paintings by such giants as Tintoretto, Veronese, and Tiepolo. Notable items include Tintoretto's *Miracle of St. Augustine*, Veronese's *The Cherub of the Balustrade* and his *Madonna and Child*, and Tiepolo's *Time and Truth*.

Tempio di Santa Corona

Via Santa Corona. ☎ **323644.** Admission is free. Mon 3:30–6pm, Tues–Sun 9:30am–12:15pm and 3:30–6pm. Bus: 1 or 7.

This church was founded in the mid-13th century, designed in the Gothic style. Much altered over the centuries, it should be visited if for no other reason than to see Giovanni Bellini's *Baptism of Christ* (fifth altar on the left). In the left transept, a short distance away, is another of Vicenza's well-known works of art—this one by Veronese, depicting the three Wise Men paying tribute to the Christ child. The high altar with its intricate marble work is also of interest. A visit to Santa Corona is more rewarding than a trek to the Duomo (cathedral), which is only of passing interest.

WHERE TO STAY
MODERATE

Hotel Campo Marzio

Viale Roma 21, 36100 Vicenza. ☎ **0444/545700.** Fax 0444/320495. 35 rms. A/C MINIBAR TV TEL. 240,000–280,000 lire ($150–$175) double. Rates include breakfast. AE, DC, MC, V. Free parking. Bus: 1 or 7.

This contemporary hotel is ideally situated in a peaceful part of the historic center of Vicenza, adjacent to a park. The hotel has undergone complete renovation. The sunny lobby has a conservatively comfortable decor that extends into the bedrooms. A cozy restaurant offers regional dining Monday through Friday.

INEXPENSIVE

⑨ Continental

Viale G. G. Trissino 89, 36100 Vicenza. ☎ **0444/505478.** Fax 0444/513319. 55 rms. MINIBAR TV TEL. 100,000–180,000 lire ($62.50–$112.50) double. Breakfast 15,000 lire ($9.40) extra. AE, DC, MC, V. Free parking. Bus: 3.

Continental is among the best choices for an overnight stopover in a town not known for its hotels. It has been renovated in a modern style and offers comfortably appointed bedrooms. About 70% of the rooms are air-conditioned. The hotel has a good restaurant where meals begin at 25,000 lire ($15.65); however, there's no meal service on Saturday, Sunday, or in August. There is a solarium on the premises.

⑨ Hotel Cristina

Corso San Felice e Fortunato 32, 36100 Vicenza. ☎ **0444/323751.** Fax 0444/543656. 34 rms (all with bath or shower). A/C MINIBAR TV TEL. 170,000 lire ($106.25) double. Rates include buffet breakfast. AE, DC, MC, V. Parking 12,000 lire ($7.50). Bus: 1 or 7.

The well-maintained, contemporary Hotel Cristina is a cozy place near the city center, with an inside courtyard where visitors can park. The decor consists of large amounts of marble and parquet flooring and lots of exposed paneling, coupled with comfortable furniture in the public rooms. The high-ceilinged bedrooms are also well furnished, although some are small. A breakfast buffet is the only meal served.

WHERE TO DINE
MODERATE

○ Cinzia e Valerio

Piazzetta Porta Padova 65-67. ☎ **505213.** Reservations required. Main courses 32,000–52,000 lire ($20–$32.50); fixed-price menu 90,000 lire ($56.25). AE, DC, V. Tues–Sat noon–2:30pm and 7:30–9:30pm. Closed Aug. Bus: 1 or 7. SEAFOOD.

By most accounts, this is the best (and perhaps the most beautiful) restaurant in Vicenza. You'll be greeted by a polite staff and views of masses of seasonal flowers before being ushered into the elegant dining rooms. The house fish specialties are time-tested recipes that originated on the Adriatic coastline. In this particular restaurant, the chef is a woman named Cinzia, and the maitre d'hôtel a man named Valerio—this combination gave the restaurant its name. Your meal might begin with mollusks and shellfish arranged into an artfully elegant platter. Other dishes might include risotto flavored with squid and squid ink, a collection of crab and lobster that might surprise you by its size and weight, and an endless procession of fish that arrives cooked any way you prefer, from Cinzia's ovens.

INEXPENSIVE

Antica Trattoria Tre Visi

Contrà Porti 6. ☎ **324868.** Reservations required. Main courses 18,000–20,000 lire ($11.25–$12.50). AE, DC, MC, V. Tues–Sun 12:30–2:30pm and 7:30–10:30pm. Closed July. Bus: 1 or 7. VICENTINO/INTERNATIONAL.

This restaurant was established as a simple tavern in the early 1600s within a building erected in 1470. After many name changes and variations, it was named "The Three Faces" more than a century ago after the rulers of Austria, Hungary, and Bavaria, whose political influence at the time was very powerful within the Veneto. The decor is in the rustic style, with a fireplace, ceramic wall decorations, baskets of fresh fruit, and tavern chairs. You can see the kitchen from the main dining area. Together with the rich choice of international dishes, you can enjoy a good selection of wines of the Vicenza region. The owner will be pleased to make suggestions and help you with your choice. Featured might be *baccalà* (salt codfish) *alla vicentina*, calves' liver, roast goat, zuppa di fagiole (bean soup), or spaghetti with duck sauce. Another specialty is *capretto alla gambalaro* (goat marinated for four days in a mixture of wine, vinegar, and spices, then roasted). The best-known dessert is *pincha alla vicentina*, the traditional cake of the region, made with yellow flour, raisins, and figs.

Ristorante Grandcaffè Garibaldi

Piazza dei Signori 5. ☎ **544147.** Reservations not necessary. Main courses 16,000–21,000 lire ($10–$13.15). AE, DC, MC, V. Restaurant, Thurs–Tues 12:30–3pm; Thurs–Mon 7:30–11pm. Café, Thurs–Tues 8am–midnight. Bus: 1 or 7. VICENTINO/INTERNATIONAL.

The most impressive café in town has a design worthy of the city of Palladio. In the heartbeat center, it has a wide terrace and ornate ceiling, marble tables, and a long glass case of sandwiches from which you can make a selection before you sit down (the waitress will bring them to your table). In the café, panini (sandwiches)

Città del Palladio

His name was Andrea di Pietro, but his friends called him "Palladio." In time he would become the most prominent architect of the Italian High Renaissance, living and working in his beloved Vicenza which remains, in spite of the destruction of 14 of his buildings during World War II air raids, a living museum to his architectural achievements. (These structures, however, were lavishly photographed and documented before their demise.) In time Vicenza would become known as Città del Palladio. Palladio was actually born in Padua where he was apprenticed to a stone carver, but fled in 1523 to Vicenza where he would live for most of his life, dying there in 1580.

In his youth, Palladio journeyed to Rome where he studied the architecture of the Roman, Vitruvius, who was to have a profound influence on him. Returning to Vicenza, Palladio in time perfected the "Palladian style," with its use of pilasters and a composite structure on a gigantic scale. The "attic" in his design was often surmounted by statues. One critic of European architecture wrote, "The noble design, the perfect proportions, the rhythm, and the logically vertical order invites devotion." Palladio's treatise on architecture, published in four volumes, is required reading for aspiring architects.

By no means was Palladio a genius, in the way the Florentine, Brunelleschi, was. No daring innovator, Palladio was more like an academician who went by the rules. That means that even though all of his buildings were harmonious, there were no surprises in them either.

One of his most acclaimed buildings is Villa Rotonda in Vicenza, a cube with a center circular hall crowned by a dome. On each of the quartet of external sides is a pillared, rectangular portico. The classic features, although dry and masquerading as a temple, captured the public's imagination. This same type of villa was to reappear all over England and America.

The main street of Vicenza, Corso Andrea Palladio, honors its most famous hometown boy, who spent much of his life building villas for the wealthy of his day. The street is a textbook illustration of the great architect's work (or that of his pupils), and a walk along the corso is one of the most memorable in Italy.

cost 4,000 lire ($2.50), or a cappuccino, 3,000 lire ($1.90). Prices are slightly lower if you stand at the bar. On the premises is an upstairs restaurant, with trays of antipasti and arrangements of fresh fruit set up on a central table. The menu's array of familiar Italian specialties is among the best in town.

Scudo di Francia

Contrá Piancoli 4. ☎ **323322.** Reservations recommended. Main courses 18,000–22,000 lire ($11.25–$13.75). AE, DC, MC, V. Tues–Sun noon–2pm; Tues–Sat 8–10pm. Closed Aug 15–25. Bus: 1 or 7. VICENTINO.

This 15th-century palace is a short walk from piazza dei Signori. The restaurant has a sunny decor accented with gilt wall sconces, high ceilings, and a garden visible through its rear windows. Menu choices change frequently, but are likely to include pasta fagiole in the style of the Veneto, ravioli stuffed with pulverized radicchio, risottos flavored with whatever is seasonal at the time, spaghetti with squid, and baccalà alla vicentina (codfish).

Trieste, the Dolomites & South Tyrol

16

The limestone Dolomites are a peculiar mountain formation of the northeastern Italian Alps. Some of their peaks soar to a height of 10,500 feet. One of Europe's greatest natural attractions, the Dolomites are a year-round pleasure destination, with two high seasons: in midsummer, and then in winter when the skiers slide in.

At times the Dolomites form fantastic shapes, combining to create a landscape that looks primordial, with chains of mountains that resemble a giant dragon's teeth. Clefts descend precipitously along jagged rocky walls, while at other points a vast flat tableland—spared by nature's fury—emerges.

The provinces of Trent and Bolzano (Bozen in German) form the Trentino–Alto Adige region. The area is rich in health resorts, attracting many German-speaking visitors to its alpine lakes and mountains. Many of its waters—some of which are radioactive—are said to have curative powers.

South Tyrol is surrounded by the Dolomite Alps. Until 1919 South Tyrol was part of Austria, and even though it today belongs to Italy, it is still very much Tyrolean in character, both in its language (German) and in its dress.

Today the Trentino–Alto Adige region functions with a great deal of autonomy.

Before I proceed to details, readers with an extra day or so to spare may first want to postpone their Dolomite or Tyrolean adventure for a detour to Trieste.

A DRIVING TOUR

Day 1   As you bid a reluctant farewell to Venice with a promise to return, head 72 miles to the northwest to Trieste on the half-moon-shaped Gulf of Trieste which spills into the Adriatic. Wander around the piazza dell'Unità d'Italia and visit the Castello di Miramare and the Grotta Gigante. Overnight in Trieste.

Days 2–3   From Trieste, head northwest into the Dolomites for a 2-day holiday in Cortina d'Ampezzo, taking in its natural attractions. It is both a summer and a winter resort.

Day 4   From Cortina, go along the 68-mile Great Dolomite Road heading west. It's one of the most scenic drives in all of Europe (see below). Overnight in Bolzano.

What's Special About Trieste, the Dolomites & South Tyrol

Great Towns/Villages
- Cortina d'Ampezzo, a splendid mountain town that's the leading ski resort of the Dolomites.
- Trieste, the former major port of the Hapsburg Empire, once the cultural and commercial center of the Adriatic.
- Merano, an old-fashioned spa town, with a rich Tyrolean character.

Religious Shrine
- The Duomo, at Trent (meeting place of the Council of Trent in 1545), in majestic Lombard Romanesque style.

Architectural Highlights
- Piazza dell'Unità d'Italia, Trieste, a neoclassic square of perfect proportions, the largest one in Italy fronting the sea.

Ace Attractions
- Tondi di Faloria, a cable car in Cortina d'Ampezzo that offers the grandest panorama of the Dolomites from its summit at 10,543 feet.
- Grotta Gigante, 9 miles from Trieste, an enormous cavern, considered Italy's most interesting phenomena of speleology.

Museums and Palaces
- Miramare, outside Trieste, former home of Archduke Maximilian, the Hapsburg ruler who became emperor of Mexico.

☕ **TAKE A BREAK**   Birreria Forsterbran, via Goethe 6 in Bolzano (☎ 0471/977243), is favored for its rib-sticking food. The kitchen takes special care with its grilled vegetables and is known for its ravioli with purple-red radicchio. At the piazza Walther, head up the via della Mostra until you reach via Goethe (go right). Hours are Monday to Saturday from 9am to midnight.

Day 5   From Bolzano, head northwest for only 18 miles to Merano, the old capital of Tyrol before Austria lost the region to Italy at the end of World War I. There are no grand attractions here, other than the site and the spa itself where visitors flock to take the "grape cure." Overnight in Merano.

Day 6   Return south to other centers in Italy but budget an overnight stopover if possible in histroic Trent, 36 miles southwest of Bolzano. This is where the Council of Trent met from 1545 to 1563.

FOOD & WINE

The cookery of Trentino and Alto Adige, whose chief towns are Trent and Bolzano, is a land of orchards and vineyards, offering a varied cuisine that is not only pleasing to the taste but colorful on the plate. Austrian and Germanic tradition prevails in the kitchen, although in the decades following the Italian takeover of the region, a more Mediterranean flavor prevails as well. You get not only strudel and würstel, but also ravioli and gnocchi.

Fish from alpine lakes, including eels from Lake Caldaro, add variety. *Arrosti* or roasts, mainly veal, form a mainstay of the diet. Some dishes are simple, such *as omelette di patate e maiale* (filled with lean pork and diced potatoes), but tasty.

Trieste, The Dolomites & South Tyrol

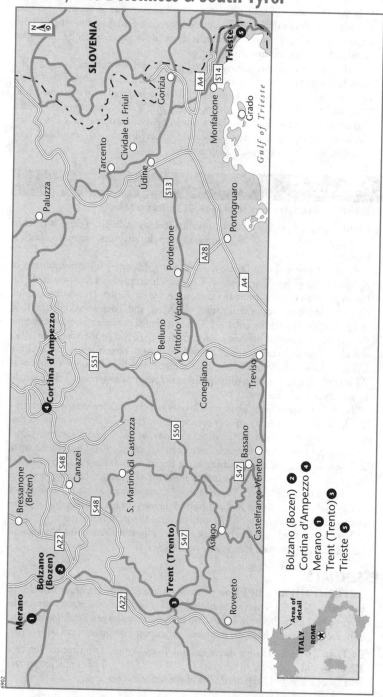

Bolzano (Bozen) ❷
Cortina d'Ampezzo ❹
Merano ❶
Trent (Trento) ❸
Trieste ❺

Area of detail

ITALY
ROME ★

6902

Some 20 varieties of wine exist, including Casteller, one of the most popular, although it is almost sweet (usually served between meals). Lagrein, ranging from a ruby red to a bright garnet in color, is served with special meals by those who enjoy its nutty, slightly aromatic flavor.

A Rheinish wine like Riesling is served with hors d'oeuvres and fish and has a straw yellow color, tending toward pale green, with a nutty, subtle flavor and a characteristic bouquet. Santa Guistina di Bolzano is served with roasts and wild fowl and has a mellow, if a bit sharp, flavor, with a slight undertone of vanilla. Teriano, a pale greenish yellow, has a subtle, persistent bouquet and a dry, harmonious and slightly aromatic flavor, and is served with both soups and hors d'oeuvres and often accompanies alpine fish.

1 Trieste

72 miles NE of Venice, 414 miles NE of Rome, 253 miles E of Milan

On the half-moon Gulf of Trieste, opening into the Adriatic, Trieste is perched at a remote point in Italy, a shimmering, bright city with many neoclassical buildings.

As an Adriatic seaport, Trieste has had a long history, with many changes of ownership. The Hapsburg emperor, Charles VI, declared it a free port in 1719, but by the 20th century it was an ocean outlet for the Austro-Hungarian Empire. Came the war and a secret deal among the Allies, and Trieste was ceded to Italy in 1918. In the late summer of 1943 Trieste again fell to foreign troops—this time the Nazis. The arrival of Tito's army from Yugoslavia in the spring of 1945 changed its destiny once more. A postwar attempt to turn it into a free territory failed. In 1954, after much hassle, the American and British troops withdrew as the Italians marched in, with the stipulation that the much-disputed Trieste would be maintained as a free port.

Trieste has known many glamorous literary associations, particularly in the pre–World War II years. As a stopover on the *Orient Express*, it became a famed destination. Dame Agatha Christie came this way, as did Graham Greene. James Joyce, eloping with Nora Barnacle, arrived in Trieste in 1904. Out of both work and money, Joyce got a job teaching at the Berlitz School. He was to live here for nearly 10 years. He wrote *A Portrait of the Artist as a Young Man* here, and may have begun his masterpiece, *Ulysses,* also. The poet Rainer Maria Rilke also lived in the Trieste area. Author Richard Burton, known for his *Arabian Nights* translations, lived in Trieste from 1871 until he died, about 20 years later.

The Teatro Verdi, the opera house, enjoys a deserved reputation throughout Italy, and many compare it favorably with La Scala.

ESSENTIALS

GETTING THERE **By Plane** Trieste is serviced by an airport at **Ronchi dei Legionari,** 21^1/$_2$ miles northwest of the city. Daily flights on Alitalia connect the airport with Linate airport in Milan (trip time: 50 minutes) and Leonardo da Vinci in Rome (trip time: 1 hour, 10 minutes). For airport information, call 0481/7731.

By Train Trieste lies on a direct rail link from Venice. Trip time to Venice is 2^1/$_2$ hours and a one-way ticket costs 12,700 lire ($7.95). Trains pull into piazza della Libertà (☎ 418207), northwest of the historic center.

By Bus   It's better to fly, drive, or take the train to Trieste. Once there, you'll find a network of local buses servicing the region at corso Cavour (☎ 3360300 for schedules).

By Car   From Venice, continue northeast along autostrada A4 until you reach the end of the line at Trieste.

VISITOR INFORMATION   The telephone area code for Trieste is 040. The tourist information office is at via San Nicolò 20 (☎ 369881).

WHAT TO SEE & DO

The heart of Trieste is the neoclassic ✪ **piazza dell'Unità d'Italia,** said to be the largest square in Italy that fronts the sea. Opening onto the square is the town hall with a clock tower, the Palace of the Government, and the main office of the Lloyd Triestino ship line. Flanking the square are numerous cafés and restaurants, popular at night with the denizens of Trieste who sip an apéritif, then later promenade along the seafront esplanade.

After visiting the main square, you may want to view Trieste from an even better vantage point. If so, head up the hill for another cluster of attractions. You can take an antiquated tram, leaving from piazza Oberdan, getting off at Obelisco. There, at the belvedere, the city of the Adriatic will spread out before you.

Cathedral of San Giusto

Piazza Cattedrale, colle Capitolino. ☎ **309666.** Admission is free. Daily 7am–noon and 4–7pm. Bus: 24.

Dedicated to the patron saint (St. Just) of Trieste, who was martyred in A.D. 303, the basilica atop Colle di San Giusto was consecrated in 1330, incorporating a pair of churches that had been separate until then. The front is in the Romanesque style, enhanced by a rose window. Inside, the nave is flanked by two pairs of aisles. To the left of the main altar are the best of the Byzantine mosaics in Trieste (note especially the blue-robed madonna and her child). The main altar and the chapel to the right contain less interesting mosaics. To the left of the basilica entrance is a small campanile from the 14th century, which you can scale for a view of Trieste and its bay. At its base are preserved the remains of a Roman temple from the 1st century A.D. I prefer to take a taxi to the top, then walk back down, allowing a leisurely 15 minutes. From the basilica you can walk to the nearby Castle of San Giusto.

Castle of San Giusto

Piazza Cattedrale 3. ☎ **308300.** Admission to castle, 1,000 lire (65¢); museum, 2,000 lire ($1.25). Castle, Mar–Oct daily 9am–8pm; off-season daily 9am–5pm. Museum, Tues–Sun 9am–12:45pm. Bus: 24.

Constructed in the 15th century by the Venetians on the site of a Roman fort, this fortress maintained a sharp eye on the bay, watching for unfriendly visitors arriving by sea. From its bastions, panoramic views of Trieste unfold. Inside is a **museum** (☎ 766056) with a collection of arms and armor.

In July and August, open-air performances are staged at the castle.

✪ Castello di Miramare

Viale Miramare, Grignano. ☎ **224143.** Admission to castle, 8,000 lire ($5) adults, free for children 12 and under; grounds, free. Castle, Apr–Sept daily 9am–6pm; off-season daily 9am–4pm. Grounds, Apr–Sept daily 9am–7pm; off-season daily 9am–5pm. Bus: 36 from the center.

Overlooking the Bay of Grignano, this castle was erected by Archduke Maximilian, the brother of Franz Joseph, the Hapsburg emperor of Austria. Maximilian, who married Princess Charlotte of Belgium, was the commander of the Austrian navy in 1854. In an ill-conceived move, he and "Carlotta" sailed to Mexico in 1864, where he became the emperor in an unfortunate reign. He was shot in 1867 in Querétaro, Mexico. His wife lived until 1927 in a château outside Brussels, driven insane by the Mexican episode. You may remember the movie, probably on late at night, about Maximilian and Carlotta, called *Juárez,* starring Bette Davis and Paul Muni. On the ground floor of the castle, you can visit the bedroom of Maximilian (built like a ship's cabin) and that of Charlotte, as well as an impressive receiving room and more parlors, including a chinoiserie salon.

Enveloping the castle are magnificently designed park grounds (Parco di Miramare), ideal for pleasant strolls. In summer, a sound-and-light presentation in the park of the castle depicts Maximilian's tragedy in Mexico. Tickets to the presentation, which is staged in July and August, begin at 15,000 lire ($9.40).

✪ Giant Cave

In the heart of the limestone plateau called Carso that surrounds the city, you can visit the **Grotta Gigante** (☎ 327312), an enormous cavern and one of the most interesting phenomena of speleology. First explored in 1840 via the top ceiling entrance, this huge room, some 380 feet deep, was opened to the public in 1908. It's the biggest single-room cave ever opened to tourists and one of the word's largest underground rooms. A visit can be made only with a guide and takes 40 minutes. Near the entrance is the **Man and Caves Museum,** which is unique in Italy.

Tours of the cave are given Tuesday through Sunday; in March and October, every 30 minutes from 9am to noon and 2 to 5pm; November to February, every hour from 10am to noon and 2:30 to 4:30pm; April to September, every 30 minutes from 9am to noon and 2 to 7pm. Tours cost 9,000 lire ($5.65) for adults, 7,000 lire ($4.40) for children 6 to 12. From April to September you can purchase a ticket for 10,000 lire ($6.25), which includes a return ride on the old-fashioned railway cars of transit line no. 2 to the suburb of Villa Opincina, a round-trip ride to the cave on bus no. 45, and an entrance ticket to the cave, allowing a substantial saving. If you're driving, take strada del Friuli beyond the white marble Victory Lighthouse as far as Prosecco. On the freeway you can take the exit at Prosecco.

WHERE TO STAY
EXPENSIVE

Savoia Excelsior Palace
Riva del Mandracchio 4, 34124 Trieste. ☎ **040/7690.** Fax 040/77733. 146 rms, 5 suites. A/C MINIBAR TV TEL. 290,000–315,000 lire ($181.25–$196.90) double; 365,000 lire ($228.15) suite. Rates include breakfast. AE, DC, MC, V. Parking 40,000 lire ($25). Bus: 8, 9, 17, 18, 24, or 30.

This leading choice stands next to the headquarters of the Lloyd Triestino shipping palazzo, right off piazza dell'Unità d'Italia. Fronting the water, the hotel has witnessed much of the pageantry of Trieste. It was originally built by the Austrians in 1912, and still retains many Hapsburg-style frills in its ornate decor. The rooms in this first-class hotel are equipped with radio and other amenities, and many are furnished in bold modern designs. In respect to the past, there's a tea room, but an American bar adds a contemporary touch. The hotel has an excellent restaurant serving meals for 40,000 to 50,000 lire ($25 to $31.25).

MODERATE

✪ Hotel Duchi d'Aosta

Piazza dell'Unità d'Italia 2, 34121 Trieste. ☎ **040/7600011.** Fax 040/366092. 52 rms, 2 suites. A/C MINIBAR TV TEL. 275,000 lire ($171.90) double; from 560,000 lire ($350.00) suite. AE, DC, MC, V. Parking 37,000 lire ($23.15). Bus: 8, 9, 17, 18, 24, or 30.

This now-glamorous hotel began about 200 years ago as a restaurant for the dock workers who toiled at the nearby wharves. In 1873 one of the most beautiful facades in Trieste was erected to cover the existing building in a white neoclassical shell with delicate carving, arched windows, and a stone crown of heroic sculptures. The design is a lot like that of an 18th-century palace, an effect enhanced by views over the fountains and lamps of the major square of Trieste and the sea beyond it. The hotel was practically rebuilt from the inside in the 1970s. Today the bedrooms are a favorite with business travelers, who appreciate the food in the ground-floor restaurant (see my recommendation for Ristorante Harry's Grill in "Where to Dine," below) and the 19th-century ambience of the Victorian-style public rooms. Each accommodation has a well-stocked minibar concealed behind panels, antiqued walls, a built-in radio, and tasteful furniture.

INEXPENSIVE

⑤ Hotel al Teatro

Capo di piazza G. Bartoli 1, 31131 Trieste. ☎ **040/366220.** Fax 040/366560. 46 rms (34 with bath or shower). TEL. 108,000 lire ($67.50) double without bath, 140,000 lire ($87.50) double with bath. Rates include breakfast. AE, MC, V. Bus: 8, 9, 17, 18, 24, or 30.

The theatrical mask carved into the stone arch above the entrance is an appropriate symbol of a hotel favored by many of Trieste's visiting opera stars. Behind a beige neoclassical facade, a few steps from the seaside panorama of piazza dell'Unità d'Italia and about a 10-minute walk from the station, the hotel has comfortable rooms reached by a stone stairwell. The simply furnished and slightly old-fashioned rooms have parquet floors, lots of space, comfortable but minimal furniture, and a tub or shower in the rooms with bath. The hotel was built in 1830 as a private house and later served as a headquarters of the British army in the aftermath of World War II.

WHERE TO DINE
MODERATE

Al Bragozzo

Riva Nazario Sauro 22. ☎ **303001.** Reservations required. Main courses 20,000–35,000 lire ($12.50–$21.90); fixed-price all-you-can-eat menu 60,000 lire ($37.50). AE, DC, MC, V. Tues–Sat 11am–3pm and 7pm–midnight. Closed June 15–July 1. Bus: 8, 9, or 10. SEAFOOD.

This is one of the best-known fish restaurants at the port, established in the late 1960s within a *Jugenstil* building originally constructed by the Austro-Hungarians as a private house a century ago. The outdoor tables, sheltered by a canopy, are popular in summer, although the paneled dining room is better during inclement weather. Specialties include spaghetti al'Giorgio (with tomatoes and herbs), ravioli stuffed with herbs, and many different preparations of salmon and shrimp.

Ristorante Harry's Grill

In the Hotel Duchi d'Aosta, piazza dell'Unità d'Italia 2. ☎ **7351.** Reservations required. Main courses 28,000–36,000 lire ($17.50–$22.50). AE, DC, MC, V. Mon–Sat 12:15–3pm; daily 7:15–10:30pm. Bus: 8, 9, 17, 18, 24, or 30. INTERNATIONAL.

Set within Trieste's most upscale hotel, this restaurant manages to be both elegant and relaxed at the same time, a venue where a newcomer could have a correctly prepared American-style martini followed by either a simple plate of pasta or a complete, well-orchestrated and rather sumptuous meal. Despite the similarity of its name with other Harry's Bars in other parts of Italy, it is not associated with any of those other establishments in any way. The adjoining bar is one of the most popular rendezvous spots in town, particularly for the business community (although it's not related to any of the many other Harry's restaurants or bars scattered throughout Italy). The big lace-covered curtains complement the paneling, the polished brass, and the chandeliers of blue glass from Murano. In summer, tables are set up in the central traffic-free piazza dell'Unità d'Italia. Illuminated with light from the carriage lamps set into the stonework of the hotel, the outdoor terrace, with a separate area for bar clients, is sheltered by a canopy to protect clients from the Adriatic winds that sometimes sweep in from the sea.

The Mediterranean-inspired cuisine includes fresh shrimp with oil and lemon, pasta and risotto dishes, boiled salmon in sauce, veal in Madeira sauce, butter-fried calves' liver with onions, and an array of beef and fish dishes.

INEXPENSIVE

⑤ Ai Due Triestini

Via Cadorna 10. ☎ **303759.** Reservations not necessary. Main courses 7,500–18,000 lire ($4.70–$11.25). No credit cards. Mon–Sat noon–2:30pm. Closed Sept. Bus: 8, 9, or 10. ITALIAN/AUSTRIAN.

For one of the best luncheon bargains in Trieste, I suggest this tavern behind piazza dell'Unità d'Italia. Run by a husband-and-wife team, the little trattoria covers its tablecloths with plastic and doesn't even bother to print a menu. Some of the cookery leans heavily on the influence of neighboring Austria. Try, for example, spezzatino, chunks of beef in a goulash ragoût, with fresh peas and potatoes. The Hungarian goulash is quite good, as is a rich strudel in the tradition of Budapest. Many diners order beer with their meals, and others come in for a glass of wine, served from one of the casks that line the wall. It's in the center near the sea, near the Stazione Marittima.

⑤ Al Granzo

Piazza Venezia 7. ☎ **306788.** Reservations recommended. Main courses 18,000–26,000 lire ($11.25–$16.25). Fixed-price menus 30,000–65,000 lire ($18–$39). AE, DC, MC, V. Thurs–Tues 12:30–3pm and 7:30–10pm. Bus: 8, 9, or 10. SEAFOOD.

This restaurant was established in 1923, before any of its competitors along the harborfront, by the ancestors of the three brothers who run it today. It began life as a simple fish house, serving seafood stews and grilled fish to the mariners who worked in the then-nearby dockyards. Today, it's one of the leading seafood restaurants of Trieste, serving flavorful versions of that curious mixture of Italian, Austrian, and Yugoslav cuisines known as Triestino. Menu items include *brodetto*, a traditional bouillabaisse spiced with saffron and other herbs; vermicelli with black mussels; and risotto with seafood. You can select any of the fish from a wagon where fresh fish are displayed on a bed of crushed ice. There is an impressive array of fresh *contorni* (vegetables, sold individually), including all the seasonal bounty of nearby farms such as spinach, fresh peas or beans, asparagus, sautéed radicchio, and garlic-enriched rapini. A suitable wine might be a local *Tocai Friulano*, aromatic, harmonious, and somewhat tart, its color a lemon yellow to pale green. Dessert might be homemade strudel.

Antica Trattoria Suban

Via Comici 2, at San Giovanni. ☎ **54368.** Reservations recommended. Main courses 18,000–25,000 lire ($11.25–$15.65). AE, DC, MC, V. Wed–Sun 12:30–2:30pm and 7:30–10pm. Closed Aug 1–18. Bus: 8, 9, or 35. ITALIAN/AUSTRO/HUNGARIAN.

In 1865 the founder established a country tavern with a spacious terrace opening onto a view of the hills 2 miles north of Trieste in the district of San Giovanni. Today the surrounding landscape contains glimpses of the industrial age, but the brick and stone walls, the terrace, and the country feeling are still intact. The cuisine is both hearty and delicate. In the true Triestino tradition, the food offered within this place draws its inspiration from Northeastern Italy, as well as from the far Slavic, Hungarian, and Germanic recesses of what used to be the Austro-Hungarian empire. The chefs concoct specialties from fresh ingredients gathered from surrounding farmlands. Specialties include a flavorful risotto with herbs, basil-flavored crêpes, beef with garlic sauce, a perfectly prepared chicken Kiev, and veal croquettes with Parmesan and egg yolks. The chef's handling of grilled meats, is adept, and the rich pastries are worth the extra calories.

2 Cortina d'Ampezzo

100 miles N of Venice, 82 miles E of Bolzano, 255 miles NE of Milan

This fashionable resort is your best center for exploring the snowy Dolomites. Its reputation as a tourist mecca dates back to before World War I, but its recent growth has been phenomenal. Cortina d'Ampezzo draws throngs of nature lovers in summer and both Olympic-caliber and neophyte skiers in winter. It's a hotel owner's Shangri-la, charging maximum prices in July and August as well as in the three months of winter.

The town *signora* of public relations once insisted; "Just say Cortina has everything." Statements of propaganda chiefs, even when they come from charming Italian ladies, are suspect—but in this case she's nearly right. "Everything," in the Cortina context, means—first and foremost— people of every shape and hue; New York socialites rub elbows in late-night spots with frumpy Bremen hausfraus. Young Austrian men, clad in Loden jackets and stout leather shorts, walk down the streets with feathers in their caps and gleams in their eyes. French women in red ski pants sample Campari at café tables, while the tweedy English sit at rival establishments drinking "tea like mother made."

Then, too, "everything" means location. Cortina is in the middle of a valley ringed by enough Dolomite peaks to cause Hannibal's elephants to throw up their trunks and flee in horror. Regardless of which road you choose for a motor trip, you'll find the scenery rewarding. Third, "everything" means good food. Cortina sets an excellent table, inspired by the cuisine of both Venice and Tyrol. Fourth, "everything" means summer and winter sporting facilities—chiefly golf, horseback riding, curling, tennis, fishing, mountain climbing, skiing, skating, and swimming. The resort not only has an Olympic ice stadium, but an Olympic bobsled track and ski jump (the 1956 Olympics were held at Cortina, publicizing the resort all over the world). In addition, it has a skiing school, a large indoor swimming pool, an Olympic downhill track, and a cross-country track.

Finally, "everything" means top-notch hotels, pensioni, private homes, and even mountain huts for the rugged. The locations, facilities, types of service, price structures, and decor in these establishments vary considerably, but I've never inspected an accommodation here that wasn't clean. Most of the architecture of Cortina, incidentally, seems more appropriate to Zell am See, Austria, than to an Italian town.

ESSENTIALS

GETTING THERE   By Train   Frequent trains run between Venice and Calalzo di Cadore (trip time: 2 hours, 20 minutes), 19 miles south of Cortina. You proceed the rest of the way by bus. For information about schedules, call 0435/32300 in Calalzo.

By Bus   About 14 to 16 buses a day connect Calalzo di Cadore with Cortina. Buses arrive at the Cortina bus station on viale Marconi (☎ 0436/2741 for information about schedules).

By Car   Take Hwy. A13 from Venice to Pian de Vedoia, continuing north along Route 51 all the way to Cortina d'Ampezzo.

VISITOR INFORMATION   The telephone area code for Cortina d'Ampezzo is 0436. The tourist information office is at piazzetta San Francesco 8 (☎ 3231). They can assist you in arranging accommodations (see "Where to Stay," below).

WHAT TO SEE & DO

The Faloria-Cristallo area in the surroundings of Cortina is known for its 18$\frac{1}{2}$ miles of ski slopes and 10 miles of fresh-snow runs.

One of the main attractions in Cortina is to take a cable car "halfway to the stars," as the expression goes. On one of them, at least, you'll be just a yodel away from the pearly gates. It's the **Freccia Nel Cielo** (or "arrow of the sky"). For departure information, phone 0436/5052. Beginning at 9am, departures are every 20 minutes, July 12 to September 28 and December 16 to May 1. A round-trip costs 38,000 lire ($23.75). The first station is Col Druscie at 5,752 feet; the second station, Ra Valles, stands at 8,027 feet; and the top station, Tofana di Mezzo, is at 10,543 feet. At Tofana on a clear day, you can see as far as Venice.

WHERE TO STAY

The **tourist information office,** piazzetta San Francesco 8 (☎ 0436/3231), has a list of all the private homes in Cortina that take in paying guests, lodging them family style for a moderate cost. It's a good opportunity to live with a Dolomite family in comfort and informality. Even though there are nearly 4,700 hotel beds available, it's best to reserve in advance, especially from August 1 to 20 and December 20 to January 7. The tourist office, however, will not personally book you into a private home. Those arrangements you must make independently.

VERY EXPENSIVE

De la Poste

Piazza Roma 14, 32043 Cortina d'Ampezzo. ☎ **0436/4271.** Fax 0436/868435. 77 rms, 3 suites. TV TEL. 640,000 lire ($400) double; 790,000 lire ($493.75) suite. Rates include half-board. AE, DC. Parking 25,000 lire ($15.65). Closed Oct 10–Dec 20. Bus: 1 or 2.

Built like a Tyrolean mountain chalet, this hotel enjoys a central and sunny position in a pedestrian zone. It was originally constructed in the 18th century and opened as a hotel shortly after World War II. It has long been a celebrity favorite, attracting such guests as Hemingway and King Hussein of Jordan and his American-born wife, Queen Noor. Its amenities are top-rate. Open wooden balconies and terraces encircle the building, giving bedrooms sun porches. All

Frommer's Nature Notes

The very existence of the high, snowy peaks of the Dolomites comes as a surprise to foreigners who assume that Italy is an exclusively maritime country of rolling hills, steamy flatlands, and sunflooded harbors. The Dolomites add verticality and alpine charm to Italy, contributing a distinctive high-altitude wealth and Germanic overtones to the peninsula's diversity of cultures. Both the rock of which they're composed (dolomitic limestone) and the peaks themselves are named after an 18th-century French geologist, Déodat Guy Silvani Trancrède Gratet de Domolieu, who spent most of his life analyzing their mineral content. Considered part of the eastern Alps, the Dolomites stretch along the northwestern tier of Italy, following the line of the Austrian border between the valleys of the Adige and the Brenta Rivers. Although the highest peak is the Marmolada (a few feet shy of 11,000 feet above sea level), the range contains an additional 17 peaks within Italian territory which each rise above 10,000 feet. Escaping from the often intense heat of other parts of their country, Italians travel from more low-lying regions to breathe the Dolomites' cool mountain air and to ski and play in such glitteirng resorts as Cortina.

The mountains' mixture of limestone and porphyry, combined with the angle of the rising and setting sun, contributes to dramatic coloration of the mountain peaks. Most pronounced in the morning and at dusk, their colors range from soft pinks to brooding tones of russet. When the sun shines directly overhead, the hues fade to a homogenized and rather dull tone of gray. Fortunately for holidaymakers, trekkers, and skiers, the climate isn't as bone-chillingly cold as it is in the alpine regions of western Italy, and in the Alps of the Tyrol, farther to the north.

As you explore the Dolomites, don't expect lush vegetation. When not camouflaged with snow, the slopes tend to be stony and relatively bare of groundcovers. And don't rush out to gather hillside bouquets for your beloved, as many of the wildflowers (including the Austrian national flower, the edelweiss) are endangered species. Picking flowers or destroying vegetation is punishable with stiff fines.

Obviously, the Dolomites are redolent with natural beauty and trekking opportunities. Networks of hiking trails are clearly marked with painted signs, and any local tourist office (as well as most hotel reception staffs) are well-versed in the length, duration, and degree of difficulty of most treks within their neighborhood. Maps of hiking trails are broadly distributed, and any local tourist office will refer mail to the nearest branch of whatever *Associazione Guide Alpine* which proliferate within the region.

If you decide to ramble across the Dolomites for a day or two, remember to wear stout shoes, warm clothing, and a waterproof jacket (storms erupt quickly in these altitudes), and never leave the relative safety of a designated hiking path. Chair lifts, cog railways, and alpine gondolas usually operate in both summer and winter, and offer an alternative means of enjoying sweeping views over ferociously beautiful mountain scenery. Networks of hiking trails usually radiate outward from the top and bottom of most mechanical lifts, and rustically charming *refugios* (mountain huts, sometimes with dining and overnight facilities) offer the opportunity for overnight stay.

the bedrooms have double windows and French doors, chintz draperies and bedspreads, and built-in wardrobes—many homelike touches. About 45% of the rooms have minibars. The get-acquainted, woodsy bar, evoking a country tavern, is one of the liveliest spots in town. The hotel, once a postal inn, is the most popular place in Cortina for après-ski drinks.

✪ Miramonti Majestic Grand Hotel

Via Pezzie 103, 32043 Cortina d'Ampezzo. ☎ **0436/4201.** Fax 0436/867019. 106 rms, 11 suites. MINIBAR TV TEL. 460,000–900,000 lire ($287.50–$562.50) double; from 800,000 lire ($500) suite for two. Rates include half-board. AE, DC, MC, V. Free parking outside, 30,000 lire ($18) in garage. Closed Apr 1–July 16 and Sept 1–Dec 19. Hotel shuttle bus to/from the town center every 30 minutes.

Built in 1893, one of the grandest hotels in the Dolomites consists of two ochre-colored buildings with alpine hipped roofs set a short distance from the center of town. There's a gazebo built in the same style as the hotel on the right as you ascend the curved driveway leading up to the dignified facade, and a backdrop of jagged mountains behind the thick stucco walls and the dozens of gingerbread balconies. The rustic interior is filled with warmly appealing colors, lots of exposed timbers, and about the most elegant clientele in Cortina. The well-furnished bedrooms look like the accommodations in a private home, complete with matching accessories, built-in closets, and all the modern amenities.

A sports facility is on the premises, with an indoor swimming pool, exercise and massage equipment, a sauna, hydrotherapy, and physical therapy. Other sports facilities for winter and summer exercises are nearby.

MODERATE

Ancora

Corso Italia 62, 32040 Cortina d'Ampezzo. ☎ **0436/3261.** Fax 0436/3265. 64 rms, 6 suites. TV TEL. 220,000–320,000 lire ($137.50–$200) double; 400,000–660,000 lire ($250–$412.50) suite for two. Rates include half-board. AE, DC, MC, V. Parking 40,000 lire ($25). Closed Sept 15–Dec 20 and after Easter to June. Bus: 1 or 2.

This "Romantik Hotel," originally a private home back in 1826, is the domain of that hearty empress of the Dolomites, Flavia Bertozzi, who attracts sporting guests from all over the world and plays host to modern art exhibitions and classical concerts. This "hostess with the mostest" believes in her guests having a good time. The antique sculptures and objets d'art filling the hotel were gathered from Signora Flavia's trips to every province of Italy. Hers is a revamped hotel flanked on two sides by terraces with outdoor tables and umbrellas—the town center for sipping and gossiping. Garlanded wooden balconies encircle the five floors, and most bedrooms open directly onto these sunny porches. The bedrooms are all well furnished, comfortable, and especially pleasant—many with sitting areas—and you sleep under brightly colored woolen blankets. All is kept shiny clean, the service is polite and efficient, and the food is reason enough to check in.

Hotel Corona

Via Val di Sotto 12, 32040 Cortina d'Ampezzo. ☎ **0436/3251.** Fax 0436/867339. 44 rms. TV TEL. 200,000–280,000 lire ($125–$175) per person. Rates include half-board. MC, V. Free parking. Closed Apr–June and Sept 11–Dec 19. Bus: 1 or 2.

Dating from 1935, the Corona is one of the first hotels built at the resort. Its loyal clients would stay nowhere else during a stopover in Cortina. For anyone interested in modern Italian art, a stopover here is an event. The interior walls are painted a neutral white as a foil for the hundreds of carefully inventoried artworks displayed, all acquisitions of Luciano Rimoldi, the athletic manager, over the past quarter of a century. (He is also a ski instructor who coached Princess Grace in her downhill technique shortly before her death. He later served as head of the Italian ice-hockey team during the 1988 Winter Olympics at Calgary.)

Many of the most important artists of Italy (and a few from France) from 1948 to 1963 are represented here with artwork—not only painting, but sculpture and ceramic bas-reliefs. The hotel doesn't overlook sports either. It was chosen for the World Cup competition by a U.S. ski team just before they headed for the Sarajevo Olympics. The hotel prefers guests to take half-board.

⊛ Menardi

Via Majon 110, 32043 Cortina d'Ampezzo. ☎ **0436/2400.** Fax 0436/862183. 51 rms. TEL. 105,000–200,000 lire ($65.65–$125) per person. Rates include half-board. MC, V. Free parking. Closed Apr 10–June 21 and Sept 15–Dec 20. Bus: 1.

This eye-catcher in the upper part of Cortina looks like a great country inn, with its wooden balconies and shutters. Its rear windows open onto a meadow of flowers and a view of the rough Dolomite crags. The inn is 100 years old and is run by the Menardi family, who still know how to speak the old Dolomite tongue, Ladino. Decorated in the Tyrolean fashion, each bedroom has its distinct personality. Considering what you get—the quality of the facilities, the reception, and the food—I'd rate this one as the best for the money in Cortina. The living rooms and dining rooms have homelike furnishings: lots of knickknacks, pewter, antlers, spinning wheels.

Should this hotel be full, the family will book you into their second accommodations, containing only eight rooms, each with a private bath and a balcony opening onto the Dolomites.

Parc Hotel Victoria

Corso Italia 1, 32043 Cortina d'Ampezzo. ☎ **0436/3246.** Fax 0436/4734. 42 rms, 4 suites. MINIBAR TV TEL. 120,000–340,000 lire ($75–$212.50) double; from 400,000 lire ($250) suite. Rates include half-board. AE, DC, MC, V. Free parking. Closed Apr 10–July 10 and Sept 18–Dec 20. Bus: 1 or 2.

Parc Hotel Victoria is one of the best hotels in the center of town, a modern structure created in the Tyrolean style, with many good-size balconies opening onto views of the mountaintops. It's a successful place, combining the old chalet decor with contemporary, roomy areas, and lots of amenities. In the winter, all the well-furnished rooms have plenty of steam heat. The various living rooms and dining rooms are furnished with reproductions of old country furniture (bare-pine tables, peg-legged chairs). The regional fireplace with a raised hearth is the focal point for after-dinner gatherings.

INEXPENSIVE

Hotel Agip

Via Roma 118, 32043 Cortina d'Ampezzo. ☎ **0436/861400.** Fax 0436/862140. 42 rms (all with shower). TV TEL. 120,000 lire ($75) double. Rates include breakfast. AE, DC, MC, V. Parking 5,000 lire ($3.15). Bus: 1 or 2.

Hotel Agip, a member of this popular Italian chain, offers many amenities. It's a good bet if you arrive in Cortina in the off-season, when virtually everything else is closed. Its convenient location on the main road just outside the center of town—coupled with its clean, comfortable, contemporary, and no-nonsense format—have gained increasing favor with its many visitors. The bedrooms are predictably furnished and fairly quiet, the management helpful. The restaurant serves good food, featuring regional specialties.

⑤ Da Beppe Sello

Via Ronco 68, 32043 Cortina d'Ampezzo. ☎ **0436/3236.** Fax 0436/3237. 12 rms (8 with bath). 120,000 lire ($75) double without bath, 200,000 lire ($125) double with bath. Breakfast 15,000 lire ($9.40) extra. AE, DC, V. Closed Mar 31–May 15 and Sept 30–Oct 31. Bus: 2.

A third-class hotel set at the edge of the resort, Da Beppe Sello is one of the best bargains there. It's named after the nickname of its founder and expressed in alpine dialect. It was built in a chalet style in the 1950s, and offers cozily comfortable alpine-style bedrooms, each well maintained and inviting. Its restaurant (see "Where to Dine," below), is recognized as one of the finest at the resort.

WHERE TO DINE
MODERATE

Da Beppe Sello

Via Ronco 68. ☎ **3236.** Reservations recommended. Main courses 18,000–32,000 lire ($11.25–$20). AE, DC, MC, V. Daily 12:30–2pm and 7:30–10pm. Closed Mar 31–May 15 and Sept 30–Oct 31. Bus: 2. ALPINE ITALIAN.

When you grow tired of the sometimes oppressive glamour of more expensive restaurants within Cortina, you might consider heading for this simple but charming, Tyrolean-style restaurant within a simple hotel at the edge of the village.

Named after the double nicknames of the hotel's founder, Joseph (Beppe) Menardi (Sello); and run today by his multilingual niece, Elisa, it's considered a bastion of superb regional cuisine, and often visited by some of the resort's most elegant clients. Food items include filet of venison from the Dolomites served with pear, polenta, and *marmelata di mirtilli* (marmalade made from an alpine berry resembling a huckleberry or blueberry); diners get to keep the plate the dish was served on as a souvenir of their visit. Other dishes include pappardelle with rabbit sauce; tagliolini with porcini mushrooms; roast chicken with bay leaves, or filet steak flavored with bacon.

El Toulà

Località Ronco 123. ☎ **3339.** Reservations required. Main courses 22,000–32,000 lire ($13.75–$20). AE, DC, MC, V. Tues–Sat 12:30–2:30pm and 8–11pm. Closed Easter–late July and Sept 1–Christmas. Bus: 2. ITALIAN/VENETIAN.

Two miles east of Cortina, this was the first member of El Toulà chain, which today has around 10 other restaurants scattered throughout Italy and the world. (Considered as ambassadors abroad, El Toulà has branches in both Tokyo and Beijing.) Established in the early 1960s, and dubbed with a name that in the dialect of Cortina translates as "The Hayloft," it's a wood-framed structure with picture window views and an outside terrace. It's perched about a five-minute drive from the center of town, toward Pocol. The restaurant commands a panoramic view. You get excellently prepared dishes here, including squab grilled to perfection and served with an expertly seasoned sauce and veal braised with a white truffle sauce. The filet of beef is also recommended. A fritatta of sea crabs in the "Saracen" style is served as are pasta e fagiole in the style of Veneto, a pasticcio of eggplant; and Venetian-style calves liver. In the 1960s, this place was terribly chic, tied in almost exclusively with the jet set crowd of Cortina who, always dieting, ordered only carpaccio and ungarnished filet steaks. (Tourists, especially the barbaric ones, weren't really seen here a lot back then.) Despite the constant diets of the cliente, in the more realistic 90s, the cuisine is rich, flavorful, and appreciated by less stratospherically rich clients who know how to eat. The cuisine is that of the Veneto, not exclusively of Venice.

Ristorante Bellavista-li Meloncino

Località Gillardon 17A. ☎ **861043.** Reservations recommended. Main courses 20,000–25,000 lire ($12.50–$15.65). AE, MC, V. Wed–Mon 12:30–2:30pm and 8–11pm. Closed June and Nov. Follow the signs to Falzarego, stopping in the satellite suburb of Gillardon. ITALIAN.

The sweeping view of Cortina and the mountains beyond is only one of the attractions of this small, rustic restaurant set at the top of one of the village's easiest ski runs, 2 miles east of Cortina. The building looks like little more than a log hut, although the owners have added wind-sheltered terraces and a nearby barbecue grill on wheels that looks like an adaptation of a Conestoga wagon. You're likely to meet the more experienced members of the Cortina social scene here, all of whom enjoy the unusual Italian specialties prepared in the establishment's tiny kitchen—risotto with fruit (offered from June to September only), homemade liver pâté, scaloppine dishes, roast mountain goat, grilled beef in several variations, ample use of fresh mushrooms, and homemade ice cream.

✪ Ristorante Tivoli

Località Lacedel. ☎ **866400.** Reservations required. Main courses 22,000–32,000 lire ($13.75–$20). AE, DC, MC, V. Tues–Sun 12:30–2:30pm and 7:30–10pm. Closed May–June and Oct–Nov. Bus: 1. ITALIAN.

My favorite restaurant in Cortina, and one of the finest in the area, is this low-slung alpine chalet whose rear seems almost buried in the slope of the hillside. Standing high above the resort, about a mile from the center, it's beside the road leading to the hamlet of Pocol. Vastly popular with an athletic European clientele, it derives its excellence from the hard-working efforts of the gracious Calderoni family, who make this place one of the most fun and interesting at the resort.

Full meals might include stuffed rabbit in an onion sauce, wild duck with honey and orange, veal filet with basil and pine nuts, or salmon flavored with saffron. The pastas are made in the kitchen the day they are consumed. Examples include ravioli stuffed with spinach, cream, mushrooms, and truffles, or tagliatelle with goose liver. For dessert, you might sample an aspic of exotic fruit. The bustling kitchens are visible from the vestibule as you enter, adding to the warmth of the restaurant.

✪ EN ROUTE TO BOLZANO VIA THE GREAT DOLOMITE ROAD

From Cortina d'Ampezzo in the east to Bolzano in the west is a circuitous route of about 68 miles. It ranks among the grandest scenic drives in all of Europe. The first pass you'll cross (Falzarego) is about 11 miles from Cortina. At 6,900 feet above sea level, it offers a panoramic view. The next great pass is called Pordoi, at about 7,350 feet above sea level, the loftiest point along the highway (you can take a cable car to the top). You'll find restaurants, hotels, and cafés. In the spring, edelweiss grows in the surrounding fields. After crossing the pass, you'll descend to the little resort of Canazei, then much later pass by sea-blue Carezza Lake.

3 Bolzano

177 miles NE of Milan, 298 miles N of Rome, 95 miles N of Verona

The terminus of the Great Dolomite Road (or the gateway, depending on your approach), Bolzano is a town of mixed blood, reflecting the long rule that Austria enjoyed until 1919. Many names, including that of the town (Bozen), appear in German. As the recipient of considerable Brenner Pass traffic (55 miles north), the city is a melting pot of Italians and both visitors and residents from the Germanic lands. The capital of a province of the same name, Bolzano lies in the center of the Alto Adige region. It is traversed by two rivers, the Isarco and Talvera, one of which splits the town into two sections.

Bolzano is a modern industrial town, yet a worthwhile sightseeing attraction in its own right. It has many esplanades for promenading along the river. The most interesting street is the colonnaded via dei Portici. You can begin your stroll down this street of old buildings at either **piazza Municipio** or **piazza delle Erbe,** the latter a fruit market for the orchards of the province.

Bolzano makes a good headquarters for exploring the Dolomites and the scenic surroundings, such as **Renon** (Ritten in German) on the alpine plateau, with its cog train; the village of **San Genesio,** reached by cable north of Bolzano; and **Salten,** 4,355 feet up, an alpine tableland.

ESSENTIALS

GETTING THERE   By Train   Bolzano is a $2^{1}/_{2}$-hour train ride north of Verona; a one-way fare is 10,900 lire ($6.80). The Austrian city of Innsbruck, which is reached via the Brenner Pass, lies about a 95-minute train ride north of Bolzano.

By Bus   Bolzano can be reached by bus from Cortina d'Ampezzo (see above). Four buses a day make the 3-hour trip at a one-way cost of 14,500 lire ($9.05).

By Car   From Trent (see below), continue north to Bolzano on the A22; or head west from Cortina d'Ampezzo along Route 48 until you reach the signposted junction with Route 241, which covers the final circuitous lap into Bolzano.

VISITOR INFORMATION   Bolzano's telephone area code is 0471. The tourist information center is at piazza Walther 8 (☎ 970660).

WHERE TO STAY
EXPENSIVE

✪ Park Hotel Laurin
Via Laurin 4, 39100 Bolzano. ☎ **0471/311000** or 800/223-5652 in the U.S. Fax 0471/970953. 96 rms, 3 suites. A/C MINIBAR TV TEL. 315,000–375,000 lire ($196.90–$234.40) double; from 415,000 lire ($259.40) suite. Rates include breakfast. AE, DC, V. Parking 19,000 lire ($11.90). Bus: 1.

A choice place to stay, the Park Laurin captures the glamour of the past. It's the only superior first-class hotel in the Bolzano, and its rooms and suites have been refurbished, with baths in Italian marble. This has made the Park Hotel among the top first-class hotels in the Dolomites. The private garden is dominated by old shade trees and a flagstone-enclosed swimming pool.

The garden terrace is a sun pocket, ideal for lunches or dinners. A lunch costs 38,000 lire ($23.75), with a dinner going for 54,000 lire ($33.75) and up. The Laurin Bar offers piano entertainment daily, with jazz performances every Friday.

INEXPENSIVE

Hotel Alpi

Via Alto Adige 35, 39100 Bolzano. ☎ **0471/971929.** Fax 0471/970535. 110 rms. A/C MINIBAR TV TEL. 230,000 lire ($143.75) double. Rates include breakfast. AE, DC, MC, V. Parking 15,000 lire ($9.40). Bus: 1.

The exterior of this tastefully contemporary hotel is dotted with recessed balconies, large aluminum-framed windows, and the flags of many nations. The spacious public rooms are richly covered with paneling, exposed stone, and ceramic wall sculptures, which, with the comfortable upholstered seating areas, make for a pleasant hotel. In the commercial center of town, the hotel has a bar, a restaurant, a well-trained staff, and cozy rooms. Meals begin at 35,000 lire ($21.90) in the hotel's restaurant.

Scala Hotel Stiegl

Via Brennero 11 (Brennerstrasse 11), 39100 Bolzano. ☎ **0471/976222.** Fax 0471/976222. 60 rms. 200,000 lire ($125) double; from 250,000 lire ($156.25) suite. Breakfast 15,000 lire ($9.40) extra. AE, DC, V. Free parking outside, 12,000 lire ($7.50) in garage. Bus: 1.

The Scala is one of the best of the middle-bracket hotels of Bolzano. Its trilingual staff speaks fluent English, among other languages, and keeps the interior spotless. The neobaroque yellow-and-white facade is well maintained, with plenty of ornamentation scattered symmetrically over its five-story expanse. On the premises is an outdoor pool, plus a summer-garden restaurant specializing in Tyrolean dishes. The hotel affords easy access to the train station and the historic center of town. The rooms are well furnished and most contain minibars and TVs. Meals begin at 35,000 lire ($21.90). The hotel has parking spaces for 50 cars.

WHERE TO DINE
INEXPENSIVE

Da Abramo

Piazza Gries 16 (Grieserplatz 16). ☎ **280141.** Reservations recommended. Main courses 20,000–24,000 lire ($12.50–$15). AE, DC, MC, V. Mon–Sat 12:30–2:30pm and 7:30–9:30pm. Closed 2 weeks in Aug. Bus: 1. MEDITERRANEAN.

In a century-old Liberty-style villa, the most elegant restaurant in Bolzano took great pains to introduce a chic modern airiness to its physical decor. In a sienna–colored villa across the river from the historic center of town, the restaurant offers a summer garden covered with vine arbors, plus a labyrinthine arrangement of rooms. Full meals range upward from 45,000 lire ($28.15) and might include, depending on the mood of the chef, veal in a sauce of tuna and capers, roast quail with polenta, fish soup, warm seafood antipasti, codfish Venice style, a vast array of shellfish with seafood, tagliatelle with prosciutto, and beefsteak flambé with cognac.

Zur Kaiserkron

Piazza della Mostra 1 (Mustergasse 1). ☎ **970770.** Reservations recommended. Main courses 23,000–30,000 lire ($14.40–$18.75). AE, DC, MC, V. Mon–Sat noon–2:30pm; Mon–Fri 7–9:30pm. Bus: 1. SOUTH TYROLEAN/FRENCH.

The food is excellent, the decor appealing, and the multilingual management preserves the bicultural ambience for which Bolzano is known. The restaurant is housed a block from the cathedral in a yellow-and-white baroque building originally built in 1740 as the home of a wealthy Austrian merchant. For warm-weather dining, there's a canopy-covered wooden platform in front surrounded with greenery. You'll be welcomed by a member of the staff and ushered to a table under vaulted ceilings and wrought-iron chandeliers. Favorite dishes include an assortment of alpine-dried charcuterie; pâté of minced pheasant and duck liver; ravioli stuffed with spinach and minced beef; homemade tagliatelle with truffles; a traditional recipe of grüstl made from minced veal fried together with onions, eggs and potatoes; home-smoked salmon; filet of venison with rosemary, pine nuts, and sweet-and-sour sauce; roast lamb or kid; and beef goulash with polenta.

4 Merano

18 miles NW of Bolzano, 202 miles NE of Milan

Once the capital of Tyrol (before Innsbruck), Merano (Meran) was ceded to Italy at the end of World War I, but it retains much of its Austrian heritage. In days gone by it was one of the most famous resorts in Europe, drawing kings and queens and a vast entourage from many countries, who were attracted to the alpine retreat by the grape cure. (The eating of luscious Merano grapes is supposed to have medicinal value.) After a slump, Merano now enjoys popularity, especially in autumn when the grapes are harvested. Before the last war Merano also became known for its radioactive waters, in which ailing bathers supposedly secured relief for everything from gout to rheumatism.

The Passirio River cuts through the town (and along it are many promenades, evoking the heyday of the resorts of the 19th century). In the Valley of the Adige at the foot of Kuchelberg, Merano makes a good base for excursions in several directions, particularly to Avelengo. A bus from Sandplatz will deliver you to a funicular connection, in which you can ascend 3,500 feet above sea level to Avelengo, with its splendid vista and mountain hotels and pensions.

Merano is richly endowed with tourist facilities and attractions, such as open-air swimming pools at its Lido, tennis courts, and a race track.

ESSENTIALS

GETTING THERE   By Train   Five trains per day make the short run from Bolzano (see Section 3, above) to Merano, the trip taking 40 minutes and costing 3,200 lire ($2) for a one-way passage.

By Bus   From Bolzano, buses run frequently throughout the day northwest to Merano, at a one-way fare of 4,200 lire ($2.65). Buses leave from via Perathoner 4 (☎ 0471/971259) in Bolzano.

By Car   From Bolzano, head northwest along Route 38.

VISITOR INFORMATION   The telephone area code for Merano is 0473. The tourist information center is at corso della Libertà 45 (☎ 235223).

WHAT TO SEE & DO

On the Tappeinerweg promenade, the **Museo Agricolo Brunnenburg,** Ezra Pound Weg 6 (☎ 93533), is housed in a castle owned by the daughter and grandson of Ezra Pound, who lived in Merano from 1958 to 1964. The museum has displays of Tyrolean country life, including a blacksmith's shop and grain mill. There are also ethnology exhibits, plus a room dedicated to Pound. Open

Wednesday through Monday from 9:30 to 11:30am and 2 to 5pm. Admission is 2,000 lire ($1.25) for adults, 1,000 lire (65¢) for children. You can reach the castle by taking bus no. 3 to Dorf Tirol, every hour on the hour from Merano, or by climbing the Tappeinerweg. The house is closed November through March.

WHERE TO STAY
EXPENSIVE

✪ Kurhotel Palace

Via Cavour 2–4 (Cavourstrasse 2), 39012 Merano. ☎ **0473/211300.** Fax 0473/234181. 120 rms, 7 suites. MINIBAR TV TEL. 260,000–320,000 lire ($162.50–$200) double; 370,000–470,000 lire ($231.25–$293.75) suite. Rates include breakfast. Special packages for health and diet available. AE, DC, MC, V. Free parking. Closed Jan 6–Mar 19 and Nov 10–Dec 18. Bus: 4.

This deluxe hotel is a turn-of-the-century re-creation of a baroque palace set into the most beautiful formal gardens in town. The ceilings of the gilt- and cream-colored public rooms are supported by Corinthian columns similar to the ones adorning the yellow-and-white facade. The furniture, in part, seems to be good-quality copies of the 18th-century designs, and the crystal chandeliers are massive. From the rear terrace there's a view of the large marble slabs that have been arranged into a chessboard on the lawn. From there you'll be able to see the groupings of small cherubs set onto the hotel's ornate roofline that appear to be squinting down into the gardens. These contain a free-form pool whose waters flow below a tile annex for an indoor extension of the swimming area.

Many of the bedrooms have their own stone or wrought-iron balconies, which look over roses, palms, and palmettos. Although it has been in business for decades, the hotel has up-to-date comforts, and most of the units are air-conditioned. Accommodations vary widely, and rates depend on the size, season, and view.

Dining/Entertainment: Guests gather in the piano bar before going into the Tiffany Grill restaurant, where both regional and international cuisine are served, with meals costing 80,000 lire ($50) and up. In addition to the grill, there is a hotel dining room serving both lunch and dinner.

Services: Room service; babysitting; laundry; valet; medical supervision for spa, health, and fitness programs.

Facilities: Fitness equipment, indoor pool, sauna, solarium, hot whirlpool, thermal treatments, beauty farm.

Moderate

Castel Labers (Schloss Labers)

Via Labers 25, 39012 Merano. ☎ **0473/234484.** Fax 0473/234146. 30 rms, 1 suite. TEL. 200,000–250,000 lire ($125–$156.25) double; 400,000 lire ($250) suite. Rates include breakfast. Half-board 120,000–150,000 lire ($75–$93.75) per person. AE, DC, MC, V. Closed Nov 1–Apr 1. Bus: 3

Its earliest documentation dates from the 11th century, when the feudal lords of the region, the von Labers, erected a modest fortress here. Since around 1890, much enlarged and improved from its earlier role, the site has functioned as a hotel, attracting visitors from around the Italian and German-speaking world. The establishment is one of the highest hotels in Merano, located on a hillside about 2 miles east of the center of town. Some visitors compare its design of red-tiled gables and towers, darkened ceiling beams, and painted frescoes to something they'd have found in mountainous regions of Austria. The hotel, which has been owned and managed by the same family for over a century, maintains solid traditions and comfortably rustic bedrooms, usually with panoramas and simple but solid accessories. There's an on-site tennis court, and outdoor swimming pool, and a flowered patio for outside drinking and dining.

Hotel Fragsburg

Postfach 210, via Fragsburg 3 (Fragsburgerstrasse 3), 39012 Merano. ☎ **0473/244071.** Fax 0473/244493. 20 rms, 2 suites. TV TEL. 225,000–350,000 lire ($140.60–$218.75) double; 250,000–370,000 lire ($156.25–$231.25) suite. Rates include half-board. No credit cards. Closed Nov 5–Apr 13.

Rich with the Teutonic trappings of its baronial history, this hotel perches midway up the side of a sun-flooded mountainside high above Merano, a 15-minute drive away. As you'd expect, panoramas from its well-maintained verandas and decks are spectacular. It was originally built around 1520 as a hunting lodge and hideaway for the Count of Memmingen, but later suffered several centuries of neglect and decay. Its role as a hotel began in 1904, when an Austrian entrepreneur built (at his own expense) a road leading up to the place from the town center, brought in electricity, and transformed the building into summertime lodgings for guests from throughout the Hapsburg empire. Since 1932, the hotel has been progressively restored and improved to the point where it resembles an impeccably maintained historic chalet similar to something you might find in the Tyrol region of Austria. You'll find pinewood paneling, hunting trophies, art nouveau accessories, elegantly rustic bedrooms (each with a safe and an outdoor balcony), and facilities for the amusement and entertainment of families with children. On the premises is a heated swimming pool, a cocktail lounge, access to nearby tennis courts, and a dining room serving Italian-style meals. What's said to be the highest waterfall in Italy lies within a 20-minute trek from the hotel.

INEXPENSIVE

⑤ Hotel Minerva

Via Cavour 95, 39012 Merano. ☎ **0473/236712.** Fax 0473/230460. 45 rms. TV TEL. 180,000 lire ($112.50) double. Rates include breakfast. AE, DC, MC, V. Closed end of Oct–Apr 1. Bus: 3.

Built in 1909 in the Teutonic style favored by the then-rulers of Merano, this hotel is large, comfortable, and just antique enough to give its clients a sense of tradition. Surrounded by a private garden, near several more expensive hotels, it can be reached after a 10-minute pedestrian trek eastward from the center of town. All but a few of the rooms have balconies with views over the town. On the premises is an outdoor pool and an unpretentious dining room.

WHERE TO DINE
MODERATE

✪ Andrea

Via Galilei 44. ☎ **237400.** Reservations required. Main courses 32,000–35,000 lire ($20–$21.90); five-course menu regional 67,000 lire ($41.90); six-course menu dégustation 78,000 lire ($48.75). AE, DC, MC, V. Tues–Sun noon–2pm and 7–10pm. Closed Feb. Bus: 3. TYROLEAN.

Set within an art nouveau (*Jugendstil*) building erected in the town center around 1880, this restaurant was established in 1967, but soared into a role as one of the best in the region after its purchase in 1984 by the multilingual partners Pepi

Nothdurfter and Walter Oberrauch. Well-entrenched and charming, it's known to gastronomes on both sides of the Alps as one of the most respected dining spots in the region, and a sought-after resource for less experienced chefs who enroll in the cooking classes which are held here every November and January. Menu items change with the seasons, but are likely to include a terrine of foie gras served on a fresh brioche; fresh asparagus with a chervil-flavored cream sauce; risotto seasoned with whatever flavorful vegetable is in season at the time; a parfait of smoked trout with fresh horseradish sauce; tagliolini with shrimp sauce; black lasagne studded with shrimp and mussels; and a filet of sea bass with sesame seeds and zucchini.

Flora

Via Portici 75. ☎ **231484**. Reservations required. Main courses 16,500–32,000 lire ($10.30–$20). AE, DC, MC, V. Tues–Sat noon–2pm; Mon–Sat 7pm–midnight. Closed Jan 15–Feb 28. Bus: 3. ITALIAN.

Flora serves a Tyrolean and Italian cuisine of consistently good quality in its conservative, elegant confines. Full meals, costing around from 40,000 to 70,000 lire ($25 to $43.75), are likely to include ravioli stuffed with chicken and exotic mushrooms, pasta blackened with squid ink, rack of lamb cooked in a shell of salt, and marinated trout with fine herbs. The menu changes seasonally.

5 Trent (Trento)

36 miles S of Bolzano, 144 miles NE of Milan

A northern Italian city that basks in its former glory, this medieval town on the left bank of the Adige is known throughout the world as the host of the Council of Trent (1545–63). Beset with difficulties, such as the rising tide of "heretics," the Ecumenical Council convened at Trent, a step that led to the Counter-Reformation. Trent lies on the main rail line from the Brenner Pass, and many visitors like to stop off here before journeying farther south into Italy.

ESSENTIALS

GETTING THERE   By Train   Trent enjoys excellent rail connections. It lies on the Bologna–Verona–Brenner–Munich rail link, and trains pass through here day and night. The trip from Milan takes 2 hours and 40 minutes, and Rome is a 7-hour rail journey. Trains also connect Trent with Bolzano (see above) once every hour. Seven trains per day make the 3½ hour run from Venice.

By Bus   It's better to take the train to Trent and then rely on local buses once you get there. The local bus station is next to the train station (☎ 821000 for schedules), and has service to such places as Riva del Garda (see Chapter 17). Buses to Riva depart once an hour during the day.

By Car   From Bolzano (see above), head south to Trent along the A22. From Verona, continue north to Trent on the A22.

VISITOR INFORMATION   The telephone area code for Trent is 0461. The tourist information center is at via Alfieri (☎ 983880)

WHAT TO SEE & DO

The city has much old charm, offset somewhat by unbridled industrialization. For a quick glimpse of the old town, head for **piazza del Duomo,** dominated by the **Cathedral of Saint Vergilio.** Built in the Romanesque style and much restored over the years, it dates from the 12th century. It's open daily from 6:30am to noon and 2:30 to 8pm. In the center of the square is a mid-18th-century Fountain of Neptune, who is armed with a trident.

The ruling prince-bishops of Trent, who held sway until they were toppled by the French in the early 19th century, resided at the medieval **Castello del Buonconsiglio** (☎ 233770), reached from via Bernardo Clesio 3. Now the old castle has been turned into a provincial museum, with a collection of paintings and fine art, some quite ancient, including early medieval mosaics. The **Museo del Risorgimento,** also at the castle, is a museum containing mementos related to the period of national unification between 1796 and 1948. The museums are open Tuesday through Sunday from 10am to 7pm. Admission is 4,000 lire ($2.50).

Trent still makes a good base for exploring the sports resort of **Monte Bondone,** with its panoramic view (chair lifts), about 22 miles from the city center; **Paganella,** slightly more than 12 miles from Trent (the summit is nearly 7,000 feet high); and the **Brenta Dolomites.** The latter excursion, which will require at least a day for a good look, will reward you with some of the finest mountain scenery in Italy. From Trent, you'll pass by **Lake Toblino,** then travel a winding, circuitous road for much of the way, past jagged boulders. A 10-minute detour from the main road is suggested at the turnoff to the Genova valley, with its untamed scenery—at least to the thunderous **Nardis waterfall.** A good stopover point is the fast-rising little resort of Madonna di Campiglio.

WHERE TO STAY
MODERATE

Albergo Accademia
Vicolo Colico 6, 38100 Trento. ☎ **0461/233600.** Fax 0461/230174. 41 rms, 2 suites. A/C MINIBAR TV TEL. 245,000 lire ($153.15) double; from 250,000 lire ($156.25) suite. Rates include breakfast. AE, DC, MC, V. Free parking on the street. Bus: 2.

This is an alpine inn in the center of town made up of three buildings that have been joined to make a comfortable and attractive hostelry. One of the buildings is believed to be of 11th- or 12th-century origin, based on a brick wall similar to the city walls found during renovation work. According to legend, the older part of the Accademia housed church leaders who attended the Council of Trent in the 16th century. The inn stands behind the Renaissance Church of Santa Maria Maggiore. The rooms are done in light natural wood. A suite at the top of the house has a terrace from which you can see the town and the mountains.

The alpine influence is carried out in the bar and the restaurant. You can get a good meal for 40,000 lire ($25).

Hotel Buonconsiglio
Via Romagnosi 16–18, 38100 Trento. ☎ **0461/980089.** Fax 0461/980038. 45 rms, 1 suite. A/C MINIBAR TV TEL. 180,000–224,000 lire ($112.50–$140) double; 270,000 lire ($168.75) suite. Rates include breakfast. AE, DC, MC, V. Parking 10,000 lire ($6.25). Bus: 2.

Originally built shortly after World War II as the Hotel Alessandro Vittorio, and renamed Buonconsiglio in 1990 at the time of a massive renovation, this is a clean, well-administered hotel with pleasant bedrooms and a location on a busy street near the railway station. The staff speaks English. In the lobby is a collection of abstract modern paintings. Each bedroom contains a personal safe, satellite TV reception, and soundproofing against traffic noises from outside.

INEXPENSIVE

Hotel America

Via Torre Verde 50, 38100 Trento. ☎ **0461/983010.** Fax 0461/230603. 50 rms.
A/C MINIBAR TV TEL. 160,000 lire ($100) double. Breakfast 12,000 lire ($7.50) extra. AE, DC,
MC, V. Parking 15,000 lire ($9.40). Bus: 2.

This simple, attractive hotel is located in the heart of the historic old town of
Trent, and is a short walk from the rail station. Iron balconies look out to the
Dolomite mountains and a vine-wreathed arbor shelters the main entrance. Rooms
are clean and comfortable. The founder of the hotel worked in Wyoming from
1909 to 1923 and named the hotel after the country that afforded him the possibility to build it.

WHERE TO DINE
MODERATE

Orso Grigio

Via degli Orti 19. ☎ **984400.** Reservations recommended. Main courses 16,000–30,000 lire
($10–$18.75). AE, DC, MC, V. Wed–Mon 12:30–2:30pm and 7:30–9:30pm. Closed first week
of Apr and Aug 1–15. Bus: 2. ITALIAN/INTERNATIONAL.

This elegant and spacious restaurant lies about 30 yards from piazza Fiera, within
an old building whose origins may go back to the 1500s. When you see the immaculate table linen, the well-cared-for-plants, and the subdued lighting, you know
something is going right. Menus are seasonally adjusted to take in the finest of fresh
produce. The place enjoys local popularity—a good sign, since the Trentino is
noted for a refined palate. Couscous is a specialty, served with Italian grilled vegetables. Another delectable dish is a medley of four kinds of grilled fish. Other
dishes are warm lobster salad with a mustard sauce, fried Tunisian-style ravioli, and
a galette of black truffles with foie gras. Finish the feast with a chocolate mousse.
Wines of the province are a special feature of the restaurant.

✪ Restaurant Chiesa

Via San Marco 64. ☎ **238766.** Reservations recommended. Main courses 27,000–30,000
lire ($16.90–$18.75); fixed price "apple menu" 75,000 lire ($46.90). AE, DC, MC, V. Mon–
Sat 12:30–2:30pm; Mon–Tues and Thurs–Sat 7:30–9:30pm. Bus: 2. TRENTINE.

Restaurant Chiesa offers the largest array of dishes I've ever seen made with apples.
Owners Allesandro and Alberto recognized that Eve's favorite fruit, which grows
more abundantly around Trent than practically anywhere else, was the base of
dozens of traditional recipes. This popular restaurant was established in 1974 by
the parents of the present owners in the 17th-century home of County
Wolkenstein. The restaurant stands at the back of a large walled garden (you'll have
to ring the bell set into the iron gate to get in). Once inside, you can choose one
of the three large, rustically appointed rooms, with ceiling beams, stone columns,
and baskets and barrels filled with the owners' favorite fruit.

Specialties include risotto with apple, liver pâté with apple, filet of perch with
apple, and a range of other well-prepared specialties (a few of which, believe it or
not, do not contain apples). However, several meat dishes are cooked in cider. A
rich dessert might be followed by apple cider.

17 The Lake District

With its flower-bedecked promenades, lemon trees and villas, parks and gardens, and crystal-clear blue waters, the lake district may sound a bit dated, like a penny-farthing bicycle or an aspidistra in the bay window. But the lakes—notably Garda, Como, and Maggiore—continue to form one of the most enchanting splashes of scenery in northern Italy.

Like the lake district in northwestern England, the Italian lakes have attracted poets and writers—everybody from Goethe to Gabriele d'Annunzio. But after World War II the Italian lakes seemed to be largely the domain of matronly English and German types. In our more recent swings through the district, however, we've noticed an increasing joie de vivre and a rising influx of the 25 to 40 age group, particularly at such resorts as Limone on Lake Garda. Even if your time is limited, you'll want to have at least a look at Lake Garda.

DRIVING TOURS

LAKE GARDA

Day 1 From Brescia the A4 and S11 run to the southwestern corridor of Lake Garda, largest of all the lakes in Italy, its shores bordering the Veneto, Trentino–Alto Adige regions, and Lombardy. Begin your tour at Desenzano del Garda, with its old town and scenic harbor. Most visitors take the road along the western shore (S572) north.

If you're not running late, follow the first turnoff signposted to Salò, 12¹/₂ miles north of Desenzano. Mussolini's puppet government, backed by Hitler, was established here in September of 1943.

☕ **TAKE A BREAK**   Laurin, viale Landi 9 (☎ 0365/22022), in Salò, is a *Jugendstil* villa that used to be the headquarters of Mussolini's Ministry of Foreign Affairs in the war years. Now restored, it makes an ideal choice on the lake, either for rooms, costing 160,000 lire ($100) in a single or 250,000 lire ($156.25) in a double, or for meals. The restaurant is first class, both in service and appointments, with meals costing from 65,000 lire ($40.65). Try the fresh lake trout. Closed from December 20 to January 20.

What's Special About the Lake District

Great Towns/Villages
- Riva del Garda on Lake Garda, the oldest and most traditional resort along the lake.
- Sirmione, jutting out 2¹/₂ miles into Lake Garda and noted for its thermal baths.
- Bellagio, sitting on a promontory at the point where Lake Como forks, a town rich in aristocratic memories.
- Stresa, on the western shore of Lake Maggiore, the best center for exploring this beautiful lake.

Ace Attractions
- The Borromean Islands, Lake Maggiore, whose major sight is Isola Bella (Beautiful Island), dominated by a 17th-century palace.
- Villa Carlotta, the most-visited attraction at Lake Como, dating from 1847 and set in an exotic garden.

Parks/Gardens
- Villa Tartanto, Lake Maggiore, a botanical garden spread over more than 50 acres of the Castagnola Promontory.

Museum
- Vittoriale, the former home of the poet and military adventurer, Gabriele d'Annunzio, outside Gardone Riviera, on Lake Garda.

Gardone Riviera, with its memories of Gabriele d'Annunzio, who died there in 1938, lies just 3 miles north of Salò. Anchor in at this lakeside resort for an overnight stay.

Day 2   SS45B continues for 7¹/₂ miles north to Gargnano where Mussolini occupied a villa, the Feltrinelli (closed to the public). From here, another 12 miles leads you to one of the most charming spots along the lake, Limone sul Garda, where you may want to stop for lunch and explore the town. In the days when Goethe frequented the place, it was accessible only by boat. After Limone, named for its lemon groves, continue on SS45B north to Riva del Garda, as the road passes through tunnel after tunnel blasted out of rock. Overnight at Riva, at the top of the lake.

Day 3   The following day, leave Riva but this time drive along the less touristy side of the lake, the eastern shore bordering the Veneto. This route is called Gardesana Orientale (S249). It passes through Malcesine, 11 miles south of Riva, a favorite holiday target for Greta Garbo who called herself Harriet Browne when visiting. At the town of San Vigilio you can stop for lunch at the Locanda San Vigilio, which Churchill chose as a spot to paint and hibernate. Consider a luncheon at this hotel.

From here drive south for 14 miles to Peschiera del Garda, joining the S11 for a 6-mile drive to Colombare where you can follow the signposts heading north on a promontory jutting out into the lake and leading you to the little walled resort town of Sirmione where you'll regret you may be able to spend only one night.

LAKE COMO

Day 1   Begin your tour in the city of Como at the southern tip of the lake, only 25 miles north of Milan. Visit its cathedral and perhaps shop for some fashions in silk before journeying north along the western side of the lake to Cernobbio, a distance of 3 miles to the northwest. Here you might stop for a look at the Grand Hotel Villa d'Este, one of the most splendid hotels on earth. You should call ahead (see below) and request to see the grounds. If you can't afford to stay here, perhaps a luncheon will do.

Continue to Tremezzo, 48 miles north of Milan and 18 miles north of Como. Overnight at this lakeside resort, or else drive up to Menaggio, a town of equal interest.

Day 2   From Tremezzo the following morning—you can still base there if you wish—take a car ferry across the lake to visit the attractions on the eastern shore. These include mainly the Villa Carlotta, but you can also explore Villa Serbelloni and Villa Melzi if your day is long enough. Return to Tremezzo for the night, or else seek lodgings in the equally enticing resort of Bellagio.

LAKE MAGGIORE

Days 1–2   Follow Route S33 up the west side of Lake Maggiore—the Piedmont side—to Arona. You'll pass some of the most panoramic scenery on the lake. Many villas open onto beautiful gardens. At Stresa you can plan a two-night stopover, as it is the base for taking boats to the Borromean Islands.

Day 3   The following day, you can take S33 north for $12^{1}/_{2}$ miles to Verbania, from which you can take a lakeside road all the way around the lake. The route becomes S34 on its way to the Swiss town of Locarno, a distance of about 25 miles. If you want to encircle the lake you'll have to clear Swiss customs before passing through such famed tourist resorts at Ascona and eventually Locarno. From Switzerland you can head south again along the eastern or less touristy part of the lake, going through the fishing village of Luino before you reach the autostrada headed southeast to Milan where you can overnight.

☕ **TAKE A BREAK**   Camin, viale Dante 35, Luino (☎ 0332/530118), offers both 13 bedrooms and one of the best restaurants in the area. Only 13 rooms are rented, going for 246,000 lire ($153.75) in a double. However, most motorists stop for the food, partaking of such dishes as mountain lamb roasted with herbs. A meal goes for 50,000 lire ($31.25), and it's worth it.

1 Lake Garda

The most easterly of the northern Italian lakes, Garda is also the largest, stretching 32 miles in length and $11^{1}/_{2}$ miles in width at its fattest point. Sheltered by mountains, its scenery, especially the part on the western shore that reaches from Limone to Salo, has often been compared to that of the Mediterranean; you'll see olive, orange, and lemon trees, even palms. The almost-transparent lake is ringed with four art cities: Trent to the northeast, Brescia to the west, Mantua (Mantova) to the south, and Verona to the east.

The eastern side of the lake is more rugged, less trampled, but the resort-studded western strip is far more glamorous to the first-timer. On the western side, a circuitous road skirts the lake through one molelike tunnel after another. You can park your car at several secluded belvederes for a panoramic lakeside view. In spring the scenery is splashed with color, everything from wild poppy beds to oleander. Garda is well served by buses, or you can traverse the lake on steamers or motorboats, leaving from a number of harbors.

A Warning to Motorists: The twisting roads that follow the shores of Lake Garda would be enough to rattle even the most experienced driver. Couple the frightening turns, dimly lit tunnels, and emotional local drivers (who know every bend in the road—and you don't) with convoys of tour buses and trucks that rarely stay in their lane, and you have one of the more frightening drives in Italy.

Be especially careful, and don't be afraid to use your horn around blind curves. Also, be warned that Sunday is an especially risky time to drive, since everyone on the lake and from the nearby cities seems to take to the roads after a long lunch with lots of heady wine.

RIVA DEL GARDA

Some 27 miles southwest of Trent, 105 miles east of Milan, and 124 miles north-west of Venice, astride the narrowing northern point of Garda is the province of Trento, 195 feet above sea level, Riva is the oldest and most traditional resort along the lake. It consists of both an expanding new district and an old town, the latter centered at piazza III Novembre. On the harbor are the Tower of Apponale, dating from the 13th century, and the Rocca, built in 1124 and once owned by the ruling Scaligeri princes of Verona (it has been turned into a museum).

On the northern banks of the lake, between the Benacense plains and towering mountains, Riva offers the advantages of the Riviera and the Dolomites. Its climate is classically Mediterranean—mild in winter and moderate in summer. Vast areas of rich vegetation combine with the deep blue of the lake. Many come for health cures; others for business conferences, meetings, and fairs. Riva is popular with tour groups from the Germanic lands and from England.

Riva del Garda is linked to the Brenner–Modena motorway (Rovereto Sud/Garda Nord exit) and to the railway (Rovereto station), and is near Verona's Airport Villafranca.

Tourist information is available at the Palazzo dei Congressi, Parco Lido (☎ 554444). The telephone area code for Riva del Garda is 0464.

WHERE TO STAY
Expensive

✪ Hotel du Lac et du Parc
Viale Rovereto 44, 38066 Riva del Garda. ☎ **0464/551500.** Fax 0464/555200. 172 rms, 6 suites. MINIBAR TV TEL. 220,000–400,000 lire ($137.50–$250) double; from 460,000 lire ($287.50) suite for two. Rates include half-board. AE, DC, MC, V. Free parking. Closed Oct 20–Mar 26. Bus: Atesina.

This deluxe Spanish-style hotel is the best in town. Set back from the busy road behind a shrub-filled parking lot dotted with stone cherubs, the hotel has several outbuildings closer to the street containing restaurants and additional rooms. The interior of the main building is freshly decorated, with arched windows, lots of spacious comfort, and an enclosed and manicured lawn visible from the lobby. There's a huge dining room, two additional restaurants, an attractive bar, unusual accessories, and a comfortably sprawling format, each corner of which gives the impression of being part of a large private home. It was established as a hotel 100 years ago, though the current structure is from 1953. It was renovated by the Zontini family. The well-trained staff speaks a variety of languages, and seems genuinely concerned with the well-being of their guests. A garden stretches behind the hotel, containing a swimming pool, lakeside beach, and two tennis courts. The bedrooms are well furnished, each with private bath or shower, and 54 are air-conditioned.

Moderate

Hotel Sole

Piazza III Novembre no. 35, 38066 Riva del Garda. ☎ **0464/552686.** Fax 0464/552811. 52 rms (all with shower or bath), 3 suites. MINIBAR TV TEL. 200,000–250,000 lire ($125–$156.25) single or double; from 300,000 lire ($187.50) suite. Rates include breakfast. AE, DC, MC, V. Parking 20,000 lire ($12.50). Closed Nov–Feb. Bus: Atesina.

The medium-priced Hotel Sole apparently had far-sighted founders who snared the best position on the waterfront. Although rated second class by the government, and charging second-class prices, the hotel has amenities worthy of a first-class rating. It's an overgrown villa and has a large stack of rooms with arched windows and surrounding colonnades. Its interior has time-clinging traditional rooms. The lounge has a beamed ceiling and centers around a cone-sloped hooded fireplace; clusters of antique chairs sit on islands of Oriental carpets. The character and quality of the bedrooms vary considerably according to their position (most of them have views of the lake). Some are almost suites, with living-room areas; the smaller ones are less desirable. Nevertheless, all rooms are comfortable and spotless. You can dine in the formal interior room or on the flagstone lakeside terrace.

Lido Palace Hotel

Viale Carducci 10, 38066 Riva del Garda. ☎ **0464/552664.** Fax 0464/551957. 62 rms. A/C TV TEL. 210,000–270,000 lire ($131.25–$168.75) double. Rates include breakfast. AE, DC, MC, V. Free parking. Closed Nov–Mar. Bus: Atesina.

A first-class choice, the Lido Palace is a grand lakeside retreat, surrounded by gardens and only a 5-minute walk to the town center. The formal tree-lined drive reinforces the feeling of entering a private estate. The hotel was completely renovated and reopened in 1983. It has well-maintained rooms with modern furnishings and private bath or shower. A swimming pool is set on the parklike grounds. The hotel restaurant, Orient Express, serves mainly an Italian cuisine, with meals beginning at 40,000 lire ($25). Room service (7:30am to 11pm) and laundry service are available.

Inexpensive

Hotel Luise

Viale Rovereto 9, 38066 Riva del Garda. ☎ **0464/552796.** Fax 0464/554250. 58 rms. TEL. 90,000 lire ($56.25) double. Breakfast 7,000 lire ($4.40) extra. MC, V. Free parking. Closed Nov 3–Mar. Bus: Atesina.

This contemporary hotel is a few hundred yards away from the shore of the lake. It has its own free-form swimming pool as well as a nearby tennis court. The paneled interior contains big windows and comfortable furniture. All units are functionally restrained, with built-in necessities. A stopover here should be considered mainly for the price, and don't expect too much in the way of services.

Ⓢ Hotel Venezia

Viale Rovereto 62, 38066 Riva del Garda. ☎ **0464/552216.** Fax 0464/556031. 24 rms (all with bath or shower). TV TEL. 120,000–150,000 lire ($75–$93.75) double. Rates include breakfast. DC, MC, V. Free parking. Closed Nov 1–Mar 20. Bus: Atesina.

One of the most attractive budget-category hotels in town, the Venezia is housed in an angular modern building whose main section is raised on stilts above a private parking lot. Set back from the lakefront promenade, the hotel was designed as a villa in 1968. In the early 1990s it was renovated and remains a small, personalized, and unpretentious hotel. The complex is surrounded by trees on a quiet street bordered with flowers and private homes. The reception area is at the top of a flight of red marble steps. There's a private pool surrounded by palmettos, and a clean and sunny dining room with Victorian reproduction chairs. The rooms are pleasantly furnished.

WHERE TO DINE
Inexpensive

Most guests in Riva del Gorda dine at their hotels. However, there are a few good independent eateries; none better than the San Marco.

Ristorante San Marco

Viale Roma 20. ☎ **554477**. Reservations recommended. Main courses 20,000–30,000 lire ($12.50–$18.75). AE, DC, MC, V. Tues–Sun noon–2:30pm and 7–10pm. Closed Feb. Bus: 1 or 2. ITALIAN.

San Marco lies on one of the main shopping streets of the resort, set back from the lake. Originally built in the 19th century as a hotel, the property in 1979 was converted exclusively into a restaurant. If you arrive early for your reserved table, you can enjoy an apéritif at the bar up front. The food is classically Italian, and the cookery and service are excellent. You might begin with a pasta selection, such as spaghetti with clams or tortellini with prosciutto. Many good fish dishes are presented daily, including sole (prepared several ways) and grilled scampi. Among the meat selections, try the tournedos opera or the veal cutlet bolognese. The restaurant charges 40,000–75,000 lire ($25–$46.90) for a complete dinner. The owners speak English.

LIMONE SUL GARDA

Leaving Riva, the first resort you'll approach while heading south on the western shore of Lake Garda is Limone Sul Garda, 6 miles south of Riva, 99 miles northeast of Milan, and 364 miles northwest of Rome. Characteristic of the shore is the limonaie, hillside terraces of lemon and orange groves. Taking its name from the fruit of the lemon tree, Limone is one of the liveliest resorts along the lake. The resort was praised by Goethe and D.H. Lawrence.

Snuggling close to the lake, Limone is reached by descending a narrow, steep road. The village nestles on a narrow hunk of land. Shopkeepers, faced with no building room, dug right into the rock (in one such resulting grotto, you can get a cavewoman coiffure).

For those seeking recreation, there are $2^1/2$ miles of beach from which you can bathe, sail, or surf. Playing fields, tennis courts, soccer, and other sports activities, as well as discos, are available to the visitor who wants to make Limone a holiday base. The only way to get about is on foot.

If you're bypassing Limone, you may still want to make a detour south of the village to the turnoff to Tignale, in the hills. You can climb a modern highway to the town for a sweeping vista of Garda, one of the most scenic spots on the entire lake.

From April to September, a tourist information center is operated at via Piazzale Alcide De Gasperi (☎ 954265). The Limone sul Garda telephone area code is 0365.

WHERE TO STAY & DINE
Expensive
Hotel Capo Reamol
Via IV Novembre 92, 25010 Limone sul Garda. ☎ **0365/954040**. Fax 0365/954262. 60 rms (all with bath or shower). MINIBAR TV TEL. 310,000–350,000 lire ($193.75–$218.75) double. Rates include half-board. MC, V. Free parking. Closed Nov–Mar.

You won't even get a glimpse of this 1960s hotel from the main highway between Riva del Garda and Limone, because it nestles on the side of the lake well below road level. Be alert to traffic as you pull into a roadside area indicated by a sign 1¼ miles north of Limone, and then follow the driveway down a steep and narrow hill into a lower-level parking lot. Since the hotel is built on a series of terraces stretching down to the edge of the lake, you'll have to go down, not up, to your freshly decorated bedroom after registering at the reception desk. The bar, restaurant, and sports facilities are on the lowest level, sheltered from the lakeside breezes by windbreaks. Many of the public rooms are painted in pastel shades. Clients can swim in the lake or in the pool, and rent windsurfers on the graveled beach. A tavern profits, like everything else in the hotel, from views of the water. The rooms are well furnished.

Inexpensive
⊗ Hotel le Palme
Via Porto 36, 25010 Limone sul Garda. ☎ **0365/954681**. Fax 0365/954120. 28 rms. TEL. 126,000–189,000 lire ($78.12–$117.18) double. Rates include breakfast. AE, MC, V. Free parking. Closed Nov–Mar.

Completely renovated, this well-known antique Venetian-style villa, with period furniture, stands in the shade of two centuries-old palm trees in the historic center of Limone, opening directly onto the shores of Lake Garda. Although extensively remodeled for the installation of more private baths, this four-star hotel retains many of its original architectural features. The hotel offers well-furnished bedrooms, each individually decorated, containing a radio. On the second floor is a comfortable reading room with a TV set, while on the floor above is a wide terrace in the open air. On the ground floor is a large dining room with decorative sculpture, opening onto a wide terrace where in fair weather you can order meals and drinks. The cuisine, backed up by a good wine list, is excellent. Because of the popularity of the hotel, it's best to make reservations.

GARDONE RIVIERA
In the province of Brescia, 60 miles east of Milan and 20 miles northeast of Brescia, the western shore of Gardone Riviera is well equipped with a number of good hotels and sporting facilities. Its lakeside promenade attracts a wide range of predominantly European tourists for most of the year. When it used to be chic for patrician Italian families to spend their holidays by the lake, many of the more prosperous built elaborate villas not only in Gardone Riviera, but in neighboring Fasano (some of these have been converted to receive guests). The town also has the major attraction along the lake, which you may want to visit even if you're not lodging for the night.

The tourist information office is at corso della Repubblica 35 (☎ 20347). Gardone Riviera's telephone area code is 0365.

WHAT TO SEE & DO

Vittoriale, via Vittoriale 12 (☎ 20130), was once the private home of Gabriele d'Annunzio (1863–1938), the poet and military adventurer, another Italian who believed in la dolce vita, even when he couldn't afford it. Most of the celebrated events in d'Annunzio's life occurred before 1925, including his love affair with Eleonora Duse and his bravura takeover as a self-styled commander of a territory being ceded to Yugoslavia. In the later years of his life, until he died in the winter before World War II, the national hero lived the grand life at his private estate on Garda.

North of the town, Vittoriale is open year round, Tuesday through Sunday from 9am to 12:30pm and 2 to 6pm (to 5pm in spring and autumn). Admission to the grounds is 7,000 lire ($4.40), or 15,000 lire ($9.40) to the house and grounds. The furnishings and decor passed for avant garde in their day, but evoke the Radio City Music Hall of the '30s when viewed now. D'Annunzio's death mask is of morbid interest, and his bed with a "Big Brother" eye adds a curious touch of Orwell's 1984 (over the poet's bed is a faun casting a nasty sneer). The marble bust of Duse seems sadly out of place, but the manuscripts and old uniforms perpetuate the legend. In July and August, d'Annunzio plays are presented at the amphitheater on the premises. To sum up, it's a bizarre museum to a dated hero of yesteryear. To reach it, head out via Roma, connecting with via Colli.

WHERE TO STAY

Expressive

Expensive

✪ **Grand Hotel**

Via Zanardelli 72, 25083 Gardone Riviera. ☎ **0365/20261.** Fax 0365/22695. 180 rms, 10 suites. MINIBAR TV TEL. 230,000–320,000 lire ($143.75–$200) double; from 350,000–400,000 lire ($218.75–$250) suite. Rates include breakfast. Half-board 25,000 lire ($15.65) per person extra. AE, DC, MC, V. Parking 25,000 lire ($15.65). Closed Oct 15. Bus: SIA.

When it was built in 1881, this was the most fashionable hotel on the lake and one of the biggest resort hotels of its kind in Europe. Its massive tower is visible for miles around. In World War II the elegantly proportioned bedrooms served as hospital accommodations, first for the Germans and then for the Americans. Later the hotel's reputation as a glamorous resting place convinced Churchill to stay for an extended period in 1948, where he fished, wrote letters, and recovered from his frantic lifestyle. Today the establishment still boasts a distinguished clientele with regulars who return year after year.

The hotel is one of northern Italy's great reminders of turn-of-the-century grandeur. It isn't difficult to get lost in the almost-endless high-ceilinged corridors, although the focus of your visit will usually bring you back to the main salon, whose sculpted ceilings, parquet floors, and elegantly comfortable chairs make it an ideal spot for reading or watching the lake. The dining room offers the kind of good food and old-time splendor. An Italian historical film, *Mussolini and I*, was shot here.

All the rooms face the lake, avoiding the roadside noise. A series of garden terraces, a private beach, and a swimming pool are scattered throughout the extensive gardens.

Yesterday's Hero

It's sad and a bit melancholy to visit the former private villa of Gabriele d'Annunzio (1863–1938) at Gardone Riviera and relfect on fleeting fame and the legends of yesterday. Perhaps the young Italians of modern Italy don't even know who this poet and military adventurer was, but in d'Annunzio's heyday he was a legend of towering interest throughout the country.

The writer was notorious in his time, both for his lavish living and particularly for his liaison with Eleonora Duse, considered the greatest actress of her day, the Sarah Bernhardt of Italy. D'Annunzio broke her heart, along with many other hearts.

As a journalist on the staff of the *Tribuna* in Rome, and a deputy in parliament from 1897 to 1900, d'Annunzio became famous, although the years from 1910 to 1915 saw him living in France to escape his debts. D'Annunzio dominated Italian poetry at the turn of the century and became a leader of the cult of aestheticism. He made no distinction between his poetry and his life. One critic wrote, "He made poetry out of life and life out of poetry." He had an amazing gift for the use of the Italian language, as reflected in the passionate strength of the drama, *Francesca da Rimini* (1902) or the charm of La Figlia di Iorio (1904). His writings made him the most popular poet in all of Italy for three decades. He had great influence on young Italian writers of his time. But, sadly, he declined. One long-ago critic put it this way, "Patriotism degenerated into politics, politics into violent dilettantism; national sovereignty became imperialism; love a lascivious sensuality; words became ornamentation."

He ardently advocated Italian entry into World War I, and served in the army, navy, and finally air force (he was to lose an eye in aerial combat). Sensational exploits, including a 1918 reconnaissance flight over Vienna, won him world headlines. In the controversy between Italy and Yugoslavia over the status of Fiume, he led a band of Italian soldiers and occupied the city in September of 1919. He did this without the consent of the Italian government. Proclaiming Fiume an "Italian regency of the Carnaro," d'Annunzio ruled as a virtual dictator until the Italian government booted him in December of 1920.

It was rumored that Mussolini would eventually purchase Vittoriale for d'Annunzio to shut up his "poetic mouth." The poet filled the villa with mementos and souvenirs of his conquests in love and war, even dry-docking the prow of the battleship, *Puglia,* in the grounds.

Until his death, d'Annunzio continued to collect souvenirs and bizarre objects, often expensive ones, for which he went into excessive debt. In his *Sala del Lebbroso,* he would lie in a coffin contemplating his own upcoming death. After the war when his "souvenirs" were first inspected by the American press, one reviewer called them "a fascist rummage-sale."

Inexpensive

Ⓢ Bellevue Hotel

Via Zanardelli 81, 25083 Gardone Riviera. ☎ **0365/290088.** Fax 0365/290088. 33 rms (all with bath or shower). TEL. 80,000–90,000 lire ($50–$56.25) per person. Rates include half-board. V. Free parking. Closed Oct 11–Mar. Bus: Cosino.

This villa perched up from the main road has many terraces surrounded by trees and flowers—and an unforgettable view. You can stay here even on a budget, enjoying the advantages of lakeside villa life. On the grounds is a swimming pool. The lounges are comfortable, and the dining room affords a view through the arched windows. The quality of the meals is excellent (no skimpy helpings here). Meals begin at 38,000 lire ($23.75) and in fair weather are served in a large garden.

A Nearby Place to Stay

Fasano del Garda is a satellite resort of Gardone Riviera, lying 1 1/4 miles to the north. Many prefer it to Gardone.

✪ Hotel Villa del Sogno (Villa of Dreams)

Via Zanardelli 107, Fasano del Garda, 25080 Gardone Riviera. ☎ **0365/290181.** Fax 0365/290230. 33 rms, 5 suites. TV TEL.. 320,000–360,000 lire ($200–$225) double; from 460,000 lire ($287.50) suite. Rates include breakfast. AE, DC, MC, V. Free parking. Closed Oct 20–Apr 1. Bus: Cosino.

This 1920s re-creation of a Renaissance villa offers sweeping views of the lake and spaciously comfortable old-fashioned bedrooms. Set a few hundred yards above the water, with easy access to its private beach, the hotel also has a pool and is ringed with terraces filled with café tables and pots of petunias and geraniums, which combine with bougainvillea and jasmine to brighten the surroundings. The baronial stairway of the interior, as well as many of the ceilings and architectural details, were crafted from wood. The bedrooms are well furnished, each with private bath or shower. Nine rooms are air-conditioned.

Where to Dine

Most visitors to this resort take their meals at their hotels. However, there are some good independent dining selections.

Expensive

✪ Villa Fiordaliso

Via Zanardelli 132. ☎ **20158.** Reservations required. Main courses 28,000–50,000 lire ($17.50–$31.25); fixed-price menus 65,000 lire ($40.65) for five courses, 90,000 lire ($56.25) for seven courses. AE, DC, MC, V. Wed–Sun 12:30–2:30pm, Tues–Sun 7:30–10:30pm. Closed Oct 28–Dec 20. Bus: SIA. ITALIAN.

This deluxe establishment is a Liberty-style (art nouveau) villa from 1924 with gardens stretching down to the edge of the lake. The chef's cuisine is personalized, likely to include a terrine of eel and salmon in an herb-and-onion sauce, a timbale of rice and shellfish with curry, and several succulent fish and meats grilled over a fire. Other specialties include ravioli with Bergoss cheese (a salty regional cheese), sardines from a nearby lake baked in an herb crust, and scampi in a sauce of tomatoes and wild onions. Not including wine, the bill ranges from 62,000 to 105,000 lire ($38.75 to $65.65). This little bastion of fine food has impeccable service to match.

Moderate

Ristorante la Stalla

Strade per il Vittoriale. ☎ **21038.** Reservations recommended. Main courses 12,000–26,000 lire ($7.50–$16.25). AE, DC, MC, V. Wed–Mon 12:30–2:30pm and 7:30–9:30pm. Closed Jan. Bus: SIA. INTERNATIONAL.

This charming restaurant is frequented by local families, who sometimes drive for miles just to dine here. In a handcrafted stone building with a brick-columned porch, outdoor tables, and an indoor ambience loaded with rustic artifacts and crowded tables, the restaurant is set in a garden ringed with cypresses on a hill above the lake. To get there, follow the signs up il Vittoriale, as if you were going to d'Annunzio's former home, to a quiet street with singing birds and residential houses. The building was commissioned by d'Annunzio as a stable for his horses. Sunday afternoon is the most crowded time to visit.

Specialties will be recited by one of the uniformed waiters. Depending on the shopping that day, they might include a selection of freshly prepared antipasti, risotto with cuttlefish, or crêpes fondue. Polenta is served with Gorgonzola and walnuts, or you may prefer filet of beef in a beer sauce. Meals cost 38,000 to 80,000 lire ($23.75 to $50).

SIRMIONE

Perched at the tip of a narrowing strip of land 80 miles east of Milan and 25 miles east of Brescia, Sirmione juts out for $2^1/_2$ miles into Lake Garda. Noted for its thermal baths (used in the treatment of deafness), the town is a major resort that blooms in spring and wilts in late autumn. It's reached by heading north after veering from the autostrada connecting Milan and Verona.

The resort was a favorite of Giosuè Carducci, the Italian poet who won the Nobel prize for literature in 1906. In Roman days it was frequented by still another poet, Catullus. Today the Grotto di Catullo is the chief sight, an unbeatable combination of Roman ruins and a panoramic view of the lake. You can wander at leisure through the remains of this once-great villa. The attraction is open April through September, Tuesday through Sunday from 9am to 6pm; off-season, Tuesday through Sunday from 9am to 4pm. The admission is 6,000 lire ($3.75). For more information, phone 916157. To reach the grotto, take via Catullo.

At the entrance to the town stands the moated 13th-century Rocca Scalingera castle, piazza Castello (☎ 916148), that once belonged to the powerful Scaligeri princes of Verona. Architecturally, the medieval castle is distinguished by its crenellated battlements. You can climb to the top and walk the ramparts. It is open April through October, Tuesday through Sunday from 9am to 6:30pm; off-season, Tuesday through Sunday from 9am to 12:30pm. Admission is 6,000 lire ($3.75).

The tourist information center is at viale Marconi 2 (☎ 916245). The telephone area code for Sirmione is 030.

WHERE TO STAY

During the peak summer season, motorists need a hotel reservation to take their vehicles into the crowded confines of the town. However, there is a large parking area at the entrance to the town. Accommodations are plentiful. The only way to visit Sirmione is on foot. All the hotels below are in the center of town.

Very Expensive

✪ Villa Cortine Palace

Via Grotte 12, 25019 Sirmione. ☎ **030/990-58-90.** Fax 030/91390. 53 rms, 2 suites. A/C TV TEL. 480,000–660,000 lire ($300–$412.50) double; 900,000–1,100,000 lire ($562.50–$687.50) suite. Rates include half-board. AE, DC, MC, V. Free parking. Closed Oct 22–Apr 1. Bus: SIA.

This first-class choice is luxuriously set apart from the town center, surrounded by imposing, sumptuous gardens that would be the pride of any hotel in the world. The hotel was originally built in 1905, although in 1957 a new wing greatly increased its amenities and capacities. Today, all but a handful of its bedrooms lie within this new wing, with only the bar and reception area contained within the original hotel. The century-old landscaping in the hotel's park contains a formal entrance through the fluted columns of a colonnade, and winding lanes lined with cypress trees, wide-spreading magnolias, and flower-bordered marble fountains with classic sculpture. In comfort and convenience, the bedrooms are unequaled in Sirmione. Each has a private bath or shower, and some offer a minibar. The interior has one formal drawing room, with much gilt and marble—it's positively palatial.

Expensive

Grand Hotel Terme

Viale Marconi 1, 25019 Sirmione. ☎ **030/916261.** Fax 030/916568. 58 rms, 1 suite. A/C MINIBAR TV TEL. 350,000–400,000 lire ($218.75–$250) double; from 700,000 lire ($437.50) suite. Rates include breakfast. AE, DC, MC, V. Free parking. Closed Nov–Mar. Bus: SIA.

This rambling, three-story hotel at the entrance of the old town is on the lake next to the Scaligeri Castle. The wide marble halls and stairs lead to well-furnished, balconied bedrooms. Constructed in 1948, the hotel has contemporary furnishings, plus a number of spa and physical-therapy facilities and a swimming pool. The food served in the indoor-outdoor dining room is excellent, with such offerings as prosciutto and melon, risotto with snails, fettuccine with fresh porcini, and a wide choice of salads and fruits. Meals begin at 60,000 lire ($37.50).

Inexpensive

⑤ Flaminia Hotel

Piazza Flaminia 8, 25019 Sirmione. ☎ **030/916078.** Fax 030/916193. 48 rms. TV TEL. 148,000–170,000 lire ($92.50–$106.25) double. Rates include breakfast. AE, DC, MC, V. Free parking. Bus: SIA.

This is one of the best little hotels in Sirmione, with a number of facilities and amenities, including air conditioning in some of the rooms. One of the more modern accommodations, it lies near the town center right on the lakefront, with a terrace extending out into the water. The bedrooms are made attractive by French doors opening onto private balconies. The lounges are furnished in a functional modern style. Breakfast is the only meal served.

⑤ Hotel Eden

Piazza Carducci 17, 25019 Sirmione. ☎ **030/916481.** Fax 030/916483. 33 rms. A/C TV TEL. 190,000 lire ($118.75) double. Rates include breakfast. AE, MC, V. Parking 17,000 lire ($10.65). Closed Nov–Feb. Bus: SIA.

The exterior of the Hotel Eden, whose foundations date from the 12th century, is covered with pink stucco with stone trim around each of the big windows. The awning-covered entrance opens into a beautifully polished hall, where the gray and pink marble covering the floors came from India. Breakfast or drinks can be enjoyed on a flagstone-covered terrace surrounded with flowers. A winding stone staircase leads to the tastefully contemporary bedrooms. Each of the units is outfitted with pastel shades, and has its own marble-trimmed bath and radio—these are among the most up-to-date bedrooms in Sirmione. Fifteen rooms have a minibar. The location is in the center of the old city.

⑤ Olivi

Via San Pietro 5, 25019 Sirmione. ☎ **030/9905365.** Fax 030/916472. 60 rms. A/C TV TEL. 165,000–195,000 lire ($103.15–$121.90) double. Rates include breakfast. AE, MC, V. Free parking. Closed Dec. Bus: SIA.

This hotel is the creation of its sun-loving owner, Cerini Franco. Its location is excellent, on the rise of a hill in a grove of olive trees, at the edge of town. The all-glass walls of the major rooms never let you forget you're in a garden spot of Italy. Even the compact and streamlined bedrooms have walls of glass leading out onto open balconies. Facilities include an outdoor swimming pool and a solarium. Laundry and room service are also provided. The hotel serves typically Italian meals for 50,000 lire ($31.25). Sometimes live music is featured, even country music when the hotel stages a barbecue.

WHERE TO DINE

Ristorante Grifone da Luciano

Via delle Bisse 5. ☎ **916097.** Reservations not necessary. Main courses 18,000–32,000 lire ($11.25–$20). AE, DC, MC, V. Thurs–Tues noon–2:30pm and 7–10:30pm. Closed Nov–mid-Mar. Bus: SIA. INTERNATIONAL.

One of the most attractive restaurants in town is separated from the castle by a row of shrubbery, a low stone wall, and a moat. From your seat on the flagstone terrace, you'll have a view of the crashing waves and the plants that ring the dining area. The headquarters of this establishment is technically an old stone house surrounded with olive trees. Many of the diners gravitate toward the low-lying glass-and-metal extension stretching toward the lake. The tables inside are covered with candles and flowers. Food items include many varieties of fish and many of the standard dishes of the classic Italian kitchen.

La Rucola

Vicolo Strentelle 5. ☎ **916326.** Reservations recommended. Main courses 23,000–25,000 lire ($14.40–$15.65). AE, MC, V. Fri–Wed 12:15–2:30pm and 7:15–10:30pm. Closed Jan 7–Feb 15. Bus: SIA. ITALIAN.

In the heart of town, this restaurant lies on a small alley a few steps from the main gate leading into Sirmione. The building looks like a vine-laden, sienna-colored country house and was originally a stable 150 years ago. Full meals, served in a modernized interior, cost around 60,000 lire ($37.50) and could include fresh salmon, langoustines, mixed grilled fish, and a more limited meat selection. Meats are most often grilled or flambéed, including Florentine beefsteak. Newer items on the menu include gnocchetti de riso with baby squid and squid ink and filet of turbot with potatoes and a zabaglione of spinach. Good pasta dishes include spaghetti with clams and several local specialties. Many of the desserts are made for two diners, including crêpes Suzette and banana flambé.

2 Lake Como

Everything noble, everything evoking love—that was how Stendhal characterized fork-tongued Lake Como. Others have called it "the looking glass of Venus," and Virgil pronounced it as "our greatest lake." More than 30 miles north of Milan, it is next to Garda, the most visited of Italian lakes. A shimmering deep blue, the lake spans 2¹/₂ miles at its widest point. With its flower-studded gardens, its villas built for the wealthy of the 17th and 18th centuries, its mild climate, Larius (as it was known to the Romans) is among the most scenic spots in all of Italy.

COMO

This is the name of both the lake and its principal city. At the southern tip of the lake, 25 miles north of Milan and 388 miles north of Rome, Como is known for its silk industry. Most visitors will pass through here to take a boat tour of the lake. If you do so, you'll cross piazza Cavour, the lakeside square and the center of local life.

Because Como is also an industrial city, I have generally shunned it for overnighting, preferring to anchor into one of the more attractive resorts along the lake, including Bellagio. However, train passengers who don't plan to rent a car may prefer Como (the city, that is) for convenience.

For centuries the destiny of the town has been linked to that of Milan. This means that Como prospered along with Milan, but also shared many of its misfortunes.

Como is called the world capital of silk, the silkmakers of the city joining communal hands with the fashion designers of Milan. Como has been making silk since Marco Polo first returned with silkworms from China. However, Como today isn't engaged in mulberry and worm cultivation, and hasn't been since the end of World War II. Those arduous labors, including the spinning of raw silk, are done in China. Como imports its thread from China.

Designers such as Giorgio Armani and Bill Blass pass through Como, discussing the patterns they want with silk manufacturers.

The tourist information center is at piazza Cavour 17 (☎ 269712). Como's telephone area code is 031.

WHAT TO SEE & DO

Before rushing off on a boat for a tour of the lake, you may want to look at the Cattedrale de Como, piazza del Duomo (☎ 300610), which dates from the 14th century when the master builders of the city began its construction in the Lombard-Gothic style. Before it was finished the Renaissance was in flower, and it wasn't until the 1700s that the Duomo was officially "crowned." The exterior of the cathedral, frankly, is more interesting than the interior. Dating from 1487, it is lavishly decorated with statues, including those of Pliny the Elder (A.D. 23–79) and the Younger (A.D. 62–113), whom one writer once called "the beautiful people of ancient Rome." Inside, look for the 16th-century tapestries depicting scenes from the Bible.

WHERE TO STAY

Hotel Barchetta Excelsior

Piazza Cavour 1, 22100 Como. ☎ **031/3221.** Fax 031/302622. 82 rms, 3 suites. A/C MINIBAR TV TEL. 210,000–239,000 lire ($131.25–$149.40) double; 296,000 lire ($185) suite. Rates include breakfast. AE, DC, MC, V. Parking 25,000 lire ($15.65). Bus: 1 or 2.

This first-class hotel is set at the edge of the main square in the commercial section of town. Its original construction was a century ago, but it was demolished and reconstructed in a more modern format in 1957. Major additions have been made to the hotel, including the alteration of its restaurant and an upgrading of the bedrooms, which are comfortably furnished, often with a balcony overlooking this heartbeat square and the lake. All accommodations have radios, among other amenities, and most have lake views. There's a parking lot behind the hotel, plus a covered garage just over 50 yards away.

Metropole & Suisse

Piazza Cavour 19, 22100 Como. ☎ **031/269444.** Fax 031/300808. 71 rms, 3 suites. A/C MINIBAR TV TEL. 220,000 lire ($137.50) double; 250,000 lire ($156.25) suite. Breakfast 20,000 lire ($12.50) extra. AE, DC, MC, V. Parking 20,000 lire ($12.50). Bus: 1 or 2.

This hotel offers good value in clean, convenient accommodations. Near the cathedral on this major lake-fronting square, it's composed of three lower floors dating from around 1700, plus upper floors that were added about 60 years ago. The hotel began life as a waterfront store at the edge of what was then part of the lake (the square you see today is a landfill dating from 1850). The Swiss creator of the hotel was photographed with the staff in 1892, a picture that still hangs behind the reception desk. Each of the bedrooms is different, rich with character for the most part. Many repeat clients have staked out their favorite rooms. A parking garage and the city marina are nearby. A popular restaurant, Imbarcadero, under separate management, fills most of the ground floor of the hotel.

WHERE TO DINE

Ristorante Imbarcadero

Piazza Cavour 20. ☎ **270166.** Reservations recommended. Main courses 22,000–35,000 lire ($13.75–$21.90). AE, DC, MC, V. Daily 12:30–2:30pm and 7:30–10pm. Closed Jan 1–8. Bus: 1 or 2. INTERNATIONAL.

Established more than a decade ago in a 300-year-old building near the edge of the lake, this restaurant is filled with a pleasing blend of carved Victorian chairs, panoramic windows with marina views, and potted palms. You'll be greeted near the long, streamlined bar area by a member of the uniformed staff. The outdoor terrace set up on the square in summer is ringed with shrubbery and illuminated with evening candlelight. The chef makes his own tagliatelle, or you may want to order spaghetti with garlic, oil, and red pepper. Main courses include beef alla Rossini, veal cutlet milanese, sea bass with olives and wine, and whitefish direct from the lake. Desserts are often lavish productions, including banana flambé and crêpes Suzette.

CERNOBBIO

Cernobbio, 3 miles northwest of Como, 391 miles northwest of Rome, and 33 miles north of Milan, is a small, fashionable resort frequented by the wealthy of Europe because of its deluxe hotel, the 16th-century Villa d'Este. But its idyllic anchor on the lake has also attracted a less affluent tourist, who'll find a number of third- and even fourth-class accommodations as well.

The tourist information center is at via Regina 33B (☎ 510198) and is open from Easter to October. The telephone area code for Cernobbio is 031.

WHERE TO STAY

Very Expensive

✪ Grand Hotel Villa D'Este

22010 Cernobbio. ☎ **031/3481.** Fax 031/348844. 108 rms, 48 suites. A/C MINIBAR TV TEL. 600,000–700,000 lire ($375–$437.50) double; 1,150,000–1,450,000 lire ($718.75–$906.25) suite. Rates include breakfast. AE, DC, MC, V. Free parking. Closed end Oct–Mar 1. Bus: 6

One of Italy's most legendary hotels, Villa d'Este was originally built in 1568 as a lakeside home and pleasure pavilion for the cardinal Tolomeo Gallio. One of the most famous Renaissance-era hotels in the world, designed in the neoclassical style by Pellegrino Pellegrini di Valsolda, it passed from owner to illustrious owner for 300 years until it was transformed into a hotel in 1873.

Today, the hotel remains a kingdom in itself, a historic and splendid palace surrounded by 10 acres of some of the finest hotel gardens in Italy. The interior lives up to the almost enthralling beauty of the grounds. Noteworthy public areas include the Salon Napoleone, whose silken wallcoverings were embroidered especially for the emperor's visit; the Canova room, centered around a statue of Venus by the room's namesake; a Grand Ballroom suitable for some of the most festive banquets in Europe; and a bar outfitted in shades of gold and white. Throughout, frescoed ceilings, impeccable antiques, and attentive service create one of the world's most envied hotels. Each bedroom has a decor of its own, and a roster of historically famous former occupants. Thirty-four of the hotel's 156 accommodations lie within the Queen's Pavilion, an elegant annex originally built in 1856.

Dining/Entertainment: The hotel contains two restaurants (The Grill Room and The Verandah), both of culinary merit. Both serve à la carte dinners for around 100,000 lire ($62.50) each. Lunches are less expensive, especially in summer when light buffets are set on long tables within view of the gardens. Throughout the year, there's always at least a live pianist on most nights, and in midsummer, there's a small orchestra that plays dance music three evenings a week.

Services: Room service, babysitting, laundry, valet, hairdresser, massage, concierge.

Facilities: A swimming pool whose filtered waters float atop Lake Como; access to the world-class golf course at nearby Montofano; red-clay tennis courts; gym, sauna, Turkish bath; squash court; waterskiing and other sports.

Inexpensive

Hotel Asnigo

Via Noseda 2, 22012 Cernobbio. ☎ **031/510062.** Fax 031/510249. 30 rms, 3 suites. MINIBAR TV TEL. 175,000 lire ($109.40) double; 230,000 lire ($143.75) suite for three. Rates include breakfast. AE, DC, MC, V. Free parking. Bus: 6.

Asnigo, 1 mile northeast of the center of Cernobbio, calls itself un piccolo Grand Hotel. Commanding a view of Como from its hillside perch at piazza Santo Stefano, this is a good little first-class hotel set in its own garden. Its special and subtle charms have long been known to a lake-loving set of British visitors as it dates from 1914.

An Englishwoman writes: "Last summer I did something not recommendable to your readers: I went on a trip to Italy with my nephew and his wife from America, who quite frankly patronize a higher type of establishment than I do. Naturally, they were lured to the Villa d'Este on Como. I, fortunately, was able to find a splendid little hotel in the hills, the Asnigo. The proprietor was most helpful, the meals flawless and beautifully served, the room spotlessly clean and comfortable. After being a dinner guest one night at the Villa d'Este, I returned the hospitality the following evening by inviting my relatives for a most enjoyable meal at my hotel. At least they learned that good food and comfort are not the sole domain of a deluxe hotel." We echo her sentiments. Meals here begin at 45,000 lire ($28.15).

BELLAGIO

Sitting on a promontory at the point where Lake Como forks, 48 miles north of Milan and 18 miles northeast of Como, Bellagio is with much justification given the label of "The Pearl of Larius." It has also been called "the prettiest town in Europe." A sleepy veil hangs over the town's arcaded streets and its little shops. Bellagio is rich in memories, having attracted fashionable, even royal visitors, such as King Leopold I of Belgium, who used to own the 18th-century Villa Giulia. Bellagio is a 45-minute drive north from Como.

The tourist information center is at piazza della Chiesa 14 (☎ 950204). The Bellagio telephone area code is 031.

WHAT TO SEE & DO

To reach many of the places in Bellagio, you must climb streets that are really stairways. Its lakeside promenade blossoms with flowering shrubbery. From the town, visitors can take tours of Lake Como and enjoy several sports such as rowing and tennis, or else they can lounge at Bellagio Lido.

If time allows, try to explore the gardens of the Villa Serbelloni, piazza della Chiesa (☎ 950204, same as the tourist office), the Bellagio Study and Conference Center of the Rockefeller Foundation (not to be confused with the Grand Hotel Villa Serbelloni by the waterside in the village). The villa is not open to the public, but the park can be visited on guided tours starting at 10:30am and 4pm, and lasting for 1^{1}/$_{2}$ hours. Tours are conducted daily except Monday from mid-April to mid-October at a cost of 5,000 lire ($3.15) per person; the proceeds go to local charities.

The most important tourist attraction of Bellagio is the garden of the Villa Melzi museum and chapel, at lungolario Marconi (☎ 950318). The villa was built in 1808 for Duke Francesco Melzi d'Eril, vice-president of the Italian republic founded by Napoleon. Franz Liszt and Stendhal are among the illustrious guests who have stayed here. The park has many well-known sculptures, and if you're here in the spring you can enjoy the azaleas. Today it's the property of Count Gallarti Scotti, who opens it from April to the end of October, daily from 9am to 6pm. Admission is 5,000 lire ($3.15).

NEARBY ATTRACTIONS

From Como, car-ferries ply back and forth across the lake to Cadenabbia on the western shore. Cadenabbia is another lakeside resort, with hotels and villas, the most important of which you'll surely want to visit is the Villa Carlotta.

Directly south of Cadenabbia on the run to Tremezzo, Villa Carlotta (☎ 0344/40405) is the most-visited attraction of Lake Como—and with good reason. In a serene setting, the villa is graced with gardens of exotic flowers and blossoming shrubbery, especially rhododendrons and azaleas. Its beauty is tame, cultivated, much like a fairytale that recaptures the halcyon life available only to the very rich of the 19th century. Dating from 1847, the estate was named after a Prussian princess, Carlotta, who married the Duke of Sachsen-Meiningen. Inside the villa are a number of art treasures including Canova's Cupid and Psyche, and a number of neoclassical statues by Bertel Thorvaldsen, the Danish sculptor who died in 1844. Also displayed are neoclassical paintings, furniture, and a stone-and-bronze table ornament that belonged to Viceroy Eugene Beauharnais. From March 15 to March

31 and in October, it is open daily from 9am to noon and 2 to 4:30pm; from the first of April through September, daily from 9am to 6pm. Admission is 8,000 lire ($5) for adults, 4,000 lire ($2.50) for children 7 to 14.

WHERE TO STAY & DINE

Expensive

✪ Grand Hotel Villa Serbelloni

Via Roma 1, 22021 Bellagio. ☎ **031/950216,** or 800/223-6620 in the U.S. Fax 031/951529. 95 rms, 5 suites. MINIBAR TV TEL. 395,000–430,000 lire ($246.90–$268.75) double; 780,000–995,000 lire ($487.50–$621.90) suite. Rates include breakfast. AE, DC, MC, V. Free parking. Closed Nov–Mar. Bus: Bellagio bus from Como.

This lavish old hotel is for those born to the grand style of life. Prominently placed, it stands proud and serene at the edge of town against a backdrop of hills. Surrounded by its own gardens of flowers and semitropical plants, it's perched on the lakefront, and guests sunbathe on the waterside terrace or doze under a willow tree. Inside, the public rooms rekindle the spirit of the baroque: the grand drawing room with a painted ceiling, marble columns, a glittering chandelier, and ornate gilt furnishings and the mirrored neoclassical dining room. The bedrooms are wide-ranging, from elaborate suites with a recessed tile bath, baroque furnishings, and lake-view balconies to more chaste quarters. The most desirable rooms open onto the lake; 13 rooms are air-conditioned. The hotel is surrounded by a beautiful lakeside garden and park that are often visited by the general public. In 1993 it opened a fitness and beauty center.

Inexpensive

Hotel du Lac

Piazza Mazzini 32, 22021 Bellagio. ☎ **031/950320.** Fax 031/951624. 48 rms (all with bath or shower). A/C MINIBAR TV TEL. 180,000 lire ($112.50) double. Rates include breakfast. MC, V. Parking 12,000 lire ($7.50). Closed Nov 1–Mar 25. Bus: Bellagio bus from Como.

Hotel du Lac was built 150 years ago, when the waters of the lake came directly up to the front door of the ochre facade. Landfill was dumped into the lake to create the piazza Mazzini. Today there's a generous terraced expanse of flagstones in front, on which are café tables and an arched arcade. The bedrooms are comfortably furnished, containing such amenities as satellite TV, minibar, hairdryers, and air-conditioning. On the second floor is a glassed-in terrace restaurant, and guests can also bask in the sun or relax in the shade on the rooftop garden, opening onto panoramic views of the lake.

⑤ Hotel Florence

Piazza Mazzini 45, 22021 Bellagio. ☎ **031/950342.** Fax 031/951722. 36 rms. TV TEL. 185,000 lire ($115.60) double. Rates include breakfast. MC, V. Closed Nov–Mar. Bus: Bellagio bus from Como.

The entrance to this green-shuttered 19th-century villa is under a vaulted arcade near the ferryboat-landing stage. Wisteria climbs over the iron balustrades of the lake-view terraces. The Florence is one of the most charming middle-bracket choices in the resort. The reception desk is at one end of an entrance hall whose ceilings are supported by massive timbers, old vaulting, and Doric columns made of granite. There's even a Tuscan fireplace, with finely chiseled carving and a globelike wrought-iron chandelier. The main section of this hotel was built around

1720, although most of what you see today was added around 1880. For 150 years the hotel has been run by a member of the Ketzlar family, who originally acquired it as a private villa, turning it into one of the artistic centers of the lake area. Today you'll probably be welcomed by the charming Roberta Ketzlar (who studied foreign languages and worked for a short time as a Milanese radio announcer), her brother Ronald, and their mother, Friedl. The bedrooms are scattered amid spacious upstairs sitting and dining areas, and often have high ceilings, antiques, and lake views. In the '90s the hotel was vastly improved, with the addition of a gourmet restaurant and an America Bar, which becomes a kind of jazz club on Sunday evenings.

TREMEZZO

Reached by frequent ferries from Bellagio, Tremezzo, 48 miles north of Milan and 18 miles north of Como, is another popular west-shore resort that opens onto a panoramic view of Lake Como. Around the town is a district know as Tremezzina, with luxuriant vegetation that includes citrus trees, palms, cypresses, and magnolias. Tremezzo is the starting point for many excursions. Its accommodations are much more limited than those in Bellagio.

From May to October, there is a tourist information center at piazzale Trieste 3 (☎ 40493). The telephone area code for Tremezzo is 0344.

WHERE TO STAY
Moderate

Grand Hotel Tremezzo Palace
Via Regina 8, 22019 Tremezzo. ☎ **0344/40446.** Fax 0344/40201. 98 rms, 2 suites. MINIBAR TV TEL. 240,000–280,000 lire ($150–$175) double; from 350,000 lire ($218.75) suite. Rates include breakfast. AE, DC, MC, V. Free parking. Closed Nov 15–Mar 1. Transportation: Ferry from Bellagio or hydrofoil from Como.

Built in 1910 on a terrace several feet above the traffic of the lakeside road, this hotel is considered one of the region's best examples of the Italian Liberty (art nouveau) style. In 1990, most of the pale-yellow hotel was discreetly modernized, and bedrooms on two of the hotel's four floors were garnished with air conditioning. (This allows guests to have a choice. Many reject the air conditioning despite the fact that there's no additional charge for it, preferring open-windowed access to lakefront breezes instead.) Bedrooms are comfortable, traditionally furnished, and high-ceilinged, and are priced according to views of either the lake or the park and garden extending from the back of the hotel to the top of the nearby hills. Rooms that face the lake are the more expensive in the above-mentioned price range, and usually have private balconies.

Dining/Entertainment: The hotel contains two restaurants as well as an outdoor dining terrace that closes during inclement weather. Both serve regional and international cuisines, with meals priced from 65,000 lire ($40.65) per person. On a platform beside the lake is the Club l'Escale, a bar that is popular with hotel guests and residents of surrounding communities. There's also a billiard room, heliport, and conference facilities.

Services: Room service, babysitting, laundry, valet.

Facilities: A very large park, a large and elegant pool in back of the hotel, and a slightly less desirable one in front; a tennis court, a lido beside the lake, and a jogging track.

Inexpensive

Hotel Bazzoni & du Lac

Via Regina 26, 22019 Tremezzo. ☎ **0344/40403.** Fax 0344/41651. 123 rms. TEL. 123,000–147,000 lire ($76.90–$91.90) double. Rates include breakfast. AE, DC, MC, V. Free parking. Closed Oct 15–Apr 12. Transportation: Ferry from Ballagio or hydrofoil from Como.

There was an older hotel on this spot during Napoleon's era, although it was bombed by the British five days after the official end of World War II. Today the reconstructed hotel is a collection of glass-and-concrete walls, with prominent balconies at the edge of the lake. It's one of the best hotels in a resort town filled with hotels with grander formats but much less desirable accommodations. The main restaurant on the ground floor has a baronial but unused fireplace, contemporary wall frescoes of the boats on the lake, and scattered carvings. The pleasantly furnished sitting rooms include antique architectural elements from older buildings. A summer restaurant near the hotel's entrance is constructed like a small island of glass walls.

A NEARBY PLACE TO STAY

✪ Grand Hotel Victoria

Via lungolago Castelli 7–11, 22017 Menaggio. ☎ **0344/32003.** Fax 0344/32992. 49 rms, 4 junior suites. A/C MINIBAR TV TEL. 280,000 lire ($175) double; from 400,000 lire ($250) suite. Rates include breakfast. Half-board 50,000 lire ($31.25) per person. AE, DC, MC, V. Free parking. Transportation: Ferry from Bellagio or hydrofoil from Como.

This is one of the best hotels on the lake, built in 1806 along a lakeside road bordered with chestnut trees. It was renovated in 1983 into a format almost as luxurious as the original, with attention paid to the preservation of ornate plasterwork whose tendrils and curlicues entwine the ceiling vaults. Architectural details include lavish use of marble, big windows, and carving on the white facade that resembles the heads of what look like water sprites.

Some sections of the establishment have been purchased for private use by vacationing individuals, but the majority of the rooms are available to rent. The modern furniture and amenities in the bedrooms include a radio, plus a private bath with wall tiles designed by Valentino. The beach in front of the hotel is the best spot on Lake Como for windsurfing, especially between 3 and 7pm.

Dining/Entertainment: Guests enjoy drinks on the outdoor terrace near the stone columns of the tree-shaded portico, or in the antique-filled public rooms. The restaurant has well-prepared food, art nouveau chandeliers, and an embellished ceiling showing all the fruits of an Italian harvest scattered amid representations of lyres and mythical beasts. Expect to spend from 50,000 to 70,000 lire ($31.25 to $43.75) for full meals.

Services: Room service, babysitting, laundry, valet.

Facilities: Swimming pool, beach, tennis court, private boats.

WHERE TO DINE

Al Veluu

Via Rogaro 11, Rogaro di Tremezzo. ☎ **40510.** Reservations recommended. Main courses 23,000–26,000 lire ($14.40–$16.25). AE, MC, V. Wed–Mon noon–2pm and 7:30–9:30pm. Closed Nov 11–Mar 19. Bus: 10. LOMBARD/INTERNATIONAL.

Al Veluu, 1 mile north of the resort in the hills, is an ideal stopover for visitors looking for a regional restaurant with plenty of charm and lots of personalized attention. Owner Carlo Antonini is an important element in the relaxed format of this excellent restaurant. Al Veluu (which means "the sail" in the local dialect) is a reminder to him of the time he spends with his friends sailing his boat on Lake Como, which is visible in a panoramic sweep from the terrace's well-prepared tables. The rustic dining room with its fireplace and big windows is a welcome refuge in inclement weather. But in summer the terrace lures all.

Most of the vegetables and produce come freshly picked from the garden, which lies just across the curving road leading up from the lake. Even the butter is home-made, and the best cheeses come from a local farmer whose home is visible among the rocks and trees of a nearby mountain. Menu items include gamberoni (giant shrimp) and fresh fish prepared in several different ways, plus pasta with salmon or in a pesto sauce, carpaccio, grilled beef, veal cutlet milanese or piccata style, and luscious desserts that might include banana flambé, zabaglione, or crêpes Suzette. On weekends the menu is augmented with lake fish and meats in many varieties from the outdoor grill.

3   Lake Maggiore

The waters of this lake wash up on the banks of Piedmont and Lombardy in Italy, but its more austere northern basin (Locarno, for example) lies in the mountainous region of Switzerland. At its longest point it streches a distance of more than 40 miles, and it's 6^1/$_2$ miles at its widest stretch.

A wealth of natural beauty awaits the visitor: mellowed lakeside villas, dozens of gardens with lush vegetation, sparkling waters, panoramic views. A veil of mist seems to hover at times, especially in the early spring and late autumn.

Maggiore is a most rewarding lake to visit from Milan, especially because of the Borromean Islands in its center (most easily reached from Stresa). The fortunate visitor will be able to drive around the entire basin. But those on a more limited schedule may find the western, resort-studded shore the most scenic. From Milan, a drive northwest for about 51 miles will take you to Stresa, the major resort on Lake Maggiore.

STRESA

On the western shore, 407 miles northwest of Rome and 51 miles northwest of Milan, Stresa has skyrocketed from a simple village of fisherfolk to a first-class international resort. Its vantage on the lake is almost unparalleled, and its level of hotel accommodations is superior to that of the Maggiore resorts of Italy. Scene of sporting activities and an international Festival of Musical Weeks (beginning in late August), it swings into action in April, then dwindles in popularity at the end of October. Depending on traffic, Stresa is reached in an hour from Milan on the Simplon Railway. There are no buses for getting about town, but Stresa is small and can easily be walked.

The tourist information center is at via Principe Tomaso 70-72 (☎ 30150). Stresa's telephone area code is 0323.

WHERE TO STAY
Very Expensive

☼ **Grand Hotel des Iles Borromées**
Corso Umberto 1 no. 67, 28049 Stresa. ☎ **0323/30431.** Fax 0323/32405. 172 rms, 13 suites. A/C MINIBAR TV TEL. 490,600–550,000 lire ($306.65–$343.75) double;

699,000–1,595,000 lire ($437.25–$996.90) suite. Rates include breakfast. AE, DC, MC, V. Free parking.

Set on the edge of the lake in a flowering garden, this hotel has an ornate facade looking over the water. The Borromean Islands are visible from many of the bedrooms. All the accommodations have been furnished in an Italian/French Empire style, including rich ormolu, burnished hardwoods, plush carpets, and pastel color schemes. Each room has a private bath or shower, which look as if every quarry in Italy has been scoured for matched marble. The hotel opened its doors for the first time in 1863, attracting titled notables. Alexandra, the grand duchess of Russia, carved her name into one of the hotel's windowpanes with a diamond ring in 1870. But it wasn't until the opening of the Sempione Tunnel in 1906 that the hotel (and Stresa) could profit from the beginning of mass tourism. Famous guests of yesterday have included J. P. Morgan and Eleanora Duse. Hemingway ordained that the hero of *A Farewell to Arms* should stay here to escape from World War I.

The public rooms, elegantly capped with two-tone ornate plasterwork and crystal chandeliers, were even the scene of a top-level meeting among the heads of state of Italy, Great Britain, and France in an attempt to stave off World War II. Today all this splendor can be part of your vacation, but it won't come cheaply.

In addition, the hotel also operates the Residenza, with 27 rooms in a building separate from the main hotel. Prices here are 20% less than those charged in the hotel. Each room in the Residenza is decorated in a modern style, with air conditioning, TV, minibar, and private bath or shower.

Dining/Entertainment: The hotel restaurant serves a cuisine based on specialties of Lombardy and Piedmont, with meals costing 93,500 lire ($58.45) and up. Special dishes include filet of perch with sage and tenderloin cooked on a black stone.

Services: Room service, laundry, babysitting.

Facilities: A medically supervised health and exercise program in the Centro Benessere, two outdoor swimming pools, a tennis court.

Moderate

Hotel Astoria

Corso Umberto I no. 31, 28049 Stresa. ☎ **0323/32566.** Fax 0323/933785. 100 rms. MINIBAR TV TEL. 180,000–260,000 lire ($112.50–$162.50) double. Rates include breakfast. AE, DC, MC, V. Free parking. Closed end Oct–Easter.

Midway between the railway station and the center of Stresa, this hotel lies about a 5-minute walk from either. Fronting the lake, it was rebuilt partially in 1993, giving an even more modern gloss to an already contemporary hotel. A medium-price establishment, it is expressly for sun-seekers wanting an accommodation with its own heated swimming pool, Turkish bath, small gym, roof garden, and Jacuzzi. It features triangular balconies—one to each bedroom—jutting out for the view. The bedrooms are streamlined and spacious. The public lounges have walls of glass opening toward the lake view and the garden. The portion of the dining room favored by most guests is the wide-paved, open-air, front terrace, where under shelter you dine on good cuisine while enjoying Maggiore as the chef d'oeuvre. An Italian and international cuisine is served with meals beginning at 45,000 lire ($28.15).

Regina Palace

Corso Umberto I no. 33, 28049 Stresa. ☎ **0323/933777.** Fax 0323/933776. 167 rms, 7 suites. MINIBAR TV TEL. 290,000–310,000 lire ($181.25–$193.75) double;

330,000–550,000 lire ($206.25–$343.75) suite. Rates include breakfast. AE, DC, MC, V. Free parking outside, 15,000 lire ($9.40) in garage. Closed Dec–Mar.

Regina Palace was built in 1908 in a boomerang-shaped design whose central curve faces the lakefront. The hotel looks almost like the spinnaker of a sailboat running downwind. Foremost among its architectural features are the art deco illuminated-glass columns (lit from within) that are capped with gilded Corinthian capitals. A wide marble stairwell is flanked with carved oak lions, while the elaborately patterned ceiling of the main lobby is illuminated with natural light. There's a swimming pool in the rear, and a guest roster that has included George Bernard Shaw, Ernest Hemingway, King Umbert I of Italy, Princess Margaret, and Gina Lollobrigida. Lately, about half of the guests are American, many of them with tour groups that stream through Stresa. Tennis courts are on the premises, and there is ample parking. Other facilities include squash courts, a Jacuzzi, saunas, a health club, and a Turkish bath. Bedrooms are equipped with all the modern comforts, and many have views of the Borromean Islands, so famous in Italian romantic novels. The hotel also has two dining rooms, one reserved only for residents, where fixed-price meals cost 55,000 lire ($34.40). The other dining choice is the Charleston, an à la carte restaurant.

Inexpensive

⑤ Albergo Ariston

Corso Italia 60, 28049 Stresa. ☎ **0323/31195.** Fax 0323/31195. 12 rms. 100,000 lire ($62.50) double. Rates include breakfast. Half-board 85,000 lire ($53.15) per person. AE, DC, MC, V. Free parking. Closed Dec 1–Apr 1.

Here is a good bargain. The hotel is listed as third class, but its comfort is superior. The rooms are well kept and attractively furnished. Nonresidents can stop in for a meal, ordering a lunch or dinner with wine for 26,000 lire ($16.25) and up. The food is served on the terrace, which has a panoramic view of the lake and gardens. Your hosts are the Balconi family.

Hotel Moderno

Via Cavour 33, 28049 Stresa. ☎ **0323/30468.** Fax 0323/933775. 53 rms (all with bath or shower). MINIBAR TV TEL. 160,000–200,000 lire ($100–$125) double. Rates include breakfast. AE, DC, MC, V. Free parking. Closed Nov–Mar.

A block from the lake and boat-landing stage, Moderno lies in the center of Stresa. Dating from the turn of the century, subsequent modernization, including the most recent one in 1989, has rendered the building's original lines unrecognizable. Bedrooms each have a personalized decor, with good beds and phones for direct dialing and automatic wakeup calls. Moderno has three restaurants, which is unusual for such a small hotel. These include the hotel dining room, reserved for hotel guests only, the Gazebo, and Damigiana. In all three, a set menu is offered for 30,000 lire ($18.75).

WHERE TO DINE

Moderate

✪ Ristorante Emiliano

Corso Italia 50. ☎ **31396.** Reservations required. Main courses 15,000–35,000 lire ($9.40–$21.90); fixed-price menu 55,000 lire ($34.40). AE, DC, MC, V. Wed–Mon 12:30–2:30pm and 7:30–10pm. Closed Jan 10–Feb 16 and Nov 15–Dec 5. EMILIANA.

As its name suggests, the cuisine comes directly from the Emilia-Romagna region of Italy. The restaurant's decor makes it the most elegant nonhotel restaurant in

Stresa. It also serves the best food on Lake Maggiore. The entrance is sheltered by a wrought-iron and glass canopy, which extends partially over the outdoor tables with their view of the lake. Changing menu specialties might include slices of fresh goose liver served with a fondant of onions; pink cannelloni stuffed with a purée of fish; braised Piedmont pigeon in wine and herb sauce; roast duckling with rosemary sauce; or roulades of filet of lakefish prepared with saffron. Desserts include several kinds of crêpes and cassatas.

Inexpensive

Ⓢ Taverna del Pappagallo

Via Principessa Margherita 46. ☎ **30411.** Reservations not accepted. Main courses 15,000–18,000 lire ($9.40–$11.25); pizzas 7,000–15,000 lire ($4.40–$9.40). No credit cards. Thurs–Mon 11:30am–2:30pm and 6:30pm–midnight. ITALIAN.

This formal little garden restaurant and tavern is operated by the Ghiringhelli brothers, who turn out some of the least expensive meals in Stresa. Specialties include gnocchi (semolina dumplings), many types of scaloppine, scalamino allo spiedoe fagioli (grilled sausage with beans), and saltimbocca alla romana (a veal-and-ham dish). At night pizza is king (try the pizza Regina). A complete meal will cost from 35,000 lire ($21) up. The service has a personal touch.

BORROMEAN ISLANDS

The heart of Lake Maggiore is occupied by this chain of tiny islands, which were turned into sites of lavish villas and gardens by the Borromeo clan. From the harbor at Stresa, you can buy an excursion ticket on a boat that will take you to the three major islands. Boats leave about every 30 minutes in summer, and the trip takes 3 hours. The navigation offices at Stresa's center port (☎ 44555) are open daily from 8am to 8pm. The best deal is to purchase an excursion ticket for 11,200 lire ($7), entitling you to go back and forth during the day.

The telephone area code for the islands is 0323.

WHAT TO SEE & DO

The major stopover is on the ✪ Isola Bella (Beautiful Island), which should be visited if you have time for only one sight. Dominating the island is the 17th-century Borromeo Palazzo (☎ 30556). When approached from the front, the figurines in the garden evoke the appearance of a wedding cake. On conducted tours, you are shown through the light and airy palace, from which the views are remarkable. Napoleon slept here. A special feature is the six grotto rooms, built piece by piece like a mosaic. In addition, there is a collection of quite good tapestries, with gory cannibalistic animal scenes. Outside, the white peacocks in the garden enchant year after year. The palace and its grounds are open March to October, daily from 9am to noon and 1:30 to 5:30pm; the annual closing is October 25 to March 26. To visit the palace and its gardens costs 10,000 lire ($6.25) for adults, 5,000 lire ($3.15) for children 6 to 15.

The largest of the chain, ✪ Isola Madre (Mother Island) is visited chiefly because of its botanical gardens. You wander through a setting ripe with pomegranates, camellias, wisteria, rhododendrons, bougainvillea, hibiscus, hydrangea, magnolias, even a cypress tree from the Himalayas. The 17th-century palace (☎ 31261) on the grounds may also be visited. It contains a rich collection of 17th- and 18th-century furnishings. Of particular interest is a collection of 19th-century French and German dolls belonging to Countess Borromeo. Livery of various kinds belonging to the House of Borromeo is also exhibited. The unique 18th-century marionette theater of the House of Borromeo, complete with scripts, stage scenery, and devices for sound, light, and other special effects, is on display. Peacocks, pheasants, and other birds live and roam freely on the grounds. Visiting hours are 9am to noon and 1:30 to 5:30pm daily from March 27 to October 24. Admission to both palace and grounds is 10,000 lire ($6.25) for adults, 5,000 lire ($3.15) for children 6 to 15.

Isola del Pescatori (Fisher's Island) is without major sights or lavish villas, but in many ways it is the most colorful. Less a stage setting than its two neighbors, it's inhabited by fisherfolk who live in cottages. Good walks are possible in many directions.

VILLA TARANTO

Back on the mainland near the resort of Pallanza, north of Stresa, the ✪ Giardini Botanici at Villa Taranto, via Vittorio Veneto 111, Verbania-Pallanza (☎ 0323/ 556667), are spread over more than 50 acres of the Castagnola Promontory, which juts out into Lake Maggiore. In this dramatic setting between the mountains and the lake, more than 20,000 species of plants from all over the world thrive in a well-tended and cultivated institution, begun in 1931 by a Scotsman, Capt. Neil McEacharn. Plants range from rhododendrons and azaleas to specimens from such faraway places as Louisiana and Canada. Seasonal exhibits include fields of Dutch tulips (80,000 of them), Japanese magnolias, giant water lilies, cotton plants, and rare varieties of hydrangeas. The formal gardens of the villas are carefully laid out with ornamental fountains, statues, and reflection pools. Among the more ambitious creations of the gardens is the elaborate irrigation system that pumps water from the lake to all parts of the gardens, and the Terrace Gardens, complete with waterfalls and swimming pool.

The villa gardens are open April 1 through October 31, every day from 8:30am to 6:30pm. Professional guides will take you on tours, which last more than an hour. You may also take a round-trip boat ride from Stresa, which docks at the Villa Taranto pier adjoining the entrance to the gardens. You pay an admission of 10,000 lire ($6.25) for adults, 9,000 lire ($5.60) for children 6 to 14.

Milan & Lombardy 18

The vicissitudes of Italy's history are reflected in Lombardy as perhaps in no other region. Conquerors from barbarians to Napoleon have marched across its plain. Even Mussolini came to his end here. He and his mistress—both already dead—were strung up in a Milan square as war-weary residents vented their rage upon the two bodies.

Among the most progressive of all the Italians, the Lombards have charted an industrial empire unequaled in Italy. Often the dream of the underfed and jobless worker in the south is to go to Milano for the high wages and the good life, although thousands end up finding neither.

Lombardy isn't all manufacturing. Milan, as we'll soon see, is filled to the brim with important attractions, and nearby are old Lombard art cities—Bergamo, Cremona, and Mantua (Mantova), as well as the Carthusian Monastery of Pavia.

DRIVING TOUR

Days 1–2: Milan, 355 miles northwest of Rome, can be your gateway to Lombardy. Take in the panoramic sweep of the city, the industrial and artistic center of the north of Italy, and go on several shopping binges. Take in such major attractions as Il Duomo, Pinacoteca di Brera, Museo Poldi-Pezzoli, and Biblioteca-Pinacoteca Ambrosiana. Count yourself lucky if you get a hard-to-obtain ticket to attend an opera at La Scala.

Day 3 From Milan, take autostrada E64 east for a visit to Bergamo, lying 31 miles to the northeast. Explore its Città Alta or Upper Town and visit the Galleria dell'Accademia Carrara.

☕ **TAKE A BREAK** If you'd like a simple lunch, try Trattoria al Castello, via Castello 14, in Bergamo (☎ 035/259607), at the foot of the castle. The food is plain and straightforward, the main courses costing from 10,000 lire ($6.25), but the views are among the most panoramic in the area.

Continue east on the autostrada toward Brescia, cutting south on A21 to Cremona for the night.

Day 4 At a point 59 miles southeast of Milan, Cremona is the "city of the violin." In the morning, take in the piazza del Comune

---

What's Special About Milan & Lombardy

Great Towns/Villages

- Milan, the major city of northern Italy, with a history going back 2,500 years.
- Mantua, ancient seat of the Gonzagas, hometown of Virgil; the great Mantegna was court painter here for 50 years.
- Bergamo, acclaimed for its Città Alta or Upper Town, fortified by the Venetians during their long centuries of control.
- Cremona, on the Po River, the city of the violin, birthplace of Monteverdi and Stradivari.

Museums/Galleries

- The Brera Palace and Picture Gallery, in Milan, rich in the works of Lombard and northern Italian painters.
- The Poldi Pezzoli Museum, Milan, with three major galleries filled with masterpieces, devoted to the Renaissance Lombard school.

Religious Shrines

- The Duomo of Milan, begun in 1386, a marvel of white marble loaded with belfries, gables, statues, and pinnacles.
- The Duomo at Cremona, a magnificent Lombard building begun in the Romanesque style and famed for its Torrazzo, a beautiful campanile, the tallest in Italy.

Palace

- The Ducal Palace, in Mantua, with luxuriously and sumptuously decorated apartments from the 16th to the 18th century.

Ace Attraction

- La Scala, in Milan, acclaimed by some as the world's greatest opera house, with a season lasting from mid-December to May.

---

and the Museo Stradivariano. Enjoy lunch at either Aquila Nera (Black Eagle) or Ceresole. Even though starred restaurants, they are reasonable in price. For the night cut east along SS10 to Mantua (Mantova). If you arrive late, plan a morning visit to its Museo di Palazzo Ducale.

FOOD & WINE

The distinctive cookery of Lombardy, which relies heavily on country butter, reaches its finest levels of achievement in Milan. Even the minestrone tastes different here from the way it does in other parts of Italy. The specialty is risotto, rice cooked in consommé and flavored with saffron. A land of mountains, valleys, and lakes, the region of Lombardy is fertile, and every village has its own wine, some of which has won the praise and poetry of such big names as Pliny and Virgil. Even Leonardo da Vinci and Carducci have tasted the food and wine of Lombardy, and given it their blessing.

A tasty, aromatic, and refined cookery, the Lombardy cuisine relies on smoked meats, beef, dairy products, and the inevitable rice (as opposed to pasta). The most famous dish is the celebrated veal cutlet milanese (in Vienna they call it Wiener schnitzel). Osso buco is another highly praised dish—shinbone of veal cooked in a ragoût). Polenta made with corn meal always wins praise—"one bite of polenta, one bit of crunchy delight?"—and sometimes its served with *osei* (little roast birds). *Stufato* is stewing beef cooked in a savory sauce made with tomatoes and other vegetables.

The vines of Lombardy yield tender grapes which are transformed into such aromatic wines as Barbagallo, Buttafucco, and something called "Inferno." Barbagallo, usually served with poultry, has a strong red color, with a delicate bouquet and fruity quality. Buttafucco is a fairly full-bodied, bright-red wine, with a lively bouquet. Its served with roasts. Inferno is much more appealing than it sounds, a deep ruby red in color, with a penetrating bouquet and a nutty aftertaste. It's served with all lunches and dinners.

Other wines include Rosso Riviera del Garda, a brilliant light ruby red in color with a nutty, fruity bouquet, and Sassella, also a bright ruby red in color with a bouquet of roses, served with red-meat roasts and rare game.

1 Milan

355 miles NW of Rome, 87 miles NE of Turin, 88 miles N of Genoa

Italians in the south, perhaps resentful of the hard-earned prosperity of the north, sometimes declare that the Milanese are not unlike their nearby neighbors, the no-nonsense Swiss. With two million inhabitants, Milan doesn't evoke the languor and garrulousness of the rest of Italy, it doesn't muck about with excessive manners, and it doesn't snooze somnolently in the midday heat. It works, it moves, and it bustles. It's Italy's window on Europe, its most advanced showcase, devoid of the dusty and musty history that sometimes seems to paralyze modern developments in Rome or Florence, or the watery rot that seems to pervade the sublimely beautiful Venice with an inevitable sense of decay.

Part of the work ethic that has catapulted Milan toward the 21st century may stem from the Teutonic origins of the Lombards (originally from northwestern Germany) who occupied Milan and intermarried with its population after the collapse of the Roman Empire. Later, the Teutonic influence was strengthened during the 18th-century occupation by the Austrians.

Today, however, Milan is a commercial powerhouse and, partly because of the 400 banks and the major industrial companies headquartered here, the most influential city in Italy. It's the center of the country's publishing industry, its silk industry, its television and advertising industries, and its design industry; and it lies very close to the densest collection of automobile-assembly plants, rubber and textile factories, and chemical plants in Italy. It also boasts La Scala, one of the most prestigious opera houses in Europe, a major commercial university (the alma mater of most of Italy's corporate presidents), and the site of several world-renowned annual trade fairs.

Since its beginning Milan has, with unashamed capitalistic style, purchased more art than it has produced, and lured to its borders what is probably the most energetic and hard-working group of creative intellects in all of Italy. To make it in Milan, in either business or the arts, is to have made it to the top of the pecking order in modern Italy. Milan is, in effect, the New York of Italy. If you came to Italy to find sun-flooded piazzas and somnolent afternoons, you probably won't find them amid the fogs and rains of Milan. You will, however, have placed your finger on the pulse of modern Italy.

Throughout history Milan has had to succeed by its wits. Set on one of the most fertile plains in Europe, with few natural defenses other than the skill of its diplomats and traders, the city has always more or less successfully negotiated through the labyrinth of European politics. Since the A.D. 313 proclamation by Constantine the Great of the Edict of Milan (which declared the Roman Empire officially Christian), Milan has been in the center of events.

In the 14th century the Visconti family, through their wits, wealth, and a series of astute marriages with the royal families of England and France, made Milan the strongest state in Italy. Realizing its dependence on agriculture early in its history, Milan initiated a continuing campaign of drainage and irrigation of the Po Valley that helped to make it one of the most fertile regions in the world.

Later, in the 1700s, Milan was dominated by the Hapsburgs, a legacy that left it with scores of neoclassical buildings in its inner core and an abiding appreciation for music and (perhaps) work. In 1848 Milan was at the heart of the northern Italian revolt against its Austro-Hungarian rulers. To buttress its claims of legitimacy, Milan encouraged the development of a pan-Italian dialect (through the novelist Manzoni) that could be understood by everyone in Italy, regardless of their native dialects. Milan (with neighbor Piedmont) was at the center of the 19th-century nationalistic passion that swept through Italy and laid the groundwork for the country's eventual unification. By the turn of the century thousands of workers had immigrated to Milan from the south; they swelled its population and raised its industrial output to envied figures.

Milan both elected and then helped to destroy Mussolini, who, after being shot repeatedly by Milanese partisans, was hung by his heels on a meat hook, with his mistress, in the town's main square.

Today Milan is the only Italian city other than Rome that receives transatlantic flights. The city is elegant and prosperous; its inhabitants are tuned in to developments in Paris, London, and New York, and proud of their dynamic and unusual city.

ESSENTIALS

GETTING THERE   By Plane   Milan is serviced by two airports, the **Aeroporto di Linate,** $4^1/2$ miles east of the inner city, and the **Aeroporto della Malpensa,** 31 miles to the northwest. In general, the Malpensa airport is used for most transatlantic flights, whereas Linate is for flights within Italy and Europe. For general flight information about both airports, call 74852200. Buses for Linate leave from the Porta Garibaldi station every 20 minutes from 5:40am to 7pm and every 30 minutes from 7 to 9pm. Buses for Malpensa leave from the Stazione Centrale every $2^1/2$ hours before international and intercontinental flight departures. (Buses run in both directions, so they're the best bet for new arrivals.) This, I assure you, is much cheaper than taking a taxi.

By Train   Milan is serviced by the finest rail connections in Italy. The main rail station for arrivals is Mussolini's mammoth **Stazione Centrale,** piazza Duca d'Aosta (☎ 67500), where you'll find the National Railways information office open daily from 7am to 10:30pm. One train per hour arrives from either Genoa or Turin (trip time: $1^1/2$–2 hours from either city); a one-way fare from either point is 12,000 lire ($7.50). Twenty trains arrive each day from Venice (trip time: 3 hours), at a one-way fare of 18,700 lire ($11.70); and one train per hour arrives from Florence (trip time: 3 hours), with a one-way cost of 59,300 lire ($37.05).

Trains from Rome arrive every hour, taking 5 hours for the journey and costing from 59,300 lire ($35.60) each way.

By Bus   Buses link Milan with Pavia, Bergamo, and other cities of Lombardy. Some of these companies are privately owned and others are under the control of Regione Lombardia. For information about various routings in the province, ask at the A.T.M. Information Office, on the departures floor of Stazione Centrale, at piazza Duca d'Aosta (☎ 6697032).

By Car   The A4 autostrada is the principal east–west route for Milan, with the A8 coming in from the northwest, the A1 from the southeast, and the A7 from the southwest. The A22 is another major north–south artery, running just east of Lake Garda.

ORIENTATION

Piazza del Duomo lies in the heart of historical Milan. This square, which contains the cathedral, is also the geographical heart of the ever-growing city. Milan is encircled by three "rings," one of which is the **Cerchia dei Navigli,** a road that more or less follows the outline of the former medieval walls. The road runs along what was formerly a series of canals—hence the name *navigli.* The second ring is known both as **Bastioni** or **Viali,** and it follows the outline of the Spanish Walls from the 16th century. It is now a tram route (take no. 29 or 30). A much more recent ring is the **Circonvallazione Esterna,** which connects you with the main roads coming into Milan.

If you're traveling within the Cerchia dei Navigli, which is relatively small, you can do so on foot. It's not recommended that you attempt to drive within this circle unless you're heading for a garage. All the major attractions, including Leonardo's *Last Supper,* La Scala, and the Duomo, lie within this ring.

One of Milan's most important streets, **via Manzoni,** begins near the Teatro alla Scala, and will take you to piazza Cavour, a key point for the traffic arteries of Milan. The **Arch of Porta Nuova** marks the entrance to via Manzoni. This *archi,* as they call it in Italian, is a remnant of the medieval walls. To the northwest of piazza Cavour lie the Giardini Pubblici, and to the northwest of these important gardens is **piazza della Repubblica.** From this square, via Vittorio Pisani leads into **piazza Duca d'Aosta,** site of the cavernous Stazione Centrale.

Back at piazza Cavour, you can head west along via Fatebenefratelli into the **Brera district,** whose major attraction is the Accademia di Brera at via Brera 28. This district in recent years has become a major center in Milan for offbeat shopping and after-dark diversions.

GETTING AROUND

A special 3,800 lire ($2.40) one-day travel pass, good for unlimited use on the city's tram, bus, and subway network, is available in Milan at the tourist office, Ente Provinciale per il Turismo, at piazza del Duomo at via Marconi 1 (☎ 02/980662). Those planning a longer stay can purchase a weekly pass, costing 8,400 lire ($5.25) and requiring a photo.

The city bus system covers most destinations in Milano, at a cost of 1,100 lire (70¢), as does the subway at the same fare. Some subway tickets are good for continuing trips on city buses at no extra charge, but they must be used within 75 minutes of purchase. These fares are presented only for your general guidance and may go up during the lifetime of this edition.

To phone a taxi, dial 6767 or 8388; fares start at 4,000 lire ($2.50), with a nighttime surcharge of 4,000 lire ($2.50).

FAST FACTS: Milan

American Express   There is an American Express bank at via Brera 3 (☎ 85571), open Monday through Friday from 9am to 5pm.

Area Code   The telephone area code is 02.

Consulates   The **U.S. Consulate,** largo Donegani 1 (☎ 02/29001841), is open Monday through Friday from 8:30am to 12:30pm and 2 to 4:30pm. The consulate of **Canada** is at via Vittor Pisani 19 (☎ 6697451), open Monday through Friday from 9am to 5pm. Citizens of the **United Kingdom** will find their consulate at via San Paolo 7 (☎ 8693442), open Monday through Friday from 9:15am to 12:15pm and 2:30 to 4:30pm. **Australia** has a consulate at via Borgogna 2 (☎ 777041), open Monday through Friday from 9am to noon and 2 to 4:30pm. Citizens of **New Zealand** should contact their consulate in Rome.

Emergencies   For the police, call 77271; for an ambulance, 7733; for an emergency, 113.

Hospital   About a 5-minute ride from the Duomo of Milan, the Ospedale Maggiore Policlinico, via Francesco Sforza 35 (☎ 581655), should serve your medical needs. It has English-speaking doctors.

Laundry   Self-Service Lavanderia Automatica, corso Porta Vittoria 51 (☎ 55192315), is one of the most centrally located. Otherwise, ask your hotel or look in the yellow pages for a *lavanderia* near you.

Newspapers   Foreign newspapers can be found at all major newsstands, among them those at the Stazione Centrale and piazza del Duomo. If you read Italian (even just a little bit), you can pick up information about present attractions and coming events, such as cinema and theater schedules, by buying the daily *La Repubblica*, a useful newspaper. If you're seeking secondhand bargains, you can learn about sales in *Secondamano*, which comes out only on Monday and Thursday.

Pharmacies   If you need a drugstore, you can find an all-night pharmacy by phoning 192 for information. A pharmacy (☎ 6690735) at the Stazione Centrale never closes.

Post Offices   Most branches are open from 8:30am to 1:30pm Monday through Saturday. The Central Post Office is at via Cordusio 4 (☎ 8692069), and is open Monday through Friday from 8:30am to 5:30pm and Saturday from 8:30am to 1pm. To reach it, take the subway to the Cordusio stop.

Religious Services   Roman Catholic services in English are conducted at Santa Maria Annunciata, piazza del Duomo 18 (☎ 804441). Protestant worship is at Cristiana Protestante, via M. de Marchi 9 (☎ 6552858), and at Cristiana Protestante, via P.L. da Palestrina 14 (☎ 66987408).

Telephone   If you need to make long-distance calls, try, if possible, to avoid going through your hotel switchboard, which will impose staggering surcharges. The best place is the Central Post Office (see above), where telephone booths and operators maintain a 24-hour service.

Tourist Offices   One of the first things you may need in Milan is some information. If so, you'll find the **Azienda di Promozione Turistica del Milanese,** on piazza del Duomo at via Marconi 1 (☎ 809662), particularly helpful, dispensing free maps and whatever advice they can. There is a branch at the Stazione Centrale (☎ 6690532) for arriving train passengers.

WHAT TO SEE & DO
THE TOP ATTRACTIONS

Despite its modern architecture and industry, Milan is a city of great art. The serious sightseer will give the metropolis at least two days for exploration. If your schedule is frantic, see the Duomo, and the important Brera Picture Gallery.

✪ Il Duomo

Piazza del Duomo. ☎ **870907.** Admission is free. June–Sept daily 7am–7pm; Oct–May daily 9am–4:30pm. Subway: Duomo. Tram: 1, 4, or 8.

In the very center of Milan, opening onto the heart of the city's life, is piazza del Duomo. Its impressive lacy Gothic cathedral ranks with St. Peter's in Rome and the cathedral at Seville, Spain, among the largest in the world. It's 479 feet long and 284 feet wide at the transepts. The cathedral, which dates from 1386, has seen numerous architects and builders. The conqueror of Milan, Napoleon, even added his own decorating ideas to the facade in the early years of the 19th century. The imposing structure of marble is the grandest and most flamboyant example of the Gothic style in Italy.

Built in the shape of a Latin cross, the cathedral is divided by soaring pillars into five naves. The overall effect is like a marble-floored Grand Central Terminal—that is, in space—with far greater dramatic intensity. In the crypt rests the tomb of San Carlo Borromeo, the cardinal of Milan. To experience the Duomo at its most majestic, you must ascend to the roof, either by elevator for 7,000 lire ($4.40) or by steps for 4,000 lire ($2.50), from which you can walk through a "forest" of pinnacles, turrets, and marble statuary—like a promenade in an early Cocteau film. The gilded Madonna towers over the tallest spire.

Museo del Duomo

In the Palazzo Reale, piazza del Duomo 14. ☎ **860358.** Admission 8,000 lire ($5). Tues–Sun 9:30am–12:30pm and 3–6pm. Subway: Duomo.

Museo del Duomo is housed in the Palazzo Reale (Royal Palace). It's like a picture storybook of the cathedral's six centuries of history. The museum has exhibits of statues and decorative sculptures, some of which date from the 14th century. Also shown are antique art objects, stained-glass windows (some from the 15th century), and ecclesiastical vestments, many as old as the 16th century. The museum also houses the Museo d'Arte Comtemporanea upstairs, with a permanent exhibition of Italian Futurist art, along with some Picasso works.

✪ Santa Maria delle Grazie *(The Last Supper)*

Piazza Santa Maria delle Grazie. ☎ **4987588.** Admission to church, free; *Last Supper*, 12,000 lire ($7.50). Viewers admitted 25 at a time are required to pass through antechambers designed to remove pollutants on their bodies. After they view the painting for 10 minutes only, visitors must walk through two additional filtration chambers. Mon–Sat 6:50am–noon and 3–7pm, Sun 3–7pm; *Last Supper*, Tues–Sun 8:15am–1:45pm. Subway: Cadorna. Bus: 21 or 24.

Off corso Magenta, on piazza Santa Maria delle Grazie, this Gothic church was erected by the Dominicans in the mid-15th century. A number of its more outstanding features, such as the cupola, were designed by the great Bramante. But tourists from all over the world flock here to gaze upon a mural in the convent next door. In what was once a refectory, the incomparable Leonardo da Vinci adorned one wall with *The Last Supper*. Commissioned by Ludovico the Moor, the painting was finished about 1497. The gradual erosion of the painting makes for one of the most intriguing stories in art. It narrowly escaped being bombed in 1943, and is now being restored. What remains today, however, is Leonardo's "outline"—and even it is suffering badly. As one Italian newspaper writer puts it: "If you want to see 'Il Cenacolo,' don't walk—run!" A painting of grandeur, the composition protrays Christ at the moment he announces to his shocked apostles that one of them will betray him. Vasari called the portrait of Judas "a study in perfidy and wickedness."

✪ Pinacoteca di Brera

Via Brera 28. ☎ **864-63-501.** Admission 8,000 lire ($4.80). Tues–Sat 9am–5pm; Sun 9am–1pm. Subway: Lanza.

Pinacoteca di Brera, one of Italy's finest art galleries, contains an exceptionally good collection of works by both Lombard and Venetian masters. Like a Roman emperor, Canova's nude Napoleon—a toga draped over his shoulder—stands in the courtyard (fittingly, a similar statue ended up in the Duke of Wellington's house in London).

Among the notable artworks, a *Pietà* by Lorenzo Lotto is a work of great beauty, as is Gentile Bellini's *St. Mark Preaching in Alexandria* (it was finished by his brother, Giovanni). Seek out Andrea Mantegna's *Virgin and the Cherubs*, a great work from the Venetian school. Two of the most important prizes at the Brera are Mantegna's *Dead Christ* and Giovanni Bellini's *La Pietà*, as well as Carpaccio's *St. Stephen Debating*.

Other paintings include Titian's *St. Jerome*, as well as such Lombard art as Bernardino Luini's *Virgin of the Rose Bush* and Andrea Solario's *Portrait of a Gentleman*. One of the greatest panels is Piero della Francesca's *Virgin and Child Enthroned with Saints and Angels and the Kneeling Duke of Urbino in Armor*. Seek out, in addition, the *Christ* by Bramante. One wing, devoted to modern art, offers works by such artists as Boccioni, Carrà, and Morandi. One of my favorite paintings in the gallery is Raphael's *Wedding of the Madonna*, with a dancelike quality. *The Last Supper at Emmaus* is another moving work, this one by Caravaggio.

MORE ATTRACTIONS

✪ Museo Poldi-Pezzoli

Via Manzoni 12. ☎ **794889.** Admission 10,000 lire ($6.25). Tues–Fri 9:30am–12:30pm and 2:30–6pm; Sat 9:30am–12:30pm and 2:30–7:30pm; Sun 9:30am–12:30pm. Closed Apr–Sept Sun 2:30–7:30pm. Subway: Montenapoleone. Tram: 1 or 4. Bus: 61, 96, or 97.

This fabulous museum is done in great taste and is rich with antique furnishings, tapestries, frescoes, and Lombard wood carvings. It also displays a remarkable collection of paintings by many of the old masters of northern and central Italy, including Andrea Mantegna's *Madonna and Child*, Giovanni Bellini's *Cristo Morto*, and Filippo Lippi's *Madonna, Angels, and Saints* (superb composition). One room is devoted entirely to Flemish artists, and there is a collection of ceramics and also one of clocks and watches. The museum grew out of a private collection donated to the city in 1881.

Milan

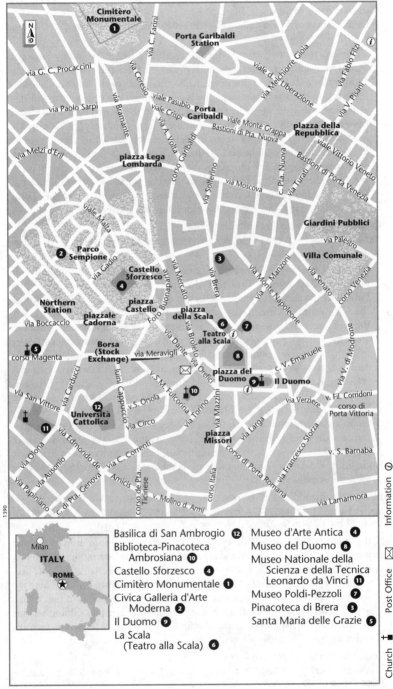

Cimitèro Monumentale ①
Porta Garibaldi Station
via C. Farini
via G. C. Procaccini
via Ceresio
viale Pasubio
viale Crispi
Porta Garibaldi
viale Monte Grappa
Bastioni di Pta. Nuova
viale di Melchiorre Gioia
via Fabio Filzi
via V. Pisani
(i)
via Paolo Sarpi
via Bramante
via A. Volta
corso Garibaldi
piazza della Repubblica
viale Vittorio Veneto
via Melzi d'Eril
piazza Lega Lombarda
via Solferino
via Moscova
c. Pta. Nuova
via Turati
Bastioni di Porta Venezia
viale Malta
Giardini Pubblici
via Palestro
② **Parco Sempione**
③
Villa Comunale
via Senato
corso Venezia
via Gadio
Castello Sforzesco
④
via Mercato
via Brera
via Manzoni
via Monte Napoleone
Northern Station
via Boccaccio
piazza Castello
Foro Bonaparte
piazzale Cadorna
piazza della Scala
⑥ ⑦
(i)
Teatro alla Scala
⑤ ✝
corso Magenta
Borsa (Stock Exchange)
via Meravigli
via Dante
via Broletto
via Orefici
⑧
✉
piazza del Duomo
⑨ ✝ **Il Duomo**
(i)
C. V. Emanuele
via V. di Modrone
via San Vittore
via Carducci
Luini
via Cappuccio
V. S.M. Fulcorina
V. S. Orsola
✝⑩
via Mazzini
via Verzière
v. Fil. Corridoni
corso di Porta Vittoria
✝
⑪
⑫ **Università Cattolica**
via Torino
via Circo
piazza Missori
via Larga
corso di Porta Romana
via Francesco Sforza
via Olona
via Edmondo de Amicis
via Ausonio
via C. Correnti
piazza Missori
via Italia
v. S. Barnaba
via Papiniano
c. di Pta. Genova
corso de Pta. Ticinese
v. Molino d. Armi
via Lamarmora

1390

Basilica di San Ambrogio ⑫	Museo d'Arte Antica ④
Biblioteca-Pinacoteca Ambrosiana ⑩	Museo del Duomo ⑧
Castello Sforzesco ④	Museo Nationale della Scienza e della Tecnica Leonardo da Vinci ⑪
Cimitèro Monumentale ①	
Civica Galleria d'Arte Moderna ②	Museo Poldi-Pezzoli ⑦
Il Duomo ⑨	Pinacoteca di Brera ③
La Scala (Teatro alla Scala) ⑥	Santa Maria delle Grazie ⑤

ITALY
Milan
ROME ★

Church ✝ Post Office ✉ Information (i)

Museo d'Arte Antica

In Castello Sforzesco, piazza Castello. ☎ **62083940.** Admission 8,000 lire ($5). Tues–Sun 9:30am–5:30pm. Subway: Cairoli.

Castle Sforzesco, the Castle of Milan, is an ancient fortress rebuilt by Francesco Sforza, who launched another governing dynasty. It is believed that both Bramante and Leonardo da Vinci contributed architectural ideas to the fortress. Following extensive World War II bombings, it was painstakingly restored and continued its activity as a Museum of Ancient Art. Displayed on the ground floor are sculpture from the 4th century A.D., medieval art mostly from Lombardy, and armor. The most outstanding exhibit, however, is Michelangelo's *Rondanini Pietà*, on which he was working the week he died. In the rooms upstairs, besides a good collection of ceramics, antiques, and bronzes, is the important picture gallery, rich in paintings from the 14th to the 18th century, including works by Lorenzo Veneziano, Mantegna, Lippi, Bellini, Crivelli, Foppa, Bergognone, Cesare da Sesto, Lotto, Tintoretto, Cerano, Procaccini, Morazzone, Guardi, and Tiepolo.

○ Biblioteca-Pinacoteca Ambrosiana

Piazza Pio XI no. 2. ☎ **86451436.** Admission 8,000 lire ($5). Tues–Sun 9:30am–4:50pm. Subway: Duomo-Cordusio.

Near the Duomo, the Ambrosiana Picture Gallery and Library were founded in the early 17th century by Cardinal Federico Borromeo. On the second floor, the Pinacoteca contains a remarkable collection of art, mostly from the 15th through the 17th century. Among the notable works are a *Madonna and Angels* by Botticelli; works by Brueghel (which have impressive detail, and are among the best art in the gallery); paintings by Lombard artists, including Bramantino's *Presepe*, in earthy, primitive colors; plus a curious miniature *St. Jerome with Crucifix* by Andrea Solario, along with works by Bernardino Luini. The museum owns a large sketch by Raphael on which he labored before painting *The School of Athens* for the Vatican. The most celebrated treasures are the productions of Leonardo da Vinci's *Codice Atlantico.* (In Milan, the master had as a patron the powerful Ludovico Sforza, known as "The Moor.") After seeing the sketches (in facsimile), you can only agree with Leonardo's evaluation of himself as a genius without peer. Attributed to him is a portrait of a musician, believed to have been Franchino Gaffurio. The Library contains many medieval manuscripts, which are shown for scientific examination only.

Museo Nazionale della Scienza e della Tecnica Leonardo da Vinci

Via San Vittore 21. ☎ **485551.** Admission 10,000 lire ($6.25) ages 18–60, 6,000 lire ($3.75) under 18 and 60 or more. Tues–Sun 9am–5pm. Subway: S. Ambrogio.

If you're a fan of Leonardo da Vinci, as I am, you may want to drop by this vast museum complex where you could practically spend a week devouring the exhibits. For the average visitor the most interesting section is the Leonardo da Vinci Gallery, which displays copies and models from the Renaissance genius. There is a reconstruction pharmacy from a convent, along with a monastic cell, even a sewing-machine collection. You'll also see antique carriages plus exhibits relating to astronomy, telecommunications, watchmaking, goldsmithery, motion pictures, and the subjects of classic physics.

Civica Galleria d'Arte Moderna

Via Palestro 16. ☎ **760-02-819.** Admission is free. Tues–Sun 9:30am–5:30pm. Subway: Palestro. Bus: 61, 65, 96, or 97.

Civica Galleria d'Arte Moderna (Civic Modern Art Gallery) used to be known as the royal villa before its name was changed to the Villa Comunale. Constructed between 1790 and 1793, it was designed by the architect Leopold Pollack. For a short time it was the residence of Napoleon and Eugène de Beauharnais. The gallery has a large collection of works from the Milanese neoclassical period, along with many paintings that show the development of Italian Romanticism. It's predictably rich in the works of Lombard artists. Important collections that have been donated are those of Carlo Grassi and the Vismara art accumulation. Also important is the Marino Marini Museum, which was opened in 1973. Marini, a famous Italian sculptor, has some 200 works displayed, including not only sculpture, but paintings and graphics, all a gift of the artist himself. You'll recognize the names of many artists on parade: Picasso, Matisse, Rouault, Renoir, Modigliani, Corot, Millet, Manet, Cèzanne, Bonnard, and Gauguin.

Basilica di Sant'Eustorgio

Piazza Sant'Eustorgio 1. ☎ **5810183.** Admission 1,000 lire (65¢). Daily 8am–noon and 3–7pm. Tram: 3.

The bell tower of the 4th-century Basilica of Sant'Eustorgio dates from the 13th century; it was built in the Romantic style by patrician Milanese families. It has the first tower clock in the world, made in 1305. Originally, this was the tomb of the Three Kings (4th century A.D.). Inside, its greatest treasure is the Capella Portinari, designed by the Florentine Michelozzo in Renaissance style. The chapel is frescoed and contains a bas-relief of angels at the base of the cupola. In the center is an intricately carved tomb, supported by marble statuary of the 13th century by Balduccio of Pisa. Inside are the remains of St. Peter Martyr. The basement has a Roman crypt.

Basilica di San Ambrogio

Piazza di Sant'Ambrogio 15. ☎ **86450895.** Admission to church, free; museum, 3,000 lire ($1.90). Church, Mon–Sat 7am–noon and 2:30–7pm; Sun 7am–1pm. Museum, Mon–Sat 10am–noon and 3–5pm; Sun 3–5pm. Closed Aug. Subway: San Ambrogio. Bus: 50, 54, 96, or 97.

This was originally erected by St. Ambrose in the later years of the 4th century A.D. The present structure was built in the 12th century in the Romanesque style. The remains of St. Ambrose rest in the crypt. The church, entered after passing through a quadrangle, is rather stark and severe, in the style of its day. The atrium is its most distinguishing architectural feature. In the apse are interesting mosaics from the 12th century. The Lombard tower at the side dates from 1128, and the facade, with its two tiers of arches, is impressive.

In the church is the **Museo della Basilica di S. Ambrogio,** containing some frescoes, 15th-century wood paneling, silver and gold objects originally for the altar, paintings, and sculpture, including Flemish tapestries.

Cimitèro Monumentale

Piazzale Cimitèro Monumentale 1. ☎ **659-9938.** Admission is free. Apr–Sept, Tues–Sun 8:30am–6pm; Oct–Mar, Tues–Sun 8:30am–5pm. Tram: 4, 8, 12, or 14.

Cimitèro Monumentale (Monumental Cemetery) has catered for more than 100 years to the whims of Milan's elite society. Actually, the only requirements for burial in the cemetery are, first, that you are dead, and second, that you can buy your way into a plot. Some families have paid up to 200 million lire just for the privilege of burying their dead here. The graves are marked not only with brass plates or granite markers, but also with Greek temples, elaborate obelisks, or such original works as an abbreviated version of Trajan's Column.

This outdoor museum has become such an attraction that a superintendent has compiled an illustrated guidebook—a sort of "Who *was* who." Among the cemetery's outstanding sights is a sculpted version of *The Last Supper.* Several fine examples of art nouveau sculpture dot the hillside, and there's a tasteful example of Liberty-style architecture (Italy's version of art nouveau) in a tiny chapel designed to hold the remains of Arturo Toscanini's son, who died in 1906. Among the notables buried here are Toscanini himself and novelist Alessandro Manzoni. In the Memorial Chapel is the tomb of Salvatore Quasimodo, who won the 1959 Nobel prize in literature. Here also rest the ashes of Ermann Einstein, father of the scientist. In the Palanti Chapel is a monument commemorating the 800 Milanese citizens slain in Nazi concentration camps. (A model of this monument is displayed in the Museum of Modern Art in New York.) The location is a few blocks east of Stazione Porta Garibaldi.

WHERE TO STAY

In the city are some deluxe as well as a superabundance of first- and second-class hotels, most of which are big on comfort but short on romance. In the third- and fourth-class bracket and on the pensione (boarding house) level there are dozens of choices—many of which rank at the bottom of the totem pole of comparably classed establishments in all of Italy's major cities, with the exception of Naples. Some places are outright dangerous, and others so rock-bottom and unappealing as to hold little interest for the average visitor. In several places, men sit around in the lobby in their bathrobes watching soccer games on the one TV set.

Our recommendation is—if you can afford it—to stay in a better grade of hotel in Milan, and to leave your serious budgeting to such tourist meccas as Rome, Florence, and Venice, which have clean, comfortable, and often architecturally interesting third- and fourth-class hotels and pensioni. However, for the serious economizer we have included some budget recommendations for Milan, which, we are told, represent the best of the lot. They are presented as safe and (hopefully) clean shelters, but with no particular enthusiasm on our part.

VERY EXPENSIVE

Four Seasons Hotel Milano

Via Gesù 8, 20121 Milano. ☎ **02/77088.** Fax 02/770850000. 77 rms, 16 suites. A/C MINIBAR TV TEL. 632,000–768,400 lire ($395–$480.25) double; from 813,600 lire ($508.50) suites. Breakfast 40,000–45,000 lire ($25–$28.15) extra. AE, DC, MC, V. Subway: Lanza.

Milan's most exciting five-star hotel opened in 1993 in a location beloved by any shopper—a side street opening onto the most elegant concentration of upscale boutiques in Italy, via Montenapoleone. Housed within the walls of what was originally built as a monastery in the 14th century, its acquisition was considered a real estate coup by the Toronto-based Four Seasons group. The building once functioned as the residence for the Hapsburg-appointed governor of northern Italy in the 1850s, and later, as luxury apartments. The medieval facade, many of the frescoes and columns, and the original monastic details were incorporated into a modern edifice flooded with sunlight and accented with bronze, stone floors, glass, pearwood cabinetry, Murano chandeliers, and acres of Fortuny fabrics. Accommodations are cool, conservative, spacious, and discreetly outfitted in tones of beige and pale green, always with a sense of understated luxury.

Dining/Entertainment: The hotel lounge contains the architectural renderings for stage sets that were later used at the nearby La Scala opera house. Nearby is the hotel's gastronomic showcase, Il Teatro, where meals cost from 100,000 lire ($62.50), and are served only at dinner, every day from 8pm to midnight. A less formal dining area, La Veranda, serves meals continuously every day from 7am to 11pm for around 60,000 lire ($37.50) per person.

Services: 24-hour room service, concierge.

Facilities: A high-tech fitness center was in place at presstime, although during the lifetime of this edition, additional spa facilities will probably become available. A business center provides virtually any service you'd expect from your own office.

Milano Hilton

Via Galvani 12, 20124 Milano. ☎ **02/69831** or 800/445-8667 in the U.S. or Canada. Fax 02/66-71-08-10. 303 rms, 18 suites. A/C MINIBAR TV TEL. 384,000–596,000 lire ($240–$372.50) double; 900,000–1,360,000 lire ($562.50–$850) suite. Breakfast 25,000–35,000 lire ($15.65–$21.90) extra. Children stay free in parents' room. AE, DC, MC, V. Parking 45,000 lire ($28.15). Subway: Stazione Centrale.

Milano Hilton, built in 1969, is a modern glass-and-steel cube a few blocks from the main railway station. Its comfortable furnished bedrooms contain everything you'd expect in terms of high-quality accommodations, as well as many extras. This all-purpose hotel could suit either a tourist or a businessperson, and the mix of clients in the London Bar, with its richly upholstered chairs, contains both. The marble-trimmed lobby has four elevator banks.

Dining/Entertainment: The hotel spent millions of lire renovating the upstairs restaurant, Da Guiseppe, whose warmly chosen shades of gilt and brown, along with its Belle Epoque accessories, recall the era of Verdi, whose portrait hangs behind a frequently used grand piano. A portrait of Verdi's mistress, Guiseppina Strepponi, hangs on the opposite wall. Their juxtaposition helps to create the kind of intimacy that goes well with the Italian and international dishes that are the specialties of the house. À la carte meals range from 35,000 to 75,000 lire ($21.90 to $46.90). The London Bar is like an elegant English pub.

Services: Room service, babysitting, laundry, valet.

Facilities: Facilities for the disabled, business center.

Palace Hotel

Piazza della Repubblica 20, 20124 Milano. ☎ **02/6336** or 800/221-2340 in the U.S., or 800/955-2442 in Canada. Fax 02/654485. 220 rms, 6 suites. A/C MINIBAR TV TEL. 530,000 lire ($331.25) double; 700,000–1,600,000 lire ($437.50–$1,000) suite. Breakfast 25,000–40,000 lire ($15.65–$25). AE, DC, MC, V. Parking 48,000–80,000 lire ($30–$50). Subway: Repubblica. Tram: 1, 4, 11, 29, or 30.

Palace Hotel, blithely ignoring the pell-mell commercial world around it, stands aloof on a hill near the railway station; it has a formal car entrance and a facade of 11 floors with tiers of balconies. Primarily a business hotel catering to some of Europe's most prominent figures, the Palace also welcomes tourists and occasional entertainers. The bedrooms are furnished with pastel upholstery and carpeting, and reproductions of Italian antiques. Modern conveniences include heated towel racks and minibars concealed behind mahogany chests.

Dining/Entertainment: The hotel bar attracts an international clientele, and the Grill Casanova is acclaimed as one of the finest in Milan, offering both regional and international dishes, with meals costing 90,000 lire ($56.25) and up.

Services: Room service, babysitting, laundry, valet.
Facilities: Fitness center.

Prìncipe di Savoia

Piazza della Repubblica 17, 20124 Milano. ☎ **02/6230** or 800/325-3535 in the U.S. and Canada. Fax 02/6595838. 297 rms, 47 suites. A/C MINIBAR TV TEL. 561,000–693,000 lire ($350.65–$433.10) double; from 1,045,000–2,200,000 lire ($653.10–$1,375) suite. Breakfast 30,800–48,400 lire ($18.75–$30.25) extra. AE, DC, MC, V. Parking 50,000 lire ($31.25) and up. Subway: Repubblica. Tram: 1, 4, 11, 29, 30.

The Prìncipe was built in 1927 to fill the need for a luxurious hotel near the Stazione Centrale. It was completely restored in 1991. Substantial and luxurious, it offers good solid comfort amid crystal, detailed plasterwork, fine carpets, and polished marble. The bedrooms are spacious and modernized and decorated in a 19th-century Lombard style. Many are paneled in hardwoods, and all contain leather chairs, stylish furniture, and modern bath with all the accessories. The Prìncipe, whose elaborately ornamented wings date from 1947 and 1954, has housed what might be a "Who's Who" of 20th-century Western society. Notable guests have included Luciano Pavarotti, Ingrid Bergman, Alexander Haig, Julio Iglesias, Henry Ford, a wide assortment of the Rockefellers, Evita Peron, Maria Callas, Jerry Lewis, and the Duke of Windsor.

Dining/Entertainment: The spacious bar area off the main lobby is the social focal point of the hotel. The hotel has a notable restaurant, Galleria, serving both regional and international dishes with meals beginning at 90,000 lire ($56.25). It also offers the popular Doney café (see "Where to Dine," below).

Services: Room service, babysitting, laundry, valet.

Facilities: Limited facilities for the disabled, sauna, health club, solarium, indoor swimming pool.

MODERATE

Carlton Hotel Senato

Via Senato 5, 20121 Milano. ☎ **02/760-15-535.** Fax 02/783300. 79 rms. A/C MINIBAR TV TEL. 310,000 lire ($193.75) double. Breakfast 20,000 lire ($12.50) extra. AE, MC, V. Parking 30,000–60,000 lire ($18.75–$37.50). Closed Aug. Subway: San Babila.

The facade of this hotel appears like a collection of private ochre-fronted villas joined into a single unit behind an iron fence. The modernized interior is set up to receive the dozens of traveling businesspeople who check in weekdays from other sections of Europe and from America. Each of the well-furnished bedrooms contains wall-to-wall carpeting and a high-ceilinged format. The hotel has a restaurant and bar on the premises, and also has a parking garage. Laundry service, babysitting, and room service are also provided.

✓ Casa Svizzera

Via San Raffaele 3, 20121 Milano. ☎ **02/8692246.** Fax 02/72004690. 45 rms. A/C MINIBAR TV TEL. 230,000 lire ($143.75) double. Rates include breakfast. AE, DC, MC, V. Parking 30,000 lire ($18.75). Subway: Duomo.

Casa Svizzera, right off piazza del Duomo, is one of the most serviceable hotels in the city, following a reconstruction in 1970. Two elevators service five floors of rooms. Features include paneled double windows and soundproofing to keep out the noise. The bedrooms, furnished in a homelike fashion, have air conditioning that can be independently regulated.

Excelsior Gallia

Piazza Duca d'Aosta 9, 20124 Milano. ☎ **02/6785** or 800/225-5843 in the U.S. and Canada. Fax 02/66713239. 220 rms, 6 suites. A/C MINIBAR TV TEL. 381,500–425,000 lire ($238.45–$265.65) double; 959,000–1,350,000 lire ($599.40–$843.75) suite. Breakfast 22,000–35,000 lire ($13.75–$21.90) extra. AE, DC, MC, V. Parking 35,000 lire ($21.90). Subway: Stazione Centrale. Tram: 1, 2, or 9.

Originally completed in 1933 by members of the Gallia family, this hotel was built in the Liberty (art nouveau) style and has ever since been a monument on the piazza Duca d'Aosta. Enlarged in the 1960s, it was bought by the British-based Forte chain in 1989, and in 1994, additional renovations combined some of the smaller rooms into larger and more comfortable accommodations. Set near the main railway station, the hotel is one of the most expensive and visible hotels in Milan. Bedrooms fall into two categories: modern and comfortable in the newer wing and more graciously old-fashioned in the original core. All are soundproofed against the roar of traffic in the massive plaza outside.

Dining/Entertainment: The hotel contains a noted restaurant, Gallia's, serving regional and international dishes. The Baboon Bar (also recommended separately) offers a stylish place for a rendezvous. A piano player performs in a corner of the lobby on some evenings.

Services: Room service, babysitting, laundry, valet.

Facilities: Concierge, business center, fitness club with a massage center, gym, whirlpool, sauna.

Hotel Galles-Milano

Via Ozanam 1 (corso Buenos Aires), Milano 20129. ☎ **02/204841** or 800/528-1234 in the U.S. and Canada. Fax 02/29404872. 100 rms, 5 suites. A/C MINIBAR TV TEL. 170,000–540,000 lire ($106.25–$337.50) double; 250,000–750,000 lire ($156.25–$468.75) suite. Rates include breakfast. AE, DC, MC, V. Subway: Lima.

The walls that contain this hotel were originally built in 1901 as one of the then-most-glamorous hotels in Milan. In 1990, a consortium of Italian investors poured millions of dollars into an elegant rehabilitation, producing an aggressively marketed hotel that is much favored by businesspeople, conventioneers, and temporary visitors to Milan looking for safe, comfortable, and unpretentious lodgings. The interior lacks the art nouveau glamour of many of its competitors, although this omission doesn't seem to bother the many clients who approve of the establishment's functional lines and conservatively modern bedrooms. The hotel contains a big-windowed rooftop restaurant (La Terrazza) with additional seating on a canopy-covered terrace, and a cocktail bar with a drink for virtually everyone's taste. In use in spring or summer is a roof garden with a solarium and Jacuzzi.

Windsor

Via Galileo Galilei 2, 20124 Milano. ☎ **02/6346.** Fax 02/659-0663. 118 rms, 7 suites. A/C MINIBAR TV TEL. 260,000 lire ($162.50) double; from 320,000 lire ($200) suite. Rates include breakfast. AE, DC, MC, V. Parking 16,000 lire ($10). Subway: Repubblica. Bus: 1, 9, 29, 30, or 33.

Windsor was erected and furnished in 1968. In spite of its "moderno," it maintains a warm ambience. A generous use of vibrant colors, plus a wise selection of traditional furnishings, with an accent on comfort, have made the Windsor a satisfactory hotel in its price range. A corner building of sienna-colored marble, it was built midway between the railway station and the Duomo on a tree-lined boulevard. The accommodations contain wall-to-wall draperies and built-in headboards and chests. Public facilities include a cozy bar, as well as a breakfast room, with tall panels of wood and walls of curtained glass. The Windsor Grill serves an international cuisine, with meals starting at 35,000 lire ($21.90). It's located near piazza Repubblica; there's a parking garage. Services include laundry, babysitting, and room service.

INEXPENSIVE

⊗ Antica Locanda Solferino

Via Castelfidardo 2, 20121 Milano. ☎ **02/6592706.** Fax 02/6571361. 11 rms (all with bath). TV TEL. 150,000 lire ($93.75) double. Rates include breakfast. V. Parking 25,000–30,000 lire ($15.65–$18.75) nearby. Subway: Moscova.

When this country-style hotel was opened in 1976, the surrounding neighborhood was considered a depressed backwater of downtown Milan. Since then, however, the location has improved into an avant-garde community of actors, writers, and poets, and this inn deserves some of the credit for the transformation. The hotel got off to a fortuitous beginning soon after it opened when members of the editorial staff of *Gentleman's Quarterly* stayed here while working on one of their fashion features in Milan. Since then, Lindsay Kemp and Marcello Mastroianni have been among the fashionable clients who either stay in one of the old-fashioned bedrooms or who dine at the ground-floor restaurant (see my recommendation in "Where to Dine," below). The restaurant is under separate management.

Each bedroom is different, which reflects the floor plan of the 19th-century building that houses it. There are no singles. The furnishings include Daumier engravings, art nouveau or late 19th-century bourgeois pieces, and various armoires purchased from a nearby hotel that went out of business. But the baths are modern. Since the hotel is small and often fully booked, it's wise to make reservations as far in advance as possible.

Hotel Bolzano

Via Boscovich 21, 20124 Milano. ☎ **02/6691451.** Fax 02/6691455. 35 rms (all with bath or shower). A/C MINIBAR TV TEL. 190,000 lire ($118.75) double. Rates include breakfast. AE, DC, MC, V. Parking 28,000 lire ($17.50). Subway: Stazione Centrale.

This hotel, about 500 feet from the main railway station, has been considerably renovated and upgraded. English is spoken, and the hotel has a helpful management, which makes this a welcome oasis. Ideal for families, some triple and quadruple units are also rented. The hotel has a patio and a comfortable lounge as well. Laundry service is provided. There is also a private garden and a garage in front of the hotel.

⊗ Hotel Gran Duca di York

Via Moneta 1A (piazza Cordusio), 20123 Milano. ☎ **02/874863.** Fax 02/869-0344. 33 rms. TV TEL. 220,000 lire ($137.50) double; 260,000 lire ($162.50) triple. Rates include breakfast. AE, V. Parking 35,000 lire ($21.90). Closed Aug. Subway: Cordusio.

When it was built by the Catholic church in the 1890s, this Liberty-style palace was used as a residence for dozens of priests who staffed the nearby Duomo. Among them was the cardinal of Milan, who later became Pope Pius XI. Today visitors can rent one of the pleasantly furnished and well-kept bedrooms, each with a private bath sheathed with patterned tiles. There are only three singles. Behind the ochre-and-stone facade, visitors will find a bar in an alcove of the severely elegant lobby, where a suit of armor and leather-covered armchairs contribute to the restrained tone.

⑤ Hotel Manzoni

Via Santo Spirito 20, 20121 Milano. ☎ **02/760-05-700.** Fax 02/784212. 52 rms. TEL. 198,000 lire ($123.75) double. Breakfast 19,000 lire ($11.90) extra. AE, DC, MC, V. Parking 30,000–35,000 lire ($18.75–$21.90). Subway: San Babila.

Hotel Manzoni charges reasonable prices considering its location near the most fashionable shopping streets of Milan. It lies behind a facade of stone slabs on a fairly quiet one-way street. Each of its bedrooms is outfitted with comfortable functional furniture and carpeting, which are color coordinated. Many of the accommodations contain TVs. A brass-trimmed winding staircase leads from the lobby into a bar and TV lounge. The cooperative English-speaking staff will point the way to the hotel's garage.

Hotel Star

Via dei Bossi, 20121 Milano. ☎ **02/801501.** Fax 02/861787. 30 rms (all with shower). A/C TV TEL. 202,000 lire ($126.25) double. Rates include buffet breakfast. AE, MC, V. Closed Aug. Parking 20,000–25,000 lire ($12.50–$15.65). Subway: Duomo.

The Ceretti family welcome guests to their well-run little hotel on a narrow street positioned a few blocks from La Scala and the Duomo. The lobby has been refurbished, making it brighter than before, and the bedrooms are comfortably furnished. Amenities such as hairdryers have been installed in the bathrooms. Double glass windows cut down on the noise from the street. A rich buffet breakfast is served, including jams, pâté, yogurts, cheese, eggs, ham, and fruit salad, along with cereal, croissants, and various teas, juices, and coffee.

WHERE TO DINE

The wide economic levels of the population—from textile manufacturer to factory worker—are reflected in the prices in the restaurants, which range from the haute-cuisine type to the pizza parlor.

EXPENSIVE

✪ Giannino

Via Amatore Sciesa 8. ☎ **55195582.** Reservations required. Main courses 42,000–66,000 lire ($26.25–$41.25). AE, DC, MC, V. Tram: 12 or 60. MILANESE.

Giannino continues to enchant its loyal patrons and to win new adherents every year who sing its praises. Rightly, it's considered one of the top restaurants in all of Lombardy, and has been since its founding in 1899. It has a chef who approaches every day as if he must make his reputation anew. Diners have a choice of several attractively styled rooms, but eyes rivet on the tempting underglass offerings of the *specialità gastronomiche milanesi* from the behind-the-glass kitchen. The choice is excellent, including such characteristic Lombard dishes as the tender, breaded veal cutlet and the risotto simmered in broth and coated with Parmesan cheese. It's difficult to recommend any specific dish, as everything we've ordered, or even seen going by, piqued my taste. However, we have special affection for the tagliolini con scampi al verde, fresh homemade noodles with prawn tails in green herb sauce. Also superb are the cold fish and seafood salad and the beautifully seasoned *orata al cartoccio* (a fish baked in a brown paper bag with shrimp butter along with fresh herbs.)

Il Teatro

In the Four Seasons Hotel Milano, via Gesù 8. ☎ **77088.** Reservations recommended. Main courses 30,000–36,000 lire ($18.75–$22.50). Set price dinner 75,000 lire ($46.90). AE, DC, MC, V. Mon–Sat 7:30pm–midnight. Closed Aug. INTERNATIONAL.

This is the culinary showcase of the shopping district's newest and most glamorous hotel (see "Where to Stay.") Favored since its opening in 1993 by such luminaries as Versace, Missoni, Calvin Klein, and members of the Agnelli family, the restaurant lies one floor below the lobby level of a Milanese palazzo that was originally built in the 1400s as a cloister. Containing no more than 50 places, the restaurant has an outdoor patio overlooking a garden for warm-weather dining, and a dining room whose walls are sheathed in burnished paneling and nut-colored leather. Overhead is suspended a tented ceiling of champagne-colored silk.

Prices are less expensive than you might have thought, considering the setting and the degree of elegance. A seasonal menu changes at least four times a year, but might include an *involtini* of eggplant with ricotta and mint; crispy crayfish with a purée of tomatoes; potato gnocchi stuffed with caviar and fresh dill; and a filet of red mullet with essence of tomato and black truffles. Dessert might be a *mille-feuille croquante* layered with walnuts, chocolate mousse, and raspberries.

St. Andrews

Via Sant'Andrea 23. ☎ **798236.** Reservations required. Main courses 32,000–60,000 lire ($20–$37.50). AE, DC, MC, V. Mon–Sat 12:30–3:30pm and 8pm–1am. Closed Aug. Bus: 65, 96, or 97. INTERNATIONAL.

This restaurant has given much pleasure to many people for many years. It offers one of the finest kitchens in Lombardy, preparing both international and regional food. The cuisine is superior. Menu items include an unusual appetizer of steak tartare mixed with caviar and seasonings, John Dory in a salt crust, and rack of lamb in the provençal style. The dessert specialty is a *tartatelli*, which is composed of pastry with a honey and strawberry sauce. At lunch it has somewhat the atmosphere of a private club and is apt to be filled with businesspeople. The armchairs are covered in black leather, the paneling is dark wood, and the lighting is discreet from hooded lamps. Formally attired waiters give superb service to regular guests and to such celebrities as famous Italian fashion stylists, which are likely to include Gianfranco Ferré, Armani, Versace, Mariuccia Mandelli (Krizia), and Missoni Fendi.

MODERATE

Al Chico di Uva

Via Sirtori 24, ☎ **29406883.** Reservations recommended. Main courses 16,000–35,000 lire ($10–$21.90). AE, DC, MC, V. Mon–Fri noon–2:30pm; Mon–Sat 7–10:30pm. Closed Aug 3–27. Subway: Porta Venezia. TUSCAN/ITALIAN.

Al Chico, a good neighborhood restaurant specializing in such fare as onion soup and fondue bourguignonne, was established in the 1970s in a much-renovated, century-old building. Tuscan specialties such as Florentine beefsteak are also featured, and portions are tasty and satisfying. The chef is rightly proud of his pappardelle with porcini mushrooms, branzini (sea bass) cooked in a salt crust, and spaghetti with mushrooms and spring onions. The place is usually crowded, but it's worth the wait for a table. The service is good, and the basic materials that go into the dishes are fresh and well selected at the market. Of course, you'll want to order chianti, that most typical of all Italian wines, to go with your meal. Good house wines from Tuscany are stocked. In summer, you can eat in a garden.

Alfio-Cavour

Via Senato 31. ☎ **76000633.** Reservations recommended. Main courses 25,000–35,000 lire ($15.60–$21.90). AE, DC, MC, V. Mon–Fri 12:30–3pm; Sun–Fri 7:30–11pm. Closed Aug. Subway: San Babila. ITALIAN/INTERNATIONAL.

There's a luminous quality to the lavish displays of antipasti served with relish at this family-run restaurant. It stems partly from the Tahitian-style decor, where trees grow through the glass panels of a greenhouselike roof and vines entwine themselves among bamboo lattices. You'll be seated in the clear light of what used to be a private garden. The restuarant is best known for its serve-yourself display of antipasti, where the polite but sharp-eyed staff bills you for what you select. A pasta specialty is the flavorful spaghetti pescatore, with bits of seafood. You might follow with large grilled shrimp or a "gran misto" fish fry, or else one of the many excellent beef or veal dishes.

Al Porto

Piazzale Generale Cantore. ☎ **8321481.** Reservations required. Main courses 25,000–40,000 lire ($15.65–$25). AE, DC, MC, V. Tues–Sat 12:30–2:30pm; Mon–Sat 7:30–10:30pm. Closed Dec 24–Jan 3 and Aug. Subway: S. Agostino. Bus: 8 or 19. SEAFOOD/ITALIAN.

Established in 1907 within a building that functioned during the 18th century as one of the city's customs houses, this restaurant is among the most popular seafood restaurants in Milan. To enter this pavilion, lying in the Navigli district of the city, you pass by tanks of "demons of the deep" (some of which might later end up on your plate). The glassed-in garden room is the most sought after by the loyal habitués of this place. By some estimates, reservations are sometimes necessary several days in advance because of its popularity, especially with a clientele of business patrons who consider its setting conducive to good business. Menu items include orata (dorado) with pink peppercorns, bavette with scampi and fresh tomatoes, and branzini (sea bass) with white Ligurian wine and olives. Many patrons come here for just one dish: risotto ai fruitti di mare, the classic Lombard dish served with an assortment of sea creatures. One of the staff confided that the "best patrons" begin with a selection from the warm antipasti, then follow with one of the risotto offerings, and, finally, order the traditional fritto misto, sautéed shellfish and fish, although many diners find this far too much food. Of the fritto misto, almost anything that swims is likely to turn up on the plate. Everything tastes better with one of the Friuli wines.

A Santa Lucia

Via San Pietro all'Orto 3. ☎ **76023155.** Reservations recommended. Main courses 22,000–35,000 lire ($13.75–$21.90). V. Tues–Sun noon–2:30pm and 3:30pm–3am. Closed Aug. Subway: San Babila. ITALIAN/SEAFOOD.

A Santa Lucia pulls out hook, line, and sinker to lure you with some of the best fish dinners in Milan. A festive place at which to dine, the restaurant is decked out with photographs of pleased celebs, who attest to the skill of its kitchen. You can order such specialties as a savory fish soup, which is a meal in itself; fried baby squid; or good-tasting sole. Spaghetti alle vongole evokes the tang of the sea with its succulent clam sauce. Pizza also reigns supreme. Try either the calzone of Naples or the pizza napoletana, the classic dish of the city on the bay. Both are made with mozzarella.

Bistrot di Gualtiero Marchesi

Via San Raffaele 2. ☎ **877120.** Reservations required. Main courses 20,000–30,000 lire ($12.50–$18.75); fixed-price menus 44,000 lire ($27.50); vegetarian menu, 54,000 lire ($33.75); Milanese menu, 63,000 lire ($39.40); fish menu. AE, DC, MC, V. Mon–Sat 12:30–2:30pm and 7:30–10:30pm. Closed Aug 8–29. Subway: Duomo. LOMBARD.

Near the Duomo, this bistro was created by Signor Gualtiero Marchesi, the patron saint of *cucina nuova* in Italy. Once hailed by *Time* magazine as among the

10 top chefs in the world, he operated a very expensive restuarant at another location. He moved his major restaurant to the town of Erbusco, near Brescia, but this bistro was left as a love token to Milan. It boasts one of the best views of the cathedral in all the city. Set on the top floor of the Rinascente Center, which rises seven stories across a narrow street from the cathedral ("almost within touching distance"), the bistro has big walls of glass to better admire the view. The menu is likely to depend on the inspiration of the chef. Dishes enjoyed in the past have included an unusual form of half-opened ravioli, or crayfish cooked very al dente with cucumbers. You are almost certain to find a perfectly done veal cutlet milanese.

Boeucc Antico Ristorante

Piazza Belgioioso 2. ☎ **76020224.** Reservations required. Main courses 25,000–32,000 lire ($15–$19.20). AE. Mon–Fri 12:40–2:30pm; Sun–Fri 7:40–10:40pm. Closed August. Subway: Duomo. INTERNATIONAL.

This restaurant, established in 1696, is a trio of rooms in a severely elegant old palace, within walking distance of the Duomo and the major shopping streets of Milan. Throughout you'll find soaring stone columns and modern art. In summer, guests gravitate to a terrace for open-air dining. The hearty specialties, the standard of the kitchen, come from regions of Italy. You might enjoy a spaghetti in clam sauce, a salad of shrimp with arugula and artichokes, or grilled liver, veal, or beef with aromatic herbs. In season, sautéed zucchini flowers accompany some dishes.

Doney

In the Principe di Savoia hotel, piazza della Repubblica 17. ☎ **6230.** Reservations not necessary. Main courses 15,000–29,000 lire ($9.40–$18.15); afternoon tea 23,000 lire ($14.40). AE, DC, MC, V. Daily noon–12:30am and 4–7pm. Subway: Repubblica. Tram: 1, 4, 11, 29, or 30. LIGHT. INTERNATIONAL/AFTERNOON TEA.

Its burnished paneling, plush upholstery, and soaring frescoed ceiling are considered some of the high points of one of Milan's most recent (and most expensive) hotel restorations. Part of the $40-million restoration of one of the city's most visible hotels, Doney borrowed its name from a historic café in Rome, and much of its decorative allure from the turn-of-the-century "Liberty" style of Italy's gilded age. Its menu features elegant but simple preparations of salads (lobster, artichokes, and pear), and sandwiches (smoked salmon on brown bread). Also available are steaks. During teatime, the English-inspired service might include any of nine kinds of tea, and pastries and finger sandwiches from a trolley. At any hour, the place functions gracefully as a popular meeting point.

La Scaletta

Piazza Stazione Genova 3. ☎ **58100290.** Reservations required. Main courses 28,000–36,000 lire ($17.50–$22.50). AE. Tues–Sat noon–1:15pm and 8–9:30pm. Closed one week at Easter, Aug, and Dec 24–Jan 6. Subway: Stazione Genova. ITALIAN.

La Scaletta emerges near the top in the highly competitive world of Milanese restaurants, and it's housed in a Liberty-style building dating from around the turn of the century. Here, modern Italian cuisine is practiced by the chefs with a certain flair. In an elegant setting, which some diners have likened to a small and exclusive London club, the restaurant serves in two rooms. Because this place is so popular with the business community of the city, reservations are essential, as far in advance as possible. The quality of the ingredients is superb. The chefs demand that every item be fresh, whether it be fish or vegetables. The veal dishes are heavenly. You might begin with a tripe terrine in gelatin or a scampi salad, before giving serious attention to your main course. A specialty is a risotto made with green peas and wild mushrooms. Other special dishes include a carpaccio with herbs, tagliatelle with clams and broccoli, sautéed kidneys with mushrooms, and a pâté of snails. The signature dessert is freshly made *gelati* with rosemary and sage.

✪ Peck's Restaurant

Via Victor Hugo 4. ☎ **876775.** Reservations not necessary. Main courses 28,000–36,000 lire ($17.50–$22.50); fixed price menus 60,000–80,000 lire ($37.50–$50). AE, DC, MC. V. Mon–Sat 12:15–2:30pm and 7:15–10:30pm. Closed Sun July 1–20. Subway: Duomo. MILANESE/ITALIAN.

Peck's is owned by the famous delicatessen of Milan, which many gastronomes consider the Milanese equivalent of Fauchon's in Paris. It was established by Francesco Peck, who came to Milan from Prague in the 19th century. His small restaurant eventually became a food empire. In an environment filled with shimmering marble and modern Italian paintings, an alert staff will serve you an elegant cuisine. The fresh specialties include a classic version of risotto milanese, rack of lamb with fresh rosemary, ravioli alla fonduata, and lombo di vitello (veal) with artichokes, followed by chocolate meringue for dessert. Its cured meats are said to be the richest in Italy.

✪ Savini

Galleria Vittorio Emanuele 11. ☎ **72003433.** Reservations required: Main courses 35,000–45,000 lire ($21.90–$28.15); fixed-price lunch with wine 65,000 lire ($40.65); fixed price dinner without wine 80,000 lire ($50). AE, DC, MC, V. Mon–Fri noon–3pm; Mon–Sat 7:30–11pm. Closed Dec 23–Jan 6 and Aug. 10–21. Subway: Duomo. LOMBARD.

Savini provides a heavenly introduction to the aromatic cookery of Lombardy and has attracted everybody from Puccini to Pavarotti. Perched in the heart of the great glass-enclosed arcade opposite the Duomo, the "classico" restaurant, which dates from 1867, draws both the out-of-towner and the discriminating local who wants some of the most savory viands in the city. Guests sit on the terrace outside, or dine in the old-world room, with its crystal chandeliers and glittering silverware. Waiters in black jackets hover over you to see that you enjoy every mouthful. Many of the most memorable dishes are unassuming, for example, the specialty of Lombardy—costoletta alla milanese, the most tender veal coated with egg batter and breadcrumbs, then fried a rich brown. The pièce de résistance of Milan, most often ordered before the main course, is risotta alla milanese—that is, rice simmered in a broth and dressed with whatever the artiste in the kitchen selects that night. Savini is excellently stocked with a wide range of wine (the staff will gladly assist you).

✪ Trattoria Bagutta

Via Bagutta 14. ☎ **76002767.** Reservations required. Main courses 20,000–50,000 lire ($12.50–$31.25). AE, DC, MC, V. Mon–Sat 12:30–2:30pm and 7:30–10:30pm. Closed Sat–Sun in July–Aug. Subway: San Babila. INTERNATIONAL.

Patronized by artists, this restaurant is the most celebrated of the trattorie in Milan. A venerable-looking establishment, which dates from 1927, it's slightly hard to find in its side-street location. The Bagutta is known for the caricatures—framed and frescoed—that cover its walls. Of the many large and bustling dining rooms, the rear one with its picture windows is most enticing.

The tempting food draws on the kitchens of Lombardy, Tuscany, and Bologna for inspiration. Assorted antipasti are offered. Main-dish specialties include fried squid and scampi, *lingua e pure* (tongue with mashed potatoes), linguine with shrimp in a tomato cream sauce, and scaloppine alla Bagutta. The Bagutta enjoys a vogue among out-of-towners, who consider it chic to patronize the sophisticated little trattoria, as opposed to the more deluxe restaurants.

INEXPENSIVE

Al Tempio d'Oro

Via delle Leghe 23. ☎ **26145709.** Reservations not necessary. Main courses 10,000–17,000 lire ($6.25–$10.65). No credit cards. Mon–Sat 8pm–2am. Closed two weeks in Aug. Subway: Pasteur. ITALIAN/INTERNATIONAL.

This restaurant, near the central railway station, offers inexpensive and well-prepared meals in an ambience similar to what you might have found if an ancient Greek temple had decided to serve beer on tap along with international food specialties. The chef is proud of his fish soup, Spanish paella, and North African couscous. The crowd scattered among the ceiling columns is relaxed, and they contribute to an atmosphere that's somewhat like that of a beer hall. No one will mind if you stop by just for a drink.

⑤ La Magolfa

Via Magolfa 15. ☎ **8321696.** Reservations required. Main courses 17,000–22,000 lire ($10.65–$13.75); fixed-price meal 60,000 lire ($37.50). AE, DC, MC, V. Mon–Sat 8pm–midnight. Closed Aug. Subway: Porta Genova. MILANESE/LOMBARD.

La Magolfa, one of the city's dining bargains, offers a gargantuan fixed-price meal. The building is a country farmhouse, whose origins go back to the 1500s, although the restaurant opened only in 1960. It's likely to be crowded, as is every other restaurant in Milan that offers such value. If you don't mind its location away from the center of town, in Zona Ticinese in the southern part of the city, you'll be treated to some very good regional cookery that emerges fresh from battered pots and pans. A general air of conviviality reigns. There is music of local origin nightly.

⑤ Peck

Via Victor Hugo 4. ☎ **876774.** Reservations required. Main courses 18,000–22,000 lire ($11.25–$13.75). AE, DC, MC, V. Mon–Sat 7:30am–9pm. Subway: Duomo. MILANESE/LOMBARD.

Peck offers one of the best mealtime values in Milan, served in a glamorous cafeteria associated with the most famous delicatessen in Italy—a high-priced restaurant in the basement offers meals beginning at 70,000 lire ($43.75); see the listing above under "Moderate." Only a short walk from the Duomo, Peck has a stand-up bar in front, and, in the rear, well-stocked display cases that contain specialties fresh from the establishment's treasure trove of produce. Armed with a plastic tray, you can sample such temptations as artichoke-and-Parmesan salad, seafood salads, marinated carpaccio, slabs of tender veal in an herb sauce, risotto marinara, and selections from a carving table laden with a juicy display of roast meats.

Ristorante Solferino

Via Castelfidaro 2. ☎ **6599886.** Reservations recommended. Main courses 20,000–28,000 lire ($12.50–$17.50). AE, DC, MC, V. Mon–Sat noon–2pm and 7–11pm. Subway: Moskava. MILANESE.

This is a country-style inn, built 150 years ago, with all the accoutrements you'd expect to find in a farming community rather than in the center of a busy city. A restaurant was founded here in 1950. Below a beamed ceiling, next to racks of wine bottles and among the fashion stars, you can dine on such specialties as risotto Grande Milano, Milanese veal with potatoes, gnocchi with salmon, carpaccio, osso buco, tagliatelle with grilled vegetables, and follow with a dessert known as "Milanese Custard." The establishment maintains a limited number of bedrooms upstairs (see "Where to Stay," above), as well as a less formal and much less expensive buffet-style restaurant just around the corner.

⑤ Taverna del Gran Sasso
Piazza Principessa Clotilde 10. ☎ **6597578.** Reservations not necessary. Lunch main courses 10,000–13,000 lire ($6.25–$8.15); all-you-can-eat dinner 58,000 lire ($36.25). MC, V. Mon–Fri 12:30–2pm; Mon–Sat 7:30–10:30pm. Closed Jan 1 and Aug. Tram: 29 or 30. ABRUZZI.

This old tavern, dating from 1962, provides regional meals, and a visit here is a joyride as well. Filled with lots of sentimental baubles, its walls are crowded ceiling to floor with copper molds, ears of corn, strings of pepper and garlic, and cart wheels. A tall, open hearth burns with a charcoal fire, and a Sicilian cart is laden with baskets of bread, dried figs, nuts, and kegs of wine. As you enter, you'll find a mellowed wooden keg of wine with a brass faucet (you're supposed to help yourself, using glass mugs). The cuisine features a number of specialties from the Abruzzi district in the south of Italy—regional dishes such as maccheroni alla chitarra, a distinctively shaped macaroni with a savory meat sauce. The first course offers at least 10 choices; the second, 2; the third, 4; the fourth, 5; and there are six or seven desserts to choose from for the final selection. Dinner is an all-you-can-eat feast, although at lunch courses are only à la carte.

SHOPPING

London has Harrods, Paris has all the big-name boutiques you can think of, and Rome and Florence instill an acquisitional fever in the eyes of anyone who even window-gazes. Milan, however, is blessed with one of the most unusual concentrations of shopping possibilities in Europe. Most of the boutiques are infused with the style, humor, and sophistication that has made Milan the dynamo of the Italian fashion industry, a place where the sidewalks sizzle with the hard-driving entrepreneurial spirit that has been part of the northern Italian textile industry for centuries.

One well-heeled shopper from Florida recently spent the better part of her vacation in Italy shopping for what she called "the most unbelievable variety of shoes, clothes, and accessories in the world." A walk on the fashion subculture's focal point, **via Montenapoleone,** one of Italy's three great shopping streets, a mile-long strip that has become a showcase for famous (and high-priced) makers of clothes and shoes, with excursions into the side streets, will quickly confirm that impression.

Note carefully that beauty does not come cheaply in the garment industry, and the attention you receive will often be based directly on the salesperson's impression of how much money you plan to spend. But as a handful of American models, along with design imitators from around the world, know, there are indeed riches to be discovered.

Early-morning risers will be welcomed only by silent streets and closed gates. Most shops are closed all day Sunday and Monday (although some open on Monday afternoon). Some stores open at 9am unless they're very chic, and then they're not likely to open until 10:30am. They remain open, for the most part, until 1pm, reopening again between 3:30 and 7:30pm.

Books

American Bookstore
Via Camperio 16. ☎ **878920**.

There are bigger and flashier bookstores in Rome, but this one will probably stock that paperback novel you always wanted to read, or the scholarly exegesis of Milanese artwork you should have reviewed before your trip and never did. Only English-language books are stocked, as well as an assortment of periodicals. Open Monday from 3 to 7:30pm, Tuesday through Friday from 10am to 7:30pm, and Saturday from 10am to 1pm and 3 to 7pm.

Department Stores

La Rinascente
Piazza del Duomo. ☎ **88521**.

La Rinascente bills itself with accuracy as Italy's largest fashion department store. In addition to clothing, the basement carries a wide variety of giftware for the home, including handwork from all regions of Italy. The information desk on the ground floor will answer your questions. On the establishment's seventh floor there's a bank, a travel agency, Rolando hairdresser, Estée Lauder Skincare Center, a coffee-bar, and the Brunch and Bistro restaurants.

Incidently, the name of the store was suggested by the poet Gabriele d'Annunzio, for which he received a compensation of 5,000 lire. The store was officially opened right before Christmas in the closing year of World War I, but it burned down on Christmas Eve. Rebuilt, it later met total destruction in an Allied bombing raid in 1943. But it has always rallied from disaster and now is better than ever. Open Monday from 1 to 7:30pm and Tuesday through Saturday from 9:30am to 7:30pm.

Fashion

For Men

Giorgio Armani
Via San Andrea 9. ☎ **76003234**.

Giorgio Armani is housed with the style we've come to expect from Armani, in a large showroom vaguely reminiscent of a very upscale aircraft hangar. Armani's trademark is a look that incorporates loosely fitting, unstructured, and unpadded clothing draped loosely over firm bodies. Though there's a bit more structure to the clothes since Richard Gere made the look popular in *American Gigolo*, Armani still creates elegant upholstery for elegant people. Open Monday from 3:30 to 5pm and Tuesday through Saturday from 10am to 1:30pm and 3:30 to 5pm.

Galtrucco
Via Montenapoleone 27. ☎ **76002978**.

This store is a two-floor collection of elegant men's suits, shirts, and knitwear. The ready-to-wear clothes are well-made and attractively conservative. Also available are a battalion of tailors prepared to create a custom-made suit, laden with details that a discerning eye will pick up immediately, complete with a label by Brioni. Open Monday from 3 to 7pm and Tuesday through Saturday from 10am to 7pm.

Shopping Secrets of Milan

- **Prada,** via della Spiga 1 (☎ 76002019), has the best leather goods and other stylish accessories for women in Milan. *Travel & Leisure* called it "a fashion industry phenomenon." The black nylon backpack is the most popular item.
- **Salmoiraghi Vigano,** Corso Matteotti 22 (☎ 76000100), is known for having the best-looking sunglasses in Italy, attracting all trendoids. It's for those who want to look like Marcello Mastroianni in the Fellini flick, *La Dolce Vita*.
- **Sebastian,** via Borgospesso 18 (☎ 780532), has been called the most "eccentric" shoe store for women and men in Milan. More than 150 styles and a wide range of materials, from fabric to leather and suede, await discriminating shoppers who'd like to have their shoes custom-made.
- **G. Lorenzi,** via Montenapoleone 9 (☎ 76022848), has been called "an Italian Library of Congress" for small gift items. In this tiny store, you'll find everything you were looking for in the way of small gifts—and a lot of stuff you've never seen before. Many are one-of-a-kind items.
- **Nanna Strada,** via Gesù 4 (☎ 76014310), offers one of the most exciting assortments of women's wear in Milan. The setting is like an art gallery, and the clothing is highly individualistic, for both day and evening.
- **Lo Scarabeo d'Oro,** via Sant Andrea 3 (☎ 760000547), fashions one-of-a-kind pieces of jewelry from exotic items such as antique coins. Unusual metals are also fashioned into jewelry.
- **Dom,** Corso Matteotti 3 (☎ 76023410), offers the finest selection of silver, crystal, and porcelain in Milan.
- **Primavera,** via Torino 47 (☎ 8053069). When the high prices of Milano fashion are beyond your means, go here for stylish clothing (both women and men) at bargain basement prices.
- **R&G Falzone,** via Edmondo de Amicis 51 (☎ 89403714), offers stacks of designer clothing for the women with a full figure. Discounts about 25% off regular boutique prices.

Gemelli
Corso Vercelli 16. ☎ **433404.**

This store sells well-made clothes for men, women, babies, and teenagers, which, while stylish and serviceable, are neither as glamorous nor as chillingly expensive as some of the city's more famous clothiers. Everything here is off the rack; there is no custom-tailoring service. Open Monday from 3 to 7:30pm and Tuesday through Saturday from 9:15am to 1pm and 3 to 7:30pm.

Mila Schön
Via Montenapoleone 2. ☎ **781190.**

The sophisticated men's line of the successful female designer is inventoried here. The look is casually chic, hip, and expensive. If you're male, thin, and relatively muscular, you'll probably look terrific in Mila Schön. Mila's women's line is on the ground floor. Even the somewhat-flippant accessories are stratospherically expensive. Open Monday from 3:30 to 7:30pm and Tuesday through Saturday from 10:30am to 7:30pm.

Ermengildo Zegna
Via Pietro Verri 3. ☎ **795521.**

This shop, which opened in 1985, offers a complete range of menswear, beginning with the Sartorial line, the Zenga *haute couture* offering of suits, jackets, trousers, and accessories. The "soft line" is dedicated to a younger customer, and the sportswear collection and yachting line allows you to wander the globe with the right apparel. The shop also offers a "made-to-measure" service with a selection of 300 fabrics per season. An outfit can be made in about four weeks, then shipped to any destination in the world. Open Monday from 3 to 7pm and Tuesday through Saturday from 9:30am to 7pm.

For Women

Gianfranco Ferré
Via della Spiga 11–13. ☎ **76000385.**

This is the only outlet in Milan for a famous designer whose women's fashions are worn by some of the world's most elegant dressers. The range is wide—perfect tailleurs and soft knitwear, feminine organza shirts, or sensual evening dresses, along with refined leather accessories, bijoux, and foulards. Next door to the women's shop is an outlet for men's clothing by the same designer, keeping the same hours. Open Monday from 3 to 7pm and Tuesday through Saturday from 10am to 1pm and 2:30 to 7pm (closed in August).

Spiga 31 di R. Bilancioni
Via della Spiga 31. ☎ **76023502.**

The inventory here includes an unusual look that the casually elegant nightowl might like. Clothing ranges somewhere between sportswear and formal evening wear, without really fitting into either category. If you choose to show off a purchase from the sometimes flamboyant, sometimes discreet inventory at the country club, you probably won't need to worry that another woman will be wearing the same dress. Open Monday from 3:30 to 7:30pm and Tuesday through Saturday from 10am to 1pm and 3:30 to 7:30pm.

JEWELRY

Mario Buccellati
Via Montenapoleone 4. ☎ **76002153.**

Mario Buccellati offers the best-known—and probably the most expensive—silver and jewels in Italy. The designs of the cast-silver bowls, tureens, and christening cups are nothing short of rhapsodic, and the quality is among the finest in the world. You'll be ushered into the tastefully appointed showroom within what turns out to be a formidable security system. Open Monday from 3 to 7:15pm and Tuesday through Saturday from 9am to 12:30pm and 3 to 7:15pm.

Meru
Via Solferino 3. ☎ **86460700.**

Meru sells consciously avant-garde jewelry, rumored to have been worn and privately publicized by young and beautiful European film stars. Many of the pieces are set into enameled backgrounds and often include unusual types of gemstones such as rose quartz, coral, and amber. All pieces are made by Meru themselves, in a style quite different from the usual traditional jewelry sold in many other stores. Open Monday from 3:30 to 7:30pm and Tuesday through Saturday from 9:30am to 1pm and 3:30 to 7pm (closed July 30 to September 10).

LACE

Jesurum
Via Verri 4. ☎ **76015045.**

This is the Milanese outlet of a Venice-based company that has been famous since 1870 for making and selling lace in many different applications. Set on a very short street where none of the buildings has an obvious street number, it sells all-lace or lace-edged tablecloths, lace doilies, and all the handmade textiles that a bride might like to add to her trousseau. They also sell lace blouses, even a swimming suit (which might be better suited to a photo session than to a game of water polo) and lace by the meter for trimming curtains or whatever. Open Monday 3 to 7pm and Tuesday through Saturday from 10am to 7pm.

LEATHER GOODS & SHOES

Beltrami
Via Montenapoleone 16. ☎ **76023422.**

Prices are chillingly high, but the leather goods for men and women are among the best you'll find anywhere. The showroom is appropriately glamorous, the merchandise appropriately chic. Beltrami has another shop, which has the same hours, at piazza Santa Babila 4A (☎ 76000546). Open Monday from 3:30 to 7:30pm and Tuesday through Saturday from 10am to 1pm and 3:30 to 7:30pm.

Salvatore Ferragamo
Via Montenapoleone 3. ☎ **76006660.**

The label is instantly recognizable and the quality high at this shop that has created and designed shoes since the 1930s for the fashion goddesses and gods of Europe and Hollywood. The establishment, which is rigidly controlled by a large and extended second generation of the original founders, is still a leader in style and allure. The store contains inventories of shoes, luggage, and accessories for women and men. Also for sale are Ferragamo leather jackets, pants, and a small selection of clothing. Open Monday from 3 to 7pm and Tuesday through Saturday from 10am to 1:30pm and 3 to 7pm.

Alfonso Garlando
Via Madonnina 2. ☎ **86463733.**

The prices on the merchandise here range up to the very expensive, but the shop's size and lack of concern with a stylish showroom almost guarantees a reasonable choice of merchandise for a reasonable price. They sell shoes for men and women, but not children. Open Monday from 12:30 to 7:30pm and Tuesday through Saturday from 10am to 7:30pm.

Gucci
Via Montenapoleone 5. ☎ **76013050.**

Gucci is the Milanese headquarters for the most famous leather-goods distributor in Italy. Its shoes, luggage, and wallets for men and women, handbags, and leatherware accessories usually have the colors of the Italian flag (olive and crimson) stitched in the form of a more-or-less discreet ribbon across the front of most of the company's merchandise. Open Monday from 3:30 to 7pm and Tuesday through Saturday from 10am to 7pm.

Sebastian
Via Borgospesso 18. ☎ **780532.**

Sebastian sells excellent shoes for men and women from a ready-made stockpile of fashionable models, which Sebastian makes in its own factories. For almost the same price (if you don't mind waiting two months or more) you can order custom-made shoes, which will be shipped to whatever address you specify. Custom-made shoes are usually available only in women's styles. This is a boon for clients with wide, narrow, large, or small feet, who consider Sebastian something of a sartorial and orthopedic blessing. Open Monday from 3 to 7pm and Tuesday through Saturday from 9:30am to 7pm.

Tanino Crisci
Via Montenapoleone 3. ☎ **76021264.**

Its showroom evokes the interior of a private club in London because of its oiled paneling and conservative leather chairs. Its inventory includes elegantly conservative footwear for men and women, but its most famous products are the leather boots that will make you look like an ace equestrian, polo player, or stalker of big game—even if they haven't been your lifelong hobbies. Open Monday from 3 to 7pm and Tuesday through Saturday from 10am to 7pm.

LINGERIE

B. Finzi
Galleria Vittorio Emanuele. ☎ **86460920.**

Styles of underwear have changed since this shop was established in 1859, but the Milanese demand for both practical and frivolous "unmentionables" has continued unabated. (The polite Italian word for these is *biancheria intima*.) Most of the stock here is for all kinds and types of women (look especially for the satin-trimmed silk camisoles), but there's also a selection of underwear for men (most of which is bought for them by their wives or companions). Open Monday from 3 to 7:30pm and Tuesday through Saturday from 9:30am to 1pm and 3 to 7pm.

MALLS

Caffè Moda
Via Durini 14. ☎ **76021188.**

Despite the implications of its name, this is actually a shopping complex filled with the deliberately informal offshoots of some of the most renowned clothing designers in Italy. Its focal point is the ground-floor café and bar that gives the complex its name, around which all the gossip of the neighborhood seems to ebb and flow. Radiating outward, and stretching over three different levels, are at least 20 different shops. These include jeans outlets of both Valentino and Gianfranco Ferré, and informal (but still expensive) outlets for Missoni, Valentino Uomo, and Krizia Poi. Each boutique maintains its own hours, but most of them are open nonstop Monday through Saturday from 10am to 7pm. A few of the smaller shops might close briefly for lunch. The complex is located about a block behind the Palazzo Reale.

PAPER

I Giorni Di Carta

Corso Garibaldi 81. ☎ **6552514.**

This is one of the city's most unusual outlets for writing paper and stationery, with dozens of different colors, textures, and weights. Much of the inventory is made from ecologically conscious recycled paper. The establishment also sells briefcases to carry your letters, pens and ink, and ornamental paperweights. Open Monday through Saturday from 10:30am to 2pm and 3:30 to 7:30pm.

PERFUMES

Profumo

Via Brera 6. ☎ **72023334.**

Profumo sells some of Italy's most exotic perfumes for women, plus cologne and aftershave lotions for men. Some Italian scents are exclusively distributed here near the American Express office. Open Monday from 3 to 7pm and Tuesday through Saturday from 10am to 7pm.

PORCELAIN & CRYSTAL

Richard-Ginori

Corso Buenos Aires 1. ☎ **29516611.**

Since 1735 this company has manufactured and sold porcelain to dukes, duchesses, and ordinary bourgeois consumers. Considered a household word in Italy, Ginori sells ovenproof porcelain in both modern and traditional themes, as well as crystal and silverware that they either make themselves or inventory from other manufacturers such as Baccarat or Wedgwood. There is another branch, slightly larger, at via Dante 9 (☎ 864-600-82). Open Monday from 3 to 7:30pm and Tuesday through Saturday from 9am to 12:30pm and 3 to 7:30pm.

PRINTS & ENGRAVINGS

Raimondi Di Pettinaroli

Corso Venezia 6. ☎ **76002412.**

This is considered the finest shop in Milan for antique prints and engravings, plus reprints of old engravings made from the original copper places. It was originally established in 1776, a date dear to the heart of many U.S. readers. Of particular interest are the engravings of Italian cityscapes during the 19th century, and the many treasures worth framing after you return home. Open Monday from 3 to 7pm and Tuesday through Saturday from 9:30am to 12:30pm and 3 to 7pm.

MILAN AFTER DARK

As in Rome, many of the top nightclubs in Milan shut down for the summer, when the cabaret talent and the bartenders pack their bags and head for the hills or the seashore. However, Milan is a big city, and there's always plenty of after-dark diversions. This sprawling metropolis is also one of the cultural centers of Europe.

THE PERFORMING ARTS

The most complete list of cultural events appears in the large Milan newspaper, the left-wing *Repubblica*. If you're in town, try for a Thursday edition, usually with the most complete listings.

Teatro alla Scala

Piazza della Scala. ☎ **72003744.** Tickets 30,000–300,000 lire ($18.75–$187.50).

If you have only a night for Milan and are here between mid-December and May, try to attend a performance at the world-famous Teatro alla Scala. Built to the designs of Piermarini, the neoclassic opera house was restored after World War II bomb damage. The greatest opera stars appear here, and the Milanese first-night audience is considered among the hardest to please in the world. Tickets are also extremely hard to come by and are sold out weeks in advance. However, you do stand a chance of getting gallery tickets, seats so far up they should be called "celestial." The box office is open Tuesday through Sunday from noon to 7pm. Tickets are not sold on the telephone.

Opera lovers will also want to visit the **Museo Teatrale alle Scala** (☎ 805-3418) in the same building. Established in 1913, it contains a rich collection of historical mementoes and records of the heady world of opera. Among them are busts and portraits of such artists as Beethoven, Chopin, Donizetti, Verdi, and Puccini. Two halls are devoted to Verdi alone, with objects including scores written in his own hand and the spinet on which he learned to play. Rossini's eyeglasses and his pianoforte tuning key are in a vitrine, and there are many other such treasures, including a death-cast of Chopin's left hand. A small gallery honors Toscanini, with his batons, medals, and pince-nez on display. One of the greatest thrills for opera lovers who may not be in Milan at the time of a performance at La Scala—or may not be able to get tickets—will be the view from the third floor. From here, you can look down on the theater's ornate auditorium with its velvet draperies. Charging 5,000 lire ($3.15) for admission, it is open May through September, Monday through Saturday from 9am to noon and 2 to 6pm and on Sunday from 9:30am to 12:30pm and 2 to 6pm. In the off-season, hours are Monday through Saturday from 9am to noon and 2 to 6pm. Subway: Duomo.

Conservatorio

Via del Conservatorio 12. ☎ **76001755.** Tickets 25,000–60,000 lire ($15.65–$37.50).

The finest in classical music is performed at the Conservatorio in the San Babila sector. Year round, a high-quality program of classical concerts—widely varied—is showcased here for a cultured Milanese audience. Subway: San Babila.

Piccolo Teatro

Via Rovello 2. ☎ **72333222.** Tickets 46,000 lire ($28.75).

The Piccolo Teatro, near via Dante, became a socialist theater in the years after World War II, but now the city of Milan is the landlord. Programs are varied today, and performances are in Italian. Its director, Giorgio Strehler, is acclaimed as one of the most avant garde and talented in the world. The theater lies between the Duomo and the Castle of the Sforzas. It's sometimes hard to obtain seats here. No shows are presented on Monday; closed in August. Subway: Cordusio or Cairoli.

THE CLUB & MUSIC SCENE

Ca' Bianca Club

Via Lodovico il Moro 117. ☎ **89125777.** Cover 25,000 lire ($15.65) including show and one drink, 90,000–100,000 lire ($56.25–$62.50) with dinner.

Ca' Bianca has a changing venue of live music, which ranges—depending on the availability of the musicians—from folk music to cabaret to Dixieland jazz on

Wednesday night. Technically, this is considered a private club, but no one at the door will prevent you from entering if you aren't a member. The show—whatever it may consist of on the night of your visit—begins at 11pm. The club is open Monday through Saturday from 8:30pm to 1am; closed in August.

Club Astoria

Piazza Santa Maria Beltrade 2. ☎ **86463710.** No cover.

This popular nightclub is one of the most frequented in town, especially by the expense-account-junket crowd. When there's a floor show, a drink might cost around 40,000 lire ($25), which takes the place of a cover charge. Otherwise, drinks begin at 25,000 lire ($15.65). Open daily from 10:30pm to 4am; closed in August.

Facsimile

Via Tallone 11. ☎ **7380635.** No cover, but first drink obligatory.

This is a popular rendezvous point where rock-conscious Milanese can commune with their favorite video stars in living color. The decor is almost entirely gray and red, and the rock videos might be the same kinds of images a New Yorker might view on a lonely Friday night. There are outdoor tables for star-gazing. Drinks range upward from 9,000 lire ($5.65). The bar is open Tuesday through Sunday from 6:30pm to 2am.

Rolling Stone

Corso XXII Marzo no. 32. ☎ **7381000.** Cover 20,000–25,000 lire ($12.50–$15.65) depending on the event.

This club was originally established for the Beat Generation of the 1950s, later attracting *la dolce vita* people of the 1960s. In 1984, it adopted its present rock-and-roll preoccupation which it maintains to this day, featuring heavy-metal rock and an ocean of aggressively energetic groups in their 20s. Its open every night, usually from 10:30pm to 4am, but don't even consider showing up here until at least midnight (otherwise you will have the place to yourself). On some selected concerts, the place doesn't open until 1am. Drinks cost from 8,000 to 10,000 lire ($5 to $6.25). Closed in July and August.

GAY CLUBS

Nuova Idea International

Via de Castillia 30. ☎ **69007859.** Cover (including one free drink) 20,000 lire ($12.50) Thurs, Fri, and Sun; 25,000 lire ($15.65) Sat.

This is the largest, oldest, most active, and most fun gay disco in Italy, very much tied in to the urban bustle of modern Milan. Its sense of freedom would be unthinkable in smaller towns in the provinces. It prides itself on mimicking the examples of the large, all-gay discos of Northern Europe. It draws a patronage of young and not-so-young men, many of whom are film or theater actors. There's a large video screen, and sometimes live entertainment is presented. Drinks cost from 9,000 lire ($5.65) each. It's open Thursday through Sunday from 9:30pm to 2:30am.

Zip

Corso Sempione 76 at via Salvioni. ☎ **3314904.** Cover (including one drink) 50,000 lire ($31.25). Tram: 1, 9, or 33.

One of the most deliberately raunchy gay clubs in southern Europe, Zip is a *club privato* although non-Italian newcomers can enter upon presentation of a passport.

This dive contains a labyrinth of inner rooms devoted to a disco with a clientele of gay males, a late-night cafeteria, a screen showing gay porno, and a "dark room" where the action is uninhibited. The disco opens nightly at midnight and often reaches its peak at 3am or 4am, before shutting down for a much-needed rest at 6am. The establishment lies in back of Castello Sforzesco. If you attend, be alert to the neighborhood at this late hour, and exercise caution once you're inside. Drinks cost 10,000 lire ($6.25).

THE BAR SCENE

Al Teatro
Corso Garibaldi 16. ☎ **864222.**

Decorated a bit like a bohemian parlor of the last century, this is a popular bar set across the street from one of Milan's most visible theaters, the Teatro Fossati. It opens for morning coffee every day except Monday at 7am, and closes (after several changes of ambience) at 2am. At night there is sometimes some kind of musical entertainment, but most of the time clients seem perfectly happy to drink their drinks, gossip, and flirt. Cocktails cost 6,000–11,000 lire ($3.75–$6.90). In addition to coffee and drinks, the establishment serves toasts and tortes. In fine weather tables are sometimes set outside on corso Garibaldi.

Bar Giamaica
Via Brera 32. ☎ **876723.**

The place is loud and bustling, and seats its potential diners with a no-nonsense kind of gruff humor. That, however, is part of the allure of a bar that has attracted writers and artists for many years, and that today is considered one of the mainstays of the Milanese night scene. The personalities who work here haven't changed in many years. If you want only a drink, you'll have lots of company among the office workers who jostle around the tiny tables, often standing rather than sitting because of the lack of room. It's open as a restaurant Monday to Saturday from noon to 2:30pm and for dinner Monday to Saturday from 7:30 to 10pm. Meals cost from 20,000 lire ($12.50) (for a salad and a beer) to as much as 45,000 lire ($28.15) (for a full Italian regalia). Reservations are not accepted in advance, but you won't lack company while waiting at the bar for a table. The bar opens at 9am every day except Sunday, and remains open until around 12:30am or later, depending on the crowd.

Grand Hotel Pub
Via Ascanio Sforza 75. ☎ **89511586.**

Despite its name, this establishment does not rent bedrooms, or even pretend to be grand. Instead, it's a large, animated restaurant and pub where live music or cabaret is frequently performed. In summer, crowds can move quickly from the smoky interior out into a sheltered garden. Depending on the venue for the night you arrive, the evening's entertainment might consist of either vocal or instrumental music, or Italian-language cabaret/comedy. Most visitors come here only for a drink, which is priced between 6,000 to 10,000 lire ($3.75 to $6.25), but if you're hungry, a restaurant on the premises charges around 50,000 lire ($31.25) for a full meal. The place is open Tuesday through Sunday from 8pm to 2am. On Sunday lunch is also served from 12:30 to 2:30pm. Entrance is usually free.

THE CAFE SCENE

Every city in Italy seems to have a café filled with 19th-century detailing and memories of Verdi or some such famous person. It usually offers a wide variety of pastries and a particular kind of clientele who gossip, sip espresso, munch in-between-meals snacks, and compare notes on shopping. In Milan the establishments listed below are popular for this activity.

Berlin Café

Via Gian Giacomo Mora 9. ☎ **8394336.**

As its name implies, the decor emulates a café in turn-of-the-century Berlin; the ambience is enhanced with etched glass and marble-top tables. No one will mind if you come just for coffee or a drink (available Tuesday through Sunday from 8am to 2am), but if you want a meal, the establishment serves lunch from noon to 3pm and dinner from 6pm to 2am. Food is predominantly vegetarian, using very little meat or fish (perhaps a bit of ham for flavor). A meal might include platters of pasta, a torte de verdura, rice pilaf, or pastries. An à la carte dinner begins at 28,000 lire ($17.50); and a Sunday brunch (served from 8am to 4pm) costs 28,000 lire ($17.50). Drinks range from 9,000 to 13,000 lire ($5.65 to $8.15). The establishment is also the occasional setting for an exhibition of paintings by local artists.

Café Cova

Via Montenapoleone 8. ☎ **76000578.**

Amid a chic assemblage of garment-district personnel, along with the shoppers who support them, the café follows a routine it established back in 1817. This involves concocting gallons of the heady espresso to keep everyone's nerves jumping. They also dispense staggering amounts of pralines, chocolates, brioches, and sandwiches from behind a glass display case. The more elegant sandwiches contain smoked salmon and truffles. Clients drink their espresso from fragile gold-rimmed cups at one of the small tables in an elegant inner room or while standing up at the prominent bar. Most of the action takes place at the bar, so you don't really need a table unless you're exhausted from too much shopping. Coffee at the bar costs 1,500 lire (95¢), or 5,000 lire ($3.15) at a table. Hot and cold food items are priced from 500 to 30,000 lire (30¢ to $18.75) Open Monday through Saturday from 8am to 8pm; closed in August.

Caffè Milano

Via Montebello 7. ☎ **29003300.**

In summer, the crowed sometimes spills outside onto the small plaza, turning the pavement in front of the establishment into an extension of the interior. Most visitors consider it a pleasant mixing pot and rendezvous point, with relaxing music and flattering lighting. Drinks cost 6,000 to 12,000 lire ($3.75 to $7.50).

The establishment also has a restaurant that serves classic Milanese cuisine, such as risotto, fresh pasta, and veal dishes. Full meals cost from 55,000 lire ($34.40), including wine, and are served from noon to 2:30pm and 7:45pm to 1am. The bar is open from 10:30am to 3pm and 5pm to 2am. Both the bar and the restaurant are closed on Sunday.

Pasticceria Taveggia

Via Visconti di Modrone 2. ☎ **76021257.**

Established in 1910, this is one of the oldest and most historic cafés of Milan. Behind ornate glass doors set into the 19th-century facade, Taveggia is reputed to make the best cappuccino and espresso in town. To match this quality, a variety of brioches, pastries, candies, and tortes is offered. Freshly made on the premises, they can be enjoyed while standing at the bar or seated in the Victorian tea room. All service at the tables is slightly more expensive, as is the rule in Europe. A cappuccino costs 1,800 lire ($1.15) at the bar, 5,500 lire ($3.45) at a table. Food items range from 7,000 to 15,000 lire ($4.40 to $9.40). Taveggia is open Tuesday through Sunday from 7:30am to 8:30pm; closed in August.

EASY EXCURSIONS

The ✪ Certosa **(Charter House)** of Pavia, via Monumento 4 (☎ 0382/925613), marks the pinnacle of the Renaissance statement in Lombardy. The Carthusian monastery is 5 miles north of the town of Pavia and 19 miles south of Milan. Gian Galeazzo Visconti founded the Certosa in 1396, but it was not completed until years after. The result is one of the most harmonious structures in Italy.

The facade, studded with medallions and adorned with colored marble and sculptural work, was designed in part by Amadeo, who worked on the building in the late 15th century. Inside, much of its rich decoration is achieved by frescoes reminiscent of an illustrated storybook. You'll find works by Perugino (*The Everlasting Father*) and Bernardino Luini (*Madonna and Child*). Gian Galeazzo Visconti, the founder of the Certosa, is buried in the south transept.

Through an elegantly decorated portal you enter the cloister, noted for its exceptional terra-cotta decorations. In the cloister is a continuous chain of elaborate "cells," attached villas with their own private gardens and loggia. Admission is free, but donations are requested. The charterhouse keeps its longest hours from May to August when it's open daily from 9 to 11:30am and 2:30 to 6pm. In March and April and again in Septermber and October, it's open Tuesday through Sunday from 9 to 11:30am and 2:30 to 5pm; from November through February, its hours are Tuesday through Sunday from 9 to 11:30am and 2:30 to 4:30pm.

Buses run between Milan and Pavia every hour from 5am to 10pm daily, taking 50 minutes and costing 4,100 lire ($2.55) one way. Trains leave Milan bound for Pavia once every hour, at a one-way fare of 3,200 lire ($2). Motorists can take Route 35 south from Milan or take A7 to Binasco and continue on Route 35 to Pavia and its Certosa.

2 Bergamo

31 miles NE of Milan, 373 miles NW of Rome

Known for its defenses and for its wealth since the Middle Ages, Bergamo is considered one of the most characteristic of the Lombardian hill towns. Many of the town's stone fortifications were built on Roman foundations by the medieval Venetians, who considered Bergamo one of the gems of their trading network during several centuries of occupation. Set on a hilltop between the Seriana and the Brembana valleys, Bergamo lies in the alpine foothills, in a setting similar to what you might expect in the hills of Umbria or Tuscany. The Old Town (*Città Alta*), set 900 feet above sea level, is buttressed by and terraced upon the original Venetian fortifications. About a half-mile downhill is the New Town (usually identified by residents simply as "Bergamo,"), with many 19th- and early-20th-century buildings. A settlement of wide streets and Northern Italian bourgeois prosperity, it contains the bus and railway stations, most hotels, and the town's commercial and administrative center. The two-in-one aspect of Bergamo, as well as its role in the mercantile history of Lombardy, was analyzed and praised by one of its strongest champions, the 19th-century French novelist Stendahl.

ESSENTIALS

GETTING THERE By Train Trains arrive from Milan once every hour. The trip takes an hour, and a one-way ticket costs 4,500 lire ($2.80). For information about rail connections in Bergamo, call 247624.

By Bus The bus station in Bergamo is across from the train station. For bus information or schedules in the area, call 248150. Buses arrive from Milan once every 30 minutes; a one-way ticket costs 6,500 lire ($4.05).

By Car From Milan, head east on the autostrada A4.

VISITOR INFORMATION The telephone area code for Bergamo is 035. The tourist information office is at Papa Giovanni XXIII no. 106 (☎ 242226).

WHAT TO SEE & DO
THE UPPER TOWN

For the sightseer, the higher the climb the more rewarding the view. The ✪ **Città Alta** is replete with narrow circuitous streets, old squares, splendid monuments, and imposing and austere medieval architecture that prompted d'Annunzio to call it "a city of muteness." To reach the Upper Town, take bus no. 1 or 3, then a 10-minute walk up viale Vittorio Emanuele.

The heart of the Upper Town is **piazza Vecchia,** which has witnessed most of the town's upheavals and a parade of conquerors ranging from Attila to the Nazis. On the square is the Palazzo della Ragione, the town hall; an 18th-century fountain; and the Palazzo Nuovo of Scamozzi, the library of Bergamo.

A vaulted arcade connects piazza Vecchia with piazza del Duomo. Opening onto the latter is the cathedral of Bergamo, which has a baroque overlay. An interesting church on this square is the **Basilica di Santa Maria Maggiore.** D'Annunzio (roughly translated) said it seemed "to blossom in a rose-filtered light." Built in the Romanesque style, the church was founded in the 12th century. Much later it was baroqued on its interior, and given a disturbingly busy ceiling. There are exquisite Flemish and Tuscan tapestries displayed that incorporate such themes as the Annunciation and the Crucifixion. The choir dates from the 16th century, and was designed by Lotto. In front of the main altar is a series of inlaid panels depicting such themes as Noah's Ark and David and Goliath. It is open Monday through Saturday from 8am to noon and 3 to 6pm; Sunday, 9am to 12:45pm and 3 to 6pm.

Also opening onto piazza del Duomo is the ✪ **Colleoni Chapel,** which honors the already-inflated ego of the Venetian military hero. The Renaissance chapel, with an inlaid marble facade reminiscent of Florence, was designed by Giovanni Antonio Amadeo, who is chiefly known for his creation of the Certosa in Pavia, south of Milan. For the *condottiere,* Amadeo built an elaborate tomb, surmounted by a gilded equestrian statue (Colleoni, of course, was the subject of one of the world's most famous equestrian statues, which now stands on a square in Venice). The tomb sculpted for the soldier's daughter, Medea, is much less elaborate. Giovanni Battista Tiepolo painted most of the frescoes on the ceiling. It's open daily from 9am to 12:30pm and 2 to 6pm. Admission is free.

Facing the cathedral is the baptistery, which dates from the mid-14th century and was rebuilt at the end of the 19th century. The original architect of the octagonal building was Giovanni da Campione.

THE LOWER TOWN

○ Galleria dell'Accademia Carrara

Piazza Giacomo Carrara 82A. ☎ **399643.** Admission 3,000 lire ($1.90) adults, free for children under 18. Wed–Mon 9:30am–12:30pm and 2:30–5:30pm. Bus: 2, 9, 12, or 14.

Filled with a wide-ranging collection of the works of home-grown artists, as well as Venetian and Tuscan masters, the academy draws art lovers from all over the world. The most important works are on the top floor—so head there first if your time is limited. The Botticelli portrait of *Giuliano di Medici* is well known, and another room contains three different versions of Giovanni Bellini's favorite subject, the *Madonna and Child*. It's interesting to compare his work with that of his brother-in-law, Andrea Mantegna, whose *Madonna and Child* is also displayed, as is Vittore Carpaccio's *Nativity of Maria*, which was seemingly inspired by Flemish painters.

Farther along you encounter a most original treatment of the old theme of the "Madonna and Child"—this one the work of Cosmé Tura of Ferrara. Also displayed are three tables of a predella by Lotto, a portrait of the *Holy Family with St. Catherine* (wonderful composition) by Lotto, and Raphael's St. Sebastian. The entire wall space of another room is taken up with paintings by Moroni (1523–78), a local artist who seemingly did portraits of everybody who could afford it. In the salons to follow, foreign masters, such as Rubens, van der Meer, and Jan Brueghel, are represented, along with Guardi's architectural renderings of Venice and Longhi's continuing parade of Venetian high society.

WHERE TO STAY
MODERATE

Hotel Excelsior San Marco

Piazza della Repubblica 6, 24122 Bergamo. ☎ **035/366111.** Fax 035/223201. 163 rms. A/C MINIBAR TV TEL. 301,000 lire ($188.15) double. Rates include breakfast. AE, DC, MC, V. Parking 30,000 lire ($18.75) indoors, 20,000 lire ($12.50) outdoors. Bus: 1, 3, 7, or 9.

This is a 32-year-old establishment at the edge of a city park dotted with flowers. It's actually about midway between the old and new towns, both of which might be visible from the balcony of your room. The lobby area contains a small bar, reddish stone accents, and low-slung leather chairs. The most prominent theme of the ceiling frescoes is that of the lion of St. Mark. The bedrooms are attractively furnished and comfortable.

INEXPENSIVE

Agnello d'Oro

Via Gombito 22, 24100 Bergamo. ☎ **035/249883.** Fax 035/235612. 20 rms (all with bath or shower). TV TEL. 100,000 lire ($62.50) double. Breakfast 12,000 lire ($7.50) extra. AE, DC, MC, V. Bus: 1 or 3.

Agnello d'Oro is an intimate, old-style country inn right in the heart of Città Alta, facing a handkerchief square with a splashing fountain. It's an atmospheric background for good food or an adequate bedroom, all of which were refurbished in 1995. When you enter the cozy reception lounge, you should ring an old bell to bring the owner away from the kitchen. You dine at wooden tables, and sit on carved ladderback chairs. Among the à la carte offerings are three worthy regional specialties. Try casoncelli alla bergamasca, a succulent ravioli dish, or quaglie farcite (quail stuffed and accompanied by slices of polenta). If you choose the risotto al profumo di bosco (with mushrooms and truffle cream), you'll be presented with a dish painted by the manager. A complete meal costs 55,000 to 65,000 lire ($34.40 to $40.60). The room becomes the tavern lounge between meals. Wine is served in unusual pitchers. The restaurant is closed Monday and Sunday night.

Hotel Cappello d'Oro

Viale Papa Giovanni XXIII no. 12, 24100 Bergamo. ☎ **035/232503.** Fax 035/242946. 124 rms. MINIBAR TV TEL. 201,000 lire ($125.65) double. Rates include breakfast. AE, DC, MC, V. Parking 30,000 lire ($18.75). Bus: 1, 3, 7, or 9.

Hotel Capello d'Oro is a renovated 150-year-old corner building on a busy street in the center of the newer section of town, at Porta Nuova near the railway station. The 19th-century facade has been covered with stucco, and the public rooms and the bedrooms are functional, high-ceilinged, and clean, and might be suitable for an overnight stopover. Rooms are adequately furnished, and 80 of them are air-conditioned. If you need a parking space, its better to reserve it when you make your room booking.

WHERE TO DINE

EXPENSIVE

✪ Ristorante da Vittorio

Viale Papa Giovanni XXIII no. 21. ☎ **218060.** Reservations required. Main courses 25,000–40,000 lire ($15.65–$25); fixed-priced menu 60,000 lire ($37.50), 95,000 lire ($59.40), and 130,000 lire ($81.25). AE, DC, MC, V. Thurs–Tues noon–2:30pm and 7:30–9:30pm. Closed Aug 5–27. Bus: 1, 3, or 6. INTERNATIONAL.

This is a well-known and popular restaurant on the main boulevard of the newer section of town. In this location, it has thrived since the 1960s. Set on a corner, the establishment lights its entrance with lanterns. You enter a long and narrow hallway, which is richly paneled with striped pearwood, and in summer, lined with tables laden with all the fruits of the Italian harvest. The menu is amazingly complete; it offers more than a dozen kinds of risotto, more than 20 kinds of pasta, and around 30 meat dishes, as well as just about every kind of fish that swims, somewhere, in the waters around Italy. Examples include grilled "fantasy of the sea" with fresh seasonal vegetables, a breast of goose with a tapenade of black olives, a tartare of salmon with avocado and a scallopine of veal with basil and thyme sauce. The service is efficient, all of it directed by members of the Cerea family who by now are among the best-known citizens of Bergamo.

MODERATE

Taverna dei Colleoni

Piazza Vecchia 7. ☎ **232596.** Reservations required. Main courses 22,000–40,000 lire ($13.75–$25); fixed-price lunch including wine 50,000 lire ($31.25); fixed-price dinner without wine 90,000 lire ($56.25). AE, DC, MC, V. Tues–Sun 12:30–3pm; Tues–Sat 7:30–10pm. Closed Aug 1–20. Bus: 1 or 3. INTERNATIONAL/LOMBARDO.

In the heart of the Città Alta, this restaurant is known to many a gourmet who journeys here to try regional dishes of exceptional merit. Its walls date from the 11th century, and it is the most historic restaurant in Bergamo. Architecturally it continues the design concept on the medieval plaza that contains it. The sidewalk tables are popular in summer, and the view is part of the reward for dining there. Inside, the decor suggests medievalism, but with a fresh approach. The ceiling is vaulted, the chairs are leather, and there's a low-floor dining room with a wood-burning fireplace. Known for its creative interpretations of Lombardian cuisines, the establishment features such dishes as a casserole of jumbo shrimp with polenta, homemade flat pasta with a delicate ragoût of wild duck, and Adriatic turbot on a bed of crispy potatoes.

3 Cremona

59 miles SE of Milan, 61 miles S of Bergamo

This city of the violin is found on the Po River plain. Music lovers from all over the world flock here, as it was the birthplace of Monteverdi (the father of modern opera), and of Stradivari (latinized to Stradivarius), who made violin-making an art. Born in Cremona in 1644, Antonio Stradivari became the most famous name in the world of violin-making; he far exceeded the skill of his teacher, Nicolò Amati. The third great family name associated with the craft, Guarneri, was also of Cremona.

ESSENTIALS

GETTING THERE   By Train   At least nine trains per day run between Milan and Cremona (trip time: 1¹/₂ hours), at a one-way fare of 7,500 lire ($4.70). Train information is available at the rail station in Cremona at via Dante 68 (☎ 22237).

By Bus   Seven buses a day make the run from Milan to Cremona, at a one-way fare of 5,800 lire ($3.65). The bus station is on via Dante (☎ 29212 for schedules and information).

By Car   From Milan, take Route 415 southeast of Milan.

VISITOR INFORMATION   The telephone area code is 0372. The tourist information office is at piazza del Comune 5 (☎ 23233).

WHAT TO SEE & DO

Most of the attractions of the city are centered on the harmonious **piazza del Comune.** The Romanesque cathedral dates from 1107, although its actual consecration was in 1190. Over the centuries, Gothic, Renaissance, even baroque elements were incorporated. In the typical Lombard style, the pillars of the main portal rest on lions, an architectural detail matched in the nearby octagonal baptistery from the 13th century. Surmounting the portal are some marble statues in the vestibule, with a Madonna and Bambino in the center. The rose window over it, from the 13th century, is inserted in the facade like a medallion.

Inside, the cathedral consists of one nave flanked by two aisles. The pillars are draped with Flemish tapestries. Five arches on each side of the nave are admirably frescoed by such artists as Boccaccio Boccaccino (see his *Annunciation* and other scenes from the life of the Madonna, painted in the early 16th century). Other artists who worked on the frescoes were Gian Francesco Bembo (*Adoration of the Wise Men* and *Presentation at the Temple*), Gerolamo Romanino (scenes from the life of Christ), and Altobello Melone (a *Last Supper*). It's open Monday through

Saturday from 7am to noon and 3 to 7pm, and Sunday from 7am to 1pm and 4 to 7pm. Admission is free.

Beside the cathedral is the **Torrazzo,** which dates from the late 13th century and enjoys a reputation as the tallest campanile (bell tower) in Italy. The tower soars to a height of 353 feet. It's open Monday through Saturday from 10:30am to noon and 3 to 6pm, and Sunday from 10:30am to 12:30pm and 3 to 7pm; from December to mid-March, however, it's open only on Sunday and holidays. Admission is 5,000 lire ($3.15) for adults and 3,000 lire ($1.90) for children.

From the same period, and also opening onto the piazza, are the **Loggia dei Militi** and the **Palazzo Comunale** in the Gothic style as uniquely practiced in Lombardy.

Museo Stradivariano

Via Palestro 17. ☎ **29349.** Admission 5,000 lire ($3.15) adults, 3,000 lire ($1.90) children. Tues–Sat 9:30am–12:15pm and 3–5:45pm, Sun 9:30am–12:15pm. Bus: 1.

At this museum you can see a collection of models, designs, and shapes and tools of Stradivari (1644–1737). This Italian violin maker produced more than 1,000 strong instruments, many of which are considered among the best ever made. He learned his craft from Nicolò Amati.

WHERE TO STAY
INEXPENSIVE

Hotel Agip

Località San Felice, 26100 Cremona. ☎ **0372/450490.** Fax 0372/451097. 77 rms. A/C MINIBAR TV TEL. 160,000 lire ($100) double. Rates include breakfast. AE, DC, MC, V. Free parking. Motorists take autostrada A21 to the Casello exit for 1¹/₂ miles.

This motel, part of a nationwide chain, is at the San Felice exit of the superhighway between Piacenza and Brescia. Many a late-night traveler in this part of Italy has been rescued by the availability of a room here. Checking in has a certain ease. The motel is a modern establishment with comfortable bedrooms outfitted with hairdryers and soundproofed against the noise of the nearby highway. A good restaurant on the premises serves copious amounts of food, with a fixed-price menu costing 30,000 lire ($18.75). Parking is also easy here.

Hotel Continental

Piazza della Libertà 26, 26100 Cremona. ☎ **0372/434141.** Fax 0372/434141. 57 rms, 7 suites. A/C MINIBAR TV TEL. 160,000 lire ($100) double; from 180,000 lire ($112.50) suite. Rates include breakfast. AE, DC, MC, V. Parking 15,000–20,000 lire ($9.40–$12.50). Bus: 1 or 2.

Roads from many parts of northern Italy converge on the busy square on which the comfortably 1980s Hotel Continental stands. There isn't that much of a difference between this hotel and scores of other pleasantly up-to-date hotels in Italy, except for the obvious pride in the musical history of Cremona that is displayed by the staff. They will be eager to point out the illuminated glass cases built into the lobby walls. These contain early 20th-century copies of violins by Amati and Stradivari. There are also instruments made by master luthiers of Cremona, some of whom seem to be on a first-name basis with the management. A bronze bust of Claudio Monteverdi, the 17th-century composer, looks out over the lobby, and a restaurant that can seat 500 people is on the premises. Each of the hotel's comfortably furnished bedrooms has sound-insulated windows.

WHERE TO DINE
MODERATE

✪ Aquila Nera (Black Eagle)

Via Sicardo 3. ☎ **25646**. Reservations recommended. Main courses 20,000–35,000 lire ($12.50–$21.90). AE, DC, MC, V. Tues–Sun 12:15–2:30pm; Tues–Sat 8–10pm. Closed Jan 1–10 and July 29–Aug 26. CREMONESE.

This restaurant, established around 1986, occupies the street level of a 16th-century palace at the edge of Cremona's main square, overlooking its cathedral. Inside, an array of regional specialties is flavorfully prepared using fresh local ingredients. Many items change with the season, but might include risotto with seafood, breast of pigeon in puff pastry served with a foie gras sauce, filet of dorado with an orange sauce, fricassee of sturgeon in mustard sauce, tagliatelle with lobster, and roasted lamb with spring onions. Desserts might include a nougat-flavored mousse with chocolate sauce.

✪ Ceresole

Via Ceresole 4. ☎ **30990**. Reservations required. Main courses 20,000–25,000 lire ($12.50–$15.65). DC, MC, V. Tues–Sat noon–2:30pm and 8–10:30pm. Closed Jan 22–30 and Aug 6–28. Bus: 1 or 2. ITALIAN.

Near the Duomo, Ceresole is an elegant and well-known culinary institution, lying in a century-old building in the historic heart of Cremona. Behind a masonry facade on a narrow street, it has windows covered with elaborate wrought-iron grills. Specialties include rice with rhubarb, a wide array of delicately seasoned fish (some of them served with fresh seasonal mushrooms and truffles), whiting with a green-peppercorn-flavored cream sauce, and grilled baby piglet. Some of the dishes are based on time-honored regional recipies, including spaghetti alla marinara, straccotto di manza (a regional form of beef stew), and grilled filets of eel, and ravioli with radicchio.

4 Mantua (Mantova)

25 miles S of Verona. 95 miles SE of Milan, 291 miles NW of Rome

Once a duchy, Mantua had a flowering of art and architecture under the Gonzaga dynasty that held sway over the town for nearly four centuries. Originally an Etruscan settlement, later a Roman colony, it has known many conquerors, including the French and Austrians in the 18th and 19th centuries. Virgil, the great Latin poet, has remained its most famous son (he was born outside the city in a place called Andes). Verdi set his *Rigoletto* here; Romeo (Shakespeare's creation, that is) took refuge here; and writer Aldous Huxley called Mantua "the most romantic city in the world."

Mantua is an imposing, at times even austere city, despite its situation near three lakes, Superior, di Mezzo, and Inferiore. It's very much a city of the past and is easily reached from a number of cities in northern Italy.

The historic center is traffic free, but there are buses outside the rail station. Take bus no. 3 to the center.

ESSENTIALS

GETTING THERE By Train Mantua has excellent rail connections, lying on direct lines to such cities as Milan, Cremona, Modena, and Verona. Six trains a day arrive from Milan, taking $2^1/_4$ hours; a one-way ticket costs 20,600 lire ($12.90). From Cremona, trains arrive every hour (trip time: 1 hour), a one-way ticket costing 8,600 lire ($5.40). The train station is at piazza Don Leoni (☎ 321646).

By Bus Most visitors arrive by train, but Mantua has good bus connections with Brescia; 15 buses a day make the 4-hour journey at a cost of 6,000 lire ($3.75) for a one-way ticket. The bus station is on piazza Mondadori (☎ 327237).

By Car From Cremona (see above), continue east along Route 10.

VISITOR INFORMATION The telephone area code is 0376. The tourist information center is at piazza Andrea Mantegna 6 (☎ 328253).

WHAT TO SEE & DO

✪ Museo di Palazzo Ducale

Piazza Sordello 40. ☎ **320283.** Admission 10,000 lire ($6.25) adults, free for children 17 and under. Mar–Sept, Sun–Mon 9am–1pm, Tues–Sat 9am–1pm and 2:30–4pm; Oct–Feb, Tues–Sat 9am–1pm and 2:30–3:30pm. Bus: 3.

At piazza Sordello, the ducal apartments of the Gonzagas may be visited. With more than 500 rooms and 15 courtyards, the group of palaces is considered by many to be the most remarkable in Italy—certainly when judged from the standpoint of size. Like Rome, the compound wasn't built in a day, or even in a century. The earlier buildings, erected to the specifications of the Bonacolsi family, date from the 13th century. The later 14th and early 15th centuries saw the rise of the Castle of St. George, designed by Bartolino da Novara. The Gonzagas also added the Palatine Basilica of St. Barbara by Bertani.

Over the years the historic monument of Renaissance splendor has suffered the loss of many of the art treasures collected by Isabella d'Este during the 15th and 16th centuries, in her efforts to turn Mantua into "La Città dell'Arte." Her descendants, the Gonzagas, sold the most precious objects to King Charles I of England in 1628, and two years later most of the remaining rich collection was looted during the sack of Mantua. Even Napoleon did his bit by carting off some of the objects still there.

The painting collection is rich, including works by Tintoretto and Sustermans, and a "cut-up" Rubens. The display of classical statuary is impressive, gathered mostly from the various Gonzaga villas at the time of Maria Theresa of Austria. Among the more inspired sights are the Zodiac Room, the Hall of Mirrors with a vaulted ceiling constructed at the beginning of the 17th century, the River Chamber, the Apartment of Paradise, the Apartment of Troia with frescoes by Giulio Romano, and a scale reproduction of the Holy Staircase in Rome. The most interesting and best-known room in the castle is the Camera degli Sposi (bridal chamber), frescoed by Andrea Mantegna. Winged cherubs appear over a balcony at the top of the ceiling. Look for a curious dwarf and a mauve-hatted portrait of King Christian I of Denmark. There are many paintings by Domenico Fetti, along with a splendid series of nine pieces of tapestry woven in Brussels and based on cartoons by Raphael. A cycle of frescoes on the age of chivalry by Pisanello has been recently discovered. A guardian takes visitors on a tour to point out the many highlights.

Basilica of Sant'Andrea

Piazza Mantegna. ☎ **328504.** Admission is free. Daily 7am–7pm. Bus: 3.

Built to the specifications of Leon Battista Alberti, this church opens into piazza Mantegna, just off piazza delle Erbe, where you'll find fruit vendors. The actual work on the basilica, started in the 15th century, was carried out by a pupil of Alberti's, Luca Fancelli. However, before Alberti died in 1472, it is said that architecturally speaking—he knew he had "buried the Middle Ages." The church was finally completed in 1782 after Juvara crowned it with a dome. As you enter, the first chapel to your left contains the tomb of the great Mantegna (the paintings are by the artist's son, except for the *Holy Family* by the old master himself). The sacristan will light it for you. In the crypt you'll encounter a representation of one of the more fanciful legends in the history of church relics: St. Andrew's claim to possess the blood of Christ, "the gift" of St. Longinus, the Roman soldier who is said to have pierced his side. Beside the basilica is a campanile (bell tower), which dates from 1414.

Palazzo Te

Viale Te 1. ☎ **323266.** Admission 10,000 lire ($6.25) adults, 5,000 lire ($3.15) children and those over 60. Tues–Sun 9am–5:30pm. Bus: 3.

This Renaissance palace, built in the 16th century, is known for its frescoes by Giulio Romano and his pupils. At the edge of the city, it's reached on viale Te. Federigo II, one of the Gonzagas, ordered the villa built as a place where he could slip away to see his mistress. The name is said to have been derived from the word *Tejeto*, which in the local dialect means "a cut to let the waters flow out." This was once marshland drained by the Gonzagas for their horse farm. The frescoes in the various rooms, dedicated to everything from horses to Psyche, rely on mythology for subject matter. The Room of the Giants, the best known, has a scene that depicts heaven venting its rage on the giants who have moved threateningly against it.

WHERE TO STAY
INEXPENSIVE

❺ Hotel Dante

Via Corrado 54, 46100 Mantua. ☎ **0376/326425.** Fax 0376/221141. 40 rms. TV TEL. 130,000–135,000 lire ($81.25–$84.40) double. Rates include breakfast. AE, DC, MC, V. Parking 20,000 lire ($12.50). Bus: 3.

Built in 1968, this boxy, modern hotel was constructed with a parking area under the recessed entrance area and a marble-accented interior, parts of which look out over a flagstone-covered courtyard. The hotel's location is on a narrow street in the busy commercial center. Some of the rooms have air conditioning and a minibar.

Mantegna Hotel

Via Fabio Filzi 10B, 46100 Mantua. ☎ **0376/350315.** Fax 0376/368564. 34 rms, 3 suites. A/C TV TEL. 130,000 lire ($81.25) double; 180,000 lire ($112.50) suite. Rates include breakfast. AE, DC, MC, V. Free parking. Closed Dec 24–Jan 5. Bus: 3.

Mantegna is in a commercial section of town, a few blocks from one of the entrances to the old city. This six-story hotel has bandbox lines and a facade of light-gray tiles. The lobby is accented with gray and red marble slabs, along with enlargements of details of paintings by (as you probably guessed) Mantegna. About half the units look out over a sunny rear courtyard, although the rooms facing the street are fairly quiet as well. The hotel is a good value for the rates charged.

Rechigi Hotel

Via P. F. Calvi 30, 46100 Mantua. ☎ **0376/320781.** Fax 0376/220291. 50 rms, 6 suites. A/C TV TEL. 200,000 lire ($125) double; 230,000 lire ($143.75) suite. Breakfast 18,000 lire ($11.25) extra. AE, DC, MC, V. Parking 25,000 lire ($15.60). Bus: 3.

Near the center of the old city stands the Rechigi, a comforable modern hotel, one of the best in Mantua. Its lobby is warmly furnished, with an alcove bar. The owners maintain the property well, and they have decorated the attractively furnished rooms in good taste. There's a parking garage. Only breakfast is served.

WHERE TO DINE
MODERATE

✪ Il Cigno Trattoria dei Martini

Piazza Carlo d'Arco 1. ☎ **327101.** Reservations recommended. Main courses 22,000–32,000 lire ($13.75–$20). AE, DC, MC, V. Wed–Sun 12:30–2pm and 7:30–9:30pm. Closed Jan 12–16 and Aug 1–17. Bus: 3. MANTOVANO.

This trattoria overlooks a cobblestone square in the old part of Mantua. The exterior of the building is a faded ochre, with wrought-iron cross-hatched window bars within sight of the easy parking on the piazza outside. After passing through a large entrance hall studded with frescoes, you'll come upon the bustling dining rooms. Both freshwater and saltwater fish are featured, as are such dishes as agnoli (a form of pasta) in a light sauce or risotto. Bollito misto (a medley of boiled meats) is served with various sauces, including one made of mustard. One excellent pasta, tortelli di zucca, is stuffed with pumpkin.

✪ L'Aquila Nigra (The Black Eagle)

Vicolo Bonacolsi 4. ☎ **327180.** Reservations recommended. Main courses 18,000–22,000 lire ($11.25–$13.75). AE, DC, MC, V. Tues–Sat noon–2pm and 8–10pm. Closed Jan 1–15 and Aug 8–28. Bus: 3. MANTOVANO/ITALIAN.

This restaurant is in a Renaissance mansion on a narrow passageway by the Bonacolsi Palace. The building that contains it actually had its foundations back in the 1200s, although the restaurant dates from 1984. Among the excellent food served in the elegant rooms, which may come as a surprise after going through the more mundane entrance hall, you can choose from such dishes as pike from the Mincio River, called luccio, served with salsa verde (green sauce) and polenta, as well as other specialties of the region. You might order a pasta or the gnocchi alle ortiche (potato dumplings tinged with puréed nettles) as part of your meal. Eel marinated in vinegar, one of the most distinctive specialties of Mantova, is also served, as is tortelli di zucca (with a pumpkin base), and a delectable pasta, maccheroni ducale, made with minced pork and fagioli (beans).

INEXPENSIVE

Ristorante Pavesi

Piazza delle Erbe 13. ☎ **323627.** Reservations recommended. Main courses 12,000–21,000 lire ($7.50–$13.15). AE, MC, V. Fri–Wed 12:30–2:30pm and 7:30–9:30pm. MANTOVANO.

Ristorante Pavesi has the advantage of being located under an ancient arcade on what might be the most beautiful square in Mantua. The walls of this place partially date from the 1200s, although the restaurant itself dates from before World War II. It's a cozy, intimate family-run establishment whose decor consists of hundreds of antique copper pots hanging randomly from the single barrel vault of the plaster ceiling. A well-stocked antipasti table is placed near the door, and it's loaded with delicacies. In summer, tables spill out into the square, offering guests a chance to drink in the surrounding architecture as well as the aromas from the kitchen. Specialties include agnolotti (a form of Mantovano tortellini) with meat, cheese, sage, and butter, as well as risotto alla mantovana (with pesto). Other palatable dishes include noodles with mushrooms or salmon, roast filet of veal (deboned and rolled), and a well-made blend of fagioli (white beans) with onions.

Piedmont & Valle d'Aosta

19

Towering, snow-capped alpine peaks; oleander, poplar, and birch trees; sky-blue lakes; river valleys and flower-studded meadows; the chamois and the wild boar; medieval castles; Roman ruins and folklore; the taste of vermouth on home ground; Fiats and fashion—northwestern Italy is a fascinating area to explore.

Piedmont is largely agricultural, although its capital, Turin, is one of Italy's front-ranking industrial cities (with more mechanics per square foot than any other location in Europe). The influence of France is strongly felt, both in the dialect and in the kitchen.

Valle d'Aosta (really a series of valleys) has traditionally been associated with Piedmont, but in 1948 it was given wide-ranging autonomy. Most of the residents (in this least-populated district in Italy) speak French. Closing in Valle d'Aosta to the north on the French and Swiss frontiers are the tallest mountains in Europe, including Mont Blanc (15,780 ft.), the Matterhorn (14,690 ft.), and Monte Rosa (15,200 ft.). The road tunnels of Great St. Bernard and Mont Blanc (opened in 1965) connect France and Italy.

The best-known wines of the region are Asti Spumante, a brilliant straw color with a delicate bouquet and abundant foam, considered the prototype of Italian sparkling wines and served with desserts. Barolo often accompanies the red-meat roasts so popular in the area. It's aged for about seven years, emerging the color of an orange-yellow brick, with a delicate bouquet of violets. Ranked along with Barbera and Chianti, it is considered one of the finest wines in Italy.

Barbera, served with game and spicy dishes is a dark ruby red in color, with the tonic taste of the vine, its bouquet evocative of both the cherry and the violet. The region's fabled apéritif is Vermouth di Torino, often served iced. It's made from the base of a neutral white wine flavored with Moscato d'Asti, herbs, and spices, along with spirits, bitters, sugar, and tonic. Its color ranges from tawny to dark yellow.

A DRIVING TOUR

Day 1 Turin, 140 miles southwest of Milan, is the gateway to the region. The autostrada network of Italy links Piedmont and the Valle d'Aosta with the rest of the country and with neighboring France. Travelers from France can go through the Mont Blanc Tunnel

---

What's Special About Piedmont & Valle d'Aosta

Great Towns/Villages
- Turin, home of the Fiat auto works, and the great industrial and cultural center of northwestern Italy.
- Aosta, the major town of one of Italy's most beautiful valleys, with a history going back to the 1st century B.C.
- Courmayeur, Italy's best all-around ski resort, but excellent for summer mountain exploration, too.

Architectural Highlight
- Piazza San Carlo in Turin, considered the loveliest and most unified square in northern Italy, covering some $3^1/_2$ acres.

Museum
- The Egyptian Museum, in Turin, rated second only to that of Cairo, and including a famed statue of Ramses II.

Ace Attractions
- The cable-car lift in Courmayeur, taking you across Mont Blanc all the way to Chamonix, France, for the ride of a lifetime.
- Skiing at Courmayeur. It's not the most challenging in Europe, but the stunning alpine backdrops of Mont Blanc are almost unequaled.
- The Valle d'Aosta, a series of valleys that are rich in scenery, folklore, regional food, and handcrafts.

Religious Shrine
- The Chapel of the Holy Shroud, Cathedral of San Giovanni, in Turin, where the life-size image of a crucified body (was it Christ?) has mystified the world for ages.

---

outside Chamonix. From the south of Italy the A21 autostrada cuts northwest into Turin. Once in Turin visit the Egyptian Museum and the Capella della Santa Sindone (unless it's closed for repairs), the latter housing the Holy Shroud. See, if possible, the Royal Palace—all too much for one day, but perhaps that's all the time you have.

🍵 **TAKE A BREAK**   Porta Di Savona, piazza Vittorio Veneto 2 in Turin (☎ 011/831453), is one of the city's oldest restaurants, opening onto a view of the Po valley. Turin has far finer restaurants than this, but if you're a first-time visitor, you can order some of the most typical dishes of Piedmont here, including bagna cauda and bollito misto, the latter a mixed medley of boiled meats with an excellent sauce.

Day 2   From Turin take the A5 autostrada to Aosta to acquaint yourself with its surrounding scenic valley. The old town is still contained within its Roman walls. Visit its major Roman monuments and dine in a typical tavern that night.

Day 3   For a final look at the region, continue on the route west (SS26) to the resort of Courmayeur, 22 miles northwest of Aosta. Although primarily a ski resort, it is visited chiefly for those wanting to take the cable-car lift across Mont Blanc all the way to Chamonix, France. This is one of the most thrilling aerial experiences in northern Italy and will occupy your day. You can return to

Piedmont & Valle D'Aosta

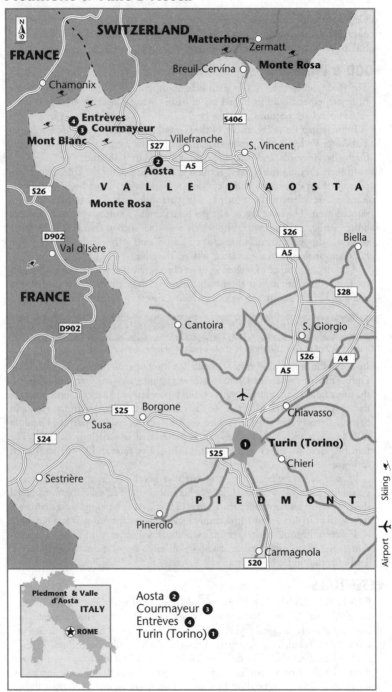

Courmayeur for the night—or, perhaps better yet—anchor in the satellite resort of Entrevès where you can visit La Maison de Filippo or "Chalet of Gluttony," and fill up on all the specialties of the region.

FOOD & WINE

The Piedmont kitchen is a fragrant delight, differing in many respects from the Milanese, especially in its liberal use of garlic. What it lacks in subtlety is often made up in large portions of hearty fare.

In the upper Po valley, an arc of the Central and Western Alps, the Piedmont and Aosta Valley is often industrial in part but has a rich agricultural bounty. Orchards, vineyards, and fields of grass for cattle raising abound.

In such a setting the cookery is often hearty, suitable for the cold, bracing alpine air. First-rate roasts and plenty of stews (heavily flavored with garlic) are featured. Agnoletti is the most popular pasta dish, a small ravioli stuffed with minced meat. The most savory fare is a bagna cauda, a sauce made with olive oil, butter, garlic, and anchovies, into which vegetables such as chard sticks or celery sticks are dipped. Chamois meat, often served with a wine sauce flavored with herbs and anchovies, is the choicest dish on the table.

A fonduta is a sauce of melted Fontina cheese, flavored with white truffles, often from Alba. Although frighteningly expensive, these truffles are sprinkled over many an elegant dish in the region, including risotto or sliced turkey breasts.

1 Turin (Torino)

140 miles SW of Milan, 108 miles NW of Genoa, 414 miles NW of Rome

In Turin, the capital of Piedmont, the Italian Risorgimento (unification) was born. During the years when the United States was fighting its Civil War, Turin became the first capital of a unified Italy, a position it later lost to Florence. Turin was once the capital of Sardinia. Much of the city's history is associated with the House of Savoy, a dynasty that reigned for nine centuries, even presiding over the kingdom of Italy when Victor Emmanuel II was proclaimed king of Italy in 1861. The family ruled, at times in name only, until the monarchy was abolished in 1946.

In spite of having been subject to extensive bombings, Turin found renewed prosperity after World War II, largely because of the Fiat manufacturers based there. The city has been called the Detroit of Italy. Many buildings were destroyed, but much of its 17th- and 18th-century look remains. Turin is well laid out, with wide streets, historic squares, churches, and parks. For years it has had a reputation as the least-visited and least-known of Italy's major cities. Easily reached, Turin (Torino in Italian) is on the Po River.

ESSENTIALS

GETTING THERE **By Plane** Alitalia and ATI fly into the Caselle International Airport (☎ 5676361), about 9 miles north of Turin. This important airport receives international flights as well, from the principal European cities: London, Paris, Frankfurt, Stuttgart, Düsseldorf, Munich, Barcelona, Lisbon, Amsterdam, Brussels, Madrid, Thessaloniki, Vienna, and Zurich. Turin Airport is linked with direct scheduled flights to 24 destinations (10 domestic and 14 international cities); it is used by 14 scheduled carriers that operate regular flights. SAGAT SPA (Turin Airport Management Company) is responsible for all aspects of airport activities. In December 1993, it inaugurated the New Air Passenger Terminal, one of the most technologically advanced structures in Europe covering a total area of more than 36,000 square miles, with five operational levels and six loading bridges. The New Air Terminal handles up to three million passengers a year.

By Train Turin is a major rail terminus, with arrivals at Stazione di Porta Nuova (☎ 5613333) or Stazione Centrale (central station), corso Vittorio Emanuele II (☎ 517551), in the heart of the city. It takes 1 hour and 15 minutes to reach Milan by train from Turin, but anywhere from 9 to 11 hours to reach Turin from Rome, depending on the connection. The one-way fare from Milan is 12,100 lire ($7.55), 96,800 lire ($60.50) from Rome.

By Bus It's possible to catch a bus in Chamonix (France) and go to Turin. Three buses a day run through the Mont Blanc Tunnel, taking $3^1/_2$ hours and costing 28,500 lire ($17.80) for a one-way ticket. There are also 15 buses a day arriving from Milan, taking 2 hours and costing 17,500 lire ($10.95) one way.

By Car If you're coming from France via the Mont Blanc Tunnel, you can pick up the autostrada at Aosta. You can also reach Turin by autostrada from both the French and Italian Rivieras, and there is an easy link from Milan.

SPECIAL EVENTS Turin stages two major cultural fêtes every year, including the Sere d'Estate festival in July, with programs devoted to dance, music, and theater. Classical music reigns supreme in September at the month-long Settembre Musica with performances at various parts of the city. For details about these festivals, contact Assesorato per la Cultura, piazza San Carlo 161 (☎ 5765573).

ORIENTATION

VISITOR INFORMATION If you're seeking specific information about Turin, go to the office of A.P.T., via Roma 226 (☎ 011/535901), open Monday through Saturday from 9am to 7:30pm. There's another office at the train station, Porta Nuova (☎ 531327), open the same hours.

CITY LAYOUT The Stazione di Porta Nuova is in the very center of town. The Po River, which runs through Turin, lies to the east of the station. One of the main arteries running through Turin is corso Vittorio Emanuele II, directly north of the station. Turin is also a city of fashion, with excellent merchandise in its shops, and you'll want to walk along the major shopping street, via Roma, which begins north of the station, leading eventually to two squares that join each other, piazza Castello and piazza Reale. In the middle of via Roma, however, is piazza San Carlo, which many consider the heartbeat of Turin.

FAST FACTS: TURIN

American Express The representative of American Express in Turin, Malan Viaggi, is at via Accademia delle Scienze 1 (☎ 513841). It's closed Saturday afternoon and all day Sunday. Some services are not available on Saturday.

Area Code Turin's telephone area code is 011.

Drugstore If you need an all-night drugstore, try Pharmacie, corso Vittoria Emanuele II no. 66 (☎ 541271).

Emergencies In a life-threatening emergency, dial 113. To seek first aid or to call an ambulance, phone 5747. A major police station is at Corso Vinzaglia 110 (☎ 55881).

Medical Care   For a medical problem, call Mauriziano Umberto, Largo Turati 62 (☎ 50801).

Post Office   The main post office is at via Alfieri 10 (☎ 535891); closed on Sunday.

Religious Services   English-language ecumenical services are conducted every Sunday at 10am at the Chiesa Evangelica Valdese of Turin, Corso Vittorio Emanuele II no. 23. (☎ 6692838).

Taxis   To summon a taxi, phone 5737.

Telephone   Public telephones are at via Roma 18 bis, via Arsenale 13, and the Stazione di Porta Nuova.

WHAT TO SEE & DO

Begin your explorations at ✪ **piazza San Carlo.** Although heavily bombed during World War II, it's still the loveliest and most unified square in the city. It was designed by Carlo di Castellamonte in the 17th century, and covers about 3¹/₂ acres. The two churches are those of Santa Cristina and San Carlo. Some of the most prestigious figures in Italy once sat on this square, sipping coffee and plotting the unification of Italy.

✪ Egyptian Museum

Palazzo dele' Accademia delle Scienze, via Accademia della Scienze 6. ☎ **5617776.** Admission 10,000 lire ($6.25) adults, free for children 18 and under or for those 60 and over. Tues–Sun 9am–2pm. Bus: 56 or 61.

You'll find the most interesting museums housed in the Guarini-designed, 17th-century Science Academy Building. The Egyptian Museum's collection is so vast that it's rated second only to the one at Cairo. Of the statuary, that of Ramses II is the best known, but there is one of Amenhotep II as well. A room nearby contains a rock temple consecrated by Thutmose III in Nubia. In the crowded wings upstairs, the world of the pharaohs lives on (one of the prize exhibits is the "Royal Papyrus," with its valuable chronicle of the Egyptian monarchs from the 1st through the 17th Dynasty). The funerary art is exceptionally rare and valuable, especially the chapel built for Maia and his young wife, and an entirely reassembled tomb (that of Kha and Merit, 18th Dynasty), discovered in good condition at the turn of the century.

Galleria Sabauda

Palazzo dell'Accademia delle Scienze, via Accademia delle Scienze 6. ☎ **547440.** Admission 8,000 lire ($5), free under 18 and over 60. Tues–Sun 9am–2pm. Bus: 1 or 4.

In the same building as the Egyptian Museum, you can see one of the richest art collections in Italy, acquired over a period of centuries by the House of Savoy. The gallery's largest exhibition is of the Piedmontese masters, but it has many fine examples of Flemish art as well. Of the latter, the best-known painting is Sir Anthony van Dyck's *Three Children of Charles I.* Other important works include Botticelli's *Venus,* Memling's *Passion of Christ,* Rembrandt's *Sleeping Old Man,* Duccio's *Virgin and Child,* Mantegna's *Holy Conversation,* Jan van Eyck's *The Stigmata of Francis of Assisi,* Veronese's *Dinner in the House of the Pharisee,* Bellotto's *Views of Turin,* intriguing paintings by Brueghel, and a section of the royal collections between 1730 and 1832.

✪ Capella della Santa Sindone (Cathedral of San Giovanni)

Piazza San Giovanni. ☎ **4366101.** Admission is free. Chapel, Tues–Sat 9am–noon and 3–5:30pm; cathedral, daily 7am–noon and 3–5:30pm.

The Holy Shroud

Listed as one of the world's greatest mysteries, the *Santissima Sindone* (Holy Shroud) is one of the most famous and controversial religious artifacts on earth. It is housed in the Capella della Santa Sindona (closed indefinitely for restoration) in the Cathedral of San Giovanni in the Piedmont city of Turin. The shroud is said to be the one that Joseph of Arimathea wrapped around the body of Christ when he was removed from the cross following crucifixion.

The shroud—really a sheet—reveals the agonized features of a man who suffered crucifixion, almost in photographic detail. The face of the bearded man is complete with a crown of thorns, and the marks by a thonged whip and bruises are compatible with the torment of carrying a cross. The shroud is a four-yard length of linen. No one has successfully put forth a scientific explanation as to why the imprint of the man on the cloth exists, or even how its image became impregnated in the threads of the cloth. Photography, of course, had not yet been invented.

Turin did not always possess this relic. First mentioned in the Gospel of Matthew, the cloth disappeared to history until it mysteriously "turned up" in Cyprus, centuries after the death of Christ. From Cyprus, it was taken to France, where it was first exhibited in 1354, and was immediately denounced as a fraud by a French bishop at the time. In 1578, it was acquired by Duke Emanuele Filiberto, of the house of Savoy, who took the shroud to Turin in 1578.

For centuries, the church did not allow scientists to conduct carbon-dating tests of the shroud. The first scientific testing of the shroud suggested that it was a fraud, probably dating from the 12th century. In 1988, three teams of scientists—from the United States, Britain, and Italy—each announced that the shroud was a clever forgery, except that they estimated the time frame of its fabrication as between 1260 and 1390.

The Archbishop of Turin has presented the shroud to the Holy See, and the fact that the Vatican accepted it as a holy relic has increased some world belief in the shroud's validity. However, the Vatican has refrained from pronouncing it as "the true shroud." The shroud remains encased within a silver casket held within an iron box in the Turin chapel. Only two keys can unlock the casket, one held by the Archbishop of Turin, another by the Palatine Cardinals, church seniors based permanently in the Vatican. The key unlocks only the casket—not the mystery of the shroud.

The Renaissance Cathedral of San Giovanni, dedicated to John the Baptist, is of major interest to visitors since it houses Guarini's Chapel of the Holy Shroud. The chapel, crowned by a baroque dome, is only a short walk from the entrance to the Royal Palace. Acquired by Emanuele Filiberto (the subject of the equestrian statue in piazza San Carlo), the shroud is purported to be the one that Joseph of Arimathea wrapped around the body of Christ when he was removed from the cross. Detailed charts in front of the holy relic claim to show evidence of a hemorrhage produced by the crown of thorns. Scientific testing, however, dated the shroud from the 12th century, or even much later.

The shroud, which rests in a silver box behind bulletproof glass, has always been the subject of controversy. When it was first exhibited in 1354, a French bishop denounced it as a fraud. The life-sized image of a crucified body looks like a photographic negative; since photography had not yet been invented, how the image was imprinted remains a mystery. You can rest assured that the final word has not been sounded in this matter.

Palazzo Reale (Royal Palace)

Piazza Castello. ☎ **4361455**. Admission 6,000 lire ($3.75). Tues–Sun 9am–5pm. Bus: 1, 4, 57, or 63.

The palace that the Savoys called home was begun in 1645. The halls, the columned ballroom by Palagi, the tea salon, and the "Queen's Chapel" are richly baroque in style. The original architect was Amedeo de Castellamonte, but numerous builders supplied ideas and effort before the palazzo was finally complete. As in nearly all ducal residences of that period, the most bizarre room is the one bedecked with flowering chinoiserie. The Throne Room is of interest, as is the tapestry-draped Banqueting Hall. Le Nôtre, the famous Frenchman, mapped out the gardens, which may also be visited. In the building you can also visit the Royal Armory (America Reale), with its large collection of arms and armor and many military mementos.

WHERE TO STAY

Like Milan, Turin is an industrial city first and a tourist center second. Most of its hotels were built after 1945 with an eye toward modern comfort but not necessarily style. Generally the hotels lack distinction, except in the expensive range.

EXPENSIVE

Hotel Concord

Via Lagrange 47, 10123 Torino. ☎ **011/5176756**. Fax 011/5176305. 139 rms, 4 suites. A/C MINIBAR TV TEL. Mon–Thurs 335,000 lire ($209.40) double; Fri–Sun 190,000 lire ($118.75) double. Suite all week from 435,000 lire ($271.90). Rates include breakfast. AE, DC, MC, V. Parking 30,000 lire ($18.75). Bus: 1 or 4.

The Concord is across from the hysterical traffic of a street that runs alongside the Porta Nuova train station. Its large facade is decorated with bas-reliefs, and dotted with cast-iron balconies. The entire hotel was modernized in 1982, and many of the guests here are business travelers. The lobby is covered in marble. The comfortable rooms feature individually controlled air conditioning and double-glazed, soundproof windows. A bank of elevators leads to a stylish bar and restaurant one floor above street level. Additional hotel amenities include room service, babysitting, laundry, valet, and facilities for the disabled.

Jolly Hotel Principi di Piemonte

Via Gobetti 15, 10123 Torino. ☎ **011/5629693** or 212/685-3700 in New York. Fax 011/5620270. 107 rms, 8 suites. A/C MINIBAR TV TEL. 353,300–413,800 lire ($220.80–$258.65) double; from 655,000 lire ($409.40) suite. Rates include breakfast. AE, DC, MC, V. Parking 20,000–25,000 lire ($12.50–$15.65). Bus: 1 or 4.

A favorite choice of Fiat executives, this hotel is in the center of the city, near the railway station. This building itself is from 1939. Owned by the country's Jolly chain, it employed some of Italy's finest architects and designers in its wholesale revamping. In general, a variety of styles has been used, utilizing antiques and reproductions, as well as modern items. The public rooms are grand in style and furnishings, with bas-relief ceilings, gold wall panels, silk draperies, Louis XVI–style chairs, and baroque marble sideboards.

Dining/Entertainment: There are several dining rooms, both formal and informal, as well as a fashionable drinking lounge.

Services: Room service, babysitting, laundry, valet.

✪ **Turin Palace Hotel**

Via Sacchi 8, 10128 Torino. ☎ **011/5625511.** Fax 011/5612187. 123 rms, 2 suites. A/C MINIBAR TV TEL. 250,000–295,000 lire ($156.25–$184.40) double; from 550,000 lire ($343.75) suite. Rates include breakfast. AE, DC, MC, V. Parking 32,000 lire ($20). Bus: 9.

This graceful hotel, with glass doors and a white marble facade, has a tradition of attentive service in plush surroundings. It is convenient to the center of town; its entrance is across from the Porta Nuova train station. Its fashionable address prompted Empress Elizabeth of Austria to stay here in 1893, accompanied by a baron, a countess, three friends, and eight servants. Today the clientele is likely to include top-level management from General Motors headquarters in Detroit on business trips to Turin. The public rooms contain a scattering of full-size oil portraits as well as opulent chairs and console tables of massively carved and gilded woods. These have been supplemented with an assortment of tasteful contemporary furniture as well. The bedrooms and baths are soundproof, with conveniences that include radios.

Dining/Entertainment: Guests, mostly businesspeople, gather in the American Bar for drinks before heading for the hotel restaurant where Piedmont and international cuisine are served with meals ranging from 60,000 to 100,000 lire ($37.50 to $62.50). The restaurant is closed August 1–22.

Services: Room service, babysitting, laundry, valet.

Facilities: A garage is on the premises, as are facilities for the disabled.

✪ **Villa Sassi**

Via Traforo del Pino 47, 10132 Torino. ☎ **011/8980556.** 15 rms, 2 suites. MINIBAR TV TEL. 300,000 lire ($187.50) double; 400,000 lire ($250) suite. Rates include breakfast. AE, DC, MC, V. Free parking. Bus: 15 or 61.

This classic 17th-century-style estate lies 4 miles east of the center and is surrounded by park grounds and approached by a winding driveway. It was converted long ago into a top-grade hotel and restaurant. The original, impressive architectural details are still intact, including the wooden staircase in the entrance hall. The drawing room features an overscale mural and life-size sculpted baroque figures holding bronze torchiers. Each bedroom has been individually decorated (the furniture is a combination of antiques and reproduction). The manager sees that it's run in a personal way, with "custom-made" service.

Dining/Entertainment: The intimate drinking salon is elegantly decorated with its draped red-velvet walls, bronze chandelier, black dado, and low seat cushions. See "Where to Dine," below, for a recommendation of the hotel restaurant.

MODERATE

Hotel Victoria

Via Nino Costa 4, 10123 Torino. ☎ **011/5611909.** Fax 011/5611806. 90 rms. MINIBAR TV TEL. 200,000–260,000 lire ($125–$162.50) double. Rates include breakfast. AE, DC, MC, V. Parking 25,000 lire ($15.65). Bus: 61.

This small but substantial hotel has better accommodations than its second-class designation would lead one to expect. The bedrooms are well designed, and each one has a different monochromatic color scheme. Rooms come in two different categories: standard and deluxe. Graceful furniture and large stained-glass windows contribute to a feeling of luxury in the public rooms. Breakfast is the only meal served.

INEXPENSIVE

Hotel Genio

Corso Vittorio Emanuele II no. 47, 10125 Torino. ☎ **011/6505771.** Fax 011/6508264. 90 rms. MINIBAR TV TEL. Mon–Thurs 200,000 lire ($125) double; Fri–Sun 130,000 lire ($81.25) double. Rates include breakfast. AE, DC, MC, V. Parking 30,000 lire ($18.75). Bus: 1, 9, 52, or 67.

Originally built at the end of the 19th century, this four-story hotel in the center of town was renovated into a streamlined, modern format in 1990. Set close to the railway station, its accommodations contain a comfortable blend of contemporary and early 20th-century furniture, and have double-paned windows for soundproofing. About 40 of the bedrooms are air-conditioned, and sell for a daily supplement of 2,000 lire ($1.25) extra per day. Other than breakfast, no meals are served.

Hotel Goya

Via Principe Amedeo 41 bis, 10123 Torino. ☎ **011/8174951.** Fax 011/8174953. 30 rms. A/C MINIBAR TV TEL. 140,000 lire ($87.50) double. Rates include breakfast. AE, DC, MC, V. Bus: 1 or 4.

This hotel, like many others in the Turin chain that owns it, is named after a famous artist. Located on a fairly quiet street in the historic core of the city center, this century-old hotel was renovated in 1993. Breakfast is the only meal served, but the lobby contains a small bar area just behind the reception desk. There's no garage on the premises, so parking on the street might be a problem.

Hotel Piemontese

Via Berthollet 21, 10125 Torino. ☎ **011/6698101.** Fax 011/6690571. 35 rms, 5 suites. A/C MINIBAR TV TEL. Mon–Thurs 175,000–190,000 lire ($109.40–$118.75) double; Fri–Sun 140,000 lire ($87.50) double. Suite all week 210,000 lire ($131.25). Rates include breakfast. AE, DC, MC, V. Parking 15,000 lire ($9.400). Bus: 1, 18, 34, 35, 61, or 67.

Hotel Piemontese is in a 19th-century building near the historical center and the Stazione Centrale. The facade is covered with iron balconies and ornate stone trim. The restructured interior is well maintained, and the comfortable bedrooms and public places have undergone a complete restoration. Breakfast, taken in an airy, sunny room, is the only meal served at the hotel, but nearby restaurants are willing to offer ample fixed-price menus to guests of the Piemontese for 30,000 lire ($18.75) per person. Laundry and 24-hour room service are available. Guests can patronize a nearby sports center with a swimming pool.

WHERE TO DINE
EXPENSIVE

Del Cambio

Piazza Carignano 2. ☎ **546690.** Reservations required. Main courses 25,000–40,000 lire ($15.65–$25). AE, DC, MC, V. Mon–Sat noon–2:30pm and 7:45–10:30pm. Bus: 4, 58, or 63. PIEDMONT/MEDITERRANEAN.

Del Cambio is a classic, traditional restaurant of old Turin, often attracting members of the Agnelli family. Here, you can dine in comparative grandeur, in an old-world setting of white-and-gilt walls, crystal chandeliers, and gilt mirrors.

The restaurant was founded in 1757; it's the oldest restaurant in Turin, and possibly in all of Italy. The stateman Camillo Cavour was one of its loyal patrons, and his much-frequented corner is immortalized with a bronze medallion.

The white truffle of Piedmont is featured in many specialties of the chef, who has received many culinary honors. To begin with, the assorted antipasti are excellent; the best pasta dish is the regional agnolotti piemontesi. Among the main dishes to be singled out for special praise are fondue with truffles from Alba and beef braised in Barolo wine. Some of this establishment's trademark specialties derive from very old recipes of the southwestern Alps, and include artichokes stewed with bone marrow and truffles; girello aromatizato all Piemontese (flank steak marinated for several days in a mixture of sugar, salt, and aromatic herbs, sliced paper-thin, and served with Parmesan and such seasonal vegetables as artichokes or arugula); and tonno di coniglio à la manière antica (rabbit cooked according to ancient traditions). Rounding out the repast is a homemade tart.

✪ Due Lampioni da Carlo

Via Carlo Alberto 45. ☎ **8179380.** Reservations required. Main courses 22,000–52,000 lire ($13.75–$32.50). AE, V. Mon–Sat 12:30–3pm and 7:30–11pm. Closed Aug. Bus: 61. PIEDMONT/INTERNATIONAL.

Giovanni Agnelli, the head of Fiat, has a gift for finding the best restaurants in Turin; that's why he has been known to patronize this elegant 17th-century palace in the heart of the city, run by chef Carlo Bagatin. Specialties are from the Piedmont district, and only the finest of ingredients go into the tasty dishes. The antipasto selection is among the very best in Turin, and you can follow with a choice of agnolotti, stuffed with duck and cooked with local white truffles, or perhaps tournedos with olive purée. Other favorite dishes include tripe soup, ravioli stuffed with ricotta and pesto, brains fried in an herb liqueur, a mosaic of fish served as a beautiful antipasti, and a bollito misto (medley of boiled meats) in the "style of the stockbrokers." Men are required to wear a jacket and tie.

✪ El Toulà–Villa Sassi

Via Traforo del Pino 47. ☎ **8980556.** Reservations required. Main courses 32,000–45,000 lire ($20–$28.15). AE, DC, MC, V. Mon–Sat noon–2pm and 8–10:30pm. Closed Aug. Bus: 15 or 61. PIEDMONT.

This spacious 17th-century villa is on the rise of a hill 4 miles east of the center on the road to Chieri. The stylish, antique-decorated establishment has seen the addition of a modern dining room, with glass walls extending toward the gardens (most of the tables have an excellent view). Some of the basic food-stuff is brought in from the villa's own farm—not only the vegetables, fruit, and butter, but the beef as well. For an appetizer, try the frogs' legs cooked with broth-simmered rice, or fonduta, a Piedmont fondue, made with fontina cheese and local white truffles. Another local dish is agnolotti, a meat-stuffed pasta like ravioli. If it's featured, you may want to try the prized specialty of the house: camoscio in salmi—that is, chamois (a goatlike antelope) prepared in a sauce of olive oil, anchovies, and garlic, laced with wine and served with polenta.

MODERATE

⑨ Ristorante C'Era Una Volta

Corso Vittorio Emanuele II no. 41. ☎ **655498.** Reservations required. Fixed-price dinner 35,000–45,000 lire ($21.90–$28.15). AE, DC, MC, V. Mon–Sat 8:30pm–midnight. Closed Aug. Bus: 1, 9, 18, 52, or 67. PIEDMONT.

Near the Porta Nuova Stazione, this restaurant is entered from the busy street through carved doors; you take an elevator one floor above ground level. Because the restaurant adheres to the classic dishes of the Piedmontese cuisine, it is a good introduction to the food of the Italian alpine regions. Many clients are faithful devotees. The decor is in the typical Piedmontese style, with hanging copper pots and thick walls of stippled plaster. Fixed-price meals feature an apéritif, a choice of seven or eight antipasti, and two first and two main courses, with vegetables, dessert, and coffee. Typical regional fare includes polenta, crêpes, rabbit, and guinea fowl. The translation of the restaurant's name is "Once upon a time."

✪ Ristorante Vecchia Lanterna

Corso Re Umberto 21. ☎ **537047.** Reservations required. Main courses 30,000–45,000 lire ($18.75–$28.15). DC, MC, V. Mon–Fri noon–3pm; Mon–Sat 8pm–midnight. Closed Aug 10–20. Bus: 1 or 9. PIEDMONT/INTERNATIONAL.

This is one of Turin's most popular upper-bracket restaurants, and it usually proves to be a rewarding gastronomic experience. It's housed in a building from 1740. The bar area near the entrance has Belle Epoque lighting fixtures, heavy gilt mirrors, ornate 19th-century furniture, and Oriental rugs over carpeting. The dining room reminds guests of old Venice. Most of the furnishings were completed during the reign of the king whose name also supplied the street addresses.

The antipasti selection is a treat—king crab Venetian style, asparagus flan, pâté de foie gras, grilled snails on a skewer, and marinated trout. This could be followed by ravioli stuffed with duck and served with a truffle sauce, your choice of risotto, or snail soup. Main courses change seasonally, but often include goose-liver piccata on a bed of fresh mushrooms, sea bass Venetian style, garnished frogs' legs, and many other tempting dishes. The seafood grill is especially delectable here; each element is prepared individually and then assembled afterward.

INEXPENSIVE

Caffè Torino

Piazza San Carlo 204. ☎ **545118.** Reservations not necessary. Main courses 16,000–22,000 lire ($10–$13.75). AE, DC, MC, V. Daily 7am–1am. Bus: 72 to piazza Castello. ITALIAN.

Established in 1903, this famous coffeehouse is the best re-creation in Turin of the days of Vittorio Emanuele, decorated with faded frescoes, brass and marble inlays, and a somewhat battered kind of 19th-century formality. Set on one of the most elegant squares in northern Italy, it has a staff that adheres to a confusing series of rules about where and when clients can and should be seated. There's a stand-up bar near the entrance, a rather formal dining room off to the side, display cases filled with snack food, and a café area with tiny tables and unhurried service.

Ⓢ Da Mauro

Via Maria Vittoria 21. ☎ **8170604.** Reservations not accepted. Main courses 10,000–16,000 lire ($6.25–$10). No credit cards. Tues–Sun noon–2:30pm and 7:30–10pm. Closed July. Bus: 18. ITALIAN/TUSCAN.

Within walking distance of piazza San Carlo, the best of the town's low-cost trattorie is generally packed (everybody loves a bargain). The food is conventional, but it does have character; the chef borrows freely from most of the gastronomic centers of Italy, although the cuisine is mainly Tuscan. An excellent pasta specialty is the cannelloni. Most main dishes consist of well-prepared fish, veal, and poultry. Desserts such as Italian cheesecake and ice cream are consistently enjoyable.

§ Trattoria Ostu Bacu

Corso Vercelli 226. ☎ **2464579.** Reservations recommended. Main courses 16,000–30,000 lire ($10–$18.75). DC, MC, V. Mon–Sat noon–2pm and 7:30–10pm. Bus: 51. PIEDMONT.

This bustling trattoria—established in 1968—is owned by the Barla family, who prepare the regional specialties that have made the place so popular. These include agnolotti (ravioli stuffed with spinach and beef), rolled veal, and other savory main dishes such as a fritto misto di carne (home-style mixed grill) and risotto al barbera (made with wine and spring onions). There is also a full array of homemade pastries from time to time. The ambience attracts an upscale local crowd, who might show up when they want to avoid the formality of deluxe spots such as Villa Sassi. The wines are excellent vintages from Piedmont.

TURIN AFTER DARK

This city of Fiat is also the cultural center of northwestern Italy. Turin is considered a major stopover for concert artists performing between Genoa and Milan. The daily newspaper of Piedmont, La Stampa, will list complete details of any cultural events occurring during your stay.

Classical music concerts are presented at Auditorium della RAI, via Rossini 15 (☎ 5710), throughout the year, although mainly in the winter months. Tickets range from 30,000 to 200,000 lire ($18.75 to $125), depending on the production.

One of the country's leading opera houses, **Teatro Regio,** piazza Castello 215 (☎ 8815241), is in Turin. Concerts and leading ballets are also presented here. The box office is open Tuesday through Sunday from 1 to 6:30pm. Tickets cost 20,000–200,000 lire ($12.50–$125); closed in August.

Opera and other classical productions are presented in summer outside the gardens of the Palazzo Reale.

2 Aosta

114 miles NW of Milan, 78 miles N of Turin, 463 miles NW of Rome

In the capital of Valle d'Aosta stands the Arch of Augustus, built in 24 B.C., the date of the Roman founding of the town. Via Sant'Anselmo, part of the old city from the Middle Ages, leads to the arch. Even more impressive are the ruins of a Roman theater, reached by the Porta Pretoria, a major gateway that dates from the 1st century B.C. and was built of huge blocks. A Roman forum is today a small park with a crypt, lying off piazza San Giovanni near the cathedral. The ruins of the theater are open year round Monday through Friday from 9am to 6:30pm and Saturday and Sunday from 9am to noon and 2 to 5pm. The forum is open May through September, daily from 9am to 6:30pm; October through April, daily from 9am to noon and 2 to 5pm.

The town is also enriched by its medieval relics. The Gothic Church of Sant'Orso, founded in the 12th century, is characterized by its landmark steeple designed in the Romanesque style. You can explore the crypt, but the cloisters, with capitals of some three dozen pillars depicting biblical scenes, are more interesting. The church lies directly off via Sant'Anselmo, and is open daily from 9am to 5pm. Admission is free.

Lying as it does on a major artery, Aosta makes for an important stopover point, either for overnighting or as a base for exploring Valle d'Aosta or taking the cable car to the Conca di Pila, the mountain that towers over the town.

ESSENTIALS

GETTING THERE   By Train   Eleven trains per day run directly from Turin to Aosta (trip time: 2 hours); a one-way ticket costs 10,500 lire ($6.55). From Milan, the trip involves a change of trains at Chiuasso, takes 4½ hours, and costs 15,400 lire ($9.65) one way.

By Bus   Twelve buses a day travel between Turin and Aosta, taking 2½ hours, and four to six buses a day arrive from Milan (trip time: 4 hours).

By Car   From Turin, continue north along the A5. The autostrada comes to an end just to the east of Aosta.

VISITOR INFORMATION   The telephone area code is 0165. The tourist information center is at piazza Chanoux 8 (☎ 236627).

WHERE TO STAY
MODERATE

Hotel Valle d'Aosta

Corso Ivrea 146, 11100 Aosta. ☎ **0165/41845.** Fax 0165/236660. 104 rms. MINIBAR TV TEL. 150,000–210,000 lire ($93.75–$131.25) double. Rates include breakfast. AE, DC, MC, V. Free parking. Closed Dec 15–27. Bus: 2.

This modern hotel with its zigzag conrete facade is one of the leading choices in Aosta. Located on a busy road leading from the old town to the entrance of the autostrada, it's a prominent stopover for motorists using the Great Saint Bernard and Mont Blanc tunnels into Italy. The sunny lobby has beige stone floors, paneled walls, and deep leather chairs. All bedrooms have double windows and views angled toward the mountains. A restaurant is on the premises, under a different management (see "Ristorante Le Foyer" in "Where to Dine," below). The lobby contains an oversized bar area. The hotel also offers room service, babysitting, laundry, and a garage.

INEXPENSIVE

Hotel Roma

Via Torino 7, 11100 Aosta. ☎ **0165/41000.** Fax 0165/32404. 33 rms. TEL. 90,000–110,000 lire ($56.25–$68.75) double. Breakfast 10,000 lire ($6.25) extra. AE, DC, MC, V. Parking 10,000 lire ($6.25). Bus: 2.

Silvio Lepri and Graziella Nicoli are the owners of this hotel, which is on a peaceful alleyway behind a cubist-style white stucco building; it's surrounded by the balconies and windows of what appear to be private apartments. The entrance is at the top of an exterior concrete stairwell. The public rooms include a warmly paneled bar area, big windows, and a homelike decor filled with bright colors and rustic accessories. There's a garage on the premises, plus public parking nearby.

✪ Le Pageot

Via Giorgio Carrel 31, 11100 Aosta. ☎ **0165/32433.** Fax 0165/33217. 18 rms. TV TEL. 110,000 lire ($68.75) double; 142,000 lire ($88.75) triple. Breakfast 13,000 lire ($8.10) extra. AE, DC, MC, V. Parking 10,000 lire ($6.25). Bus: 2.

Built in 1985, this is one of the best-value hotels in town. It has a modern, angular facade of brown brick with big windows, and floors crafted from carefully polished slabs of mountain granite. Bedrooms are clean and functional, and the well-lit public areas include a breakfast room and TV room. The hotel's name translates from an antiquated local dialect into the word for bed. There's no restaurant.

WHERE TO DINE
MODERATE

Ristorante Le Foyer

Corso Ivrea 146. ☎ **32136.** Reservations recommended. Main courses 20,000–40,000 lire ($12.50–$25). AE, DC, MC, V. Wed–Mon 12:15–1:50pm; Wed–Sun 7:30–9:30pm. Closed Jan 15–31 and July 5–20. Bus: 2. VALLE D'AOSTAN/INTERNATIONAL.

This restaurant sits beside a traffic artery on the outskirts of town. The full Valdostan meals you get here are both flavorful and cost-conscious. In a wood-paneled dining room that's illuminated by a wall of oversized windows, you can dine on specialties such as salmon trout, beef tagliata with balsamic vinegar, vegetable flan with fondue, or fresh noodles with smoked salmon and asparagus. There is also a good selection of French and Italian wines.

⑤ Vecchia Aosta

Piazza Porta Pretoria 4. ☎ **361186.** Reservations recommended. Main courses 15,000–20,000 lire ($9.40–$12.50); fixed-price menus 28,000–35,000 lire ($17.50–$21.90). AE, DC, MC, V. Thurs–Tues noon–3pm and 7:30–10pm. Closed June 15–30 and Nov 15–30. Bus: 2. VALLE D'AOSTAN/INTERNATIONAL.

What is probably the most unusual restaurant in Aosta lies in the narrow niche between the inner and outer Roman walls of the Porta Pretoria. It's in an old building which, although modernized, still bears evidence of the superb building techniques of the Romans, whose chiseled stones are sometimes visible between patches of modern wood and plaster. Full meals are served on at least two different levels in a labyrinth of nooks and isolated crannies, and might include homemade ravioli, filet of beef with mushrooms, pepperoni flan, eggs with cheese fondue and truffles, and a cheese-laden version of Valdostan fondue.

INEXPENSIVE

⑤ Ristorante Piemonte

Via Porta Pretoria 13. ☎ **40111.** Reservations not necessary. Main courses 15,000–20,000 lire ($9.40–$12.50); fixed-price menus 25,000–28,000 lire ($15.65–$17.50). MC, V. Sat–Thurs noon–3pm and 7–10pm. Closed Aug. Bus: 2. VALLE D'AOSTAN/INTERNATIONAL.

On a relatively traffic-free street lined with shops, this family-run place is one of the best of the low-cost trattorie inside the walls of the old town. Established in 1910, it has been popular and unpretentious ever since. In a setting of vaulted ceilings and tile floors, you can savor bagna cauda, cannelloni of the chef, risotto with roast pork, sautéed octopus with ginger, and an array of refreshing desserts, which could include fresh strawberries with lemon.

3 Courmayeur & Entrèves

COURMAYEUR

Courmayeur, a 22-mile drive northwest of Aosta, is Italy's best all-around ski resort, with a "high season" attracting the alpine excursionist in summer, the ski enthusiast in winter. Its popularity was given a considerable boost with the opening of the Mont Blanc road tunnel, feeding traffic from France into Italy (estimated time for the trip: 20 minutes). The cost for an average car is 40,000 lire ($25) one way.

With Europe's highest mountain in the background, Courmayeur sits snugly in a valley. Directly to the north of the resort is the alpine village of Entrèves, sprinkled with a number of chalets (some of which take in paying guests).

In the vicinity, you can take a cable-car lift—one of the most unusual in Europe—across Mont Blanc all the way to Chamonix, France. It's a ride across glaciers that's altogether frightening, altogether thrilling—for steel-nerved adventure seekers only. This is a spectacular achievement in engineering. Departures on the Funivie Monte Bianco are from La Palud, near Entrèves. The three-stage cable car heads for the intermediate stations, Pavillon and Rifugio Torino, before reaching its peak at Punta Helbronner at 11,254 feet. At the latter, you'll be on the doorstep of the glacier and the celebrated 11½-mile Vallée Blanche ski run to Chamonix (France), which is most often open at the beginning of February every year. The round-trip price for the cable ride is 45,000 lire ($28.15) per person. Departures are every 20 minutes, and service is daily from 8am to 1pm and 2 to 5pm. At the top is a terrace for sunbathing, a bar, and a snack bar. Panoramic views unfold of 40 alpine peaks. Bookings are possible at Esercizio Funivie, Franzione La Palud 22 (☎ 0165/89925).

ORIENTATION

GETTING THERE   Proceed to Aosta by rail. In Aosta at the bus terminal, piazza Narbonne (☎ 362027), adjacent to the train station, you can take any of 11 buses leaving daily for Courmayeur. Trip time is 1 hour, and a one-way ticket costs 3,600 lire ($2.25). Motorists should continue west from Aosta on Route 26 heading for Mont Blanc; Courmayeur lies on the way there.

VISITOR INFORMATION   The telephone area code for Courmayeur and Entrèves is 0165. The tourist information center for Courmayeur is at piazzale Monte Bianco (☎ 842060).

Once you arrive in the center of Courmayeur, you walk, as the resort is rather compact. However, if you're going somewhere in the environs, such as Entrèves or La Palud (to catch the cable car for Mont Blanc), then the buses will be labeled with the geographic destination. The tourist office (see above) has a complete schedule, and buses depart from just outside the office.

WHERE TO STAY

Courmayeur has a number of good and attractive hotels, many of which are open seasonally. Always reserve ahead in high season, either summer or winter.

Expensive

Grand Hotel Royal e Golf

Via Roma 87, 11013 Courmayeur. ☎ **0165/846787.** Fax 0165/842093. 87 rms, 4 suites. A/C MINIBAR TV TEL. 290,000–560,000 lire ($181.25–$350) double; 470,000–930,000 lire ($293.75–$581.25) suite. Rates include breakfast. AE, DC, MC, V. Free parking outside, 18,000 lire ($11.25) inside. Closed Easter–June 20 and Sept 15–Nov. Hotel shuttle transports guests about.

Built in 1950, this hotel is in a dramatic location above the heart of the resort between the most fashionable pedestrian walkway and a thermally heated outdoor swimming pool. Much of its angular facade is covered with rocks, so that it fits in neatly with the surrounding mountainous landscape. Rooms are generally large, with built-in furnishings and streamlined bathrooms.

Dining/Entertainment: The hotel's social center is a large and comfortable lounge, flanked on one side by a bar and on another by a dais where a pianist provides nightly entertainment in season. One of the resort's pockets of posh, La Grill dell'Hotel Royal e Golf is on the lobby level; see my recommendation in "Where to Dine," below. The hotel also has a regular dining room that is open daily.

Services: Room service, babysitting, laundry, valet, hydromassage.

Facilities: Swimming pool, sauna, Jacuzzi.

✪ Hotel Pavillon

Strada Regionale 60, 110113 Courmayeur. ☎ **0165/846120.** Fax 0165/846122. 50 rms, 10 suites. MINIBAR TV TEL. 320,000–390,000 lire ($200–$243.75) double; 480,000–800,000 lire ($300–$500) suite. Rates include half-board. AE, DC, MC, V. Parking 10,000 lire ($6.25). Closed May 1–June 15 and Sept 30–Dec 1.

A selection of the prestigious Relais & Châteaux, this is easily the swankiest and most important hotel at the resort, in spite of its small size. Many of the clients warming themselves around the stone fireplace are from England, Germany, and France, which adds a continental allure. Built in 1965, renovated in 1990, and designed like a chalet, the hotel is located a 4-minute walk south of Courmayeur's inner-city pedestrian zone. The bedrooms, which are entered through leather-covered doors, feature built-in furniture and a comfortable conservative decor; all but two have private balconies. The hotel is only a short walk to the funicular that goes to Plan Checrouit.

Dining/Entertainment: One of my favorite restaurants in town is Le Bistroquet, found on these premises (see "Where to Dine," below).

Services: Room service, babysitting, laundry, valet.

Facilities: In the basement is a full array of hydrotherapy facilities; there's also a covered swimming pool that is visible from the entrance vestibule.

Moderate

✪ Palace Bron

Località Plan Gorret 41, 11013 Courmayeur. ☎ **0165/846742.** Fax 0165/844015. 26 rms, 1 suite. TV TEL. 230,000–340,000 lire ($143.75–$212.50) double; 520,000–690,000 lire ($325–$431.25) suite. Breakfast 25,000 lire ($15.65) extra. AE, DC, MC, V. Free parking. Closed Oct–Nov and May–June. Bus: Plan Gorret.

About 1¼ miles from the heart of the resort, this tranquil oasis is one of the plushest addresses in town. The white-walled chalet is the most noteworthy building on the pine-studded hill, and it has a commanding view over all of Courmayeur and the mountains beyond. Guests are often made to feel like members of a baronial private household rather than patrons of a hotel.

The bedrooms are handsomely furnished and well maintained. Winter visitors appreciate its proximity to the many ski lifts in the area. Walking from the chalet to the center of town is a good way to exercise after dining on the kitchen's filling cuisine. There's a nearby parking lot for motorists who prefer to drive the long, steep distance up from town.

Dining/Entertainment: The hotel's piano bar is especially lively in winter, hosting skiers from all over Europe and America. The restaurant has a refined international cuisine, with formal service. Meals cost 55,000–75,000 lire ($34.40–$46.90).

Services: Room service, babysitting, laundry, valet.

Inexpensive

Bouton d'Or

Strada Traforo del Monte Bianco 10, 11013 Courmayeur. ☎ **0165/846729.** Fax 0165/842152. 35 rms (all with bath or shower). TV TEL. 140,000–160,000 lire ($87.50–$100) double. Rates include breakfast. AE, DC, MC, V. Free parking. Closed Nov and June.

Named after the buttercups that cover the surrounding hills in summer, this hotel off piazzale Monte Bianco is owned by the Casale family, who built it in 1970 and renovated it in 1990. It features an exterior painted yellow and gray, stone trim, and a flagstone roof. French windows lead from the clean, comfortable bedrooms onto small balconies. Each of the rooms has radio, among other amenities. The hotel is about 100 yards (toward the Mont Blanc Tunnel to France) from the most popular restaurant in Courmayeur, Le Vieux Pommier, which is owned by the same family. The hotel also has a garage, sauna, solarium, and garden.

⊗ Hotel Courmayeur

Via Roma 158. 11013 Courmayeur. ☎ **0165/846732.** Fax 0165/845125. 26 rms (all with bath or shower). TV TEL. 85,000–110,000 lire ($53.15–$68.75) per person in single or double. Rates include half-board. V. Closed end of Apr–June 18 and Oct–Nov.

Hotel Courmayeur, right in the center of the resort, was constructed so that most of its rooms would have unobstructed views of the nearby mountains. A number of the bedrooms, furnished in the mountain chalet style, also have wooden balconies. Nonresidents can visit the hotel restaurant, paying 38,000 lire ($23.75) for a meal. Regional food is served.

Hotel Del Viale

Viale Monte Bianco 74, 11013 Courmayeur. ☎ **0165/846712.** Fax 0165/844513. 23 rms (all with bath or shower). MINIBAR TV TEL. 150,000–180,000 lire ($93.75–$112.50) double. Rates include breakfast. AE, DC, MC, V. Free parking outside, 10,000 lire ($6.25). Closed May and Nov.

This old-style mountain chalet at the edge of town is a good place to enjoy the indoor-outdoor life. There's a front terrace with tables set out under trees in fair weather, and the rooms inside are cozy and pleasant in the chillier months. In the winter, guests can gather in the taproom to enjoy après-ski life, drinking at pine tables and warming their feet before the open fire. The house is filled with such pieces as a large wooden pillar rescued from a wine press, hanging copper kettles, pewter, exposed beams, and pots of flowers in the window. The clean and comfortable bedrooms, with natural wood, have a rustic air about them.

WHERE TO DINE

Expensive

✪ La Grill dell'hotel Royal e Golf

In the Grand Hotel Royal e Golf, via Roma 87. ☎ **846787.** Reservations required in winter. Main courses 40,000–65,000 lire ($25–$40.65). AE, DC, MC, V. Tues–Sun 7:30–10pm. Closed Apr 18–July 1 and Sept 15–Dec 10. INTERNATIONAL/ITALIAN.

On the lobby level of this previously recommended hotel is the most fashionable— and certainly the most expensive—restaurant in town. It has only 30 places for diners interested in the cultivated cuisine inspired by the legacy of "Harry" Cipriani, of Harry's Bar fame. It's sparely decorated, with a carved Gothic screen from an English church standing against one wall. The relatively simple but fresh and well-prepared dishes include pasta e fagioli, carpaccio, risotto with radicchio, and rosettes of veal Cipriani style. The hotel's foie gras—served on a brioche—is said to be the "best anywhere." The menu changes daily.

Inexpensive

◎ Cadran Solaire

Via Roma 122. ☎ **844609.** Reservations required. Main courses 18,000–25,000 lire ($11.25–$15.65); fixed-price menu 30,000 lire ($18.75). AE, DC, MC, V. Wed–Sun 12:30–3pm and 7:30–11pm. Closed May and Sept 30–Nov 15. VALLE D'AOSTAN.

In the center of town is the most interesting restaurant in Courmayeur. Named after the sundial (cadran solaire) that embellishes the upper floor of its chalet facade, it's owned by Leo Garin, whose also-recommended La Maison de Filippo (see under Entrèves, below) is the most popular restaurant in the Valle d'Aosta. The restaurant is as unusual architecturally as it is gastronomically. Try to come for a before-dinner drink in the vaulted bar; its massive stones were crafted into almost alarmingly long spans in the 16th century using construction techniques that the Romans perfected. A few steps away, the rustically elegant dining room has its own stone fireplace, a beamed ceiling, and wide plank floors.

Specialties change with the season but are likely to include warm goat cheese blended with a salad, noodles with seasonal vegetables, a baked cheese and spinach casserole, and duck breast with plums. Desserts are sumptuous.

Leone Rosso

Via Roma 73. ☎ **846726.** Reservations recommended. Main courses 16,000–26,000 lire ($10–$16.25). MC, V. Fri–Wed noon–2:30pm and 7:30–10:30pm. Closed mid-May to mid-June and Oct. VALLE D'AOSTAN.

Leone Rosso is in a stone- and timber-fronted house in a slightly isolated courtyard, a few paces from the busy pedestrian traffic of via Roma. It serves well-prepared and seasoned Valdostan specialties, including fondues, a thick and steaming regional version of minestrone, tagliatelle with mushrooms and en papillotte, and an array of rich, creamy desserts. Some meats are grilled right at your table by yourself. This place is not to be confused with The Red Lion pub, which is recommended separately (see "Evening Entertainment," below).

◉ Le Vieux Pommier

Piazzale Monte Bianco 25. ☎ **842281.** Reservations recommended. Main courses 18,000–26,000 lire ($11.25–$16.25). AE, DC, MC, V. Tues–Sun noon–2pm and 7–9:30pm. Closed for 10 or 15 days in May, and Oct. VALLE D'AOSTAN.

The apple tree that was cut down so that construction on the restaurant could begin is now the focal point of this establishment, which is located on the main square of town. One of its guests was filmmaker Ingmar Bergman, who, like everyone else, appreciated the exposed stone, the copper-covered bar, the heavy ceiling beams, and thick pine tables arranged in an octagon around the heavily ornamented tree.

Today Alessandro Casale, the son of the woman who established the restaurant, directs the kitchen. He's assisted by his wife, Lydia, and they have traveled on tours of Europe, teaching the technique of their regional cuisine. Your meal might consist of three kinds of dried alpine beef, followed by noodles in a ham-studded cream sauce, and an arrangement of three kinds of pasta or four types of fondue, including a regional variety with fontina, milk, and egg yolks. Then it's on to chicken suprême en papillote or four or five unusual meat dishes that are cooked mountain style, right at your table. Six kinds of grilled meats are also offered, all of them tasty and flavored with aromatic herbs. Desserts are refreshingly sweet, especially the chocolate-cream parfait. Your meal is usually finished off by coffee served in the style of the Valle d'Aosta.

COURMAYEUR AFTER DARK

The life expectancy of the average disco in an alpine resort such as Courmayeur is about that of a snow crystal in July. The local clubs can be fun, however, and might offer a chance to meet someone. As of this writing, the après-ski crowd is attracted to the electronic rhythms at the following establishments.

American Bar
Via Roma 43. ☎ **846707.**

Not to be confused with a less desirable bar with the same name at the end of the same street, this is one of the most popular bars on the après-ski circuit. It's rowdy and sometimes outrageous, but most often a lot of fun. You might want to peruse the message board for notes from long-departed friends, but most guests end up in one of the two rooms, beside either an open fireplace or a long, crowded bar. The place is open in winter daily from 9am to 1am; it's sometimes closed on Tuesday, but never in ski season. A small beer costs 4,000 lire ($2.50); a glass of white wine goes for 3,000 lire ($1.90) and up.

Café Posta
Via Roma 51. ☎ **842272.**

Café Posta is as sedate as its neighbor, the American Bar, is unruly. Many guests prefer to remain in the warmly decorated bar area, never venturing into the large and comfortable salon with a glowing fireplace in an adjacent room. A piano provides live entertainment nightly in season from 8:30pm to 1:30am. The place changes its stripes throughout the day, opening as a morning café at 8:30am. A whisky and soda costs from 10,000 lire ($6.25).

Le Clochard
Route de Frazione Dolonne. ☎ **846766.** Cover 20,000 lire ($12.50).

"The Drunkard" is one of the most popular discos in town, catering to an over-25 crowd of skiers, hikers, and sports enthusiasts who enjoy unwinding with electrically amplified music. It lies at the edge of the resort. Near the busy bar and a blazing wintertime fireplace you'll find a warm and comfortable spot to watch the international goings-on. It's open every evening in winter from 9:30pm to 1:30am. In summer, its schedule varies with business at the resort.

ENTRÈVES

Even older than Courmayeur, Entrèves is an ancient community that's small and compact, really a mountain village of wood houses. Many discriminating clients prefer its alpine charm to the more bustling resort of Courmayeur. It's reached by a steep and narrow road. Many gourmets book in here just to enjoy the regional fare, for which the village is known.

Just outside Entrèves on the main highway lies the Val Veny cable car, which skiers take in winter to reach the Courmayeur lift system.

Entrèves is located 2 miles north of Courmayeur (signposted off Route 26). Buses from the center of Courmayeur run daily to Entrèves.

There is no local tourist office (ask at the tourist office in Courmayeur; see above). The telephone area code is the same for both resorts: 0165.

WHERE TO STAY

Note that La Brenva, listed under "Where to Dine," below, also offers accommodations.

Inexpensive

⑤ La Grange

11013 Courmeyeur-Entrèves. ☎ **0165/869733.** Fax 0165/869744. 21 rms, 2 suites. MINIBAR TV TEL. 180,000–200,000 lire ($112.50–$125) double; from 300,000 lire ($187.50) suite. Rates include breakfast. AE, DC, MC, V. Free parking. Closed May–June and Oct–Nov.

This will be one of the first buildings you'll see as you enter this rustic alpine village, a short distance from Courmayeur, toward the Mont Blanc Tunnel. A few stones of the foundation probably date from as early as the 1300s, when the building was used as a barn for the cows that grazed on the neighboring slopes. What you'll see today is a stone building whose balconies and gables are outlined against the steep hillside into which it's built. The Berthod family transformed a dilapidated property into a rustic and comfortable hotel in 1979, surrounding the establishment with summer flowerbeds. Today it's managed by Bruna Berthod Perri and her nephew, Stefano Pellin, whose enthusiasm is evident. The unusual decor includes a grandfather clock in the lobby, along with a collection of antique tools and a rhythmic series of thick timbers, stucco, and exposed stone walls. Music is played in the bar, which is open only to residents of the hotel. There is also an exercise room and a sauna. A rich breakfast is the only meal served, but you can choose your menu in different restaurants cooperating with Le Grange. Facilities include a solarium, sauna, and gym.

WHERE TO DINE

Moderate

⑤ La Brenva

Frazione Entrèves di Courmayeur, 11013 Courmeyeur-Entrèves. ☎ **0165/89285.** Fax 0165/869780. Reservations required. Main courses 20,000–32,000 lire ($12.50–$20). DC, MC, V. VALLE D'AOSTAN/FRENCH.

Many skiers from Courmayeur make a special trek to Entrèves just to have a drink at the old-fashioned bar area of this hotel and restaurant, where a copper espresso machine is topped by a brass eagle, and many of the decorative accessories are at least a century old. The core of the building was constructed in 1884 as a rustic hunting lodge for Victor Emmanuel. In 1897 it became a hotel, the closest one to the base of Mont Blanc, and in 1980 the owners enlarged its stone foundations with the addition of extra bedrooms and a larger eating area.

The restaurant consists of three rooms, each with exposed stone walls, wide flooring planks, hunting trophies, copper pots, and straw-bottomed chairs. Fires burn almost all the time in winter, and many diners prefer an apéritif in the unusual salon, within view of the well-chosen paintings. On any given day the menu could include prosciutto, fonduta for two, carbonada with polenta, scaloppine with fresh mushrooms, Valle d'Aostan beefsteak, and zabaglione for dessert.

Each of the 14 simple and comfortable bedrooms has a private bath, TV, phone, and lots of peace and quiet. Many of them have covered loggias. With half-board included, they rent for 130,000 to 200,000 lire ($81.25 to $125) per person daily. La Brenva is a Provençal word for the thousands of larches that cover the surrounding mountainside. The inn takes a vacation in either May or June (dates vary, so call first).

Ⓢ La Maison de Filippo

Frazione Entrèves di Courmayeur. ☎ **869797.** Reservations required. Fixed-price menu 55,000 lire ($34.40). MC, V. Wed–Mon 12:30–2:30pm and 7:30–10:30pm. Closed June and Nov. VALLE D'AOSTAN.

Since 1965 this restaurant has offered the complete gastronomic experience of the regional kitchen in a typical atmosphere. A colorful tavern, it's the creation of Leo Garin, who has been featured in both *Playboy* and *Town & Country*. His establishment is for those who enjoy a rustic, festive atmosphere and bountiful regional food. Many French people ride through the Mont Blanc Tunnel just to dine here. Inside, the three-story open hallway seems like a rustic barn, with an open worn wooden staircase leading to the various dining nooks. You pass casks of nuts, baskets of fresh fruits, window ledges with bowls of salad, fruit tarts, wooden boxes spilling over with spices, onions, gourds, and loaves of freshly baked bread. It's one of the most charming inns in all the valley.

The fare is served either in the mellowed rooms inside, or in the beer garden in summer, which has a full view of Mont Blanc. Mr. Garin features local specialties on an all-you-can-eat basis. Some call his mansion the "Chalet of Gluttony." A typical meal? It might begin with a selection of antipasti, followed by a 2-foot-long platter of about 60 varieties of sausage, with a cutting board and knife. Then there will be a parade of pasta dishes. For a main course, you can pick everything from fondue to camoscio (chamois meat) to trout with an almond-and-butter sauce, to roast duck with an orange glaze. You may even prefer the local boiled dinner, with pungent hamhock, cabbage, and potatoes. Accompanying are huge hunks of coarse country bread from a wicker basket (the size of a laundry bin). For dessert, crêpes Suzette are an ever-popular favorite, along with a selection of regional cheeses.

Genoa & the Italian Riviera

20

For years the retreat of the wintering wealthy, the Italian Riviera now enjoys a broad base of tourism. Even in winter (the average temperature in January hovers around the 50° Fahrenheit mark) the Riviera is popular, although not for swimming. The protection provided by the Ligurian Apennines that loom in the background makes the balmy weather possible.

The winding coastline of the Rivieras, particularly the one that stretches from the French border to San Remo, is especially familiar to moviegoers as the background for countless flicks about sports-car racing, jewel thieves, and spies. Over the years the northwestern coast of Italy has seen the famous and the infamous, especially literary figures: the poet Shelley (who drowned off the shore), d'Annunzio, Byron, Katherine Mansfield, George Sand, and D. H. Lawrence.

The Mediterranean vegetation is characterized by pines, olives, citrus trees, and cypresses. The Western Riviera—the **Riviera di Ponente,** from the border to Genoa—is sometimes known as the Riviera of Flowers because of its profusion of blossoms. Starting at the French border, Ventimiglia is the gateway city to Italy. Along the way you'll encounter the first big resort, Bardighera, followed by San Remo, the major center of Riviera tourism.

Genoa, which divides the Riviera into two parts, is the capital of the Ligurian region—a big, bustling port city that has charm for those willing to spend the time to seek out its treasures.

On the **Riviera di Levante** (eastern) are three small, dramatically situated resorts—Rapallo, Santa Margherita, and Portofino (the favorite of the yachting set).

A DRIVING TOUR

Day 1   Let San Remo, lying east of Monaco and the French resort of Menton, be your gateway to the Italian Riviera. The so-called capital of the *Riviera di Fiori* (Riviera of Flowers), evokes an Edwardian aura, and has been fashionable since the turn of the century, when it attracted German and Russian aristocrats. Visit its *Mercato dei Fiori* (Flower Market), test your luck at its Municipal Casino, and explore the old town. For a panoramic view of the coast

What's Special About Genoa & the Italian Riviera

Great Towns/Villages

- Genoa, prominent between the 11th and 15th centuries and still a major port city.
- San Remo, the capital and major resort of the Italian Riviera, made famous by the wintering wealthy of the Belle Epoque era.
- Rapallo, overlooking the Gulf of Tiguillio, still a leading resort, although its heyday was before World War II.
- Portofino, called the "Pearl of the Riviera," a former fishing village that today is the rendezvous of the rich and famous.

Beaches

- Riviera di Ponente, a narrow coastal strip with rocky outcrops between dozens of sandy coves that open onto wide bays.
- Riviera di Levante, a wild, rugged coastline that also contains compact bays and inlets for swimming.

Ace Attractions

- The Mercato dei Fiori, San Remo, the most colorful flower market in Italy, known for its roses, carnations, and mimosa active from October to June.
- The Port at Genoa, the largest in Italy, with a sailors' quarter and five major basins; best seen by taking a boat ride.

Architectural Highlights

- The Città Vecchia (Old Town), San Remo, a maze of winding alleys and staircases that preserve the life of the fisherfolk of yesterday.
- Via Garibaldi, Genoa, a street of palaces that form the most important architectural holdover from the days of the Genovese aristocrats.

(sometimes you can see as far as Cannes) take the funicular to Monte Bignone. Overnight in San Remo.

Day 2: Leave San Remo heading for Genoa. A good stopover en route would be Savona, the largest town on the Riviera di Ponente, and largely industrial.

☕ TAKE A BREAK   La Farinata, via Montesisto 15, in Savona (☎ 019/826458), makes a good luncheon stopover, especially if you want to sample fresh fish. Platters are accompanied by *farinata*, flat cakes made from chick-pea flour and roasted. Closed weekends and also for two weeks in August.

From Savona it is a 29-mile drive to Genoa, the major port of Italy. Overnight there.

Day 3   Since you will have had little time to explore the port, spend this day taking in its attractions, include a stroll down via Garibaldi and a visit to its most important museums, including Galleria Nazionale. Take a boat tour of the port and spend another night.

Day 4   From Genoa, drive south along the cost for about 17 miles until you reach Rapallo, one of the most fashionable resorts in Italy. Take a cable car to the Sanctuary of di Montallegro and walk along Monte Rosa for one of the most panoramic views of the Ligurian coastline. Perhaps consider a summer boat trip to Portofino.

The Genoese manner . . . is exceedingly animated and pantomimic; so that two friends of the lower class conversing pleasantly in the street, always seem on the eve of stabbing each other forthwith, and a stranger is immensely astonished at their not doing it.
—Charles Dickens, Letter to John Forster, July 20, 1844.

Day 5   To avoid checking in and out of another hotel, you can base in Rapallo and use it as a center for exploring Santa Margherita Ligure, lying only 19 miles east of Genoa. It's a rival of Rapallo, opening onto the Gulf of Tiguillio. After exploring the town, drive about 4 miles south to Portofino, where you'll want to spend the entire day, exploring the village and its hillsides, perhaps dining in a local restaurant before returning to Rapallo for the night.

FOOD & WINE

Opening onto the Ligurian Sea, the area around Genoa and the Italian Riviera is rich with vegetation and filled with seaside towns and winter resorts. It is the land of the pesto sauce, made with fresh basil, cheese, garlic, olive oil and walnuts.

This sauce dresses all forms of pasta, such as trenette (thin noodles), as well as many other dishes, including gnocchi (little dumplings of dough or potato flour). Buridda is the regional fish soup (seasoned with hot spices)—it's the Ligurian form of bouillabaisse.

One of the most famous dishes of Genoa is *cima alla genovese*, beef filled with fat, sweetbreads, chopped pork, and fresh peas—all flavored with onion and garlic, then stewed on a slow fire. The most favored rice dish is riso arrosto alla genovese, a timbale of sausage, peas, rice, mushrooms, artichokes, cheese, and onion—all browned in an oven.

Although not as numerous as the wines in other regions of Italy, there are a number of good wines, including Cinqueterre, one of the most important. Served often with fish, it is golden yellow in color, with an aromatic bouquet. The wine is also known as Sciacchetra. Other well-known wines include Coronata, a pale straw yellow in color, with a delicate bouquet (sometimes, however, it verges upon sweetness). It too is often served with fish. Two others include Polcevera, a light straw yellow, with a delicate bouquet and somewhat nutty flavor, a favorite with fish, and Vermentino Ligure, also a pale yellow in color, with a good bouquet and refreshing flavor. Served with fish and last courses, the wine is sometimes semi-sparkling.

1 San Remo

10 miles E of the French border, 85 miles SW of Genoa, 397 miles NW of Rome

San Remo's reputation has grown ever since Emperor Frederick William wintered in a villa here. It initially attracted the turn-of-the-century wealthy, including the French, the English, and later, the Americans. The flower-filled resort has been considerably updated, and its casino, race track, 18-hole golf course, and deluxe Royal Hotel still on occasion attract the fashionable. Its climate is considered the mildest on the entire western Riviera.

ESSENTIALS

GETTING THERE   By Train   Since San Remo lies on the coast between Ventimiglia and Imperia—6 miles from each—it's a major stop for many trains in Italy or (for running to or from France). A train leaves Genoa heading for the French border once per hour, stopping in San Remo. Rome is 8 hours by train from San Remo. For train information and schedules in Genoa, call 284081 from 7am to 11pm.

By Bus   If you've arrived in Italy from France in the gateway town of Ventimiglia, you'll find a bus leaving for San Remo about every 15 minutes. The trip takes 30 minutes, and a one-way ticket costs 2,400 lire ($1.50). It's also possible to take one of three buses per day from Monaco (trip time: 1¹/₂ hours). On Monday, Wednesday, and Saturday a bus departs Milan for San Remo at 8am, arriving at 1:30pm.

By Car   Autostrada A10, which runs east–west along the Riviera, is the fastest way for motorists to reach San Remo from either the French border or Genoa.

VISITOR INFORMATION   The telephone area code for San Remo is 0184. The tourist information center is at Corso Nuvoloni (☎ 571571).

WHAT TO SEE & DO

Even if you're just passing through, you might want to stop off and visit **La Città Vecchia** (also known as La Pigna), the Old City on the top of the hill. Far removed in spirit from the burgeoning, sterile-looking town near the water, old San Remo blithely ignores the present, and its tiny houses on narrow, steep lanes seem to capture the past. In the new town, the palm-flanked **passeggiata dell'Imperatrice** attracts the promenader. For a scenic view, you can reach **San Romolo** and **Monte Bignone** at 4,265 feet by car.

From October to June, you can visit the most famous flower market in Italy, the ✪ **Mercato di Fiori,** open daily from 6 to 8am. It's held in the market hall between corso Garibaldi and piazza Colombo. In this market you'll see some 20,000 tons of roses, mimosa, and carnations, which are grown along the balmy climate of the Riviera in winter before shipment to all parts of Europe.

WHERE TO STAY
EXPENSIVE

✪ Royal Hotel

Corso Imperatrice 80, 18038 San Remo. ☎ **0184/5391.** Fax 0184/661445. 151 rms, 12 suites. A/C MINIBAR TV TEL. 280,000–448,000 lire ($175–$280) double; from 500,000 lire ($312.50) suite. Rates include breakfast. AE, DC, MC, V. Parking 13,000–24,000 lire ($8.15–$15). Closed Oct 20–Dec 21. Bus: 20.

This place is almost like a mirror reflection of the Beverly Hills Hotel, complete with terraces and gardens, a heated free-form saltwater swimming pool, a forest of palm trees, bright flowers, and hideaway nooks for shade. The activity centers around the garden terrace, since little emphasis is put on the public lounges (which are decked out in the grand old dowager style). The bedrooms vary considerably—some are of tennis-court size with private balconies, many have sea views, and others face the hills. The furnishings range from traditional to modern. Rooms on the fifth floor—all doubles—are more expensive, because they have the best views and are more luxuriously appointed.

Italian Riviera

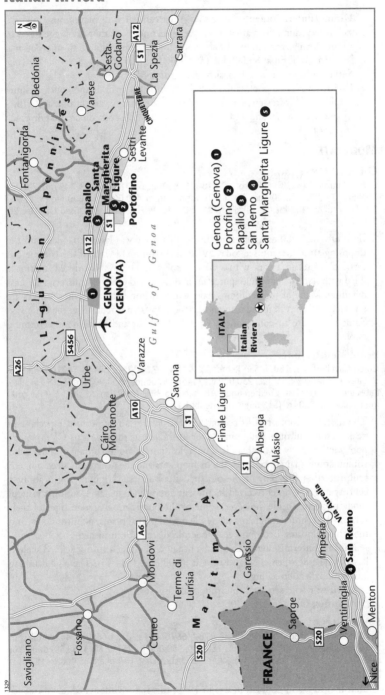

Dining/Entertainment: There's an American bar with piano music nightly. Lunch is served in fair weather on the veranda under an arbor of orange roses. In the more formal restaurant, diners enjoy both a regional and an international cuisine. Meals begin at 85,000 lire ($53.15).

Services: Room service, babysitting, laundry, valet.

Facilities: Heated pool, sauna, solarium, minigolf, gym, tennis court, facilities for children, hairdressers, covered and open-air parking areas, a garage with a mechanic, a car wash, and a gas pump, plus an 18-hole golf course and horseback riding nearby.

MODERATE

✪ Grand Hotel Londra

Corso Matuzia 2, 18038 San Remo. ☎ **0184/668000.** Fax 0184/668073. 149 rms, 7 suites. MINIBAR TV TEL. 235,000 lire ($146.90) double; from 450,000–500,000 lire ($281.25–$312.50) suite. Rates include breakfast. AE, DC, MC, V. Free parking. Closed Oct–Dec 20. Bus: U.

Built around 1900 as a two-story hotel, this place was later expanded into the imposing structure you see today. Within a 10-minute walk of the commercial district, it's set in a park with a view of the sea. The well-furnished interior is filled with framed engravings, porcelain in illuminated cases, gilt mirrors, and brass detailing. Many of the bedrooms have wrought-iron balconies whose curves are repeated in the art nouveau iron-and-glass canopy that extends over the entryway. Some rooms are air-conditioned. There's also a bar and an outdoor swimming pool.

Hotel Méditerranée

Corso Cavallotti 76, 18038 San Remo. ☎ **0184/571000.** Fax 0184/541106. 62 rms, 3 suites. A/C MINIBAR TV TEL. 250,000 lire ($156.25) double; 350,000 lire ($218.75) suite. Rates include breakfast. Children under 18 receive a 30% reduction. AE, MC, V. Free parking outside; 25,000 lire ($15.65) in garage. Bus: U.

The traffic in front of this steel-and-glass structure can be profuse, especially in peak season, but once you're inside, or in the rear garden with its Olympic-size pool you'll scarcely be aware of it. The stylish public rooms contain pleasing color combinations that go well with the many plants and the generously sized modern sculpture that fills part of the polished floor space. Originally built about a century ago, the hotel received its present appearance in 1974 during a tasteful modernization. Inside, however, some of the public rooms retain signs of their turn-of-the-century grandeur and are filled with potted plants, polished floors, and modern sculptures. Bedrooms are modernized and well furnished.

Dining/Entertainment: The Aloha restaurant, under a rustic inclined shelter, has a Polynesian theme. Meals begin at 55,000 lire ($34.40). There's a drinking area with a metallic ceiling.

Services: Room service, babysitting, laundry, valet.

Facilities: Olympic-size pool.

Suite Hotel Nyala

Strada Solaro 134, 18038 San Remo. ☎ **0184/667668.** Fax 0184/666059. 44 rms (all with bath), 36 suites. A/C MINIBAR TV TEL. 180,000–260,000 lire ($112.50–$162.50) double or suite. Season, 180,000 lire ($112.50). Rates include breakfast. Half-board 45,000 lire ($28.15) per person. AE, DC, MC, V.

Built in 1984, and doubled in size in 1993, this is a well-designed, comfortable, and modern hotel which lies among the venerable trees of what served a century ago as the English-style park for a since-demolished private villa. Set within a residential neighborhood containing some impressive antique villas, on a street which interconnects with the Corso Matuzia, one of the town's main arteries, it's considered the most modern hotel in San Remo.

Most rooms have a view over the sea, and a terrace which receives lots of sunlight thanks to the fact that the hotel's outside walls slope, in the style of a Mayan pyramid, inward. About half of the accommodations are junior suites, with a separate sitting area and a balcony that's larger than those within the bedrooms (Suites and double rooms, incidentally, cost the same.) On the premises is a dining room, a palm-fringed outdoor swimming pool, a bar, and a staff who works hard to make holidays successful. Nonresidents pay 60,000 lire ($37.50) for a fixed-price menu in the dining room, which overlooks a view of the Ligurian sea.

INEXPENSIVE

Hotel Belsoggiorno Juana

Corso Matuzia 41, 18038 San Remo. ☎ **0184/667631.** Fax 0184/667471. 43 rms (all with bath or shower). TV TEL. 120,000 lire ($75) double. Rates include breakfast. Half-board 95,000 lire ($59.40) per person. DC, MC, V. Free parking. Closed Oct–Nov. Bus: U.

This centrally located hotel is near Imperatrice, the main sea promenade, and the beaches. Attractively furnished and inviting, it contains a large reception area, plenty of living rooms for lounging, and TV rooms. Manager Luciana Maurizi De Benedetti has also provided a nice garden in which to sit and enjoy the sun and plants. Because the food is good, you may prefer to order the fixed-price menu for 35,000 lire ($21.90) if you're not staying here on half-board. Facilities include a garage.

✪ Hotel Eletto

Corso Matteotti 44 18038 San Remo. ☎ **0184/531548.** 29 rms. TV TEL. 120,000 lire ($75) double. Half-board 100,000 lire ($62.50) per person. AE, MC, V. Free parking. Bus: U.

This hotel is on the main artery of town, near more expensive hotels. It has a 19th-century facade with cast-iron balconies and ornate detailing. The rear of the hotel is set in a small garden with perhaps the biggest tree in San Remo casting a welcome shade over the flowerbeds. This pleasant stopover point has public rooms filled with carved panels, old mirrors, and antique furniture, as well as windows on two sides. Bedrooms are old-fashioned and comfortable. The sunny and well-maintained dining room serves inexpensive meals beginning at 40,000 lire ($25).

Hotel Mariluce

Corso Matuzia 3, 16038 San Remo. ☎ **0184/667805.** 23 rms (19 with bath or shower). 56,000–76,000 lire ($35–$47.50) double without bath; 80,000–95,000 lire ($50–$59.40) double with bath. Rates include breakfast. MC, V. Free parking. Closed Nov–Dec 20. Bus: U.

As you're walking along the flowered promenade away from the commercial center of town, you'll notice a flowering garden that's enclosed on one side by the neighboring walls of a Polish Catholic church; one of the walls is emblazoned with a gilded coat-of-arms. Behind the garden is the building that until 1945 housed a refugee center that Poles throughout Europe used as a base for finding friends and relatives. Today it's one of the most reasonably priced hotels in the resort, a bargain for San Remo, offering simply furnished but comfortable bedrooms. The furniture in the public rooms is bathed in sunlight from the big windows. From the flowering garden, visitors can see the grounds and facades of surrounding hotels, which are far more expensive. The Mariluce lies 300 yards from the main rail station. A passage under the street leads from the garden to the beach.

Hotel Miramare Continental Palace

Corso Matuzia 9, 18038 San Remo. ☎ **0184/667601.** Fax 0184/667655. 60 rms, 6 suites. TEL. 370,000–430,000 lire ($231.25–$268.75) double, including full board. 340,000–600,000 lire ($212.50–$375) suite, plus full board supplement 100,000 lire ($62.50) per person. AE, DC, MC, V. Free parking. Closed Sept 30–Dec 22. Bus: U.

This well-maintained traditional building is set behind semitropical gardens, which border a busy thoroughfare. A curved driveway leads past palmettos to the front entrance, where the lobby is filled with marble floors, gilt-frame mirrors, French portrait busts, 19th-century bronzes, and an art nouveau painting above the reception desk. After passing through the public rooms, you'll discover a seaside garden with sculptures and plenty of verdant hideaways. The bedrooms are clean and comfortable; some are in a neighboring annex with views of the garden. The hotel has a good restaurant. A covered swimming pool is in one of the outbuildings. There's also a sauna, solarium, and gym.

WHERE TO DINE

In San Remo you'll be introduced to the Ligurian cuisine, a table characterized by the Genovese style of cooking, with a reliance on seafood dishes. If it's featured on the menu, try the buridda, which is the Ligurian version of Mediterranean bouillabaisse. The white wines from the five villages (the Cinque Terre) are highly valued.

EXPENSIVE

✪ Da Giannino

Lungomare Trento e Trieste 23. ☎ **504014.** Reservations recommended. Main courses 30,000–40,000 lire ($18.75–$25). AE, DC, MC, V. Tues–Sun 12:30–2:30pm; Tues–Sat 7:30–10pm. Closed May 15–June 1. Bus: U. ITALIAN.

In spite of increasing competition, this is still acclaimed as the finest restaurant in San Remo. In a conservatively comfortable and elegant setting, you can enjoy such specialties as a warm seafood antipasti, a flavorful risotto laced with cheese and a pungently aromatic green sauce, and a selection of main courses that change with the availability of ingredients. Some of the more exotic selections are likely to include a marinated cuttlefish gratinée. The wine list includes many of the better vintages of both France and Italy.

✪ Paolo e Barbara

Via Roma 47. ☎ **53-16-53.** Reservations recommended. Main courses 33,000–44,000 lire ($20.65–$27.50); *menu degustazione* 90,000 lire ($56.25), without wine. AE, DC, MC, V. Thurs–Tues 12:30–2:15pm and 8–10pm. Closed Thurs lunch in summer. Bus: U. LIGURIAN/ITALIAN.

Named after the husband-and-wife team who owns it (the Masieri family), this restaurant has caught the imagination of San Remo since it was established in 1987. Contained within a dignified building near the casino, it specializes in both traditional recipes from the region, as well as a handful of innovative dishes created by its staff. Meals here tend to be drawn-out affairs, so allow adequate time before you decide to visit. Depending on the season, the menu might feature a tartare of raw marinated mackerel served with a garlic mousse and a potato-tomato and basil-flavored garnish; trenette (a regional pasta) with freshly pulverized pesto;

grilled crayfish served on a bed of onion purée with fresh herbs, olive oil, and pine nuts; and a wide array of fresh fish and freshly made desserts.

INEXPENSIVE

Il Bagatto

Via Matteotti 145. ☎ **531925.** Reservations not necessary. Main courses 15,000–35,000 lire ($9.40–$21.90); fixed-price menus 40,000–60,000 lire ($25–$37.50). AE, DC, MC, V. Mon–Sat noon–3pm and 7:30–10pm. Closed June 15–July 15. Bus: U. LIGURIAN.

Il Bagatto provides good meals in the 16th-century home of an Italian duke, with dark beams, provincial chairs, and even oversized pepper grinders brought to the tables. The location is in the shopping district of the town, about two blocks from the sea. My most recent dinner began with a choice of creamy lasagne or savory hors d'oeuvres. The scaloppine with artichokes and asparagus was especially pleasing, as was (on another occasion) a mixed grill of Mediterranean fish. All orders were accompanied by potatoes and a choice of vegetables, then followed by crème caramel for dessert. Many kinds of Ligurian fish are served here, including filet of sea bass in a sauce made with fresh peppers, and a *gallinella*, the quintessential white-flesh Ligurian fish, roasted with potatoes and olives.

La Lanterna

Via Molo di Ponente al Porto 16. ☎ **506855.** Reservations required Sat–Sun. Main courses 15,000–31,000 lire ($9.40–$19.40). AE, DC, MC, V. Fri–Wed 12:30–2:30pm and 7:30–10pm. Closed Nov 15–Jan 15. Bus: U. SEAFOOD.

In a building near the harbor, La Lanterna is a nautically decorated enclave of good seafood that is well recommended by many local residents. Established around 1917, it is one of the few restaurants that has survived in San Remo from the heady days of the resort's Edwardian grandeur. The clientele can get very fashionable here, especially in summer, when outdoor tables are set beneath parasols within view of the harbor's many yachts. Meals might include an excellent version of fish soup (*brodetto di pesce con crostini*), a Ligurian fish fry, and such meat dishes as scaloppine in marsala wine sauce. Sea bass and red snapper are both readily available and might be proposed either grilled; fried with olive oil, herbs, and lemon; or baked in an oven with artichokes, olives, and white wine sauce.

SAN REMO AFTER DARK

The high life holds forth at the **San Remo Casino,** Corso Inglesi 18 (☎ 534001), in the very center of San Remo; the casino is built in a turn-of-the-century style known as "Liberty," an ornate mixture of classical and art nouveau. For decades, fashionable visitors have dined in high style in the elegant restaurant, reserved tables at the roof garden's cabaret, or tested their luck at the gaming tables. Like a white-walled palace, the pristine-looking casino stands at the top of a steep flight of stone steps above the main artery of town.

Visitors today can attend a variety of shows, fashion parades, concerts, and theatrical presentations staged throughout the year. The entrance fee is 15,000 lire ($9.40) for the French and American gaming rooms, which are open daily from 2:30pm to 3am. Presentation of a passport is required, and a jacket and tie are requested as proper attire for men. For the slot machines section, entrance is free and there is no particular dress code; it's open daily from 10am to 3am. The casino's restaurant is open nightly from 8:30pm to 1:30am, charging 60,000 to 100,000 lire ($37.50 to $62.50) per person for dinner, which consists of international specialties. The restaurant has an orcherstra playing everything from waltzes to rock music. A roof-garden cabaret is open only on Friday and Saturday nights, with shows beginning at 10pm. If you visit for drinks only (and not dinner), the cost is 35,000 lire ($21.90) per drink.

2 Genoa (Genova)

88 miles SW of Milan, 311 miles NW of Rome, 120 NE of Nice (France)

It was altogether fitting that "Genoa the Proud" (Superba) gave birth to Christopher Columbus. Its link with the sea dates back to ancient times. However, Columbus did his hometown a disservice. By blazing the trail to the New World, he dealt a devastating blow to Mediterranean ports in general, as the balance of trade shifted to newly developing centers on the Atlantic.

Even so, Genoa today is Italy's premier port, and ranks with Marseilles in European importance. In its heyday (the 13th century), its empire, extending from colonies on the Barbary Coast to citadels on the Euphrates, rivaled that of Venice. Apart from Columbus, its most famous son was Andrea Doria (the ill-fated oceanliner was named after him), who wrested his city from the yoke of French domination in the early 16th century.

Like a half moon, the port encircles the Gulf of Genoa. Its hills slope right down to the water, so walking is likely to be an up- and downhill affair. Because of the terrain, the Christopher Columbus Airport opened quite late in Genoa's development.

The center of the city's maritime life, the ✪ **harbor of Genoa** makes for an interesting stroll, particularly in the part of the old town bordering the water. Sailors from many lands search for adventure and women to entertain them in the little bars and cabarets that occupy the back alleyways. Often the streets are merely medieval lanes, with foreboding buildings closing in.

A Word of Warning: The harbor, particularly after dark, is not for the squeamish. It can be dangerous. If you go wandering, don't go alone and leave as many valuables in safekeeping as possible. Genoa is rougher than Barcelona, more comparable to Marseilles. Not only in the harbor area, but on any side street that runs downhill, a woman is likely to lose her purse.

The present harbor is the result of extensive rebuilding, following massive World War II bombardments that crippled its seaside installations. The best way to view the overall skyline is from a harbor cruise, which departs daily from the area of the Genoa Aquarium at 3:15pm. The trip lasts an hour. Along the way you pass naval yards, shipbuilders, steelworkers, and warehouses (yachters anchor at Duca degli Abruzzi)—not a pretty picture entirely, but a fascinating landscape of industrial might. Purchase tickets at Cooperatica Battellieri del Porto di Genova (☎ 265712). Tours depart from the Stazione Marittima daily at 10am and 2pm, costing 10,000 lire ($6.25) adults, 6,000 lire ($3.75) children under 14 and those over 60.

ESSENTIALS

GETTING THERE By Plane　Alitalia and other carriers fly into **Aeroporto Internazionale de Genova Cristoforo Colombo,** 4 miles west of the city center in Sestri Ponente. For information about flights, call 6015410.

By Train　Genoa has good rail connections with the rest of Italy; it lies only $1^1/_2$ hours from Milan, 3 hours from Florence, and $1^1/_2$ hours from the French border. Genoa has two major rail stations, the **Stazione Prìncipe** and the **Stazione**

Brignole. Chances are you'll arrive at the Prìncipe, which is nearest to the harbor and the old part of the city. However, both trains and municipally operated buses run between the two stations. For information about trains, call 284081.

By Bus   SITA buses (☎ 313851), originating in Genoa, service the full length of the Ligurian coast in both directions. It's best to arrive in Genoa by car, plane, or rail, then rely on the bus to take you up or down the coast.

By Car   Motorists will find Genoa right along the main autostrada (A10) that begins its run at the French border and continues along the Ligurian coastline.

By Ferry   It's highly likely that you'll find yourself in Genoa waiting for the ferryboat to take you to such offshore destinations as Sardinia or Sicily. If so, the number to call for information is the **Stazione Marittima** (☎ 261466). You can also arrive in Genoa by ferry. There is a 22-hour service to Genoa originating in Palermo (Sicily), costing 310,000 lire ($193.75) per person for a one-way ticket. Ferries also leave from Porto Torres (Sardinia), going to Genoa, at a one-way fare of 53,500 lire ($33.45).

ORIENTATION

VISITOR INFORMATION   Visitors can get information at the major office of **Azienda Di Promozione Turistica,** via Roma 11 (☎ 010/541541). It's open Monday through Friday from 8am to 1:15pm and 2 to 6:30pm, and Saturday from 8am to 1:15pm. Information booths dispensing tourist literature can also be found at the rail stations, Porta Principe and at the airport. The rail station office is open Monday through Saturday from 8am to 8pm; at the airport Monday through Saturday 10am to 4pm.

CITY LAYOUT   Genoa opens onto the Porto di Genova, and most of the section of interest to visitors lies between two main rail stations, **Stazione Prìncipe,** on the western fringe of the town, near the port, and **Stazione Brignole,** to the northeast, which opens onto piazza Verdi. A major artery is **via XX Settembre,** which runs between piazza Ferrari in the west and piazza della Vittoria in the east. **Via Balbi** is another major artery, beginning its run east of the Stazione Prìncipe, off piazza Acquaverde. At the end of Genoavia Balbi you'll come to piazza Nunziata. From there, a short walk along via Cairola leads to the most important touristic street of Genoa, the palazzo-flanked **via Garibaldi** (but more about that later).

FAST FACTS: Genoa

American Express   The representative of American Express in Genoa is Viatur, piazza Fontane Marose 3 (☎ 561241). But you should be a client—that is, carry an American Express card or use the company's traveler's checks—before you have your mail sent to them. Hours are Monday through Friday from 9am to 2:30pm and 3 to 6:45pm.

Area Code   The telephone area code is 010.

Currency Exchange   To exchange money, you'll find service at Delfino, via Balbi 161R. However, both the Brignole and Prìncipe railway stations have exchange offices open daily from 7am to 10pm.

Drugstores   Genoa has several all-night pharmacies, including Pescetto, via Balbi 185R (☎ 262697). Need a pharmacy at night? Dial 192.

Emergencies Dial 113 for assistance in a general emergency. If it's automobile trouble, call A.C.I., Soccorso Stradale (☎ 116). For an ambulance, call 570-5951.

Gas Station If you don't mind self-service, there's an Agip gas station that's open at night, located along viale Brigate Partigiane. You must have the right change.

Lost Property The lost-and-found office is the Comune, via Garibaldi 9 (☎ 20981).

Medical Care If you're in need of a doctor, try Ospedale San Martino, viale Benedetto XV no. 10 (☎ 35351).

Police Dial 113.

Post Office The post office, at via Dante and piazza de Ferrari (☎ 160), has a telex and fax. It's open Monday through Saturday from 8:15am to 7:40pm.

Religous Services If you're Roman Catholic, you can go into almost any church in Genoa. If you're Protestant, there's the Chiesa Evangelica Metodista, via Fabio Da Persico 40 (☎ 887225), and if you're Jewish, there's the Tempio Israelitico on via Bertora (☎ 891513).

Taxi To call a radio taxi, dial 2696.

Telephone If you need to make a long-distance call, it's cheapest to go to the office at via XX Settembre no. 139, which is open 24 hours a day (your hotel is likely to impose heavy surcharges). You can also place calls at both the Brignole and Prìncipe railroad stations until 9pm.

WHAT TO SEE & DO

In the heart of the city, you can stroll down ✪ **via Garibaldi,** the street of patricians, on which noble Genovese families erected splendid palazzi in late Renaissance times. The guiding hand behind the general appearance and most of the architecture was Alessi, who grew to fame in the 16th century (he studied under Michelangelo).

Civica Galleria di Palazzo Rosso

Via Garibaldi 18. ☎ **282641.** Admission 6,000 lire ($3.75), free for children under 17 or seniors over 60. Tues, Thurs–Fri, Sun 9am–6pm; Wed and Sat 9am–7pm. Bus: 18, 19, 20, 35, 39, or 40.

This 17th-century palace was once the home of the Brignole-Sale, a local aristocratic family who founded a Genovese dynasty. It was restored after having been bombed in World War II, and contains a good collection of paintings, with such exceptional works as *Giuditta* by Veronese, St. Sebastian by Reni, and *Cleopatra* by Guercino. Perhaps the best-known exhibit is Sir Anthony van Dyck's portrait of Pauline and Anton Giulio Brignole-Sale from the original collection, and the magnificent frescoes by Gregorio De Ferrari (*Spring* and *Summer)* and Domenico Piola (*Autumn* and *Winter)*. There are also collections of ceramics and sculpture and a display of gilded baroque statuary. Across from this red palace is the white palace, the Palazzo Bianco Gallery.

Civica Galleria di Palazzo Bianco

Via Garibaldi 11. ☎ **291803.** Admission 6,000 lire ($3.75) adults, free for children 17 and under and seniors over 60. Tues, Thurs, Fri, and Sun 9am–1pm; Wed and Sat 9am–7pm. Bus: 18, 19, 20, 35, 39, or 40.

The Duchess of Gallier donated this palace, along with her collection of art, to the city. Although the palace originally dates from the 16th century, its appearance today is the work of later architects. Gravely damaged during the war, the restored palace reflects the most recent advances in museum planning. The most significant paintings—from the Dutch and Flemish schools—include Gerard David's *Polittico della Cervara* and Memling's *Jesus Blessing the Faithful*, as well as works by Sir Anthony van Dyck and Peter Paul Rubens. A wide-ranging survey of European and local artists is presented—with paintings by Caravaggio, Zurbarán, and Murillo, and works by Bernardo Strozzi (a whole room) and Alessandro Magnasco (excellent painting of a scene in a Genovese garden).

Galleria Nazionale (National Gallery)

In the Palazzo Spinola, piazza della Pellicceria 1. ☎ **294661.** Admission 8,000 lire ($5) adults, free for children 18 and under and seniors over 60. Monday 9am–1pm, Tues–Sat 9am–7pm, Sun 2–7pm. Bus: 18, 19, or 20.

The National Gallery houses a major painting collection. (This palace was designed for the Grimaldi family in the 16th century as a private residence, although the Spinolas took it over eventually.) Its notable works include Joos van Cleve's *Madonna in Prayer*, Antonello da Messina's *Ecce Homo*, and Giovanni Pisano's *Guistizia*. The gallery is also known for its decorative arts collection (furniture, silver, and ceramics, among other items).

Galleria di Palazzo Reale (Royal Palace Gallery)

Via Balbi 10. ☎ **247-06-40.** Admission 8,000 lire ($5) adults, free for children 18 or under and over 60. Mon–Tues 9am–1:30pm; Wed–Sun 9am–7pm. Bus: 18, 19, or 20. Train: 5-minute walk from Stazione Principe.

The Royal Palace was started about 1650, and work continued until the early years of the 18th century. It was built for the Balbi family, then sold to the Durazzos. It later became one of the royal palaces of the Savoias in 1824. King Charles Albert modified many of the rooms around 1840. As in all Genovese palazzi, some of these subsequent alterations marred original designs. Its Galleria is filled with paintings and sculpture, works of art by van Dyck, Tintoretto, G. F. Romanelli, and L. Giordano. Frescoes and antiques from the 17th to the 19th century are displayed. Seek out, in particular, the Hall of Mirrors and the Throne Room.

Cathedral of San Lorenzo

Piazza San Lorenzo (Lawrence), via Tommaso Reggio 17. ☎ **296695.** Admission to Cathedral, free; treasury, 1,000 lire (65¢). Tues–Sat 9–11:30am and 3–5:30pm. Bus: 18, 19, or 39.

Although Genoa is noted for its medieval churches, this one towers over all of them. The cathedral is distinguished by its bands of black and white marble adorning the facade in the Pisan style. In its present form it dates from the 13th century, although it was erected upon the foundation of a much earlier structure. Alessi, referred to earlier, designed the dome, and the campanile (bell tower) dates from the 16th century. The Chapel of John the Baptist, with interesting Renaissance sculpture, is said to contain the remains of the saint for whom it is named. The treasury is worth a visit, especially for its Sacred Bowl, thought to be the Holy Grail when Crusaders brought it back from Caesarea in the early 12th century (Eastern traders probably made goodly sums off naive Christians pursuing relics for the church back home.)

WHERE TO STAY

Generally, hotels in Genoa are second rate, but some good finds await those who search diligently. *Warning:* Some of the cheap hotels and pensions in and around the waterfront are to be avoided. My recommendations, however, are suitable even for women traveling alone.

EXPENSIVE

Bristol-Palace

Via XX Settembre no. 35, 16121 Genova. ☎ **010/592541.** Fax 010/561756. 128 rms, 5 suites. A/C MINIBAR TV TEL. 270,000 lire ($168.75) double; 350,000 lire ($218.75) suite. Rates include breakfast. AE, DC, MC, V. Parking 30,000 lire ($18.75). Bus: 18, 19, or 20.

Bristol-Palace, dating from the late 19th century, has a number of features that will make your stay in Genoa special. Its obscure entrance behind colonnades on a commercial street is misleading; the salons and drawing rooms within are furnished nicely with traditional pieces—many antiques are utilized, some of which appear to be of museum caliber. The dining room, in the Louis XVI style, is the most inspired, an ornately carved ceiling highlighting a mural of cloud-riding cherubs in the center. The larger of the bedrooms have an old-fashioned elegance, are spacious and comfortable, and are tastefully furnished. The hotel's stairway is one of the most stunning in Genoa. The English bar is a favorite rendezvous point, and a small but elegant restaurant, Il Caffè de Bristol, offers daily lunches or dinners for 45,000 lire ($28.15) per person.

Jolly Hotel Plaza

Via Martin Piaggio 11, 16122 Genova. ☎ **010/839-3641** or 800/221-2626 in the U.S., or 800/237-0319 in Canada. Fax 010/8391850. 149 rms, 1 suite. A/C MINIBAR TV TEL. 270,000–350,000 lire ($168.75–$218.75) double; 490,000 lire ($306.25) suite. Rates include breakfast. AE, DC, MC, V. Parking 30,000 lire ($18.75). Bus: 18, 37, 46, or 47.

A four-star member of the prestigious Jolly chain, this hotel is newer than its modified classic facade would suggest. Centrally located near the piazza Corvetto, it was built in 1950 to replace an older hotel destroyed during an air raid in World War II. In 1992, the hotel was renovated, upgraded, and enlarged by incorporating a neighboring building into its premises. Today, it offers comfortably furnished bedrooms, outfitted in soothing colors that appeal to a clientele of business travelers from throughout Europe. On the premises are an American-style bar and a grill room, La Villetta di Negro, where meals cost around 70,000 to 110,000 lire ($43.75 to $68.75) each. During periods when the hotel isn't particularly full, management sometimes opts not to open the restaurant on weekends.

MODERATE

City Hotel

Via San Sebastiano 6, 16123 Genova. ☎ **010/5545.** Fax 010/586301. 64 rms, 1 suite. A/C MINIBAR TV TEL. 170,000–340,000 lire ($106.25–$212.50) double; 200,000–500,000 lire ($125–$312.50) suite. Rates include breakfast. AE, DC, MC, V. Parking 30,000 lire ($18.75). Bus: 18, 19, 20, 21, 31, or 41.

One of the best hotels in its category is located in a starkly angular stucco and travertine postwar building, surrounded by a crumbling series of town houses. The hotel itself was last renovated in 1990. The convenient location, near piazza Corvetto and via Garibaldi, is one of the hotel's best features. The staff will welcome you upon your arrival in the warm and comfortable wood-and-granite

Genoa

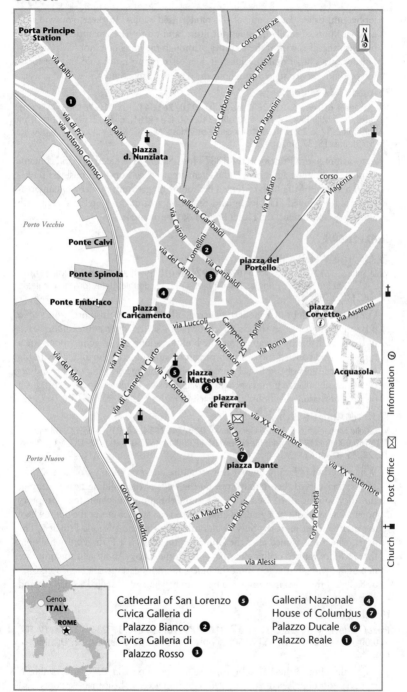

Porta Principe Station

via Balbi
via di Prè
via Antonio Gramsci
via Balbi

1

piazza d. Nunziata

corso Firenze
corso Firenze
corso Carbonara
corso Paganini

Galleria Garibaldi

via Caffaro

corso Magenta

Porto Vecchio

Ponte Calvi

Ponte Spinola

Ponte Embriaco

via Cairoli
Lomellini
via del Campo
via Garibaldi

2
3
4

piazza del Portello

piazza Caricamento

via Luccoli

via di Canneto Il Curto

Campetto
Vico Indurati
25 Aprile
via Roma

piazza Corvetto
i

via Assarotti

Acquasola

via Turati

via del Molo

5
via S. Lorenzo
piazza G. Matteotti
6

piazza de Ferrari

via XX Settembre

via Dante

Porto Nuovo

7
piazza Dante

via XX Settembre

corso M. Quadrio

via Madre di Dio
via Fieschi

Corso Podestà

via Alessi

N

Information ⊖

Post Office ⊠

Church ✝

Genoa
ITALY

★ ROME

Cathedral of San Lorenzo **5**
Civica Galleria di
  Palazzo Bianco **2**
Civica Galleria di
  Palazzo Rosso **3**

Galleria Nazionale **4**
House of Columbus **7**
Palazzo Ducale **6**
Palazzo Reale **1**

lobby, and usher you to one of the modernized rooms. In these, you will find parquet floors, specially designed furniture, and up-to-date amenities. A cocktail bar with snacks is part of the facilities. Although the hotel does not have a restaurant for meals other than breakfast, it does offer a short list of cold and hot foods served room-service style throughout the day and early evening.

Hotel Savoia Majestic

Via Arsenale di Terra 5, 16126 Genova. ☎ **010/261641.** Fax 010/261883. 123 rms, 5 suites. A/C MINIBAR TV TEL. 290,000–340,000 lire ($181.25–$212.50) double; from 410,000 lire ($256.25) suite. Rates include breakfast. AE, DC, MC, V. Parking 30,000 lire ($18.75). Bus: 18, 37, 46, or 47.

Across from piazza Prìncipe is the 1887 Hotel Savoia Majestic, which still contains some of its original accessories. The clients tend to be European business travelers. The decor of the high-ceilinged bedrooms ranges from modern to conservatively old-fashioned. The lobby and reception area of this hotel is shared with another establishment, the Hotel Londra & Continentale.

INEXPENSIVE

✪ Albergo Viale Sauli

Viale Sauli 5, 16121 Genova. ☎ **010/561397.** Fax 010/590092. 56 rms. A/C MINIBAR TV TEL. 110,000 lire ($68.75) single; 150,000 lire ($93.75) double. Rates include breakfast. AE, DC, MC, V. Bus: 18.

On the second floor of a modern concrete office building, this hotel is just off a busy shopping street in the center of town. It's scattered over three floors, each of them reachable by elevator from the building's lobby. The public rooms are a high-ceilinged paneled trio of bar, breakfast room, and reception area, all with big windows and lots of comfort. Enore Sceresini is the opera-loving owner, and his clients usually include businesspeople who appreciate cleanliness and comfort. Each of the units has marble floors and a spacious bath.

⑤ Hotel Agnello d'Oro

Vico delle Monachette 6, 16126 Genova. ☎ **010/2462084.** Fax 010/2462327. 38 rms. TV TEL. 150,000 lire ($93.75) double. Breakfast 12,000 lire ($7.50) extra. AE, DC, MC, V. Bus: 18, 20, 35, 37, or 41.

When the Doria family owned this structure and everything around it in the 1600s, they carved their family crest on the walls of the building near the top of the alley so that all of Genoa would know the point at which their property began. The symbol was a golden lamb, and you can still see one at the point where the narrow street joins the busy boulevard leading to the Stazione Prìncipe. The hotel, which was named after the animal on the crest, is a 17th-century building that includes vaulted ceilings and paneling in the lobby. About half the units are in a newer wing, but if you want the oldest accommodations, ask for Room 6, 7, or 8. Today the hotel is maintained by a family who have installed a small bar and restaurant off the lobby.

Hotel Astoria

Piazza Brignole 4, 16122 Genova. ☎ **010/873316.** Fax 010/817236. 73 rms. TV TEL. 120,000–180,000 lire ($75–$112.50) double. Rates include breakfast. AE, DC, MC, V. Bus: 18.

Originally built in the 1920s but opened as a hotel only in 1978, this establishment has lots of polished paneling, wrought-iron accents, beige marble floors, and a baronial carved fireplace in one of the public rooms. Rooms are comfortably furnished and the maintenance is high. The hotel sits on an uninspiring square that contains a filling station and whose view encompasses a traffic hub and many square blocks of apartment buildings. There's a bar on the premises, but no restaurant. There is no garage; street parking only.

Hotel Vittoria Orlandi

Via Balbi 33–45, 16126 Genova. ☎ **010/261923.** Fax 010/262656. 56 rms. TV TEL. 100,000–130,000 lire ($62.50–$81.25) double. Breakfast 5,000 lire ($3.15) extra. AE, DC, MC, V. Parking 30,000 lire ($18.75). Bus: 18 or 37.

Since this hotel is constructed on one of the hillsides for which Genoa is famous, its entrance is under a tunnel that opens at a point about a block from the Stazione Prìncipe. An elevator will take you up to the reception area. The establishment, built in 1926, welcomes a wide variety of guests, some of them staying for only one night, in the simple but clean rooms. Many of the units have balconies. About half the units are air-conditioned and contain a minibar. Best of all, the hotel is quiet because of the way it's sheltered by other buildings from the busy boulevards.

WHERE TO DINE

Genoa, which has been praised for its cuisine, has lots of restaurants and trattorie, many of which are strung along the harbor. The following recommendations will give you several opportunities to judge it for yourself.

MODERATE

✪ Da Giacomo

Corso Italia 1R. ☎ 362-9647. Reservations required. Main courses 25,000–40,000 lire ($15.65–$25). AE, DC, MC, V. Daily 12:30–2:30pm and 7:30–10pm. Closed Aug. Bus: 17, 18, or 37. LIGURIAN.

Try for a table with a view of the sea at what many food critics regard as the premier restaurant of Genoa, decorated in an elegant modern style. The service is deluxe, as is the ambience, graced with plants. Eating has been called "an art" at this refined restaurant, established in 1965. Ligurian cooking is dominated by the sea and so is the menu here, beginning with a superb seafood antipasti, some of which is raw but cut and carved with the exquisite care you find in Tokyo. Meat, fish, and poultry dishes are prepared with unusual flair. The fabled pesto sauce accompanies many dishes, especially the pasta. This sauce in Ligure is made of pine nuts (sometimes walnuts), olive oil, basil, and cheese, and during the Crusades it was reported that the Genoese contingent could always be identified by the aroma of pesto surrounding them. Some of the finest regional wines in Italy are offered, and desserts are made fresh daily on the premises.

✪ Gran Gotto

Viale Brigate Bisagno 69R. ☎ 564344. Reservations recommended. Main courses 32,000–36,000 lire ($20–$22.50). AE, MC, V. Mon–Fri 12:30–2:30pm; Mon–Sat 7:30–10pm. Closed Aug 12–31. Bus: 17, 18, or 37. SEAFOOD.

Although it was established in 1937, and has been in the same family ever since, this restaurant moved to new quarters in 1995. Today, amid a setting of modern art and vaguely Austrian accessories, it is considered one of the most top-notch restaurants of Genoa. Its name translates from Genovese dialect as "large glass" (as in a glass of wine). The emphasis is on seafood, but the meat and pasta dishes aren't neglected. In fact, the most typical offering, trenette al pesto, is quite famous, a pasta of paper-thin noodles (depending on the artistry of the chef) that's served with the characteristic pesto. The delicately simmered risotto is also tempting. The main dishes are most reasonably priced and of high standard, including the mixed fish fry or the French baby squid. The zuppa di pesce, like a Mediterranean bouillabaisse, has made many a luncheon for many a gourmet. The rognone al cognac is another superb choice—tender calves' kidneys that have been cooked and delicately flavored in cognac. Roast lamb flavored with thyme is another favorite dish.

Ristorante Saint Cyr

Piazza Marsala 4. ☎ **886897.** Reservations required. Main courses 30,000–32,000 lire ($18.75–$20). AE, DC, MC, V. Mon–Fri noon–2:30pm; Mon–Sat 7:30–10pm. Closed Dec 23–Jan 7. Bus: 18, 20, 35, 37, or 41. LIGURIAN/PIEDMONTESE.

My favorite time to come to this restaurant is at night, when some of the most discriminating palates in Genoa might be seen enjoying dishes generously adapted from regional recipes. The location is near piazza Corvetto in a building that in 1900 was a printing factory. The restaurant was established here in 1971. The food items change every day, although a recent menu featured rice with truffles and cheese, a timpale of fresh spinach, a charlotte of fish, and a variety of braised meats, each delicately seasoned and perfectly prepared. Specialties include *scamone* (a certain cut of beef) cooked in Barolo wine and *ravioli al sugo do carne* (ravioli with sauce made from meat juices). Another specialty is fresh sturgeon with baby vegetables. The restaurant is open for lunch, when the clientele is likely to be conservatively dressed businesspoeple discussing shipping contracts. There's a good selection of wines to accompany your meal.

Ristorante Zeffirino

Via XX Settembre no. 20. ☎ **591990.** Reservations recommended. Main courses 25,000–40,000 lire ($15.65–$25); fixed-price menu 60,000 lire ($37.50). AE, DC, MC, V. Thurs–Tues noon–3pm and 7pm–midnight. Bus: 17, 18, 20, 29, 31, or 36. LIGURIAN.

In a cul-de-sac just off one of the busiest boulevards of Genoa, this place has hosted celebrities ranging from Frank Sinatra to Luciano Pavarotti, from Pope John Paul II to Liza Minelli. Established in the 1930s, it moved to its present location in the 1950s. At least 14 members of the Zeffirino family prepare what is said to be the best pasta in the city, from recipes collected from all over Italy. These include lesser-known varieties such as quadrucci, pettinati, and cappelletti, as well as the more familiar taglietelle and lasagne. Following one of these platters, you can select from a vast array of meat and fish, along with 1,000 kinds of wine. Ligurian specialties, including risotto alla pescatore and beef stew with artichokes, are featured. Try a wide array of shellfish—either baked or steamed—and served with seasonal vegetables.

INEXPENSIVE

Il Cucciolo

Viale Sauli 33. ☎ **561321.** Reservations recommended. Main courses 19,000–28,000 lire ($11.90–$17.50). AE, DC, MC, V. Mon–Sat noon–3pm and 7:30–10:30pm. Bus: 17, 18, 20, 36, 37, or 45. TUSCAN.

When you're in Genoa, you may want to try excellent fish and Ligure dishes, as well as various international dishes, and dine in a refined atmosphere, as the Genovese do. That is, if you can find it. Go armed with a good map, as Il Cucciolo lies on one of those "hidden" squares in the center of the city, where parking your car is possible since the restaurant has a private lot. Should you be in the area at night, you'll find lanterns placed festively outside, adorning this ground-floor restaurant in a 19th-century building. The restaurant was established here in 1934. You not only get good Ligure food, but well chosen wines as well. Specialties include seafood antipasti, both warm and cold; ravioli with veal and a butter-sage sauce; fish baked in *cartoccio* (in a paper bag); and calf's liver prepared in the style of Venice. The service is efficient and the reception is gracious.

3 Rapallo

296 miles NW of Rome, 17 miles SE of Genoa, 100 miles S of Milan

Atop seaside resort—known for years to the chic and wealthy crowd who live in villas studding the hillside—Rapallo occupies a remarkable site overlooking the Gulf of Tiguillio. In summer, the crowded heart of Rapallo takes on a carnival air, as hordes of bathers occupy the rocky sands along the beach. In the area is an 18-hole golf course, as well as an indoor swimming pool, a riding club, and a modern harbor. You can also take a cable car to the **Sanctuary di Montallegro,** then walk to **Monte Rosa** for what is considered one of the finest views of the Ligurian coast. There are many opportunities for summer boat trips, not only to Portofino but to the Cinque Terre.

Rapallo's long history is often likened to Genoa's. It became part of the Repubblica Superba in 1229, but Rapallo had existed long before that. Its cathedral dates from the 6th century when it was founded by the bishops of Milan. Walls once enclosed the medieval town, but now only the Saline Gate remains. Rapallo has also been the scene of many an international meeting, the most notable of which was the 1917 conference of wartime allies.

ESSENTIALS

GETTING THERE By Train Three trains from Genoa stop off here each hour, at a one-way fare of 2,600 lire ($1.65). Service is daily from 4:30am to midnight.

By Bus Buses operated by SITA (☎ 010/313851 in Genoa for information and schedules) link Rapallo with Genoa.

By Car From Genoa, continue southeast along the A12 autostrada.

VISITOR INFORMATION The telephone area code for Rapallo is 0185. The tourist center is at via Diaz 9 (☎ 51282).

Once you arrive in Rapallo by public or private transportation, you can walk around to the following hotels and restaurants.

WHERE TO STAY
EXPENSIVE

✪ Grand Hotel Bristol

Via Aurelia Orientale 369, 16035 Rapallo. ☎ **0185/273313.** Fax 0185/55800. 85 rms, 6 suites. A/C MINIBAR TV TEL. 280,000–360,000 lire ($175–$225) double; from 440,000 lire ($275) suite. Rates include breakfast. AE, MC, V. Parking 20,000 lire ($12.50).

This hotel, one of the Riviera's grand old buildings, has undergone a sparkling renovation; it's easily one of the most glamorous hotels along the coast. Originally built in 1908, it was reopened in 1984 as the personal brainchild of a multimillionaire who died shortly after its transformation. The turn-of-the-century pink-and-white facade, with surrounding shrubbery and iron gates, was spruced up but basically unchanged during the five-year rebuilding program. The interior, however, which was mostly gutted, now contains five elegant restaurants in several degrees of formality, and a pool whose inviting waters are visible from many of the bedrooms. The kitchens are about the most modern anywhere, and the polite staff is dressed in formal morning suits. The lush, modern decor includes tasteful colors and stylish accessories.

Some of the bedrooms have private terraces, and all contain electronic window blinds, lots of mirrors, and tree-of-life motifs wallpapered onto the spaces above the oversize beds.

Dining/Entertainment: The most formal of all the hotel's five restaurants, Le Cupole, lies under the hotel's twin Victorian towers. Fixed-price lunches and dinners cost around 75,000 lire ($46.90).

Services: Room service, babysitting, laundry, valet, hairdresser, beautician, massage salon.

Facilities: The hotel's free-form swimming pool is one of the biggest in the region. There's also a series of conference rooms.

MODERATE

Eurotel

Via Aurelia di Ponente 22, 16035 Rapallo. ☎ **0185/60981.** Fax 0185/50635. 65 rms. A/C MINIBAR TV TEL. 180,000–210,000 lire ($112.50–$131.25) double. Rates include breakfast. AE, DC, MC, V. Free parking outdoors; 20,000 lire ($12.50) in garage.

With seven floors and three elevators, this vivid sienna-colored structure is one of the tallest hotels in town, set above the port at the top of a winding road where you'll have to negotiate the oncoming traffic with care. In addition to its room accommodations, the hotel contains about 35 privately owned condominiums that are usually occupied during part of each year by their owners. The lobby has marble floors and a helpful staff. All units contain built-in cabinets, arched loggias with views over the gulf of Rapallo, and beds that fold, Murphy style, into the walls. A bar and a second-floor panoramic restaurant, Antica Aurelia, are on the premises, as is a swimming pool set within a verdant garden.

INEXPENSIVE

✪ Hotel Giulio Cesare

Corso Cristoforo Colombo 52, 16035 Rapallo. ☎ **0185/50685.** Fax 0185/60896. 53 rms. TV TEL. 130,000 lire ($81.25) double; 95,000 lire ($59.40) per person with half-board. AE, MC, V. Free parking. Closed Nov–Dec 8.

This modernized, four-story villa is a bargain for the Italian Riviera. When the genial owner skillfully renovated the establishment, he kept expenses down to keep room rates lower. The hotel, which lies on the coast road about 90 feet from the sea, offers bedrooms with a homelike atmosphere, which feature good views of the Gulf of Tiguillio and are furnished with tasteful reproductions (most of the rooms have sunny balconies). Ask for the rooms on the top floor if you want a better view and quieter surroundings. The meals are prepared with fine ingredients (the fresh fish dishes are superb).

Hotel Miramare

Lungomare Vittorio Veneto 27, 16035 Rapallo. ☎ **0185/230261.** Fax 0185/273570. 22 rms, 6 suites. MINIBAR TV TEL. 100,000–150,000 lire ($62.50–$93.75) double; 150,000–170,000 lire ($93.75–$106.25) suite. Half-board 110,000–150,000 lire ($62.50-$93.75) per person. AE, DC, MC, V. Parking 15,000 lire ($9.40). Closed Nov.

On the water near a stone gazebo is this jazz age (1929) re-creation of a Renaissance villa, with exterior frescoes that have faded in the salt air. The gardens in front have been replaced by a glass extension that contains a clean and contemporary restaurant where an aquarium bubbles near the entrance (see "Where to Dine," below). The accomodations inside are clean and simple, comfortable, and high-ceilinged. Many on them have iron balconies that stretch toward the harbor.

WHERE TO DINE
MODERATE

Ristorante da Monique

Lungomare Vittorio Veneto 6. ☎ **50541.** Reservations required. Main courses 15,000–25,000 lire ($9.40–$15.65). AE, DC, MC, V. Wed–Mon 12:30–2:30pm and 7:30–10pm. Closed Jan 10–Feb 8. SEAFOOD.

This is one of the most popular seafood restaurants along the harbor, especially in summer when the tavern chairs are almost completely filled. It's been a local favorite since the 1930s. It features nautical decor in a big-windowed setting, which overlooks the boats of the marina. As you'd expect, fish is the specialty, including seafood salad, fish soup, risotto with shrimp, spaghetti with clams or mussels, grilled fish, and both tagliatelle and scampi "Monique."

INEXPENSIVE

Ristorante Elite

Via Milite Ignoto 19. ☎ **50551.** Reservations not necessary. Main courses 12,000–30,000 lire ($7.50–$18.75); fixed-price menu 35,000 lire ($21.90). AE, DC, MC, V. Fri–Wed noon–2:30pm and 7:30–10pm. Closed Nov. SEAFOOD.

This restaurant is set back from the water on a busy commercial street in the center of town. It was established in the 1960s in a building from the 1930s. Mainly fish is served; the offering depends on the catch of the day. Your dinner might consist of mussel marinara, minestrone Genovese style, risotto marinara, trenette al pesto, scampi, zuppa di pesci, sole meunière, turbot, or a mixed fish fry from the Ligurian coast. A limited selection of the standard meat dishes is available, too. At the peak of the midsummer tourist invasion, the restaurant is likely to remain open every day.

Ristorante Miramare

In the Hotel Miramare, lungomare Vittorio Veneto 27. ☎ **230261.** Reservations recommended. Main courses 15,000–35,000 lire ($9.40–$21.90). AE, DC, MC, V. Daily 12:30–2pm and 7:30–9:30pm. SEAFOOD/LIGURIAN.

Set within a previously recommended hotel, a building originally conceived as a private villa, this restaurant serves well-prepared and unpretentious food. In a modern brown, blue, and white dining room overlooking the sea, you can order fried calamari, spaghetti with clams, sea bass or turbot baked with potatoes and artichokes, veal in marsala sauce, and flavorful versions of fish soup.

4 Santa Margherita Ligure

19 miles E of Genoa, 3 miles S of Portofino, 296 miles NW of Rome

A resort rival to Rapallo, Santa Margherita Ligure also occupies a beautiful position on the Gulf of Tiguillio. Its attractive harbor is usually thronged with fun seekers, and the resort offers the widest range of accommodations in all price levels on the eastern Riviera. It has a festive appearance, with a promenade, flower beds, and palm trees swaying in the wind. As is typical of the Riviera, its beach combines rock and sand. Santa Margherita Ligure is linked to Portofino by a narrow road. It's on the Rome–Genoa rail link. The climate of Santa Margherita Ligure is mild, even in the winter months, when many elderly clients visit the resort.

The town dates back to A.D. 262. The official name of Santa Margherita Ligure was given to the town by King Victor Emmanuel II in 1863. Before that, it had many other names, including Porto Napoleone, an 1812 designation from Napoleon.

You can visit the richly embellished **Sanctuary of Santa Maria della Rosa,** piazza Caprera, with its Italian and Flemish paintings, along with relics of the saint for whom the town was named.

ESSENTIALS

GETTING THERE **By Train** Three trains per hour arrive from Genoa daily from 4:30am to midnight, charging 2,600 lire ($1.65) for a one-way ticket. Telephone 286630 in Santa Margherita Ligure for rail information. The station is at piazza Federico Raoul Nobili.

By Bus Buses run frequently between Portofino and Santa Margherita Ligure daily, charging 1,700 lire ($1.05) for a one-way ticket. You can also catch a bus in Rapallo bound for Santa Margherita; during the day one leaves Rapallo every 20 minutes on the 10-minute run.

By Car Take Route 227 southeast from Genoa.

VISITOR INFORMATION The telephone area code for Santa Margherita Ligure is 0185. The tourist information center is at via 25 Aprile 2B (☎ 287485).

Santa Margherita Ligure is relatively compact, and once you reach the place—by either public or private transportation—you can walk to the following recommendations.

WHERE TO STAY
VERY EXPENSIVE

Imperiale Palace Hotel

Via Pagana 19, 16038. Santa Margherita Ligure. ☎ **0185/288991.** Fax 0185/284223. 86 rms, 11 junior suites. A/C MINIBAR TV TEL. 360,000–515,000 lire ($225–$321.90) double; from 650,000 lire ($406.25) suite. Rates include breakfast. AE, DC, MC, V. Parking 15,000 lire ($9.40). Closed Dec–Mar.

The Imperial looks like an ornate gilded palace, and many guests like its faded grandeur to spend their "season on the Riviera." Located at the edge of the resort, it's built against a hillside and surrounded by semitropical gardens. Bikini-clad women and men of the international set feel at home here. The public rooms of the Imperial Palace live up to the hotel's name—old courtly splendor dominates, with vaulted gilt and painted ceilings, satin-covered antiques, ornate mirrors, and inlaid marble floors.

The bedrooms vary widely, from royal suites to simple singles away from the sea. Many of the rooms have elaborate ceilings, balconies, brass beds, chandeliers, and white antique furniture. Others are rather rawboned, so your opinion of this hotel will likely depend on your room assignment.

Dining/Entertainment: The dining room is formal, with white colonnades and arches and mahogany chairs, an appropriate background for Ligurian and international meals. There's also a two-decker open-air restaurant, and the music room, with its grand piano and satin chairs, is still enjoyed at teatime. In summer live music is presented on the terrace.

Service: Room service, babysitting, laundry, valet.

Facilities: All along the water's edge, a festive recreation center has been created, with an oval flagstone swimming pool on a terrace, an extended stone wharf for sunbathing, and cabañas.

EXPENSIVE

✪ Grand Hotel Miramare

Via Milite Ignoto 30, 16038 Santa Margherita Ligure. ☎ **0185/287013** or 800/223-6800 in the U.S. Fax 0185/284651. 75 rms, 9 suites. A/C MINIBAR TV TEL. 339,000–399,000 lire ($211.90–$249.40) double; 540,000–667,000 lire ($337.50–$416.90) suite. Rates include breakfast. Reduced rates available for children under 12 in parents' room. AE, MC, V. Parking 20,000 lire ($12.50).

It was on the terrace of this hotel in 1933 that Marconi succeeded in transmitting for the first time, by means of microwaves, telegraphic, and telephonic signals to a distance of more than 90 miles. Today the building has a festive confectionary look that's enhanced by the blue shutters and dazzling white facade. Separated from a stony beach by a busy boulevard, it's a 3-minute walk from the center of town. The hotel is surrounded by gardens whose meticulously maintained rear side is visible through huge plate-glass windows. To one side is a curved outdoor swimming pool with heated sea water. This adjoins a raised sun terrace dotted with parasols and iron tables. Bedrooms are well furnished.

Dining/Entertainment: The hotel restaurant has many Victorian touches, including fragile chairs and blue-and-white porcelain set into the plaster walls. Meals begin at 80,000 lire ($50).

Services: Room service, babysitting, laundry, valet.

Facilities: Heated sea water outdoor pool, private beach, Miramare Skywater School.

MODERATE

Hotel Continental

Via Pagana 8, 16038 Santa Margherita Ligure. ☎ **0185/286512.** Fax 0185/284463. 76 rms. A/C MINIBAR TV TEL. 275,000 lire ($171.90) double, including breakfast; 160,000-195,000 lire ($100-$121.90) per person with half-board. AE, DC, MC, V. Parking 12,000–20,000 lire ($7.50–$12.50).

From the winding road leading into town you'll see this hotel's grandiose facade, with its Doric portico, balustrades, and fancy carvings. After you enter the high-ceilinged and airy public rooms, however, you'll see the terraced gardens that stretch down to a private beach. In fair weather, the hotel operates a snack bar there, where guests enjoy light lunches while admiring a view of Santa Margherita bay. The bedrooms are filled with conservative furnishings, and often have tall French windows that lead onto wrought-iron balconies. A nearby annex contains additional lodging. The view from the restaurant encompasses the curved harbor in the center of town, a few miles away. The bedrooms are comfortably furnished. Since the turn of the century, the Ciana family has managed this year-round property. They also operate the Regina Elena (see below), Metropole, and Laurin.

With such a command of rooms, they can almost always accommodate you in any season.

Hotel Regina Elena

Lungomare Milite Ignoto 44, 16038 Santa Margherita Ligure. ☎ **0185/287003.** Fax 0185/284473. 103 rms. A/C MINIBAR TV TEL. 232,000–275,000 lire ($145–$171.90) double, including breakfast; 164,000–208,000 lire ($102.50–$130) per person with half-board. AE, DC, MC, V. Free parking.

In a building painted in pastel shades, this hotel is by the sea, along the scenic thoroughfare leading to Portofino. Rooms are furnished with modern styling and are well maintained, most of them opening onto a balcony with a view of the sea. An annex in the garden contains additional rooms. The hotel was built in 1908, and many turn-of-the-century details remain, including a marble staircase and the lounge. The hotel is operated by the Ciana family, which has been receiving guests since the turn of the century. They also operate the Continental (see above) and the Metropole and Laurin.

Dining/Entertainment: The dining room is the most interesting part of the hotel, in a 12-sided structure with walls made almost entirely of glass. The half-board plan features an excellent cuisine.

Services: Room service, babysitting, laundry, valet.

Facilities: Conference center, garden leading to private beach that can be reached by an underpass; roof garden pool with Jacuzzi.

Park Hotel Suisse

Via Favale 31, 16038 Santa Margherita Ligure. ☎ **0185/289571.** Fax 0185/281469. 85 rms (all with bath or shower). TV TEL. 140,000–340,000 lire ($87.50–$212.50) double. Rates include breakfast. No credit cards. Parking 10,000 lire ($6.25).

Set in a garden above the town center, the Park Hotel Suisse features a panoramic view of the sea and harbor. It has seven floors, all modern in design, with deep private balconies that are like al fresco living rooms for some of the bedrooms. On the lower terrace is a large, free-form, saltwater swimming pool surrounded by semitropical vegetation. A modernistic water chute, diving boards, a café with parasol tables for refreshments—all give one the advantages of seaside life and then some. The comfortable bedrooms that open onto the rear gardens, without sea view, cost slightly less; the rooms are decked out with contemporary furnishings in bold colors. The hotel, although built in 1957, has been renovated many times since. The hotel restaurant serves an international menu, with dinners costing from 40,000 lire ($25). The hotel lies 800 yards from the rail station above a small harbor about 100 yards from the sea. You have to cross a small street to reach the water, or you can use the outdoor pool.

INEXPENSIVE

Ⓢ Albergo Conte Verde

Via Zara 1, 16038 Santa Margherita Ligure. ☎ **0185/287139.** Fax 0185/284211. 35 rms (27 with shower). 95,000 lire ($59.40) double without shower, 125,000–135,000 lire ($78.15–$84.40) double with shower. Rates include breakfast. AE, DC, MC, V. Free parking. Closed Mar 1–15 and Dec 1–Dec 25.

This place offers one of the warmest welcomes in town to the budget traveler. Only two blocks from the sea, this third-class hotel has been revamped, and its rooms are simple but adequate. The terrace in front of the hotel has swing gliders, and the lounge has period furnishings, including rockers. All is consistent with the villa exterior of shuttered windows, flower boxes, and a small front garden and lawn where tables are set out for refreshments. Open year-round, the hotel also has a good and inexpensive restaurant, where you can order a complete menu costing 30,000 to 35,000 lire ($18.75 to $21.90).

⑤ Albergo Fasce

Via Bozzo 3, 16038 Santa Margherita Ligure. ☎ **0185/286435.** Fax 0185/283580. 16 rms. TV TEL. 57,500 lire ($35.95) per person with breakfast; 85,000 lire ($53.15) per person with half-board. AE, DC, MC, V. Parking 15,000 lire ($9.40).

A family-run hotel, the Fasce is functional yet welcoming. Each of its streamlined modern rooms has a private bath, color TV, safety deposit box, and phone. On the roof is a panoramic solarium. English-born Jane McGuffie Fasce runs the hotel along with her husband, Aristide. Everything functions in a homelike way, and many guests have praised the cuisine, which is available only to hotel guests. Extra amenities include 4-hour laundry service. The hotel also provides free bicycles for touring the area.

Hotel Jolanda

Via Luisito Costa 6, 10 16038 Santa Margherita Ligure. ☎ **0185/287-513.** Fax 0185/284763. 40 rms. TV TEL. 126,000–136,000 lire ($78.75-$85) double, including breakfast; 85,000–110,000 lire ($53.15-$68.75) per person with half-board. AE, V.

For more than 40 years, the Pastine family has been welcoming visitors to their little hotel, a short walk from the sea. A patio serves as a kind of open-air living room. The pensione lies on a peaceful little street, away from the noise of traffic. Rooms are comfortably furnished, with private bath, TV, and phone. Guests often gather in the bar before preceding to the restaurant, where an excellent Ligurian cuisine is served.

WHERE TO DINE
MODERATE

Ristorante la Ghiaia

In the Lido Palace Hotel, via Andrea Doria 5. ☎ **283708.** Reservations recommended. Main courses 18,000–35,000 lire ($11.25–$21.90). AE, DC, MC, V. Thurs–Tues 12:30–2pm and 8–10pm. Closed Nov. SEAFOOD.

This establishment's name in translation means "sea rocks," and that's precisely what you'll see from the windows that provide multifaceted views of the water. It's set on the ground floor of one of the town's most centrally located hotels, and the modern decor includes clear colors and paintings throughout the sunny dining rooms. Outdoor tables are shielded from the pedestrian traffic by rows of shrubbery. Your meal might begin with *antipasti di mare, tagliolini al pesto, zuppa di pesce* (fish soup), *risotto di mare* (rice with seafood), or spaghetti with lobster sauce. Fresh fish, including turbot, scampi, gamberini, and sea bass, is priced by the gram.

INEXPENSIVE

Trattoria Cesarina

Via Mameli 2C. ☎ **286059.** Reservations recommended, especially in midsummer. Main courses 25,000–35,000 lire ($15.65–$21.90). AE, DC, MC, V. Thurs–Tues 12:30–2:30pm and 7:30–10pm. LIGURIAN.

This trattoria lies beneath the arcade of a short but monumental street that runs into piazza Fratelli Bandiere. In an atmosphere of bentwood chairs and discreet lighting, you can enjoy an endless array of Ligurian dishes. Specialties include arrays of meat, vegetables, and seafood antipasti, along with classical Italian dishes

Cinque Terrace

North of La Spezia is Cinque Terre, or Five Lands—five little cliffside-hugging towns which originated as fishing villages in the Middle Ages, built at the locations of natural harbors along what is known as the Riviera di Levante, between Genoa and La Spezia where the Apuane Alps send high ridges right to the sea. The alpine ridges and rugged country inland from the harbors caused the five towns to be inaccessible by land for centuries after their origin. The towns are **Riomaggiore, Manarola, Corniglia, Vernazza,** and **Monterosso al Mare,** this last a town popular among sandy-beach devotees.

Today the Cinque Terre towns can be reached by train or (except for Corniglia and Vernazza) by car. To drive here, take the autostrada A12, going from Genoa to Livorno, then exit at Brugnato, some 20 miles from Monterosso al Mare, going via Pignone. At Monterosso is a large parking area for use of beach crowds. A local highway leads from La Spezia to Riomaggiore and Manarola, but cars are not allowed to enter the village and must park outside. Trains stop hourly at all five towns, taking 4 minutes to go from one to the other. Purchase your ticket at the local station.

Many visitors to the Cinque Terre prefer to walk but the trail in part goes around coastal ledges and cliff overhangs and is for the adventurous only. A leaflet about the paths in the area that are considered safe for walking is available form the **Tourist Information Center** at via Fegina Monterosso al Mare (☎ 0187/817506). This office is open only from Easter to October.

Among sights along the way are a 1622 Capuchin convent, a crenellated fortress, ancient buildings, and the fishing boats in the harbor at Monterosso. Vernazza has a plaza on the harbor. Labyrinthine steps lead through the ancient town, and you can see an elegant Renaissance campanile with an octagonal balustrade. Corniglia is not at the water's edge, as are the other four towns. Instead, it is on a promontory that juts out, with a long stairway leading down to the quay where fishing boats tie up. In the town stands a Renaissance chapel built in layers of black basalt and white travertine, giving it a striped effect seen mainly in Tuscany. Corniglia was built in a ravine and has houses climbing both sides of the declivity, with fishing boats lining the one street of the town.

Manarola welcomes visitors to its sidewalk cafés, where you can rest. The path leading from it to Riomaggiore is called via dell'Amore. Riomaggiore rests in the natural valleys, with both an old and a new town. Instead of cars, fishing boats are parked on the street, and a weekly market is held every Thursday. All five towns are known for their wines.

---

as taglierini with seafood and pappardella in a fragrant sausage sauce, plus seasonal fish such as red snapper or dorado, best when grilled, that has been caught off the nearby coast.

5 Portofino

22 miles SE of Genoa, 106 miles S of Milan, 301 miles NW of Rome

About 4 miles south of Santa Margherita Ligure, along one of the most beautiful coastal roads in all of Italy, is Portofino.

Favored by the yachting set, the resort is in an idyllic location on a harbor, where the water reflects all the pastel-washed little houses that run along it. In the 1930s, it enjoyed a reputation with artists; later, a chic crowd moved in—and they're still there, occupying villas in the hills and refusing to surrender completely to tourists who pour in during the day.

The thing to do in Portofino: During the day—but preferably before sunset—start on a walk that leads toward the tip of the peninsula. You'll pass the entrance to an old castle (where a German baron once lived), old private villas, towering trees, and much vegetation, before you reach the lighthouse. Allow an hour at least. When you return to the main piazza, proceed to one of the two little drinking bars on the left side of the harbor that rise and fall in popularity.

Once Portofino was a sleepy fishing village, but its history goes back to Roman times. Pliny called it "Portus Deophini." It was the private domain of Benedictines before it was incorporated into the Republic of Genoa in 1414, becoming in 1815 a part of the Kingdom of the Two Sicilies.

Before beginning that walk to the lighthouse, as mentioned, you can climb steps from the port leading to the little parish Church of St. George. A panoramic view of the port and bay is possible from the terrace here. In summer, you can also take boat rides around the coast to such points as San Fruttuoso.

Portofino is tiny and you can walk wherever you want to go.

ESSENTIALS

GETTING THERE By Train Go first to Santa Margherita Ligure (see above), then continue the rest of the way by bus.

By Bus Tiguillio buses leave Santa Margherita Ligure once every 30 minutes bound for Portofino. The one-way ticket is 1,700 lire ($1.05), and you can purchase tickets aboard the bus.

By Car From Santa Margherita Ligure, continue south along the only road, which hugs the promontory until you reach Portofino. In summer traffic is likely to be heavy.

VISITOR INFORMATION The telephone area code for Portofino is 0185. The tourist information center is at via Roma 35 (☎ 269024).

WHERE TO STAY

Portofino is severely limited in hotels. Therefore, in July and August you may be forced to book a room in nearby Santa Margherita Ligure or Rapallo.

EXPENSIVE

✪ Albergo Splendido

Viale Baratta 13, 16034 Portofino. ☎ **0185/269551** or 800/992-5055 in the U.S. Fax 0185/269614. 63 rms, 27 suites. A/C MINIBAR TV TEL. 455,000–560,000 lire ($284.40–$350) double; 715,000–915,000 lire ($446.90–$571.90) suite for two. Rates include half-board. AE, DC, MC, V. Closed Oct 23–Apr 6.

This Relais & Châteaux selection provides a luxury base for those who moor their yacht in the harbor below, or have closed down their Palm Beach residence for the summer. Originally built as a monastery during the Middle Ages, this four-story building was attacked with such frequency by Saracen pirates that the monks abandoned it. In the 19th century, Baron Baratta revived the wreck, converting it into a family summer home. It had been built on an east-west axis following the hill's

The Rich and the Infamous

Even though today overrun by day-trippers eating ice cream, Portofino has gone down in the annals of world chicdom as a haven for the elite who occupy villas in the hills and arrive on yachts. They only appear at the portside bars and piazzetta of Portofino when the day trippers have mercifully departed. The resident locals call the visitors "barbarians," although most working people in Portofino live exclusively off them.

No one seems to know for sure who launched this tiny fishing village into fashion, making it known worldwide as "the Pearl of the Italian Riviera." Perhaps it was Guy de Maupassant arriving in 1889 aboard his sailboat *Bel-Ami*, titled after the French author's frivolous but successful novel.

Critics—snobbish ones, that is—claim Portofino was never chic but more like a circus. Consider these notes from this reporters impressions of travel in the 1960s and make your own judgment.

"There I was at La Gritta American Bar, entertaining a party of three villa owners (two from England and one from Germany) when Rex Harrison (alone for a change) appeared to occupy the only reserved table. He knew both of the Brits and acknowledged our table briefly with weak handshakes before assuming a seat at his empty table. He occupied center position before asking the bartender to 'do something about the lighting.' It was a bit harsh, and 'Sexy Rexy' appeared to have had a bad night.

Within moments we knew Harrison wasn't going to be drinking alone. He was at the bar to greet Taylor & Burton arriving on a yacht. All three actors had finally recovered from the debacle, *Cleopatra*, in which the trio had starred. After hugs and kisses, with a promise to return, Taylor made her way through the village whereas Burton began heavy drinking at the bar with Harrison.

As Taylor made the rounds of boutiques—she was then at her most unfashionable and worst dressed look—women from the village crowded around her as she emerged from various boutiques. They held up their babies for her to admire, often aggressively thrusting them in her face.

contour, offering sea views and sun throughout the day. The building opened as a hotel in 1901, set on 4 acres of semitropical gardens.

The hotel is reached from the village by a steep and winding road that's flanked by twisting, silvery olive trees and banks of flowers growing against stone walls. From one of the hotel's pergola verandas you can enjoy a panorama of the sea and rugged Riviera coastline.

Inside, a refreshing, informal country-house flavor prevails. The villa is rambling, with several levels of public rooms, terraces, and "oh, that view" bedrooms. Each private room is furnished in a personal way—no two alike. Traditional old pieces include antique desks and comfortable sofas and armchairs in small sitting areas. Prices are high, and vary according to the room.

Dining/Entertainment: The bilevel dining room is divided by a row of arches and furnished with Biedermeier chairs, flower bouquets, and a fine old tapestry. The restaurant terrace not only enjoys a view but also serves traditional dishes of typical Ligurian cooking, plus international specialties.

It soon became apparent they were actually trying to sell their babies to the fabled star, and were quoting amounts in lire. Taylor didn't purchase any babies that night, but did spend more than $5,000 in one boutique alone.

Anytime her drink got low, meaning one inch below the rim of the glass, a bartender from aboard her yacht rushed her a fresh one.

Finally, Taylor entered the bar to join Harrison and Burton. These revelations were overheard: Burton had called Taylor 'Miss Tits' and 'Fat Little' before and after meeting her. Eddie Fisher was known as 'the busboy.' Burton gloated to Harrison that he'd earned "more money on that bloody film than you did.' And what he hated most in all the world was being called 'England's Brando' or 'the working man's Laurence Olivier.' Between revelations, he broke into recitations of the poetry of Dylan Thomas, a fellow Welshman.

Taylor revealed this: She'd confided to Harrison her determination not to let Burton 'bag her,' as he did most of his leading ladies. Until the devastating reviews came out, she fully believed that her role as Cleopatra was 'the greatest woman's part ever written,' and she fully expected to receive a second Academy Award for her role. She admitted that she used Mike Todd as her role model to imagine the relationship between Julius Caesar and Cleopatra."

Such are the happenings and events likely to occur at the harbor of Portfino and in the Splendido on the hill, one of the most famous and expensive hotels in all of Italy. The hotel too would have its stories to tell, especially after the departure of such illustrious guests of yesterday as the Duke and Duchess of Windsor, Ernest Hemingway, Greta Garbo, Ingrid Bergman, Aristotle Onassis, Clark Gable, John Wayne, and even Larry Hagman who as J.R. Ewing in "Dallas" won fame throughout Italy.

Today a lot of villas remain unoccupied in the hills around Portfino. Continuing corruption scandals in Italy have meant that some of the powerful elite are laying low and avoiding such high-profile resorts as Portofino which has just too many paparazzi.

Services: Room service, babysitting, laundry, valet, massage.

Facilities: Hotel speedboat, saltwater heated swimming pool, beauty center, solarium, sauna.

MODERATE

Albergo Nazionale

16034 Portofino. ☎ **0185/269575.** Fax 0185/269578. 2 rms, 10 suites. MINIBAR TV TEL. 200,000 lire ($125) double; 350,000–400,000 lire ($218.75–$250) suite. Breakfast 20,000 lire ($12.50) extra. MC, V. Closed Nov 15–Mar 15.

At stage center, right on the harbor, this old villa with many roof levels, is modest, yet well laid out. The suites here are tastefully decorated, and the little lounge has a brick fireplace, coved ceiling, antique furnishings, and good reproductions. Most of the bedrooms, furnished in a mixture of styles (hand-painted Venetian in some of the rooms), have a view of the harbor. There are no singles.

⑤ Hotel Eden

Vico Dritto 18, 16034 Portofino. ☎ **0185/269091.** Fax 0185/269047, 9 rms. MINIBAR TV TEL. 180,000–260,000 lire ($112.50–$162.50) double. Rates include breakfast. AE, DC, MC, V. Public parking 27,000 lire ($16.90). Closed Dec 1–20.

Just 150 feet away from the harbor in the heart of the village is a little albergo, a budget holdout in an otherwise high-fashion resort. Set in a garden (hence its name), it's a good place to stay. While there is no view of the harbor, there's a winning vista from the front veranda, where breakfast is served. The hotel is run by Mr. Ferruccio, and life here is decidedly casual.

WHERE TO DINE

EXPENSIVE

Il Pitosforo

Molo Umberto I no. 9. ☎ **269020.** Reservations required. Main courses 35,000–78,000 lire ($21.90–$48.75). AE, DC, MC, V. Wed–Mon noon–2:30pm and 7:30–11pm. Closed lunch July–Aug. LIGURIAN/ITALIAN.

Reached by climbing steps, Il Pitosforo draws a raft of raves and, most likely, cries of protest when the tab is presented. While not blessed with an especially distinguished decor, its position right on the harbor gives it all the native chic it needs, and has ever since Bogey and Bacall or Taylor and Burton came this way long ago. The food is worthy. Zuppa di pesce is a delectable Ligurian fish soup, or you may prefer the bouillabaisse, which is always reliable here. The pastas are especially recommendable, and include lasagne al pesto, wide noodles prepared in the typical Genovese sauce. Fish dishes include mussels alla marinara and paella valenciana for two, saffron-flavored rice studded with sea fruit and chicken. Some meat and fish dishes are grilled over hot stones, others over charcoal. Men should wear jackets.

MODERATE

Da U'Batti

Vico Nuovo 17. ☎ **269379.** Reservations recommended. Main courses 40,000–45,000 lire ($25–$28.15). AE, MC, V. Tues–Sun noon–3pm and 8–11pm. Closed Nov 15–Jan 15. SEAFOOD.

Informal, chic, and colorful, this place is on a narrow cobblestone-covered piazza a few steps above the port. Founded in 1963, it still perpetuates some of the *La Dolce Vita* aura of that heady time. A pair of barnacle-encrusted anchors, hanging above the arched entrance, hint at the seafaring specialties that have become this establishment's trademark. Owner and sommelier Giancarlo Foppiano serves delectable dishes, which might include trenette with pesto sauce, a soup of "hen clams," spaghetti with olives, rice with shrimp or crayfish, or fish alla Battista. It has a good selection of grappa, as well as French and Italian wines.

Delfino

Piazza Martiri delli Olivetta 40. ☎ **269081.** Reservations recommended Sat. Main courses 34,000–46,000 lire ($21.25–$28.75). AE, DC. MC, V. Tues–Sun noon–3pm and 7–11pm. Closed Nov–Dec. SEAFOOD.

Right on the village square that fronts the harbor is Delfino, Portofino's most fashionable dining spot (along with Il Pitosforo; see above). It's located in a sienna-colored harborside building with forest-green shutters. It is both nautically rustic and informally chic. Less expensive than Il Pitosforo, it offers virtually the same type of food, such as lasagne al pesto. Again, the fish dishes provide the best reason for lifting your fork: zuppa di pesce (a soup made of freshly caught fish with a secret spice blend), risotto with shrimp, sole, squid, and other sea creatures. If you can't stand fish but are trapped into dining with those who love it, then know that the chef at Delfino prides himself on his sage-seasoned *vitello all'uccelletto*, a roast veal with a gamey taste. Depending on your choice of fish dishes, expect a final tab ranging upward from 75,000 to 105,000 lire ($46.90 to $65.65) per person. Try to get a table near the front so as to enjoy or at least be amused by the parade of visitors and villagers.

Ristorante da Puny

Piazza Martiri delli Olivetta. ☎ **269037.** Reservations required. Main courses 25,000–42,000 lire ($15.65–$26.25). No credit cards. Fri–Wed noon–3pm and 7–11pm. Closed Dec 15–Feb 20. SEAFOOD.

This place competes successfully with the established leaders of Portofino's portside restaurants. Da Puny is set up on the stone square that opens onto the harbor. Because of its location, it's practically in the living room of Portofino, within sight of the evening activities that make the town famous as a hangout for the chic and tan yachting set. Green-painted tables are set under trees at night on a slate-covered outdoor terrace. Inside, the nautical decor includes walls of stippled stucco, with a zodiac theme inlaid in brass above the bar area. The menu includes pappardelle Portofino, antipasto of the house, spaghetti with clams, baked fish with potatoes and olives, fried zucchini flowers, and an array of freshly caught fish.

PORTOFINO AFTER DARK

La Gritta American Bar

Calata Marconi 20. ☎ **269126.**

La Gritta vies for business with its rival a few storefronts away. Between the two of them, they have attracted the biggest names in show business and elsewhere: from Onassis to Frank Sinatra to John Wayne. It is said that Rex Harrison, while drinking in this bar with the Duke of Windsor, excused himself to go and purchase a package of cigarettes. He never came back. On the way for the cigarettes, he ran into actress Kay Kendal and the two eloped. These celebrities have intermingled with dozens of tourists and a collection of U.S. Navy personnel in this small, well-appointed restaurant. As James Jones, author of *From Here to Eternity*, noted: "This is the nicest waterfront bar this side of Hong Kong." That's true, but it's always wise to check your bar tab carefully before you stagger out looking for a new adventure. La Gritta means "The Crab" in Genovese dialect. Long drinks cost 13,000 to 18,000 lire ($8.15 to $11.25) a piece. Open Friday through Wednesday from 8:30pm to 3am.

Scafandro American Bar

Calata Marconi 10. ☎ **269105.**

This is one of the village's chic rendezvous points, a place that has attracted an array of yachting guests. The seating arrangements inside contribute to the general feeling of well-being, since they're three-quarter-round banquettes, pulled up to teakwood tables with brass detailing. The members of your party will be illuminated by hanging dome lights, while in a corner sits a brass-and copper headset removed from a 19th-century diver's costume. If one of the world's celebrities doesn't happen to come in while you're here, you can always study one of the series of unusual nautical engravings adorning the walls. Most drinks cost 13,000 to 18,000 lire ($8.15 to $11.25). Open Wednesday through Monday from 8:30 to 3am.

21 Naples & Pompeii

Campania is in many ways the most eerie, memorable, and beautiful region of Italy, sociologically different from anything else in Europe—haunting, confusing, and satisfying, all at the same time. Campania forms a fertile crescent around the Bays of Naples and Sorrento, and stretches inland into a landscape of limestone rocks dotted with patches of fertile soil. It was off the shores of Campania that Ulysses ordered his crew to tie him, ears unstopped, to the mast of his ship, so that he alone would hear the songs of the sirens without throwing himself overboard to sample their pleasures. Today the siren song of Campania still lures, with a chemistry that some visitors insist is an aphrodisiac.

The geological oddities of Campania include a smoldering and dangerous volcano (already famous for having destroyed Pompeii and Herculaneum), sulfurous springs that belch steam and smelly gases, and lakes that ancient myths refer to as the gateway to Hades. Its seaside highway is the most beautiful in the world (and probably the most treacherous); it combines danger at every hairpin turn with some of Italy's most reckless drivers. Despite such dark images, Campania is one of the most captivating regions of Italy, sought out by native Italians and visitors alike for its combination of earth, sea, and sky. Coupled with this are what might well be the densest collection of ancient ruins in Europe, each celebrated by classical scholars as among the very best of its kind.

The ancient Romans dubbed the land Campania Felix, which may reflect their satisfaction with the district that inspired the construction of hundreds of private villas for their rulers. In some ways the beauty of Campania contributed to the decay of the Roman Empire, as Caesars, their senators, and their courtiers spent more and more time pursuing its pleasures and abandoning the cares of Rome's administrative problems.

Even today, seafront land in Campania is so desirable that hoteliers have poured their life savings into foundations of buildings that are sometimes bizarrely cantilevered above rock-studded cliffs. Despite their numbers, these hotels tend to be profitably overbooked in summer.

Although residents of Campania sometimes stridently extol the virtues of its cuisine, it's not the most renowned in Italy. Its produce, however, is superb and its wine heady.

What's Special About Naples & Pompeii

Great Cities/Towns
- Naples, one of the world's most beautiful seaports.
- Pompeii, an archaeological treasure trove, unearthed from volcanic ash, rates as one of the top sights of the ancient world.

Museums
- The National Archaeological Museum, Naples, offering one of Europe's most valuable collections—many treasures removed from long-buried Pompeii.
- The Museo e Gallerie Nazionali di Campodimonte, Naples, one of Italy's best collections of paintings from the 14th through the 16th century.

Ace Attractions
- Herculaneum, an archaeological site smaller than Pompeii, but in many ways even more interesting; it, too, was buried under volcanic ash.
- Vesuvius, a volcano that has struck terror across the Campania, looming menacingly over the Bay of Naples.

Ancient Monuments
- The Phlaegrean Fields (Campi Flegrei), an explosive land of myth and legend, lying near Naples.
- Lago d'Averno, 10 miles west of Naples, a lake in an extinct volcano crater that the ancients called the Gateway to Hades.

Today Campania typifies the conditions that northern Italians label "the problem of the south." Although the inequities are the most pronounced in Naples, the entire region, outside the resorts along the coast, has a lower standard of living and education, and higher crime rates, plus less developed standards of health care, than the more affluent north.

Television has contributed to leveling regional differences. Nevertheless, Campania is still rife with superstitious myths, vendettas, and restrictive problems. It is also home to a people who can sometimes overwhelm you with kindnesses and spontaneity. Despite, or perhaps because of, these tendencies, it's worth investing your vacation time in Campania. In some way, it captures the soul and soulfulness of southern Italy.

A DRIVING TOUR

Day 1 Naples is the traditional gateway to Campania, as the city lies on the major north-south line from Milan down Italy's western coastline to Reggio di Calabria and Messina. There are two routes from Rome—one going via Latina and Formia, the other going via Frosinone and Caserta. Motorists find the quickest route from Rome is the Rome-Naples A2 autostrada, which passes Caserta 18 miles north of Naples, or the Naples-Reggio di Calabria A3, which goes by Salerno, 33 miles south of Naples. Arrive in Naples for a late lunch and visit the Museo Archeologico Nazionale. At sunset stroll along the waterfront, dining in a sea-bordering tavern there at night.

☕ **TAKE A BREAK** One of the best places for pizza—the most celebrated culinary offering of Naples—is Pizzeria Trianon da Ciro, via Pietro

Collette 44–46 in Naples (☎ 081/5539426), where pies cost from 8,000 to 13,000 lire ($5 to $8.15). The staff is rude but the pizza is savory and tasty. You can select from nearly 20 different concoctions emerging from the fiery ovens. Hours are Monday through Saturday from 10am to 3:30pm and 6:30 to 11pm; Sunday, only 6:30 to 11pm.

Day 2   The following morning see some more sights of Naples, especially the Museo e Gallerie Nazionali di Capodimonte. In the late morning begin your tour of the Phlaegrean Fields (see below), land of myth and legend. These sights lie west of Naples, begining at Solfatara, 7½ miles away. This is an ancient volcano. Other sights include Pozzuoli, a mile and a half from Solfatara, where you can visit the ruins of Anfiteatro Flavio and the Temple of Serapis. Other major sights in the area include Baia, a former imperial retreat; Lago dAverno, a lake occupying an extinct volcano crater, and ancient Cuma, site of one of the first outposts of Greek colonization in Italy, with the cave of the legendary Cumaean Sibyl. Return to Naples for the night.

Day 3   You can continue to be based at Naples or else move south to a hotel at Pompeii (although the choices are very limited). On Day 3, visit Herculaneum in the morning which was destroyed when Vesuvius erupted in August of A.D. 79. Later in the day you can explore Vesuvius and Pompeii.

Day 4   The ancient city of Pompeii, also destroyed by Vesuvius, is so rich in attractions that many visitors plan to spend another day here exploring the ruins.

FOOD & WINE

This is the land of spaghetti and pizza, two dishes that have gained popularity around the world. Although once thought to be "anti-digestion," pasta now enjoys acceptability everywhere, certainly on its home ground of Campania, including Naples and Salerno among its chief towns. Many Neapolitans prefer it simple— spaghetti al pomodoro, cooked al dente and served with a light sauce made of fresh tomatoes cooked in oil and spiced with basil. Spaghetti alle vongole (with baby clams) always has that tang of the sea.

The chief stew of the region is zuppa alla marinara, varieties of fish flavored with pepper, salt, parsley, tomatoes, and garlic. The classic pizza alla napoletana is the most famous dish of Naples. Its usually covered with mozarrella, olive oil, anchovies, marjoram, and tomato sauce before popped into a fiery oven.

Fritto misto is a golden brown fry of fish, cheese, cauliflower, sweetbreads, and potatoes, but even more popular is melanzane alla parmigiana—eggplant, thinly sliced, and cooked with mozzarella, tomato sauce, olive oil, spices, and Parmesan cheese. Beefsteak or veal is often served "alla pizzaiola" style—with tomato, olive oil, garlic, and marjoram.

The wines of Campania were the most highly placed from ancient days. Pliny put Falerno at the top of his list, and even Horace acclaimed the wine as generous, robust, and fiery. Martial pronounced it "immortal." Virgil and others sang the praise of this vivid ruby-red wine, with a distinctive bouquet, evocative of flowers, and with a dry but fruity flavor. As it ages, it gets better. It is the preferred wine with roasts, poultry, red meat, and game.

Other wines include Biancolella d'Ischia, one of the finest wines produced on that island, and often served with fish. It has a mellow, harmonious flavor, with a delicate bouquet. Gragnana, served with all meats, is a dark mulberry in color, with a purplish foam and a bouquet evocative of faded violets. Nutty and generally mellow, it is the wine that has played a role in the literature and legend of Naples.

1 Naples (Napoli)

136 miles SE of Rome, 162 miles W of Bari

Its city government is reportedly corrupt, many of its businesses dominated by the Mafia; it has indisputably the worst air pollution and traffic in Italy; and its hordes of street children make it the juvenile delinquent capital of Europe. Naples is Italy's most controversial city: You'll either love it or hate it. It is louder, more intense, more unnerving, but perhaps ultimately more satisfying for the traveler than almost anywhere in Italy.

Naples has changed a lot since the cholera outbreak of 1973, when the world discovered that the city had no sewers and was basking on the edge of a picturesque but poisoned bay. New civic centers have been planned, and some of the city's baroque palaces have been restored. But to the foreigner unfamiliar with the complexities of the multifarious "Italys" and their regional types, the Neapolitan is still the quintessence of the country—easy to caricature ("O Sole Mio," "Mamma Mia," bel canto). If Sofia Loren (a native who moved elsewhere) evokes the Italian woman for you, you'll find more of her look-alikes here than in any other city. Perhaps more visible are the city's children. In one of the most memorable novels to come out of World War II, *The Gallery* by John Horne Burns, there is this passage: "But I remember best of all the children of Naples, the *scugnizzi*. Naples is the greatest baby plant in the world. Once they come off the assembly line, they lose no time in getting onto the streets. They learn to walk and talk in the gutters. Many of them seem to live there." If Burns were writing this novel today, he might also have warned you that these scugnizzi specialize in *lo scippo* (local dialect for petty thievery). Of course, if it's your purse or wallet that has been stolen, it may be no petty crime to you. Guard your person and your valuables carefully as you explore the tangled, often dangerous streets of Naples.

A LOOK AT THE PAST Neapolitan legends claim that the city was founded after the body of Parthenope (a nymph who committed suicide after being spurned by Ulysses) washed ashore in the nearby bay. Archaeological evidence suggests that it was founded by Greek colonists late in the 5th century B.C.

During the height of the Roman Empire, Naples was only one of dozens of important cities that surrounded the famous bay. Roman emperors, especially Nero, perhaps in order to show that they appreciated the finer (Greek-inspired) things in life, treated Naples as a resort, away from the pressure of imperial Rome. They also used it as a departure point for their nearby villas on Capri. It was visited by poets (Virgil wrote the *Georgics* here) and sybarites alike. Under the Byzantine administration of the remnants of the Roman Empire, Naples actually grew and prospered—unlike many of its Italian neighbors. This was in part because of its excellent harbor, and in part because many of its competitors (Pompeii and

Herculaneum, for example) were destroyed by economic stagnation or by cascades of molten lava and ash.

Over the centuries Naples has known many conquerors, and lived in constant fear of the potential for a volcanic eruption that might annihilate the city. These facts might help to explain its "live for today" philosophy. Among its conquerors and leaders have been everyone from the Normans in 1139, Charles of Anjou in 1266, the Aragonese of Spain under Alfonso V in 1435, Archduke Charles of Austria in 1707, French Bourbons in 1734, the pan-Italian nationalist armies of Garibaldi in 1861, and, after the fiasco of Mussolini's brand of fascism during World War II, the Americans.

During the 18th and 19th centuries, French, English, and German tourists visited the Bay of Naples as an essential part (perhaps the highlight) of their grand European tour. They flooded the northern European consciousness with legends and images of Naples as the most beautiful and carefree city in the world. "See Naples and die," the popular wisdom claimed. Some historians write that the unabashed sexual permissiveness of the 18th- and 19th-century Naples was more of a lure to northern Europeans than the region's archaeology.

AND ON TO THE PRESENT   Today the only "dying" you're likely to experience is being run over by a car. Each of the city's 2.2 million inhabitants seems to have a beat-up Fiat, battalions of which speed erratically and incessantly over hopelessly narrow roads originally laid our more than 2,000 years ago. To add to the confusion, hordes of Neapolitan children will blithely throw lit firecrackers into moving traffic, stop traffic to beg or smear your windshield with a soiled towel, or (sometimes more or less endearingly) try to pick your pocket.

Surely, the Neapolitans are the most spontaneous people on earth, wearing their emotions on the surface of their skin. No Neapolitan housewife gets overheated running up and down steps to convey a message to someone on the street—she handles the situation by screaming out the window.

Both arguments and love happen spontaneously, and are sometimes just as quickly forgotten. The Neapolitan dialect is considered one of the most distinctive and difficult in all of Italy, with an almost alarming number and diversity of words (a source of pride) for describing intimate body parts and functions. This richness of expressions might have been grudgingly respected by Dante. Naples even bears the dubious honor of having introduced syphilis to the world in 1495 (history's first recorded version), the outbreak of which was immediately blamed on a group of French soldiers quartered there at the time.

Today Naples is a city to be savored in bits and pieces. It comes at you like a runaway car, with tour-ticket sellers, car thieves, hotel hawkers, and pimps and hustlers, and a series of human encounters that seesaw between extraordinary warmth and kindness and a kind of surrealistic nightmare.

With its almost total absence of parks, its lack of space (it has the highest population density of any city in Europe), and the constant and unrelieved perception that it will disintegrate into total anarchy at any moment, it's not a destination for queasy palates and weak hearts. Add to this the 35% unemployment rate, the unending prevalence of both major and minor larceny, the highest infant-mortality rate in Italy, the heat, and the pollution, and you have a destination many visitors rush through quickly on their way to somewhere else.

Still, the tattered splendor of baroque palaces (whose charm is enhanced by shrubs and bushes growing from cracks in their cornices), the sense of history, and the unalloyed spectacle of humanity struggling, with humor and perserverance, to survive, makes Naples one of the most memorable places you'll visit in Italy. Only one thing, *don't show up on Monday*, when most attractions are closed.

Naples is a fantastic adventure. The best approach, from its bay, is idyllic—a port set against the backdrop of a crystal-blue sky and volcanic mountains. The rich attractions inside the city and in the environs (Pompeii, Ischia, Capri, Vesuvius, the Phlaegrean Fields, Herculaneum) make Naples one of the five top tourist meccas of Italy. The inexperienced may have difficulty coping with it. The seasoned explorer will find it worthy ground, and might even try venturing down side streets, some of which teem with prostitutes and a major source of their upkeep: the ubiquitous sailor.

ESSENTIALS

GETTING THERE　By Plane　The quickest way to get to Naples from Rome and other major Italian cities, including Milan, is to fly there on a domestic flight, which will put you into **Aeroporto Capodichino,** via Umberto Maddalena (☎ 7803235), four miles north of the city. A city ATAN bus (no. 14) makes the 15-minute run between the airport and Naples' piazza Garibaldi in front of the main rail terminus. The bus fare is 1,000 lire (65¢), or about 20,000 lire ($12.50) if you take a taxi. Domestic flights are available on Alitalia, Alisarda, and Ati. Flying time from Milan is 1 hour, 20 minutes; from Palermo, 1 hour, 15 minutes; from Rome, 50 minutes; and from Venice, 1 hour, 15 minutes. For flight information about departures, call 081/7803235.

By Train　Frequent trains connect Naples with the rest of Italy. For example, one or two trains per hour arrive from Rome, taking $2^1/2$ hours and costing 16,000 lire ($10) for a one-way passage. It's also possible to reach Naples from Milan in about 7 hours, costing 61,000 lire ($38.15) for a one-way ticket. Trains also run back and forth to the port city of Brindisi on the Rome-Leone line (used by visitors taking ferries from Greece), taking $6^1/2$ hours and costing 31,200 lire ($19.50) for a one-way ticket.

The city has two main rail terminals, **Stazione Centrale,** at piazza Garibaldi, and **Stazione Margellina,** at piazza Amadeo. If you want rail information, call 5534188.

Alitalia, in collaboration with FS, the Italian State Railways, links Naples with Rome's Leonardo da Vinci International Airport without intermediate stops. Twice a day, seven days a week, the "Alitalia Airport Train by FS," departs from Stazione Margellina, heading north to Rome and the airport. To travel on the airport train, you must have an Alitalia airline ticket.

By Bus　Take either private or public transportation (airlines, rail) to reach Naples. Once there, various provincial bus companies service all the towns and villages throughout the region. The SITA buses, departing from via Pisanelli 3 (☎ 5522176), are your best bet, as they run to such popular tourist spots as Amalfi, Pompeii, Ravello, and Salerno.

By Car　In the old days the custom was to sail into the Bay of Naples, but today's traveler is more likely to drive there, heading down the autostrada from Rome. The Rome–Naples autostrada (A2) passes Caserta 18 miles north of Naples and the Naples–Reggio di Calabria autostrada (A3) runs by Salerno, 33 miles north of Naples.

By Ferry　If you're already in Sicily, you can go on a ferry to Naples from Palermo on **Tirrenia Lines,** Molo Angionio, Stazione Marritima (☎ 7613688), in the port area of Palermo. A one-way ticket costs 68,400 lire ($42.75) per person for the $10^1/2$-hour boat trip to Naples.

ORIENTATION

ARRIVING If you arrive by train at the Stazione Centrale, in front of piazza Garibaldi, you'll want to escape from that horror by taking one of the major arteries of Naples, **corso Umberto,** in the direction of the Santa Lucia district. Along the water, many boats, such as those heading for Capri and Ischia, leave from **Porto Beverello.**

TOURIST INFORMATION Visitors can ask for information at the **Ente Provinciale per il Turismo** at the Stazione Centrale (☎ 268779). There's another office at piazza del Gesù Nuovo 7 (☎ 5523328). They're open Monday through Saturday from 9am to 2pm and 3 to 7pm and on Sunday from 9am to 3pm.

CITY LAYOUT Many visitors to Naples confine their visit to the bayside **Santa Lucia** area, and perhaps venture into another section to see an important museum. Most of the major hotels lie along via **Partenope,** which looks out not only to the Gulf of Naples but the Castel dell'Ovo. To the west is the **Mergellina** district, site of many restaurants and dozens of apartment houses. The far western section of the city is known as **Posillipo.**

One of the most important squares of Naples is **piazza del Plebiscito,** north of Santa Lucia. The Palazzo Reale opens onto this square. On a satellite square, you can visit **piazza Trento y Trieste,** with its Teatro San Carlo and entrance to the famed Galleria Umberto I. To the east is the third most important square, **piazza Municipio.** From piazza Trento y Trieste, you encounter the main shopping street of Naples, **via Toledo/via Roma,** on which you can walk as far as piazza Dante. From that square, take via Enrico Pessina to the most important museum in Naples, located on piazza Museo Nazionale.

GETTING AROUND   By Train If you're planning to rely on public transportation, chances are you'll use the suburban rail line, the **Circumvesuviana,** to reach the major towns in the environs, including Pompeii (the chief destination of sightseers), Sorrento, and Herculaneum.

By Subway The **Metropolitana** (subway) line will deliver you from the Stazione Centrale in the west, all the way to the Stazione Mergellina. Get off at piazza Amadeo if you wish to take the funicular to Vómero. Fares are reasonable on public transportation, costing 1,500 lire (95¢) per trip.

By Bus or Tram It's dangerous to ride buses at rush hours. Never have I seen such pushing, shoving, and jockeying for position. On one recent trip, I saw a middle-aged woman fall from a too-crowded bus, injuring her leg. I was later told that this was a routine occurrence. If you're a linebacker, take your chances. Many prefer to leave the buses to the battle-hardened Neapolitans and take the subway or tram no. 1 or 4, which run from the Stazione Centrale to the Mergellina station. (It will also let you off at the quayside points where the boats depart for Ischia and Capri.)

By Taxi If you survive the reckless driving (someone once wrote that all Neapolitans drive like the anarchists they are), you'll only have to do battle over the bill. You will inevitably be overcharged. Many cab drivers claim that the meter is broken, and they then proceed to assess the cost of the ride, always to your disadvantage. Some legitimate surcharges are imposed, including night drives and extra luggage. However, many taxi drivers deliberately take you "the long way there" to run up your costs. In repeated visits to Naples, I have never yet been quoted an honest fare. I no longer bother with the meter; instead, I estimate what the fare would be worth, negotiate with the driver, and take off into the night. If you want to take a chance, you can call a radio taxi at 5564444.

By Car Getting around Naples can be a nightmare! Motorists should pay particular attention, as Neapolitans are fond of driving the wrong way on one-way streets and speeding hysterically along lanes reserved for public transportation, sometimes cutting into your lane without warning. Red lights, if they are turned on at all, seem to hold no terror for a Neapolitan driver. In fact, you may want to park your car and walk. There are two dangers in that. One is that your car can be stolen, as mine once was, even though apparently "guarded" by an attendant in front of a deluxe hotel. The other danger is that you're likely to get mugged (nearly a third of the city is unemployed, and people have to live somehow).

By Funicular Funiculars take passengers up and down the steep hills of Naples. The **Funicolare Centrale** (☎ 7632504), for example, connects the lower part of the city to Vómero. Departures are from piazzetta Duca d'Aosta, just of via Roma. Cable cars run daily, from 7am to 10pm. Watch that you don't get stranded by missing the last car back.

By Horse & Buggy Another means of transport, more expensive but far more romantic than a taxi, is a horse and buggy. They're still in service, most often taking visitors along the waterfront in Santa Lucia. Fares are to be negotiated.

FAST FACTS: Naples

Area Code For Naples and its environs, the telephone area code is 081.

Consulates You'll find the consulate of the **United States** on piazza della Repubblica (☎ 5838111) where the staff has long ago grown weary of hearing about another stolen passport. Its consular services are open from July to mid-September, Monday through Friday from 8am to 1:30pm. From mid-September to June, hours are Monday through Friday from 9am to 12:30pm and 3 to 5:30pm. The consulate of the **United Kingdom** is at via Francesco Crispi 122 (☎ 663511), open in summer Monday through Friday from 7 to 11am and 1 to 4pm; and in off-season, Monday through Friday from 9am to 12:30pm and 3 to 5:30pm.

Citizens of Canada, Australia, and New Zealand will need to go to the embassies and consulates of their home countries in Rome (see "Fast Facts: Rome," in Chapter 4).

Drugstores If it's a drugstore you want, go to Farmacia Helvethia, piazza Garibaldi 11, near Stazione Centrale (☎ 5548894).

Emergencies If you have an emergency, dial 113. To reach the police or carabinieri, call 112. For an ambulance, call 7520696.

Medical Care If you are in need of medical services, try the Guarda Medica Permanente, piazza del Municipio (☎ 7513177).

Post Office The main post office is on piazza G. Matteotti (☎ 5520067). Look for the Posta Telegrafo sign outside. It is open Monday through Friday from 8:15am to 1:30pm and on Saturday from 8:15am to 12:10pm.

Whoever it was who said (I believe it was Nelson), "See Naples and die," perpetrated one of the greatest hoaxes in history. Or perhaps I am unlucky when I go there.
— Geoffrey Harmsworth, *Abyssinian Adventure,* 1935

Telephone   If you need to make a long-distance call, you can do so at the Stazione Centrale, where an office is open 24 hours; if you make calls from your hotel, you will likely be hit with an excessive surcharge.

WHAT TO SEE & DO

Before striking out for Pompeii or Capri, you should try to see some of the sights inside Naples. If you're hard-pressed for time, then settle for the first three museums of renown.

THE TOP ATTRACTIONS

Reconfirm any museum hours before going there. A book issued annually can't keep up with the changes—they've been known to change from month to month, depending on how much or how little money is in the city treasury.

✪ Museo Archeologico Nazionale

Piazza Museo 18–19. ☎ **440166.** Admission 8,000 lire ($5) adults, 4,000 lire ($2.50) children 18 and under. June–Aug Tues–Sat 9am–7pm, Sun 9am–1pm; Sept–May Tues–Sat 9am–2pm, Sun 9am–1pm. Metropolitana: Piazza Cavour.

With its Roman and Greek sculpture, this museum contains one of the most valuable archaeological collections in Europe—the select Farnese acquisitions are notable in particular, as are mosaics and sculpture excavated at Pompeii and Herculaneum. The building dates from the 16th century, and was turned into a museum some two centuries later by Charles and Ferdinand IV Bourbon.

On the ground floor is one of the treasures of the Farnese collections: The nude statues of Armodio and Aristogitone are the most outstanding in the room. A famous bas-relief (from an original of the 5th century B.C.) in a nearby salon depicts Orpheus and his wife, Eurydice, with Mercury.

The nude statue of the spear-bearing *Doryphorus*, copied from a work by Polyclitus the Elder and excavated at Pompeii, enlivens another room. Also see the gigantic but weary *Hercules*, a statue of remarkable boldness; it's a copy of an original by Lysippus, the 4th-century B.C. Greek sculptor for Alexander the Great, and was discovered in the Baths of Caracalla in Rome. On a more delicate pedestal is the decapitated but exquisite *Venus* (Aphrodite). The *Psyche of Capua* shows why Aphrodite was jealous. The *Group of the Farnese Bull* presents a pageant of violence from the days of antiquity. A copy of either a 2nd- or 3rd-century B.C. Hellenistic statue—one of the most frequently reproduced of all sculptures—it was also discovered at the Baths of Caracalla. The marble group depicts a scene in the legend of Amphion and Zethus, who tied Dirce, wife of Lycus of Thebes, to the horns of a rampaging bull. After this, you'll have seen the best of the works on this floor.

The galleries on the mezzanine are devoted to mosaics excavated from Pompeii and Herculaneum. These include scenes of cock fights, dragon-tailed satyrs, an aquarium, and the finest one of all, *Alexander Fighting the Persians.*

On the top floor are some of the celebrated bronzes, which were dug out of the Pompeii and Herculaneum lava and volcanic mud. Of particular interest is a

Hellenistic portrait of Berenice, a comically drunken satyr, a statue of a *Sleeping Satyr*, and *Mercury on a Rock*.

✪ Museo e Gallerie Nazionali di Capodimonte

Parco di Capodimonte (off Amedeo di Savoia), via Milano 1. ☎ **7441307**. Admission 8,000 lire ($5) adults, free for children 18 and under. July–Sept Tues–Sat 9am–7:30pm, Sun 9am–1pm; Oct–June Tues–Sat 9am–2pm, Sun 9am–1pm. Bus: 110 or 127 from the rail station.

The gallery and museum are in the 18th-century Palace of Capodimonte (built in the time of Charles III), which stands in a park. It houses one of Italy's finest picture galleries (an elevator takes visitors to the top floor).

On display are seven Flemish tapestries, which were made according to the designs of Bernart van Orley, and show grand-scale scenes from the Battle of Pavia (1525), in which the forces of Francis I of France—more than 25,000 strong—lost to those of Charles V. Van Orley, who lived in a pre-*Guernica* day, obviously didn't consider war a horror, but a romantic ballet.

One of the pinacoteca's greatest possessions is Simone Martini's *Coronation* scene, which depicts the brother of Robert of Anjou being crowned king of Naples by the bishop of Toulouse. You'll want to linger over the great Masaccio's *Crucifixion*, a bold expression of grief. The most important room is literally filled with the works of Renaissance masters, notably an *Adoration of the Child* by Luca Signorelli, a *Madonna and Child* by Perugino, a panel by Raphael, a *Madonna and Child with Angels* by Botticelli, and—the most beautiful of all—Fillipino Lippi's *Annunciation and Saints*.

Look for Andrea Mantegna's *St. Eufemia* and his portrait of Francesco Gonzaga, his brother-in-law Giovanni Bellini's *Transfiguration*, and Lotto's *Portrait of Bernardo de Rossi* and his *Madonna and Child with St. Peter*.

In one room is Raphael's *Holy Family and St. John*, and a copy of his celebrated portrait of Pope Leo X. Two choice sketches include Raphael's *Moses* and Michelangelo's *Three Soldiers*. Displayed farther on are the Titians, with Danae taking the spotlight from Pope Paul III.

Another room is devoted to Flemish art: Pieter Brueghel's *Blind Men* is an outstanding work, and his *Misanthope* is devilishly powerful. Other foreign works include Joos van Cleve's *Adoration of the Magi*. You can climb the stairs for a panoramic view of Naples and the bay, a finer landscape than any you'll see inside.

The state apartments downstairs deserve inspection. Room after room is devoted to gilded mermaids, Venetian sedan chairs, ivory carvings, a porcelain chinoiserie salon (the best of all), tapestries, the Farnese armory, and a large glass and china collection.

Museo Nazionale di San Martino

Largo San Martino 5 (in the Vómero residential district). ☎ **5781769**. Admission 6,000 lire ($3.75) adults, free for children 17 and under. Tues–Sat 9am–2pm, Sun 9am–1pm. Bus: 49 or 42. Funicular: Centrale from via Toledo.

Magnificently situated on the grounds of the Castel Sant'Elmo, this museum was founded in the 14th century as a Carthusian monastery, but fell into decay until the 17th century, when it was reconstructed by architects in the Neapolitan baroque style. Now a museum for the city of Naples, it displays stately carriages, historical documents, ship replicas, china and porcelain, silver, Campagna paintings of the 19th century, military costumes and armor, and the lavishly adorned crib by Cuciniello. A balcony opens onto a panoramic view of Naples and the bay, as well as Vesuvius and Capri. Many come to the museum just to stand on this belvedere in space and drink in the view. The colonnaded cloisters have curious skull sculpture on the inner balustrade.

MORE ATTRACTIONS

Palazzo Reale (Royal Palace)

Piazza del Plebiscito 1. ☎ **413888.** Admission 6,000 lire ($3.75) adults, free for children 17 and under. Tues–Sat 9am–1:30pm, Sun 9am–1pm. Tram: 1 or 4.

This palace was designed by Domenico Fontana in the 17th century. The eight statues on the facade are of Neapolitan kings. Located in the heart of the city, the square is one of the most architecturally interesting in Naples, with a long colonnade and a church, San Francesco di Paolo, that evokes the style of the Pantheon in Rome. Inside the Palazzo Reale you can visit the royal apartments, lavishly and ornately adorned in the baroque style with colored marble floors, paintings, tapestries, frescoes, antiques, and porcelain. Charles de Bourbon, son of Philip IV of Spain, became king of Naples in 1734. A great patron of the arts, he installed a library in the Royal Palace, one of the greatest of the south, with more than 1,250,000 volumes.

Castel Nuovo (New Castle)

Piazza del Municipo. Admission 5,000 lire ($3.15). Mon–Fri 9am–2pm; Sat 9am–1pm. Tram: 1 or 4.

The New Castle, which houses municipal offices, was built in the late 13th century on orders from Charles I, king of Naples, as a royal residence for the House of Anjou. It was badly ruined, and virtually rebuilt in the mid-15th century by the House of Aragon. The castle is distinguished by a trio of three round imposing battle towers at its front. Between two of the towers, and guarding the entrance, is an arch of triumph designed by Francesco Laurana to commemorate the expulsion of the Angevins by the forces of Alphonso I in 1442. It has been described by art historians as a masterpiece of the Renaissance. The Palatine Chapel in the center dates from the 14th century, and the city commission of Naples meets in the Barons' Hall, designed by Segreta of Catalonia.

In the castle some frescoes and sculptures (of minor interest) from the 14th and 15th centuries are displayed.

Castel dell'Ovo (Castle of the Egg)

☎ **7645688.** Follow via Console along the seafront from piazza del Plebiscito to the port of Santa Lucia; Castel dell'Ovo is at the end of the promontory there. Tram: 1 or 4.

This 2,000-year-old fortress overlooks the Gulf of Naples. The site of the castle was important centuries before the birth of Christ, and was fortified by early settlers. In time, a major stronghold to guard the bay was erected and duly celebrated by Virgil. In one epoch of its long history, it served as a state prison. The view from here is panoramic. It's not open to the public except for special exhibits.

Acquario

Villa Comunale 1, via Caracciolo. ☎ **5833111.** Admission 3,000 lire ($1.90) adults, 1,500 lire (95¢) children. Mar–Oct, Tues–Sat 9am–5pm, Sun 10am–6pm; Nov–Feb, Tues–Sat 9am-5pm, Sun 9am–2pm. Tram: 1 or 4.

The Aquarium is in a municipal park, Villa Comunale, between via Caracciolo and the Riviera di Chiaia. Established by a German naturalist in the 1800s, the Aquarium is the oldest in Europe. It is said to display about 200 species of marine plants and fish, all found in the Bay of Naples (they must be a hardy lot).

Naples

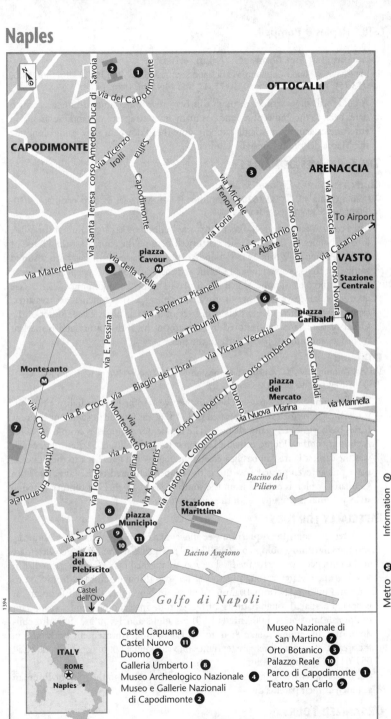

Castel Capuana ⑥
Castel Nuovo ⑪
Duomo ⑤
Galleria Umberto I ⑧
Museo Archeologico Nazionale ④
Museo e Gallerie Nazionali
  di Capodimonte ②

Museo Nazionale di
  San Martino ⑦
Orto Botanico ③
Palazzo Reale ⑩
Parco di Capodimonte ①
Teatro San Carlo ⑨

ITALY
ROME
Naples •

Information ⓘ

Metro Ⓜ

Catacombs of San Gennaro (St. Januarius)

In the Chiesa del Buon Consiglio, via di Capodimonte 16. ☎ **7411071.** Admission 5,000 lire ($3.15). Tours Fri–Sun at 9:30, 10:15, 11, and 11:45am. Tram: 1 or 4.

A guide will show visitors through this two-story underground cemetery, which dates back to the 2nd century and has many interesting frescoes and mosaics. You enter the catacombs on via di Capodimonte (head down an alley going alongside the Madre del Buon Consiglio Church).

THE CHURCHES OF NAPLES

Church of Santa Chiara (Clare)

Via Santa Chiara 49. ☎ **5526209.** Admission is free. Mon–Sat 8:30am–noon and 4:30–6:30pm; Sun 8:30am–noon. Tram: 1 or 4.

On a palazzo-flanked street, this church was built on orders from Robert the Wise, king of Naples, in the early 14th century. It became the church for the House of Anjou. Although World War II bombers heavily blasted it, it has been restored somewhat to its original look, a Gothic style as practiced by Provençal architects. The altarpiece by Simone Martini is displayed at the Capodimonte Galleries (see above), which leave the Angevin royal sarcophagi as the principal art treasures, especially the tomb of King Robert in back of the main altar. The Cloister of the Order of the Clares was restored by Vaccaro in the 18th century and is marked by ornate adornment, particularly in the tiles.

Il Duomo

Via del Duomo 147. ☎ **449097.** Admission is free. Daily 7:30am–12:30pm and 4:30–7:30pm. Metropolitana: Piazza Cavour.

The Duomo of Naples may not be as impressive as some in other Italian cities, but it is visited nevertheless. Consecrated in 1315, it was Gothic in style, but the centuries have witnessed many changes. The facade, for example, is from the 1800s. A curiosity of the Duomo is that it has access to the Basilica of St. Restituta, which was the earliest Christian basilica erected in Naples and goes back to the 4th century. But an even greater treasure is the chapel dedicated to St. Januarius (San Gennaro), which is entered from the south aisle. In a rich 17th-century baroque style, it contains ampullae with the saint's blood.

ESPECIALLY FOR KIDS

Children can enjoy the **Aquarium** (see above) in a city park called Villa Comunale, and the **Giardino Zoologico** (☎ 5833111), which is in the Mostra d'Oltremare at the entrance to viale Kennedy. The zoo, established by a German naturalist in 1873, is open March through October, Tuesday through Saturday, from 9am to 5pm and on Sunday from 10am to 6pm. From November through February, it is open Tuesday through Saturday, from 9am to 5pm and on Sunday from 9am to 2pm. Admission is 3,000 lire ($1.90) for adults and 1,500 lire (95¢) for children. And, to cap it off, take them to the **Edenlandia Amusement Park,** also in the area of Mostra d'Oltremare (entrance on viale Kennedy). It's open all year. Call 081/611182 for information.

In the Naples area, children delight in wandering through the ruins of **Pompeii** as much as their parents do.

ORGANIZED TOURS

If you want to visit points of interest in the environs, and don't relish the prospect of driving yourself around in difficult traffic or depending on public transportation, you can take a guided tour. The most popular jaunts are to Pompeii, but you can also take a hydrofoil to Capri. Sometimes lunch is included in these tours; at other times it is extra. Some tours are offered year round, although all travel agencies feature their full program only from June through September. Prices tend to be standardized from agency to agency. The most complete tours and services are offered by **CIT,** piazza Municipio 72 (☎ 5545426), with a branch office at Stazione Marittima (☎ 5522960). Hours are Monday through Friday from 9am to 1pm and 2:30pm to 6pm.

WHERE TO STAY

With some exceptions, the accommodations in Naples are a sad lot. Most of the large hotels are in the popular (also dangerous) district of Santa Lucia. Many of the so-called first-class establishments line via Partenope along the water. In and around the central railway station are other clusters, many built in the late 1950s (and some that seemingly haven't been changed since that faraway time).

Regardless of the price range in which you travel, there's a bed waiting for you in Naples. Regrettably, that bed often isn't clean or comfortable. I'll present a selection of what are generally conceded to be the "best" hotels in Naples, but know that with an exception or two, none of the other candidates leaves me with much enthusiasm. Many of the innkeepers I've encountered seem an indifferent lot.

EXPENSIVE

Grande Albergo Vesuvio
Via Partenope 45, 80121 Napoli. ☎ **081/7640044** or 800/223-6800 in the U.S. Fax 081/ 7640044. 167 rms, 16 suites. A/C MINIBAR TV TEL. 390,000 lire ($243.75) double; from 650,000 lire ($406.25) suite. Rates include breakfast. AE, DC, MC, V. Parking 30,000 lire ($18.75). Bus: 102, 112, 128, or 140.

Originally built in 1882, the Vesuvio was restored about 50 years later and features a marble- and stucco-sheathed facade evocative of art deco. When it was constructed, it was the first and foremost hotel along the fabled bay, and many aristocratic members of English society flocked here. Curved balconies extend toward the Castel dell'Ovo (the Castle of the Egg). The overhauled hotel remains one of the best in Naples. Today, each of its rooms has a lofty ceiling, rich cove moldings, parquet floors, a renovated tiled bathroom with lots of space, and large closets. You'll also find a scattering of antiques throughout the echoing hallways.

Dining/Entertainment: The hotel also has a first-class restaurant, Caruso; a roof garden; and a comfortable bar that evokes the most stylish decor of the 1950s. Meals begin at 60,000 lire ($37.50).

Hotel Excelsior
Via Partenope 48, 80121 Napoli. ☎ **081/7640111** or 800/325-3535 in the U.S. and Canada. Fax 081/7649743. 124 rms, 12 suites. A/C MINIBAR TV TEL. 335,000–370,000 lire ($209.40–$231.25) double; 600,000–1,000,000 lire ($375–$625) suite. Breakfast 25,000–39,000 lire ($15.65–$24.40) extra. AE, DC, MC, V. Parking 28,000–32,000 lire ($17.50–$20). Tram: 1 or 4.

The Excelsior is situated in a most dramatic position right on the waterfront, with views of Santa Lucia and Vesuvius. It has been restored and refurbished. There are many elegant details, such as Venetian chandeliers, Doric columns, wall-size murals, and bronze torchiers. This same taste prevails in the bedrooms, where Oriental rugs blend with tradtional elements. Most of them are, in reality, bed/ sitting rooms. Each room contains a well-maintained private bath.

Dining/Entertainment: When you dine at the Excelsior, expect to pay 70,000 lire ($43.75) and up for a meal. The cuisine is both Neapolitan and international. Breakfast can be ordered on a covered roof terrace.

Services: Room service, babysitting, laundry, valet.

Facilities: 24-hour garage, solarium.

MODERATE

Grand Hotel Parker's

Corso Vittorio Emanuele 135, 80121 Napoli. ☎ **081/7612474.** Fax 081/663527. 73 rms, 10 suites. A/C TV TEL. 290,000–330,000 lire ($181.25–$206.25) double; from 750,000 lire ($468.75) suite. Rates include breakfast. AE, DC, MC, V. Parking 20,000 lire ($12.50). Bus: 118, 120, or 128.

The hotel sits up and away from the harbor commotion, and many guests check in just to enjoy the view of Naples from its window. Some even maintain that Naples looks much better from this perch than it does when you get down into its teeming life. This gracious accommodation on one of the better hillside avenues of Naples was built in 1870. It has now been fully restored, and once again has reclaimed its position as one of the finest hotels in Naples. It was created when architects cared about the beauty of their work—neoclassic walls, fluted pilasters, and ornate ceilings. Bedrooms are traditionally furnished, some quite formal. Naturally, all guests try for a "room with a view."

Dining/Entertainment: Its roof garden restaurant offers a fine view of Naples and the bay. An international Mediterranean cuisine is served here Monday through Saturday, with meals beginning at 50,000 lire ($31.25).

Services: Laundry, valet, babysitting, room service.

Facilities: Foreign-currency exchange, business center.

✪ Hotel Britannique

Corso Vittorio Emanuele 133, 80121 Napoli. ☎ **081/7614145.** Fax 081/669760. 88 rms, 10 suites. A/C TV TEL. 250,000 lire ($156.25) double; from 320,000 lire ($200) suite. Breakfast 15,000 lire ($9.40) extra. AE, DC, MC, V. Parking 15,000–30,000 lire ($9.40–$18.75). Bus: 118, 120, or 128.

This remake of a former aristocratic villa has a hillside view of the Bay of Naples. The Britannique is on the curve of a wide hillside boulevard, away from the harbor; it has a panoramic view of the harbor from a distance. Furnishings and carpets are sober but elegant, and each room contains some antiques. The hotel also has a garden blooming with tropical flowers and plants. Guests gather for drinks in the cocktail lounge and bar in the Louis XVI style. The hotels restaurant specializes in a continental cuisine, and in summer guests can order meals on the roof terrace.

Hotel Majestic

Largo Vasto a Chiaia 68, 80121 Napoli. ☎ **081/416500.** Fax 081/416500. 129 rms, 6 junior suites. MINIBAR TV TEL. 270,000 lire ($168.75) double; 300,000–450,000 lire ($187.50–$281.25) suite. Rates include breakfast. AE, DC, MC, V. Parking 22,000 lire ($13.75). Metrpolitana: Piazza Amedo.

This is one of Naples's finest four-star hotels. Built in 1959 on 10 floors, this renovated hotel is now one of the most up-to-date hostelries in a city too often filled with decaying mansions. A favorite with the conference crowd, it lies in the antiques district of Naples—at your doorstep will be dozens of fashionable boutiques. Reservations are important, as this hotel is often fully booked. There's a cozy American bar and a restaurant, Magic Grill, which serves both Neapolitan dishes and international specialties Monday through Saturday. Since the garage is so small, its better to reserve space at the time you book your room.

Hotel Miramare

Via Nazario Saura 24, 80132 Napoli. ☎ **081/7647589.** Fax 081/7640775. 31 rms. A/C MINIBAR TV TEL. 240,000–290,000 lire ($150–$181.25) double. Rates include breakfast. AE, DC, MC, V. Parking 25,000–35,000 lire ($15.65–$21.90). Bus: 106 or 150.

In a superb location, seemingly thrust out toward the harbor on a dockside boulevard, the Miramare is central and sunny. Originally the hotel was an aristocratic villa, but in 1944 it was transformed into a hotel after serving for a short period as the American consulate. At the end of World War II, it was the only hotel in Naples, as the others had been damaged by the war. Its lobby evokes a little Caribbean hotel, with a semitropical look. The bedrooms have been renovated, and now are pleasantly furnished and well maintained by the management. Bedrooms have soundproof windows to protect against the traffic noise outside. On the premises is an American bar, a restaurant-tavern, and a roof garden.

Hotel Paradiso

Via Catullo 11, 80122 Napoli. ☎ **081/7614161,** or 800/528-1234 in the U.S. Fax 081/7613449. 71 rms, 2 suites. A/C MINIBAR TV TEL. 260,000 lire ($162.50) double; from 350,000 lire ($218.75) suite. Rates include breakfast. AE, DC, MC, V. Parking 24,000 lire ($15). Bus: 23, 106, or 140.

This hotel might be paradise, but only after you reach it. If you arrive at the central station and head for this address in the Posillipo section, the distance is some $3^1/2$ miles. One irate driver claimed that it took about the same amount of time— $3^1/2$ hours, that is—to reach this address. Once there, however, your nerves are soothed by the view, one of the most panoramic of any hotel in Italy. The Bay of Naples unfolds before you, and in the distance Mount Vesuvius looms menacingly. On a clear day you can even see the promontory of Sorrento. The hotel is one of the best in Naples, with well-furnished and comfortably equipped bedrooms. When you take your breakfast, you may want to linger here before facing the traffic of Naples again.

Should you elect not to go out at night, you can patronize the fine restaurant at the Paradiso, which serves both Neapolitan and Italian specialties, with meals beginning at 43,000 lire ($26.90).

Hotel Royal

Via Partenope 38, 80121 Napoli. ☎ **081/7644800.** Fax 081/7645707. 273 rms, 14 suites. A/C MINIBAR TV TEL. 230,000–340,000 lire ($143.75–$212.50) double; 560,000 lire ($350) suite. Rates include breakfast. AE, DC, MC, V. Parking 26,000 lire ($16.25). Bus: 106, 140, or 150.

Hotel Royal, built in 1955, is in a desirable location on this busy street, which runs beside the bay in Santa Lucia. You park in an underground garage, then enter a greenery-filled vestibule, where the stairs that lead to the modern lobby are flanked by a pair of stone lions. Each of the bedrooms has a balcony and contemporary furniture. Some, but not all, offer a water view. A seawater pool with an adjacent flower-dotted sun terrace is on the hotel's roof.

Hotel Santa Lucia

Via Partenope 46, 80121 Napoli. ☎ **081/7640666.** Fax 081/7648580. 95 rms, 12 suites. A/C MINIBAR TV TEL. 250,000–320,000 lire ($156.25–$200) double; from 380,000 lire ($237.50) suite. Rates include breakfast. AE, DC, MC, V. Parking 25,000 lire ($15.65). Tram: 1 or 4.

Santa Lucia's imposing neoclassical facade overlooks a sheltered marina that extends off the Bay of Naples. From the windows of about half the bedrooms you can watch motorboats and yachts bobbing at anchor, fishermen repairing nets, and all the waterside life that Naples is famous for. The interior has undergone extensive renovations, and is decorated in a family-conscious Neapolitan style, with terrazzo floors, and lots of upholstered chairs scattered throughout the lobby. The bedrooms are large and high-ceilinged, with French doors that open onto tiny verandas. The noisier rooms overlook the traffic of via Santa Lucia. There's an American-inspired bar on the premises plus the Restaurant Jardin, serving a superb Mediterranean cuisine.

INEXPENSIVE

Albergo San Germano

Via Beccadelli 41, 80125 Napoli. ☎ **081/570-5422** or 800/528-1234 in the U.S. Fax 081/570-1546. 104 rms. A/C MINIBAR TV TEL. 200,000–230,000 lire ($125–$143.75) double. Rates include breakfast. AE, DC, MC, V. Free parking. Bus: 102 or 152.

Designed like an Italian version of a Chinese pagoda, this brick-and-concrete hotel is ideal for late-arriving motorists who are reluctant to negotiate the traffic of Naples. A terraced swimming pool and garden are welcome respites after a day in Naples. The hotel's bedrooms are clean, and each has a tile bath. The hotel serves meals only to residents. There is a lobby bar, along with a modern restaurant.

From the autostrada, follow the signs to Tangenziale Napoli (toward Napoli); exit eight miles later at Agnano Terme. After paying the toll, drive less than a mile toward Naples, where you'll see the hotel on your right. You can park your car here and take bus no. 102 or 152 into the center of Naples, a distance of about four miles.

Hotel Rex

Via Palepoli 12, 80132 Napoli. ☎ **081/764-9389.** Fax 081/764-9227. 40 rms. A/C TV TEL. 160,000 lire ($100) double. Rates include breakfast. AE, DC, V. Parking 30,000 lire ($18.75). Bus: 106 or 150.

The most famous budget hotel in Santa Lucia, Hotel Rex has played host to lira-watchers around the world since its opening in 1938. Some like it and others don't (the mail tends to be mixed). Nevertheless, proof of its popularity is that its bedrooms are often fully booked when other hotels have many vacancies. The building itself is lavishly ornate architecturally, but the bedrooms are simple. Breakfast is the only meal served.

Hotel Serius

Viale Augusto 74, 80125 Napoli. ☎ **081/239-4844.** Fax 081/239-4844. 69 rms. A/C MINIBAR TV TEL. 165,000 lire ($103.15) double. Rates include breakfast. AE, MC, V. Free parking. Tram: 1 or 4. Bus: 144, 150, or 152.

Built in 1974 to provide well-organized comfort, this hotel is on a palm-lined street of a relatively calm neighborhood known as Fuorigrotto, lying a short bus ride north of the center. The paneled split-level lobby contains an intimate bar and several metal sculptures of horses and birds. The bedrooms are simply furnished with boldly patterned fabrics and painted furniture. In addition to the bar, there's a pleasant, contemporary dining room.

WHERE TO DINE

A mixed reaction. Naples is the home of pizza and spaghetti. If you're mad for either of those items, then you'll delight in sampling the authentic versions.

However, if you like subtle cooking and have an aversion to olive oil or garlic, you won't fare as well.

One of the major problems is overcharging. It's not uncommon for four foreign visitors to have a dinner in a Naples restaurant, particularly those once-famous ones in Santa Lucia, and be billed for five dinners. Service in many restaurants tends to be poor. Again, as in the hotels, I will attempt to pick out the best of the lot.

EXPENSIVE

✪ Giuseppone a Mare
Via Ferdinando Russo 13. ☎ **5756002**. Reservations required. Main courses 28,000–34,000 lire ($17.50–$21.25). AE, DC, MC, V. Mon–Sat 12:30–3:30pm and 8–midnight. Closed Dec 23–31 and Aug 9–15. Bus: 140. SEAFOOD.

Here you can dine in Neapolitan sunshine on an open-air terrace with a view of the bay. The restaurant at Capo Posillipo is known for serving the best and the freshest seafood in Campania. Diners make their selections from a trolley in the center of the dining room, which is likely to include everything from crabs to eels. You might precede your fish dinner with some antipasti, such as fritters (a batter whipped up with seaweed and fresh squash blossoms). Naturally, there is linguine with clams, a dish familiar enough in restaurants in North America, except that the chef here adds squid and mussels. Much of the day's catch is deep-fried a golden brown. The pièce de résistance is an octopus casserole (try it if you dare!). If the oven's going, you can also order a pizza. Some fine southern Italian wines are served too, especially those from Ischia and Vesuvio.

✪ La Cantinella
Via Cuma 42. ☎ **7648684**. Reservations required. Main courses 35,000–42,000 lire ($21.90–$26.25). AE, DC, MC, V. Mon–Sat 12:30–3pm and 7:30pm–midnight. Closed Dec 24–Jan 6 and Aug 13–31. Tram: 1 or 4. Bus: 106 or 140. SEAFOOD.

You get the impression of Chicago in the 1920s as you approach this place, and speakeasy-style doors open after you ring. The restaurant is on a busy street that skirts the bay in Santa Lucia, with a terrace overlooking the sea. Inside, you'll find a well-stocked antipasto table and—get this—a phone on each table. The menu includes four different preparations of risotto (including one with champagne), many kinds of pasta (including penne with vodka, and linguine with scampi and seafood), and most of the classic beef and veal dishes of Italy. Best known for its fish, Cantinella serves grilled seafood at its finest.

MODERATE

Don Salvatore
Strada Mergellina 4A. ☎ **681817**. Reservations recommended. Main courses 19,000–29,000 lire ($11.90–$18.15). AE, DC, MC, V. Thurs–Tues 1–4pm and 8pm–1am. Metropolitana: Mergellina. SEAFOOD.

This is no simple, lowly pizzeria, but the creative statement of a serious restaurateur, who directs his waterfront establishment with passion and dedication. Antonio Aversano takes his wine as seriously as his food. The latter is likely to include linguine with shrimp or with squid, or a linguine facetiously named "Cosa Nostra," another name for the Mafia. There's also an array of fish served daily, along with a marvelous assortment of fresh Neapolitan vegetables grown in the surrounding countryside. Fish dishes are priced according to weight based on daily market quotations. Rice comes flavored in a delicate fish broth, and you can get a reasonably priced bottle from the wine cellar, said to be the finest in Campania. The location is on the seafront near the departure point of hydrofoils for Capri.

Il Gallo Nero

Via Torquato Tasso 466. ☎ **643012.** Reservations recommended. Main courses 18,000–32,000 lire ($11.25–$20). AE, DC, MC, V. Sun 12:30–3pm; Tues–Sat 7pm–midnight. Closed Aug. Metropolitana: Mergellina. PASTA/NEAPOLITAN.

Dinner here is almost like a throwback to the mid-19th century. Gian Paolo Quagliata is the owner who, with a capable staff, maintains the hillside villa with its period furniture and accessories. In summer, the enthusiastic clientele is served on an elegant outdoor terrace. Many of the dishes are based on 100-year-old recipes from the classical Neapolitan repertoire, although a few are more recent inventions of the chef himself. You might enjoy the Neapolitan linguine with pesto, rigatoni with fresh vegetables, tagliatelle primavera, or macaroni with peas and artichokes. Fish dishes are usually well prepared, whether grilled, broiled, or sautéed. Meat dishes include slightly more exotic creations such as prosciutto with orange slices, veal cutlets with artichokes, and a savory array of beef dishes.

La Sacrestia

Via Orazio 116. ☎ **7611051.** Reservations required. Main courses 18,000–28,000 lire ($11.25–$17.50). AE, DC, MC, V. Tues–Sat 12:30–4:30pm and 7:40–11:30pm. Closed two weeks in Aug; closes Sun (not Mon) in July–Aug. Funicular: From Mergel-lina. PASTA/SEAFOOD.

The trompe-l'oeil frescoes in this establishment's two-story interior, as well as the name La Sacrestia, vaguely suggest something ecclesiastical. But that's not the case here. Reputed to be the best restaurant in Naples, La Sacrestia is a bustling place, sometimes called "the greatest show in town." It's perched near the top of one of the belvederes of Naples, and is reached by going along a seemingly endless labyrinth of winding streets from the port. In summer, an outdoor terrace with its flowering arbor provides seating with a view over the lights of the harbor. Meals emphasize well-prepared dishes, often with strong doses of Neapolitan drama. You might, for example, try what is said to be the most luxurious macaroni dish in Italy ("Prince of Naples"), concocted with truffles and mild cheeses. The fettuccine alla Gran Caruso is made from fresh peas, mushrooms, prosciutto, and tongue. Less ornate selections include a full array of pastas and dishes composed of octopus, squid, and shellfish. Main courses include carpaccio and veal. Food is served "until the last diner finishes." The place is best reached by taxi.

Rosolino

Via Nazario Sauro 5–7. ☎ **7640547.** Reservations required. Main courses 12,000–18,000 lire ($7.50–$11.25). AE, DC, MC, V. Mon–Sat 12:30–3:30pm and 8pm–midnight. Tram: 1 or 4. SEAFOOD.

This stylish, place is not defined as a nightclub by its owners, but rather as a restaurant with dancing. Set on the waterfront, it's divided into two distinct areas; there's a piano bar near the entrance, where you might have a drink before passing into a much larger dining room. There, in interiors ringed with stained glass set into striking patterns, you can dine within sight of a bandstand reminiscent of the Big Band era. Live music is offered only on Saturday night. Dishes include rigatoni with zucchini and meat sauce, an impressive array of fresh shellfish, and such beef dishes as tournedos and veal scaloppine. Most fresh fish is priced according to weight. There are three different wine lists, including one for French wines and champagne.

INEXPENSIVE

Dante e Beatrice

Piazza Dante 44–45. ☎ **5499438.** Reservations recommended. Main courses 10,000–21,000 lire ($6.25–$13.15). No credit cards. Tues–Sun 12:30–3:30pm and 7:30–11pm. Closed Aug 15–30. Tram: 1 or 4. NEAPOLITAN.

Gregarious and unpretentious, and named after the players in one of the great romantic tragedies of the Renaissance, Dante e Beatrice was established in 1956 and remains one of the best restaurants in its neighborhood. Specializing in all the staples of the Neapolitan cuisine, it serves simple, flavorful, and filling portions of lasagne, minestrone, spaghetti with clams, tagliatelle, pasta fagiole, and grilled fish to the many workday clients who seek this place out.

Ristorante la Fazenda

Via Marechiaro 58A. ☎ **5757420.** Reservations required. Main courses 15,000–28,000 lire ($9.40–$17.50). AE, V. Tues–Sat 1–4pm; Mon–Sat 7:30pm–12:30am. Closed Aug 12–18. SEAFOOD.

It would be hard to find a more typically Neapolitan restaurant than this one, offering a panoramic view that on a clear day can include the island of Capri. The decor is rustic, loaded with agrarian touches and filled with an assortment of Neapolitan families, lovers, and visitors who have made it one of their preferred dining locales since it opened in 1973. In summer the overflow from the dining room spills onto the terrace. Menu speciaties include linguine with scampi, an array of fresh grilled fish, sautéed clams, a mixed Italian grill, several savory stews, and many chicken dishes, along with lobster with fresh grilled tomatoes.

ⓢ Umberto

Via Alabardieri 30. ☎ **418555.** Reservations required. Main courses 10,000–22,000 lire ($6.25–$13.75). AE, DC, V. Thurs–Tues 12:30–3:30pm and 7:30–10:30pm. Closed Aug. Bus: 106 or 150. NEAPOLITAN.

Located off piazza dei Martiri, Umberto might be one of the most atmospheric places to dine in all of Naples. The tasteful dining room has been directed for many a year by the same interconnected family. There's likely to be an evening dance band playing. The excellent Italian specialties served here include pizzas, gnocchi with potatoes, and grilled meats and fishes, as well as savory stews and a host of pasta dishes. The bel canto era lives on here.

ⓢ Vini e Cucina

Corso Vittorio Emanuele 761. ☎ **660302.** Reservations not accepted. Main courses 10,000–12,000 lire ($6.25–$7.50). No credit cards. Mon–Sat noon–4:30pm and 7pm–midnight. Closed Aug. Metropolitana: Mergellina.

The best ragú sauce in all of Naples is said to be made at this trattoria, which has only 10 tables and is known for its home-cookery. You can get a really satisfying meal here, but I must warn you—it's almost impossible to get in. Dedicated diners might do as I do: arrive early and wait for a table. The cooking is the best home-style version of the Neapolitan cuisine we have been able to find in this tricky city. The spaghetti, along with that fabulous sauce, is served *al dente*. The restaurant is in front of the Mergellina station.

A HISTORIC PIZZERIA

ⓢ Brandi

Via Miano 27–29. ☎ **7410455.** Reservations required. Main courses 9,000–20,000 lire ($5.65–$12.50). No credit cards. Tues–Sun noon–3pm and 6:30pm–midnight. Tram: 1 or 4. NEAPOLITAN.

A Sweet Shop

Giovanni Scaturchio, at piazza San Domenico Maggiore 19 (☎ 5516944), offers the most caloric collection of pastries in Naples, and is famous for both satisfying and fattening local residents since around 1900. Representative pastries include the entire selection of Neapolitan sweets, cakes, and candies, including brioches soaked in liqueur, pound cake (cassate) filled with layered ricotta, Moor's heads, and cheesy-ricotta pastries known as sfogliatelle, dear to the heart of most Neapolitans, who fondly remember them from childhood. Another specialty is ministeriale, a chocolate cake filled with liqueur and chocolate cream. There are tables where you can sit. Pastries cost from 1,600 lire ($1) if consumed standing up or from 3,500 lire ($2.20) if enjoyed at a table. It's open Monday and Wednesday through Sunday from 7:30am to 8:30pm.

Considered the most historic pizzeria in Italy, Brandi was established by Pietro Colicchio in the 19th century. His successor, Raffaele Esposito, who enjoyed the reputation that his hard work had earned, was requested one day to prepare a banquet for Margherita di Savoia, the queen of Italy. So successful was the reception of the pizza made with tomato, basil, olive oil, and mozzarella, that the queen accepted the honor of having it named after her. Thus was pizza Margherita born from the kitchens of Naples's Restaurant Brandi.

Today you can order the pizza that pleased a queen, as well as such other specialties as linguine with scampi, fettuccine "Regina d'Italia," and a full array of seafood dishes.

SHOPPING

Naples is hardly the shopper's paradise that Milan, Venice, Florence, and Rome are. Nevertheless, there are some good buys here for the shopper willing to seek them out. The finest shopping area lies around **piazza dei Martiri** and along such streets as via dei Mille, via Calabritto, and via Chiaia. There's more commercial shopping between piazza Trieste e Trento and piazza Dante along **via Toledo/via Roma.**

Coral is much sought-after by collectors. Much of the coral is now sent to Naples from Thailand, but it's still shaped into amazing jewelry at one of the workrooms at Torre del Greco, on the outskirts of Naples, off the Naples–Pompeii highway. Cameos are also made there.

ANTIQUES

Arte Antica
Via Domenico Morelli 6. ☎ **7643704.**

Considered one of the finest antiques stores in Naples, Arte Antica has been at this address since 1900. The Falanga family, the owners, specialize in Italian antiques. Their speciality is the kind of florid and exquisitely detailed porcelain that has always been prized in Naples. Open Monday from 4 to 8pm; Tuesday through Saturday from 9:30am to 1:30pm and 4 to 8pm.

Salvatore Iermano
Via Domenico Morelli 30. ☎ **7643913.**

The speciality here is antiques, particularly antique versions of an art form prac-ticed in southern Italy for hundreds of years, the crèche. usually sold as a set of wood or terra-cotta figures that represent all the important characters at the birth of Jesus, they are sought-after as antiques. Open Monday from 4:30 to 8pm and Tuesday through Saturday from 10am to 1:30pm and 4:30 to 8pm (closed Saturday afternoon in summer).

BOOKS

De Perro
Via dei Mille 17. ☎ **418687.**

Most of the books here are in Italian. Many deal with the art and architecture of southern Italy, with photographs that might be considered souvenirs in their own right. Open Monday through Friday from 9am to 1:30pm and 4:30 to 8pm, and Saturday from 9am to 1:30pm.

DEPARTMENT STORES

Coin
Via Alessandro Scarlatti 100. ☎ **5780111.**

Coin is a department store that's known to virtually everybody in Naples. It sells everything from housewares to clothing. Open Monday from 4:10 to 8pm and Tuesday through Saturday from 9:15am to 1:15pm and 4:10 to 8pm.

La Rinascente
Via Toledo 343. ☎ **411511.**

This is the Neapolitan branch of Italy's most interesting department-store chain. Open Monday from 4 to 7:45pm and Tuesday through Saturday from 9am to 1:30pm and 4 to 7:45pm.

FABRIC

La Tienda
Via dei Mille 63. ☎ **415249.**

La Tienda is one of the best-known fabric shops in Naples. If you've ever been tempted to take up sewing, you'll find all the tools you'll need right here. some of the fabrics are the same as those used by Italy's well-known designers. Open

---

A Grand Cafe

The decor of the **Gran Caffè Gambrinus,** via Chiaia 1 (☎ 417582), the oldest café in Naples, dating from 1860, would fit easily into a grand Bourbon palace. Along the vaulted ceiling of an inner room, Empire-style caryatids spread their togas in high relief above frescoes of mythological playmates. The café is known for its espresso and cappuccino, as well as pastries and cakes whose variety dazzles the eye. These pastries are probably the most famous in Naples. You can also order potato and rice croquettes and fried pizzas for a light lunch. Tea costs 3,500 lire ($2.20); cappuccino goes for 4,000 lire ($2.50) at a table. The café is open Wednesday through Monday from 7am to 11pm, although it remains open on Saturday until 1am. It's near the Galleria Umberto. Closed Aug 15–31.

Monday through Saturday from 9am to 1:30pm and 4:30 to 8pm (closed Monday morning in winter and Saturday afternoon in summer).

FASHION

Eddy Monetti
Piazza Santa Catarina 7. ☎ **403229.**

This is the women's branch of a fine clothing empire still owned by Signor Eddy Monetti. The men's branch, at via dei Mille 45 (☎ 407064), sells elegant men's clothing, well tailored and well selected. Both branches are open Monday from 4:30 to 8pm and Tuesday through Saturday from 9am to 1:30pm and 4:30 to 8pm.

Salvatore Balbi
Via Chiaia 258. ☎ **418551.**

Here you can get underwear, nightshirts, socks, and shirts for men, in a shop filled with colorfully artistic underwear displays, and crowds of women making their selections. Many of their garments, especially the bathrobes, are very elegant. Open Monday from 4:30 to 7pm and Tuesday through Saturday from 9am to 1:30pm and 4:30 to 7pm.

Stefanel
Via Chiaia 195. ☎ **407562.**

Stefanel sells fun and informal sports clothes and casual clothes in bright colors for women and men. Open Monday from 4 to 8pm and Tuesday through Saturday from 9am to 1:30pm and 4 to 8pm.

FOOD

Codrington & Co.
Via Chiaia 94. ☎ **418257.**

Codrington & Co. was founded about a century ago by a British family, and has a reputation in Naples as a purveyor of mostly English foodstuffs, sold and displayed from a briskly English-inspired shop near the Ponte di Chiaia. There are food and spices from throughout the world, as well as Devonshire marmalade, Stilton cheese, and old-fashioned chutney, but along with these edibles you'll find an array of small household objects, kitchen utensils, soap, and those gadgets that—once you discover them—you might not want to do without. Open Monday from 4:30 to 7:30pm and Tuesday through Saturday from 9am to 1:30pm and 4:30 to 7:30pm.

GIFTS

Bottega Della Carta
Via Cavallerizza a Chiaia 22–23. ☎ **421903.**

The specialty here is party supplies, carnival masks, and writing supplies, plus unusual gifts to take back home. Open Monday from 4:30 to 7:30pm and Tuesday through Saturday from 9am to 1:15pm and 4:30 to 7:30pm.

JEWELRY

Theo Brinkmann
Piazza Municipio 21. ☎ **5520555.**

Theo Brinkmann is one of the leading jewelers of Naples, a strictly local, Naples-based establishment with a long history and no other branches. Open Monday through Friday from 9am to 1:30pm and 4:30 to 8pm, and Saturday from 9am to 1:30pm.

Del Porto

Via Santa Lucia 165. ☎ **7640093**.

The specialty here is jewelry made from coral, much of which is carved into beautifully intricate designs. These include cameos, rings, necklaces, and ear ornaments. Open Monday through Friday from 9am to 1pm and 4:30 to 8pm, and Saturday from 9am to 1pm; closed in August.

LEATHER & SHOES

D'Aria

Via dei Mille 71. ☎ **415309**.

This is a large and well-stocked shoe outlet that sells Italian and other shoes for both men and women. Open Monday from 4:30 to 8pm and Tuesday through Saturday from 9am to 1:30pm and 4:30 to 8pm.

Salvatore Spatarella

Via Calabritto 1. ☎ **7643794**.

Here you can inspect a full array of well-made leather goods such as purses, luggage, shoes, handbags, and wallets. It's run by the Spatarella family, who also have a carefully selected array of women's clothing. Open Monday from 4:30 to 8pm and Tuesday through Saturday from 9:30am to 1:30pm and 4:30 to 8pm.

LINENS

D'Andrea

Via Santa Brigida 34. ☎ **5510621**.

D'Andrea is a well-stocked outlet for tablecloths, napkins, and towels, a few of which are hand-embroidered, though most are machine-made. The establishment also sells undergarments for men, women, and children. Open Monday from 4:30 to 8pm and Tuesday through Saturday from 9:30am to 1:30pm and 4:30 to 7:30pm.

NAPLES AFTER DARK

A sunset **walk through Santa Lucia** and along the waterfront never seems to dim in pleasure, even if you've lived in Naples for 40 years straight. Visitors are also fond of riding around town in one of the **carrozzelle (horse-drawn wagons)**.

Or you can stroll by the glass-enclosed **Galleria Umberto,** off via Roma in the vicinity of the Theater of San Carlo. The 19th-century gallery, which evokes many a memory for aging former G.I.s, is still standing today, although a little the worse for wear. It's a kind of social center for Naples. John Horne Burns used it for the title of his novel *The Gallery,* in which he wrote: "In August 1944, everyone in Naples sooner or later found his way into this place and became like a picture on the wall of the museum."

On its nightclub and cabaret circuit, Naples probably offers more sucker joints than any other port along the Mediterranean. If you're starved for action, you'll find plenty of it, and you're likely to end up paying for it dearly.

OPERA

Teatro San Carlo

Via San Carlo. ☎ **7972331**. Tickets, 20,000–175,000 lire ($12.50–$109.40). Box office Dec–June, Tues–Sun 10am–1pm and 4:30–6:30pm.

Across from the Galleria Umberto, this is one of the largest opera houses in Italy, with some of the best acoustics. Built in only six months time for King Charles's birthday in November 1737, it was restored in a gilded neoclassical style. Grand-scale productions are presented here on the main stage.

A NIGHTCLUB

Chez Moi

Via dei Parco Margherita 13. ☎ **407526**.

This is considered one of the city's best-managed nightclubs, with a strict policy of refusing entrance to anyone who looks like he or she might cause trouble inside. This is appreciated by the designers, government ministers, and visiting socialites who seem to enjoy the place. Clients tend to be over 25 years old, and have included the mayor of Naples. You'll be ushered to a table in an interior with a decor of soft blues and greens, where you'll order your first drink. This will cost 25,000 lire ($15.65). The place is open Friday through Sunday from 10:30pm until "as long as people continue to enjoy themselves." Occasionally the management will present a cabaret act or a live pianist at the bar, but more frequently the music is highly danceable disco.

A DISCO

Kiss Kiss

Via Sgambati 47. ☎ **5466566**. Cover 20,000 lire ($12.50) Fri and Sun; 25,000 lire ($15.65) Sat.

Kiss Kiss is huge—probably the largest disco in Naples. The youngish crowd, which is usually between 18 and 25, mingle and dance and generally have an uninhibited good time. If you tire of the human melee going on at the several bars or on the dance floor, you can watch video movies or videotaped rock concerts on one of several different screens. There's a restaurant and piano bar on the premises, called the Kiss Kiss Café, set up in a separate (and quieter) room. The place is open only on Friday and Saturday from 10pm to 3am and on Sunday from 8pm to 2am. The Friday-night crowd tends to be older and slightly more sedate.

2 The Environs of Naples

PHLAEGREAN FIELDS

One of the bizarre attractions of southern Italy, the Phlaegrean Fields (Campi Flegrei), as they are known, form a backdrop for a day's adventure of exploring west of Naples and along its bay. An explosive land of myth and legend, the fiery fields contain a semi-extinct volcano (Solfatara), the cave of the Cumaean Sibyl, Virgil's gateway to the "Infernal Regions," the ruins of thermal baths and amphitheaters built by the Romans, deserted colonies left by the Greeks—and lots more.

If you're depending on public transportation, the best center for exploring the area is **Pozzuoli,** which is reached by Metropolitana (subway) from the Stazione Centrale in Naples. The fare is 1,200 lire (75¢). Once in Pozzuoli, you can take one of the SEPSA buses at any bus stop, which will take you to places such as Baia

Impressions

The museum is full, as you know, of lovely Greek bronzes. The only bother is that they all walk about the town at night.

—Oscar Wilde, letter to Ernest Dowson, October 11, 1897

in 20 minutes. You can also go to Cumae on one of these buses, or to Solfatara or Lago d'Averno.

✪ SOLFATARA   About 7¹/₂ miles west of Naples, near Pozzuoli, is the ancient Vulcano Solfatara, via Solfatara 161 (☎ 5267413), the crater of Solfatara. It hasn't erupted since the final year of the 12th century, but it has been threatening ever since. It gives off sulfurous gases and releases scalding vapors through cracks in the earth's surface. In fact, the activity—or inactivity—of Solfatara has been observed for such a long time that the crater's name is used by Webster's dictionary to define any "dormant volcano" emitting vapors.

The crater may be visited daily from 8:30am to sunset, at a cost of 4,800 lire ($3) for adults, 2,700 lire ($1.70) for children. To reach it, take bus no. 152 from Naples or the Metropolitana line from the Stazione Centrale to Solfatara. Once you get off at the train station, you can board one of the city buses that go up the hill, or you can walk to the crater in about 20 minutes.

POZZUOLI   Located a mile and a half away from Solfatara, the seaport of Pozzuoli opens onto a gulf of the same name, and is screened from the Bay of Naples by a promontory. The ruins of the **Anfiteatro Flavio,** via Nicola Terracciano, built in the last part of the 1st century A.D., testify to past greatness. Considered one of the finest surviving examples of the arenas of antiquity, it is particularly distinguished by its "wings"—which, considering their age, are in good condition. You can see the remains where exotic beasts from Africa were caged before being turned loose in the ring to test their jungle skill against a gladiator. The amphitheater (☎ 5266007), which may be visited daily from 9am to 1 hour before sunset, is said to have entertained 40,000 spectators at the height of its glory. An admission fee of 4,000 lire ($2.50) is charged.

In another part of town, the **Tempio di Serapide** was really the "Macellum," or market square, and some of its ruined pillars still project upward today. It was erected during the reign of the Flavian emperors.

Pozzuoli can be reached by subway leaving from the Stazione Centrale in Naples.

BAIA   In the days of Imperial Rome, the emperors—everybody from Julius Caesar to Hadrian—came here to frolic in the sun while enjoying the comforts of their luxurious villas and Roman baths. Nero is said to have murdered his mother, Agrippina, at nearby Bacoli, with its Pool of Mirabilis. (The ancient "Baiae" was named for Baios, helmsman for Ulysses.) Parts of its illustrious past have been dug out. Ruins of scope and dimension were revealed, including both the Temple of Baiae and the Thermal Baths, said to have been among the greatest erected in Italy.

You can explore this archaeological district daily from 9am to two hours before sunset. Admission is 4,000 lire ($2.50). The town is reached in 15 minutes by rail from Cumana Station.

LAGO D'AVERNO   Ten miles west of Naples, a bit to the north of Baia, is a lake occupying an extinct volcanic crater. Known to the ancients as the Gateway

Vesuvius

Stand at the bottom of the great market-place of Pompeii, and look up at the silent streets, . . . over the broken houses with their inmost sanctuaries open to the day, away to Mount Vesuvius, bright and snowy in the peaceful distance; and lose all count of time, and heed of other things, in the strange and melancholy sensation of seeing the Destroyed and the Destroyer making this quiet picture in the sun.

—Charles Dickens, *Pictures from Italy*

A volcano that has struck terror in Campania, the towering, pitch-black Vesuvius looms menacingly over the Bay of Naples. The date—August 24, A.D. 79—is well known, for it was then that Vesuvius burst forth and buried Pompeii, Herculaneum, and Stabiae under its mass of lava and volcanic mud. Many fail to realize that Vesuvius has erupted periodically ever since (thousands were killed in 1631): the last major spouting of lava occurred in this century (it blew off the ring of its crater in 1906). The last spectacular eruption was March 31, 1944. The approach to Vesuvius is dramatic, with the terrain growing forlorn and foreboding as you near the top. Along the way you'll see villas rising on its slopes and vineyards (the grapes produce an amber-colored wine known as Lacrimae Christi; the citizens of Pompeii enjoyed wine from this mountainside, as excavations revealed). Closer to the summit, the soil becomes the color of puce and an occasional wildflower appears.

Although it may sound like a dubious invitation to some (Vesuvius, after all, is an active volcano), it's possible to visit the rim—or lips, so to speak—of the crater's mouth. As you look down into its smoldering core, you may recall that Spartacus, in a century before the eruption that buried Pompeii, hid in the hollow of the crater, which was then covered with vines.

To reach Vesuvius from Naples, you can take the Circumvesuviana Railway, or (in summer only) a motor-coach service from piazza Vittoria, which hooks up with bus connections at Pugliano. You get off the train at the Ercolano station, the 10th stop. Since inexpensive bus service to the top has been discontinued, you'll have to take a taxi to a point near the top—but always negotiate the fare in advance. It's obligatory to hire a guide for 5,000 lire ($3.15) to take you to the top.

to Hades, it was for centuries shrouded in superstition. Its vapors were said to produce illness and even death, and Averno could well have been the source of the expression "still waters run deep." Facing the lake are the ruins of what has been known as the Temple of Apollo from the 1st century A.D., and what was once commonly identified as the Cave of the Cumaean Sibyl. According to legend, the Sibyl is said to have ferried Aeneas, son of Aphrodite, across the lake, where he traced a mysterious spring to its source, the River Styx. In the 1st century B.C., Agrippa turned it into a harbor for Roman ships by digging out a canal.

From Baia, the site is reached by bus on the Napoli–Torre Gaveta line.

CUMA   Ancient Cumae was one of the first outposts of Greek colonization in what is now Italy. Twelve miles west of Naples, it's of interest chiefly because it is said to have contained the cave of the legendary Cumaean Sibyl. The **cave of the oracle,** really a gallery, was dug by the Greeks in the 5th century B.C. and was a sacred spot to them. Beloved by Apollo, the Sibyl is said to have written the *Sibylline Oracles,* a group of books of prophecy purchased, according to tradition, by Tarquin the Proud. You may visit not only the caves, but also the ruins of temples dedicated to Jupiter and Apollo (later converted into Christian churches), daily from 9am to two hours before sunset, for 4,000-lire ($2.50) admission. On via Domitiana, to the east of Cuma, you'll pass the **Arco Felice,** an arch about 64 feet high, built by Emperor Domitian in the 1st century A.D.

The Ferrovia Cumana train line runs here.

✪ HERCULANEUM

The builders of Herculaneum, Ercolano in Italian, were still working to repair the damage caused by an A.D. 62 earthquake when Vesuvius erupted on that fateful August day in A.D. 79. Herculaneum, a much smaller town (about one-fourth the size of Pompeii), didn't start to come to light again until 1709, when Prince Elbeuf launched the unfortunate fashion of tunneling through it for treasures. The prince was more intent on profiting from the sale of objets d'art than in uncovering a dead Roman town.

Subsequent excavations at the site, **Ufficio Scavi di Ercolano,** corso Resina, Ercolano (☎ 081/7390963), have been slow and sporadic. In fact, Herculaneum is not completely dug out today. One of the obstacles has been than the town was buried under lava, which was much heavier than the ash and pumice stone that piled onto Pompeii. Of course, this formed a greater protection for the buildings buried underneath—many of which were more elaborately constructed than those at Pompeii, as Herculaneum was a seaside resort for patrician families. The complication of having the slum of Resina resting over the yet-to-be-excavated district has further impeded progress and urban renewal.

Although all the streets and buildings of Herculaneum hold interest, some ruins merit more attention than others. The baths (*terme*) are divided between those at the forum and those on the outskirts (Terme Suburbane, near the more elegant villas). The municipal baths, which segregated the sexes, are larger, but the ones at the edge of town are more lavishly adorned. The Palestra was a kind of sports arena, where games were staged to satisfy the spectacle-hungry denizens.

The typical plan for the average town house was to erect it around an uncovered atrium. In some areas, Herculaneum possessed the forerunner of the modern apartment house. Important private homes to seek out include the "House of the Bicentenary," the "House of the Wooden Cabinet," the "House of the Wooden Partition," and the "House of Poseidon (Neptune) and Amphitrite," the last containing what is perhaps the best-known mosaic discovered in the ruins.

The finest example of how the aristocracy lived is provided by a visit to the "Casa dei Cervi," named the House of the Stags because of sculpture found inside. Guides are fond of showing their male clients a statue of a drunken Hercules urinating. Some of the best of the houses are locked and can be seen only by permission.

The ruins may be visited daily from 9am to one hour before sunset, for 8,000-lire ($5) admission. To reach the archaeological zone, take the regular train service from Naples on the Circumvesuviana Railway, a 20-minute ride leaving about every half hour from corso Garibaldi 387; or take bus no. 255 from piazza Municipio. Otherwise, it's a 4¹/₂-mile drive on the autostrada to Salerno (turn off at Ercolano).

3 Pompeii

15 miles S of Naples, 147 miles SE of Rome

When Vesuvius erupted in A.D. 79, Pliny the Younger, who later recorded the event, thought the end of the world had come. For our next adventure, we head south from Naples to the scene of the long-ago excitement.

The ruined Roman city of Pompeii (Pompei in Italian), dug out from the inundation of volcanic ash and pumice stone rained on it by Vesuvius in the year A.D. 79, has sparked the imagination of the world. At the excavations, the life of 19 centuries ago is vividly experienced.

Numerous myths have surrounded Pompeii, one of which is that a completely intact city was rediscovered. Actually the Pompeiians—that is, those who escaped—returned to their city when the ashes had cooled and removed some of the most precious treasures from the thriving resort. They were the forerunners of the later archaeologists. But they left plenty behind to be uncovered at a later date and carted off to museums throughout Europe and America.

After a long medieval sleep, Pompeii was again brought to life in the late 16th century, quite by accident, by the architect Domenico Fontana. However, it was in the mid-18th century that large-scale excavations were launched. Somebody once remarked that Pompeii's second tragedy was its rediscovery, that it really should have been left to slumber for another century or two, when it might have been taken better care of. The comment was prompted by the sad state of some of the present ruins and the poor maintenance in general.

ESSENTIALS

GETTING THERE   By Train   The Circumvesuviana Railway in Naples departs every half hour from piazza Garibaldi. A round-trip fare is 2,500 lire ($1.55); trip time: 45 minutes each way.

By Bus   At the railway station in Pompeii, bus connections take you to the entrance to the excavations. There is an entrance about 50 yards from the railway station at Villa Misteri.

By Car   To reach Pompeii from Naples, take the 13 1/2-mile drive on the autostrada to Salerno.

VISITOR INFORMATION   The telephone area code is 081. The tourist information center is at via Sacra 1 (☎ 8507255).

WHAT TO SEE & DO

The best preserved 2,000-year-old ruins in Europe, ✪ **Ufficio Scavi di Pompei,** piazza Esedra (☎ 081/8611051), is most often visited on a day trip from Naples (allow at least four hours for a superficial look at the archaeological site). The most elegant of the patrician villas, the **House of Vettii** has a courtyard, statuary (such as a two-faced Janus), paintings, and a black-and-red Pompeiian dining room frescoed with cupids. The house was occupied by two brothers named Vettii, both of whom were wealthy merchants. As you enter the vestibule, you'll see a painting of Priapus resting his gargantuan phallus on a pair of scales. The guard will reveal other erotic fertility drawings and statuary, although most such material has been removed from Pompeii to the Archaeological Museum in Naples. This house is considered the best example of a villa and garden that have been restored. The house is also known for its frescoes of delicate miniature cupids.

The second important villa, near the Porto Ercolano (Herculaneum Gate), lies outside the walls. The **House of Mysteries** (Villa dei Misteri) is reached by going out viale alla Villa dei Misteri. What makes the villa exceptional, aside from its architectural features, are its remarkable frescoes, depicting scenes associated with the sect of Dionysus (Bacchus), one of the cults that was flourishing in Roman times. Note in some of the backgrounds the Pompeiian red. The largest house, called the **House of the Faun** (Casa del Fauno) because of a bronze statue of a dancing faun found there, takes up a city block and has four different dining rooms and two spacious peristyle gardens. It sheltered the celebrated Battle of Alexander the Great mosaic, which is now in a museum in Naples.

In the center of town is the **Forum**—though rather small, it was the heart of Pompeiian life, known to bakers, merchants, and the wealthy aristocrats who lived luxuriously in the villas. Parts of the Forum were severely damaged in an earthquake 16 years before the eruption of Vesuvius and had not been repaired when the final destruction came. Three buildings that surround the Forum are the **basilica** (the largest single structure in the city) and the temples of Apollo and Jupiter. The **Stabian Thermae** (baths)—where both men and women lounged and relaxed in between games of knucklebones—are in good condition, among the finest to come down to us from antiquity. Here you'll see some skeletons. In a building called Lupanare, erotic paintings are displayed. These frescoes are the source of the fattest tips to guides.

In the **Antiquarium** is a number of objects used in the day-to-day life of the Pompeiians, including kitchen utensils and pottery, as well as mosaics and sculpture. Note the cast of a dog caught in the agony of death.

The excavations may be visited daily from 9am until about one hour before sunset for an admission fee of 10,000 lire ($6.25). At the entrance you can hire a guide at a prescribed rate.

WHERE TO STAY

Accommodations appear to be for earnest archaeologists only. The best of the lot follow. Villa Laura is the only really suitable hotel in town; the otherchoices are barely passable and are suggested only as emergency stopovers. Some hotels in Pompeii are not considered safe, because of robberies. Protect your valuables and your person and don't wander the streets at night.

Because the hotel situation here is so poor, most visitors look at the excavations, then seek better accommodations at either Naples (see above) or Sorrento (see Chapter 22), for the night.

INEXPENSIVE

Hotel del Santuario

Piazza Bartolo Longo 2–6, 80045 Pompei. ☎ **081/850-6165.** Fax 081/850-2822. 52 rms. TEL. 90,000 lire ($56.25) double. Rates include breakfast. AE, MC, V.

This hotel in town is in the very center of Pompeii, and opens onto the major square. The entrance faces a small park. The hotel rents simply furnished bedrooms. Across from the major basilica of Pompeii, the hotel also offers a ristorante, pizzeria, gelateria, and tea room. Reasonably priced meals range from 18,000 to 30,000 lire ($11.25 to $18.75). You can enjoy such dishes as beefsteak pizzaiola or a mixed fry of shrimp and squid. Limited parking is available.

Hotel Villa Dei Misteri

Via Villa dei Misteri 11. 80045 Pompei-Scavi. ☎ **081/861-3593.** 41 rms (all with bath or shower). 70,000 lire ($43.75) double. Breakfast 5,000 lire ($3.15) extra. No credit cards. Free parking. Transportation: From the Pompeii rail station, take the Sorrento train and get off at the Villa dei Misteri stop.

Located 250 yards from the Scavi Station, this 1930s' hotel is suitable for motorists. About a mile and half south of the center of town, it features a swimming pool, a little garden, and a place to park your car. The family-style welcome may compensate for a certain lack of facilities and amenities. The place could stand a facelift, but many readers have expressed their fondness for it. Only doubles are rented.

WHERE TO DINE
INEXPENSIVE

✪ Il Prìncipe

Piazza Bartolo Longo 8. ☎ **8505566.** Reservations required. Main courses 18,000–28,000 lire ($11.25–$17.50). AE, DC, MC, V. Tues–Sun 12:30–3pm and 7:30–11:30pm. Closed Aug 1–15. CAMPANIAN/MEDITERRANEAN.

The leading restaurant of Pompeii, Il Prìncipe is also acclaimed as one of the best restaurants in Campania. The decor, though relatively recent, incorporates the best decorative features of ancient Pompeii, including an intelligent scattering of brightly colored frescoes and mosaics. Guests can dine inside its beautiful interior, or select a sidewalk table at the corner of the most important square in Pompeii, with views of the basilica. For your first course, you might start with carpaccio or a salad of porcini (mushrooms); then follow with one of the pasta dishes, perhaps spaghetti vongole (with baby clams). Superb fish dishes, such as sea bass and turbot, are served, and you can also order saltimbocca (sage-flavored veal with ham) or steak Diane.

Zi Caterina

Via Roma 20. ☎ **8507447.** Reservations recommended. Main courses 8,000–20,000 lire ($5–$12.50). AE, DC, MC, V. Wed–Mon noon–11pm. Closed June 28–July 8. SEAFOOD/ NEAPOLITAN.

This good choice is conveniently located in the center of town near the basilica, with two spacious dining rooms. The antipasto table might tempt you with its seafood, although the pasta e fagiole with mussels might also be what you'd want to start your meal with. The chef's special rigatoni, with tomatoes and prosciutto, is tempting, as is the array of fish or one of the live lobsters fresh from the tank.

Amalfi Coast & Capri 22

When the English say "See Naples and die," they mean the city and the bay, with majestic Mt. Vesuvius in the background. When the Germans use the expression, they mean the Amalfi Drive. And, indeed, several motorists do die each year while seeing the Amalfi Coast, for the road is dangerous and too narrow to accommodate the heavy stream of summer traffic, especially the large tour buses that almost sideswipe each other as they try to pass. Moreover, in driving along the coast you sometimes find it difficult to concentrate on the road because of the view. The drive, remarked André Gide, "is so beautiful that nothing more beautiful can be seen on this earth."

Capri and Sorrento have long been known to international travelers. But the popularity of the resort-studded Amalfi Drive has been a more recent phenomenon. Perhaps it was discovered by German officers in World War II, then later by American and English servicemen (Positano was a British rest camp in the last months of the war). Later, when the war was over, many returned, often bringing their families. The little fishing villages in time became major tourism centers, with hotels and restaurants in all catagories. Sorrento and Amalfi are in the vanguard, with the widest range of facilities; Positano has more snob appeal and remains popular with artists; Ravello is still the choice of the discriminating few, such as Gore Vidal, who desire relative seclusion. To cap off an Amalfi Coast adventure, you can take a boat from Sorrento to Capri, which needs no advance billing. Three sightseeing attractions in this chapter—in addition to the towns and villages—are worthy of a special pilgrimage: The Emerald Grotto between Amalfi and Positano, the Blue Grotto of Capri, and the Greek temples of the ancient Sybarite-founded city of Paestum, south of Salerno.

A DRIVING TOUR

Day 1   Begin your tour of the Amalfi Drive in Sorrento, 31 miles south of Naples. Subject of song and legend as the home of the Sirens, the town stands on a cliff overlooking the Bay of Naples. Its shopping is also the best along the coast so you can easily occupy the minimum of a day here (more if you have time).

What's Special About the Amalfi Coast & Capri

Great Towns/Villages

- Capri, a tiny jewel of an island in the Bay of Naples that attracts some two million tourists a year.
- Positano, a holiday town that for decades has been the retreat of celebrities, such as director Franco Zeffirelli.
- Amalfi, a once-great maritime power, now a holiday resort known for its Duomo.
- Ravello, a tiny town with spectacular panoramas filled with narrow "step streets," a retreat of the rich and famous.
- Sorrento, the subject of song, story, and legend, the former "home of the Sirens" with a clifftop position overlooking the Bay of Naples.

Ace Attractions

- The Emerald Grotto, outside Amalfi, a millenia-old chamber of stalagmites and stalactites.
- The Blue Grotto, at Capri, known to the ancients, a grotto visited for its stunning cerulean waters.
- The Amalfi Coast, a corniche road following a rocky coast between Sorrento and Salerno, with innumerable bends and wild landscape.

Ancient Monument

- The ancient Sybarite city of Paestum, 25 miles south of Salerno, known for its impressive Greek ruins and Temple of Neptune.

☕ **TAKE A BREAK**   Taverna dell800, via dellAccademia 29, in Sorrento (☎ **081/8785970**), is a pub/restaurant, operated by a friendly chap everybody calls "Tony." Mercifully air conditioned, it offers such lunchtime fare as sausage with broccoli or pasta with Parmesan cheese, although you can order more substantial fare in the evening. It's also a good place to visit for a beer on a hot day.

Day 2   A narrow, curvy, and twisting highway stretches for 11 miles around the Amalfi peninsula to the enchanting little resort of Positano. Although the scenery is panoramic, this drive may be too scary for most. In that case you can reach Positano another way: From Sorrento head back toward Naples on the S145. At Meta you can get on the S163 which cuts across mountainous terrain until youre delivered to the Costa Amalfitana on the south side of the peninsula. The S163 will continue its hellish way all the way to Salerno. Follow this treacherous drive until you come to Positano which hopefully will be worth the effort of reaching it. This holiday town certainly deserves an overnight, or a lot more time if your schedule permits. At least stop for lunch, perhaps at:

☕ **TAKE A BREAK**   O Caporale, via Regina Giovanni 12 (☎ **089/875374**), where you get a wide assortment of seafood and pasta dishes. A specialty is La Caporalesa, pasta whipped up with capers and eggplant. You eat under a vine-covered canopy opening onto the water. Closed November through February.

The Amalfi Coast

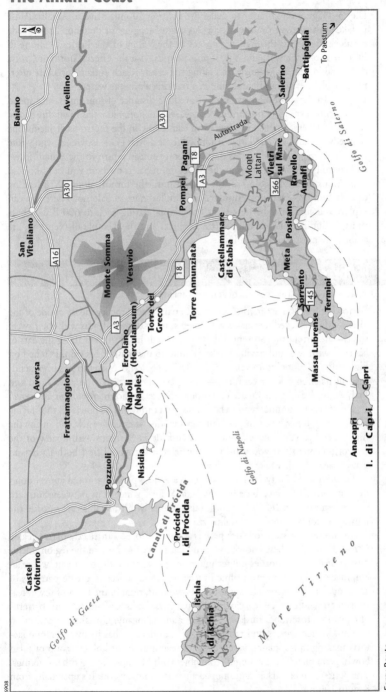

Ferry Route — — —

Day 3 Figure on an hour to make the twisting 10-mile drive to Amalfi. Pause to take in the views from the village or Vettica Maggiore or Praiano. The cliffside corniche takes you through the gorges of the Valley of the Furies (Vallone di Furore). Along the way, and only if time permits, visit the Green Grotto or Grotta di Smeraldo, the major attraction along the coast. Reach Amalfi for a late afternoon stroll of exploration and dine in a trattoria along the water.

Day 4 In the morning drive up to Ravello, a distance of four miles, and spend the morning exploring this hilltop village, with panoramic vistas in all directions. In a place where "poets go to die," you can follow in the footsteps of Jacqueline Kennedy Onassis, Greta Garbo, Andre Gide, and even D.H. Lawrence who wrote *Lady Chatterley's Lover* here. In the afternoon you can return to the Amalfi Drive and continue along the coast in the direction of Salerno where you can hook up with Autostrada E45 going south. Take it until the turnoff along SS18 leading directly south to Paestum, a distance of 25 miles south of Salerno. There you can explore the ancient Sybarite city of Poseidonia, dating back to 600 B.C. These ruins, including a Doric temple (the basilica) and the Temple of Neptune, are among the most evocative in Italy.

1 Sorrento

31 miles S of Naples, 159 miles SE of Rome, 31 miles W of Salerno

Borrowing from Greek mythology, the Romans placed the legendary abode of the Sirens—those wicked mermaids who lured seamen to their deaths with their sweet songs—at Surrentum (Sorrento). Ulysses resisted their call by stuffing the ears of his crew with wax and having himself bound to the mast of his ship. Perched on high cliffs, overlooking the Bays of Naples and Salerno, Sorrento has been sending out its siren call for centuries—luring everybody from Homer to Lord and Lady Astor. It is the birthplace of Torquato Tasso, author of *Jerusalem Delivered.*

The streets in summer tend to be as noisy as a carnival. The hotels on the "racing strip," corso Italia, need to pass out earplug kits when they tuck you in for the night. Perhaps you'll have a hotel on a cliffside in Sorrento with a view of the "sea of the sirens." If you want to swim in that sea, you'll find both paths and private elevators that take guests down.

To enjoy the beauty of the Amalfi Drive, whose perils are noted above, don't drive it yourself. Take a blue bus marked "SITA," which runs between Sorrento and Salerno or Amalfi. In Sorrento, bus stations with timetables are outside the railway station and in the central piazza.

An interesting stop for shoppers is **A Gargiulo & Jannuzzi,** piazza Tasso (☎ 8781041), the best-known maker of marquetry furniture in the region. Demonstrations of the centuries-old technique are presented in the basement, where an employee will combine multihued pieces of wood veneer to create patterns of arabesques and flowers. The sprawling showrooms, right in the heart of town, feature an array of card tables, clocks, and partners' desks, each inlaid with patterns of elmwood, rosewood, bird's-eye maple, and mahogany. Upstairs is a collection of embroidered napery and table linen. The outlet also has its own ceramic factory, making mugs, plates, vases, cups, tile pictures, plant holders, soup or salad bowls, pizza plates, and wrought-iron tables with tile tops, among other offerings. The pottery can be packed and shipped anywhere in the world. It's open daily from 8am to 10pm.

ESSENTIALS

GETTING THERE   By Train   Sorrento is served by frequent express trains from Naples (trip time: one hour). The high-speed train, called Ferrovia Circumvesuviana, leaves from one floor underground at the Stazione Centrale. For information about schedules to Sorrento, call 5534188 in Naples.

By Bus   From Naples, take the Ferrovia Circumvesuviana (see above), which is the fastest and cheapest way to get to Sorrento. Once at the Sorrento train station, you will find SITA buses servicing the Amalfi Coast. Buses depart from the Circumvesuviana station. Take any blue bus headed for Amalfi or Salerno. For information about schedules, call 8782708 in Sorrento.

By Car   From Naples, head south on Route 18, cutting west at the junction with Route 145.

VISITOR INFORMATION   The telephone area code is 081. The tourist information office is at via De Maio 35 (☎ 8074033), which winds down to the port where ships to Capri and Naples anchor.

WHERE TO STAY

In its first- and second-class hostelries, Sorrento is superior to almost any resort in the south, and offers accommodations in all price ranges.

EXPENSIVE

Grand Hotel Ambasciatori

Via Califano 18, 80067 Sorrento. ☎ **081/878-2025.** Fax 081/8071021. 103 rms, 6 suites A/C TV TEL. 310,000–340,000 lire ($193.75–$212.50) double; from 375,000 lire ($234.40) suite. Rates include breakfast. AE, MC, V. Free parking. Bus: SITA.

The heavily buttressed foundation that prevents this cliffside hotel from plunging into the sea looks like something from a medieval monastery. Built in a style reminiscent of a private villa, it was landscaped to include several rambling gardens whose edges conform to the edge of the precipice. A set of steps and a private elevator lead to the wooden deck of a bathing wharf. A barbecue is also available in this area. Inside, a substantial collection of Oriental carpets, marble floors, and well-upholstered armchairs provide plush enclaves of comfort.

    Dining/Entertainment: The main restaurant offers both regional and international specialties, with meals beginning at 55,000 lire ($34.40). There's also a snack bar by the pool. Twice a week a live-music program of Neapolitan songs is presented.

    Services: Room service, babysitting, laundry, valet.

    Facilities: A garage on the premises provides much-needed parking; there's also a heart-shaped swimming pool. An elevator takes guests down the cliff to the beach.

Grand Hotel Excelsior Vittoria

Piazza Tasso 34, 80067 Sorrento. ☎ **081/807-1044.** Fax 081/877-1206. 106 rms, 12 suites. MINIBAR TV TEL. 365,000–470,000 lire ($228.15–$293.75) double; 600,000–1,000,000 lire ($375–$625) suite. Rates include breakfast. AE, DC, MC, V. Free parking. Bus: SITA.

This place, built between 1834 and 1882, on the edge of a cliff, and surrounded by semitropical gardens with lemon and orange trees, combines 19th-century glamour with modern amenities. The grounds were designed and planted when grandeur was a prerequisite for a resort hotel. The terrace theme predominates, especially on the water side where you can enjoy the cold drinks served at sunset while gazing at Vesuvius across the bay. Three elevators take bathers down to the harbor. Inside, the atmosphere is old worldish, especially in the mellow dining room (see below). The hotel has 12 luxury suites, including the one named for Enrico Caruso, who stayed in it in 1921. The bedrooms have their own drama, some with balconies that open onto the perilous cliffside drop. The rooms have a wide mixture of furnishings, with many antique pieces.

Dining/Entertainment: The dining room is festive and formal, with ornate, hand-painted ceilings that depict clouds, sprays of flowers, and clusters of cherubs. You'll sit in ivory and cane provincial chairs while you enjoy a top-notch Sorrento cuisine. But it's the panoramic view that makes dining here memorable. Meals begin at 75,000 lire ($46.90). In summer you can dine in the open air. Live entertainment is presented twice a week.

Services: Room service, babysitting, laundry, valet.

Facilities: Large swimming pool.

MODERATE

Hotel Bristol

Via del Capo 22, 80067 Sorrento. ☎ **081/8784522.** Fax 081/8071910. 134 rms, 5 suites. A/C TV TEL. 210,000–330,000 lire ($131.25–$206.25) double; 280,000–430,000 lire ($175–$268.75) suite. Rates include breakfast. AE, DC, MC, V. Free parking. Bus: SITA.

The Bristol was built pueblo style in 1958 on a hillside at the edge of town, and every room has a view of Vesuvius and the Bay of Naples. The hotel lures with its contemporary decor and spaciousness, and with well-appointed public and private rooms. The bedrooms are warm and inviting, with bright covers and built-in niceties. Most have balconies that overlook the sea, and some contain minibars.

Dining/Entertainment: The attraction of the dining room with its terrace and all-glass facade is really the bay and view. There's an outer sun-shaded terrace for afternoon drinks from the winter-garden bar. A summer-only Discoteca is near the large pool.

Services: Room service, babysitting, laundry, valet.

Facilities: Swimmng pool, Finnish sauna.

Parco Dei Principi

Via Rota 1, 80067 Sorrento. ☎ **081/8784644.** Fax 081/8783786. 93 rms, 3 suites. A/C MINIBAR TV TEL. 280,000–350,000 lire ($175–$218.75) double; from 500,000 lire ($312.50) suite. Rates include breakfast. AE, DC, MC, V. Free parking. Closed Nov–Mar. Bus: SITA.

In 1962, the owner of one of Italy's well-respected hotel chains commissioned the construction of an elegant and well-coordinated new hotel by noted Milanese architect Gio Ponti. The setting was the park surrounding the 18th-century villa of Prince Leopold of Bourbon Sicily. Whereas the original palace was intended for the private use of the hotel chain's owners, the modern annex quickly became respected as one of Sorrento's best hotels. An additional building, set inland from the sea, near the park's entrance, caters only to bus tours and groups.

Today, Gio Ponti's hotel design occupies a desirable seafront position on cliffs above the water, ringed with gardens filled with towering palms, acacias, olives, scented lemons, and magnolias.

A private elevator takes swimmers down the cliff, which affords views of the Bay of Naples and Vesuvius, to the private beach. There's a mooring pier for yachts and motorboats, and for waterskiing. The public rooms are spacious, with blue-and-white herringbone tile floors and cerulean-blue furniture. The bedrooms continue the sky-blue theme, with striped floors, walls of glass leading to private balconies, and built-in furniture.

Dining/Entertainment: The hotel restaurant has both a formal dining room and a terrace with a view of the water. Both regional and international dishes are offered. Meals begin at 55,000 lire ($34.40).

Services: Room service, babysitting, laundry, valet.

Facilities: Swimming pool.

INEXPENSIVE

⑤ Hotel Désirée

Via del Capo 31 bis, 80067 Sorrento. ☎ **081/8781563.** 22 rms (all with bath or shower). TEL. 115,000–120,000 lire ($71.90–$75) double. Rates include breakfast. No credit cards. Free parking. Closed Nov–Mar. Bus: SITA.

Désirée is half a mile from the center of town at the beginning of the Amalfi Drive. This tranquil hotel is directed by the Gargiulo family, who speak English. The establishment is ringed with terraces, whose flowered masonry overlooks the Bay of Naples and nearby trees. This used to be an upper-class private home before it was transformed into the good-value hotel it is today. Many of the attractive personal touches remain in the decor. You'll recognize the hotel by its green glass lanterns in front and the welcoming awning stretched over the front entrance. A private beach can be reached by elevator.

⑤ Hotel Regina

Via Marina Grande 10, 80067 Sorrento. ☎ **081/8782722.** Fax 081/8782721. 36 rms. A/C TEL. 136,000 lire ($85) double. Rates include breakfast. AE, V. Parking 8,000 lire ($5). Closed Nov–Mar 14. Bus: SITA.

Evenly spaced rows of balconies jut out over the Regina's well-tended garden. On its uppermost floor, a glassed-in dining room and an outdoor terrace encompass views of the Mediterranean extending as far as Naples and Vesuvius. Only breakfast is served. The clean, functional bedrooms have tile floors and private terraces.

Villa di Sorrento

Via Fuorimura 4, 80067 Sorrento. ☎ **081/8781068.** Fax 081/8072679. 20 rms (all with bath or shower). TEL. 180,000 lire ($112.50) double. Rates include breakfast. AE, DC, MC, V. Bus: SITA.

This is a pleasant villa right in the center of town. Architecturally romantic, it attracts travelers with its petite wrought-iron balconies, tall shutters, and vines climbing the facade. The rooms have such small niceties as bedside tables and lamps, and some accommodations have terraces. There's an elevator as well.

WHERE TO DINE
MODERATE

L'Antica Trattoria

Via. P.R. Giuliani 33. ☎ **8071082.** Reservations recommended. Main courses 13,000–28,000 lire ($8.15–$17.50); set menus 28,000–50,000 lire ($17.50–$31.25). No credit cards. Tues–Sun noon–3pm and Tues–Sun 7pm–midnight. Closed Jan. CAMPANESE/INTERNATIONAL.

Set within the weatherbeaten walls of what was originally built 300 years ago as a dignified private villa, this restaurant is warm, charming, and polite. Although all of its food is well-prepared, and faithful to the tenets of the Italian repertoire, its real virtue lies within its antipasti. Each of these is homemade, and features fish and a daunting array of pastas which include lasagne, fettuccine, tortelloni, and ravioli which in its best version is stuffed with seafood. Sea bass or red mullet can be baked in a salt crust, a process that produces a beautifully cooked and firm-fleshed final product. The assortment of ice creams is especially tempting, some of the best in town.

INEXPENSIVE

La Favorita–O'Parrucchiano

Corso Italia 71. ☎ **8781321.** Reservations required. Main courses 10,000–16,000 lire ($6.25–$10). MC, V. Daily noon–4pm and 7pm–midnight. Closed Wed from Oct 30–June 30. Bus: SITA. NEAPOLITAN.

This is a good choice on the busiest street in Sorrento. The building is like an old tavern, with an arched ceiling in the main dining room. On the terrace in the rear you can dine in a garden of trees, rubber plants, and statuary. Among the à la carte dishes, classic Italian fare is offered, including ravioli Caprese (filled with fresh cheese and covered with a tomato sauce), cannelloni, a mixed fish fry from the Bay of Naples, and a veal cutlet milanese. The chef will also prepare a pizza for you.

2 Positano

35 miles SE of Naples, 10 miles E of Sorrento, 165 miles SE of Rome

A hillside, Moorish-style village—on the southern strip of the Amalfi Drive, Positano opens onto the Tyrrhenian Sea with its legendary islands of the sirens. The Sirenuse Islands, mentioned in Homer's *Odyssey,* form the mini-archipelago of Li Galli. Still privately owned, these islands were once purchased by Leonid Massine, the Russian-born choreographer. It is said that the town was "discovered" after World War II when Gen. Mark Clark stationed troops in nearby Salerno. When the U.S. soldiers went on holiday, they learned of the glories of Positano. It has jackrabbited along the classic postwar route of many a European resort: a sleeping fishing village that was visited by painters and writers (Paul Klee, Tennessee Williams), and then was taken over by bohemia-sampling visitors.

Once Positano was part of the powerful Republic of the Amalfis, a rival of Venice as a sea power in the 10th century. Today smart boutiques dot the village, and bikinis add vibrant colors to the mud-gray beach where you're likely to get pebbles in your sand castle. Prices have been rising sharply over the past few years. The 500-lire-a-night rooms popular with sunset-painting artists have gone the way of your baby teeth.

The topography of the village, you'll soon discover, is impossible. If you learn to climb the landscape with relative ease, you'll be qualified to hire out as a "scab" during the next donkey sit-down strike. John Steinbeck once wrote: "Positano bites deep. It is a dream place that isn't quite real when you are there and becomes beckoningly real after you have gone."

ESSENTIALS

GETTING THERE   By Bus   Positano has no rail connections, but is reached by a rather thrilling bus ride from Sorrento. SITA buses leave from Sorrento frequently throughout the day, more often in summer than in winter; a one-way fare is 1,800 lire ($1.15). For information about schedules in Sorrento, call SITA at 8782708.

By Car Positano lies along the Amalfi Drive (Route 145, which becomes Route 163 at the approach to the resort).

VISITOR INFORMATION The telephone area code is 089. The tourist information center is at via del Saracino 4 (☎ 875067).

WHERE TO STAY
VERY EXPENSIVE

✪ San Pietro

Via Laurito 2, 84017 Positano. ☎ **089/875455**. Fax 089/811449. 52 rms, 5 suites. A/C MINIBAR TV TEL. 450,000–650,000 lire ($281.25–$406.25) double; 525,000–1,600,000 lire ($328.15–$1,000) suite. Rates include breakfast. AE, DC, MC, V. Free parking. Closed Nov–Mar. Bus: 3.

A mile from Positano toward Amalfi, San Pietro has only a miniature 15th-century chapel, which projects out on a high cliff, for identification. A behind-the-scenes elevator takes you down to the cliff ledges of what is the chicest resort along the Amalfi Coast. By changing elevators at the reception lounge, you can descend even farther to the swimming and boating cove, where you can sunbathe and enjoy the water in seclusion. The suitelike bedrooms are super-glamorous, and many have a picture window beside the bathtub (there's even a huge sunken Roman bath in one suite). Bougainvillea from the terraces reaches into the ceilings of many of the living rooms. The collection of antiques and reproductions fills the living room. San Pietro neither advertises nor posts signs, and the privacy of guests is zealously guarded. Many have been distinguished, including, in times past, Lord Laurence Olivier, Rudolf Nureyev, and Gregory Peck.

Dining/Entertainment: Guests gather at sunset in the piano bar. A dining room has been cut into the cliff, and features picture windows the length of the room. A refined international cuisine is featured, costing from 75,000–100,000 lire ($46.90–$62.50) on the à la carte menu.

Services: Room service, babysitting, laundry, valet.

Facilities: Swimming pool, private beach, tennis court.

✪ Le Sirenuse

Via Colombo 30, 84017 Positano. ☎ **089/875066**. Fax 089/811798. 58 rms, 2 suites. A/C MINIBAR TV TEL. 380,000–600,000 lire ($237.50–$375) double; 610,000–1,200,000 lire ($381.25–$750) suite. Rates include breakfast. AE, DC, MC, V. Free parking. Bus: 3.

Good taste reigns supreme at Le Sirenuse. Everything exists for its sophisticated clientele, which includes numerous artists and writers. The hotel, an old villa only a few minutes' walk up from the bay, is owned by the aristocratic Sersale family and was their private family residence until 1951. The marchesa personally selects all the furnishings, which include fine carved chests, 19th-century paintings and old prints, a spinet piano, upholstered pieces in bold colors, and a Victorian cabinet, taken from an old jewelry shop. The bedrooms, all with private bath and many with Jacuzzi, are varied, and all have terraces that overlook the village. Your room may have an iron bed, high and ornate and painted red, as well as a carved chest and refectory tables.

Dining/Entertainment: Meals are well served on one of the three terraces, and the chef caters to the international palate with a regional cuisine. Meals start at 65,000 lire ($40.65).

Services: Room service, babysitting, laundry, valet.

Facilities: Swimming pool, sauna, gym.

EXPENSIVE

✪ Hotel Poseidon

Via Pasitea 148, 84017 Positano. ☎ **089/875213.** Fax 089/875833. 46 rms, 2 suites.
A/C MINIBAR TV TEL. 230,000–320,000 lire ($143.75–$200) double; 450,000–520,000
lire ($281.25–$325) suite. Rates include breakfast. AE, DC, MC, V. Parking 30,000 lire
($18.75). Closed Nov 4–Mar 29. Bus: 3.

This hotel, among the very finest in Positano, was built in 1950 by the Aonzo family as their summer residence. In 1955, it was enlarged and transformed into a
hotel. Today, this first-class, four-star hotel is still owned and managed by the
Aonzo family, who provide one of the most hospitable welcomes at the resort.
Centrally located, it is charming, discreet, and elegant, with tastefully selected antique furniture and objects. Bedrooms are traditionally furnished and beautifully
maintained.

Dining/Entertainment: Along with its terraces and garden, the hotel offers both
indoor and outdoor dining; its chefs feature both a regional and continental cuisine in La Terrazza del Poseidon, with its antique terra-cotta floors, walnut fixtures,
and wrought-iron window frames. From May until the end of September, meals,
costing from 60,000 lire ($37.50), are served on the panoramic terrace, covered
with a portico of bougainvillea and ivy.

Services: Room service, laundry, babysitting, massages, facials.

Facilities: Freshwater swimming pool, health club (the first and only one in
Positano), with a sauna, hydromassage spa, and gym with a professional trainer.

MODERATE

⑤ Albergo l'ancora

Via Colombo 36, 84017 Positano. ☎ **089/875318.** Fax 089/811784. 18 rms. MINIBAR TV
TEL. 180,000–210,000 lire ($112.50–$131.25) double. AE, DC, MC, V. Free parking. Closed
Nov 1–Apr 1. Bus: 3.

This is a stand-out choice in its classification. A hillside villa turned hotel, it has
the atmosphere of a private club. It's fresh and sunny here, with each room like a
bird's nest on a cliff. All rooms are doubles, and 11 are air-conditioned. Designed
to accommodate the maximum of sun terraces and sheltered loggias for shade, the
hotel is a 5-minute climb from the beach (maybe longer if you're past 35). Its main
lounge has clusters of club chairs, tile floors, and teardrop chandeliers. But the
bedrooms—which cater to couples only—are the stars, with their individualized
treatments. Well-chosen antiques, such as fine inlaid desks, are intermixed with
more contemporary pieces. The bathrooms in each of the double rooms are tiled
and contain a bidet, and each room opens onto a private terrace. Meals are served
on the informal outdoor terrace, under a vine-covered sun shelter, but only to hotel
guests.

⑤ Albergo Miramare

Via Trara Genoino 31, 84017 Positano. ☎ **089/875002.** Fax 089/875219. 18 rms, 4 suites.
TEL. 200,000–310,000 lire ($125–$193.75) double; 250,000–350,000 lire ($156.25–
$218.75) triple; 270,000–310,000 lire ($168.75–$193.75) suite. Rates include breakfast.
AE, MC, V. Free parking. Closed Jan 5–Mar 10. Bus: 3.

This is one of the most charming accommodations in Positano, suitable for those
who like the personalized touch that only a small, individualized inn can provide.
The hotel was converted from a private mansion, which is now well on its way
toward a century of life. Located in the heart of town on a cliff, the hotel attracts

a discriminating clientele who appreciate the terraces, both public and private, where one can sip Campari and soda and contemplate the sea. Guests, who reach the hotel after a steep climb, are housed in one of two tastefully furnished buildings in a setting of citrus trees, with lots of flamboyant bougainvillea. Your bed will most likely rest under a vaulted ceiling, and the white walls will be thick. Even the bathrooms are romantic. Some rooms have air conditioning.

The conversation piece of the hotel is a glass bathtub on a flowery terrace. What might seem like questionable taste in Los Angeles—a pink porcelain clamshell serving as a wash basin—becomes charming at the Miramare, even when the water rushes from a sea-green ceramic fish with coral-pink gills. The hotel lies about a 3-minute walk from the beach, which you reach by going down a series of stairs.

Albergo Ristorante Covo dei Saraceni

84017 Positano. ☎ **089/875400.** Fax 089/875878. 58 rms. A/C MINIBAR TV TEL. 220,000–360,000 lire ($137.50–$225) double. Rates include buffet breakfast. Half-board 50,000 lire ($31.25) per person. AE, DC, MC, V. Parking 20,000–25,000 lire ($12.50–$15.65). Closed Nov–Mar. Bus: 3.

You'll find this rambling yellow-ochre building a few steps above the port. It's a desirable choice for those who want to be in the swim of the summer action. The side closest to the water culminates in a rounded tower of rough-hewn stone, inside of which is an appealing restaurant open to the breezes and a firsthand view of the crashing waves. Meals range from 30,000 to 60,000 lire ($18.75 to $37.50). The hotel rents comfortably furnished bedrooms, doubles only.

Buca di Bacco

Via Rampa Teglia 8, 84017 Positano. ☎ **089/875699.** Fax 089/875731. 54 rms. A/C MINIBAR TV TEL. 216,000–256,000 lire ($135–$160) double. Rates include breakfast. AE, DC, MC, V. Parking 25,000 lire ($15.65). Closed Oct 31–Mar. Bus: 3.

This is one of the best moderately priced hotels at the resort, also housing one of the best restaurants in the area (see "Where to Dine," below). On the main beach of Positano, it often draws guests who patronize only its bar, one of the best-known rendezvous points along the Amalfi Drive. A large terrace opens onto the beach, and you can enjoy a Campari and soda while still in your bathing suit. The oldest and most expensive part, the Buca Residence, was an old seaside mansion constructed at the dawn of the 19th century. Rooms are well furnished, with many facilities, including balconies that face the sea. Air conditioning is included.

INEXPENSIVE

Casa Albertina

Via Tavolozza 4, 84017 Positano. ☎ **089/875143.** Fax 089/811540. 20 rms, 3 suites. A/C MINIBAR TV TEL. 300,000 lire ($187.50) double; 340,000 lire ($212.50) suite for two. Rates include half-board. AE, DC, MC, V. Bus: 3.

This villa guesthouse is reached by climbing a steep and winding road. It offers a view of the coastline from its perch on the side of a hill. Each bedroom is a gem, color coordinated in either mauve or blue. The rooms are furnished with well-selected pieces, such as gilt mirrors, fruitwood end tables, and bronze bed lamps. Each accommodation has wide French doors that lead out to a private balcony. You can have breakfast on the terra-cotta-tile terrace on your own garden furniture. A few rooms have a Jacuzzi. The hotel also has a good restaurant that specializes in fresh grilled fish. Meals, if ordered separately, range from 40,000 to

55,000 lire ($25 to $34.40). Laundry service and a babysitter are available on request, and the hotel has both a bar and a solarium.

✪ Palazzo Murat

Via dei Mulini 23, 84017 Positano. ☎ **089/875177.** Fax 089/811419. 28 rms. MINIBAR TV TEL. 210,000–270,000 lire ($131.25–$168.75) double. Rates include breakfast. AE, DC, MC, V. Parking 25,000 lire ($15.65). Closed Nov–Easter. Bus: 3.

For nostalgic atmosphere and baroque style, this place has no equal in all of Positano. The jasmine and bougainvillea are so profuse in its garden that they spill over their enclosing wall onto the arbors of the narrow street outside. Once this was the sumptuous retreat of Napolean I's brother-in-law, the king of Naples. Considered the most dashing cavalry leader of his age, he was eventually court-martialed and shot. Today, shell designs cap the villa windows, which look out over a cluster of orange trees and the wrought-iron tendrils of the gate that leads into the garden. To enlarge the property, a previous owner erected a comfortable annex in a style compatible with the original villa. Only breakfast is served. Nineteen rooms are air-conditioned.

WHERE TO DINE
INEXPENSIVE

Buca di Bacco

Via Ramp Teglia 8. ☎ **875699.** Reservations required. Main courses 15,000–34,000 lire ($9.40–$21.25). AE, DC, MC, V. Daily 12:30–3:30pm and 8–11pm. Closed Oct 20–Mar. Bus: 3. CAMPANIA/ITALIAN.

Right on the beach you'll find one of Positano's top restaurants. Guests often stop for a before-dinner drink in the bar downstairs then head for the dining room on a big covered terrace that faces the sea. The tone of the *buca* is apparent as you enter. On display are various fresh fish, special salads, and fruit, including luscious black figs and freshly peeled oranges soaked in caramel. An exciting opener is a salad made with fruits of the sea, or you may prefer the zuppa di cozze (mussels), prepared with flair in a tangy sauce. Pasta dishes are homemade, and meats are well prepared with fresh ingredients.

Chez Black

Via del Brigantino. ☎ **875036.** Reservations required in summer. Main courses 16,000–26,000 lire ($10–$16.25). AE, DC, MC, V. Daily 12:30–3pm and 7:30–11pm. Closed Jan 8–Feb 8. Bus: 3. SEAFOOD.

The owner is Salvatore Russo, but for his restaurant he uses the suntan-inspired name that his friends gave him in college. Founded after World War II, the restaurant occupies a desirable position near the beach. In summer, it's in the "eye of the hurricane" of action. Its varnished ribbing, glowing sheath of softwood and brass, and yacht-inspired semaphore symbols make it one of the most beautiful restaurants in town. A stone-edged aquarium holds fresh lobsters, while rack upon rack of local wines give diners a choice. Seafood is the specialty, as well as a wide selection of pizzas fresh from a circular oven. Most diners order substantial meals. The best-known dish is the spaghetti with crayfish, but you might also be tempted by linguine with fresh pesto, grilled swordfish, sole, or shrimp, along with an array of veal, liver, chicken, and beef dishes.

3 Amalfi

38 miles SE of Naples, 21 miles W of Salerno, 169 miles SE of Rome

From the 9th to the 11th century the seafaring Republic of Amalfi rivaled those great maritime powers, Genoa and Venice. Its maritime code, the *Tavole Amalfitane*, was used in the Mediterranean for centuries. But raids by Saracens and a flood in the 14th century devastated the city. Its power and influence weakened, until it rose again in modern times as the major resort on the Amalfi Drive.

From its position at the slope of the steep Lattari hills, it overlooks the Bay of Salerno. The approach to Amalfi is most dramatic, whether you come from Positano or from Salerno. Today Amalfi depends on tourist traffic, and the hotels and pension in dead center are right in the milling throng of holiday makers. The finest and most highly rated accommodations are on the outskirts.

ESSENTIALS

GETTING THERE   By Bus   SITA buses run every two hours during the day from Sorrento, for a one-way fare of 3,200 lire ($2). There are also SITA bus connections from Positano, a one-way ticket costing 1,800 lire ($1.15). Information about schedules is available in Sorrento by calling SITA at 8782708. In Amalfi, the bus terminal is at the waterfront on piazza Flavio Gioia (☎ 871009 for information about schedules).

VISITOR INFORMATION   The telephone area code is 089. The tourist information center is at corso delle Repubbliche Marinare 19-21 (☎ 871107).

WHAT TO SEE & DO

Evoking a rich past is the **Duomo** (cathedral), piazza del Duomo, named in honor of St. Andrew (Sant'Andrea), whose remains are said to be buried inside the crypt. Reached by climbing steep steps, the cathedral is characterized by its black-and-white facade and its mosaics. Inside, the one nave and two aisles are all richly baroqued. The cathedral dates back to the 11th century, although the present structure has been rebuilt. Its bronze doors were made in Constantinople, and its campanile (bell tower) is from the 13th century, erected partially in the Romanesque style. The Duomo is open daily from 7am to 1:30pm and 3 to 8pm. You can also visit the **"Cloister of Paradise" (Chiostro Paradiso),** to the left of the cathedral, originally a necropolis for members of the Amalfitan "establishment." This graveyard dates from the 1200s and contains the broken columns and statues, as well as sarcophagi, of a long-gone civilization. The cloister is open daily from 9am to 1:30pm and 3 to 8pm and charges 1,000 lire (65¢) for admission.

For your most scenic walk in Amalfi, start at piazza del Duomo and head up via Genova. The classic stroll will take you to the **Valle dei Mulini** (the Valley of the Mills), so called because of the paper mills along its rocky reaches. (The seafaring republic is said to have acquainted Italy with the use of paper.) You'll pass by fragrant gardens and scented citrus groves.

And for the biggest attraction of all, head west to the ✪ **Emerald Grotto (Grotta della Smeraldo).** This ancient cavern, known for its light effects, is a millenia-old chamber of stalagmites and stalactites. Three miles west of Amalfi, the grotto is reached from the coastal road via a descent by elevator, which costs 5,000 lire ($3.15), including the boat ride. Then you board a boat that traverses the eerie world of the grotto. The stalagmites, unique in that some are underwater, rise up in old formations. Visits are possible daily from 9am to 5pm in March and April, from 8:30am to 6pm May through September, and from 10am to 4pm October through February. Take the SITA bus in Amalfi going toward Sorrento.

WHERE TO STAY
EXPENSIVE

Hotel Luna Convento
Via Pantoleone Comite 19, 84011 Amalfi. ☎ **089/871002.** Fax 089/871333. 45 rms. TV TEL. 360,000 lire ($225) double. Rates include half-board. AE, DC, MC, V. Parking 20,000 lire ($12.50). Bus: SITA.

This hotel boasts a 13th-century cloister said to have been founded by St. Francis of Assisi. Most of the building you see today was constructed in 1975. Now converted into a modern hotel, it's a sun trap. The long corridors, where monks of old used to tread, are lined with sitting areas, which are used by the most unmonastic guests. The bedrooms have sea views, terraces, and modern furnishings. All rooms are doubles.

Dining/Entertainment: The rather formal dining room has a coved ceiling, high-backed chairs, arched windows that open toward the water, and good food (Italian and international) served in an efficient manner. The hotel also has a night-club that projects toward the sea. In summer, an orchestra plays for dancing.

Services: Room service, babysitting, laundry, valet.

Facilities: A free-form swimming pool is nestled on the rocks, near the sound of the surf and sea gulls.

✪ Santa Caterina
Strada Amalfitana, 84011 Amalfi. ☎ **089/871012.** Fax 089/871351. 70 rms, 11 suites. A/C MINIBAR TV TEL. 340,000–480,000 lire ($212.50–$300) double; from 600,000 lire ($375) suite. Rates include breakfast. Half-board 70,000 lire ($43.75) per person. AE, DC, MC, V. Free parking outside, 20,000 lire ($12.50) in garage. Bus: SITA.

Perched on top of a cliff, the Santa Caterina has an elevator that will take you down to a private beach. This "saint" is one of the most scenic accommodations around, dating from 1902. You are housed in the main structure or in one of the small "villas" in the citrus groves along the slopes of the hill. The accommodations are furnished in good taste, with an eye toward the comfort of all guests. Most of the rooms have private balconies that face the sea, a sea that was once filled with the powerful fleet of the Amalfi Republic when it was a formidable maritime power. The furniture respects the tradition of the house, and in every room there's an antique piece. The bathrooms are spacious, with luxurious fittings, and each of them has a hairdryer.

Dining/Entertainment: The food here is among the best at the resort, so the boarding arrangement is no hardship. Many of the vegetables are grown in the hotel's own garden, and the fish tastes so fresh that I suspect the chef has an agreement with local fishermen to bring in the "catch of the day" earmarked for the pampered guests of Santa Caterina. Also, once or twice a week, a special evening buffet accompanied by music is held. Nonresidents can order lunch or dinner, which costs 70,000 to 85,000 lire ($43.75 to $53.15).

Services: Room service, babysitting, laundry, valet.

Facilities: Saltwater pool.

MODERATE

Excelsior Grand Hotel

Via Pogerola, 84011 Amalfi. ☎ **089/830015.** Fax 089/830255. 97 rms. TEL. 100,000–175,000 lire ($62.50–$109.40) per person. Rates include full-board. AE, DC, MC, V. Free parking. Bus: SITA.

Two miles north of Amalfi at Pogerola, the Excelsior is a modern first-class hotel built in 1962 on the coast. This extravaganza on a high mountain perch outdoes the positions of the nearby cliff-hanging monasteries, and all its rooms are angled toward the view. You get the first glimmer of sunrise and the last rays of golden light. The social center is the 100-foot terrazzo-edged swimming pool filled with filtered mountain spring water. For the lazier folk, there's a nearby garden shaded by umbrellas and a private beach. The hotel structure is unconventional; the core is a high octagonal glass tower that rises above the central lobby, with exposed mezzanine lounges and an open staircase that leads to the view.

The bedrooms are individually designed, with plenty of room, and the furnishings are chosen with flair. The many good reproductions, some antiques, king-size beds, and tile floors all contrast with the white walls. The private balconies, complete with garden furniture, are the most important feature.

Dining/Entertainment: The dining room, with mirrored pillars and ornate blue-and-white tile floors, is a dignified place in which to sample the Italian cuisine with Gallic overtones. Several spots were especially created for a festive stay, notably Bar del Night, where musicians play for dancing on weekends.

Services: Transportation to and from the beach is provided by boat and bus for 15,000 lire ($9.40).

Facilities: Swimming pool.

INEXPENSIVE

Hotel Belvedere

Via Smeraldo, Conca dei Marini, 84011 Amalfi. ☎ **089/831282.** Fax 089/831439. 36 rms. TEL. 150,000–200,000 lire ($93.75–$125) double. Breakfast 15,000 lire ($9.40) extra. AE, MC, V. Free parking. Closed Oct 15–Easter. Bus: SITA.

Lodged below the coastal road outside Amalfi on the drive to Positano, the aptly named Belvedere has one of the best swimming pools in the area. It's in a prime location, hidden from the view and noise of the heavily traveled road, and thrust out toward the sea. Rooms have terraces that overlook the water. Signor Lucibello, who owns the hotel, sees to it that guests are content, and provides, among other things, parking space for your car (a bus takes you into Amalfi). The facilities are serviceable and comfortable.

Dining/Entertainment: Well-prepared Italian meals are served either inside (where walls of windows allow for views of the coast) or on the front terrace, with its garden furniture. There is also a cocktail bar.

Services: Room service, babysitting, laundry, valet.

Facilities: Swimming pool, outdoor parking space.

⑤ Hotel Lidomare

Largo Piccolomini 9, 84011 Amalfi. ☎ **089/871332.** Fax 089/857972. 13 rms. TV TEL. 60,000–75,000 lire ($37.50–$46.90) double. Breakfast 10,000 lire ($6.25) extra. AE, DC, MC, V. Parking 12,000 lire ($7.50). Bus: SITA.

This pleasant, small hotel is just a few steps from the sea, and its building dates from the 13th century. The high-ceilinged bedrooms are airy and clean, and contain a scattering of modern furniture mixed with Victorian-era antiques. The Camera family are the owners, and they extend a warm welcome to their never-ending stream of foreign visitors. They offer 12 double bedrooms (there is only one single), 7 of which have air conditioning. Breakfast is extra and is the only meal served, but you can order it until 11:30am. This hotel is one of the best bargains in Amalfi.

Hotel Miramalfi

Via Quasimodo 3, 84011 Amalfi. ☎ **089/871588.** Fax 089/871588. 43 rms (all with bath or shower), 3 suites. MINIBAR TV TEL. 150,000–195,000 lire ($93.75–$121.90) double; 250,000–295,000 lire ($156.25–$184.40) suite. Rates include breakfast. Half-board 100,000–140,000 lire ($62.50–$87.50) per person. Air conditioning 10,000 lire ($6.25) supplement per room. AE, DC, MC, V. Free parking. Bus: SITA.

On the western edge of Amalfi, the Miramalfi lies below the coastal road and beneath a rocky ledge on its own beach. The rooms at this family-owned and managed hotel are wrapped around the curving contour of the coastline, and have unobstructed views of the sea. The stone swimming pier—used for sunbathing, diving, and boarding motor launches for waterskiing—is reached by a winding cliffside path, past terraces of grapevines. A space saver is the rooftop parking area. The dining room has glass windows and a few semitropical plants; the food is good and served in abundant portions. Breakfast is provided on one of the main terraces or on your own balcony. Each bedroom is well equipped, with built-in headboards, fine beds, cool tile floors, and efficient maintenance. There is a swimming pool and an elevator to the beach.

Marina Riviera

Via Comite 9, 84011 Amalfi. ☎ **089/871024.** Fax 089/871024. 20 rms (all with bath or shower). MINIBAR TV TEL. 150,000–180,000 lire ($93.75–$112.50) double. Rates include breakfast. AE, DC, MC, V. Parking 20,000 lire ($12.50). Closed Oct 31–Mar 31. Bus: SITA.

Fifty yards from the beach, this hotel offers rooms with terraces that overlook the sea. Directly on the coastal road, it rises against the foot of the hills, with side ve-randas and balconies. There's a gracious dining room with high-backed provincial chairs, but meals in the open air are preferred. A restaurant called Eolo opened in the spring of 1995 right below the hotel itself and is under the same management. Meals range in price from 40,000 to 60,000 lire ($25 to $37.50). Two adjoining public lounges are traditionally furnished, and a small bar provides drinks when-ever you want them. The refurbished rooms are comfortable, with a balcony and such amenities as a hairdryer. Half the rooms are air-conditioned. The hotel was originally built around 1900 and was enlarged twice with modern wings set above and below the original core during the 1980s.

WHERE TO DINE
INEXPENSIVE

La Caravella-Amalfi

Via Matteo Camera 12. ☎ **871029.** Reservations required. Main courses 18,000–26,000 lire ($11.25–$16.25). AE, V. Daily 12:30–2:30pm and 7:30–11pm. Closed Tues from Sept 15–June 15, and Nov. Bus: SITA. CAMPANIA.

La Caravella is a leading restaurant and, happily, it's inexpensive. A grottolike, air-conditioned place, it's off the main street next to the road tunnel, only a minute from the beach. You get well-cooked, authentic Italian specialties, such as spaghetti

Caravella with a seafood sauce. Scaloppine alla Caravella is served with a tangy clam sauce, and a healthy portion of zuppa di pesce (fish soup) is also ladled out. You can have a platter of the mixed fish fry, with crisp, tasty bits of shrimp and squid, followed by an order of fresh fruit served at your table in big bowls.

Da Gemma

Via Frà Gerardo Sassi 9. ☎ **871345.** Reservations required. Main courses 20,000–32,000 lire ($12.50–$20). AE, DC, MC, V. Daily 1–3pm and 8pm–midnight. Closed Wed Sept–June and Jan 15–Feb 15. Bus: SITA. SEAFOOD.

One of the best restaurants in town, Da Gemma takes inspired liberties with the regional cuisine and gives diners a strong sense of the family unity that makes this place popular. The kitchen sends out plateful after plateful of savory spaghetti, sautéed mixed shellfish, fish casserole, and a full range of other "sea creature" dishes. In summer, the intimate dining room more than doubles with the addition of an outdoor terrace.

4 Ravello

171 miles SE of Rome, 41 miles SE of Naples, 18 miles W of Salerno

Known to long-ago personages ranging from Richard Wagner to Greta Garbo, Ravello is the choice spot along the Amalfi Drive. Its reigning celebrity at the moment is Gore Vidal, who purchased a villa as a writing retreat. The village seems to hang 1,100 feet up, between the Tyrrhenian Sea and some celestial orbit. From Amalfi, 4 miles to the southwest, the sleepy (except for summer tour buses) village is approached by a wickedly curving road that cuts through the villa- and vine-draped hills that hem in the Valley of the Dragone. Celebrated in poetry, song, and literature are Ravello's major attractions, two villas.

ESSENTIALS

GETTING THERE **By Bus** Buses from Amalfi leave for Ravello every hour from 7am to 10pm. Buses leave from the terminal at the waterfront at piazza Flavio Gioia (☎ 871009 for schedules and information). The one-way fare to Ravello is 1,500 lire (95¢).

By Car From Amalfi, take a circuitous mountain road north of the town (the road is signposted to Ravello).

ESSENTIALS The telephone area code is 089. The tourist information center is at piazza del Duomo 10 (☎ 857096).

WHAT TO SEE & DO

Villa Cimbrone

Via Santa Chiara 26. ☎ **857459.** Admission 5,000 lire ($3.15) adults, 3,000 lire ($1.90) children. Daily 9am–sunset.

A long walk past grape arbors and private villas takes you to the Villa Cimbrone. After ringing the bell for admission, you'll be shown into the vaulted cloisters (on the left as you enter); note the grotesque bas-relief. Later, you can stroll (everybody "strolls" in Ravello) through the gardens, past a bronze copy of Donatello's *David*. Along the rose-arbored walkway is a tiny, but roofless, chapel. At the far end of the garden is a cliffside view of the Bay of Salerno, a scene that the devout might claim was the spot where Satan took Christ to tempt him with the world.

Villa Rufolo

Piazza Vescovado. ☎ **857866.** Admission 4,000 lire ($2.50) adults, 2,000 lire ($1.25) children. Year round, daily 9:30am–1pm year round; May–Sept daily 3–7pm, Oct–Mar daily 2–5pm. Bus: SITA.

Located near the Duomo, Villa Rufolo was named for the patrician family who founded it in the 11th century. Once the residence of kings and popes, such as Hadrian IV, it is now remembered chiefly for its connection with Wagner. He composed an act of *Parsifal* here in a setting he dubbed the "Garden of Klingsor." Boccaccio was so moved by the spot that he included it as background in one of his tales. The Moorish-influenced architecture evokes the Alhambra at Granada. The large tower was built in what is known as the "Norman-Sicilian" influence. You can walk through the flower gardens that lead to lookout points over the memorable coastline.

WHERE TO STAY

The choice of accommodations at Ravello is limited in number, but large on charm.

VERY EXPENSIVE

✪ Hotel Palumbo/Palumbo Residence

Via San Giovanni del Toro 28, 84010 Ravello. ☎ **089/857244.** Fax 089/858133. 27 rms, 3 suites. A/C MINIBAR TV TEL. Hotel, 450,000–545,000 lire ($281.25–$340.65) double; 600,000–1,090,000 lire ($375–$681.25) suite. Residence, 240,000–290,000 lire ($150–$181.25) double. Rates include breakfast. AE, DC, MC, V. Parking 20,000 lire ($12.50). Bus: SITA.

This elite retreat on the Amalfi Coast, a 12th-century palace, has been favored by the famous ever since Richard Wagner (who did a lot of composing here) persuaded the Swiss owners, the Vuilleumier family, to take in paying guests. If you stay here you'll understand why Max Reinhardt, Humphrey Bogart (filming *Beat the Devil*), Henry Wadsworth Longfellow, Ingrid Bergman, Zsa Zsa Gabor, Tennessee Williams, Richard Chamberlain, and a young John and Jacqueline Kennedy found its situation in the village ideal. D. H. Lawrence even wrote part of *Lady Chatterley's Lover* while staying here.

The hotel offers gracious living in its series of drawing rooms, furnished with English and Italian antiques. Most of the snug but elegantly decorated bedrooms have a tile bath and their own terrace. Although the original Hotel Palumbo contains by far the more glamorous and better-accessorized accommodations, about seven of the hotel's rooms lie within a modern annex in the garden. Built in the 1950s, and modernized in the 1970s, the annex rooms contain TV, telephone, minibar, functional furniture, and a few offer views of the sea.

Dining/Entertainment: Meals begin at 85,000 lire ($53.15) and are served in a 17th-century dining room with baroque accents and a dining terrace opening to the panoramic outdoors. "Fill-in'"bookings are accepted. The cuisine, the finest in Ravello, shows the influence of the Swiss-Italian ownership. It would be worth it to come here just to enjoy the hotel's lemon and chocolate soufflés. The Palumbo also produces its own Episcopio wine, served on the premises. The wine originated in 1860 and is stored in 50,000-liter casks in a vaulted cellar.

Services: Room service, babysitting, laundry, valet.

Facilities: Solarium overlooking the Gulf of Salerno.

EXPENSIVE

Hotel Caruso Belvedere

Via San Giovanni del Toro, 84010 Ravello. ☎ **089/857111.** Fax 089/857372. 24 rms. TEL. 169,000–217,000 lire ($105.65–$135.65) double. Rates include breakfast. AE, DC, MC, V. Free parking outside, 10,000 lire ($6.25) in garage. Bus: SITA.

This spacious clifftop hotel, built into the 11th-century remains of what was once the d'Afflitto Palace, is now operated as a hotel by the Caruso family. It has semitropical gardens and a belvedere that overlooks the Bay of Salerno. From here, you can look down the terraced mountain slopes and see the rows of grapes used to make the "Grand Caruso" wine on the premises. The atmosphere is gracious. The bedrooms have character, some with paneled doors, some with antiques, and some with a private terrace. You'll never forget the arcaded walks, the Gothic arches, the pots of geraniums, the orange and purple bougainvillea, and the wine press with its large vats.

Dining/Entertainment: The indoor dining room has the original coved ceiling, plus tile floors. It opens onto a wide terrace where meals are also served under a canopy. The cuisine is special here. Naturally, the locally produced wines are served: red, white, or rosé. For nonresidents, a fixed-price menu costs 42,000 lire ($26.25).

Services: Room service, babysitting, laundry, valet.

MODERATE

Hotel Giordano e Villa Maria

Piazza del Duomo, via S. Chiara 2, 84010 Ravello. ☎ **089/857170.** Fax 089/857071. 51 rms (all with bath or shower), 2 suites. A/C TV TEL. 199,000–210,000 lire ($124.40–$131.25) double; 299,000–420,000 lire ($186.90-$262.50) suite. Rates include breakfast. AE, MC, V. Free parking. Bus: SITA.

The older, but more obviously modernized, of these two hotels is the Hotel Giordano, which was originally built in the late 1700s as a private manor house of the family who continues to run it today. In the 1970s, the owners bought the then-available neighboring house, the Villa Maria, a late 19th-century vacation home of an aristocratic family from Rome. Today, the two buildings operate as quasi-independent, jointly owned hotels whose facilities are open to residents of either establishment.

Accommodations in the Villa Maria are probably more glamorous than those in the Hotel Giordano, and usually contain high ceilings, a scattering of antiques, and sea views. Accommodations in the Hotel Giordano have garden views and conservative reproductions of traditional furniture. On the premises is a large heated swimming pool set near the Giordano, at least two bars, and a pair of restaurants where full meals cost from around 50,000 lire ($31.25) each. (Unlike its twin, the restaurant within the Villa Maria remains open throughout the winter and has a panoramic view of the sea.) After a 15-minute walk, guests can reach the beach by walking along ancient pathways or by taking one of the public buses departing from Ravello's central square every hour. Plenty of parking is available.

☉ Hotel Parsifal

Via G. D'Anna 5, 84010 Ravello. ☎ **089/857144.** Fax 089/857972. 19 rms (all with bath or shower). TV TEL. 100,000–120,000 lire ($62.50–$75) per person, single or double. Rates include half-board. AE, DC, MC, V. Free parking on street only. Closed Oct 15–Easter. Bus: SITA.

This little hotel incorporates portions of the original convent, founded in 1288 by Augustinian monks who had an uncanny instinct for picking the best views, and the most inspiring situations in which to build their retreats. The cloister, with stone arches and a tile walk, has a multitude of potted flowers and vines, and the garden spots, especially the one with a circular reflection pool, are the favorites of all. Chairs are placed for guests to watch the setting sun and fiery lights that illuminate the twisting shoreline. Dining is on the trellis-covered terrace where bougainvillea and wisteria scents mix with that of lemon blossoms. The living rooms have bright and comfortable furnishings, set against pure white walls. The bedrooms, while small, are tastefully arranged. A few rooms have terraces.

Hotel Rufolo

Via San Francesco 3, 84010 Ravello. ☎ **089/857133.** Fax 089/857935. 30 rms, 2 suites. MINIBAR TV TEL. 190,000–260,000 lire ($118.75–$162.50) double; 350,000 lire ($218.75) suite. Rates include breakfast. AE, DC, MC, V. Free parking. Bus: SITA.

This little gem, run by the hospitable Schiavo family, housed D. H. Lawrence for a long while in 1926. The view from the sun decks is superb, and chairs are placed on a wide terrace and around the swimming pool. The bedrooms are cozy and immaculate, some with air conditioning. Recently enlarged and modernized, the hotel lies in the center between cloisters of pine trees of the Villa Rufolo, from which the hotel takes its name, and the road that leads to the Villa Cimbrone. Mr. Schiavo and his family take good care of their guests.

Dining/Entertainment: Food served in the restaurant is quite good, and the service is efficient. Meals begin at 45,000 lire ($28.10).

Services: Room service, babysitting, laundry.

Facilities: Swimming pool, solarium.

INEXPENSIVE

ⓢ Albergo Toro

Viale Wagner 3, 84010 Ravello. ☎ **089/857211.** Fax 089/857211. 9 rms. TEL. 75,000–85,000 lire ($46.90–$53.15) per person. Rates include half-board. AE, MC, V. Closed Nov 15–Mar 15. Bus: SITA.

This place is a real bargain. It's a small, charming villa that has been converted to receive paying guests. The Toro—entered through a garden—lies just off the village square with its catheral. It has semimonastic architecture, with deeply set arches, long colonnades, and a tranquil character. The rooms are decent, and the owner is especially proud of the meals he serves.

WHERE TO DINE

INEXPENSIVE

Most guests take meals at their hotels. But try to escape the board requirement at least once to sample the goods at the following establishments.

ⓢ Cumpa' Cosimo

Via Roma. ☎ **857156.** Reservations recommended. Main courses 12,000–24,000 lire ($7.50–$15). AE, V. Daily 12:30–3pm and 7:30–10pm. Closed Monday Nov–Mar. Bus: SITA. CAMPANIA.

This restaurant's clientele is likely to include everyone from the electrician down the street to a well-known movie star searching for the best home cooking in town. It was established as an offshoot to a nearby butcher shop in 1929 by a town patriarch known affectionately as Cumpa' (godfather) Cosima and his wife Cumma' (godmother) Chiara. Today, their daughter, the kindly Netta Bottone, runs the place, turning out well-flavored regional food in generous portions. Menu items include homemade versions of seven different pastas, served with your choice of seven different sauces. Any of these might be followed by a mixed grill of fish, giant prawns, or roasted lamb well seasoned with herbs. The seasonal availability of vegetables is respected, as the restaurant offers, according to the calendar, artichokes, asparagus, or mushrooms. Certain fish dishes are priced according to weight, the price based on daily market quotations.

Ristorante Garden

Via Boccacio 4. ☎ **857226.** Reservations not necessary. Main courses 13,000–22,000 lire ($8.15–$13.75). MC, V. Daily noon–2:30pm and 7:30–10pm. Bus: SITA. CAMPANIA.

Perhaps this pleasant restaurant's greatest claim to fame occurred in 1962 when Jacqueline Onassis, then the wife of President Kennedy, came from a villa where she was staying to dine here with the owner of Fiat. Today some of that old glamour is still visible on the verdant terrace, which was designed to cantilever over the cliff below. The Mansi family offers well-prepared meals, which might include one of four kinds of spaghetti, cheese crêpes, and an array of soups, a well-presented antipasto table, brochettes of grilled shrimp, a mixed fish fry, and sole prepared in several ways. One of the local wines will be recommended.

On the premises are 10 well-scrubbed rooms, each with its own bath and terrace. Singles rent for 70,000 lire ($43.75); doubles for 95,000 lire ($59.40), including breakfast.

5 Paestum

25 miles S of Salerno, 62 miles SE of Naples, 189 miles SE of Rome

The ancient Sybarite city of Paestum (Poseidonia) dates back to 600 B.C. It was abandoned for centuries and fell to ruins. But the remnants of its past, excavated in the mid-18th century, are glorious—the finest heritage left from the Greek colonies that settled in Italy. The roses of Paestum, praised by the ancients, bloom two times yearly, splashing the landscape of the city with a scarlet red, a good foil for the salmon-colored temples that still stand in the archaeological garden.

ESSENTIALS

GETTING THERE   By Train   Paestum is within easy reach of Salerno, an hour away. Both buses and trains service the route. You can catch a southbound train, which departs Salerno with a stop at Paestum about every two hours. For schedules, call 252200 in Salerno. A one-way fare is 39,000 lire ($24.40).

By Bus   You can also take a bus in Salerno from piazza Concordia (near the rail station); one leaves for Paestum about every 30 minutes. The bus station in Salerno is at via Irno 2–4 (☎ 795021). A one-way fare is 4,000 lire ($2.50).

By Car   From Salerno, take Route 18 south.

VISITOR INFORMATION   The telephone area code is 0828. The tourist information center is at via Magna Grecia 151–156 (☎ 811016), in the archaeological zone.

WHAT TO SEE & DO

The ✪ **basilica** is a Doric temple that dates from the 6th century B.C., the oldest temple from the ruins of the Hellenic world in Italy. The basilica is characterized by 9 columns in front and 18 on the sides. The Doric pillars are approximately 5 feet in diameter. Walls and ceiling, however, long ago gave way to decay. Animals were sacrificed to gods on the altar.

The ✪ **Temple of Neptune** is the most impressive of the Greek ruins at Paestum. It and the Temple of Haphaistos ("Theseum") in Athens remain the best-preserved Greek temples in the world, both dating from around 450 to 420 B.C. Six columns in front are crowned by an entablature, and there are 14 columns on the sides. The **Temple of Caeres,** from the 6th century B.C., has 34 columns still standing and a large altar for sacrifices to the gods.

The temple zone may be visited daily from 9am to 5pm for an admission fee of 10,000 lire ($6.25). Using the same ticket, you can visit the ✪ **Museo Archeologico Nazionale di Paestum,** via Magna Grecia 169 (☎ 811023), across the road from the Caeres Temple. It displays the metopes removed from the treasury of the Temple of Hera (Juno). Some of southern Italy's finest tomb paintings, from the 4th century B.C. are displayed here. *The Diver's Tomb* is an extraordinary example of painting from the first half of the 5th century B.C. The museum is open from 9am to 2pm (until 1pm on Sunday).

New discoveries have revealed hundreds of Greek tombs, which have yielded many Greek paintings. Archaeologists have called the find astonishing. In addition, other tombs excavated were found to contain clay figures in a strongly impressionistic vein.

WHERE TO STAY

Strand Hotel Schuhmann

Via Laura Mare, 84063 Paestum. ☎ **0828/851151.** Fax 0828/851183. 36 rms (all with bath or shower). A/C MINIBAR TV TEL. 100,000–170,000 lire ($62.50–$106.25) double. Rates include breakfast. AE, DC, MC, V. Free parking. Paestum bus from Salerno.

If you'd like to combine serious looks at Italy's archaeological past with the first-class amenities of a beachside resort, try the Strand Hotel Schuhmann, a delightful choice for a holiday. Set in a pine grove removed from traffic noises, the hotel has a large terrace with a view of the sea and a subtropical garden that overlooks the Gulf of Salerno and the Amalfi Coast to Capri. Its bedrooms are well furnished and maintained, and each has a balcony or terrace. Guests get use of the beach facilities and deck chairs. The hotel also has a restaurant, charging 40,000 lire ($25) for a meal.

WHERE TO DINE

Nettuno Ristorante

Zona Archeologica. ☎ **811028.** Reservations not necessary. Main courses 20,000–24,000 lire ($12.50–$15). AE, DC, MC, V. May–June and Sept–Oct, daily 12:30–3pm; July–Aug, daily 7:30–10pm. Closed Mon Nov–Feb. Paestum bus from Salerno. CAMPANIA.

While at Paestum, you may want to take time out for lunch. If so, you'll find the Nettuno a special place at which to dine. It stands in a meadow just at the edge of the ruins, like a country inn or villa. The interior dining room has vines growing over its arched windows, and from the tables there's a good view of the ruins. The ceilings are beamed, the room divided by three Roman stone arches. Outside is a terrace for dining that faces the temples—like a stage for a Greek drama. Under pine trees, hedged in by pink oleander, you can order such a typical selection as beefsteak or roast chicken, a vegetable or salad, plus dessert. Menu suggestions include spaghetti with filets in tomato sauce, veal cutlet, and crème caramel.

6 Capri

3 miles off the tip of the Sorrentine peninsula

The broiling dog-day July and August sun that beats down on Capri illuminates a circus of humanity. The parade of visitors would give Ripley's "Believe It or Not" material for months. In the upper town, a vast snakelike chain of gaudily attired tourists promenades through the narrow quarters (many of the lanes evoke the casbahs of North Africa).

The Greeks called Capri (pronounced *Cap*-ry, not Ca-*pree*, as in the old song) "the island of the wild boars." Before the big season rush, which lasts from Easter to the end of October, Capri is an island of lush Mediterranean vegetation (olives, vineyards, flowers) encircled by emerald waters, an oasis in the sun even before emperor Tiberius moved the seat of the empire here. Writers such as D. H. Lawrence have in previous decades found Capri a haven. Some have written of it, including Axel Munthe (*The Story of San Michele*) and Norman Douglas (*Siren Land*). The latter title is a reference to Capri's reputation as the "island of the sirens," a temptation to Ulysses. Other distinguished visitors have included Gide, Mendelssohn, Dumas, and Hans Christian Andersen.

Don't visit Capri, incidentally, for great beaches, as there aren't any. The mountainous landscape doesn't make for long sandy beaches. There are some spots for bathing, and many of these have been turned into clubs called *stabilimenti balneari*, which you must pay to visit.

Touring the island is relatively simple. You dock at unremarkable **Marina Grande,** the port area. From there, you can take the funicular to the town of **Capri** above, site of the major hotels, restaurants, cafés, and shops. From Capri, a short bus ride will deliver you to **Anacapri,** at the top of the island near Monte Solaro. The only other settlement you might want to visit is **Marina Piccola,** on the south side of the island. The major beach is here. There are also beaches at Punta Carnea and Bagni di Tiberio. The tourist office will pinpoint these locations on a map for you.

ESSENTIALS

GETTING THERE   By Boat   You can go from Naples by **hydrofoil** in just 45 minutes with boats departing from Molo Beverello. The hydrofoil (*aliscafo*) leaves several times daily (some stop at Sorrento). A one-way trip costs 16,000 lire ($10). It's cheaper, but takes longer (about 1 1/2 hours), to go by regularly scheduled ferryboat, with a one-way ticket costing 10,000 lire ($6.25). For schedules, call 081/7613688 in Naples.

VISITOR INFORMATION   There's no need to have a car in tiny Capri, and they are virtually impossible to drive on the hairpin roads anyway. The island is serviced by funiculars, taxis, and buses. Many of Capri's hotels are remotely located, especially those at Anacapri, and some are inaccessible by car. I strongly recommend that visitors to the island arrive with as little luggage as possible. However, with even minor baggage, you may need the services of a porter. You'll find the headquarters of the island's union of porters in a building connected to the jetty at Marina Grande. There you can cajole, coddle, coerce, or connive your way through the hiring process where the only rule seems to be that there are no rules.

One positive aspect to the business is that your porter will know where to find the hotel among the winding passageways and steep inclines of the island's arteries. Your best defense during your pilgrimage might be a sense of humor.

The telephone area code is 081.

MARINA GRANDE

The least attractive of the island's communities, Marina Grande is the port, and it bustles with the coming and going of hundreds of visitors daily. It has a little sand-cum-pebble beach, on which you're likely to see American sailors—on shore leave from Naples—playing ball, occasionally upsetting a Coca-Cola over mamma and bambino.

If you're just spending the day on Capri, you should leave at once for the island's biggest attraction, the ✪ **Grotto Azzurra (Blue Grotto),** open daily from 9am till one hour before sunset. In summer, boats that leave frequently from the harbor at Marina Grande transport passengers to the entrance of the grotto for 8,000 lire ($5) round trip. Once at the grotto, you'll pay 6,500 lire ($4.05) for the small rowboat that traverses the water. Admission is another 4,000 lire ($2.50).

You'll have to change boats to go under the low entrance to the cave. The toughened boatmen of the Campania are usually skilled at getting heavier passengers from the big boat into the skimpy craft with a minimum of volcanic spills.

The Blue Grotto is one of the best-known natural sights of the region, although the way passengers are hustled in and out of it makes it somewhat of a tourist trap. It is beautiful, however, but because of all the shabby commercialism that surrounds it, many passengers opt to miss it. Known to the ancients, it was later lost to the world until an artist stumbled on it in 1826. Inside the cavern, light refraction (the sun's rays entering from an opening under the water) achieves the dramatic Mediterranean cerulean color. The effect is stunning, as thousands testify yearly.

If you wish, you can take a trip around the entire island, passing not only the Blue Grotto, but the Baths of Tiberius, the "Palazzo al Mare" built in the days of the empire, the Green Grotto (less known), and the much-photographed rocks called the Faraglioni. The motorboats circle the island in about 1 1/2 hours at a cost of 36,000 lire ($22.50) per person.

Connecting Marina Grande with Capri (the town) is a frequently running funicular that charges 3,000 lire ($1.90) round-trip. However, should you arrive off-season, the funicular, really a cog railway, doesn't operate. Instead, you can take a bus from Marina Grande to Capri at a one-way cost of 1,500 lire (95¢).

For information, get in touch with the Tourist Board, piazza Umberto I no. 19 (☎ 8370686), at Capri, open daily from 9am to 1pm and 3:30 to 6:45pm.

CAPRI

The main town is the center of most of the hotels, restaurants, and elegant shops—and the milling throngs. The heart of the resort, piazza Umberto I, is like a grand living room.

WHAT TO SEE & DO

One of the most popular walks from the main square is down via Vittorio Emanuele, past the deluxe Quisisana, to the **Giardini di Augusto.** The park is the

Siren Land

Over the centuries, artists and writers have been drawn to the Isle of Capri that the Emperor Augustus called *Capri Apragopolis* ("city of sweet idleness"). The island's first bigtime "swinger" was another emperor, Tiberius, who spent the last decade of his licentious life at his Villa Jovis in Capri, wandering from bed to bed in search of some new erotic amusement. He is said to have inspired a long line of hedonists over the centuries, ranging from munitions king Baron Von Krupp to the acerbic Oscar Wilde who appreciated the golden Mediterranean youth of the island.

There's definitely a live-and-let-live attitude on Capri—perhaps that's why even Maxim Gorky settled here from 1907 to 1913, running a school for revolutionaries that is said to have been attended by Lenin and Stalin.

English writers, especially, have been fond of the island. Noël Coward, for example, pronounced it "the most beautiful operetta stage in the world." His visits to the island were noted by playwright Tennessee Williams, who notoriously satirized him in the play, *The Milk Train Doesn't Train Here Anymore*, in which the "witch of Capri" was played by Mildred Dunnock. Rather ironically, when the play was rewritten as a movie, *Boom*, starring Richard Burton and Elizabeth Taylor, the part of the "witch of Capri" was recast as a man and Coward played himself. Another, very different writer, Graham Greene found Capri an island of inspiration for his writing, and returned to his villa there frequently.

The English writer most identified with the island was Norman Douglas (1868–1952). Capri provided the inspiration for his best known novel, *South Wind*, published in 1917. He later told friends he'd fallen in love with Capri when he first saw it in full bloom in the spring of 1888.

At the age of only 28, Douglas had been forced into retirement from the Foreign Office in London because of an impending scandal that involved an aristocratic Russian woman in the court of St. Petersburg. With what money he had, he purchased a villa along the Posillipo peninsula overlooking the Bay of Naples. Calling it "Villa Maya," he lived there for four years in a disastrous marriage to his cousin, Elsa Fitzgibbon, finally divorcing her in 1904.

It was then he moved to Capri, purchasing Villa Daphne. In about three years, he'd spent all his money and told friends he'd been forced into writing because of "sheer poverty." His first book, *Siren Land* (1911) was followed by *Fountains in the Sand* (1912) and *Old Calabria* (1915). Critics hailed these almost forgotten books as among the best travel books ever penned, but the public wasn't buying until the publication of the novel, *South Wind*, with Capri as a setting.

Other works were to follow: *They Went* (1920), *Alone* (1921), *Together* (1923), *Paneros* (1931), *Looking Back* (1933), and finally, *Late Harvest* (1946). Douglas died in 1952 after writing *Footnote on Capri*. He spent the post-war years of his life at the Villa Tuoro in Capri (owned by a friend), and his tomb in the Capri cemetery can be visited.

choice spot in Capri for views and relaxation. From this perch, you can see the legendary Faraglioni, the rocks, once inhabited by the "blue lizard." At the top of the park is a belvedere that overlooks emerald waters and Marina Piccola. Nearby you can visit the **Certosa,** a Carthusian monastery erected in the 14th century in honor of St. James. The monastery is open daily except Monday from 9am to 2pm and charges no admission.

Back at piazza Umbert I, head up via Longano, then via Tiberio, all the way to Monte Tiberio. Here is **Villa Jovis,** the splendid ruin of the estate from which Tiberius ruled the empire from A.D. 27 to 37. Actually, the Jovis was one of a dozen villas that the depraved emperor erected on the island. Apparently Tiberius couldn't sleep, so he wandered from bed to bed. From the ruins there's a view of both the Bay of Salerno and the Bay of Naples, as well as of the island. The ruins of the imperial palace may be visited daily from 9am to one hour before sunset for 4,000-lire ($2.50) admission.

SHOPPING

Carthusia-Profumi di Capri
Via Camerelle 10. ☎ **8370368.**

This little shop on Capri's luxury shopping street specializes in perfume made on the island. The shop has existed since 1947, attracting such clients in days gone by as Elizabeth Taylor before she started touting her own perfume. The scents are unique, and many women consider Carthusia perfumes to be collector's items. Open daily from 9:30am to 9pm. Carthusia also has a perfume laboratory, at via Matteotti 2 (☎ 8373668), which can be visited daily from 9am to 7pm. There is another Carthusia shop in Anacapri, at via Capodimonte 26 (☎ 837-3668), next to the Villa Axel Munthe. The shops close in January and on Sunday in February and March.

WHERE TO STAY

Finding your own bed for the night can be a real problem if you arrive in July or August without a reservation. There's a far greater demand for rooms than there is a supply. Capri is also an exclusive enclave of the wealthy, and even the cheaper accommodations are able to charge high prices. Many serious economizers return to the mainland for the night, unable to pay the steep tariffs of Capri.

Very Expensive

Quisisana & Grand Hotel
Via Camerelle 2, 80073 Capri. ☎ **081/8370788.** Fax 081/8376080. 150 rms, 15 suites. A/C MINIBAR TV TEL. 380,000–650,000 lire ($237.50–$406.25) double; 850,000–1,000,000 lire ($531.25–$625) suite. Rates include breakfast. AE, DC, MC, V. Closed Nov–March. Transportation: Capri Funicular.

The deluxe choice is the Quisisana & Grand Hotel, the favorite nesting place for a regular international clientele. Opened as a small hotel around the turn of the century, the Quisisana was enlarged and became the foremost of the resort hotels here after World War II. More spacious than its central location would indicate, its private garden is shut off from the tourists passing outside its front entrance. A large, rather sprawling, but imposing structure, it has bedrooms ranging from cozy singles to spacious suites—all of which open onto wide arcades with a view of the seacoast. They vary greatly in decor, with both traditional and conservatively modern furnishings. In the main lounge the furnishings are in antique gold. Capri's social center, the terrace of the hotel, is where everybody who is anybody goes for cocktails before dinner.

Dining/Entertainment: The hotel has two restaurants, both under the supervision of the famed chef Gualtiero Marchesi. At Colombaia, ideal for lunch, the head chef is proud of his fresh-tasting and attractively displayed fish dishes, as well as his lush fruits and vegetables. In the evening, Quisi Restaurant is alluring with candlelight, serving a creative Mediterranean and local cuisine. The American bar (which seems appropriate to Berkeley Square, London) is the second-most frequented spot on the premises, and overlooks the swimming pool on the lower terrace.

Services: Room service, babysitting, laundry, valet.

Facilities: Sauna, Turkish bath and massage facilities, indoor and outdoor swimming pool, beauty shop, gymnasium, tennis courts.

✪ La Scalinatella (Little Steps)

Via Tragara 8, 80073 Capri. ☎ **081/8370633.** Fax 081/8378291. 28 rms, 8 suites. A/C MINIBAR TV TEL. 500,000 lire ($312.50) double; from 640,000 lire ($400) suite. Rates include breakfast. AE, DC, MC, V. Closed Nov 15–Mar 15. Transportation: Capri funicular.

One of the most delightful hotels in Capri is constructed above terraces that offer a panoramic view of the water and a nearby monastery. It's composed of an interconnected pair of 200-year-old houses acquired in 1962 and 1969 by the present owners, the Morgano family. The ambience is one of unadulterated luxury; rooms include a phone beside each of the bathtubs, beds set into alcoves, elaborate wrought-iron accents that ring both the inner stairwell and the ornate balconies, and a sweeping view over the establishment's surrounding gardens and its swimming pool. The hotel contains a restaurant, open only at lunchtime, where simple but flavorful dishes are served on a terrace beside the swimming pool. Meals cost from 65,000 lire ($40.65) each.

Expensive

Hotel Flora

Via Federico Serena 26, 80073 Capri. ☎ **081/837-0211.** Fax 081/837-8949. 24 rms. A/C MINIBAR TV TEL. 350,000 lire ($218.75) double. Rates include breakfast. AE, DC, MC, V. Closed Jan 9–Mar 1. Transportation: Capri funicular.

Hotel Flora overlooks the monastery of St. James and the sea, and features terraces edged with oleander, bougainvillea, and geraniums. There are several tile courtyards with garden furniture, pots of tropical flowers, and spots where you can either sunbathe or be cooled by the sea breezes. The public and private rooms are a wise blend of the old and new. The bedrooms are well furnished. There's an annex across the street. The Flora also offers a first-class restaurant La Certosa di San Giacomo with an impressive cuisine; meals are reasonably priced, ranging from 50,000 to 70,000 lire ($31.25 to $43.75), service included. Many excellent regional wines are also served.

Hotel Luna

Viale Matteotti 3, 80073 Capri. ☎ **081/8370433.** Fax 081/8377459. 54 rms. A/C MINIBAR TV TEL. 230,000–450,000 lire ($143.75–$281.25) double, including breakfast. 160,000–275,000 lire ($100–$171.90) per person with half-board. AE, DC, MC, V. Closed Oct 15 to Thurs before Easter. Transportation: Capri funicular.

This first-class hotel stands on a cliff overlooking the sea and the rocks of Faraglioni. It's almost between the Gardens of Augustus and the Carthusian monastery of St. James. The building, however, is nondescript. The furnishings are reproductions of antiques. Architecturally, the tile designs for the floor set the pace. The bedrooms, a mixture of contemporary Italian pieces and a Victorian decor, incorporate wood and padded headboards and gilt mirrors over the desk, all consistently in good style. Some of the bedrooms have arched, recessed private terraces that overlook the garden of flowers and semitropical plants. There's a clubby drinking lounge, and the dining room lures with good cuisine.

Hotel Punta Tragara

Via Tragara 57, 80073 Capri. ☎ **081/8370844.** Fax 081/8377790. 17 rms, 30 suites. A/C MINIBAR TV TEL. 280,000–350,000 lire ($175–$218.75) double; 380,000–520,000 lire ($237.50–$325) suite. Rates include breakfast. AE, DC, MC, V. Closed Nov–Easter. Transportation: Capri funicular.

This former private villa stands above rocky cliffs at the tip of the most desirable panorama in Capri, but that isn't all it has in its favor. Its sienna-colored walls and Andalusian-style accents are designed so that each of the apartment accommodations is subtly different from its neighbors. Outfitted with mottled carpeting, big windows, substantial furniture, and all the modern comforts, each unit opens onto a private terrace or a balcony studded with flowers and vines, plus a sweeping view. On the premises are two swimming pools, one of which is heated, plus multi-branched cactus plants in oval terra-cotta pots, quiet retreats near a baronial fireplace, and a grotto disco. An often-debated point on Capri involves this hotel's isolation from the other activities of the island, although many clients consider its isolation a virtue rather than a drawback. This is especially the case in high season when other sections of the island can be very crowded.

La Palma

Via Vittorio Emanuele 39, 80073 Capri. ☎ **081/8370133.** Fax 081/8376966. 70 rms. A/C MINIBAR TV TEL. 200,000–400,000 lire ($125–$250) double. Rates include breakfast. AE, DC, MC, V. Transportation: Capri funicular.

This hotel was established a century ago as one of the first symbols of modern tourism on the island. Right in the center of Capri, it caters to guests who seek first-class amenities and comforts—and who are willing to pay the piper for the privilege. Restored and renovated in an appealing style that blends modern and traditional styles, the hotel has a white-walled exterior, and a forecourt with palms and potted shrubs. Each bedroom is handsomely furnished.

Its restaurant, Relais la Palma, is one of the finest dinner choices in Capri if you'd like to make a reservation in the evening. Meals cost from 40,000 lire ($25). Although the hotel remains open in winter, the restaurant operates only from Easter through late September.

La Pineta

Via Tragara 6, 80073 Capri. ☎ **081/8370644.** Fax 081/837-6445. 45 rms, 6 suites. A/C MINIBAR TV TEL. 400,000 lire ($250) double; 500,000 lire ($312.50) suite. Rates include breakfast. Midwinter reductions of 45%. AE, DC, MC, V. Transportation: Capri funicular.

This is that rare hotel in Capri that remains open all year. Built in 1952, it has been receiving visitors ever since. A four-star hotel, it's on one of the most enchanting walks on the island. A terraced hotel, it lures with its contemporary decor and swimming pool where you can enjoy lunch daily from noon to 5pm. The swimming pool is heated during spring and autumn. Bedrooms are well kept and furnished.

Villa Brunella

Via Tragara 24, 80073 Capri. ☎ **081/8370122.** Fax 081/8370430. 18 rms. A/C TV TEL. 335,000–395,000 lire ($209.40–$246.90) double. Rates include breakfast. AE, DC, MC, V. Closed Nov 15–Mar 15.

Set within a 10-minute walk from many of Capri's largest hotels (i.e., the Quisisana), this hotel was originally built in the late 1940s as a privately owned villa. In 1963, it was transformed into a well-appointed and comfortable hotel by its present owner, Vincenzo Ruggiero, who named it after his hardworking wife, Brunella. All of the double rooms have balconies or terraces and views of the sea. On the premises is a carefully landscaped swimming pool, a bar, and a cozy restaurant.

Moderate

Regina Cristina

Via Serena 20, 80073 Capri. ☎ **081/8370744.** Fax 081/8370550. 50 rms, 5 suites. A/C MINIBAR TV TEL. 390,000 lire ($243.75) double; from 450,000 lire ($281.25) suite. Rates include breakfast. Midwinter discounts up to 45%. AE, DC, MC, V. Transportation: Capri funicular.

The white facade of the Regina Cristina rises four stories above one of the most imaginatively landscaped gardens in Capri. It was built in 1959, and renovated in 1993 in a sun-flooded design of open spaces, sunken lounges, cool tiles, and *la dolce vita* armchairs. Each accommodation has its own balcony and is very restful. Most of the rooms have Jacuzzi features in their bathtubs.

La Vega

Via Occhio Marino 10, 80073 Capri. ☎ **081/8370481.** Fax 081/8370342. 23 rms. A/C MINIBAR TV TEL. 260,000–380,000 lire ($162.50–$237.50) double. Rates include breakfast. AE, DC, MC, V. Closed Nov–Easter. Transportation: Capri funicular.

This hotel originated as the private home of the family who continues to run it today. Originally built in the 1930s, and renovated in 1992, it has a clear view of the sea and is nestled amid trees against a sunny hillside. Each of the oversize rooms of this four-level building has a shower, and a private balcony that overlooks the water. Below the rooms is a garden of flowering bushes, and on the lower edge is a free-form swimming pool with a grassy border for sunbathing and a little bar for refreshments. The rooms have decoratively tiled floors and the beds have wrought-iron headboards. Some contain TV, and most of the units have Jacuzzi features. All rooms are doubles. Breakfast is served on a terrace surrounded by trees and large potted flowers or else on your private balcony.

Inexpensive

Villa Krupp

Via Matteotti 12, 80073 Capri. ☎ **081/8370362.** Fax 081/8376489. 15 rms. TEL. 160,000–210,000 lire ($100–$131.25) double. Rates include breakfast. MC, V. Transportation: Capri funicular.

This place is a sunny villa-turned guesthouse that overlooks the Gardens of Augustus. Surrounded by shady trees, it offers a splendid view of the sea from its lofty terraces. A family-run place, it has the advantage of intimacy. The front parlor is all glass; it has views of the seaside, and semitropical plants set near Hong Kong chairs, all intermixed with painted Venetian-style pieces. Your bedroom may be large, with a fairly good bathroom. Many of the rooms have a terrace. Breakfast is the only meal offered.

Villa Sarah

Via Tiberio 3A, 80073 Capri. ☎ **081/8377817.** Fax 081/8377215. 20 rms. TV TEL. 240,000 lire ($150) double. Rates include breakfast. AE, MC, V. Closed Oct 15–Easter. Transportation: Capri funicular.

Villa Sarah, although far removed from the day-trippers from Naples, is still very central. A steep walk from the main square, it seems part of another world with its Capri garden and good views. All it lacks is a swimming pool. Considered one of the bargains of the island, it's often fully booked, so reservations are needed if you arrive in summer. The view of the sea is only from the upper floors. An old private house stands on the grounds, but is no longer in use as a hotel—the hotel section of bedrooms is in a modern building. Some bedrooms have terraces. Only breakfast is served.

WHERE TO DINE
Moderate

I Faraglioni

Via Camerelle 75. ☎ **8730320.** Reservations required. Main courses 22,000–36,000 lire ($13.75–$22.50). AE, V. Tues–Sun 12:30–3pm and 7:30pm–midnight. July–Sept open daily. Closed Nov–Mar. Transportation: Capri funicular. SEAFOOD/CONTINENTAL.

Some locals say that the food is only a secondary consideration to the social ferment that usually seems to be part of this popular restaurant. In any event, the kitchen turns out a well-prepared collection of European specialties, which is usually based on seafood from the surrounding waters. Examples might include linguine with lobster, seafood crêpes, rice Créole, spaghetti with clams, grilled or baked fish of many different varieties, and a wide assortment of meat dishes. Desserts might be made of one of the regional pastries mixed with fresh fruit.

La Capannina

Via Le Botteghe 14. ☎ **8370732.** Reservations required for dinner. Main courses 18,000–38,000 lire ($11.25–$23.75). AE, MC, V. Thurs–Tues noon–3pm and 7:30–10:30pm. Aug open daily. Closed Nov 11–Mar 14. Transportation: Capri funicular. CAMPANA/ITALIAN.

This restaurant is not pretentious, although it's patronized by a host of famous people, ranging from film actresses to dress designers to royalty. A trio of inside rooms is decorated in a tavern manner, although the main draw in summer is the inner courtyard, with its ferns and hanging vines. At a table covered with a colored cloth, you can select the finest meals on the island. Wine is from vineyards owned by the restaurant. If featured, a fine opener is Sicilian macaroni. Main-dish specialties include baby shrimp au gratin, pollo (chicken) alla Capannina, and scaloppine Capannina. However, the most savory skillet of goodies is the zuppa di pesce, a soup made with fish from the bay. Some of the dishes, however, were obviously inspired by the nouvelle cuisine school.

✪ La Pigna

Via Roma 30. ☎ **837-0280.** Reservations recommended. Main courses 16,000–30,000 lire ($10–$18.75). AE, DC, MC, V. Wed–Mon (daily Aug) noon–3pm; Wed–Mon (daily July–Sept) 8pm–2am. Closed 1 or 2 months in winter (dates vary). Transportation: Capri funicular. NEAPOLITAN.

A short walk from the bus station, La Pigna serves the finest meals for the money on the entire island, outside of the hotel dining rooms. Dining here is like attending a garden party in Capri, and this has been true since 1875. The owner loves flowers almost as much as good food. The ambience is one of a greenhouse, with purple petunias, red geraniums, bougainvillea, and lemon trees that flourish in abundance. Much of the produce comes from the restaurant's gardens in Anacapri. The food is excellent, regardless of what you select, but try in particular the penne tossed in a sauce made of eggplant, and the chicken suprême with mushrooms, the house specialty. Another dish I can recommend is the rabbit, which was raised on the farm; it's stuffed with herbs. The dessert specialty is an almond-and-chocolate torte. Another feature of the restaurant is homemade liquors, one of which is distilled from local lemons. The waiters are courteous and efficient, and the atmosphere is nostalgic, as guitarists stroll by singing sentimental Neapolitan ballads.

Inexpensive

Al Geranio

Giardini Augusto, viale Matteotti 8. ☎ **8370616.** Reservations required Fri–Sat. Main courses 18,000–32,000 lire ($11.25–$20). AE, DC, MC, V. Wed–Mon 12:30–3pm and 7:30–10pm. Closed Oct 30–Easter. Transportation: Capri funicular. FRENCH/MEDITERRANEAN.

One of the most scenically located restaurants in Capri, Al Geranio stands in the Gardens of Augustus en route to the Villa Krupp. It can be easily reached from two of the leading hotels, the Quisisana and the Luna. Arrive early to enjoy an apéritif in the piano bar, which is furnished in a modern style. The earlier you arrive in the summer, the better chance you have of getting an outdoor table. The kitchen turns out a good Mediterranean cuisine, which is likely to include such dishes as fish soup, fried shrimp, swordfish, crêpes with cheese, and cannelloni. A savory dish to order is zuppa di cozze (mussel soup). You might also try Capri-style ravioli. Look for the daily specials.

Ⓢ Casanova

Via Le Botteghe 46. ☎ **8377642.** Reservations required at dinner in summer. Main courses 12,000–28,000 lire ($7.50–$17.50). AE, DC, MC, V. Fri–Wed noon–3pm and 7pm–midnight. July–Sept open daily. Closed Jan–Mar. Transportation: Capri funicular. NEAPOLITAN/ITALIAN.

Run by the D'Alessio family, and only a short walk from piazza Umberto I, this is one of the finest dining rooms in Capri. Its cellar offers a big choice of Italian wines, with most of the favorites of the Campania, and its cooks turn out a savory blend of Neapolitan and Italian specialties. You might begin with a cheese-filled ravioli, then go on to veal Sorrento or even red snapper "crazy waters" (with baby tomatoes). The seafood is always fresh and well prepared. A large and tempting buffet of antipasti is at hand. In a small wine cellar you can enjoy a good selection of Italian and foreign wines with a variety of cheeses.

Da Gemma

Via Madre Serafina 6. ☎ **8377113.** Reservations required. Main courses 14,000–26,000 lire ($8.75–$16.25). AE, DC, MC, V. Tues–Sun 12:30–3pm and 7:30pm–midnight. Closed Nov–Dec 15. Transportation: Capri funicular. REGIONAL/SEAFOOD.

Long a favorite with painters and writers, this place is reached from piazza Umberto I by going up an arch-covered walkway, reminiscent of Tangier, Morocco. Some tables are arranged for the view. Everything's cozy and atmospheric. The cuisine is provincial, with a reliance on fish dishes. The best beginning is the mussel soup, and pizzas are also featured in the evening. The finest main dish to order is the boiled fish of the day with creamy butter, priced according to weight. Desserts are mouthwatering. It has an annex across the street that remains open in winter.

Ⓢ La Cisterna

Via Madre Serafina 5. ☎ **8375620.** Reservations required. Main courses 12,000–22,000 lire ($7.50–$13.75). AE, DC, MC, V. Fri–Wed 11:45am–3:30pm and 7pm–midnight. Closed Jan–Feb. Transportation: Capri funicular. SEAFOOD.

This excellent, small restaurant is run by two brothers, Francesco and Salvatore Trama. The warm welcome extended by the owners sets the atmosphere in which to enjoy the fine food. Ask what the evening specials are. They might be mama's green lasagne, or a fish main dish of whatever was freshest at the dock that afternoon, marinated in wine, garlic, and ginger and broiled. The lightly breaded and deep-fried baby squid and octopus, a mouth-watering saltimbocca, spaghetti with clams, and a filling zuppa di pesce are usually on the menu. La Cisterna lies only a short walk from piazza Umberto I and is reached via a labyrinth of covered "tunnels."

Ⓢ Ristorante al Grottino

Via Longano 27. ☎ **8370584.** Reservations not necessary. Main courses 14,000–24,000 lire ($8.75–$15). AE, V. Wed–Mon noon–3pm and 7–11pm. Closed Jan 8–Mar 25 and Nov 5–Dec 20. Transportation: Capri funicular. SEAFOOD/NEAPOLITAN.

In its *la dolce vita* heyday, this was the retreat of the rich and famous, and some can still remember appearances here by Ted Kennedy, the late Ginger Rogers, or Princess Soraya. That crowd has long departed or died, but the place remains popular among ordinary folk. To reach it you must walk down a narrow alleyway that branches off from piazza Umberto I to an establishment not unlike a bistro in North Africa. The chef knows how to rattle his pots and pans. Bowing to the influence of the nearby Neapolitan cuisine, he offers four different dishes of fried mozzarella cheese, any one highly recommended. A big plate of the mixed fish fry from the seas of the Campania is a favored main dish. The zuppa di cozze (clam soup) is a savory opener, as is the ravioli alla caprese. Truly succulent is linguine with scampi.

SPECIALTY DINING

One of the major pastimes in Capri is to occupy an outdoor table at one of the cafés on the piazza Umberto I. Each arriving visitor picks his or her own favorite, although they're all about the same. Even some permanent residents (and this is a good sign) patronize **Bar Tiberio,** piazza Umberto I (☎ 8370268), which is open daily from 7am to 2am, sometimes until 3 or 4am if business merits it. Larger and a little more comfortable than some of its competitors, this café has tables both inside and outside that overlook the busy life of the square where virtually every visitor to Capri shows up at one time or another. A cappuccino costs 4,000 lire ($2.50) if you're sitting, but you can order many other types of drinks as well. Whiskey begins at 9,000 lire ($5.65).

ANACAPRI

Capri is the upper town of Marina Grande. To see the upper town of Capri, you have to get lost in the clouds of Anacapri—more remote, secluded, and idyllic than the main resort, and reached by a daring 3,000-lire ($1.90) round-trip bus ride, more thrilling than any roller coaster. One visitor once remarked that all bus drivers to Anacapri "were either good or dead." At one point in its history Anacapri and Capri were connected only by the Scala Fenicia, the Phoenician Stairs.

When you disembark at piazza della Victoria, you'll find a Caprian Shangri-la, a village of charming dimensions.

To continue your ascent to the top, you then hop aboard a chair lift to **Monte Solaro,** the loftiest citadel on the entire island at its lookout perch of 1,950 feet. The ride takes about 12 minutes, operates daily from 9:30am to sunset, and charges 7,000 lire ($4.40) for a round-trip ticket. At the top, the panorama of the Bay of Naples is spread before you.

You can head out to **Villa San Michele** on viale Axel Munthe to Capodimonte 34 (☎ 8371401). This was the home of Axel Munthe, the Swedish author (*The Story of San Michele*), physician, and friend of Gustav V, king of Sweden, who visited him several times on the island. The villa is as Munthe (who died in 1949) furnished it, in a harmonious and tasteful way. From the rubble and ruins of an imperial villa built underneath by Tiberius, Munthe purchased several marbles, which are displayed inside. You can walk through the gardens for another in a series of endless panoramas of the island. Tiberius used to sleep out there al fresco on hot nights. The villa, which is open daily, may be visited from 9am to 6pm from May to September, from 9:30am to 5pm in April and October, and from 9:30am to 4:30pm in March; in winter, hours are 10:30am to 3:30pm. Admission is 6,000 lire ($3.75). Villa San Michele is a 5-minute walk from piazza Monumento in Anacapri.

WHERE TO STAY

Expensive

Europa Palace

Via Capodimonte 2, 80071 Anacapri. ☎ **081/8373800.** Fax 081/8313191. 92 rms, 20 junior suites. A/C MINIBAR TV TEL. 280,000–480,000 lire ($175–$300) double; from 750,000 lire ($468.75) suite. Rates include breakfast. AE, DC, MC, V. Closed Oct 31–Easter. Transportation: Anacapri bus.

On the slopes of Monte Solaro, the first-class Europa sparkles with *moderne*, and turns its back on the past to embrace the semiluxury of today. Its designer, who had bold ideas, obviously loved wide open spaces, heroic proportions, and vivid colors. The landscaped gardens with palm trees and plenty of bougainvillea have a large swimming pool, which most guests use as their outdoor living room. Each of the bedrooms is attractively and comfortably furnished. Featured are four special suites, each with a private swimming pool.

Dining/Entertainment: The hotel's restaurant, L'Olivo, is known for its fine cuisine with Mediterranean specialties, even with some nouvelle cuisine; meals begin at 60,000 lire ($37.50). In the swimming pool area is a snack bar where light lunches and snacks are served.

Services: Room service, babysitting, laundry, valet.

Facilities: Swimming pool, beauty spa for medical and beauty treatments.

Hotel San Michele di Anacapri

Via Orlandi 1-3, 80071 Anacapri. ☎ **081/8371427.** Fax 081/8371420. 56 rms. TV TEL. 150,000–180,000 lire ($93.75–$112.50) per person, single or double. Rates include half-board. AE, DC, MC, V. Closed Nov–Mar. Transportation: Anacapri bus.

This hotel has spacious cliffside gardens and unmarred views as well as enough shady or sunny nooks to please everybody. It also has the largest swimming pool in Capri. Guests linger long and peacefully in its private and well-manicured gardens, where the green trees are softened by splashes of color from hydrangea and geraniums. The position of this contemporary, well-appointed hotel is just right: near Axel Munthe's Villa San Michele. The view for diners includes the Bay of Naples and Vesuvius. The lounges are furnished in an older, more traditional vein, much like the appearance of a country house in France. The bedrooms carry out the same theme, with a respect for the past, but also with sufficient examples of today's amenities, such as a tile bath in most rooms, good beds, and plenty of space.

Moderate

Ⓢ Bellavista

Via Orlandi 10, 80071 Anacapri. ☎ **081/8371821.** Fax 081/8370957. 15 rms. TEL. 130,000–140,000 lire ($81.25–$87.50) double. Rates include breakfast. Half-board 90,000–110,000 lire ($56.25–$68.75) per person. AE. Closed Oct 31–Easter. Transportation: Anacapri bus.

Only a 2-minute walk from the main piazza, this is a modern holiday retreat with a panoramic view. Lodged into a mountainside, the hotel is decorated with primary colors, has large living and dining rooms, and terraces with a view of the sea. The breakfast and lunch terrace has garden furniture and a rattan-roofed sun shelter, and the cozy lounge has an elaborate tile floor and a hooded fireplace of a raised hearth, ideal for nippy nights. The bedrooms are pleasingly contemporary (a few have a bed mezzanine, a sitting area on the lower level, and a private entrance). The restaurant is closed on Monday.

Inexpensive

Caesar Augustus

Via Orlandi 4, 80071 Anacapri. ☎ **081/8371421.** Fax 081/5560119. 50 rms. TEL. 100,000–200,000 lire ($62.50–$125) double. Rates include breakfast. Discounts available when business is slow. AE, DC, MC, V. Closed Oct 15–late Mar. Transportation: Anacapri bus.

Isolated from the island's main population centers, and set beside the road leading from Capri to Anacapri, this unpretentious modern hotel has pleased other readers of this guidebook. Its managers seem ready and able to negotiate favorable rates for stays during periods of low demand. Rooms are adequately furnished with simple contemporary furniture, and come with a wide array of views, over either the sea or a pleasant garden. Many of the guests here seem to return over the years. On the premises is a restaurant and a bar, and a genial and informal welcome from the resident managers and staff.

Hotel Loreley

Via Orlandi 12, 80071 Anacapri. ☎ **081/8371440.** 18 rms. TEL. 100,000–130,000 lire ($62.50–$81.25) double. Rates include breakfast. AE, MC, V. Closed Nov 30–Mar 15. Transportation: Anacapri bus.

The Loreley has more to offer than economy: It's a cozy, immaculately kept accommodation, with a homelike, genial atmosphere. Opened in 1963, it features an open-air veranda with a bamboo canopy, rattan chairs, and of course a good view. The rooms overlook lemon-bearing trees that have (depending on the season) either scented blossoms or fruit. The bedrooms are quite large, with unified colors and enough furniture to make for a sitting room. Each room has a balcony. The hotel is approached through a white iron gate, past a stone wall. It lies off the road toward the sea, and is surrounded by fig trees and geraniums.

MARINA PICCOLA

A little fishing village and beach on the south shore, Marina Pioccola can be reached by bus (later you can take a bus back up the steep hill to Capri). The village opens onto emerald-and-cerulean waters, with the Faraglioni rocks of the sirens jutting out at the far end of the bay. Treat yourself to a meal at **La Canzone del Mare,** Marina Piccola, ☎ 8370104.

Sicily is an ancient land of myth and legend. It is also, according to many Italians, a land unto itself, different from the rest of Italy, in customs and traditions, and proudly so. On the map, the toe of the Italian boot seems poised to kick Sicily away from the mainland, as if it did not belong to the rest of Italy. The largest of the Mediterranean islands, it is located some 80 miles from the coast of Africa and is swept by winds that dry its fertile fields every summer, crisping the harvest into a sun-blasted palette of browns. Like its landscape, Sicily is a hypnotic place of dramatic turbulence, as absurdly emotional and intense as a play by native son Luigi Pirandello.

For centuries, Sicily's beauty and charm have attracted the greedy eye of foreigners: Greeks (before the island was conquered by Rome), Vandals, Arabs, Normans, Swabians, the fanatically religious house of Aragon, the French Bourbons. Homer, in the *Odyssey*, recorded ancient myths about cannibalistic tribes (the Laestrygones) living near the site of modern Catania.

Centuries later, legends grew about Sicily's patron saint, Agatha, martyred by having her breasts cut off. The island still teems with all kinds of tales shrouded in primeval lore and legend, as well as with stories, many fervently believed, about the curative powers of water from certain caves and the harmful powers of the evil eye. That the Sicilians should have created and held on to such phantasmagoric tales and legends is not surprising, in view of their island's history of natural and political disasters.

Through the centuries, a series of plagues, ferocious family vendettas, volcanic eruptions, earthquakes, and economic hardships have threatened many times to destroy the interwoven cultures of Sicily. Always, the island has persevered. Its archaeology and richly complex architecture are endlessly fascinating, and the masses of almond and cherry trees in bloom in February make it one of the most beautiful places in Italy.

Too long neglected by travelers wooed by the art cities of the north, Sicily is today attracting greater numbers of foreign visitors. This land of volcanic islands is full of sensual sights and experiences: a sirocco whirling out of the nearby Libyan deserts, horses with plumes and bells pulling gaily painted carts, vineyards and fragrant citrus groves, Greek temples and classical dramas performed in ancient theaters, and the aromatic fragrance of a glass of Marsala.

What's Special About Sicily

Great Towns/Villages
- Taormina, one of the world's loveliest resorts, set on the blue Ionian Sea, looking out at snow-capped Mount Etna.
- Palermo, capital of Sicily, opening on the Tyrrhenian Sea, founded by sea-faring Phoenicians in the 6th century B.C.
- Agrigento, known to the Greeks, one of ancient Sicily's most beautiful and prosperous cities.
- Selinunte, ancient Selinus, founded in 682 B.C. and today one of Sicily's most important archaeological sites.

Ace Attraction
- Mount Etna, the highest point on the island, still active, the largest and most famous volcano in Europe.

Ancient Monuments
- The Valley of the Temples, Agrigento, a panoramic sweep of surviving Greek temples, including the Temple of Concord (450 B.C.), the second-best-preserved Greek temple in the world.
- Segesta, with a Doric temple from 430 B.C., with a peristyle of 36 columns.
- The archaeological zone of Syracuse, with a Greek theater from the 5th century B.C., one of the largest and best preserved of the ancient world.

Religious Shrine
- Monreale, outside Palermo, containing a Duomo known for its dazzling 12th-century mosaics.

Today the Sicilians are an intriguing and fiercely proud racial mix, less Latin than the Italians, spiritually akin in many ways to North Africa and the wild waste-lands of the Sahara. Luigi Barzini, in *The Italians*, wrote, "Sicily is the schoolroom model of Italy for beginners, with every Italian quality and defect magnified, exasperated, and brightly colored. . . . Everywhere in Italy, life is more or less slowed down by the exuberant intelligence of the inhabitants: In Sicily it is practically paralyzed by it."

There are far too many cars in Palermo, a sometimes-unpleasant reflection of the new (sometimes drug-related) prosperity that seems to have encouraged everyone on the island to buy a car. Parts of the island are heavily polluted by industrialization, but the age-old poverty still remains in the streets, home to thousands of children who seemingly grow up there.

Geologically, Sicily broke away from the mainland of Africa (not Europe) millions of years ago. Even today, the 2½-mile channel separating it from the tip

Impressions

In a sense all our thinking about the Mediterranean crystallized around the images planted here by the Greeks. . . . In Sicily one sees that the Mediterranean evolved at the same rhythm as man; they both evolved together. One interpreted itself to the other, and out of the interaction Greek culture was first born.

—Lawrence Durell, *Sicilian Carousel*, 1977

of the Italian peninsula is still a dangerously unstable earthquake zone, making hopes for the eventual construction of a bridge unfeasible. The ancient Greeks claimed that the busy strait was the lair of deadly sea monsters, Scylla and Charybdis, who, according to legend, delighted in wrecking Greek ships and devouring the flesh of the sailors aboard.

Today Sicily has a relatively stable population of around five million inhabitants. Its resorts, ancient temples, and distinctive cuisine are bringing it increasingly into the world's consciousness. Even Goethe, who traveled widely here, commented on the sometimes bizarre, always captivating, symbols he saw, but concluded, "To have seen Italy without having seen Sicily is not to have seen Italy at all, for Sicily is the clue to everything."

A DRIVING TOUR

Day 1 Arrive in tacky Messina, often by car ferry from the mainland. The third largest city of Sicily, and the setting of Shakespeares *Much Ado About Nothing*, it does not invite lingering. Take autostrada A18 down the eastern coast of Italy, about 30 miles to Taormina where one night will be all too brief. Set on Monte Tauro overlooking the Ionian Sea, this is the most majestic resort in Sicily.

Day 2 From Taormina, A18 continues south to Catania, Sicily's second largest city and a busy seaport, where you might want to have lunch.

☕ **TAKE A BREAK** La Siciliana, viale Marco Polo 52A in Catania (☎ 095/3764000), offers both folkloric inner rooms or garden setting for eating. Fresh fish is displayed in a glass case, and the choice of that and other regional Sicilian dishes is wide. One of the most typical Catanese dishes, and recommended to all first-time visitors, is rigatona alla norma, made with fresh basil, fried eggplant, and tomatoes. Closed Monday and two weeks in August.

Continue south from Catania for 36 miles to Syracuse where you'll want to overnight.

Day 3 Plan on a full day exploring the ruins and monuments of this town, opening onto the Ionian Sea in southeastern Italy. In ancient times it was the capital of Magna Graecia and was considered one of the greatest cities on earth. Hours can be spent exploring its archaeological zone and such attractions as a steep-walled quarry known as the Latomie del Paradise. Spend yet another night in Syracuse.

Day 4 After driving south from Syracuse, the autostrada soon ends and Route SS115 takes over, leading you to Noto, filled with Sicilian baroque architecture and worth some of your time. Most of the city's monuments are on the main street, Corso Vittorio Emanuele. Get back on the SS115 which will take you to Ragusa, which is encircled by large chemical plants. Hurry on from here, passing Gela until you reach your goal for the night: Agrigento.

Day 5 While still based in Agrigento, explore the Valley of the Temples, which will be one of the highlights of your tour in Italy. See them at dawn, when they are hauntingly beautiful, and again at twilight when illuminations by flood lights make for a spectacle.

Day 6 The route west (SS115) leads to Sciacca, 39 miles from Agrigento. Sciacca, which deserves a brief stopover, is known for its ceramics and its thermal baths. Continue along the SS115 for 25 miles to Selinunte. This ancient town, founded in 682 B.C., was one of the most prosperous Greek colonies in Italy. Its ruins, along with those at Agrigento, are among the highlights of a trip to Sicily. After exploring the ruins, continue on the SS115 north to Castelvetrano, then head west to Marsala for 22 miles. Marsala is known for its fortified wine, often compared to sherry. This is the site where Garibaldi landed with 1,000 men to launch his campaign to liberate Sicily from Bourbon rule.

☕ **TAKE A BREAK**   Delfino, lungomare Mediterraneo in Marsala (☎ 0923/998188), makes the best luncheon stopover. This sea-bordering restaurant features alfresco dining. Its specialties are both fish soup and fish salad. The fresh catch of the day is grilled and perfectly seasoned. The chef is also known for his seafood couscous, inspired by North Africa across the way. The location is $3^1/_2$ miles south of the town.

From Marsala take SS115 north to Trapani for the night, a distance of 19 miles.
Day 7   In the morning explore Trapani, the westernmost of the towns of Sicily. After passing through its dreary suburbs you head for the narrowing promontory which is the most interesting part of this colorful port to explore. From Trapani continue to Erice, a distance of 9 miles to the northeast. This was the ancient Eryx, founded by the Elymnians. It was mentioned in Virgil's *Aeneid*. With its fortified castles, it owes much of its present look to its Norman conquerors. Take S113 directly out of Erice east to Segesta for 12 miles. A rival of Selinunte, Segesta was founded in the 12th century B.C. It contains one of the world's great Doric temples.

From Segesta follow the autostrada signs (A29) heading for Palermo for the night.
Days 8–9   In Sicily's capital, you'll be kept busy both day and night with its many attractions. You need the 9th day to explore the sights in the environs, including Cefalù and Monreale. Try to work in some time at the beach at Mondello Lido, $7^1/_2$ miles to the east of Palermo.

FOOD & WINE

The sauces and stews are complicated and aromatic, as benefits this rugged, highly individualistic island. Good vineyards, rich vegetation (in part) and fertile soil have led to the creation of a "perfumed" cuisine on land, but many Sicilians turn to the sea, not only for their livelihood but for their food.

Local specialties include maccheroni with shelled prawns mixed into the tomatoes, or else macceroni con le sarde, spaghetti with a spicy sauce of pine nuts, fennel, spices, olive oil, and chopped sardines. Cannoli are cylindrical pastry cases, stuffed with cottage cheese, candied fruit, or chocolate, and a cassata is an ice cream cake, often with almonds and custard.

Cuscusu is one of the most nourishing items on the Sicilian menu, a fish soup with pasta (every chef makes it differently). Bottarga di tonno is tunny roe sometimes grilled, sometimes boiled, and always served with fresh lemon and oil. Farsumagru is a breast of beef or veal stuffed with hard-boiled eggs and spices. Sicilians are known for their gelati or ices, considered the best in Italy, often made with fresh fruits.

The wines are an equal of the cuisine. One of its best known wines, Mamertino, was praised by the ancient poet Martial, and was served to Caesar at the banquet

Sicily

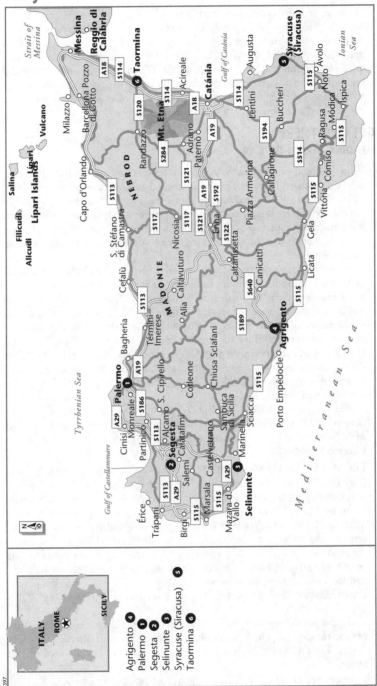

honoring his third consulship. It has a keen bouquet and is a golden yellow in color. It often accompanies fish dishes. Other famous wines of the region include Faro, ruby red in color with a fine bouquet and nutty flavor, served with meats and roasts; and Corco blanco di Casteldaccia, a straw-yellow, intense and brilliant wine with a distinctive bouquet, often served with antipasti. The most celebrated and best known Sicilian wine is Marsala, amber yellow in color with orange depths to it. With its pleasing fragrance and special bouquet, Marsala is velvety and fruity, and is served with desserts or drunk as a pick-you-up between meals.

GETTING THERE
HEADING SOUTH BY CAR

When you head south toward Sicily today, you won't have the transportation headache that plagued Goethe. The Autostrade del Sole stretches all the way from Milan to Reggio di Calabria, sticking out on the "big toe," the gateway to Sicily.

One day a bridge is supposed to connect Sicily with the mainland. The project, it is estimated, would take at least eight years and cost at least a billion dollars. A major problem is that the span is to stretch across the Strait of Messina, a prime earthquake zone.

At present, one way to reach Sicily is to take a ferryboat from Villa San Giovanni or Reggio di Calabria to Messina, costing 1,600 lire ($1) per passenger. Vessels of the state railway ferry leave daily from 3:20am to 10:05pm, and it takes less than an hour to cross. Cars are transported on these ferries, the cost depending on the size of the vehicle. Much quicker, shaving at least 22 minutes off the crossing time, is an aliscafo (hydrofoil) leaving from Reggio di Calabria. You'll pay 5,000 lire ($3.15) one way. However, the aliscafo is recommended because the higher price usually means fewer passengers—hence, less crowding. You cannot take your vehicle on a hydrofoil. Call 0965/898123, 0965/894003, or 0965/29568 for various connections.

Near Reggio di Calabria, incidentally, is a much smaller community, Scilla, famous in Homeric legend. Mariners of old, including Ulysses, crossed the Strait of Messina from here, and faced the double menace of the two monsters, Charybdis and Scylla.

FROM NAPLES TO SICILY BY SEA   One way to reach Palermo is by night ferry from Naples. The ferry leaves Naples at 8pm, arriving in Palermo the next morning at 7am. On Friday there is another departure at 10pm. The service is run by Tirrenia S.A. For information about this service, call the company's office in Naples at 081/7613688. However, if you're already in Palermo and want to take the ferry service back to Naples, dial 091/333300; unfortunately, you won't always find someone who speaks English. Sleeping compartments are often booked days in advance, and there may be space available only on deck. The cost for an average car on the ferry is 110,000 lire ($68.75). First-class passage costs 99,200 lire ($62) per person for a one-way ticket or 68,700 lire ($42.95) in second class.

It's also possible to take a hydrofoil from Naples to Palermo in summer. Most of these trips, operated by S.N.A.V., leave Naples at 3pm, the trip taking 5 hours. A one-way fare costs 28,500 lire ($17.80). Cars are not allowed on the hydrofoil.

FLYING TO SICILY   There are daily Alitalia (☎ 800/223-5730 in the U.S.) flights to Palermo from Milan, Naples, Venice, Pisa, Genoa, Bologna, Turin, and

Rome. There are around six flights a day from Rome. Flights go to Catania at least once a day from Milan, Pisa, Rome, and Turin.

1 Palermo

145 miles W of Messina

As the ferryboat docks in the Bay of Palermo, and you start spotting blond, blue-eyed bambini all over the place, don't be surprised. If the fair-haired children don't fit your conception of what a Sicilian should look like, remember that the Normans landed here in 1060, six years before William the Conqueror put in at Hastings, and launched a campaign to wrest control of the island from the Arabs. Both elements were to cross cultures, a manifestation still seen today in Palermo's architecture—a unique style, Norman-Arabic.

The city is the largest port of Sicily, its capital, and the meeting place of a regional parliament granted numerous autonomous powers in postwar Italy. Against a backdrop of the citrus-studded Conca d'Oro plain and Monte Pellegrino, it's a city of wide boulevards, old quarters in the legendary Sicilian style (laundry lapping against the wind, smudge-faced kids playing in the street), town houses, architecturally harmonious squares, baroque palaces, and modern buildings (many erected as a result of Allied bombings in 1943). It also has the worst traffic jams in Sicily.

Palermo was founded by the Phoenicians, but it has known many conquerors, some of whom established courts of great splendor (Frederick II), others of whom brought decay (the Angevins).

ESSENTIALS

GETTING THERE   By Plane   If you fly from Rome or Naples, you'll land at Cinisi–Punta Raisi (☎ 091/591414), some 19 miles west of Palermo. It's best to catch a local airport bus, which runs hourly from the airport to piazza Castelnuovo; the fare is 4,500 lire ($2.80). For the same trip a taxi is likely to charge at least 60,000 lire ($37.50)—more if the driver thinks he can get away with it.

By Train   Trains arrive in Palermo at piazza Cesare (☎ 6161806 for information) on the eastern side of town. It's possible to take a train from Rome, a 15-hour journey; a one-way ticket goes for 64,000 lire ($40). Most visitors, however, take the train from Naples, a 13-hour journey; a one-way ticket costs 52,000 lire ($32.50). Of course, a water crossing from the mainland to Sicily is involved in both trips.

By Bus   Palermo has bus connections with other major cities in Italy, operated by Autoservizi Segesta, via Balsamo 26 (☎ 6167919). For example, 16 buses a day make the $2^1/_2$-hour trip from Catania, at a one-way cost of 16,000 lire ($10). One bus a day arrives Monday through Saturday from Syracuse; the trip lasts 4 hours and a one-way ticket costs 21,200 lire ($13.25).

By Car   After your arrival from mainland Italy at Messina, head west on autostrada A20, which becomes Route 113, then A20 again, and finally A19 before its final approach to Palermo.

VISITOR INFORMATION   The telephone area code is 091. There are tourist information offices at strategic points, including the Palermo airport. The principal office, however, is the Azienda Autonoma Turismo, piazza Castelnuovo 34 (☎ 583847).

GETTING AROUND

Most municipally operated buses in Palermo charge 1,000 lire (65¢) for a ticket, which is a cheap way of getting about. Most passengers purchase their tickets at tobacco shops (tabacchi) throughout the city before getting on. Otherwise, you'll need some 100-lire coins handy. If you plan to use the buses at least three times during the day, you might want to purchase a day ticket, costing 3,000 lire ($1.90), allowing you unlimited rides on the city's bus network. These tickets are sold at the main bus station in front of the train station at piazza Cesare. For information about the city buses (AMAT), call 350111.

FAST FACTS: PALERMO

American Express   The agent for American Express is Giovanni Ruggieri e Figli, via Emerico Amari 40 (☎ 587144), which is open Monday through Friday from 9am to 1pm and 4 to 7pm, and on Saturday from 9am to 1pm.

Consulate   You'll find the U.S. Consular Agency at via Re Federico, 18 BIS 90141 (☎ 091/6110020), open Monday through Friday from 9am to 1pm.

Crime   Be especially alert. Some citizens here are the most skilled pickpockets on the continent. Keep your gems locked away (in other words, don't flaunt any sign of wealth). Women who carry handbags are especially vulnerable to purse-snatchers on Vespas. Don't leave valuables in your car. In fact, we almost want to say don't leave your car alone, even knowing how impossible that is unless you put it in a garage (highly recommendable). Police squads operate mobile centers through the town to help combat street crime.

Emergencies   In order to call police, report a fire, or summon an ambulance, dial 113.

Post Office   The major post office is on via Roma 322 (☎ 160) and is open Monday through Saturday from 8:15am to 7:30pm.

WHAT TO SEE & DO
THE TOP SIGHTS

"The four corners" of the city, the ✪ **Quattro Canti di Città,** is in the heart of the old town, at the junction of corso Vittorio Emanuele and via Maqueda. The ruling Spanish of the 17th century influenced the design of this grandiose baroque square, replete with fountains and statues. From here you can walk to piazza Bellini, the most attractive of the plazas of the old city. In an atmosphere reminiscent of the setting for an operetta, you're likely to hear strolling singers with guitars entertaining pizza eaters. Opening onto it is the Church of Santa Maria dell'Ammiraglio (also known as "La Martorana"), piazza Bellini 3 (☎ 6161692), erected in 1143 with a Byzantine cupola by an admiral to Roger II. Its decaying but magnificent bell tower was built from 1146 to 1185. It's open Monday through Saturday from 8am to 1pm and 3:30 to 7pm, and Sunday from 8am to 1pm. Admission is free.

Also fronting the square are the Church of San Cataldo, erected in 1160 in the Arab-Byzantine style with a trio of faded pink cupolas, and the Church of Santa Caterina, from the 16th century.

Adjoining the square is piazza Pretoria, dominated by a fountain designed in Florence in 1554 for a villa, but acquired by Palermo about 20 years later. A short walk will take you to the cathedral of Palermo.

Cathedral of Palermo

Corso Vittorio Emanuele. ☎ **334373.** Admission is free. Daily 7am–noon and 4–6pm. Bus: 3 or 24.

This cathedral is a curious spectacle where East meets West. It was built in the 12th century on the foundation of an earlier basilica that had been converted by the Arabs into a mosque. The cathedral—much altered over the centuries—was founded by an English archbishop known as Walter of the Mill. The "porch," built in the 15th century on the southern front in the Gothic style, is an impressive architectural feature. But the cupola, added in the late 18th century, detracts from the overall appearance, and the interior was revamped unsuccessfully at the same time, resulting in a glaring incongruity in styles. The "pantheon" of royal tombs includes that of the Emperor Frederick II, in red porphyry under a canopy of marble.

San Giovanni Degli Eremiti

Via del Benedettini Bianchi 3. ☎ **296238.** Admission is free. Daily 9am–2pm. Bus: 3 or 24.

The other church worthy of note is Saint John of the Hermits. Perhaps in an atmosphere appropriate for the recluse it honors, this little church with its twin-columned cloister is one of the most idyllic spots in all of Palermo. A medieval veil hangs heavy in the gardens, with their citrus blossoms and flowers, especially on a hot summer day as you wander around in its cloister. Ordered built by Roger II in 1132, the church adheres to its Arabic influence, surmounted by pinkish cupolas, while showing the Norman style as well. The Palace of the Normans is in the vicinity.

✪ Palazzo di Normanni

Piazza del Parlamento. ☎ **6561879.** Admission is free. Palace, Mon and Fri–Sat 9am–12:30pm; chapel, Mon–Fri 9am–noon and 3–5pm, Sat–Sun 9am–noon. Bus: 104, 105, 108, 109, or 110.

This Palace of the Normans contains one of the greatest art treasures in Sicily, the Cappella Palatina (Palatine Chapel). Erected at the request of Roger II in the 1130s, it is considered the finest example of the Arabic-Norman style of design and building. The effect of the mosaics inside is awe-inspiring. Almond-eyed biblical characters from the Byzantine art world in lush colors create a panorama of epic pageantry, illustrating such Gospel scenes as the Nativity. The overall picture is further enhanced by inlaid marble and mosaics and pillars made of granite shipped from the East. For a look at still more mosaics, this time in a more secular vein depicting scenes of the hunt, you can visit the Hall of Roger II upstairs, the seat of the Sicilian Parliament, where security is likely to be tight. Visitors are taken through on guided tours.

Galleria Regionale della Sicilia

Via Alloro 4. ☎ **6164317.** Admission 2,000 lire ($1.25) adults, free for children 17 and under and adults over 60. Mon and Sat 9am–1:30pm; Tues, Thurs, and Fri 3–7:30pm; Sun 9am–12:30pm. Closed Wed. Bus: 3, 5, or 8.

Palazzo Abatellis was built in the Gothic and Renaissance styles. Today it houses the Regional Gallery, with important collections showing the evolution of art in Sicily from the 13th to the 18th century. On the ground floor is a most famous work, a 15th-century fresco *Triumph of Death*, in all its gory magnificence. A horseback-riding skeleton, representing death, tramples his victims under hoof.

Worthy of mention are three mayolica plates, valuable specimens of "Loza dorada" manufactured in the workshops of Manises, and the "Giara" manufactured in the workshops of Málaga at the end of the 13th century.

Francesco Laurana's slanty-eyed Eleonora d'Aragona is worth seeking out, as are seven grotesque D'Roleries painted on wood. Of the paintings on the second floor, *L'Annunziata* by Antonello da Messina, a portrait of the Madonna with depth and originality, is one of the most celebrated paintings in Italy. The 13th-room contains a very good series of Flemish paintings from the 15th and 16th centuries, among which the best is the so-called *Trittico Malvagna* by Jean Gossaert, called *Mabuse*.

✪ Museo Regionale Archeologico

Piazza Olivella 4. ☎ **6620220.** Admission 2,000 lire ($1.25). Mon, Wed–Thurs, Sat, Sun 8am–1pm; Tues and Fri 8am–5pm. Bus: 101, 102, 103, 104, 107, and 122.

Located in a former convent, this is one of the greatest archaeological collections in southern Italy, where the competition's stiff. Many works displayed here were excavated from Selinunte, once one of the major towns in Magna Graecia (Greater Greece). See, in particular, the Sala di Selinunte, displaying the celebrated metopes that adorned the classical temples, as well as slabs of bas-relief. The gallery also owns important sculpture from the Temple of Himera. The collection of bronzes is exceptional, including the athlete and the stag discovered in the ruins of Pompeii (a Roman copy of a Greek original) and a bronze ram that came from Syracuse, dating from the 3rd century B.C. Among the Greek sculpture is *The Pouring Satyr*, excavated at Pompeii (a Roman copy of a Greek original by Praxiteles).

CATACOMBS

✪ Catacombe Cappuccini

Piazza Cappuccini 1. ☎ **212117.** Admission is free (donations accepted). Tours given Mon–Sat 9am–noon and 3–5pm, Sun and holidays 9am–noon. Bus: 327 from piazza Castelnuovo or 105 from Stazione Centrale.

The final attraction in the city is the most bizarre of all. Located on the outskirts of Palermo, the catacombs evoke the horrors of the Rue Morgue. The fresco you might have seen in the Galleria Regionale della Sicilia, *Triumph of Death*, dims by comparison to the real thing. The catacombs, it was discovered, contained a preservative that helped to mummify dead people. Sicilians, everyone from nobles to maids, were buried here in the 19th century, and it was the custom on Sunday to go and visit Uncle Luigi to see how he was holding together. If he fell apart, he was wired together again or wrapped in burlap sacking. The last person buried in the catacombs was placed to rest in 1920—a little girl almost lifelike in death. But many Sicilians of the 19th century are in fine shape, considering—with eyes, hair, and even clothing fairly intact (the convent could easily be turned into a museum of costume). Some of the expressions on the faces of the skeletons take the fun out of Halloween—a grotesque ballet. The catacombs may be visited on guided tours.

WHERE TO STAY

Generally you'll find a poor lot of hostelries, aided by a few fine choices that prove the exception the rule. Hunt and pick carefully, as many hotels of Palermo are not suitable for the average international wayfarer.

EXPENSIVE

○ Villa Igiea Grand Hotel

Via Belmonte 43, 90142 Palermo. ☎ **091/543744.** Fax 091/547654. 117 rms, 6 suites. A/C MINIBAR TV TEL. 350,000 lire ($218.75) double; from 600,000 lire ($375) suite. Rates include breakfast. AE, DC, MC, V. Free parking. Bus: 3, 8, 9, 21, or 31.

This deluxe hotel was originally built at the turn of the century as one of Sicily's great aristocratic estates, and today it's one of the top two luxury hotels on the island. The exterior resembles a medieval Sicilian fortress whose carefully chiseled walls include crenellated battlements and forbidding watchtowers. It was constructed of the same buff-colored stone that Greek colonists used during the Punic wars when they erected a circular temple which, although heavily buttressed with modern scaffolding, still stands in the garden. Nearby, nestled amid a grove of pines and palms, is an art nouveau statue of Igiea, goddess of flowers. Everywhere are clusters of antiques. Accommodations vary from sumptuous suites with private terraces to rooms of lesser size and glamour. The hotel, reached by passing through an industrial portside north of Palermo, sits on a cliff with a view of the open sea.

Dining/Entertainment: The hotel's bar is baronial, with a soaring stone vault. You dine in a grand and glittering room against a backdrop of paneled walls, ornate ceilings, and chandeliers. Meals, both Sicilian and classic Italian, begin at 65,000 lire ($40.65).

Services: Room service, babysitting, laundry, valet.

Facilities: Terrace overlooking the water, swimming pool, tennis court.

MODERATE

Grande Albergo Sole

Corso Vittorio Emanuele 291, 90133 Palermo. ☎ **091/581811.** Fax 091/6110182. 150 rms. A/C MINIBAR TV TEL. 172,000 lire ($107.50) double. Rates include breakfast. AE, DC, MC, V. Parking 10,000 lire ($6.25). Bus: 3 or 24.

This pleasant, second-class hotel lies in the busy historic center of Palermo. A 1960s' remake of a century-old building, it houses a helpful staff and simple and uncomplicated bedrooms, each with radio and modern furniture. On the premises are a residents' lounge, a bar, a restaurant, and a roof garden and terrace for sunbathing.

○ Hotel Sausele

Via Vincenzo Errante 12, 90127 Palermo. ☎ **091/6161308.** Fax 091/6167525. 36 rms (all with bath or shower). TEL. 125,000 lire ($78.15) double. Rates include breakfast. AE, DC, MC, V. Parking 15,000 lire ($9.40). Bus: 3 or 24.

This modern hotel near the railway station is the best in a run-down area. It's owned and managed by Swiss-born Signora Sausele, who has created a clean establishment. Run efficiently, it's a modest but quite pleasant albergo, with bedrooms adequate for a good night's rest. The hotel has an elevator, garage, bar, and TV room. The lounges are air-conditioned.

Jolly Hotel del Foro Italico

Foro Italico 22, 90133 Palermo. ☎ **091/6165090** or 800/221-2626 in the U.S., or 800/247-1277 in Canada. Fax 091/6161441. 268 rms, 5 suites. A/C MINIBAR TV. 181,700–222,100 lire ($113.55–$138.80) double or suite. Rates include breakfast. Half-board 40,400 lire ($25.25) per person. AE, DC, MC, V. Free parking. Bus: 3 or 24.

Off a busy boulevard (the Foro Italico, facing the Gulf of Palermo), this 1960s' hotel invites with shafts of pale blue supporting triangular balconies. Try for the bedrooms on the upper floors or at the rear, which are quieter. One of the best of the hotels (and popular for Sicilian wedding receptions), it offers a contemporary atmosphere and good accommodations. The public rooms have bright colors and serviceable furnishings. In the bedrooms all is well organized, with lots of built-in pieces and comfortable beds. The Jolly also has a garden.

Dining/Entertainment: On the premises are a restaurant and an American bar. The food is both Sicilian and Italian, with meals beginning at 50,500 lire ($31.55).

Services: Room service, babysitting, laundry, valet.

Facilities: Swimming pool, parking lot.

President Hotel

Via Francesco Crispi 230, 90139 Palermo. ☎ **091/580733.** Fax 091/6111588. 129 rms. A/C TV TEL. 130,000–180,000 lire ($81.25–$112.50) double. Rates include breakfast. AE, DC, MC, V. Parking 5,000 lire ($3.15). Bus: 9.

Its eight-story concrete-and-glass facade rises above the harborfront quays where ferryboats dock before sailing to Naples. This is one of the better and more up-to-date of the middle-bracket hotels in town. Built in 1978, it was renovated in the early 1990s. You'll pass beneath the facade's soaring arcade before entering the informal stone-trimmed lobby. One of the most appealing coffee shop/bars in town lies at the top of a short flight of stairs next to the reception area. There's a panoramic restaurant on the uppermost floor, plus a guarded parking garage in the basement. The bedrooms are comfortably furnished, each with a radio and TV.

INEXPENSIVE

Albergo Cavour

Via Alessandro Manzoni 11, 90133 Palermo. ☎ **091/6162759.** 9 rms (4 with bath or shower). 40,000 lire ($25) double without bath, 50,000 lire ($31.25) double with bath. No credit cards. Parking 10,000 lire ($6.25). Bus: 7 or 21.

Albergo Cavour is on the fifth floor of a 1920s' building conveniently located in front of the central station. The rooms are suitable for overnight stopovers, and the manager sees to it that they're well kept and decently furnished, with comfortable mattresses on the beds. No meals are served, but many cafés are nearby.

○ Hotel Liguria

Via Mariano Stabile 128, 90139 Palermo. ☎ **091/581588.** 16 rms (4 with bath). TV TEL. 49,000 lire ($30.65) double without bath, 64,000 lire ($40) double with bath. Breakfast 6,000 lire ($3.75) extra. No credit cards. Bus: 3 or 4.

This well-scrubbed family-run hotel has won several awards for its quality accommodations. At the upstairs reception desk, Signora Lidia Grosso de Grana will register you into one of her tile-floored accommodations, each of which is suitable for one or two people. Born in Genoa, she named the property after the region of her birth. Many of the rooms are awash with sunlight from the big windows, and each has a clothes press and comfortable bedding. The rooms are scattered over two floors.

WHERE TO DINE
MODERATE

○ L'Approdo da Renato

Via Messina Marine 224. ☎ **6302881.** Reservations required Fri–Sat. Main courses 18,000–30,000 lire ($11.25–$18.75). AE, MC, V. Mon–Sat 12:30–3pm and 8–11pm. Closed Aug 10–25. Bus: 31. SICILIAN.

This restaurant lies in an elegant villa originally built in 1880 in a position over-looking the sea. From its dining room, or from its flowering outdoor terrace, you'll have a view over the Gulf of Palermo. Run by a husband-and-wife team, it's infused with gaiety. Some visitors are invited to explore the wine cellar, whose contents are said to rival the best in all of Italy, certainly in all of Sicily. The kitchen adheres to time-tested Sicilian recipes, and they have no real specialties, as the menu depends on the season and the finest of available ingredients at any given time. Nearly all diners begin with a selection of authentic Sicilian antipasti, both vegetarian and seafood, with tuna factored in somehow. You never know what dishes are going to be offered, but memorable past meals have included fresh fish marinated in refined olive oil and flavored with herbs, crêpes filled with seafood, swordfish in a mandarin orange sauce, and roast goat flavored with Sicilian herbs.

Charleston

Piazzale Ungheria 30. ☎ **321366.** Reservations required. Main courses 22,000–28,000 lire ($13.75–$17.50). AE, DC, MC, V. Mon–Sat 1–3 or 4pm and 8–11:30pm. Closed Sun June–Sept. Bus: 3 or 24. SICILIAN/INTERNATIONAL.

For years Charleston was regarded as the finest restaurant in Sicily, although today there is far more competition for that title. Nevertheless, it remains a national culinary monument of Sicilian hospitality and old-fashioned virtues, an appealing choice in Palermo. The owners create a refined and perfect milieu for their presentation of Sicilian dishes, which naturally concentrate on fresh fish. The kitchen prepares a number of international dishes as well. Full meals cost from 70,000 lire ($43.75).

Gourmand's

Via della Libertà. ☎ **323431.** Reservations recommended. Main courses 19,000–26,000 lire ($11.90–$16.25). AE, DC, MC, V. Mon–Sat 1–3pm and 8–11pm. Closed Aug 5–25. Bus: 3 or 24. SICILIAN.

Gourmand's is among the best restaurants in Palermo for an introduction to the rich, aromatic cookery of Sicily. A corner restaurant in the most elegant commer-cial district of town, it's a light and airy room filled with original paintings and Chinese-red ceiling lattices. You'll admire the richly laden antipasto table before you're ushered to your table. For a first course, I'd suggest spaghetti Gourmand's or an involtini of eggplant. Fresh fish is always available, and you might prefer it grilled as a main course. However, the chef does many Italian dishes well, including veal escalope in the Valdostan style and pepper steak or, if available, roast quail. Risotto with salmon is often featured on the menu, as is rigatoni Henry IV. Meals range from 50,000 to 75,000 lire ($31.25 to $46.90).

La Scuderia

Viale del Fante 9. ☎ **520323.** Reservations recommended. Main courses 20,000–30,000 lire ($12.50–$18.75). AE, DC, MC, V. Mon–Sat 12:30–3pm and 8:30pm–midnight. Closed Aug 15–31. Bus: 1. ITALIAN.

Dedicated professionals direct this appealing restaurant, which is surrounded by trees at the foot of Monte Pellegrino, lying north of the city center and directly south of Parco della Favorita. The inside section is augmented in summer with one of the prettiest flowering terraces in town, a place sought after by everyone from erstwhile lovers to extended families to glamour queens in for a holiday. The sound of falling water, followed by the tunes of a piano player, greet you as you enter. The imaginative cuisine includes a mixed grill of fresh vegetables with a healthy dose of a Sicilian cheese called caciocavallo, along with stuffed turkey cutlet, a wide array of beef and veal dishes, involtini of eggplant, risotto with seafood, veal spiedino, and many tempting desserts, one known as pernice all'erotica. Full meals start at 50,000 lire ($31.25).

INEXPENSIVE

ⓢ Al Vicolo

Cortile Scimecaz. ☎ **651-2464**. Reservations recommended. Main courses 12,000–16,000 lire ($7.50–$10). No credit cards. Mon–Sat 12:30–3pm and 7–11:30pm. Closed Aug 10–25. Bus: 3 or 24. SICILIAN.

Located off piazza San Francesco Saverio, this is one of the most characteristic trattoria of the city. This regional restaurant deserves more acclaim than it traditionally receives. The dining rooms were converted from former warehouse rooms used for storing produce. For your antipasti, you might prefer panelle (chickpea or garbanzo fritters) and arancini (rice croquettes). Potato croquettes are also likely to appear on the menu. As the friendly waiters are likely to point out, if you order too much of these tasty but starchy appetizers you won't have room for the main course. That is all too true, especially if you also select sardines à beccafico (stuffed and flavored with laurel) or squid in a savory sauce as part of your antipasti.

Many of the most typical dishes of Sicily are served here, including pasta mixed with sardines and wild fennel. For some diners, this is an acquired taste; for the devotee of Sicilian cuisine, it's reason enough to visit the restaurant. Any pasta labeled "all Norma" comes with vine-ripened tomatoes and eggplant. The local fish is fresh and abundant, and always appears on the menu—grilled or sautéed, depending on your desires. Local meats including lamb and kid are always offered. You can wash down the meal—Sicilians say "irrigate"—with a selection of regional wines.

ⓢ Friend's Bar

Via Brunelleschi 138, Borgo Nuovo. ☎ **201401**. Reservations required. Main courses 19,000–24,000 lire ($11.90–$15). AE, DC, MC, V. Tues–Sun 1–3pm and 8–10pm. Closed Aug 16–31. Bus: 29 or 72. SICILIAN.

The name, in English no less, might sound like a place in a small town in New Jersey. In spite of that incongruity, this is one of the finest restaurants in Palermo, located in a suburb called Borgo Nuovo. A meal here is considered an event by many Sicilians. Friend's Bar has become one of the sought-after places on the island, one where a reservation for one of the garden seats is almost essential to get past the bar. There is indeed a bar on the premises, although most of the emphasis is on the viands served in the dining room or on the terrace. First, you might enjoy a few of the many delicacies from the antipasto table, followed by one of the many regional specialties such as subtly flavored pastas, and an array of steamed or grilled fish dishes or one of the meat dishes that have made this place so well known locally. The house wine (red) is a good accompaniment for most any meal, which will usually cost about 50,000 to 70,000 lire ($31.25 to $43.75).

PALERMO AFTER DARK

We always like to begin our evening by heading to the century-old Caffè Mazzara, via Generale Magliocco 15 (☎ 321443), where you can sample Sicilian ice cream—among the best in the world—and order coffee that's the richest in all the country. Or perhaps you'll prefer to sit quietly, sipping the heady Sicilian wines. At this café you can anchor in the corner where Giuseppe di Lampedusa in the late 1950s wrote a great many chapters of *The Leopard*, one of the finest novels to come out of Italy. Besides an espresso bar and pastry shop on the first floor, there's a so-called American grill on the second floor as well as the prestigious Restaurant Charleston. If you can't find a place to eat in Palermo on a Sunday, when virtually everything is shut, the Mazzara is a good bet. It's open daily from 7:30am to 10pm. Cappuccino costs 2,200 lire ($1.40) at the bar.

One of the most elegant discos in town, Speak Easy, viale Strasburgo 34 (☎ 518486), is open Tuesday through Sunday nights from 10:30pm to 2:30am. The cover charge is 18,000 lire ($11.25); once inside drinks cost 10,000 lire ($6.25). The disco lies on the northern edge of Palermo (at night it's better—certainly safer—to come here by taxi). Closed in summer.

EASY EXCURSIONS
MONREALE

The town of Monreale is six miles from Palermo, up Monte Caputo and on the edge of the Conca d'Oro plain. If you don't have a car, you can reach it by taking bus no. 389 from piazza Indipendenza in Palermo. The Normans under William II founded a Benedictine monastery at Monreale some time in the 1170s. Near the ruins of that monastery a great cathedral was erected.

As with the Alhambra in Granada, Spain, the ✪ **Church of Monreale** has a relatively drab facade, giving little indication of the riches inside. The interior is virtually covered throughout with shimmering mosaics, illustrating scenes from the Bible, such as the story of Adam and Eve or Noah and the Ark. The artwork provides a distinctly original interpretation to the old, rigid Byzantine form of decoration. The mosaics make for an Eastern look despite the Western-style robed Christ reigning over his kingdom. The ceiling is ornate, even gaudy. On the north and west facade of the church are two bronze doors in relief depicting biblical stories. The cloisters are also of interest. Built in 1166, they consist of twin mosaic columns, every other pair an original design (the lava inlay was hauled from the active volcano, Mount Etna). The church and cloisters are open April to September, Monday through Saturday from 9am to 7pm and Sunday from 9am to 1pm; October to March, Monday through Saturday from 9am to 2pm and Sunday from 9am to 1pm. Admission is 3,000 lire ($1.90).

It's also possible to visit the treasury and the terraces, each charging another 2,000 lire ($1.25) for admission. They are open from 7:30am to 12:30pm and 3 to 6:30pm. The terraces are actually the rooftop of the church, from which you'll be rewarded with a view of the cloisters.

Where to Stay

⑤ Park Hotel Carrubella
Corso Umberto 1, 90046 Monreale. ☎ **091/6402188.** Fax 091/6402189. 30 rms. A/C TEL. 104,000 lire ($65) double. Breakfast 10,000 lire ($6.25) extra. AE, DC, MC, V. Free parking.

The Park Hotel is one of the tallest buildings in town, its terraces providing a sweeping view over the famous church, the surrounding valleys, and the azure coastline of faraway Palermo. To reach it, follow a one-lane road originating at the plaza near the church, which takes you along a serpentine series of terraces; the hotel is 800 yards from the cathedral. The spacious interior is filled with luxurious mirrors, and deep and comfortable armchairs, along with scattered pieces of sculpture. In the public rooms, as well as in the bedrooms, the floors are covered with rows of Sicilian tiles hand-painted into flowery designs. The genial partners who own this place offer comfortably furnished accommodations, each with its own balcony. Well-prepared meals are served in the conservatively elegant dining room, costing from 35,000 lire ($21.90).

Where to Dine

La Botte

Contrada Lenzitti 416 (S.S. 186). ☎ **414051.** Reservations required Sat–Sun. Main courses 14,000–20,000 lire ($8.75–$12.50). AE, DC, MC, V. Tues–Sun 8–11pm. Closed July–Aug. Bus: 8 or 9 from Palermo. SICILIAN/ITALIAN.

Most of the dishes served here are derived from ancient recipes of Palermo, whose origins have long been forgotten. Perhaps you'll begin with an aromatic antipasto of such local ingredients as artichokes, tuna, shrimp, and about 30 different dishes. Pasta specialties are always smooth choices, followed by creative Sicilian meat dishes. Full meals cost 45,000 to 55,000 lire ($28.15 to $34.40).

MONDELLO LIDO

When the summer sun burns hot and old men on the square seek a place in the shade, and bambini tire of their toys, it's beach weather. For the denizen of Palermo, that means Mondello, $7^1/_2$ miles to the east. Originally, before this beachfront started attracting the wealthy class of Palermo, it was a fishing village (it still is), and you can see rainbow-colored fishing boats bobbing up in the harbor. A sandy beach, a good one, stretches for about a mile and a half, and it's filled to capacity on a July or August day. You might call it a Palermitan seaside experience. Some women traveling alone have found Mondello more inviting and less intimidating than downtown Palermo. In summer, an express bus (no. 6, "Beallo") goes to Mondello, leaving from the central train station in Palermo.

Where to Stay

✪ Mondello Palace Hotel

Viale Principe di Scalea 2, 90151 Mondello. ☎ **091/450001.** Fax 091/450657. 83 rms, 10 suites. A/C MINIBAR TV TEL. 240,000 lire ($150) double; from 325,000 lire ($203.15) suite. Rates include breakfast. AE, DC, MC, V. Free parking. Bus: 614 or 615 from Palermo.

Set within a garden of palms and semitropical shrubs, across the coastal road from Palermo's most popular beach, this is the most visible and most famous hotel in Mondello. Originally built in 1950, and renovated several times since then, it offers four stories of airy and comfortable bedrooms outfitted in tones of blue, red, and white. All double rooms have balconies and sea views. Clients of yesteryear have included Sofia Loren and Luchino Visconti; today the place might include families vacationing en masse from the hinterlands of Sicily or northern Europe. There's a large swimming pool set into the garden, a bar, and sea-view indoor/outdoor restaurant serving full meals for around 50,000 lire ($31.25) each.

Splendid Hotel la Torre

Via Piano di Gallo 11, 90151 Mondello. ☎ **091/450222.** Fax 091/450033. 170 rms, 9 suites. A/C TV TEL. 179,000 lire ($111.90) double; from 358,000 lire ($223.75) suite. Rates include breakfast. AE, DC, MC, V. Free parking. Bus: 614 or 615 from Palermo.

Built in 1962 and renovated in 1984, this hotel beside the beach lies half a mile north of Mondello's center, rising four floors. From your comfortable bed you can get up and walk out onto your private terrace overlooking the sea from which the

Normans came to invade. Like any Mediterranean resort hotel, La Torre is crowded during the peak summer months, so reservations are important. It offers well-furnished chambers, some quite spacious. All are well maintained (at least the 14 units I recently inspected with a maid who wanted to show me everything, including the linen closet). During the day there are many sports and recreational activities to occupy your time, including swimming pools, a tennis court, a garden, and plenty of games for children. La Torre is very much a family resort instead of a romantic retreat.

It attracts some heavy drinkers as well—the bar opens at 9am, staying open until 1am. The place is not a gourmet haven, but I've enjoyed my meals here, especially the pasta and fish dishes. The cookery is quite good, the choice is ample, and the staff takes good care of you. Expect to spend 45,000 to 55,000 lire ($28.15 to $34.40).

Where to Dine

☼ Charleston le Terrazze

Viale Regina Elena. ☎ **450171.** Reservations required. Main courses 22,000–28,000 lire ($13.75–$17.50). AE, DC, MC, V. Daily 1–3pm and 8–11pm. Closed Oct–May. Bus: 614 or 615 from Palermo. SICILIAN/INTERNATIONAL.

The best food in Mondello is served at this buff-colored seaside fantasy of art nouveau, with spires and gingerbread detailing. It fronts the sands. The kitchen, fortunately, matches the delights of the eye. The Sicilian staff who work here add to the sense of luxury and refinement. However, it's expensive, so bring lots of money—at least 70,000 to 100,000 lire ($43.75 to $62.50) per person. The chef specializes in many dishes, including such favorites as melazana (eggplant) Charleston (in my modest opinion, the Sicilians do the best eggplant dishes in the world). Try also the pesce spada (swordfish) al gratin and scaloppe Conca d'Oro. For dessert, you can have a smooth finish by ordering a parfait di caffè. For a wine, I recommend a Corvo, which comes both "blanco" and "rosso." Of course, with a name like Le Terrazze it's got to deliver the mandatory terrace with a view.

Casablanca

Via Piano di Gallo 30-32. ☎ **454685.** Reservations not necessary. Main courses 12,000–22,000 lire ($7.50–$13.75); fixed-price menu 35,000 lire ($21.90). AE, DC, MC, V. Tues–Sun noon–3:30pm and 7:30–11:30pm. Open daily in summer. Closed Jan 8–Feb 15. Bus: 614 or 615 from Palermo. SICILIAN/INTERNATIONAL.

Casablanca is a refined and reasonably priced restaurant, with a panoramic view of the Golfo Mondello. It offers almost faultless service from its well-trained staff. Both a regional and international cuisine is offered. The sauces, especially those accompanying shellfish, are delectable. Many of the dishes are also flambéed at table, and served to an appreciative audience. The wine list includes a well-chosen selection of Sicilian, Italian, and international brands. From May through October a terrace is open onto the sea, and many diners prefer to sit here, ordering drinks, crêpes, ice cream, and the like. There is also an on-site "panoramic pizzeria" and pub.

CEFALÙ

For another day's excursion, we recommend a trek east from Palermo for 43 miles to this fishing village, which is known all over Europe for its Romanesque cathedral, an outstanding achievement of the Arab-Norman architectural style. Two SAIS buses a day connect Palermo to Cefalù.

What to See & Do

Il Duomo

Piazza de Duomo, off corso Ruggero. ☎ **922021.** Admission is free. Daily 9am–noon and 3:30–7pm.

Resembling a military fortress, the Duomo was built by Roger II to fulfill a vow he made when faced with a possible shipwreck. Construction began in 1131, and in time two square towers dotted the landscape of Cefalù, curiously placed between the sea and a rocky promontory. The architectural line of the cathedral has a severe elegance, and inside are some outstanding Byzantine-inspired mosaics. Seek out especially Christ the Pantocrator in the dome of the apse. Capitals in the Sicilian-Norman style are supported by columns.

Museo Mandralisca

Via Mandralisca. ☎ **21547.** Admission 4,000 lire ($2.50). Mon–Sat 9am–12:30 and 3:30–7pm; Sun 9am–12:30pm.

Before leaving town, try to visit this museum opposite the cathedral, with its outstanding collection of art, none more notable than the 1470 Portrait of an Unknown by Antennal Messina. Some art critics have journeyed all the way down from Rome just to stare at this handsome work.

Where to Dine

Al Gabbiano da Saro

Viale Lungomare 17. ☎ **21495.** Reservations recommended Sat–Sun. Main courses 10,000–30,000 lire ($6.25–$18.75). AE, DC, MC, V. June 15–Sept 15, daily noon–3pm and 7pm–midnight. Sept 16–June 14, Thurs–Tues noon–3pm and 7pm–midnight. Closed mid-Jan to mid-Feb. SICILIAN.

In a century-old building, this trattoria is typical of the area, attracting both locals and visitors in almost equal measure. Fresh fish is the thing to order at this rustic trattoria on the seaside, making your way through a list of unpronounceable sea creatures. You might begin with zuppa di cozze, a savory mussel soup. The vegetables and pastas are good too, especially pennette alla Norma (with eggplant). Involtini of swordfish is another specialty. The cookery is consistent, as is the service. If you speak a little Italian, it helps. Expect to spend at least 35,000 lire ($21.90).

Da Nino al Lungomare

Viale Lungomare 11. ☎ **22582.** Reservations required. Main courses 12,000–22,000 lire ($7.50–$13.75); fixed-price menu 21,000 lire ($13.15). AE, DC, MC, V. June–Sept, daily noon–3pm and 7–11pm. Oct–May, Wed–Mon noon–3pm and 7–11pm. Closed Nov. SOUTHERN ITALIAN/SICILIAN.

In a century-old building, this is a reasonably good choice for southern Italian and Sicilian cuisine. That means that the kitchen is in no way influenced by trends or food fads. Time-tested recipes are served here, including a delectable risotto marinara or fisher's rice or else an involtini of meat. Fresh fish, however, is the featured item.

2 Segesta

41 miles SW of Palermo, 91 miles NW of Agrigento

Segesta was the ancient city of the Elymi, a people of mysterious origin, although they have been linked by some to the Trojans. As the major city in western

Sicily, it was brought into a series of conflicts with the rival power nearby, Selinus (Selinunte). From the 6th through the 5th century B.C. there were near-constant hostilities. The Athenians came from the east to aid the Segestans in 415 B.C., but the expedition ended in disaster, forcing the city to turn eventually for help to Hannibal of Carthage.

Twice in the 4th century B.C. it was besieged and conquered, once by Dionysius and again by Agathocles, the latter a particularly brutal victor who tortured, mutilated, or made slaves of most of the citizenry. Recovering eventually, Segesta in time turned on its old (but dubious) ally, Carthage. Like all Greek cities of Sicily, it ultimately fell to the Romans.

ESSENTIALS

GETTING THERE   By Bus   If you're going to see one of the classical plays (see below), you can take a bus leaving from piazza Politeama in Palermo approximately two hours before the show is presented. You should purchase your ticket in advance in Palermo, however; most travel agents sell such tickets, costing 15,000–25,000 lire ($9.40–$15.65).

By Car   Continue west from Palermo along autostrada A29.

VISITOR INFORMATION   Consult the tourist information office in Palermo (see Section 1 of this chapter).

WHAT TO SEE & DO

Today Segesta is visited for its remarkable ✪ **Doric temple,** dating from the 5th century B.C. Although never completed, it's in an excellent state of preservation (the entablature still remains). The temple was far enough away from the ancient town to have escaped leveling during the "scorched earth" days of the Vandals and Arabs.

From its position on a lonely hill, the Doric temple commands a majestic setting. Although you can scale the hill on foot, you're likely to encounter Sicilian boys trying to hustle you for a donkey ride. From mid-July until the first of August, classical plays are performed at the temple. Ask at the tourist information office in Palermo for details. Local travel agents in Palermo sell tickets.

In another spot on Mount Barbaro, a theater, built in the Greek style into the rise of the hill, has been excavated. It was erected in the 3rd century B.C.

In the car park leading to the temple is a café for refreshments. Otherwise, Segesta is bereft of dining or accommodation selections.

3 Selinunte

76 miles SW of Palermo. 70 miles W of Agrigento

One of the lost cities of ancient Sicily, ✪ Selinunte traces its history to the 7th century B.C. when immigrants from Megara Hyblaea (Syracuse) set out to build a new colony. They succeeded, erecting a city of power and prestige adorned with many temples. But that was like calling attention to a good thing. As earlier mentioned, much of Selinunte's fate was tied up with seemingly endless conflicts with the Elymi people of Segesta. Siding with Selinunte's rival, Hannibal virtually leveled the city in 409 B.C. Despite an attempt, the city was never to recover its former glory, and fell into ultimate decay.

Today it's an archaeological garden, its temples in scattered ruins, the mellowed stone, the color of honey, littering the ground as if an earthquake had struck (as one did in ancient times). From 9am to dusk daily, you can walk through the monument zone, exploring such relics as the remains of the Acropolis, the heart of old Selinunte. Parts of it have been partially excavated and reconstructed, as much as is possible with the bits and fragments remaining. Admission is 2,000 lire ($1.25).

The temples, in varying states of preservation, are designated by alphabetical lettering. Temple E, in the Doric style, contains fragments of an inner temple. Standing on its ruins before the sun goes down, you can look across the water that washes up again on the shores of Africa, from which the Carthaginian fleet emerged to destroy the city. The temples are dedicated to such mythological figures as Apollo and Hera (Juno). Most of them date from the 6th and 5th centuries B.C. Temple G, in scattered ruins, was one of the largest erected in Sicily, and was built in the Doric style.

ESSENTIALS

GETTING THERE   By Train   From Palermo, Trapani, or Marsala, you can make rail connections to Castelveltrano. Once at Castelveltrano, you must board a bus for Selinunte. Most passengers reach Selinunte from Palermo (call 6161806 in Palermo for more information).

By Bus   Buses (about five per day) depart from in front of the rail terminal at Castelveltrano heading for Selinunte. A one-way fare is 2,000 lire ($1.25).

By Car   Selinunte is on the southern coast of Sicily and is best explored by car, as public transportation is awkward. From Segesta, continue south on autostrada A29 until Castelveltrano. From there, follow the signposted secondary road marked "Selinunte" which leads south to the sea.

VISITOR INFORMATION   There are no tourist offices in the area. The telephone area code for Selinunte is 0924.

PLACES TO STAY & DINE IN NEARBY MARINELLA

The site of the ruined temple of Selinunte contains virtually no hotels, restaurants, or watering holes of note. Most visitors stop at the temple for a daylight visit, heading on to other locales at night. There are a handful of overnight accommodations, however, in the little seafront village of Marinella, which lies about a mile east of Selinunte. To reach Marinella, you'll travel along a narrow country road lined in part with stone walls.

Impressions

There is in the Sicilian . . . a great deal of Arab solemnity as a background to Italian vivacity.

—Walter Starkie, *The Waveless Plain*, 1938

I have heard it said that Sicilians can't use the telephone because they need both hands to talk with.

—Anonymous

Hotel Alceste

Via Alceste 23, 91020 Marinella di Selinunte. ☎ **0924/46184.** Fax 0924/46143. 26 rms. TEL. 78,000 lire ($48.75) double. Breakfast 10,000 lire ($6.25) extra. AE, MC, V. Free parking on street.

After they erected the concrete walls of this hotel, the builders painted it a shade of sienna and filled its three-sided courtyard with dining tables and plants. This seasonal hotel is about a 15-minute walk from the ruins. The simple bedrooms each have private bath or phone. Most visitors, however, stop only for a meal, enjoying a regional dinner costing from 25,000 lire ($15.65) and up.

4 Agrigento

80 miles S of Palermo, 109 miles SE of Trapani

Greek colonists from Gela (Caltanissetta) named it Akragas when they established a beachhead here in the 6th century B.C. In time their settlement grew to become one of the most prosperous cities in Magna Graecia (Greater Greece). A great deal of that growth is attributed to the despot Phalaris, who ruled from 571 to 555 B.C. and is said to have roasted his victims inside a brazen bull, eventually meeting the same fate himself.

Empedocles, the Greek philosopher and politician (also credited by some as the founder of medicine in Italy), was the most famous son of Akragas, born around 490 B.C. He formulated the four-elements theory (earth, fire, water, and air), modified by the agents love and strife. In modern times the town produced Luigi Pirandello, the playwright *(Six Characters in Search of an Author),* who won the Nobel Prize in literature in 1934.

Like nearby Selinunte, the city was attacked by war-waging Carthaginians, the first assault in 406 B.C. In the 3rd century B.C. the Carthaginians and Romans played Russian roulette with the city until it finally succumbed to Roman domination by 210 B.C. The city was then known as Agrigentium.

The modern part of the present town (in 1927 the name was changed from Girgenti to Agrigento) occupies a hill site. The narrow streets—casbahlike—date back to the influence of the conquering Saracens. Heavy Allied bombing in World War II necessitated much rebuilding.

Below the town stretch the long reaches of "La Valle dei Templi," containing some of the greatest Greek ruins in the world.

ESSENTIALS

GETTING THERE   By Train   Eleven trains per day arrive from Palermo, taking 1¹/₂ hours; a one-way ticket costs 10,900 lire ($6.80). For information about schedules, call 6161806 in Palermo. If you're already on the east coast of Sicily, the best connections are through Catania, with 10 trains per day arriving at Agrigento. Trip time is 3³/₄ hours, and a one-way ticket costs 14,400 lire ($9). In Catania, call 531625 for information.

By Bus   From Selinunte (see above), take the bus to Castelveltrano, at a one-way cost of 1,500 lire (95¢); then transfer to another bus bound for Agrigento. There are four daily buses from Castelveltrano to Agrigento. The trip takes 1¹/₄ hours, and a one-way ticket costs 9,600 lire ($6).

By Car   From Palermo, cut southeast along Route 121, which becomes 188 and 189 before it finally reaches Agrigento and the Mediterranean.

VISITOR INFORMATION   The telephone area code for Agrigento is 0922. The tourist information center is at via Atenea 123 (☎ 20454).

WHAT TO SEE & DO

THE VALLEY OF THE TEMPLES   Many writers are fond of suggesting that Greek ruins be viewed at either dawn or sunset. Indeed, their mysterious aura is heightened then. But for details you can search them out under the bright cobalt-blue Sicilian sky. The backdrop for the temples is idyllic, especially in spring when the striking almond trees blossom into pink.

Riding out our strada Panoramica, you'll first approach (on your left), the ✪ **Temple of Juno (Giunone).** With many of its Doric columns now restored, this temple was erected sometime in the mid-5th century B.C., at the peak of a construction boom that skipped across the celestial globe honoring the deities. As you climb the blocks, note the remains of a cistern as well as a sacrificial altar in front. There are good views of the entire valley from the perch here.

The ✪ **Temple of Concord,** next, ranks along with the Temple of Hephaistos (the "Theseum") in Athens as the best-preserved Greek temple in the world. Flanked by 13 columns on its side, along with six in front and six in back, the temple was built in the peripteral hexastyle. You'll see the clearest example in Sicily of what an inner temple was like. In the late 6th century A.D., the pagan structure was transformed into a Christian church, which may have saved it for posterity, although today it has been stripped down to its classical purity.

The ✪ **Temple of Hercules** is the most ancient, dating from the 6th century B.C. Badly ruined (only eight pillars are standing), it once ranked in size with the Temple of Zeus. At one time the temple sheltered a celebrated statue of Hercules. The infamous Gaius Verres, the Roman magistrate who became an especially bad governor of Sicily, attempted to steal the image as part of his temple-looting tear on the island.

The ✪ **Temple of Jupiter (Zeus)** was the largest in the valley, similar in some respects to the Temple of Apollo at Selinunte. In front of the structure was a large altar. The giant on the ground was one of several telamones (atlases) used to support the edifice.

The so-called ✪ **Temple of Dioscuri,** with four Doric columns intact, is a pasticcio—that is, it is composed of fragments from different buildings. At various times it has been designated as a temple honoring Castor and Pollux, the twin sons of Leda, and deities of seafarers; and Demeter (Ceres), the goddess of marriage and of the fertile earth; and Persephone, the daughter of Zeus who became the symbol of spring.

The temples can usually be visited daily from 9am till one hour before sunset. City bus nos. 8, 9, 10, or 11 leave from the train station in Agrigento, taking you to the site of the temples.

IN TOWN   The Museo Regionale Archeologico stands near the Church of Saint Nicholas (Eglisia di San Nicola), on contrada San Nicola (☎ 29008), and is open Monday through Friday from 9am to 1pm and Saturday from 9am to 5pm, charging no admission. Its single most important exhibit is a head of the god Telamon from the Temple of Jupiter. The collection of Greek vases is also impressive. Many of the artifacts on display were dug up when Agrigento was excavated. Bus: 8, 9, 10, or 11.

WHERE TO STAY

Only a fair lot of hostelries is offered, but they're compensatingly inexpensive, the best choices falling in the medium-priced range.

MODERATE

Hotel Villa Athena

Via dei Templi 33, 92100 Agrigento. ☎ **0922/596288.** Fax 0922/402180. 40 rms. A/C MINIBAR TV TEL. 250,000 lire ($156.25) double. Rates include breakfast. AE, MC, V. Free parking outdoors. Bus: 8, 9, 10, or 11.

This 18th-century former private villa, set in the Valley of the Temples less than 2 miles from town, rises from the Sicilian landscape. Its grounds have been planted with fruit trees that bloom in January. During the day, guests sit in the paved courtyard, enjoying a drink and the fresh breezes. At night from one of the villa's windows, a view of the floodlit temples, a string of Doric ruins, can be seen. In a setting of gardenia bushes and flowers, a swimming pool has been installed. The dining room is in a separate building, serving both regional specialties and international dishes. In summer, make a reservation about two weeks in advance. Rooms are modern, with Italian styling. Room 205 frames a perfect view of the Temple of Concord.

INEXPENSIVE

Hotel Tre Torri

Strada Statale 115 no. 7, Viallagio Mosè. 92100 Agrigento. ☎ **0922/606733.** Fax 0922/607839. 118 rms. A/C TEL. 160,000 lire ($100) double. Rates include breakfast. AE, DC, MC, V. Free parking. Bus: 3.

Four and a half miles south of Agrigento in the village of Villaggio Mosè, this selection lies near the better-known Jolly Hotel in an unattractive commercial district, yet some consider it among the best hotels in town. Sheltered behind a mock-medieval facade of white stucco, chiseled stone blocks, false crenellations, and crisscrossed iron balconies, the hotel, which opened in 1982, is a favorite with the Italian business traveler. A swimming pool in the small, terraced garden is visible from a restaurant. There's also a bar, sometimes with live piano music. The bedrooms are comfortable, and some contain TVs. Furnishings are modern.

WHERE TO DINE

INEXPENSIVE

Le Caprice

Strada Panoramica dei Templi 51. ☎ **26469.** Reservations required. Main courses 18,000–32,000 lire ($11.25–$20). AE, DC, MC. V. Sept–June, Sat–Thurs 12:30–3pm and 7:30–11pm. Aug daily 12:30–3pm and 7:30–11pm. Closed July 1–15. Bus: 9. SEAFOOD/ITALIAN.

A loyal clientele return to this well-directed restaurant for special celebrations as well as for everyday fun. Specialties of the house include an antipasto buffet, a mixed fish fry from the gulf, along with rolled pieces of veal in a savory sauce. Full meals cost 34,000 to 52,000 lire ($21.25 to $32.50).

Trattoria Del Vigneto

Via Cavalleri Magazzeni 11. ☎ **414319.** Reservations not necessary. Main courses 18,000–20,000 lire ($11.25–$12.50); fixed-price menus 20,000–25,000 lire ($12.50–$15.65). AE. Wed–Mon 12:30–3pm and 8–10pm. Closed Nov. Bus: 9. SICILIAN.

This is a fine place to go for a Sicilian meal after a visit to the Valley of the Temples, just a short distance away. Menu items include a mixed Sicilian grill, loaded with many kinds of meat, along with lamb cutlets and a flavor-packed beef-steak laced with cheese and local herbs. The welcome is sincere.

5   Syracuse (Siracusa)

35 miles SE of Catania

Of all the Greek cities of antiquity that flourished on the coast of Sicily, Siracusa was the most important, a formidable competitor of Athens in the West. In the heyday of its power, it dared take on Carthage, even Rome. At one time its wealth and size were unmatched by any other city in Europe.

On a site on the Ionian Sea, colonizers from Corinth founded the city in about 735 B.C. Much of its history was linked to despots, beginning in 485 B.C. with Gelon, the "tyrant" of Gela who subdued the Carthaginians at Himera. Siracusa came under attack from Athens in 415 B.C., but the main Athenian fleet was destroyed and the soldiers on the mainland captured. They were herded into the Latoma di Cappuccini at piazza Cappuccini, a stone quarry. The "jail," from which there was no escape, was particularly horrid, as the defeated soldiers weren't given food and were packed together like cattle and allowed to die slowly.

Dionysius I was one of the greatest despots, reigning over the city during its particular glory in the 4th century B.C., when it extended its influence as a sea power. But in 212 B.C., the city fell to the Romans who, under Marcellus, sacked its riches and art. Incidentally, in this rape Siracusa lost its most famous son, the Greek physicist and mathematician Archimedes, who was slain in his study by a Roman soldier.

Before you go, you might want to read Mary Renault's novel *The Mask of Apollo*, set in Syracuse of the 5th century B.C. As one critic put it, "It brings the stones to life."

The most famous of the ancient quarries, the ✪ **Latomia del Paradiso** is one of four or five latomies from which stones were hauled to erect the great monuments of Siracusa in its day of glory. On seeing one of the caves, Michelangelo de Caravaggio is reputed to have dubbed it "The Ear of Dionysius," because of its unusual shape, like that of a human ear. But what an ear! It's nearly 200 feet long. You can enter the inner chamber of the grotto where the tearing of paper sounds like a gunshot. It is said that the despot Dionysius used to force his prisoners into the "ear" at night, where he was able to hear every word they said. But this story, widely reported, is dismissed by some scholars as fanciful. Nearby is the Grotta dei Cordari, where ropemakers plied their ancient craft.

Today, the city's harborfront is lined with a distinguished collection of 18th- and 19th-century town houses, each brightly painted in a spectrum of colors, whose ensemble provides one of the most charming vistas in Sicily.

ESSENTIALS

GETTING THERE   By Train   From other major cities in Sicily, you'll find Syracuse best reached by train: 1¹/₂ hours from Catania, 2 hours from Taormina (coming up), and 5 hours from Palermo (see above).

By Bus   If you're in Catania, you can continue south by SAIS bus to Syracuse. Eight buses make the 1¹/₂-hour trip per day, costing 6,500 lire ($4.05) one way. Phone SAIS in Syracuse at 66710 for information and schedules.

By Car From Catania, continue south along Route 114.

VISITOR INFORMATION The telephone area code for Syracuse is 0931. The tourist information center is at via San Sebastiano 45 (☎ 67710), facing the Church of San Giovanni, with a branch office at the entrance to the archaeological park, on largo Anfiteatro Romano (☎ 60510).

OTHER SIGHTS

✪ Museo Paolo Orsi

Viale Teocrito 66. ☎ **464022.** Admission 2,000 lire ($1.25) adults, free for children 17 and under and seniors over 60. Tues–Sat 9am–1pm; Wed and Fri 3–6:30pm. Bus: 1.

One of the most important archaeological museums in southern Italy, the Museo Paolo Orsi made its debut in 1988, replacing an early archaeological museum. Here, in these modern quarters, you can survey the Greek, Roman, and early Christian epochs in sculpture and fragments of archaeological remains. The museum also has a rich coin collection. Of the statues here (and there are several excellent ones), the best known is the headless Venus Anadyomene (arising from the sea). This work of art dates from the Hellenistic period in the 2nd century B.C. One of the earliest-known works is of an earth mother suckling two babes, from the 6th century B.C. The pre-Greek vases have great style and elegance. The museum stands in the gardens of Villa Landolina in Akradina.

✪ Catacombe di San Giovanni (St. John)

At the end of viale San Giovanni. Admission 2,000 lire ($1.25) adults; free for 17 or under or over 60. Mar 15–Nov 4, Thurs–Tues 9am–1pm and 3–6pm; off-season Thurs–Tues 10am–noon. Bus: 1.

These honeycombed tunnels of empty coffins evoke the catacombs along the Appian Way in Rome. The world down below is approached from the Chiesa di San Giovanni, from the 3rd century A.D., and the present building is of a much later date. Included in the early Christian burial grounds is the crypt of St. Marcianus, which lies under what was reportedly the first cathedral erected in Sicily. *Warning:* Make sure you exit in plenty of time before closing. Two women readers who entered the catacombs after 5pm were accidentally locked in for the night, and managed to escape, only after a harrowing and dangerous ordeal of wandering around in the dark.

ORTYGLA ISLAND

Ortygla, inhabited for many thousands of years, is also named Citta Vecchia, and contains the town's cathedral, many rows of houses spanning 500 years of building styles, most of the city's medieval and baroque monuments, and some of the most charming vistas in Sicily. Its beauties praised by Pindar, the island, reached by crossing the Ponte Nuova, was the heart of Siracusa, having been founded by the Greek colonists from Corinth. In Greek mythology, it is said to have been ruled by Calypso, daughter of Atlas, the sea nymph who detained Ulysses (Odysseus) for seven years on the island. The island is about a mile long and half again as wide.

Heading out the Foro Italico, you'll come to the Fountain of Arethusa, also famous in mythology. Alpheius, the river god, son of Oceanus, is said to have fallen in love with the sea nymph Arethusa. The nymph turned into this spring or fountain, but Alpheius became a river and "mingled" with his love. According to legend, the spring ran red when bulls were sacrificed at Olympus.

At piazza del Duomo, the Cathedral of Syracuse, with a baroque facade, was built over the ruins of the Temple of Minerva, and employs the same Doric columns. The temple was erected after Gelon the Tyrant defeated the Carthaginians at Himera in the 5th century B.C. The Christians converted it into a basilica in the 7th century A.D.

The Palazzo Bellomo, fronting via Capodieci, off Foro Vittorio Emanuele II, dates from the 13th century, with many alterations, and is today the home of the Galleria Regionale, via Capodieci 14 (☎ 69511). Not only is the palace fascinating, with its many arches, doors, and stairs, but it also has a fine collection of paintings. The most notable is *Annunciation* by Antennal da Messina from 1474. There is also a noteworthy collection of antiques and porcelain. It is open Monday through Saturday 9am to 2pm; Sunday 9am to 1pm, charging an admission of 2,000 lire ($1.25).

WHERE TO STAY

Moderate

Jolly

Corso Gelone 46, 96100 Siracusa. ☎ **0931/461111** or 800/221-2626 in the U.S., or 800/237-0319 in Canada. Fax 0931/461126. 100 rms (all with bath or shower). A/C MINIBAR TV TEL. 230,000 lire ($143.75) double. Rates include breakfast. AE, DC, MC, V. Free parking. Bus: 1.

The best place to stay is the Jolly, a member of a chain that is the Holiday Inn of Italy. You get no surprises here—clean, modern, functional rooms, short on soul but good on comfort. The hotel restaurant offers lunch or dinner for 50,000 lire ($31.25) in its restaurant, Il Giardinetto.

Inexpensive

Hotel Bellavista

Via Diodoro Siculo 4, 96100 Siracusa. ☎ **0931/411355.** Fax 0931/37927. 45 rms (all with bath or shower). TV TEL. 138,000 lire ($86.25) double. Rates include breakfast. AE, DC, MC, V. Free parking. Bus: 1.

Family owned and run, this hotel was built in a four-story format in 1960, then renovated several times. It lies in the commercial center, close to the archaeological zone. There's an annex in the garden for overflow guests. The main lounge has a sense of space, with leather chairs and semitropical plants. The bedrooms are informal and comfortable, often furnished with traditional pieces. Most rooms feature a sea-view balcony.

Hotel Forte Agip

Viale Teracati 30–32, 96100 Siracusa. ☎ **0931/463232.** Fax 0931/67115. 87 rms. A/C MINIBAR TV TEL. 149,000 lire ($93.15) single or double. Rates include breakfast. AE, DC, MC, V. Free parking. Bus: 2, 8, or 11.

Located a short drive inland from the medieval Citta Vecchia, in a position near the ancient Greek theater and most of the city's classical monuments, this member of a national hotel chain is designed for ease of access and convenience to motorists. Each of the monochromatic bedrooms is simple, streamlined, and similar to other chain-motel rooms throughout Europe. The in-house restaurant is often visited by residents of Syracuse who consider the generous portions, unpretentious service, and flavorful specialties worth the trip. Menu items include pastas, stuffed veal, American-style tournedos, salads, and a changing array of fresh fish. Full meals begin at around 35,000 lire ($21.90).

Ⓢ Panorama

Via Necropoli Grotticalle 33, 98100 Siracusa. ☎ **0931/412188.** 51 rms (all with bath or shower). TV TEL. 95,000 lire ($59.40) double. Breakfast 8,000 lire ($5) extra. AE, MC, V. Free parking. Bus: 1.

Near the entrance to the city, on a rise of Temenite Hill, is this bandbox-modern hotel, built on a busy street, about 5 minutes from the Greek theater or Roman amphitheater. It's not a motel, but does provide parking space. Inside, a contemporary accommodation awaits you. The bedrooms are pleasant and up-to-date, with comfortable but utilitarian pieces. On the premises is a hotel dining room serving only a continental breakfast (not included in the room prices).

WHERE TO DINE

Inexpensive

Arlecchino

Via dei Tolomei 5. ☎ **66386.** Reservations recommended. Main courses 16,000–30,000 lire ($10–$18.75). AE, DC, MC, V. Tues–Sun 12:30–3:30pm and 7:30pm–midnight. Closed Sun July–Sept. Bus: 1. SEAFOOD.

This restaurant, founded in 1967, occupies the street level of a 250-year-old palace in the heart of the Città Vecchia, a short walk from the cathedral. Despite its understated decor, Arlecchino is considered by some gourmets the best restaurant in town. Many specialties emerge from this fragrant kitchen. These include a wide array of homemade pastas, a cheese-laden crespelline of the house, pasta with sardines, spiedini with shrimp, and a selection of pungent beef, fish, and veal dishes. Full meals cost 40,000 to 60,000 lire ($25 to $37.50).

Ⓢ Darsena da Ianuzo

Riva Garibaldi 6. ☎ **66104.** Reservations required. Main courses 12,000–20,000 lire ($7.50–$12.50). AE, MC, V. Thurs–Tues 12:30–3pm and 8–10pm. Bus: 1. SEAFOOD.

This might not differ all that much from dozens of other seafood restaurants in the Città Vecchia, except that the food here seems to be exceptionally good and the welcome warm. Specialties include fresh shellfish, spaghetti with clams, a side collection of fresh grilled and baked fish, and the ever-present fish soup. A full meal costs 30,000 to 40,000 lire ($18.75 to $25).

Gambero Rosso

Via Eritrea 2. ☎ **68546.** Reservations recommended. Main courses 14,000–22,000 lire ($8.75–$13.75). AE, MC, V. Fri–Wed 12:30–3pm and 8–10pm. Bus: 1. SICILIAN/ MEDITERRANEAN.

Ideal for those who want to dine at an old tavern, this restaurant is near the entrance to the bridge leading to the Città Vecchia (Old Town). Restored, it's a mellow building, close to the fishing boats. It has a certain charm, and the cuisine is dedicated to the best of Sicilian dishes. A reliable dish is the zuppa di pesce (fish soup). An alternative choice is the zuppa di cozze, a plate brimming with fresh mussels in a savory marinade. Among the asciutte, the Sicilian cannelloni is good. The meat dishes feature a number of choices from the kitchens of Latium, Tuscany, and Emilia-Romagna. A complete meal will cost 25,000 to 30,000 lire ($15.65 to $18.75).

Ristorante Jonico E Rutta E Ciauli

Riviera Dionisio il Grande 194. ☎ **65540.** Reservations recommended. Main courses 20,000–25,000 lire ($12.50–$15.65). AE, DC, MC, V. Wed–Mon 12:30–3pm and 8–10pm. Bus: 1. SICILIAN.

This is one of the best restaurants on the island for serving the typical cuisine and local wines of Sicily. The restaurant offers a veranda and garden setting right on the sea, with a panoramic view (the location is about 100 yards from the Latomia dei Cappuccini). The decoration is in the typical Sicilian style. The antipasto array alone is dazzling. Superb homemade pasta dishes are served (ask one of the English-speaking waiters to explain some of the many variations or settle for spaghetti with caviar). One of the most interesting fish dishes I recently sampled was spada a pizzaiola (a swordfish in a savory, garlic-flavored sauce). Meat specialties include polpettone (rolled meat) alla siracusana, and a delectable stew made of various fish. The dessert specialty is a cassatine siciliana. Expect to pay 50,000 to 60,000 lire ($31.25 to $37.50).

❸ Ristorante Rossini

Via Savoia 6. ☎ **24317.** Reservations recommended. Main courses 16,000–20,000 lire ($10–$12.50). AE, DC, MC, V. Wed–Mon 12:30–3:30pm and Wed–Mon 8–10pm. Bus: 1. MEDITERRANEAN.

Ristorante Rossini is a homelike and comfortable enclave of regional gastronomy, offering meals to 50 fortunate diners a night, from 50,000 lire ($31.25) for a complete meal. You might begin with an assortment from the amply stocked buffet table of antipasti, then select one of many main dishes, including a mousse of fish with fresh shrimp, perhaps a shellfish risotto with roast peppers and tomato purée. A twice-roasted swordfish is also a specialty.

6 Taormina

33 miles N of Catania, 33 miles S of Messina, 155 miles E of Palermo

Runaway bougainvillea, silvery olive branches, a cerulean sky, cactuses adorning the hills like modern sculpture, pastel plastered walls, garden terraces of geraniums, trees laden with oranges and lemons, ancient ruins—all that and more is Taormina, Sicily's most desirable oasis.

Dating from the 4th century B.C., Taormina hugs close to the edge of a cliff overlooking the Ionian Sea. Writers for English Sunday supplements rave of its unspoiled charms and enchantment. The sea, even the railroad track, lie down below, connected by bus routes. Looming in the background is Mount Etna, the active volcano. Noted for its mild climate, the town enjoys a year-round season.

A lot of people contributed to putting Taormina on the tourist map. Since it was first inhabited by a tribe known as the Siculi, it has known many conquerors, including Greeks, Carthaginians, Romans, Saracens, French, and Spanish. Its first tourist was said to have been Goethe, who arrived in 1787. He recorded his impressions in his *Journey to Italy.* Other Germans were to follow in the centuries to come, including a red-haired Prussian, Otto Geleng. Arriving at the age of 20 in Taormina, he recorded its beauties in his painted landscapes. These were exhibited in Paris and caused much excitement—people had to go themselves to find out if Taormina was all that beautiful.

Another German, Wilhelm von Gloeden, arrived to photograph not only the town, but also nude boys crowned with laurel wreaths. These pictures sent

European high society flocking to Taormina. Von Gloeden's photographs, some of which are even printed in official tourist literature to this day, form one of the most enduring legends of Taormina. Souvenir shops still sell his pictures, which, although considered scandalous in their day, would be tame, even innocent, by today's X-rated standards.

Following in the footsteps of von Gloeden came a host of international celebrities hoping to see what all the excitement was about: Truman Capote, Tennessee Williams, Marlene Dietrich, Joan Crawford, Rita Hayworth, and Greta Garbo, to name only some of the more stellar personalities of yesterday. Always in disguise, sometimes as Harriet Brown, Ms. Garbo used Taormina as a vacation retreat from 1950 until her last mysterious arrival in 1979. Many of these stars, including Garbo, stayed at a villa on the road to Castel Mola owned by Gayelord Hauser, the celebrated dietician to Hollywood stars back in the golden age. In time another wave of stars were to arrive: Taylor and Burton, Cary Grant, and the woman who turned him down, Sofia Loren.

The rich and famous still come here, along with a lot of middle-class visitors as well. Taormina remains chic.

ESSENTIALS

GETTING THERE   By Train   You can make rail connections on the Messina line to Syracuse. Telephone 51511 in Taormina for schedules. The train station at Taormina, however, is a mile from the heart of the resort, but buses waiting there will take you up a hill.

By Bus   Most visitors arrive in Messina, their "gateway" to Sicily. There they can board a Taormina-bound bus; 13 leave per day, taking 1½ hours. More details are available in Messina by calling SAIS, the bus company (☎ 090/771914).

By Car   From Messina, head south along autostrada A18. From Catania, continue north along the A18.

VISITOR INFORMATION   The Taormina telephone area code is 0942. A tourist information center is in the Palazzo Corvaja, largo Santa Caterina (☎ 23243).

Once you arrive in the center of Taormina, you can walk to the following recommendations. If you arrive at the train station, you'll find a bus taking you up to the center of Taormina every 15 to 45 minutes (schedules vary throughout the year), daily from 9am to 9pm; a one-way ticket costs 2,500 lire ($1.55).

WHAT TO SEE & DO

✪ **The Greek and Roman Theater,** via Teatro Greco (☎ 23220), is the most visited monument, offering a view of rare beauty of Mount Etna and the seacoast. At an unrecorded time the Greeks hewed the theater out of rock on the slope of Mount Tauro, but the Romans remodeled and modified it greatly for their amusement. The conquering Arabs, who seemed intent on devastating the town in the 10th century, slashed away at it. On the premises is an antiquarium, containing not only artifacts from the classical period but early Christian ones as well. The theater is open Tuesday through Sunday from 9am to 2 hours before sunset. Admission is 2,000 lire ($1.25) for adults; children 17 and under and seniors over 60 are admitted free.

The other thing to do in Taormina is to walk through the Giardino Pubblico, via Bagnoli Croce, a flower-filled garden overlooking the sea, a choice spot for views as well as a place to relax. At a bar in the park, you can order drinks. Take bus no. 1 or 2 to reach these attractions.

WHERE TO STAY

The hotels in Taormina are the best in Sicily—in fact, the finest in southern Italy after you head south of Amalfi. All price levels and accommodations are offered, from sumptuous suites to army cots.

VERY EXPENSIVE

✪ San Domenico Palace

Piazza San Domenico 5, 98039 Taormina. ☎ **0942/23701.** Fax 0942/625506. 101 rms, 8 suites. A/C MINIBAR TV TEL. 620,000 lire ($387.50) double; from 1,560,000 lire ($975) suite. Half-board 400,000–450,000 lire ($250–$281.25) per person. AE, DC, MC, V. Parking 30,000 lire ($18.75). Bus: 1 or 2.

This is one of the great old hotels of Europe, converted from a 14th-century Dominican monastery, complete with cloisters. Overhauled, it almost begrudgingly boasts air conditioning and a flower-edged swimming pool. Its position is legend to discriminating travelers—high up from the sea coast, on several different levels surrounded by terraced gardens of almond, orange, and lemon trees. In the 19th century it blossomed as a hotel, with no expense spared, and was a favorite of the elite: kings, artists, writers, statesmen.

The large medieval courtyard is planted with semitropical trees and flowers. The encircling enclosed loggia, the old vaulted-ceilinged cloister, is decorated with potted palms and ecclesiastical furnishings (high-backed carved choir stalls, wooden angels and cherubs, religious paintings in oil). Off the loggia are great refectory halls turned into sumptuously furnished lounges. While antiques are everywhere, the atmosphere is not museumlike, but gracious, with traditional upholstered chairs and sofas. Ornate ceilings climb high, and arched windows look out onto the view.

The bedrooms, opening off the cloister, would surely impress a cardinal. One-of-a-kind furniture has been utilized, including elaborate carved beds, gilt, Chinese red, provincial pieces, Turkish rugs, Venetian chairs and dressers.

Dining/Entertainment: The cuisine, a combination of Sicilian and Italian dishes, is the most refined in Taormina. Dining in the main hall is an event, with meals costing from 95,000 lire ($59.40). The cuisine is supervised by a masterful chef.

Services: Room service, babysitting, laundry, valet.

Facilities: Swimming pool.

MODERATE

Bristol Park Hotel

Via Bagnoli Croce 92, 98039 Taormina. ☎ **0942/23006.** Fax 0942/24519. 50 rms, 2 suites. A/C MINIBAR TV TEL. 200,000–250,000 lire ($125–$156.25) double; 250,000–310,000 lire ($156.25–$193.75) suite. Rates include breakfast. Half-board 110,000–170,000 lire ($68.75–$106.25) per person. AE, DC, MC, V. Parking 15,000 lire ($9.40). Closed mid-Nov to Feb. Bus: 1 or 2.

This is one of the all-out comfort hotels, built high on the cliffside at the edge of Taormina. Close to the public gardens of Duca di Cesaro, it offers a spectacular view of the coastline and Mount Etna from most of its private sun balconies. The interior decor is amusing: with tufted satin, plush and ornate. In contrast, the bedrooms are traditional, with private bath. Meals, ordered separately, begin at 50,000 lire ($31.25). The dining room, with arched windows framing the view, offers international meals, with an occasional Sicilian dish. There's a private beach with free deck chairs and parasols, plus bus service to the beach from June 1 to September 30. The hotel has a swimming pool, and there's a private garage.

Excelsior Palace

Via Toselli 8, 98039 Taormina. ☎ **0942/23975.** Fax 0942/23978. 89 rms. A/C TV TEL. 250,000 lire ($156.25) double. Rates include breakfast. Half-board 170,000–195,000 lire ($106.25–$121.90) per person. AE, DC, MC, V. Free parking. Bus: 1 or 2.

The Excelsior seems like a Moorish palace, lost on the end ridge of the mountain fringe of Taormina. It's as foreboding as a fortress on two sides, but the severity dissolves inside into style and comfort. The gardens at the back have terraces of scented semitropical flowers, date palms, yucca, and geraniums. The view of Etna and the seacoast below is of a rare enchantment. Renovated successfully, the hotel is managed so that superior facilities and service await all guests. The bedrooms have plenty of space and are decorated in a traditional manner. You can swim at the hotel's seaside annex, and the kitchen staff will pack you a picnic lunch.

Hotel Monte Tauro

Via Madonna delle Grazi 3, 98039 Taormina. ☎ **0942/24402.** Fax 0942/24403. 30 rms, 40 junior suites. A/C MINIBAR TV TEL. 240,000 lire ($150) double; from 280,000 lire ($175) suite. Rates include breakfast. AE, DC, MC, V. Free parking. Bus: 1 or 2.

Engineering skills and tons of poured concrete went into the construction of this dramatic hotel built into the side of a scrub-covered hill rising high above the sea, within view of the coastline. Each bedroom has a circular balcony, often festooned with flowers. The social center is the many-angled swimming pool, whose cantilevered platform is ringed with a poolside bar, dozens of plants, and comfortable deck chairs. The velvet-covered chairs of the modern, tile-floored interior are upholstered in the same blues, grays, and violets of the sunny bedrooms where Mondrian-style rectangles and stripes decorate the bedspreads and accessories. The hotel rents well-furnished bedrooms and suites, each with private bath or shower.

Jolly Hotel Diodoro

Via Bagnoli Croce 75, 98039 Taormina. ☎ **0942/23312** or 800/221-2626 in the U.S., or 800/237-0319 in Canada. Fax 0942/23391. 102 rms. A/C MINIBAR TV TEL. 191,800–240,000 lire ($119.90–$150) double. Rates include breakfast. Half-board 130,000–225,000 lire ($81.25–$140.65) per person. AE, DC, MC, V. Free parking. Bus: 1 or 2.

The Jolly is one of the most luxurious of the first-class hotels. Actually it was built and designed privately, and then taken over by the Jolly chain. The design of everything—the public lounges, the bedrooms—is well coordinated, on a high taste level. The dining room, with tall windows on three sides, is projected toward the sea and Mount Etna. If there's a sun in Taormina, you'll find it here. The outdoor swimming pool is also a sun trap; you can bathe, swim, and enjoy the view of mountains, trees, and flowers. The bedrooms are tasteful and comfortable, with well-designed furniture and the latest gadgets. Each has a private bath or shower. Many of the rooms are angled toward the sea, with wide-open windows.

INEXPENSIVE

⑤ Ariston

Via Bagnoli Croce 128, 98039 Taormina. ☎ **0942/23838.** Fax 0942/21137. 176 rms. A/C MINIBAR TEL. 75,000–130,000 lire ($46.90–$81.25) per person. Rates include half-board. AE, MC, V. Free parking. Bus: 1 or 2.

Substantial and cost-conscious, and favored by families from Italy and the rest of Europe, this modern hotel was built in 1975 with four stories rising above a verdant park about 400 yards from the center of Taormina. About 36 of its rooms lie within a low-rise garden annex nearby. Although the hotel is located inland, a short walk from the sea, there's a swimming pool on the premises, a piano bar, and a restaurant with efficient service and both Sicilian and international specialties.

La Campanella

Via Circonvallazione 3, 98039 Taormina. ☎ **0942/23381.** Fax 0942/625248. 12 rms. TEL. 120,000 lire ($75) double. Rates include breakfast. No credit cards. Bus: 1 or 2.

This hotel offers an environment rich in the aesthetics of gardening, painting, and hospitality. It sits at the top of a seemingly endless flight of stairs, which begin at a sharp curve of the main road leading into town. You climb past terra-cotta pots and dangling tendrils of a terraced garden, eventually arriving at the house. The owners maintain clean and uncluttered bedrooms, each with its own bath.

Pensione Svizzera

Via Pirandello 26, 98039 Taormina. ☎ **0942/23790.** Fax 0942/625906. 20 rms (all with shower). TEL. 80,000 lire ($50) double. Rates include breakfast. AE, DC, MC, V. Free parking. Closed Jan–Feb.

This is a pleasant place to stay, about an eighth of a mile from the center of town. The recently restored pensione is owned and operated by Antonino Vinciguerra and his German-born wife, both of whom speak English. Try to get a room that overlooks the sea and Isola Bella. All bedrooms have a shower and toilet. There's also a garden with shady palm trees where breakfast is served in summer. The funicular going down to the beach at Mazzarò is a little over 100 yards from the pensione, as is the bus terminal.

Villa Belvedere

Via Bagnoli Croci 79, 98039 Taormina. ☎ **0942/23791.** Fax 0942/625830. 44 rms. TEL. 213,000 lire ($133.15) double. Rates include breakfast. MC, V. Parking 5,000 lire ($3.15). Closed Nov–Mar. Bus: 1 or 2.

This is a gracious old villa bathed in Roman gold near the Giardino Pubblico. In its garden is a heated swimming pool. From the cliffside terrace in the rear—a social center for guests—is that view: the clear blue sky, the gentle Ionian Sea, the cypress-studded hillside, and menacing Mount Etna looking as if it's about to blow its top. It's the same view, incidentally, enjoyed by clients at the more expensive first-class hotels nearby. The formal entrance is enhanced by potted plants and wall-covering vines, and the interior living rooms of this generations-old, family-run establishment would captivate Elizabeth Barrett Browning. The bedrooms have been restored, and 15 of them are air-conditioned. Breakfast is served, and there are two bars. Lunch is served at a snack bar by the pool.

⑤ Villa Fiorita

Via Pirandello 39, 98039 Taormina. ☎ **0942/24122.** Fax 0942/625967. 24 rms, 2 suites. A/C MINIBAR TV TEL. 145,000 lire ($90.65) single or double; from 179,000 lire ($111.90) suite. Rates include breakfast. AE, MC, V. Parking 15,000 lire ($9.40). Bus: 1 or 2.

One of the most charming hotels in its category, Villa Fiorita stretches toward the town's Greek theater from its position beside the road leading up to the top. Designed in 1976, its imaginative decor includes a handful of ceramic stoves, which the owner delights in collecting. A well-maintained garden is bordered by an empty but ancient Greek tomb whose stone walls have been classified as a national treasure. The bedrooms are arranged in a steplike labyrinth of corridors and stairwells, some of which bend to correspond to the rocky slope on which the hotel was built. Each unit contains some kind of antique, as well as a tile bath, radio, and usually a flowery private terrace. There are no single rooms.

⊗ Villa Nettuno

Via Pirandello 33, 98039 Taormina. ☎ **0942/23797.** Fax 0942/626035. 13 rms. 90,000 lire ($56.25) double. Breakfast 5,000 lire ($3.15) extra. MC, V. Parking 5,000 lire ($3.15). Bus: 1 or 2.

What's probably our favorite budget accommodation in town is a geranium-colored villa with Renaissance-style stone trim. It lies near the city center, opposite a cableway that transports passengers down to the sea. Visitors must climb several flights of steps after leaving the traffic of the main street leading into town. They pass beneath an archway whose keystone is carved with a grotesque stone face. The villa was acquired by the Sciglio family in 1887 and converted into a pensione by the warm-hearted but highly discerning Maria Sciglio in 1953. Guests enjoy breakfast in a garden with hibiscus and night-blooming jasmine. The dining room is like the rococo living quarters of an elegant Sicilian family. Each of the attractive, well-scrubbed bedrooms contains its own modernized bath and panoramic terrace (all but two of the terraces look out to sea).

⊗ Villa Paradiso

Via Roma 2, 98039 Taormina. ☎ **0942/23922.** Fax 0942/625800. 35 rms (all with bath or shower). A/C TV TEL. 140,000–240,000 lire ($87.50–$150) double. Rates include breakfast. AE, DC, MC, V. Parking 20,000 lire ($12.50). Closed Nov 4–Dec 20.

This charming five-story hotel is at one end of the main street of town, near the Greek theater and overlooking the public gardens and tennis courts. The creation of Signor Salvatore Martorana, it's a moderately priced choice for those who want to live well. He loves his establishment, and that attitude is reflected in the personal manner in which the living room is furnished, with antiques and reproductions. Each of the bedrooms is individually decorated, containing a balcony. Guests spend many sunny hours on the rooftop solarium, or in the informal drinking bar and lounge where wallflowers are rare. There's also a TV room for guests, plus two elevators. Prices include transportation to and from the Paradise Beach Club in Letojanni, use of sun umbrellas, deck chairs, and showers, plus changing cabins, swimming pool, hydromassage, and garden. The beach is private. Guests can play tennis free year round.

Villa Schuler

Piazzetta Bastione, via Roma, 98039 Taormina. ☎ **0942/23481.** Fax 0942/23522. 27 rms. TEL. 115,000 lire ($71.90) double. Rates include breakfast. AE, MC, V. Free parking outside, 11,000 lire ($6.90) in garage.

Family owned and run, this hotel was converted from a Sicilian villa in 1905. High above the Ionian Sea, it offers views of snowcapped Mount Etna and the Bay of Naxos. The hotel lies only a 2-minute stroll from the central corso Umberto, and about a 15-minute walk from the cable car taking guests down to the beach below. It's also near the ancient theater of Taormina. Surrounded by its own gardens and filled with the fragrance of bougainvillea and jasmine, the hotel is an ideal retreat. Bedrooms are comfortably furnished and many have a small balcony or terrace opening onto a view of the sea. Breakfast can be served in your room or else taken on a panoramic palm terrace overlooking the coastline. Facilities and

The Aeolian Islands

The Greeks who came this way in the 6th century B.C. believed that the Aeolian, or Lipari, Islands were the home of Aeolus, god of the winds. Volcanic activity on these islands has been reported since ancient times. In Messina province, the islands cluster into a Y shape, the northern tip formed by **Stromboli,** with **Vulcano** at the southern tip. Both these islands have volcanic activity, the crater at Stromboli being the most spectacular. The largest island in the archipelago is **Lipari,** which produces a malmsey-type wine.

For the reader willing to make the journey, the islands form one of the most exciting itineraries in southern Italy. After the peak of the summer season is over, you'll have the Aeolians almost to yourself, except for the local people.

The best way to reach these islands is by a surface-skimming hydrofoil departing from Milazzo, about 20 miles west of Messina. There is also regular ferry service to the islands. Ferry schedules change rapidly, depending on the season, so you must check locally about actual departure times. By ferry, Vulcano is reached in only 1 1/2 hours, Lipari in 2 hours. A ferry to Stromboli means that you must first go to Lipari and make connections from there. It is also possible to take hydrofoil (*aliscafi*) service from Naples. The hydrofoil is more expensive than the ferry, but much quicker.

Lipari is the chief town of the chain, with an important Aeolian archeological museum, **Museo Archeologico Eoliano,** housed in the former bishop's palace. The museum is open daily from 9am to 2pm (from 9am to 1pm on Sunday). Formed of volcanic rock, the town is framed by two beaches, Marina Lunga, which is the port and Marina Corta.

The town is dominated by the castle on the site that was the seat of prehistoric settlements from the Neolithic to the Bronze Age and the acropolis of the Greek and Roman towns. The encircling wall of the castle is of the Spanish period (16th century), but it encloses the ruins of the Greek and Norman forti-fications.

According to mythology, Vulcano was the actual home of the god of the winds, Aeolus mentioned earlier. The island is wild and desolate, attracting only the most adventurous to its rugged, rocky shores who soak in mud baths and lie on black sand beaches. Vulcano is the crater of a volcano that last saw action in 1890. Prehistoric sites have been discovered on the island, but the major interest is in looking at the volcanic formations, the sulfur vapors, and the hot mud flows. Instead of potentially dangerous climbing, We suggest that you negotiate with one

services include a roof terrace solarium, small library, 24-hour bar and room service, and laundry.

PLACES TO STAY IN NEARBY MAZZARÒ

If you arrive in Taormina in summer, you may prefer to stay at Mazzarò, which is about 3 miles form the heart of the more famous resort (same telephone area code). This is the major beach of Taormina, and has some fine hotels, as reflected by those recommended below. A bus for Mazzarò leaves from the center of Taormina every 30 minutes daily from 8am to 9pm, charging 1,500 lire (95¢).

of the local fishermen, arranging for a tour around Vulcano by boat. It's much easier that way.

Stromboli is the most distant of the Aeolian Islands, about 50 miles north of the coastal town of Milazzo. If you've heard of it, you probably only associate it with the Ingrid Bergman movie made there in 1949 during that so-called scandalous period in her life. That movie put Stromboli on the tourist map. Throughout the year, hydrofoils run daily from Milazzo to the major islands in the Aeolians, turning around at Stromboli.

Your first impression as you approach the island is that it is simply a huge black rock jutting out into the sea. The 3,000-foot cone silhouetted against the sky is the only active volcano in the Aeolians, but its activity is more like that of a wheezing old codger than an explosive juvenile. In the late-afternoon sun, the volcanic rock reflects its orange-and-red highlights, giving the approaching visitor an exciting, almost Fourth of July display.

As you near the "lee" side—the part of the island away from the volcano activity—you'll see the tiny houses standing out in the glaring whiteness against the hillside. The volcanic soil is rich, and bougainvillea, geraniums, petunias, roses, and fig trees grow in profusion.

The real experience in Stromboli is outside. Activities on the island are limited to hiking, swimming, fishing, boating—and eating. You can dine, perhaps, on the terrace of a hotel, overlooking the deep blue of the Tyrrhenian Sea, with the black backdrop of the Stromboli volcano behind you. The food is always good and plentiful—freshly caught fish and local vegetables make up a great part of the diet.

If you want to get a closer look at the volcano during your stay, you can take a motorlaunch—the hotels usually have boats available (for a fee to be negotiated)—around the island. Fortunately, Stromboli pours its molten rock down the side opposite the inhabited portion, and its exciting to watch the lava as it hisses into the sea. The more energetic may prefer to hike up the hillside. Guides are available for the 3-hour trek, about 3,000 feet over rock and volcanic ash. Swimming in Stromboli is a rare pleasure. Scuba-diving is especially popular, since the waters are uncommonly calm and crystal clear. Fishing is an alternative sport, and spearfishing in scuba gear can be a rewarding experience—especially if you take your catch back to your hotel for dinner.

No cars are allowed on Stromboli—only bicycles, mopeds, and three-wheel vehicles, used by locals for transporting goods and guests.

EXPENSIVE

Grande Albergo Capotaormina

Via Nazionale 105, 98039 Mazzarò. ☎ **0942/24000.** Fax 0942/625467. 207 rms, 3 suites. A/C MINIBAR TV TEL. 323,000 lire ($201.90) double; from 365,000 lire ($228.15) suite. Rates include breakfast. AE, DC, MC. V. Parking 15,000 lire ($9.40). Closed Jan–Mar 19.

Grande Albergo is a world unto itself, nestled atop a rugged cape projecting into the Ionian Sea. It was designed by one of Italy's most famous architects, Minoletti. There are five floors on five wide sun terraces, plus a saltwater swimming pool at the edge of the cape. Elevators take you through 150 feet of solid rock to the beach below. Bedrooms are handsomely furnished and well proportioned, with wide glass doors opening onto private sun terraces. There are two bars—one intimate, the other more expansive with an orchestra for dancing. The lobby blends the cultures of Rome, Carthage, and Greece, and an open atrium reaches skyward through the center. The food is lavishly presented, and is effectively enhanced by Sicilian wines.

✪ Mazzarò Sea Palace

Via Nazionale 147, 98030 Mazzarò. ☎ **0942/24004.** Fax 0942/626237. 84 rms, 3 suites. A/C MINIBAR TV TEL. 310,000–550,000 lire ($193.75–$343.75) double; 410,000–700,000 lire ($256.25–$437.50) suite. Rates include half-board. AE, DC, MC, V. Parking 22,000 lire ($13.75). Closed Nov–Mar.

The Sea Palace is a leading four-star hotel in this little satellite resort of Taormina. It opens onto perhaps the most beautiful bay in Sicily. Its modern design was completed in the early 1970s, and graced with big windows to let in cascades of light and offer views of the coastline. Candlelight dinners are served on the restaurant terrace. The food is served on fine china and crystal, and guests are pampered by the staff. The piano bar is a popular nighttime spot. There is also a private beach for guests. The rooms are well furnished, most opening onto panoramic views. It is customary to stay here on the half-board plan.

Villa Sant'Andrea

Via Nazionale 137, 98030 Mazzarò. ☎ **0942/23125.** Fax 0942/24838. 67 rms (all with bath or shower). A/C TV TEL. 370,000–560,000 lire ($231.25–$350) double. Rates include half-board. AE, DC, MC, V. Parking 20,000 lire ($12.50).

This hotel stands at the base of the mountain, directly on the sea, where you can swim off its own private beach. A villa was converted into a first-class hotel. A cable car, just outside the front gates of the hotel, will whisk you to the heart of Taormina. The villa receives guests year round. You'll feel like part of a house party. The rooms are informal, with a homelike prettiness, and there is a winning dining terrace where you can enjoy good food. Even if you're not a guest, you might want to try the hotel restaurant, Oliviero, which is one of the finest on the island, having won many awards. Meals range from 65,000 to 70,000 lire ($40.65 to $43.75).

WHERE TO DINE
MODERATE

Giova Rosy Senior

Corso Umberto 38. ☎ **24411.** Reservations recommended. Main courses 18,000–32,000 lire ($11.25–$20). AE, DC, V. July–Sept daily 12:30–3pm and 8–10:30pm; off-season, Fri–Wed 12:30–3pm and 8–10:30pm. Closed Jan 6–Feb 15. Bus: 1 or 2. SICILIAN.

This rustically old-fashioned place serves a variety of local specialties, including, for example, an array of linguine, risotto dishes, and a spiedini with shrimp and lobster dosed with a generous shot of cognac. You might also enjoy Sicilian antipasti or eggplant with ricotta. You'll have a view of the ancient theater, while giving your order to a member of the staff. Full meals cost from 50,000 lire ($31.25).

Ristorante Da Lorenzo

Via Michele Amari 4. ☎ **23480.** Reservations required. Main courses 14,000–30,000 lire ($8.75–$18.75). AE, DC, MC, V. Thurs–Tues noon–3pm and 6:30–11pm. Closed Nov 15–Dec 15. Bus: 1 or 2. SICILIAN/ITALIAN.

This is a clean and bright restaurant on a quiet street near the landmark San Domenico Hotel, in front of the town hall. The restaurant has a terrace shaded by an 850-year-old tree, which is the botanical pride of the town. You can enjoy meals that might include a fresh selection of antipasti, spaghetti with sea urchins, scaloppine mozzarella, grilled swordfish, filet of beef with Gorgonzola, and bean soup. Some of the oil paintings that decorate the white walls add an aesthetic element to your dinner. Full meals cost 28,000 to 58,000 lire ($17.50 to $36.25).

INEXPENSIVE

⑤ Il Ciclope

Corso Umberto. ☎ **23263.** Reservations recommended. Main courses 14,000–23,000 lire ($8.75–$14.40). AE, MC, V. Thurs–Tues 12:30–3pm and 7:30–10pm. Closed Jan 8–Feb 8. Bus: 1 or 2. SICILIAN/ITALIAN.

This is one of the best of the low-priced trattorie of Taormina. Set back from the main street, it opens onto the pint-sized piazzetta Salvatore Leone. In summer, try for an outside table if you'd like both your food and yourself inspected by the passing parade. Meals are fairly simple but the ingredients are fresh, the dishes well prepared. Try, for example, the fish soup or Sicilian squid. If that doesn't interest you, then go for the entrecôte Ciclope, or perhaps the grilled shrimp. Most diners begin their meal with a selection from the antipasti di mare, a savory collection of seafood hors d'oeuvres. Meals cost 30,000 lire ($18.75) and up.

Ristorante La Griglia

Corso Umberto 54. ☎ **23980.** Reservations recommended. Main courses 14,000–26,000 lire ($8.75–$16.25). AE, DC, MC, V. Wed–Mon 12:30–2:30pm and 7:30–11:30pm. Closed Nov. Bus: 1 or 2. SICILIAN/INTERNATIONAL.

Opened in 1974, this restaurant is one of the best in town. The vestibule that funnels visitors from the main street of the old city into the interior contains a bubbling aquarium and a menagerie of carved stone lions. The masses of plants inside almost conceal the terra-cotta floors and big-windowed views over the feathery trees of a garden. Your meal might include a selection from the antipasto display, a carpaccio fresh fish, and an involtini of spaghetti and eggplant.

Ristorante Luraleo

Via Bagnoli Croce 27. ☎ **24279.** Reservations recommended. Main courses 15,000–22,000 lire ($9.40–$13.75). AE, DC, MC, V. Thurs–Tues noon–3pm and 7–11pm. Closed Jan. Bus: 1 or 2. SICILIAN/INTERNATIONAL.

Acclaimed by a handful of city residents as the best place in town, Ristorante Luraleo is eager to offer excellent value for an attractive price. Many diners prefer the flowering terrace, where pastel tablecloths are shaded by the vine-covered arbor overhead. Of course, if you prefer to dine indoors, there's a not-very-large country-rustic dining room with tile accents, flowers, evening candlelight, racks of wine bottles, and richly laden antipasto table. The grilled fish is good here, as are the pastas, regional dishes, and herb-flavored steak. Risotto with salmon and pistachio nuts is a specialty, as is the house tortellini and involtini siciliana. Full meals, including wine and all the extras, cost from 45,000 lire ($28.15) per person.

⑤ Ristorante U'Bossu

Via Bagnoli Croce 50. ☎ **23311.** Reservations required. Main courses 12,000–22,000 lire ($7.50–$13.75); fixed-price menu 20,000 lire ($12.50). MC, V. Tues–Sun 12:30–3pm and 7:30–10pm. Bus: 1 or 2. SICILIAN.

Vines are entwined around the facade of this small and crowded restaurant in a quiet part of town. Amid a pleasing decor of fresh flowers, wagon-wheel chandeliers, prominently displayed wine bottles, and burnished wooden panels, you can enjoy a meal pungent with all the aromas of an herb garden. Specialties include antipasti from the buffet, pasta with sardines, homemade ravioli, grilled shrimp, fish soup, and grilled swordfish. Full à la carte meals begin at 35,000 lire ($21).

PLACES TO DINE IN NEARBY MAZZARÒ
INEXPENSIVE

Ristorante Angelo A Mare—Il Delfino
Via Nazionale, Mazzarò. ☎ **23004.** Reservations not necessary. Main courses 14,000–22,000 lire ($8.75–$13.75). AE, DC, MC, V. Daily noon–3pm and 7pm–midnight. Closed Nov–Mar 31. Transportation: Cable car. MEDITERRANEAN/ITALIAN.

Located in Mazzarò, about 3 miles from Taormina, this restaurant offers a flowering terrace with a view over the bay. Both the decor and the menu items are inspired by the sea, and carefully supervised by the chef and owner. Mussels are a specialty, as well as a house-style steak, along with involtini of fish, cannelloni, and risotto marinara (fisher's rice). Complete meals cost 35,000 to 45,000 lire ($21.90 to $28.15).

TAORMINA AFTER DARK
Caffè Wunderbar
Piazza IX Aprile no. 7, corso Umberto. ☎ **625302.**

During the years he came to Taormina, this popular spot was a favorite watering hole of Tennessee Williams and his companion, Frank Merlo. It's in two areas of the most delightful square in town. Beneath a vine-entwined arbor, the outdoor section is perched as close as is safely possible to the edge of the cliff. I prefer one of the Victorian armchairs of the elegant interior, where an impressionistic pair of sculpted figures fill symmetrical wall niches beneath chandeliers. There's also a well-stocked bar, as well as a piano bar. An espresso costs 3,900 lire ($2.45), and a cappuccino, 4,800 lire ($3) if you sit. Open Wednesday through Monday from 8:30am to 2:30am. From July through September it's open daily.

Tiffany
Van San Pancrazio 5 (Porto Messina). ☎ **625430.** Cover (including one drink) 20,000 lire ($12.50).

A gridwork of illuminated lattices stretches above the glossy dance floor of this underground air-conditioned disco, in the historic center of Taormina. Open daily from 10pm to 3:30 or 4am. The disco stands at the entrance to town.

EASY EXCURSIONS
CASTEL MOLA

Once this little hamlet, 3 miles northwest of Taormina, rivaled the resort itself in importance. But it long ago retired to a happy slumber. Castel Mola is reached only from Taormina. Many visitors walk the entire goat-climbing distance, enjoying panoramic sea views and making a day of it. Five buses a day run between Taormina and Castel Mola.

Castle walls surround Castel Mola, and all the medieval fortification commands today is a view of the coast, Taormina, and formidable Etna, that repository of a thousand fearsome myths.

Even if it weren't for that view, it would be worth coming to Castel Mola to enjoy the superb food at Il Faro.

Where to Dine

⑤ Il Faro

Contrada Petralia (via Rotabile Castel Mola). ☎ **28193.** Reservations recommended. Main courses 13,000–22,000 lire ($8.15–$13.75). No credit cards. Thurs–Tues 12:30–3pm and 7:30–10pm. SICILIAN.

The proprietor is charming, and inquiring if everything is pleasing. You'll see him going between the dining terrace and the inside room, filling glasses of wine, whatever. At his ristorante/bar, half a mile before Castel Mola, homemade Sicilian cookery is the specialty of the kitchen, and it's done with consummate skill. The food seems to reflect the rugged character of the people who inhabited this part of Sicily. Aromatic sauces cover the pastas, and the stews are complicated. Of course, everyone overindulges in the wine. Expect to spend 25,000 to 30,000 lire ($15.65 to $18.75) per person for a complete meal, including wine. Never make the excursion on Wednesday, when Il Faro is closed.

MOUNT ETNA

Looming menacingly over the coast of eastern Sicily, ✪ Mount Etna is the highest and largest active volcano in Europe, and I do mean active! The peak changes in size over the years, but is currently listed somewhere in the neighborhood of 10,800 feet. Etna has been active in modern times (in 1928 the little village of Mascali was burned under its lava), and eruptions in 1971 rekindled the fears of Sicilians, as did those in 1992.

Etna has figured in history and in Greek mythology. Empedocles, the 5th-century B.C. Greek philosopher, is said to have jumped into its crater as a sign that he was being delivered directly to Mount Olympus to take his seat among the gods. It was under Etna that Zeus crushed the multiheaded, viper-riddled dragon Typhoeus, thereby securing domination over Olympus. Hephaestus, the god of fire and blacksmiths, was believed to have made his headquarters in Etna, aided by the single-eyed Cyclopes.

The Greeks warned that whenever Typhoeus tried to break out of his "jail," lava erupted and earthquakes cracked the land. Granted that, the monster must have nearly escaped on March 11, 1669, the date of one of the most violent eruptions recorded, destroying Catania about 17 miles away.

Always get the latest report from local tourist offices before contemplating a trip to Mount Etna.

For a good view of the ferocious, lava-spewing mountain, take one of the trains operated by Ferrovia Circumetnea, which circumnavigate the base of the mighty volcano. Trains can be boarded at the Stazione Borgo, via Caronda, 350 (☎ 095/54124), in Catania, lying off the viale Leonardo da Vinci. A 5-hour circular tour from Catania costs 12,000 lire ($7.50).

If you'd prefer not to attempt this rather cumbersome do-it-yourself means of seeing Etna, you should consider a package tour deal from Taormina. Campagnia Siciliana turismo, corso Umberto 101 (☎ 23301), each headquartered at Taormina, offers package deals, ranging in price from 33,000 to 75,000 lire ($20.65 to $46.90), the latter and costlier jaunt taking you all the way to the top.

Appendix

Italian Menu Terms

Agnolotti A crescent-shaped pasta shell stuffed with a mixture of chopped meat, spices, vegetables, and cheese; when prepared in rectangular versions, the same combination of ingredients is identified as ravioli.

Amaretti Crunchy, very sweet, almond-flavored macaroons.

Antipasti Succulent tidbits served at the beginning of a meal (before the pasta), whose ingredients might include slices of cured meats, seafood (especially shellfish), and cooked and seasoned vegetables.

Aragosta Lobster.

Arrosto Roasted meat.

Baccalà Dried and salted codfish.

Bistecca alla fiorentina Florentine-style steaks, coated before grilling with olive oil, pepper, lemon juice, salt and parsley.

Bollito misto Assorted boiled meats served on a single platter.

Braciola Pork chop.

Bresaola Air-dried spiced beef.

Bruschetta Toasted bread, heavily slathered with olive oil and garlic and often topped with tomatoes.

Bucatini Hollow, coarsely textured spaghetti.

Cabretto ripieno al forno Oven-roasted stuffed baby goat.

Cacciucco ali livornese Seafood stew.

Calzone Pizza dough rolled with the chefs choice of sausage, tomatoes, cheese, etc., then baked into a kind of savory turnover.

Cannelloni Tubular dough stuffed with meat, cheese, or vegetables, then baked in a creamy white sauce.

Cappellacci alla ferrarese Pasta stuffed with pumpkin.

Cappelletti Small ravioli ("little hats") stuffed with meat or cheese.

Carciofi Artichokes.

Carpaccio Thin slices of raw cured beef, sometimes in a piquant sauce.

Cassatta alla siciliana A richly caloric dessert combining layers of sponge cake, sweetened ricotta cheese, and candied fruit, bound together with an icing of chocolate buttercream.

Cervello al burro nero Brains in black-butter sauce.

Coppa Cured morsels of pork filet encased in sausage skins, served in slices.

Costoletta alla milanese Veal cutlet dredged in bread crumbs, fried, and sometimes flavored with cheese.

Cozze Mussels.

Fagioli White beans.

Fave Fava beans.

Fettuccine Flat noodles.

Foccacia Ideally, concocted from potato-based dough left to rise slowly for several hours, then garnished with tomato sauce, garlic, basil, salt, and pepper drizzled with olive oil; similar to a high-pan, deep-dish pizza most popular in the deep south, especially Bari.

Fontina Rich cows-milk cheese.

Frittata Italian omelet.

Fritto misto A deep-fried medley of whatever small fish, shellfish, and squid are available in the marketplace that day.

Fusilli Spiral-shaped pasta.

Gelato (produzione propria) Ice cream (homemade).

Gnocchi Dumplings usually made from potatoes (*gnocchi alla patate*) or from semolina (*gnocchi alla romana*), often stuffed with combinations of cheese, spinach, vegetables, or whatever combinations strike the chef's fancy.

Gorgonzola One of the most famous blue-veined cheeses of Europe; strong, creamy, and aromatic.

Granita Flavored ice, usually with lemon or coffee.

Insalata di frutti di mare Seafood salad (usually including shrimp and squid) garnished with pickles, lemon, olives, and spices.

Lasagne An oven-baked pasta dish which incorporates thin layers of green (*lasagne verde*) or white dough alternating with sausage or ground meat, grated cheese, and white sauce; in certain regions this dish is laced with ricotta.

Minestrone A rich and savory vegetable soup usually sprinkled with grated Parmesan cheese and studded with noodles.

Mortadella Mild pork sausage, fashioned into large cylinders and served sliced.

Mozzarella A non-fermented cheese, made from the fresh milk of a buffalo (or, if unavailable, from a cow), boiled and then kneaded into a rounded ball, served fresh.

Mozzarella con pomodori (also **"caprese"**) Fresh tomatoes with fresh mozzarella, basil, pepper, and olive oil.

Osso buco Beef or veal knuckle slowly braised until the cartilage is tender, and then served with a highly flavored sauce.

Panettone Sweet, yellow-colored bread baked in the form of a brioche.

Panna Heavy cream.

Parmigiano Parmesan, a hard and salty yellow cheese usually grated over pastas and soups but also eaten alone; also known as *granna*.

Peperoni Green, yellow, or red sweet peppers.

Pesci al cartoccio Fish baked in a parchment envelope with onions, parsley, and herbs.

Pesto A flavorful green sauce concocted from basil leaves, cheese, garlic, marjoram, and (if available) pine kernels.

Piccata al marsala Thin escalope of veal braised in a pungent sauce flavored with Marsala wine.

Piselli al prosciutto Peas with strips of ham.

Pizza Specific varieties include: *capricciosa* (its ingredients depend on the whim of the chef), *margherita* (incorporates tomato sauce, cheese, fresh basil, and memories of the first queen of Italy, Marguerite di Savoia), *napoletana* (ham, capers, tomatoes, oregano, cheese, and the distinctive taste of anchovies), *quatro stagione* (translated as "four seasons," fresh vegetables, ham, and bacon), and *siciliana* (contains black olives, capers, and cheese).

Pizzaiola   A process whereby something (usually a beefsteak) is covered in a tomato-and-oregano sauce.

Polenta   Thick porridge or mush made from cornmeal flour.

Polenta de uccelli   Assorted small birds roasted on a spit and served with polenta.

Polenta e coniglio   Rabbit stew served with polenta.

Polla alla cacciatore   Chicken with tomatoes and mushrooms cooked in wine.

Pollo all diavola   Highly spiced grilled chicken.

Ragu   Meat sauce.

Ricotta   A soft and bland cheese, often used in cooking, made from cow's or sheep's milk.

Rigatoni   Large macaroni designed with ridges to more effectively absorb sauce.

Risotto   Italian rice.

Risotto alla milanese   Rice with saffron and wine.

Salsa verde   "Green sauce," made from capers, anchovies, lemon juice and/or vinegar, and parsley.

Saltimbocca   Veal scallop layered with prosciutto and sage; its name literally translates as "jump in your mouth," a reference to its tart and savory flavor.

Salvia   Sage.

Scaloppina alla Valdostana   Escalope of veal stuffed with cheese and ham.

Scaloppine   Thin slices of veal coated in flour and sautéed in butter.

Semifreddo   A frozen dessert; usually ice cream with sponge cake.

Seppia   Cuttlefish (a kind of squid); its black ink is used for flavoring in certain sauces for pasta, and also in risotto dishes.

Sogliola   Sole.

Spaghetti   A long, round, thin pasta, variously served: *alla bolognese* (with ground meat, mushrooms, peppers, etc.), *alla carbonara* (with bacon, black pepper, and eggs), *al pomodoro* (with tomato sauce), *al sugo/ragù* (with meat sauce), and *alle vongole* (with clam sauce).

Spiedini   Pieces of meat grilled on a skewer over an open flame.

Stufato   Beef braised in white wine with vegetables.

Tagliatelle   Flat egg noodles.

Tiramisu   Richly caloric dessert containing layers of triple-crème cheeses and rum-soaked sponge cake.

Tonno   Tuna.

Tortelli   Pasta dumplings stuffed with ricotta and greens.

Tortellini   Rings of dough stuffed with minced and seasoned meat and served either in soups or a full-fledged pasta covered with sauce.

Trenette   Thin noodles served with pesto sauce and potatoes.

Trippe alla fiorentina   Beef tripe (intestines).

Vermicelli   Very thin spaghetti.

Vitello tonnato   Cold sliced veal covered with tuna-fish sauce.

Zabaglione/zabaione   Egg yolks whipped into the consistency of a custard, flavored with Marsala, and served warm as a dessert.

Zampone   Pigs trotter stuffed with spicy seasoned port, boiled and sliced.

Zuppa inglese   Sponge cake soaked in custard sauce and rum.

Index

The following Frommer's guides are available from your favorite bookstore, or you can use the order form on the preceding page to request them as part of your membership in Frommer's Travel Book Club.

FROMMER'S COMPLETE TRAVEL GUIDES

(Comprehensive guides to sightseeing, dining and accommodations, with selections in all price ranges—from deluxe to budget)

FROMMER'S $-A-DAY GUIDES

(Dream Vacations at Down-to-Earth Prices)

FROMMER'S COMPLETE CITY GUIDES

(Comprehensive guides to sightseeing, dining, and accommodations in all price ranges)

Amsterdam, 8th Ed.	S176	Minneapolis/St. Paul, 4th Ed.	S159
Athens, 10th Ed.	S174	Montréal/Québec City '95	S166
Atlanta & the Summer Olympic		Nashville/Memphis, 1st Ed.	S141
Games '96 (avail. 11/95)	S181	New Orleans '96 (avail. 10/95)	S182
Atlantic City/Cape May, 5th Ed.	S130	New York City '96 (avail. 11/95)	S183
Bangkok, 2nd Ed.	S147	Paris '96 (avail. 9/95)	S180
Barcelona '93-'94	S115	Philadelphia, 8th Ed.	S167
Berlin, 3rd Ed.	S162	Prague, 1st Ed.	S143
Boston '95	S160	Rome, 10th Ed.	S168
Budapest, 1st Ed.	S139	St. Louis/Kansas City, 2nd Ed.	S127
Chicago '95	S169	San Antonio/Austin, 1st Ed.	S177
Denver/Boulder/Colorado Springs,		San Diego '95	S158
3rd Ed.	S154	San Francisco '96 (avail. 10/95)	S184
Disney World/Orlando '96 (avail. 9/95)	S178	Santa Fe/Taos/Albuquerque '95	S172
Dublin, 2nd Ed.	S157	Seattle/Portland '94-'95	S137
Hong Kong '94-'95	S140	Sydney, 4th Ed.	S171
Las Vegas '95	S163	Tampa/St. Petersburg, 3rd Ed.	S146
London '96 (avail. 9/95)	S179	Tokyo '94-'95	S144
Los Angeles '95	S164	Toronto, 3rd Ed.	S173
Madrid/Costa del Sol, 2nd Ed.	S165	Vancouver/Victoria '94-'95	S142
Mexico City, 1st Ed.	S175	Washington, D.C. '95	S153
Miami '95-'96	S149		

FROMMER'S FAMILY GUIDES

(Guides to family-friendly hotels, restaurants, activities, and attractions)

California with Kids	F105	San Francisco with Kids	F104
Los Angeles with Kids	F103	Washington, D.C. with Kids	F102
New York City with Kids	F101		

FROMMER'S WALKING TOURS

*(Memorable strolls through colorful and historic neighborhoods,
accompanied by detailed directions and maps)*

Berlin	W100	Paris, 2nd Ed.	W112
Chicago	W107	San Francisco, 2nd Ed.	W115
England's Favorite Cities	W108	Spain's Favorite Cities (avail. 9/95)	W116
London, 2nd Ed.	W111	Tokyo	W109
Montréal/Québec City	W106	Venice	W110
New York, 2nd Ed.	W113	Washington, D.C., 2nd Ed.	W114

FROMMER'S AMERICA ON WHEELS

*(Guides for travelers who are exploring the U.S.A. by car, featuring a brand-new
rating system for accommodations and full-color road maps)*

Arizona/New Mexico	A100	Florida	A102
California/Nevada	A101	Mid-Atlantic	A103

FROMMER'S SPECIAL-INTEREST TITLES

Arthur Frommer's Branson!	P107	Frommer's Where to Stay U.S.A.,	
Arthur Frommer's New World		11th Ed.	P102
of Travel (avail. 11/95)	P112	National Park Guide, 29th Ed.	P106
Frommer's Caribbean Hideaways		USA Today Golf Tournament Guide	P113
(avail. 9/95)	P110	USA Today Minor League	
Frommer's America's 100 Best-Loved		Baseball Book	P111
State Parks	P109		

FROMMER'S BEST BEACH VACATIONS

*(The top places to sun, stroll, shop, stay, play, party, and swim—with each
beach rated for beauty, swimming, sand, and amenities)*

California (avail. 10/95)	G100	Hawaii (avail. 10/95)	G102
Florida (avail. 10/95)	G101		

FROMMER'S BED & BREAKFAST GUIDES

*(Selective guides with four-color photos and full descriptions of
the best inns in each region)*

California	B100	Hawaii	B105
Caribbean	B101	Pacific Northwest	B106
East Coast	B102	Rockies	B107
Eastern United States	B103	Southwest	B108
Great American Cities	B104		

FROMMER'S IRREVERENT GUIDES

*(Wickedly honest guides for sophisticated travelers
and those who want to be)*

Chicago (avail. 11/95)	I100	New Orleans (avail. 11/95)	I103
London (avail. 11/95)	I101	San Francisco (avail. 11/95)	I104
Manhattan (avail. 11/95)	I102	Virgin Islands (avail. 11/95)	I105

FROMMER'S DRIVING TOURS

*(Four-color photos and detailed maps outlining
spectacular scenic driving routes)*

Australia	Y100	Italy	Y108
Austria	Y101	Mexico	Y109
Britain	Y102	Scandinavia	Y110
Canada	Y103	Scotland	Y111
Florida	Y104	Spain	Y112
France	Y105	Switzerland	Y113
Germany	Y106	U.S.A.	Y114
Ireland	Y107		

FROMMER'S BORN TO SHOP

*(The ultimate travel guides for discriminating
shoppers—from cut-rate to couture)*

Hong Kong (avail. 11/95)	Z100	London (avail. 11/95)	Z101